*Copyright
in a
Global Information
Economy*

ASPEN CASEBOOK SERIES

Copyright in a Global Information Economy

Fourth Edition

Julie E. Cohen

Mark Claster Mamolen Professor of Law
and Technology
Georgetown University Law Center

Lydia Pallas Loren

Robert E. Jones Professor of Advocacy and Ethics
Lewis and Clark Law School

Ruth L. Okediji

William L. Prosser Professor of Law
University of Minnesota Law School

Maureen A. O'Rourke

Dean & Professor of Law
Michaels Faculty Research Scholar
Boston University School of Law

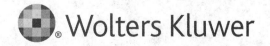 Wolters Kluwer

To contact Customer Service, e-mail customer.service@wolterskluwer.com, call 1-800-234-1660, fax 1-800-901-9075, or mail correspondence to:

Wolters Kluwer
Attn: Order Department
PO Box 990
Frederick, MD 21705

Printed in the United States of America.

2 3 4 5 6 7 8 9 0

ISBN 978-1-4548-5201-8

Library of Congress Cataloging-in-Publication Data

Copyright in a global information economy / Julie E. Cohen, Mark Claster Mamolen Professor of Law and Technology Georgetown University Law Center; Lydia Pallas Loren, Robert E. Jones Professor of Advocacy and Ethics Lewis and Clark Law School; Ruth L. Okediji, William L. Prosser Professor of Law, University of Minnesota Law School; Maureen A. O'Rourke, Dean & Professor of Law, Michaels Faculty Research Scholar, Boston University School of Law. —Fourth Edition.
      p. cm
Includes bibliographical references and index.
    ISBN 978-1-4548-5201-8 (alk. paper)
1. Copyright—United States. 2. Copyright, International. 3. International and municipal law—United States.
I. Cohen, Julie E. II. Loren, Lydia. III. Okediji, Ruth L. IV. O'Rourke, Maureen A.

    KF2996.C67 2015
    346.7304′82—dc23

                                                                2015006678

About Wolters Kluwer Law & Business

Wolters Kluwer Law & Business is a leading global provider of intelligent information and digital solutions for legal and business professionals in key specialty areas, and respected educational resources for professors and law students. Wolters Kluwer Law & Business connects legal and business professionals as well as those in the education market with timely, specialized authoritative content and information-enabled solutions to support success through productivity, accuracy and mobility.

Serving customers worldwide, Wolters Kluwer Law & Business products include those under the Aspen Publishers, CCH, Kluwer Law International, Loislaw, ftwilliam.com and MediRegs family of products.

CCH products have been a trusted resource since 1913, and are highly regarded resources for legal, securities, antitrust and trade regulation, government contracting, banking, pension, payroll, employment and labor, and healthcare reimbursement and compliance professionals.

Aspen Publishers products provide essential information to attorneys, business professionals and law students. Written by preeminent authorities, the product line offers analytical and practical information in a range of specialty practice areas from securities law and intellectual property to mergers and acquisitions and pension/benefits. Aspen's trusted legal education resources provide professors and students with high-quality, up-to-date and effective resources for successful instruction and study in all areas of the law.

Kluwer Law International products provide the global business community with reliable international legal information in English. Legal practitioners, corporate counsel and business executives around the world rely on Kluwer Law journals, looseleafs, books, and electronic products for comprehensive information in many areas of international legal practice.

Loislaw is a comprehensive online legal research product providing legal content to law firm practitioners of various specializations. Loislaw provides attorneys with the ability to quickly and efficiently find the necessary legal information they need, when and where they need it, by facilitating access to primary law as well as state-specific law, records, forms and treatises.

ftwilliam.com offers employee benefits professionals the highest quality plan documents (retirement, welfare and non-qualified) and government forms (5500/PBGC, 1099 and IRS) software at highly competitive prices.

MediRegs products provide integrated health care compliance content and software solutions for professionals in healthcare, higher education and life sciences, including professionals in accounting, law and consulting.

Wolters Kluwer Law & Business, a division of Wolters Kluwer, is headquartered in New York. Wolters Kluwer is a market-leading global information services company focused on professionals.

For Andrew and Eli.
> —J.E.C.

*For Mom and Dad, thanks for keeping me sane . . . and
a little crazy.*
> —L.P.L.

*For Tade, Francis, Aaron and Anna . . . . my "good and perfect"
gifts from the Lord.*
> —R.L.O.

For James, always and forever.
> —M.A.O.

Summary of Contents

Contents

PART II
The Subject Matter of Copyright

2   *Requirements for Copyright Protection*   *49*

3   *Authorship*   *137*

PART III
The Statutory Rights of Copyright Owners

Copyright in Musical Works and Sound Recordings   409

Moral Rights and Performers' Rights   449

PART IV
Indirect Infringement and Lawful Use

9   *The Different Faces of Infringement*   *483*

10   *Fair Use*   563

PART V
Practical Considerations in Licensing and Enforcing Copyrights

PART VI
New Enforcement Strategies and Public Policy Limits

14 *Technological Protections* *861*

Preface

As this casebook moves into its fourth edition, the relentless pace of technological innovation, particularly with respect to digital communication technologies, continues to challenge well-settled copyright doctrines, creating new opportunities to contest the nature and scope of the various interests implicated by copyright. This edition therefore continues to emphasize the evolving nature of copyright law, and the copyright system more generally, in response to technological change and the pressures of globalization. We provide students with not only a firm foundation in the traditional precepts of copyright law, but also a strong theoretical background with which to evaluate the public policy implications of the ongoing changes. Each chapter includes material carefully selected and arranged to help students appreciate how the law has evolved over time and the complexities introduced by new technologies and/or new theoretical approaches.

As is expected of a new edition, we have updated all the chapters to reflect new legislation and case law, including materials reflecting international trends. Our website at www.coolcopyright.com contains background materials (including additional pictures) for the cases in the book, as well as some alternative cases, including some that appeared in the third edition but have now been replaced. We trust that students and teachers will find these materials useful to augment the text or to provide resources for deeper study of a particular topic.

The fourth edition differs from the third in several important respects. Most notably, we have reorganized the material into six parts: (1) Introduction to Copyright Law, (2) The Subject Matter of Copyright, (3) The Statutory Rights of Copyright Owners, (4) Indirect Infringement and Lawful Use, (5) Practical

Considerations in Licensing and Enforcing Copyrights, and (6) New Enforcement Strategies and Public Policy Limits. This structure introduces students to the exclusive rights of copyright owners earlier in the course, and enables them to study the materials on formalities and duration in the context of an integrated unit on copyright due diligence, licensing, and enforcement.

The fourth edition also has some new features to help both teachers and students navigate the material. Recognizing the ever-increasing complexity of copyright law, we have used the terminology "Diving Deeper" to flag sections addressing detailed provisions of the law that not all teachers may wish to cover. We have included text boxes for greater ease of reading and to help students link various themes that may appear across different chapters. The boxes highlight practice tips; remind students of what they have read in past chapters or sections and highlight what is to come; provide comparative perspectives; explain technological concepts; and give information on the later history of some of the excerpted cases. Perhaps most important, we have added "Problems" and "Practice Exercises" to give students a sense of the types of issues they may face in practice. "Problems" generally ask the students to apply statutory sections directly, while "Practice Exercises" ask them to think about how to advise a client, develop and argue a case, or draft a legal document.

We continue to believe that understanding the role of copyright law in the information economy requires more than a study of the Copyright Act and copyright case law. To understand why copyright law is the way it is, and to develop an appreciation for what it might become, one must consider the history and evolution of technologies for creating and distributing copyrighted works; the structure and political influence of the major copyright industries and user groups; and the availability of other legal regimes (such as contract law) to supplement or even supplant copyright protection. We include introductory materials on these topics and then give substantial consideration throughout the book to the historical, technological, political, and legal contexts within which copyright law operates.

We have retained the use of secondary source materials that offer insights about the evolution of copyright and contemporary information policy. However, in response to feedback from students and teachers, we have streamlined the use of secondary materials and asked questions designed to facilitate a firmer understanding of the ways that theory and practice converge. We have condensed the Notes and Questions in service of those goals. Suggestions for additional reading on various topics can be found on our website, www.coolcopyright.com.

In addition, we continue to emphasize the importance of international developments for U.S. copyright law and policy. We integrate both international and comparative materials throughout the text, rather than leaving those materials until the end of the book or treating them as advanced topics. Throughout the book, we discuss relevant treaty provisions and, in many instances, ask students to compare specific domestic copyright rules with the corresponding rules of other countries.

Our hope is that students who use this book and our supporting website will come to understand and appreciate the copyright system as a work-in-progress, and recognize that copyright is not simply a regime of private law, but rather one that implicates both private and public interests. We believe that we offer students a unique text that will help them develop the skills necessary to identify and think critically about both contested issues in particular cases and larger patterns of change within the copyright system as a whole. Our expectation is that students will emerge from this process of exploration well-informed and better equipped to practice copyright law in a world in which continual change is the norm.

Julie E. Cohen
Lydia Pallas Loren
Ruth L. Okediji
Maureen A. O'Rourke

February 2015

Acknowledgments

We gratefully acknowledge the assistance of many people who have helped us since we began work on this book. The first edition benefited greatly from the many helpful and generous suggestions offered by Richard Chused, Shubha Ghosh, Paul Goldstein, Dennis Karjala, David Lange, Mark Lemley, Jessica Litman, Michael Meurer, Harvey Perlman, Pamela Samuelson, and a number of anonymous colleagues. In addition, we acknowledge the research assistance of Teeshna Bahadur, Stacy Blasberg, Casey Caldwell, Mitzi Chang, Cyrus Christenson, Olivia Farrar-Wellman, Sally Garrison, Stephen Goldberg, Michael Green, Scott Katz, Anne Koch, Charles McLawhorn, Ilana Safer, Julie Short, Stephanie Smith, and Victor Wandres, and the secretarial and administrative assistance of Melissa Adamson, Suzan Benet, Sue Morrison, and Irene Welch. We would also like to thank John Showalter for his expert assistance in obtaining permission to reproduce excerpts from the various books, law review articles, and other secondary sources quoted in the text of the first edition; Andy Marion for word processing wizardry; and Lisa Bowles, Tracey Bridgman, Stephanie Burke, Raquel Ortiz, Russ Sweet, and Joel Wegemer for library services.

For their assistance with our preparation of the second edition, we would like to thank Robert Brauneis, Richard Chused, Wendy Gordon, Jessica Litman, Peter Maggs, James Speta, Rebecca Tushnet, Philip Weiser, and a number of anonymous colleagues who generously provided Aspen with detailed reviews based on their experiences teaching from the first edition. We also gratefully acknowledge the research assistance of Andrew Crouse, Robert Dowers, Tomas Felcman, Laura Hayes, David Hesford, Jon Putman, Duke Tufty, Kathryn Ward, Marci Windsheimer, and Matthew Windsor; the secretarial and administrative assistance of Melissa Adamson, Suzan Benet, Liz Cerrato, and Michael Mercurio; and the library assistance of Steve Donweber, Terri Gallego O'Rourke, Mary Rumsey, and David Zopfi-Jordan. In addition, we would like to extend special thanks to Matthew Windsor for the comprehensive redesign of the book's companion website, www.coolcopyright.com.

The third edition benefited considerably from the detailed, insightful feedback offered by Margreth Barrett, Mark Bartholomew, Annemarie Bridy, Wendy Gordon, James Grimmelmann, Rita Heimes, Jessica Litman, Michael Madison, Kenneth L. Port, Pam Samuelson, and John G. Sprankling. In addition, we acknowledge the research assistance of Emily Adams, Theresa Coughlin, Ryan Houck, Robert Insley, Andrew Jacobs, Christopher Klimmek, Jack Mellyn, John Rankin, and Dan Roberts; the secretarial and administrative assistance of Margaret Flynn, Julie F. Hunt, and Pamela Malone; and the library assistance of David Bachman, Raquel Ortiz, Mary Rumsey, and Stefanie Weigmann.

For their feedback on matters pertaining to the fourth edition, we thank James Burger, Wendy Gordon, James Grimmelmann, Melissa Levine, Jessica Litman, David Olson, Pamela Samuelson, and a number of anonymous colleagues who generously provided Aspen with feedback based on their experiences teaching from the third edition. We also gratefully acknowledge the research assistance of Sarvesh Desai, Allegra Funsten, Amanda Gomm, Tricia Juettemeyer, Jonathan Upchurch, Carla Virlee, Chris Visentin, and Cong Yao; the secretarial and administrative assistance of Sharon Capuano-George, Jenny Carron, Liz Cerrato, Bria Goldman, Anna Selden, and Kathryn Ticknor; and the library assistance of David Bachman, Barbara Monroe, Suzanne Thorpe, Stefanie Weigmann, and David Zopfi-Jordan.

In keeping with Aspen style guidelines, omissions of citations and footnotes are not noted with ellipses, while omission of text is appropriately indicated. Omission of entire paragraphs is indicated with ellipses at the end of the preceding paragraph or text. Finally, we acknowledge the authors and/or copyright owners of the following excerpts and images, used in this book with their permission.

Books and Articles

Cohen, Julie E., *The Place of the User in Copyright Law*, 74 Fordham Law Review 347 (2005). Reprinted courtesy of Julie Cohen.

Goldstein, Paul, *Derivative Rights and Derivative Works in Copyright*, 30 Journal of the Copyright Society 209 (1983). Reprinted courtesy of Paul Goldstein.

Gordon, Wendy J., *Fair Use as Market Failure: A Structural and Economic Analysis of the Betamax Case and Its Predecessors*, 82 Columbia Law Review 1600 (1982). Reprinted courtesy of Wendy Gordon.

Hardy, Trotter, *Property (and Copyright) in Cyberspace*, 1996 University of Chicago Legal Forum 217 (1996). Reprinted courtesy of the University of Chicago Legal Forum.

Lee, Edward, *Warming Up to User-Generated Content*, 2008 University of Illinois Law Review 1459. Reproduced by permission of the publisher from 2008 *University of Illinois Law Review* 1459. Copyright 2008 by The Board of Trustees of the University of Illinois.

Litman, Jessica, *The Public Domain*, 39 Emory Law Journal 965 (1990). Reprinted courtesy of Jessica Litman.

Netanel, Neil Weinstock, *Copyright and a Democratic Civil Society*, 106 Yale Law Journal 283 (1996). Reprinted courtesy of Neil Netanel and by permission of The Yale Law Journal Company and William S. Hein Company.

Samuelson, Pamela. *The Quest for a Sound Conception of Copyright's Derivative Work Right*, 101 Georgetown Law Journal 1505 (2013). Reprinted courtesy of Pamela Samuelson.

Illustrations

Borgman, Jim, editorial cartoon, "No More Packing in the Middle of the Night!"© 1984 King Features. Reprinted with special permission of King Features Syndicate.

Gere, Joanne, photograph of "RIBBON Rack in Shadow." Reprinted courtesy of Brandir International, Inc.

Graylock, Jennifer, photograph of Batmobile. Photo © Jennifer Graylock. Reprinted with permission.

Kieselstein-Cord, Barry, "Winchester" and "Vaquero" belt buckles. © 1976 (Winchester) and 1978 (Vaquero) Kieselstein-Cord. Reprinted courtesy of Barry Kieselstein-Cord.

IBM Corporation, screen shot of Lotus 1-2-3 release 2.01. Reprint Courtesy of International Business Machines Corporation, © International Business Machines Corporation.

Mannion, Jonathan, photographs of Kevin Garnett, "Iced Out Comp Board" and infringing detail from Coors Billboard. Original photograph of Kevin Garnett © Jonathan Mannion. Photographs reprinted courtesy of Jonathan Mannion.

Martin, Jan, "Symphony #1."© 1987 Jan Martin. Photograph reprinted courtesy of Jan Martin.

Nelson-Salabes, Inc. Architects/Planners, photographs of Satyr Hill assisted living facility as proposed by Nelson-Salabes, Inc. and as built by Morningside Holdings. Photographs reprinted courtesy of Nelson-Salabes, Inc. Architects/Planners.

Reid, James Earl, "Third World America: A Contemporary Nativity."© 1985 James Earl Reid. Photograph reprinted courtesy of James Earl Reid, Sculptor.

Steinberg, Saul, "View of the World from 9th Avenue," cover image from the March 29, 1976 issue of *The New Yorker*. Original Artwork by Saul Steinberg. © 1976 The Saul Steinberg Foundation/Artists Rights Society (ARS), New York. Cover reprinted with permission of *The New Yorker* magazine. All rights reserved.

Ty, Inc., "Squealer" beanbag toy. © 1993 Ty, Inc. Reprinted courtesy of Ty, Inc. Photograph of "Squealer" and "Preston" beanbag toys reprinted courtesy of Banner & Witcoff, Ltd.

I

INTRODUCTION TO COPYRIGHT LAW

1

Copyright in Context

Copyright law is a pervasive feature of our information society, and its role and effect on the ordinary lives of citizens are often the subjects of heated debate. Our present law is derived from a set of rules first adopted in the eighteenth century, when no one could foresee either the extent to which information technologies would evolve or the role that information industries would eventually play in the national and global economies. Today, copyright law confronts the realities of the continuously evolving modern networked world, one in which individuals, corporations and governments have seemingly unlimited capacity to communicate ideas, share information, and access vast amounts of data. As new technologies challenge the traditional copyright framework, it is essential that those who study, practice, and make copyright law understand the fundamental policies underlying the copyright system. Additionally, it is imperative to consider U.S. copyright law and policy within the larger context of international copyright relations and norm-setting processes.

The materials in this chapter situate U.S. copyright law in its theoretical, historical, and global contexts. We begin with a brief summary of the major principles of U.S. copyright law and their organization within this book.

Copyright law in the U.S. is a federal statute, codified in Title 17 of the U.S. Code. The authority for Congress to enact the copyright law derives from an express grant of power in Article I of the Constitution:

> The Congress shall have Power . . . To promote the Progress of Science and useful Arts, by securing for limited Times to Authors and Inventors the exclusive Right to their respective Writings and Discoveries.

KEEP IN MIND

The phrase "intellectual property" did not come into vogue until the last several decades of the twentieth century. For many years, Art. I, §8, cl. 8 was known as the Patent and Copyright Clause. Today, some commentators prefer the "Exclusive Rights Clause" or the "Progress Clause" because those labels are more faithful to the literal constitutional text.

U.S. Const., Art. I, §8, cl. 8. Throughout this book, we refer to this clause as the "Intellectual Property Clause." To get a feel for the current Copyright Act (the "Act"), adopted in 1976 and amended many times since then, spend a few minutes examining its table of contents.

The remaining chapters in Part I explore copyrightable subject matter and authorship. The Act imposes certain threshold requirements a work must meet before it is entitled to protection. In Chapter 2, we consider those requirements and why the Act imposes them. Generally, the Act grants a limited statutory monopoly in *original* works of authorship that are *fixed* in a tangible medium of expression. In addition, the Act codifies the principle known as the *idea/expression distinction*, which excludes from protection ideas, facts, methods of operation, and the like. Such items are part of what is called the *public domain*, a concept we discuss in more detail later in this chapter and throughout this book. Chapter 3 examines the concept of *authorship* and who is entitled to claim rights under the Act. Chapter 4 considers certain categories of works—applied art, architecture, and computer software—that closely meld *form and function* and therefore test the outer boundaries of copyright protection.

Part II introduces the *exclusive rights* granted to copyright owners. In the language of property law, these exclusive rights make up the "sticks" in the copyright owner's bundle of rights. For all categories of works, the Act grants copyright owners the rights to (1) reproduce the work, (2) prepare derivative works based on the work, and (3) publicly distribute copies of the work. The Act also grants copyright owners of certain categories of works the right(s) to publicly display the work and/or to publicly perform it. For one category of works, sound recordings, the Act limits the right of public performance to performance by digital transmission. We explore these rights, including their justifications and limits, in Chapters 5, 6, and 7. Chapter 5 considers the *reproduction* and *derivative work* rights. Chapter 6 discusses the rights of *distribution*, *public display*, and *public performance*. Chapter 7 explores the exclusive rights in musical works and sound recordings; in particular, it focuses on the ways that participants in the *music industry* have structured business models around those rights and on how new technologies have continually disrupted those arrangements. Finally, when the U.S. acceded to the Berne Convention for the Protection of Literary and Artistic Works, the foremost international copyright treaty, it became obligated to protect certain *moral rights* of authors. In Chapter 8, we examine how Congress provided some measure of moral rights protection in the Act, as well as certain protections for performers required by another international treaty, the Agreement on Trade Related Aspects of Intellectual Property Rights (TRIPS Agreement).

Part III considers two important sets of doctrines that help to define the reach of copyright infringement liability. In Chapter 9 we discuss who may be held liable for *civil copyright infringement*, focusing particularly on a set of doctrines that establish *secondary liability* for parties that facilitate infringement and on certain special rules that apply to online service providers. At the same time, many *limiting doctrines* authorize users of copyrighted works and certain intermediaries, such as libraries, to copy, distribute, or publicly display or perform portions of works and sometimes even entire works without incurring liability for infringing the copyright owner's exclusive rights. A number of limiting doctrines that authorize specific activities are discussed in Part III. The essential, judicially-created doctrine of *fair use* is the subject of Chapter 10.

Part IV explores the practical considerations that attend claiming, licensing, and enforcing copyrights. Many people believe that one must register a work in order to "have" a copyright or that, at a minimum, there must be a symbol, "©", appearing on the work for it to be copyrighted. However, the Copyright Act does not require *registration* as a condition of copyright protection and, since 1989, it has not required that any *notice* of copyright be placed on the work itself. Once an original work of authorship is fixed in a tangible medium of expression, that work is protected by federal copyright law. There are, however, good reasons for both registering copyright and using a copyright notice, and we discuss them in Chapter 11. In addition, Chapter 11 discusses the *duration* of copyright, and introduces the due diligence requirements that surround the use of older works copyrighted when notice and renewal were required. Chapter 12 discusses issues related to the use of *contracts* and *licenses* in the copyright context. We explore the rules that govern transfer of ownership of a copyright, the arrangements that may give rise to implied licenses, and the increasingly ubiquitous use of shrinkwrap licenses. Chapter 12 also addresses new forms of licenses, including Open Source and Creative Commons licenses, that seek to change copyright's default rules to make more user activities permissible. Chapter 13 considers the *copyright infringement lawsuit*. Litigating (or settling) a copyright dispute requires understanding a variety of procedural matters ranging from federal subject matter jurisdiction to standing to the right to jury trial. Chapter 13 also discusses the remedies available in a civil infringement action under the Copyright Act. Finally, Chapter 13 explores the requirements that are necessary to support a prosecution for *criminal copyright infringement*.

Part V considers the use of additional measures beyond copyright law to protect copyright interests. Faced with the advent of digital technologies, which enable instantaneous, mass distribution of perfect copies, the copyright industries have sought additional protection both through *technological protection measures*, such as encryption, and *expanded legal rights*. Chapter 14 addresses those efforts and the legal battles that have ensued as a result. The final chapter, Chapter 15, considers the use of contract and other rights created by state law to augment the protection available under copyright law. Understanding the interplay between copyright law and state law requires mastery of *federal preemption* principles. Chapter 15 explores these principles and their application in the specific context of copyright law.

Before delving into the details of the Act in Chapters 2 through 15, we turn in the remainder of this chapter to the theoretical justifications for copyright law, the history of U.S. copyright law, and an overview of how U.S. copyright law fits within the international copyright system.

A. THE THEORETICAL UNDERPINNINGS OF COPYRIGHT LAW

Many people believe that the reason copyright exists is to protect those who create works from those who would pilfer their works. While this is, in many ways, the effect of copyright law, and indeed it is copyright law's intended effect, it is not exactly the reason that copyright law exists. As stated in the Constitution's Intellectual Property Clause, the fundamental purpose of the U.S. copyright system is to "promote . . . Progress." Simply pointing to the constitutional language, however, masks the complexity of why copyright exists. What did the Framers mean by "Progress"? Why do other countries, not guided by the U.S. Constitution, grant copyright protection?

1. Incentives for Authors and Publishers

To understand why copyright might be necessary, consider a world in which no copyright protection exists. An author may spend months or even years writing a novel that, once completed, she hopes will earn her a comfortable income as recompense for her efforts. Imagine that the author's publisher decides to sell copies of her novel for a modest $20. That price will allow the publisher to recover the costs of reproduction, distribution, marketing, and, of course, the author's compensation. In a world without copyright, once the novel is publicly available, no legal rule would prevent others from freely copying it. In fact, another publisher could take our hypothetical author's novel, reproduce copies of it, and sell them for less than $20, say $16. Sales at $16 still would be profitable because this publisher need not pay the author. Who would buy the $20 copies from the author's publisher when the exact same novel is available elsewhere for $16? Next, another company could begin selling copies for even less than $16, and so on, until the price approached the cost of the cheapest way to make and distribute the copies. While the copyists might be able to recover their full costs of production, in this hypothetical world, the author will not receive anywhere near the same level of compensation that she would receive in a world with copyright. She will receive payments from her publisher, but the amount will decrease toward zero over time as copyists make cheaper versions of her work available. The total she receives may no longer provide her with sufficient compensation to write the novel in the first place. While at first glance the public might seem to benefit from lower prices in a world without copyright, in fact it might be harmed if, on the whole, fewer works were produced.

This example illustrates what economists call the public goods problem in intangibles. The cost of creating new works is often high, but the cost of reproducing them is low and, once the work is created, reproducing it in no way depletes the original. This latter characteristic is referred to as "nonrivalrous" consumption: One party's use of the good does not interfere with another party's use. Intangible goods, including copyrighted works, are not like tangible goods with rivalrous consumption characteristics. For example, if one person eats an apple, it interferes with another person's ability to eat the same apple. In contrast, if one person sings a song, it does not interfere with another person's ability to sing the same song. Similarly, one person reading a novel does not interfere with another person's ability to read the same novel. The second person may not be able to use the same *copy* of the book at the same time, but once the work has been released to the public, an unlimited number of people may "consume" the work without depleting it.

Importantly, public goods also have the characteristic of nonexcludability. Once the good is produced, there is no way to exclude others from enjoying its benefits. The classic example of national defense best illustrates the nonexcludability principle. When a country's citizens' tax dollars pay for the national defense, there is no way to exclude non-taxpaying citizens from the benefits of that defense system. Similarly, once a copyrightable song is released to the public, it is impossible to exclude non-paying members of the public from hearing and enjoying it. And unless the manuscript of a novel is kept under lock and key, it will be impossible to restrict appreciation of its plot, characters, and wording only to those who have paid for a copy.

One explanation for copyright protection is that it is necessary to solve the public goods problem. By granting the bundle of rights enumerated above, copyright law provides a legal entitlement to the copyright owner to exclude others from enjoying certain benefits of the work. This enables an author to recoup her investment in the creation of the work. This legal protection will also encourage disclosure and dissemination of the work because the author no longer needs to fear the copyist; the law will provide a remedy to stop unauthorized copying and to compensate for the harm caused by it. By solving the public goods problem, copyright law furnishes appropriate incentives to creators and publishers and thereby prevents underproduction of creative works.

As thus described, copyright's purpose is purely utilitarian. Copyright law exists to provide a marketable right for the creators and distributors of copyrighted works, which in turn creates an incentive for production and dissemination of new works. As we discuss in Section B.2, *infra*, the Framers of the U.S. Constitution embraced this utilitarian rationale for copyright protection when they granted Congress the power to enact the copyright laws. Granting a limited monopoly to the authors of creative works provided a means for the fledgling country to encourage progress in knowledge and learning.

This is not to suggest that the only (or primary) reason authors create is the promise of monetary reward. To the contrary, creators report a wide variety of motivations, including passion and dedication to their craft. *See, e.g.,* Jessica Silbey, The Eureka Myth: Creators, Innovators, and Everyday Intellectual Property (2014). Even so, there are economic costs associated with creative activity (e.g., materials and promotion costs) as well as opportunity costs that arise when authors choose to invest time in creative endeavors rather than pursuing other, more immediately lucrative, activities. Copyright establishes a baseline set of rights that authors may choose to exercise.

Focusing solely on the incentive to create works of authorship, moreover, neglects the role that copyright plays in encouraging dissemination of those works. Because copyright law provides remedies to stop unauthorized copying and compensate for the monetary harm it has caused, it furnishes incentives for publishers and other production intermediaries to invest in cultural production. Viewed this way, copyright "creates a foundation for predictability in the organization of cultural production, something particularly important in capital-intensive industries like film production, but important for many other industries as well." Julie E. Cohen, *Copyright as Property in the Post-Industrial Economy: A Research Agenda*, 2011 Wisc. L. Rev. 141, 143.

As you will learn, utilitarian thinking about copyright must carefully consider the appropriate scope of the rights to be granted. Granting copyright may solve the public goods problem, but only if the rights are calibrated well enough. Rights that are too weak will not correct the public goods problem, and rights that are too extensive in scope will introduce costs of their own. Keep in mind that no work is truly original. Rather, all works build to some extent on earlier creations: Would Suzanne Collins have written *The Hunger Games*, or Merian C. Cooper *The Most Dangerous Game*, if not for the Greek myth of Theseus? Exclusionary rights that are too strong may result in robust levels of production initially, followed by less-than-optimal production of subsequent-generation works.

The state of technology for copying and distributing works also affects the optimal scope of copyright protection because technology determines the ease with which a copyright may be enforced or infringed. The development of networked digital technologies has affected—and, according to some, jeopardized—the efficacy of the exclusive rights. Paradoxically, at the same time such technologies have caused some to question the assumptions that lead to the conclusion that copyright protection is necessary for progress. Consider the following excerpt.

Trotter Hardy, Property (and Copyright) in Cyberspace
1996 U. Chi. Legal F. 217, 220-28.

Conventional wisdom argues that informational works, because they exhibit such a low ratio of copying-to-creating costs, must be protected by copyright, or else no one will take the time or trouble to produce them in the first place. . . . At best, however, this conclusion is a half truth. It is more accurate to say that information works—and for that matter, any nontrivial creative efforts—require the existence of an incentive for their creation. Whether the incentive necessarily must be copyright is a different matter. To make that determination, we must look at other types of incentives. . . .

We can find the typical incentives that face most information producers by asking what information producers need to overcome their fears of cheap copying. The general answer is not "copyright law," because that reflects too narrow a conception. The better answer is that would-be producers of information need *some assurance that copying will be limited*. The notion of "some assurance" rather than "complete assurance" reflects the fact that 100 percent assurance of anything—or zero risk—has never been a requirement of any business. Similarly, I use the deliberately vague notion of "limited" copying rather than "no copying" because the exact amount of copying that an information producer will tolerate will vary widely depending on the type of information being produced, the goals of the producer, and so on. . . .

Given, then, that producers of information products need some assurance that copying will be limited, the next question is how producers obtain that assurance. In other words, how do they "limit" copying? This question is best answered by looking at the aggregate combination of four factors: 1) entitlement-like protection; 2) contract-like protection; 3) state-of-the-art limitations; and 4) special-purpose technical limitations. Other factors also could be listed; I do not mean that these four are exclusive, but rather that they seem intuitively important enough to merit particular attention. In any event, nothing will be lost by a simplified analysis because my essential points do not depend on the exact number of factors.

. . . The first factor is "entitlement-like protection." By this I mean the wide recognition that informational products have an "owner" and that this owner has some "rights" that would be violated by unauthorized copying of the product. Such rights inhere in the product or the owner and are binding on the world in general; they are not a matter of contract. . . .

The second limitation on copying arises from contract. In contrast to the entitlement regime, a contract regime protects information only because two or more parties have agreed to treat the product as protected. Those who are not a party to any such contract are not bound by its terms. . . .

. . . This happens, for example, when users of an information service such as Lexis or Westlaw sign an access agreement. Much of the information on these services consists of public-domain material: cases and statutes. Without a contract limiting the practice, the user of such a service could copy and resell the material. Contracts with the services provide otherwise, of course, and these contracts are based not on any entitlement to the public-domain information, but rather on the consideration of allowing access to the service. . . .

After entitlements and contracts comes a third form of limitation on copying— the state-of-the-copying art. For any medium of expression, making a copy entails costs, yet obviously different media entail very different copying costs. Technological changes affect this cost. For example, if a manuscript must be written out by hand to make a copy, the cost of doing so—in time, money, and "trouble"— imposes a natural limit on how many copies one will make of the manuscript. Similarly, a glossy magazine like the *National Geographic* can be photocopied on a photocopier, but this fact seems almost irrelevant to the *National Geographic*'s plans for distribution. Readily accessible, inexpensive copy machines only produce black and white copies on poor quality paper. Photographs reproduce especially poorly. . . .

Finally, special-purpose technological restrictions can limit copying. A typical example of such self-help measures is the use by cable companies of signal "scrambling." For a home viewer to have access to certain channels, the viewer must pay the cable company for a piece of electronic equipment that will "descramble" the signal and render it viewable. This has nothing to do with the state-of-the-cable art: cable companies are able with present technology to send a signal down the cable wire for viewing. Rather, it is the result of individual effort by the information owner (or transmitter) to overcome what otherwise might be too little limitation from entitlement-like rules, unenforceable contracts, or a state-of-the-art that permits ready copying. . . .

It is helpful to think of this four-part "aggregate assurance" of limited copying in the form of a pie chart. One slice of the "pie" represents the limitations inhering in the "state-of-the-copying art," another represents "entitlement-like" protection, and so on. The overall size of the pie—the sum of all four factors—is what matters to information producers, because the overall size determines how limited the unauthorized copying of their product will be.

. . . The taxonomy implies that if one of the "slices" of the pie grows or shrinks, other slices must shrink or grow proportionally if the producer is to preserve the same overall assurance of limited copying. . . .

NOTES AND QUESTIONS

1. Professor Hardy's "slices of the pie" metaphor is one way to understand recent movements in copyright law. Another way to conceptualize these issues is to consider the slices of the pie as different kinds of "fences." As you learned in property law, a legal system for delineating and protecting property rights can be efficient. Without legal entitlements, individuals would spend considerable resources fencing in "their" property. Legal entitlements provide a certain level of protection, thereby reducing the need to build the most secure fence possible. Legal entitlements, however, are not perfect. People do disobey laws for a variety of reasons. Consider the kinds of copying that occur via the Internet. When copying becomes prevalent enough, a copyright owner may feel that she cannot rely solely on legal entitlements as her only fence and that other fences, such as technological and/ or contractual restrictions that make copying more difficult, are needed. Are there informal fences that can also serve to delineate property rights? Consider, for example, ethics that define appropriate behavior in a particular community (e.g., academic norms regarding plagiarism and citations). Do such social norms merely reinforce existing fences or constitute a separate fence altogether?

2. The pie to which Professor Hardy refers effectively provides authors with property rights to avoid the underproduction problem associated with public goods. Could Professor Hardy's pie ever result in creators receiving too many property rights? What would be the costs associated with such rights? According to Professor Julie Cohen, "Hardy's 'pie' is incomplete, in that it omits the slice consisting of 'no-protection,' or entitlements belonging to the public—a slice not currently conceived as 'property' in the same sense as the interest belonging to the copyright owner." Julie E. Cohen, Lochner *in Cyberspace: The New Economic Orthodoxy of "Rights Management,"* 97 Mich. L. Rev. 462, 510 (1998). Professor Cohen argues that the public's "slice" of the pie is essential to achieving copyright's goal of promoting "progress":

> . . . [T]he current market for creative and informational works generates at least two different kinds of ancillary social benefit. First, society . . . realizes benefits from the

content of certain works. Creative and informational works educate and inform the public, shape individual and community perceptions of the world, and set the parameters of public debate. . . . Second, social benefit accrues from the rights to access and use unprotected, public domain elements of existing works, and to re-use and transform existing works in certain settings and circumstances. These rights and practices lead to the development of creative and scholarly talents and, ultimately, to the creation of new works. . . .

. . . [B]oth types of uncompensated positive externality are woven into the fabric of the existing market for creative and informational works; they are the background conditions against which the market operates.

. . . Th[is] analysis suggests . . . that public access and use privileges do not in fact represent a tax on copyright owners to subsidize the reading public, as some copyright owners have claimed. If anything, they represent a tax on the reading public to subsidize the creative public, both present and future.

Id. at 547-49. Can you reconcile Professor Hardy's and Professor Cohen's views? Within Professor Hardy's model, is it possible to take into account the public's interests to which Professor Cohen refers? Would Professor Hardy object if a copyright owner could employ technological measures to make copying impossible? Would Professor Cohen?

3. It is important to view copyright as one of many options for providing incentives for creation and dissemination of new works. Can you think of other government incentives that would encourage individuals to create new works? Governments often use tax breaks and/or direct subsidies to encourage investment in activities they view as desirable. If the purpose behind copyright law is to promote progress in knowledge and learning, would tax breaks, subsidies, or other non-copyright incentives likely be sufficient to achieve that goal? As you go through this course, consider as well whether there are circumstances in which such incentives might be more efficient than copyright.

2. Authors' Rights

The utilitarian justification for copyright protection is not the only possible rationale for granting exclusive rights to authors of creative works. Some argue that such rights are morally required. The countries of Continental Europe generally subscribe to the notion that an author's natural right in her creation is the principal justification for copyright protection. For example, Professor Jane Ginsburg explains the French understanding of authors' rights as follows:

. . . [P]ost-revolutionary French laws and theorists portray the existence of an intimate and almost sacred bond between authors and their works as the source of a strong literary and artistic property right. Thus, France's leading modern exponent of copyright theory, the late Henri Desbois, grandly proclaimed: "The author is protected as an author, in his status as a creator, because a bond unites him to the object of his creation. In the French tradition, Parliament has repudiated the utilitarian concept of protecting works of authorship in order to stimulate literary and artistic activity."

Jane C. Ginsburg, *A Tale of Two Copyrights: Literary Property in Revolutionary France and America*, 64 Tul. L. Rev. 991, 992 (1990).

Other strands of Continental European thinking about copyright derive from the works of the philosophers Immanuel Kant and G. W. F. Hegel, who argued that literary works were external embodiments of authorial personality or will. Particularly under Hegelian thought, literary and artistic productions can be the subject of economic transactions, but the relationship between the author and the work remains specially deserving of protection. Professor Margaret Jane Radin supplies this explanation of a Hegelian approach in the context of tangible property:

> A person cannot be fully a person without a sense of continuity of self over time. To maintain that sense of continuity over time and to exercise one's liberty or autonomy, one must have an ongoing relationship with the external environment, consisting of both "things" and other people. . . . One's expectations crystallize around certain "things," the loss of which causes more disruption and disorientation than does a simple decrease in aggregate wealth. For example, if someone returns home to find her sofa has disappeared, that is more disorienting than to discover that her house has decreased in market value by 5%.

Margaret Jane Radin, *Property and Personhood*, 34 Stan. L. Rev. 957, 1004 (1982). According to Professor Radin, this view of the origin of property rights justifies stronger property rights in the objects that are most closely bound up with one's sense of personhood.

The European authors' rights approach to copyright includes a concept called moral rights that protects certain non-economic interests of authors. Authors have rights to prevent distortion, destruction, or even misattribution of a work. As we discuss later (in Chapter 8), despite global harmonization efforts, U.S. copyright law with its utilitarian underpinnings does not fully embrace protection for moral rights.

Even in the United States, one can detect in copyright law strands of the idea that authors have certain natural rights in their works. Unlike Continental Europe's conception of an almost sacred bond of personality between an author and her work, however, to the extent that American law incorporates a natural rights theory, it relies in large measure on premises derived from the writings of John Locke, particularly his *Two Treatises on Government*.

John Locke, *Two Treatises on Government*
Book II, ch. V (1690)

God, who hath given the World to Men in common, hath also given them reason to make use of it to the best advantage of Life, and convenience. . . . [Y]et being given for the use of Men, there must of necessity be a means *to appropriate* [the earth and its contents] some way or other before they can be of any use. . . .

Though the Earth, and all inferior Creatures be common to all Men, yet every Man has a *Property* in his own *Person*. This no Body has any Right to but himself. The *Labour* of his Body, and the *Work* of his Hands, we may say, are properly his. Whatsoever he then removes out of the State that Nature hath provided, and left it in, he hath mixed his *Labour* with, and joyned to it something that is his own, and thereby makes it his *Property*. . . . [I]t hath by this *labour* something annexed to it, that excludes the common right of other Men. For this *Labour* being the unquestionable Property of the Labourer, no Man but he can have a right to what that is once joyned to, at least where there is enough, and as good left in common for others.

He that is nourished by the Acorns he pickt up under an Oak, or the Apples he gathered from the Trees in the Wood, has certainly appropriated them to himself. . . . I ask then, When did they begin to be his? . . . And 'tis plain, if the first gathering made them not his, nothing else could. That *labour* put a distinction between them and common. . . . And will any one say he had no right to those Acorns or Apples he thus appropriated, because he had not the consent of all Mankind to make them his? Was it a Robbery thus to assume to himself what belonged to all in Common? If such a consent as that was necessary, Man had starved, notwithstanding the Plenty God had given him. . . .

It will perhaps be objected to this, That if gathering the Acorns, or other Fruits of the Earth, &c. makes a right to them, then any one may *ingross* as much as he will. To which I Answer, Not so. The same Law of Nature, that does by this means give us Property, does also *bound* that *Property* too. . . . As much as any one can make use of to any advantage of life before it spoils; so much he may by his labour fix a Property in. Whatever is beyond this, is more than his share, and belongs to others. Nothing was made by God for Man to spoil or destroy. . . .

Professor Wendy Gordon supplies this explanation of how Locke's arguments translate into our time and, specifically, to the intellectual property context:

> Locke's property theory has many strands, some of which are overtly utilitarian and others of which draw on varying notions of desert. To the extent that his theory purports to state a nonconsequentialist natural right in property, it is most firmly based on the most fundamental law of nature, the "no-harm principle." The essential logic is simple: Labor is mine and when I appropriate objects from the common I join my labor to them. If you take the objects I have gathered you have also taken my labor, since I have attached my labor to the objects in question. This harms me, and you should not harm me. You therefore have a duty to leave these objects alone. Therefore I have property in the objects.
>
> Similarly, if I use the public domain to create a new intangible work of authorship or invention, you should not harm me by copying it and interfering with my plans for it. I therefore have property in the intangible as well. . . .

Wendy J. Gordon, *A Property Right in Self-Expression: Equality and Individualism in the Natural Law of Intellectual Property*, 102 Yale L.J. 1533, 1544-45 (1993).

NOTES AND QUESTIONS

1. How might the difference between tangible objects and intangible "labors of the mind" affect the types of rights that society should grant to a "laborer"? In general, copyright law does not ask how hard someone worked in creating a particular work and then assign rights commensurate with that effort. In fact, some creative works that are afforded copyright protection are the result of mere fortuity. *See, e.g., Time, Inc. v. Bernard Geis Assocs.*, 293 F. Supp. 130 (S.D.N.Y. 1968) (acknowledging copyright protection for a home movie of the presidential motorcade during which JFK was shot). Other works are not granted protection despite painstaking effort exerted in their creation. *See, e.g., Hearn v. Meyer*, 664 F. Supp. 832 (S.D.N.Y. 1987) (refusing to recognize copyright protection in reproduction of public domain art prints completed through an exacting and time-consuming process). Is this consistent with Lockean labor theory? Is it more consistent with the utilitarian justification for copyright?

2. As you have learned, under an authors' rights approach to copyright, rights in literary and artistic production exist not because of the labor that has been invested, but instead because of the close relationship between the work and authorial personality or will. Does the authors' rights approach supply a more plausible justification for copyright in works of authorship than the Lockean labor theory approach? Why, or why not?

3. In the United States, the utilitarian justification for copyright protection predominates. There are, however, pronounced strains of authors' rights reasoning in U.S. copyright law as well. As you read the material in this book, consider how differences in theoretical justifications might influence matters such as the scope of copyright, its duration, and the use of limiting doctrines.

3. A Robust Public Domain

The existence of the public domain is a foundational principle of the U.S. copyright system. Unfortunately, the term "public domain" is not amenable to a simple definition. Certainly, it includes works for which copyright protection has expired. Recall that the Intellectual Property Clause expressly states that rights may be granted to authors only for "limited Times." Passage into the public domain is thus mandated by the Constitution itself. But what else does the public domain include, and what purposes does it serve?

Jessica Litman, The Public Domain
39 Emory L.J. 965, 965-67, 975-77 (1990)

Our copyright law is based on the charming notion that authors create something from nothing, that works owe their origin to the authors who produce them. Arguments for strengthening copyright protection, whether predicated on a theory of moral deserts or expressed in terms of economic incentives, often begin with the premise that copyright should adjust the balance between the creative individuals who bring new works into being and the greedy public who would steal the fruits of their genius.

The process of authorship, however, is more equivocal than that romantic model admits. To say that every new work is in some sense based on the works that preceded it is such a truism that it has long been a cliché, invoked but not examined. But the very act of authorship in *any* medium is more akin to translation and recombination than it is to creating Aphrodite from the foam of the sea. Composers recombine sounds they have heard before; playwrights base their characters on bits and pieces drawn from real human beings and other playwrights' characters; novelists draw their plots from lives and other plots within their experience; software writers use the logic they find in other software; lawyers transform old arguments to fit new facts; cinematographers, actors, choreographers, architects, and sculptors all engage in the process of adapting, transforming, and recombining what is already "out there" in some other form. This is not parasitism: it is the essence of authorship. . . .

The lay understanding of the public domain in the copyright context is that it contains works free from copyright. Works created before the enactment of copyright statutes, such as Shakespeare's *Macbeth* or Pach[el]bel's *Canon*, are available for fourth grade classes across the nation to use for school assemblies without permission from any publisher or payment of any royalties. Another class of old works in the public domain are works once subject to copyright, but created so long ago that the copyright has since expired, such as Mark Twain's *Huckleberry Finn*. . . .

But the class of works not subject to copyright is, in some senses, the least significant portion of the public domain. The most important part of the public domain is a part we usually speak of only obliquely: the realm comprising aspects of copyrighted works that copyright does not protect. Judge Learned Hand discussed this facet of the public domain in connection with an infringement suit involving a play entitled *Abie's Irish Rose*:

> We assume that the plaintiff's play is altogether original, even to an extent that in fact it is hard to believe. We assume further that, so far as it has been anticipated by earlier plays of which she knew nothing, that fact is immaterial. Still, as we have already said, her copyright did not cover everything that might be drawn from her play; its content went to some extent into the public domain.

The concept that portions of works protected by copyright are owned by no one and are available for any member of the public to use is such a fundamental one that it receives attention only when something seems to have gone awry. Although the public domain is implicit in all commentary on intellectual property, it rarely takes center stage. Most of the writing on the public domain focuses on other issues: Should the duration of copyright be extended? Should we recognize new species of intellectual property rights? Should federal intellectual property law cut a broad preemptive swathe or a narrow one? Copyright commentary emphasizes that which is protected more than it discusses that which is not. But a vigorous public domain is a crucial buttress to the copyright system; without the public domain, it might be impossible to tolerate copyright at all. . . .

NOTES AND QUESTIONS

1. What do you think Professor Litman means by "aspects of copyrighted works that copyright does not protect"? Remember the idea/expression distinction that we mentioned at the outset of this chapter. The ideas contained in a work are not protected by copyright, but their expression is. Ideas, then, are among the "aspects of copyrighted works that copyright does not protect." Why shouldn't copyright law protect ideas? We return to this question, and also consider other unprotected aspects of copyrighted works, in Chapter 2.

2. Is Professor Litman's account of the public domain consistent with the utilitarian theory of protection as articulated by Professor Hardy? By Professor Cohen?

3. In what ways is the importance of a rich public domain consistent with Lockean labor theory justifications for copyright law? According to Professor Gordon:

> [R]ecall how the laborer's claim to deserve property is itself justified. . . . [T]he same no-harm principle dictates that the laborer should not do harm to other peoples' claim to the common. When the two conflict, the common must prevail. . . .
>
> Thus no natural right to property could exist where a laborer's claims would conflict with the public's claim in the common. . . . Locke's own resolution is to declare the conditions under which a natural right to property *is* justified: if there is "enough, and as good left in common for others" after the appropriator has taken up his share, then no one has grounds for complaint. . . .

Wendy J. Gordon, *A Property Right in Self-Expression: Equality and Individualism in the Natural Law of Intellectual Property*, 102 Yale L.J. 1533, 1561-62 (1993). In this excerpt Professor Gordon highlights what is sometimes referred to as Locke's proviso: Property rights are only appropriate when there is enough left in common for others. Does the authors' rights theory discussed by Professor Ginsburg yield a similar conclusion?

4. An Uncensored Marketplace of Ideas

Those who emphasize the importance of the public domain in copyright law seek to understand copyright in the context of the creative practices that occur within society. A different approach to the social context of copyright law views copyright as effectuating purposes more commonly associated with the modern First Amendment. This approach draws on the fact that the constitutional grant of authority to enact copyright protection is the only part of the original Constitution to address the issue of freedom of expression. Remember, the Bill of Rights, including the First Amendment, came later.

Professor Neil Netanel argues that copyright is best understood as a system intended to support our democratic civil society. *See* Neil Weinstock Netanel, *Copyright and a Democratic Civil Society*, 106 Yale L.J. 283 (1996).[1] He argues that copyright fulfills both a "production function" and a "structural function" that

1. Excerpts reprinted by permission of the author and of The Yale Law Journal and William S. Hein Company from The Yale Law Journal, Vol. 106, pages 347, 350, 353, 356-58, 360-61.

together create a marketplace characterized by a diversity of expression. Such diversity supports and, indeed, is a necessary condition of, a democratic regime.

According to Professor Netanel, copyright law's production function "encourages creative expression on a wide array of political, social, and aesthetic issues. The activity of creating and communicating such expression and the expression itself constitute vital components of a democratic civil society." *Id.* at 347. He stresses that by encouraging production and dissemination of works, copyright law helps to ensure that the body politic has the information it needs to participate in democratic processes. His reasoning applies not only to factual works but also to creative ones, on the ground that "[m]any creative works have broad political and social implications even if they do not appear or even seek to convey an explicit ideological message." *Id.* at 350.

In Professor Netanel's model, copyright law also performs a structural function by encouraging the creation of copyright industries that are independent of government control:

> Prior to the first modern copyright statutes in the eighteenth century, writers and artists were heavily dependent on royal, feudal, and church patronage for their livelihoods. This dependency undermined expressive autonomy and thwarted the development of a vital, freethinking intelligentsia. . . .
>
> When the Framers drafted the Copyright Clause and the Copyright Act of 1790, they took as self-evident that the diffusion of knowledge and exchange of view through a market for printed matter was a pillar of public liberty. . . .
>
> Part and parcel of this vision was an understanding that democratic governance requires not simply the diffusion of knowledge per se, but also an autonomous sphere of print-mediated citizen deliberation and public education. . . . It was only by maintaining their fiscal independence that authors and publishers could continue to guard public liberty. . . .

Id. at 353, 356-58.

NOTES AND QUESTIONS

1. Do you read Professor Netanel to be arguing that the Framers originally conceived copyright as a means for social engineering or that the modern state should use copyright that way to effectuate the Framers' more general purpose? Do you agree with either argument?

2. Do modern government grant programs that subsidize the production of creative works pose structural risks to freedom of expression similar to those identified by Professor Netanel? Does public university funding of various creative endeavors pose such risks?

Some countries have dedicated tax revenue to support their film industries. For example, Canada has the Canada Feature Film Fund, administered by Telefilm Canada, which provides assistance for screenwriting, production, marketing, and promotion of feature films. Do you think national film industry subsidies threaten or encourage expressive freedoms?

3. Professor Netanel makes the following observations regarding the private-sector copyright industries:

> Our public discourse is far more dissonant and eclectic than that envisioned by the Framers. The political elite of the early Republic abhorred expressions of ideological faction and generally disdained fiction and "light" entertainment. Such works, however, form a major part of our copyright-supported discursive universe. From our perspective, the Framers' watchdog view of literature and the press also seems somewhat simplistic. Today's media conglomerates have attained an agenda-setting power that rivals that of state officials and, in the view of some commentators, undermines the democratic character of public discourse by skewing it towards those with the financial wherewithal to obtain access or buy advertised products.

Netanel, *supra* at 358. He concludes that, on balance, the copyright market continues to function as the Framers envisioned:

> But the copyright market also contains room for highly innovative and provocative expression, as well as that targeted for specialized or minority audiences. Significantly, copyright's fundamental capacity to support expressive diversity will likely grow dramatically in the digital age. The ease and low cost of digital production and dissemination has the potential of enabling authors, for the first time, to communicate directly with audiences throughout the world. As a result, many authors will be able to bypass media conglomerates, creating a copyright market characterized by an even greater multiplicity of view.

Id. at 360-61. As you continue through the book, consider whether you agree. Consider also what effects different copyright doctrines have on expressive freedoms.

5. A Theory of Users' Rights?

Within the traditional framework of copyright regulation, the law is addressed either to authors on whom the law confers protection or to users whose activities the law purports to constrain. In today's networked information economy, the central role of users in the production and exchange of creative materials has given rise to a nascent theory of users' rights as an important justification for copyright law. Professor Jessica Litman observes:

> We sometimes talk and write about copyright law as if encouraging the creation and dissemination of works of authorship were the ultimate goal, with nothing further required to "promote the Progress of Science." We have focused so narrowly on the production half of the copyright equation that we have seemed to think that the Progress of Science is nothing more than a giant warehouse filled with works of authorship. When we do this, we miss, or forget, an essential step. In order for the creation and dissemination of a work of authorship to mean anything at all, someone needs to read the book, view the art, hear the music, watch the film, listen to the CD, run the computer program, and build and inhabit the architecture. . . .

Copyright law is intended to create a legal ecology that encourages the creation and dissemination of works of authorship, and thereby "promote the Progress of Science." . . . [L]aws that discourage book reading end up being bad for book authors. Thus, it isn't difficult to frame an argument that copyright law cannot properly encourage authors to create new works if it imposes undue burdens on readers. . . . [C]opyright law encourages authorship at least as much for the benefit of the people who will read, view, listen to, and experience the works that authors create, as for the advantage of those authors and their distributors.

Jessica Litman, *Lawful Personal Use*, 85 Tex. L. Rev. 1871, 1879-82 (2007).

Other scholars have argued for a more accurate representation of users and their interests in copyright law. According to Professor Julie Cohen, "users play two important roles within the copyright system: Users receive copyrighted works, and (some) users become authors. Both roles further the copyright system's larger project to promote the progress of knowledge." Julie E. Cohen, *The Place of the User in Copyright Law*, 74 Fordham L. Rev. 347, 348 (2007). Professor Cohen identifies three models of the user in copyright jurisprudence and in the academic literature:

[T]he economic user, who enters the market with a given set of tastes in search of the best deal; the "postmodern" user, who exercises limited and vaguely oppositional agency in a world in which all meaning is uncertain and all knowledge relative; and the romantic user, whose life is an endless cycle of sophisticated debates about current events, discerning quests for the most freedom-enhancing media technologies, and home production of high-quality music, movies, and open-source software.

Id.

Characterizing these models of the user as artificial, she advances a fourth model, the "situated user," who "deserves copyright law's solicitude precisely because neither her tastes nor her talents are . . . well formed." *Id*. at 349. According to Professor Cohen:

[T]his imperfect being requires our attention because she must nevertheless become the vehicle by and through which copyright's collective project is advanced. The situated user engages cultural goods and artifacts found within the context of her culture through a variety of activities, ranging from consumption to creative play. The cumulative effect of these activities, and the unexpected cultural juxtapositions and interconnections that they both exploit and produce, yield what the copyright system names, and prizes, as "progress." This model of the situated user suggests that the success of a system of copyright depends on both the extent to which its rules permit individuals to engage in creative play and the extent to which they enable contextual play, or degrees of freedom, within the system of culture more generally. . . . [For the situated user, b]oth her patterns of consumption and the extent and direction of her own authorship will be shaped and continually reshaped by the artifacts, conventions and institutions that make up her cultural environment. . . .

Id. She argues that "[s]cholars and policymakers should ask how much latitude the situated user needs to perform her functions most effectively, and how the current entitlement structure of copyright law might change to accommodate that need." *Id*. at 374.

Other scholars, however, assert that users exert powerful influence on accepted practice with respect to copyrighted works. According to Professor Edward Lee:

> The most significant copyright development of the twenty-first century has not arisen through any law enacted by Congress or opinion rendered by the Supreme Court. Nor has it come from an organized group, movement, or industry seeking to effectuate a change to the copyright system. Instead, it has come from the unorganized, informal practices of various, unrelated users of copyrighted works, many of whom probably know next to nothing about copyright law. . . .
>
> . . . Whether in blogs, fan fiction, videos, music, or other mashups, many users freely use the copyrighted works of others without prior permission and even beyond our conventional understandings of fair use. Yet, often, as in the case of noncommercial uses of copyrighted works on blogs or in fan fiction, the copyright holders do not seem to care, and, in some cases, publicly condone the general practice. Moreover, the mass practices of many users of popular Web 2.0[*] sites, like YouTube, of ignoring the need to obtain permission before using someone else's copyrighted work have even prompted the securing of commercial licenses between Web 2.0 sites and the copyright holders in order to ratify the mass practices of users. Thus, instead of being condemned as infringement, the unauthorized mass practices of users may have, in some instances, turned out to be the catalyst for subsequent ratification of those practices, albeit in some bargained-for exchange not even involving the users themselves.
>
> Put simply, copyright law as we know it "on the books" is not exactly how copyright law operates in practice. Instead of being defined a priori by statute or at a single snapshot in time, the contours of an author's exclusive rights in the Web 2.0 world are being defined by a much messier and more complex process involving a loose, unorganized "give and take" of sorts among users, copyright holders, and intermediaries. . . .

Edward Lee, *Warming Up to User-Generated Content*, 2008 U. Ill. L. Rev. 1459, 1460-62.

NOTES AND QUESTIONS

1. Is developing a theory of users' rights a credible constitutional exercise? To the modern eye, the Intellectual Property Clause makes no mention of users at all, yet among the eighteenth-century meanings of the word "progress" was dissemination. *See* Malla Pollack, *What Is Congress Supposed to Promote? Defining "Progress" in Article I, Section 8, Clause 8 of the U.S. Constitution, or Introducing the Progress Clause*, 80 Neb. L. Rev. 754 (2002).

2. Can users' rights be conceptualized using other theories of copyright discussed in this section? Can you articulate a theory of users' rights using the tools of economic analysis, the Lockean proviso, or Professor Netanel's argument about the role of copyright in a democratic civil society? Should a theory of the user inform the

---

[*] "Web 2.0" is a term that was used to refer to the movement from the original static manner in which users viewed websites (Web 1.0) to platforms that allow users to engage more interactively with content and with other users.—Eds.

rights that copyright confers on authors, or should it merely inform defenses to claims of copyright infringement?

3. What do you make of the four models of the copyright user outlined by Professor Cohen? Into which model do you fit?

4. Is the difference between Professor Lee and Professor Cohen simply one of form? If users have as much freedom within the interstices of copyright law as Professor Lee argues, is a theory of users' rights needed?

6. What Progress, and Whose Welfare?

Although the authors quoted above offer different views about exactly how copyright law should be structured, all would agree that copyright law is intended to promote the general public welfare. But is copyright law *necessary* to promote general welfare? "Public welfare" is a slippery concept, and particularly so when one adopts a global perspective. As the following excerpt explores, western-style copyright systems do not fully account for some other cultures' understandings of what "progress" and "welfare" mean.

≣   *William P. Alford, To Steal a Book Is an Elegant Offense*
≣   *28-29 (1995)*

[Professor Alford describes the cultural acceptance of copying in China prior to the imposition of western notions of intellectual property protection in the late nineteenth and early twentieth centuries. Chinese culture develops with significant reference to the past. The importance of this interaction with the past for further cultural development makes copying of earlier works a culturally valuable activity.]

. . . Nor, as was often the case in the West, was such use accepted grudgingly and then only because it served as a vehicle through which apprentices and students developed their technical expertise, demonstrated erudition, or even endorsed particular values, although each of these phenomena also existed in imperial China. On the contrary, in the Chinese context, such use was at once both more affirmative and more essential. It evidenced the user's comprehension of and devotion to the core of civilization itself, while offering individuals the possibility of demonstrating originality within the context of those forms and so distinguishing their present from the past.

In view of the foregoing, there was what Wen Fong has termed a "general attitude of tolerance, or indeed receptivity, shown on the part of the great Chinese painters towards the forging of their own works." Such copying, in effect, bore witness to the quality of the work copied and to its creator's degree of understanding and civility. Thus Shen Zhou (1427-1509) is reported to have responded to the suggestions that he put a stop to the forging of his work by remarking, in comments that were not considered exceptional, "if my poems and painting, which are only small efforts to me, should prove to be of some aid to the forgers, what is there for me to grudge about?" Much the same might be said of literature, where the

Confucian disdain for commerce fostered an ideal, even if not always realized in practice, that true scholars wrote for edification and moral renewal rather than profit. Or, as it was expressed so compactly in a famed Chinese aphorism, "Genuine scholars let the later world discover their work [rather than promulgate and profit from it themselves]."

NOTES AND QUESTIONS

1. As the excerpt from Professor Alford's book demonstrates, perspectives on the legitimacy and social value of copying others' creations can vary significantly. During the many centuries in which China fully ascribed to the views described by Professor Alford, Chinese civilization produced a rich bounty of scientific, technical, and artistic creations. Can that reality be squared with the utilitarian justification for copyright protection? Can it be squared with justifications for copyright protection based on authors' rights? What does this suggest about the adequacy of those justifications?

2. To what extent should copyright law reflect or accommodate different cultural conceptions regarding the value of creativity and copying? Should differences in cultures affect the scope of protection afforded authors?

3. Article 27(2) of the Universal Declaration of Human Rights ("UDHR") (1948) recognizes the right of an individual to the "protection of the moral and material interests resulting from any scientific, literary or artistic production of which he is the author." Article 27(1), however, provides that "[e]veryone has the right freely to participate in the cultural life of the community, to enjoy the arts and to share in scientific advancement and its benefits." UDHR art. 27. If copyright protection and cultural participation are both considered human rights, how should copyright law respond? Is a human rights perspective consistent with the utilitarian justification for copyright? For analysis of the implications flowing from a human rights conception of intellectual property, see Laurence R. Helfer, *Towards a Human Rights Framework for Intellectual Property*, 40 U.C. Davis L. Rev. 971 (2007). For an argument that human rights norms are implicit in the design of intellectual property laws, see Ruth L. Okediji, *Securing Intellectual Property Objectives: New Approaches to Human Rights Considerations*, in Casting the Net Wider: Human Rights, Development and New Duty-Bearers (Margot E. Salomon, Arne Tostensen, & Wouter Vandenhole eds., 2007).

PRACTICE EXERCISES

Consider how copyright law should resolve the following situations. How much does the underlying policy rationale that you emphasize influence your desired outcome?

a. A researcher combs through libraries and archives, conducts a number of interviews, and develops a new theory about the death of the infamous criminal John Dillinger. In a series of books, he contends that the FBI did not kill Dillinger in 1934. Instead, Dillinger escaped and retired to the West Coast where he lived until at least 1979. A network television station produces an episode of a popular detective series set in California, in which the protagonists investigate the possibility that Dillinger is still alive. The TV show cites some of the evidence the researcher used to support his theory. The researcher sues for copyright infringement.

b. Alice Randall writes a book, *The Wind Done Gone*, that retells the story of Margaret Mitchell's classic novel, *Gone With the Wind*, from the perspective of Scarlett O'Hara's black half-sister, who is a slave on the family plantation. Mitchell's estate sues to block publication of the book.

c. A teenager creates a video of himself lip-synching to Beyoncé's hit song "Crazy in Love" and posts the video on YouTube. The copyright owner of the song requests YouTube remove the video.

d. Jimmy Fallon, host of *The Tonight Show*, takes clips of Brian Williams broadcasting the NBC Nightly News, and sets them to the tune of "Rapper's Delight," a hip hop song. The owner of the copyright in "Rapper's Delight" sues *The Tonight Show*.

e. A company partners with a number of leading libraries to create a fully searchable database of all the books in their collections. Entire books are scanned into the database, and the search engine allows full-text searches and full-text search returns. Publishers that do not want their books included can opt out. The company informs users of where they may purchase or borrow the books. The publishers sue the search engine.

f. A carpet manufacturer reproduces traditional designs originating from an indigenous people. The carpet manufacturer copied the designs directly from paintings created by living artists of native descent without permission from anyone. The designs in the paintings are sacred images that date back many centuries. In the culture of these indigenous people, only certain individuals who know and adhere to traditional laws and rituals are permitted to reproduce ancestral images. The carpets are mass produced and sold in the country now encompassing the lands of the indigenous people as well as in other countries. One of the living artists sues the carpet manufacturer.

B. THE HISTORY OF U.S. COPYRIGHT LAW

The basic copyright framework devised over 200 years ago has weathered dramatic changes in the means of producing and distributing creative works. This section reviews the history of copyright law in the context of these changes.

1. From Censorship to Markets

The history of copyright law in the United States begins, not surprisingly, in England. What *is* surprising to many students of copyright law is that the first real copyright statutes were tools for government censorship and press control. Copyright did not become a tool for promoting knowledge and learning until later.

In the years before the printing press, reproducing a work involved the laborious task of hand copying. This fact, along with an extremely low literacy rate, made legal regulation of unauthorized copying practically unnecessary. When William Caxton introduced the printing press in England in 1476, the economics of copying changed drastically. Booksellers felt this advance to be a mixed blessing. The printing press reduced both the time it took to bring a book to market and the cost to print copies. If a book was popular, however, other printers could quickly copy it.

The English booksellers and others in related trades had been organized as a guild prior to the introduction of the printing press, but guild rules could not be invoked to prevent copying by nonmembers. The threat of encroachment by outsiders caused the guild to seek ways of making its system of private law enforceable against nonmembers as well. Printing patents, granted by the sovereign at his royal prerogative, offered one such method of enforcement, but their availability was limited. Therefore, the printers also sought a more robust governing body in the form of the royally chartered Stationers' Company, created in 1557. The booksellers' desires for greater enforcement ability coincided with the Crown's desire to gain control over the dangerous possibilities of the printed word and to prevent the publication of "seditious and heretical material." Lyman Ray Patterson, Copyright in Historical Perspective 20-29 (1968). The 1557 charter reserved the printing of most works to members of the Stationers' Company and granted the company the right to search out and destroy unlawfully printed books. In the sixteenth and seventeenth centuries, several Star Chamber decrees and the Licensing Act of 1662 continued the regime of press control using the members of the Stationers' Company as enforcers. By agreeing to assist in the censorship desired by the Crown, the members of the Company obtained a mechanism for preventing nonmembers from publishing works owned by members.

The system of copyright protection for members of the Stationers' Company was designed to benefit the publishers and the Crown, not authors, and became widely criticized. In a now-famous passage, author John Milton wrote in protest that ideas were not "a staple commodity . . . to [be] mark[ed] and license[d] like our broadcloth and our woolpacks." John Milton, Areopagitica: A Speech for the Liberty of Unlicensed Printing 29 (1644) (H.B. Cotterill ed. 1959). After the Glorious Revolution of 1688, the royal licensing laws were allowed to lapse. In 1695, the last of the legally sanctioned censorship acts ended and the Stationers were unsuccessful in convincing Parliament to reinstate their control.

After their defeat in Parliament, the publishers changed their tactics and sought to obtain legal protection for writings on behalf of authors—who, of course, would have to assign their rights to the publishers in order to be paid. In 1710, Parliament enacted the Statute of Anne, which granted an assignable right to authors to control the publication of their writings. The new copyright act was fundamentally different from the previous proclamations and licensing laws in two important ways. Instead of a tool of censorship, the Statute of Anne was expressly meant to be, as its title stated, "[a]n act for the encouragement of learning."[1] Additionally, the Statute of

---

1. The statute's preamble stated:

> WHEREAS Printers, Booksellers, and other Persons have of late frequently taken the Liberty of printing, reprinting and publishing, or causing to be printed, reprinted and published, Books and other Writings, without the Consent of the Authors or Proprietors

Anne granted rights of limited duration (two 14-year terms), whereas previously the Stationers' right had endured in perpetuity.

Of course, a copyright of limited duration does not hold the same profit potential for authors and publishers as one that extends in perpetuity. Before the English courts, the publishers sought ways to obtain a copyright of longer duration than the statute provided. For a number of years, they were successful in persuading the courts that they also had a common law copyright, separate from the statutory copyright, that lasted forever. However, in the case of *Donaldson v. Becket*, 98 Eng. Rep. 257 (H.L. 1774), the House of Lords rejected perpetual copyright. *Donaldson* established beyond a doubt that copyrights in published works were subject to the durational limits of the Statute of Anne.

For a detailed account of the historical development of copyright law, see Patterson, *supra*. *See also* Ronan Deazley, On the Origin of the Right to Copy (2004); Tomás Gómez-Arostegui, *Copyright at Common Law in 1774*, 47 Conn. L. Rev. 1 (2014) (discussing the *Donaldson* case).

2. "Progress," Incentives, and Access

England had taken centuries to arrive at a copyright law that embodied a public purpose and reduced the threat that copyright could be used as a tool for government censorship. That history was not lost on the Framers of the Constitution, who expressly incorporated the requirement that copyright must serve a public purpose in the wording of the Intellectual Property Clause: "The Congress shall have Power . . . *To promote the Progress of Science and useful Arts*, by securing for limited Times to Authors and Inventors the exclusive Right to their respective Writings and Discoveries." U.S. Const., Art. I, §8, cl. 8 (emphasis added).[2] The Constitution, like the Statute of Anne, also makes explicit the guarantee of a public domain; the "exclusive Right" granted to authors may only be for "limited Times."

> **KEEP IN MIND**
>
> Note that under principles of parallel construction, the exclusive rights granted to "Authors" in their "Writings" are to "promote the Progress of Science." At the time of the Constitution's adoption, the word "Science" had a different meaning than it does today. Today, "Science" conjures up images of laboratories, test tubes, and microscopes. Then, "Science" broadly connoted knowledge and learning.

In 1790, the first Congress embraced the idea of copyright having an educational purpose, entitling the first copyright law "An act for the encouragement of learning" and providing for two 14-year terms of protection. Act of 1790, 1st

---

of such Books and Writings, to their very great Detriment, and too often to the Ruin of them and their Families: For preventing therefore such Practices for the future, and for the Encouragement of learned Men to compose and write useful Books [this statute is therefore enacted].

Statute of Anne, 8 Anne, c. 19 (1710).

2. Before the adoption of the Constitution, each of the original 13 states except Delaware enacted its own copyright statute. Many followed the example of the Statute of Anne, and many began with a preamble that stated the public purposes that the grant of copyright was intended to serve.

Cong., 2d Sess., ch. 15, 1 Stat. 124 (1790). To receive this Act's protection, an author had to comply with various formalities, including registration of title, publication of the registration in a local newspaper, and deposit of a copy of the work with the secretary of state within six months of publication.

The deposit requirement effectively meant that the federal government came into possession of a great store of knowledge. In 1800, Congress passed legislation authorizing the establishment of a library for its own use. This institution evolved into the Library of Congress, which today is the de facto national library of the United States. Beginning in 1846, the Library became the repository for copies of works deposited under the Copyright Act. The Copyright Act of 1870 centralized all registration and deposit activities in the Library of Congress. Finally, in 1897, Congress established the Copyright Office as a department of the Library of Congress and created the position of Register of Copyrights to oversee the administration of the copyright system.

In the United States, as in England's *Donaldson* case, litigants presented arguments to courts claiming the existence of a perpetual, common law copyright. In the famous case of *Wheaton v. Peters*, 33 U.S. (8 Pet.) 591 (1834), the Supreme Court addressed the question of copyright protection for reports of the Court's opinions. The Court recognized that the opinions themselves could not be copyrighted, but other material added by the Court's reporter, such as summaries of the parties' arguments, was eligible for protection. However, the reporter had failed to comply with the statutory formalities required for protection. Thus, if there were to be any copyright protection for the reporter's material, it would have to arise outside the bounds of the federal statute. As in *Donaldson v. Beckett*, the plaintiff asserted common law copyright protection; as in *Donaldson*, the high court rejected it:

> That an author, at common law, has a property in his manuscript, and may obtain redress against any one who deprives him of it, or by improperly obtaining a copy endeavours to realise a profit by its publication, cannot be doubted; but this is a very different right from that which asserts a perpetual and exclusive property in the future publication of the work, after the author shall have published it to the world.
>
> The argument that a literary man is as much entitled to the product of his labour as any other member of society, cannot be controverted. And the answer is, that he realises this product by the transfer of his manuscripts, or in the sale of his works, when first published. . . .
>
> In what respect does the right of an author differ from that of an individual who has invented a most useful and valuable machine? In the production of this, his mind has been as intensely engaged, as long; and, perhaps, as usefully to the public, as any distinguished author in the composition of his book.
>
> The result of their labours may be equally beneficial to society, and in their respective spheres they may be alike distinguished for mental vigour. Does the common law give a perpetual right to the author, and withhold it from the inventor? And yet it has never been pretended that the latter could hold, by the common law, any property in his invention, after he shall have sold it publicly. . . .
>
> That every man is entitled to the fruits of his own labour must be admitted; but he can enjoy them only, except by statutory provision, under the rules of property, which regulate society, and which define the rights of things in general.

Id. at 657-58.

The *Wheaton* Court's rejection of any kind of common law copyright in published works effectively meant that copyright in such works would be governed exclusively by the federal statute adopted by Congress. That is the rule today. As you will see later, Congress has extended the exclusive scheme of federal protection to unpublished works as well.

Court opinions from the nineteenth century also recognized that not every piece of written expression is subject to copyright protection. As already noted, the *Wheaton* Court observed that the opinions of the Court could not be copyrighted but were part of the public domain—free for anyone to copy. Several years later, in *Emerson v. Davies*, 8 F. Cas. 615 (1845), Justice Story reasoned that the nature of authorship requires some freedom to build on certain aspects of past works:

> In truth, in literature, in science and in art, there are, and can be, few, if any, things, which, in an abstract sense, are strictly new and original throughout. Every book in literature, science and art, borrows, and must necessarily borrow, and use much which was well known and used before. No man creates a new language for himself, at least if he be a wise man, in writing a book. He contents himself with the use of language already known and used and understood by others. No man writes exclusively from his own thoughts, unaided and uninstructed by the thoughts of others. The thoughts of every man are, more or less, a combination of what other men have thought and expressed, although they may be modified, exalted, or improved by his own genius or reflection. If no book could be the subject of copy-right which was not new and original in the elements of which it is composed, there could be no ground for any copy-right in modern times, and we should be obliged to ascend very high, even in antiquity, to find a work entitled to such eminence. Virgil borrowed much from Homer; Bacon drew from earlier as well as contemporary minds; Coke exhausted all the known learning of his profession; and even Shakespeare and Milton, so justly and proudly our boast as the brightest originals would be found to have gathered much from the abundant stores of current knowledge and classical studies in their days.

Id. at 619.

Courts further reasoned that the same policies required some leeway to use copyrighted material produced by others. Four years prior to his opinion in *Emerson*, in the case of *Folsom v. Marsh*, 9 F. Cas. 342 (1841), Justice Story expressly recognized that using selections from a preexisting work "fairly" did not constitute an infringement of copyright. That recognition marked the beginning of the venerable fair use doctrine in U.S. copyright law.

By the end of the nineteenth century, copyright protection was firmly established in U.S. law as a means of encouraging progress in knowledge and learning. The protection afforded by copyright law was subject to important limits, and those limits were also seen as necessary for encouraging the creation of new works. The rapid technological changes that began at the start of the twentieth century, however, posed difficult challenges for the basic copyright framework.

3. Copyright Law and Technological Change

The copyright system established by the First Congress has expanded considerably beyond its original bounds. As new forms of creative expression have developed, Congress has extended copyright protection accordingly. The current Copyright Act thus covers a much greater variety of creative output than the original Act of 1790. And as new technologies have emerged for disseminating creative products, Congress has revised the protections afforded by copyright law to reach these new distribution and communication media.

a. New Methods of Creating New Works

The first Copyright Act, enacted in 1790, extended copyright protection to authors of maps, charts, and books. Over the next century, Congress gradually expanded the list to include engravings, etchings, and prints (1802); musical compositions (1831); dramatic compositions (1856); photographs and negatives (1865); and paintings, drawings, chromolithographs, statuary, and "models or designs intended to be perfected as works of the fine arts" (1870).

As this brief history illustrates, continuing change in the prevailing methods of producing creative works required numerous amendments to keep the list of protected works current. This legislative practice continued in the 1909 overhaul of the Copyright Act, which stated that copyrightable works included "all the writings of an author," but then proceeded to list the following as classes of works protected by copyright:

(a) Books, including composite and cyclopaedic works, directories, gazetteers, and other compilations;
(b) Periodicals, including newspapers;
(c) Lectures, sermons, addresses, prepared for oral delivery;
(d) Dramatic or dramatico-musical compositions;
(e) Musical compositions;
(f) Maps;
(g) Works of art; models or designs for works of art;
(h) Reproductions of a work of art;
(i) Drawings or plastic works of a scientific or technical character;
(j) Photographs;
(k) Prints and pictorial illustrations.

Almost immediately, Congress amended this list to include "motion-picture photoplays" and "motion pictures other than photoplays" (1912). Still later, Congress added "prints or labels used for articles of merchandise" (1939) and, finally, sound recordings (1971).

In the 1976 Act, Congress chose a new approach to enumerating the works protected by copyright. This approach was intended "to free the courts from rigid or outmoded concepts of the scope of particular categories." H.R. Rep. No. 94-1476, 94th Cong., 2d Sess. at 53 (1976), *reprinted in* 1976 U.S.C.C.A.N. 5659, 5666. Rather than listing works according to the particular form or medium in which they were expressed (e.g., "books" and "periodicals"), the Act set forth broad categories of content that the law protects. Section 102(a) of the 1976 Act listed seven such nonexclusive categories: "(1) literary works; (2) musical works, including any accompanying words; (3) dramatic works, including any accompanying music;

(4) pantomimes and choreographic works; (5) pictorial, graphic, and sculptural works; (6) motion pictures and other audiovisual works; and (7) sound recordings." These categories subsume many of the kinds of works that were listed separately in the 1909 Act and have proved more adaptable to change. Congress did not, for example, need to amend the Act when digital audio recordings and later DVD movies became available, because the statutory definitions of "sound recordings" and "audiovisual works" were already worded broadly enough to encompass the new media. Since 1976, Congress has added only one more category to the list in §102(a)—architectural works (1990).

b. New Technologies for Distributing and Copying Works

In addition to enabling new forms of creative expression, technological changes have transformed the ways in which creative works are produced, distributed, and accessed by members of the public. These changes have greatly complicated the task of defining a copyright owner's rights.

For hundreds of years, the only viable means of making copies of creative works for mass distribution was the printing press, and proximity to a physical copy was required to read or view a work. Musical compositions were distributed in the form of sheet music, which musically inclined customers could play on instruments of their own.

Near the start of the twentieth century, however, the print-based copyright landscape began to change rapidly. First came methods for distributing and playing recorded sounds and displaying moving images. The late 1800s and early 1900s witnessed the commercial marketing of both the mechanical player piano and motorized players for phonograph records. In 1894, the motion picture was invented and the first films were exhibited to the public. Shortly thereafter, in the 1920s and 1930s, first radio and then television provided means for transmitting sounds and images over great distances. Both radio and television penetration increased sharply after World War II. By 1950, radio ownership averaged 2.3 sets per household, and more than 50 percent of U.S. households owned a television.

Next, in the mid-twentieth century came inexpensive, readily available methods of reproducing texts, images, and sounds that did not require the assistance of the customary publishing intermediaries. In 1948, Bing Crosby produced the first professional sound recordings on magnetic audiotape; by the late 1970s, analog audiotape equipment capable of recording as well as playing pre-recorded tapes was widely available in consumer markets. A U.S. government study conducted in 1989 found that 41 percent of respondents had engaged in home audiotaping during the previous year. U.S. Congress, Office of Technology Assessment, Copyright and Home Copying: Technology Challenges the Law 151 (1989). The automatic plain-paper photocopier, first marketed by the Xerox Corporation in 1959, was in widespread use in offices by the 1960s. By 1966, 14 billion photocopies were made each year; by 1985, the annual total exceeded 700 billion. The first videocassette recorders were marketed in the United States in the early 1960s; by 1987, VCRs were in use in 50 percent of U.S. homes.

The digital technologies that emerged in the late twentieth century accelerated these trends. The introduction of the personal computer in the late 1970s and early

1980s was followed in rapid succession in the late 1980s and 1990s by pre-recorded compact discs; digital audio recording media; digital multimedia technology; sophisticated desktop publishing software; pre-recorded and recordable digital versatile discs; the Internet; the World Wide Web; digital compression formats for storing and transmitting high-fidelity audio and video files; and software-based audio and video players, "rippers," and recording tools. These technologies provide enormous versatility. Once a work consisting of text, sounds, and/or images has been rendered in digital form, it can be reproduced instantaneously without the degradation in quality that characterizes analog reproduction technologies such as traditional tape recorders. Anyone with access to the Internet can transmit such works instantaneously, with a few taps on a keyboard, to anywhere else in the country or the world, and anyone with access to a Web server can display the works for others to see, modify, and forward to others with access to the Internet. More recently, the emergence of densely networked communication platforms that facilitate the sharing and tagging of media files has empowered users to engage in a wide variety of activities that utilize creative works available in digital formats. As you will see, copyright law has attempted to respond to all these changes.

c. Legal Responses to New Technologies

Nineteenth-century copyright law generally granted copyright owners the rights to control printing and publication of their works. The law additionally granted the right to control public performances to the owners of copyright in dramatic compositions. As public performances of first live, and then recorded, music grew in popularity and sales of sheet music declined, however, the owners of copyrights in musical compositions demanded broader protection.

In 1909, Congress enacted a comprehensive revision of the copyright law. The Copyright Act of 1909 extended rights of public performance to musical compositions and granted owners of musical composition copyrights a limited right to compensation, via a compulsory license, from those who prepared "mechanical" sound recordings of their works. (At the time, this meant phonograph records and player piano rolls.) The 1909 Act also extended the term of copyright protection, which had evolved over time from a maximum of 28 years in 1790 to a maximum of 42 years in 1908, to a new maximum of 56 years.

The new media of the twentieth century rapidly tested the limits of the new statute. Public performance rights had to be extended to other works enabled by new technologies, such as motion pictures and television broadcasts. Owners of copyright in pictorial works such as drawings and photographs argued that they deserved analogous rights to control the broadcasting of these works. Meanwhile, the existing formal requirements for copyright protection, which were based on concepts like publication of copies with notice of copyright, could not easily be applied to the new broadcast technologies.

These and other perceived inadequacies ultimately led to enactment of the 1976 Copyright Act, which took effect on January 1, 1978. The 1976 Act defined five exclusive rights of copyright owners. Those rights included not only the traditional rights of reproduction and distribution, but also broadened rights of public performance and display and a newly defined right to create derivative works based on the copyrighted work. In addition, it abandoned the 1909 Act's focus on publication as the trigger for federal copyright protection and provided that protection would attach from the moment that a work was fixed in a tangible medium of expression—which, for broadcast works, could be the making of a contemporaneous recording. Finally, the 1976 Act substantially lengthened the copyright term once again. Although, as you will soon see, the 1976 Act has undergone numerous changes in recent years, it provides the basic structure for U.S. copyright law today. Note, though, that many works under copyright today were created before 1978, so it will be necessary for you to study certain provisions of the 1909 Act as well.

4. The Political Economy of Copyright Law

The 1976 Act is a curious amalgam of broad, general rights; open-ended exceptions like the fair use doctrine; and complex, technical licensing provisions. In part, this facially odd mesh of different types of provisions reflects the continuing challenges posed by new technologies. In part, however, it reflects an unusual degree of involvement by affected constituencies in the drafting process and in the negotiation of subsequent amendments.

a. The Copyright Legislative Process

The process of copyright revision that culminated in the 1976 Act witnessed the full-fledged emergence of a novel interest-group model for drafting copyright legislation. As Professor Jessica Litman describes:

> A review of the 1976 Copyright Act's legislative history demonstrates that Congress and the Registers of Copyrights actively sought compromises negotiated among those with economic interests in copyright and purposefully incorporated those compromises into the copyright revision bill, even when they disagreed with their substance. Moreover, both the Copyright Office and Congress intended from the beginning to take such an approach, and designed a legislative process to facilitate it.
>
> One might argue that this was an improper way to create a statute, on the ground that it involved an egregious delegation of legislative authority to the very interests the statute purports to regulate. Alternatively, one might argue that the process constituted an ingenious solution to the problem of drafting a statute for an area so complicated that no member of Congress could acquire meaningful expertise.

Jessica Litman, *Copyright, Compromise, and Legislative History*, 72 Cornell L. Rev. 857, 879 (1987).

Professor Litman identifies two principal drawbacks to this process. The first concerns the extent to which it addressed the concerns of all relevant industries:

> [O]f course, it wasn't possible to invite every affected interest. Some interests lacked organization and had no identifiable representatives. . . . In the conferences convened in the 1960s, painters and sculptors did not attend and the Copyright Office's efforts to seek them out proved unavailing. Choreographers, theatrical directors, and

computer programmers sent no representatives because they had no representatives to send. Other interests that would have profound effect on copyright did not yet exist at the time of the conferences. . . . [T]here were no video cassette manufacturers, direct satellite broadcasters, digital audio technicians, motion picture colorizers, or on-line database users to invite in 1960.

Jessica Litman, *Copyright Legislation and Technological Change*, 68 Or. L. Rev. 275, 311-12 (1989). In part for this reason, although participants in the drafting process hoped that the eventual result would be a statute both sufficiently flexible and sufficiently enduring for the modern era, the result has been somewhat different. Technologies have continued to change, putting pressure on copyright law, and the demands of globalization have increased, adding to that pressure. In the 39 years since the 1976 Act, it has been amended over 27 times. Today, the Copyright Act is a complex and ungainly document. The Copyright Act of 1909 was 14 pages long. The Copyright Act of 1976 was 62 pages long when enacted; after all the intervening amendments, the current Act is closer to 300 pages.

Professor Litman's second critique is different:

Nor could the rest of us be there. . . . Many of us are consumers of copyrighted songs and also consumers of parodies of copyrighted songs, watchers of broadcast television and subscribers to cable television, patrons of motion picture theatres and owners of videotape recorders, purchasers and renters and tapers of copyrighted sound recordings. Although a few organizations showed up at the conferences purporting to represent the "public" with respect to narrow issues, the citizenry's interest in copyright and copyrighted works was too varied and complex to be amenable to interest group championship. Moreover, the public's interests were not somehow approximated by the push and shove among opposing industry representatives.

Id. at 312. We will return to this critique below.

b. The Traditional Copyright Industries

As Professor Litman's investigation of the copyright legislative process suggests, no study of modern copyright law would be complete without consideration of the economic and political roles of the copyright industries and the resulting effects on copyright law and policy. As information and entertainment goods have assumed increasing importance within the United States and global economies, the industries that produce and disseminate those goods have grown correspondingly. It should come as no surprise, then, that those industries wield considerable political power, both domestically and in international trade matters.

Throughout the twentieth century, technological developments facilitated the domestic growth and global expansion of the traditional copyright industries. By 2012, the traditional "core copyright industries" ("motion pictures, sound recordings, music publishing, print publishing, computer software, theater, advertising, radio, television, and cable broadcasting") accounted for 6.71 percent of U.S. GDP, adding value in excess of $1.1 trillion dollars. Stephen E. Siwek, *Copyright Industries in the U.S. Economy: The 2014 Report*, at 2 (2014). Meanwhile, as technology has brought the world closer together, foreign consumers increasingly have demanded the products of American copyright industries. One estimate of the foreign sales/ exports of selected copyright industries ("recorded music; motion pictures, television and video; software publishing; and non-software publications including newspapers, books and periodicals") was $129.5 billion in 2009, $142.1 billion in 2011, and $156.3 billion in 2013. *Id.* at 15. These foreign sales/export numbers have outstripped those of many other sectors. *Id.* at 16-17.

As the economic power of the core copyright industries has continued to grow, so too has their domestic political power. Each industry is represented on Capitol Hill by at least one, and often more than one, major trade association. These associations have large budgets and considerable clout. New copyright legislation is often initiated at the copyright industries' request, and the relevant legislative committees routinely invite representatives of the copyright industries to submit proposed statutory language. Trade associations representing the major copyright industries also play a significant role in both international and regional trade negotiations, as well as in norm-setting activities at various international fora. *See* Susan Sell, Private Power, Public Law: The Globalization of Intellectual Property Rights, Cambridge University Press (2003).

c. The Rise and Importance of New Intermediaries

From its earliest origins, the effective functioning of the copyright system has required the involvement of third parties—intermediaries—to help move copyrighted content to consumers, ensuring that the public has optimal access to copyrighted works through a variety of channels. Bookstores and libraries are examples of classic intermediaries, as are museums and archives. Intermediaries also facilitate licensing processes, ensuring that users have lawful and cost-effective methods of accessing and paying for uses of copyrighted works. ASCAP and BMI, created in the early twentieth century to facilitate licensing of public performance rights in the music industry, are good examples of this type of intermediary. Whether intermediaries are public institutions such as libraries and museums or private actors like ASCAP and BMI, the roles they play in achieving the copyright system's objectives are important considerations that shape copyright law. International copyright treaties and the copyright statutes of many countries contain explicit provisions specifically directed at intermediaries that balance their interests with those of copyright owners.

With the proliferation of networked information technologies and user platforms, new intermediaries have emerged. The resulting conflicts have required fresh consideration of intermediaries' role in the copyright system. Online intermediaries, such as Internet service providers (ISPs)—e.g., Comcast and Time Warner—and online service providers (OSPs)—e.g., YouTube, Facebook, and Google—distribute, host, and help users locate content on the Internet, much of which is protected by copyright. These intermediaries play a vital role in our information-driven society by providing the infrastructure through which information is transmitted, shared, and experienced. The services they provide, however, have raised questions about who should be liable for infringing uses of copyrighted works and about the appropriate extent of intermediaries' responsibility for enforcing copyright rules in the digital environment. How intermediaries are treated within the copyright system greatly affects the overall strength and stability of the protection afforded by copyright law.

The topic of intermediary liability also raises questions about the effect of the copyright system on technological innovation. In an attempt to balance the competing interests in copyright protection and innovation, Congress amended the Copyright Act in ways that attempt to impose some responsibility for copyright infringement while also preserving the business models on which many of the new intermediaries are based. But with the constant development of new online services and business models, the traditional copyright industries have continued vigorous lobbying and litigation efforts to strengthen intermediary liability.

In these ongoing discussions, the new digital intermediaries wield considerable economic and political power of their own, and now are routinely invited to the legislative bargaining table alongside the traditional copyright industries. In response to copyright industry-sponsored reports regarding the value of copyright protection to U.S. industries, the Computer & Communications Industry Association (CCIA) published a competing report that highlighted the economic importance of the "fair use industries," i.e., industries that benefit from and/or rely on limits to copyright. *See* Thomas Rogers & Andrew Szamosszegi, *Fair Use in the U.S. Economy: Economic Contribution of Industries Relying on Fair Use*, CCIA, 2011. According to the authors, these industries include manufacturers of consumer devices that allow individual copying of copyrighted programming, educational institutions, software developers, and Internet search and Web hosting providers. *Id.* at 6. The fair use economy in 2009 accounted for $4.5 trillion in revenues, representing a 42 percent increase over the 2002 figure of $3.4 trillion. *Id.* at 18. According to the report, the fair use industries in 2009 accounted for about 17 percent of the total U.S. GDP. *Id.* at 20.

NOTES AND QUESTIONS

1. What do you think of the method of legislative drafting described by Professor Litman? What is your response to her criticisms? The branch of economic analysis known as public choice theory would predict that legislation on copyright issues would be shaped by the parties who have the greatest interest in, and set the highest monetary value on, the outcome. *See, e.g.,* Daniel A. Farber & Philip P. Frickey, Law and Public Choice: A Critical Introduction (1991). Is it practical to expect all relevant constituencies to be represented whenever new legislation is drafted?

2. Who is "the public," and who should represent its interests? Large media conglomerates are both producers and users of copyrighted works. For example, a movie studio may need to seek permission to use a copyrighted song and/or copyrighted materials owned by others in its motion picture for which it seeks its own copyright protection. Are there any reasons why such companies would not be adequate proxies for consumer interests?

3. How would you reconcile the important role of intermediaries with the constitutional mandate that the copyright system grant authors "exclusive rights" in their writings? Should intermediaries be considered a vital part of the copyright system? To what extent do you think a users' rights justification for copyright can be anchored in the technological infrastructures and services provided by intermediaries?

4. ISPs and OSPs generate a significant amount of revenue from new business models, many of which revolve around advertising revenues. Content owners have argued for a long time that they should be entitled to a share of those revenues given that much online activity involves copyrighted content. Do you agree? Does a utilitarian justification for copyright imply such a stake in the revenue streams of ISPs and OSPs?

5. In recent years, a number of independent, nonprofit organizations have become involved in copyright lawmaking and policy. Some of those organizations, such as the American Library Association and the Association of American Universities, represent longstanding copyright constituencies that, like the core copyright industries, play central roles in the production and distribution of creative works. Others, such as the Home Recording Rights Coalition, represent electronics companies that are concerned about proposals to regulate equipment that might be used to infringe copyrights. Still other organizations, such as the Future of Music Coalition and Public Knowledge, were formed expressly to engage in copyright-related lobbying and public relations.

C. THE ROLE OF INTERNATIONAL TREATIES AND INSTITUTIONS

Congress has made some of the most significant changes to U.S. copyright law in the last two decades in response to international treaties or legislative developments in other countries. The United States has also initiated several multilateral and regional treaties, all intended to raise international standards for copyright protection and enforcement. There is considerable irony in these developments. As the following materials reveal, the United States has evolved from a copyright isolationist to a leader in setting global copyright policy. Below, we trace that evolution as well as that of the international copyright system generally.

1. From Pirate to Holdout to Enforcer: International Copyright and the United States

Following passage of the Statute of Anne in England in 1710, other European countries began to enact legislation to protect the rights of authors in their creative works. The intra-European wars that accompanied empire building and the resulting conquests of other nation-states helped expose new countries to the emerging system of copyright protection. In more peaceful times, trade relations with countries that lacked domestic copyright protection typically led to recognition of such protection on a *reciprocal* basis: Two countries would agree that each would protect copyrighted works of the others' citizens, but each would remain free to provide that protection under its own substantive law. Meanwhile, countries such as England, Germany, and France that had significant colonial territories in Africa, Asia, and the Americas typically extended domestic copyright legislation to overseas territories. These developments signaled the beginnings of an international system of copyright protection.

To say that some form of copyright protection existed in many parts of the world from the eighteenth century onward, however, is not to say that authors could obtain protection for their works in any part of the world. Instead, the copyright law of most countries explicitly excluded foreign authors and their works from protection.

The United States was no different. For more than a century after independence, foreign works could be freely copied and sold. This rule allowed U.S. publishers to pirate popular works of foreign authors such as Charles Dickens, Sir Walter Scott, William Makepeace Thackeray, and William Wordsworth. Indeed, much of Dickens's tour of the United States in the 1840s was devoted to arguing for protection for his works.

Discrimination against the works of foreign, non-U.S.-domiciled authors continued to be the rule until 1891. The Copyright Act of 1891 extended copyright protection to works of non-U.S.-domiciled, foreign authors if their home countries accorded comparable protection to works of U.S. authors. With this change, the United States took an important first step toward the national treatment principle that is the cornerstone of modern trade agreements, including international copyright agreements. Under a national treatment principle, member countries cannot discriminate against foreign authors but must agree to accord the same protection to foreign authors as to their own authors. The 1891 Act also extended protection to works of foreign authors if the United States joined an international agreement that required reciprocal protection of the works of citizens of other countries that were parties to the agreement.

The 1891 Act, however, conditioned protection for foreign authors (and for U.S. authors) on *production* of their works within the United States. The statute required that deposited copies "be printed from type set within the United States, or from plates made therefrom, or from negatives, or drawings on stone made within the limits of the United States, or from transfers made therefrom," and prohibited importation of copies made outside the country for the duration of the copyright. Act of Mar. 3, 1891, §3, 26 Stat. 1106, 1107 (1891). This provision became known as the "Manufacturing Clause." Although amendments over the years narrowed its scope, it remained in force until July 1, 1986.

The 1909 and 1976 revisions to the copyright law retained the then-existing three categories of foreign authors whose works the copyright law would protect: (1) foreign authors domiciled in the United States at the time of first publication of their works in the United States, (2) foreign authors whose countries afforded comparable protection to the works of U.S. authors, and (3) foreign authors from countries that were parties to an international agreement ratified by the United States. For most of the twentieth century, however, the United States declined to join the preeminent international copyright treaty, the Berne Convention for the Protection of Literary and Artistic Works (1886), for reasons discussed in section C.2 below. Instead, in 1954, the United States joined the Universal Copyright Convention (UCC), a less rigorous agreement developed by the United Nations Educational, Scientific, and Cultural Organization (UNESCO) whose members primarily included developing countries. Consistent with the provisions of the 1909 Act, the United States then extended protection to works of citizens of UCC member states.

As international trade flows became more and more important to the U.S. economy, and particularly as intellectual goods became major export commodities, the United States gradually grew more interested in international enforcement of intellectual property rights. The U.S. Trade Representative (USTR) negotiated several bilateral trade agreements that included provisions for protection of intellectual property rights. In the 1980s, reliance on this strategy increased dramatically. The Omnibus Trade and Competitiveness Act of 1988 amended §301 of the Trade Act of 1974 to authorize the USTR to identify nations that have violated a trade agreement with the United States or whose policies unjustifiably burden or restrict U.S. commerce. This amendment, known as "special 301," authorizes the USTR to target violations of U.S. intellectual property rights in foreign countries by publicly listing such countries and using the listings to press for strengthened intellectual property protection and enforcement. Finally, the United States embarked on a process to accede to the Berne Convention.

2. The Berne Convention

Prior to the mid-nineteenth century, bilateral trade agreements were the most common and effective method for a country to ensure protection of its citizens' creative works outside its own boundaries. The proliferation of such agreements, and the uncertainty and confusion they generated, ultimately led European states to form a multilateral agreement regarding copyright protection. In 1886, ten countries signed this agreement, known as the Berne Convention.[1] The signatory countries included the greatest colonial powers, so the Berne Convention encompassed a significant part of the world.

For a number of reasons, however, the United States did not join the Berne Convention for over 100 years. First, the Berne Convention imposes certain minimum substantive standards that its members must meet. While both the UCC and Berne Convention called for national treatment, the United States did not wish to be obligated to provide all foreign works with a uniformly high substantive standard of protection on a national treatment basis. Second, the Berne Convention provides that the enjoyment of copyright "shall not be subject to any formality," Berne Conv., art. 5(2), and the United States did not want to abandon

---

1. These countries were Belgium, France, Germany, Haiti, Italy, Liberia, Spain, Switzerland, the United Kingdom, and Tunisia. The United States and Japan attended the final drafting conference as observers only.

the formalities, such as publication with notice of copyright, that it had chosen to impose on authors who wished to gain federal copyright protection. Third, the Berne Convention required protection for some works, such as architectural works, that were not currently protected under U.S. copyright law. Finally, it required protection for noneconomic or "moral" rights of authors, which the United States, with its emphasis on economic rights, had never explicitly protected in its copyright law.

In the 1980s, as international protection of intellectual property rights became a high priority for the United States, and as the U.S. copyright industries agitated for U.S. adherence to the Berne Convention, Congress reconsidered its resistance to ratification. However, Congress also sought to respond to the concerns of groups that opposed ratification. In the Berne Convention Implementation Act of 1988, Congress adopted a "minimalist" approach to ratification, making only those changes to copyright law that were absolutely necessary to qualify it for membership. The legislative history of the Berne Convention Implementation Act (BCIA), which took effect on March 1, 1989, observed: "Adherence to the [Berne] Convention . . . will ensure a strong, credible U.S. presence in the global marketplace" and "is also necessary to ensure effective U.S. participation in the formulation and management of international copyright policy." S. Rep. No. 100-352, 100th Cong., 2d Sess. 2-5 (1988), *reprinted in* 1988 U.S.C.C.A.N. 3706, 3707-10.

> **LOOKING FORWARD**
>
> This minimalist approach has left some international copyright scholars questioning whether the U.S. is in full compliance with the Berne Convention in key areas such as protection of moral rights, the fair use doctrine, and formalities. We consider those questions in Chapters 8, 10, and 11.

Once the United States ratified the Berne Convention, it turned its attention to one of its principal motivations for joining: strengthening the international intellectual property system. Together with the European Union and Japan, the United States commenced negotiations for a comprehensive intellectual property agreement to be adopted within the context of the multilateral trade system of the General Agreement on Tariffs and Trade (GATT).

3. The TRIPS Agreement

The Agreement on Trade Related Aspects of Intellectual Property Rights (TRIPS Agreement or TRIPS) is one of a number of agreements that comprise the Final Act of the 1994 Uruguay Round of multilateral trade negotiations under the auspices of the GATT. This celebrated round of negotiations, which involved the majority of the trading nations of the world, commenced in 1986 and concluded in 1994. The Final Act created a new institution, the World Trade Organization (WTO), to provide a forum for ongoing trade negotiations and to oversee the administration and implementation of the various agreements that constitute the Final Act. As of June 26, 2014, 160 countries are members of the WTO.

The TRIPS Agreement is premised on the position, advanced primarily by the United States, that intellectual property protection is a trade issue. According to this view, in a global economy increasingly characterized by trade in information goods, failure to protect intellectual property rights distorts the flow of trade and undermines the welfare benefits flowing from the GATT system. Thus, the TRIPS Agreement's preamble states that an overall concern is "to reduce distortions and impediments to international trade . . . taking into account the need to promote effective and adequate protection of intellectual property rights, and to ensure that measures and procedures to enforce intellectual property rights do not themselves become barriers to legitimate trade. . . ."

To that end, the TRIPS Agreement establishes minimum universal substantive standards for the protection of intellectual property. It covers all of the major categories of intellectual property—copyrights, patents, and trademarks—as well as ancillary categories such as geographical indications, industrial designs, layout designs of integrated circuits, and trade secrets. Member countries may choose to enact protection that exceeds the level specified by the TRIPS Agreement's provisions and also may adopt enforcement measures more stringent than TRIPS requires.

Part I of the TRIPS Agreement sets forth the basic rules that apply to all categories of intellectual property protection. These include the classic international trade standard requiring national treatment (art. 3) and the related concept of most-favored-nation (MFN) treatment (art. 4). Like the national treatment principle, the MFN principle is one of nondiscrimination; it requires each member nation to accord other members the same level of treatment that it currently extends to the nation with which it has the best relations (in other words, its most favored nation). Finally, and importantly, Article 8 of the TRIPS Agreement sets forth the agreement's goal:

> The protection and enforcement of intellectual property rights should contribute to the promotion of technological innovation and to the transfer and dissemination of technology, to the mutual advantage of producers and users of technological knowledge and in a manner conducive to social and economic welfare, and to a balance of rights and obligations.

Part II of the TRIPS Agreement outlines the substantive requirements for copyright protection. Article 9 requires members to comply with the substantive provisions of the Berne Convention, thus explicitly incorporating the Berne Convention's standards into the TRIPS Agreement. Article 9, however, does not require recognition of moral rights; consequently, countries that have not ratified the Berne Convention can join the WTO without having to provide protection for moral rights. In addition, the TRIPS Agreement mandates protection for some subject matter not covered by the Berne Convention, such as computer programs and compilations of data. Article 12 sets the minimum duration of copyright protection at life of the author plus 50 years. Finally, Article 13 sets forth the standard for permissible limitations or exceptions to owners' rights, indicating that such limitations should be confined to "certain special cases which do not conflict with a normal exploitation of the work and do not unreasonably prejudice the legitimate interests of the right holder." As you will see, this provision, known as the "three-step test," is proving particularly important in defining the scope of copyright law in the post-WTO era.

The TRIPS Agreement represents an important departure from the Berne Convention framework because it prescribes both standards of adequacy for domestic enforcement and mechanisms for international resolution of disputes between member countries. The Berne Convention's failure to provide enforcement mechanisms had been a major source of dissatisfaction for industrialized countries. The United States and other nations that pushed for adoption of a trade agreement on intellectual property rights argued that both types of enforcement are necessary for effective protection on a global basis. Under the TRIPS Agreement, member nations are obligated to provide procedures for copyright owners to secure enforcement of both the rights enumerated in the Berne Convention and those added by the TRIPS Agreement within their domestic legal systems. Disputes between member nations about compliance with the TRIPS standards are subject to the dispute settlement system of the WTO, which we discuss in section 4.a, *infra*.

NOTES AND QUESTIONS

1. Why do you think Congress was reluctant to extend reciprocal copyright protection to works by European nationals for so long?

2. What was the purpose of the Manufacturing Clause? Did it protect authors?

3. Generally, a treaty may or may not be *self-executing*. A self-executing treaty is one whose terms have the force of law domestically once the United States agrees to be bound by it. A nonself-executing treaty is one for which Congress must enact implementing legislation. A U.S. litigant, therefore, can only sue to enforce rights arising from such a treaty that has been incorporated into federal law through the implementing legislation passed by Congress. Most treaties that the United States enters into are nonself-executing, and the Berne Convention and the TRIPS Agreement are consistent with that pattern. In both cases, Congress had to enact implementing legislation to bring the United States into compliance with the new treaty obligations and to provide a domestic source of rights for individual copyright owners.

> **LOOKING FORWARD**
>
> As we discuss in Chapter 11, there are important practical reasons that such authors should consider registering in the U.S. even though they are not required to do so to obtain protection.

4. Note the practical effect of the international agreements. Works by U.S. authors that are protected by copyright in the United States are protected by copyright in Berne Convention and TRIPS countries without the authors having to take any additional steps. Whether a work by a U.S. author would be protected in a non-Berne, non-TRIPS country would depend on whether the United States has an agreement with that country. If not, the U.S. author would have to comply with the individual country's copyright law. Foreign authors from Berne or TRIPS countries, meanwhile, are protected under U.S. law without registering their copyrights here.

4. International Copyright Lawmaking and Enforcement Under the Berne Convention and the TRIPS Agreement

As described above, the Berne Convention offered important substantive protections, but those protections were not effective because the Convention lacked a mechanism to ensure the compliance of member countries. The TRIPS Agreement supplies such a mechanism, and the dispute settlement system of the WTO has influenced the relationship between international and domestic copyright law in important ways. In addition, the advent of the Internet spurred a new round of treaty making and domestic implementing legislation outside of the WTO framework.

a. The World Trade Organization

Established in 1995, the WTO is the international organization responsible for administering the multilateral trade agreements concluded in the Uruguay Round, including the TRIPS Agreement. The functions of the WTO also include providing a forum for negotiations for member states and administering the Dispute Settlement Understanding (DSU). Commentators regard the DSU as one of the most important accomplishments of the Uruguay Round, particularly because of its implications for intellectual property enforcement. In essence, all WTO member countries have agreed to limit their sovereignty by submitting to a binding international process for the settlement of disputes, including those relating to TRIPS obligations. As you have learned in other law school courses, the power to settle disputes is rooted in the authority to interpret rules. The WTO, through its dispute settlement process, is responsible for interpreting the TRIPS Agreement, and thus, as a practical matter, for setting the level of international protection for copyright owners.

The DSU establishes a Dispute Settlement Body (DSB) charged with administering the rules and procedures of the DSU. The DSB establishes panels to hear disputes, adopts the reports of the panels, and oversees the disputing parties' implementation of panel rulings and recommendations. In many ways, the DSU hearing process resembles a typical lawsuit in an American court, except that the parties are countries. Parties have strict time limits for all submissions, and ex parte communication with the panel members is forbidden. Citizens of countries that are parties to a dispute are disqualified from serving on the panel. Panels may seek information, technical advice, and expert counsel on aspects of the dispute. In addition, the DSU provides for third-party submissions from countries that have interests in a disputed issue. Finally, and importantly, there is appellate review. Both panels and the DSU's appellate body are charged with resolving disputes promptly.

The DSB will adopt the panel's report or, if applicable, the appellate body's report unless it decides by consensus not to do so. Afterward, the member nation whose laws or measures were ruled inconsistent with the TRIPS Agreement must inform the DSB of its intentions. If a member asserts that it cannot comply immediately with the ruling, the member is required to state a reasonable time period in which it will do so. Failure to comply with the DSB's ruling may lead to the suspension of concessions or other trade privileges by the aggrieved member until the offending country corrects the problem or the parties reach a mutually satisfactory agreement. A panel may also award the aggrieved party compensation for the value of lost benefits under the TRIPS Agreement.

Several copyright-related disputes have been submitted to the WTO to date, including two that involve the United States as the defendant. The first, which involves public performance rights in musical compositions, is discussed in Chapter 7, *infra*. In the second, the European Union filed a complaint against the United States, alleging that the "special 301" process discussed in section C.1 above is inconsistent with the WTO dispute settlement process. The WTO panel ruled in favor of the United States but noted that its decision was based "in full or in part" on undertakings by the U.S. executive branch that the United States would not use §301 to violate international obligations. The panel noted that "should [these undertakings] be repudiated or in any other way removed by the U.S. Administration or another branch of the U.S. Government, the findings of conformity contained in these conclusions would no longer be warranted." Panel Report, *United States— Section 301-310 of the Trade Act of 1974*, WT/DS152/R, at 351 (Dec. 22, 1999).

b. The World Intellectual Property Organization (WIPO)

The World Intellectual Property Organization (WIPO) is the oldest and most well known of the international intellectual property institutions. WIPO's origins date back to 1883, when European nations adopted the major international patent treaty, the Paris Convention for the Protection of Industrial Property. Both the Paris Convention and the Berne Convention provided for international secretariats. These secretariats were placed under the supervision of the Swiss government and located in Berne, Switzerland. In 1893, the two organizations were integrated; over the next several years, the new organization went through several name changes. The Convention Establishing the World Intellectual Property Organization was signed in 1967 and entered into force in 1970. Today, WIPO is located in Geneva, Switzerland, and is one of the specialized agencies of the United Nations. It operates autonomously, with its own membership, budget, staff, programs, and governing bodies.

In 1996, WIPO sponsored two important treaties designed to address copyright protection and related rights in the digital age. These are the WIPO Copyright Treaty, which we discuss in Chapter 14, *infra*, and the WIPO Performances and Phonograms Treaty. The United States ratified both treaties and passed implementing legislation in 1998.

An obvious question is how a post-1994 WIPO treaty fits within the framework of the TRIPS Agreement. As discussed in section C.3 above, the TRIPS Agreement explicitly incorporates the Berne Convention's standards (except those relating to moral rights). Under Article 20 of the Berne Convention, member countries may enter into "special agreements among themselves, in so far as such agreements grant to authors more extensive rights than those granted by the Convention." Thus, TRIPS members may agree to other intellectual property treaties that implement higher standards of protection. Additionally, countries that are not members of TRIPS may sign WIPO treaties on particular topics. WIPO has become a forum for ongoing discussion of the substantive policy questions concerning the optimal scope of intellectual property rights. WIPO regularly convenes expert panels on a range of intellectual property-related topics within the context of its mandate "to promote the protection of intellectual property throughout the world through cooperation among States and, where appropriate, in collaboration with any other international organization." Convention Establishing the World Intellectual Property Organization, art. 3.

NOTES AND QUESTIONS

1. A copyright owner may not directly invoke the WTO's DSU to challenge a country's domestic implementing legislation as inconsistent with TRIPS but must pursue such a grievance through its own country's representatives to the WTO. Another alternative for a copyright owner is to sue a private party in the other country's courts under its TRIPS-implementing legislation and raise the issue of TRIPS compliance during the litigation. As we shall see, however, such arguments rarely have been successful in U.S. courts.

2. Should other countries be in a position to influence the content of U.S. copyright law? Why, or why not? Some scholars, concerned about the use of international agreements and enforcement proceedings to expand the scope of copyright protection, have suggested that the Constitution may limit Congress' ability to implement continued expansion. Certainly, both history and theory suggest that the Framers, who adopted a utilitarian rationale for intellectual property rights and expressed distaste for perpetual protection, would wish to see some limits on copyright. It is difficult, however, to determine exactly what those limits should be. As a political matter, do you think that Congress is likely to recognize constitutional limits on its authority to implement international copyright treaties? Are courts likely to recognize such limits?

c. The WTO, WIPO and Developing Countries

The negotiations that led to the Final Act of the Uruguay Round often pitted developing countries against developed ones. The TRIPS Agreement, in particular, posed difficulties for developing countries. Like the United States in its first century of independence, developing countries today are interested in inexpensive access to copyrighted works; developed countries generally are not. States that wished to accede to the Final Act of the Uruguay Round by joining the WTO, however, had to accept all of the agreements included therein. This "single package" rule corrected what was perceived as a major deficiency in the previous GATT system whereby member states could join the system à la carte, choosing which rules they would accept and which ones they would reject. Ultimately, developing countries agreed to the TRIPS Agreement in exchange for liberalized trade rules regarding agricultural goods and textiles.

Developing countries continue to argue, however, that the high standards in the TRIPS Agreement do not promote their domestic welfare and raise the costs of access to protected works necessary for economic development. As Professor Ruth Okediji explains:

> Notwithstanding intellectual property laws, developing countries remained marginalized in the global economy. . . . Overall, the experiment with intellectual property laws in developing countries was broadly regarded as a failure in terms of accomplishing economic development goals. The persistent economic malaise in many developing countries, despite elaborate technology transfer regimes, gradually diminished the legitimacy of national intellectual property laws and, ultimately, of the international system. Dominant issues of concern included the prohibitive costs of licenses for copyrighted works, the strict terms of use imposed by licensing agreements over patented products, and the disparate levels of bargaining power between users of protected goods and intellectual property owners. Countries at the margins experienced the social and economic costs associated with intellectual property rights, but none of the perceived systemic benefits—in particular, the stimulation of local inventiveness.

Ruth Gana Okediji, *Copyright and Public Welfare in Global Perspective*, 7 Ind. J. Global Legal Stud. 117, 149-50 (1999).

In 2007, in response to concerns expressed by developing countries about the need for a more balanced approach to WIPO's fundamental mission of promoting the harmonization of international intellectual property rights, the WIPO General Assembly adopted the "Development Agenda." It consists of 45 recommendations divided into 6 clusters, many directed at re-orienting WIPO's operational philosophy and its technical assistance programs. *See* <http://www.wipo.int/ip-development/en/agenda/recommendations.html>. The Development Agenda is viewed by scholars, commentators, and many international consumer advocacy groups as an important response to longstanding complaints by developing and least-developed countries about WIPO's singular dedication to achieving stronger levels of protection globally without consideration of the public policy objectives that inform the regulation of intellectual property rights in most industrially advanced countries. Although the Development Agenda has been widely regarded as a victory for the developing and least-developed countries, it remains unclear how its adoption will transform substantive treaty obligations that embody high standards for global intellectual property protection. There are also questions about the extent to which WIPO's core mission to strengthen and promote intellectual property protection can be realistically altered to accommodate norms that promote access to, and dissemination of, knowledge-based goods.

NOTES AND QUESTIONS

1. Are copyright systems transplantable? Developing countries were given a five-year grace period to implement the TRIPS requirements. TRIPS, art. 65(1)(2). Certain "least-developed countries" (LDCs) were given a grace period of ten years, until January 1, 2006. *Id.* at art. 66(1). In November 2005, WTO member countries agreed to extend the deadline for compliance for LDCs until

2013 when it was again extended to 2021. Do you think that developing countries made a good bargain?

2. Since the conclusion of the TRIPS Agreement, the United States and the European Union have embarked on an aggressive program of bilateral and regional trade agreements with developing and least-developed countries. These bilateral and regional free trade agreements (RTAs) characteristically feature provisions requiring the developing countries to implement substantive and procedural standards that are more stringent than those imposed by the TRIPS Agreement. These so-called "TRIPS-plus" provisions also include requirements that the countries ratify the WIPO Copyright Treaty (WCT) and WIPO Performances and Phonograms Treaty (WPPT), both concluded within a few years of the TRIPS Agreement. Why do you think the United States has pursued these bilateral/regional agreements? Can you think of any benefits of incorporating intellectual property protection in regional agreements that would not be available through the TRIPS Agreement? What factors might contribute to the willingness of developing and least-developed countries to agree to TRIPS-plus provisions?

5. New Approaches to International Copyright Lawmaking

As you have learned in this chapter, copyright lawmaking involves more than just questions of legal doctrine and policy. Many actors are involved in the debates and proposals that lead to any new copyright legislation. Often, legislative outcomes are the result of compromises reached between competing interest groups, but the rapid evolution of technology has consistently challenged settled compromises.

The same complex web of actors, interests, and alliances is reflected in the international copyright system. In the view of some copyright industry groups, stronger copyright enforcement is needed in the digital environment. These groups have pressured the United States to seek stronger copyright enforcement standards, including new standards for intermediary liability. As one example of the scope of the challenge, consider that as of 2014, YouTube has over 1 billion unique visitors each month watching over 6 billion hours of video. Every minute, 100 hours of video are uploaded. Eighty percent of YouTube traffic comes from outside the United States, and the platform is localized in 61 countries across 61 languages. As these numbers suggest, consumption of copyrightable material is difficult to restrict territorially, and this creates tension between countries that regulate digital goods differently. Moreover, countries may view each others' domestic enforcement regimes as inadequate to effectively address infringement in the online context.

Copyright industry groups have pressured the United States to seek stronger copyright enforcement standards, including standards for intermediary liability, in new bilateral and regional trade agreements. So-called plurilateral trade agreements such as the Trans-Pacific Partnership Agreement (TPP) and the Transatlantic Trade and Investment Partnership (TTIP), both under negotiation as of 2014, have emerged as important potential sources of international copyright lawmaking, introducing new challenges of their own. Each of these agreements has been characterized by secrecy with no drafts of the negotiating text officially released to the public.

Negotiations also take place outside of the more traditional and transparent fora of the WTO and WIPO, raising concerns that any resulting norms will be skewed in favor of private industry groups. If successfully concluded, the TPP and TTIP combined will cover products comprising over 60 percent of global GDP.

The influence exerted by the copyright industries has, however, prompted pushback from the public and the new online intermediaries described in section B.4.c, *supra*. For example, in 2012, proposed domestic legislation to expand intermediary liability suffered a major defeat at the hands of an unprecedented global coalition of users and intermediaries. The Stop Online Piracy Act (SOPA), H.R. 3261, 112th Cong. (2011), and its counterpart in the Senate, The PROTECT-IP Act (PIPA), S. 968, 112th Cong. (2011), would have allowed the U.S. Justice Department to obtain court orders *in rem* against owners of foreign websites that were suspected of enabling or facilitating copyright violations and would have expanded liability for advertisers, financial institutions, and other intermediaries who interacted with such websites. Opposition and outright resistance was swift and unequivocal. Opponents organized an Internet "blackout" in which Wikipedia, Google, and over 115,000 other websites replaced their homepages with an all-black page protesting SOPA and PIPA. Congress tabled SOPA and PIPA shortly after the blackout protest.

The public protests against SOPA and PIPA were echoed in Europe and other parts of the world, coordinated and orchestrated by some of the same groups that participated in the U.S. protest. Such international coordination by a "global public" is another new feature of international copyright lawmaking. Stakeholders from all sides are demanding access to negotiating fora and transparency about the positions taken by their governments.

NOTES AND QUESTIONS

1. How well do you think the public can be represented in international lawmaking fora? What do you make of the fact that plurilateral trade agreements are negotiated in secrecy?

2. Does it make sense to negotiate copyright standards as part of larger international economic agreements that may include tradeoffs reflecting a variety of goals?

3. As the world moves towards greater harmonization, how should the different justifications for copyright law shape global copyright policy? What difference do the justifications make if so much policy is, in the end, shaped by private actors acting in global concert across national borders?

II

THE SUBJECT MATTER
OF COPYRIGHT

2

Requirements for Copyright Protection

Chapter 1 introduced some of the reasons that society might find it desirable to implement a legal rule that grants creators certain exclusive rights in their works. Translating theory into practice, however, raises a number of important questions. In this chapter, we consider the basic requirements for copyright protection. As you read the materials, think about the policies underlying the requirements. Keep in mind also that a determination of copyrightability says little or nothing about the value of the copyright or the underlying work to the creator or to society. Whether a copyright is valuable or not depends on a number of factors, including the nature of the work, the scope of the copyright and other rights in the work, whether the creator chooses to exploit the work commercially, and whether the public values the work.

A. THE ELEMENTS OF COPYRIGHTABLE SUBJECT MATTER

Over time, Congress has changed its answer to the question of what works should be protected by copyright. What has not changed, however, is Congress' starting point—the Constitution:

> The Congress shall have Power . . . To promote the Progress of Science and the useful Arts, by securing for limited Times to Authors and Inventors the exclusive Right to their respective Writings and Discoveries.

U.S. Const., Art. I, §8, cl. 8. As you will see, Congress has broad (although not infinite) leeway in defining what the terms in the clause mean. Thus, the congressional decision about which "writings" should be the subject matter of copyright protection is primarily one of policy.

From an economic perspective, the grant of exclusive rights entails a variety of costs. First, any system of rights entails costs of administration and enforcement. In the particular case of copyright, the cost of administration (compared especially to patent law that has an extensive pre-grant examination process) is not especially significant, but the cost of enforcement, particularly if litigation is required, can be steep. Additionally, the copyright system results in so-called deadweight losses because copyright enables creators to price above the marginal cost of their works.[1] Indeed, for the rights to achieve the goal of correcting the public goods problem discussed in Chapter 1, they must allow such pricing. However, the higher price means that some consumers will not be able to purchase copies of the protected work. This limits dissemination of the knowledge contained within the work— knowledge that might provide the basis for further progress. This is a second cost of a copyright system, albeit one that is hard to quantify.

Simple economic theory would hold that a system of exclusive rights should not incur these costs unless the benefits it produces exceed them. Granting exclusive rights in a work that would have been created in their absence imposes a loss on society; granting stronger exclusive rights than necessary to induce creation of a work also imposes a loss. Conversely, of course, failing to grant rights or granting weaker ones than necessary to induce creation also imposes a loss. Further complicating matters, different types of works and different industries have widely varying incentive structures. Is the incentive required to encourage the efficient level of software production the same as that required for novels? Should policymakers conduct a cost-benefit analysis for each individual work, for each type of work, or in the aggregate? As you will see in this and later chapters, the Act speaks in general terms but does also sometimes provide quite detailed rules for particular types of works, partly to acknowledge differences among them and the industries that produce or market them.

In reality, of course, the decision to grant exclusive rights in particular works does not depend entirely on cost-benefit analysis. Other, noneconomic considerations also will militate for (or against) grants of copyright protection. Is the work of a sort that appears to require creativity to produce? Does copyright protection for that work therefore seem theoretically justified? Would extending protection to a particular kind of subject matter interfere too much with the creation of new works?

---

1. Marginal cost is the additional cost to produce one more unit of output. Standard economic theory holds that in a competitive market, sellers will price their products at marginal cost. Deadweight loss is the loss associated with noncompetitive pricing (i.e., non-marginal cost pricing) or other factors that move the market away from the competitive output.

In the case of copyrighted works, the marginal cost is the expense to produce and distribute one more unit of the medium embodying the work. Pricing at marginal cost, however, does not permit the creator of the work to recoup the fixed costs incurred in creating the work initially. Copyright gives the rightholder some market power to enable pricing above marginal cost. Copyright thus produces some amount of deadweight loss. Note that the grant of copyright protection will not necessarily result in the rightholder obtaining an economic monopoly, because market substitutes for the work may exist. The deadweight losses associated with above marginal-cost pricing will increase as the rightholder's market power increases.

Finally, once the initial cost-benefit decision to create a copyright system has been made, decisions about which works should benefit may simply reflect considerations of equity and consistency. Once some works are designated to receive copyright protection, it may seem only fair that other, similar works also receive it. As technology has developed, leading to opportunities to create works in new ways, copyright law has repeatedly had to confront the question whether to expand protection to new works. As you will see, the answer has almost always been "yes." Do you think that Congress should routinely require empirical evidence before granting new rights (or introducing limits on existing ones)?

Section 102 of the Copyright Act represents the congressional judgment as to what works merit the grant of the exclusive copyright rights, identifies some of the categories of subject matter eligible for protection, and places limits on the elements of a work eligible for protection:

> **LOOKING FORWARD**
>
> Note that neither registration with the Copyright Office nor use of the © symbol is required to obtain or maintain copyright protection. We address the benefits of both registration and notice in Chapter 11.

§102. Subject matter of copyright: In general

(a) Copyright protection subsists, in accordance with this title, in original works of authorship fixed in any tangible medium of expression, now known or later developed, from which they can be perceived, reproduced or otherwise communicated, either directly or with the aid of a machine or device. Works of authorship include the following categories:

(1) literary works;
(2) musical works, including any accompanying words;
(3) dramatic works, including any accompanying music;
(4) pantomimes and choreographic works;
(5) pictorial, graphic, and sculptural works;
(6) motion pictures and other audiovisual works;
(7) sound recordings; and
(8) architectural works.

(b) In no case does copyright protection for an original work of authorship extend to any idea, procedure, process, system, method of operation, concept, principle, or discovery, regardless of the form in which it is described, explained, illustrated, or embodied in such work.

Thus, §102 establishes three requirements for copyrightable subject matter. First, the work for which protection is sought must be "fixed" in a tangible medium of expression. Second, it must be an "original work of authorship." The third and final requirement is a negative one: Copyright protection for a work that is both fixed and original will not extend to elements of the work that constitute ideas, procedures, and the like. In other words, copyright protection does not attach to every element of a work. Section 102 also provides a nonexclusive categorization of works of authorship eligible for protection so long as they meet the three requirements. As you will see in later chapters, categorization can be important in determining the scope of protection. For now, as you read the cases, think about how the work at issue would be classified.

<table>
<tr><td>

KEEP IN MIND

Always look first to the statute for a definition of terms used in the Act. You will find many terms – e.g., "fixed," and most of the subject matter categories – defined in §101. Other terms are defined elsewhere in the Act. Sometimes, however, as in the case of "original works of authorship," there is no definition in the Act.

</td></tr>
</table>

1. Fixation

Section 102(a) requires that a work be "fixed in a tangible medium of expression" to be eligible for copyright protection. The Berne Convention leaves the decision about whether to require fixation to member countries (*see* Berne Conv. Art. 2(2)), and neither the WIPO Copyright Treaty nor the TRIPS Agreement requires fixation. Many, if not most, countries' copyright laws do not include a fixation requirement. As you read the following, consider why the U.S. requires fixation as a condition of copyright protection.

Congress defined "fixed" in the 1976 Copyright Act in §101:

> A work is "fixed" in a tangible medium of expression when its embodiment in a copy or phonorecord, by or under the authority of the author, is sufficiently permanent or stable to permit it to be perceived, reproduced, or otherwise communicated for a period of more than transitory duration. A work consisting of sounds, images, or both, that are being transmitted, is "fixed" for purposes of this title if a fixation of the work is being made simultaneously with its transmission.

17 U.S.C. §101.

Under §101, there are only two types of media in which a work may be fixed: copies and phonorecords. Read the definitions of "copies" and "phonorecords" in §101 now, and consider what the differences are between them and what types of works are likely to embodied in each.

As Congress explained when enacting the 1976 Act, it chose the concept of fixation as a high level approach to the problem of identifying when a copy of a work could be said to exist. It also intentionally drafted the new statutory definition of "fixed" to accommodate new technologies:

> [The] broad language is intended to avoid the artificial and largely unjustifiable distinctions, derived from [some cases] under which statutory copyrightability has been made to depend upon the form or medium in which the work is fixed. Under the bill it makes no difference what the form, manner, or medium of fixation may be—whether it is in words, numbers, notes, sounds, pictures, or any other graphic or symbolic indicia, whether embodied in a physical object in written, printed, photographic, sculptural, punched, magnetic, or any other stable form, and whether it is capable of perception directly or by means of any machine or device "now known or later developed."

H.R. Rep. No. 94-1476, 94th Cong., 2d Sess. 52 (1976), *reprinted in* 1976 U.S.C.C.A.N. 5659, 5665. Note, however, that in the §101 definitions of "phonorecords" and "copies," Congress preserved the distinction between media embodying sounds and other fixed embodiments of copyrighted works.

Some complexities remained, however. Re-read the first sentence of the definition of "fixed." Despite its breadth, it did not clearly cover live transmissions of, for example, a comedy routine or song performed over the airwaves, which might not exist in a copy sufficiently stable to be perceived for a period of more than transitory duration. Yet broadcasts clearly are able to be perceived by their intended audiences and it would be paradoxical if no one could claim a copyright interest in a means of dissemination capable of reaching millions of listeners or viewers simultaneously. This problem also illustrates the difference between U.S. copyright law and that of other countries that accord protection to perceptible works regardless of fixation.

To solve the problem of live broadcasts while still retaining a fixation requirement in U.S. copyright law, Congress added a second sentence to the statutory definition. That sentence adopts a narrow, situation-specific solution to resolve:

> the status of live broadcasts—sports, news coverage, live performances of music, etc.— that are reaching the public in unfixed form but that are simultaneously being recorded. . . . The further question to be considered is whether there has been a fixation. If the images and sounds to be broadcast are first recorded (on a video tape, film, etc.) and then transmitted, the recorded work would be considered a "motion picture" subject to statutory protection against unauthorized reproduction or retransmission of the broadcast. If the program content is transmitted live to the public while being recorded at the same time, the case would be treated the same; the copyright owner would not be forced to rely on common law rather than statutory rights in proceeding against an infringing user of the live broadcast.
>
> Thus, assuming it is copyrightable—as a "motion picture" or "sound recording," for example—the content of a live transmission should be regarded as fixed and should be accorded statutory protection if it is being recorded simultaneously with its transmission.

H.R. Rep. No. 94-1476, 94th Cong., 2d Sess. 52-53 (1976), *reprinted in* 1976 U.S.C.C.A.N. 5659, 5665-66.

This clarification of the copyright status of live transmissions, however, raised another question: What about a contemporaneous recording of a live performance that is not also simultaneously being transmitted? Arguably, a contemporaneous recording of a live performance that is not being transmitted still could qualify as a fixation of the work being performed under the first sentence of the statutory definition as long as it is prepared by or under the authority of the author. However, the leading treatise on copyright law takes the opposite view. *See* Melville B. Nimmer & David Nimmer, 1 Nimmer on Copyright §1.08[C][2], at 1-115 (asserting that the second sentence of the definition sets forth the only circumstances in which "the simultaneous recordation concept" can effect a fixation). If a performer cannot cause copyright to subsist in a live performance by making a simultaneous recording, an unauthorized bootleg recording made by an audience member would not violate any copyright rights belonging to the performer.[2]

---

2. If the *work* being performed—e.g., a musical composition or dramatic monologue—were protected by copyright, the bootlegger would need permission from the copyright owner of that work to make copies of the recording and distribute them. You will learn about the complicated field of music copyrights in Chapter 7.

> **LOOKING FORWARD**
>
> In Chapter 8.B.1 we will consider whether Congress has the power to protect "unfixed" works.

In 1994, Congress enacted an amendment to the Copyright Act to implement the TRIPS Agreement, which requires protection for live musical performances. Section 1101(a) prohibits the fixation or transmission of a live musical performance without the consent of the performer, and also prohibits the reproduction or distribution of copies or phonorecords of an unauthorized fixation of a live musical performance.

The meaning of "fixed" seemed obvious enough both in terms of the media in which works would be embodied (e.g., books and sheet music, cassette tapes, film, and hard disks) and as a test for the initial creation of a copyrightable work. For example, a traditional literary work such as a novel exists, for purposes of federal copyright protection, from the moment that the author causes it to be fixed on paper or in a word processing file. But how should courts interpret the statutory language in the case of digital images that seem to have an ephemeral existence or that change depending on user interaction?

Williams Electronics, Inc. v. Artic International, Inc.
685 F.2d 870 (3d Cir. 1982)

SLOVITER, J.: . . . Plaintiff-appellee Williams Electronics, Inc. manufactures and sells coin-operated electronic video games. A video game machine consists of a cabinet containing, inter alia, a cathode ray tube (CRT), a sound system, hand controls for the player, and electronic circuit boards. The electronic circuitry includes a microprocessor and memory devices, called ROMs (*R*ead *O*nly *M*emory), which are tiny computer "chips" containing thousands of data locations which store the instructions and data of a computer program. The microprocessor executes the computer program to cause the game to operate. . . .

In approximately October 1979 Williams began to design a new video game, ultimately called DEFENDER, which incorporated various original and unique audiovisual features. The DEFENDER game was introduced to the industry at a trade show in 1980 and has since achieved great success in the marketplace. One of the attractions of video games contributing to their phenomenal popularity is apparently their use of unrealistic fantasy creatures, a fad also observed in the popularity of certain current films. In the DEFENDER game, there are symbols of a spaceship and aliens who do battle with symbols of human figures. The player operates the flight of and weapons on the spaceship, and has the mission of preventing invading aliens from kidnapping the humans from a ground plane.

Williams obtained three copyright registrations relating to its DEFENDER game: one covering the computer program . . . the second covering the audiovisual effects displayed during the game's "attract mode"[3] . . . and the third covering the audiovisual effects displayed during the game's "play mode."[4] . . .

Defendant-appellant Artic International, Inc. is a seller of electronic components for video games in competition with Williams. The district court made the following relevant findings which are not disputed on this appeal. Artic has sold circuit boards, manufactured by others, which contain electronic circuits including a microprocessor and memory devices (ROMs). These memory devices incorporate a computer program which is virtually identical to Williams' program for its DEFENDER game. The result is a circuit board "kit" which is sold by Artic to others and which, when connected to a cathode ray tube, produces audiovisual effects and a game almost identical to the Williams DEFENDER game including both the attract mode and the play mode. The play mode and actual play of Artic's game, entitled "DEFENSE COMMAND," is virtually identical to that of the Williams game, i.e., the characters displayed on the cathode ray tube including the player's spaceship are identical in shape, size, color, manner of movement and interaction with other symbols. Also, the attract mode of the Artic game is substantially identical to that of Williams' game, with minor exceptions such as the absence of the Williams name and the substitution of the terms "DEFENSE" and/or "DEFENSE COMMAND" for the term "DEFENDER" in its display. Based on the evidence before it, the district court found that the defendant Artic had infringed the plaintiff's computer program copyright for the DEFENDER game by selling kits which contain a computer program which is a copy of plaintiff's computer program, and that the defendant had infringed both of the plaintiff's audiovisual copyrights for the DEFENDER game by selling copies of those audiovisual works.

In the appeal before us, defendant does not dispute the findings with respect to copying but instead challenges the conclusions of the district court with respect to copyright infringement and the validity and scope of plaintiff's copyrights. . . .

With respect to the plaintiff's two audiovisual copyrights, defendant contends that there can be no copyright protection for the DEFENDER game's attract mode and play mode because these works fail to meet the statutory requirement of "fixation." . . . Defendant claims that the images in the plaintiff's audiovisual game are transient, and cannot be "fixed." Specifically, it contends that there is a lack of "fixation" because the video game generates or creates "new" images each time the attract mode or play mode is displayed, notwithstanding the fact that the new images are identical or substantially identical to the earlier ones.

We reject this contention. The fixation requirement is met whenever the work is "sufficiently permanent or stable to permit it to be . . . reproduced, or otherwise communicated" for more than a transitory period. Here the original audiovisual features of the DEFENDER game repeat themselves over and over. The identical

---

3. The "attract mode" refers to the audiovisual effects displayed before a coin is inserted into the game. It repeatedly shows the name of the game, the game symbols in typical motion and interaction patterns, and the initials of previous players who have achieved high scores.

4. The "play mode" refers to the audiovisual effects displayed during the actual play of the game, when the game symbols move and interact on the screen, and the player controls the movement of one of the symbols (e.g., a spaceship).

contention was previously made by this defendant and rejected by the court in *Midway Manufacturing Co. v. Artic International, Inc., supra,* slip op. at 16-18. Moreover, the rejection of a similar contention by the Second Circuit is also applicable here. The court stated:

> The [video game's] display satisfies the statutory definition of an original "audiovisual work," and the *memory devices of the game satisfy the statutory requirement of a "copy" in which the work is "fixed."* The Act defines "copies" as "material objects . . . in which a work is fixed by any method now known or later developed, and from which the work can be perceived, reproduced, or otherwise communicated, either directly or with the aid of a machine or device" and specifies that a work is "fixed" when "its embodiment in a copy . . . is sufficiently permanent or stable to permit it to be perceived, reproduced, or otherwise communicated for a period of more than transitory duration." 17 U.S.C. App. §101 (1976). *The audiovisual work is permanently embodied in a material object, the memory devices,* from which it can be perceived with the aid of the other components of the game.

Stern Electronics, Inc. v. Kaufman, 669 F.2d [852,] 855-56 [(2d Cir. 1982)] (footnote omitted; emphasis added).

Defendant also apparently contends that the player's participation withdraws the game's audiovisual work from copyright eligibility because there is no set or fixed performance and the player becomes a co-author of what appears on the screen. Although there is player interaction with the machine during the play mode which causes the audiovisual presentation to change in some respects from one game to the next in response to the player's varying participation, there is always a repetitive sequence of a substantial portion of the sights and sounds of the game, and many aspects of the display remain constant from game to game regardless of how the player operates the controls. *See Stern Electronics, Inc. v. Kaufman,* 669 F.2d at 855-56. Furthermore, there is no player participation in the attract mode which is displayed repetitively without change. . . .

NOTES AND QUESTIONS

1. Why require fixation as a condition of copyright protection? Do works that are not fixed qualify as "writings" in the constitutional sense? Are there policy considerations that militate in favor of requiring fixation?

2. *Williams* says that player participation that changes the screen display does not make the audiovisual work "unfixed" for copyright purposes. Do you agree with the court's reasoning? What criterion does the court use to determine whether the fixation requirement has been satisfied? How would that criterion apply to newer generations of games in which artificial intelligence and virtual reality techniques allow the player to "create" the game as he or she plays? If the display may never be repeated exactly (because the same interaction may never occur), is the display copyrightable?

3. Why do you think Congress included the phrase "by or under the authority of the author" in the definition of "fixed"? If your copyright professor gives an off-the-cuff lecture and you make an audiotape of it, is the recording a work "fixed in a tangible medium of expression" for purposes of obtaining copyright protection?

The fixation question rarely arises in the context of copyrightability; more often, it arises in cases involving alleged infringement. Infringement of the exclusive right of reproduction (covered in detail in Chapter 5) can occur only if the allegedly infringing material is itself fixed in either a copy or a phonorecord. We turn here to a case involving alleged infringement in the context of digital embodiments of works, which often have a more ephemeral existence than the embodiments with which legislators drafting the 1976 Act were familiar.

Cartoon Network LP v. CSC Holdings, Inc.
536 F.3d 121 (2d Cir. 2008), cert. denied, *557 U.S. 946 (2009)*

WALKER, J.: . . .

[Cablevision provides its subscribers with a Remote Storage DVR System (the RS-DVR) to allow customers who do not own DVRs to record and play back content. Cablevision split its programming data stream into two identical streams. One is transmitted to Cablevision's customers and the other routed through a buffering device called the Broadband Media Router (BMR) (in 1.2 second increments). The BMR reformats the data stream and sends it to the Arroyo Server, which in turn consists of two data buffers and high-capacity hard disks. The data then moves through the "primary ingest buffer" (in 0.1 second increments). If a customer requests a recording of the program, the data moves from the primary ingest buffer ultimately to a part of a hard disk allocated to that customer. Otherwise, the programming data continues to pass through buffer memory, and is overwritten by new programming data.]

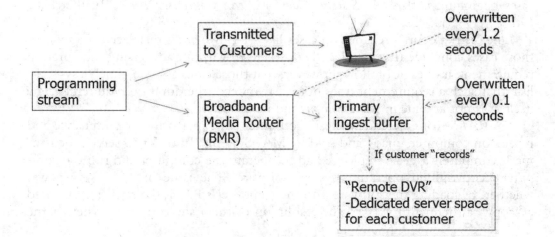

Discussion . . .

I. *The Buffer Data*

It is undisputed that Cablevision, not any customer or other entity, takes the content from one stream of programming, after the split, and stores it, one small piece at a time, in the BMR buffer and the primary ingest buffer. As a result, the information is buffered before any customer requests a recording, and would be buffered even if no such request were made. The question is whether, by buffering the data that make up a given work, Cablevision "reproduce[s]" that work "in copies," 17 U.S.C. §106(1), and thereby infringes the copyright holder's reproduction right.

"Copies," as defined in the Copyright Act, "are material objects . . . in which a work is fixed by any method . . . and from which the work can be . . . reproduced." *Id*. §101. The Act also provides that a work is " 'fixed' in a tangible medium of expression when its embodiment . . . is sufficiently permanent or stable to permit it to be . . . reproduced . . . *for a period of more than transitory duration*." *Id*. (emphasis added). We believe that this language plainly imposes two distinct but related requirements: the work must be embodied in a medium, i.e., placed in a medium such that it can be perceived, reproduced, etc., from that medium (the "embodiment requirement"), and it must remain thus embodied "for a period of more than transitory duration" (the "duration requirement"). *See* 2 Melville B. Nimmer & David Nimmer, Nimmer on Copyright §8.02[B][3], at 8–32 (2007). Unless both requirements are met, the work is not "fixed" in the buffer, and, as a result, the buffer data is not a "copy" of the original work whose data is buffered.

The district court mistakenly limited its analysis primarily to the embodiment requirement. As a result of this error, once it determined that the buffer data was "[c]learly . . . capable of being reproduced," i.e., that the work was embodied in the buffer, the district court concluded that the work was therefore "fixed" in the buffer, and that a copy had thus been made. In doing so, it relied on a line of cases beginning with *MAI Systems Corp. v. Peak Computer Inc.*, 991 F.2d 511 (9th Cir.1993). . . .

The district court's reliance on cases like *MAI Systems* is misplaced. In general, those cases conclude that an alleged copy is fixed without addressing the duration requirement; it does not follow, however, that those cases assume, much less establish, that such a requirement does not exist. Indeed, the duration requirement, by itself, was not at issue in *MAI Systems* and its progeny. . . .

In *MAI Systems*, defendant Peak Computer, Inc., performed maintenance and repairs on computers made and sold by MAI Systems. In order to service a customer's computer, a Peak employee had to operate the computer and run the computer's copyrighted operating system software. The issue in *MAI Systems* was whether, by loading the software into the computer's RAM, the repairman created a "copy" as defined in §101. The resolution of this issue turned on whether the software's embodiment in the computer's RAM was "fixed," within the meaning of the same section. The Ninth Circuit concluded that

> by showing that Peak loads the software into the RAM and is then able to view the system error log and diagnose the problem with the computer, MAI has adequately shown that the representation created in the RAM is "sufficiently permanent or stable to permit it to be perceived, reproduced, or otherwise communicated for a period of more than transitory duration."

Id. at 518 (quoting 17 U.S.C. §101).

The *MAI Systems* court referenced the "transitory duration" language but did not discuss or analyze it. The opinion notes that the defendants "vigorously" argued that the program's embodiment in the RAM was not a copy, but it does not specify the arguments defendants made. *Id.* at 517. This omission suggests that the parties did not litigate the significance of the "transitory duration" language, and the court therefore had no occasion to address it. This is unsurprising, because it seems fair to assume that in these cases the program was embodied in the RAM for at least several minutes.

Accordingly, we construe *MAI Systems* and its progeny as holding that loading a program into a computer's RAM *can* result in copying that program. We do not read *MAI Systems* as holding that, as a matter of law, loading a program into a form of RAM *always* results in copying. Such a holding would read the "transitory duration" language out of the definition, and we do not believe our sister circuit would dismiss this statutory language without even discussing it. It appears the parties in *MAI Systems* simply did not dispute that the duration requirement was satisfied; this line of cases simply concludes that when a program is loaded into RAM, the embodiment requirement is satisfied—an important holding in itself, and one we see no reason to quibble with here.

At least one court, relying on *MAI Systems* in a highly similar factual setting, has made this point explicitly. In *Advanced Computer Services of Michigan, Inc. v. MAI Systems Corp.,* the district court expressly noted that the unlicensed user in that case ran copyrighted diagnostic software "for minutes or longer," but that the program's embodiment in the computer's RAM might be too ephemeral to be fixed if the computer had been shut down "within seconds or fractions of a second" after loading the copyrighted program. 845 F. Supp. 356, 363 (E.D. Va. 1994). We have no quarrel with this reasoning. . . .

Cablevision does not seriously dispute that copyrighted works are "embodied" in the buffer. Data in the BMR buffer can be reformatted and transmitted to the other components of the RS–DVR system. Data in the primary ingest buffer can be copied onto the Arroyo hard disks if a user has requested a recording of that data. Thus, a work's "embodiment" in either buffer "is sufficiently permanent or stable to permit it to be perceived, reproduced," (as in the case of the ingest buffer) "or otherwise communicated" (as in the BMR buffer). The result might be different if only a single second of a much longer work was placed in the buffer in isolation. In such a situation, it might be reasonable to conclude that only a minuscule portion of a work, rather than "a work" was embodied in the buffer. Here, however, where every second of an entire work is placed, one second at a time, in the buffer, we conclude that the work is embodied in the buffer.

Does any such embodiment last "for a period of more than transitory duration"? No bit of data remains in any buffer for more than a fleeting 1.2 seconds. And unlike the data in cases like *MAI Systems,* which remained embodied in the computer's RAM memory until the user turned the computer off, each bit of data here is rapidly and automatically overwritten as soon as it is processed. While our inquiry is necessarily fact-specific, and other factors not present here may alter the duration analysis significantly, these facts strongly suggest that the works in this case are embodied in the buffer for only a "transitory" period, thus failing the duration requirement.

Against this evidence, plaintiffs argue only that the duration is not transitory because the data persist "long enough for Cablevision to make reproductions from them." Br. of Pls.-Appellees the Cartoon Network et al. at 51. As we have explained above, however, this reasoning impermissibly reads the duration language out of the statute, and we reject it. Given that the data reside in no buffer for more than 1.2 seconds before being automatically overwritten, and in the absence of compelling arguments to the contrary, we believe that the copyrighted works here are not "embodied" in the buffers for a period of more than transitory duration, and are therefore not "fixed" in the buffers. Accordingly, the acts of buffering in the operation of the RS–DVR do not create copies, as the Copyright Act defines that term. . . .

NOTES AND QUESTIONS

1. Do you agree with the *Cartoon Network* court's reasoning? Why, or why not? Does the court convincingly distinguish *MAI*?

2. The House Report accompanying the 1976 Act states:

[T]he definition of fixation would exclude from the concept purely evanescent or transient reproductions such as those projected briefly on a screen, shown electronically on a television or other cathode ray tube, or captured momentarily in the memory of a computer.

H.R. Rep. No. 94-1476, 94th Cong., 2d Sess. 53 (1976), *reprinted in* 1976 U.S.C.C.A.N. 5659, 5666. Does *Cartoon Network* or *MAI* seem more faithful to the legislative intent expressed in this passage?

PROBLEMS

a. Andy takes photos with his iPhone and sends them via Snapchat to his distribution list. The photos are only temporarily stored on Snapchat's servers and the recipients' devices. A "snap" is deleted from Snapchat's and the recipients' systems after all recipients have viewed it, although a Snapchat user may set his or her device to store the photo indefinitely. Are the snaps fixed? Do Andy's settings matter to this inquiry?

b. Would your answer to Question a change if Andy uses Instagram instead? Assume that Instagram stores images on its own servers and in the sender's account (at the sender's option) but not on the recipients' devices.

2. Originality

The second requirement for copyrightability is that a work be an "original work[] of authorship." 17 U.S.C. §102(a). Once again, neither the Berne Convention nor the TRIPS Agreement expressly imposes any requirement of originality or creativity, although both agreements assume an authorial presence. Nonetheless, nearly all countries require some level of creativity as a prerequisite for copyright protection. To see why, consider whether it would make sense to grant exclusive rights to someone who merely copies a preexisting work. From an economic perspective, the mere copyist has supplied nothing to justify the cost of a grant of copyright; from a noneconomic perspective, the copyist has supplied nothing of his or her "own." But it is difficult to quantify the level of originality that is most likely to accomplish copyright law's goals. Indeed, as you will see, it is possible to define the term "originality" in different ways.

a. Classic Cases

Although U.S. copyright law has always required originality as a condition of copyright protection, it has not always done so expressly. Instead, courts found an originality requirement implicit in the statutes and in the underlying language of the constitutional grant of authority to enact copyright laws. The following three cases, while now quite old, are part of every copyright lawyer's lexicon and good examples of early judicial approaches to defining originality.

Burrow-Giles Lithographic Co. v. Sarony
111 U.S. 53 (1884)

MILLER, J.: . . . The suit was commenced by an action at law in which Sarony was plaintiff and the lithographic company was defendant, the plaintiff charging the defendant with violating his copyright in regard to a photograph, the title of which is "Oscar Wilde No. 18." . . . [The defendant assigns as error the finding of] the court below . . . that Congress had and has the constitutional right to protect photographs and negatives thereof by copyright. . . .

The constitutional question is not free from difficulty. . . . The argument here is, that a photograph is not a writing nor the production of an author. Under the acts of Congress designed to give effect to this section, the persons who are to be benefited are divided into two classes, authors and inventors. The monopoly which is granted to the former is called a copyright, that given to the latter, letters patent. . . . It is insisted in argument, that a photograph being a reproduction on paper of the exact features of some natural object or of some person, is not a writing of which the producer is the author.

Section 4952 of the Revised Statutes places photographs in the same class as things which may be copyrighted with "books, maps, charts, dramatic or musical compositions, engravings, cuts, prints, paintings, drawings, statues, statuary, and models or designs intended to be perfected as works of the fine arts." "According to the practice of legislation in England and America," says Judge Bouvier, 2 Law Dictionary, 363, "the copyright is confined to the exclusive right secured to the author or proprietor of a writing or drawing which may be multiplied by the arts of printing in any of its branches."

The first Congress of the United States, sitting immediately after the formation of the Constitution, enacted that the "author or authors of any map, chart, book, or books, being a citizen or resident of the United States, shall have the sole right and liberty of printing, reprinting, publishing, and vending the same for the period of fourteen years from the recording of the title thereof in the clerk's office, as afterwards directed." 1 Stat. 124, 1. This statute not only makes maps and charts subjects of copyright, but mentions them before books in the order of designation. The second section of an act to amend this act, approved April 29, 1802, 2 Stat. 171, enacts that from the first day of January thereafter, he who shall invent and design, engrave, etch, or work, or from his own works shall cause to be designed and engraved, etched or worked, any historical or other print or prints shall have the same exclusive right for the term of fourteen years from recording the title thereof as prescribed by law. . . .

The construction placed upon the Constitution by the first act of 1790, and the act of 1802, by the men who were contemporary with its formation, many of whom were members of the convention which framed it, is of itself entitled to very great weight, and when it is remembered that the rights thus established have not been disputed during a period of nearly a century, it is almost conclusive.

Unless, therefore, photographs can be distinguished in the classification on this point from the maps, charts, designs, engravings, etchings, cuts, and other prints, it is difficult to see why Congress cannot make them the subject of copyright as well as the others. These statutes certainly answer the objection that books only, or writing in the limited sense of a book and its author, are within the constitutional provision. Both these words are susceptible of a more enlarged definition than this. An author in that sense is "he to whom anything owes its origin; originator; maker; one who completes a work of science or literature." Worcester. So, also, no one would now claim that the word writing in this clause of the Constitution, though the only word used as to subjects in regard to which authors are to be secured, is limited to the actual script of the author, and excludes books and all other printed matter. By writings in that clause is meant the literary productions of those authors, and Congress very properly has declared these to include all forms of writing, printing, engraving, etching, &c., by which the ideas in the mind of the author are given visible expression. The only reason why photographs were not included in the extended list in the act of 1802 is probably that they did not exist, as photography as an art was then unknown, and the scientific principle on which it rests, and the chemicals and machinery by which it is operated, have all been discovered long since that statute was enacted. . . .

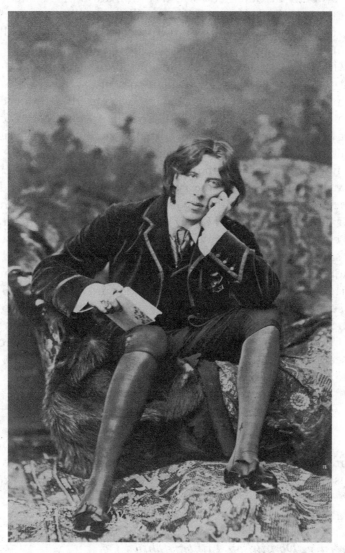

Oscar Wilde No. 18

We entertain no doubt that the Constitution is broad enough to cover an act authorizing copyright of photographs, so far as they are representatives of original intellectual conceptions of the author.

But it is said that an engraving, a painting, a print, does embody the intellectual conception of its author, in which there is novelty, invention, originality, and therefore comes within the purpose of the Constitution in securing its exclusive use or sale to its author, while the photograph is the mere mechanical reproduction of the physical features or outlines of some object, animate or inanimate, and involves no originality of thought or any novelty in the intellectual operation connected with its visible reproduction in shape of a picture. That while the effect of light on the prepared plate may have been a discovery in the production of these pictures, and patents could properly be obtained for the combination of the chemicals, for their application to the paper or other surface, for all the machinery by which the light reflected from the object was thrown on the prepared plate, and for all the improvements in this machinery, and in the materials, the remainder of the process is merely mechanical, with no place for novelty, invention or originality. It is simply the manual operation, by the use of these instruments and preparations, of transferring to the plate the visible representation of some existing object, the accuracy of this representation being its highest merit. This may be true in regard to the ordinary production of a photograph, and, further, that in such case a copyright is no protection. On the question as thus stated we decide nothing. . . .

The third finding of facts says, in regard to the photograph in question, that it is a "useful, new, harmonious, characteristic, and graceful picture, and that plaintiff made the same . . . entirely from his own original mental conception, to which he gave visible form by posing the said Oscar Wilde in front of the camera, selecting and arranging the costume, draperies, and other various accessories in said photograph, arranging the subject so as to present graceful outlines, arranging and disposing the light and shade, suggesting and evoking the desired expression, and from such disposition, arrangement, or representation, made entirely by plaintiff, he produced the picture in suit." These findings, we think, show this photograph to be an original work of art, the product of plaintiff's intellectual invention, of which plaintiff is the author, and of a class of inventions for which the Constitution intended that Congress should secure to him the exclusive right to use, publish and sell, as it has done by section 4952 of the Revised Statutes. . . .

Does the standard of originality identified by the *Burrow-Giles* Court suggest that copyright protects unposed photographs? How about representational art intended for use in advertising? Consider the Supreme Court's next pronouncement on originality.

Bleistein v. Donaldson Lithographing Co.
188 U.S. 239 (1903)

HOLMES, J.: This case comes here from the United States Circuit Court of Appeals for the Sixth Circuit by writ of error. It is an action brought by the plaintiffs in error to recover the penalties prescribed for infringements of copyrights. The alleged infringements consisted in the copying in reduced form of three chromolithographs prepared by employees of the plaintiffs for advertisements of a circus owned by one Wallace. Each of the three contained a portrait of Wallace in the corner and lettering bearing some slight relation to the scheme of decoration, indicating the subject of the design and the fact that the reality was to be seen at the circus. One of the designs was of an ordinary ballet, one of a number of men and women, described as the Stirk family, performing on bicycles, and one of groups of men and women whitened to represent statues. The Circuit Court directed a verdict for the defendant on the ground that the chromolithographs were not within the protection of the copyright law, and this ruling was sustained by the Circuit Court of Appeals. *Courier Lithographing Co. v. Donaldson Lithographing Co.*, 104 Fed. Rep. 993. . . .

We shall do no more than mention the suggestion that painting and engraving unless for a mechanical end are not among the useful arts, the progress of which Congress is empowered by the Constitution to promote. The Constitution does not limit the useful to that which satisfies immediate bodily needs. *Burrow-Giles Lithographing Co. v. Sarony*, 111 U.S. 53. It is obvious also that the plaintiffs' case is not affected by the fact, if it be one, that the pictures represent actual groups—visible things. They seem from the testimony to have been composed from hints or description, not from sight of a performance. But even if they had been drawn from the life, that fact would not deprive them of protection. The opposite proposition would mean that a portrait by Velasquez or Whistler was common property because others might try their hand on the same face. Others are free to copy the original. They are not free to copy the copy. The copy is the personal reaction of an individual upon nature. Personality always contains something unique. It expresses its singularity even in handwriting, and a very modest grade of art has in it something irreducible, which is one man's alone. That something he may copyright unless there is a restriction in the words of the act. . . .

We assume that the construction of Rev. Stat. §4952, allowing a copyright to the "author, inventor, designer, or proprietor . . . of any engraving, cut, print . . . [or] chromo" is affected by the act of 1874, c. 301, §3, 18 Stat. at L. 78, 79. That section provides that, "in the construction of this act the words 'engraving,' 'cut' and 'print' shall be applied only to pictorial illustrations or works connected with the fine arts." We see no reason for taking the words "connected with the fine arts" as qualifying anything except the word "works," but it would not change our decision if we should assume further that they also qualified "pictorial illustrations," as the defendant contends.

These chromolithographs are "pictorial illustrations." The word "illustrations" does not mean that they must illustrate the text of a book, and that the etchings of Rembrandt or Steinla's engraving of the Madonna di San Sisto could not be protected today if any man were able to produce them. Again, the act however construed, does not mean that ordinary posters are not good enough to be considered within its scope. The antithesis to "illustrations or works connected with the fine arts" is not works of little merit or of humble degree, or illustrations addressed to the less educated classes; it is "prints or labels designed to be used for any other articles of manufacture." Certainly works are not the less connected with the fine arts because their pictorial quality attracts the crowd and therefore gives them a real use—if use means to increase trade and to help to make money. A picture is none the less a picture and none the less a subject of copyright that it is used for an advertisement. And if pictures may be used to advertise soap, or the theatre, or monthly magazines, as they are, they may be used to advertise a circus. Of course, the ballet is as legitimate a subject for illustration as any other. A rule cannot be laid down that would excommunicate the paintings of Degas.

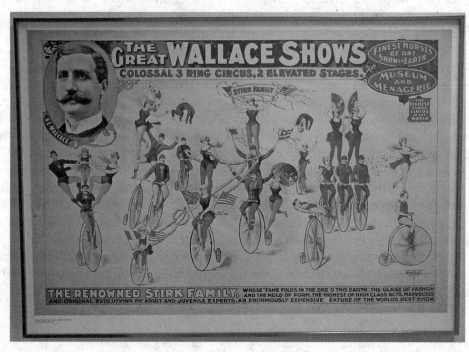

Circus Poster

Finally, the special adaptation of these pictures to the advertisement of the Wallace shows does not prevent a copyright. That may be a circumstance for the jury to consider in determining the extent of Mr. Wallace's rights, but it is not a bar. Moreover, on the evidence, such prints are used by less pretentious exhibitions when those for whom they were prepared have given them up.

It would be a dangerous undertaking for persons trained only to the law to constitute themselves final judges of the worth of pictorial illustrations, outside of the narrowest and most obvious limits. At the one extreme, some works of genius would be sure to miss appreciation. Their very novelty would make them repulsive until the public had learned the new language in which their author spoke. It may be more than doubted, for instance, whether the etchings of Goya or the paintings of Manet would have been sure of protection when seen for the first time. At the other end, copyright would be denied to pictures which appealed to a public less educated than the judge. Yet if they command the interest of any public, they have a commercial value—it would be bold to say that they have not an aesthetic and educational value—and the taste of any public is not to be treated with contempt. It is an ultimate fact for the moment, whatever may be our hopes for a change. That these pictures had their worth and their success is sufficiently shown by the desire to reproduce them without regard to the plaintiffs' rights. We are of opinion that there was evidence that the plaintiffs have rights entitled to the protection of the law.

NOTES AND QUESTIONS

1. Identify and compare the originality standards that *Burrow-Giles* and *Bleistein* employ. Which makes more sense in light of the copyright system's goals?

2. Focus on the statement in *Bleistein*: "Others are free to copy the original. They are not free to copy the copy." Why not? Suppose, for example, that an artist travels to Colorado and paints a landscape of the Colorado Rockies. A company based in New York wishes to use the landscape to advertise its product. Why should the company incur the costs of sending someone to Colorado to paint the same landscape?

3. In *Bleistein*, the court states, "That these pictures had their worth and their success is sufficiently shown by the desire to reproduce them without regard to the plaintiffs' rights. . . . We are of the opinion that there was evidence that the plaintiffs have rights entitled to the protection of the law." Should evidence of value be relevant to the question of copyrightability? Why, or why not?

4. Perhaps the most famous part of the *Bleistein* opinion is Justice Holmes's discussion of the dangers of requiring judges to evaluate aesthetic merit. His conclusion that judges should not do so has become known as the *Bleistein* nondiscrimination principle. Is this principle justified for all types of works? In particular, why should the artwork in advertisements be protected by copyright? Are copyright incentives required for the creation of advertisements?

The first time that Congress attempted a comprehensive statement of the sorts of works entitled to copyright protection, it chose language that mirrored that of the constitutional grant. Section 4 of the 1909 Act provided that "[t]he works for which copyright may be secured under this title shall include all the writings of the author." Cases decided under the 1909 Act continued to follow the Court's guidance about the nature of the originality requirement implicit in that formulation.

Alfred Bell & Co. v. Catalda Fine Arts, Inc.
191 F.2d 99 (2d Cir. 1951)

[The plaintiff asserted copyrights in eight mezzotint engravings of paintings from the late eighteenth and early nineteenth centuries. The mezzotint process involved drawing a hand tool across a copper plate, tracing a photograph of the original work, pressing the tracing on the copper plate, and hand-scraping the picture on the plate to produce images of light and shadow. The plate was then covered with steel. Color would be applied by hand before the production of each print. The artist's goal was to reproduce the paintings as accurately as possible in the mezzotints. The paintings on which the mezzotints were based were no longer protected by copyright. The defendants produced and sold color lithographs of the mezzotints.

The district court found that

> [i]t is possible by this [mezzotint] process to make quite a satisfactory reproduction of the original painting in whatever size desired . . . preserving the softness of line which is characteristic of the oil painting. It is not, however, possible to make a photographic copy of the painting by this method exact in all its details. The work of the engraver upon the plate requires the individual conception, judgment and execution by the engraver on the depth and shape of the depressions in the plate to be made by the scraping process in order to produce in this other medium the engraver's concept of the effect of the oil painting. No two engravers can produce identical interpretations of the same oil painting.

74 F. Supp. 973, 975 (S.D.N.Y. 1947). The district court found the plaintiff's copyright valid and infringed. Defendant appealed.]

FRANK, J.: Congressional power to authorize both patents and copyrights is contained in Article 1, §8 of the Constitution. In passing on the validity of patents, the Supreme Court recurrently insists that this constitutional provision governs. On this basis, pointing to the Supreme Court's consequent requirement that, to be valid, a patent must disclose a high degree of uniqueness, ingenuity and inventiveness, the defendants assert that the same requirement constitutionally governs copyrights. As several sections of the Copyright Act—e.g., those authorizing copyrights of "reproductions of works of art," maps, and compilations—plainly dispense with any such high standard, defendants are, in effect, attacking the constitutionality of those sections. But the very language of the Constitution differentiates (a) "authors" and their "writings" from (b) "inventors" and their "discoveries." Those who penned the Constitution,[2] of course, knew the difference. The pre-revolutionary English statutes had made the distinction. In 1783, the Continental Congress had passed a resolution recommending that the several states enact legislation to "secure" to authors the "copyright" of their books. Twelve of the thirteen states (in 1783-1786) enacted such statutes. Those of Connecticut and North Carolina covered books, pamphlets, maps, and charts.

Moreover, in 1790, in the year after the adoption of the Constitution, the first Congress enacted two statutes, separately dealing with patents and copyrights. The patent statute, enacted April 10, 1790, 1 Stat. 109, provided that patents should issue only if the Secretary of State, Secretary of War and the Attorney General, or any two of them "shall deem the invention or discovery sufficiently useful and important"; the applicant for a patent was obliged to file a specification "so particular" as "to distinguish the invention or discovery from other things before known and used . . ."; the patent was to constitute *prima facie* evidence that the patentee was "the first and true inventor or . . . discoverer . . . of the thing so specified." The Copyright Act, enacted May 31, 1790, 1 Stat. 124, covered "maps, charts, and books." A printed copy of the title of any map, chart or book was to be recorded in the Clerk's office of the District Court, and a copy of the map, chart or book was to be delivered to the Secretary of State within six months after publication. Twelve years later, Congress in 1802, 2 Stat. 171, added, to matters that might be copyrighted, engravings, etchings and prints.

---

2. Many of them were themselves authors.

Thus legislators peculiarly familiar with the purpose of the Constitutional grant, by statute, imposed far less exacting standards in the case of copyrights. They authorized the copyrighting of a mere map which, patently, calls for no considerable uniqueness. They exacted far more from an inventor. And, while they demanded that an official should be satisfied as to the character of an invention before a patent issued, they made no such demand in respect of a copyright. . . . [T]he Constitution, as so interpreted, recognizes that the standards for patents and copyrights are basically different.

The defendants' contention apparently results from the ambiguity of the word "original." It may mean startling, novel or unusual, a marked departure from the past. Obviously this is not what is meant when one speaks of "the original package," or the "original bill," or (in connection with the "best evidence" rule) an "original" document; none of those things is highly unusual in creativeness. "Original" in reference to a copyrighted work means that the particular work "owes its origin" to the "author."[8] No large measure of novelty is necessary. . . .

. . . [N]othing in the Constitution commands that copyrighted matter be strikingly unique or novel. Accordingly, we were not ignoring the Constitution when we stated that a "copy of something in the public domain" will support a copyright if it is a "distinguishable variation"; or when we rejected the contention that "like a patent, a copyrighted work must be not only original, but new," adding, "That is not . . . the law as is obvious in the case of maps or compendia, where later works will necessarily be anticipated." All that is needed to satisfy both the Constitution and the statute is that the "author" contributed something more than a "merely trivial" variation, something recognizably "his own." Originality in this context "means little more than a prohibition of actual copying." No matter how poor artistically the "author's" addition, it is enough if it be his own. *Bleistein v. Donaldson Lithographing Co.*, 188 U.S. 239. . . .

We consider untenable defendants' suggestion that plaintiff's mezzotints could not validly be copyrighted because they are reproductions of works in the public domain. Not only does the Act include "Reproductions of a work of art," but—while prohibiting a copyright of "the original text of any work . . . in the public domain"—it explicitly provides for the copyrighting of "translations, or other versions of works in the public domain." The mezzotints were such "versions." They "originated" with those who made them, and—on the trial judge's findings well supported by the evidence—amply met the standards imposed by the Constitution and the statute.[22] There is evidence that they were not intended to, and did not,

---

8. *Burrow-Giles Lithographic Co. v. Sarony*, 111 U.S. 53, 57-58.

22. See Copinger, The Law of Copyrights (7th ed. 1936) 46: "Again, an engraver is almost invariably a copyist, but although his work may infringe copyright in the original painting if made without the consent of the owner of the copyright therein, his work may still be original in the sense that he has employed skill and judgment in its production. He produces the resemblance he is desirous of obtaining by means very different from those employed by the painter or draughtsman from whom he copies: means which require great labour and talent. The engraver produces his effects by the management of light and shade, or, as the term of his art expresses it, the *chiaroscuro*. The due degrees of light and shade are produced by different lines and dots; he who is the engraver must decide on the choice of the different lines or dots for himself, and on his choice depends the success of his print."

imitate the paintings they reproduced. But even if their substantial departures from the paintings were inadvertent, the copyrights would be valid.[23] A copyist's bad eyesight or defective musculature, or a shock caused by a clap of thunder, may yield sufficiently distinguishable variations. Having hit upon such a variation unintentionally, the "author" may adopt it as his and copyright it.

Accordingly, defendants' arguments about the public domain become irrelevant. They could be relevant only in their bearing on the issue of infringement, i.e., whether the defendants copied the mezzotints. But on the findings, again well grounded in the evidence, we see no possible doubt that defendants, who did deliberately copy the mezzotints, are infringers. For a copyright confers the exclusive right to copy the copyrighted work—a right not to have others copy it. Nor were the copyrights lost because of the reproduction of the mezzotints in catalogues. . . .

NOTES AND QUESTIONS

1. Should copyright protect the result of "[a] copyist's bad eyesight or defective musculature, or a shock caused by a clap of thunder"?

2. What role did the provisions of the 1909 Act play in the Second Circuit's determination of copyrightability?

3. Should the fact that the creator is copying a preexisting work that is in the public domain affect the evaluation of what is required to obtain a copyright in the new work? How does the court resolve this question? We return to this question, which involves what are known in copyright law as "derivative works," later in this chapter.

Note on Nonobviousness and Originality

In *Burrow-Giles*, the Court hinted at some of the differences between copyright law and patent law, which offers protection to certain technological innovations. Copyright law requires that a work of expression be "original" to be protected. Patent law, in contrast, requires that an invention be new, useful, and nonobvious to qualify for protection. Section 103 of the Patent Act, which defines nonobviousness, specifies that a patent may not issue "if the differences between the subject matter sought to be patented and the prior art are such that the subject matter as a whole would have been obvious . . . to a person having ordinary skill in the art to which said subject matter pertains." 35 U.S.C. §103(a). Under the 1976 Copyright Act,

---

23. See Kallen, Art and Freedom (1942) 977 to the effect that "the beauty of the human singing voice, as the western convention of music hears it, depends upon a physiological dysfunction of the vocal cords. . . ."

Plutarch tells this story: A painter, enraged because he could not depict the foam that filled a horse's mouth from champing at the bit, threw a sponge at his painting; the sponge splashed against the wall—and achieved the desired result.

no prior assessment of the work's level of originality is required; instead, copyright automatically subsists in an original work of authorship at the time the work is fixed in a tangible medium of expression. In contrast, to obtain a patent, the inventor must file an application with the Patent and Trademark Office (PTO). An examiner will assess whether the application meets the statutory requirements. Often, the examiner will determine that the application as written does not meet the nonobviousness standard, and the inventor will need to narrow the claims to avoid rejection.

As both the Patent Act and the patent practice of examination make clear, the requirement of nonobviousness is significantly more stringent than the copyright requirement of originality. In *Graham v. John Deere Co.*, 383 U.S. 1 (1966), the Supreme Court indicated that the nonobviousness threshold for patentability is constitutionally mandated:

> The [Intellectual Property] clause is both a grant of power and a limitation. This qualified authority, unlike the power often exercised in the sixteenth and seventeenth centuries by the English Crown, is limited to the promotion of advances in the "useful arts." It was written against the backdrop of the practices—eventually curtailed by the Statute of Monopolies—of the Crown in granting monopolies to court favorites in goods or businesses which had long before been enjoyed by the public. *See* Meinhardt, Inventions, Patents and Monopoly, pp. 30-35 (London, 1946). The Congress in the exercise of the patent power may not overreach the restraints imposed by the stated constitutional purpose. Nor may it enlarge the patent monopoly without regard to the innovation, advancement or social benefit gained thereby. Moreover, Congress may not authorize the issuance of patents whose effects are to remove existent knowledge from the public domain, or to restrict free access to materials already available. Innovation, advancement, and things which add to the sum of useful knowledge are inherent requisites in a patent system which by constitutional command must "promote the Progress of . . . useful Arts." This is the *standard* expressed in the Constitution and it may not be ignored. And it is in this light that patent validity "requires reference to a standard written into the Constitution." *A. & P. Tea Co. v. Supermarket Corp.*, [340 U.S. 147,] 154 [(1950)] (concurring opinion).

383 U.S. at 5-6.

One consequence of the difference in threshold standards for protectability is that the copyright and patent systems have very different rules about the treatment of independently created works and inventions, respectively. Recall again Justices Holmes's statement in *Bleistein* that "[o]thers are free to copy the original. They are not free to copy the copy." Because copyright law requires simply that a work not have been copied, a copyright owner cannot obtain relief against another author who independently generates expression that replicates the copyrighted work. Instead, a second comer who is an independent creator may receive her own copyright. Because patent law requires that a patentable invention represent a nonobvious advance over all existing prior art, a second comer who independently generates an already patented invention may not receive a patent. Further, a patent confers the exclusive right to make, use, or sell the invention; thus, the second comer who independently generates a patented invention may not make, use, or sell it without infringing the patent.

NOTES AND QUESTIONS

1. Why do you think patent law and copyright law have such different threshold standards and such different rules about independent creation? If patented works are more expensive to develop than copyrighted works, might that explain the differences? *See* Dan L. Burk, *Patenting Speech*, 79 Tex. L. Rev. 99, 153 (2000). Or do the threshold requirements reflect a trade-off between quality (patent) and quantity (copyright)? *See* Paul Goldstein, *Infringement of Copyright in Computer Programs*, 47 U. Pitt. L. Rev. 1119, 1121 (1986). If so, why choose this trade-off? Does copyright law's threshold standard differ from that of patent law because copyright protects aesthetic works rather than useful ones? *See* Douglas Y'Barbo, *The Heart of the Matter: The Property Right Conferred by Copyright*, 49 Mercer L. Rev. 643, 665-66 (1998).

2. Consider, again, whether a higher standard of originality would be appropriate. Should the copyright originality standard perform the sort of gatekeeping function that the patent nonobviousness standard performs? For discussion of this question, see Joseph Scott Miller, *Hoisting Originality*, 31 Cardozo L. Rev. 451 (2009) (arguing that the social cost of copyright protection has grown as copyright's reach has expanded, and that such cost can be mitigated by recalibrating originality to reward the production of unconventional expression).

b. Establishing the Modern Originality Standard

In the 1976 Act, Congress deliberately chose new language to describe the sorts of works eligible for copyright protection: "original works of authorship." 17 U.S.C. §102(a). As the legislative history of the Act explains:

> [A] recurring question [under the 1909 Act] has been whether the statutory and the constitutional provisions are coextensive. If so, the courts would be faced with the alternative of holding copyrightable something that Congress clearly did not intend to protect, or of holding constitutionally incapable of copyright something that Congress might one day want to protect. To avoid these equally undesirable results, the courts have indicated that "all the writings of an author" under the [1909 Act] is narrower in scope than the "writings" of "authors" referred to in the Constitution. The bill avoids this dilemma by using a different phrase—"original works of authorship"—in characterizing the general subject matter of statutory copyright protection.

H.R. Rep. No. 94-1476, 94th Cong., 2d Sess. 51 (1976), *reprinted in* 1976 U.S.C.C.A.N. 5659, 5664. In other words, the intent of the 1976 Act was to "avoid exhausting the constitutional power of Congress to legislate in [the] field" of copyrightable subject matter. *Id.*

But the 1976 Act does not indicate exactly what Congress meant by "original works of authorship." According to the legislative history, "[t]he phrase 'original works of authorship,' which is purposely left undefined, was intended to incorporate without change the standard of originality established by the courts under the [1909 Act]. This standard does not include requirements of novelty, ingenuity, or esthetic merit, and there is no intention to enlarge the standard of copyright protection to require them." *Id.* The task of interpreting the scope of the statutory grant of copyright protection was thus left, once again, to the courts.

In the United States, both as a statutory matter and as a constitutional matter, the modern definition of "originality" requires more than mere independent creation, but not much more. In the following case, the Supreme Court articulated the modern definition of originality.

Feist Publications, Inc. v. Rural Telephone Service Co.
499 U.S. 340 (1991)

O'CONNOR, J.: . . .

I

Rural Telephone Service Company, Inc., is a certified public utility that provides telephone service to several communities in northwest Kansas. It is subject to a state regulation that requires all telephone companies operating in Kansas to issue annually an updated telephone directory. Accordingly, as a condition of its monopoly franchise, Rural publishes a typical telephone directory, consisting of white pages and yellow pages. The white pages list in alphabetical order the names of Rural's subscribers, together with their towns and telephone numbers. The yellow pages list Rural's business subscribers alphabetically by category and feature classified advertisements of various sizes. Rural distributes its directory free of charge to its subscribers, but earns revenue by selling yellow pages advertisements.

Feist Publications, Inc., is a publishing company that specializes in area-wide telephone directories. Unlike a typical directory, which covers only a particular calling area, Feist's areawide directories cover a much larger geographic range, reducing the need to call directory assistance or to consult multiple directories. The Feist directory that is the subject of this litigation covers 11 different telephone service areas in 15 counties and contains 46,878 white pages listings—compared to Rural's approximately 7,700 listings. Like Rural's directory, Feist's is distributed free of charge and includes both white pages and yellow pages. Feist and Rural compete vigorously for yellow pages advertising. . . .

Of the 11 telephone companies, only Rural refused to license its listings to Feist. Rural's refusal created a problem for Feist, as omitting these listings would have left a gaping hole in its area-wide directory, rendering it less attractive to potential yellow pages advertisers. . . .

Unable to license Rural's white pages listings, Feist used them without Rural's consent. Feist began by removing several thousand listings that fell outside the geographic range of its area-wide directory, then hired personnel to investigate the 4,935 that remained. These employees verified the data reported by Rural and sought to obtain additional information. As a result, a typical Feist listing includes the individual's street address; most of Rural's listings do not. Notwithstanding these additions, however, 1,309 of the 46,878 listings in Feist's

1983 directory were identical to listings in Rural's 1982-1983 white pages. Four of these were fictitious listings that Rural had inserted into its directory to detect copying. . . .

II

A

This case concerns the interaction of two well-established propositions. The first is that facts are not copyrightable; the other, that compilations of facts generally are. Each of these propositions possesses an impeccable pedigree. . . .

There is an undeniable tension between these two propositions. Many compilations consist of nothing but raw data—i.e., wholly factual information not accompanied by any original written expression. On what basis may one claim a copyright in such a work? Common sense tells us that 100 uncopyrightable facts do not magically change their status when gathered together in one place. . . .

The key to resolving the tension lies in understanding why facts are not copyrightable. The *sine qua non* of copyright is originality. To qualify for copyright protection, a work must be original to the author. . . . Original, as the term is used in copyright, means only that the work was independently created by the author (as opposed to copied from other works), and that it possesses at least some minimal degree of creativity. 1 M. Nimmer & D. Nimmer, Copyright §§2.01[A], [B] (1990) (hereinafter Nimmer). To be sure, the requisite level of creativity is extremely low; even a slight amount will suffice. The vast majority of works make the grade quite easily, as they possess some creative spark, "no matter how crude, humble or obvious" it might be. *Id.*, §1.08[C][1]. . . .

Originality is a constitutional requirement. The source of Congress' power to enact copyright laws is Article I, §8, cl. 8, of the Constitution, which authorizes Congress to "secur[e] for limited Times to Authors . . . the exclusive Right to their respective Writings." In two decisions from the late 19th century—*The Trade-Mark Cases*, 100 U.S. 82 (1879); and *Burrow-Giles Lithographic Co. v. Sarony*, 111 U.S. 53 (1884)—this Court defined the crucial terms "authors" and "writings." In so doing, the Court made it unmistakably clear that these terms presuppose a degree of originality. . . .

It is this bedrock principle of copyright that mandates the law's seemingly disparate treatment of facts and compilations. "No one may claim originality as to facts." [Nimmer], §2.11[A], p. 2-157. This is because facts do not owe their origin to an act of authorship. The distinction is one between creation and discovery: The first person to find and report a particular fact has not created the fact; he or she has merely discovered its existence. . . .

Factual compilations, on the other hand, may possess the requisite originality. The compilation author typically chooses which facts to include, in what order to place them, and how to arrange the collected data so that they may be used effectively by readers. These choices as to selection and arrangement, so long as they are made independently by the compiler and entail a minimal degree of creativity, are sufficiently original that Congress may protect such compilations through the copyright laws. . . .

This inevitably means that the copyright in a factual compilation is thin. Notwithstanding a valid copyright, a subsequent compiler remains free to use the facts contained in another's publication to aid in preparing a competing work, so long as the competing work does not feature the same selection and arrangement. . . .

It may seem unfair that much of the fruit of the compiler's labor may be used by others without compensation. As Justice Brennan has correctly observed, however, this is not "some unforeseen byproduct of a statutory scheme." *Harper & Row*, 471 U.S., at 589 (dissenting opinion). It is, rather, "the essence of copyright," *ibid.*, and a constitutional requirement. The primary objective of copyright is not to reward the labor of authors, but "[t]o promote the Progress of Science and useful Arts." Art. I, §8, cl. 8. Accord, *Twentieth Century Music Corp. v. Aiken*, 422 U.S. 151, 156 (1975). To this end, copyright assures authors the right to their original expression, but encourages others to build freely upon the ideas and information conveyed by a work. *Harper & Row, supra*, 471 U.S., at 556-557. This principle, known as the idea/expression or fact/expression dichotomy, applies to all works of authorship. As applied to a factual compilation, assuming the absence of original written expression, only the compiler's selection and arrangement may be protected; the raw facts may be copied at will. This result is neither unfair nor unfortunate. It is the means by which copyright advances the progress of science and art. . . .

B

As we have explained, originality is a constitutionally mandated prerequisite for copyright protection. The Court's decisions announcing this rule predate the Copyright Act of 1909, but ambiguous language in the 1909 Act caused some lower courts temporarily to lose sight of this requirement. . . .

. . . [T]hese courts developed a new theory to justify the protection of factual compilations. Known alternatively as "sweat of the brow" or "industrious collection," the underlying notion was that copyright was a reward for the hard work that went into compiling facts. The classic formulation of the doctrine appeared in *Jeweler's Circular Publishing Co.* [*v. Keystone Publishing Co.*], 281 F. [83 (2d Cir. 1922)], at 88:

> The right to copyright a book upon which one has expended labor in its preparation does not depend upon whether the materials which he has collected consist or not of matters which are publici juris, or whether such materials show literary skill *or originality*, either in thought or in language, or anything more than industrious collection. The man who goes through the streets of a town and puts down the names of each of the inhabitants, with their occupations and their street number, acquires material of which he is the author (emphasis added).

The "sweat of the brow" doctrine had numerous flaws, the most glaring being that it extended copyright protection in a compilation beyond selection and arrangement—the compiler's original contributions—to the facts themselves. Under the doctrine, the only defense to infringement was independent creation. A subsequent compiler was "not entitled to take one word of information previously published," but rather had to "independently wor[k] out the matter for himself, so as to arrive at the same result from the same common sources of information."

Id., at 88-89. . . . "Sweat of the brow" courts thereby eschewed the most fundamental axiom of copyright law—that no one may copyright facts or ideas. . . .

Without a doubt, the "sweat of the brow" doctrine flouted basic copyright principles. Throughout history, copyright law has "recognize[d] a greater need to disseminate factual works than works of fiction or fantasy." *Harper & Row*, 471 U.S., at 563. Accord, Gorman, *Fact or Fancy: The Implications for Copyright*, 29 J. Copyright Soc. 560, 563 (1982). But "sweat of the brow" courts took a contrary view; they handed out proprietary interests in facts and declared that authors are absolutely precluded from saving time and effort by relying upon the facts contained in prior works. In truth, "[i]t is just such wasted effort that the proscription against the copyright of ideas and facts . . . [is] designed to prevent." *Rosemont Enterprises, Inc. v. Random House, Inc.*, 366 F.2d 303, 310 (CA2 1966), *cert. denied*, 385 U.S. 1009 (1967). "Protection for the fruits of such research . . . may in certain circumstances be available under a theory of unfair competition. But to accord copyright protection on this basis alone distorts basic copyright principles in that it creates a monopoly in public domain materials without the necessary justification of protecting and encouraging the creation of 'writings' by 'authors.'" Nimmer §3.04, p. 3-23.

C . . .

. . . In enacting the Copyright Act of 1976, Congress dropped the reference to "all the writings of an author" and replaced it with the phrase "original works of authorship." 17 U.S.C. §102(a). In making explicit the originality requirement, Congress announced that it was merely clarifying existing law. . . .

To ensure that the mistakes of the "sweat of the brow" courts would not be repeated, Congress took additional measures. For example, §3 of the 1909 Act had stated that copyright protected only the "copyrightable component parts" of a work, but had not identified originality as the basis for distinguishing those component parts that were copyrightable from those that were not. The 1976 Act deleted this section and replaced it with §102(b), which identifies specifically those elements of a work for which copyright is not available. . . . Section 102(b) is universally understood to prohibit any copyright in facts. . . .

Congress took another step to minimize confusion by deleting the specific mention of "directories . . . and other compilations" in §5 of the 1909 Act. As mentioned, this section had led some courts to conclude that directories were copyrightable *per se* and that every element of a directory was protected. In its place, Congress enacted two new provisions. First, to make clear that compilations were not copyrightable per se, Congress provided a definition of the term "compilation." Second, to make clear that the copyright in a compilation did not extend to the facts themselves, Congress enacted §103. . . .

The purpose of the statutory definition is to emphasize that collections of facts are not copyrightable *per se*. It conveys this message through its tripartite structure. . . . The statute identifies three distinct elements and requires each to be met for a work to qualify as a copyrightable compilation: (1) the collection and assembly of pre-existing material, facts, or data; (2) the selection, coordination, or arrangement of those materials; and (3) the creation, by virtue of the particular selection, coordination, or arrangement, of an "original" work of authorship. . . .

. . . It is not enough for copyright purposes that an author collects and assembles facts. To satisfy the statutory definition, the work must get over two additional hurdles. In this way, the plain language indicates that not every collection of facts receives copyright protection. Otherwise, there would be a period after "data." . . .

Not every selection, coordination, or arrangement will pass muster. This is plain from the statute. It states that, to merit protection, the facts must be selected, coordinated, or arranged "in such a way" as to render the work as a whole original. This implies that some "ways" will trigger copyright, but that others will not. . . .

As discussed earlier, however, the originality requirement is not particularly stringent. A compiler may settle upon a selection or arrangement that others have used; novelty is not required. Originality requires only that the author make the selection or arrangement independently (i.e., without copying that selection or arrangement from another work), and that it display some minimal level of creativity. Presumably, the vast majority of compilations will pass this test, but not all will. There remains a narrow category of works in which the creative spark is utterly lacking or so trivial as to be virtually nonexistent. Such works are incapable of sustaining a valid copyright. Nimmer §2.01[B].

Even if a work qualifies as a copyrightable compilation, it receives only limited protection. This is the point of §103 of the Act. Section 103 explains that "[t]he subject matter of copyright . . . includes compilations," §103(a), but that copyright protects only the author's original contributions—not the facts or information conveyed:

> The copyright in a compilation . . . extends only to the material contributed by the author of such work, as distinguished from the preexisting material employed in the work, and does not imply any exclusive right in the preexisting material. §103(b).

As §103 makes clear, copyright is not a tool by which a compilation author may keep others from using the facts or data he or she has collected. . . . The 1909 Act did not require, as "sweat of the brow" courts mistakenly assumed, that each subsequent compiler must start from scratch and is precluded from relying on research undertaken by another. Rather, the facts contained in existing works may be freely copied because copyright protects only the elements that owe their origin to the compiler—the selection, coordination, and arrangement of facts.

In summary, the 1976 revisions to the Copyright Act leave no doubt that originality, not "sweat of the brow," is the touchstone of copyright protection in directories and other fact-based works. Nor is there any doubt that the same was true under the 1909 Act. The 1976 revisions were a direct response to the Copyright Office's concern that many lower courts had misconstrued this basic principle, and Congress emphasized repeatedly that the purpose of the revisions was to clarify, not change, existing law. The revisions explain with painstaking clarity that copyright requires originality, §102(a); that facts are never original, §102(b); that the copyright in a compilation does not extend to the facts it contains, §103(b); and that a compilation is copyrightable only to the extent that it features an original selection, coordination, or arrangement, §101. . . .

III . . .

The selection, coordination, and arrangement of Rural's white pages do not satisfy the minimum constitutional standards for copyright protection. As mentioned at the outset, Rural's white pages are entirely typical. . . . In preparing its white pages, Rural simply takes the data provided by its subscribers and lists it alphabetically by surname. The end product is a garden-variety white pages directory, devoid of even the slightest trace of creativity.

Rural's selection of listings could not be more obvious: It publishes the most basic information—name, town, and telephone number—about each person who applies to it for telephone service. This is "selection" of a sort, but it lacks the modicum of creativity necessary to transform mere selection into copyrightable expression. Rural expended sufficient effort to make the white pages directory useful, but insufficient creativity to make it original.

We note in passing that the selection featured in Rural's white pages may also fail the originality requirement for another reason. Feist points out that Rural did not truly "select" to publish the names and telephone numbers of its subscribers; rather, it was required to do so by the Kansas Corporation Commission as part of its monopoly franchise. Accordingly, one could plausibly conclude that this selection was dictated by state law, not by Rural. . . .

NOTES AND QUESTIONS

1. If the originality threshold is so low, what is its point? How does such a low standard fit with the justifications for copyright discussed in Chapter 1?

2. We will return to the *Feist* opinion in Section B.2, *infra*, which addresses the copyrightability of compilations like those involved in *Feist*. For now, note that the originality standard announced in *Feist* applies generally, not only in the context of compilations.

PROBLEMS

Consider whether the following items meet the modern standard of originality and, if so, whether copyright's goals are served by providing protection (remember, for the item to be copyrighted it must be fixed as well as original):

a. A tweet that expresses your opinion about the New York Yankees offseason: "NYY got Beltran, McCann & Tanaka; BoSox need to watch out" Tweets are limited generally to 140 characters and Twitter stores every users' tweet on its servers for 30 days after a user deactivates its account. Neither the sender's nor followers' devices store tweets.

b. A comment that you have posted on a travel website reviewing a restaurant at which you recently dined: "Went to this restaurant for a special occasion and was so disappointed – it was almost a parody. Just because it's a celebrity chef doesn't mean that it's automatically great. The flavors didn't work together and every dish was over-salted.

The chef was flirting with customers – who was running the kitchen? Maybe it is great but on this night, it was a waste of time and money that I found offensive."

    c. A label on a shampoo bottle that reads, "Directions for use: Lather. Rinse. Repeat."

c. Some Contemporary Originality Problems

After *Feist*, just how minimal can an author's creative contribution be and still qualify as copyrightable? Photography and digital technology can capture reality in exact detail. The following cases address originality in these contexts.

Mannion v. Coors Brewing Company
377 F. Supp. 2d 444 (S.D.N.Y. 2006)

KAPLAN, J.: . . .

FACTS

Jonathan Mannion is a freelance photographer who specializes in portraits of celebrity athletes and musicians in the rap and rhythm-and-blues worlds. In 1999 he was hired by SLAM, a basketball magazine, to photograph basketball star Kevin Garnett in connection with an article. . . . The article, entitled "Above the Clouds," appeared as the cover story of the December 1999 issue of the magazine. It was accompanied by a number of Mannion's photographs of Garnett, including the one at issue here (the "Garnett Photograph"), which was printed on a two-page spread introducing the article.

The Garnett Photograph . . . is a three-quarter-length portrait of Garnett against a backdrop of clouds with some blue sky shining through. The view is up and across the right side of Garnett's torso, so that he appears to be towering above earth. He wears a white T-shirt, white athletic pants, a black close-fitting cap, and a large amount of platinum, gold, and diamond jewelry ("bling bling" in the vernacular), including several necklaces, a Rolex watch and bracelet on his left wrist, bracelets on his right wrist, rings on one finger of each hand, and earrings. His head is cocked, his eyes are closed, and his heavily-veined hands, nearly all of which are visible, rest over his lower abdomen, with the thumbs hooked on the waistband of the trousers. The light is from the viewer's left, so that Garnett's right shoulder is the brightest area of the photograph and his hands cast slight shadows on his trousers. As reproduced in the magazine, the photograph cuts off much of Garnett's left arm.

In early 2001, defendant Carol H. Williams Advertising ("CHWA") began developing ideas for outdoor billboards that would advertise Coors Light beer to young black men in urban areas. One of CHWA's "comp boards"—a "comp board" is an image created by an advertising company to convey a proposed design—used a manipulated version of the Garnett Photograph and superimposed on it the words "Iced Out" ("ice" being slang for diamonds) and a picture of a can of Coors Light beer (the "Iced Out Comp Board"). CHWA obtained authorization from Mannion's representative to use the Garnett Photograph for this purpose.

The Iced Out Comp Board . . . used a black-and-white, mirror image of the Garnett Photograph, but with the head cropped out on top and part of the fingers cropped out below. CHWA forwarded its comp boards to, and solicited bids for the photograph for the Coors advertising from, various photographers including Mannion, who submitted a bid but did not receive the assignment.

Coors and CHWA selected for a Coors billboard a photograph (the "Coors Billboard") . . . that resembles the Iced Out Comp Board. The Coors Billboard depicts, in black-and-white, the torso of a muscular black man, albeit a model other than Garnett, shot against a cloudy backdrop. The pose is similar to that in the Garnett Photograph, and the view also is up and across the left side of the torso. The model in the billboard photograph also wears a white T-shirt and white athletic pants. The model's jewelry is prominently depicted; it includes a necklace of platinum or gold and diamonds, a watch and two bracelets on the right wrist, and more bracelets on the left wrist. The light comes from the viewer's right, so that the left shoulder is the brightest part of the photograph, and the right arm and hand cast slight shadows on the trousers.

Mannion subsequently noticed the Coors Billboard at two locations in the Los Angeles area. He . . . brought this action for infringement in February of 2004. . . . The parties each move for summary judgment.

Garnett Photograph

Iced Out Comp Board

Coors Billboard and Billboard Detail

DISCUSSION

DETERMINING THE PROTECTIBLE ELEMENTS OF THE GARNETT PHOTOGRAPH

The first question must be: in what respects is the Garnett Photograph protectible?

1. *Protectible Elements of Photographs . . .*

It sometimes is said that "copyright in the photograph conveys no rights over the subject matter conveyed in the photograph." But this is not always true. It of course is correct that the photographer of a building or tree or other pre-existing object has no right to prevent others from photographing the same thing. That is because originality depends upon independent creation, and the photographer did not create that object. By contrast, if a photographer arranges or otherwise creates the subject that his camera captures, he may have the right to prevent others from producing works that depict that subject.

Almost any photograph "may claim the necessary originality to support a copyright." Indeed, ever since the Supreme Court considered an 1882 portrait by the celebrity photographer Napoleon Sarony of the 27-year-old Oscar Wilde, courts have articulated lists of potential components of a photograph's originality. These lists, however, are somewhat unsatisfactory.

First, they do not deal with the issue, alluded to above, that the nature and extent of a photograph's protection differs depending on what makes that photograph original.

Second, courts have not always distinguished between decisions that a photographer makes in creating a photograph and the originality of the final product. Several cases, for example, have included in lists of the potential components of photographic originality "selection of film and camera," "lens and filter selection," and "the kind of camera, the kind of film, [and] the kind of lens." Having considered the matter fully, however, I think this is not sufficiently precise. Decisions about film, camera, and lens, for example, often bear on whether an image is original. But the fact that a photographer made such choices does not alone make the image original. "Sweat of the brow" is not the touchstone of copyright. Protection derives from the features of the work itself, not the effort that goes into it. . . .

A photograph may be original in three respects. They are not mutually exclusive.

a. Rendition

First, "there may be originality which does not depend on creation of the scene or object to be photographed . . . and which resides [instead] in such specialties as angle of shot, light and shade, exposure, effects achieved by means of filters, developing techniques etc." I will refer to this type of originality as originality in the rendition because, to the extent a photograph is original in this way, copyright protects not *what* is depicted, but rather *how* it is depicted. . . .

b. Timing

A photograph may be original in a second respect. "[A] person may create a worthwhile photograph by being at the right place at the right time." I will refer to this type of originality as originality in timing.

. . . A modern work strikingly original in timing might be *Catch of the Day,* by noted wildlife photographer Thomas Mangelsen, which depicts a salmon that appears to be jumping into the gaping mouth of a brown bear at Brooks Falls in Katmai National Park, Alaska. An older example is Alfred Eisenstaedt's photograph of a sailor kissing a young woman on VJ Day in Times Square, the memorability of which is attributable in significant part to the timing of its creation.

Copyright based on originality in timing is limited by the principle that copyright in a photograph ordinarily confers no rights over the subject matter. Thus, the copyright in *Catch of the Day* does not protect against subsequent photographs of bears feasting on salmon in the same location. Furthermore, if another photographer were sufficiently skilled and fortunate to capture a salmon at the precise moment that it appeared to enter a hungry bear's mouth—and others have tried, with varying degrees of success—that photographer, even if inspired by Mangelsen, would not necessarily have infringed his work because Mangelsen's copyright does not extend to the natural world he captured.

In practice, originality in timing gives rise to the same type of protection as originality in the rendition. In each case, the image that exhibits the originality, but not the underlying subject, qualifies for copyright protection.

c. Creation of the Subject

The principle that copyright confers no right over the subject matter has an important limitation. A photograph may be original to the extent that the photographer created "the scene or subject to be photographed." This type of originality, which I will refer to as originality in the creation of the subject, played an essential role in *Rogers v. Koons* [960 F.2d 301 (2d Cir. 1992)] and *Gross v. Seligman* [212 F. 930 (2d Cir. 1914)].

In *Rogers,* the court held that the copyright in the plaintiff's photograph *Puppies,* which depicted a contrived scene of the photographer's acquaintance, Jim Scanlon, and his wife on a park bench with eight puppies on their laps, protected against the defendants' attempt to replicate precisely, albeit in a three dimensional sculpture, the content of the photograph. Although the Circuit noted that *Puppies* was original because the artist "made creative judgments concerning technical matters with his camera and the use of natural light"—in other words, because it was original in the rendition—its originality in the creation of the subject was more salient. The same is true of the works at issue in *Gross v. Seligman,* in which the Circuit held that the copyright in a photograph named *Grace of Youth* was infringed when the same artist created a photograph named *Cherry Ripe* using "the same model in the identical pose, with the single exception that the young woman now wears a smile and holds a cherry stem between her teeth."

* * * * * *

To conclude, the nature and extent of protection conferred by the copyright in a photograph will vary depending on the nature of its originality. Insofar as a photograph is original in the rendition or timing, copyright protects the image but does not prevent others from photographing the same object or scene. . . .

By contrast, to the extent that a photograph is original in the creation of the subject, copyright extends also to that subject. Thus, an artist who arranges and then photographs a scene often will have the right to prevent others from duplicating that scene in a photograph or other medium.[65]

2. Originality of the Garnett Photograph

There can be no serious dispute that the Garnett Photograph is an original work. The photograph does not result from slavishly copying another work and therefore is original in the rendition. Mannion's relatively unusual angle and distinctive lighting strengthen that aspect of the photograph's originality. His composition—posing man against sky—evidences originality in the creation of the subject. Furthermore, Mannion instructed Garnett to wear simple and plain clothing and as much jewelry as possible, and "to look 'chilled out.'" His orchestration of the scene contributes additional originality in the creation of the subject.

Of course, there are limits to the photograph's originality and therefore to the protection conferred by the copyright in the Garnett Photograph. For example, Kevin Garnett's face, torso, and hands are not original with Mannion, and Mannion therefore may not prevent others from creating photographic portraits of Garnett. Equally obviously, the existence of a cloudy sky is not original, and Mannion therefore may not prevent others from using a cloudy sky as a backdrop.

The defendants, however, take this line of reasoning too far. They argue that it was Garnett, not Mannion, who selected the specific clothing, jewelry, and pose. In consequence, they maintain, the Garnett Photograph is not original to the extent of Garnett's clothing, jewelry, and pose. They appear to be referring to originality in the creation of the subject.

There are two problems with the defendants' argument. The first is that Mannion indisputably orchestrated the scene, even if he did not plan every detail before he met Garnett, and then made the decision to capture it. The second difficulty is that the originality of the photograph extends beyond the individual clothing, jewelry, and pose viewed in isolation. It is the entire image—depicting man, sky, clothing, and jewelry in a particular arrangement—that is at issue here, not its individual components. . . .

Meshwerks, Inc. v. Toyota Motor Sales U.S.A., Inc.
528 F.3d 1258 (10th Cir. 2008)

GORSUCH, J.: . . . [Toyota and its advertising agency, Saatchi & Saatchi, hired Grace & Wild, Inc., to supply digital models of Toyota's vehicles for its model-

---

65. I recognize that the preceding analysis focuses on a medium—traditional print photography—that is being supplanted in significant degree by digital technology. These advancements may or may not demand a different analytical framework.

year 2004 advertising campaign.] . . . G&W subcontracted with Meshwerks to assist with two initial aspects of the project—digitization and modeling. Digitizing involves collecting physical data points from the object to be portrayed. In the case of Toyota's vehicles, Meshwerks took copious measurements of Toyota's vehicles by covering each car, truck, and van with a grid of tape and running an articulated arm tethered to a computer over the vehicle to measure all points of intersection in the grid. Based on these measurements, modeling software then generated a digital image resembling a wire-frame model. . . .

At this point, however, the on-screen image remained far from perfect and manual "modeling" was necessary. Meshwerks personnel fine-tuned or, as the company prefers it, "sculpted," the lines on screen to resemble each vehicle as closely as possible. Approximately 90 percent of the data points contained in each final model, Meshwerks represents, were the result not of the first-step measurement process, but of the skill and effort its digital sculptors manually expended at the second step. For example, some areas of detail, such as wheels, headlights, door handles, and the Toyota emblem, could not be accurately measured using current technology; those features had to be added at the second "sculpting" stage, and Meshwerks had to recreate those features as realistically as possible by hand, based on photographs. Even for areas that were measured, Meshwerks faced the challenge of converting measurements taken of a three-dimensional car into a two-dimensional computer representation; to achieve this, its modelers had to sculpt, or move, data points to achieve a visually convincing result. The purpose and product of these processes, after nearly 80 to 100 hours of effort per vehicle, were two-dimensional wire-frame depictions of Toyota's vehicles that appeared three-dimensional on screen, but were utterly unadorned—lacking color, shading, and other details. Attached to this opinion as Appendix A are sample screen-prints of one of Meshwerks' digital wire-frame models.

With Meshwerks' wire-frame products in hand, G&W then manipulated the computerized models by, first, adding detail, the result of which appeared on screen as a "tightening" of the wire frames, as though significantly more wires had been added to the frames, or as though they were made of a finer mesh. Next, G&W digitally applied color, texture, lighting, and animation for use in Toyota's advertisements. . . .

[Meshwerks sued Toyota, Saatchi & Saatchi, and G&W, asserting that it had contracted for only a one-time use of its models and that subsequent, unauthorized uses infringed its copyrights in the models. The district court granted defendants' motion for summary judgment, and Meshwerks appealed.]

II . . .

A . . .

The parties focus most of their energy in this case on the question whether Meshwerks' models qualify as independent creations, as opposed to copies of

Toyota's handiwork. But what can be said, at least based on received copyright doctrine, to distinguish an independent creation from a copy? And how might that doctrine apply in an age of virtual worlds and digital media that seek to mimic the "real" world, but often do so in ways that undoubtedly qualify as (highly) original? . . .

[P]hotography was initially met by critics with a degree of skepticism: a photograph, some said, "copies everything and explains nothing," and it was debated whether a camera could do anything more than merely record the physical world. . . . [In *Burrow-Giles*], the Court indicated [that] photographs are copyrightable, if only to the extent of their original depiction of the subject. Wilde's image [was] not copyrightable; but to the extent a photograph reflects the photographer's decisions regarding pose, positioning, background, lighting, shading, and the like, those elements can be said to "owe their origins" to the photographer, making the photograph copyrightable, at least to that extent.

As the Court more recently explained in *Feist*, the operative distinction is between, on the one hand, ideas or facts in the world, items that cannot be copyrighted, and a particular expression of that idea or fact, that can be. . . . So, in the case of photographs, for which Meshwerks' digital models were designed to serve as practically advantageous substitutes, authors are entitled to copyright protection only for the "incremental contribution," *SHL Imaging, Inc.* [*v. Artisan House, Inc.*], 117 F. Supp. 2d at 311 [(S.D.N.Y. 2000)] (internal quotation omitted), represented by their interpretation or expression of the objects of their attention.

B

Applying these principles, evolved in the realm of photography, to the new medium that has come to supplement and even in some ways to supplant it, we think Meshwerks' models are not so much independent creations as (very good) copies of Toyota's vehicles. . . .

1

Key to our evaluation of this case is the fact that Meshwerks' digital wire- frame computer models depict Toyota's vehicles without any individualizing features: they are untouched by a digital paintbrush; they are not depicted in front of a palm tree, whizzing down the open road, or climbing up a mountainside. Put another way, Meshwerks' models depict nothing more than un-adorned Toyota vehicles—the car *as* car. *See* Appendix A. . . . [I]n short, its models reflect none of the decisions that can make depictions of things or facts in the world, whether Oscar Wilde or a Toyota Camry, new expressions subject to copyright protection.

The primary case on which Meshwerks asks us to rely actually reinforces this conclusion. In *Ets-Hokin v. Skyy Spirits, Inc.*, 225 F.3d 1068 (9th Cir. 2000) (*Skyy I*), the Ninth Circuit was faced with a suit brought by a plaintiff photographer who alleged that the defendant had infringed on his commercial photographs of a Skyy-brand vodka bottle. The court held that the vodka bottle, as a "utilitarian object," a fact in the world, was not itself (at least usually) copyrightable. *Id*. at 1080 (citing 17 U.S.C. §101). At the same time, the court recognized that plaintiff's photos reflected decisions regarding "lighting, shading, angle, background, and so forth," *id*. at 1078, and to the extent plaintiff's photographs reflected such original contributions the court held they could be copyrighted. In so holding, the Ninth Circuit reversed a district court's dismissal of the case and remanded the matter for further proceedings, and Meshwerks argues this analysis controls the outcome of its case.

But *Skyy I* tells only half the story. The case soon returned to the court of appeals, and the court held that the defendant's photos, which differed in terms of angle, lighting, shadow, reflection, and background, did not infringe on the plaintiff's copyrights. *Ets-Hokin v. Skyy Spirits, Inc.*, 323 F.3d 763, 765 (9th Cir.2003) (*Skyy II*). Why? The only constant between the plaintiff's photographs and the defendant's photographs was the bottle itself, *id*. at 766, and an accurate portrayal of the unadorned bottle could not be copyrighted. . . .

The teaching of *Skyy* I and II, then, is that the vodka bottle, because it did not owe its origins to the photographers, had to be filtered out to determine what copyrightable expression remained. And, by analogy—though not perhaps the one Meshwerks had in mind—we hold that the unadorned images of Toyota's vehicles cannot be copyrighted by Meshwerks and likewise must be filtered out. To the extent that Meshwerks' digital wire-frame models depict only those unadorned vehicles, having stripped away all lighting, angle, perspective, and "other ingredients" associated with an original expression, we conclude that they have left no copyrightable matter.

Confirming this conclusion as well is the peculiar place where Meshwerks stood in the model-creation pecking order. On the one hand, Meshwerks had nothing to do with designing the appearance of Toyota's vehicles, distinguishing them from any other cars, trucks, or vans in the world. . . . On the other hand, how the models Meshwerks created were to be deployed in advertising—including the backgrounds, lighting, angles, and colors—were all matters left to those (G & W, Saatchi, and 3D Recon) who came after Meshwerks left the scene. . . .[8]

It is certainly true that what Meshwerks accomplished was a peculiar kind of copying. It did not seek to recreate Toyota vehicles outright—steel, rubber, and all; instead, it sought to depict Toyota's three-dimensional physical objects in a two-dimensional digital medium. But we hold, as many before us have already suggested, that, standing alone, "[t]he fact that a work in one medium has been copied from a work in another medium does not render it any the less a 'copy.'" Nimmer on Copyright §8.01[B]. After all, the putative creator who merely shifts the medium in which another's creation is expressed has not necessarily added anything beyond the expression contained in the original.

In reaching this conclusion, we do not for a moment seek to downplay the considerable amount of time, effort, and skill that went into making Meshwerks'

---

8. We are not called upon to, and do not, express any view on the copyrightability of the work products produced by those who employed and adorned Meshwerks' models.

digital wire-frame models. But, in assessing the originality of a work for which copyright protection is sought, we look only at the final product, not the process, and the fact that intensive, skillful, and even creative labor is invested in the process of creating a product does not guarantee its copyrightability. *See Feist*, 499 U.S. at 359-60. . . .

2

Meshwerks' intent in making its wire-frame models provides additional support for our conclusion. "In theory, the originality requirement tests the putative author's state of mind: Did he have an earlier work in mind when he created his own?" Paul Goldstein, Goldstein on Copyright §2.2.1.1. If an artist affirmatively sets out to be unoriginal—to make a copy of someone else's creation, rather than to create an original work—it is far more likely that the resultant product will, in fact, be unoriginal. Of course, this is not to say that the accidental or spontaneous artist will be denied copyright protection for not intending to produce art; it is only to say that authorial intent sometimes can shed light on the question of whether a particular work qualifies as an independent creation or only a copy.

In this case, the undisputed evidence before us leaves no question that Meshwerks set out to copy Toyota's vehicles, rather than to create, or even to add, any original expression. The purchase order signed by G & W asked Meshwerks to "digitize and model" Toyota's vehicles, and Meshwerks' invoice submitted to G & W for payment reflects that this is exactly the service Meshwerks performed. Aplt's App. at 113, 115. Meshwerks itself has consistently described digitization and modeling as an attempt accurately to depict real-world, three-dimensional objects as digital images viewable on a computer screen. *See, e.g., id.* at 369 ("the graphic sculptor is not intending to 'redesign' the product, he or she is attempting to depict that object in the most realistic way"). . . .

C

Although we hold that Meshwerks' digital, wire-frame models are insufficiently original to warrant copyright protection, we do not turn a blind eye to the fact that digital imaging is a relatively new and evolving technology and that Congress extended copyright protection to "original works of authorship fixed in any tangible medium of expression, *now known or later developed.*" 17 U.S.C. §102(a) (emphasis added). . . .

Digital modeling can be, surely is being, and no doubt increasingly will be used to create copyrightable expressions. Yet, just as photographs *can be*, but are not *per se*, copyrightable, the same holds true for digital models. There's little question that digital models *can* be devised of Toyota cars with copyrightable features, whether by virtue of unique shading, lighting, angle, background scene, or other choices. The problem for Meshwerks in this particular case is simply that the uncontested facts reveal that it wasn't involved in any such process. . . . For this reason, we do not envision any "chilling effect" on creative expression based on our holding today. . . .

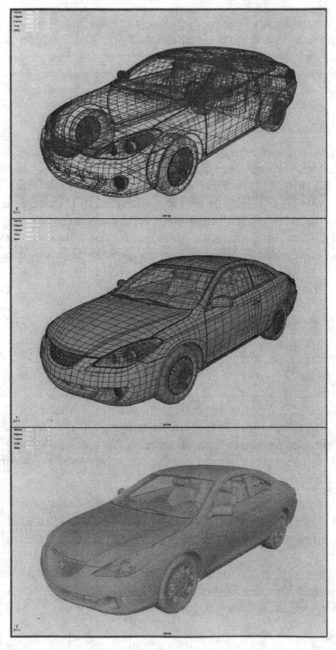

Appendix A

NOTES AND QUESTIONS

1. How distinct are the different dimensions of originality described by the decision in *Mannion*? Was the photograph in *Burrow-Giles* original in rendition, original in creation of the subject, or both? Does assessment of originality in "rendition" or "creation of the subject" violate the *Bleistein* nondiscrimination principle? Should the *Mannion* taxonomy, or one like it, be used for other types of works? Would it have been helpful in evaluating the lithographs in *Bleistein*? How about the digital models in *Meshwerks*?

2. Is the decision in *Meshwerks* consistent with that in *Alfred Bell*? What explains the different results in the two cases? Why aren't the features added by hand by Meshwerks at the "sculpting" stage sufficient to establish originality?

3. Is it appropriate to consider intent in determining originality? Why, or why not? If so, what type of intent is relevant? If Meshwerks had created its digital models for an art exhibit rather than for an advertising campaign, should the result change?

4. In *Bridgeman Art Library, Ltd. v. Corel Corp.*, 36 F. Supp. 2d 191 (S.D.N.Y. 1999), Bridgeman had been authorized to prepare and sell color reproductions of public domain paintings residing in museums and private collections. Corel allegedly copied Bridgeman's color transparencies to produce its own CD-ROM product. The court dismissed Bridgeman's copyright infringement claim, ruling that the transparencies did not contain the required "distinguishable variation," but reflected only "slavish copying." Do you agree with the court's conclusion? Why, or why not?

Many photographs, including a large number in the public domain, are held in private collections and made available to the public only as digital replicas. For example, Corbis, a company founded by Bill Gates, acquired the Bettman Archive's collection of 16.5 million photographs, including 30 years' worth of United Press International photographs. To preserve the original photographs, Corbis stores them in an underground, climate-controlled storage facility. Digital reproductions are available via license. Can Corbis copyright the digital images? Would it make any difference to your answer if Corbis digitally watermarks each image? If Corbis cannot copyright the images under the Copyright Act, should it be able to place contractual restrictions on access to and use of them?

5. Is an Andy Warhol painting of a Campbell's soup can original? If yes, how does it differ from the reproductions at issue in *Bridgeman Art Library* and *Meshwerks*?

PROBLEMS

Consider whether and to what extent copyright would (or should) protect the following:

a. A photograph by acclaimed documentary photographer Walker Evans of riders on the New York City subway.

b. Photographs on a restaurant menu depicting dishes available at the restaurant.

c. A digital photograph of a dining room table taken for the purpose of offering the table for sale on craigslist.org.

d. A live broadcast of the Super Bowl, recorded simultaneously with its transmission.

3. The "Idea/Expression Distinction"

The third requirement for copyrightable subject matter is a negative one: Certain items are categorically excluded from receiving copyright protection. According to §102(b) of the Act: "In no case does copyright protection for an original work of authorship extend to any idea, procedure, process, system, method of operation, concept, principle, or discovery, regardless of the form in which it is described, explained, illustrated, or embodied in such work." 17 U.S.C. §102(b). Many countries' laws have similar provisions, and the rule mandating exclusion of certain items from copyright protection also is expressly recognized in international copyright agreements. Both the TRIPS Agreement and WIPO Copyright Treaty specify that copyright protection extends "to expressions and not to ideas, procedures, methods of operation or mathematical concepts as such." TRIPS, art. 9(2); WIPO Copyright Treaty, art. 2.

Courts and commentators often describe §102(b) as implementing a venerable precept of copyright law: An idea can never be copyrightable, but its expression may be. In fact, §102(b) seems to have two purposes: (1) to define the line between what is eligible for copyright protection and what belongs to the public domain; and (2) to define the line between copyrightable and patentable subject matter. The phrase "idea/expression distinction" is thus shorthand for a rule requiring the exclusion of a variety of elements of a work from copyright protection.

Both economic and noneconomic approaches to copyright view the items listed in §102(b) as basic building blocks of copyrightable expression, and hold that granting copyright in these items would be counterproductive. Consider, for example, the idea of a pair of doomed lovers whose families oppose their marriage, or the scientific concepts embodied in Einstein's theory of relativity, or the steps that need to be performed to change a tire or bake an apple pie. Would it be efficient to give exclusive rights in any of these "ideas" to the first person to write about it? Would it be fair, or morally justifiable, to do so?

While the goal of protecting "expression" rather than "idea" is simple enough to state, implementing it in practice is much harder. As in the case of §102(a)'s originality requirement, the legislative history of §102(b) is somewhat vague, indicating primarily that the provision was intended to continue the status quo: "Section 102(b) in no way enlarges or contracts the scope of copyright protection under the present law. Its purpose is to restate . . . that the basic dichotomy between expression and idea remains unchanged." H.R. Rep. No. 94-1476, 94th Cong., 2d Sess. 57 (1976), *reprinted in* 1976 U.S.C.C.A.N. 5659, 5670. Once again, therefore, the courts must develop their own guiding principles. As you read the cases in this section, keep §102(b)'s twofold purpose in mind, and think about whether that helps to explain the results in particular cases that might otherwise seem difficult to understand.

a. The Classic Case

The landmark Supreme Court decision on the "idea/expression distinction" is *Baker v. Selden*, 101 U.S. 99 (1879). Indeed, the legislative history of §102(b) indicates that Congress intended §102(b) in part to codify the holding of *Baker*. H.R. Rep. No. 94-1476, 94th Cong., 2d Sess. 57 (1976), *reprinted in* 1976 U.S.C.C.A.N. 5659, 5670. As you read the case, try to identify where the Court draws the line between copyrightable and uncopyrightable subject matter.

Baker v. Selden
101 U.S. 99 (1879)

BRADLEY, J.: Charles Selden, the testator of the complainant in this case, in the year 1859 took the requisite steps for obtaining the copyright of a book, entitled "Selden's Condensed Ledger, or Book-keeping Simplified," the object of which was to exhibit and explain a peculiar system of book-keeping. In 1860 and 1861, he took the copyright of several other books, containing additions to and improvements upon the said system. The bill of complaint was filed against the defendant, Baker, for an alleged infringement of these copyrights. The latter, in his answer, denied that Selden was the author or designer of the books, and denied the infringement charged, and contends on the argument that the matter alleged to be infringed is not a lawful subject of copyright. . . .

The book or series of books of which the complainant claims the copyright consists of an introductory essay explaining the system of book-keeping referred to, to which are annexed certain forms or blanks, consisting of ruled lines, and headings, illustrating the system and showing how it is to be used and carried out in practice. This system effects the same results as book-keeping by double entry; but, by a peculiar arrangement of columns and headings, presents the entire operation, of a day, a week, or a month, on a single page, or on two pages facing each other, in an account-book. The defendant uses a similar plan so far as results are concerned; but makes a different arrangement of the columns, and uses different headings. If the complainant's testator had the exclusive right to the use of the system explained in his book, it would be difficult to contend that the defendant does not infringe it, notwithstanding the difference in his form of arrangement; but if it be assumed that the system is open to public use, it seems to be equally difficult to contend that the books made and sold by the defendant are a violation of the copyright of the complainant's book considered merely as a book explanatory of the system. Where the truths of a science or the methods of an art are the common property of the whole world, any author has the right to express the one, or explain and use the other, in his own way. As an author, Selden explained the system in a particular way. It may be conceded that Baker makes and uses account-books arranged on substantially the same system; but the proof fails to show that he has violated the copyright of Selden's book, regarding the latter merely as an explanatory work; or that he has infringed Selden's right in any way, unless the latter became entitled to an exclusive right in the system.

The evidence of the complainant is principally directed to the object of showing that Baker uses the same system as that which is explained and illustrated in Selden's books. It becomes important, therefore, to determine whether, in obtaining the copyright of his books, he secured the exclusive right to the use of the system or method of book-keeping which the said books are intended to illustrate and explain. It is contended that he has secured such exclusive right, because no one can use the system without using substantially the same ruled lines and headings which he has appended to his books in illustration of it. In other words, it is contended that the ruled lines and headings, given to illustrate the system, are a part of the book, and, as such, are secured by the copyright; and that no one can make or use similar ruled lines and headings, or ruled lines and headings made and arranged on substantially the same system, without violating the copyright. And this is really the question to be decided in this case. Stated in another form, the question is, whether the exclusive property in a system of book-keeping can be claimed, under the law of copyright, by means of a book in which that system is explained? The complainant's bill, and the case made under it, are based on the hypothesis that it can be. . . .

There is no doubt that a work on the subject of book-keeping, though only explanatory of well-known systems, may be the subject of a copyright; but, then, it is claimed only as a book. Such a book may be explanatory either of old systems, or of an entirely new system; and, considered as a book, as the work of an author, conveying information on the subject of book-keeping, and containing detailed explanations of the art, it may be a very valuable acquisition to the practical knowledge of the community. But there is a clear distinction between the book, as such, and the art which it is intended to illustrate. The mere statement of the proposition is so evident, that it requires hardly any argument to support it. The same distinction may be predicated of every other art as well as that of book-keeping. A treatise on the composition and use of medicines, be they old or new; on the construction and use of ploughs, or watches, or churns; or on the mixture and application of colors for painting or dyeing; or on the mode of drawing lines to produce the effect of perspective,—would be the subject of copyright; but no one would contend that the copyright of the treatise would give the exclusive right to the art or manufacture described therein. The copyright of the book, if not pirated from other works, would be valid without regard to the novelty, or want of novelty, of its subject-matter. The novelty of the art or thing described or explained has nothing to do with the validity of the copyright. To give to the author of the book an exclusive property in the art described therein, when no examination of its novelty has ever been officially made, would be a surprise and a fraud upon the public. That is the province of letters-patent, not of copyright. The claim to an invention or discovery of an art or manufacture must be subjected to the examination of the Patent Office before an exclusive right therein can be obtained; and it can only be secured by a patent from the government. . . .

. . . The very object of publishing a book on science or the useful arts is to communicate to the world the useful knowledge which it contains. But this object would be frustrated if the knowledge could not be used without incurring the guilt of piracy of the book. And where the art it teaches cannot be used without employing the methods and diagrams used to illustrate the book, or such as are similar to them, such methods and diagrams are to be considered as necessary incidents to the art, and given therewith to the public; not given for the purpose of publication in other works explanatory of the art, but for the purpose of practical application.

Of course, these observations are not intended to apply to ornamental designs, or pictorial illustrations addressed to the taste. Of these it may be said, that their form is their essence, and their object, the production of pleasure in their contemplation. This is their final end. They are as much the product of genius and the result of composition, as are the lines of the poet or the historian's periods. On the other hand, the teachings of science and the rules and methods of useful art have their final end in application and use; and this application and use are what the public derive from the publication of a book which teaches them. But as embodied and taught in a literary composition or book, their essence consists only in their statement. This alone is what is secured by the copyright. The use by another of the same methods of statement, whether in words or illustrations, in a book published for teaching the art, would undoubtedly be an infringement of the copyright.

Recurring to the case before us, we observe that Charles Selden, by his books, explained and described a peculiar system of book-keeping, and illustrated his method by means of ruled lines and blank columns, with proper headings on a page, or on successive pages. Now, whilst no one has a right to print or publish his book, or any material part thereof, as a book intended to convey instruction in the art, any person may practise and use the art itself which he has described and illustrated therein. The use of the art is a totally different thing from a publication of the book explaining it. The copyright of a book on book-keeping cannot secure the exclusive right to make, sell, and use account-books prepared upon the plan set forth in such book. Whether the art might or might not have been patented, is a question which is not before us. It was not patented, and is open and free to the use of the public. And, of course, in using the art, the ruled lines and headings of accounts must necessarily be used as incident to it.

The plausibility of the claim put forward by the complainant in this case arises from a confusion of ideas produced by the peculiar nature of the art described in the books which have been made the subject of copyright. In describing the art, the illustrations and diagrams employed happen to correspond more closely than usual with the actual work performed by the operator who uses the art. Those illustrations and diagrams consist of ruled lines and headings of accounts; and it is similar ruled lines and headings of accounts which, in the application of the art, the book-keeper makes with his pen, or the stationer with his press; whilst in most other cases the diagrams and illustrations can only be represented in concrete forms of wood, metal, stone, or some other physical embodiment. But the principle is the same in all. The description of the art in a book, though entitled to the benefit of copyright, lays no foundation for an exclusive claim to the art itself. The object of the one is explanation; the object of the other is use. The former may be secured by copyright. The latter can only be secured, if it can be secured at all, by letters-patent. . . .

[BAKER'S FORM.]

AUDITOR'S REGISTER

RECEIPTS.

Date.	No.	From.	For.	County.						Total.
			Total							

DISBURSEMENTS.

Date.	No.	To.	For.	By.	County.	Poor.	Bridge.			Total.
			Total.							

BALANCE SHEET

FUNDS	Rec'd to 186	[Dist'd] to 186	To Rec. to 186	To Dis. to 186	Balance 186	Ov'r Pd 186
County.						
Poor.						
Bridge.						
School.						
Township.						
Corporation.						
Redemption of Lands.						
Teachers' Institute.						
Show Licenses.						
Peddlers' Licenses.						
Volunteer Relief.						
Section 16.						
State Fund.						
Road Taxes.						
Building.						
Rail Road.						
Ministry.						
Soldiers' Pay.						
Bounty.						
Balance in Treasury.						
Total.						
County Treasurer-General Acct.						

ADDITIONAL RECEIPTS.

Floating Order.

ADDITIONAL DISBURSEMENTS.

Exhibit.

RIGHT HAND PAGE

LEFT HAND PAGE

[SELDEN'S FORM]

AUDITOR'S RECORD.   CONDENSED LEDGER.

DISBURSEMENTS.

County Fund.

Date.	No.	Amount.	Fo.	For.	Authority.

RECEIPTS.

Date.	No.	Amount.	Of.	For.	Authority.

Date: from ...... to ...... inclusive.

Bro'ght Forward.		Distri- bution.		Sundries to Sundries. TREASURER.			Total.		Balan- ces.	
Dr.	Cr.	Dr.	Cr.	Dr. $	Cr. $	Cr.	Dr.	Cr.	Dr.	Cr.

Floating Order

County Fund.
Bridge Fund.
County Infirmary.
Building Fund.
Internal Fund.
Kind Fund.
Sale Redemptions.
Refunders.
Tax Omissions.
Forfeitures.
Duplicate.
Section 16.
Section 29.
Peddlers' License.
Show License.
State Fund.
School Fund.
Corporation Fund.
Township Fund.
Treasurer's Fees.
State Relief Fund.
Soldiers' Fund.
Militia Fund.
Bounty Fund.
School Examiners' Fund.
CARRIED FORWARD.

LEFT HAND PAGE

RIGHT HAND PAGE

NOTES AND QUESTIONS

1. What exactly is the *Baker* holding? What (if anything) in Selden's book is copyrightable and what is not?

2. While *Baker* is often cited as the foundational case establishing the idea/expression distinction, does it in fact do so? According to Professor Pamela Samuelson, "[T]he main message the Court was trying to convey was that bookkeeping systems and other useful arts were beyond the scope of copyright protection in any text that might explain them or any drawing that might illustrate them." Pamela Samuelson, *Why Copyright Excludes Systems and Processes from the Scope of Its Protection*, 85 Tex. L. Rev. 1921, 1926 (2007). Do you agree? Examine §102(b) again. Which of the listed items are most closely related to the *Baker* Court's holding? Does *Baker* mean that the more useful a work is, the less likely it is to be copyrightable? If courts interpret *Baker* in the way that Professor Samuelson recommends, will they inevitably have to evaluate artistic merit?

3. In *Baker* the defendant was a direct competitor of the copyright holder. Should that matter to the copyright analysis?

4. Section 101 of the Patent Act defines patentable subject matter to include "any new and useful process" that meets the statute's requirements. Selden's bookkeeping system could be considered a process, but courts during Selden's time most likely would have held the system unpatentable based on a judicially created doctrine excluding business methods from patent protection. In *Bilski v. Kappos*, 561 U.S. 593 (2010), the Court held that "the Patent Act leaves open the possibility that there are at least some processes that can be fairly described as business methods that are within patentable subject matter under §101." *Id.* at 609.

Note on the Merger Doctrine and Thin Copyright

Closely related to the exclusionary principle expressed in §102(b) is the doctrine of merger: Where only one or a limited number of ways exist to express an idea, the idea and expression merge, and copyright cannot be used to prevent another from using the same or similar expression. The merger doctrine commands universal agreement, but courts differ in the way they apply it. Some decisions treat merger as a bar to copyrightability. For example, in *Morrissey v. Procter & Gamble Co.*, 379 F.2d 675 (1st Cir. 1967), the court held that instructions for a sweepstakes contest could not be copyrighted:

> When the uncopyrightable subject matter is very narrow, so that "the topic necessarily requires" . . . if not only one form of expression, at best only a limited number, to permit copyrighting would mean that a party or parties, by copyrighting a mere handful of forms, could exhaust all possibilities of future use of the substance. In such circumstances it does not seem accurate to say that any particular form of expression comes from the subject matter. However, it is necessary to say that the subject matter would be appropriated by permitting the copyrighting of its expression. We cannot recognize copyright as a game of chess in which the public can be checkmated. Cf. *Baker v. Selden*. . . .

379 F.2d at 679. According to others, the doctrine supplies a defense to copyright infringement liability. *See, e.g.*, *Kregos v. Associated Press*, 937 F.2d 700, 705 (2d Cir. 1991) ("Assessing merger in the context of alleged infringement will normally provide a more detailed and realistic basis for evaluating the claim that protection of expression would invariably accord protection to an idea.").

Sometimes, there are more than a few ways to express an idea, but the scope for variation is quite limited. In such cases, a court may conclude that the particular expression is copyrightable but that the scope of the copyright is "thin"—so thin that infringement only occurs in the case of a virtually identical copy. *See, e.g.*, *Johnson Controls, Inc. v. Phoenix Control Sys., Inc.*, 886 F.2d 1173, 1175 (9th Cir. 1989) ("Where an idea and the expression 'merge,' or are 'inseparable,' the expression is not given copyright protection. . . . In addition, where an expression is, as a practical matter, indispensable, or at least standard, in the treatment of a given idea, the expression is protected only against verbatim, or virtually identical copying.").

Finally, note that in its regulations, the Copyright Office has indicated its view that certain items should always be excluded from copyright protection:

§202.1 Material not subject to copyright

The following are examples of works not subject to copyright and applications for registration of such works cannot be entertained:

(a) Words and short phrases such as names, titles, and slogans; familiar symbols or designs; mere variations of typographic ornamentation, lettering or coloring; mere listing of ingredients or contents;

(b) Ideas, plans, methods, systems, or devices, as distinguished from the particular manner in which they are expressed or described in a writing;

(c) Blank forms, such as time cards, graph paper, account books, diaries, bank checks, scorecards, address books, report forms, order forms and the like, which are designed for recording information and do not in themselves convey information;

(d) Works consisting entirely of information that is common property containing no original authorship, such as, for example: Standard calendars, height and weight charts, tape measures and rulers, schedules of sporting events, and lists or tables taken from public documents or other common sources.

(e) Typeface as typeface.

37 C.F.R. §202.1.

NOTES AND QUESTIONS

1. What are the practical differences, if any, to litigants of the different approaches to the merger doctrine? What incentives does the "thin copyright" approach create?

2. Section 102(b) explains some, but not all, of the items on the Copyright Office's list of excluded items. Does the merger doctrine explain all of the others?

PRACTICE EXERCISE: COUNSEL A CLIENT

If Selden's book were still under copyright, how would you advise a client who wanted to do the following:

a. implement an accounting system requiring the client to use exact copies of the forms;

b. publish a book of blank forms containing exact copies of Selden's forms;

c. publish a book comparing different accounting systems, and including (i) a description of Selden's system, (ii) exact copies of the forms, and (iii) examples of how to modify the forms to meet different needs.

---

b. Complications

Baker and §102(b) might be read to suggest that information separates neatly into three categories: copyrightable, patentable, and public domain. The reality is more complicated. As we noted at the outset of this section, the phrase "idea/expression distinction" is shorthand for a rule requiring the exclusion of a variety of elements of a work from copyright protection. Within copyright law, the conceptual difficulties in separating those elements from protectable expression can be substantial.

We begin by considering the line between fact and fiction. Some works blend the two, making the scope of copyright protection in such works difficult to assess. Many nonfictional historical works, meanwhile, include some material that rests, at least in part, on hypothesis or conjecture. Additionally, many expressive works, both fictional and nonfictional, employ standard expressions to conjure up certain images. Does copyright bar duplication of such expressions? Consider what the next case has to say about these questions.

A.A. Hoehling v. Universal City Studios, Inc.
618 F.2d 972 (2d Cir.), cert. denied, *449 U.S. 841 (1980)*

KAUFMAN, C.J.: A grant of copyright in a published work secures for its author a limited monopoly over the expression it contains. The copyright provides a financial incentive to those who would add to the corpus of existing knowledge by creating original works. Nevertheless, the protection afforded the copyright holder has never extended to history, be it documented fact or explanatory hypothesis. The rationale for this doctrine is that the cause of knowledge is best served when history is the common property of all, and each generation remains free to draw upon the discoveries and insights of the past. Accordingly, the scope of copyright in historical accounts is narrow indeed, embracing no more than the author's original expression of particular facts and theories already in the public domain. As the case before us illustrates, absent wholesale usurpation of another's expression, claims of copyright infringement where works of history are at issue are rarely successful.

I.

This litigation arises from three separate accounts of the triumphant introduction, last voyage, and tragic destruction of the Hindenburg, the colossal dirigible constructed in Germany during Hitler's reign. The zeppelin, the last and most sophisticated in a fleet of luxury airships, which punctually floated its wealthy passengers from the Third Reich to the United States, exploded into flames and disintegrated in 35 seconds as it hovered above the Lakehurst, New Jersey Naval Air Station at 7:25 P.M. on May 6, 1937. Thirty-six passengers and crew were killed but, fortunately, 52 persons survived. Official investigations conducted by both American and German authorities could ascertain no definitive cause of the disaster, but both suggested the plausibility of static electricity or St. Elmo's Fire, which could have ignited the highly explosive hydrogen that filled the airship. Throughout, the investigators refused to rule out the possibility of sabotage. . . .

The final pages of the airship's story marked the beginning of a series of journalistic, historical, and literary accounts devoted to the Hindenburg and its fate. Indeed, weeks of testimony by a plethora of witnesses before the official investigative panels provided fertile source material for would-be authors. Moreover, both the American and German Commissions issued official reports, detailing all that was then known of the tragedy. A number of newspaper and magazine articles had been written about the Hindenburg in 1936, its first year of trans-Atlantic service, and they, of course, multiplied many fold after the crash. In addition, two passengers, Margaret Mather and Gertrud Adelt, published separate and detailed accounts of the voyage, C. E. Rosendahl, commander of the Lakehurst Naval Air Station and a pioneer in airship travel himself, wrote a book titled *What About the Airship?*, in which he endorsed the theory that the Hindenburg was the victim of sabotage. In 1957, Nelson Gidding, who would return to the subject of the Hindenburg some 20 years later, wrote an unpublished "treatment" for a motion picture based on the deliberate destruction of the airship. In that year as well, John Toland published *Ships in the Sky* which, in its seventeenth chapter, chronicled the last flight of the Hindenburg. In 1962, Dale Titler released *Wings of Mystery*, in which he too devoted a chapter to the Hindenburg.[1]

Appellant A. A. Hoehling published *Who Destroyed the Hindenburg?*, a full-length book based on his exhaustive research in 1962. Mr. Hoehling studied the investigative reports, consulted previously published articles and books, and conducted interviews with survivors of the crash as well as others who possessed information about the Hindenburg. His book is presented as a factual account, written in an objective, reportorial style.

---

1. Titler's account was published after the release of appellant's book. In an affidavit in this litigation, Titler states that he copied Hoehling's theory of sabotage. Hoehling, however, has never instituted a copyright action against Titler.

The first half recounts the final crossing of the Hindenburg, from Sunday, May 2, when it left Frankfurt, to Thursday, May 6, when it exploded at Lakehurst. Hoehling describes the airship, its role as an instrument of propaganda in Nazi Germany, its passengers and crew, the danger of hydrogen, and the ominous threats received by German officials, warning that the Hindenburg would be destroyed. The second portion, headed *The Quest*, sets forth the progress of the official investigations, followed by an account of Hoehling's own research. In the final chapter, spanning eleven pages, Hoehling suggests that all proffered explanations of the explosion, save deliberate destruction, are unconvincing. He concludes that the most likely saboteur is one Eric Spehl, a "rigger" on the Hindenburg crew who was killed at Lakehurst.

According to Hoehling, Spehl had motive, expertise, and opportunity to plant an explosive device, constructed of dry-cell batteries and a flashbulb, in "Gas Cell 4," the location of the initial explosion. An amateur photographer with access to flashbulbs, Spehl could have destroyed the Hindenburg to please his ladyfriend, a suspected communist dedicated to exploding the myth of Nazi invincibility.

Ten years later appellee Michael MacDonald Mooney published his book, *The Hindenburg*. Mooney's endeavor might be characterized as more literary than historical in its attempt to weave a number of symbolic themes through the actual events surrounding the tragedy. His dominant theme contrasts the natural beauty of the month of May, when the disaster occurred, with the cold, deliberate progress of "technology." The May theme is expressed not simply by the season, but also by the character of Spehl, portrayed as a sensitive artisan with needle and thread. The Hindenburg, in contrast, is the symbol of technology, as are its German creators and the Reich itself. The destruction is depicted as the ultimate triumph of nature over technology, as Spehl plants the bomb that ignites the hydrogen. Developing this theme from the outset, Mooney begins with an extended review of man's efforts to defy nature through flight, focusing on the evolution of the zeppelin. This story culminates in the construction of the Hindenburg, and the Nazis' claims of its indestructibility. Mooney then traces the fateful voyage, advising the reader almost immediately of Spehl's scheme. The book concludes with the airship's explosion.

Mooney acknowledges, in this case, that he consulted Hoehling's book, and that he relied on it for some details. He asserts that he first discovered the "Spehl-as-saboteur" theory when he read Titler's *Wings of Mystery*. Indeed, Titler concludes that Spehl was the saboteur, for essentially the reasons stated by Hoehling. Mooney also claims to have studied the complete National Archives and New York Times files concerning the Hindenburg, as well as all previously published material. Moreover, he traveled to Germany, visited Spehl's birthplace, and conducted a number of interviews with survivors.

After Mooney prepared an outline of his anticipated book, his publisher succeeded in negotiations to sell the motion picture rights to appellee Universal City Studios. Universal then commissioned a screen story by writers Levinson and Link, best known for their television series, *Columbo*, in which a somewhat disheveled, but wise detective unravels artfully conceived murder mysteries. In their screen story, Levinson and Link created a Columbo-like character who endeavored to identify the saboteur on board the Hindenburg. Director Robert Wise, however, was not satisfied with this version, and called upon Nelson Gidding to write a final screenplay. Gidding, it will be recalled, had engaged in preliminary work on a film about the Hindenburg almost twenty years earlier.

The Gidding screenplay follows what is known in the motion picture industry as a "Grand Hotel" formula, developing a number of fictional characters and subplots involving them. This formula has become standard fare in so-called "disaster" movies, which have enjoyed a certain popularity in recent years. In the film, which was released in late 1975, a rigger named "Boerth," who has an anti-Nazi ladyfriend, plans to destroy the airship in an effort to embarrass the Reich. Nazi officials, vaguely aware of sabotage threats, station a Luftwaffe intelligence officer on the zeppelin, loosely resembling a Colonel Erdmann who was aboard the Hindenburg. This character is portrayed as a likable fellow who soon discovers that Boerth is the saboteur. Boerth, however, convinces him that the Hindenburg should be destroyed and the two join forces, planning the explosion for several hours after the landing at Lakehurst, when no people would be on board. In Gidding's version, the airship is delayed by a storm, frantic efforts to defuse the bomb fail, and the Hindenburg is destroyed. The film's subplots involve other possible suspects, including a fictional countess who has had her estate expropriated by the Reich, two fictional confidence men wanted by New York City police, and an advertising executive rushing to close a business deal in America. . . .

[Hoehling sued Universal and Mooney for copyright infringement. The district court granted summary judgment in favor of the defendants.]

II. . . .

A

Hoehling's principal claim is that both Mooney and Universal copied the essential plot of his book—i.e., Eric Spehl, influenced by his girlfriend, sabotaged the Hindenburg by placing a crude bomb in Gas Cell 4. . . .

[A]ppellees . . . argue that Hoehling's plot is an "idea," and ideas are not copyrightable as a matter of law. *See Sheldon v. Metro-Goldwyn Pictures Corp.*, 81 F.2d 49, 54 (2d Cir.), *cert. denied*, 298 U.S. 669. . . .

Hoehling, however, correctly rejoins that while ideas themselves are not subject to copyright, his "expression" of his idea is copyrightable. *Id.* at 54. . . .

. . . But, where, as here, the idea at issue is an interpretation of an historical event, our cases hold that such interpretations are not copyrightable as a matter of law. In *Rosemont Enterprises, Inc. v. Random House, Inc.*, 366 F.2d 303 (2d Cir. 1966), *cert. denied*, 385 U.S. 1009 . . . , we held that the defendant's biography of Howard Hughes did not infringe an earlier biography of the reclusive alleged billionaire. Although the plots of the two works were necessarily similar, there could be no infringement because of the "public benefit in encouraging the development of historical and biographical works and their public distribution." *Id.* at 307; *accord, Oxford Book Co. v. College Entrance Book Co.*, 98 F.2d 688 (2d Cir. 1938). To avoid a chilling effect on authors who contemplate tackling an historical issue or event, broad latitude must be granted to subsequent authors who make use of historical subject matter, including theories or plots. Learned Hand counseled in *Myers v. Mail & Express Co.*, 36 C.O. Bull. 478, 479 (S.D.N.Y. 1919), "[t]here cannot be any such thing as copyright in the order of presentation of the facts, nor, indeed, in their selection."[5]

In the instant case, the hypothesis that Eric Spehl destroyed the Hindenburg is based entirely on the interpretation of historical facts, including Spehl's life, his girlfriend's anti-Nazi connections, the explosion's origin in Gas Cell 4, Spehl's duty station, discovery of a dry-cell battery among the wreckage, and rumors about Spehl's involvement dating from a 1938 Gestapo investigation. Such an historical interpretation, whether or not it originated with Mr. Hoehling, is not protected by his copyright and can be freely used by subsequent authors.

B

The same reasoning governs Hoehling's claim that a number of specific facts, ascertained through his personal research, were copied by appellees.[6] The cases in this circuit, however, make clear that factual information is in the public domain. *See, e.g., Rosemont Enterprises, Inc., supra*, 366 F.2d at 309; *Oxford Book Co., supra*, 98 F.2d at 691. Each appellee had the right to "avail himself of the facts contained" in Hoehling's book and to "use such information, whether correct or incorrect, in his own literary work." *Greenbie v. Noble*, 151 F. Supp. 45, 67 (S.D.N.Y. 1957). Accordingly, there is little consolation in relying on cases in other circuits holding that the fruits of original research are copyrightable. *See, e.g., Toksvig v. Bruce Publications Corp.*, 181 F.2d 664, 667 (7th Cir. 1950); *Miller v. Universal City Studios, Inc.*, 460 F. Supp. 984 (S.D. Fla. 1978). Indeed, this circuit has clearly repudiated *Toksvig* and its progeny. In *Rosemont Enterprises, Inc., supra*, 366 F.2d at 310, we refused to "subscribe to the view that an author is absolutely precluded from saving

---

5. This circuit has permitted extensive reliance on prior works of history. *See, e.g., Gardner v. Nizer*, 391 F. Supp. 940 (S.D.N.Y. 1975) (the story of the Rosenberg trial not copyrightable); *Fuld v. National Broadcasting Co.*, 390 F. Supp. 877 (S.D.N.Y. 1975) ("Bugsy" Siegel's life story not copyrightable); *Greenbie v. Noble*, 151 F. Supp. 45 (S.D.N.Y. 1957) (the life of Anna Carroll, a member of Lincoln's cabinet, not copyrightable). The commentators are in accord with this view. *See, e.g.,* 1, Nimmer on Copyright §2.11[A] (1979); Chafee, *Reflections on the Law of Copyright: I*, 45 Colum. L. Rev. 503, 511 (1945).

6. In detailed comparisons of his book with Mooney's work and Universal's motion picture, Hoehling isolates 266 and 75 alleged instances of copying, respectively. Judge Metzner correctly pointed out that many of these allegations are patently frivolous. The vast majority of the remainder deals with alleged copying of historical facts. It would serve no purpose to review Hoehling's specific allegations in detail in this opinion. The following ten examples, however, are illustrative: (1) Eric Spehl's age and birthplace; (2) Crew members had smuggled monkeys on board the Graf Zeppelin; (3) Germany's ambassador to the U.S. dismissed threats of sabotage; (4) A warning letter had been received from a Mrs. Rauch; (5) The Hindenburg's captain was constructing a new home in Zeppelinheim; (6) Eric Spehl was a photographer; (7) The airship flew over Boston; (8) The Hindenburg was "tail heavy" before landing; (9) A member of the ground crew had etched his name in the zeppelin's hull; and (10) The navigator set the Hindenburg's course by reference to various North Atlantic islands.

time and effort by referring to and relying upon prior published material. . . . It is just such wasted effort that the proscription against the copyright of ideas and facts . . . are designed to prevent." *Accord*, 1 Nimmer on Copyright §2.11 (1979).

C

The remainder of Hoehling's claimed similarities relate to random duplications of phrases and sequences of events. For example, all three works contain a scene in a German beer hall, in which the airship's crew engages in revelry prior to the voyage. Other claimed similarities concern common German greetings of the period, such as "Heil Hitler," or songs, such as the German National anthem. These elements, however, are merely *scenes à faire*, that is, "incidents, characters or settings which are as a practical matter indispensable, or at least standard, in the treatment of a given topic." *Alexander* [*v. Haley*], 460 F. Supp. [40, 45 S.D.N.Y.1977]; *accord, Bevan v. Columbia Broadcasting System, Inc.*, 329 F. Supp. 601, 607 (S.D.N.Y. 1971). Because it is virtually impossible to write about a particular historical era or fictional theme without employing certain "stock" or standard literary devices, we have held that *scenes à faire* are not copyrightable as a matter of law. *See Reyher v. Children's Television Workshop*, 533 F.2d 87, 91 (2d Cir.), *cert. denied*, 429 U.S. 980 (1976). . . .

D

All of Hoehling's allegations of copying, therefore, encompass material that is non-copyrightable as a matter of law, rendering summary judgment entirely appropriate. We are aware, however, that in distinguishing between themes, facts, and *scenes à faire* on the one hand, and copyrightable expression on the other, courts may lose sight of the forest for the trees. By factoring out similarities based on non-copyrightable elements, a court runs the risk of overlooking wholesale usurpation of a prior author's expression. A verbatim reproduction of another work, of course, even in the realm of nonfiction, is actionable as copyright infringement. *See Wainwright Securities, Inc. v. Wall Street Transcript Corp.*, 558 F.2d 91 (2d Cir. 1977), *cert. denied*, 434 U.S. 1014. . . . Thus, in granting or reviewing a grant of summary judgment for defendants, courts should assure themselves that the works before them are not virtually identical. In this case, it is clear that all three authors relate the story of the Hindenburg differently.

In works devoted to historical subjects, it is our view that a second author may make significant use of prior work, so long as he does not bodily appropriate the expression of another. *Rosemont Enterprises, Inc., supra*, 366 F.2d at 310. This principle is justified by the fundamental policy undergirding the copyright laws— the encouragement of contributions to recorded knowledge. The "financial reward guaranteed to the copyright holder is but an incident of this general objective, rather than an end in itself." *Berlin v. E.C. Publications, Inc.*, 329 F.2d 541, 543-44 (2d Cir.), *cert. denied*, 379 U.S. 822 (1964). . . . Knowledge is expanded as well by granting new authors of historical works a relatively free hand to build upon the work of their predecessors. . . .

NOTES AND QUESTIONS

1. Why should the plot of a fictional work receive copyright protection? Why isn't it enough for copyright to extend only to the literal textual wording?

2. Examine the text of §102(b) again. Which word or words in the statute exclude facts from copyright protection? According to the *Feist* Court:

> [t]o borrow from *Burrow-Giles*, one who discovers a fact is not its "maker" or "originator." . . . 'The discoverer merely finds and records." Census takers, for example, do not "create" the population figures that emerge from their efforts; in a sense, they copy these figures from the world around them. . . . The same is true of all facts—scientific, historical, biographical, and news of the day. "[T]hey may not be copyrighted and are part of the public domain available to every person."

Feist, 499 U.S. at 347-48. Are historical theories also "discoveries"? Are historians less creative than painters or novelists? Should a work that is held out to the public as a work of historical fiction receive stronger copyright protection than a work that is held out to the public as a work of history?

3. The *Hoehling* court notes that it is attempting to avoid the wasted effort incurred when a second comer is required to research factual events anew. How is this wasted effort any different from that discussed in Question 2, Section A.2.9 *supra*, in which two artists each had to travel to Colorado to depict the same landscape? Each was free to copy the original but the second artist was not free to copy the copy painted by the first. Why doesn't the same rule apply to historical facts? Why doesn't it apply to historical theories?

Note that historians are subject to separate ethical norms that prohibit plagiarism and require citation of sources. Do these norms serve the same purposes that copyright law serves?

4. The merger doctrine applies when it is necessary to copy expression because the underlying idea may not be effectively expressed in another way. The doctrine of *scenes à faire* protects a second comer's use of literary devices that are not literally necessary to express an idea, but that the audience has come to expect. What are the justifications for these doctrines? Are they equally compelling?

Next, we consider how the law should separate unprotectable systems or processes from copyrightable expression. Many industries develop new approaches to classifying information. When, if ever, are the results of such efforts copyrightable? Put differently, is §102(b) simply an elaboration of §102(a) or does it add something—i.e., could there be subject matter that qualifies for copyright protection under §102(a) (because it is sufficiently original), but that nevertheless is excluded by §102(b)?

ATC Distribution Group, Inc. v. Whatever It Takes Transmissions & Parts, Inc.
402 F.3d 700 (6th Cir. 2005)

Opinion

Boggs, C.J.

[ATC, a company selling transmission parts, had purchased another firm's assets, including a catalog with illustrations and a numbering system for transmission parts. Kenny Hester, a former ATC employee, formed his own competitive company, Whatever It Takes Transmissions ("WITT"). Hester obtained an electronic version of the catalog and developed a similar one. ATC sued for copyright infringement and the court granted summary judgment for WITT. This appeal followed.]

II

We review a district court's order granting summary judgment *de novo,* and its findings of fact for clear error.

A. Copyright infringement. . . .

ATC claims that WITT and Hester infringed its copyrights in the parts catalog, the individual part numbers contained in the catalog, the illustrations contained in the catalog, and its self-described "Numbering System Manual." Appellees do not contest the allegation that they copied these works and items. Rather, they raise the affirmative defense that . . . none of the works or items listed are eligible for copyright protection.

The district court . . . agreed that the catalog, part numbers, illustrations, and the manual lacked the originality required for copyright protection, and that Appellees' admitted copying of these works and items could not have constituted copyright infringement as a matter of law. The district court therefore held that Appellees were entitled to summary judgment on ATC's claim of copyright infringement. . . . [W]e agree. . . .

1. Catalog and Part Numbers.

. . . ATC argues that its catalog is a creative classification scheme, or taxonomy, which sorts parts into categories and sub-categories, and allocates numbers to each part. Under this theory, the individual part numbers would be protected as the copyrightable expressions of the overall taxonomy. . . .

ATC's parts-classification scheme divides transmission parts into a series of categories and sub-categories. There are three basic categories: brand, transmission type, and type of part. In addition, a suffix field is available to further sub-divide a particular part when appropriate. Within each category, several sub-categories have been created. In the brand category the sub-categories are relatively obvious: the transmissions are listed by manufacturer. In the part category the sub-categories are less obvious, and require decisions such as whether to have a single category of rings, of which some are sealing rings and some are O-rings, or to have two distinct categories, sealing rings and O-rings. Each of the three basic categories and the optional suffix are represented in each part number by a two-digit or three-digit field (with the occasional letter), within which the transmission types or parts are numbered in order, with gaps being left in each sub-category to accommodate new parts in the future. Although all parts within a sub-category are numbered sequentially, the ordering of the sub-categories within a field, or the parts within a sub-category appears to be random. As such, the fact that an "O-ring pump" and an "O-ring pump bolt" are in the same general range of numbers is no accident. But the fact that O-rings in general are numbered in the 300's, and the fact that these two parts are numbered 311 and 312 rather than 341 and 342, are accidental. Each discrete transmission part will have a number that is between five and nine digits and/or letters.

ATC claims that its numbering scheme involves several different types of creativity: (1) deciding what kind of information to convey in part numbers; (2) predicting future developments in the transmission parts industry and deciding how many slots to leave open in a given sub-category to allow for those developments; (3) deciding whether an apparently novel part that does not obviously fit in any of the existing classifications should be assigned a new category of its own or placed in an existing category, and, if the latter, which one; (4) designing the part numbers; and (5) devising the overall taxonomy of part numbers that places the parts into different categories. An example of this last type of creativity would be the decision to include in the catalog entries for "Pressure Plate, Intermediate (Top)" (assigned number 144) and "Pressure Plate, Intermediate (Bottom)" (145), as opposed to using one unitary entry for "Pressure Plate, Intermediate," but adding a suffix to that part number that differentiates between top (1441) and bottom (1442) plates.

a. The ATC Catalog as a Taxonomy.

Classification schemes can in principle be creative enough to satisfy the originality requirement of copyright protection. *See Am. Dental Ass'n v. Delta Dental Plans Ass'n,* 126 F.3d 977, 979 (7th Cir.1997) ("Facts do not supply their own principles of organization. Classification is a creative endeavor. . . . There can be multiple, and equally original, biographies of the same person's life, and multiple original taxonomies of a field of knowledge."). None of ATC's claimed creative endeavors seem particularly creative when compared to a great painting or novel, but the Supreme Court has made clear that only a bare minimum amount of creativity is required to satisfy the constitutional originality requirement. *See Feist,* 499 U.S. at 345. At least some of the decisions made by ATC are arguably "non-obvious choices" made from "among more than a few options." *See Matthew Bender & Co. v. West Publ'g Co.,* 158 F.3d 674, 682 (2d Cir.1998).

Original and creative *ideas,* however, are not copyrightable, [under] 17 U.S.C. §102(b). . . . And all of the creative aspects of the ATC classification scheme are just that: ideas. ATC cannot copyright its prediction of how many types of sealing ring will be developed in the future, its judgment that O-rings and sealing rings should form two separate categories of parts, or its judgment that a new part belongs with the retainers as opposed to the pressure plates.

The *expression* of ATC's ideas about part classification and the future of the transmission parts market is not barred from copyright protection by the idea-expression distinction. It is barred, however, in part by the "merger doctrine," and in part by the originality requirement. For almost all of the types of creativity claimed by ATC, there is only one reasonable way to express the underlying idea. For example, the only way to express the prediction that a maximum of four additional types of sealing ring might be developed is to leave four numbers unallocated, and the only way to express the idea that a novel part should be placed with the sealing rings rather than with the gaskets is to place that part with the sealing rings. Under the merger doctrine, "when there is essentially only one way to express an idea, the idea and its expression are inseparable [i.e., they merge,] and copyright is no bar to copying that expression." *Kohus v. Mariol,* 328 F.3d 848, 856 (6th Cir.2003) (alteration in original, internal citation omitted).

The only aspect of the numbering system that does not merge with the under-lying idea is the allocation of numbers to each sub-category, and ultimately to each part. ATC argues that its individual part numbers are copyright protected as expressions of the catalog as a whole, and cites as authority the Seventh Circuit's holding in *American Dental,* which held that the American Dental Association's *Code on Dental Procedures and Nomenclature* was copyrightable. *See* 126 F.3d at 979. The *Code* classified dental procedures into groups, with each procedure receiving a number, a short description, and a long description. *Id.* at 977. . . . The Seventh Circuit held that the numbers assigned to each procedure were copyrightable, in addition to the long and short descriptions of each procedure. *Id.* at 979.

The *American Dental* court's rationale for holding that the individual proce-dure numbers were copyrightable is rather opaque:

> Number 04267 reads "guided tissue regeneration-nonresorbable barrier, per site, per tooth" but could have read "regeneration of tissue, guided by nonresorbable barrier, one site and tooth per entry." Or "use of barrier to guide regeneration of tissue, without regard to the number of sites per tooth and whether or not the barrier is resorbable." The first variation is linguistic, the second substantive; in each case the decision to use the actual description is original to the ADA, not knuckling under to an order imposed on language by some "fact" about dental procedures. Blood is shed in the ADA's commit-tees about which description is preferable. The number assigned to any one of the three descriptions could have had four or six digits rather than five; guided tissue regeneration could have been placed in the 2500 series rather than the 4200 series; again any of these choices is original to the author of a taxonomy, and another author could do things differently. Every number in the ADA's Code begins with zero, assuring a large supply of unused numbers for procedures to be devised or reclassified in the future; an author could have elected instead to leave wide gaps inside the sequence. A catalog that initially assigns 04266, 04267, 04268 to three procedures will over time depart substantively

from one that initially assigns 42660, 42670, and 42680 to the same three procedures. So all three elements of the Code-numbers, short descriptions, and long descriptions, are copyrightable subject matter under 17 U.S.C. §102(a).

Ibid. Almost all of this passage concerns either the wording of the descriptions, or the creative thought that went into the underlying taxonomy, such as the decision to leave gaps in the numbering system. The discussion of the numbers themselves is limited to two immaterial observations: that numbers in the 4200's rather than the 2500's were assigned to guided tissue regeneration; and that the numbers assigned to a particular procedure in a catalog will differ depending on the prior allocation of numbers to other procedures. Neither of these facts evidences any creativity by the ADA that would render the numbers eligible for copyright protection. The mere fact that numbers are attached to, or are a by-product of categories and descriptions that are copyrightable does not render the numbers themselves copyrightable.

Even assuming, *arguendo,* that some strings of numbers used to designate an item or procedure could be sufficiently creative to merit copyright protection, the parts numbers at issue in the case before us do not evidence any such creativity. ATC's allocation of numbers to parts was an essentially random process, serving only to provide a useful shorthand way of referring to each part. The only reason that a "sealing ring, pump slide" is allocated number 176 is the random ordering of sub-categories of parts, and the random ordering of parts within that sub-category. Were it not for a series of random orderings within each category field, a given part could be 47165 or 89386. As such, the particular numbers allocated to each part do not *express* any of the creative ideas that went into the classification scheme in any way that could be considered eligible for copyright protection. These numbers are no more copyrightable than would be the fruit of an author's labors if she wrote a book and then "translated" it into numbers using a random number generator for each letter in every word. Even if the text in English was copyrightable, the randomly generated list of numbers that comprised the "translation" could not be.

Originality aside, there are other sound reasons for denying copyright protection to short "works," such as part numbers. Although the fact that ATC had a copyright in the number 45607 might not ultimately preclude other people or entities from using that number in other contexts, given the defenses of fair use and independent creation available to those accused of copyright infringement, anyone using that number in a commercial context would face the time-consuming and expensive prospect of having to defend themselves against such claims. This would not only be extremely inefficient, but would provide a way for the creators of otherwise uncopyrightable ideas or works to gain some degree of copyright protection through the back door simply by assigning short numbers or other shorthand phrases to those ideas or works (or their component parts). Indeed, the Copyright Office will not register a short name, phrase, or expression, such as the name of a product or service, even if it is novel or distinctive. *See* 37 C.F.R. §202.1 While the use without compensation of one's labors may seem unfair, "this is not 'some unforeseen byproduct of a statutory scheme.' It is, rather, 'the essence of copyright,' and a constitutional requirement. The primary objective of copyright is not to reward the labor of authors, but 'to promote the Progress of Science and useful

Arts.'" *Feist*, 499 U.S. at 349 (internal citations omitted). Permitting uncopyrightable materials to receive protection simply by virtue of adding a number or label would allow an end run around that constitutional requirement.

As a last resort, ATC suggested during oral argument that even if neither the ideas that gave rise to the parts numbers, nor the individual part numbers, *qua* expressions of those ideas, are copyrightable, the part numbers taken as a whole were somehow copyrightable as a middle ground between the two, much in the same way that while neither the basic idea behind a novel nor the individual words used to write it are protected, the story that those words form when taken together is copyrightable. The flaw in this argument is that there is no such middle ground in this case. Unlike the words that comprise a novel, which add up to a story, the numbers used in ATC's catalog only add up to a long list of numbers. Putting all the numbers together does not make them expressive in the way that putting words together makes a narrative. . . .

NOTES AND QUESTIONS

1. Why didn't the merger doctrine dictate the same result in *American Dental* that it did in *ATC*? The *American Dental* court did not simply address the copyrightability of the plaintiff's procedure numbers, but also considered the accompanying short descriptions and the classification system as a whole. It observed: "Dental procedures could be classified by complexity, or by the tools necessary to perform them, or by the parts of the mouth involved, or by the anesthesia employed, or in any of a dozen different ways. The Code's descriptions don't 'merge with the facts' any more than a scientific description of butterfly attributes is part of a butterfly." *Am. Dental Ass'n v. Delta Dental Plans Ass'n*, 126 F.3d 977, 979 (7th Cir. 1997). Which reasoning—the *ATC* court's or the *American Dental* court's—do you find more persuasive and why?

2. Should a taxonomy be considered a "process" or "method of operation" and therefore categorically barred from copyrightability under §102(b)? Should this be the rule even if the taxonomy is highly original—in other words, is there a kind of originality that is noncopyrightable?

3. Might the *scenes a faire* doctrine be relevant in a taxonomy case? If a taxonomy becomes an industry standard, should that militate against copyright protection?

B. TWO SPECIAL CASES: DERIVATIVE WORKS AND COMPILATIONS

In addition to the basic copyrightable subject matter provisions of §102, the Copyright Act contains a separate section that accords copyright protection to two special types of works:

§103. Subject matter of copyright: Compilations and derivative works

(a) The subject matter of copyright as specified by section 102 includes compilations and derivative works, but protection for a work employing preexisting material in which copyright subsists does not extend to any part of the work in which such material has been used unlawfully.

(b) The copyright in a compilation or derivative work extends only to the material contributed by the author of such work, as distinguished from the preexisting material employed in the work, and does not imply any exclusive right in the preexisting material. The copyright in such work is independent of, and does not affect or enlarge the scope, duration, ownership, or subsistence of, any copyright protection in the preexisting material.

As you read the following materials, consider whether authors of compilations and derivative works are or should be held to different standards of originality than authors of other works.

1. Derivative Works

U.S. copyright law has long recognized copyrights in works based on other works. For example, the Copyright Act of 1909 extended copyright protection to "[r]eproductions of a work of art" and to "abridgements, adaptations, arrangements, dramatizations, translations, or other versions" of preexisting works. Pub. L. No. 60-349, 60th Cong., 2d Sess. §§5(h), 6, 35 Stat. 1075, 1077 (1909). In the 1976 Act, Congress adopted the term *derivative work* and set forth a broad definition that encompasses any work based on or derived from another work:

> A "derivative work" is a work based upon one or more preexisting works, such as a translation, musical arrangement, dramatization, fictionalization, motion picture version, sound recording, art reproduction, abridgement, condensation, or any other form in which a work may be recast, transformed, or adapted. A work consisting of editorial revisions, annotations, elaborations, or other modifications which, as a whole, represent an original work of authorship, is a "derivative work."

17 U.S.C. §101.

International copyright treaties similarly require protection of works based on other works, but the international copyright community has not adopted the "derivative work" terminology. The Berne Convention mandates protection for "[t]ranslations, adaptations, arrangements of music and other alterations of a literary or artistic work." Berne Conv., art. 2(3). The TRIPS Agreement incorporates this provision by reference.

Section 103(b) of the Act indicates that copyright in a derivative work subsists only in the new material contributed by the author of the derivative work. Neither §103(b) nor the definition in §101, however, indicates when the derivative material is sufficiently distinguishable from the underlying work to constitute a copyrightable work in its own right. Review the excerpt from *Feist*, *supra* page 73, which sets forth the standard that a work must satisfy to be considered an "original work of authorship." Then consider the standards of originality applied in the following cases.

L. Batlin & Son, Inc. v. Snyder
536 F.2d 486 (2d Cir.) (en banc), cert. denied, 429 U.S. 857 (1976)

OAKES, J.: . . . Uncle Sam mechanical banks have been on the American scene at least since June 8, 1886, when Design Patent No. 16,728, issued on a toy savings bank of its type. The basic delightful design has long since been in the public domain. The banks are well documented in collectors' books and known to the average person interested in Americana. . . . Uncle Sam, dressed in his usual stove pipe hat, blue full dress coat, starred vest and red and white striped trousers, and leaning on his umbrella, stands on a four- or five-inch wide base, on which sits his carpetbag. A coin may be placed in Uncle Sam's extended hand. When a lever is pressed, the arm lowers, and the coin falls into the bag, while Uncle Sam's whiskers move up and down. . . .

Appellant Jeffrey Snyder doing business as "J.S.N.Y." obtained a registration of copyright on a plastic "Uncle Sam bank" in Class G ("Works of Art") as "sculpture" on January 23, 1975. According to Snyder's affidavit, in January, 1974, he had seen a cast metal antique Uncle Sam bank with an overall height of the figure and base of 11 inches. In April 1974, he flew to Hong Kong to arrange for the design and eventual manufacture of replicas of the bank as Bicentennial items. . . . Snyder wanted his bank to be made of plastic and to be shorter than the cast metal sample "in order to fit into the required price range and quality and quantity of material to be used." The figure of Uncle Sam was thus shortened from 11 to nine inches, and the base shortened and narrowed. It was also decided, Snyder averred, to change the shape of the carpetbag and to include the umbrella in a one-piece mold for the Uncle Sam figure "so as not to have a problem with a loose umbrella or a separate molding process." . . .

[Batlin, a competing importer of novelty Uncle Sam mechanical banks, filed suit against Snyder after the U.S. Customs Service refused entry to a shipment of banks ordered by Batlin from a Hong Kong trading company. Batlin sought a declaration that Snyder's copyright was invalid. The district court granted Batlin a preliminary injunction under the 1909 Act.]

This court has examined both the appellants' plastic Uncle Sam bank made under Snyder's copyright and the uncopyrighted model cast iron mechanical bank which is itself a reproduction of the original public domain Uncle Sam bank. Appellant Snyder claims differences not only of size but also in a number of other very minute details: the carpetbag shape of the plastic bank is smooth, the iron bank rough; the metal bank bag is fatter at its base; the eagle on the front of the platform in the metal bank is holding arrows in his talons while in the plastic bank he clutches leaves, this change concededly having been made, however, because "the arrows did not reproduce well in plastic on a smaller size." The shape of Uncle Sam's face is supposedly different, as is the shape and texture of the hats, according to the Snyder affidavit. In the metal version the umbrella is hanging loose while in the plastic item it is included in the single mold. The texture of the clothing, the hairline, shape of the bow ties and of the shirt collar and left arm as well as the flag carrying the name on the base of the statue are all claimed to be different, along with the shape and texture of the eagles on the side. Many of these differences are not perceptible to the casual observer. Appellants make no claim for any difference based on the plastic mold lines in the Uncle Sam figure which are perceptible. . . .

The test of originality is concededly one with a low threshold in that "[a]ll that is needed . . . is that the 'author' contributed something more than a 'merely trivial' variation, something recognizably 'his own.' " *Alfred Bell & Co. v. Catalda Fine Arts, Inc.*, 191 F.2d at 103. But as this court said many years ago, "[w]hile a copy of something in the public domain will not, if it be merely a copy, support a copyright, a distinguishable variation will. . . ." *Gerlach-Barklow Co. v. Morris & Bendien, Inc.*, 23 F.2d 159, 161 (2d Cir. 1927). . . .

A reproduction of a work of art obviously presupposes an underlying work of art. . . . The underlying work of art may as here be in the public domain. But even to claim the more limited protection given to a reproduction of a work of art (that to the distinctive features contributed by the reproducer), the reproduction must contain "an original contribution not present in the underlying work of art" and be "more than a mere copy." 1 M. Nimmer, [The Law of Copyright (1975)], §20.2, at 93. . . .

Nor can the requirement of originality be satisfied simply by the demonstration of "physical skill" or "special training" . . . required for the production of the plastic molds that furnished the basis for appellants' plastic bank. A considerably *higher* degree of skill is required, true artistic skill, to make the reproduction copyrightable. . . . Here on the basis of appellants' own expert's testimony it took [Snyder's Hong Kong contractor] "[a]bout a day and a half, two days work" to produce the plastic mold sculpture from the metal Uncle Sam bank. If there be a point in the copyright law pertaining to reproductions at which sheer artistic skill and effort can act as a substitute for the requirement of substantial variation, it was not reached here.

Appellants rely heavily upon *Alva Studios, Inc. v. Winninger*, [177 F. Supp. 265 (S.D.N.Y. 1959)], the "Hand of God" case, where the court held that "great skill and originality [were required] to produce a scale reduction of a great work with exactitude." 177 F. Supp. at 267. There, the original sculpture [Auguste Rodin's *Hand of God*—Eds.] was, "one of the most intricate pieces of sculpture ever created" with "[i]nnumerable planes, lines and geometric patterns . . . interdependent in [a] multi-dimensional work." *Id*. Originality was found primarily by the district court to consist primarily in the fact that "[i]t takes 'an extremely skilled sculptor' many hours working directly in front of the original" to effectuate a scale reduction. *Id*. at 266. The court, indeed, found the exact replica to be so original, distinct, and creative as to constitute a work of art in itself. The complexity and exactitude there involved distinguishes [sic] that case amply from the one at bar. As appellants themselves have pointed out, there are a number of trivial differences or deviations from the original public domain cast iron bank in their plastic reproduction. Thus concededly the plastic version is not, and was scarcely meticulously produced to be, an exactly faithful reproduction. Nor is the creativity in the underlying work of art of the same order of magnitude as in the case of the "Hand of God." Rodin's sculpture is, furthermore, so unique and rare, and adequate public access to it such a problem that a significant public benefit accrues from its precise, artistic reproduction. No such benefit can be imagined to accrue here from the "knock-off" reproduction of the cast iron Uncle Sam bank. Thus appellants' plastic bank is neither in the category of exactitude required by *Alva Studios* nor in a category of substantial originality; it falls within what has been suggested by the amicus curiae is a copyright no-man's land. . . .

. . . To extend copyrightability to minuscule variations would simply put a weapon for harassment in the hands of mischievous copiers intent on appropriating and monopolizing public domain work. . . .

Uncle Sam Bank

MESKILL, J., dissenting: . . . [T]he author's reasons for making changes should be irrelevant to a determination of whether the differences are trivial. As noted in *Alfred Bell, supra*, 191 F.2d at 105, even an inadvertent variation can form the basis of a valid copyright. After the fact speculation as to whether Snyder made changes for aesthetic or functional reasons should not be the basis of decision.

. . . Granting Snyder a copyright protecting [his] variations would ensure only that no one could copy his particular version of the bank now in the public domain, i.e., protection from someone using Snyder's figurine to slavishly copy and make a mold. . . .

This approach seems quite in accord with the purpose of the copyright statute to promote progress by encouraging individual effort through copyright protection. . . .

≡≡≡   *Schrock v. Learning Curve International, Inc.*
≡≡≡   *586 F.3d 513 (7th Cir. 2009)*

S YKES, J.: . . .

I. Background

HIT is the owner of the copyright in the "Thomas & Friends" properties, and Learning Curve is a producer and distributor of children's toys. HIT and Learning Curve entered into a licensing agreement granting Learning Curve a license to create and market toys based on HIT's characters. . . .

In 1999 Learning Curve retained Daniel Schrock to take product photographs of its toys, including those based on HIT's characters, for use in promotional materials. On numerous occasions during the next four years, Schrock photographed several lines of Learning Curve's toys, including many of the "Thomas & Friends" toy trains, related figures, and train-set accessories. . . . Schrock invoiced Learning Curve for this work, and some of the invoices included "usage restrictions" purporting to limit Learning Curve's use of his photographs to two years. Learning Curve paid the invoices in full—in total more than $400,000.

Learning Curve stopped using Schrock's photography services in mid-2003 but continued to use some of his photos in its printed advertising, on packaging, and on the internet. In 2004 Schrock registered his photos for copyright protection and sued HIT and Learning Curve for infringement;. . . . HIT and Learning Curve moved for summary judgment, arguing primarily that Schrock's photos were derivative works and not sufficiently original to claim copyright protection, and that neither HIT nor Learning Curve ever authorized Schrock to copyright the photos. . . .

The district court granted summary judgment for the defendants. . . . [The judge concluded that the photographs were derivative works.] Then, following language in *Gracen* [*v. Bradford Exchange*, 698 F.2d 300 (7th Cir. 1983)], the judge held that Learning Curve's permission to make the photos was not enough to trigger Schrock's copyright in them; the judge said Schrock must also have Learning Curve's permission to copyright the photos. Schrock did not have that permission, so the judge concluded that Schrock had no copyright in the photos and dismissed his claim for copyright infringement. Schrock appealed.

II. Discussion . . .

A. Photographs as Derivative Works

Whether photographs of a copyrighted work are derivative works is the subject of deep disagreement among courts and commentators alike. *See* 1 Melville B. Nimmer & David Nimmer, Nimmer on Copyright §3.03[C][1], at 3-20.3 (Aug. 2009). . . .

We need not resolve the issue definitively here. The classification of Schrock's photos as derivative works does not affect the applicable legal standard for determining copyrightability, although as we have noted, it does determine the scope of copyright protection. Accordingly, we will assume without deciding that each of Schrock's photos qualifies as a derivative work within the meaning of the Copyright Act.

B. *Originality and Derivative Works . . .*

Our review of Schrock's photographs convinces us that they do not fall into the narrow category of photographs that can be classified as "slavish copies," lacking any independently created expression. To be sure, the photographs are accurate depictions of the three-dimensional "Thomas & Friends" toys, but Schrock's artistic and technical choices combine to create a two-dimensional image that is subtly but nonetheless sufficiently his own.[3] This is confirmed by Schrock's deposition testimony describing his creative process in depicting the toys. Schrock explained how he used various camera and lighting techniques to make the toys look more "life like," "personable," and "friendly." He explained how he tried to give the toys "a little bit of dimension" and that it was his goal to make the toys "a little bit better than what they look like when you actually see them on the shelf." The original expression in the representative sample is not particularly great (it was not meant to be), but it is enough under the applicable standard to warrant the limited copyright protection accorded derivative works under §103(b).

Aside from arguing that the works fail under the generally accepted test for originality, Learning Curve and HIT offer two additional reasons why we should conclude that Schrock's photographs are not original. First, they claim that the photos are intended to serve the "purely utilitarian function" of identifying products for consumers. The purpose of the photographs, however, is irrelevant. *See Bleistein v. Donaldson Lithographing Co.,* 188 U.S. 239, 251-52 (1903).

The defendants' second and more substantial argument is that it is not enough that Schrock's photographs might pass the ordinary test for originality; they claim that as derivative works, the photos are subject to a higher standard of originality. A leading copyright commentator disagrees. The Nimmer treatise maintains that the quantum of originality required for copyright in a derivative work is the same as that required for copyright in any other work. *See* 1 Nimmer on Copyright §3.01, at 3-2, §3.03[A], at 3-7. More particularly, Nimmer says the relevant standard is whether a derivative work contains a "nontrivial" variation from the preexisting work "sufficient to render the derivative work distinguishable from [the] prior work in any meaningful manner." *Id.* §3.03[A], at 3-10. The caselaw generally follows this formulation. *See, e.g., Eden Toys, Inc. v. Florelee Undergarment Co.,* 697 F.2d 27, 34-35 (2d Cir.1982) (holding that numerous minor changes in an illustration of Paddington Bear were sufficiently nontrivial because they combined to give Paddington a "different, cleaner 'look'"); *Millworth Converting Corp. v. Slifka,*

---

3. We note, however, that a mere shift in medium, without more, is generally insufficient to satisfy the requirement of originality for copyright in a derivative work. *Durham Indus., Inc. v. Tomy Corp.,* 630 F.2d 905, 910 (2d Cir.1980) (noting that circuit's rejection of "the contention that the originality requirement of copyrightability can be satisfied by the mere reproduction of a work of art in a different medium"); *L. Batlin & Son, Inc. v. Snyder,* 536 F.2d 486, 491 (2d Cir.1976) (same).

276 F.2d 443, 445 (2d Cir.1960) (holding that embroidered reproduction of a public-domain embroidery of Peter Pan was sufficiently distinguishable because the latter gave a "three-dimensional look" to the former embroidery).

Learning Curve and HIT argue that our decision in *Gracen* established a more demanding standard of originality for derivative works. *Gracen* involved an artistic competition in which artists were invited to submit paintings of the character Dorothy from the Metro-Goldwyn-Mayer ("MGM") movie *The Wizard of Oz*. Participating artists were given a still photograph of Dorothy from the film as an exemplar, and the paintings were solicited and submitted with the understanding that the best painting would be chosen for a series of collector's plates. *Gracen*, 698 F.2d at 301. Plaintiff Gracen prevailed in the competition, but she refused to sign the contract allowing her painting to be used in the collector's plates. The competition sponsor commissioned another artist to create a similar plate, and Gracen sued the sponsor, MGM, and the artist for copyright infringement. We held that Gracen could not maintain her infringement suit because her painting, a derivative work, was not "substantially different from the underlying work to be copyrightable." *Id*. at 305.

Gracen drew this language from an influential Second Circuit decision, *L. Batlin & Son, Inc. v. Snyder,* 536 F.2d 486 (2d Cir.1976). Read in context, however, the cited language from *L. Batlin* did not suggest that a heightened standard of originality applies to derivative works.[4] To the contrary, the Second Circuit said only that to be copyrightable a work must "'contain some substantial, not merely trivial originality.'" *Id*. at 490 (quoting *Chamberlin v. Uris Sales Corp.,* 150 F.2d 512, 513 (2d Cir.1945)). The court explained that for derivative works, as for any other work, "[t]he test of originality is concededly one with a low threshold in that all that is needed is that the author contributed something more than a merely trivial variation, something recognizably his own." *Id*. (internal quotation marks and ellipsis omitted).

The concern expressed in *Gracen* was that a derivative work could be so similar in appearance to the underlying work that in a subsequent infringement suit brought by a derivative author, it would be difficult to separate the original elements of expression in the derivative and underlying works in order to determine whether one derivative work infringed another. The opinion offered the example of artists A and B who both painted their versions of the Mona Lisa, a painting in the public domain. *See Gracen,* 698 F.2d at 304. "[I]f the difference between the original and A's reproduction is slight, the difference between A's and B's reproductions will also be slight, so that if B had access to A's reproductions the trier of fact will be hard-pressed to decide whether B was copying A or copying the Mona Lisa itself." *Id*.

No doubt this concern is valid. But nothing in the Copyright Act suggests that derivative works are subject to a more exacting originality requirement than other

---

4. To the extent that *Gracen*'s reading of *L. Batlin* and its "substantial difference" language can be understood as establishing a more demanding standard of originality for derivative works, it has received mixed reviews. Some commentators have suggested that *Gracen* may have inappropriately narrowed the copyrightability of derivative works without a statutory basis. . . . The Third Circuit has agreed and explicitly rejected *Gracen*'s interpretation of *L. Batlin*. *Dam Things from Denmark v. Russ Berrie & Co.,* 290 F.3d 548, 564 (3d Cir.2002).

works of authorship. Indeed, we have explained since *Gracen* that "the only 'originality' required for [a] new work to [be] copyrightable . . . is enough expressive variation from public-domain or other existing works to enable the new work to be readily distinguished from its predecessors." *Bucklew* [*v. Hawkins, Ash, Baptie & Co., LLP*, 329 F.3d 923, 929 (7th Cir. 2003)]. We emphasized in *Bucklew* that this standard does not require a "high degree of [incremental] originality." *Id.*

We think *Gracen* must be read in light of *L. Batlin*, on which it relied, and *Bucklew*, which followed it. And doing so reveals the following general principles: (1) the originality requirement for derivative works is not more demanding than the originality requirement for other works; and (2) the key inquiry is whether there is sufficient nontrivial expressive variation in the derivative work to make it distinguishable from the underlying work in some meaningful way. This focus on the presence of nontrivial "distinguishable variation" adequately captures the concerns articulated in *Gracen* without unduly narrowing the copyrightability of derivative works. It is worth repeating that the copyright in a derivative work is thin, extending only to the incremental original expression contributed by the author of the derivative work. *See* 17 U.S.C. §103(b).

As applied to photographs, we have already explained that the original expression in a photograph generally subsists in its rendition of the subject matter. If the photographer's rendition of a copyrighted work varies enough from the underlying work to enable the photograph to be distinguished from the underlying work (aside from the obvious shift from three dimensions to two, *see supra* n.3), then the photograph contains sufficient incremental originality to qualify for copyright. Schrock's photos of the "Thomas & Friends" toys are highly accurate product photos but contain minimally sufficient variation in angle, perspective, lighting, and dimension to be distinguishable from the underlying works; they are not "slavish copies." Accordingly, the photos qualify for the limited derivative-work copyright provided by §103(b). . . .

C. Authorization and Derivative Works

To be copyrightable, a derivative work must not be infringing. *See* 17 U.S.C. §103(a). The owner of the copyright in the underlying work has the exclusive right to "prepare derivative works based upon the copyrighted work," 17 U.S.C. §106(2), and "it is a copyright infringement to make or sell a derivative work without a license from the owner of the copyright on the work from which the derivative work is derived," *Bucklew*, 329 F.3d at 930. This means the author of a derivative work must have permission to make the work from the owner of the copyright in the underlying work; *Gracen* suggested, however, that the author of a derivative work must *also* have permission to *copyright* it. 698 F.2d at 303-04 ("[T]he question is not whether Miss Gracen was licensed to make a derivative work but whether she was also licensed to exhibit [her] painting and to copyright it. . . . Even if [Gracen] was authorized to exhibit her derivative works, she may not have been authorized to copyright them."). The district court relied on this language from *Gracen* to conclude that Schrock has no copyright in his photos because he was not authorized by Learning Curve to copyright them. This was error.

. . . *Gracen*'s language presupposing a permission-to-copyright requirement was dicta; the case was actually decided on nonoriginality grounds. *Id.* at 305. More importantly, the dicta was mistaken; there is nothing in the Copyright Act requiring the author of a derivative work to obtain permission to copyright his work from the owner of the copyright in the underlying work. To the contrary, the Act provides that copyright in a derivative work, like copyright in any other work, arises by operation of law once the author's original expression is fixed in a tangible medium. . . .

. . . [B]ecause the owner of a copyrighted work has the exclusive right to control the preparation of derivative works, the owner could limit the derivative-work author's intellectual-property rights in the contract, license, or agreement that authorized the production of the derivative work. . . .

In this case, the evidence submitted with the summary-judgment motion does not establish [whether] the parties adjusted Schrock's rights by contract . . .

Accordingly, for all the foregoing reasons, we REVERSE the judgment of the district court and REMAND for further proceedings consistent with this opinion.

[Images reproduced from the court's opinion.]

Circled Photo by Dan Schrock Photography
Rescue Hospital   2002

Circled Photo by Dan Schrock Photography
Rescue Hospital   2002

NOTES AND QUESTIONS

1. Do *L. Batlin* and *Schrock* employ the same standard of originality?

2. Compare the result in *L. Batlin* with those in *Alva Studios v. Winninger* (discussed in the *L. Batlin* opinion) and *Alfred Bell & Co. v. Catalda Fine Arts, Inc.*, Section A.2.a *supra*. Can the three decisions be reconciled? Both of the latter cases involved fine art reproductions. Was the *L. Batlin* court discriminating based on a perceived lack of artistic content? What else might explain the *L. Batlin* court's reluctance to find copyrightable originality in the plastic reproductions?

3. Should the standard of originality for derivative works be the same as the basic standard set forth in *Feist, supra*? The *L. Batlin* court and the *Gracen* court were both anxious to avoid giving the first creator of a derivative work "a de facto monopoly" on all subsequent derivative works. *Gracen v. Bradford Exch.*, 698 F.2d 300, 304 (7th Cir. 1983). At the same time, however, the *L. Batlin* court noted that allowing a derivative copyright in *Alva Studios* produced "significant public benefit." Are these conclusions reconcilable?

According to the *Gracen* court, the concern about de facto monopolies is based in part on a desire to protect the rights of the owner of copyright in the underlying work. *Gracen*, 698 F.2d at 304. Are there also reasons to be concerned about de facto monopolies on derivative works based on underlying public domain works? Should a different originality standard apply depending on whether the underlying work is copyrighted or in the public domain?

4. Are photographs derivative works of what they depict? Courts have differed on the proper approach to that question. *See Ets-Hokin v. Skyy Spirits, Inc.*, 225 F.3d 1068 (9th Cir. 2000) (photograph of vodka bottle was not a derivative work because bottle was not copyrightable); *SHL Imaging, Inc. v. Artisan House, Inc.*, 117 F. Supp. 2d 301 (S.D.N.Y. 2000) (photographs of ornamental picture frames were not derivative works because they did not recast, transform, or adapt those works, but merely depicted them). Which approach do you prefer? Should a photograph be considered a derivative work whenever the subject of the photograph is itself copyrightable? Are there reasons to treat photography differently than other methods of art reproduction?

> **KEEP IN MIND**
>
> The right to prepare derivative works is one of the exclusive rights of the copyright owner, so unauthorized preparation of a derivative work may infringe the copyright. The copyrightability and infringement inquiries differ in focus. The copyrightability inquiry is concerned with what the second comer has added, while the infringement inquiry (which we consider in Chapter 5) is concerned with what the second comer has taken.

5. Section 103(a) of the Act indicates that "protection for a work employing preexisting material in which copyright subsists does not extend to any part of the work in which such material has been used unlawfully." *Schrock* holds that the requirement of lawful use can be satisfied by a showing that the second comer had permission to create the derivative work, and does not require an additional showing of permission to assert a derivative copyright. Of course, as the court notes, asserting copyright protection for the derivative work could be prohibited by contract. Do you agree with the court's reasoning? The district court had held that without express permission from the copyright owner, no copyright could be asserted in the derivative work. Which is the better default rule?

Under §103(a), can a derivative work prepared without the copyright owner's permission qualify for copyright protection? Under what circumstances? (Hint: do "unlawfully" and "without permission" mean the same thing?)

PRACTICE EXERCISE: ADVOCACY

Movie Maven, LLP, buys the master reels of old, public domain films, restores them, and creates "panned and scanned" versions that adapt the films to a format more suitable for home viewing. Movie Maven has filed copyright registrations for its versions of the films, identifying them as derivative works. A new competitor, Regis Films, has begun copying Movie Maven's versions of the films and selling them as its own. Movie Maven has sued Regis Films for copyright infringement, and Regis Films has hired your firm to represent it. The supervising partner has asked you to draft a summary judgment motion. Prepare an outline of the main points you will make.

Note on Blocking Patents

The patent system follows a very different set of rules for allocating rights in initial inventions and subsequent patentable improvements. The second comer who invents a patentable improvement may apply for and receive a patent regardless of whether the first inventor authorized the improvement. The first inventor and the improver are said to hold "blocking patents." The improver may not practice his invention without permission from the original inventor, but the first inventor may not practice the improvement without permission from the improver. Such patents are frequently the subjects of cross-licensing agreements between the two inventors. *See Standard Oil Co. v. United States*, 283 U.S. 163, 172 n.5 (1931); *Carpet Seaming Tape Licensing v. Best Seam, Inc.*, 616 F.2d 1133, 1142 (9th Cir. 1980), *cert. denied*, 464 U.S. 818 (1983); 5 Donald S. Chisum, Chisum on Patents §16.02[1][a] (2001).

The blocking patents rule has been justified in terms of efficiency. According to Professor Merges, the rule encourages the original patentee to bargain with improvers, and therefore avoids potentially significant holdout costs that might impede valuable innovation. Robert Merges, *Intellectual Property Rights and Bargaining Breakdown: The Case of Blocking Patents*, 62 Tenn. L. Rev. 75 (1994); *see generally* Ian Ayres & Eric Talley, *Solomonic Bargaining: Dividing a Legal Entitlement to Facilitate Coasean Trade*, 104 Yale L.J. 1027 (1995). More generally, a number of legal scholars have concluded that society benefits most when would-be improvers compete with one another and with the original patentee to produce and disclose to the public valuable inventions, even if this rule results in some duplicative research. *See, e.g.*, Robert P. Merges & Richard R. Nelson, *On the Complex Economics of*

Patent Scope, 90 Colum. L. Rev. 839, 877-908 (1990); Mark A. Lemley, *The Economics of Improvement in Intellectual Property Law*, 75 Tex. L. Rev. 989 (1997).

Some commentators, however, have criticized the blocking patents rule. In an influential article published in 1977, Professor Edmund Kitch argued that giving patentees broad rights to control subsequent improvements to their inventions would result in a more efficient allocation of research efforts. Kitch analogized such rights to nineteenth-century mining claims, which reserved for first comers the right to explore (or license others to explore) the land described in the claim deed. He argued that adopting a similar regime for patent law would reduce wasteful duplication and ensure optimal allocation of licenses to develop improvements, and therefore would promote greater overall progress. Edmund W. Kitch, *The Nature and Function of the Patent System*, 20 J.L. & Econ. 265, 276-78 (1977); *see also* Mark F. Grady & Jay I. Alexander, *Patent Law and Rent Dissipation*, 78 Va. L. Rev. 305 (1992). Professor Kitch's "prospect" model actually is quite similar to the copyright rule granting first comers the right to control the preparation of derivative works.

If blocking patents promote efficient bargaining between first comers and improvers, would not a regime of "blocking copyrights" also be efficient? Or is the "prospect" model more appropriate for copyright law? For an extended discussion of this question, see Lemley, *supra*.

2. Compilations

The Copyright Act of 1909 recognized copyright in "compilations," but did not supply a general definition of the term. The 1976 Act remedied that omission. Section 101 provides: "A 'compilation' is a work formed by the collection and assembling of preexisting materials or of data that are selected, coordinated, or arranged in such a way that the resulting work as a whole constitutes an original work of authorship." The TRIPS Agreement similarly mandates copyright protection for "[c]ompilations of data or other material . . . which by reason of the selection or arrangement of their contents constitute intellectual creation." TRIPS Agreement, art. 10(2).

a. Selection, Arrangement, and Coordination of Data

As you know from reading *Feist Publications, Inc. v. Rural Telephone Service Co.*, Section A.2.b *supra*, the Supreme Court there rejected the "sweat of the brow" theory as a basis for copyright protection of compilations, and explained that the Copyright Act's definition of an eligible "compilation" indicates how a compilation may satisfy the constitutionally mandated originality requirement:

> Factual compilations . . . may possess the requisite originality. The compilation author typically chooses which facts to include, in what order to place them, and how to arrange the collected data so that they may be used effectively by readers. These choices as to selection and arrangement, so long as they are made independently by the

compiler and entail a minimal degree of creativity, are sufficiently original that Congress may protect such compilations through the copyright laws. . . .

Feist, 499 U.S. at 348.

The use of the disjunctive "or" in the definition of a compilation indicates that original expression can be found in the selection of the items to include in the compilation, regardless of their coordination or arrangement. Originality also can subsist in the arrangement or coordination of the items selected, regardless of whether the selection itself is also original. The *Feist* Court indicated, however, that even when an arrangement or selection of data is sufficiently original, the copyright in such compilations is thin. To infringe, the defendant must copy the compilation's original elements (i.e., its selection or arrangement) exactly or almost exactly. In addition, separating the idea of a particular compilation's selection or arrangement from its expression can be a particularly vexing problem. Consider the following cases:

CCC Information Services, Inc. v. Maclean Hunter Market Reports, Inc.
44 F.3d 61 (2d Cir. 1994), cert. denied, *516 U.S. 817 (1995)*

Leval, J.:

Background

. . . The appellant is Maclean Hunter Market Reports, Inc. ("Maclean"). Since 1911, Maclean, or its predecessors, have published the *Automobile Red Book—Official Used Car Valuations* (the "Red Book"). The Red Book, which is published eight times a year, in different versions for each of three regions of the United States (as well as a version for the State of Wisconsin), sets forth the editors' projections of the values for the next six weeks of "average" versions of most of the used cars (up to seven years old) sold in that region. These predicted values are set forth separately for each automobile make, model number, body style, and engine type. Red Book also provides predicted value adjustments for various options and for mileage in 5,000 mile increments.

The valuation figures given in the Red Book are not historical market prices, quotations, or averages; nor are they derived by mathematical formulas from available statistics. They represent, rather, the Maclean editors' predictions, based on a wide variety of informational sources and their professional judgment, of expected values for "average" vehicles for the upcoming six weeks in a broad region. The introductory text asserts, "You, the subscriber, must be the final judge of the actual value of a particular vehicle. Any guide book is a supplement to and not a substitute for expertise in the complex field of used vehicle valuation."

. . . Appellee CCC Information Services, Inc. ("CCC"), is also in the business of providing its customers with information as to the valuation of used vehicles. Rather than publishing a book, however, CCC provides information to its customers through a computer data base. Since at least 1988, CCC has itself been systematically loading major portions of the Red Book onto its computer network and republishing Red Book information in various forms to its customers.

. . . CCC's "VINguard Valuation Service" ("VVS") provides subscribers with the average of a vehicle's Red Book valuation and its valuation in the NADA Official Used Car Guide (the "Bluebook"), the other leading valuation book, published by the National Automobile Dealers Association ("NADA"). The offer of this average of Red Book and Bluebook satisfies a market because the laws of certain states use that average figure as a minimum for insurance payments upon the "total loss" of a vehicle. . . .

. . . CCC brought this action in 1991, seeking, inter alia, a declaratory judgment that it incurred no liability to Maclean under the copyright laws by taking and republishing material from the Red Book. Maclean counterclaimed alleging infringement. . . . [The district court granted summary judgment of noninfringement for CCC; Maclean appealed.]

Discussion

1. *Does the Red Book manifest originality so as to be protected by the copyright laws?* The first significant question raised by this appeal is whether Maclean holds a protected copyright interest in the Red Book. CCC contends, and the district court held, that the Red Book is nothing more than a compilation of unprotected facts, selected and organized without originality or creativity, and therefore unprotected under the Supreme Court's teachings in *Feist*. We disagree. . . .

The protection of compilations is consistent with the objectives of the copyright law, which are . . . dictated by the Constitution. . . . Compilations that devise new and useful selections and arrangements of information unquestionably contribute to public knowledge by providing cheaper, easier, and better organized access to information. Without financial incentives, creators of such useful compilations might direct their energies elsewhere, depriving the public of their creations and impeding the advance of learning. . . .

The thrust of the Supreme Court's ruling in *Feist* was not to erect a high barrier of originality requirement. It was rather to specify, rejecting the strain of lower court rulings that sought to base protection on the "sweat of the brow," that *some* originality is essential to protection of authorship, and that the protection afforded extends only to those original elements. Because the protection is so limited, there is no reason under the policies of the copyright law to demand a high degree of originality. To the contrary, such a requirement would be counterproductive. The policy embodied into law is to encourage authors to publish innovations for the common good—not to threaten them with loss of their livelihood if their works of authorship are found insufficiently imaginative. . . .

The district court was simply mistaken in its conclusion that the Red Book valuations were, like the telephone numbers in *Feist*, pre-existing facts that had merely been discovered by the Red Book editors. To the contrary, Maclean's evidence demonstrated without rebuttal that its valuations were neither reports of historical prices nor mechanical derivations of historical prices or other data. Rather, they represented predictions by the Red Book editors of future prices estimated to cover specified geographic regions.[6] According to Maclean's evidence, these predictions were based not only on a multitude of data sources, but also on professional judgment and expertise. The testimony of one of Maclean's deposition witnesses indicated that fifteen considerations are weighed; among the considerations, for example, is a prediction as to how traditional competitor vehicles, as defined by Maclean, will fare against one another in the marketplace in the coming period. The valuations themselves are original creations of Maclean.

Recognizing that "[o]riginality may also be found in the selection and ordering of particular facts or elements," the district court concluded that none had been shown. . . . This was because the Red Book's selection and arrangement of data represents "a logical response to the needs of the vehicle valuation market." . . . The fact that an arrangement of data responds *logically* to the needs of the market for which the compilation was prepared does not negate originality. To the contrary, the use of logic to solve the problems of how best to present the information being compiled is independent creation. . . .

We find that the selection and arrangement of data in the Red Book displayed amply sufficient originality to pass the low threshold requirement to earn copyright protection. This originality was expressed, for example, in Maclean's division of the national used car market into several regions, with independent predicted valuations for each region depending on conditions there found. A car model does not command the same value throughout a large geographic sector of the United States; used car values are responsive to local conditions and vary from place to place. A 1989 Dodge Caravan will not command the same price in San Diego as in Seattle. In furnishing a single number to cover vast regions that undoubtedly contain innumerable variations, the Red Book expresses a loose judgment that values are likely to group together with greater consistency within a defined region than without. The number produced is necessarily both approximate and original. Several other aspects of the Red Book listings also embody sufficient originality to pass *Feist*'s low threshold. These include: (1) the selection and manner of presentation of optional features for inclusion; (2) the adjustment for mileage by 5,000 mile increments (as opposed to using some other breakpoint and interval); (3) the use of the abstract concept of the "average" vehicle in each category as the subject of the valuation; and (4) the selection of the number of years' models to be included in the compilation.

We conclude for these reasons that the district court erred in ruling that the Red Book commands no copyright protection by reason of lack of originality.

2. *The idea-expression dichotomy and the merger of necessary expression with the ideas expressed*. CCC's strongest argument is that it took nothing more than ideas, for which the copyright law affords no protection to the author. According to this argument, (1) each entry in the Red Book expresses the authors' *idea* of the value of a particular vehicle; [and] (2) to the extent that "expression" is to be found in the

---

6. That they are expressed in numerical form is immaterial to originality. . . . The Act broadly defines literary works to include "works, other than audiovisual works, expressed in words, numbers, or other verbal or numerical symbols. . . ."

Red Book's valuations, such expression is indispensable to the statement of the idea and therefore merges with the idea. . . .

The argument is not easily rebutted, for it does build on classically accepted copyright doctrine. . . .

Given the nature of compilations, it is almost inevitable that the original contributions of the compilers will consist of *ideas*. Originality in *selection*, for example, will involve the compiler's idea of the utility to the consumer of a limited selection from the particular universe of available data. One compiler might select out of a universe of all businesses those he believes will be of interest to the Chinese-American community, *see Key Publications,* [*Inc. v. Chinatown Today Pub'l Enterp., Inc.,*] 945 F.2d [509,] 514 [(2d Cir. 1991)], another will select those statistics as to racehorses or pitchers that are believed to be practical to the consumers in helping to pick winners, *see Kregos v. Associated Press,* 937 F.2d [700,] 706-07 [(2d Cir. 1991)] . . . ; another will offer a list of restaurants he suggests are the best, the most elegant, or offer the best value within a price range. Each of these exercises in selection represents an *idea*.

In other compilations, the original contribution of the compiler will relate to ideas for the coordination, or arrangement of the data. Such ideas for arrangement are generally designed to serve the consumers' needs . . . [such as] a listing of New York restaurants . . . broken down by geographic areas of the city, specialty or type (e.g., seafood, steaks and chops, vegetarian, kosher, Chinese, Indian); price range; handicapped accessibility, etc.

It is apparent that virtually any independent creation of the compiler as to selection, coordination, or arrangement will be designed to add to the usefulness or desirability of his compendium for targeted groups of potential customers, and will represent an idea. In the case of a compilation, furthermore, such structural ideas are likely to be expressed in the most simple, unadorned, and direct fashion. If, as CCC argues, the doctrine of merger permits the wholesale copier of a compilation to take the individual expression of such ideas, so as to avoid the risk that an idea will improperly achieve protection, then the protection explicitly conferred on compilations by Section 103 of the U.S. Copyright Act will be illusory.

We addressed precisely this problem in *Kregos,* 937 F.2d 700. The plaintiff Kregos had created a form to be used to help predict the outcome of a baseball game by filling in nine statistics of the competing pitchers. . . .

[*Kregos* described] different categories of ideas. It distinguished between, on the one hand, those ideas that undertake to advance the understanding of phenomena or the solution of problems, such as the identification of the symptoms that are the most useful in identifying the presence of a particular disease; and those, like the pitching form there at issue, that do not undertake to explain phenomena or furnish solutions, but are infused with the author's taste or opinion. *Kregos* postulated that the importance of keeping ideas free from private ownership is far greater for ideas of the first category. . . .

. . . To the extent that protection of the Red Book would impair free circulation of any ideas, these are ideas of the weaker category, infused with opinion; the valuations explain nothing, and describe no method, process, or procedure. Maclean Hunter makes no attempt, for example, to monopolize the basis of its economic forecasting or the factors that it weighs. . . . As noted above, the Red Book specifies in its introduction that "[y]ou, the subscriber, must be the final judge of the actual value of a particular vehicle." . . .

The balancing of interests suggested by *Kregos* leads to the conclusion that we should reject CCC's argument seeking the benefit of the merger doctrine. . . .

Conclusion

Because Maclean has demonstrated a valid copyright, and an infringement thereof, we direct the entry of judgment in Maclean's favor. We remand to the district court for further proceedings.

Matthew Bender & Co. v. West Publishing Co.
158 F.3d 693 (2d Cir. 1998), cert. denied, 526 U.S. 1154 (1999)

JACOBS, C.J.: Defendants-appellants West Publishing Co. and West Publishing Corp. (collectively "West") create and publish printed compilations of federal and state judicial opinions. Plaintiff-appellee Matthew Bender & Company, Inc. and intervenor-plaintiff-appellee HyperLaw, Inc. (collectively "plaintiffs") manufacture and market compilations of judicial opinions stored on compact disc-read only memory ("CD-ROM") discs, in which opinions they embed (or intend to embed) citations that show the page location of the particular text in West's printed version of the opinions (so-called "star pagination").[1] Bender and HyperLaw seek judgment declaring that star pagination will not infringe West's copyrights in its compilations of judicial opinions. West now appeals from a judgment of the United States District Court for the Southern District of New York (Martin, J.), granting summary judgment of noninfringement to Bender and partial summary judgment of noninfringement to HyperLaw.

West's primary contention on appeal is that star pagination to West's case reporters allows a user of plaintiffs' CD-ROM discs (by inputting a series of commands) to "perceive" West's copyright-protected arrangement of cases, and that plaintiffs' products (when star pagination is added) are unlawful copies of West's arrangement. We reject West's argument. . . .

Discussion . . .

. . . [C]opyright protection in compilations "may extend only to those components of a work that are original to the author." [*Feist*, 499 U.S. 340,] 348. . . . The "originality" requirement encompasses requirements both "that the work was independently created . . . , *and* that it possesses at least some minimal degree of

---

1. This cross-reference method is called "star pagination" because an asterisk and citation or page number are inserted in the text of the judicial opinion to indicate when a page break occurs in a different version of the case.

creativity." *Id*. at 345 . . . (emphasis added). At issue here are references to West's volume and page numbers distributed through the text of plaintiffs' versions of judicial opinions. West concedes that the pagination of its volumes—i.e., the insertion of page breaks and the assignment of page numbers—is determined by an automatic computer program, and West does not seriously claim that there is anything original or creative in that process. As Judge Martin noted, "where and on what particular pages the text of a court opinion appears does not embody any original creation of the compiler." Because the internal pagination of West's case reporters does not entail even a modicum of creativity, the volume and page numbers are not original components of West's compilations and are not themselves protected by West's compilation copyright.[9]

Because the volume and page numbers are unprotected features of West's compilation process, they may be copied without infringing West's copyright. However, West proffers an alternative argument based on the fact (which West has plausibly demonstrated) that plaintiffs have inserted or will insert *all* of West's volume and page numbers for certain case reporters. West's alternative argument is that even though the page numbering is not (by itself) a protectible element of West's compilation, (i) plaintiffs' star pagination to West's case reporters embeds West's arrangement of cases in plaintiffs' CD-ROM discs, thereby allowing a user to perceive West's protected arrangement[11] through the plaintiffs' file-retrieval programs, and (ii) that under the Copyright Act's definition of "copies," 17 U.S.C. §101, a work that allows the perception of a protectible element of a compilation through the aid of a machine amounts to a copy of the compilation. We reject this argument. . . .

. . . West's definition of a copy, as applied to a CD-ROM disc, would expand the embedded work to include all arrangements and *re* arrangements that could be made by a third-party user who manipulates the data on his or her own initiative. But the relevant statutory wording refers to material objects in which "a work" readable by technology "is fixed," not to another work or works that can be created, unbidden, by using technology to alter the fixed embedding of the work, by rearrangement or otherwise. The natural reading of the statute is that the arrangement of the work is the one that can be perceived by a machine without an uninvited manipulation of the data. . . .

---

9. The same conclusion can be arrived at using a different chain of reasoning. There is a fundamental distinction under the Copyright Act between the original work of authorship and the physical embodiment of that work in a tangible medium. . . . The embedding of the copyrightable work in a tangible medium does not mean that the features of the tangible medium are also copyrightable. Thus, here, the original element of West's compilation, its arrangement of cases, is protectable, while the features of the physical embodiment of the work, *i.e.,* the page numbers, are not.

11. . . . [B]ecause we find that West's arrangement has not been copied through the insertion of star pagination to West's case reporters, we can assume without deciding that West's case reporters contain an original and copyrightable arrangement.

In addition, this opinion will not address any copying by plaintiffs of the *selection* of cases included in West's case reporters. First, West argued below that Bender had copied West's arrangement of cases, not its selection. Second, it is uncontested that plaintiffs' compilations include many more opinions than West's case reporters. . . . Accordingly, we cannot find that the selection of cases in plaintiffs' compilations is substantially similar to West's selection. . . .

Conclusion

We hold that Bender and HyperLaw will not infringe West's copyright by inserting star pagination to West's case reporters in their CD-ROM disc version of judicial opinions. The judgment of the district court is affirmed.

SWEET, J., dissenting: . . . The majority concludes that because the volume and page numbers are "unprotected features" of West's compilation process, they may be copied without infringing West's copyright. The majority reasons that, pursuant to the Copyright Act, the "embedding of the copyrightable work in a tangible medium does not mean that the features of the tangible medium are also copyrightable." Therefore, West's arrangement of cases is protectible, but the page numbers are not. The classification of page numbers as physical embodiment rather than the result of originality is the foundation stone of the majority's interpretation of the authorities dealing with the copyright statute.

In my view West's case arrangements, an essential part of which is page citations, are original works of authorship entitled to copyright protection. Comprehensive documentation of West's selection and arrangement of judicial opinions infringes the copyright in that work.

This reasoning is consistent with *Feist*. As discussed above, the majority notes that the compiler's copyright is "thin." *Feist*, 499 U.S. 340, 350-51. Therefore, "a subsequent compiler remains free to use the facts contained in another's publication to aid in preparing a competing work, *so long as the competing work does not feature the same selection and arrangement.*" *Id.* at 349, . . . (emphasis added). In this case, allowing plaintiffs to use the page numbers contained in West's publication enables them to feature West's same selection and arrangement. Indeed, were it not for the ability to reproduce West's arrangement, its pagination would be of limited (if any) use. . . .

. . . [T]he pagination results from West's arrangements, selections, syllabi, headnotes, key numbering, citations and descriptions. The page number, arbitrarily determined, is the sole result of the West system, appears nowhere else, and is essential to its coordinated method of citation. It is, so to speak, an original fact resulting from West's creativity. . . .

According to the majority, a more fundamental reason to reject West's argument that plaintiffs have copied its arrangement is that the arrangement can be perceived only after a person uses the machine to rearrange the material.

Some of the most seminal developments in copyright law have been driven by technological change. There was a time when people questioned whether photographs, *see Burrow-Giles Lithographic Co. v. Sarony*, 111 U.S. 53 (1884), or advertisements, *see Bleistein v. Donaldson Lithographing Co.*, 188 U.S. 239 (1903), were copyrightable. Here again it is necessary to reconcile technology with pre-electronic principles of law. Clearly, plaintiffs' CD-ROM disks are not "copies" in the traditional sense. Yet, plaintiffs provide the ability for a user to push a button or two and obtain West's exact selection and arrangement. This technological capacity presents a new question. The majority's answer threatens to eviscerate copyright protection for compilations.

NOTES AND QUESTIONS

1. Why did MacLean Hunter's compilation manifest originality in selection, arrangement, or coordination? Are you persuaded that the items the court identifies are items that copyright should protect? How do you think the *Baker v. Selden* Court would have responded to a claim for copyright protection of numbers based on a selection of variables? Should the court have considered items like the selection of optional features, the abstract concept of an "average" vehicle, and the use of 5,000 mile increments to be *scenes a faire* for purposes of automobile valuation?

2. Are you persuaded by the *CCC* court's distinction between ideas that "explain phenomena or furnish solutions" and those that are "are infused with the author's taste or opinion"? Is that court right to conclude that the language of the Copyright Act requires such a distinction?

In *ATC Distribution Group v. Whatever It Takes Transmissions and Parts*, Section A.3. *supra*, the court rejected the plaintiff's argument that its catalog could be copyrightable as a compilation: "[T]he only aspect of the catalog that differs from the [earlier] catalog is the choice of headings and arrangement of the parts into categories—two minor differences . . . insufficiently creative to justify copyright protection." *ATC Distribution Group, Inc. v. Whatever It Takes Transmissions & Parts, Inc.*, 402 F.3d 700, 711 (6th Cir. 2005). Is that decision consistent with *Feist*? Are *CCC* and *ATC* consistent?

3. If the *Matthew Bender* court had needed to decide whether West's underlying selection or arrangement of cases were copyrightable, how do you think it would have ruled?

4. In *Matthew Bender*, is the majority effectively concluding that West's arrangement of cases has become a fact? Should that necessarily preclude copyright protection for the page numbers? In *CCC* the defendant argued that the selection of variables factoring into the price of used vehicles was itself a fact. Why did the court reject that argument? Was the court right to do so? Some facts, such as the atomic weight of oxygen or the altitude of Denver, exist in nature. Others exist only because of some creative effort—e.g., "Katniss Everdeen volunteered to represent District 12 in the Hunger Games and won them, along with District 12's male tribute, Peeta Mellark." Even atomic weight and altitude, however, are human-created ways of measuring natural phenomena. Should copyright recognize a distinction between "natural" and "created" facts? If so, on which side of the line should numbers based on a selection of variables fall?

PRACTICE EXERCISE: COUNSEL A CLIENT

William Beane has developed a computer program that makes creative use of known statistics to calculate a "Personal Productivity Indicator" for each individual baseball player. Historical data suggest that the PPI is highly accurate, and therefore quite valuable in predicting a player's worth. Beane wants to publish a *Guide to the Personal Productivity Indicator* that gives the results of the calculation for each player. He seeks your advice on what, if anything, he has that is copyrightable. What is your advice?

Note on Alternative Modes of Protection for Databases

The copyright in databases may be thin, but databases are nonetheless susceptible to the public goods problem. A compiler may spend substantial sums collecting the data and if others can freely copy it, the compiler will not be able to recoup his expenses, let alone make a profit. In addition, in the information age databases play increasingly important roles in commerce, research, and public discourse. Many commentators therefore conclude that compilers of such works should receive some sort of protection to provide them with an incentive to collect and aggregate data. If that is right, the critical inquiry is what form such protection should take.

In Europe, the EU Database Directive requires member states to provide copyright protection for databases that "by reason of the selection or arrangement of their contents, constitute the author's own intellectual creation" and that required substantial qualitative or quantitative investment in the "obtaining, verification or presentation of the contents." Directive 96/9/EC of the European Parliament and of the Council of March 11, 1996 on the Legal Protection of Databases, 1996 O.J. (L 77) 20. The Directive established a new right to "prevent extraction and/or re-utilization of the whole or of a substantial part . . . of the contents of the database." Article 10 provides for a 15-year term of protection. Upon additional investment in the database, a new 15-year term arises, resulting in the potential for perpetual protection for databases that are continually updated. The benefits of the Directive extend only within the European Community and to residents of countries that provide a reciprocal level of protection.

In the United States, a recurring issue in the controversy over database protection has been whether Congress can constitutionally provide protection to "unoriginal" compilations of data. Given that originality is a constitutional requirement for protection of the "writings" of authors, Congress cannot rely on the Intellectual Property Clause as the basis of its authority to enact such protection. Some commentators argue that Congress may rely on the Commerce Clause instead, and that such legislation would not violate the Constitution if it granted rights with more limited scope than those afforded under the patent and copyright laws. J. H. Reichman & Pamela Samuelson, *Intellectual Property Rights in Data?*, 50 Vand. L. Rev. 51, (1997) (outlining a model that borrows from unfair competition principles).

Over the past two decades, proponents of database protection have several times convinced members of Congress to propose legislation modeled on the EU Database Directive or on a misappropriation tort theory. Other constituencies have opposed such legislation, arguing that *sui generis* protection for databases would increase transaction costs for data users, deter value-added uses, and undermine First Amendment freedoms. In addition, they have noted the prospect of anticompetitive conduct by sole-source data providers and the resulting (even if unintended) adverse effects on innovation and competition.

NOTES AND QUESTIONS

1. Do you think there is a need for legal protection for collections of data? What data would you want to obtain to help you answer that question?

2. Today, computerized databases often derive their value from comprehensiveness rather than original selection and it can be difficult to identify a particular arrangement or coordination when the data are stored electronically. Do these developments suggest an answer one way or the other on the question of copyright versus *sui generis* protection for databases?

3. According to the *Feist* Court, copyright law "encourages others to build freely upon the ideas and *information* conveyed by a work," and this is so by design. *Feist Publ'ns. Inc. v. Rural Tel. Serv. Co.*, 499 U.S. 340, 350 (1991). How might *sui generis* protection for insufficiently original works affect this important copyright objective?

b. Selection, Arrangement, and Coordination of Elements Other Than Data

Prior to the TRIPS Agreement, the international copyright norm required copyright protection only for "[c]ollections of literary and artistic works such as encyclopedias and anthologies." Berne Conv., art. 2(5). The U.S. Copyright Act calls such works "collective works" and indicates that they are a type of "compilation." *See* 17 U.S.C. §101. Therefore, encyclopedias, anthologies, periodical issues, and similar works are copyrightable to the extent that they manifest originality in the selection, arrangement, or coordination of their components.

> **KEEP IN MIND**
>
> Each component of an encyclopedia, anthology, periodical issue, or similar work typically will be protected by a separate copyright.

What else does the definition of a compilation cover? Can a textual or pictorial work be viewed as a compilation of its elements? If so, how does that affect the determination of copyrightability? Consider the following cases:

Roth Greeting Cards v. United Card Co.
429 F.2d 1106 (9th Cir. 1970)

HAMLEY, J.: . . . Roth's claim involves the production and distribution by United of seven greeting cards which bear a remarkable resemblance to seven of Roth's cards on which copyrights had been granted. . . .

. . . [T]he trial court found that the art work in plaintiff's greeting cards was copyrightable, but not infringed by defendant. The trial court also found that, although copied by defendant, the wording or textual matter of each of the plaintiff's cards in question consist of common and ordinary English words and phrases which are not original with Roth and were in the public domain prior to first use by plaintiff.

Arguing that the trial court erred in ruling against it on merits, Roth agrees that the textual material involved in their greeting cards may have been in the public domain, but argues that this alone did not end the inquiry into the copyrightability of the entire card. Roth argues that "[I]t is the arrangement of the words, their combination and plan, together with the appropriate artwork . . ." which is original, the creation of Roth, and entitled to copyright protection. . . .

United argues, and we agree, that there was substantial evidence to support the district court's finding that the textual matter of each card, considered apart from its arrangement on the cards and its association with artistic representations, was not original to Roth and therefore not copyrightable.[2] However, proper analysis of the problem requires that all elements of each card, including text, arrangement of text, art work, and association between art work and text, be considered as a whole.

Considering all of these elements together, the Roth cards are, in our opinion, both original and copyrightable. In reaching this conclusion we recognize that copyright protection is not available for ideas, but only for tangible expression of ideas. *Mazer v. Stein*, 347 U.S. 201, 217 (1954). We conclude that each of Roth's cards, considered as a whole, represents a tangible expression of an idea and that such expression was, in totality, created by Roth. . . .

It appears to us that in total concept and feel the cards of United are the same as the copyrighted cards of Roth. With the possible exception of one United card . . . , the characters depicted in the art work, the mood they portrayed, the combination of art work conveying a particular mood with a particular message, and the arrangement of the words on the greeting card are substantially the same as in Roth's cards. In several instances the lettering is also very similar. . . .

The remarkable similarity between the Roth and United cards in issue . . . is apparent to even a casual observer. For example, one Roth card . . . has, on its front, a colored drawing of a cute moppet suppressing a smile and, on the inside, the words "i wuv you." With the exception of minor variations in color and style, defendant's card . . . is identical. Likewise, Roth's card entitled "I miss you already," depicts a forlorn boy sitting on a curb weeping, with an inside message reading ". . . and You Haven't even Left . . ." . . . , is closely paralleled by United's card with the same caption, showing a forlorn and weeping man, and with the identical inside message. . . .

Roth Cards (left) and United Cards (right)

2. Thus, if United had copied only the textual materials, which were not independently copyrightable, United might have been able to do so with impunity. . . .

≡ *Satava v. Lowry*
323 F.3d 805 (9th Cir.), cert. denied, *540 U.S. 983 (2003)*

GOULD, J. . . .

Plaintiff Richard Satava is a glass artist from California. In the late 1980s, Satava was inspired by the jellyfish display at an aquarium. He began experimenting with jellyfish sculptures in the glass-in-glass medium and, in 1990, began selling glass-in-glass jellyfish sculptures. . . .

Satava describes his sculptures as "vertically oriented, colorful, fanciful jellyfish with tendril-like tentacles and a rounded bell encased in an outer layer of rounded clear glass that is bulbous at the top and tapering toward the bottom to form roughly a bullet shape, with the jellyfish portion of the sculpture filling almost the entire volume of the outer, clearglass shroud." Satava's jellyfish appear lifelike. They resemble the *pelagia colorata* that live in the Pacific Ocean.

During the 1990s, defendant Christopher Lowry, a glass artist from Hawaii, also began making glass-in-glass jellyfish sculptures. Lowry's sculptures look like Satava's, and many people confuse them.

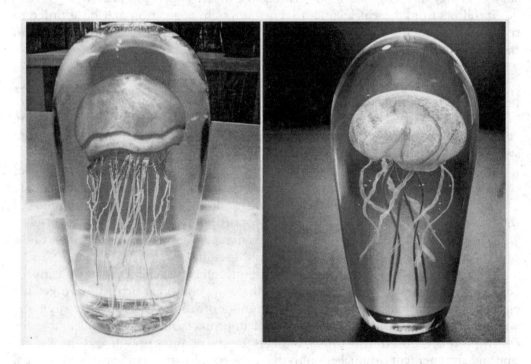

In Hawaii, Satava's sculptures have appeared in tourist brochures and art magazines. The sculptures are sold in sixteen galleries and gift shops, and they appear in many store windows. Lowry admits he saw a picture of Satava's jellyfish sculptures in *American Craft* magazine in 1996. And he admits he examined a Satava jellyfish sculpture that a customer brought him for repair in 1997.

Glass-in-glass sculpture is a centuries-old art form that consists of a glass sculpture inside a second glass layer, commonly called the shroud. The artist creates an inner glass sculpture and then dips it into molten glass, encasing it in a solid outer glass shroud. The shroud is malleable before it cools, and the artist can manipulate it into any shape he or she desires.

Satava filed suit against Lowry accusing him of copyright infringement. Satava requested, and the district court granted, a preliminary injunction, enjoining Lowry from making sculptures that resemble Satava's. . . .

II . . .

Any copyrighted expression must be "original." *Feist Pubs., Inc. v. Rural Tel. Serv. Co.,* 499 U.S. 340, 345 (1991). Although the amount of creative input by the author required to meet the originality standard is low, it is not negligible. *See Feist,* 499 U.S. at 362. . . .

The originality requirement mandates that objective "facts" and ideas are not copyrightable. *Baker v. Selden,* 101 U.S. (11 Otto) 99 (1879); *Feist,* 499 U.S. at 347. . . . Similarly, expressions that are standard, stock, or common to a particular subject matter or medium are not protectable under copyright law.[3]

It follows from these principles that no copyright protection may be afforded to the idea of producing a glass-in-glass jellyfish sculpture or to elements of expression that naturally follow from the idea of such a sculpture. . . .

Satava may not prevent others from depicting jellyfish with tendril-like tentacles or rounded bells, because many jellyfish possess those body parts. He may not prevent others from depicting jellyfish in bright colors, because many jellyfish are brightly colored. He may not prevent others from depicting jellyfish swimming vertically, because jellyfish swim vertically in nature and often are depicted swimming vertically. . . .

Satava may not prevent others from depicting jellyfish within a clear outer layer of glass, because clear glass is the most appropriate setting for an aquatic animal. He may not prevent others from depicting jellyfish "almost filling the entire volume" of the outer glass shroud, because such proportion is standard in glass-in-glass sculpture. And he may not prevent others from tapering the shape of their shrouds, because that shape is standard in glass-in-glass sculpture. . . .

It is true, of course, that a *combination* of unprotectable elements may qualify for copyright protection. But it is not true that *any* combination of unprotectable elements automatically qualifies for copyright protection. Our case law suggests, and we hold today, that a combination of unprotectable elements is eligible for copyright protection only if those elements are numerous enough and their selection and arrangement original enough that their combination constitutes an original work of authorship.

The combination of unprotectable elements in Satava's sculpture falls short of this standard. The selection of the clear glass, oblong shroud, bright colors, proportion, vertical orientation, and stereotyped jellyfish form, considered together,

---

3. Standard elements sometimes are called "*scenes a faire,*" vaguely French for "scenes which 'must' be done." The Ninth Circuit treats *scenes a faire* as a defense to infringement rather than as a barrier to copyrightability.

lacks the quantum of originality needed to merit copyright protection. These elements are so commonplace in glass-in-glass sculpture and so typical of jellyfish physiology that to recognize copyright protection in their combination effectively would give Satava a monopoly on lifelike glass-in-glass sculptures of single jellyfish with vertical tentacles. *See Feist,* 499 U.S. at 363 (noting that the selection, coordination, and arrangement of phone numbers in a directory "is not only unoriginal, it is practically inevitable"). . . .[5]

We do not mean to suggest that Satava has added nothing copyrightable to his jellyfish sculptures. He has made some copyrightable contributions: the distinctive curls of particular tendrils; the arrangement of certain hues; the unique shape of jellyfishes' bells. To the extent that these and other artistic choices were not governed by jellyfish physiology or the glass-in-glass medium, they are original elements that Satava theoretically may protect through copyright law. Satava's copyright on these original elements (or their combination) is "thin," however, comprising no more than his original contribution to ideas already in the public domain. Stated another way, Satava may prevent others from copying the original features he contributed, but he may not prevent others from copying elements of expression that nature displays for all observers, or that the glass-in-glass medium suggests to all sculptors. Satava possesses a thin copyright that protects against only virtually identical copying. . . .

NOTES AND QUESTIONS

1. Does *Roth Greeting Cards* effectively treat the greeting cards as "compilations"? If copyright did not protect compilations, would the cards be considered copyrightable after taking into account the exclusions mandated by §102(b)? How would the *Satava* court answer this question?

Although *Roth Greeting Cards* predates *Feist,* courts today frequently invoke the "total concept and feel" standard in both copyrightability and infringement contexts. Is that standard consistent with *Feist*?

---

5. We reach this conclusion based in part on our examination of the dozens of photographs of glass-in-glass jellyfish sculptures in the record. Some of the sculptures depict almost colorless jellyfish. Some of the sculptures have spherical shrouds. Some have shrouds encased in opaque black glass with clear windows cut through. Though none of the sculptures are identical, all of them are substantially similar. They differ only insofar as an artist has added or omitted some standard element. To give Satava a copyright on this basic combination of elements would effectively give him a monopoly on the idea of glass-in-glass sculptures of single vertical jellyfish. Congress did not intend for artists to fence off private preserves from within the public domain, and, if we recognized Satava's copyright, we would permit him to do exactly that.

Our analysis above suggests that the "merger doctrine" might apply in this case. Under the merger doctrine, courts will not protect a copyrighted work from infringement if the idea underlying the copyrighted work can be expressed in only one way, lest there be a monopoly on the underlying idea. In light of our holding that Satava cannot prevent other artists from using the standard and stereotyped elements in his sculptures, or the combination of those elements, we find it unnecessary to consider the application of the merger doctrine.

2. Does viewing a textual or graphic work as a compilation of its elements, rather than simply as a literary or pictorial work, make sense as an analytical matter? Does that approach make a finding of originality more or less likely? As a practical matter, in what kinds of cases are litigants asserting copyrights likely to characterize their works as compilations?

3. Is there a minimum number of preexisting elements that a creator must combine in order for the result to manifest copyrightable originality? The Compendium of U.S. Copyright Office Practices §312.2 (3d Ed. 2014) states that the Copyright Office "generally will not register a compilation containing only two or three elements, because the selection is necessarily *de minimis*." It also provides that "[g]enerally, a selection consisting of less than four items will be scrutinized for sufficient authorship." *Id*. What do you think of these rules?

PRACTICE EXERCISE: COUNSEL A CLIENT

Tara McNeely created and published a set of maps of hiking trails in rural Virginia. She began by taking public domain topographical maps published by the U.S. Geological Survey and tracing them. She then added data culled from other sources to them (e.g., boundary information about private property abutting hiking trails, taken from records at local property offices; information about trailheads and available parking taken from maps published by local wilderness groups, and so on), added color and shading to give the maps a three-dimensional effect, and selected different fonts for labeling different items. You represent the Shenandoah Back-Country Association, a nonprofit organization. Your client would like to copy some of the McNeely maps and distribute them free of charge to its members, and has asked for your opinion on whether it would incur copyright liability by doing so. Are the maps copyrightable? Review the materials in this chapter, including particularly the Copyright Office regulation listing material not subject to copyright, page 97 *supra*, and then provide your answer.

3

Authorship

In Chapter 2, you studied the requirements for copyrightability that flow from the constitutional authorization to grant exclusive rights in "Writings." We turn now to the equally important question of who should be entitled to claim copyright protection. The Intellectual Property Clause specifies that rights are to be granted to "Authors." What does it mean to be an "author"? Does this wording impose additional threshold requirements for the grant of copyright?

Determination of authorship is important because the Copyright Act vests initial ownership of copyright in the work in the party or parties deemed the "author" or "authors" of the work. Determination of authorship also has ongoing practical importance. Although the author of a work may assign ownership of the copyright to another, the Copyright Act contains provisions enabling certain authors to recapture their ownership rights.

> ### LOOKING FORWARD
>
> In Chapter 11 you will learn about the provisions that allow authors to terminate transfers of copyright ownership.

The Copyright Act recognizes three kinds of authorship: sole authorship, joint or co-authorship, and employer authorship of "works made for hire":

§201. Ownership of copyright

(a) **Initial ownership.** Copyright in a work protected under this title vests initially in the author or authors of the work. The authors of a joint work are co-owners of copyright in the work.

(b) **Works made for hire.** In the case of a work made for hire, the employer or other person for whom the work was prepared is considered the author for purposes of this title, and, unless the parties have expressly agreed otherwise in a written instrument signed by them, owns all of the rights comprised in the copyright.

Given the practical importance of authorship status, it may be surprising to learn that the Copyright Act does not define the term, nor do the major international copyright instruments. All refer simply to "authors." In fact, conceptions of

137

authorship differ considerably worldwide. As you will see, in the U.S. copyright system, determinations of authorship reflect both cultural and economic values. In particular, the "works made for hire" provision of the U.S. Copyright Act in §201(b) stands in stark contrast to the copyright laws of many other countries, which recognize only natural persons as authors notwithstanding the existence of an employment relationship.

As you read this chapter, identify the different understandings of authorship embodied in the Copyright Act's categories and consider the extent to which they are consistent with each other and with the policies incorporated in the Intellectual Property Clause.

A. SOLE AUTHORSHIP

In the absence of a statutory definition of authorship, how should courts decide who is an author? What factors should be relevant to the inquiry? Consider the following case.

Lindsay v. The Wrecked and Abandoned Vessel R.M.S. Titanic
52 U.S.P.Q.2d 1609 (S.D.N.Y. 1999)

BAER, J.: . . . In 1994, the plaintiff, under contract with a British television company, filmed and directed the British documentary film, "Explorers of the *Titanic*," a chronicle of [defendant] RMST's third salvage expedition of the *Titanic*. . . . To film this documentary, Lindsay sailed with RMST and the salvage expedition crew to the wreck site and remained at sea for approximately one month. . . . The plaintiff alleges that during and after filming this documentary in 1994, he conceived a new film project for the *Titanic* wreck using high illumination lighting equipment. . . .

As part of his pre-production efforts, the plaintiff created various story boards for the film, a series of drawings which incorporated images of the *Titanic* by identifying specific camera angles and shooting sequences "that reflected Planitff's [*sic*] creative inspiration and force behind his concept for shooting the Subject Work." . . . The plaintiff also alleges that he, along with members of his film team, designed the huge underwater light towers that were later used to make the film. . . . Lindsay also "personally constructed the light towers" and thereafter "for approximately 3-4 weeks directed, produced, and acted as the cinematographer of the Subject Work, underwater video taping of the *Titanic* wreck site, and otherwise participated in the 1996 salvage operation." . . . He also directed the filming of the wreck site from on board the salvage vessel "Ocean Voyager" after leading daily planning sessions with the crew of the *Nautile*, the submarine used to transport the film equipment and photographers to the underwater wreck site. . . . The purpose of the sessions was to provide the photographers with "detailed instructions for positioning and utilizing the light towers." . . .

[Plaintiff asserted a copyright infringement claim against defendants based on their licensing of the footage to The Discovery Channel. The defendant moved to dismiss.]

The defendants . . . argue that the plaintiff cannot have any protectable right in the illuminated footage since he did not dive to the ship and thus did not himself actually photograph the wreckage. This argument, however, does not hold water. . . .

For over 100 years, the Supreme Court has recognized that photographs may receive copyright protection in "so far as they are representatives of original intellectual conceptions of the author." *Burrow-Giles Lithographic Co. v. Sarony*, 111 U.S. 53, 58 (1884). An individual claiming to be an author for copyright purposes must show "the existence of those facts of originality, of intellectual production, of thought, and conception." . . . Taken as true, plaintiff's allegations meet this standard. Lindsay's alleged storyboards and the specific directions he provided to the film crew regarding the use of the lightowers [sic] and the angles from which to shoot the wreck all indicate that the final footage would indeed be the product of Lindsay's "original intellectual conceptions." . . .

All else being equal, where a plaintiff alleges that he exercised such a high degree of control over a film operation—including the type and amount of lighting used, the specific camera angles to be employed, and other detail-intensive elements of a film—such that the final product duplicates his conceptions and visions of what the film should look like, the plaintiff may be said to be an "author" within the meaning of the Copyright Act. . . .

NOTES AND QUESTIONS

1. Recall *Alfred Bell & Co. v. Catalda Fine Arts, Inc.*, 191 F.2d 99 (2d Cir. 1951), which you read in Chapter 2.A.2.a. Would the engravings in that case, which reproduced paintings by Old Masters, meet the standard of authorship described in *Lindsay*? Is there a difference between "originality" and "authorship"?

2. If "originality" and "authorship" are indeed distinct concepts, does the requirement of authorship translate into a separate, and perhaps higher, threshold for copyright protection? The Supreme Court's decision in *Feist* notwithstanding, should the constitutional reference to "Authors" be read to require this result?

3. In the United States, authorship is limited to human authors. The Compendium of U.S. Copyright Office Practices (3d ed. 2014), provides that the Copyright Office "will register an original work of authorship, provided that the work was created by a human being. . . . Because copyright law is limited to 'original intellectual conceptions of the author,' the Office will refuse to register a claim if it determines that a human being did not create the work." *Id.* at §306. Do you agree with the position adopted by the Copyright Office? Is this position supported by the holding in *Burrow-Giles Lithographic Co. v. Sarony*, 111 U.S. 53 (1884), which you read in Chapter 2.A.2.a, *supra*? The Compendium goes on to state "[s]imilarly, the

Office will not register works produced by a machine or mere mechanical process that operates randomly or automatically without any creative input or intervention from a human author." See *id*. Is there any basis in the Intellectual Property Clause for this position?

4. Professor Peter Jaszi argues that an individualistic conception of authorship developed during the Romantic era played, and continues to play, an important role in shaping Anglo-American copyright law. In particular, he argues that "[t]he 'authorship' concept, with its roots in notions of individual self-proprietorship, provided the rationale for thinking of literary productions as personal property with various associated attributes including alienability." Peter Jaszi, *Toward a Theory of Copyright: The Metamorphoses of "Authorship,"* 1991 Duke L.J. 455, 472. According to Professor Oren Bracha, the eventual transformation of copyright from a limited right to print and vend to a more general right of ownership also reflects the influence of nineteenth-century commercial values and the publisher interest groups that advanced them. Oren Bracha, *The Ideology of Authorship Revisited: Authors, Markets, and Liberal Values in Early American Copyright*, 108 Yale L.J. 186 (2008). As a result of these processes of abstraction and commodification, contemporary copyright law—the law that protects Viacom as well as J. K. Rowling—confronts a tension between protecting economic rights in "works" and protecting "authors."

B. JOINT AUTHORSHIP

Section 101 defines a "joint work" as "a work prepared by two or more authors with the intention that their contributions be merged into inseparable or interdependent parts of a unitary whole." 17 U.S.C. §101. Under this definition, what level of contribution is sufficient to qualify a party as a co-author?

Erickson v. Trinity Theatre, Inc.
13 F.3d 1061 (7th Cir. 1994)

RIPPLE, J.: . . . [Karen Erickson, a founding member of the Trinity Theatre, prepared three plays for the company. After a dispute developed between the parties, Trinity stopped paying royalties to Erickson for performances of the plays. Trinity argued that it was a co-author and co-owner of copyright in the plays because various Trinity actors had made suggestions that Erickson incorporated during development of the plays.]

Even if two or more persons collaborate with the intent to create a unitary work, the product will be considered a "joint work" only if the collaborators can be considered "authors." Courts have applied two tests to evaluate the contributions of authors claiming joint authorship status: Professor Nimmer's de minimis test and Professor Goldstein's copyrightable subject matter ("copyrightability") test. The de minimis and copyrightability tests differ in one fundamental respect. The de minimis test requires that only the combined product of joint efforts must be copyrightable. By contrast, Professor Goldstein's copyrightability test requires that each author's contribution be copyrightable. . . .

[Professor Nimmer's] position has not found support in the courts. . . . First, . . . [it] is not consistent with one of the Act's premises: ideas and concepts standing alone should not receive protection. Because the creative process necessarily involves the development of existing concepts into new forms, any restriction on the free exchange of ideas stifles creativity to some extent. Restrictions on an author's use of existing ideas in a work, such as the threat that accepting suggestions from another party might jeopardize the author's sole entitlement to a copyright, would hinder creativity. Second, contribution of an idea is an exceedingly ambiguous concept. Professor Nimmer provides little guidance to courts or parties regarding when a contribution rises to the level of joint authorship except to state that the contribution must be "more than a word or a line." . . .

We agree that the language of the Act supports the adoption of a copyrightability requirement. Section 101 of the Act defines a "joint work" as a "work prepared by two or more *authors*" (emphasis added). To qualify as an author, one must supply more than mere direction or ideas. . . .

. . . This test also enables parties to predict whether their contributions to a work will entitle them to copyright protection as a joint author. . . .

[Because Trinity could not identify any specific copyrightable contributions made by its actors, the court concluded that Trinity could not qualify as a joint author of the plays.]

Some works, like motion pictures, incorporate the copyrightable contributions of many people, each of whom intends that his or her contribution be merged with the others to form a unitary whole. Is each of these individuals therefore an "author"?

Aalmuhammed v. Lee
202 F.3d 1227 (9th Cir. 1999)

KLEINFELD, J.: . . . In 1991, Warner Brothers contracted with Spike Lee and his production companies to make the movie *Malcolm X*, to be based on the book, *The Autobiography of Malcolm X*. Lee co-wrote the screenplay, directed, and co-produced the movie, which starred Denzel Washington as Malcolm X. Washington asked Jefri Aalmuhammed to assist him in his preparation for the starring role because Aalmuhammed knew a great deal about Malcolm X and Islam. Aalmuhammed, a devout Muslim, was particularly knowledgeable about the life of Malcolm X, having previously written, directed, and produced a documentary film about Malcolm X.

. . . [Aalmuhammed] reviewed the shooting script for Spike Lee and Denzel Washington and suggested extensive script revisions. Some of his script revisions were included in the released version of the film; others were filmed but not included in the released version. Most of the revisions Aalmuhammed made were to ensure the religious and historical accuracy and authenticity of scenes depicting Malcolm X's religious conversion and pilgrimage to Mecca.

Aalmuhammed submitted evidence that he directed Denzel Washington and other actors while on the set, created at least two entire scenes with new characters, translated Arabic into English for subtitles, supplied his own voice for voice-overs, selected the proper prayers and religious practices for the characters, and edited parts of the movie during post production. Washington testified in his deposition that Aalmuhammed's contribution to the movie was "great" because "he helped to rewrite, to make more authentic." . . .

During the summer before *Malcolm X's* November 1992 release, Aalmuhammed asked for a writing credit as a co-writer of the film, but was turned down. When the film was released, it credited Aalmuhammed only as an "Islamic Technical Consultant," far down the list. . . .

[Aalmuhammed sought a declaratory judgment that the movie was a "joint work" and that he was a co-owner of the copyright and entitled to an accounting of the profits. The Ninth Circuit affirmed the district court's grant of summary judgment to defendants.]

. . . The statutory language establishes that for a work to be a "joint work" there must be (1) a copyrightable work, (2) two or more "authors," and (3) the authors must intend their contributions be merged into inseparable or interdependent parts of a unitary whole. A "joint work" in this circuit "requires each author to make an independently copyrightable contribution" to the disputed work. *Malcolm X* is a copyrightable work, and it is undisputed that the movie was intended by everyone involved with it to be a unitary whole. . . . Aalmuhammed has . . . submitted evidence that he rewrote several specific passages of dialogue that appeared in *Malcolm X*, and that he wrote scenes relating to Malcolm X's Hajj pilgrimage that were enacted in the movie. If Aalmuhammed's evidence is accepted, as it must be on summary judgment, these items would have been independently copyrightable. . . .

But there is another element to a "joint work." A "joint work" includes "two or more authors." Aalmuhammed established that he contributed substantially to the film, but not that he was one of its "authors." We hold that authorship is required under the statutory definition of a joint work, and that authorship is not the same thing as making a valuable and copyrightable contribution. . . .

Who, in the absence of contract, can be considered an author of a movie? The word is traditionally used to mean the originator or the person who causes something to come into being, or even the first cause, as when Chaucer refers to the "Author of Nature." For a movie, that might be the producer who raises the money. Eisenstein thought the author of a movie was the editor. The "auteur" theory suggests that it might be the director, at least if the director is able to impose his artistic judgments on the film. . . .

The Supreme Court dealt with the problem of defining "author" in new media in *Burrow-Giles Lithographic Co. v. Sarony*. . . . The Court decided that the photographer was the author, quoting various English authorities: "the person who has superintended the arrangement, who has actually formed the picture by putting the persons in position, and arranging the place where the people are to be—the man who is the effective cause of that"; " 'author' involves originating, making, producing, as the inventive or master mind, the thing which is to be protected"; "the man who really represents, creates, or gives effect to the idea, fancy, or imagination." The Court said that an "author," in the sense that the Founding Fathers used the term in the Constitution, was " 'he to whom anything owes its origin; originator; maker; one who completes a work of science or literature.' "

Answering a different question, what is a copyrightable "work," as opposed to who is the "author," the Supreme Court held in *Feist Publications* that "some minimal level of creativity" or "originality" suffices. But that measure of a "work" would be too broad and indeterminate to be useful if applied to determine who are "authors" of a movie. So many people might qualify as an "author" if the question were limited to whether they made a substantial creative contribution that that test would not distinguish one from another. Everyone from the producer and director to casting director, costumer, hairstylist, and "best boy" gets listed in the movie credits because all of their creative contributions really do matter. It is striking in *Malcolm X* how much the person who controlled the hue of the lighting contributed, yet no one would use the word "author" to denote that individual's relationship to the movie. A creative contribution does not suffice to establish authorship of the movie.

Burrow-Giles, in defining "author," requires more than a minimal creative or original contribution to the work. *Burrow-Giles* is still good law, and was recently reaffirmed in *Feist Publications*. *Burrow-Giles* and *Feist Publications* answer two distinct questions; who is an author, and what is a copyrightable work. . . .

The Second and Seventh Circuits have likewise concluded that contribution of independently copyrightable material to a work intended to be an inseparable whole will not suffice to establish authorship of a joint work.[24] Although the Second and Seventh Circuits do not base their decisions on the word "authors" in the statute, the practical results they reach are consistent with ours. These circuits have held that a person claiming to be an author of a joint work must prove that both parties intended each other to be joint authors. In determining whether the parties have the intent to be joint authors, the Second Circuit looks at who has decision making authority, how the parties bill themselves, and other evidence.

In *Thomson v. Larson*, an off-Broadway playwright had created a modern version of *La Boheme*, and had been adamant throughout its creation on being the sole author. He hired a drama professor for "dramaturgical assistance and research," agreeing to credit her as "dramaturg" but not author, but saying nothing about "joint work" or copyright. The playwright tragically died immediately after the final dress rehearsal, just before his play became the tremendous Broadway hit, *Rent*. The dramaturg then sued his estate for a declaratory judgment that she was an author of *Rent* as a "joint work," and for an accounting. The Second Circuit noted that the dramaturg had no decision making authority, had neither sought nor was billed as a co-author, and that the defendant entered into contracts as the sole author. On this

---

24. *Thomson v. Larson*, 147 F.3d 195 (2d Cir. 1998); *Erickson v. Trinity Theatre, Inc.*, 13 F.3d 1061 (7th Cir. 1994); *Childress v. Taylor*, 945 F.2d 500 (2d Cir. 1991).

reasoning, the Second Circuit held that there was no intent to be joint authors by the putative parties and therefore it was not a joint work. . . .

Aalmuhammed did not at any time have superintendence of the work. Warner Brothers and Spike Lee controlled it. . . .

Also, neither Aalmuhammed, nor Spike Lee, nor Warner Brothers, made any objective manifestations of an intent to be coauthors. Warner Brothers required Spike Lee to sign a "work for hire" agreement, so that even Lee would not be a co-author and co-owner with Warner Brothers. . . .

The Constitution establishes the social policy that our construction of the statutory term "authors" carries out. . . . Progress would be retarded rather than promoted, if an author could not consult with others and adopt their useful suggestions without sacrificing sole ownership of the work. Too open a definition of author would compel authors to insulate themselves and maintain ignorance of the contributions others might make. Spike Lee could not consult a scholarly Muslim to make a movie about a religious conversion to Islam, and the arts would be the poorer for that. . . .

NOTES AND QUESTIONS

1. Review the questions posed following the excerpt from the *Lindsay* decision, *supra* Section A. Have your answers to any of those questions changed? Do the attributes of authorship identified by the *Aalmuhammed* court matter more when one is resolving claims of co-authorship? Why, or why not?

> **COMPARATIVE PERSPECTIVE**
>
> Some countries, e.g., France and the Republic of Korea, require that all co-authors consent to any exploitation of the work. Those countries, though, are more likely than the United States to furnish express safeguards against unreasonable behavior by co-authors. Thus, the Korean copyright law directs that consent may not be unreasonably withheld, while France authorizes its courts to resolve disagreements.

2. Recall the statutory definition of a joint work: "a work prepared by two or more authors with the intention that their contributions be merged into inseparable or interdependent parts of a unitary whole." 17 U.S.C. §101. Are *Erickson* and *Aalmuhammed* simply focusing on different elements of the definition, or are they interpreting the same element differently?

3. The Copyright Act does not specify how rights should be apportioned among joint authors. According to judge-made doctrine, all authors of a joint work receive equal interests in the work. Thus, for example, if there are two joint authors, each author receives a one-half undivided interest. Upon an author's death, her interest passes to her heirs (*see* Chapter 11, *infra*). Permission of all co-authors is required for an assignment or an exclusive license of the copyright, but any co-author may grant a nonexclusive license without her co-authors' consent, subject to a duty to account for any profits received from the license. Are these judge-made rules the right ones? How might they have affected judicial evaluation of the co-authorship claims asserted in *Aalmuhammed*?

4. Should Aalmuhammed instead have claimed sole authorship in his separate contributions to *Malcolm X*? How should such a claim be resolved?

PRACTICE EXERCISE: COUNSEL A CLIENT

Carol Knight, an award-winning director, wrote a short "treatment" for what became a Broadway show exploring the coming of age of an orphan who had suffered much as a youth and turned to a life of crime as an adult. The initial show, based on a script written by Knight was a critical failure during a long-running preview period. The producers hired a new writer to work with Knight to revise the production by transforming what was a dark, adult show to one that was more family friendly, appealing to children and adults alike. The show was transformed into a musical in which the orphan as an adult became a rock star with a philanthropic nature. Knight objected to many of the changes and resigned after the new script was completed and before previews began. Some changes were made after the previews and before the Broadway opening. The show is a smash. The producers refuse to pay royalties to Knight. Knight seeks your advice. What questions would you ask Ms. Knight and what facts would you seek to establish? How would your advice change depending on the answers you receive?

Note on the Intent to Merge Requirement and Implications for Collaborative Works

For a work to qualify as a joint work, all of the authors must have intended at the time they prepared their contributions that those contributions be merged to form a unitary whole. This requirement, like the requirement that each would-be author must contribute a copyrightable contribution, sometimes is justified on grounds of predictability and efficiency. Knowing the identities of other authors helps the parties structure their relationships more efficiently ex ante, and protects them against ex-post claims of authorship.

The intent to merge requirement creates difficulties for works that are collaborative and evolve over time. Notable examples include open source software and Wikipedia. Open source software is written and distributed with a license that allows others to modify the software and distribute their modified versions, provided they do so under the terms of the original license. Wikipedia is an online reference source whose entries are written and edited by users on an ad hoc basis. Authors who contribute to open source software and Wikipedia often contribute copyrightable expression, but those individuals typically are not identified in advance and their contributions may not be made contemporaneously. The contributors to such works know that others will be adding creative expression, and indeed expect such future contributions. Does that expectation amount to an intent that the contributions be merged?

What about works in the realms of folklore and indigenous arts that represent the cumulative creativity of generations, and that also may have religious

> **KEEP IN MIND**
>
> Generally speaking, an "inseparable" work is one in which the various contributions are blended together, as in the case of computer software or even this casebook. An "interdependent" work is one in which the work can be broken into separate components, such as lyrics and music.

significance? The creation of such works typically is not premised on economic returns, and so the logic that makes predictability and efficiency important policy objectives is difficult to apply. Should the intent-to-merge requirement (and the other requirements for joint authorship) apply in the same way to such works? Note that many of these works are also very old, making it difficult to ascertain the extent to which copyright attaches.

Another way to understand the role of the intent-to-merge requirement, then, is that it establishes clear boundaries around the kinds of works that copyright law is willing to recognize as jointly authored. One might conceive of the requirement as a type of legal formality (akin to the requirement of a "writing" for certain types of contracts) that forces parties to acknowledge and demarcate their creative relationship.

NOTES AND QUESTIONS

1. How should copyright law view the status of contributors whose expressions are combined with those of others sequentially rather than contemporaneously? Some courts have held that an author in such a case retains her ownership rights in her contribution and may have a claim for infringement if it is used without permission in combination with contributions from others. *See Maurizio v. Goldsmith*, 84 F. Supp. 2d 455 (S.D.N.Y. 2000); *Ulloa v. Universal Music and Video Distribution Corp.*, 303 F. Supp. 2d 409 (S.D.N.Y. 2004). Another way to approach the problem is to treat the combined work as a derivative work. Which approach do you prefer?

2. Should the intent to merge be specific to a particular contribution? In the case of open source software, should it matter that all programmers involved in the creation are contractually bound to permit others to modify or add to the software? In the case of Wikipedia, should it matter that collaborative editing is the norm?

3. If no one qualifies as an "author" of the end product resulting from large-scale sequential collaboration, is the work a "work of authorship" at all? *See generally* Peter Jaszi, *On the Author Effect: Contemporary Copyright and Collective Creativity*, *in* Martha Woodmansee & Peter Jaszi, eds., The Construction of Authorship: Textual Appropriation in Law and Literature 29 (1994).

C. WORKS MADE FOR HIRE

Predictable rules about joint authorship status are one way to allocate copyright rights in works created by multiple contributors. The "work made for hire" provisions of the Copyright Act establish another way for copyright ownership to be allocated. In *Aalmuhammed*, the Ninth Circuit observed in passing that Warner Brothers, not Spike Lee, was the "author" of *Malcolm X* pursuant to a "'work [made] for hire agreement." Given the court's description of the qualities necessary for authorship, that might seem to be a curious result. We turn now to the "work made for hire" provisions of the Act.

The 1909 Copyright Act specified that "the word 'author' shall include an employer in the case of works made for hire," Copyright Act of 1909, §62, 17 U.S.C. §26 (1976 ed.), but did not define the term "works made for hire." The 1976 Act rectified that omission:

> A "work made for hire" is—
>   (1) a work prepared by an employee within the scope of his or her employment; or
>   (2) a work specially ordered or commissioned for use as a contribution to a collective work, as a part of a motion picture or other audiovisual work, as a translation, as a supplementary work, as a compilation, as an instructional text, as a test, as answer material for a test, or as an atlas, if the parties expressly agree in a written instrument signed by them that the work shall be considered a work made for hire. For the purpose of the foregoing sentence, a "supplementary work" is a work prepared for publication as a secondary adjunct to a work by another author for the purpose of introducing, concluding, illustrating, explaining, revising, commenting upon, or assisting in the use of the other work, such as forewords, afterwords, pictorial illustrations, maps, charts, tables, editorial notes, musical arrangements, answer material for tests, bibliographies, appendixes, and indexes, and an "instructional text" is a literary, pictorial, or graphic work prepared for publication and with the purpose of use in systematic instructional activities.

17 U.S.C. §101. This definition, however, soon raised interpretative issues of its own.

1. Works Created by Employees Within the Scope of Their Employment

The Copyright Act's first definition of a work made for hire has two requirements that must be satisfied. First, the creator of the work must be an employee, and second the work must be prepared within the scope of his or her employment. We address each of these requirements in turn.

a. Who Is an "Employee"?

Community for Creative Non-Violence v. Reid
490 U.S. 730 (1989)

MARSHALL, J.:

I

. . . In the fall of 1985, CCNV decided to participate in the annual Christmastime Pageant of Peace in Washington, D.C., by sponsoring a display to dramatize the plight of the homeless. As the District Court recounted:

> [CCNV trustee Mitch] Snyder and fellow CCNV members conceived the idea for the nature of the display: a sculpture of a modern Nativity scene in which, in lieu of the

traditional Holy Family, the two adult figures and the infant would appear as contemporary homeless people huddled on a streetside steam grate. The family was to be black (most of the homeless in Washington being black); the figures were to be life-sized, and the steam grate would be positioned atop a platform "pedestal," or base, within which special-effects equipment would be enclosed to emit simulated "steam" through the grid to swirl about the figures. They also settled upon a title for the work—"Third World America"—and a legend for the pedestal: "and still there is no room at the inn." 652 F. Supp. 1453, 1454 (DC 1987).

Snyder made inquiries to locate an artist to produce the sculpture. He was referred to respondent James Earl Reid, a Baltimore, Maryland, sculptor. In the course of two telephone calls, Reid agreed to sculpt the three human figures. CCNV agreed to make the steam grate and pedestal for the statue. Reid proposed that the work be cast in bronze, at a total cost of approximately $100,000 and taking six to eight months to complete. Snyder rejected that proposal because CCNV did not have sufficient funds, and because the statue had to be completed by December 12 to be included in the pageant. Reid then suggested, and Snyder agreed, that the sculpture would be made of a material known as "Design Cast 62," a synthetic substance that could meet CCNV's monetary and time constraints, could be tinted to resemble bronze, and could withstand the elements. The parties agreed that the project would cost no more than $15,000, not including Reid's services, which he offered to donate. The parties did not sign a written agreement. Neither party mentioned copyright.

After Reid received an advance of $3,000, he made several sketches of figures in various poses. At Snyder's request, Reid sent CCNV a sketch of a proposed sculpture showing the family in a creche-like setting: the mother seated, cradling the baby in her lap; the father standing behind her, bending over her shoulder to touch the baby's foot. Reid testified that Snyder asked for the sketch to use in raising funds for the sculpture. Snyder testified that it was also for his approval. Reid sought a black family to serve as a model for the sculpture. Upon Snyder's suggestion, Reid visited a family living at CCNV's Washington shelter but decided that only their newly born child was a suitable model. While Reid was in Washington, Snyder took him to see homeless people living on the streets. Snyder pointed out that they tended to recline on steam grates, rather than sit or stand, in order to warm their bodies. From that time on, Reid's sketches contained only reclining figures.

Throughout November and the first two weeks of December 1985, Reid worked exclusively on the statue, assisted at various times by a dozen different people who were paid with funds provided in installments by CCNV. On a number of occasions, CCNV members visited Reid to check on his progress and to coordinate CCNV's construction of the base. CCNV rejected Reid's proposal to use suitcases or shopping bags to hold the family's personal belongings, insisting instead on a shopping cart. . . .

On December 24, 1985, 12 days after the agreed-upon-date, Reid delivered the completed statue to Washington. There it was joined to the steam grate and pedestal prepared by CCNV and placed on display near the site of the pageant. Snyder paid Reid the final installment of the $15,000. The statue remained on display for a month. In late January 1986, CCNV members returned it to Reid's studio in

Baltimore for minor repairs. Several weeks later, Snyder began making plans to take the statue on a tour of several cities to raise money for the homeless. Reid objected, contending that the Design Cast 62 material was not strong enough to withstand the ambitious itinerary. He urged CCNV to cast the statue in bronze at a cost of $35,000, or to create a master mold at a cost of $5,000. Snyder declined to spend more of CCNV's money on the project.

In March 1986, Snyder asked Reid to return the sculpture. Reid refused. He then filed a certificate of copyright registration for "Third World America" in his name and announced plans to take the sculpture on a more modest tour than the one CCNV had proposed. Snyder, acting in his capacity as CCNV's trustee, immediately filed a competing certificate of copyright registration.

Snyder and CCNV then commenced this action against Reid. . . . After a 2-day bench trial, the District Court declared that "Third World America" was a "work made for hire" under §101 of the Copyright Act. . . . The court reasoned that Reid had been an "employee" of CCNV within the meaning of §101(1) because CCNV was the motivating force in the statue's production. . . .

[The D.C. Circuit reversed and remanded, holding that under traditional principles of agency law, Reid was an independent contractor, and that therefore the work was not "prepared by an employee" as required by §101(1). The court further held that the statue could not be a "work made for hire" under §101(2).] We granted certiorari to resolve a conflict among the Courts of Appeals over the proper construction of the "work made for hire" provisions of the Act. . . . We now affirm.

II

A . . .

The dispositive inquiry . . . is whether "Third World America" is "a work prepared by an employee within the scope of his or her employment" under §101(1). The Act does not define these terms. In the absence of such guidance, four interpretations have emerged. The first holds that a work is prepared by an employee whenever the hiring party retains the right to control the product. . . . A second, and closely related, view is that a work is prepared by an employee under §101(1) when the hiring party has actually wielded control with respect to the creation of a particular work. This approach was formulated by the Court of Appeals for the Second Circuit, *Aldon Accessories Ltd. v. Spiegel, Inc.*, 738 F.2d 548, *cert. denied,* 469 U.S. 982 (1984), and adopted by the Fourth Circuit, *Brunswick Beacon, Inc. v. Schock-Hopchas Publishing Co.*, 810 F.2d 410 (1987), the Seventh Circuit, *Evans Newton, Inc. v. Chicago Systems Software*, 793 F.2d 889, *cert. denied,* 479 U.S. 949 (1986), and, at times, by petitioners. . . . A third view is that the term "employee" within §101(1) carries its common-law agency law meaning. This view was endorsed by the Fifth Circuit in *Easter Seal Society for Crippled Children & Adults of Louisiana, Inc. v. Playboy Enterprises*, 815 F.2d 323 (1987), and by the Court of Appeals below. Finally, respondent and numerous *amici curiae* contend that the term "employee" only refers to "formal, salaried" employees. The Court of Appeals for the Ninth Circuit recently adopted this view. *See Dumas v. Gommerman*, 865 F.2d 1093 (1989).

The starting point for our interpretation of a statute is always its language. *Consumer Product Safety Comm'n v. GTE Sylvania, Inc.*, 447 U.S. 102, 108 (1980). The Act nowhere defines the terms "employee" or "scope of employment." It is, however, well established that "[w]here Congress uses terms that have accumulated settled meaning under . . . the common law, a court must infer, unless the statute otherwise dictates, that Congress means to incorporate the established meaning of these terms." *NLRB v. Amax Coal Co.*, 453 U.S. 322, 329 (1981). . . . In the past, when Congress has used the term "employee" without defining it, we have concluded that Congress intended to describe the conventional master-servant relationship as understood by common-law agency doctrine. . . . Nothing in the text of the work for hire provisions indicates that Congress used the words "employee" and "employment" to describe anything other than " 'the conventional relation of employer and employee.' " . . . On the contrary, Congress' intent to incorporate the agency law definition is suggested by §101(1)'s use of the term, "scope of employment," a widely used term of art in agency law. *See* Restatement (Second) of Agency §228 (1958). . . .

In contrast, neither test proposed by petitioners is consistent with the text of the Act. The exclusive focus of the right to control the product test on the relationship between the hiring party and the product clashes with the language of §101(1), which focuses on the relationship between the hired and hiring parties. The right to control the product test also would distort the meaning of the ensuing subsection, §101(2). Section 101 plainly creates two distinct ways in which a work can be deemed for hire: one for works prepared by employees, the other for those specially ordered or commissioned works which fall within one of the nine enumerated categories and are the subject of a written agreement. The right to control the product test ignores this dichotomy by transforming into a work for hire under §101(1) any "specially ordered or commissioned" work that is subject to the supervision and control of the hiring party. Because a party who hires a "specially ordered or commissioned" work by definition has a right to specify the characteristics of the product desired, at the time the commission is accepted, and frequently until it is completed, the right to control the product test would mean that many works that could satisfy §101(2) would already have been deemed works for hire under §101(1). Petitioners' interpretation is particularly hard to square with §101(2)'s enumeration of nine specific categories of specially ordered or commissioned works eligible to be works for hire. . . .

The actual control test . . . fares only marginally better when measured against the language and structure of §101. . . . Under the actual control test, a work for hire could arise under §101(2), but not under §101(1), where a party commissions, but does not actually control, a product which falls into one of the nine enumerated categories. Nonetheless, we agree with the Court of Appeals for the Fifth Circuit that "[t]here is simply no way to milk the 'actual control' test . . . from the language of the statute." . . .

We therefore conclude that the language and structure of §101 of the Act do not support either the right to control the product or the actual control approaches.[8]

The structure of §101 indicates that a work for hire can arise through one of two mutually exclusive means, one for employees and one for independent contractors, and ordinary canons of statutory interpretation indicate that the classification of a particular hired party should be made with reference to agency law.

This reading of the undefined statutory terms finds considerable support in the Act's legislative history. . . .

In 1961, the Copyright Office's first legislative proposal retained the distinction between works by employees and works by independent contractors. *See* Report of the Register of Copyrights on the General Revision of the U.S. Copyright Law, 87th Cong., 1st Sess. . . . After numerous meetings with representatives of the affected parties, the Copyright Office issued a preliminary draft bill in 1963. Adopting the Register's recommendation, it defined "work made for hire" as "a work prepared by an employee within the scope of the duties of his employment, but not including a work made on special order or commission." . . .

In response to objections by book publishers that the preliminary draft bill limited the work for hire doctrine to "employees," the 1964 revision bill expanded the scope of the work for hire classification to reach, for the first time, commissioned works. The bill's language, proposed initially by representatives of the publishing industry, retained the definition of work for hire insofar as it referred to "employees," but added a separate clause covering commissioned works, without regard to subject matter, "if the parties so agree in writing." Those representing authors objected that the added provision would allow publishers to use their superior bargaining position to force authors to sign work for hire agreements. . . .

In 1965, the competing interests reached a historic compromise, which was embodied in a joint memorandum submitted to Congress and the Copyright Office, incorporated into the 1965 revision bill, and ultimately enacted in the same form and nearly the same terms 11 years later. . . . The compromise retained as subsection (1) the language referring to "a work prepared by an employee within the scope of his employment." However, in exchange for concessions from publishers on provisions relating to the termination of transfer rights, the authors consented to a second subsection which classified four categories of commissioned works as works for hire if the parties expressly so agreed in writing: works for use "as a contribution to a collective work, as a part of a motion picture, as a translation, or as supplementary work." The interested parties selected these categories because they concluded that these commissioned works, although not prepared by employees and thus not covered by the first subsection, nevertheless should be treated as works for hire because they were ordinarily prepared "at the instance, direction, and risk of a publisher or producer." . . .

---

8. We also reject the suggestion of respondent and *amici* that the §101(1) term "employee" refers only to formal, salaried employees. While there is some support for such a definition in the legislative history, . . . the language of §101(1) cannot support it. The Act does not say "formal" or "salaried" employee, but simply "employee." Moreover, respondent and those *amici* who endorse a formal, salaried employee test do not agree upon the content of this test. . . .

Third World America: A Contemporary Nativity
Original artwork © James Earl Reid. Reprinted by permission.

[The remaining five categories in current subsection (2) were added by the House Judiciary Committee during subsequent revisions.]

Finally, petitioners' construction of the work for hire provisions would impede Congress' paramount goal in revising the 1976 Act of enhancing predictability and certainty of copyright ownership. *See* H.R. Rep. No. 94-1476, *supra*, at 129. In a "copyright marketplace," the parties negotiate with an expectation that one of them will own the copyright in the completed work. With that expectation, the parties at the outset can settle on relevant contractual terms, such as the price for the work and the ownership of reproduction rights.

To the extent that petitioners endorse an actual control test, CCNV's construction of the work for hire provisions prevents such planning. Because that test turns on whether the hiring party has closely monitored the production process, the parties would not know until late in the process, if not until the work is completed, whether a work will ultimately fall within §101(1). . . .

B

We turn, finally, to an application of §101 to Reid's production of "Third World America." In determining whether a hired party is an employee under the general common law of agency, we consider the hiring party's right to control the manner and means by which the product is accomplished. Among the other factors relevant to this inquiry are the skill required; the source of the instrumentalities and tools; the location of the work; the duration of the relationship between the parties; whether the hiring party has the right to assign additional projects to the hired party; the extent of the hired party's discretion over when and how long to work; the method of payment; the hired party's role in hiring and paying assistants; whether the work is part of the regular business of the hiring party; whether the hiring party is in business; the provision of employee benefits; and the tax treatment of the hired party. *See* Restatement §220(2) (setting forth a nonexhaustive list of factors relevant to determining whether a hired party is an employee). No one of these factors is determinative. . . .

[The Court concluded that in light of these factors, the court of appeals had correctly determined that Reid was an independent contractor rather than an employee of CCNV. It remanded for a determination of whether, under §101, the sculpture was nonetheless a joint work co-authored by Reid and CCNV.]

AFTERMATH

Following the remand, the district court assisted the parties in negotiating a settlement, under which Reid was credited with sole authorship of the work and CCNV received sole ownership of the original sculpture. Reid received the exclusive right to make three-dimensional reproductions, but the agreement authorized both parties to make two-dimensional reproductions. *See CCNV v. Reid*, 1991 Copr. L. Dec. (CCH) ¶26,753 (D.D.C. Jan. 7, 1991).

Following negotiation of the settlement and entry of the consent judgment by the district court, Reid requested access to the sculpture so that he could make a mold of it, but CCNV refused. The parties returned to court again, where the district judge found that Reid had an "implied easement of necessity" to enable him to exercise his rights under the consent judgment. *CCNV v. Reid*, 1991 WL 370138 (D.D.C. Oct. 16, 1991).

JustMed, Inc. v. Byce
600 F.3d 1118 (9th Cir. 2010)

FLETCHER, J: . . .

I

Joel Just and Michael Byce . . . together developed the idea of a digital audio larynx, a device to help laryngectomees—individuals whose larynxes have been surgically removed—produce clearer speech. . . .

Byce worked on the project between 1995 and 1998, but no one did any further work on the device from 1999—when Byce's wife, the sister of Just's wife Ann, unexpectedly died—until 2003. Then, in 2003, Joel and Ann Just formed JustMed, Inc., . . . to continue development of the product. Just recruited a former business associate, Jerome Liebler, to help work on the idea. He offered founders' options to

Byce, and Byce ultimately invested $25,000 in return for 130,000 shares. Byce also accepted a position on JustMed's board of directors, serving with the Justs.

Just and Liebler worked full time developing a new hardware prototype and writing source code for the product. Liebler wrote a majority of the code, working at his home on his own computers. . . .

Since it was not yet producing a product, the company operated financially by selling shares to family members and by relying on loans from the Justs. Just and Liebler did not receive a cash salary and instead were compensated with shares of stock.

By the summer of 2004, JustMed had a marketable product called "JusTalk." Liebler, however, moved to Kentucky, making it difficult for him to continue his work on the product. At the same time, Byce expressed interest in becoming more involved with the company. Liebler was still drawing half of his salary, but agreed to have the whole package—at that point, $90,000 per year, paid as 15,000 shares per month, each share valued at 50 cents—transferred to Byce and to have Byce take over development of the source code.

At trial, Just testified that Byce was hired as an employee to replace Liebler, who was also an employee, and that Byce agreed to be paid a salary in shares of stock. Byce, on the other hand, testified that while he expected to be adequately compensated in shares upon transferring ownership of the source code, he never understood himself to be an employee and had no "explicit knowledge" that he was accruing shares as compensation.

JustMed and Byce had no written employment agreement. Byce never filled out an I–9 employment verification form or, until 2005, a W–4 tax withholding form. At most, Just documented Byce's salary and duties in a notebook that he kept, although the notation indicating when Byce started was not recorded until several months after Byce began working on the source code. Although Byce began full-time work on the source code in September 2004 and began accruing JustMed stock in October, he never received share certificates for the stock he received as compensation. Indeed, the company generally did not keep formal records other than a series of notebooks Just maintained to track conversations and events. While Byce worked for JustMed, the company did not issue Byce a W–2 wage statement form, withhold taxes, or pay workers' compensation or unemployment insurance. Nor did the company provide benefits for Byce or report his employment to the state. Just testified that he did not think much of this was necessary because he thought of Byce as a JustMed "executive," and because JustMed was modeled on prior startup technology businesses that Just had been involved with, where employees were paid exclusively in stock and the stock was never reported as income because of its uncertain value.

Although Byce was carrying on Liebler's duties, Byce operated differently, because he did not live and work in Oregon as Liebler had. Instead, Byce worked from his home in Boise, Idaho, using his own computer. . . . Byce set his own hours, often working late into the night, and Just did not tell him how to spend his days. As Byce developed new versions of the source code, he would e-mail the new version to Just, who would compile it and load it onto the JusTalk to evaluate its performance. Whereas Just had previously worked side-by-side with Liebler, Just and Byce often communicated by phone or e-mail, and occasionally would meet in Boise or Portland or somewhere in between.. . . . Just, admittedly a poor programmer, never made changes to the source code, and by the time this dispute arose, Byce had substantially rewritten the source code Liebler had developed. . . .

While he was working on the source code, Byce was included in the company profile brochure and had a JustMed business card. He was alternatively referred to as the "Director of Research and Development" and the "Director of Engineering," the latter title supplied by Byce himself. Although he was primarily working on the source code, Byce also updated the company Web site and attended conferences, marketing meetings, and demonstrations on behalf of JustMed.

Because he was not earning money, Byce was living on credit, and by May 2005 he was worried about his financial situation. He told Just that he would soon need cash. In response, Just agreed to have JustMed pay Byce half in cash and half in shares. Byce filled out a W–4 form, and the company issued three checks for him as payment for May, June, and July 2005.

Byce, however, never cashed the checks. At this point, Byce became concerned that Just did not view him as an equal in the corporation. In order to protect what he perceived as his intellectual property, Byce changed the copyright statement on the software, so that it now read "Copyright (c) Mike Byce 2005" instead of copyright JustMed.

[After discovering that he owned many fewer shares than the Justs and Liebler, Byce deleted the source code from JustMed's systems.]

JustMed filed suit in state court, and Byce removed the case to federal court, asserting that it required determination of ownership of the software under the Copyright Act. . . .

After a bench trial, the district court found in favor of JustMed and held that Byce was an employee when he wrote the software, so that JustMed owned the copyright to the software. . . .

III . . .

A

. . . As it is relevant here, a "work made for hire" is "a work prepared by an employee within the scope of his or her employment." 17 U.S.C. §101. Thus, whether Byce owns the source code copyright turns on whether he was an employee of JustMed or an independent contractor.

The Supreme Court has explained that absent any textual indications to the contrary, when Congress uses the terms "employee," "employer," or "scope of employment," it means to incorporate principles from the general common law of agency. *CCNV*, 490 U.S. at 740-41. Accordingly, "the hiring party's right to control the manner and means by which the product is accomplished" is the central inquiry here. *Id.* at 751. Factors relevant to this inquiry include: [those listed in the *CCNV* case, citing the Restatement (Second) of Agency §220(2) (1958) – EDS.]. Because "the common-law test contains no shorthand formula or magic phrase that can be applied to find the answer, all of the incidents of the relationship must be assessed and weighed with no one factor being decisive." *Nationwide Mut. Ins. Co. v. Darden,* 503 U.S. 318, 324 (1992); *see also Aymes v. Bonelli,* 980 F.2d 857, 861 (2d Cir.1992) ("It does not necessarily follow that because no one factor is dispositive all factors are equally important, or indeed that all factors will have relevance in every case. The factors should not merely be tallied but should be weighed according to their significance in the case.").

Byce argues on appeal that the district court improperly weighed the factors and ignored crucial facts, especially JustMed's tax treatment of Byce, the failure to provide him with benefits, the failure to fill out appropriate employment forms, the lack of any written agreement regarding Byce's employment or salary, and the lack of stock certificates for shares Byce was accruing.

However, taking the various factors into account, we conclude that the district court did not err in finding that Byce was an employee. In particular, the contemplated duration of the relationship, the tasks Byce did for JustMed, the fact that Byce earned a salary from JustMed, and the nature of JustMed's business all support the finding that Byce was an employee. While no one factor is decisive, we draw some guidance in weighing the factors from JustMed's status as a technology start-up company. The evidence of the way JustMed operates gives support to the finding that Byce was an employee. Admittedly, some of the factors that Byce points to support his position, but mostly they are entitled to little weight when viewed in light of the way JustMed conducts its business.

JustMed hired Byce primarily to work on the JusTalk software, but he was not hired for a specific term or with a discretely defined end product in mind. *Cf. CCNV,* 490 U.S. at 753 (independent contractor hired for single task of producing sculpture). JustMed continuously worked on the source code to improve its effectiveness and capability. Although Byce's work on the source code lasted only nine months, it was halted not because the code's development had reached a logical termination point but because of the parties' dispute. Thus, the fact that the parties contemplated a relationship of indefinite duration cuts in favor of finding Byce an employee.

Byce did other work for JustMed as well. He updated the company's Web site and demonstrated the JusTalk units at tradeshows. Byce had previously worked on the Web site when he acted only as a director and shareholder for the company, but his continued work on tasks besides programming indicates JustMed could have assigned additional projects to Byce. Moreover, his formal title indicates that he had broad duties within JustMed, as well as a relationship with the company that was intended to be permanent.

JustMed hired Byce to replace Liebler, an employee, and paid him the same salary that Liebler received. . . . Although independent contractors are often paid upon completion of a specific job, *see CCNV,* 490 U.S. at 753 (independent contractor was to be paid upon completion of sculpture), Byce was paid a regular monthly salary in the same way as other JustMed employees. This weighs heavily in favor of finding him an employee, even though much of the salary came in the form of stock.

Also militating in favor of JustMed is the fact that its primary business was the development and marketing of the JusTalk device. Byce's work was integral to JustMed's regular business, since the JusTalk cannot work without functioning software. Indeed, there is evidence that JustMed tried to sell consumers on the JusTalk precisely by emphasizing that the software could constantly be updated. It seems highly unlikely that JustMed would leave such an important, continuous responsibility to an independent contractor who would terminate his relationship with the company upon completing a working version of the software.

While some factors initially seem to favor Byce, on closer examination they are insufficient to find him an independent contractor.

It is true, for example, that Just did not exercise much control over the manner and means by which Byce created the source code. However, this is not as important to a technology start-up as it might be to an established company. Byce was an inventive computer programmer expected to work independently. The business model and Byce's duties do not require that the project be completed in a particular manner or that Just continuously oversee Byce's work, so long as JustMed eventually found itself with a marketable product. Moreover, Just did have some input into Byce's work on the software, even if it was given by e-mail and phone. *Cf.* [*Aymes,* 980 F.2d] at 862 (input from client regarding computer program's functions "weighs heavily in favor of finding [programmer] . . . an employee"); *but see CCNV,* 490 U.S. at 752 ("[T]he extent of control the hiring party exercises over the details of the product is not dispositive.").

The nature of the business and the work similarly means that Byce's ability to set his own hours and the fact that he worked from home are not particularly relevant. As a programmer, Byce could, in essence, ply his craft at any time and from any place without significant impairment to its quality or his ability to meet JustMed's needs. So although physical separation between the hiring party and the worker is often relevant to determining employment status, it is less germane in light of the kind of work Byce was doing. Of course, computer programming is a skilled profession, which weighs in favor of finding Byce not an employee, but given the other factors and the fact that JustMed's regular business requires it to employ programmers, we find this far from conclusive.

Byce's strongest argument turns on JustMed's failure to pay benefits and fill out the appropriate employment forms, and JustMed's tax treatment of Byce. Some courts have relied heavily on these factors as "highly probative of the true nature of the employment relationship." *See Aymes,* 980 F.2d at 861, 863–64 ("[E]very case since [*CCNV*] that has applied the test has found the hired party to be an independent contractor where the hiring party failed to extend benefits or pay social security taxes."); *see also Kirk v. Harter,* 188 F.3d 1005, 1009 (8th Cir.1999) (agreeing with *Aymes* that employee benefits and tax treatment are especially significant to determination of employee status). There is a danger, however, in relying on them too heavily, because they do not bear directly on the substance of the employment relationship—the right to control. In this case, the factors do not decisively favor Byce, especially when one considers JustMed's business model.

We note Byce did eventually fill out a W–4 form and have taxes withheld once he started receiving paychecks from JustMed. The tax treatment here is therefore more ambiguous than in other copyright cases where courts have relied on the hiring party's treatment of the hired party as an independent contractor—for example, by not withholding taxes and by giving the hired party 1099 forms—and only later asserted that the individual was an employee. *See Aymes,* 980 F.2d at 859; *Kirk,* 188 F.3d at 1009. While an inherent unfairness exists in a company claiming a worker to be an independent contractor in one context but an employee in another, *see Aymes,* 980 F.2d at 859, that is not the case here.

JustMed's treatment of Byce with regard to taxes, benefits, and employment forms is more likely attributable to the start-up nature of the business than to Byce's alleged status as an independent contractor. The indications are that other employees, for example Liebler, were treated similarly. Insofar as JustMed did not comply with federal and state employment or tax laws, we do not excuse its actions, but in this context the remedy for these failings lies not with denying the firm its intellectual property but with enforcing the relevant laws.

As a small start-up company, JustMed conducted its business more informally than an established enterprise might. This fact can make it more difficult to decide whether a hired party is an employee or an independent contractor, but it should not make the company more susceptible to losing control over software integral to its product. Weighing the common law factors in light of the circumstances and JustMed's business, we conclude that the district court did not err in holding that Byce was an employee and that the source code was a work made for hire. . . .

NOTES AND QUESTIONS

1. To what extent does the test adopted by the *CCNV v. Reid* Court further the stated goals of predictability and certainty? In *Aymes v. Bonelli,* 980 F.2d 857 (2d Cir. 1992), the court reasoned:

> [T]here are some factors that will be significant in virtually every situation. These include: (1) the hiring party's right to control the manner and means of creation; (2) the skill required; (3) the provision of employee benefits; (4) the tax treatment of the hired party; and (5) whether the hiring party has the right to assign additional projects to the hired party. These factors will almost always be relevant and should be given more weight in the analysis. . . .

Id. at 861. The *JustMed* court cited *Aymes* but then took a different approach. Do you agree with its conclusion that Byce was an employee? Was the court just rescuing a small company from its failure to execute a contract? Would it have held differently if the alleged employer in the case had been, for example, Microsoft? For a comprehensive discussion of the case law applying the *CCNV v. Reid* test, see Ryan G. Vacca, *Works Made for Hire—Analyzing the Multifactor Balancing Test,* 42 Fla. St. U. L. Rev. (forthcoming 2015).

2. In 2005, the American Law Institute adopted The Restatement (Third) of Agency, intended to supersede The Restatement (Second) of Agency. The wording of many of the sections has changed significantly and a different numbering scheme has been implemented. Section 7.07 is the parallel to old §220, and it no longer contains the list of factors that the Supreme Court discussed in *CCNV* v. *Reid*; instead, it simply states: "[A]n employee is an agent whose principal controls or has the right to control the manner and means of the agent's performance of work." Restatement (Third) of Agency, §7.07(3)(a) (2005). Should a change in the Restatement affect how courts analyze whether an individual is an employee or an independent contractor for purposes of determining whether a work is a work made for hire? Note that in both Restatements, the relevant sections are intended to define the scope of liability an employer faces for the tortious acts of its employee. The provisions are not directed at ownership of work-product created by employees. Should these provisions even be relevant to determining ownership of employee-created work product?

3. Examine carefully the second subsection of the "work made for hire" definition. Why did *Third World America* not qualify as a work made for hire under §101(2)? Why did *Malcolm X* qualify as such a work? If Aalmuhammed had signed a work made for hire contract would that have put an end to his arguments concerning joint authorship?

4. Recall the *Aalmuhammed* court's discussion of the requirements for authorship. Can the works made for hire rule be reconciled with that discussion? Can it be reconciled with the constitutional language that authorizes copyright protection? For insightful discussions of the tensions between economic and creative motivations for producing, distributing, and adapting works, see Anthony J. Casey & Andres Sawicki, *Copyright in Teams*, 80 U. Chi. L. Rev. 1683 (2014); Rochelle Cooper Dreyfuss, *The Creative Employee and the Copyright Act of 1976*, 54 U. Chi. L. Rev. 590 (1987).

> ### COMPARATIVE PERSPECTIVE
>
> Countries such as France and Germany require the "author" of a work to be the natural person (or persons) who created it, and initial ownership of copyright vests in that person. Some countries have hybrid regimes for certain types of works that provide the employee with the sole right to be credited as author but assign economic rights to the employer. China uses this approach for engineering designs, product designs, maps, and computer software. For all other works, China vests copyright ownership in the employee but gives the employer a two-year exclusive right to exploit the work within the scope of the employer's business.

5. In the United States and other countries that follow the works made for hire model, the rationale for assigning authorship and initial ownership to employers is economic. When copyrightable material is prepared by an employee, the employer assumes the economic risk associated with developing and marketing the work. Is the works made for hire model therefore good economic policy? If so, wouldn't the same reasoning apply to any specially ordered or commissioned work? Would you support an amendment to §101 extending the works made for hire designation to all such works?

6. Many of the countries that lack a works made for hire rule expressly provide that the initial ownership of copyright in an employee-created work may be varied by contract. The United States also allows employers and employees to vary initial ownership of copyright by contract. *See* 17 U.S.C. §201(b). Who do you think benefits most from this rule, employees or employers? Does it depend on the particular creative market? What policy objectives should inform the evaluation of contracts that vary the initial ownership of copyright—those of contract, employment law, or copyright law? For discussion of the economic issues surrounding the

allocation of authorship and initial copyright ownership to employers, see Michael D. Birnhack, *Who Owns Bratz? The Integration of Copyright and Employment Law*, 20 Fordham Intell. Prop., Media & Ent. L.J. 95 (2009).

> ## PRACTICE EXERCISE: DRAFTING
>
> Should Congress add a definition of "employee" to §101? If so, what test should it choose, and why? Try your hand at drafting the language that you would recommend.

---

b. Determining "Scope of Employment"

The second requirement for a work to qualify as a "work made for hire" under the first definition provided in §101 is that the work must also have been created within the employee's "scope of employment." We turn now to this second requirement.

Rouse v. Walter & Associates, L.L.C.
513 F. Supp. 2d 1041 (S.D. Iowa 2007)

GRITZNER, J:. . . . [Beginning in the late 1980s two Research Professors at Iowa State University, Dr. Gene Rouse and Dr. Doyle Wilson, developed a method for determining the quality of beef on live cattle using an ultrasound machine and a computer software program called LAIPS (live animal intramuscular fat prediction software). LAIPS arose in the context of sponsored research and Rouse and Wilson had signed agreements that assigned the copyright in the software to the Iowa State University Research Foundation (ISURF). A separate program called USOFT was created later as a user interface for LAIPS. USOFT was created at the request of Rouse and Wilson by Dr. Viren Amin who worked in Rouse and Wilson's lab. Unlike LAIPS, USOFT was never expressly assigned to ISURF. ISURF licensed the use of LAIPS and USOFT to others, including the defendant Walters & Associates. In 1998 Rouse, Wilson, and Amin formed Biotronics, Inc.]

In 2002, Rouse, Wilson, and Amin, through their company, Biotronics, decided to establish a commercial business and compete in the ultrasound market. Biotronics would thus be directly competing with Walter & Associates. Biotronics does not use USOFT in the course of its ultrasound business. . . .

. . . On May 11, 2005, Rouse, Wilson, and Amin signed an Agreement Between Joint Owners that stated they are the joint owners of all right, title, and interest in the copyright to the USOFT software program. On June 8, 2005, Wilson, Rouse, and Amin filed a Certificate of Registration with the United States Copyright Office for the USOFT program. The copyright was registered on June 9, 2005. At some time during 2005, prior to the filing of the present suit, Rouse and Wilson sent a cease and desist letter to Walter, claiming USOFT was independently owned by them. Walter & Associates refused to discontinue their use of the USOFT program. [Rouse, Wilson, and Amin sued for copyright infringement.] . . .

On May 1, 2007, Defendants filed a Motion for Partial Summary Judgment contending that Rouse and Wilson's claims for copyright infringement must be dismissed because . . . USOFT was created by Amin, Rouse, and Wilson within the scope of their employment at ISU and thus is owned by ISU as work made for hire. . . .

Work Made for Hire.

. . . "In the case of a work made for hire, the employer or other person for whom the work was prepared is considered the author for purposes of this title, and, unless the parties have *expressly* agreed otherwise in a *written instrument signed by them,* owns all of the rights comprised in the copyright." 17 U.S.C. §201(b) (emphasis added). Defendants assert that ISU owns the copyright to USOFT as work made for hire. Rouse, Wilson, and Amin contend the work-for-hire doctrine does not apply in this case because Rouse, Wilson, and Amin expressly agreed otherwise in a written instrument.

Plaintiffs contend that at the commencement of their employment with ISU, they signed a "letter of intent" with the University that expressly incorporated into the letter of intent the ISU Faculty Handbook, and that this Faculty Handbook contains a policy that vests ownership rights in the authors unless assigned to ISURF. Plaintiffs further contend that even if the work-for-hire doctrine could apply in this case, the required elements are not met, and disputed issues of material fact exist that preclude summary judgment on the issue of work for hire.

The Court must therefore examine whether USOFT was "work for hire" and if so whether an express written agreement regarding the ownership of its copyright exists. In analyzing whether a creation constitutes work made for hire, the Court examines three factors.

> As expressed in Section 228 of the *Restatement,* the key principle is that a servant's conduct is within the scope of employment "only if: (a) it is of the kind he is employed to perform; (b) it occurs substantially within the authorized time and space limits; [and] (c) it is actuated, at least in part, by a purpose to serve the master."

Avtec Sys., Inc. v. Peiffer, 21 F.3d 568, 571 (4th Cir.1994). The Court will address each of these three factors in turn.

1. Was the work of the kind Amin, Rouse and Wilson were employed to perform?

Defendants assert that as ISU tenured faculty, Rouse and Wilson were expected to and did in fact engage in research activities. Rouse and Wilson argue that the creation of USOFT was not the kind of work they were expected to perform.

Rouse testified that he and Wilson devoted approximately fifteen years of their ISU careers working on the research project relating to the prediction of intramuscular fat in live cattle, bringing in over $1.6–million in sponsored research funding to support such work. Rouse's curriculum vitae shows that since as early as 1995 he has published numerous scholarly articles pertaining to real-time ultrasound image processing in relation to predicting intramuscular fat in beef cattle. Wilson's curriculum vitae similarly shows he has published numerous articles during his tenure with ISU regarding the ultrasound imaging of intramuscular fat of beef cattle. . . .

Rouse testified that at some point they determined they had to write some front-end software for LAIPS if they were going to process large numbers of images, and this front-end software is what is now known as USOFT. The record shows that using a small portion of the $1.6–million in research funding, new Windows©-based computers were purchased for use in the research project, and thus a need arose for Windows© compatible front-end software that would allow the researchers to process larger numbers of images at a faster pace on these new computers. Rouse testified he instructed Amin to put the USOFT software together on a Windows©-based platform. . . . Wilson testified Amin developed USOFT to assist and support Wilson and Rouse in their research at ISU and to speed up their research process.

Amin testified he began working with the Department of Animal Science after he graduated in 1992, working on beef ultrasound, and that he was still working in the Department of Animal Science when he was developing USOFT. Amin testified that he did research, developed algorithms to analyze the images, assisted in developing a procedure to derive information out of the images, assisted in scanning the images and, wrote source codes. Amin also assisted in making improvements to the LAIPS software program, and he developed a program to interpret images. . . . Although Amin stated in his May 24, 2007, declaration that his position was "as a scientist, not a programmer," this more recent declaration contradicts not only Amin's own deposition testimony that in performing work for the Department of Animal Science he had programmed software, but also his own curriculum vitae, in which he included, under the header "Primary areas of interest and expertise," "computer based system and software development for bio-medical and agricultural imaging applications," and under the header "Other Professional Activities," "Developed USOFT and related software products for animal ultrasound researchers."

Given these facts, there exists no genuine issue of material fact that the development of USOFT was within the scope of duties Amin was hired to perform. . . .

Rouse and Wilson argue that although part of Amin's salary was paid by grant funding, this salary was paid for his work as a scientist, not as a computer programmer. Courts have found that although not hired to program software, where the development of software occurred within the scope of the employee's employment it can be deemed work of the kind the employee was hired to perform.

An Iowa State University Proposal Data Form signed by Rouse, Wilson, and Amin on October 9, 1997, shows the three proposed a project entitled "Centralized Processing of Real Time Ultrasound Images Research Project." The project was approved by the University. There is overwhelming testimony in the record from Wilson, Rouse, and Amin that Wilson and Rouse directed Amin to develop a front-end program, USOFT, in order to provide them with a faster interface for the LAIPS software. This faster interface for LAIPS would certainly assist Rouse and Wilson in continuing their ultrasound research project at ISU and allow them to run the ultrasound processing laboratory more efficiently based on the ability to process the images more quickly. Further, ISURF licensed USOFT, along with LAIPS, to a third party, evidence that USOFT was important to the process of ultrasound imaging and clearly integral to the work and an obvious part of the research task. The Court concludes Plaintiffs have failed to generate a genuine issue of material fact regarding whether directing Amin to develop USOFT, and assisting him in that development, was the type of work Rouse and Wilson were employed to perform. . . .

2. Did the work of Amin, Rouse, and Wilson occur substantially within authorized time and space limits?

Rouse, Wilson, and Amin contend the development of USOFT did not occur substantially within authorized space and time limits, asserting Amin used his own personal computer at home for the "vast" majority of programming the USOFT program.

An employee cannot establish copyright ownership rights solely on the basis that the work was done at home on off-hours. *Avtec Sys., Inc.,* 21 F.3d at 571. . . .

Amin testified it was normal for him to perform his work both at ISU and at home, and when working on developing USOFT, he worked both at ISU and at home. Amin further testified that when he was working on USOFT at ISU, he would be working on ISU computers. Wilson also testified that some of the actual writing of the USOFT code was done with the computers at ISU. Amin testified that while he was working on the research project for Wilson and Rouse, he was a salaried employee of ISU. He further testified the testing of USOFT *must* have occurred at ISU's Department of Animal Science because he did not keep a copy of the LAIPS program at his home, and LAIPS would have been necessary in testing how USOFT functioned. . . .

. . . There exists no genuine issue regarding whether the development of USOFT occurred substantially within authorized time and space limits.

3. Were Amin, Rouse, and Wilson actuated at least in part by a purpose to serve the master?

Plaintiffs contend the evidence indicates they were self-motivated to create the USOFT program and that further ultrasound research did not require the development of new interface software. Indeed, the record shows that *further* ultrasound research did not require the development of a new interface; however, *faster* ultrasound research did necessitate that a new Windows©-based interface be developed.

"[T]he *Restatement* does not require that the servant's only motivation be to help his or her employer; the motivation need only be partial." *Genzmer* [*v. Public Health Trust of Miami-Dade County*], 219 F. Supp. 2d [1275,] 1282 [S. D. Fla. 2002]; Conduct may be considered within the scope of employment even when done in part to serve the purposes of the employee, or a third party. Restatement (Second) of Agency §236 (1958).

Rouse testified that he and Wilson spent approximately fifteen years of their careers at ISU on the development of software to predict intramuscular fat on live cattle. Wilson similarly testified that the majority of their research was in this area. The record also reveals that in 1997, Rouse, Wilson, and Amin co-authored a published article in ISU's Beef Research Reports publication entitled "USOFT: An Ultrasound Image Analysis Software for Beef Quality Research." The article states as follows, in pertinent part:

> . . . [A] personal-computer based software[-version] has been developed, which is copyrighted by the ISU Research Foundation, Inc.
> The software, USOFT, is an image analysis software . . .

Plaintiffs argue the article's reference to the software copyrighted by ISURF was with respect to LAIPS, but the plain language of the article speaks for itself. The article evidences USOFT was part of the research that was being conducted for ISU.

. . . Further, the evidence clearly shows that Amin inserted into USOFT code lines which state, "U–SOFT for Beef Quality Grading (v1.5d 9/17/98) © Iowa State University." Amin further included in the USOFT program a screen that specifically states, "This software is developed at Iowa State University (U.S.A.) and copyrighted by the ISU Research Foundation, Inc. No part of this software should be copied in any form without written permission of the copyright holder." Amin admits he wrote that into the program. Plaintiffs argue these copyright statements were included in USOFT to protect the proprietary LAIPS software, but this argument runs contrary to Plaintiffs' own assertion that USOFT and LAIPS were separate and distinct and that USOFT was capable of functioning with any program that has the appropriate MF prediction models. . . . [T]he references strongly demonstrate the understanding of the parties prior to any advocacy in the context of later claims and litigation.

The record shows there is no genuine issue regarding whether Rouse, Wilson, and Amin were motivated at least in material part by a desire to further the research of the ISU Department of Animal Science. . . .

C. Is There a Written Document Establishing Amin, Rouse, and Wilson as Owners of USOFT?

Where work is deemed "work made for hire," under the Copyright Act such work automatically vests with the employer unless an express, written agreement between the employer and employee exists. . . .

Rouse and Wilson assert they do have such a written instrument, arguing that at the time they began their employment, they signed a letter of intent with ISU. Rouse and Wilson contend this letter of intent expressly incorporated the ISU Faculty Handbook policy, stating, "I understand that this agreement is in accordance with the policies contained in the Iowa State University Faculty Handbook and I accept the position described above." Specifically, Plaintiffs contend that Sections 8.3.6.3 and 8.3.6.5 constitute the written agreement that exempts them from the work-for-hire doctrine.

The Faculty Handbook states, "The Faculty Handbook is the official statement of Iowa State University policy governing the rights, responsibilities, and performance of faculty." Section 8.3.6.[3] of the Faculty Handbook is entitled "Policies." This section states as follows:

8.3.6.3. Policies

Iowa State University encourages the development of educational materials to assist in meeting its responsibilities for academic instruction, extension, and research. . . .

The university recognizes the vested rights of an author. . . . However, if the educational materials are to be developed with university sponsorship, the author is expected to assign these rights for the benefit of the university. It is not intended that this policy affect the traditional university relationship to faculty members' ownership of books or other instructional materials whose preparation was not supported or assisted in a substantial way by the university. . . .

Plaintiffs argue that USOFT was "educational" in nature, and thus under Section 8.3.6.3 they retained the authorship to USOFT. There is no evidence in the record to demonstrate USOFT was educational in nature or otherwise used for academic instruction. . . .

Section 8.3.6.5 of the Faculty Handbook is entitled "Intellectual Property: Policies and Procedures." This section states as follows:

8.3.6.5. Intellectual Property: Policies and Procedures.

. . . [The Office of Intellectual Property and Technology Transfer (OIPTT)] provides educational services on issues related to intellectual property. ISURF owns and manages all Iowa State University intellectual property. When members of the university community apply for sponsored funding, they sign the following statement on [a required document called the Gold Sheet]: "I agree to be bound by the terms and conditions of the outside grant or contract which supports this proposed activity and, in consideration of the information and facilities made available to me by the university or the outside sponsor, to assign copyright and patent rights to the Iowa State University Research Foundation, Inc. in accordance with terms and conditions stated in the *Faculty Handbook*. I certify that I have not been debarred, suspended or declared ineligible to receive federal agency funds." In signing such a statement, the faculty member agrees that any intellectual property arising from sponsored funding will be assigned to ISURF. ISURF has the responsibility for managing all legal aspects of obtaining protection for intellectual property. [OIPTT] works closely with ISURF and with faculty and administrators within the university to obtain and evaluate disclosures, to determine the appropriate means of protection of intellectual property, and to aid in the marketing of that property. . . .

Rouse and Wilson argue that these two sections of the Faculty Handbook clearly indicate the existence of a written agreement, as defined by 17 U.S.C. §201(b), limiting "work for hire" for Rouse and Wilson in accordance with the terms of the Faculty Handbook.

"An agreement altering the statutory presumption under the Copyright Act must be *express*." *Manning v. Bd. of Tr. of Cmty. Coll. Dist. No. 505* (*Parkland Coll.*), 109 F. Supp. 2d 976, 981 (C.D. Ill. 2000) (citing *Baltimore Orioles, Inc. v. Major League Baseball Players Ass'n*, 805 F.2d 663, 672 (7th Cir. 1986)).

An employee policy is insufficient to alter the statutory presumption under the Copyright Act. *Id.* . . .

In any event, ISU expressly acknowledges the work-for-hire doctrine applies to employees and faculty members. ISURF and OIPTT policies that pertain to copyright state that the ownership of copyright in traditional scholarly works, such as poems, plays, visual arts, textbooks, and musical compositions, remain with the student or faculty authors. This policy then goes on to state as follows:

> Other types of copyrighted works such as software, instructional materials, and works of non-faculty employees are owned by the university or for the benefit of the university when:
>
> - Significant university resources are required to develop a copyrighted work. . . . Funded research is considered a use of significant university resources.
> - *Copyrighted works are produced by university employees in performance of the duties of their position at ISU. These works are considered developed under copyright's work-for-hire doctrine, under which the university is considered the author and owner of the copyright.*
> - The work may also be patented, such as the case with software. (Note that in these cases, the university reserves the right to pursue multiple forms of legal protection).
> - The work uses any of the university trademarks, including the names ISU, Iowa State, or Cyclones.

Rouse and Wilson argue they never used grant money in creating USOFT; however, both testified they raised over $1.6–million in funding for the ultrasound imaging research, and the record shows a small portion of these funds were used to purchase the computers on which USOFT was developed. Further, both Rouse and Wilson testified they spent over fifteen years at ISU conducting this research, and such a significant amount of time cannot be said to be anything but in the performance of their duties in their position at ISU. The work not only uses the name Iowa State University, USOFT actually has the internationally known copyright symbol "©" in front of Iowa State University's name on the USOFT screen displays. While it is unclear if USOFT is the type of software that actually can be patented, it appears that given the record of this case, the development of USOFT falls into practically every category ISURF and OIPTT have described as being works in which ownership in the copyright will vest in the University. . . .

Plaintiffs have failed to generate a genuine issue of material facts regarding whether an express, written agreement existed between ISU and the Plaintiffs that exempts USOFT from the "work for hire" doctrine. . . .

NOTES AND QUESTIONS

1. Do you agree with the result in *Rouse*? Under the court's reasoning, would there ever be a case in which software developed with significant grant funding would require an assignment of copyright ownership from the developer to the institution?

2. The "scope of employment" question in copyright cases is now complicated by the fact that the Restatement (Third) of Agency, completed in 2005, no longer includes the test from §228 of the Restatement (Second). According to the new Restatement:

> An employee acts within the scope of employment when performing work assigned by the employer or engaging in a course of conduct subject to the employer's control. An employee's act is not within the scope of employment when it occurs within an independent course of conduct not intended by the employee to serve any purpose of the employer.

Restatement (Third) of Agency, §7.07(2) (2005). Apply this test to the facts of *Rouse*. Would it have produced a different outcome?

3. Review the section of the *Rouse* opinion setting forth the University's intellectual property policy. Why does the University permit faculty and student authors to own the copyrights in some works but not in others?

Under the Patent Act, initial ownership of the patent vests in the inventor, although it can be assigned even before filing the patent application. *See* 35 U.S.C. §118; 37 CFR 3.73(a). Many universities (and other employers) require all patents to be assigned to the institution. Why might a university have a different policy for patentable inventions than copyrightable creations? Some faculty creations, like software, may be eligible for both types of protection. What is ISU's policy in such a case?

4. Traditionally, under a so-called teacher exception, college and university teachers were considered the owners of copyright in their scholarly writings and course materials, notwithstanding their status as fulltime employees. Because the 1976 Act did not expressly preserve this exception, there is some debate about whether it still exists. *Compare Hays v. Sony Corp.*, 847 F.2d 412, 416 (7th Cir. 1988) (Posner, J.), and *Weinstein v. University of Illinois,* 811 F.2d 1091, 1094 (7th Cir. 1987) (Easterbrook, J.) (arguing exception exists) *with Vanderhurst v. Colorado Mountain College Dist.*, 16 F. Supp. 2d 1297, 1307 (D. Colo. 1998) (ruling, based on §101(1) and *CCNV v. Reid*, that teaching outline created by instructor was work made for hire).What are the arguments for and against a teacher exception? Is it relevant that the legislative history of the 1976 Act does not discuss the exception and gives no indication that Congress ever considered it?

PRACTICE EXERCISE: COUNSEL A CLIENT

You are General Counsel to a private liberal arts college that is considering a revision to its policy regarding ownership of copyrighted works produced by faculty members. The current policy recognizes faculty ownership of the copyrights in all such works. What changes would you advise? What should be done about ownership of copyright in works whose production was supported in part by external funding? What should be done about faculty participation in open source software development?

Note on Employer Ownership of Trade Secrets

Many cases involving employee assertions of copyright ownership also present trade secrecy claims. Recall that under the 1976 Copyright Act, copyright subsists in original, fixed works created after January 1, 1978, even if the works are concealed from the general public. In particular, as discussed in greater detail in Chapter 4, computer software is copyrightable but also frequently embodies economically valuable, nonpublic innovation.[3]

The standards used in copyright law and trade secrecy law to determine whether a work was created within the scope of employment are similar, but not identical. As *Rouse* illustrates, in copyright disputes, courts have followed a three-step test based on the general scope-of-employment provision of the Restatement (Second) of Agency, §228.

In trade secrecy cases, courts have relied on a different test, originally set forth in §397 of the Restatement (Second) of Agency, that focuses more narrowly on ownership of employee-developed inventions. That test does not ask whether the employee was motivated in part by a desire to serve the employer, but only whether the invention relates to the type of work the employee was hired to perform, and in particular whether the employee's duties are "inventive" or "noninventive." Thus, if an employee

> is employed to do experimental work for inventive purposes, it is inferred ordinarily . . . that . . . ideas arrived at through the experimentation are to be owned by the employer. This is even more clear where one is employed to achieve a particular result which the invention accomplishes. On the other hand, if one is employed merely to do work in a particular line in which he is an expert, there is no inference of employer ownership.

Restatement (Second) of Agency §397, cmt. a (1958); see also Restatement (Third) of Unfair Competition §42, cmt. e (1995) (referencing this test for ownership of trade secrets). Have courts adjudicating scope-of-employment issues in copyright cases relied on the wrong Restatement provision?

Trade secrecy cases further distinguish between "specific inventive" and "general inventive" employees; employees hired for specific inventive purposes will retain ownership of innovations they make in other, unrelated fields, while "general inventive" employees will almost never retain ownership of their innovations. *See generally*, Roger M. Milgrim, Milgrim on Trade Secrets §5.02[4] (1996). In addition, an employer may acquire an equitable "shop right" to use employee-owned innovations that were developed using the employer's facilities even if the innovation is outside the scope of the employee's employment. *See id.* at §5.02[4][c].

---

3. A trade secret is any information that derives independent economic value from not being generally known to competitors and is subject to reasonable measures to maintain its secrecy. *See* Uniform Trade Secrets Act §1; Restatement (Third) of Unfair Competition §39 (1995).

NOTES AND QUESTIONS

1. The tests for ownership of employee-created copyrights versus trade secrets could lead to divergent results, for example, in a case involving an "inventive" employee who produces copyrighted material related to her work duties and then asserts, and can prove, that her efforts were not appreciably motivated by a desire to serve the employer. In such a case, the employer would own the trade secret, but the employee would own the copyright. Does that result make sense? If not, how might the law achieve greater consistency on the question of employer ownership?

2. The "scope of employment" nexus between copyright and trade secrecy claims implicates federal supremacy considerations. Should the outcome of a federal copyright claim be dictated by the outcome of a related state trade secrecy claim, or even more generally by state law? In *CCNV v. Reid, supra,* the Court observed:

> In past cases of statutory interpretation, when we have concluded that Congress intended terms such as "employee," "employer," and "scope of employment" to be understood in light of agency law, we have relied on the general common law of agency, rather than on the law of any particular State, to give meaning to these terms. . . . Establishment of a federal rule of agency, rather than reliance on state agency law, is particularly appropriate here given the Act's express objective of creating national, uniform copyright law. . . . We thus agree with the Court of Appeals that the term "employee" should be understood in light of the general common law of agency.

490 U.S. at 740-41.

PRACTICE EXERCISE: DRAFTING

Amaryllis Systems, Inc. (ASI) is a startup company working on developing software that will substantially increase the speed of downloads from the Internet. The company may seek patents on some aspects of the software, but it plans to rely heavily on trade secret and copyright laws to protect it. Cheryl is a programmer who has worked for a number of years in the software industry, and she is considering whether to accept a job with ASI. ASI wants to ensure that Cheryl does not use third-party software (including any open source software) or software she has written in her spare time in the past in ASI's product. It also wants to own whatever code Cheryl writes while employed by ASI. For her part, Cheryl wants to retain her ability to be valuable to other employers. Draft the intellectual property clause of the employment contract that ASI should offer Cheryl.

---

2. Section 101(2) and "Specially Ordered or Commissioned" Works

If the person creating the work is not an employee, the only other mechanism for the work to qualify as a work made for hire is under the second definition. Section 101(2) dictates a two-part inquiry, requiring a writing and also that the type of work be within one of the nine categories of works listed in the statute. We address each of these requirements below.

a. The Requirement of a Signed Written Instrument

For a commissioned work to be a work made for hire, the statute requires that the parties "expressly agree in a written instrument signed by them that the work shall be considered a work made for hire." But when must the writing be executed, and what must it say? Predictably, both questions have inspired litigation.

Courts have disagreed on whether the writing must be prepared before or after the work is created. In *Schiller & Schmidt, Inc. v. Nordisco Corp.*, 969 F.2d 410 (7th Cir. 1992), the Seventh Circuit held that the writing must precede creation of the work. Writing for the court, Judge Posner commented: "The requirement of a written statement . . . is not merely a statute of frauds, although that is the purpose emphasized by the cases. . . . [The writing requirement also serves] to make the ownership of property rights in intellectual property clear and definite, so that such property will be readily marketable." *Id.* at 412. The Ninth Circuit has also held that the written work made for hire agreement must precede the creation of the work. *Gladwell Gov't Servs., Inc. v. Cnty. of Marin*, 265 Fed. Appx. 624, 626 (9th Cir.2008). Other Circuits, however, have held that the parties could memorialize their agreement after the fact, so long as the evidence showed that they actually had agreed on a work made for hire relationship before the work's creation. *See e.g. Eden Toys, Inc. v. Florelee Undergarment Co.*, 697 F.2d 27 (2d Cir. 1982); *Playboy Enterprises, Inc. v. Dumas*, 53 F.3d 549 (2d Cir. 1995). The Second Circuit observed that in some circumstances, the rule adopted in *Schiller & Schmidt* "could frustrate the intent of the parties and cloud rather than serve the goal of certainty." *Dumas*, 53 F.3d at 559.

Courts also have disagreed on whether the writing must actually use the words "work made for hire." According to the *Dumas* court, it must. *Dumas*, 53 F.3d at 560 (holding that language referring to an "assignment . . . of all right, title and interest" was insufficient to satisfy §101(2)). But in *Armento v. Laser Image, Inc.*, 950 F. Supp. 719 (W.D.N.C. 1996), the court concluded that given the circumstances surrounding the parties' relationship, the written agreement requirement was satisfied by language that provided that the commissioned maps and artwork "remain the sole property of [defendants], and cannot be reproduced or used for any other purpose by [the artist] without the written consent of [defendants]." *Id.* at 729. Echoing the *Dumas* court's own reasoning on the timing issue, the *Armento* court reasoned that a bright-line rule requiring the "magic words" might work injustice in some cases. *Id.* at 731-32. Likewise, the Ninth Circuit has held that "there is no requirement, either in the [Copyright] Act or the caselaw, that work-for-hire contracts include any specific wording." *Warren v. Fox Family Worldwide, Inc.*, 328 F.3d 1136, 1141 (9th Cir.2003)

b. The Categories of Eligible Works

Even with a signed written agreement, the work must fall within one of the nine listed categories. The categories in §101(2) were identified during the lengthy consultation process that produced the 1976 Copyright Act. Review the *CCNV v. Reid* Court's discussion of the legislative history of the statutory definition of "works made for hire." Note that the negotiations over what to include in the list of categories of works eligible to be works made for hire through contracting took place initially in the 1960s. Likely for that reason, there was no discussion about including either software or sound recordings.

One of the more interesting recent episodes involving §101(2) relates to sound recordings. In 1999, at the request of the recording industry, Congress briefly added sound recordings to the list of categories of commissioned works as part of an amendment appended, without discussion or testimony, to an omnibus bill intended to amend the patent, trademark, and telecommunications laws. Intellectual Property and Communications Omnibus Reform Act of 1999, §1011(d), *as enacted by* Pub. L. 106-113, §1000(a)(9), 113 Stat. 1501A-521, -544 (1999). Recording artists greeted the news with outrage, and accused the recording industry of staging a copyright grab. Less than a year later, Congress repealed the amendment. The repeal directed courts and the Copyright Office to proceed as though both pieces of legislation had never been enacted. Work Made for Hire and Copyright Corrections Act of 2000, Pub. L. 106-379, §2, 114 Stat. 1444, 1444 (2000).

One category that is on the list is "compilations." As you saw in Chapter 2, just what constitutes a compilation can vary widely. At least one court has used this category to find that computer software may be a work made for hire. *See e.g.*, Logicam Inclusive, Inc. v. W.P. Stewart & Co., 72 U.S.P.Q.2d 1632 (S.D.N.Y. 2004). Courts have, however, rejected the argument when it comes to sound recordings. *See e.g. Lulirama Ltd. v. Axcess Broadcast Services, Inc.*, 128 F.3d 872, 878 (5th Cir.1997).

NOTES AND QUESTIONS

1. Do you agree with the *Schiller* court or the *Dumas* court regarding the timing of the written agreement? Do you agree with the *Dumas* court or the *Armento* court regarding the use of the literal words "work made for hire"?

2. Based on your review of *CCNV v. Reid*, what do you think of the process by which the §101(2) categories were selected? Consider also the economics of the situation. Is there a transaction cost justification for the nine categories, or for some of them? In light of economic considerations, should sound recordings be added to the list? Should software?

3. Record labels typically require recording artists to sign contracts that state that their contributions are works made for hire, and (in the alternative) assign the copyrights in their sound recordings to the record company. Given this standard industry practice, why were recording artists so outraged at the addition of sound recordings to the list of works eligible to be works made for hire? As you will learn in Chapter 11, under other provisions of the Copyright Act, individual authors have the right to terminate transfers of their copyrights after a prescribed period of time. Individuals who create works made for hire have no such right, because they are not considered authors. If sound recordings were eligible to be works made for hire under §101(2), recording artists would give up potentially valuable termination rights.

PRACTICE EXERCISE: ADVOCACY

You are counsel to The Software Alliance, a trade association of software firms. Hiring independent contractors is common practice in the software industry. Many of these programmers argue that they are de facto employees and should receive the same employee benefits and other advantages as their salaried co-workers. Do you think that your organization's membership would support an amendment adding contributions to computer programs to the categories of works eligible for "work made for hire" status under §101(2)? Why, or why not? If your membership desired it, how would you make the case for such an amendment?

D. GOVERNMENT WORKS

On its face, subsection (1) of the "works made for hire" definition would encompass works created by government employees in the scope of their employment. In fact, however, the Act excludes U.S. government works—defined in §101 as "work[s] prepared by an officer or employee of the United States government as part of that person's official duties"—from copyright protection entirely:

> §105. Subject matter of copyright: United States Government works
> Copyright protection under this title is not available for any work of the United States Government, but the United States Government is not precluded from receiving and holding copyrights transferred to it by assignment, bequest, or otherwise.

The rule codified in §105 has a long history. Recall from Chapter 1 that in 1834, in litigation between two Supreme Court reporters over the reproduction of annotated volumes of the Court's opinion, the Court observed, "no reporter has or can have any copyright in the written opinions delivered by this Court." *Wheaton v. Peters*, 33 U.S. (8 Pet.) 591, 668 (1834). There are, however, several types of government documents to which §105 by its terms does not apply.

COMPARATIVE PERSPECTIVE

Article 2(4) of the Berne Convention provides that the copyright status of official texts is for member countries to determine. Many foreign governments, particularly in common law countries, claim copyright in works prepared by their employees under a concept known as "Crown Copyright." Materials covered by Crown Copyright may include legislation, government codes of practice, government reports, official press releases, government forms, and other public records. International organizations, including the United Nations and its specialized agencies, also routinely claim copyright in their documents.

Note first that the statute does not directly address the copyright status of works prepared pursuant to a contract with the federal government. The legislative history explains that omission:

> The bill deliberately avoids making any sort of outright, unqualified prohibition against copyright in works prepared under Government contract or grant. There may well be cases where it would be in the public interest to deny copyright in the writings generated by Government research contracts and the like; it can be assumed that, where a Government agency commissions a work for its own use merely as an alternative to having one of its own employees prepare the work, the right to secure a private copyright would be withheld. However, there are almost certainly many other cases where the denial of copyright protection would be unfair or would hamper the production and publication of important works. Where, under the particular circumstances, Congress or the agency involved finds that the need to have a work freely available outweighs the need of the private author to secure copyright, the problem can be dealt with by specific legislation, agency regulations, or contractual restrictions.

H.R. Rep. No. 94-1476, 94th Cong., 2d Sess. 59 (1976), *reprinted in* 1976 U.S.C.C.A.N. 5659, 5672.

Next, §105 does not by its terms apply to state and local legal systems, or to the products of foreign legal systems. The Copyright Office has indicated, however, that it will not register "edicts of government," whether federal, state, local, or foreign. Compendium II of Copyright Office Practices, §305.08(d).

Section 105 also does not apply to laws or regulatory codes drafted by private organizations like the American Law Institute (ALI) which drafts Restatements. In *Veeck v. Southern Building Code Congress Int'l* (SBCCI), 293 F.3d 791 (5th Cir. 2002) (en banc), *cert. denied*, 539 U.S. 969 (2003), the Fifth Circuit held that when a state adopts a privately drafted code as law, such law is not copyrightable. Citing *Wheaton v. Peters*, 33 U.S. (Pet.) 591 (1834), and its progeny, the *Veeck court* held that legislative enactments are not meaningfully different from judicial opinions with respect to copyrightability. The court also held that the enacted codes were facts, ineligible for copyright protection: ". . . The codes are . . . the unique, unalterable expression of the 'idea' that constitutes local law. . . . It should be obvious that for copyright purposes, laws are 'facts': the U.S. Constitution is a fact; the Federal Tax Code and its regulations are facts; the Texas Uniform Commercial Code is a fact. . . ." 293 F.3d at 801-02.

The *Veeck* court distinguished cases in which the law requires citizens to refer to a copyrighted work. For example, a statute might refer to the Red Book, a car valuation guide. Citizens examining the statute would have to look outside of the statute itself—to the copyrighted Red Book—

> in the process of fulfilling their obligations. The copyrighted works do not "become law" merely because a statute refers to them. . . . Equally important, the referenced works or standards [in those cases] were created by private groups for reasons other than incorporation into law. To the extent incentives are relevant to the existence of copyright protection, the authors in these cases deserve incentives. . . . In the case of a model code, on the other hand, the text of the model serves no other purpose than to become law.

Id. at 804-05.

Finally, note that both the federal government and state governments may receive submissions that include copyrighted works—e.g., regulatory filings and briefs and other submissions in court cases. Copyright owners challenging the copying of their works as supporting exhibits in legal proceedings have been uniformly rebuffed. *See Bond v. Blum*, 317 F.3d 385 (4th Cir. 2003); *Healthcare Advocates, Inc. v. Harding, Earley, Follmer & Frailey*, 497 F. Supp. 2d. 627 (E.D. Pa. 2007); *see also American Inst. of Physics v. Schwegman, Lundberg & Woessner*, Civ. No. 12-528 (D. Minn. Aug. 30, 2013), 2013 WL 4666330 (rejecting claims of infringement for including copies of journal articles establishing prior art in patent firm's internal document management system). A recent lawsuit against Westlaw and LEXIS-NEXIS for reproducing legal briefs drafted by private attorneys met a similar fate. *White v. West Publ'g Corp.*, No. 12-CV-01340, 2013 WL 544057 (S.D.N.Y. Feb. 11, 2013).

LOOKING BACK—AND FORWARD

In Chapter 2 you learned that facts are ineligible for copyright protection. Arguably, legal briefs filed with courts and copyrighted materials reproduced in supporting exhibits should be considered "facts" for copyright purposes, like the enacted codes in *Veeck*. Generally, however, courts and commentators have employed a different analysis, concluding that uses of copyrighted material as supporting exhibits are fair uses. You will learn about fair use in Chapter 10.

What about subsequent disclosures of copyrighted materials that the government receives? The Freedom of Information Act (FOIA) requires that U.S. government agencies make their records available for public inspection and copying, 5 U.S.C. §552(a), and many states have enacted FOIA-like disclosure requirements. May the government provide copies of copyrighted documents without incurring copyright infringement liability? Generally, courts seem unwilling to endorse either an agency's claim for a blanket exemption from FOIA requirements or a private party's claim that FOIA requires an agency to release information regardless of the economic interests involved. For example, in analyzing claims under the FOIA exemption for trade secrets, courts balance "the public interest in disclosure against the interest Congress intended the exemption to protect." *Gilmore v. U.S. Dept. of Energy*, 4 F. Supp. 2d 912, 922 (N.D. Cal. 1998). In *Gilmore* the court held that computer software was not an agency record subject to FOIA's disclosure requirements, while also noting that if the software were made available under FOIA, the value of the "copyright effectively [would be] reduced to zero." *Id.* at 923.

NOTES AND QUESTIONS

1. Recall Chapter 1's discussion of the policies underlying copyright law. By excluding works of the federal government from copyright protection, Congress is making a judgment that those policies are not implicated for such works (or that other, more important policies are). What are the relevant policies implicated by §105?

2. In Chapter 2 you learned that West Publishing Company claims copyright in both the print and electronic versions of its federal case reports as compilations manifesting originality in selection, coordination, and/or arrangement. From time to time, smaller publishers of federal judicial decisions have challenged the wisdom of allowing private parties to claim copyright in published federal case reports, particularly where those reports have been given official status. Is there a "need to have [these] works freely available"?

3. Do you agree with the *Veeck* decision? It was extremely close: 8-6. What arguments do you think the dissent made? The majority emphasized that SBCCI continued to hold a copyright in its model codes. 293 F.3d at 794. Veeck did not copy the laws from the local statute books; rather, he copied it from a disk of model codes sold by SBCCI. *Id.* at 793. The court still found no infringement. Of what value is SBCCI's copyright?

The issues raised in the *Veeck* case are likely to continue to arise as various organizations seek to make statutory materials available online. In 2013, the American Society of Heating, Refrigerating and Air-Conditioning Engineers, the American Society for Testing and Materials, and the National Fire Protection Association sued the operator of the website public.resource.org for publishing standards incorporated into statutes and regulations. *See American Society for Testing and Materials v. Public.Resource.Org, Inc.*, No. 1:13-cv-01215-EGS (D. D.C. filed Aug. 6, 2013). Should *Veeck* determine the outcome of this case?

4. What are the implications of *Veeck* for proposed uniform laws and accompanying reporters' notes drafted by the Uniform Law Commission (ULC) and the American Law Institute (ALI)? For example, ULC and ALI promulgate the Uniform Commercial Code (UCC), which includes both proposed legislative text and comments by the relevant drafting committee. Some states adopt only the text as law; some also adopt the comments as law. Do the ULC and the ALI have a copyright in anything? If not, would that result undermine the incentive to create model uniform laws?

In 2013, at least three states—Georgia, Idaho, and Mississippi—sent cease and desist letters to Public.Resource.Org, *supra* note 3, for posting state statutory material on-line. Should it matter whether the website posts the state codes only or includes the uniform annotations?

4

Form Versus Function: Useful Articles, Architectural Works, and Software

Over two centuries, copyright law has expanded to embrace an increasingly wide variety of subject matter, requiring courts to apply the requirements of fixation, originality, and the idea/expression distinction across vastly different kinds of works. This chapter explores the various tests developed by the courts to determine whether certain kinds of creative works that are also functional satisfy the requirements for copyrightability. The problem of distinguishing possibly copyrightable form from uncopyrightable function raises legal questions about the proper scope of the copyright system and policy questions about the implications of extending protection to works that embody both creative and functional elements. As you read the following materials, consider whether copyright is the proper protection for the type of work at issue. For example, assuming that some form of legal protection is needed for, say, the design of a lamp or the innovations embodied in a computer program, should that legal protection be copyright?

A. USEFUL ARTICLES WITH PICTORIAL, GRAPHIC, AND SCULPTURAL DIMENSIONS

As prior chapters have made clear, three-dimensional works of art that are original and fixed are copyrightable. Does eligibility for copyright change when the work is incorporated into a product with a utilitarian function? For example, is a "Hello Kitty" piggy bank copyrightable? Under modern copyright law, the answer depends on the extent to which a product's expressive aspects are separable from its useful ones. We begin by tracing the evolution of the separability requirement and then explore its application in the context of contemporary applied art and industrial design.

1. The Classic Case

Prior to the 1976 Act, the Supreme Court addressed the question of copyright protection for useful articles with expressive aspects in the following case.

Mazer v. Stein
347 U.S. 201 (1954)

REED, J.: . . .

Respondents are partners in the manufacture and sale of electric lamps. One of the respondents created original works of sculpture in the form of human figures by traditional clay-model technique. From this model, a production mold for casting copies was made. The resulting statuettes, without any lamp components added, were submitted by the respondents to the Copyright Office for registration as "works of art" or reproductions thereof under §5(g) or §5(h) of the copyright law, and certificates of registration issued. Sales (publication in accordance with the statute) as fully equipped lamps preceded the applications for copyright registration of the statuettes. Thereafter, the statuettes were sold in quantity throughout the country both as lamp bases and as statuettes. The sales in lamp form accounted for all but an insignificant portion of respondents' sales. . . .

. . . [Petitioners Mazer, et al., copied the statuettes and sold their own lamps embodying the copies. They contended that the statuettes, when "intended primarily to [be] use[d] . . . in the form of lamp bases to be made and sold in quantity," were not proper subject matter of copyright. Respondents brought a copyright infringement lawsuit. T]he District Court dismissed the complaint. The Court of Appeals reversed and held the copyrights valid. It said: "A subsequent utilization of a work of art in an article of manufacture in no way affects the right of the copyright owner to be protected against infringement of the work of art itself." 204 F.2d [472, 477 (4th Cir. 1952)].

. . . The case requires an answer, not as to a manufacturer's right to register a lamp base but as to an artist's right to copyright a work of art intended to be reproduced for lamp bases. . . . Petitioners question the validity of a copyright of a work of art for "mass" production. "Reproduction of a work of art" does not mean to them unlimited reproduction. Their position is that a copyright does not cover industrial reproduction of the protected article. . . .

. . . [The Court reviewed the history of legislation defining categories of copyrightable subject matter, beginning with the Act of 1790 and ending with the 1909 Copyright Act. We summarize this history in Chapter 1.B.3.a *supra*.] In 1909 Congress again enlarged the scope of the copyright statute. . . . Significant for our purposes was the deletion of the fine-arts clause of the 1870 Act. Verbal distinctions between purely aesthetic articles and useful works of art ended insofar as the statutory copyright language is concerned. . . .

The successive acts, the legislative history of the 1909 Act and the practice of the Copyright Office unite to show that "works of art" and "reproductions of works of art" are terms that were intended by Congress to include the authority to copyright

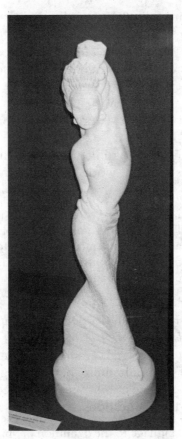

Lamp Base

these statuettes. Individual perception of the beautiful is too varied a power to permit a narrow or rigid concept of art. . . .

The economic philosophy behind the clause empowering Congress to grant patents and copyrights is the conviction that encouragement of individual effort by personal gain is the best way to advance public welfare through the talents of authors and inventors in "Science and useful Arts." Sacrificial days devoted to such creative activities deserve rewards commensurate with the services rendered.

Affirmed.

DOUGLAS, J., concurring: . . . The Copyright Office has supplied us with a long list of such articles which have been copyrighted—statuettes, book ends, clocks, lamps, door knockers, candlesticks, inkstands, chandeliers, piggy banks, sundials, salt and pepper shakers, fish bowls, casseroles, and ash trays. Perhaps these are all "writings" in the constitutional sense. But to me, at least, they are not obviously so. It is time that we came to the problem full face. I would accordingly put the case down for reargument.

NOTES AND QUESTIONS

1. Are door knockers, fish bowls, and the other things that Justice Douglas lists "art" (or "Science")? Are they "Writings" or "Discoveries"? Is protection of these items the inevitable consequence of the nondiscrimination principle articulated by Justice Holmes in *Bleistein*, Chapter 2.A.2.a, *supra* ?

2. Does protection of the lamps in *Mazer* and the examples listed in the concurrence advance the goals of the copyright law discussed in Chapter 1, *supra*?

2. Defining Useful Articles and Determining Separability

Congress sought to codify the holding of *Mazer* in the 1976 Act. The definition of "pictorial, graphic, and sculptural works" states, in part:

> Such works shall include works of artistic craftsmanship insofar as their form but not their mechanical or utilitarian aspects are concerned; the design of a useful article, as defined in this section, shall be considered a pictorial, graphic, or sculptural work only if, and only to the extent that, such design incorporates pictorial, graphic, or sculptural features that can be identified separately from, and are capable of existing independently of, the utilitarian aspects of the article.

17 U.S.C. §101. A "useful article," in turn, is "an article having an intrinsic utilitarian function that is not merely to portray the appearance of the article or to convey information." *Id.*

Thus, Congress subjected pictorial, graphic, and sculptural elements of useful articles to an "extra" test of copyrightability beyond originality and fixation: that of separability. Why? What is the separability test intended to do? In an attempt to provide some guidance on these questions, the House Report noted:

> The Committee has added language to the definition of "pictorial, graphic, and sculptural works" in an effort to make clearer the distinction between works of applied art protectable under the bill and industrial designs not subject to copyright protection. . . .
>
> In adopting this amendatory language, the Committee is seeking to draw as clear a line as possible between copyrightable works of applied art and uncopyrightable works of industrial design. A two-dimensional painting, drawing, or graphic work is still capable of being identified as such when it is printed on or applied to utilitarian articles such as textile fabrics, wallpaper, containers, and the like. The same is true when a statue or carving is used to embellish an industrial product or, as in the *Mazer* case, is incorporated into a product without losing its ability to exist independently as a work of art. On the other hand, although the shape of an industrial product may be aesthetically satisfying and valuable, the Committee's intention is not to offer it copyright protection under the bill. Unless the shape of an automobile, airplane, ladies' dress, food processor, television set, or any other industrial product contains some element that, physically or conceptually, can be identified as separable from the utilitarian aspects of that article, the design would not be copyrighted under the bill. The test of separability and independence from "the utilitarian aspects of the article" does not depend upon the nature of the design—that is, even if the appearance of an article is determined by esthetic (as opposed to functional) considerations, only elements, if any, which can be identified separately from the useful article as such are copyrightable. And, even if the three-dimensional design contains some such element (for example,

a carving on the back of a chair or a floral relief design on silver flatware), copyright protection would extend only to that element, and would not cover the over-all configuration of the utilitarian article as such.

H.R. Rep. No. 94-1476, 94th Cong., 2d Sess. 54-55 (1976), *reprinted in* 1976 U.S.C.C.A.N. 5659, 5667-68.

Applying the statutory definitions has proved troublesome in practice, with cases requiring courts to make difficult line-drawing decisions between an artifact's utilitarian function and its design. The statuette in *Mazer* was physically separable from the lighting fixture. Think of the variety of decorative techniques that you have seen employed in lamps today. Many of those techniques are nonrepresentational, and many incorporate design elements into the overall configuration of the article. In such cases, it can be quite difficult to identify the precise location of the line between form and function, and thus to determine whether separable, copyrightable features exist. These cases require courts to determine what is meant by the other kind of separability mentioned in the House Report: *conceptual separability*. Read the following case and consider how effectively the court resolves the separability question.

≡≡≡ *Pivot Point International, Inc. v. Charlene Products, Inc.*
≡≡≡ 372 F.3d 913 (7th Cir. 2004)

RIPPLE, J: . . .

Pivot Point International, Inc. ("Pivot Point"), brought this cause of action against Charlene Products, Inc., and its president Peter Yau for copyright infringement. . . . The district court granted summary judgment for the defendants on the ground that the copied subject matter, a mannequin head, was not copyrightable. . . . For the reasons set forth in the following opinion, we reverse the judgment of the district court and remand the case for proceedings consistent with this opinion.

I. Background

A. Facts

Pivot Point develops and markets educational techniques and tools for the hair design industry. It was founded in 1965 by Leo Passage, an internationally renowned hair designer. One aspect of Pivot Point's business is the design and development of mannequin heads, "slip-ons" (facial forms that slip over a mannequin head) and component hair pieces.

In the mid–1980s, Passage desired to develop a mannequin that would imitate the "hungry look" of high-fashion, runway models. Passage believed that such a mannequin could be marketed as a premium item to cutting-edge hair-stylists and to stylists involved in hair design competitions. Passage then worked with a German artist named Horst Heerlein to create an original sculpture of a female human head. Although Passage discussed his vision with Heerlein, Passage did not give Heerlein any specific dimensional requirements. From Passage's description, Heerlein created a sculpture in plaster entitled "Mara."

Wax molds of Mara were made and sent to Pivot Point's manufacturer in Hong Kong. The manufacturer created exact reproductions of Mara in polyvinyl chloride ("PVC"). The manufacturer filled the PVC form with a liquid that expands and hardens into foam. The process of creating the Mara sculpture and of developing the mannequin based on the sculpture took approximately eighteen months.

In February of 1988, when Pivot Point first inspected the PVC forms of Mara, it discovered that the mannequin's hairline had been etched too high on the forehead. The manufacturer corrected the mistake by adding a second, lower hairline. Although the first, higher hairline was visible upon inspection, it was covered with implanted hair. The early PVC reproductions of Mara, and Pivot Point's first shipment of the mannequins in May of 1988, possessed the double hairlines.

About the same time that it received its first shipment of mannequins, Pivot Point obtained a copyright registration for the design of Mara, specifically the bareheaded female human head with no makeup or hair. Heerlein assigned all of his rights in the Mara sculpture to Pivot Point. Pivot Point displayed the copyright notice in the name of Pivot Point on each mannequin.

Pivot Point enjoyed great success with its new mannequin. To respond to customer demand, Pivot Point began marketing the Mara mannequin with different types and lengths of hair, different skin tones and variations in makeup; however, no alterations were made to the facial features of the mannequin. For customer ease in identification, Pivot Point changed the name of the mannequin based on its hair and skin color; for instance, a Mara mannequin implanted with yak hair was called "Sonja," and the Mara mannequin implanted with blonde hair was called "Karin."

At a trade show in 1989, Charlene, a wholesaler of beauty products founded by Mr. Yau, displayed its own "Liza" mannequin, which was very close in appearance to Pivot Point's Mara. In addition to the strikingly similar facial features, Liza also exhibited a double hairline that the early Mara mannequins possessed.

On September 24, 1989, Pivot Point noticed Charlene for copyright infringement. When Charlene refused to stop importing and selling the Liza mannequin, Pivot Point filed this action. . . .

II. Analysis . . .

B. Copyrightability

The central issue in this case is whether the Mara mannequin is subject to copyright protection. This issue presents, at bottom, a question of statutory interpretation. . . . If an article is not "useful" as the term is defined in §101, then it is a pictorial, graphic and sculptural work entitled to copyright protection (assuming the other requirements of the statute are met).

1. Usefulness

Pivot Point submits that the Mara mannequin is not a "useful article" for purposes of §101 because its "inherent nature is to portray the appearance of runway models. Its value," continues Pivot Point, "resides in how well it portrays the appearance of runway models, just as the value of a bust—depicting Cleopatra, for example, . . . —would be in how well it approximates what one imagines the subject looked like." Appellant's Br. at 19. . . .

Charlene presents us with a different view. It suggests that . . . the Mara mannequin does have a useful function other than portraying an image of a high-fashion runway model. According to Charlene, Mara also is marketed and used for practicing the art of makeup application. Charlene points to various places in the record that establish that Mara is used for this purpose and is, therefore, a useful article subject to the limiting language of §101. . . .

. . . [W]e shall assume that the district court correctly ruled that Mara is a useful article and proceed to examine whether, despite that usefulness, it is amenable to copyright protection.

2. Separability

We return to the statutory language. A useful article falls within the definition of pictorial, graphic or sculptural works "*only if, and only to the extent that, such design incorporates pictorial, graphic, or sculptural features that can be identified separately from, and are capable of existing independently of, the utilitarian aspects of the article.*" 17 U.S.C. §101. It is common ground between the parties and, indeed, among the courts that have examined the issue, that this language, added by the 1976 Act, was intended to distinguish creative works that enjoy protection from elements of industrial design that do not. Although the Congressional goal was evident, application of this language has presented the courts with significant difficulty. . . .

Even though the words of the statute do not yield a definitive answer, we believe that the statutory language nevertheless provides significant guidance in our task. We therefore shall examine in more detail what that language has to tell us, and we return to the necessary starting point of our task, §101. . . .

Certainly, one approach to determine whether material can be "identified separately," and the most obvious, is to rely on the capacity of the artistic material to be severed physically from the industrial design. When a three-dimensional article is the focus of the inquiry, reliance on physical separability can no doubt be a helpful tool in ascertaining whether the artistic material in question can be separated from the industrial design. As Professor Denicola points out, however, such an approach really is not of much use when the item in question is two-dimensional. *See* [Robert C.] Denicola, [*Applied Art & Industrial Design: A Suggested Approach to Copyright in Useful Articles,* 67 Minn. L. Rev. 707, 744 (1983)]. Indeed, because this provision, by its very words, was intended to apply to two-dimensional material, it is clear that a physical separability test cannot be the exclusive test for determining copyrightability.

It seems to be common ground between the parties and, indeed, among the courts and commentators, that the protection of the copyright statute also can be secured when a conceptual separability exists between the material sought to be copyrighted and the utilitarian design in which that material is incorporated. The difficulty lies not in the acceptance of that proposition, which the statutory language clearly contemplates, but in its application. As noted by Pivot Point, the following tests have been suggested for determining when the artistic and utilitarian aspects of useful articles are conceptually separable: 1) the artistic features are "primary" and the utilitarian features "subsidiary," *Kieselstein-Cord v. Accessories by Pearl, Inc.*, 632 F.2d 989, 993 (2d Cir. 1980); 2) the useful article "would still be marketable to some significant segment of the community simply because of its aesthetic qualities," Melville B. Nimmer & David Nimmer, 1 Nimmer on Copyright §2.08[B][3], at 2–101 (2004); 3) the article "stimulate[s] in the mind of the beholder a concept that is separate from the concept evoked by its utilitarian function," *Carol Barnhart Inc. v. Econ. Cover Corp.*, 773 F.2d 411, 422 (2d Cir. 1985) (Newman, J., dissenting); 4) the artistic design was not significantly influenced by functional considerations, *see Brandir Int'l, Inc. v. Cascade Pac. Lumber Co.*, 834 F.2d 1142, 1145 (2d Cir. 1987) (adopting the test forwarded in Denicola, *supra*, at 741); 5) the artistic features "can stand alone as a work of art traditionally conceived, and . . . the useful article in which it is embodied would be equally useful without it," Paul Goldstein, 1 Copyright §2.5.3, at 2:67 (2d ed.2004).; and 6) the artistic features are not utilitarian, *see* William F. Patry, 1 *Copyright Law & Practice* 285 (1994). . . .

Among the circuits, the Court of Appeals for the Second Circuit has had occasion to wrestle most comprehensively with the notion of "conceptual separability." Its case law represents, we believe, an intellectual journey that has explored the key aspects of the problem. We therefore turn to a study of the key stages of doctrinal development in its case law.

a.

The Second Circuit first grappled with the issue of conceptual separability in *Kieselstein–Cord v. Accessories by Pearl, Inc.*, 632 F.2d 989 (2d Cir. 1980). In that case, Kieselstein–Cord, a jewelry designer, had created a line of decorative and jeweled belt buckles inspired by works of art; he obtained copyright registrations for his designs. When the line was successful, Accessories by Pearl, Inc., ("Pearl") copied the designs and marketed its own, less-expensive versions of the belt buckles. Kieselstein–Cord then sued Pearl for copyright infringement; however, Pearl claimed that the belt buckles were not copyrightable because they were " 'useful articles' with no 'pictorial, graphic, or sculptural features that can be identified separately from, and are capable of existing independently of, the utilitarian aspects' of the buckles." *Id*. at 991–92. The Second Circuit disagreed. Although it did not articulate a specific test for evaluating conceptual separability, it focused on the "primary" and "subsidiary" elements of the article and concluded:

> We see in appellant's belt buckles conceptually separable sculptural elements, as apparently have the buckles' wearers who have used them as ornamentation for parts of the

body other than the waist. The primary ornamental aspect of the Vaquero and Winchester buckles is conceptually separable from their subsidiary utilitarian function. This conclusion is not at variance with the expressed congressional intent to distinguish copyrightable applied art and uncopyrightable industrial design. Pieces of applied art, these buckles may be considered jewelry, the form of which is subject to copyright protection.

Id. at 993 (internal citations omitted).

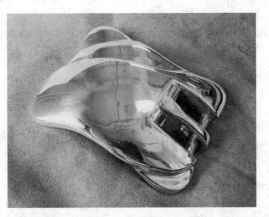

© *1978 Kieselstein-Cord. Reprinted by permission.*
Vaquero Buckle

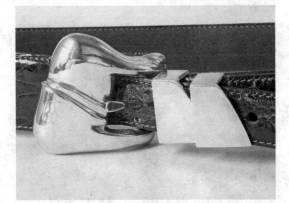

© *1976 Kieselstein-Cord. Reprinted by permission.*
Winchester Buckle

b.

The Second Circuit revisited the issue of conceptual separability in *Carol Barnhart Inc. v. Economy Cover Corp.,* 773 F.2d 411 (2d Cir.1985). In that case, Carol Barnhart, a provider of retail display items, developed four mannequins consisting of human torsos for the display of shirts and jackets. It obtained copyright registrations for each of the forms. When a competitor, Economy Cover, copied the designs,

Carol Barnhart claimed infringement of that copyright. The Second Circuit held that the designs were not copyrightable. It explained:

> [W]hile copyright protection has increasingly been extended to cover articles having a utilitarian dimension, Congress has explicitly refused copyright protection for works of applied art or industrial design which have aesthetic or artistic features that cannot be identified separately from the useful article. Such works are not copyrightable regardless of the fact that they may be "aesthetically satisfying and valuable."
>
> Applying these principles, we are persuaded that since the aesthetic and artistic features of the Barnhart forms are inseparable from the forms' use as utilitarian articles the forms are not copyrightable. . . . [Barnhart] stresses that the forms have been responded to as sculptural forms, and have been used for purposes other than modeling clothes, e.g., as decorating props and signs without any clothing or accessories. While this may indicate that the forms are "aesthetically satisfying and valuable," it is insufficient to show that the forms possess aesthetic or artistic features that are physically or conceptually separable from the forms' use as utilitarian objects to display clothes. On the contrary, to the extent the forms possess aesthetically pleasing features, even when these features are considered in the aggregate, they cannot be conceptualized as existing independently of their utilitarian function.

Id. at 418 (internal citations omitted). The court also rejected the argument that *Kieselstein–Cord* was controlling. The majority explained that what distinguished the Kieselstein–Cord buckles from the Barnhart forms was "that the ornamented surfaces of the buckles were not in any respect required by their functions; the artistic and aesthetic features would thus be conceived as having been added to, or superimposed upon, an otherwise utilitarian article." *Id.* at 419. . . .

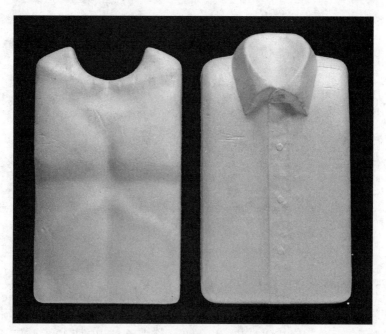

Torso Forms

c.

The Second Circuit soon addressed conceptual separability again in *Brandir International, Inc. v. Cascade Pacific Lumber Co.*, 834 F.2d 1142 (2d Cir.1987). That case involved the work of an artist, [Steven] Levine; specifically, Levine had created a sculpture of thick, interwoven wire. A cyclist friend of Levine's realized that the sculpture could, with modification, function as a bicycle rack and thereafter put Levine in touch with Brandir International, Inc. ("Brandir"). The artist and the Brandir engineers then worked to modify the sculpture to produce a workable and marketable bicycle rack. Their work culminated in the "Ribbon Rack," which Brandir began marketing in 1979. Shortly thereafter, Cascade Pacific Lumber Co. ("Cascade") began selling a similar product, and, in response, Brandir applied for copyright protection and began placing copyright notices on its racks. The Copyright Office, however, rejected the registration on the ground that the rack did not contain any element that was "capable of independent existence as a copyrightable pictorial, graphic or sculptural work apart from the shape of the useful article." *Id.* at 1146.

The court first considered the possible tests for conceptual separability in light of its past decisions and, notably, attempted to reconcile its earlier attempts:

> Perhaps the differences between the majority and the dissent in Carol Barnhart might have been resolved had they had before them the Denicola article on *Applied Art and Industrial Design: A Suggested Approach to Copyright in Useful Articles*, [67 Minn. L. Rev. 707 (1983)]. . . . Denicola argues that . . . "Copyrightability . . . should turn on the relationship between the proffered work and the process of industrial design." *Id.* at 741. He suggests that "the dominant characteristic of industrial design is the influence of nonaesthetic, utilitarian concerns" and hence concludes that copyrightability "ultimately should depend on the extent to which the work reflects artistic expression uninhibited by functional considerations." *Id.* To state the Denicola test in the language of conceptual separability, if design elements reflect a merger of aesthetic and functional considerations, the artistic aspects of a work cannot be said to be conceptually separable from the utilitarian elements. Conversely, where design elements can be identified as reflecting the designer's artistic judgment exercised independently of functional influences, conceptual separability exists.

> We believe that Professor Denicola's approach provides the best test for conceptual separability and, accordingly, adopt it here for several reasons. First, the approach is consistent with the holdings of our previous cases. In *Kieselstein–Cord*, for example, the artistic aspects of the belt buckles reflected purely aesthetic choices, independent of the buckles' function, while in *Carol Barnhart* the distinctive features of the torsos—the accurate anatomical design and the sculpted shirts and collars—showed clearly the influence of functional concerns. . . . Second, the test's emphasis on the influence of utilitarian concerns in the design process may help . . . "alleviate the de facto discrimination against nonrepresentational art that has regrettably accompanied much of the current analysis." *Id.* at 745.

Id. at 1145 (footnotes omitted).

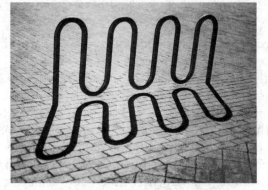

Photo by Joanne Gere.
RIBBON Rack in Shadow

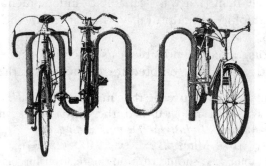

RIBBON is a registered trademark of
Brandir International, Inc.
Reprinted by permission.

Applying Professor Denicola's test to the Ribbon Rack, the court found that the rack was not copyrightable. The court stated that, "[h]ad Brandir merely adopted one of the existing sculptures as a bicycle rack, neither the application to a utilitarian end nor commercialization of that use would have caused the object to forfeit its copyrighted status." *Id.* at 1147. However, when the Ribbon Rack was compared to earlier sculptures, continued the court, it was "in its final form essentially a product of industrial design." *Id.*

> In creating the RIBBON Rack, the designer . . . clearly adapted the original aesthetic elements to accommodate and further a utilitarian purpose. These altered design features of the RIBBON Rack, including the spacesaving, open design achieved by widening the upper loops . . . the straightened vertical elements that allow in- and above-ground installation of the rack, the ability to fit all types of bicycles and mopeds, and the heavy-gauged tubular construction of rustproof galvanized steel, are all features that combine to make for a safe, secure, and maintenance-free system of parking bicycles and mopeds.
> . . .
> . . . While the RIBBON Rack may be worthy of admiration for its aesthetic qualities alone, it remains nonetheless the product of industrial design. Form and function are

inextricably intertwined in the rack, its ultimate design being as much the result of utilitarian pressures as aesthetic choices. . . . Thus there remains no artistic element of the RIBBON Rack that can be identified as separate and "capable of existing independently, of, the utilitarian aspects of the article."

Id. at 1146–47. . . .

C. Application . . .

The Second Circuit cases exhibit a progressive attempt to forge a workable judicial approach capable of giving meaning to the basic Congressional policy decision to distinguish applied art from uncopyrightable industrial art or design. In *Kieselstein–Cord,* the Second Circuit attempted to distinguish artistic expression from industrial design by focusing on the present use of the item, i.e., the "primary ornamental aspect" versus the "subsidiary utilitarian function" of the object at issue. 632 F.2d at 993. In *Carol Barnhart,* the Second Circuit moved closer to a process-oriented approach:

> What distinguishes those [Kieselstein–Cord] buckles from the Barnhart forms is that the ornamented surfaces of the buckles were not in any respect required by their utilitarian functions; the artistic and aesthetic features could thus be conceived of as having been added to, or superimposed upon, an otherwise utilitarian article. The unique artistic design was wholly unnecessary to performance of the utilitarian function. In the case of the Barnhart forms, on the other hand, the features claimed to be aesthetic or artistic, e.g., the life-size configuration of the breasts and the width of the shoulders, are inextricably intertwined with the utilitarian feature, the display of clothes. Whereas a model of a human torso, in order to serve its utilitarian function, must have some configuration of the chest and some width of shoulders, a belt buckle can serve its function satisfactorily without any ornamentation of the type that renders the Kieselstein–Cord buckles distinctive.

773 F.2d at 419. Thus, it was the fact that the creator of the torsos was driven by utilitarian concerns, such as how display clothes would fit on the end product, that deprived the human torsos of copyright protection.

This process-oriented approach for conceptual separability—focusing on the process of creating the object to determine whether it is entitled to copyright protection—is more fully articulated in *Brandir* and indeed reconciles the earlier case law pertaining to conceptual separability.

> [T]he approach is consistent with the holdings of our previous cases. In *Kieselstein–Cord,* for example, the artistic aspects of the belt buckles reflected purely aesthetic choices, independent of the buckles' function, while in *Carol Barnhart* the distinctive features of the torsos—the accurate anatomical design and the sculpted shirts and collars—showed clearly the influence of functional concerns. Though the torsos bore artistic features, it was evident the designer incorporated those features to further the usefulness of the torsos as mannequins.

Brandir, 834 F.2d at 1145. . . .

Conceptual separability exists, therefore, when the artistic aspects of an article can be "conceptualized as existing independently of their utilitarian function." *Carol Barnhart,* 773 F.2d at 418. This independence is necessarily informed by "whether the design elements can be identified as reflecting the designer's artistic judgment exercised independently of functional influences." *Brandir,* 834 F.2d at 1145. If the elements do reflect the independent, artistic judgment of the designer, conceptual separability exists. Conversely, when the design of a useful article is "as much the result of utilitarian pressures as aesthetic choices," *id.* at 1147, the useful and aesthetic elements are not conceptually separable.

Applying this test to the Mara mannequin, we must conclude that the Mara face is subject to copyright protection. It certainly is not difficult to conceptualize a human face, independent of all of Mara's specific facial features, i.e., the shape of the eye, the upturned nose, the angular cheek and jaw structure, that would serve the utilitarian functions of a hair stand and, if proven, of a makeup model. Indeed, one is not only able to conceive of a different face than that portrayed on the Mara mannequin, but one easily can conceive of another visage that portrays the "hungry look" on a high-fashion runway model. Just as Mattel is entitled to protection for "its own particularized expression" of an "upturned nose[ ], bow lips, and widely spaced eyes," *Mattel,* [*Inc. v. Goldberger Doll Manufacturing Co.,*] 365 F.3d [133,] 136 [(2d Cir. 2004)], so too is Heerlein (and, therefore, Pivot Point as assignee of the copyright registration) entitled to have his expression of the "hungry look" protected from copying.

Mara can be conceptualized as existing independent from its use in hair display or make-up training because it is the product of Heerlein's artistic judgment. When Passage approached Heerlein about creating the Mara sculpture, Passage did not provide Heerlein with specific dimensions or measurements; indeed, there is no evidence that Heerlein's artistic judgment was constrained by functional considerations. . . . Such considerations, had they been present, would weigh against a determination that Mara was purely the product of an artistic effort. By contrast, after Passage met with Heerlein to discuss Passage's idea for a "hungry-look" model, Heerlein had carte blanche to implement that vision as he saw fit. . . . Thus, because Mara was the product of a creative process unfettered by functional concerns, its sculptural features "can be identified separately from, and are capable of existing independently of," its utilitarian aspects. It therefore meets the requirements for conceptual separability and is subject to copyright protection.

Conclusion

The Mara mannequin is subject to copyright protection. We therefore must reverse the summary judgment . . . .

KANNE J., dissenting. . . . I cannot join the majority opinion because I am not persuaded that the "Mara" mannequin is copyrightable. All functional items have aesthetic qualities. If copyright provided protection for functional items simply because of their aesthetic qualities, Congress's policy choice that gives less protection in patent than copyright would be undermined.

The majority rightly assumes that Mara is a "useful article." . . . To receive copyright protection as a "sculptural work," then, Mara must come within the narrow restrictions placed on "useful articles" in the definition of pictorial, graphic, and sculptural works. . . .

The majority, concluding that Congress intended "to state a single, integrated standard," deduced that the standard must be "conceptual separability." This may be correct, as it is very difficult to divine the distinction between physical and conceptual separability if those standards are properly stated. In my view, however, the majority's explanation of conceptual separability lacks a basis in the statute. . . .

. . . The statute asks two questions: Does the useful article incorporate "sculptural features that can be identified separately from the utilitarian aspects" of the article? And are these features "capable of existing independently" from the utilitarian aspects? The copyright statute is concerned with protecting only non-utilitarian features of the useful article. To be copyrightable, the statute requires that the useful article's functionality remain intact once the copyrightable material is separated. In other words, Pivot Point needs to show that Mara's face is not a utilitarian "aspect" of the product "Mara," but rather a separate non-utilitarian "feature." The majority, by looking only to whether the features could also "be conceptualized as existing independently of *their utilitarian function*" and ignoring the more important question of whether the features themselves are utilitarian *aspects* of the useful article, mistakenly presupposes that utilitarian aspects of a useful article can be copyrighted. If we took away Mara's facial features, her functionality would be greatly diminished or eliminated, thus proving that her features cannot be copyrighted. . . .

NOTES AND QUESTIONS

1. Which approach to conceptual separability in *Pivot Point* is more faithful to the language of the House Report, the majority's or the dissent's? How well do the statutory definitions and the accompanying legislative history delineate the dividing line between copyrightable "applied art" and uncopyrightable "industrial design"?

2. Is conceptual separability more appropriately considered a question of fact or a question of law?

3. Recall the nondiscrimination principle articulated by Justice Holmes in *Bleistein*, Chapter 2.A.2.a, *supra*. Professor Alfred Yen has argued that it is impossible to undertake a conceptual separability analysis without making judgments about what is art and what is not. *See* Alfred C. Yen, *Copyright Opinions and Aesthetic Theory*, 71 S. Cal. L. Rev. 247 (1998). He argues that judges would be better served by being conscious of the problem of "subjective censorship" and purposefully being more open-minded to alternate aesthetic sensibilities about what constitutes art. *Id*. at 300-01. Do you agree?

4. Remember that the threshold determination of whether something is a "useful article" is important, because something that is not a "useful article" need not be subjected to a separability analysis. Do belt buckles, mannequin forms or heads, and bicycle racks satisfy the §101 definition of "useful article"? Read the definition of "useful article" again and then consider whether the following would qualify:

  a. A collection of blank forms in a personal organizer
  b. A Statue of Liberty foam novelty hat
  c. A slipper shaped like a bear foot

5. Section 113 of the Copyright Act places some additional limits on the scope of copyright in a pictorial, graphic, or sculptural work. Examine §§113(b)-(c) now. Why do you think those limitations are in the statute?

PRACTICE EXERCISE: ADVOCACY

Comic book publisher DC Comics has sued Mark Towle, the owner-operator of Gotham Garage, a business that customizes cars to resemble famous television and movie vehicles. The complaint alleges that Towle and Gotham Garage have been producing and selling vehicle modification kits based on the design of the Batmobile that appeared in television shows and films based on the original Batman comic. Defendant has filed a motion to dismiss arguing that the Batmobile is a useful article and that the features in question are not copyrightable. You represent DC Comics. Prepare an outline of the arguments that you will make in opposition to the motion and draft your argument headings.

The Original Batmobile

Note on Alternative Modes of Protection

Article 25 (1) of the TRIPS Agreement requires all WTO member countries to provide protection for "independently created industrial designs that are new or original." Countries have the option of meeting this obligation through industrial design law or copyright law. *See* TRIPS Agreement, Art. 25 (2). As you read the following materials, consider whether the United States is in compliance with its international obligations, and whether any of the regimes described are (or could be) adequate complements to, or substitutes for, copyright protection in this area.

a) Design Patents

Under the Patent Act, a design patent is available for "any new, original, and ornamental design for an article of manufacture." 35 U.S.C. §171. If granted, the design patent lasts for 14 years from the date of issuance. *Id.* §173 During that period, the patentee may prevent others from making, using, importing, or selling an article embodying the patented design. *Id.* §271. There are few limitations on the subject matter of design patents. In re *Koehring*, 37 F.2d 421 (C.C.P.A. 1930), is illustrative. There, the court reasoned that in enacting design patent protection, Congress "had in mind the elimination of much of the unsightly repulsiveness that characterizes many machines and mechanical devices which have a tendency to depress rather than excite the esthetic sense." *Id.* at 422. The court concluded that the statutory grant of protection could extend to any man-made article, with or without moving parts, as long as the appearance of that article was "a matter of concern to anybody." *Id.* at 423. The design, however, cannot be governed solely by function. *See Seiko Epson Corp. v. Nu-Kote Int'l, Inc.*, 190 F.3d 1360, 1368 (Fed. Cir. 1999).

Although the numbers of design patent applications and issued design patents have increased significantly in recent years, reliance on copyright protection for useful articles is far more common. Given the stronger protection afforded by a design patent and the ability to elect both forms of protection simultaneously, this might strike the student of intellectual property law as curious. The reasons for this pattern are largely practical. First, design patent infringement is more difficult to prove than copyright infringement, although the Federal Circuit recently modified the patent test for infringement. *See Egyptian Goddess, Inc. v. Swisa, Inc.*, 543 F.3d 665 (2008) (en banc) (describing test as whether ordinary observer familiar with the prior art would be deceived into believing the accused product is the same as the patented design); *see* James Juo, *Egyptian Goddess: Rebooting Design Patents and Resurrecting* Whitman Saddle, 18 Fed. Cir. B.J. 429, 450 (2009). Second, and more significantly, obtaining design patent protection is expensive and time-consuming. The average examination time is 14 months, U.S. Patent & Trademark Office (USPTO), Design Patents: January 1988—December 2012 (2013), and protection does not attach until the patent is granted. Many mass-marketed products have relatively short life cycles. Submitting a design patent application before a design proves profitable may not make sense, but marketing the product while the application is pending invites copying before legal protection is available.

Recent changes in design patent law may make design patents more attractive to creators. Once fully in effect on May 13, 2015, the Patent Law Treaties Implementation Act of 2012 will increase the design patent term from 14 to 15 years, and establish a cost effective international design patent application filing system. *See* Patent Law Treaty Implementation Act of 2012, Pub. L. No. 112-211, 126 Stat. 1527 (2012). Design patent applications and grants have increased in recent years. In 2005, the USPTO received 25,553 design patent applications and granted 12,951 design patents. In 2012, applications were up to 32,799 with 21,951 grants.

b) Trade Dress

Another option for design protection developed relatively recently. In 1992 the Supreme Court upheld a jury verdict in favor of Taco Cabana, a Mexican restaurant chain that charged a competitor with imitating its "trade dress"—the external and internal decor of its restaurants—thereby creating an impression of joint ownership or affiliation. Importantly, the Court held that Taco Cabana did not need to prove that its trade dress had acquired "secondary meaning"—i.e., that customers in its target market recognized the decor as an indicator of source. *Two Pesos, Inc. v. Taco Cabana, Inc.*, 505 U.S. 763 (1992).

Two Pesos set off a torrent of trade dress infringement litigation, but the boom was short-lived. Almost immediately, courts were confronted with novel questions about what features of a product could be protected as trade dress. The Supreme Court answered this question in *Wal-Mart Stores, Inc. v. Samara Bros., Inc.*, 529 U.S. 205 (2000), and substantially limited the scope of its earlier *Two Pesos* decision. The Court distinguished product design from words or packaging that might be attached to a product, reasoning that although consumers might be "predisposed" to regard the latter as symbols of source, the same predisposition did not exist with respect to product features. It observed: "Consumers should not be deprived of the benefits of competition with regard to the utilitarian and esthetic purposes that product design ordinarily serves by a rule of law that facilitates plausible threats of suit against new entrants. . . ." *Id.* at 213. The Court concluded that secondary meaning must be proved for trade dress protection to apply to product configuration.

In addition, as is the case with design patent protection, trade dress protection is not permitted for functional features of product design. In trademark parlance, trade dress is considered functional if it is essential to the use or purpose of the product or if it affects the cost or quality of the article, or "if exclusive use of the feature would put competitors at a significant non-reputation-related disadvantage," *Qualitex Co. v. Jacobson Prod. Co.*, 514 U.S. 159, 165 (1995). Moreover, a manufacturer wishing to claim trade dress protection for a product feature disclosed in an expired patent (utility, not design) must overcome a strong presumption that the feature is functional and not protectible as trade dress. *TrafFix Devices, Inc. v. Marketing Displays, Inc.*, 532 U.S. 23 (2001).

c) Industrial Design Protection

Many countries have adopted *sui generis* industrial design protection laws. In the United States, the last several decades have witnessed repeated attempts to secure passage of industrial design protection legislation. Although substantial interests have supported such proposals, equally powerful lobbies have opposed them. To date, Congress has shown greater willingness to enact *sui generis* protection for specific subcategories of industrial design perceived to merit special attention than to enact general purpose industrial design legislation.

Not surprisingly, given its economic importance, the computer industry was the first beneficiary of efforts to establish industry-specific design protection. By the early 1980s, newly developed techniques enabled relatively inexpensive copying of the integrated circuit designs embedded in semiconductor chips, which required great effort and expense to develop. In 1984, Congress enacted the first *sui generis* design protection law, the Semiconductor Chip Protection Act (SCPA), Pub. L. No. 98-620, 98 Stat. 3335 (1984) (codified at 17 U.S.C. §§901-914), which granted limited protection for the designs of semiconductor chips, also known as "mask works."

Later, boat manufacturers lobbied successfully for passage of the Vessel Hull Design Protection Act (VHDPA), Pub. L. No. 105-304, Title V, 112 Stat. 2860, 2906 (1998) (codified at 17 U.S.C. §§1301-1332). The VHDPA extended federal protection to the design of a "useful article," defined as "a vessel hull or deck . . . which in normal use has an intrinsic utilitarian function that is not merely to portray the appearance of the article or to convey information. . . ." 17 U.S.C. §1301(b)(2). Owners of original designs were protected for 10 years from another's making, selling or importing for sale a hull or deck embodying the design. *See id*. §1308. The VHDPA was drafted in a way that would make it easy to amend into a more general design protection law (e.g., by removing the restriction to "vessel hull or deck" in the definition of "useful article.") So far, however, no such amendment has been forthcoming.

NOTES AND QUESTIONS

1. Would a general purpose industrial design protection regime be desirable for the United States? Why, or why not? Given what you have learned thus far about the values underlying the U.S. intellectual property system, how would you design a regime of intellectual property protection for industrial designs? Under what constitutional power would Congress enact such *sui generis* protection?

2. If Congress were to enact a general design protection law, what, if anything, should it do about designs that are also eligible for protection under copyright and/or design patent law? Would allowing a designer to claim protection under more than one legal regime result in overprotection? Should Congress draw boundaries between different legal regimes or require claimants to elect one form of protection or the other?

3. In general, clothing is considered functional for copyright purposes, and most design features do not survive the separability test. Numerous attempts to convince Congress to enact *sui generis* protection for fashion design have failed. Should Congress enact such legislation? If you were a member of Congress, what information would you want to have before forming your opinion?

PRACTICE EXERCISE: COUNSEL A CLIENT

Your client, a consumer electronics company, wishes to produce a line of mobile phones and tablets. The company has drawn up designs for its products as pictured below and has approached you for advice on how best to protect this new line of products. What factors should you keep in mind as you consider possible legal regimes for protecting these goods? Draft an opinion letter setting forth your recommendation and reasoning.

B. ARCHITECTURAL WORKS

Section 102 of the Copyright Act lists eight different categories of works of authorship eligible for protection. Prior to the addition of architectural works to that list in 1990, architectural *plans* were protected as graphic works, but finished *buildings* were not. Finished buildings generally were not considered protected because no matter how aesthetically pleasing, buildings are functional. More precisely, as useful articles, buildings would be subject to the separability analysis discussed in Section A.2 *supra*. Congress and the courts refused to acknowledge any separability that would permit protection for a building itself, although particular nonfunctional features like gargoyles might be protected. The legislative history of §102 indicates that Congress intended copyright to protect "[p]urely nonfunctional or monumental structures" and "artistic sculpture or decorative ornamentation or embellishment added to a structure." H.R. Rep. No. 94-1476 at 55, *reprinted in* 1976 U.S.C.C.A.N. at 5668. Thus, for example, if both the Statue of Liberty and the Empire State Building had been constructed after January 1, 1978, copyright protection might extend to the Statue of Liberty as a monumental work, but not to the Empire State Building because of its functionality.

The pre-1990 exclusion of buildings from copyright protection had an important consequence for owners of copyrights in architectural plans: Although copying the plans would infringe the copyrights, building from the plans would not.

The copyright status of buildings changed in 1990 following U.S. accession to the Berne Convention. Article 2 of the Berne Convention defines literary and artistic works to include "illustrations, maps, plans, sketches and three dimensional works relative to geography, topography, architecture or science." Without modifying the protection that was already available for architectural plans, Congress passed the Architectural Works Copyright Protection Act (AWCPA), which added architectural works as the eighth category of works in §102(a). Section 101 defines an "architectural work" as

> the design of a building as embodied in any tangible medium of expression, including a building, architectural plans, or drawings. The work includes the overall form as well as the arrangement and composition of spaces and elements in the design, but does not include individual standard features.

17 U.S.C. §101.

After the AWCPA, an author of architectural plans can use those plans as deposit copies to register an architectural work. Because Congress did not exclude architectural plans from the definition of "pictorial, graphic, and sculptural works," the plans can also be registered as graphic works. Using the plans to register the *architectural work* protects against another's building the structure described in the plans; registering the plans as *graphic works* does not. Second, the building can be registered separately as an architectural work. *See* 37 C.F.R. §202.11.

1. What Is a "Building"?

The Copyright Act defines "architectural work" as "the design of a building . . .", §101, but does not define "building." The House Report accompanying the AWCPA states that the term encompasses "habitable structures such as houses and office buildings. It also covers structures that are used, but not inhabited, by human beings, such as churches, pergolas, gazebos, and garden pavilions." *See* H.R. Rep. 101-735, *reprinted in* 1990 U.S.C.C.A.N. 6935, 6951. The regulations pertinent to architectural work registration promulgated by the Copyright Office pursuant to its authority under §702 of the Copyright Act implements that language:

> The term *building* means humanly habitable structures that are intended to be both permanent and stationary, such as house and office buildings, and other permanent and stationary structures designed for human occupancy, including but not limited to churches, museums, gazebos, and garden pavilions.

37 C.F.R. §202.11(b)(2) (1997). The regulations further prohibit registration of "[s]tructures other than buildings, such as bridges, cloverleafs, dams, walkways, tents, recreational vehicles, mobile homes, and boats." *Id.* (d)(1).

While in many cases it may be clear that the work at issue qualifies as a building, in other cases it is not so obvious. For example, one court found that a shopping mall store located within the larger structure of the shopping mall did not qualify as a building. *Yankee Candle Co. v. New England Candle Co.*, 14 F. Supp. 2d 154 (D. Mass. 1998), *vacated by settlement*, 29 F. Supp. 2d 44 (1998). In another case, a multistory parking garage with stairwells and areas for vending machines was found to qualify as a building. *Moser Pilon Nelson Architects, LLC v. HNTB Corp.*, 80 U.S.P.Q. 2d 1085 (D. Conn. 2006).

2. Are Buildings "Compilations"?

Once the issue of what constitutes a building has been resolved, how is the originality required of all copyrightable works to be judged? When a building is protected as an architectural work, it is not subject to the statutorily mandated separability analysis employed for useful articles. Does the last sentence of the definition of "architectural work" achieve the same purpose as the separability analysis? Consider the following cases:

Nelson-Salabes, Inc. v. Morningside Holdings
2001 WL 419002 (D. Md. 2001), aff'd in part, rev'd in part on other grounds, 284 F.3d 505 (4th Cir. 2002)

[Plaintiff, Nelson-Salabes, Inc., was hired by developers to provide architectural design work for a proposed assisted living facility, Satyr Hill Catered Living (Satyr Hill). Nelson-Salabes created four drawings depicting the footprint, floor plans, and elevations of the Satyr Hill site. These drawings were integrated into the overall development plan and submitted to Baltimore County for approval of the required special exception, a lengthy but necessary step in the development of any assisted living center in Baltimore County. Subsequent to the county's approval, the original developers sold the project to the defendant, Morningside Holdings, a company that already owned other assisted living centers. Morningside Holdings was particularly interested in the site because it had an approved development plan. After being told that they were not going to be retained as architects on the project, Nelson-Salabes informed the managing agent for Morningside that he "could proceed with another architect, but if he did so, he could not use Nelson-Salabes's design, including the footprint and elevations." The new architects that Morningside hired were told to design Satyr Hill to conform to another of Morningside's assisted living centers. The new plans were submitted to the county for approval as amended development plans, stating the reasons for the amendment as "minor footprint revisions" and "minor changes to architectural elevations of buildings."]

BLACK, J.: . . . As designed by Nelson-Salabes, the Satyr Hill site has a three-story building configured in [a] "Y" shape. The front elevation features an octagonal shaped silo in the center, where two arms of the "Y" intersect. The first floor of the silo serves as an entrance. A porte-cochere extends from the entrance to a traffic circle in front of the building. The second and third floors of the silo serve as common areas and contain large windows. The first floor of the vertical element is brick, and the remainder of the building is vinyl siding. Both ends of the front elevation contain a vertical element protruding from the building with bay windows and a gable roof. There are also vertical elements with gable roofs located between the silo and the ends of the building. These elements protrude from the building and aesthetically break up the length of the building. . . .

. . . Nelson-Salabes presented a certificate of registration for its architectural work for the Satyr Hill site.[*] Consequently, the burden shifts to the defendants to rebut plaintiff's *prima facie* case of validity.

The defendants assert that neither the footprint of the building, nor the elevations are copyrightable. More specifically, defendants assert that the Y-shaped footprint is neither original nor an expression of artistic merit. Rather, they argue that it is utilitarian and within the public domain. According to the defendants, the "Y" shape is commonly used for architectural structures and, in this case, was dictated by zoning regulations, building codes, and physical attributes of the site. Similarly, the defendants assert that the various elements of the front elevation, such as brick, siding, gables, the octagonal entrance, and bay windows are common features of similar buildings in the area. Defendants further assert that the height of the building and the elevations were dictated by the Baltimore County zoning ordinance.

The Court agrees that Nelson-Salabes's use of certain individual features, such as the bay windows or the octagonal entrance, is neither original nor an expression of artistic merit. Nonetheless, "[t]he mere fact that component parts of a collective work are neither original to the plaintiff nor copyrightable by the plaintiff does not preclude a determination that the combination of such component parts as a separate entity is both original and copyrightable." Moreover, 17 U.S.C. §101 provides that an "architectural work" includes "the overall form as well as the arrangement and composition of spaces and elements in the design, but does not include individual standard features." 17 U.S.C. §101.

Here, the Court finds that Nelson-Salabes's combination of common features such as a Y-shaped footprint, bay windows, the octagonal silo entrance, and gables created a unique design. To be sure, Paul Seiben, plaintiff's expert in architecture, testified that he had never seen the same combination of elements used by

---

* As authorized by the definition of "architectural work," Nelson-Salabes obtained the registration based on the design as embodied in its plans.—EDS.

© 1998 Nelson-Salabes, Inc. Architects/Planners. Reprinted by permission.
Defendants' nursing home, as built

© 1998 Nelson-Salabes, Inc. Architects/Planners. Reprinted by permission.
Computer simulation based on Nelson-Salabes design

Nelson-Salabes on any other building. Further, the footprint and front elevation used by Nelson-Salabes were not the only feasible designs. Consequently, the Court further finds that the defendants have failed to rebut the *prima facie* validity of plaintiff's copyright, and that Nelson-Salabes's selection and arrangement of common architectural features is unique and exhibits artistic expression. Therefore, the Court further finds that Nelson-Salabes owns a valid copyright in its architectural work for the Satyr Hill site. . . .

. . . [The court determined that the defendants had infringed the plaintiff's copyrighted architectural work.] [T]he Court finds that both works contain the same unique combination of design elements including the use of an octagonal entrance, protruding gables, and bay windows on the ends of the building. The Court recognizes that differences do exist between the two designs. . . . Further supporting the Court's conclusion is the fact that Turner, Morningside's managing agent,] told his architect that he wanted the design to fit within the approved plan. It is also undisputed that only minor changes could be made to the plan or it would require a new special exception. Moreover, the defendants noted on their amended development plans that they only made "minor" changes to the footprint and elevations. . . .

Intervest Construction, Inc. v. Canterbury Estate Homes, Inc.
554 F.3d 914 (11th Cir. 2008)

BIRCH, J.: In this copyright infringement action the appellant contends that the district court erred when it examined the two floor-plans at issue . . . emphasizing the differences between the two . . .

I. Background

. . . [T]he floor plan for The Westminster was created in 1992 as a work-made-for-hire by Intervest Construction, Inc. ("Intervest"). The putatively infringing floor-plan, The Kensington, was created in 2002 by Canterbury Estate Homes, Inc. ("Canterbury"). Each floor-plan depicts a four-bedroom house, with one bedroom being denominated as a "master" bedroom or suite. Each floor plan includes a: two-car garage; living room; dining room; "family" room; foyer; "master" bathroom; kitchen; second bathroom; nook; and porch/patio. Each floor-plan also reflects certain "elements" common to most houses: doors; windows; walls; bathroom fixtures (toilet, tub, shower, and sink); kitchen fixtures (sink, counter, refrigerator, stovetop, and pantry/cabinets); utility rooms and fixtures (washer, dryer, and sink); and closets. A cursory examination of the two floor-plans reveals that the square footage of both is approximately the same. Also, as is common to houses, there are placements of entrances, exits, hallways, openings, and utilities (furnace, air conditioner, hot water heater, and telephone hardware).

After identifying all of these unassigned components and elements of the floor-plans, the district court undertook a careful comparative analysis of the selection, coordination, and arrangement of these common components and elements.

The district court focused upon the dissimilarities in such coordination and arrangement: [The court then proceeded with a lengthy comparison of the floor plans. A few excerpts from that comparison are included below.]

First, Canterbury represents that the square footage of the rooms in the two designs is different, and visual examination of the floor plans appears to confirm that. . . .

Second, the garage in The Westminster has a front entrance, while The Kensington's has a side entrance. Further, Intervest's design has an attic access from the garage, while Canterbury's version has a "bonus room" above the garage, something The Westminster lacks entirely. Moreover, the inside air conditioning unit and water heater are placed differently in the two floor plans. Additionally, The Kensington has two windows in the garage, while The Westminster has none. In The Westminster, there is a bedroom closet to the left of the utility room, whereas in The Kensington, there is a hallway in that location. . . .

Proceeding to the center portion of the homes, the nooks in the two plans are markedly different. In that regard, [The Westminster's] nook feeds into a ninety degree angle adjacent to the Porch and has windows looking both to the outside and to the Porch. On the other hand, [The Kensington's] design is rounded into the porch and is completely made of glass. There is no window to the outside or into the Covered Patio. Moreover, the entrance from the Nook into the Living Room in [The Westminster's] design has an elongated wall which travels much further into the Living Room than in [The Kensington's] design, and also fails to break inward at a ninety degree angle like in [The Kensington's] design. . . .

The kitchens in the two plans are also substantially different. In that connection, the wall placement in the southeast corner of the kitchens is significantly different. [The Kensington's] design pushes this wall further into the Living Room and pushes the Kitchen Counter much further north than in [The Westminster's] design. This allows [The Kensington's] design to have a much larger Pantry than [The Westminster's] design. . . .

. . . Additionally, in The Kensington's master bath, "the doors to the walk-in closets . . . are solid and open in different directions than those [in the Westminster], which uses a retractable door." Finally, the sinks in the master bath are placed differently in the two designs. In The Kensington, the sinks are centered; in The Westminster, they are not." . . .

II Discussion

Since we are dealing with a specific type of copyrightable work, here an architectural work, we begin by examining the statutory definition of an "architectural work," to wit: "the design of a building as embodied in any tangible medium of expression, including a building, architectural plans or drawings. The work includes the overall form as well as the arrangement and composition of spaces and elements in the design, but does not include individual standard features." 17 U.S.C. §101 (2008). A review of the legislative history discloses that such "individual standard features" include "common windows, doors, and other staple building components." H.R. Rep. No. 101-735 (1990) *as reprinted in* 1990 U.S.C.C.A.N. 6935, 6949. Including the phrase "the arrangement and composition of spaces and elements in the design" demonstrates Congress' appreciation that "creativity in architecture frequently takes the form of a selection, coordination, or arrangement of unprotectible elements into an original, protectible whole." *Id.* Accordingly, while individual standard features and architectural elements classifiable as ideas or concepts are not themselves copyrightable, an architect's original combination or arrangement of such elements may be. Thus, the definition of an architectural work closely parallels that of a "compilation" under the statute, that is: "[A] work formed by the collection and assembling of preexisting materials or of data that are selected, coordinated, or arranged in such a way that the resulting work as a whole constitutes an original work of authorship." 17 U.S.C. §101. The Supreme Court . . . and our court . . . [have] indicated that the compiler's choices as to selection[,] coordination, or arrangement are the only portions of a compilation, or here, architectural work, that are even entitled to copyright protection. Accordingly, any similarity comparison of the works at issue here must be accomplished at the level of protected expression—that is, the *arrangement* and *coordination* of those common elements ("selected" by the market place, i.e., rooms, windows, doors, and "other staple building components"). In undertaking such a comparison it should be recalled that the copyright protection in a compilation is "thin." Moreover, as the Second Circuit has noted, the substantial similarity inquiry is "narrowed" when dealing with a compilation.

Thus, when viewed through the narrow lens of compilation analysis only the original, and thus protected arrangement and coordination of spaces, elements and other staple building components should be compared.[3] . . . [A]s noted above, while a creative work is entitled to the most protection, a compilation is entitled to the least, narrowest or "thinnest" protection. Accordingly, when courts have examined copyright infringement claims involving compilations the definition of "substantial similarity" has been appropriately modified to accentuate the narrower scope of protection available. . . .

3.

> There are three types of work that are entitled to copyright protection—creative, derivative, and compiled. Copyrights in these three distinct works are known as creative, derivative, and compilation copyrights. An example of a creative work is a novel. An example of a derivative work is a screenplay based on a novel; it is called "derivative" because it is based on a preexisting work that has been recast, transformed, or adapted. An example of a compilation is [the floor plans at issue in this case.] The [Copyright] Act has created a hierarchy in terms of the protection afforded to these different types of copyrights. A creative work is entitled to the most protection, followed by a derivative work, and finally by a compilation. This is why the *Feist* Court emphasized that the copyright protection in a factual compilation is "thin."

Warren Publishing, Inc. v. Microdos Data Corp., 115 F.3d 1509, 1515 n. 16 (11th Cir. 1997) (citation omitted).

III Conclusion

. . . Given that the plans at issue were protected by compilation copyrights which were "thin," the district court correctly determined that the differences in the protectable expression were so significant that, as a matter of law, no reasonable properly instructed jury of lay observers could find the works substantially similar. . . .

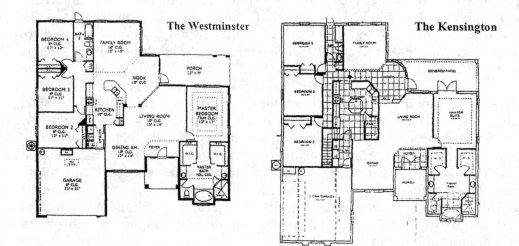

NOTES AND QUESTIONS

1. The standard employed for determining the copyrightability of architectural works again highlights the significance of the categories listed in §102. The definition of architectural work clearly envisions a compilation analysis: an architectural work "includes the overall form as well as the arrangement and composition of spaces and elements in the design, but does not include individual standard features." 17 U.S.C. §101. The legislative history of the AWCPA states:

> The phrase "arrangement and composition of spaces and elements" recognizes that: (1) creativity in architecture frequently takes the form of a selection, coordination, or arrangement of unprotectible elements into an original, protectible whole; (2) an architect may incorporate new, protectible design elements into otherwise standard, unprotectible building features; and (3) interior architecture may be protected.

H.R. Rep. No. 101-735, 101st Cong., 2d Sess. 20-21 (1990), *reprinted in* 1990 U.S.C.C.A.N. 6935, 6949. The legislative history of the AWCPA also indicates a two-step analysis for determining copyrightability:

> First, an architectural work should be examined to determine whether there are original design elements present, including overall shape and interior architecture.

If such design elements are present, a second step is reached to examine whether the design elements are functionally required. If the design elements are not functionally required, the work is protectible without regard to physical or conceptual separability.

H.R. Rep. No. 101-735, 101st Cong., 2d Sess. 20-21 (1990), *reprinted in* 1990 U.S.C.C.A.N. 6935, 6951-52.

Would the issue in *Nelson-Salabes* have been decided differently if the court had applied a conceptual separability approach? Why should pictorial, graphic, or sculptural works and architectural works be treated differently? Do the different standards for these categories of works relate somehow to the availability of other forms of protection?

2. Once the court determines that the structure is a building, copyrightable elements for architectural works can be found in either the exterior plans or the interior floor plan, or both. Consider the floor plan of your house or apartment. Is it subject to copyright protection as an architectural work? Did you remember to consider when it was "constructed"?

3. Section 120 places some additional limits on the copyright in an architectural work. Read §120 now. Do the limitations listed there seem appropriate? Do they seem fair to the author/copyright owner, to the owner of a covered building, and to the public? Do they seem consistent with the utilitarian justification for copyright? Does economic theory, particularly the role of transaction costs, provide a rationale for the §120 limitations?

4. Prior to the AWCPA it was clear that monuments were to be protected, if at all, as sculptural works. Now that architectural works are granted protection, it is unclear whether the classification for certain monumental works has changed or whether dual categorization is possible. The legislative history is not particularly helpful on this topic. The implications of this debate about categorization are, however, significant. Consider the Statue of Liberty, the St. Louis Arch, or the Vietnam Veterans Memorial. Are these and similar works copyrightable as sculptural works? If they had been constructed after 1990, would they be copyrightable as architectural works? For monuments constructed after 1990, their categorization for copyright purposes may affect both the scope of protection afforded the copyright owner and the rights of the public to make certain uses of the works. In particular §120 does not apply to sculptural works. How should courts resolve the question of categorization? For exploration of the copyright issues related to monumental works of architecture, see Melissa M. Mathis, Note, *Function, Nonfunction, and Monumental Works of Architecture: An Interpretive Lens in Copyright Law,* 22 Cardozo L. Rev. 595 (2001).

PRACTICE EXERCISE: COUNSEL A CLIENT

Miller's Ale House has approximately 50 restaurant/sports bar locations, and has registered copyrights for 5 different floor plans, each containing a different arrangement of various decorative elements. Boynton Carolina, prior to opening its restaurant called Boynton Ale House a mile from one of Miller's establishments (located in Boynton Beach, FL), renovated its building's interior. It added many of the features of Miller's restaurants, including walls paneled with dock wood, an exposed kitchen, a bar located at the center of the restaurant topped with a soffit, "high-top" tables in a portion of the restaurant, and the color red for the restaurant's name on its exterior and menus. Boynton's restaurant also differs in a number of ways, most notably in that Boynton Carolina is in a stand-alone building, while Miller's Boynton Ale House is connected to other shops. Other differences include the bar's location relative to each restaurant's entry, the configuration of booth seating, and the arrangement of games inside the restaurant. The outdoor areas also differ: Boynton Carolina has an outside corner bar and outside seating whereas Miller's Boynton Ale House has no outdoor seating.

Miller's Ale House has consulted you to discuss suing Boynton Carolina for copyright infringement. Please write a letter discussing the arguments that might be made and providing your assessment of the strength of the case.

C. COMPUTER SOFTWARE

Like the other categories of works you have just studied, software presents unique questions for copyright law. As a functional work—one that ultimately tells a device what to do—software is unlike other works traditionally protected by the Copyright Act that are created to communicate directly to users. Moreover, it is possible to write two completely different programs that, from the user's vantage point, behave in exactly the same way. *See* Pamela Samuelson et al., *A Manifesto Concerning the Legal Protection of Computer Programs*, 94 Colum. L. Rev. 2308, 2316-19 (1994). At the same time, software also reflects creative decisions. Some have argued that a programmer's written code is analogous to the text of a novel, with its organizational structure akin to the novel's plot. *See* Anthony L. Clapes et al., *Silicon Epics and Binary Bards: Determining the Proper Scope of Copyright Protection for Computer Programs*, 34 UCLA L. Rev. 1493, 1533-38 (1987). Indeed, Congress itself seized on this analogy, choosing to protect computer programs as literary works under the 1976 Act. Although the Berne Convention does not mention computer programs, the U.S. approach influenced the drafters of the TRIPS Agreement, which requires that computer programs be protected as literary works. *See* TRIPS Agreement, art. 10.

In the early days of computer technology, copyright law did not clearly protect computer software. Firms relied on trade secret law to protect source code and contract law to define the terms of use of the object code that they distributed to customers. This changed when Congress passed the 1976 Copyright Act. The Act's legislative history suggested that programs could be copyrightable as literary works and explained the underlying reasoning: "The term 'literary works' does not connote any criterion of literary merit or qualitative value: it includes . . . computer programs to the extent that they incorporate authorship in the programmer's expression of original ideas, as distinguished from the ideas themselves." H.R. Rep. No. 94-1476, 94th Cong., 2d Sess. 54 (1976), *reprinted in* 1976 U.S.C.C.A.N. 5659, 5667.

During the revision process that culminated in the 1976 Act, Congress established the Commission on New Technological Uses of Copyrighted Works (CONTU) to investigate a variety of issues, including those associated with computers and computer programs. CONTU's final report, ultimately published in 1980, concluded that computer programs could be "writings" for constitutional purposes and that §102(b) of the new Act did not bar protection: "Programs should no more be considered machine parts than videotapes should be considered parts of projectors. . . . When a program is copied into the memory of a computer it still exists in a form in which a human-readable version may be produced. . . ." CONTU's Final Report and Recommendations 41, 45, *in* Copyright, Congress, and Technology: The Public Record, vol. 5 (Oryx Press 1980) [hereinafter CONTU Report].

CONTU's recommendations were not unanimous. Commissioner John Hersey, then president of the Authors' League, wrote a strong dissent. Hersey particularly objected to copyright protection for the machine-readable versions of programs: "Works of authorship have always been intended to be circulated to human beings and to be used by them—to be read, heard, or seen, for either pleasurable or practical ends. Computer programs, in their mature phase, are addressed to machines. . . . Printed instructions tell how to do; programs are able to do." *Id.* at 56, 58. Noting that the principal supporters of copyright protection for software were large corporations, he predicted that firms would "lock their software into their own hardware," *id.* at 72-73, adversely affecting independent software vendors.

As the CONTU majority had recommended, Congress added the definition of "computer program" to §101 to make its intent to protect programs as literary works clear in the statutory language itself. Read the definitions of "computer program" and "literary works" in §101 now to understand how Congress achieved its goal. As you will see, the analogy to literary works has presented difficulties for courts, and Commissioner Hersey's concerns about lock-in and barriers to entry have surfaced in the cases, requiring the courts to consider the extent to which copyright law's protections and exclusions reflect competition policy.

UNDERSTANDING THE TECHNOLOGY

Particularly when coding a complex system, programmers begin by defining the system's desired functionalities and mapping out its structure (producing plans that are akin to architects' blueprints). They then use a programming language to write the source code (i.e., the human-readable code) that will implement the desired functionality according to the structure they have designed.

A device (i.e., the hardware) cannot execute source code. Rather, the programmers must use another program, often called a compiler, to translate the source code into machine-readable code, called object code. Object code is often represented as binary numbers (1s and 0s) that indicate the states of microprocessor switches (on or off) in the device. Generally, firms market only the object code to end users.

An operating system is a program that "talks" directly to the hardware. An application, in turn, "talks" to the operating system. So, for example, your desktop

> may run the Microsoft Windows operating system. Word for Windows is an application that runs on the Windows operating system. In the early days of computer software, an application written for one operating system could not run on another operating system without modification. As you will see, over time, programming methodologies have evolved to permit applications to run on multiple operating systems without modifications and, as a result, it has become easier for programmers to write source code that is reusable across devices.

1. Source Code Versus Object Code

In the first generation of cases litigated under the 1976 Act, courts addressed the questions whether copyright law protects both source and object code and whether it should apply differently to operating system software and application programs. Consider the following case:

Apple Computer, Inc. v. Franklin Computer Corp.
714 F.2d 1240 (3d Cir. 1983), cert. dismissed, *464 U.S. 1033 (1984)*

SLOVITER, J.: . . . Franklin [Computer Corp.], the defendant below, manufactures and sells the ACE 100 personal computer [that is] designed to be "Apple compatible," so that peripheral equipment and software developed for use with the Apple II computer could be used in conjunction with the ACE 100. Franklin's copying of Apple's operating system computer programs in an effort to achieve such compatibility precipitated this suit. [The district court denied plaintiff Apple Computer's request for a preliminary injunction and Apple appealed.] . . .

A computer program can be stored or fixed on a variety of memory devices, two of which are of particular relevance for this case. The ROM (Read Only Memory) is an internal permanent memory device consisting of a semi-conductor "chip" which is incorporated into the circuitry of the computer. A program in object code is embedded on a ROM before it is incorporated in the computer. Information stored on a ROM can only be read, not erased or rewritten. The ACE 100 apparently contains EPROMS (Erasable Programmable Read Only Memory) on which the stored information can be erased and the chip reprogrammed, but the district court found that for purposes of this proceeding, the difference between ROMs and EPROMs is inconsequential. 545 F. Supp. [812, 813 n.3 (E.D. Pa. 1983)]. The other device used for storing the programs at issue is a diskette or "floppy disk", an auxiliary memory device consisting of a flexible magnetic disk resembling a phonograph record, which can be inserted into the computer and from which data or instructions can be read. . . .

Franklin did not dispute that it copied the Apple programs. . . . [Franklin's Vice President David] McWherter concluded that use of the identical signals was necessary in order to ensure 100 percent compatibility with application programs created to run on the Apple computer. . . . Apple introduced evidence that Franklin could have rewritten programs, . . . and that there are in existence operating programs written by third parties which are compatible with Apple II.

Franklin's principal defense . . . is primarily a legal one, directed to its contention that the Apple operating system programs are not capable of copyright protection. . . .

Copyrightability of a Computer Program Expressed in Object Code

Certain statements by the district court suggest that programs expressed in object code, as distinguished from source code, may not be the proper subject of copyright. We find no basis in the statute for any such concern. . . .

The district court also expressed uncertainty as to whether a computer program in object code could be classified as a "literary work."[7] However, the category of "literary works", one of the seven copyrightable categories, is not confined to literature in the nature of Hemingway's *For Whom the Bell Tolls*. The definition of "literary works" in section 101 includes expression not only in words but also "numbers, or other . . . numerical symbols or indicia", thereby expanding the common usage of "literary works." Thus a computer program, whether in object code or source code, is a "literary work" and is protected from unauthorized copying, whether from its object or source code version. . . .

Copyrightability of Computer Operating System Programs . . .

1. "Process", "System" or "Method of Operation" . . .

Franklin's attack on operating system programs as "methods" or "processes" seems inconsistent with its concession that application programs are an appropriate subject of copyright. Both types of programs instruct the computer to do something. Therefore, it should make no difference for purposes of section 102(b) whether these instructions tell the computer to help prepare an income tax return (the task of an application program) or to translate a high level language program from source code into its binary language object code form (the task of an operating system program such as "Applesoft"). Since it is only the instructions which are protected, a "process" is no more involved because the instructions in an operating system program may be used to activate the operation of the computer than it would be if instructions were written in ordinary English in a manual which described the necessary steps to activate an intricate complicated machine. There is, therefore, no reason to afford any less copyright protection to the instructions in an operating system program than to the instructions in an application program.

Franklin's argument, receptively treated by the district court, that an operating system program is part of a machine mistakenly focuses on the physical

7. The district court stated that a programmer working directly in object code appears to think more as a mathematician or engineer, that the process of constructing a chip is less a work of authorship than the product of engineering knowledge, and that it may be more apt to describe an encoded ROM as a pictorial three-dimensional object than as a literary work. 545 F. Supp. at 821-22. . . . Apple does not seek to protect the ROM's architecture but only the program encoded upon it.

characteristics of the instructions. But the medium is not the message. We have already considered and rejected aspects of this contention. . . . The mere fact that the operating system program may be etched on a ROM does not make the program either a machine, part of a machine or its equivalent. Furthermore, as one of Franklin's witnesses testified, an operating system does not have to be permanently in the machine in ROM, but it may be on some other medium, such as a diskette or magnetic tape, where it could be readily transferred into the temporary memory space of the computer. In fact, some of the operating systems at issue were on diskette. As the CONTU majority stated,

> Programs should no more be considered machine parts than videotapes should be considered parts of projectors or phonorecords parts of sound reproduction equipment. . . . That the words of a program are used ultimately in the implementation of a process should in no way affect their copyrightability.

CONTU Report at 21. . . .

Perhaps the most convincing item leading us to reject Franklin's argument is that the statutory definition of a computer program as a set of instructions to be used in a computer in order to bring about a certain result, 17 U.S.C. §101, makes no distinction between application programs and operating programs. Franklin can point to no decision which adopts the distinction it seeks to make. . . .

2. Idea/Expression Dichotomy . . .

We . . . focus on whether the idea is capable of various modes of expression. If other programs can be written or created which perform the same function as an Apple's operating system program, then that program is an expression of the idea and hence copyrightable. In essence, this inquiry is no different than that made to determine whether the expression and idea have merged, which has been stated to occur where there are no or few other ways of expressing a particular idea. . . .

The district court made no findings as to whether some or all of Apple's operating programs represent the only means of expression of the idea underlying them. Although there seems to be a concession by Franklin that at least some of the programs can be rewritten, we do not believe that the record on that issue is so clear that it can be decided at the appellate level. Therefore, if the issue is pressed on remand, the necessary finding can be made at that time.

Franklin claims that whether or not the programs can be rewritten, there are a limited "number of ways to arrange operating systems to enable a computer to run the vast body of Apple-compatible software", Brief of Appellee at 20. This claim has no pertinence to either the idea/expression dichotomy or merger. The idea which may merge with the expression, thus making the copyright unavailable, is the idea which is the subject of the expression. The idea of one of the operating system programs is, for example, how to translate source code into object code. If other methods of expressing that idea are not foreclosed as a practical matter, then there is no merger. Franklin may wish to achieve total compatibility with independently developed application programs written for the Apple II, but that is a commercial and competitive objective which does not enter into the somewhat metaphysical issue of whether particular ideas and expressions have merged. . . .

NOTES AND QUESTIONS

1. In the early days of computer technology, many machines were special purpose devices with functionality built into the hardware—i.e., there was no need for software. Why do you think that over time functionality began to move out of hardware and into software? The hardware most likely would not have been copyrightable. Why should the software be copyrightable? Should creativity automatically translate to copyright protection? Few would dispute that Albert Einstein was creative, but could he have obtained copyright protection for $E=mc^2$? Is a novel different from a computer program in ways that should influence the copyright analysis?

2. Compiled code does not necessarily—or even usually—have the same sequence as the source code from which it was derived. Should that fact matter to the copyright analysis?

3. Do you agree with the court that Franklin's desire for compatibility with Apple's operating system is irrelevant to the copyright analysis? The relevance of compatibility to the copyright analysis is an issue that continues to arise, as you will see in the material that follows.

2. Program Structure

The second generation of cases, which continues to the present, involves claims directed toward program structure. Rather than copying literal elements of the code, another programmer could copy the structure of a program and write code in a different language from the original. That code would perform exactly the same function in exactly the same way as the original, but would not copy the original's literal code. Does that second program infringe the copyright in the first program's design? After all, the plot of a novel is protected; by analogy, shouldn't the design of a program be protected? Answering this question requires courts to grapple with the implications of treating software as a literary work and applying traditional doctrines to new technology.

What would motivate a second programmer to copy structural elements of an earlier program, often described as nonliteral copying? The later programmer may wish to avoid doing her own creative work. Or she might wish to offer her own product that is attractive to users who have become accustomed to the earlier program. For example, once users store files in Word format and become accustomed to using the Word user interface, they are unlikely to switch to a new word-processing program unless it will read their stored files and work in roughly the same way. Or, most minimally, the second programmer might wish simply to offer her own product that is compatible, or "interoperable," with an existing operating system and/or with other existing programs designed to run on that system. Unlike most other copyrighted works, software typically is designed to work with other software. For example, many users would like to edit their files stored in Microsoft Word seamlessly on their desktop, laptop, tablet, and phone. For Word to work on each of these devices, however, it must communicate with their operating systems. New applications and utilities also must run within existing software environments if they are to succeed commercially.

In this section, we consider the case that has become the majority approach to addressing claims of nonliteral infringement that depend on the copyrightability of program structure.

Computer Associates International, Inc. v. Altai, Inc.
982 F.2d 693 (2d Cir. 1992)

WALKER, J.: . . .

Among other things, this case deals with the challenging question of whether and to what extent the "non-literal" aspects of a computer program, that is, those aspects that are not reduced to written code, are protected by copyright. . . .

Background . . .

I. Computer Program Design

Certain elementary facts concerning the nature of computer programs are vital to the following discussion. The Copyright Act defines a computer program as "a set of statements or instructions to be used directly or indirectly in a computer in order to bring about a certain result." 17 U.S.C. §101. In writing these directions, the programmer works "from the general to the specific." *Whelan Assocs., Inc. v. Jaslow Dental Lab., Inc.*, 797 F.2d 1222, 1229 (3d Cir. 1986), *cert. denied*, 479 U.S. 1031 (1987). *See generally* Steven R. Englund, Note, *Idea, Process, or Protected Expression?: Determining the Scope of Copyright Protection of the Structure of Computer Programs*, 88 Mich. L. Rev. 866, 867-73 (1990) (hereinafter "Englund"); Peter S. Menell, *An Analysis of the Scope of Copyright Protection for Application Programs*, 41 Stan. L. Rev. 1045, 1051-57 (1989) (hereinafter "Menell"); Mark T. Kretschmer, Note, *Copyright Protection For Software Architecture: Just Say No!*, 1988 Colum. Bus. L. Rev. 823, 824-27 (1988) (hereinafter "Kretschmer"); Peter G. Spivack, Comment, *Does Form Follow Function? The Idea/Expression Dichotomy in Copyright Protection of Computer Software*, 35 U.C.L.A. L. Rev. 723, 729-31 (1988) (hereinafter "Spivack").

The first step in this procedure is to identify a program's ultimate function or purpose. An example of such an ultimate purpose might be the creation and maintenance of a business ledger. Once this goal has been achieved, a programmer breaks down or "decomposes" the program's ultimate function into "simpler constituent problems or 'subtasks,'" Englund, at 870, which are also known as subroutines or modules. *See* Spivack, at 729. In the context of a business ledger program, a module or subroutine might be responsible for the task of updating a list of outstanding accounts receivable. Sometimes, depending upon the complexity of its task, a subroutine may be broken down further into sub-subroutines.

Having sufficiently decomposed the program's ultimate function into its component elements, a programmer will then arrange the subroutines or modules into what are known as organizational or flow charts. Flow charts map the interactions between modules that achieve the program's end goal. *See* Kretschmer, at 826.

In order to accomplish these intra-program interactions, a programmer must carefully design each module's parameter list. A parameter list, according to the expert appointed and fully credited by the district court, Dr. Randall Davis, is "the information sent to and received from a subroutine." *See* Report of Dr. Randall Davis, at 12. The term "parameter list" refers to the form in which information is passed between modules (e.g. for accounts receivable, the designated time frame and particular customer identifying number) and the information's actual content (e.g. 8/91-7/92; customer No. 3). *Id*. With respect to form, interacting modules must share similar parameter lists so that they are capable of exchanging information.

"The functions of the modules in a program together with each module's relationships to other modules constitute the 'structure' of the program." Englund, at 871. . . .

In fashioning the structure, a programmer will normally attempt to maximize the program's speed, efficiency, as well as simplicity for user operation, while taking into consideration certain externalities such as the memory constraints of the computer upon which the program will be run. *See id*.; Kretschmer, at 826; Menell, at 1052. "This stage of program design often requires the most time and investment." Kretschmer, at 826.

Once each necessary module has been identified, designed, and its relationship to the other modules has been laid out conceptually, the resulting program structure must be embodied in a written language that the computer can read. This process is called "coding," and requires two steps. *Whelan*, 797 F.2d at 1230. First, the programmer must transpose the program's structural blue-print into a source code. . . . Once the source code has been completed, the second step is to translate or "compile" it into object code. . . .

After the coding is finished, the programmer will run the program on the computer in order to find and correct any logical and syntactical errors. This is known as "debugging" and, once done, the program is complete. *See* Kretschmer, at 826-27.

II. *Facts*

[Computer Associates (CA) developed and marketed a program called CA-SCHEDULER, which was intended to schedule when the computer should perform certain functions, and to control the computer's operation while it executed the schedule. Another program, ADAPTER, was a module within CA-SCHEDULER that translated CA-SCHEDULER's language to allow it to run on the operating system installed on the user's computer. This saved CA the time and expense of writing different versions of CA-SCHEDULER for different operating systems, and saved its customers the expense of buying multiple copies for each operating system their machines might use. Altai sought to modify its own scheduling software, ZEKE, to run on operating systems other than the one for which it was designed. Altai hired a programmer (Arney) away from CA, not knowing that Arney had worked on ADAPTER and had also brought home a copy of its source code. Arney copied about 30 percent of ADAPTER's source code into OSCAR 3.4, Altai's first implementation of a compatibility component analogous to ADAPTER's. The lower court found copyright infringement and Altai did not appeal that holding. On discovering the infringement, Altai gave eight new programmers who had not worked on OSCAR 3.4 a description of what function-ality the software required. These programmers wrote new code, replacing OSCAR 3.4 with a new compatibility component, OSCAR 3.5. The district court held that Altai's OSCAR 3.5 did not infringe any CA copyrights. CA appealed. The portion of the opinion that we have reproduced here focuses on determining the protectible elements of CA's program. Chapter 5.A.3.b.4 contains the portion of the opinion considering whether Altai infringed.] . . .

Discussion . . .

I. Copyright Infringement . . .

As a general matter, and to varying degrees, copyright protection extends beyond a literary work's strictly textual form to its non-literal components. As we have said, "[i]t is of course essential to any protection of literary property . . . that the right cannot be limited literally to the text, else a plagiarist would escape by immaterial variations." *Nichols v. Universal Pictures Co.*, 45 F.2d 119, 121 (2d Cir. 1930) (L. Hand, J.), *cert. denied*, 282 U.S. 902 (1931). Thus, where "the fundamental essence or structure of one work is duplicated in another," 3 Nimmer, §13.03[A][1], at 13-24, courts have found copyright infringement. This blackletter proposition is the springboard for our discussion.

A. Copyright Protection for the Non-literal Elements of Computer Programs . . .

CA argues that, despite Altai's rewrite of the OSCAR code, the resulting program remained substantially similar to the *structure* of its ADAPTER program. . . . In addition to these aspects, CA contends that OSCAR 3.5 is also substantially similar to ADAPTER with respect to the list of services that both ADAPTER and OSCAR obtain from their respective operating systems. We must decide whether and to what extent these elements of computer programs are pro-tected by copyright law. . . .

[The court noted that the Copyright Act protects original works of authorship, including literary works, and that Congress intended to protect computer programs as literary works.]

The syllogism that follows from the foregoing premises is a powerful one: if the non-literal structures of literary works are protected by copyright; and if computer programs are literary works, as we are told by the legislature; then the non-literal structures of computer programs are protected by copyright. . . .

1) Idea vs. Expression Dichotomy . . .

The essentially utilitarian nature of a computer program . . . complicates the task of distilling its idea from its expression. *See SAS Inst.* [*Inc. v. S & H Computer Sys., Inc.*], 605 F. Supp. [816,] 829 [(M.D. Tenn. 1985)]; *cf.* Englund, at 893. In order to describe both computational processes and abstract ideas, its content "combines creative and technical expression." *See* Spivack, at 755. The variations of expression found in purely creative compositions, as opposed to those contained in utilitarian works, are not directed towards practical application. For example, a narration of Humpty Dumpty's demise, which would clearly be a creative composition, does not serve the same ends as, say, a recipe for scrambled eggs—which is a more process oriented text. Thus, compared to aesthetic works, computer programs hover even more closely to the elusive boundary line described in §102(b).

The doctrinal starting point in analyses of utilitarian works, is the seminal case of *Baker v. Selden*, 101 U.S. 99 (1879). In *Baker,* the Supreme Court faced the question of "whether the exclusive property in a system of bookkeeping can be claimed, under the law of copyright, by means of a book in which that system is explained?" . . .

To the extent that an accounting text and a computer program are both "a set of statements or instructions . . . to bring about a certain result," 17 U.S.C. §101, they are roughly analogous. In the former case, the processes are ultimately conducted by human agency; in the latter, by electronic means. In either case, as already stated, the processes themselves are not protectable. But the holding in *Baker* goes farther. The Court concluded that those aspects of a work, which "must necessarily be used as incident to" the idea, system or process that the work describes, are also not copyrightable. 101 U.S. at 104. . . . From this reasoning, we conclude that those elements of a computer program that are necessarily incidental to its function are similarly unprotectable.

While *Baker v. Selden* provides a sound analytical foundation, it offers scant guidance on how to separate idea or process from expression, and moreover, on how to further distinguish protectable expression from that expression which "must necessarily be used as incident to" the work's underlying concept. . . .

2) Substantial Similarity Test for Computer Program Structure: Abstraction-Filtration-Comparison

. . . As the cases that we shall discuss demonstrate, a satisfactory answer to this problem [of separating idea from expression] cannot be reached by resorting, *a priori,* to philosophical first principals [sic]. . . .

Step One: Abstraction

[T]he theoretic framework for analyzing substantial similarity expounded by Learned Hand in the *Nichols* case is helpful in the present context. In *Nichols*, we enunciated what has now become known as the "abstractions" test for separating idea from expression:

Upon any work . . . a great number of patterns of increasing generality will fit equally well, as more and more of the incident is left out. The last may perhaps be no more than the most general statement of what the [work] is about, and at times might consist only of its title; but there is a point in this series of abstractions where they are no longer protected, since otherwise the [author] could prevent the use of his "ideas," to which, apart from their expression, his property is never extended. *Nichols*, 45 F.2d at 121.

. . . [T]he abstractions test "implicitly recognizes that any given work may consist of a mixture of numerous ideas and expressions." 3 Nimmer §13.03[F], at 13-62.34-63.

As applied to computer programs, the abstractions test will comprise the first step in the examination for substantial similarity. Initially, in a manner that resembles reverse engineering on a theoretical plane, a court should dissect the allegedly copied program's structure and isolate each level of abstraction contained within it. This process begins with the code and ends with an articulation of the program's ultimate function. Along the way, it is necessary essentially to retrace and map each of the designer's steps—in the opposite order in which they were taken during the program's creation.

As an anatomical guide to this procedure, the following description is helpful:

> At the lowest level of abstraction, a computer program may be thought of in its entirety as a set of individual instructions organized into a hierarchy of modules. At a higher level of abstraction, the instructions in the lowest-level modules may be replaced conceptually by the functions of those modules. At progressively higher levels of abstraction, the functions of higher-level modules conceptually replace the implementations of those modules in terms of lower-level modules and instructions, until finally, one is left with nothing but the ultimate function of the program. . . . A program has structure at every level of abstraction at which it is viewed. At low levels of abstraction, a program's structure may be quite complex; at the highest level it is trivial.

Englund, at 897-98; *cf.* Spivack, at 774.

Step Two: Filtration

. . . Professor Nimmer suggests, and we endorse, a "successive filtering method" for separating protectable expression from non-protectable material. *See generally* 3 Nimmer §13.03[F]. This process entails examining the structural components at each level of abstraction to determine whether their particular inclusion at that level was "idea" or was dictated by considerations of efficiency, so as to be necessarily incidental to that idea; required by factors external to the program itself; or taken from the public domain and hence is nonprotectable expression. *See also* Kretschmer, at 844-45 (arguing that program features dictated by market externalities or efficiency concerns are unprotectable). The structure of any given program may reflect some, all, or none of these considerations. Each case requires its own fact specific investigation. . . .

(a) Elements Dictated by Efficiency

The portion of *Baker v. Selden,* discussed earlier, . . . appears to be the cornerstone for what has developed into the doctrine of merger. The doctrine's underlying principle is that "[w]hen there is essentially only one way to express an idea, the idea and its expression are inseparable and copyright is no bar to copying that expression." . . . Under these circumstances, the expression is said to have "merged" with the idea itself. In order not to confer a monopoly of the idea upon the copyright owner, such expression should not be protected. . . .

. . . [W]hen one considers the fact that programmers generally strive to create programs "that meet the user's needs in the most efficient manner," Menell, at 1052, the applicability of the merger doctrine to computer programs becomes compelling. In the context of computer program design, the concept of efficiency is akin to deriving the most concise logical proof or formulating the most succinct mathematical computation. Thus, the more efficient a set of modules are, the more closely they approximate the idea or process embodied in that particular aspect of the program's structure.

While, hypothetically, there might be a myriad of ways in which a programmer may effectuate certain functions within a program,—i.e., express the idea embodied in a given subroutine—efficiency concerns may so narrow the practical range of choice as to make only one or two forms of expression workable options. *See* 3 Nimmer §13.03[F][2], at 13-63; *see also Whelan,* 797 F.2d at 1243 n.43 ("It is true that for certain tasks there are only a very limited number of file structures available, and in such cases the structures might not be copyrightable. . . ."). Of course, not all program structure is informed by efficiency concerns. *See* Menell, at 1052 (besides efficiency, simplicity related to user accommodation has become a programming priority). It follows that in order to determine whether the merger doctrine precludes copyright protection to an aspect of a program's structure that is so oriented, a court must inquire "whether the use of *this particular set* of modules is necessary efficiently to implement that part of the program's process" being implemented. Englund, at 902. If the answer is yes, then the expression represented by the programmer's choice of a specific module or group of modules has merged with their underlying idea and is unprotected. *Id.* at 902-03. . . .

(b) Elements Dictated By External Factors

We have stated that where "it is virtually impossible to write about a particular historical era or fictional theme without employing certain 'stock' or standard literary devices," such expression is not copyrightable. *Hoehling v. Universal City Studios, Inc.,* 618 F.2d 972, 979 (2d Cir.), *cert. denied,* 449 U.S. 841 (1980). . . .

Professor Nimmer points out that "in many instances it is virtually impossible to write a program to perform particular functions in a specific computing environment without employing standard techniques." 3 Nimmer §13.03[F][3], at 13-65. This is a result of the fact that a programmer's freedom of design choice is often circumscribed by extrinsic considerations such as (1) the mechanical specifications of the computer on which a particular program is intended to run; (2) compatibility requirements of other programs with which a program is designed to operate in conjunction; (3) computer manufacturers' design standards; (4) demands of the industry being serviced; and (5) widely accepted programming practices within the computer industry. *Id.* at 13-66-71. . . .

Building upon . . . existing case law, we conclude that a court must also examine the structural content of an allegedly infringed program for elements that might have been dictated by external factors.

(c) Elements taken From the Public Domain

Closely related to the non-protectability of *scenes a faire,* is material found in the public domain. Such material is free for the taking and cannot be appropriated by a single author even though it is included in a copyrighted work. . . .

Step Three: Comparison

The third and final step of the test for substantial similarity that we believe appropriate for non-literal program components entails a comparison. Once a court has sifted out all elements of the allegedly infringed program which are "ideas" or are dictated by efficiency or external factors, or taken from the public domain, there may remain a core of protectible expression. In terms of a work's copyright value, this is the golden nugget. . . .

3) Policy Considerations . . .

Feist [*Publ'ns, Inc. v. Rural Tel. Serv. Co.,* 499 U.S. 340 (1991)] teaches that substantial effort alone cannot confer copyright status on an otherwise uncopyrightable work. As we have discussed, despite the fact that significant labor and expense often goes into computer program flow-charting and debugging, that process does not always result in inherently protectable expression. . . .

Furthermore, we are unpersuaded that the test we approve today will lead to the dire consequences for the computer program industry that plaintiff and some *amici* predict. To the contrary, serious students of the industry have been highly critical of the sweeping scope of copyright protection engendered by . . . [a rule that] "enables first comers to 'lock up' basic programming techniques as implemented in programs to perform particular tasks." Menell, at 1087.

To be frank, the exact contours of copyright protection for non-literal program structure are not completely clear. We trust that as future cases are decided, those limits will become better defined. Indeed, it may well be that the Copyright Act serves as a relatively weak barrier against public access to the theoretical interstices behind a program's source and object codes. This results from the hybrid nature of a computer program, which, while it is literary expression, is also a highly functional, utilitarian component in the larger process of computing.

Generally, we think that copyright registration—with its indiscriminating availability—is not ideally suited to deal with the highly dynamic technology of computer science. Thus far, many of the decisions in this area reflect the courts' attempt to fit the proverbial square peg in a round hole. The district court, *see Computer Assocs.,* 775 F. Supp. [544, 560 (E.D.N.Y. 1991)], and at least one commentator have suggested that patent registration, with its exacting up-front novelty and non-obviousness requirements, might be the more appropriate rubric of protection for intellectual property of this kind. . . .

In the meantime, Congress has made clear that computer programs are literary works entitled to copyright protection. Of course, we shall abide by these instructions, but in so doing we must not impair the overall integrity of copyright law. . . .

NOTES AND QUESTIONS

1. The *Altai* case was the second major case to address claims of infringement based on software's structure. The first was *Whelan Assocs., Inc. v. Jaslow Dental Lab., Inc.,* 797 F.2d 1222 (3d Cir. 1986), *cert. denied,* 479 U.S. 1031 (1987). The *Whelan* court stated that the "idea" of a program is its "purpose or function . . . *and everything that is not necessary to that purpose or function would be part of the expression of the idea.*" *Id.* at 1236 (emphasis added). The *Altai* court and most others have rejected *Whelan's* test for separating idea from expression in the case of program structure as overbroad—i.e., it provides "too much" protection for a program's structure. Do you agree with this criticism? Why, or why not? Do you think *Altai* provides too much, too little, or the right amount of copyright protection?

2. The *Altai* court points out that much, if not most, of the investment in creating a program is made in designing it. Actual coding is not that expensive. If the practical implication of *Altai* is that copyright protects the literal code but little of the structure that the programmer designed, is that result consistent with the policy bases for copyright discussed in Chapter 1?

3. Is *Altai* consistent with *Apple Computer, Inc. v. Franklin Computer Corp., supra* Section C.1, in its treatment of compatibility considerations? Economic and legal commentators often describe the software market as characterized by network effects. In its simplest terms, a network market is one in which the value of a product grows as more people purchase it. As the number of applications running on an operating system increases, the value of the system goes up, causing more developers to write applications for it and more consumers to adopt it, and so on. Commentators call this phenomenon a "positive feedback effect," and that effect helps to explain why large first-mover advantages characterize network markets. (For a more detailed description of network effects, see Mark A. Lemley & David McGowan, *Legal Implications of Network Economic Effects,* 86 Cal. L. Rev. 479 (1998).) In *Altai,* many similarities between the programs at issue were dictated by a third party not involved in the litigation—IBM. IBM had the dominant share of the mainframe operating system market and both Altai and Computer Associates sought to have their programs run on the most popular IBM systems. Thus, both had to write their scheduling programs to fit with IBM's interfaces, necessitating at least some similarities between the two programs. In contrast, in *Apple*, Franklin essentially sought to "clone" Apple's operating system and compete directly with it by offering a compatible environment for applications written for the Apple operating system.

As *Altai* and *Apple* suggest, there are different kinds of compatibility. Should it matter to the copyright analysis what type of compatibility is involved in a particular case?

4. From whose perspective and at what point in time would you assess whether compatibility is required? Is the relevant perspective that of the first programmer or the alleged infringer, and is the relevant time that of creation of the initial program or that of the alleged infringement? What policy goals might be furthered by adopting the alleged infringer's perspective?

5. For an argument that policy considerations do not support copyright protection for a program's structure, see Dennis S. Karjala, *The Relative Roles of Patent and Copyright in the Protection of Computer Programs*, 17 J. Marshall J. Computer & Info. L. 41 (1998). Nevertheless, Professor Karjala applauds the *Altai* decision. In his view, "[i]n fact, a court that applies the *Computer Associates* filters honestly will soon realize that *everything* in the [structure, sequence and organization of a program] is present for the purpose of making the program function better, that is, for efficiency reasons. Consequently, under *Computer Associates*, after filtering for efficiency there is very little, if anything, to protect besides the code." *Id.* at 54.

Do you agree? Are efficiency considerations monolithic? Put differently, programmers make efficiency trade-offs. Some, for example, might choose to optimize use of the computer's memory or processing capacity; others the usability of the program. Program structure varies depending on those choices. Do such choices evidence the sort of creativity that copyright protects?

PRACTICE EXERCISE: ADVOCACY

PrintCo, a manufacturer of digital printers, includes in its printers a toner loading program that measures the amount of toner remaining in a cartridge. The program, which consists of eight commands, also prevents a PrintCo printer from accepting a toner cartridge that does not include the proper set of complementary commands. ChipComm sells microprocessors containing the PrintCo code to third-party toner cartridge manufacturers, enabling them to sell consumers low-cost cartridges that are compatible with PrintCo printers. PrintCo has sued ChipComm for copyright infringement. Your firm has been retained to represent ChipComm. The supervising attorney has asked you to draft a Rule 12(b)(6) motion to dismiss. Prepare an outline of the points you will cover in the motion and draft the argument headings.

3. User Interfaces

The question of copyright protection for user interfaces also has bedeviled courts, commentators, and software firms. The next case addresses that question.

≡ ***Lotus Development Corp. v. Borland International, Inc.***
≡ *49 F.3d 807 (1st Cir. 1995)*, aff'd by an equally divided court, *516 U.S. 233 (1996)*

STAHL, J:

This appeal requires us to decide whether a computer menu command hierarchy is copyrightable subject matter. In particular, we must decide whether, as the district court held, plaintiff-appellee Lotus Development Corporation's copyright in Lotus 1-2-3, a computer spreadsheet program, was infringed by defendant-appellant Borland International, Inc., when Borland copied the Lotus 1-2-3 menu command hierarchy into its Quattro and Quattro Pro computer spreadsheet programs.

I. Background

Lotus 1-2-3 is a spreadsheet program that enables users to perform accounting functions electronically on a computer. Users manipulate and control the program via a series of menu commands, such as "Copy," "Print," and "Quit." Users choose commands either by highlighting them on the screen or by typing their first letter. In all, Lotus 1-2-3 has 469 commands arranged into more than 50 menus and submenus.

Lotus 1-2-3, like many computer programs, allows users to write what are called "macros." By writing a macro, a user can designate a series of command choices with a single macro keystroke. Then, to execute that series of commands in multiple parts of the spreadsheet, rather than typing the whole series each time, the user only needs to type the single pre-programmed macro keystroke, causing the program to recall and perform the designated series of commands automatically. Thus, Lotus 1-2-3 macros shorten the time needed to set up and operate the program.

Borland released its first Quattro program to the public in 1987, after Borland's engineers had labored over its development for nearly three years. Borland's objective was to develop a spreadsheet program far superior to existing programs, including Lotus 1-2-3. In Borland's words, "[f]rom the time of its initial release . . . Quattro included enormous innovations over competing spreadsheet products."

. . . Borland included in its Quattro and Quattro Pro version 1.0 programs "a *virtually identical* copy of the entire 1-2-3 menu tree." *Borland III*, 831 F. Supp. [202, 212 (D. Mass. 1993)] (emphasis in original). In so doing, Borland did not copy any of Lotus's underlying computer code; it copied only the words and structure of Lotus's menu command hierarchy. Borland included the Lotus menu command hierarchy in its programs to make them compatible with Lotus 1-2-3 so that spreadsheet users who were already familiar with Lotus 1-2-3 would be able to switch to the Borland programs without having to learn new commands or rewrite their Lotus macros.

In its Quattro and Quattro Pro version 1.0 programs, Borland achieved compatibility with Lotus 1-2-3 by offering its users an alternate user interface, the "Lotus Emulation Interface." By activating the Emulation Interface, Borland users would see the Lotus menu commands on their screens and could interact with Quattro or Quattro Pro as if using Lotus 1-2-3, albeit with a slightly different looking screen and with many Borland options not available on Lotus 1-2-3. In effect, Borland allowed users to choose how they wanted to communicate with Borland's spreadsheet programs: either by using menu commands designed by Borland, or by using the commands and command structure used in Lotus 1-2-3 augmented by Borland-added commands. . . .

. . . [Lotus sued Borland for copyright infringement. Both parties moved for summary judgment.] [T]he district court denied Borland's motion and granted Lotus's motion in part. The district court ruled that the Lotus menu command hierarchy was copyrightable expression because

> [a] very satisfactory spreadsheet menu tree can be constructed using different commands and a different command structure from those of Lotus 1-2-3. In fact, Borland has constructed just such an alternate tree for use in Quattro Pro's native mode. Even if one holds the arrangement of menu commands constant, it is possible to generate literally millions of satisfactory menu trees by varying the menu commands employed.

Borland II, 799 F. Supp. [203, 217 (D. Mass. 1992)]. The district court demonstrated this by offering alternate command words for the ten commands that appear in Lotus's main menu. *Id*. For example, the district court stated that "[t]he 'Quit' command could be named 'Exit' without any other modifications." . . . Because so many variations were possible, the district court concluded that the Lotus developers' choice and arrangement of command terms, reflected in the Lotus menu command hierarchy, constituted copyrightable expression. . . .

Immediately following the district court's summary judgment decision, Borland removed the Lotus Emulation Interface from its products. . . . Borland retained what it called the "Key Reader" in its Quattro Pro programs. Once turned on, the Key Reader allowed Borland's programs to understand and perform some Lotus 1-2-3 macros. . . . Accordingly, people who wrote or purchased macros to shorten the time needed to perform an operation in Lotus 1-2-3 could still use those macros in Borland's programs. The district court permitted Lotus to file a supplemental complaint alleging that the Key Reader infringed its copyright. . . .

. . . [T]he district court found that Borland's Key Reader file included "a virtually identical copy of the Lotus menu tree structure, but represented in a different form and with first letters of menu command names in place of the full menu command names." . . . The district court held that "the Lotus menu structure, organization, and first letters of the command names . . . constitute part of the protectible expression found in [Lotus 1-2-3]." Accordingly, the district court held that with its Key Reader, Borland had infringed Lotus's copyright. . . . The district court then entered a permanent injunction against Borland from which Borland appeals.

This appeal concerns only Borland's copying of the Lotus menu command hierarchy into its Quattro programs. . . .

II. Discussion

On appeal, Borland does not dispute that it factually copied the words and arrangement of the Lotus menu command hierarchy. Rather, Borland argues that it "lawfully copied the unprotectable menus of Lotus 1-2-3." . . .

B. Matter of First Impression

Whether a computer menu command hierarchy constitutes copyrightable subject matter is a matter of first impression in this court. . . .

Borland vigorously argues, however, that the Supreme Court charted our course more than 100 years ago when it decided *Baker v. Selden,* 101 U.S. 99 (1879). . . . Borland argues:

> The facts of *Baker v. Selden,* and even the arguments advanced by the parties in that case, are identical to those in this case. The only difference is that the "user interface" of Selden's system was implemented by pen and paper rather than by computer.

. . . Borland even supplied this court with a video that, with special effects, shows Selden's paper forms "melting" into a computer screen and transforming into Lotus 1-2-3.

We do not think that *Baker v. Selden* is nearly as analogous to this appeal as Borland claims. . . . [U]nlike Selden, Lotus does not claim to have a monopoly over its accounting system. Rather, this appeal involves Lotus's monopoly over the commands it uses to operate the computer. Accordingly, this appeal is not, as Borland contends, "identical" to *Baker v. Selden.*

C. Altai . . .

While the *Altai* test may provide a useful framework for assessing the alleged nonliteral copying of computer code, we find it to be of little help in assessing whether the literal copying of a menu command hierarchy constitutes copyright infringement. . . .

D. The Lotus Menu Command Hierarchy: A "Method of Operation"

Borland argues that the Lotus menu command hierarchy is uncopyrightable because it is a system, method of operation, process, or procedure foreclosed from copyright protection by 17 U.S.C. §102(b). . . .

We think that "method of operation," as that term is used in §102(b), refers to the means by which a person operates something, whether it be a car, a food processor, or a computer. Thus a text describing how to operate something would not extend copyright protection to the method of operation itself; other people would be free to employ that method and to describe it in their own words. Similarly, if a new method of operation is used rather than described, other people would still be free to employ or describe that method.

We hold that the Lotus menu command hierarchy is an uncopyrightable "method of operation." The Lotus menu command hierarchy provides the means by which users control and operate Lotus 1-2-3. If users wish to copy material, for example, they use the "Copy" command. If users wish to print material, they use the "Print" command. Users must use the command terms to tell the computer what to do. Without the menu command hierarchy, users would not be able to access and control, or indeed make use of, Lotus 1-2-3's functional capabilities.

The Lotus menu command hierarchy does not merely explain and present Lotus 1-2-3's functional capabilities to the user; it also serves as the method by which the program is operated and controlled. The Lotus menu command hierarchy is different from the Lotus long prompts, for the long prompts are not necessary to the operation of the program; users could operate Lotus 1-2-3 even if there were no long prompts.[9] The Lotus menu command hierarchy is also different from the Lotus screen displays, for users need not "use" any expressive aspects of the screen displays in order to operate Lotus 1-2-3; because the way the screens look has little bearing on how users control the program, the screen displays are not part of Lotus 1-2-3's "method of operation."[10] The Lotus menu command hierarchy is also different from the underlying computer code, because while code is necessary for the program to work, its precise formulation is not. In other words, to offer the same capabilities as Lotus 1-2-3, Borland did not have to copy Lotus's underlying code (and indeed it did not); to allow users to operate its programs in substantially the same way, however, Borland had to copy the Lotus menu command hierarchy. Thus the Lotus 1-2-3 code is not a[n] uncopyrightable "method of operation." . . .

Accepting the district court's finding that the Lotus developers made some expressive choices in choosing and arranging the Lotus command terms, we nonetheless hold that that expression is not copyrightable because it is part of Lotus 1-2-3's "method of operation." We do not think that "methods of operation" are limited to abstractions; rather, they are the means by which a user operates something. If specific words are essential to operating something, then they are part of a "method of operation" and, as such, are unprotectable. This is so whether they must be highlighted, typed in, or even spoken, as computer programs no doubt will soon be controlled by spoken words.

The fact that Lotus developers could have designed the Lotus menu command hierarchy differently is immaterial to the question of whether it is a "method of operation." In other words, our initial inquiry is not whether the Lotus menu command hierarchy incorporates any expression. Rather, our initial inquiry is whether the Lotus menu command hierarchy is a "method of operation."

9. As the Lotus long prompts [(short text appearing under the highlighted menu command that explains what the command does)] are not before us on appeal, we take no position on their copyrightability, although we do note that a strong argument could be made that the brief explanations they provide "merge" with the underlying idea of explaining such functions. . . .

10. As they are not before us on appeal, we take no position on whether the Lotus 1-2-3 screen displays constitute original expression capable of being copyrighted.

Concluding, as we do, that users operate Lotus 1-2-3 by using the Lotus menu command hierarchy, and that the entire Lotus menu command hierarchy is essential to operating Lotus 1-2-3, we do not inquire further whether that method of operation could have been designed differently. The "expressive" choices of what to name the command terms and how to arrange them do not magically change the uncopyrightable menu command hierarchy into copyrightable subject matter. . . .

In many ways, the Lotus menu command hierarchy is like the buttons used to control, say, a video cassette recorder ("VCR"). . . . Users operate VCRs by pressing a series of buttons that are typically labelled "Record, Play, Reverse, Fast Forward, Pause, Stop/Eject." That the buttons are arranged and labeled does not make them a "literary work," nor does it make them an "expression" of the abstract "method of operating" a VCR via a set of labeled buttons. Instead, the buttons are themselves the "method of operating" the VCR.

When a Lotus 1-2-3 user chooses a command, either by highlighting it on the screen or by typing its first letter, he or she effectively pushes a button. . . .

That the Lotus menu command hierarchy is a "method of operation" becomes clearer when one considers program compatibility. Under Lotus's theory, if a user uses several different programs, he or she must learn how to perform the same operation in a different way for each program used. For example, if the user wanted the computer to print material, then the user would have to learn not just one method of operating the computer such that it prints, but many different methods. We find this absurd. The fact that there may be many different ways to operate a computer program, or even many different ways to operate a computer program using a set of hierarchically arranged command terms, does not make the actual method of operation chosen copyrightable; it still functions as a method for operating the computer and as such is uncopyrightable.

Consider also that users employ the Lotus menu command hierarchy in writing macros. Under the district court's holding, if the user wrote a macro to shorten the time needed to perform a certain operation in Lotus 1-2-3, the user would be unable to use that macro to shorten the time needed to perform that same operation in another program. Rather, the user would have to rewrite his or her macro using that other program's menu command hierarchy. This is despite the fact that the macro is clearly the user's own work product. . . .

We also note that in most contexts, there is no need to "build" upon other people's expression, for the ideas conveyed by that expression can be conveyed by someone else without copying the first author's expression. In the context of methods of operation, however, "building" requires the use of the precise method of operation already employed; otherwise, "building" would require dismantling, too. Original developers are not the only people entitled to build on the methods of operation they create; anyone can. Thus, Borland may build on the method of operation that Lotus designed and may use the Lotus menu command hierarchy in doing so. . . .

BOUDIN, J., concurring:. . . .
Most of the law of copyright and the "tools" of analysis have developed in the context of literary works such as novels, plays, and films. In this milieu, the principal problem—simply stated, if difficult to resolve—is to stimulate creative expression

without unduly limiting access by others to the broader themes and concepts deployed by the author. The middle of the spectrum presents close cases; but a "mistake" in providing too much protection involves a small cost: subsequent authors treating the same themes must take a few more steps away from the original expression.

The problem presented by computer programs is fundamentally different in one respect. The computer program is a *means* for causing something to happen; it has a mechanical utility, an instrumental role, in accomplishing the world's work. Granting protection, in other words, can have some of the consequences of *patent* protection in limiting other people's ability to perform a task in the most efficient manner. Utility does not bar copyright (dictionaries may be copyrighted), but it alters the calculus.

Of course, the argument *for* protection is undiminished, perhaps even enhanced, by utility: if we want more of an intellectual product, a temporary monopoly for the creator provides incentives for others to create other, different items in this class. But the "cost" side of the equation may be different where one places a very high value on public access to a useful innovation that may be the most efficient means of performing a given task. Thus, the argument for extending protection may be the same; but the stakes on the other side are much higher. . . .

Requests for the protection of computer menus present the concern with fencing off access to the commons in an acute form. A new menu may be a creative work, but over time its importance may come to reside more in the investment that has been made by *users* in learning the menu and in building their own mini-programs—macros—in reliance upon the menu. Better typewriter keyboard layouts may exist, but the familiar QWERTY keyboard dominates the market because that is what everyone has learned to use. . . .

Thus, to assume that computer programs are just one more new means of expression, like a filmed play, may be quite wrong. The "form"—the written source code or the menu structure depicted on the screen—look hauntingly like the familiar stuff of copyright; but the "substance" probably has more to do with problems presented in patent law or, as already noted, in those rare cases where copyright law has confronted industrially useful expressions. Applying copyright law to computer programs is like assembling a jigsaw puzzle whose pieces do not quite fit. . . .

. . . [I]t is very hard to see that Borland has shown any interest in the Lotus menu except as a fall-back option for those users already committed to it by prior experience or in order to run their own macros using 1-2-3 commands. At least for the amateur, accessing the Lotus menu in the Borland Quattro or Quattro Pro program takes some effort.

Put differently, it is unlikely that users who value the Lotus menu for its own sake—independent of any investment they have made themselves in learning Lotus' commands or creating macros dependent upon them—would choose the Borland program in order to secure access to the Lotus menu. Borland's success is due primarily to other features. Its rationale for deploying the Lotus menu bears the ring of truth.

Now, any use of the Lotus menu by Borland is a commercial use and deprives Lotus of a portion of its "reward," in the sense that an infringement claim if allowed would increase Lotus' profits. But this is circular reasoning: broadly speaking, every limitation on copyright or privileged use diminishes the reward of the original creator. Yet not every writing is copyrightable or every use an infringement. The provision of reward is one concern of copyright law, but it is not the only one. If it were, copyrights would be perpetual and there would be no exceptions.

The present case is an unattractive one for copyright protection of the menu. The menu commands (*e.g.,* "print," "quit") are largely for standard procedures that Lotus did not invent and are common words that Lotus cannot monopolize. What is left is the particular combination and sub-grouping of commands in a pattern devised by Lotus. This arrangement may have a more appealing logic and ease of use than some other configurations; but there is a certain arbitrariness to many of the choices.

If Lotus is granted a monopoly on this pattern, users who have learned the command structure of Lotus 1-2-3 or devised their own macros are locked into Lotus, just as a typist who has learned the QWERTY keyboard would be the captive of anyone who had a monopoly on the production of such a keyboard. Apparently, for a period Lotus 1-2-3 has had such sway in the market that it has represented the *de facto* standard for electronic spreadsheet commands. So long as Lotus is the superior spreadsheet—either in quality or in price—there may be nothing wrong with this advantage.

But if a better spreadsheet comes along, it is hard to see why customers who have learned the Lotus menu and devised macros for it should remain captives of Lotus because of an investment in learning made by the users and not by Lotus. Lotus has already reaped a substantial reward for being first; assuming that the Borland program is now better, good reasons exist for freeing it to attract old Lotus customers: to enable the old customers to take advantage of a new advance, and to reward Borland in turn for making a better product. If Borland has not made a better product, then customers will remain with Lotus anyway.

Thus, for me the question is not whether Borland should prevail but on what basis. . . .

A different approach would be to say that Borland's use is privileged because, in the context already described, it is not seeking to appropriate the advances made by Lotus' menu; rather, having provided an arguably more attractive menu of its own, Borland is merely trying to give former Lotus users an option to exploit their own prior investment in learning or in macros. . . .

. . . Some solutions (e.g., a very short copyright period for menus) are not options at all for courts but might be for Congress. In all events, the choices are important ones of policy, not linguistics, and they should be made with the underlying considerations in view.

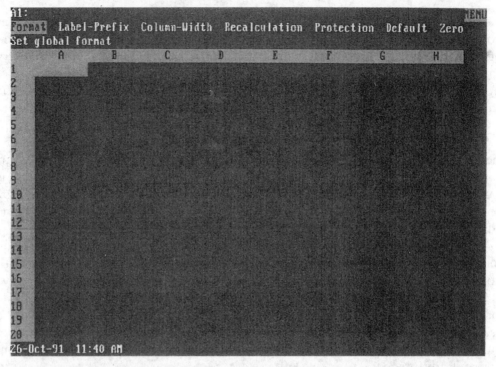

Lotus 1-2-3 release 2.01 Screen Captures © 1987 IBM Corporation. Used with permission
of IBM Corporation. Lotus and 1-2-3 are trademarks of IBM Corporation,
in the United States, other countries, or both.
Screen Shot of Lotus 1-2-3 2.01

NOTES AND QUESTIONS

1. How is the approach of the *Lotus* court different from that of the *Altai* court?
Do you agree with the *Lotus* court that *Altai*'s analysis was not relevant in its case?
(Try applying the *Altai* test to the Lotus menu command hierarchy.) Would the
Apple court have agreed with the *Lotus* court's approach?

2. Should the law use different tests for the copyrightability of program-to-
program interfaces and user interfaces? Keep in mind that the term "interface" is
broad, and "program-to program interfaces" may encompass how applications con-
nect to operating systems, how modules of the same program communicate with
each other, and even sometimes how operating systems work with hardware. The
nature and extent of compatibility considerations may vary depending on the type of
interface. Should that matter to the copyright analysis?

3. As the *Lotus* case illustrates, somewhat weaker network effects characterize the
market for applications. Customers invest time and money in acquiring the skills
necessary to operate a system. If customers cannot transfer that investment to another
system, at least some of them will not incur the costs to switch even to a superior system.
Should this sort of lock-in have any relevance to the copyright analysis? Does permitting
a second comer to copy a successful user interface penalize the first company for its
success? For an excellent discussion of the *Lotus* case and the problems of "user holdup"
and lock-in, see Robert P. Merges, *Who Owns the Charles River Bridge?: Intellectual
Property and Competition in the Software Industry* (working paper 1999), http://
www.law.berkeley.edu/institutes/bclt/pubs/merges/criver.pdf.

4. Many user interfaces use icons instead of words—consider the mail icon on an Android operating system as compared to the mail icon on a Windows system. What if Lotus had used fancifully designed icons instead of words on its menus for program commands, and a competitor copied those icons? Should the result of a copyrightability analysis change? An entire industry is devoted to analyzing the most efficient way to design user interfaces. Would idea and expression inevitably merge?

5. User interfaces can also be registered as pictorial or graphic works. In such cases, the copyright owner can assert two separate infringement claims. Consider first the Lotus user interface and then the Android or iPhone user interface in light of the materials you read in Section A *supra* on useful articles with pictorial, graphic, or sculptural aspects. How does the copyrightability analysis change?

4. Application Programming Interfaces

In the years since both *Altai* and *Lotus*, computer programming languages and programming practices have continued to evolve. Programming languages similar to the one at issue in *Altai* are still in use, but newer programming languages are structured to be compatible with a wide array of hardware and software configurations. This is done using what are known as virtual machines: sets of programming routines and subroutines that interact directly with the specific hardware and software configuration of a type of device (e.g., computer, tablet, smartphone, etc.), thus insulating the application programs themselves from the specific details of the hardware and software environments in which those applications are actually running. Application programming interfaces (APIs) define doorways to the various preexisting functions contained in the virtual machine. Additionally, programmers often employ reusable blocks of code—i.e., code written once to perform particular functions and then incorporated into many products; APIs define doorways to this code as well. Sometimes the code is available as open source; other times it is licensed by the original author. To what extent are APIs and their component parts copyrightable? Consider the following case:

> ### LOOKING FORWARD
>
> Open source software is software developed using contracts to reorder the default entitlements specified by copyright law in a way that permits copying, distribution, and modification by members of the public. We discuss open source software in Chapter 12.

 Oracle America, Inc. v. Google Inc.
750 F.3d 1339 (Fed. Cir. 2014),
petition for cert. filed, *83 U.S.L.W. 3240 (U.S. Oct. 6, 2014)*
(No. 14-410)

O'MALLEY, J.: . . .

Background

A. *The Technology*

Sun [, the predecessor of Oracle,] developed the Java "platform" for computer programming and released it in 1996. The aim was to relieve programmers from the burden of writing different versions of their computer programs for different operating systems or devices. "The Java platform, through the use of a virtual machine, enable[d] software developers to write programs that [we]re able to run on different types of computer hardware without having to rewrite them for each different type." [*Oracle Am., Inc. v. Google Inc.*, 872 F. Supp. 2d 974, 977 (N.D. Cal. 2012) ("*Copyrightability Decision*")] With Java, a software programmer could "write once, run anywhere."

The Java virtual machine ("JVM") plays a central role in the overall Java platform. The Java programming language itself—which includes words, symbols, and other units, together with syntax rules for using them to create instructions—is the language in which a Java programmer writes source code. . . . In the Java system, "source code is first converted into 'bytecode,' an intermediate form, before it is then converted into binary machine code by the Java virtual machine" that has been designed for that device. *Id.* The Java platform includes the "Java development kit (JDK), javac compiler, tools and utilities, runtime programs, class libraries (API packages), and the Java virtual machine." *Id.* at 977 n.2.

Sun wrote a number of ready-to-use Java programs to perform common computer functions and organized those programs into groups it called "packages." These packages, which are the application programming interfaces at issue in this appeal, allow programmers to use the pre-written code to build certain functions into their own programs, rather than write their own code to perform those functions from scratch. They are shortcuts. Sun called the code for a specific operation (function) a "method." It defined "classes" so that each class consists of specified methods plus variables and other elements on which the methods operate. To organize the classes for users, then, it grouped classes (along with certain related "interfaces") into "packages." *See id.* at 982. . . . Oracle's collection of API packages is like a library, each package is like a bookshelf in the library, each class is like a book on the shelf, and each method is like a how-to chapter in a book. *Id.* at 977.

The original Java Standard Edition Platform ("Java SE") included "eight packages of pre-written programs." *Id.* at 982. The district court found, and Oracle concedes to some extent, that three of those packages—java.lang, java.io, and java.util—were "core" packages, meaning that programmers using the Java language had to use them "in order to make any worthwhile use of the language." *Id.* By 2008, the Java platform had more than 6,000 methods making up more than 600 classes grouped into 166 API packages. There are 37 Java API packages at issue in this appeal, three of which are the core packages identified by the district court. These packages contain thousands of individual elements, including classes, subclasses, methods, and interfaces.

Every package consists of two types of source code—what the parties call (1) declaring code; and (2) implementing code. Declaring code is the expression that identifies the prewritten function and is sometimes referred to as the "declaration" or "header." As the district court explained, the "main point is that this header line of code introduces the method body and specifies very precisely the inputs, name and other functionality." 872 F. Supp. 2d at 979-80. The expressions used by the programmer from the declaring code command the computer to execute the associated implementing code, which gives the computer the step-by-step instructions for carrying out the declared function.

To use the district court's example, one of the Java API packages at issue is "java.lang." Within that package is a class called "math," and within "math" there are several methods, including one that is designed to find the larger of two numbers: "max." The declaration for the "max" method, as defined for integers, is: "public static int max(int x, int y)," where the word "public" means that the method is generally accessible, "static" means that no specific instance of the class is needed to call the method, the first "int" indicates that the method returns an integer, and "int x" and "int y" are the two numbers (inputs) being compared. [*Id.*] at 980-82. A programmer calls the "max" method by typing the name of the method stated in the declaring code and providing unique inputs for the variables "x" and "y." The expressions used command the computer to execute the implementing code that carries out the operation of returning the larger number. . . .

B. Google's Accused Product: Android

The accused product is Android, a software platform that was designed for mobile devices and competes with Java in that market. Google acquired Android, Inc. in 2005 . . . . Later that same year, Google and Sun began discussing the possibility of Google "taking a license to use and to adapt the entire Java platform for mobile devices." [*Id.*] at 978. . . . The parties negotiated for months but were unable to reach an agreement. . . .

When the parties' negotiations reached an impasse, Google decided to use the Java programming language to design its own virtual machine—the Dalvik virtual machine ("Dalvik VM")—and "to write its own implementations for the functions in the Java API that were key to mobile devices." *Id.* Google developed the Android platform, which grew to include 168 API packages—37 of which correspond to the Java API packages at issue in this appeal.

With respect to the 37 packages at issue, "Google believed Java application programmers would want to find the same 37 sets of functionalities in the new Android system callable by the same names as used in Java." *Id.* To achieve this result, Google copied the declaring source code from the 37 Java API packages verbatim, inserting that code into parts of its Android software. In doing so, Google copied the elaborately organized taxonomy of all the names of methods, classes, interfaces, and packages—the "overall system of organized names—covering 37 packages, with over six hundred classes, with over six thousand methods." [*Id.*] at 999. The parties and district court referred to this taxonomy of expressions as the "structure, sequence, and organization" or "SSO" of the 37 packages. It is undisputed, however, that Google wrote its own implementing code except with respect to [certain functions and eight decompiled files.] . . .

Google released the Android platform in 2007, and the first Android phones went on sale the following year. Although it is undisputed that certain Android software contains copies of the 37 API packages' declaring code at issue, neither the district court nor the parties specify in which programs those copies appear.

Oracle indicated at oral argument, however, that all Android phones contain copies of the accused portions of the Android software. . . .

Discussion

I. Oracle's Appeal

It is undisputed that the Java programming language is open and free for anyone to use. Except to the limited extent noted below regarding three of the API packages, it is also undisputed that Google could have written its own API packages using the Java language. Google chose not to do that. Instead, it is undisputed that Google copied 7,000 lines of declaring code and generally replicated the overall structure, sequence, and organization of Oracle's 37 Java API packages. The central question before us is whether these elements of the Java platform are entitled to copyright protection. The district court concluded that they are not, and Oracle challenges that determination on appeal. . . .

. . . On this record, . . . we find that the district court failed to distinguish between the threshold question of what is copyrightable—which presents a low bar—and the scope of conduct that constitutes infringing activity. The court also erred by importing fair use principles, including interoperability concerns, into its copyrightability analysis.

For the reasons that follow, we conclude that the declaring code and the structure, sequence, and organization of the 37 Java API packages are entitled to copyright protection. . . .

A. Copyrightability . . .

. . . Circuit courts have struggled with, and disagree over, the tests to be employed when attempting to draw the line between what is protectable expression and what is not. When assessing whether the non-literal elements of a computer program constitute protectable expression, the Ninth Circuit has endorsed an "abstraction-filtration-comparison" test formulated by the Second Circuit and expressly adopted by several other circuits. *Sega Enters. Ltd. v. Accolade, Inc.*, 977 F.2d 1510, 1525 (9th Cir.1992). This test rejects the notion that anything that performs a function is necessarily uncopyrightable. And it also rejects as flawed [an] assumption that, once any separable idea can be identified in a computer program everything else must be protectable expression, on grounds that more than one idea may be embodied in any particular program. [*Computer Assocs. Int'l, Inc. v. Altai, Inc.*, 982 F.2d 693, 705–06 (2d Cir. 1992)].

. . . As the Second Circuit explains, this test has three steps. In the abstraction step, the court "first break[s] down the allegedly infringed program into its constituent structural parts." *Id.* at 706. In the filtration step, the court "sift[s]

> **KEEP IN MIND**
>
> The Federal Circuit does not have exclusive authority over copyright matters as it does over patent. In copyright cases, the Federal Circuit applies its interpretation of the law of the relevant regional circuit to which the case would have been appealed if it had not also involved a patent infringement claim. In *Oracle*, the relevant regional circuit is the Ninth – thus, the court applies Ninth Circuit law. Federal Circuit interpretations of circuit law are nonbinding on courts in that circuit.

out all non-protectable material," including ideas and "expression that is necessarily incidental to those ideas." *Id*. In the final step, the court compares the remaining creative expression with the allegedly infringing program.[4]

In the second step, the court is first to assess whether the expression is original to the programmer or author. The court must then determine whether the particular inclusion of any level of abstraction is dictated by considerations of efficiency, required by factors already external to the program itself, or taken from the public domain—all of which would render the expression unprotectable. These conclusions are to be informed by traditional copyright principles of originality, merger, and scenes a faire.

In all circuits, it is clear that the first step is part of the copyrightability analysis and that the third is an infringement question. It is at the second step of this analysis where the circuits are in less accord. Some treat all aspects of this second step as part of the copyrightability analysis, while others divide questions of originality from the other inquiries, treating the former as a question of copyrightability and the latter as part of the infringement inquiry. We need not assess the wisdom of these respective views because there is no doubt on which side of this circuit split the Ninth Circuit falls.

In the Ninth Circuit, while questions regarding originality are considered questions of copyrightability, concepts of merger and scenes a faire are affirmative defenses to claims of infringement. *Ets–Hokin* [*v. Skyy Spirits, Inc.*], 225 F.3d [1068,] 1082 [(9th Cir. 2000)]; *Satava v. Lowry*, 323 F.3d 805, 810 n. 3 (9th Cir. 2003) ("The Ninth Circuit treats scenes a faire as a defense to infringement rather than as a barrier to copyrightability.")....

With these principles in mind, we turn to the trial court's analysis and judgment and to Oracle's objections thereto. While the trial court mentioned the abstraction-filtration-comparison test when describing the development of relevant law, it did not purport to actually apply that test. Instead, it moved directly to application of familiar principles of copyright law when assessing the copyrightability of the declaring code and interpreted Section 102(b) to preclude copyrightability for any functional element "essential for interoperability" "regardless of its form." *Copyrightability Decision*, 872 F.Supp.2d at 997.

Oracle asserts that all of the trial court's conclusions regarding copyrightability are erroneous. . . . For the reasons explained below, we agree with Oracle . . . .

1. Declaring Source Code

First, Oracle argues that the district court erred in concluding that each line of declaring source code is completely unprotected under the merger and short phrases doctrines. . . . Google argues that, because there is only one way to write the names and declarations, the merger doctrine bars copyright protection. . . .

4. Importantly, this full analysis only applies where a copyright owner alleges infringement of the non-literal aspects of its work. Where "admitted literal copying of a discrete, easily-conceptualized portion of a work" is at issue—as with Oracle's declaring code—a court "need not perform a complete abstraction-filtration-comparison analysis" and may focus the protectability analysis on the filtration stage, with attendant reference to standard copyright principles.

a. Merger . . .

Under the merger doctrine, a court will not protect a copyrighted work from infringement if the idea contained therein can be expressed in only one way. For computer programs, "this means that when specific [parts of the code], even though previously copyrighted, are the only and essential means of accomplishing a given task, their later use by another will not amount to infringement." *Altai*, 982 F.2d at 708 (citation omitted). We have recognized, however, applying Ninth Circuit law, that the "unique arrangement of computer program expression . . . does not merge with the process so long as alternate expressions are available." *Atari* [*Games Corp. v. Nintendo of Am.*, Inc., 975 F.2d 832, 840 (Fed. Cir. 1992)]. . . .

. . . The evidence showed that Oracle had "unlimited options as to the selection and arrangement of the 7000 lines Google copied." Appellant Br. 50. Using the district court's "java.lang.Math.max" example, Oracle explains that the developers could have called it any number of things, including "Math. maximum" or "Arith. larger." This was not a situation where Oracle was selecting among preordained names and phrases to create its packages. As the district court recognized, moreover, "the Android method and class names could have been different from the names of their counterparts in Java and still have worked." *Copyrightability Decision*, 872 F. Supp. 2d at 976. Because "alternative expressions [we]re available," there is no merger. *See Atari*, 975 F.2d at 840.

We further find that the district court erred in focusing its merger analysis on the options available to Google at the time of copying. It is well-established that copyrightability and the scope of protectable activity are to be evaluated at the time of creation, not at the time of infringement. The focus is, therefore, on the options that were available to Sun/Oracle at the time it created the API packages. Of course, once Sun/Oracle created "java.lang.Math.max," programmers who want to use that particular package have to call it by that name. But, as the court acknowledged, nothing prevented Google from writing its own declaring code, along with its own implementing code, to achieve the same result. In such circumstances, the chosen expression simply does not merge with the idea being expressed.[7] . . .

b. Short Phrases

The district court also found that Oracle's declaring code consists of uncopyrightable short phrases. Specifically, the court concluded that, "while the Android method and class names could have been different from the names of their counterparts in Java and still have worked, copyright protection never extends to names or short phrases as a matter of law." *Copyrightability Decision*, 872 F. Supp. 2d at 976.

---

7. The district court did not find merger with respect to the structure, sequence, and organization of Oracle's Java API packages. Nor could it, given the court's recognition that there were myriad ways in which the API packages could have been organized. Indeed, the court found that the SSO is original and that "nothing in the rules of the Java language . . . required that Google replicate the same groupings." *Copyrightability Decision*, 872 F.Supp.2d at 999. As discussed below, however, the court nonetheless found that the SSO is an uncopyrightable "method of operation."

. . . The [district] court failed to recognize, however, that the relevant question for copyrightability purposes is not whether the work at issue contains short phrases—as literary works often do—but, rather, whether those phrases are creative. And, by dissecting the individual lines of declaring code at issue into short phrases, the district court further failed to recognize that an original combination of elements can be copyrightable.

By analogy, the opening of Charles Dickens' *A Tale of Two Cities* is nothing but a string of short phrases. Yet no one could contend that this portion of Dickens' work is unworthy of copyright protection because it can be broken into those shorter constituent components. The question is not whether a short phrase or series of short phrases can be extracted from the work, but whether the manner in which they are used or strung together exhibits creativity.

Although the district court apparently focused on individual lines of code, Oracle is not seeking copyright protection for a specific short phrase or word. Instead, the portion of declaring code at issue is 7,000 lines, and Google's own "Java guru" conceded that there can be "creativity and artistry even in a single method declaration." Because Oracle "exercised creativity in the selection and arrangement" of the method declarations when it created the API packages and wrote the relevant declaring code, they contain protectable expression that is entitled to copyright protection. Accordingly, we conclude that the district court erred in applying the short phrases doctrine to find the declaring code not copyrightable.

c. Scenes a Faire

. . . In the computer context, "the scene a faire doctrine denies protection to program elements that are dictated by external factors such as 'the mechanical specifications of the computer on which a particular program is intended to run' or 'widely accepted programming practices within the computer industry.'".

The trial court rejected Google's reliance on the scenes a faire doctrine. It did so in a footnote, finding that Google had failed to present evidence to support the claim that either the grouping of methods within the classes or the code chosen for them "would be so expected and customary as to be permissible under the scenes a faire doctrine." *Copyrightability Decision*, 872 F. Supp. 2d at 999 n. 9. . . .

On appeal, Google refers to scenes a faire concepts briefly, as do some amici, apparently contending that, because programmers have become accustomed to and comfortable using the groupings in the Java API packages, those groupings are so commonplace as to be indispensable to the expression of an acceptable programming platform. As such, the argument goes, they are so associated with the "idea" of what the packages are accomplishing that they should be treated as ideas rather than expression. *See* Br. of Amici Curiae Rackspace US, Inc., et al. at 19–22.

Google cannot rely on the scenes a faire doctrine as an alternative ground upon which we might affirm the copyrightability judgment of the district court. . . . [A]s noted, like merger, in the Ninth Circuit, the scenes a faire doctrine is a component of the infringement analysis [not the copyrightability analysis].

Second, Google has not objected to the trial court's conclusion that Google failed to make a sufficient factual record to support its contention that the groupings and code chosen for the 37 Java API packages were driven by external factors or premised on features that were either commonplace or essential to the idea being expressed. . . .

. . . Google's reliance on the doctrine below and the amici reference to it here are premised on a fundamental misunderstanding of the doctrine. Like merger, the focus of the scenes a faire doctrine is on the circumstances presented to the creator, not the copier. The court's analytical focus must be upon the external factors that dictated Sun's selection of classes, methods, and code—not upon what Google encountered at the time it chose to copy those groupings and that code. . . .

2. The Structure, Sequence, and Organization of the API Packages

The district court found that the SSO of the Java API packages is creative and original, but nevertheless held that it is a "system or method of operation . . . and, therefore, cannot be copyrighted" under 17 U.S.C. §102(b). *Copyrightability Decision*, 872 F. Supp. 2d at 976-77. In reaching this conclusion, the district court seems to have relied upon language contained in a First Circuit decision: *Lotus Development Corp. v. Borland International, Inc.*, 49 F.3d 807 (1st Cir. 1995), *aff'd without opinion by equally divided court*, 516 U.S. 233 (1996). . . .

On appeal, Oracle argues that the district court's reliance on *Lotus* is misplaced because it is distinguishable on its facts and is inconsistent with Ninth Circuit law. We agree. First, while the defendant in *Lotus* did not copy any of the underlying code, Google concedes that it copied portions of Oracle's declaring source code verbatim. Second, the *Lotus* court found that the commands at issue there (copy, print, etc.) were not creative, but it is undisputed here that the declaring code and the structure and organization of the API packages are both creative and original. Finally, while the court in *Lotus* found the commands at issue were "essential to operating" the system, it is undisputed that—other than perhaps as to the three core packages—Google did not need to copy the structure, sequence, and organization of the Java API packages to write programs in the Java language.

More importantly, however, the Ninth Circuit has not adopted the court's "method of operation" reasoning in *Lotus*, and we conclude that it is inconsistent with binding precedent. Specifically, we find that *Lotus* is inconsistent with Ninth Circuit case law recognizing that the structure, sequence, and organization of a computer program is eligible for copyright protection where it qualifies as an expression of an idea, rather than the idea itself. *See Johnson Controls[, Inc. v. Phoenix Control Sys.]*, 886 F.2d [1173,] 1175-76 [(9th Cir. 1989)]. And, while the court in *Lotus* held "that expression that is part of a 'method of operation' cannot be copyrighted," 49 F.3d at 818, this court—applying Ninth Circuit law—reached the exact opposite conclusion, finding that copyright protects "the expression of [a] process or method," *Atari*, 975 F.2d at 839.

We find, moreover, that the hard and fast rule set down in *Lotus* and employed by the district court here—i.e., that elements which perform a function can never be copyrightable—is at odds with the Ninth Circuit's endorsement of the abstraction-filtration-comparison analysis discussed earlier. As the Tenth Circuit concluded in expressly rejecting the *Lotus* "method of operation" analysis, in favor of the Second

Circuit's abstraction-filtration-comparison test, "although an element of a work may be characterized as a method of operation, that element may nevertheless contain expression that is eligible for copyright protection." *Mitel,* [*Inc. v. Iqtel, Inc.,* 124 F.3d 1366, 1372 (10th Cir. 1997)]. Specifically, the court found that Section 102(b) "does not extinguish the protection accorded a particular expression of an idea merely because that expression is embodied in a method of operation at a higher level of abstraction." *Id.* . . .

Courts have likewise found that classifying a work as a "system" does not preclude copyright for the particular expression of that system.

Here, the district court recognized that the SSO "resembles a taxonomy," but found that "it is nevertheless a command structure, a system or method of operation—a long hierarchy of over six thousand commands to carry out preassigned functions." *Copyrightability Decision,* 872 F. Supp. 2d at 999–1000.[12] In other words, the court concluded that, although the SSO is expressive, it is not copyrightable because it is also functional. The problem with the district court's approach is that computer programs are by definition functional—they are all designed to accomplish some task. . . . If we were to accept the district court's suggestion that a computer program is uncopyrightable simply because it "carr[ies] out pre-assigned functions," no computer program is protectable. . . .

While it does not appear that the Ninth Circuit has addressed the precise issue, we conclude that a set of commands to instruct a computer to carry out desired operations may contain expression that is eligible for copyright protection. *See Mitel,* 124 F.3d at 1372. We agree with Oracle that, under Ninth Circuit law, an original work—even one that serves a function—is entitled to copyright protection as long as the author had multiple ways to express the underlying idea. . . .

As the district court acknowledged, Google could have structured Android differently and could have chosen different ways to express and implement the functionality that it copied. Specifically, the court found that "the very same functionality could have been offered in Android without duplicating the exact command structure used in Java." *Copyrightability Decision,* 872 F. Supp. 2d at 976. The court further explained that Google could have offered the same functions in Android by "rearranging the various methods under different groupings among the various classes and packages." *Id.* The evidence showed, moreover, that Google designed many of its own API packages from scratch, and, thus, could have designed its own corresponding 37 API packages if it wanted to do so.

Given the court's findings that the SSO is original and creative, and that the declaring code could have been written and organized in any number of ways and still have achieved the same functions, we conclude that Section 102(b) does not bar the packages from copyright protection just because they also perform functions.

---

12. This analogy by the district court is meaningful because taxonomies, in varying forms, have generally been deemed copyrightable. *See, e.g., Practice Mgmt. Info. Corp. v. Am. Med. Ass'n,* 121 F.3d 516, 517-20 (9th Cir. 1997); *Am. Dental* [*Ass'n v. Delta Dental Ass'n,* 126 F.3d 977, 978-81 (7th Cir. 1997)].

3. Google's Interoperability Arguments are Irrelevant to Copyrightability . . .

Because copyrightability is focused on the choices available to the plaintiff at the time the computer program was created, the relevant compatibility inquiry asks whether the plaintiff's choices were dictated by a need to ensure that its program worked with existing third-party programs. Whether a defendant later seeks to make its program interoperable with the plaintiff's program has no bearing on whether the software the plaintiff created had any design limitations dictated by external factors. Stated differently, the focus is on the compatibility needs and programming choices of the party claiming copyright protection—not the choices the defendant made to achieve compatibility with the plaintiff's program. . . .

> **LOOKING FORWARD**
>
> In a part of its opinion not reproduced here, the *Oracle* court noted that Google's arguments regarding interoperability would be relevant to a fair use analysis. We consider fair use in Chapter 10.

Given this precedent, we conclude that the district court erred in focusing its interoperability analysis on Google's desires for its Android software. *See Copyrightability Decision*, 872 F. Supp. 2d at 1000 ("Google replicated what was necessary to achieve a degree of interoperability" with Java.). Whether Google's software is "interoperable" in some sense with any aspect of the Java platform (although as Google concedes, certainly not with the JVM) has no bearing on the threshold question of whether Oracle's software is copyrightable. It is the interoperability and other needs of Oracle—not those of Google—that apply in the copyrightability context, and there is no evidence that when Oracle created the Java API packages at issue it did so to meet compatibility requirements of other pre-existing programs.

. . . Google wanted to capitalize on the fact that software developers were already trained and experienced in using the Java API packages at issue. . . . Google's interest was in accelerating its development process by "leverag[ing] Java for its existing base of developers." Although this competitive objective might be relevant to the fair use inquiry, we conclude that it is irrelevant to the copyrightability of Oracle's declaring code and organization of the API packages.

Finally, to the extent Google suggests that it was entitled to copy the Java API packages because they had become the effective industry standard, we are unpersuaded. Google cites no authority for its suggestion that copyrighted works lose protection when they become popular, and we have found none. In fact, the Ninth Circuit has rejected the argument that a work that later becomes the industry standard is uncopyrightable. *See Practice Mgmt. Info. Corp. v. Am. Med. Ass'n*, 121 F.3d 516, 520 n.8 (9th Cir. 1997). Google was free to develop its own API packages and to "lobby" programmers to adopt them. Instead, it chose to copy Oracle's declaring code and the SSO to capitalize on the preexisting community of programmers who were accustomed to using the Java API packages. That desire has nothing to do with copyrightability. For these reasons, we find that Google's industry standard argument has no bearing on the copyrightability of Oracle's work. . . .

III. *Google's Policy–Based Arguments*

Many of Google's arguments, and those of some amici, appear premised on the belief that copyright is not the correct legal ground upon which to protect intellectual property rights to software programs; they opine that patent protection for such programs, with its insistence on non-obviousness, and shorter terms of protection, might be more applicable, and sufficient. . . .

Importantly for our purposes, the Supreme Court has made clear that "[n]either the Copyright Statute nor any other says that because a thing is patentable it may not be copyrighted." *Mazer v. Stein*, 347 U.S. 201 (1954). . . . Until either the Supreme Court or Congress tells us otherwise, we are bound to respect the Ninth Circuit's decision to afford software programs protection under the copyright laws. We thus decline any invitation to declare that protection of software programs should be the domain of patent law, and only patent law. . . .

NOTES AND QUESTIONS

1. What is the appropriate focus of the merger analysis in the context of software? The court identifies two types of source code—declaring code and implementing code. Should they be treated the same way in the merger analysis? Do you agree with the court that compatibility considerations should not affect the copyrightability analysis but rather may become relevant only later on, in the infringement analysis?

2. Do you agree with the court that an individual line of code is not a short phrase? Is the short phrases doctrine useful in assessing the copyrightability of source code? A snippet of code may be quite small but quite complex. Should that matter to the copyrightability analysis?

3. Does the *scenes a faire* doctrine translate well into the software context? If so, from whose perspective should the doctrine be considered—the initial developer's or the alleged infringer's?

4. Should the court have treated the three "core" packages differently for purposes of assessing copyrightability? According to the court,

> It seems possible that the merger doctrine, when properly analyzed, would exclude the three packages identified by the district court as core packages from the scope of actionable infringing conduct. This would be so if the Java authors, at the time these packages were created, had only a limited number of ways to express the methods and classes therein if they wanted to write in the Java language. In that instance, the idea may well be merged with the expression in these three packages. Google did not present its merger argument in this way below and does not do so here, however. Indeed, Google does not try to differentiate among the packages for purposes of its copyrightability analysis . . .

Oracle America, Inc. v. Google, Inc., 750 F.3d 1339, 1362 (Fed. Cir. 2014), *petition for cert. filed*, 83 U.S.L.W. 3240 (U.S. Oct. 6, 2014) (No. 14-410). Did Google make a mistake in litigating the case? How would you hold with respect to the copyrightability of the three core packages?

5. Do you agree with the *Oracle* court's holding regarding the copyrightability of Java's structure? Is that holding consistent with *Altai*?

6. In a portion of the *Oracle* opinion not excerpted above, the court indicated that Oracle and Google were unable to conclude a licensing arrangement because Google did not want "to make the implementation of its programs compatible with the Java Virtual Machine or interoperable with other Java programs." *Id.* at 1350. Instead, Google wanted the apps written by developers for Java to run without modification on Android. Review the Notes and Questions after both *Altai* and *Lotus* that discuss the different types of compatibility. What type of compatibility was Google interested in? Did Franklin have similar motivations in the *Apple* case? Should any of this matter to the copyrightability analysis?

Note on Alternative Modes of Protection for Computer Software

As you have seen in this section, much of the difficulty courts have had in applying copyright law to computer programs arises from computer programs' particular characteristics as works that behave and perform a useful function. In *Altai*, the court suggested that patent protection for software might be more suitable than copyright. In addition, state trade secret protection continues to operate in the background for some aspects of software. Another option would be for Congress to enact *sui generis* legislation that specifically addresses software. As you read the following materials, consider whether any of these options has advantages over copyright protection and what, if anything, Congress should do.

a) Patents

The Patent Act provides that "processes" meeting the Act's requirements are patentable subject matter. 35 U.S.C. §101. Early in the life of the software industry, both legal precedent and policy considerations presented barriers to patenting software, although firms were filing applications anyway to keep their options open. Courts had long held that neither mathematical algorithms nor methods of doing business were patentable. A program is, of course, a type of mathematical algorithm, and many programs implemented methods of doing business. On the policy side, many commentators, including CONTU, questioned whether patent protection for software might unduly restrict competition and inhibit desirable dissemination of information. *See* Pamela Samuelson, Benson *Revisited: The Case Against Patent Protection for Computer Programs and Other Computer-Related Inventions*, 39 Emory L.J. 1025 (1990); CONTU Report at 32-33. Yet what is a computer program if not a "process" for accomplishing a useful result?

The Supreme Court case that paved the way for recognition of aspects of computer programs as patentable subject matter was *Diamond v. Diehr*, 450 U.S. 175 (1981). In *Diehr*, the Court upheld a patent on a process that used a well-known equation (i.e., a mathematical algorithm) to monitor the temperature inside a synthetic rubber mold and produce a useful result—cured rubber. A series of decisions from the exclusive court for patent appeals, the Court of Appeals for the Federal Circuit, gradually whittled away at *Diehr*'s ostensible requirement that a process including a software-based algorithm must produce a physical result to be patentable. Ultimately, in *Bilski v. Kappos*, 561 U.S. 593 (2010), the Supreme Court clarified that a process may be eligible for patent protection even if it is not tied to a machine and it does not transform an article to a different state or thing. *Id.* at 603-04. While patent law, like copyright, does not protect ideas, it may protect the applications of abstract ideas "'to a new and useful end,'" *Alice Corp. v. CLS Bank Int'l*, 134 S. Ct. 2347, 2354 (2014). The difficulty comes in distinguishing an abstract idea from a patentable claim. Under both *Bilski* and *Alice*, an idea does not become patentable merely because it is implemented on a general purpose computer.

Note, finally, that patent protection for some types of functionality instantiated in software may not be available on a worldwide basis because a number of countries have restricted the scope of software patent protection. Article 52(2) of the European Patent Convention (EPC) states that "schemes, rules and methods for performing mental acts, playing games or doing business, and programs for computers" shall not be regarded as inventions.

b) Trade Secrets

The CONTU Report concluded that the availability of copyright protection for software should not preclude trade secret protection, and software firms have continued to take advantage of the trade secrecy laws. CONTU Report at 35. The 1976 Act's abandonment of the publication requirement for copyright protection enabled software firms to claim both copyright and trade secret protection simultaneously. The Copyright Office took an additional step to help firms maintain secrecy by adopting less rigorous deposit requirements for computer programs in which copyright was registered. *See* 37 C.F.R. §202.20.

Trade secrecy law protects only against misappropriation of the secret. This includes discovery of the secret by "improper means" such as corporate espionage or inducing breach of contract, but does not include independent creation. It also does not include discovery of the information through reverse engineering of a publicly available product. *See* Unif. Trade Secrets Act §1 (defining misappropriation). The rule allowing reverse engineering makes it difficult to maintain trade secrecy protection in features of products that are distributed on a widespread basis and, as you will learn in Chapter 10, courts have held that copyright law allows reverse engineering of software in certain circumstances. For all of these reasons, many modern software firms have adopted the tactic of attempting to prevent reverse engineering by attaching licenses to every copy of their programs. Software firms also use contracts to control what departing employees can take with them to their new employers. The interaction of federal copyright law and state trade secrecy and contract laws raises difficult questions, which are addressed in Chapters 12 and 15.

Note, finally, that a grant of patent protection for a particular functionality precludes continued trade secret protection for that functionality because the public disclosures required by the patent law eliminate the secrecy required under trade secrecy law.

c) *Sui Generis* Protection

In Europe, the Member States of what is now the EU did not have uniform laws protecting intellectual property rights in software. In 1991, the European Community adopted its Directive on the Legal Protection of Computer Programs to harmonize the disparate approaches and ensure adequate protection. *See* Council Directive of 14 May 1991 on the Legal Protection of Computer Programs, 1991 O.J. (L-122) 42 (EU Software Directive). One express goal of the EU Software Directive was to create a legal environment that would encourage the growth of a European software industry. At the time, the software industry in Europe lagged far behind that of the United States.

Many provisions of the EU Software Directive resemble U.S. law. The EU Software Directive provides that Member States must protect computer programs as literary works under copyright law. *See id.*, art. 1(1). Computer programs must be original to merit protection but the originality standard does not include an assessment of "the qualitative or aesthetic merits of the program." *See id.*, pmbl. As in the United States, the idea/expression distinction applies to computer programs as to other copyrighted works. *See id.*, art. 1(2).

The EU Software Directive contains some other provisions that do not have direct statutory counterparts in U.S. law. For example, it lists certain acts that a licensor of computer software may not forbid. A licensor may not restrict the right of a person to make a back-up copy. *See id.*, art. 5(2). Nor, ostensibly, may it restrict a person's right to observe, study, and test the functioning of a program to understand its ideas so long as such person is engaging in a permitted act. *See id.*, art. 5(3). Under certain circumstances, the EU Software Directive also permits a person in rightful possession of a program to reverse engineer it by decompiling the object code to obtain information necessary to ensure interoperability between the decompiled program and another independently created one. *See id.*, art. 6. The right to engage in such conduct is limited to cases in which the necessary information is not available elsewhere. *See id.*, art. 6(1).

Some commentators have recommended that the United States consider adopting a *sui generis* regime of legal protection for software that departs from the copyright model. For one such proposal, featuring a shortened term of protection, greater leeway for reverse engineering, and a system of liability rules, see Pamela Samuelson et al., *A Manifesto Concerning the Legal Protection of Computer Programs,* 94 Colum. L. Rev. 2308, 2417-18 (1994).

NOTES AND QUESTIONS

1. Software patents have posed difficulties for the PTO, both because the abstract nature of the claimed inventions makes software patent applications particularly difficult to evaluate and because the PTO has had difficulty simply processing the flood of patent applications claiming software inventions. *See generally* James Bessen & Michael J. Meurer, Patent Failure: How Judges, Bureaucrats, and Lawyers Put Innovators at Risk 187-214 (2008). Estimates of the number of software patents vary, but they surely number in the hundreds of thousands. *See* Christina Mulligan & Timothy B. Lee, *Scaling the Patent System*, 68 N.Y.U. Ann. Surv. Am. L. 289, 304 (2012) ("[T]he number of software patents issued [] is around 40,000 in a typical year (and growing)."). Many argue that the sheer number of applications, combined with gaps in examiner expertise, has resulted in the grant of some patents that are invalid—i.e., the invention claimed does not, in fact, meet the Patent Act's requirements of novelty, utility, and nonobviousness. Rather than challenging such patents, however, many companies will pay to license them. Why do you think that is the case? What is the cost to society of invalid patents?

2. If you were a software developer who had developed new and useful functionality, how would you evaluate the relative benefits and costs of maintaining trade secrecy versus seeking patent protection?

3. Why do you think the EU permits the limited copying involved in decompilation when the decompiler's goal is to achieve interoperability? What behavior on the part of dominant providers might the decompilation provision of the EU Software Directive be intended to induce?

4. In light of what you have learned in this section, do you think that developing a *sui generis* model of legal protection for software should be a priority for the United States? Is there anything else that Congress should do regarding intellectual property protection for software?

III

THE STATUTORY RIGHTS OF COPYRIGHT OWNERS

5

The Reproduction Right and the Right to Prepare Derivative Works

In previous chapters, we considered the subject matter that copyright does and does not protect and the rules that govern the inception of copyright ownership. Many of the cases you read in those chapters involved claims of copyright infringement. In §501(a), the Act provides, "Anyone who violates any of the exclusive rights of the copyright owner as provided by sections 106 through 122 . . . is an infringer of the copyright. . . ."

A plaintiff in a copyright infringement case has the initial burden of producing sufficient evidence demonstrating (1) ownership (or other entitlement to enforce) of a valid copyright and (2) violation of one of the exclusive rights reserved to the copyright owner by §106. If the plaintiff meets its burden, the defendant may then raise one or more defenses.

Section §106 sets forth the exclusive rights of a copyright owner:

§106. Exclusive rights in copyrighted works

Subject to sections 107 through 122, the owner of copyright under this title has the exclusive rights to do and to authorize any of the following:

> **KEEP IN MIND**
>
> Ultimately, the decision whether to sue for infringement of any of the exclusive rights is a business decision. The copyright owner will have to consider a number of factors, including the expense of litigation, the probability of winning the case (and whether that would occur in a time frame that makes any remedy meaningful) and the public relations consequences of bringing suit against the particular defendant.

   (1) to reproduce the copyrighted work in copies or phonorecords;
   (2) to prepare derivative works based upon the copyrighted work;
   (3) to distribute copies or phonorecords of the copyrighted work to the public by sale or other transfer of ownership, or by rental, lease, or lending;
   (4) in the case of literary, musical, dramatic, and choreographic works, pantomimes, and motion pictures and other audiovisual works, to perform the copyrighted work publicly;

(5) in the case of literary, musical, dramatic, and choreographic works, pantomimes, and pictorial, graphic, or sculptural works, including the individual images of a motion picture or other audiovisual work, to display the copyrighted work publicly; and

(6) in the case of sound recordings, to perform the copyrighted work publicly by means of a digital audio transmission.

In this chapter, we focus on §§106(1)-(2).

A. REPRODUCTION

Historically, the exclusive right to reproduce the copyrighted work in copies or phonorecords has been understood as the core right of the copyright owner. Policymakers have perceived copying as one of the most serious threats to creative incentives and, as a practical matter, copying is often implicated when a second comer wishes to use a copyrighted work in some way, permissible or otherwise.

In this section, we consider first the relatively easy case of exact copying. We then turn to the doctrine of *de minimis* copying: Generally, only copying that is material can give rise to infringement. We conclude the section by considering the harder cases that involve nonexact copies and questions of "substantial similarity."

1. The Exact Copy

Generally, the most straightforward cases under §106(1) are those that involve exact copying—e.g., the defendant obtains a copy of the plaintiff's novel, photocopies it and sells the copies in competition with the plaintiff. Absent some defense, the defendant will be liable for infringing the reproduction right.

a. The Basics

Traditionally, exact copying cases have included two groups. In the first group are the cases sometimes called "piracy" cases—e.g., the case above involving the photocopied novel, or cases involving the defendant who has burned 5,000 unauthorized copies of a chart-topping album onto CDs or has replicated 10,000 unauthorized copies of a popular software program. For cases in this group, infringement liability is usually clear. The difficult issues, if any, are procedural or remedial, including discovery issues that arise during the process of tracing the infringing copies back to their source, issues concerning the computation of damages, and so on.

> **KEEP IN MIND**
>
> The conduct of selling unauthorized reproductions of the copyrighted work would infringe the exclusive right to distribute the work in copies under §106(3). The copyright rights are both cumulative and separable–i.e., one may infringe more than one right or one may infringe by violating only one of the §106 rights.

The second group of exact copying cases concerns very different sorts of conduct. The defendants are engaged in arguably privileged activities, and infringement liability hinges on the rules that govern the various limitations and exceptions to copyright (set forth primarily in §§107-122) or the rules provided by other law (e.g., contract). The Act's defenses serve a variety of purposes:

- Public policy defenses—Some sections of the Act, like §107 (fair use), §108 (permitting certain copying by nonprofit libraries and archives), and §121 (permitting certain reproductions for the blind or others with disabilities), provide defenses to liability under §106(1) because Congress has decided that copyright policy and/or other public policies such as freedom of expression are best served by permitting the described uses.
- Defenses based on the type of work—Some sections of the Act limit the scope of copyright in particular types of works. For example, as you know from Chapter 4, §113 limits the scope of copyright in pictorial, graphic, and sculptural works and §120 limits the scope of copyright in architectural works. As we discuss in this chapter, §117 limits the scope of copyright in computer programs. Chapter 7 discusses the limitations that §§114-16 place on the scope of copyright in sound recordings and certain musical works.
- Broadcast industry defenses—Sections 112 and 118 exclude qualifying private and public broadcasters, respectively, from infringement liability for making "ephemeral" copies—i.e., copies that aid in the transmission of certain otherwise licensed broadcast content. Section 111 exempts certain secondary transmissions of broadcast programming by cable systems from liability and §§119 and 122 address secondary transmissions by satellite of distant and local television programming respectively.

More recently, the advent of digital technologies has created an additional group of exact copying cases, involving copies that are made automatically during the processes of reading, viewing, hearing, and using copyrighted works in digital form. Re-read §106(1) and note especially its reference to "copies or phonorecords." As you know from Chapter 2, "copies" and "phonorecords" are material objects in which works are fixed. As described in *Cartoon Network LP v. CSC Holdings, Inc.*, Chapter 2.A.1, *supra*, courts have held that temporary reproduction of a computer program in RAM that enables use of the program creates a "copy" for purposes of the Copyright Act. *See, e.g., MAI Systems v. Peak Computer, Inc.*, 991 F.2d 511 (9th Cir. 1993), *cert. dismissed*, 510 U.S. 1033 (1994). That conclusion has sweeping implications for the routine practices of computer and Internet users with respect to all kinds of copyrighted works. Whenever you visit a website, you

> **COMPARATIVE PERSPECTIVE**
>
> An EU Directive provides an exception from liability for "[t]emporary acts of reproduction . . . which are transient or incidental [and] an integral and essential part of a technological process" when the sole purpose is to enable either "a transmission in a network between third parties by an intermediary" or "a lawful use of a work," and when the temporary reproductions "have no independent economic significance." Directive 2001/29/EC of the European Parliament and of the Council of 22 May 2001 on the harmonization of certain aspects of copyright and related rights in the Information Society, 2001 O.J. (L. 167) 10, art. 5(1).

are able to view the materials hosted there because your browser software copies them into your device's RAM. If surfing the web makes one a copyright infringer, there are millions of infringements occurring every hour of every day.

Section 117 of the Act permits certain reproductions of computer programs, but its scope is limited, sheltering from liability only the "owner of a copy of a computer program" and certain maintenance organizations. Moreover, §117's exceptions apply only to computer programs. They provide no protection for routine reproductions in RAM of other copyrighted works.

NOTES AND QUESTIONS

1. Review the *Cartoon Network* court's discussion of the reference to "transitory duration" in the statutory definition of "fixed." When you use your Internet browser to view copyrighted content that has been placed on the Internet, do the copies in your computer's RAM qualify as fixed? If you forward an email or retweet a message, have you reproduced the email or tweet in a copy?

For material posted on the Internet by copyright owners or their licensees, an implied license may shield users from liability for temporary copying. This may help explain why the temporary copying decisions have not spawned a large amount of litigation or fundamentally altered the way the Internet functions. It also may point to a need to rethink the wording of some of the Act's most basic definitions. What do you think?

2. Would any of the acts described in Question 1 constitute infringement under the EU Directive?

3. Read §117 now. Then examine the license agreement for the operating system or word processing program installed on your PC. According to the license agreement, do you "own" your copy of that software? At the time *MAI Systems* was decided, §117 excluded nonowners (i.e., licensees) from its benefits. Congress subsequently amended §117 to authorize third-party service organizations to maintain or repair any computer "that lawfully contains an authorized copy" of the software if certain conditions are met; therefore, the specific conduct at issue in *MAI* no longer constitutes infringement. During the process that led to enactment of this amendment, Congress considered, but ultimately declined to adopt, broader language that would have extended the privileges authorized by §117 to any "rightful possessor" of a copy of a computer program. Should Congress have adopted that language instead?

PRACTICE EXERCISE: DRAFTING

You are a staff counsel to the House Committee on the Judiciary. A committee member has asked you to draft an exemption from infringement liability for automatic reproduction of copyrighted works in a computer's RAM. Draft the proposed legislation, along with an outline of the points to be included in the legislative history. What constituencies are likely to oppose the bill, and how will you address their concerns?

b. "Innocent" Infringement

Examine §106 again. Notice that it is not a defense to a charge of infringement (whether of the exclusive right to reproduce or any of the other §106 rights) for the infringer to claim she did not know that the material was protected by copyright law or that she did not intend to infringe. This strict liability approach often comes as a surprise to law students, not to mention laypeople, particularly in light of the substantial copying that occurs in the course of using the Internet.

The Act does provide a few different references to an "innocent infringement" defense. Section 405(b) provides:

> Any person who innocently infringes a copyright, in reliance upon an authorized copy or phonorecord from which the copyright notice has been omitted and which was publicly distributed by authority of the copyright owner before the effective date of the Berne Convention Implementation Act of 1988, incurs no liability for actual or statutory damages . . . before receiving actual notice that registration for the work has been made . . . if such person proves that he or she was misled by the omission of notice.

LOOKING FORWARD

The Berne Convention Implementation Act made the Act's notice provisions permissive. A copyright owner may choose to include notice of copyright, but doing so is not a condition of copyright protection. You will learn about the BCIA and copyright formalities in Chapter 11.

---

17 U.S.C. §405(b).

In addition, §504(c)(2) provides that "[i]n a case where the infringer sustains the burden of proving, and the court finds, that such infringer was not aware and had no reason to believe that his or her acts constituted an infringement . . . the court in its discretion may reduce the award of statutory damages to a sum of not less than $200." Sections 401(d) and 402(d) indicate, however, that this argument is unavailable if the copies or phonorecords at issue contained proper notice of copyright.

NOTES AND QUESTIONS

1. Review Question 1, Section 5.A.1.a *supra*, and consider the case of an Internet user who views or downloads material that was posted without the copyright owner's authorization. Would you expect the defense provided in §405(b) to be available to many such individuals?

2. Should an innocent infringement defense be available whenever copyrighted content has been distributed or made available on the Internet without notice? Would that effectively reinstate a copyright notice requirement?

3. Are there any other circumstances in which you would afford an innocent infringement defense?

c. Diving Deeper: Ephemeral Copies Under Sections 112 and 118

The challenges to copyright law caused by automatic reproduction in computer memory are not entirely unprecedented. Within the broadcast industries (e.g., television and radio), simultaneous recording of broadcast transmissions has been common practice for years. Although such reproduction is not technically inevitable as it is in the case of RAM copies, it serves a variety of purposes that are important from a business perspective. (Can you think of what those might be?) Congress responded to this practice by enacting §§112 and 118 of the 1976 Act, which exclude qualifying broadcasters from infringement liability for making certain "ephemeral" copies.

According to the legislative history of §112, Congress considered ephemeral recordings to include "copies or phonorecords of a work made for purposes of later transmission by a broadcasting organization legally entitled to transmit the work." H.R. Rep. No. 94-1476, 94th Cong., 2d Sess. 101 (1976), *reprinted in* 1976 U.S.C.C.A.N. 5659, 5716. The issue, as Congress framed it, was whether a broadcaster licensed to perform or display a work should be able to record the performance or display to aid in its transmission. *See id.* Congress concluded that "practical exigencies of broadcasting" supported an exemption from liability for such a copy but that the *scope* of the exemption remained controversial. *Id.*

Section 112(a) exempts a "transmitting organization" entitled to transmit a display or performance of the work to the public from liability for making one copy or phonorecord of a "transmission program" (defined in §101) embodying the display or performance. This exemption from liability is conditioned on the transmitting organization's refraining from making any other copy, and is limited to use of the authorized copy solely for the "transmitting organization's own transmissions within its local service area." 17 U.S.C. §112(a). The transmitting organization may not retain the copy of the transmission program for more than six months after the date of the transmission program's first broadcast to the public unless that copy is used solely for archival purposes. *See id.* The exemption does not apply to motion pictures and audiovisual works. Furthermore, under §112(g), the transmission program is not eligible for copyright protection as a derivative work under §103 unless the owner of the copyright in the preexisting material consents. Subsections 112(b)-(d) define more lenient exemptions for the reproduction of ephemeral copies by governmental bodies and other nonprofit organizations in certain circumstances. In 1998, as part of its enactment of the Digital Millennium Copyright Act (DMCA), Congress amended §112 by adding special provisions governing ephemeral copies of sound recordings. We consider the rules governing reproduction and public performance of sound recordings in Chapter 7.

Section 118(d) provides an additional exemption for ephemeral recordings made by a public broadcasting entity. The legislative history explains that "encouragement and support of noncommercial broadcasting is in the public interest." H.R. Rep. No. 94-1476, 94th Cong., 2d Sess. 117 (1976), *reprinted in* 1976 U.S.C.C.A.N. 5659, 5732. It also emphasizes that "public broadcasting may encounter problems not confronted by commercial broadcasting enterprises, due to such factors as the special nature of programming, repeated use of programs, and, of course, limited financial resources." *Id.*

The §118 exemption applies only to "published nondramatic musical works and published pictorial, graphic, and sculptural works." 17 U.S.C. §118(b).

As under §112, the public broadcasting entity must be entitled to transmit the work to qualify for the exemption. However, if the public broadcasting entity cannot reach a voluntary license agreement with the copyright owner, it may broadcast the work pursuant to a compulsory license, with rates and terms set by the Copyright Royalty Judges (CRJs) who are charged with administering the statutory and compulsory licenses under the Act. *Id.* §118(b); *see also* 37 C.F.R. §§253.1-253.11 (2005) (setting forth royalty rates for certain activities by public broadcasting entities). Unlike §112, §118 does not limit the number of copies or phonorecords that may be made of the transmission program embodying the work; does not restrict the exchange of copies or phonorecords between various public broadcasting companies; and does not require destruction of the copies after a period of time. Thus, these recordings are not "ephemeral" in the ordinary sense of the word. Finally, §118 permits a governmental body or nonprofit institution to record a program transmitted by a public broadcasting company for use in connection with classroom teaching activities so long as the recording entity destroys the copy within seven days from the date of transmission. *See* 17 U.S.C. §118(c).

NOTES AND QUESTIONS

1. Why do you think Congress excluded motion pictures and audiovisual works from §112? Why did it limit the §118 exemption to an even narrower class of works?

2. Is the statute's different treatment of commercial and public broadcast entities warranted in light of the underlying purposes of copyright law? Why, or why not?

3. In what ways are large industry players, like the radio and television broadcasters §§112 and 118 address, different from individuals who browse the web for whom there is no "ephemeral" copy exception from infringement liability? Should these differences matter to copyright law?

2. The *De Minimis* Copy

Under a longstanding doctrine of copyright law, courts will not find infringement if what the defendant took was *de minimis*—i.e., too little to justify a finding of copyright infringement. How should courts define "*de minimis*"? Consider the following case:

Gottlieb Development LLC v. Paramount Pictures Corp.
590 F. Supp. 2d 625 (S.D.N.Y. 2008)

CHIN, J.: In the motion picture "What Women Want," released by defendant Paramount Pictures Corporation ("Paramount") in 2000, Mel Gibson plays an advertising executive who acquires the ability to "hear" what women are thinking. In one scene, Gibson and his co-star Helen Hunt brainstorm with other employees to develop ideas for marketing certain consumer products to women. At various points during the scene, as shown, for example, in the photograph [below], a pinball machine—the "Silver Slugger"—appears in the background. The Silver Slugger is distributed by plaintiff Gottlieb Development LLC ("Gottlieb"), and Paramount used the pinball machine in the scene without Gottlieb's permission.

In this case, Gottlieb sues Paramount, alleging that Paramount engaged in [*inter alia*] copyright . . . infringement. . . . Paramount moves to dismiss the complaint pursuant to Fed. R. Civ. P. 12(b)(6), arguing principally that its use of the pinball machine was *de minimis* and therefore not actionable. I agree. Accordingly, Paramount's motion is granted and the complaint is dismissed.

Background . . .

1. The Silver Slugger

Gottlieb distributes and sells the "Silver Slugger" pinball machine. The Silver Slugger features three original designs (the "Designs"): (1) a depiction of a baseball diamond on the backglass, which is the upright back portion of the pinball machine; (2) another baseball diamond on the playfield, which is the playing surface of the machine; and (3) the layout of the parts of the playfield. The Designs are copyrighted, and Gottlieb has owned the copyrights since 1998. . . .

2. The Film

In December 2000, Paramount released the motion picture "What Women Want" (the "Film"). Paramount has shown the Film in theaters and sold and otherwise distributed it worldwide since then on DVD and VHS tapes and on television. . . . The Film runs for a little over two hours, and the scene at issue occurs approximately thirty-seven minutes into the Film.

The three-and-a-half minute scene depicts a brainstorming meeting in the office of the advertising agency. The meeting takes place in a large room with a relaxed and casual atmosphere—the room contains recliner chairs and bar stools, and on the far wall there is a large poster board prominently displaying the word "PLAY." A mini basketball hoop appears on one side of the room, and a statue of a penguin appears on the other. Approximately eight people are sitting in a circle. Behind one woman is a table soccer—or "foosball"—game. As Gibson's character pitches various ideas for advertisements, the "Silver Slugger" appears intermittently in the background, next to another pinball machine. It appears only for seconds at a time, always in the background, and always partially obscured by Gibson, a recliner chair, or a bar stool. The "Silver Slugger" does not appear in any shot by itself, nor is it part of the plot. It does not appear anywhere else in the Film, nor does any character ever refer to it. It is simply part of the background in one limited scene. . . .

Screen shot from "What Women Want"
[Image reproduced from the court's opinion.]

Discussion . . .

B. The Merits

1. Copyright Infringement

It is undisputed as a factual matter that Paramount copied the Silver Slugger, as an actual Silver Slugger appears in the Film. Paramount argues, however, that the use of the pinball machine was so trivial that the copying is not actionable.

a. Applicable Legal Standards

A copyright holder enjoys the right to reproduce and display publicly a copyrighted work. 17 U.S.C. §106(1), (5). To prevail on a claim of copyright infringement, a plaintiff must prove that . . . the infringing work is substantially similar. *Tufenkian Import/Export Ventures, Inc. v. Einstein Moomjy, Inc.*, 338 F.3d 127, 131 (2d Cir. 2003). To prove substantial similarity, a plaintiff must show "'(i) that it was protected expression in the earlier work that was copied and (ii) that the amount that was copied is 'more than de minimis.'" Id. . . .

. . . To determine whether the quantitative threshold of substantial similarity is met in cases involving visual works, courts consider the extent to which the copyrighted work is copied in the allegedly infringing work. The observability of the copyrighted work is critical, and courts will consider the length of time the copyrighted work is observable as well as factors such as focus, lighting, camera angles, and prominence. . . .

Courts in this district have dismissed copyright infringement claims on Rule 12(b)(6) motions where no substantial similarity was found.

b. Application

Based on the facts alleged in the complaint, and on a viewing of the Film, I conclude that there is no plausible claim of copyright infringement here. Although Gottlieb has sufficiently pled unauthorized copying of its Designs, the use of the Silver Slugger was *de minimis* as a matter of law. Hence, no reasonable juror could find substantial similarity in the legal sense, and thus the copying is not actionable.

The scene in question lasts only three-and-a-half minutes, and the Silver Slugger appears in the scene sporadically, for no more than a few seconds at a time. More importantly, the pinball machine is always in the background; it is never seen in the foreground. It never appears by itself or in a close-up. It is never mentioned and plays no role in the plot. It is almost always partially obscured (by Gibson and pieces of furniture), and is fully visible for only a few seconds during the entire scene. The Designs (on the backglass and playfield of the pinball machine) are never fully visible and are either out of focus or obscured. Indeed, an average observer would not recognize the Designs as anything other than generic designs in a pinball machine.

Gottlieb cites to *Ringgold* [*v. Black Entm't T.V. Inc.*, 126 F.3d 70 (2d Cir. 1997)] in support of its claim, but the facts of that case are inapposite. *Ringgold* involved the unauthorized use of a copyrighted poster in an episode of a HBO television series. The poster was shown, in whole or in part, nine times during a five-minute scene at the end of the episode. The poster (or a portion thereof) was seen for 1.86 to 4.16 seconds at a time, for a total of 26.75 seconds. In some instances, the poster appeared at the center of the screen. 126 F.3d at 72-73. As the Second Circuit held, the poster was "plainly observable." *Id.* at 76.

More importantly, there was a qualitative connection between the poster and the show. The poster included a painting depicting a Sunday School picnic held by the Freedom Baptist Church in Atlanta, Georgia, in 1909, and was intended to convey "aspects of the African-American experience in the early 1900s." *Id.* at 72. The show was "ROC," a television "sitcom" series about a middle-class African-American family living in Baltimore, and the scene in question was of a gathering in a church hall with a minister. *Id.* at 72-73. The Second Circuit noted that HBO's production staff "evidently thought that the poster was well suited as a set decoration for the African-American church scene of a ROC episode." *Id.* at 77. The Second Circuit concluded:

> From the standpoint of a quantitative assessment of the segments, the principal four-to-five second segment in which almost all of the poster is clearly visible, albeit in less than perfect focus, reenforced by the briefer segments in which smaller portions are visible, all totaling 26 to 27 seconds, are not *de minimis* copying.
> . . . The painting component of the poster is recognizable as a painting, and with sufficient observable detail for the "average lay observer" . . . to discern African-Americans in Ringold's colorful, virtually two-dimensional style. The *de minimis* threshold of actionable copying of protected expression has been crossed.

Id. at 77 (citation omitted).

In the present case, the "average lay observer" would not be able to discern any distinctive elements of Gottlieb's Designs—the baseball players clad in stylized, futuristic gear. The best that the average lay observer could make out in the background is a typical home-plate layout with baseball players arrayed around it.

The unique expressive element of the Designs is not discernable in those brief moments when the backglass is visible. . . .

Moreover, while use of a copyrighted work in the background may still be a basis for an infringement claim, *see Ringgold*, 126 F.3d at 77, where the use is *de minimis,* the copying will not be actionable, even where the work was chosen to be in the background for some thematic relevance. As the Second Circuit explained in *Ringgold*, "in some circumstances, a visual work, though selected by production staff for thematic relevance, or at least for its decorative value, might ultimately be filmed at such distance and so out of focus that a typical program viewer would not discern any decorative effect that the work of art contributes to the set." 126 F.3d at 77. Here, undoubtedly the Silver Slugger was chosen by the production staff because it fit in with the "sporty" theme of the background in the scene; but the Silver Slugger was one of numerous background items, and it was filmed in such a manner and appears so fleetingly that I conclude there is no plausible claim for copyright infringement here. Accordingly, Gottlieb's copyright infringement claim is dismissed. . . .

NOTES AND QUESTIONS

1. Where is the copy that allegedly violates the right of reproduction? Paramount bought the pinball machine—it didn't make copies of the machine in the course of producing its film–so, where's the copy?

2. What exactly is *de minimis*: how much the defendant took of plaintiff's work? How much the defendant took in relation to its own work? Something else?

> **LOOKING FORWARD**
>
> The fact pattern in the *Gottlieb* case also implicated the exclusive right to display the copyrighted work publicly (§106(5)). We discuss the public display right in Chapter 6.

3. Why shouldn't defendants be liable for *de minimis* copying? It is, after all, still copying and arguably not *de minimis* from the plaintiff's perspective. How well does the doctrine of *de minimis* copying fit with the theoretical justifications for copyright law that you studied in Chapter 1?

4. What if the distinctive elements of Gottlieb's Designs had been recognizable to the average lay observer? Copying that is more than *de minimis* occurs frequently in the motion picture and television industries. Such copying typically is licensed, with the major production companies each employing large numbers of people to negotiate and memorialize the agreements. In other words, the industry standard practice of clearing rights in recognizable content generates significant transaction costs. Do you agree that obtaining such clearance should be necessary any time an audiovisual work incorporates copyrighted content that is recognizable?

3. The Substantially Similar Copy

Section 106(1) would provide little protection to a copyright owner if the reproduction right were infringed only by exact copying. At the same time, it would provide too much protection if it were construed to hold liable those who take only unprotectable elements of the copyrighted work or who take so little of what is protected that the goals of copyright law are not implicated. In cases involving nonexact copying, therefore, the question is whether the defendant has engaged in actionable copying (i.e., copying in violation of §106(1)) by taking too much of what is protected by copyright in the plaintiff's work. Courts often refer to this inquiry as whether the plaintiff's and defendant's works are "substantially similar."

a. Copying in Fact

Sometimes, proving that the defendant violated the copyright owner's exclusive right of reproduction requires a special preliminary inquiry. Because copyright law affords the copyright owner no rights against the author of an independently created work, the plaintiff must show that the defendant in fact obtained protected expression of the plaintiff's and used that expression in the defendant's work. Put differently, the plaintiff must show that the defendant's allegedly infringing work does not simply represent expression originated by the defendant that coincidentally resembles the expression in the copyrighted work. As a shorthand, we use the term "copying in fact" to describe this showing. In many cases, especially those involving parties formerly in a contractual relationship with one another, the defendant's copying in fact is clear and undisputed. In other cases, though, proving copying in fact can be quite difficult.

Suppose that the defendant in a copyright infringement case has produced a novel that is similar, but not identical, to the plaintiff's, and that the defendant denies ever having read the plaintiff's novel. Discovery requests have failed to turn up any direct evidence of copying—e.g., evidence that the defendant purchased and read the plaintiff's book immediately before writing his own—but there are other ways that the defendant might have encountered the book. Is this a case of independent creation, or is the defendant lying (or simply forgetful)? How should the law decide? In general, one can imagine two kinds of circumstantial evidence that might be relevant to this question: (1) evidence suggesting that the defendant had *access* to the plaintiff's work; and (2) the degree of *similarity* between the two works. Should either kind of circumstantial evidence be sufficient to establish copying in fact? The cases in this subsection address these questions.

A word of caution before you begin reading the cases that follow: The terminology that courts use in assessing claims for infringement of the reproduction right can be confusing. First, some courts do not use the term "copying in fact," instead labeling the first part of the inquiry as whether the defendant "copied" the plaintiff's work. They then proceed to consider whether the defendant also engaged in "infringing copying" or "improper appropriation"—i.e., copying prohibited by §106(1). Second, the "substantial similarity" terminology is used by courts in determining whether the defendant copied enough of the plaintiff's protected expression to constitute infringement of the §106(1) reproduction right. It is also used, sometimes in combination with other factors, in determining whether the defendant copied from the plaintiff (copying in fact). Make sure that you understand which aspect of the copyright infringement inquiry the court is discussing when it uses terms like "copying" and "substantial similarity."

≣ *Three Boys Music Corp. v. Michael Bolton*
212 F.3d 477 (9th Cir. 2000), cert. denied, 531 U.S. 1126 (2001)

D. NELSON, J.: . . .

I. Background

The Isley Brothers, one of this country's most well-known rhythm and blues groups, have been inducted into the Rock and Roll Hall of Fame. They helped define the soul sound of the 1960s with songs such as "Shout," "Twist and Shout," and "This Old Heart of Mine," and they mastered the funky beats of the 1970s with songs such as "Who's That Lady," "Fight the Power," and "It's Your Thing." In 1964, the Isley Brothers wrote and recorded "Love is a Wonderful Thing" for United Artists. . . . The following year, they switched to the famous Motown label and had three top-100 hits including "This Old Heart of Mine."

Hoping to benefit from the Isley Brothers' Motown success, United Artists released "Love is a Wonderful Thing" in 1966. The song was not released on an album, only on a 45-record as a single. Several industry publications predicted that "Love is a Wonderful Thing" would be a hit. . . . On September 17, 1966, Billboard listed "Love is a Wonderful Thing" at number 110 in a chart titled "Bubbling Under the Hot 100." The song was never listed on any other Top 100 charts. In 1991, the Isley Brothers' "Love is a Wonderful Thing" was released on compact disc. *See* Isley Brothers, *The Isley Brothers—The Complete UA Sessions*, (EMI 1991).

Michael Bolton is a singer/songwriter who gained popularity in the late 1980s and early 1990s by reviving the soul sound of the 1960s. Bolton has orchestrated this soul-music revival in part by covering* old songs such as Percy Sledge's "When a Man Loves a Woman" and Otis Redding's "(Sittin' on the) Dock of the Bay." Bolton also has written his own hit songs. In early 1990, Bolton and [songwriting partner Andrew] Goldmark wrote a song called "Love is a Wonderful Thing." Bolton released it as a single in April 1991, and as part of Bolton's album, "Time, Love and Tenderness." Bolton's "Love is a Wonderful Thing" finished 1991 at number 49 on Billboard's year-end pop chart. . . .

[Three Boys Music Corp., the owner of the copyright in the Isley Brothers' song, sued Bolton, Goldmark, and their record companies for copyright infringement. After a jury trial, Three Boys was awarded $5.4 million.]

II. Discussion

Proof of copyright infringement is often highly circumstantial, particularly in cases involving music. A copyright plaintiff must prove (1) ownership of the copyright; and (2) infringement—that the defendant copied protected elements

---

* A "cover" is a recording by an artist of a musical work written by someone else and previously released on an album by a different recording artist. As we discuss in Chapter 7, *infra*, covers are the subject of a compulsory license under §115 of the Copyright Act.—EDS.

of the plaintiff's work. Absent direct evidence of copying, proof of infringement involves fact-based showings that the defendant had "access" to the plaintiff's work and that the two works are "substantially similar."

Given the difficulty of proving access and substantial similarity, appellate courts have been reluctant to reverse jury verdicts in music cases. . . .

Proof of access requires "an opportunity to view or to copy plaintiff's work." This is often described as providing a "reasonable opportunity" or "reasonable possibility" of viewing the plaintiff's work. We have defined reasonable access as "more than a 'bare possibility.'" *Jason* [*v. Fonda*, 698 F.2d 966, 967 (9th Cir. 1983)]. Nimmer has elaborated on our definition: "Of course, reasonable opportunity as here used, does not encompass any bare possibility in the sense that anything is possible. Access may not be inferred through mere speculation or conjecture. There must be a reasonable possibility of viewing the plaintiff's work—not a bare possibility." 4 Nimmer, §13.02[A], at 13-19. "At times, distinguishing a 'bare' possibility from a 'reasonable' possibility will present a close question." *Id.* at 13-20.

Circumstantial evidence of reasonable access is proven in one of two ways: (1) a particular chain of events is established between the plaintiff's work and the defendant's access to that work (such as through dealings with a publisher or record company), or (2) the plaintiff's work has been widely disseminated. *See* 4 Nimmer, §13.02[A], at 13-20-13-21; 2 Paul Goldstein, *Copyright: Principles, Law, and Practice* §8.3.1.1., at 90-91 (1989). Goldstein remarks that in music cases the "typically more successful route to proving access requires the plaintiff to show that its work was widely disseminated through sales of sheet music, records, and radio performances." 2 Goldstein, §8.3.1.1, at 91. . . .

Proof of widespread dissemination is sometimes accompanied by a theory that copyright infringement of a popular song was subconscious. Subconscious copying has been accepted since Learned Hand embraced it in a 1924 music infringement case: "Everything registers somewhere in our memories, and no one can tell what may evoke it. . . . Once it appears that another has in fact used the copyright as the source of this production, he has invaded the author's rights. It is no excuse that in so doing his memory has played him a trick." *Fred Fisher, Inc. v. Dillingham*, 298 F. 145, 147-48 (S.D.N.Y. 1924). In *Fred Fisher*, Judge Hand found that the similarities between the songs "amount[ed] to identity" and that the infringement had occurred "probably unconsciously, what he had certainly often heard only a short time before." *Id.* at 147.

In modern cases, however, the theory of subconscious copying has been applied to songs that are more remote in time. *ABKCO Music, Inc. v. Harrisongs Music, Ltd.*, 722 F.2d 988 (2d Cir. 1983) is the most prominent example. In *ABKCO*, the Second Circuit affirmed a jury's verdict that former Beatle George Harrison, in writing the song "My Sweet Lord," subconsciously copied The Chiffons' "He's So Fine," which was released six years earlier. *See id.* at 997, 999. Harrison admitted hearing "He's So Fine" in 1963, when it was number one on the Billboard charts in the United States for five weeks and one of the top 30 hits in England for seven weeks. *See id.* at 998. The court found: "the evidence, standing alone, 'by no means compels the conclusion that there was access . . . it does not compel the conclusion that there was not.'" In *ABKCO*, however, the court found that "the similarity was so striking and where access was found, the remoteness of that access provides no basis for reversal." *Id.* . . .

The Isley Brothers' access argument was based on a theory of widespread dissemination and subconscious copying. They presented evidence supporting four principal ways that Bolton and Goldmark could have had access to the Isley Brothers' "Love is a Wonderful Thing":

(1) Bolton grew up listening to groups such as the Isley Brothers and singing their songs. In 1966, Bolton and Goldmark were 13 and 15, respectively, growing up in Connecticut. Bolton testified that he had been listening to rhythm and blues music by black singers since he was 10 or 11, "appreciated a lot of Black singers," and as a youth was the lead singer in a band that performed "covers" of popular songs by black singers. . . .

(2) Three disk jockeys testified that the Isley Brothers' song was widely disseminated on radio and television stations where Bolton and Goldmark grew up. . . .

(3) Bolton confessed to being a huge fan of the Isley Brothers and a collector of their music. Ronald Isley testified that when Bolton saw Isley at the Lou Rawls United Negro College Fund Benefit concert in 1988, Bolton said, "I know this guy. I go back with him. I have all his stuff." . . .

(4) Bolton wondered if he and Goldmark were copying a song by another famous soul singer. Bolton produced a work tape attempting to show that he and Goldmark independently created their version of "Love is a Wonderful Thing." On that tape of their recording session, Bolton asked Goldmark if the song they were composing was Marvin Gaye's "Some Kind of Wonderful."

. . . [T]his is a more attenuated case of reasonable access and subconscious copying than *ABKCO*. In this case, the appellants never admitted hearing the Isley Brothers' "Love is a Wonderful Thing." . . . Nor did the Isley Brothers ever claim that Bolton's and Goldmark's song is so "strikingly similar" to the Isley Brothers' that proof of access is presumed and need not be proven.

Despite the weaknesses of the Isley Brothers' theory of reasonable access, the appellants had a full opportunity to present their case to the jury. Three rhythm and blues experts (including legendary Motown songwriter Lamont Dozier of Holland-Dozier-Holland fame) testified that they had never heard of the Isley Brothers' "Love is a Wonderful Thing." . . . Bolton also pointed out that 129 songs called "Love is a Wonderful Thing" are registered with the Copyright Office, 85 of them before 1964.

The Isley Brothers' reasonable access arguments are not without merit. Teenagers are generally avid music listeners. It is entirely plausible that two Connecticut teenagers obsessed with rhythm and blues music could remember an Isley Brothers' song that was played on the radio and television for a few weeks, and subconsciously copy it twenty years later. . . .

. . . Although we might not reach the same conclusion as the jury regarding access, we find that the jury's conclusion about access is supported by substantial evidence. . . .

Bolton and Goldmark also contend that their witnesses rebutted the Isley Brothers' prima facie case of copyright infringement with evidence of independent creation. By establishing reasonable access and substantial similarity, a copyright plaintiff creates a presumption of copying. The burden shifts to the defendant to rebut that presumption through proof of independent creation.

The appellants' case of independent creation hinges on three factors: the work tape demonstrating how Bolton and Goldmark created their song, Bolton and Goldmark's history of songwriting, and testimony that their arranger, Walter Afanasieff, contributed two of five unprotectible elements that they allegedly copied. The jury, however, heard the testimony of Bolton, Goldmark, Afanasieff, and [appellants' expert, Anthony] Ricigliano about independent creation. The work tape revealed evidence that Bolton may have subconsciously copied a song that he believed to be written by Marvin Gaye. Bolton and Goldmark's history of songwriting presents no direct evidence about this case. And Afanasieff's contributions to Bolton and Goldmark's song were described by the appellants' own expert as "very common." Once again, we refuse to disturb the jury's determination about independent creation. The substantial evidence of copying based on access and substantial similarity was such that a reasonable juror could reject this defense. . . .

> ### Selle v. Gibb
> *741 F.2d 896 (7th Cir. 1984)*

CUDAHY, J.: The plaintiff, Ronald H. Selle, brought a suit against three brothers, Maurice, Robin and Barry Gibb, known collectively as the popular singing group, the Bee Gees, alleging that the Bee Gees, in their hit tune, "How Deep Is Your Love," had infringed the copyright of his song, "Let It End." . . . [The jury found liability, but the district court granted the Bee Gees' motion for judgment notwithstanding the verdict.]

I

Selle composed his song, "Let It End," in one day in the fall of 1975. . . . He played his song with his small band two or three times in the Chicago area and sent a tape and lead sheet of the music to eleven music recording and publishing companies. Eight of the companies returned the materials to Selle; three did not respond. . . .

The Bee Gees are internationally known performers and creators of popular music. They have composed more than 160 songs; their sheet music, records and tapes have been distributed worldwide, some of the albums selling more than 30 million copies. The Bee Gees, however, do not themselves read or write music. In composing a song, their practice was to tape a tune, which members of their staff would later transcribe and reduce to a form suitable for copyrighting, sale and performance by both the Bee Gees and others.

In addition to their own testimony at trial, the Bee Gees presented testimony by their manager, Dick Ashby, and two musicians, Albhy Galuten and Blue Weaver, who were on the Bee Gees' staff at the time "How Deep Is Your Love" was composed. These witnesses described in detail how, in January 1977, the Bee Gees and several members of their staff went to a recording studio in the Chateau d'Herouville about 25 miles northwest of Paris. There the group composed at least six new songs and mixed a live album. Barry Gibb's testimony included a detailed explanation of a work tape which was introduced into evidence and played in court. This tape preserves the actual process of creation during which the brothers, and particularly Barry, created the tune of the accused song while Weaver, a keyboard player, played the tune which was hummed or sung by the brothers. Although the tape does not seem to preserve the very beginning of the process of creation, it does depict the process by which ideas, notes, lyrics and bits of the tune were gradually put together. . . .

The only expert witness to testify at trial was Arrand Parsons, a professor of music at Northwestern University who has had extensive professional experience primarily in classical music. He has been a program annotator for the Chicago Symphony Orchestra and the New Orleans Symphony Orchestra and has authored works about musical theory. Prior to this case, however, he had never made a comparative analysis of two popular songs. . . .

Dr. Parsons testified that, in his opinion, "the two songs had such striking similarities that they could not have been written independent of one another." . . . However, on several occasions he declined to say that the similarities could only have resulted from copying. . . .

III

Selle's primary contention on this appeal is that the district court misunderstood the theory of proof of copyright infringement on which he based his claim. Under this theory, copyright infringement can be demonstrated when, even in the absence of any direct evidence of access, the two pieces in question are so strikingly similar that access can be inferred from such similarity alone. . . .

One difficulty with plaintiff's theory is that no matter how great the similarity between the two works, it is not their similarity *per se* which establishes access; rather, their similarity tends to prove access in light of the nature of the works, the particular musical genre involved and other circumstantial evidence of access. . . .

As a threshold matter, therefore, it would appear that there must be at least some other evidence which would establish a reasonable possibility that the complaining work was *available* to the alleged infringer. . . .

Judge Leighton thus based his decision on what he characterized as the plaintiff's inability to raise more than speculation that the Bee Gees had access to his song. The extensive testimony of the defendants and their witnesses describing the creation process went essentially uncontradicted, and there was no attempt even to impeach their credibility. . . .

IV

. . . This decision is also supported by a more traditional analysis of proof of access based only on the proof of "striking similarity" between the two compositions. The plaintiff relies almost exclusively on the testimony of his expert witness, Dr. Parsons, that the two pieces were, in fact, "strikingly similar."[3] Yet formulating a meaningful definition of "striking similarity" is no simple task, and the term is often used in a conclusory or circular fashion. . . .

"Striking similarity" is not merely a function of the number of identical notes that appear in both compositions. An important factor in analyzing the degree of similarity of two compositions is the uniqueness of the sections which are asserted to be similar.

If the complaining work contains an unexpected departure from the normal metric structure or if the complaining work includes what appears to be an error and the accused work repeats the unexpected element or the error, then it is more likely that there is some connection between the pieces. . . .

Finally, the similarities should appear in a sufficiently unique or complex context as to make it unlikely that both pieces were copied from a prior common source, *Sheldon v. Metro-Goldwyn Pictures Corp.*, 81 F.2d 49, 54 (2d Cir.), *cert. denied*, 298 U.S. 669 (1936), or that the defendant was able to compose the accused work as a matter of independent creation, *Nichols v. Universal Pictures Corp.*, 45 F.2d 119, 122 (2d Cir. 1930), *cert. denied*, 282 U.S. 902 (1931). *See also Darrell v. Joe Morris Music Co.*, 113 F.2d 80 (2d Cir. 1940) ("simple, trite themes . . . are likely to recur spontaneously . . . and [only few] . . . suit the infantile demands of the popular ear"). . . .

. . . [T]o bolster the expert's conclusion that independent creation was not possible, there should be some testimony or other evidence of the relative complexity or uniqueness of the two compositions. Dr. Parsons' testimony did not refer to this aspect of the compositions and, in a field such as that of popular music in which all songs are relatively short and tend to build on or repeat a basic theme, such testimony would seem to be particularly necessary. . . .

[The court affirmed the district court's grant of judgment notwithstanding the verdict, concluding that the plaintiff had failed to establish a basis from which the jury could infer access by the defendants to his song, and also had not met his burden of proving striking similarity.]

Ty, Inc. v. GMA Accessories, Inc.
132 F.3d 1167 (7th Cir. 1997)

POSNER, C.J.: Ty, the manufacturer of the popular "Beanie Babies" line of stuffed animals, has obtained a preliminary injunction under the Copyright Act against the

---

3. Plaintiff also relies on the fact that both songs were played on numerous occasions in open court for the jury to hear and on the deposition testimony of one of the Bee Gees, Maurice, who incorrectly identified Theme B of Selle's song as the Bee Gees' composition, "How Deep Is Your Love."

sale by GMA . . . of "Preston the Pig" and "Louie the Cow." These are bean-bag animals manufactured by GMA that Ty contends are copies of its copyrighted pig ("Squealer") and cow ("Daisy"). Ty began selling the "Beanie Babies" line, including Squealer, in 1993, and it was the popularity of the line that induced GMA to bring out its own line of bean-bag stuffed animals three years later. GMA does not contest the part of the injunction that enjoins the sale of Louie, but asks us on a variety of grounds to vacate the other part, the part that enjoins it from selling Preston.

We have appended to our opinion five pictures found in the appellate record. The first shows Squealer (the darker pig, actually pink) and Preston (white). The second is a picture of two real pigs. The third and fourth are different views of the design for Preston that Janet Salmon submitted to GMA several months before Preston went into production. The fifth is a picture of the two bean-bag cows; they are nearly identical. A glance at the first picture shows a striking similarity between the two bean-bag pigs as well. The photograph was supplied by GMA and actually understates the similarity (the animals themselves are part of the record). The "real" Preston is the same length as Squealer and has a virtually identical snout. The difference in the lengths of the two animals in the picture is a trick of the camera. The difference in snouts results from the fact that the pictured Preston was a manufacturing botch. And GMA put a ribbon around the neck of the Preston in the picture, but the Preston that it sells doesn't have a ribbon. . . .

. . . [C]opying entails access. If, therefore, two works are so similar as to make it highly probable that the later one is a copy of the earlier one, the issue of access need not be addressed separately, since if the later work was a copy its creator must have had access to the original. *Selle v. Gibb*, [741 F.2d 896, 901 (7th Cir. 1984)]; *Gaste v. Kaiserman*, [863 F.2d 1061, 1068 (2d Cir. 1988)]; *Ferguson v. National Broadcasting Co.*, [584 F.2d 111 (5th Cir. 1978)]. Of course the inference of access, and hence of copying, could be rebutted by proof that the creator of the later work could not have seen the earlier one or (an alternative mode of access) a copy of the earlier one. But . . . we do not read our decision in *Selle* to hold or imply, in conflict with the *Gaste* decision, that no matter how closely the works resemble each other, the plaintiff must produce some (other) evidence of access. He must produce evidence of access, all right—but, as we have just said, and as is explicit in *Selle* itself, see 741 F.2d at 901, a similarity that is so close as to be highly unlikely to have been an accident of independent creation *is* evidence of access.

What troubled us in *Selle* but is not a factor here is that two works may be strikingly similar—may in fact be identical—not because one is copied from the other but because both are copies of the same thing in the public domain. In such a case—imagine two people photographing Niagara Falls from the same place at the same time of the day and year and in identical weather—there is no inference of access to anything but the public domain, and, equally, no inference of copying from a copyrighted work. A similarity may be striking without being suspicious.

But here it is both. GMA's pig is strikingly similar to Ty's pig but not to anything in the public domain—a real pig, for example, which is why we have included in our appendix a photograph of real pigs. The parties' bean-bag pigs bear little resemblance to real pigs even if we overlook the striking anatomical anomaly of Preston—he has three toes, whereas real pigs have cloven hooves. We can imagine an argument that the technology of manufacturing bean-bag animals somehow prevents the manufacturer from imitating a real pig. But anyone even slightly familiar with stuffed animals knows that there are many lifelike stuffed pigs on the market. . . .

Real pigs are not the only pigs in the public domain. But GMA has not pointed to any fictional pig in the public domain that Preston resembles. . . . In rebuttal all that GMA presented was the affidavit of the designer, Salmon, who swears, we must assume truthfully, that she never looked at a Squealer before submitting her design. But it is not her design drawing that is alleged to infringe the copyright on Squealer; it is the manufactured Preston, the soft sculpture itself, which, as a comparison of the first with the third and fourth pictures in the appendix reveals, is much more like Squealer than Salmon's drawing is. And remember that the manufactured Preston *in the photograph* is a sport, with its stubby snout and its ribbon. Interestingly, these are features of Salmon's drawing but not of the production-model Preston, suggesting design intervention between Salmon's submission and actual production.

It is true that only a few months elapsed between Salmon's submission of the drawing to GMA and the production of Preston. But the record is silent on how long it would have taken to modify her design to make it more like Squealer. For all we know, it might have been done in hours—by someone who had bought a Squealer. The Beanie Babies are immensely popular. They are also, it is true, sometimes hard to find. . . . But it is unbelievable that a substantial company like GMA which is in the same line of business as Ty could not have located and purchased a Squealer if it wanted to copy it. A glance at the last picture in the appendix shows an identity between Louie the Cow and Ty's Daisy that is so complete (and also not explainable by reference to resemblance to a real cow or other public domain figure) as to compel an inference of copying. If GMA thus must have had access to Louie, it is probable, quite apart from any inference from the evidence of similarity, that it had access to Squealer as well.

This discussion shows how . . . the true relation between similarity and access [can be] expressed. Access (and copying) may be inferred when two works are so similar to each other and not to anything in the public domain that it is likely that the creator of the second work copied the first, but the inference can be rebutted by disproving access or otherwise showing independent creation. . . .

NOTES AND QUESTIONS

1. Do "subconscious copying" claims serve copyright law's ultimate purpose of promoting progress? Should there be a distinct statute of limitations on such claims, or should courts impose conditions regarding when such claims can be asserted?

2. Are *Selle* and *Ty* consistent? If the similarities between "Let It End" and "How Deep Is Your Love" could be the fortuitous result of popular culture, why not the similarities between Squealer and Preston? If, as the *Ty* court states, the threshold for proving access is higher when similarities between two works can be

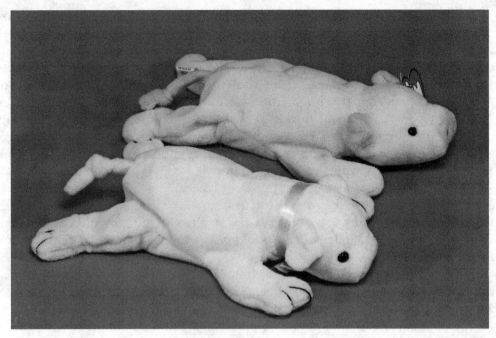

Preston and Squealer

Squealer © 1993 Ty, Inc. Reprinted by permission. Photograph provided by Banner & Witcoff, Ltd., attorneys for GMA, Inc.

attributed to public domain elements, should the threshold also be higher when the similarities can be attributed to the pervasiveness of popular culture more generally? If you had represented GMA, what arguments might you have made?

3. In *Three Boys Music Corp.*, the court observed that widespread dissemination is one way to prove "reasonable access" when trying to establish copying by the defendant. Does that approach unduly favor songs that are popular over those that never achieve any measure of success? In the digital era, how useful is the standard of widespread dissemination? For example, should the mere fact that a song is available on the Internet count as widespread dissemination? Is downloading in itself evidence of dissemination? If so, what number of downloads do you think should trigger a determination of widespread dissemination?

> **COMPARATIVE PERSPECTIVE**
>
> In the British case *Francis Day & Hunter v. Bron*, [1963] 2 All. E. R. 16 (Eng. C.A.), the court outlined a six-factor test to determine whether the defendant had copied the plaintiff's song: "[1] The degree of familiarity (if proved at all, or properly inferred) with the plaintiffs' work, [2] the character of the work, particularly its qualities of impressing the mind and memory, [3] the objective similarity of the defendants' work, [4] the inherent probability that such similarity as is found could be due to coincidence, [5] the existence of other influences on the defendant composer, and . . . [6] the quality of the defendant composer's own evidence on the presence or otherwise in his mind of the plaintiff's work."

4. How well does the "independent creation" doctrine survive cases like *Three Boys Music Corp., Selle,* and *Ty*? As the court in *Three Boys Music Corp.* explains, after the plaintiff has introduced sufficient evidence to support an inference of access, the burden shifts to the defendant to rebut that inference by proving independent creation. Practically, do the rules about proof of access articulated in the cases you read allow for such proof? In *Sheldon v. Metro-Goldwyn Pictures Corp.*, 81 F.2d 49 (2d Cir.), *cert. denied*, 298 U.S. 669 (1936), Judge Learned Hand famously observed, "[I]f by some magic a man who had never known it were to compose anew Keats's Ode on a Grecian Urn, he would be an 'author,' and, if he copyrighted it, others might not copy that poem, though they might of course copy Keats's." *Id.* at 54. Under the rules set forth in the cases above, if Keats's original "Ode on a Grecian Urn" were still protected under copyright today, would Judge Hand's hypothetical poet be considered an author or a presumptive infringer? Which result comports more closely with the policies underlying copyright law?

As discussed in Chapter 2.A.2.a, in patent law, an inventor who independently develops something that is covered by an enforceable patent still infringes that patent. Why do you think copyright law has a different rule? Should independent creation be considered a defense? Or should proving a lack of independent creation be part of the plaintiff's prima facie case?

5. The Music Genome Project is a comprehensive database of songs identified by their distinct characteristics or "genes," ranging from melody and lyrics to rhythm, tempo, harmony (including vocal harmony), arrangement and instrumentation. Founded in 2000, its goal is to establish a taxonomy of all of the musical attributes of songs to facilitate listeners' ability to identify a body of music unique to their tastes and preferences. Pandora Radio is a digital music service that relies exclusively on technology licensed from the Music Genome Project to help users identify new songs similar to the music they already enjoy. Should courts admit evidence of "genetic similarities" when considering copying in fact? In what ways might such evidence be relevant? Should such evidence trump the opinion of an expert? Of an ordinary listener? For discussion of some of the issues raised by "genetic analysis" of music, see Yvette Joy Liebesman, *Using Innovative Technologies to Analyze For similarity Between Musical Works in Copyright Infringement Disputes*, 35 AIPLA Q.J. 331 (2007). The Music Copyright Infringement Resource sponsored by Columbia Law School and the USC Gould School of Law has collected many sound files and musical scores from copyright cases involving musical works, including the works at issue in *Three Boys Music Corp.*, *Selle*, and *Arnstein*. *See* http://mcir.usc.edu/.

PRACTICE EXERCISE: COUNSEL A CLIENT

You are legislative counsel to the new Chairwoman of the House Judiciary Committee. Your boss, who is deeply critical of the "subconscious copying" doctrine, has asked you to draft a memorandum considering how best to reform it. In particular, she has asked you to analyze the possibility of expanding the innocent infringer defense that you learned about in section A.1.b, *supra*, to shelter instances of unconscious copying, either generally or in the specific case of musical works. What are the advantages and disadvantages of each approach? Would you recommend either? Is there a different solution that you think makes more sense?

Note on Access and Independent Creation in the Corporate Context

As cases like *Three Boys Music Corp.* and *Selle* suggest, documenting independent creation after the fact can be a daunting task for individual creators. The Bee Gees were able to defeat Selle's infringement claim because they could document their recording procedures, and because they and Selle traveled in very different circles. Similarly, in *Repp v. Webber*, 132 F.3d 882 (2d Cir. 1997), British composer Andrew Lloyd Webber was able to rely on geographic and social differences to defeat an infringement claim brought by an American composer of liturgical folk music. Many authors, however, cannot establish that they created their works while secluded in a French chateau or a British manor, and cannot comprehensively document their creation processes. Typically, then, when an individual defendant raises independent creation, he is arguing that the plaintiff has failed to establish the prima facie case of infringement because the plaintiff has not shown that copying in fact occurred.

Corporate creators, meanwhile, confront a slightly different set of problems. Even large companies with organized production processes cannot document every step in that process. Nonetheless, establishing procedures to document the creative process has become a matter of pressing concern for companies that create and commission copyrighted works. Under the "corporate receipt" doctrine, possession of a work by one employee of a corporation can be deemed to constitute possession by another employee or agent who allegedly infringed the copyright. *See* 4 Melville B. Nimmer & David Nimmer, Nimmer on Copyright §13.02[A] (2008). More than "bare corporate receipt" typically is required, however. *See, e.g., Jones v. Blige*, 558 F.3d 485 (6th Cir. 2009) (evidence that package containing demo CD was opened by record company insufficient to create reasonable possibility of access by another recording artist represented by the company); *Jorgensen v. Epic/Sony Records*, 351 F.3d 46, 48 (2d Cir. 2003) (bare corporate receipt insufficient to raise triable issue of access absent some connection between the recipients and the alleged infringers); *Towler v. Sayles*, 76 F.3d 579, 583 (4th Cir. 1996) (close relationship required for the corporate receipt doctrine to apply). At minimum, companies that create and commission copyrighted works require regularized procedures for handling unsolicited submissions.

Software companies have developed special procedures for documenting independent creation. Some degree of access to competitors' products often is an indispensable part of the software development process. When interoperability with an existing program is desired but that program's functional specifications are not publicly available from its developer, another developer who wants access to that information may reverse engineer the program by decompiling the object code version of the program into its human-readable

> **LOOKING BACK–AND FORWARD**
>
> As you learned in Chapter 4.C, software is more valuable to the extent that it is interoperable with other software. Courts have ruled that "intermediate copying" done during reverse engineering can be a fair use of copyrighted software; those cases are discussed in Chapter 10. Use of clean room procedures minimizes the likelihood that the final product will contain copyrightable expression that infringes the reproduction right in the first program. Altai used a clean room to produce its OSCAR 3.5 program after Computer Associates initiated litigation over OSCAR 3.4.

commands. Often, however, the developer will segregate the programmers responsible for writing the new program from those responsible for decompiling and understanding the existing program. This "clean room" process involves placing the former set of programmers in a separate room or facility and monitoring all of the technical information that goes into that room or facility. The competitor's decompiled code is excluded from the clean room. The programmers responsible for decompiling it must produce a set of specifications that simply describes the functionality that the new program must have. Those specifications are sent into the clean room, and constitute the only form of access to the competitor's product by the programming team actually writing the code for the new product.

NOTES AND QUESTIONS

1. In the patent system, documentation of inventive work is routine. Priority of invention is critical to establishing patent rights, and investigators keep detailed laboratory notebooks for precisely this purpose. Another researcher typically countersigns the notebook when the data is entered to provide additional verification of the content and date of laboratory results. Do you think that problems of proving and rebutting access would be more easily solved if authors of copyrighted works kept similar notebooks? Why, or why not?

2. What other steps might individual authors take during the creative process to bolster a defense of independent creation should they be sued for infringement?

3. Is the practical effect of the "bare corporate receipt" rule that plaintiffs have a higher evidentiary burden to satisfy than is typical for proceedings at the summary judgment stage?

PRACTICE EXERCISE: COUNSEL A CLIENT

You represent a client that produces programs for television. Your client routinely receives unsolicited submissions of screenplays, proposals for new series, and the like. What procedures would you advise your client to adopt for handling those submissions?

---

b. Substantial Similarity

In this subsection, we explore the application of the substantial similarity test to identify copying in violation of §106(1). As noted above, the question in a substantial similarity case is whether the defendant has engaged in actionable copying (i.e., copying in violation of §106(1)) by taking too much of what is protected by copyright in the plaintiff's work. The substantial similarity question is one of fact, but determining which aspects of the plaintiff's work are and are not protectable by copyright may involve questions of law.

While easily stated, the substantial similarity test has proved quite difficult to apply. In part this is because similarity also is relevant to the threshold question of copying in fact (see subsection 5.A.3.a, above). When we refer to "substantial similarity," we mean a degree of resemblance between the works that supports a finding of infringement. More fundamentally, though, substantial similarity is difficult because the judgments that are required are highly contextual.

As you read the following materials, identify the ways that different courts implement the test. Consider what each court is comparing, and how it guards against the risk of finding liability when the defendant has taken only unprotected material such as ideas and *scenes a faire* from the plaintiff. In addition, note the procedural posture of each case and consider how it affects the court's analysis.

i. Two Classic Cases

We begin with two classic cases that should be part of every copyright student's store of knowledge. As you read the cases, try to identify what test (if any) the court is using in determining wrongful appropriation.

Nichols v. Universal Pictures Corp.
45 F.2d 119 (2d Cir. 1930), cert. denied, 282 U.S. 902 (1931)

L. HAND , J.: [The plaintiff sued the defendant for copyright infringement. The district court entered a decree of dismissal from which the plaintiff appealed.]

The plaintiff is the author of a play, "Abie's Irish Rose," which it may be assumed was properly copyrighted. . . . The defendant produced publicly a motion picture play, "The Cohens and The Kellys," which the plaintiff alleges was taken from it. As we think the defendant's play too unlike the plaintiff's to be an infringement, we may assume, arguendo, that in some details

> **KEEP IN MIND**
>
> The exclusive right of reproduction protects the copyright owner not just against replication of its work in the same form (e.g., a book reproduced as a book) but also replication in another form (e.g., a play adapted into a movie as in this case). Under the 1976 Act, the reproduction right overlaps with the derivative work right, which we consider later in this chapter.

the defendant used the plaintiff's play, as will subsequently appear, though we do not so decide. It therefore becomes necessary to give an outline of the two plays.

"Abie's Irish Rose" presents a Jewish family living in prosperous circumstances in New York. The father, a widower, is in business as a merchant, in which his son and only child helps him. The boy has philandered with young women, who to his father's great disgust have always been Gentiles, for he is obsessed with a passion that his daughter-in-law shall be an orthodox Jewess. When the play opens the son, who has been courting a young Irish Catholic girl, has already married her secretly before a Protestant minister, and is concerned to soften the blow for his father, by securing a favorable impression of his bride, while concealing her faith and race. To accomplish this he introduces her to his father at his home as a Jewess, and lets it appear that he is interested in her, though he conceals the marriage.

The girl somewhat reluctantly falls in with the plan; the father takes the bait, becomes infatuated with the girl, concludes that they must marry, and assumes that of course they will, if he so decides. He calls in a rabbi, and prepares for the wedding according to the Jewish rite.

Meanwhile the girl's father, also a widower, who lives in California, and is as intense in his own religious antagonism as the Jew, has been called to New York, supposing that his daughter is to marry an Irishman and a Catholic. Accompanied by a priest, he arrives at the house at the moment when the marriage is being celebrated, but too late to prevent it and the two fathers, each infuriated by the proposed union of his child to a heretic, fall into unseemly and grotesque antics. The priest and the rabbi become friendly, exchange trite sentiments about religion, and agree that the match is good. Apparently out of abundant caution, the priest celebrates the marriage for a third time, while the girl's father is inveigled away. The second act closes with each father, still outraged, seeking to find some way by which the union, thus trebly insured, may be dissolved.

The last act takes place about a year later, the young couple having meanwhile been abjured by each father, and left to their own resources. They have had twins, a boy and a girl, but their fathers know no more than that a child has been born. At Christmas each, led by his craving to see his grandchild, goes separately to the young folks' home, where they encounter each other, each laden with gifts, one for a boy, the other for a girl. After some slapstick comedy, depending upon the insistence of each that he is right about the sex of the grandchild, they become reconciled when they learn the truth, and that each child is to bear the given name of a grandparent. The curtain falls as the fathers are exchanging amenities, and the Jew giving evidence of an abatement in the strictness of his orthodoxy.

"The Cohens and The Kellys" presents two families, Jewish and Irish, living side by side in the poorer quarters of New York in a state of perpetual enmity. The wives in both cases are still living, and share in the mutual animosity, as do two small sons, and even the respective dogs. The Jews have a daughter, the Irish a son; the Jewish father is in the clothing business; the Irishman is a policeman. The children are in love with each other, and secretly marry, apparently after the play opens. The Jew, being in great financial straits, learns from a lawyer that he has fallen heir to a large fortune from a great-aunt, and moves into a great house, fitted luxuriously. Here he and his family live in vulgar ostentation, and here the Irish boy seeks out his Jewish bride, and is chased away by the angry father. The Jew then abuses the Irishman over the telephone, and both become hysterically excited. The extremity of his feelings make the Jew sick, so that he must go to Florida for a rest, just before which the daughter discloses her marriage to her mother.

On his return the Jew finds that his daughter has borne a child; at first he suspects the lawyer, but eventually learns the truth and is overcome with anger at such a low alliance. Meanwhile, the Irish family who have been forbidden to see the grandchild, go to the Jew's house, and after a violent scene between the two fathers in which the Jew disowns his daughter, who decides to go back with her husband, the Irishman takes her back with her baby to his own poor lodgings. The lawyer, who had hoped to marry the Jew's daughter, seeing his plan foiled, tells the Jew that his fortune really belongs to the Irishman, who was also related to the dead woman, but offers to conceal his knowledge, if the Jew will share the loot. This the Jew repudiates, and, leaving the astonished lawyer, walks through the rain to his enemy's house to surrender the property. He arrives in great dejection, tells the truth, and abjectly turns to leave. A reconciliation ensues, the Irishman agreeing to share with him equally. The Jew shows some interest in his grandchild, though this is at most a minor motive in the reconciliation, and the curtain falls while the two are in their cups, the Jew insisting that in the firm name for the business, which they are to carry on jointly, his name shall stand first.

It is of course essential to any protection of literary property, whether at common-law or under the statute, that the right cannot be limited literally to the text, else a plagiarist would escape by immaterial variations. That has never been the law, but, as soon as literal appropriation ceases to be the test, the whole matter is necessarily at large, so that, as was recently well said by a distinguished judge, the decisions cannot help much in a new case. . . . Upon any work, and especially upon a play, a great number of patterns of increasing generality will fit equally well, as more and more of the incident is left out. The last may perhaps be no more than the most general statement of what the play is about, and at times might consist only of its title; but there is a point in this series of abstractions where they are no longer protected, since otherwise the playwright could prevent the use of his "ideas," to which, apart from their expression, his property is never extended. Nobody has ever been able to fix that boundary, and nobody ever can. . . . As respects plays, the controversy chiefly centers upon the characters and sequence of incident, these being the substance.

. . . [W]e do not doubt that two plays may correspond in plot closely enough for infringement. How far that correspondence must go is another matter. Nor need we hold that the same may not be true as to the characters, quite independently of the "plot" proper, though, as far as we know, such a case has never arisen. If Twelfth Night were copyrighted, it is quite possible that a second comer might so closely imitate Sir Toby Belch or Malvolio as to infringe, but it would not be enough that for one of his characters he cast a riotous knight who kept wassail to the discomfort of the household, or a vain and foppish steward who became amorous of his mistress. These would be no more than Shakespeare's "ideas" in the play, as little capable of monopoly as Einstein's Doctrine of Relativity, or Darwin's theory of the Origin of Species. It follows that the less developed the characters, the less they can be copyrighted; that is the penalty an author must bear for marking them too indistinctly.

In the two plays at bar we think both as to incident and character, the defendant took no more—assuming that it took anything at all—than the law allowed. The stories are quite different. One is of a religious zealot who insists upon his child's marrying no one outside his faith; opposed by another who is in this respect just like him, and is his foil. Their difference in race is merely an obbligato to the main theme, religion. They sink their differences through grandparental pride and affection. In the other, zealotry is wholly absent; religion does not even appear. It is true that the parents are hostile to each other in part because they differ in race; but the marriage of their son to a Jew does not apparently offend the Irish family at all, and it exacerbates the existing animosity of the Jew, principally because he has become rich, when he learns it. They are reconciled through the honesty of the Jew and the generosity of the Irishman; the grandchild has nothing whatever to do with it. The only matter common to the two is a quarrel between a Jewish and an Irish father, the marriage of their children, the birth of grandchildren and a reconciliation.

If the defendant took so much from the plaintiff, it may well have been because her amazing success seemed to prove that this was a subject of enduring popularity. Even so, granting that the plaintiff's play was wholly original, and assuming that novelty is not essential to a copyright, there is no monopoly in such a background. Though the plaintiff discovered the vein, she could not keep it to herself; so defined, the theme was too generalized an abstraction from what she wrote. It was only a part of her "ideas."

Nor does she fare better as to her characters. It is indeed scarcely credible that she should not have been aware of those stock figures, the low comedy Jew and Irishman. The defendant has not taken from her more than their prototypes have contained for many decades. If so, obviously so to generalize her copyright, would allow her to cover what was not original with her. But we need not hold this as matter of fact, much as we might be justified. Even though we take it that she devised her figures out of her brain de novo, still the defendant was within its rights.

There are but four characters common to both plays, the lovers and the fathers. The lovers are so faintly indicated as to be no more than stage properties. They are loving and fertile; that is really all that can be said of them, and anyone else is quite within his rights if he puts loving and fertile lovers in a play of his own, wherever he gets the cue. The plaintiff's Jew is quite unlike the defendant's. His obsession is his religion, on which depends such racial animosity as he has. He is affectionate, warm and patriarchal. None of these fit the defendant's Jew, who shows affection for his daughter only once, and who has none but the most superficial interest in his grandchild. He is tricky, ostentatious and vulgar, only by misfortune redeemed into honesty. Both are grotesque, extravagant and quarrelsome; both are fond of display; but these common qualities make up only a small part of their simple pictures, no more than any one might lift if he chose. The Irish fathers are even more unlike; the plaintiff's a mere symbol for religious fanaticism and patriarchal pride, scarcely a character at all. Neither quality appears in the defendant's, for while he goes to get his grandchild, it is rather out of a truculent determination not to be forbidden, than from pride in his progeny. For the rest he is only a grotesque hobbledehoy, used for low comedy of the most conventional sort, which any one might borrow, if he chanced not to know the exemplar.

. . . A comedy based upon conflicts between Irish and Jews, into which the marriage of their children enters, is no more susceptible of copyright than the outline of Romeo and Juliet.

The plaintiff has prepared an elaborate analysis of the two plays, showing a "quadrangle" of the common characters, in which each is represented by the emotions which he discovers. She presents the resulting parallelism as proof of infringement, but the adjectives employed are so general as to be quite useless. Take for example the attribute of "love" ascribed to both Jews. The plaintiff has depicted her father as deeply attached to his son, who is his hope and joy; not so, the defendant, whose father's conduct is throughout not actuated by any affection for his daughter, and who is merely once overcome for the moment by her distress when he has violently dismissed her lover. "Anger" covers emotions aroused by quite different occasions in each case; so do "anxiety," "despondency" and "disgust." It is unnecessary to go through the catalogue for emotions are too much colored by their causes to be a test when used so broadly. This is not the proper approach to a solution; it must be more ingenuous, more like that of a spectator, who would rely upon the complex of his impressions of each character. . . .

Arnstein v. Porter
154 F.2d 464 (2d Cir. 1946), cert. denied, 330 U.S. 851 (1947)

[Cole Porter (1891-1964) was among the most famous songwriters of the early twentieth century. Ira Arnstein was an eccentric (some say crazy) songwriter who had filed five separate lawsuits (all unsuccessful) against various music and film entities and individuals, often alleging wild conspiracies. In this case, Arnstein's last, Arnstein asserted that several of Cole Porter's songs infringed his compositions. At the time Arnstein filed this case one of the allegedly infringing songs, "Don't Fence Me In" was one of the most popular songs in the country, with recordings by Bing Crosby and the Andrews Sisters. – Eds.]

FRANK, J.: . . . The principal question on this appeal is whether the lower court . . . properly deprived plaintiff of a trial of his copyright infringement action [by granting defendant's motion for summary judgment]. The answer depends on whether "there is the slightest doubt as to the facts." . . .

. . . On [the issue of illicit copying (unlawful appropriation)] the test is the response of the ordinary lay hearer; accordingly, on that issue, "dissection" and expert testimony are irrelevant. . . .

[T]here can be "permissible copying," copying which is not illicit. Whether (if he copied) defendant unlawfully appropriated presents . . . an issue of fact. The proper criterion on that issue is not an analytic or other comparison of the respective musical compositions as they appear on paper or in the judgment of trained musicians. The plaintiff's legally protected interest is not, as such, his reputation as a musician but his interest in the potential financial returns from his compositions which derive from the lay public's approbation of his efforts. The question, therefore, is whether defendant took from plaintiff's works so much of what is pleasing to the ears of lay listeners, who comprise the audience for whom such popular music is composed, that defendant wrongfully appropriated something which belongs to the plaintiff.

Surely, then, we have an issue of fact which a jury is peculiarly fitted to determine.[22] Indeed, even if there were to be a trial before a judge, it would be desirable (although not necessary) for him to summon an advisory jury on this question.

We should not be taken as saying that a plagiarism case can never arise in which absence of similarities is so patent that a summary judgment for defendant would be correct. Thus suppose that Ravel's "Bolero" or Shostakovitch's "Fifth Symphony"

22. It would, accordingly, be proper to exclude tone-deaf persons from the jury. . . .

were alleged to infringe "When Irish Eyes Are Smiling." But this is not such a case. For, after listening to the playing of the respective compositions, we are, at this time, unable to conclude that the likenesses are so trifling that, on the issue of misappropriation, a trial judge could legitimately direct a verdict for defendant.

At the trial, plaintiff may play, or cause to be played, the pieces in such manner that they may seem to a jury to be inexcusably alike, in terms of the way in which lay listeners of such music would be likely to react. The plaintiff may call witnesses whose testimony may aid the jury in reaching its conclusion as to the responses of such audiences. Expert testimony of musicians may also be received, but it will in no way be controlling on the issue of illicit copying, and should be utilized only to assist in determining the reactions of lay auditors. The impression made on the refined ears of musical experts or their views as to the musical excellence of plaintiff's or defendant's works are utterly immaterial on the issue of misappropriation; for the views of such persons are caviar to the general—and plaintiff's and defendant's compositions are not caviar. . . .

. . . [R]eversed and remanded.

NOTES AND QUESTIONS

1. What is the primary purpose of Judge Hand's "abstractions" analysis? Is it helpful in assessing substantial similarity? Was the plaintiff misguided in presenting the elaborate analysis of the two works or should she have conducted that analysis differently?

2. *Arnstein* indicates that "dissection" is relevant to deciding the issue of copying in fact, but not to deciding the issue of substantial similarity. What do you think the court means by "dissection"? Why is expert testimony relevant to the issue of copying in fact but not to the issue of wrongfulness? Alternatively, why not just apply the "lay listener" test to both the issue of copying in fact and that of wrongfulness?

3. Do you think Judge Hand would agree with the *Arnstein* court's views on dissection and on the appropriate role of experts? Would the abstractions analysis of *Nichols* be useful in a case like *Arnstein*, or should the analytical tools for assessing infringement vary depending on the type of work or nature of the alleged infringement?

4. *Arnstein* instructs that courts should rely on the jury to determine "whether defendant took from plaintiff's works so much of what is pleasing to the ears of lay listeners." How does the *Arnstein* court guard against the risk of finding the defendant liable for taking only that which is unprotected? Should it matter to the court if the defendant in *Arnstein* could show that what was pleasing to the ear about plaintiff's works was a series of notes that audiologists have identified as evoking a positive response? What if the notes also appeared in Beethoven's Ninth Symphony? For a vivid and humorous demonstration of similarities in popular songs, see Axis of Awesome, "Four Chord Song," http://www.youtube.com/watch?v=oOlDewpCfZQ.

5. Note the *Arnstein* court's reference to the standard for summary judgment as "whether 'there is the slightest doubt as to the facts.'" *Arnstein v. Porter*, 154 F.2d 464, 468 (2d Cir. 1946), *cert. denied*, 330 U.S. 851 (1947). After *Arnstein*, for many years, summary judgment was difficult to obtain in infringement cases in the Second Circuit. Subsequently, however, major Supreme Court decisions articulated a standard requiring the nonmovant to produce sufficient evidence to support its position in order to survive the opposing party's motion for summary judgment. *See Anderson v. Liberty Lobby, Inc.*, 477 U.S. 242 (1986); *Celotex Corp. v. Catrett*, 477 U.S. 317 (1986).

In *Bell Atlantic Corp. v. Twombly*, 550 U.S. 544 (2007) and *Ashcroft v. Iqbal*, 556 U.S. 662 (2009), the Court ruled that for a complaint to survive a motion to dismiss under Fed. R. Civ. P. 12(b)(6), it must allege sufficient facts to make a claim for relief plausible. Some courts have used the heightened pleading standard to justify assessing substantial similarity very early in the course of litigation. *See, e.g., Peter F. Gaito Architecture, LLC v. Simone Development Corp.*, 602 F.3d 57, 64-65 (2d Cir. 2010) (summarizing the cases and affirming the district court's dismissal of a suit for infringement of copyright in an architectural work based on a visual inspection of the works).

ii. One Contemporary Approach: The Second Circuit

By now it should be apparent that the test for infringement is less exact than one might expect. In this section and the following section, we focus on more recent cases in the Second and Ninth Circuits. These circuits and their lower courts tend to be leaders in the copyright field because so many important publishing, entertainment, and software companies are located in their jurisdictions. As you read these cases, which apply the test in diverse subject matter settings ranging from illustrations to software, consider whether they are consistent with the classic cases as well as with each other. Think also about exactly what comparison the court should instruct the factfinder to conduct.

We begin with a group of cases arising in the Second Circuit.

Steinberg v. Columbia Pictures Industries, Inc.
663 F. Supp. 706 (S.D.N.Y. 1987)

STANTON, J.: In these actions for copyright infringement, plaintiff Saul Steinberg is suing the producers, promoters, distributors and advertisers of the movie "Moscow on the Hudson" ("Moscow"). Steinberg is an artist whose fame derives in part from cartoons and illustrations he has drawn for *The New Yorker* magazine. Defendant Columbia Pictures Industries, Inc. (Columbia) is in the business of producing, promoting and distributing motion pictures, including "Moscow." [The other defendants included affiliates of Columbia and newspapers publishing the alleging infringing advertisement.] . . .

Plaintiff alleges that defendants' promotional poster for "Moscow" infringes his copyright on an illustration that he drew for *The New Yorker* and that appeared on the cover of the March 29, 1976 issue of the magazine. . . .

. . . [T]his court . . . grants summary judgment on the issue of copying to plaintiff.

I ...

Summary judgment is often disfavored in copyright cases, for courts are generally reluctant to make subjective comparisons and determinations. Recently, however, this circuit has "recognized that a court may determine non-infringement as a matter of law on a motion for summary judgment." "When the evidence is so overwhelming that a court would be justified in ordering a directed verdict at trial, it is proper to grant summary judgment." ...

II

... On March 29, 1976, *The New Yorker* published as a cover illustration the work at issue in this suit, widely known as a parochial New Yorker's view of the world. The magazine registered this illustration with the United States Copyright Office and subsequently assigned the copyright to Steinberg. ...

Defendants' illustration was created to advertise the movie "Moscow on the Hudson," which recounts the adventures of a Muscovite who defects in New York. In designing this illustration, Columbia's executive art director, Kevin Nolan, has admitted that he specifically referred to Steinberg's poster, and indeed, that he purchased it and hung it, among others, in his office. Furthermore, Nolan explicitly directed the outside artist whom he retained to execute his design, Craig Nelson, to use Steinberg's poster to achieve a more recognizably New York look. Indeed, Nelson acknowledged having used the facade of one particular edifice, at Nolan's suggestion that it would render his drawing more "New York-ish." While the two buildings are not identical, they are so similar that it is impossible, especially in view of the artist's testimony, not to find that defendants' impermissibly copied plaintiff's.[1] ...

III ...

Defendants' access to plaintiff's illustration is established beyond peradventure. Therefore, the sole issue remaining with respect to liability is whether there is such substantial similarity between the copyrighted and accused works as to establish a violation of plaintiff's copyright. The central issue of "substantial similarity," which can be considered a close question of fact, may also validly be decided as a question of law. ...

The definition of "substantial similarity" in this circuit is "whether an average lay observer would recognize the alleged copy as having been appropriated from the copyrighted work." ...

There is no dispute that defendants cannot be held liable for using the *idea* of a map of the world from an egocentrically myopic perspective. ...

---

1. Nolan claimed also to have been inspired by some of the posters that were inspired by Steinberg's; such secondary inspiration, however, is irrelevant to whether or not the "Moscow" poster infringes plaintiff's copyright by having impermissibly copied it.

Even at first glance, one can see the striking stylistic relationship between the posters, and since style is one ingredient of "expression," this relationship is significant. Defendants' illustration was executed in the sketchy, whimsical style that has become one of Steinberg's hallmarks. Both illustrations represent a bird's eye view across the edge of Manhattan and a river bordering New York City to the world beyond. Both depict approximately four city blocks in detail and become increasingly minimalist as the design recedes into the background. Both use the device of a narrow band of blue wash across the top of the poster to represent the sky, and both delineate the horizon with a band of primary red.[3]

The strongest similarity is evident in the rendering of the New York City blocks. Both artists chose a vantage point that looks directly down a wide two-way cross street that intersects two avenues before reaching a river. Despite defendants' protestations, this is not an inevitable way of depicting blocks in a city with a grid-like street system, particularly since most New York City cross streets are one-way. Since even a photograph may be copyrighted because "no photograph, however simple, can be unaffected by the personal influence of the author," *Time Inc. v. Bernard Geis Assoc.,* 293 F. Supp. 130, 141 (S.D.N.Y. 1968), *quoting Bleistein, supra,* one can hardly gainsay the right of an artist to protect his choice of perspective and lay-out in a drawing, especially in conjunction with the overall concept and individual details. Indeed, the fact that defendants changed the names of the streets while retaining the same graphic depiction weakens their case: had they intended their illustration realistically to depict the streets labeled on the poster, their four city blocks would not so closely resemble plaintiff's four city blocks. Moreover, their argument that they intended the jumble of streets and landmarks and buildings to symbolize their Muscovite protagonist's confusion in a new city does not detract from the strong similarity between their poster and Steinberg's.

While not all of the details are identical, many of them could be mistaken for one another; for example, the depiction of the water towers, and the cars, and the red sign above a parking lot, and even many of the individual buildings. The shapes, windows, and configurations of various edifices are substantially similar. The ornaments, facades and details of Steinberg's buildings appear in defendants', although occasionally at other locations. In this context, it is significant that Steinberg did not depict any buildings actually erected in New York; rather, he was inspired by the general appearance of the structures on the West Side of Manhattan to create his own New York-ish structures. Thus, the similarity between the buildings depicted in the "Moscow" and Steinberg posters cannot be explained by an assertion that the artists happened to choose the same buildings to draw. The close similarity can be explained only by the defendants' artist having copied the plaintiff's work. Similarly, the locations and size, the errors and anomalies of Steinberg's shadows and streetlight, are meticulously imitated.

---

3. Defendants claim that since this use of thin bands of primary colors is a traditional Japanese technique, their adoption of it cannot infringe Steinberg's copyright. This argument ignores the principle that while "[o]thers are free to copy the original . . . [t]hey are not free to copy the copy." *Bleistein v. Donaldson Lithographing Co.,* 188 U.S. 239, 250 (1903) (Holmes, J.).

Original Artwork by Saul Steinberg, *View of the World from 9th Avenue.*

"Moscow on the Hudson" Poster

In addition, the Columbia artist's use of the childlike, spiky block print that has become one of Steinberg's hallmarks to letter the names of the streets in the "Moscow" poster can be explained only as copying. There is no inherent justification for using this style of lettering to label New York City streets as it is associated with New York only through Steinberg's poster.

While defendants' poster shows the city of Moscow on the horizon in far greater detail than anything is depicted in the background of plaintiff's illustration, this fact alone cannot alter the conclusion. "Substantial similarity" does not require identity, and "duplication or near identity is not necessary to establish infringement." Neither the depiction of Moscow, nor the eastward perspective, nor the presence of randomly scattered New York City landmarks in defendants' poster suffices to eliminate the substantial similarity between the posters. As Judge Learned Hand wrote, "no plagiarist can excuse the wrong by showing how much of his work he did not pirate."

Defendants argue that their poster could not infringe plaintiff's copyright because only a small proportion of its design could possibly be considered similar. This argument is both factually and legally without merit. "[A] copyright infringement may occur by reason of a substantial similarity that involves only a small portion of each work." Moreover, this case involves the entire protected work and an iconographically, as well as proportionately, significant portion of the allegedly infringing work.

The process by which defendants' poster was created also undermines this argument. The "map," that is, the portion about which plaintiff is complaining, was designed separately from the rest of the poster. The likenesses of the three main characters, which were copied from a photograph, and the blocks of text were superimposed on the completed map.

I also reject defendants' argument that any similarities between the works are unprotectible *scenes a faire,* or "incidents, characters or settings which, as a practical matter, are indispensable or standard in the treatment of a given topic." It is undeniable that a drawing of New York City blocks could be expected to include buildings, pedestrians, vehicles, lampposts and water towers. Plaintiff, however, does not complain of defendants' mere use of these elements in their poster; rather, his complaint is that defendants copied his *expression* of those elements of a street scene.

While evidence of independent creation by the defendants would rebut plaintiff's prima facie case, "the absence of any countervailing evidence of creation independent of the copyrighted source may well render clearly erroneous a finding that there was not copying."

Moreover, it is generally recognized that ". . . since a very high degree of similarity is required in order to dispense with proof of access, it must logically follow that where proof of access is offered, the required degree of similarity may be somewhat less than would be necessary in the absence of such proof." As defendants have conceded access to plaintiff's copyrighted illustration, a somewhat lesser degree of similarity suffices to establish a copyright infringement than might otherwise be required. Here, however, the demonstrable similarities are such that proof of access, although in fact conceded, is almost unnecessary. . . .

NOTES AND QUESTIONS

1. Are "style" and "choice of perspective and lay-out" properly considered aspects of protectable expression? Before answering, consider whether Impressionism, for example, would have been regarded as a style when it was first developed. If style is properly copyrightable, can imitating one's own style constitute copyright infringement? For example, assume an artist paints a canvas that depicts the Brooklyn Bridge. He paints the bridge in the Cubist style. He then assigns ownership of the copyright in the painting to another. Can he paint the Brooklyn Bridge again in the same style without incurring liability for copyright infringement? Can he paint other bridges in that style?

2. Should courts require a "somewhat lesser degree of similarity" when the defendant admits using the plaintiff's work for "inspiration"? Is the court confusing the two kinds of similarity at issue in a copyright infringement case?

Boisson v. Banian, Ltd.
273 F.3d 262 (2d Cir. 2001)

CARDAMONE, J.: . . . [P]laintiff [Judi Boisson] . . . designed and produced two alphabet quilts entitled "School Days I" and "School Days II." . . . [E]ach consists of square blocks containing the capital letters of the alphabet, displayed in order. The blocks are set in horizontal rows and vertical columns, with the last row filled by blocks containing various pictures or icons. The letters and blocks are made up of different colors, set off by a white border and colored edging. . . .

Defendant Vijay Rao is the president and sole shareholder of defendant Banian Ltd. . . . [H]e imported from India each of the three alphabet quilts at issue in this case[:] . . . "ABC Green Version I," . . . "ABC Green Version II" [and] "ABC Navy". . . .

[Boisson and her wholly owned company, American Country Quilts and Linens, Inc., sued Rao and Banian, alleging that the defendants had infringed the plaintiffs' copyrights in the two School Days quilts. Following a bench trial, the trial court denied the claims, ruling that Banian's quilts were not substantially similar to plaintiffs'. The court of appeals noted that the defendants had conceded the validity of the plaintiffs' copyrights and did not dispute the district court's finding of copying in fact. It then engaged in a lengthy discussion of what elements of plaintiffs' quilts were original and therefore protected by copyright, using the clearly erroneous standard to assess the district court's findings. The court found that although the alphabet itself is not copyrightable, the plaintiffs' layout was. Additionally, it held that the choice of color in combination with other creative elements can be copyrightable.]

. . . We review *de novo* the district court's determination with respect to substantial similarity because credibility is not at stake and all that is required is a visual comparison of the products—a task we may perform as well as the district court.

Generally, an allegedly infringing work is considered substantially similar to a copyrighted work if "the ordinary observer, unless he set out to detect the disparities, would be disposed to overlook them, and regard their aesthetic appeal as the same." *Folio Impressions,* [*Inc. v. Byer Cal.,*] 937 F.2d [759] at 765 [(2d Cir. 1991)]. Yet in *Folio Impressions,* the evidence at trial showed the plaintiff designer had copied the background for its fabric from a public domain document and "contributed nothing, not even a trivial variation." 937 F.2d at 764. Thus, part of the plaintiff's fabric was not original and therefore not protectible. We articulated the need for an ordinary observer to be "more discerning" in such circumstances.

> [T]he ordinary observer would compare the finished product that the fabric designs were intended to grace (women's dresses), and would be inclined to view the entire dress—consisting of protectible and unprotectible elements—as one whole. Here, since only some of the design enjoys copyright protection, the observer's inspection must be more discerning.

Id. at 765-66. Shortly after *Folio Impressions* was decided, we reiterated that a "more refined analysis" is required where a plaintiff's work is not "wholly original," but rather incorporates elements from the public domain. *Key Publ'ns, Inc. v. Chinatown Today Publ'g Enters., Inc.,* 945 F.2d 509, 514 (2d Cir. 1991). In these instances, "[w]hat must be shown is substantial similarity between those elements, and only those elements, that provide copyrightability to the allegedly infringed compilation." *Id.* . . . In the case at hand, because the alphabet was taken from the public domain, we must apply the "more discerning" ordinary observer test.

In applying this test, a court is not to dissect the works at issue into separate components and compare only the copyrightable elements. To do so would be to take the "more discerning" test to an extreme, which would result in almost nothing being copyrightable because original works broken down into their composite parts would usually be little more than basic unprotectible elements like letters, colors and symbols. This outcome—affording no copyright protection to an original compilation of unprotectible elements—would be contrary to the Supreme Court's holding in *Feist Publications* [*Inc. v. Rural Tel. Serv. Co.,* 499 U.S. 340 (1991)].

Although the "more discerning" test has not always been identified by name in our case law, we have nevertheless always recognized that the test is guided by comparing the "total concept and feel" of the contested works. For example, in *Streetwise Maps* [*Inc. v. Vandam, Inc.*], 159 F.3d [739] at 748 [(2d Cir. 1998)], we found no infringement—not because the plaintiff's map consisted of public domain facts such as street locations, landmasses, bodies of water and landmarks, as well as color—but rather "because the total concept and overall feel created by the two works may not be said to be substantially similar." . . .

. . . [W]hen evaluating claims of infringement involving literary works, we have noted that while liability would result only if the protectible elements were substantially similar, our examination would encompass "the similarities in such aspects as the total concept and feel, theme, characters, plot, sequence, pace, and setting of the [plaintiff's] books and the [defendants'] works." *Williams* [*v. Crichton*], 84 F.3d [581] at 588 [(2d Cir. 1996)]; . . .

In the present case, while use of the alphabet may not provide a basis for infringement, we must compare defendants' quilts and plaintiffs' quilts on the basis of the arrangement and shapes of the letters, the colors chosen to represent the letters and other parts of the quilts, the quilting patterns, the particular icons chosen and their placement. Our analysis of the "total concept and feel" of these works should be instructed by common sense. It is at this juncture that we part from the district court, which never considered the arrangement of the whole when comparing plaintiffs' works with defendants'. With this concept in mind, we pass to a comparison of the quilts at issue.

Comparison . . .

"School Days I" consists of six horizontal rows, each row containing five blocks, with a capital letter or an icon in each block. The groupings of blocks in each row are as follows: A-E; F-J; K-O; P-T; U-Y; and Z with four icons following in the last row. The four icons are a cat, a house, a single-starred American flag and a basket. "ABC Green Version I" displays the capital letters of the alphabet in the same formation. The four icons in the last row are a cow jumping over the moon, a sailboat, a bear and a star. "ABC Green Version II" is identical to "ABC Green Version I," except that the picture of the cow jumping over the moon is somewhat altered, the bear is replaced by a teddy bear sitting up and wearing a vest that looks like a single-starred American flag, and the star in the last block is represented in a different color.

All three quilts use a combination of contrasting solid color fabrics or a combination of solid and polka-dotted fabrics to represent the blocks and letters. The following similarities are observed in plaintiffs' and defendants' designs: "A" is dark blue on a light blue background; "B" is red on a white background; "D" is made of polka-dot fabric on a light blue background; "F" on plaintiffs' "School Days I" is white on a pink background, while the "F" on defendants' "ABC Green" versions is pink on a white background; "G" has a green background; "H" and "L" are each a shade of blue on a white background; "M" in each quilt is a shade of yellow on a white background; "N" is green on a white background; "O" is blue on a polka-dot background; "P" is polka-dot fabric on a yellow background; "Q" is brown on a light background; "R" is pink on a gray/purple background, "S" is white on a red background; "T" is blue on a white background; "U" is gray on a white background; "V" is white on a gray background; "W" is pink on a white background; "X" is purple in all quilts, albeit in different shades, on a light background; "Y" is a shade of yellow on the same light background; and "Z" is navy blue or black, in all the quilts.

Boisson also testified that defendants utilized the same unique shapes as she had given to the letters "J," "M," "N," "P," "R" and "W." With respect to the quilting patterns, "School Days I" and the "ABC Green" versions feature diamond-shaped quilting within the blocks and a "wavy" pattern in the plain white border that surrounds the blocks. The quilts are also edged with a 3/8" green binding.

From this enormous amount of sameness, we think defendants' quilts sufficiently similar to plaintiffs' design as to demonstrate illegal copying. In particular, the overwhelming similarities in color choices lean toward a finding of infringement. Although the icons chosen for each quilt are different and defendants added a green rectangular border around their rows of blocks, these differences are not sufficient to cause even the "more discerning" observer to think the quilts are other than substantially similar insofar as the protectible elements of plaintiffs' quilt are concerned. Moreover, the substitution in "ABC Green Version II" of the teddy bear wearing a flag vest as the third icon causes this version of defendants' quilt to look even more like plaintiffs' quilt that uses a single-starred American flag as its third icon. Consequently, both of defendants' "ABC Green" quilts infringed plaintiffs' copyright on its "School Days I" quilt. . . .

[The court further held that Banian's "ABC Navy" quilt did not infringe "School Days I" because the icons and colors were different. It held that the "ABC Green" quilts did not infringe "School Days II" because the "total concept and feel" were different: The letters were arranged differently and the colors (red, white, and blue in plaintiffs' quilt versus green in the defendants') did not create the same impression.]

Mannion v. Coors Brewing Company
377 F. Supp. 2d 444 (S.D.N.Y. 2006)

[Review the excerpt from the *Mannion* case, Chapter 2.A.2.c *supra*. Recall that the case involved allegations of infringement of a photograph and that both parties filed motions for summary judgment. Recall also that the court identified three different ways originality can be expressed in photographs: in rendition, timing, and creation of the subject. In the excerpt below, the court considers how to compare the photographs to determine if they are substantially similar.]

KAPLAN J.: . . .

The Idea/Expression Difficulty

Notwithstanding the originality of the Garnett Photograph, the defendants argue that the Coors Billboard does not infringe because the two, insofar as they are similar, share only "the generalized idea and concept of a young African American man wearing a white T-shirt and a large amount of jewelry."

It is true that an axiom of copyright law is that copyright does not protect "ideas," only their expression. Furthermore, when "a given idea is inseparably tied to a particular expression" so that "there is a 'merger' of idea and expression," courts may deny protection to the expression in order to avoid conferring a monopoly on the idea to which it inseparably is tied. But the defendants' reliance on these principles is misplaced.

The "idea" (if one wants to call it that) postulated by the defendants does not even come close to accounting for all the similarities between the two works, which extend at least to angle, pose, background, composition, and lighting. It is possible to imagine any number of depictions of a black man wearing a white T-shirt and "bling bling" that look nothing like either of the photographs at issue here.

This alone is sufficient to dispose of the defendants' contention that Mannion's claims must be rejected because he seeks to protect an idea rather than its expression. But the argument reveals an analytical difficulty in the case law about which more ought to be said. One of the main cases upon which the defendants rely is *Kaplan v. Stock Market Photo Agency, Inc.,* [133 F. Supp. 2d 317 (S.D.N.Y. 2001)] in which two remarkably similar photographs of a businessman's shoes and lower legs, taken from the top of a tall building looking down on a street below . . . were held to be not substantially similar as a matter of law because all of the similarities flowed only from an unprotected idea rather than from the expression of that idea.

But what is the "idea" of Kaplan's photograph? Is it (1) a businessman contemplating suicide by jumping from a building, (2) a businessman contemplating suicide by jumping from a building, seen from the vantage point of the businessman, with his shoes set against the street far below, or perhaps something more general, such as (3) a sense of desperation produced by urban professional life?

If the "idea" is (1) or, for that matter, (3), then the similarities between the two photographs flow from something much more than that idea, for it would have been possible to convey (1) (and (3)) in any number of ways that bear no obvious similarities to Kaplan's photograph. (Examples are a businessman atop a building seen from below, or the entire figure of the businessman, rather than just his shoes or pants, seen from above.) If, on the other hand, the "idea" is (2), then the two works could be said to owe much of their similarity to a shared idea. . . .

The idea/expression distinction arose in the context of literary copyright. . . . And it makes sense to speak of the idea conveyed by a literary work and to distinguish it from its expression. To take a clear example, two different authors each can describe, with very different words, the theory of special relativity. The words will be protected as expression. The theory is a set of unprotected ideas.

In the visual arts, the distinction breaks down. For one thing, it is impossible in most cases to speak of the particular "idea" captured, embodied, or conveyed by a work of art because every observer will have a different interpretation.[80] Furthermore, it is not clear that there is any real distinction between the idea in a work of art and its expression. An artist's idea, among other things, is to depict a particular subject in a particular way. As a demonstration, a number of cases from this Circuit have observed that a photographer's "conception" of his subject is copyrightable. By "conception," the courts must mean originality in the rendition, timing, and creation of the subject—for that is what copyright protects in photography. But the word "conception" is a cousin of "concept," and both are akin to "idea." In other

---

80. In cases dealing with toys or products that have both functional and design aspects, courts sometimes use "idea" to refer to a gimmick embodied in the product. . . . This case does not concern any kind of gimmick, and the Court ventures no opinion about the applicability of the idea/expression dichotomy to any product that embodies a gimmick, including toys or other objects that combine function and design.

words, those elements of a photograph, or indeed, any work of visual art protected by copyright, could just as easily be labeled "idea" as "expression." . . .

. . . [A]t what point do the similarities between two photographs become sufficiently general that there will be no infringement even though actual copying has occurred? . . . [T]this question is precisely the same, although phrased in the opposite way, as one that must be addressed in all infringement cases, namely whether two works are substantially similar with respect to their protected elements. It is nonsensical to speak of one photograph being substantially similar to another in the rendition and creation of the subject but somehow not infringing because of a shared idea. Conversely, if the two photographs are not substantially similar in the rendition and creation of the subject, the distinction between idea and expression will be irrelevant because there can be no infringement. The idea/expression distinction in photography, and probably the other visual arts, thus achieves nothing beyond what other, clearer copyright principles already accomplish. . . .

Comparison of the Coors Billboard and the Garnett Photograph

The next step is to determine whether a trier of fact could or must find the Coors Billboard substantially similar to the Garnett Photograph with respect to their protected elements.

Substantial similarity ultimately is a question of fact. "The standard test for substantial similarity between two items is whether an 'ordinary observer, unless he set out to detect the disparities, would be disposed to overlook them, and regard [the] aesthetic appeal as the same.'" The Second Circuit sometimes has applied a "more discerning observer" test when a work contains both protectible and unprotectible elements. The test "requires the court to eliminate the unprotectible elements from its consideration and to ask whether the protectible elements, standing alone, are substantially similar." The Circuit, however, is ambivalent about this test. In several cases dealing with fabric and garment designs, the Circuit has cautioned that:

> a court is not to dissect the works at issue into separate components and compare only the copyrightable elements. . . . To do so would be to take the "more discerning" test to an extreme, which would result in almost nothing being copyrightable because original works broken down into their composite parts would usually be little more than basic unprotectible elements like letters, colors and symbols. [*Boisson v. Banian, Ltd.*, 273 F.3d 262, 272 (2d Cir. 2001).]

Dissecting the works into separate components and comparing only the copyrightable elements, however, appears to be exactly what the "more discerning observer" test calls for.

The Circuit indirectly spoke to this tension in the recent case of *Tufenkian Import/Export Ventures, Inc. v. Einstein Moomjy, Inc.*[, 338 F.3d 127 (2d Cir. 2003)]. There the trial court purported to use the more discerning observer test but nonetheless compared the "total-concept-and-feel" of carpet designs. . . .

In light of these precedents, the Court concludes that it is immaterial whether the ordinary or more discerning observer test is used here because the inquiries would be identical. The cases agree that the relevant comparison is between the protectible elements in the Garnett Photograph and the Coors Billboard, but that those elements are not to be viewed in isolation.

The Garnett Photograph is protectible to the extent of its originality in the rendition and creation of the subject. Key elements of the Garnett Photograph that are in the public domain—such as Kevin Garnett's likeness—are not replicated in the Coors Billboard. Other elements arguably in the public domain—such as the existence of a cloudy sky, Garnett's pose, his white T-shirt, and his specific jewelry—may not be copyrightable in and of themselves, but their existence and arrangement in this photograph indisputably contribute to its originality. Thus the fact that the Garnett Photograph includes certain elements that would not be copyrightable in isolation does not affect the nature of the comparison. The question is whether the aesthetic appeal of the two images is the same.

Garnett

Iced Out comp Board

Coors Billboard and Billboard Detail

Original photograph of Kevin Garnett © Jonathan Mannion. Reproduced by permission.

The two photographs share a similar composition and angle. The lighting is similar, and both use a cloudy sky as backdrop. The subjects are wearing similar clothing and similar jewelry arranged in a similar way. The defendants, in other words, appear to have recreated much of the subject that Mannion had created and then, through imitation of angle and lighting, rendered it in a similar way. The similarities here thus relate to the Garnett Photograph's originality in the rendition and the creation of the subject and therefore to its protected elements.

There of course are differences between the two works. The similarity analysis may take into account some, but not all, of these. It long has been the law that "no plagiarist can excuse the wrong by showing how much of his work he did not pirate." [*Id.* at 132-33 (quoting *Sheldon v. Metro-Goldwyn Pictures Corp.*, 81 F.2d 49, 56 (2d Cir. 1936)) (internal quotation marks omitted)]. Thus the addition of the words "Iced Out" and a can of Coors Light beer may not enter into the similarity analysis.

Other differences, however, are in the nature of changes rather than additions. One image is black and white and dark, the other is in color and bright. One is the mirror image of the other. One depicts only an unidentified man's torso, the other the top three-fourths of Kevin Garnett's body. The jewelry is not identical. One T-shirt appears to fit more tightly than the other. These changes may enter the analysis because "[i]f the points of dissimilarity not only exceed the points of similarity, but indicate that the remaining points of similarity are, within the context of plaintiff's work, of minimal importance . . . then no infringement results."

The parties have catalogued at length and in depth the similarities and differences between these works. In the last analysis, a reasonable jury could find substantial similarity either present or absent. . . .

NOTES AND QUESTIONS

1. The *Boisson* court describes the ordinary observer test as focusing on aesthetic appeal: "Generally, an allegedly infringing work is considered substantially similar to a copyrighted work if the 'ordinary observer, unless he set out to detect the disparities, would be disposed to overlook them, and regard [the] aesthetic appeal [of the two works] as the same.'" *Boisson*, 273 F.3d at 272. Do you think the earlier *Arnstein* court would have agreed with this statement? Would Judge Hand have agreed with it?

2. What is the purpose of *Boisson's* "more discerning observer" test? Do you think it will achieve its purpose? Do you agree with the *Mannion* court's observation that the Second Circuit seems "ambivalent" about the test?

Can you think of a rationale for employing both a "more discerning observer" test and the "total concept and feel" test as the *Boisson* court does? What is the purpose of the total concept and feel test? Does it amount to a test for similarity of impermissible elements like ideas or concepts? If not, why not? What do you make of the *Boisson* court's reference to *Feist* and the question of originality in compilations?

3. Do you agree with the *Mannion* court's conclusion that "other, clearer copyright principles" render the idea/expression distinction superfluous in cases involving visual artworks? What are those principles? How does the court separate protectable and unprotectable elements of the Garnett photograph? How should a jury do that?

Is "rendition," as described in *Mannion*, the same as *Steinberg*'s "style" and "choice of perspective and lay-out," or is it different?

4. Consider all of the decisions from courts in the Second Circuit that you have read: *Nichols, Arnstein, Steinberg, Boisson,* and *Mannion.* Are the decisions consistent? Can differences be accounted for by the different subject matters involved: a literary work in *Nichols,* music in *Arnstein,* and pictorial, graphic, or sculptural works in *Steinberg, Boisson,* and *Mannion?*

5. In *Boisson,* the Second Circuit reversed findings of no improper appropriation made following a bench trial, made its own assessment of plaintiffs' and defendants' works, and directed that a judgment of infringement be issued. In light of what you have learned about the standard of review in copyright cases, was that appropriate? Did the court essentially conclude that the plaintiffs were entitled to judgment as a matter of law? In *Steinberg,* the district court did so conclude. Was that decision proper? Under the test articulated in *Boisson,* how likely is it that a copyright infringement case in the Second Circuit will result in summary judgment for the plaintiff? What about summary judgment for the defendant?

PRACTICE EXERCISE: ADVOCACY

James Tufenkian created the Heriz carpet (below, center) and registered the copyright with the U.S. Copyright Office. He based the Heriz design on the public domain Battilossi rug (below, left). Bashian Brothers hired former Tufenkian employee Michael Nichols-Marcy and produced the Bromley carpet (below, right) based on a design created by Nichols-Marcy. Tufenkian sued Bashian Brothers for infringement of his copyright in the Heriz. Assume that the case is to be tried to a jury, and that you represent Tufenkian. Draft proposed jury instructions on substantial similarity. If you represented Bashian Brothers, how would your proposed jury instructions differ?

Battilossi   Heriz   Bromley

iii. Another Contemporary Approach: The Ninth Circuit

Courts in the Ninth Circuit take a somewhat different approach to the problem of substantial similarity. That approach originates in *Sid & Marty Krofft Television Productions, Inc. v. McDonald's Corp.*, 562 F.2d 1157 (9th Cir. 1977). Sid and Marty Krofft had created an enormously popular children's TV show called *H.R. Pufnstuf* that featured a fantasyland and costumed characters. An ad campaign for the McDonald's fast food chain introduced a group of fanciful costumed characters inhabiting a fantasyland called McDonaldland. Based on the jury's answers to special interrogatories, the district court issued a judgment of infringement, which the Ninth Circuit upheld. Along the way, the court outlined a two-step process for determining substantial similarity:

> The determination of whether there is substantial similarity in ideas may often be a simple one. . . . [For] example . . . the idea . . . embodied [in a plaster statue of a nude] is a simple one—a plaster recreation of a nude human figure. A statue of a horse or a painting of a nude would not embody this idea and therefore could not infringe. The test for similarity of ideas is still a factual one, to be decided by the trier of fact.
>
> We shall call this the "extrinsic test." It is extrinsic because it depends not on the responses of the trier of fact, but on specific criteria which can be listed and analyzed. Such criteria include the type of artwork involved, the materials used, the subject matter, and the setting for the subject. Since it is an extrinsic test, analytic dissection and expert testimony are appropriate. Moreover, this question may often be decided as a matter of law.
>
> The determination of when there is substantial similarity between the forms of expression is necessarily more subtle and complex. As Judge Hand candidly observed, "Obviously, no principle can be stated as to when an imitator has gone beyond copying the 'idea,' and has borrowed its 'expression.' Decisions must therefore inevitably be ad hoc." If there is substantial similarity in ideas, then the trier of fact must decide whether there is substantial similarity in the expressions of the ideas so as to constitute infringement.
>
> The test to be applied in determining whether there is substantial similarity in expressions shall be labeled an intrinsic one—depending on the response of the ordinary reasonable person. It is intrinsic because it does not depend on the type of external criteria and analysis which marks the extrinsic test. . . . Because this is an intrinsic test, analytic dissection and expert testimony are not appropriate. . . .

Id. at 1164.

As described in *Krofft*, the extrinsic test envisions both a more active role for the judge and the possibility of summary disposition. At the same time, the infringement analysis is not wholly dissimilar to that conducted in the Second Circuit. After viewing representative samples of plaintiffs' and defendants' works, the *Krofft* court concluded that defendants "have captured the 'total concept and feel' of the Pufnstuf show. We would so conclude even if we were sitting as the triers of fact. There is no doubt that the findings of the jury in this case are not clearly erroneous." *Id.* at 1167 (citing *Roth Greeting Cards v. United Card Co.*, 429 F.2d 1106, 1110 (9th Cir. 1970)).

Consider the following cases, which explore the subsequent evolution of the *Krofft* test and highlight different aspects of the inquiry that a court must conduct.

Cavalier v. Random House, Inc.
297 F.3d 815 (9th Cir. 2002)

FLETCHER, J.: . . .

A. Background

[The Cavaliers developed children's stories based on a character called] Nicky Moonbeam, an anthropomorphic moon . . .

From 1995 through 1998, the Cavaliers submitted more than 280 pages of material, including their copyrighted works, to Random House and [Children's Television Workshop ("CTW")]. The first submission consisted of two stories—*Nicky Moonbeam: The Man in the Moon* and *Nicky Moonbeam Saves Christmas*—and the design for a "moon night light" to be built directly into the back cover of a "board book." A "board book" is a book with sturdy, thick pages, designed for use by young children. Later submissions in 1996 and 1998 consisted of "pitch materials," which included detailed illustrations, ideas for general story lines and television programs, specific traits of the Nicky Moonbeam characters, and goals for the Nicky Moonbeam stories.

After face-to-face meetings with the Cavaliers regarding their submissions, Random House and CTW rejected their works. Soon thereafter, in February 1999, Random House and CTW jointly published the books *Good Night, Ernie* and *Good Night, Elmo.* . . .

C. Trial Court Proceedings . . .

[The Cavaliers sued Random House and CTW for infringement of their copyrights in the Nicky Moonbeam characters, illustrations, text, and night light.]

The trial court granted Random House and CTW's motion for summary judgment on the following grounds: (1) The Cavaliers' general story lines in which anthropomorphic moon and stars ease children's fears of sleeping in the dark, and the depiction of related scenes and stock characters ("scenes-a-faire"), are not protectible by copyright; [and] (2) *Good Night, Ernie,* [and] *Good Night, Elmo* . . . were not substantially similar to the copyright-protectible material in the Cavaliers' works. . . .

II

. . . Whether a particular work is subject to copyright protection is a mixed question of fact and law subject to de novo review. "Although summary judgment is not highly favored on questions of substantial similarity in copyright cases, summary judgment is appropriate if the court can conclude, after viewing the evidence and drawing inferences in a manner most favorable to the non-moving party, that no reasonable juror could find substantial similarity of ideas and expression. . . . Where reasonable minds could differ on the issue of substantial similarity, however, summary judgment is improper." *Shaw v. Lindheim,* 919 F.2d 1353, 1355 (9th Cir. 1990) (quotation marks and citations omitted).

III

[The court noted that defendants did not dispute ownership or access.] . . . The sole issue before us is whether any of Random House's or CTW's works were substantially similar to the Cavaliers' submissions.

We employ a two-part analysis in this circuit—an extrinsic test and an intrinsic test— to determine whether two works are substantially similar. *Id.* The "extrinsic test" is an objective comparison of specific expressive elements. "[T]he test focuses on articulable similarities between the plot, themes, dialogue, mood, setting, pace, characters, and sequence of events in two works." Although originally cast as a "test for similarity of ideas," *Sid & Marty Krofft Television Prods., Inc. v. McDonald's Corp.,* 562 F.2d 1157, 1164 (9th Cir. 1977), the extrinsic test, now encompassing all objective manifestations of *expression,* no longer fits that description. The "intrinsic test" is a subjective comparison that focuses on "whether the ordinary, reasonable audience" would find the works substantially similar in the "total concept and feel of the works."

A court "must take care to inquire only whether 'the *protectible elements, standing alone,* are substantially similar.' " *Williams v. Crichton,* 84 F.3d 581, 588 (2d Cir. 1996) (emphasis in original) (citation omitted); *accord Apple Computer, Inc. v. Microsoft Corp.,* 35 F.3d 1435, 1442-43 (9th Cir. 1994). Therefore, when applying the extrinsic test, a court must filter out and disregard the non-protectible elements in making its substantial similarity determination. . . .

A. Good Night, Ernie *and* Good Night, Elmo

The Cavaliers allege that the following elements of *Good Night, Ernie* were copied by Random House and CTW from their submissions:

(1) A built-in night light with an "on" button on the inside back cover of a board book, with the light appearing as a moon with eyes, nose, and smiling benevolent expression;

(2) A character looking into the sky, wondering who and what the stars are;

(3) A character interacting with smiling, rosy-faced, bright yellow, five-pointed stars;

(4) A character sitting on a crescent moon;

(5) Smiling, bright yellow, rosy-cheeked, five-pointed stars playing and lounging on the clouds during the day and wearing colorful woolen hats;

(6) A character polishing a star with a cloth;

(7) Smiling, bright yellow, rosy-cheeked, five-pointed stars floating in a child's bedroom, glowing and comforting the child;

(8) Stars trailed by a distinctive "moondust."

The Cavaliers allege that the following elements of *Good Night, Elmo* were copied:

(1) A built-in night light comparable to that in *Good Night, Ernie;*
(2) Moonbeams shining through a window;
(3) A character saying "hop on a moonbeam and take a ride";
(4) A character interacting with smiling, yellow, rosy-cheeked, five-pointed stars trailing sparkling dust and surrounded by other stars.

We first compare the *Good Night* books to the Nicky Moonbeam stories as literary works, taken as a whole. We then compare individual art work from the *Good Night* books to that in the Cavaliers' submissions.

1. Comparison of Literary Works as a Whole

On summary judgment, only the extrinsic test matters for comparison of literary works. If the Cavaliers can show that there is a triable issue of fact under the extrinsic test, the intrinsic test's subjective inquiry must be left to the jury and Random House and CTW's motion for summary judgment must be denied. Conversely, if the Cavaliers cannot show a triable issue of fact under the extrinsic test, Random House and CTW necessarily prevail on summary judgment. A jury could not find copyright infringement because there can be no substantial similarity without evidence under both the extrinsic and intrinsic tests. We now apply the objective factors of the extrinsic test, considering only the protectible material, to determine whether *Good Night, Ernie* and/or *Good Night, Elmo,* taken as a whole, are sufficiently similar to the Cavaliers' works to raise a triable issue of fact.

The Cavaliers' Nicky Moonbeam stories and *Good Night, Elmo* share the general premise of a child, invited by a moon-type character, who takes a journey through the night sky and returns safely to bed to fall asleep. But basic plot ideas, such as this one, are not protected by copyright law. . . .

Otherwise, the actual narratives in *Good Night, Ernie* and *Good Night, Elmo* do not share much in common with the Nicky Moonbeam stories. The Nicky Moonbeam stories (2000-4000 words each) involve relatively elaborate story lines, while the text in the *Good Night* books (roughly 100 words each) describes a simple, discrete group of scenes. The stories do not share any detailed sequence of events. Moreover, although some of the Cavaliers' illustrations appear to depict events in the Nicky Moonbeam stories, the allegedly copied illustrations appear in a different context in the *Good Night* books.

The principal setting in the *Good Night* books is the night sky, which is also prevalent in the Nicky Moonbeam stories. However, this setting naturally and necessarily flows from the basic plot premise of a child's journey through the night sky; therefore, the night sky setting constitutes scenes-a-faire and cannot support a finding of substantial similarity. Furthermore, neither of the *Good Night* books involves the beach or the North Pole, the venues for significant parts of the Nicky Moonbeam stories.

The pace, dialogue, mood, and theme of the *Good Night* books differ markedly from those of the Nicky Moonbeam stories. In the *Good Night* books, the entire night journey is completed in five simple pages. There is no dialogue in *Good Night, Ernie,* and the dialogue in *Good Night, Elmo* is limited to two simple exchanges. The district court correctly characterized their mood as "fun" and "very lighthearted." There is no focused theme or message in either story.

In contrast, the Nicky Moonbeam stories progress more deliberately, with several contemplative scenes developing thematic details. There is extensive dialogue. . . . Although also written for children, the mood in the Nicky Moonbeam stories is more serious and instructional. They contain explicit messages for children. . . .

. . . [T]he main characters in the *Good Night* books are different—Sesame Street Muppets (Ernie and Elmo) rather than Nicky Moonbeam. Although *Good Night, Elmo* features Mr. Moon, he does not share any of the anthropomorphic character- istics of Nicky Moonbeam, except the ability to talk. Moreover, a moon character can be considered a stock character for children's literature, and directly flows from the idea of a journey in the night sky. None of the other characters in the Nicky Moonbeam stories are found in the *Good Night* books.

Random House and CTW contend that even if their *Good Night* books contain some protectible elements, such commonalities would not justify a finding of substantial similarity of the works. . . . We agree. . . . [A] compilation of "random similarities scattered throughout the works" is "inherently subjective and unreli- able." Th[is] argument is especially strong here since the alleged similarities are selected from over 280 pages of submissions. Further, "[c]onsideration of the total concept and feel of a work, rather than specific inquiry into plot and character development, is especially appropriate in an infringement action involving children's works[.]" Since the "total concept and feel" of the Cavaliers' stories are, as discussed above, more serious and instructional than defendants' books, a finding of infringe- ment is disfavored in this case. In sum, there is no triable issue of fact on the issue of whether either *Good Night, Ernie* or *Good Night, Elmo* is a substantially similar literary work to the Nicky Moonbeam stories under the extrinsic test.

2. Comparison of Individual Art Works

Even though we hold that the *Good Night* stories, taken as a whole, do not infringe the Cavaliers' copyright, the question remains whether protected parts of the Cavaliers' works have been copied. We therefore consider whether there exists a triable issue of substantial similarity between any of the isolated art work, as free- standing work divorced from the stories. Indeed, almost all of the allegedly copied elements are found in the Cavaliers' art work rather than in the narratives. Three of the art works present a close question of substantial similarity for summary judgment purposes: (1) the moon night light design on the extended inside back cover; (2) the illustration of stars relaxing on clouds; and (3) the illustration of stars being polished.

The basic mode of analysis for comparison of the literary elements applies to comparison of the art work. As with literary works, unprotectible elements should not be considered when applying the extrinsic test to art work. "This does not mean that at the end of the day, when the works are considered under the intrinsic test, they should not be compared as a whole. Nor does it mean that infringement cannot be based on original selection and arrangement of unprotected elements. However, the unprotectable elements have to be identified, or filtered, before the works can be considered as a whole." *Apple Computer,* 35 F.3d at 1446 (citations omitted). The precise factors evaluated for literary works do not readily apply to art works. Rather, a court looks to the similarity of the objective details in appearance. Although we do not attempt here to provide an exhaustive list of relevant factors for evaluating art work, the subject matter, shapes, colors, materials, and arrangement of the representations may be considered in determining objective similarity in appearance. . . .

A comparison of the night light designs reveals obvious similarities. The basic idea—a night light built into the inside back cover of a board book—is the same. In *Good Night, Elmo,* the night light is in the shape of a smiling moon face with pinkish cheeks and black eyes. In *Good Night, Ernie,* the exterior outline of the face on the night light is a star rather than a moon, but the features are the same. Both the moon and star faces in the *Good Night* books share these characteristics with the moon face in the Cavaliers' stories. In both of the *Good Night* books, the stars surround the night light faces in much the same manner as in the Cavaliers' stories. Both lights are positioned in the upper portion of the projecting inside back cover, as they are in the Cavaliers' design. The shape (a star enclosed in a circle) and positioning of the "on" button to the lower-right is the same. Although the concept of a built-in night light is not protectible under copyright law, the choice of a smiling moon or star face with pinkish cheeks surrounded by stars in a specific configuration, and situated above an encircled star "on" button, constitutes protectible expression. The differences—mainly that the facial features of Random House and CTW's moon and star lights have ping-pong ball-shaped eyes and bulbous nose, compared to plaintiffs' black circles and no nose—are relatively minor and do not support a grant of summary judgment for the defendant on the issue of substantial similarity.

A comparison of the two depictions of stars relaxing on clouds also reveals obvious similarities. The basic concept—stars situated on clouds—is the same. As expressed in their accompanying texts, both illustrations share the theme of exploring the stars' activities during daytime: The Cavaliers' drawing aims "to give you an idea of what stars do during the day when they are 'off work' dressing up or involved in any activity until night"; the text in *Good Night, Ernie* reads "Ernie wonders what the stars do during the day. He thinks about visiting them." Several of the stars in both illustrations are resting on clouds, appearing ready to fall asleep. Most strikingly, several of the stars in both illustrations are wearing red and green woolen (striped and solid) winter or sleeping caps. On the other hand, some of the other details differ. The stars in the Cavaliers' drawing are engaged in various activities—one is wearing a costume, one is dancing in a top hat, one is lounging, and one is yawning. In contrast, none of Random House and CTW's stars are dressed up, and all have sleepy gazes (eyelids drooping). Furthermore, the main characters in each illustration are different (*Nicky Moonbeams* v. *Ernie*) and are doing different things (reading vs. flying). Finally, as stated above, the facial features and curves of the stars are different. Despite these differences, the striking similarities in the details of the subject matter, and arrangement of the stars and the clouds, dress of the stars, and accompanying text are sufficient to survive summary judgment on the question of substantial similarity.

Finally, we compare the two depictions of stars being polished. Obvious similarities again appear. The subject matter—a star being polished—is the same. Furthermore, the stars being polished are both five-pointed, yellowish, and smiling. But the basic idea of polishing a star and the depiction of the common features of stars are unprotectible, and the two works differ significantly in the protectible details. Ernie polishes the entire star in *Good Night, Ernie,* while four smaller stars simultaneously polish the points of the star in the Cavaliers' illustration. The curves and facial details of the stars differ, as the *Good Night, Ernie* stars are rounder and have ping-pong ball-shaped eyes and red bulbous noses; moreover, there is a long line of "dirty" stars, as indicated by their brownish tint, waiting to be polished. Ernie also uses sun rays to help him polish. These significant elements are absent from the Cavaliers' work. Thus, we do not find a triable issue of substantial similarity as to this illustration. . . .

    ### *Swirsky v. Carey*
376 F.3d 841 (9th Cir. 2004)

CANBY, J.: . . .

Factual Background

This case concerns the alleged similarity between the choruses of two popular and contemporary rhythm and blues ("R & B") songs: plaintiffs' "One of Those Love Songs" ("*One*") and Mariah Carey's "Thank God I Found You" ("*Thank God*"). *One* was jointly composed by plaintiffs Seth Swirsky and Warryn Campbell (collectively "Swirsky") in 1997. . . . *One* was recorded by the musical group Xscape and released in May 1998 on Xscape's album "Traces of My Lipstick." *Thank God* was composed by defendants Carey, James Harris III, and Terry Lewis in 1999 and was released on Carey's album "Rainbow" in November 1999. *One* and *Thank God* have generally dissimilar lyrics and verse melodies, but they share an allegedly similar chorus that Swirsky claims as an infringement of *One's* copyright. Swirsky filed this action in district court against Carey, Harris, Lewis, and a number of [others] (collectively "Carey") for copyright infringement and related claims. The defendants moved for summary judgment, contending that Swirsky had failed to present a triable issue on the required first, or "extrinsic," part of our circuit's two-part test for the establishment of substantial similarity necessary to sustain a claim of copyright infringement. . . . The district court agreed . . . and granted summary judgment to Carey. . . . This appeal followed.

Substantial Similarity . . .

In determining whether two works are substantially similar, we employ a two-part analysis: an objective extrinsic test and a subjective intrinsic test. . . .

The extrinsic test considers whether two works share a similarity of ideas and expression as measured by external, objective criteria. The extrinsic test requires "analytical dissection of a work and expert testimony." *Three Boys,* 212 F.3d at 485. "Analytical dissection" requires breaking the works "down into their constituent elements, and comparing those elements for proof of copying as measured by 'substantial similarity.'" Because the requirement is one of substantial similarity to *protected* elements of the copyrighted work, it is essential to distinguish between the protected and unprotected material in a plaintiff's work.

The expert testimony on which Swirsky relied was that of Dr. Robert Walser, chair of the Musicology Department at the University of California at Los Angeles. On the basis of his aural assessment of *One* and *Thank God,* Dr. Walser opined that the two songs had substantially similar choruses.

Dr. Walser . . . stated that the two songs' choruses shared a "basic shape and pitch emphasis" in their melodies, which were played over "highly similar basslines and chord changes, at very nearly the same tempo and in the same generic style." Dr. Walser also noted that it was a "suspicious coincidence" that the two songs' choruses were both sung in B-flat. Dr. Walser further testified that the choruses in both *One* and *Thank God* shared a similar structure in that measures five through seven of each chorus were "almost exactly" the same as the first three measures of each chorus.

Dr. Walser also noted a number of differences between the two songs' choruses. Dr. Walser found that the fourth measures of the choruses were "dramatically different" from each other and noted that while the "basic, emphasized pitches and rhythms" of the basslines were alike, the basslines to both choruses were "ornamented and played slightly differently from chorus to chorus." Dr. Walser also found that certain "text-setting choices" created differences between the two songs' choruses. For example, he noted that in *Thank God,* Carey sings "D, scale degree three, for a full beat on the first beat of the first measure" while Xscape in *One* sings the same pitch "divided into two eight–note pulses." Dr. Walser ultimately concluded, however, that these differences were not enough to differentiate the songs because the overall emphasis on musical notes was the same, which "contribute[d] to the impression of similarity one hears when comparing the two songs." . . .

The district court found this evidence insufficient to survive a motion for summary judgment for four reasons. First, the district court found that Dr. Walser's expert methodology was flawed. Second, the district court, using its own analysis, found that no triable issue was raised as to the substantial similarity of measures two, three, six, seven, and eight of the two choruses. Third, the district court held that measures one and five of *One* were *scenes a faire,* and thus incapable of supporting a finding of infringement. Finally, the district court discounted any similarity between the two choruses based on key, harmony, tempo, or genre because it found no precedent for substantial similarity to be "founded solely on similarities in key, harmony, tempo or genre, either alone or in combination." We disagree with much of the district court's reasoning on all four points and conclude that Swirsky has satisfied the extrinsic test because he has provided "indicia of a sufficient disagreement concerning the substantial similarity of [the] two works."

A. Dr. Walser's Methodology

There is nothing inherently unsound about Dr. Walser's musicological methodology in this case. The district court is correct that Dr. Walser's methodology is "selective," in as much as it discounts notes that he characterizes as "ornamental." Dr. Walser, however, explained that the melody (pitch and rhythm) and bassline of a song cannot be divorced from the harmonic rhythm of a song. According to Dr. Walser, notes falling on the beat will be more prominent to the ear than notes falling off the beat. Thus, Dr. Walser opined that, even though measure three of both choruses were not identical in numerical pitch sequence or note selection, they both "emphasize[d] the second scale degree, C, over an A in the bass, resolving to the third scale degree, D, over a D in the bass in the last half of the measure." Dr. Walser provided a comparable analysis for measures one, three, and eight.

Similarly, Dr. Walser explained that some artists will ornament their notes in ways that others do not. Dr. Walser testified at deposition that both Carey and Xscape ornament their notes with "melismas" and "appoggiaturas," both of which are technical terms for moving up to the next note and then back again. Dr. Walser testified that he did not notate these ornaments in his transcriptions, or take them into account in his opinion, because he "took that to be a matter of the singer customizing the song and regarded those notes as not structural; they are ornamental." As we said in *Newton v. Diamond*, 349 F.3d 591 (2003), we can "consider only [the defendant's] appropriation of the song's compositional elements and must remove from consideration all the elements unique to [Plaintiff's] performance." *Id.* at 595. Dr. Walser's methodology sought to remove notes he perceived as performance-related.

To a certain extent, Dr. Walser's methodology does concentrate on how the two choruses sound to his expert ears, which led the district court to conclude that his testimony related to intrinsic and not extrinsic similarity. We do not agree, however, that Dr. Walser's testimony was an intrinsic rather than extrinsic analysis. He was not testifying, as the intrinsic test would require, as to whether subjectively the "ordinary, reasonable person would find the total concept and feel of the [two choruses] to be substantially similar." *Three Boys,* 212 F.3d at 485 (quoting *Pasillas v. McDonald's Corp.,* 927 F.2d 440, 442 (9th Cir. 1991)). Instead, he was stating that, although the two choruses are not exactly identical on paper, when examined in the structural context of harmony, rhythm, and meter, they are remarkably similar. We, therefore, cannot accept the district court's conclusion that Dr. Walser did not "adequately explain, based on objective criteria, why [his] particular subset of notes is more important, or more appropriately analyzed, than the other notes present in the songs." The district court erred in completely discounting Dr. Walser's expert opinion.

B. The District Court's Measure-by-Measure Analysis

The district court also erred by basing its comparison of the two choruses almost entirely on a measure-by-measure comparison of melodic note sequences from the full transcriptions of the choruses. Objective analysis of music under the extrinsic test cannot mean that a court may simply compare the numerical representations of pitch sequences and the visual representations of notes to determine that two choruses are not substantially similar, without regard to other elements of the compositions. Under that approach, expert testimony would not be required at all, for any person untrained in music could conclude that "2-2-2-2-2-2-1-2-1-3" did not match "2-2-4-3-2-3" or that a half-note is not identical to an eighth-note. Certainly, musicological experts can disagree as to whether an approach that highlights stressed notes, as Dr. Walser's does, is the most appropriate way to break down music for substantial-similarity comparison, but no approach can completely divorce pitch sequence and rhythm from harmonic chord progression, tempo, and key, and thereby support a conclusion that compositions are dissimilar as a matter of law. It is these elements that determine what notes and pitches are heard in a song and at what point in the song they are found. To pull these elements out of a song individually, without also looking at them in combination, is to perform an incomplete and distorted musicological analysis.

Furthermore, to disregard chord progression, key, tempo, rhythm, and genre is to ignore the fact that a substantial similarity can be found in a combination of elements, even if those elements are individually unprotected. Thus, although chord progressions may not be individually protected, if in combination with rhythm and pitch sequence, they show the chorus of *Thank God* to be substantially similar to the chorus of *One,* infringement can be found. *See Three Boys,* 212 F.3d at 485.

We recognize the difficulties faced by the district court in this case. . . . The application of the extrinsic test, which assesses substantial similarity of ideas and expression, to musical compositions is a somewhat unnatural task, guided by relatively little precedent. . . . The extrinsic test provides an awkward framework to apply to copyrighted works like music or art objects, which lack distinct elements of idea and expression. Nevertheless, the test is our law and we must apply it. The extrinsic test does serve the purpose of permitting summary judgment in clear cases of non-infringement, and it informs the fact-finder of some of the complexities of the medium in issue while guiding attention toward protected elements and away from unprotected elements of a composition.

In analyzing musical compositions under the extrinsic test, we have never announced a uniform set of factors to be used. We will not do so now. Music, like software programs and art objects, is not capable of ready classification into only five or six constituent elements; music is comprised of a large array of elements, some combination of which is protectable by copyright. . . . Other courts have taken account of additional components of musical compositions, including melody, harmony, rhythm, pitch, tempo, phrasing, structure, chord progressions, and lyrics. In addition, commentators have opined that timbre, tone, spatial organization, consonance, dissonance, accents, note choice, combinations, interplay of instruments, basslines, and new technological sounds can all be elements of a musical composition.

There is no one magical combination of these factors that will automatically substantiate a musical infringement suit; each allegation of infringement will be unique. So long as the plaintiff can demonstrate, through expert testimony that addresses some or all of these elements and supports its employment of them, that the similarity was "substantial" and to "protected elements" of the copyrighted work, the extrinsic test is satisfied. Swirsky has met that standard here.

C. Scenes a Faire Analysis

The district court erred in finding the first and fifth measures of *One* to be unprotectable by reason of the *scenes a faire* doctrine. *Scenes a faire* analysis requires the court to examine whether "motive" similarities that plaintiffs attribute to copying could actually be explained by the common-place presence of the same or similar "motives" within the relevant field. Under the *scenes a faire* doctrine, when certain commonplace expressions are indispensable and naturally associated with the treatment of a given idea, those expressions are treated like ideas and therefore not protected by copyright. The district court held that the first and fifth measures of *One* were not protected by copyright because Dr. Walser admitted in his deposition that the pitch sequence of the first measure of *One's* chorus was more similar to the pitch sequence in the first measure of the folk song "For He's a Jolly Good Fellow" ("*Jolly Good*") than to the pitch sequence in the first measure of *Thank God's* chorus.

The evidence does not support the district court's ruling that the first measure of *One* is a *scene a faire* as a matter of law. The songs *One* and *Jolly Good* are not in the same relevant "field" of music; *One* is in the hip-hop/R & B genre and *Jolly Good* is in the folk music genre. Thus, comparing the first measure of *One's* chorus to the first measure of *Jolly Good* does not tell the court whether the first measure of *One's* chorus is an indispensable idea within the field of hip-hop/R & B. Further, even if *One* and *Jolly Good* were in the same genre of music, a musical measure cannot be "common-place" by definition if it is shared by only two songs. *One* and *Jolly Good* are also written in different time signatures. . . .

The district court also erred in finding the fifth measure of *One* to be a *scene a faire* as a matter of law. Carey introduced no independent evidence showing that measure five of *One* was more similar to *Jolly Good* than *Thank God;* she relied exclusively on Dr. Walser's opinion that measure five was "almost identical" to measure one of *One*. As we have already pointed out, on summary judgment, "almost identical" and "identical" are not equivalents. . . . It is inappropriate to grant summary judgment on the basis of *scenes a faire* without independent evidence, unless the allegation of *scenes a faire* is uncontested. It was contested here. . . .

Conclusion

We conclude that Swirsky's expert adequately explained his methodology and provided "indicia of a sufficient disagreement concerning the substantial similarity of two works" so that the issue of the substantial similarity of the two choruses should have been presented to a jury. . . .

NOTES AND QUESTIONS

1. Under *Krofft*'s "extrinsic" test, "substantial similarity in ideas" seems intended to serve as a preliminary "filter" in the improper appropriation analysis. Does that approach make sense? Why, or why not?

2. The *Cavalier* court notes that the extrinsic test has expanded to include all "objective manifestations of expression." Why would the Ninth Circuit make that change to the *Krofft* test as originally formulated? Do you think that such a comparison is a proper first step for the court to undertake? What would the *Boisson* court say? Do you read the Second Circuit's test(s) for substantial similarity of expression as giving district courts permission to engage in an inquiry comparable to the Ninth Circuit's revised extrinsic analysis?

3. The *Swirsky* court emphasized the importance of the expert testimony regarding similarity. Review carefully the portion of the opinion that deals with the expert's methodology. How does that methodology differ from the analysis conducted by the court in *Cavalier*? Do you think the expert in *Swirsky* added any substantive analysis that a court could not undertake on its own? What was the procedural benefit to having an expert testify about substantial similarity? Were there procedural costs? Did the expert's involvement mean that the district court was accorded less authority to conduct its own analysis? Is that result appropriate?

4. How should courts treat *scenes a faire* in an infringement proceeding? Focus first on the *Cavalier* court's discussion of the common themes and visual elements in the nightlights and the two sets of drawings. Do you agree with the court's conclusions about which comparisons presented triable issues of fact and which did not? Would the *Boisson* court have analyzed the Cavaliers' copyright claims in their pictorial and sculptural works the same way?

Now consider the *Cavalier* court's affirmance of summary judgment to defendants on the Cavaliers' literary work copyright claim. Was the court correct to conclude that there was no triable issue of fact on improper appropriation of copyrightable literary expression? Would Judge Hand have agreed? In a portion of the opinion not reproduced above, the *Cavalier* court addressed the claim that the defendants infringed the plaintiffs' copyright in a series about a friendly dragon, and noted that "[t]he themes of teaching children to have confidence, to overcome their fears, and to try are not only too general to be protected but are also standard topics in children's literature." *Cavalier v. Random House, Inc.*, 297 F.3d 815, 828 (9th Cir. 2002). *See also Williams v. Crichton*, 84 F.3d 581, 589 (2d Cir. 1996) (noting that "electrified fences, automated tours, dinosaur nurseries, and uniformed workers are classic *scenes a faire* that flow from the uncopyrightable concept of a dinosaur zoo").

Finally, note the *Swirsky* court's reluctance to allow the district court to identify *scenes a faire*. Is it easier to identify *scenes a faire* in literary works and pictorial, graphic, and sculptural works than in music?

5. In recent years, as the Ninth Circuit has developed its extrinsic test, it has become more willing to allow trial courts to admit expert testimony on the substantial similarity issue. In *Swirsky*, it relied on expert testimony to reverse a grant of summary judgment. If expert testimony is important for surviving summary judgment then, at least in the Ninth Circuit, the use of experts in infringement litigation may become increasingly common. Is that a desirable state of affairs? Why, or why not?

6. Of the various substantial similarity tests you have studied in this chapter, which do you find most faithful to copyright's goals and objectives? Does your answer depend on whether you judge the risks of overprotection to be greater than the risks of underprotection?

PRACTICE EXERCISE: ADVOCACY

Review the Practice Exercise involving the Heriz and Bromley carpets, Section 5.A.3.b.ii *supra*. Assume that the case is pending in a district court in the Ninth Circuit, and that you represent the Bashian Brothers. Draft an outline for a summary judgment motion.

---

iv. Technology Cases

In technology cases, expert testimony is essential to evaluating infringement claims. Review the excerpt from the *Computer Associates v. Altai* case in Chapter 4.C.2. Recall both the factual context (a suit alleging infringement of nonliteral elements of a computer program) and the court's adoption of a three-step abstraction-filtration-comparison test for distinguishing idea from expression and determining infringement. In the following excerpt, the court considers how to assess substantial similarity.

≡ ***Computer Associates International, Inc. v. Altai, Inc.***
≡ *982 F.2d 693 (2d Cir. 1992)*

WALKER, J.: . . . Step Three: Comparison

The third and final step of the test for substantial similarity that we believe appropriate for non-literal program components entails a comparison. Once a court has sifted out all elements of the allegedly infringed program which are "ideas" or are dictated by efficiency or external factors, or taken from the public domain, there may remain a core of protectable expression. In terms of a work's copyright value, this is the golden nugget. At this point, the court's substantial similarity inquiry focuses on whether the defendant copied any aspect of this protected expression, as well as an assessment of the copied portion's relative importance with respect to the plaintiff's overall program. . . .

B. The District Court Decision . . .

1) Use of Expert Evidence in Determining Substantial Similarity Between Computer Programs

. . . [I]n deciding the limits to which expert opinion may be employed in ascertaining the substantial similarity of computer programs, we cannot disregard the highly complicated and technical subject matter at the heart of these claims. Rather we recognize the reality that computer programs are likely to be somewhat impenetrable by lay observers—whether they be judges or juries—and, thus, seem to fall outside the category of works contemplated by those who engineered the *Arnstein* test. . . .

. . . [W]e leave it to the discretion of the district court to decide to what extent, if any, expert opinion, regarding the highly technical nature of computer programs, is warranted in a given case.

In so holding, we do not intend to disturb the traditional role of lay observers in judging substantial similarity in copyright cases that involve the aesthetic arts, such as music, visual works or literature.

In this case, [the expert's] opinion was instrumental in dismantling the intricacies of computer science so that the court could formulate and apply an appropriate rule of law. While [the expert's] report and testimony undoubtedly shed valuable light on the subject matter of the litigation, Judge Pratt remained, in the final analysis, the trier of fact. The district court's use of the expert's assistance, in the context of this case, was entirely appropriate.

2) Evidentiary Analysis

The district court had to determine whether [defendant] Altai's OSCAR 3.5 program was substantially similar to [plaintiff] CA's ADAPTER. We note that Judge Pratt's method of analysis effectively served as a road map for our own, with one exception—Judge Pratt filtered out the non-copyrightable aspects of OSCAR 3.5 rather than those found in ADAPTER, the allegedly infringed program. We think that our approach—i.e., filtering out the unprotected aspects of an allegedly infringed program and then comparing the end product to the structure of the suspect program—is preferable, and therefore believe that district courts should proceed in this manner in future cases.

We opt for this strategy because, in some cases, the defendant's program structure might contain protectable expression and/or other elements that are not found in the plaintiff's program. Since it is extraneous to the allegedly copied work, this material would have no bearing on any potential substantial similarity between the two programs. Thus, its filtration would be wasteful and unnecessarily time consuming. Furthermore, by focusing the analysis on the infringing rather than on the infringed material, a court may mistakenly place too little emphasis on a quantitatively small misappropriation which is, in reality, a qualitatively vital aspect of the plaintiff's protectable expression.

The fact that the district court's analysis proceeded in the reverse order, however, had no material impact on the outcome of this case. Since Judge Pratt determined that OSCAR effectively contained no protectable expression whatso-ever, the most serious charge that can be levelled against him is that he was overly thorough in his examination.

The district court took the first step in the analysis set forth in this opinion when it separated the program by levels of abstraction. The district court stated:

> As applied to computer software programs, this abstractions test would progress in order of "increasing generality" from object code, to source code, to parameter lists, to services required, to general outline. In discussing the particular similarities, therefore, we shall focus on these levels. . . .

Moving to the district court's evaluation of OSCAR 3.5's structural compo-nents, we agree with Judge Pratt's systematic exclusion of non-protectable expres-sion. With respect to code, the district court observed that after the rewrite of OSCAR 3.4 to OSCAR 3.5, "there remained virtually no lines of code that were identical to ADAPTER." Accordingly, the court found that the code "present[ed] no similarity at all."

Next, Judge Pratt addressed the issue of similarity between the two programs' parameter lists and macros. He concluded that, viewing the conflicting evidence most favorably to CA, it demonstrated that "only a few of the lists and macros were similar to protected elements in ADAPTER; the others were either in the public domain or dictated by the functional demands of the program." As discussed above, functional elements and elements taken from the public domain do not qualify for copyright protection. With respect to the few remaining parameter lists and macros, the district court could reasonably conclude that they did not warrant a finding of infringement given their relative contribution to the overall program. . . .

The district court also found that the overlap exhibited between the list of services required for both ADAPTER and OSCAR 3.5 was "determined by the demands of the operating system and of the applications program to which it [was] to be linked through ADAPTER or OSCAR. . . ." In other words, this aspect of the program's structure was dictated by the nature of other programs with which it was designed to interact and, thus, is not protected by copyright.

Finally, in his infringement analysis, Judge Pratt accorded no weight to the similarities between the two programs' organizational charts, "because [the charts were] so simple and obvious to anyone exposed to the operation of the program[s]." CA argues that the district court's action in this regard "is not consistent with copyright law"—that "obvious" expression is protected, and that the district court erroneously failed to realize this. However, to say that elements of a work are "obvious," in the manner in which the district court used the word, is to say that they "follow naturally from the work's theme rather than from the author's crea-tivity." This is but one formulation of the *scenes a faire* doctrine, which we have already endorsed as a means of weeding out unprotectable expression. . . .

Since we accept Judge Pratt's factual conclusions and the results of his legal analysis, we affirm his denial of CA's copyright infringement claim based upon OSCAR 3.5. We emphasize that, like all copyright infringement cases, those that involve computer programs are highly fact specific. The amount of protection due structural elements, in any given case, will vary according to the protectable expression found to exist within the program at issue. . . .

NOTES AND QUESTIONS

1. Should cases like *Altai* go to the jury at all?

2. Did the *Altai* court conduct the correct comparison? If you were Computer Associates, what would you argue is the correct comparison?

3. In cases involving alleged infringement of copyright in computer program code, the approach of filtering out unprotected elements before conducting a comparison has gained widespread currency among the courts. In *Brown Bag Software v. Symantec Corp.*, 960 F.2d 1465 (9th Cir. 1992), decided the same year as *Altai*, the Ninth Circuit approved rigorous "analytic dissection" of computer program code as part of the modified "extrinsic" inquiry elaborated in its post-*Krofft* decisions.

4. In an influential decision involving competing desktop graphical user interfaces for personal computer operating systems—i.e., pictorial, graphic, or sculptural works—a district court in the Ninth Circuit warned that eliminating unprotectable elements from the substantial similarity inquiry in such cases may also create dangers:

> Because there ought to be copyright protection for an innovative melding of elements from preexisting works, elements which have been deemed "unprotectible" should not be eliminated prior to the substantial similarity of expression analysis. Suppose defendant copied plaintiff's abstract painting composed entirely of geometric forms arranged in an original pattern. The alleged infringer could argue that each expressive element (i.e., the geometric forms) is unprotectible under the functionality, merger, *scenes a faire*, and unoriginality theories and, thus, all elements should be excluded prior to the substantial similarity of expression analysis. Then, there would be nothing left for purposes of determining substantial similarity of expression. . . .
>
> [I]f it is determined that the defendant used the unprotectible elements in an arrangement which is not substantially similar to the plaintiff's work, then no copyright infringement can be found. If, on the other hand, the works are deemed substantially similar, then copyright infringement will be established even though the copyrighted work is composed of unprotectible elements. There is simply no other logical way of protecting an innovative arrangement or "look and feel" of certain works.

Apple Computer, Inc. v. Microsoft Corp., 779 F. Supp. 133, 135-36 (N.D. Cal. 1991).

The *Apple v. Microsoft* court, however, ultimately applied a quite rigorous dissection analysis to the works at issue, holding that since both works were composed primarily of unprotectable elements, the defendant's work should not be found to infringe unless it was "virtually identical" to the plaintiff's work. *See Apple Computer, Inc. v. Microsoft Corp.*, 799 F. Supp. 1006 (N.D. Cal. 1992). The Ninth Circuit affirmed, holding that such dissection does not "run afoul" of *Krofft*'s admonition to assess the "total concept and feel" of the work, because "the unprotectable elements have to be identified, or filtered, before the works can be considered as a whole. *Apple Computer, Inc. v. Microsoft Corp.,* 35 F.3d 1435, 1445-46 (9th Cir. 1994), *cert. denied,* 513 U.S. 1184 (1995). The court explained:

> Having dissected the alleged similarities and considered the range of possible expression, the court must define the scope of the plaintiff's copyright—that is, decide whether the work is entitled to "broad" or "thin" protection. Depending on the degree of protection, the court must set the appropriate standard for a subjective comparison of the works to determine whether, as a whole, they are sufficiently similar to support a finding of illicit copying.

Id. at 1443. Does the Ninth Circuit's *Apple v. Microsoft* opinion successfully reconcile the competing imperatives of dissection and holistic comparison? How does the "virtually identical" test compare to the "more discerning observer" test described in *Boisson,* section A.3.b.2 above?

5. What are the advantages and disadvantages of using different tests of substantial similarity for different types of works? Does this practice violate the nondiscrimination principle enunciated by Justice Holmes in *Bleistein v. Donaldson,* Chapter 2.A.2.a?

B. DERIVATIVE WORKS

In addition to the "core" right to reproduce the work in copies, the Copyright Act also grants to copyright owners the exclusive right "to prepare derivative works based upon the copyrighted work." 17 U.S.C. §106(2). Recall that the Act defines a derivative work as follows:

> A derivative work is a work based upon one or more preexisting works, such as a translation, musical arrangement, dramatization, fictionalization, motion picture version, sound recording, art reproduction, abridgement, condensation, or any other form in which a work may be recast, transformed, or adapted. A work consisting of editorial revisions, annotations, elaborations, or other modifications which, as a whole, represent an original work of authorship is a "derivative work."

Id. §101. Recall also that §103(a) provides that derivative works meeting the statutory standards of §102 are themselves independently copyrightable. In Chapter 2, we discussed what constitutes originality sufficient to support the *grant* of a copyright in a derivative work. In this section, we focus on a different question: the *scope* of the exclusive right of the author to prepare and to authorize others to prepare derivative works based upon the copyrighted work.

The §106(2) exclusive right to prepare derivative works based upon the copyrighted work is closely allied to the reproduction right and, as a practical matter, overlaps with it substantially. Quite often, the plaintiff will allege and the court (or jury) will find that the same conduct infringes both rights. What is the rationale for giving copyright owners the exclusive right to prepare derivative works, and how broadly should the grant be construed? In particular, how does one apply the §101 definition in real cases involving alleged infringement of the §106(2) right? Additionally, how does the derivative work right differ from the exclusive right of reproduction?

1. Reproduction or Derivative Work?

One way to view the derivative work right is on a continuum with the reproduction right: On one end are literal reproductions of entire works and on the other are derivative works reflecting substantial transformations. In the middle are new works that incorporate parts or slight modifications of underlying works. Is there a point on the continuum at which the works in question are no longer reproductions but instead (and only) derivative works? Or do the rights overlap? If the latter, how much of the continuum consists of overlapping protection?

Warner Bros. Entertainment, Inc. v. RDR Books
575 F. Supp. 2d 513 (S.D.N.Y. 2008)

PATTERSON, J.: . . .

Findings of Fact

I. *The Copyrighted Works*

Plaintiff J.K. Rowling ("Rowling") is the author of the highly acclaimed *Harry Potter* book series. Written for children but enjoyed by children and adults alike, the *Harry Potter* series chronicles the lives and adventures of Harry Potter and his friends as they come of age at the Hogwarts School of Witchcraft and Wizardry and face the evil Lord Voldemort. It is a tale of a fictional world filled with magical spells, fantastical creatures, and imaginary places and things.

Rowling published the first of seven books in the series, *Harry Potter and the Philosopher's Stone,* in the United Kingdom in 1997. In 1998, the first book was published in the United States as *Harry Potter and the Sorcerer's Stone.* Over the next ten years, Rowling wrote and published the remaining six books in the *Harry Potter* series: *Harry Potter and the Chamber of Secrets* (1998), *Harry Potter and the Prisoner of Azkaban* (1999), *Harry Potter and the Goblet of Fire* (2000), *Harry Potter and the Order of the Phoenix* (2003), and *Harry Potter and the Half-Blood Prince* (2005). The seventh and final book, *Harry Potter and the Deathly Hallows* was released on July 21, 2007. Rowling owns a United States copyright in each of the *Harry Potter* books.

The *Harry Potter* series has achieved enormous popularity and phenomenal sales. The books have won numerous awards, including children's literary awards and the British Book Award. Most gratifying to Rowling is that the *Harry Potter* series has been credited with encouraging readership among children.

As a result of the success of the *Harry Potter* books, Plaintiff Warner Bros. Entertainment Inc. ("Warner Brothers") obtained from Rowling the exclusive film rights to the entire seven-book *Harry Potter* series. . . .

In addition, Rowling wrote two short companion books to the *Harry Potter* series (the "companion books"), the royalties from which she donated to the charity Comic Relief. The first, *Quidditch Through the Ages* (2001), recounts the history and development of "quidditch," an imaginary sport featured in the *Harry Potter* series that involves teams of witches and wizards on flying broomsticks. The second, *Fantastic Beasts & Where to Find Them* (2001), is an A-to-Z encyclopedia of the imaginary beasts and beings that exist in *Harry Potter*'s fictional world. Both appear in the *Harry Potter* series as textbooks that the students at Hogwarts use in their studies, and the companion books are marketed as such. Neither of the companion books is written in narrative form; instead each book chronicles and expands on the fictional facts that unfold in the *Harry Potter* series. The companion books are both registered with the United States Copyright Office. Although the market for the companion books is not nearly as large as the market for the *Harry Potter* series, Rowling's companion books have earned more than $30 million to date.

Rowling has stated on a number of occasions since 1998 that, in addition to the two companion books, she plans to publish a *"Harry Potter* encyclopedia" after the completion of the series and again donate the proceeds to charity. . . .

II. The Allegedly Infringing Work

Defendant RDR Books is a Michigan-based publishing company that seeks to publish a book entitled "The Lexicon," the subject of this lawsuit. Steven Vander Ark, a former library media specialist at a middle school in Michigan, is the attributed author of the Lexicon. He is also the originator, owner, and operator of "The Harry Potter Lexicon" website, a popular *Harry Potter* fan site from which the content of the Lexicon is drawn.

A. *The Origins of the Lexicon . . .*

Vander Ark began work on his website, "The Harry Potter Lexicon" (the "website" or "Lexicon website"), in 1999 and opened the website in 2000. His purpose in establishing the website was to create an encyclopedia that collected and organized information from the *Harry Potter* books in one central source for fans to use for reference. At its launch, the website featured Vander Ark's descriptive lists of spells, characters, creatures, and magical items from *Harry Potter* with hyperlinks to cross-referenced entries. In response to feedback from users of the website, Vander Ark developed an A-to-Z index to each list to allow users to search for entries alphabetically.

The website presently features several indexed lists of people, places, and things from *Harry Potter,* including the "Encyclopedia of Spells," "Encyclopedia of Potions," "Wizards, Witches, and Beings," "The Bestiary," and "Gazetteer of the Wizarding World." In addition to these reference features, the website contains a variety of supplemental material pertaining to *Harry Potter,* including fan art, commentary, essays, timelines, forums, and interactive data. The website is currently run by a staff of seven or eight volunteers, including four primary editors, all of whom were recruited to help update and expand the website's content after the publication of the fifth book in the *Harry Potter* series. The website uses minimal advertising to offset the costs of operation. Use of the website is free and unrestricted. . . .

Vander Ark has received positive feedback, including from Rowling and her publishers, about the value of the Lexicon website as a reference source. In May 2004, Vander Ark read a remark by Rowling posted on her website praising his Lexicon website as follows: "This is such a great site that I have been known to sneak into an internet cafe while out writing and check a fact rather than go into a book-shop and buy a copy of Harry Potter (which is embarrassing). A website for the dangerously obsessive; my natural home." In July 2005, Vander Ark received a note from Cheryl Klein, a Senior Editor at Scholastic Inc., American publisher of the *Harry Potter* series, thanking him and his staff "for the wonderful resource [his] site provides for fans, students, and indeed editors & copyeditors of the Harry Potter series," who "referred to the Lexicon countless times during the editing of [the sixth book in the series], whether to verify a fact, check a timeline, or get a chapter & book reference for a particular event." In September 2006, Vander Ark was invited by Warner Brothers to the set of the film *The Order of the Phoenix*, where he met David Heyman, the producer of all the *Harry Potter* films. Heyman told Vander Ark that Warner Brothers used the Lexicon website almost every day. . . .

Prior to any discussions with RDR Books about publishing portions of the Lexicon website as a book, Vander Ark was aware of Rowling's public statements regarding her intention to write a *Harry Potter* encyclopedia upon completion of the seventh book in the series. In June 2007, just before the release of the seventh book, Vander Ark emailed Christopher Little Literary Agency, Rowling's literary agent in the United Kingdom, and suggested that he would be "a good candidate for work as an editor, given [his] work on the Lexicon," should Rowling start working on an encyclopedia or other reference to the *Harry Potter* series. The literary agency advised him that Rowling intended to work alone and did not require a collaborator.

B. RDR Books' Acquisition and Marketing of the Lexicon

Roger Rapoport is the president of Defendant RDR Books. Rapoport learned of Vander Ark and the Lexicon website when he read an article in his local newspaper dated July 23, 2007, profiling Vander Ark as a well known figure within the *Harry Potter* fan community and the proprietor of the Lexicon website who "holds the key to all things 'Harry Potter.'" . . .

At his first meeting with Rapoport in August 2007, Vander Ark raised his concerns regarding the permissibility of publishing the Lexicon in view of Rowling's plan to publish an encyclopedia and her copyrights in the *Harry Potter* books. Prior to August 2007, Vander Ark had developed and circulated the opinion that publishing "any book that is a guide to [the *Harry Potter*] world" would be a violation of Rowling's intellectual property rights. Vander Ark had even stated on a public internet newsgroup that he would not publish the Lexicon "in any form except online" without permission because Rowling, not he, was "entitled to that market." Vander Ark changed his mind about publishing the Lexicon after Rapoport reassured him that he had looked into the legal issue and determined that publication of content from the Lexicon website in book form was legal. Rapoport agreed to stand by this opinion by adding an atypical clause to the publishing contract providing that RDR would defend and indemnify Vander Ark in the event of any lawsuits. . . .

. . . The idea was to publish the first complete guide to the *Harry Potter* series that included information from the seventh and final *Harry Potter* novel. Vander Ark believed that there was an advantage to being the first reference guide on the market to cover all seven *Harry Potter* books. He also believed that by virtue of its completeness, the Lexicon would be most useful for the purpose it sought to serve, namely helping readers and fans to find information from the Harry Potter novels. . . .

D. The Content of the Lexicon

The Lexicon is an A-to-Z guide to the creatures, characters, objects, events, and places that exist in the world of *Harry Potter*. As received by the Court in evidence, the Lexicon manuscript is more than 400 type-written pages long and contains 2,437 entries organized alphabetically. . . .

The Lexicon manuscript was created using the encyclopedia entries from the Lexicon website. Because of space limitations for the printed work, which seeks to be complete but also easy to use, about half of the material from the website was not included in the Lexicon manuscript. . . .

The Lexicon entries cull every item and character that appears in the *Harry Potter* works, no matter if it plays a significant or insignificant role in the story. The entries cover every spell (e.g., Expecto Patronum, Expelliarmus, and Incendio), potion (e.g., Love Potion, Felix Felicis, and Draught of Living Death), magical item or device (e.g., Deathly Hallows, Horcrux, Cloak of Invisibility), form of magic (e.g., Legilimency, Occlumency, and the Dark Arts), creature (e.g., Blast-Ended Skrewt, Dementors, and Blood-Sucking Bugbears), character (e.g., Harry Potter, Hagrid, and Lord Voldemort), group or force (e.g., Aurors, Dumbledore's Army, Death Eaters), invented game (e.g., Quidditch), and imaginary place (e.g., Hogwarts School of Witchcraft and Wizardry, Diagon Alley, and the Ministry of Magic) that appear in the *Harry Potter* works. . . .

Each entry, with the exception of the shortest ones, gathers and synthesizes pieces of information relating to its subject that appear scattered across the *Harry Potter* novels, the companion books, . . . and published interviews of Rowling. The types of information contained in the entries include descriptions of the subject's attributes, role in the story, relationship to other characters or things, and events involving the subject. Repositories of such information, the entries seek to give as complete a picture as possible of each item or character in the *Harry Potter* world, many of which appear only sporadically throughout the series or in various sources of *Harry Potter* material.

The snippets of information in the entries are generally followed by citations in parentheses that indicate where they were found within the corpus of the *Harry*

Potter works. The thoroughness of the Lexicon's citation, however, is not consistent; some entries contain very few citations in relation to the amount material provided. . . . When the Lexicon cites to one of the seven *Harry Potter* novels, the citation provides only the book and chapter number. Vander Ark explained that page numbers were excluded from the citations because the various editions of the *Harry Potter* books have different pagination, but the chapter numbers remain consistent. The Lexicon neither assigns a letter to each edition nor specifies a standard edition while providing a conversion table for other editions, practices which Plaintiffs' expert Jeri Johnson testified were common for reference guides.

While not its primary purpose, the Lexicon includes commentary and background information from outside knowledge on occasion. For example, the Lexicon contains sporadic etymological references. . . . The Lexicon also points to the very few "flints," or errors in the continuity of the story, that appear in the *Harry Potter* series.

While there was considerable opining at trial as to the type of reference work the Lexicon purports to be and whether it qualifies as such (no doubt in part due to its title), the Lexicon fits in the narrow genre of non-fiction reference guides to fictional works. As Defendant's expert testified, the *Harry Potter* series is a multi-volume work of fantasy literature, similar to the works of J.R.R. Tolkien and C.S. Lewis. Such works lend themselves to companion guides or reference works because they reveal an elaborate imaginary world over thousands of pages, involving many characters, creatures, and magical objects that appear and reappear across thousands of pages. (Tr. (Sorensen) at 504:16-23; *id.* at 507:1-5 (testifying that she found 19 or 20 companion guides to J.R.R. Tolkien's works, and about 15 guides to C.S. Lewis's works).) Fantasy literature spawns books having a wide variety of purposes and formats, as demonstrated by the books about *Harry Potter* that Plaintiffs entered into evidence. (Pl. Exs. 73, 74, 75, 192; 13E-13G.) The Lexicon, an A-to-Z guide which synthesizes information from the series and generally provides citations for location of that information rather than offering commentary, is most comparable to the comprehensive work of Paul F. Ford, *Companion to Narnia: A Complete Guide to the Magical World of C.S. Lewis's* The Chronicles of Narnia, or the unauthorized A-to-Z guide by George W. Beahm, *Fact, Fiction, and Folklore in Harry Potter's World: An Unofficial Guide.*[4] . . .

Although it is difficult to quantify how much of the language in the Lexicon is directly lifted from the *Harry Potter* novels and companion books, the Lexicon indeed contains at least a troubling amount of direct quotation or close paraphrasing of Rowling's original language.[6] The Lexicon occasionally uses quotation marks to indicate Rowling's language, but more often the original language is copied without

---

4. The *Companion to Narnia,* however, is far more erudite and informative than the Lexicon. The *Harry Potter* guide by Beahm does not provide citations for the sources of its information and is less comprehensive than the Lexicon in that it covers only certain categories of information (e.g., Fabulous Beasts, Wizards, Magical Spells, etc.).

6. Some of the most extensive direct quotation occurs where the Lexicon reproduces a song or poem that appears in the novels. . . .

quotation marks, often making it difficult to know which words are Rowling's and which are Vander Ark's.

For example, in the entry for "armor, goblin made," the Lexicon uses Rowling's poetic language nearly verbatim without quotation marks.[7] The original language from *Harry Potter and the Deathly Hallows* reads:

> "Muggle-borns," he said. "Goblin-made armour does not require cleaning, simple girl. Goblins' silver repels mundane dirt, imbibing only that which strengthens it."

The Lexicon entry for "armor, goblin made" reads in its entirety:

> Some armor in the wizarding world is made by goblins, and it is quite valuable. (e.g., HBP20) According to Phineas Nigellus, goblin-made armor does not require cleaning, because goblins' silver repels mundane dirt, imbibing only that which strengthens it, such as basilisk venom. In this context, "armor" also includes blades such as swords.

Although the Lexicon entry introduces Rowling's language with the phrase, "According to Phineas Nigellus," it does not use quotation marks.

The Lexicon entry for "Dementors" reproduces Rowling's vivid description of this creature sometimes using quotation marks and sometimes quoting or closely paraphrasing without indicating which language is original expression. The original language appears in Chapters 5 and 10 of *Harry Potter and the Prisoner of Azkaban* as follows:

> . . . Its face was completely hidden beneath its hood. . . . There was a hand protruding from the cloak and it was glistening, grayish, slimy-looking, and scabbed, like something dead that had decayed in water . . .
>
> And then the thing beneath the hood, whatever it was, drew a long, slow, rattling breath, as though it were trying to suck something more than air from its surroundings.
> * * *
> Dementors are among the foulest creatures to walk this earth. They infest the darkest, filthiest places, they glory in decay and despair, they drain peace, hope, and happiness out of the air around them. Even Muggles feel their presence, though they can't see them. Get too near a dementor and every good feeling, every happy memory will be sucked out of you. If it can, the dementor will feed on you long enough to reduce you to something like itself . . . soulless and evil. . . .

The Lexicon entry for "Dementors" reads in its entirety:

> Dementors are some of the most terrible creatures on earth, flying tall black spectral humanoid things with flowing robes. They "infest the darkest, filthiest places, they glory in decay and despair, they drain peace, hope, and happiness out of the air around them," according to Lupin (PA10). Dementors affect even Muggles, although Muggles can't see the foul, black creatures. Dementors feed on positive human emotions; a large crowd is like a feast to them. They drain a wizard of his power if left with them too long. They were the guards at Azkaban and made that place horrible indeed. The Ministry used Dementors as guards in its courtrooms as well (GF30, DH13).

---

7. [In the Lexicon, i]talics are used in the block quotations to highlight the original language that is copied or paraphrased. The italics do not appear in the originals.

There are certain defenses one can use against Dementors, specifically the Patronus Charm. A Dementor's breath sounds rattling and like it's trying to suck more than air out of a room. Its hands are "glistening, grayish, slimy-looking, and scabbed." It exudes a biting, soul-freezing cold (PA5). . . .

[The court provided several additional examples of verbatim copying and close paraphrasing. – Eds.]

An example of particularly extensive direct quotation is found in the Lexicon entry for "Trelawney, Sibyll Patricia," the professor of Divination at the Hogwarts School who tells two important prophecies in the story. The Lexicon not only reproduces her prophecies word-for-word in their entirety, but in doing so, reveals dramatic plot twists and how they are resolved in the series. For example, the first prophecy reads:

> The one with the power to vanquish the Dark Lord approaches. . . . Born to those who have thrice defied him, born as the seventh month dies . . . and the Dark Lord will mark him as his equal, but he will have power the Dark Lord knows not . . . and either must die at the hand of the other for neither can live while the other survives. . . . The one with the power to vanquish the Dark Lord will be born as the seventh month dies. . . .

The Lexicon entry reproduces this prophecy exactly but in italics and indented. (Pl. Ex. 1, entry for "Trelawney, Sibyll Patricia.") The Lexicon entry continues by discussing what happens as a result of this prophecy: "Severus Snape was eavesdropping on this conversation and he reported the first part of the Prophecy to the Dark Lord. Voldemort immediately began searching for this threat, and centered his attention on the child of Lily and James Potter. (OP 37)." The entry then quotes the second prophecy, but without a citation to where it appears in the *Harry Potter* series.

A number of Lexicon entries copy Rowling's artistic literary devices that contribute to her distinctive craft as a writer. . . .

. . . [T]he Lexicon entry for "Marchbanks, Madam Griselda" uses an artful simile from the original works to describe this character. Rowling's language in *Harry Potter and the Order of the Phoenix* reads:

> . . . Harry thought Professor Marchbanks must be the tiny, stooped witch with a face so lined it looked as though it had been draped in cobwebs; Umbridge was speaking to her very deferentially. . . .

The Lexicon entry reads in part:

> . . . Madam Marchbanks in June 1996 was tiny and stooped, her face so lined it appeared draped in cobwebs. . . .

The Lexicon's close paraphrasing is not limited to the seven *Harry Potter* novels, but can be found in entries drawn from the companion books as well. For example, the entry for "Montrose Magpies" uses language from *Quidditch Through the Ages*. The original language reads:

> The Magpies are the most successful team in the history of the British and Irish League, which they have won thirty-two times. Twice European Champions. . . . The Magpies wear black and white robes with one magpie on the chest and another on the back.

The Lexicon entry reads:

> The most successful Quidditch team in history, which has won the British and Irish league thirty-two times and the European Cup twice. Their robes are black and white, with one magpie on the chest and another on the back (QA7). . . .

Aside from verbatim copying, another factual issue of contention at trial was the Lexicon entries that contain summaries of certain scenes or key events in the *Harry Potter* series. Most frequently, these are the longer entries that describe important objects, such as the "Deathly Hallows," or momentous events, such as the "Triwizard Tournament," or that trace the development of an important character, such as Harry Potter, Lord Voldemort, Severus Snape, and Albus Dumbledore. Plaintiffs' expert testified at length that in her opinion these entries constitute "plot summaries," . . . while Defendant's expert characterized them as character studies or analysis.

Neither of these characterizations is exactly apt. Without endorsing one characterization or another, such entries in the Lexicon do encapsulate elements of the very elaborate and wide ranging plot (sometimes in chronological order, sometimes not) confined to the subject of the entry. In the entries for significant characters, these plot elements are occasionally used to support an observation about the character's nature or development. . . .

Conclusions of Law . . .

B. *Copying*

. . . While acknowledging actual copying, Defendant disputes that the copying amounts to an improper or unlawful appropriation of Rowling's works. . . .

The appropriate inquiry under the substantial similarity test is whether "the copying is quantitatively and qualitatively sufficient to support the legal conclusion that infringement (actionable copying) has occurred." *Ringgold* [*v. Black Entertainment Television, Inc.*], 126 F.3d [70,] at 75 [2d Cir. 1997]. . . .

In evaluating the quantitative extent of copying in the substantial similarity analysis, the Court "considers the amount of copying not only of direct quotations and close paraphrasing, but also of all other protectable expression in the original work." *Castle Rock* [*Entertainment, Inc. v. Carol Publ'g Group, Inc.*], 150 F.3d [132,] at 140 n.6 [2d Cir. 1997]. . . .

Plaintiffs have shown that the Lexicon copies a sufficient quantity of the *Harry Potter* series to support a finding of substantial similarity between the Lexicon and Rowling's novels. The Lexicon draws 450 manuscript pages worth of material primarily from the 4,100-page *Harry Potter* series. Most of the Lexicon's 2,437 entries contain direct quotations or paraphrases, plot details, or summaries of scenes from one or more of the *Harry Potter* novels. As Defendant admits, "the Lexicon reports thousands of fictional facts from the Harry Potter works." Although hundreds of pages or thousands of fictional facts may amount to only a fraction of the seven-book series, this quantum of copying is sufficient to support a finding of substantial similarity where the copied expression is entirely the product of the original author's imagination and creation. *See Castle Rock*, 150 F.3d at 138 (concluding that a Seinfeld trivia book that copied 643 fragments from 84 copyrighted Seinfeld episodes "plainly crossed the quantitative copying threshold under *Ringgold*"); *Twin Peaks Prods., Inc. v. Publ'ns Int'l, Ltd.*, 996 F.2d 1366, 1372 (2d Cir. 1993) (upholding the district court's conclusion that "the identity of 89 lines of dialogue" between *Twin Peaks* teleplays and a guide to the television series constituted substantial similarity).

The quantitative extent of the Lexicon's copying is even more substantial with respect to *Fantastic Beasts* and *Quidditch Through the Ages*. Rowling's companion books are only fifty-nine and fifty-six pages long, respectively. The Lexicon reproduces a substantial portion of their content, with only sporadic omissions, across hundreds of entries.

As to the qualitative component of the substantial similarity analysis, Plaintiffs have shown that the Lexicon draws its content from creative, original expression in the *Harry Potter* series and companion books. Each of the 2,437 entries in the Lexicon contains "fictional facts" created by Rowling, such as the attributes of imaginary creatures and objects, the traits and undertakings of major and minor characters, and the events surrounding them. . . .

Defendant . . . argues that while a substantial similarity may be found where invented facts are "reported and arranged in such a way as to tell essentially the same story" as the original, "the order in which the fictional facts are presented in the Lexicon bears almost no resemblance to the order in which the fictional facts are arranged to create the story of Harry Potter and the universe he inhabits." Reproducing original expression in fragments or in a different order, however, does not preclude a finding of substantial similarity . . . . Here, the Lexicon's rearrangement of Rowling's fictional facts does not alter the protected expression such that the Lexicon ceases to be substantially similar to the original works.

Furthermore, the law in this Circuit is clear that "the concept of similarity embraces not only global similarities in structure and sequence, but localized similarity in language." *Twin Peaks*, 996 F.2d at 1372 (endorsing the taxonomy of "comprehensive nonliteral similarity" and "fragmented literal similarity" from the Nimmer treatise, 4 *Nimmer* §13.03[A][2]). In evaluating fragmented literal similarity, or "localized similarity in language," the Court examines the copying of direct quotations or close paraphrasing of the original work. As determined in the Findings of Fact, the Lexicon contains a considerable number of direct quotations (often without quotation marks) and close paraphrases of vivid passages in the Harry Potter works. Although in these instances, the Lexicon often changes a few words from the original or rewrites original dialogue in the third person, the language is nonetheless substantially similar. . . .

. . . To be sure, this case is different from *Twin Peaks*, where forty-six pages of the third chapter of a guidebook to the *Twin Peaks* television series were found to constitute "essentially a detailed recounting of the first eight episodes of the series. Every intricate plot twist and element of character development appear[ed] in the Book in the same sequence as in the teleplays." 996 F.2d at 1372-73. Those "plot summaries" were far more detailed, comprehensive, and parallel to the original episodes than the so-called "plot summaries" in this case. Nonetheless, it is clear that the plotlines and scenes encapsulated in the Lexicon are appropriated from the original copyrighted works. Under these circumstances, Plaintiffs have established a prima facie case of infringement.

C. Derivative Work

Plaintiffs allege that the Lexicon not only violates their right of reproduction, but also their right to control the production of derivative works. The Copyright Act defines a "derivative work" as "a work based upon one or more preexisting works, such as a translation, musical arrangement, dramatization, fictionalization, motion picture version, sound recording, art reproduction, abridgment, condensation, or any other form in which a work may be *recast, transformed, or adapted*" 17 U.S.C. §101 (emphasis added). A work "consisting of editorial revisions, annotations, elaborations, or other modifications which, as a whole, represents an original work of authorship" is also a derivative work. *Id.*

A work is not derivative, however, simply because it is "based upon" the pre-existing works.[17] If that were the standard, then parodies and book reviews would fall under the definition, and certainly "ownership of copyright does not confer a legal right to control public evaluation of the copyrighted work." *Ty, Inc. v. Publ'ns Int'l Ltd.*, 292 F.3d 512, 521 (7th Cir. 2002). The statutory language seeks to protect works that are "recast, transformed, or adapted" into another medium, mode, language, or revised version, while still representing the "original work of authorship." *See Castle Rock*, 150 F.3d at 143 n.9 (stating that "derivative works that are subject to the author's copyright transform an original work into a new mode of presentation"); *Twin Peaks*, 996 F.2d at 1373 (finding a derivative work where a guidebook based on the *Twin Peaks* television series "contain[ed] a substantial amount of material from the teleplays, transformed from one medium to another"). Thus in *Ty, Inc. v. Publications International Ltd.*, Judge Posner concluded, as the parties had stipulated, that a collectors' guide to Beanie Babies was not a derivative work because "guides don't *recast, transform, or adapt* the things to which they are guides." 292 F.3d at 520 (emphasis added).

Plaintiffs argue that based on the *Twin Peaks* decision "companion guides constitute derivative works where, as is the case here, they 'contain a substantial amount of material from the underlying work.'" This argument inaccurately states the holding of *Twin Peaks* and overlooks two important distinctions between the Lexicon and the guidebook in *Twin Peaks*. First, as mentioned earlier, the portions of the Lexicon that encapsulate plot elements or sketch plotlines bear no comparison with the guidebook in *Twin Peaks*, whose plot summaries giving "elaborate recounting of plot details" were found to constitute an "abridgement" of the original work. *See Twin Peaks*, 996 F.2d at 1373 n.2 (reproducing an excerpt of the infringing book containing a high degree of detail). Given that the Lexicon's use

---

17. The law in this Circuit has recognized that "even when one work is 'based upon' another, 'if the secondary work sufficiently transforms the expression of the original work such that the two works cease to be substantially similar, then the secondary work is not a derivative work and, for that matter, does not infringe the copyright of the original work.'" *Well-Made Toy Mfg. Corp. v. Goffa Int'l Corp.*, 354 F.3d 112, 117 (2d Cir. 2003) (quoting *Castle Rock*, 150 F.3d at 143 n.9).

of plot elements is far from an "elaborate recounting" and does not follow the same plot structure as the *Harry Potter* novels, Plaintiffs' suggestion that these portions of the Lexicon are "unauthorized abridgements" is unpersuasive. Second, and more importantly, although the Lexicon "contain[s] a substantial amount of material" from the *Harry Potter* works, the material is not merely "transformed from one medium to another," as was the case in *Twin Peaks. Id.* at 1373. By condensing, synthesizing, and reorganizing the preexisting material in an A-to-Z reference guide, the Lexicon does not recast the material in another medium to retell the story of *Harry Potter,* but instead gives the copyrighted material another purpose. That purpose is to give the reader a ready understanding of individual elements in the elaborate world of *Harry Potter* that appear in voluminous and diverse sources. As a result, the Lexicon no longer "represents [the] original work[s] of authorship." 17 U.S.C. §101. Under these circumstances, and because the Lexicon does not fall under any example of derivative works listed in the statute, Plaintiffs have failed to show that the Lexicon is a derivative work. . . .

NOTES AND QUESTIONS

1. How is infringement of the derivative work right to be determined? As described by the court, the reference guide at issue in *Twin Peaks* was found to infringe both the reproduction right and the derivative work right. The other cited Second Circuit case, *Castle Rock*, involved a quiz book concerning the characters and events in the long-running television show *Seinfeld*. The Second Circuit's opinion affirming summary judgment of infringement did not specify whether that result was based on the reproduction right, the derivative work right, or both. Instead, the court indicated that infringement of both rights should be assessed using the now-familiar test of "substantial similarity." Does that make sense? Under that approach, what independent work does the derivative work right do?

2. If infringement of the derivative work right is assessed using the substantial similarity standard, and the Lexicon infringes the reproduction right, why isn't the Lexicon also an infringing derivative work? Reread footnote 17 in the court's opinion. As you will see in Chapter 10, one of the important considerations in many fair use cases is whether the use is "transformative." A clear tension exists between the rule allowing transformative uses as fair uses and the copyright owner's right to control the preparation of derivative works. In *Castle Rock*, the court stated: "Although derivative works that are subject to the author's copyright transform an original work into a new mode of presentation, such works—unlike works of fair use—take expression for purposes that are not 'transformative.'" *Castle Rock*, 150 F.3d at 143. The *Warner Bros.* court, however, does not hold that the Lexicon is a fair use. Rather, it holds that the derivative work right is not implicated. What kinds of repurposing are fundamental enough to produce this result?

3. Would you infringe the copyright in *Harry Potter and The Sorcerer's Stone* if you wrote a book report that described the plot? Could there be a noninfringing guide to the Harry Potter books? If so, what must an author of a nonfiction reference guide do in order not to infringe the copyright in the underlying fictional work?

Would RDR Books still be liable for infringement if it had dutifully put quotation marks around each copied passage and noted its source?

4. Note that both J.K. Rowling, the author of the *Harry Potter* books, and Warner Brothers Entertainment, the exclusive licensee of the film production rights, were the plaintiffs in this litigation. Are the movies that Warner Brothers created "reproductions" of the books? Derivative works? Both?

5. Can a plaintiff state a cause of action for infringement of the copyright in a *series* of works? If the Lexicon is not substantially similar to any one of the books but substantially similar to the series taken as a whole, could that provide the basis for an infringement claim? If so, what would be the basis for the alleged similarity? You know from Chapter 2 that facts are not eligible for copyright protection. Does *Warner Bros.* hold that fictional facts receive protection?

2. Copyright, Markets, and Derivative Works

Is the derivative work right meant to give the copyright owner full creative and economic control over subsequent uses of the expression? Or are its goals more modest? The record in the *Warner Bros.* case showed that prior to entering a business relationship with RDR Books, the author of the Lexicon had developed a sense that the "market" for a Harry Potter encyclopedia belonged to J.K. Rowling. Was he right? How should a court determine whether a particular market is within a copyright owner's control? You will see in Chapter 10 that analysis of actual or potential markets for a copyrighted work is relevant to the fair use inquiry. Is such analysis relevant to determining whether something is a derivative work in the first place? Copyright scholars have developed very different views on how to answer this question, and correspondingly different views of the purpose of the derivative work right. Consider the following excerpts:

≡ ***Paul Goldstein, Derivative Rights and Derivative Works***
≡ ***in Copyright***
   30 J. Copr. Soc'y 209, 217, 227 (1983).

Taken together, sections 102(a) and 103, and sections 106(1) and 106(2), give a prospective copyright owner the incentive to make an original, underlying work, the exclusive right to make new, successive works incorporating expressive elements from the underlying work, and the incentive and exclusive right to make still newer, successive works based on these. The continuum may stretch from an underlying novel or story to the work's adaptation into a motion picture, its transformation into a television series, and the eventual embodiment of its characters in dolls, games and other merchandise. The works at the outer reaches of this continuum, and some intermediate works as well, will frequently bear scant resemblance to the expression *or* the ideas of the seminal work and will often be connected only by a license authorizing use of a title or character name.

This analysis offers some help in identifying the point at which the right "to reproduce the copyrighted work in copies" leaves off and the right "to prepare derivative works based upon the copyrighted work" begins: It is that point at which the contribution of independent expression to an existing work effectively creates a new work for a different market. . . .

Derivative rights affect the *level* of investment in copyrighted works by enabling the copyright owner to proportion its investment to the level of expected returns from all markets, not just the market in which the work first appears, as is generally the case with reproduction rights. The publisher who knows that it can license, and obtain payment for, the translation, serialization, condensation and motion picture rights for a novel will invest more in purchasing, producing and marketing the novel than it would if its returns were limited to revenues from book sales in the English language.

Derivative rights also affect the *direction* of investments in copyrighted works. By spreading the duty to pay over different markets, section 106(2) tends to perfect the information available to the copyright owner respecting the value of its works to different groups of users. It also enables choices in light of that information. Knowing that the French and German language markets belong exclusively to it, a publisher of English language works may decide to invest in works that, once translated, will appeal to these audiences as well. The publisher can acquire a work because of its motion picture potential and can comfortably invest in the work's development and marketing to increase that potential. . . .

≡ *Pamela Samuelson, The Quest for a Sound Conception*
of Copyright's Derivative Work Right
101 Geo. L.J. 1505, 1518, 1525-28, 1559-60 (2013)

. . . Relatively little attention has been given in the case law or the law-review literature to some characteristic features of the nine exemplary derivatives in the 1976 Act definition. At first blush, they seem a hodgepodge. Translation is listed first, followed by musical arrangement and then by dramatization and fictionalization. Sound recording and art reproduction are interposed between motion-picture version and abridgement, which is followed by condensation. One reason for the seemingly arbitrary nature of the examples may be the dual purpose of the definition (to identify types of works that are copyrightable and to indicate types of works that may infringe).

The nine examples seem less anomalous if one clusters them into three main categories. Abridgements and condensations represent shorter versions of works on which they are based. Translations and art reproductions generally aim to be faithful renditions of the works on which they are based. Fictionalizations, dramatizations, motion-picture versions, sound recordings, and musical arrangements involve transformation of original expression from works on which these derivatives are based, often involving transformations from one medium to another or from one genre to another. . . .

There are several reasons to believe that Congress put the nine specific types of derivatives in the statutory definition to exemplify and illustrate the kinds of derivatives it wanted rights holders to be able to control and that it did not intend to create an entirely open-ended right. For one thing, the simplification and clarification goals for the derivative work right could not be achieved if the last clause, "or any other form in which the work has been recast, transformed, or adapted," was unbounded. Had Congress intended to make the derivative work right completely open-ended, it would not have defined the term at all or would have defined it without the examples as "any work that recasts, transforms or adapts a pre-existing work."

Although the last clause of the definition of derivative work is open-ended enough to cover analogous uses and to accommodate new types of adaptations made possible by technology, the definition should be construed as a whole. It should not be construed as if it was actually two separate definitions conjoined at the hip, one that encompasses the examples and the last clause for everything else. The nine examples should instead be understood as providing some guidance about what the last clause means. Indeed, during the legislative debate, several copyright industry representatives expressed concern that use of "such as" in the derivative work and other copyright definitions would have a limiting effect on judicial interpretations of the terms under the *ejusdem generis*[100] canon of statutory construction. Some industry representatives proposed specific changes to make the definition of derivative work more open-ended and less susceptible to *ejusdem generis* limitations, but these suggestions were not adopted. . . .

The legislative history of the 1976 Act does not directly explain the rationale for granting authors a derivative work right. Drawing from insights of commentators on the derivative work right and from reflections on the exemplary derivatives, there seem to be three primary justifications for copyright law to grant some derivative work rights to authors. First, some works are created with the expectation that particular derivative markets are important to recouping investments in these works. In the absence of derivative work rights, some valuable works might not be created or disseminated to the public. Second, the grant of a derivative work right gives authors some time to decide which derivative markets to enter, with whose assistance, on what terms, and when. Third, even though many works would be created without derivative work rights, Congress could reasonably have decided that the derivative work right would avoid unjust enrichment by unlicensed exploiters of foreseeable derivative markets. Close examination of each rationale suggests that each justifies a grant of control over exemplary and analogous derivatives to achieve the intended purposes, but not beyond them. Unless carefully cabined to the kinds of foreseeable markets exemplified by the definitional

---

100. . . . . *Ejusdem generis*, meaning "of the same kind," is a canon of statutory construction. In construing a statute, when general words follow a designation of particular subjects or classes, the meaning of the general words will ordinarily be presumed to be restricted by the particular designations and as including only things or persons of the same kind, class, character, or nature as those specifically enumerated unless a contrary intention is clearly shown. . . .

derivatives, this right can unduly restrain competition and follow-on innovation, as well as interfere with free-expression interests of subsequent creators. . . .

There are important policy reasons to limit the derivative work right to foreseeable markets. Entrepreneurial second comers may perceive opportunities to create new products and markets that consumers will find attractive. Copyright owners cannot be harmed by unforeseeable uses and their incentives to invest in the underlying work and foreseen derivatives will not be affected by the new uses second comers imagine and implement. Limiting the reach of the derivative work right will encourage follow-on creators to make new works of authorship that will add to the store of knowledge, enrich culture, and entertain the public in ways that the copyright owner has not done and probably will never do. The public has a legitimate interest in the existence of new works in markets for unforeseen derivative uses of protected works. Even if there is some free riding on the plaintiffs' contributions in such cases, courts would do well to remember that free riding, as long as it is not predatory, is socially valuable. . . .

NOTES AND QUESTIONS

1. Consider the most recent family-oriented blockbuster movie. The derivative work right (typically owned by the producers as authors of a work made for hire) encompasses sequels, novelizations, video games, toys, posters, and much more. How would Professor Goldstein explain the phenomenon of movie merchandising? How would Professor Samuelson explain it? Does the derivative work right as conceptualized by Professor Goldstein encourage production of those works from which society derives the greatest benefit? Do you think Professor Goldstein would agree with Professor Samuelson's interpretation of the statute?

2. The Copyright Act provides that "The terms 'including' and 'such as' are illustrative and not limitative." 17 U.S.C. §101. Does that aid Professor Samuelson's argument concerning the interpretation of the final part of the definition of derivative work? Review the introduction to subsection 5.B.1, above, which describes a continuum of similarity ranging from literal reproductions at one end to highly transformative derivations at the other. Based on the statutory definition, do you think Congress had in mind a continuum of similarity when it adopted the derivative work right, or did Congress intend to grant a more limited right?

3. In *Warner Bros.*, the court concluded that "Under these circumstances, *and because the Lexicon does not fall under any example of derivative works listed in the statute*, Plaintiffs have failed to show that the Lexicon is a derivative work." *Warner Bros. Entertainment, Inc. v. RDR Books*, 575 F. Supp. 2d 513, 520 (S.D.N.Y. 2008) (emphasis added). The court cited *Ty, Inc.*, a case involving Beanie Baby collector guides in which the Seventh Circuit reversed a grant of summary judgment of infringement, stating that "[t]he textual portions of a collectors' guide to copyrighted works are not among the examples of derivative works listed in the statute, and guides don't recast, transform, or adapt the things to which they are guides." *Ty, Inc. v. Publ'ns Int'l Ltd.*, 292 F.3d 512, 520 (7th Cir. 2002). How does the reasoning in the two cases compare with Professor Samuelson's? With Professor Goldstein's?

4. Sometimes an alleged derivative work may substitute for the underlying work. For example, for some consumers a movie based on a book is a substitute for reading the book. Other alleged derivative works, such as the Lexicon, are complements, useful only to those who have purchased the underlying works. Might the distinction between substitute works and complementary works be a good dividing line between infringing works and noninfringing works? If so, should the distinction be made in the context of evaluating whether plaintiff has asserted a prima facie case of infringement or in the context of a defense, such as fair use?

5. The Berne Convention does not use the term "derivative work." Instead, it requires that authors be granted "the exclusive right of making and of authorizing the translation of their works" (art. 8) and "the exclusive right of authorizing adaptations, arrangements and other alterations of their works." (art. 12). The TRIPS Agreement expressly incorporates those requirements. Is U.S. copyright law more generous to copyright owners than the comparable provisions of the Berne Convention? If so, is that appropriate? Would focusing on the rights required by the Berne Convention provide a better grounding for the derivative work right?

Alternatively, would it be better for the Copyright Act to grant copyright owners one right, rather than the bundle of separate rights provided for in the current Copyright Act? *See* Zechariah Chafee, *Reflections on the Law of Copyright*, 45 Colum. L. Rev. 505 (1945) ("The essential principle is the author's right to control all the channels through which his work or any fragments of his work reach the market. It should be one right, and not just a bundle of separate rights. . . ."). How would you define the boundaries, or the "scope" of that one right?

3. Derivative Works That Do Not Involve "Copying"

Can a work be considered "recast" or "transformed," and therefore covered by the statutory definition of a "derivative work," when it has not been copied or altered but instead simply placed in a different context? Consider the following cases:

Mirage Editions, Inc. v. Albuquerque A.R.T. Company
856 F.2d 1341 (9th Cir. 1988), cert. denied, 489 U.S. 1018 (1989)

BRUNETTI, J.: Albuquerque A.R.T. (appellant or A.R.T.) appeals the district court's granting of summary judgment in favor of appellees Mirage, Dumas, and Van Der Marck (Mirage). . . .

Patrick Nagel was an artist whose works appeared in many media including lithographs, posters, serigraphs, and as graphic art in many magazines, most notably Playboy. Nagel died in 1984. His widow Jennifer Dumas owns the copyrights to the Nagel art works which Nagel owned at the time of his death. Mirage is the exclusive publisher of Nagel's works and also owns the copyrights to many of these works. . . . No one else holds a copyright in any Nagel work. Appellee Alfred Van Der Marck Editions, Inc. is the licensee of Dumas and Mirage and the publisher of the commemorative book entitled *NAGEL: The Art of Patrick Nagel* ("the book"), which is a compilation of selected copyrighted individual art works and personal commentaries.

Since 1984, the primary business of appellant has consisted of: (1) purchasing artwork prints or books including good quality artwork page prints therein; (2) gluing each individual print or page print onto a rectangular sheet of black plastic material exposing a narrow black margin around the print; (3) gluing the black sheet with print onto a major surface of a rectangular white ceramic tile; (4) applying a transparent plastic film over the print, black sheet and ceramic tile surface; and (5) offering the tile with artwork mounted thereon for sale in the retail market.

It is undisputed, in this action, that appellant did the above process with the Nagel book. The appellant removed selected pages from the book, mounted them individually onto ceramic tiles and sold the tiles at retail. . . .

The district court concluded appellant infringed the copyrights in the individual images through its tile-preparing process and also concluded that the resulting products comprised derivative works.

Appellant contends that there has been no copyright infringement because (1) its tiles are not derivative works, and (2) the "first sale" doctrine precludes a finding of infringement. . . .

The protection of derivative rights extends beyond mere protection against unauthorized copying to include the right to make other versions of, perform, or exhibit the work. . . .

What appellant has clearly done here is to make another version of Nagel's art works, and that amounts to preparation of a derivative work. By borrowing and mounting the preexisting, copyrighted individual art images without the consent of the copyright proprietors—Mirage and Dumas as to the art works and Van Der Marck as to the book—appellant has prepared a derivative work and infringed the subject copyrights.

Appellant's contention that since it has not engaged in "art reproduction" and therefore its tiles are not derivative works is not fully dispositive of this issue. Appellant has ignored the disjunctive phrase "or any other form in which a work may be recast, transformed or adapted." The legislative history of the Copyright Act of 1976 indicates that Congress intended that for a violation of the right to prepare derivative works to occur "the infringing work must incorporate a portion of the copyrighted work in *some form*." 1976 U.S. Code Cong. & Admin. News 5659, 5675 (emphasis added). The language "recast, transformed or adapted" seems to encompass other alternatives besides simple art reproduction. By removing the individual images from the book and placing them on the tiles, perhaps the appellant has not accomplished reproduction. We conclude, though, that appellant has certainly recast or transformed the individual images by incorporating them into its tile-preparing process. . . .

We recognize that, under the "first sale" doctrine as enunciated at 17 U.S.C. §109(a) . . . appellant can purchase a copy of the Nagel book and subsequently alienate its ownership in that book. However, the right to transfer applies only to the particular copy of the book which appellant has purchased and nothing else. The mere sale of the book to the appellant without a specific transfer by the copyright holder of its exclusive right to prepare derivative works, does not transfer that [derivative] right to appellant. The derivative works right, remains unimpaired and with the copyright proprietors—Mirage, Dumas and Van Der Marck. As we have previously concluded that appellant's tile-preparing process results in derivative works and as the exclusive right to prepare derivative works belongs to the copyright holder, the "first sale" doctrine does not bar the appellees' copyright infringement claims. . . .

Lee v. A.R.T. Company
125 F.3d 580 (7th Cir. 1997)

EASTERBROOK, J.: Annie Lee creates works of art, which she sells through her firm Annie Lee & Friends. Deck the Walls, a chain of outlets for modestly priced art, is among the buyers of her works, which have been registered with the Register of Copyrights. One Deck the Walls store sold some of Lee's notecards and small lithographs to A.R.T. Company, which mounted the works on ceramic tiles (covering the art with transparent epoxy resin in the process) and resold the tiles. Lee contends that these tiles are derivative works, which under 17 U.S.C. §106(2) may not be prepared without the permission of the copyright proprietor. She seeks both monetary and injunctive relief. . . .

Now one might suppose that this is an open and shut case under the doctrine of first sale, codified at 17 U.S.C. §109(a). A.R.T. bought the work legitimately, mounted it on a tile, and resold what it had purchased. Because the artist could capture the value of her art's contribution to the finished product as part of the price for the original transaction, the economic rationale for protecting an adaptation as "derivative" is absent. See William M. Landes & Richard A. Posner, *An Economic Analysis of Copyright Law,* 17 J. Legal Studies 325, 353-57 (1989). An alteration that includes (or consumes) a complete copy of the original lacks economic significance. One work changes hands multiple times, exactly what §109(a) permits, so it may lack legal significance too. But §106(2) creates a separate exclusive right, to "prepare derivative works," and Lee believes that affixing the art to the tile is "preparation," so that A.R.T. would have violated §106(2) even if it had dumped the finished tiles into the Marianas Trench. For the sake of argument we assume that this is so and ask whether card-on-a-tile is a "derivative work" in the first place.

. . . The district court concluded that A.R.T.'s mounting of Lee's works on tile is not an "original work of authorship" because it is no different in form or function from displaying a painting in a frame or placing a medallion in a velvet case. No one believes that a museum violates §106(2) every time it changes the frame of a painting that is still under copyright, although the choice of frame or glazing affects the impression the art conveys, and many artists specify frames (or pedestals for sculptures) in detail. . . . *Mirage Editions* acknowledge[s] that framing and other traditional means of mounting and displaying art do not infringe authors' exclusive right to make derivative works. Nonetheless, the ninth circuit held, what A.R.T. does creates a derivative work because the epoxy resin bonds the art to the tile. Our district judge thought this a distinction without a difference, and we agree. If changing the way in which a work of art will be displayed creates a derivative work, and if Lee is right about what "prepared" means, then the derivative work is "prepared" when the art is mounted; what happens later is not relevant, because the violation of the §106(2) right has already occurred. If the framing process does not create a derivative work, then mounting art on a tile, which serves as a flush frame, does not create a derivative work. . . .

Lee wages a vigorous attack on the district court's conclusion that A.R.T.'s mounting process cannot create a derivative work because the change to the work "as a whole" is not sufficiently original to support a copyright. Cases such as *Gracen v. The Bradford Exchange, Inc.*, 698 F.2d 300 (7th Cir. 1983), show that neither A.R.T. nor Lee herself could have obtained a copyright in the card-on-a-tile, thereby not only extending the period of protection for the images but also eliminating competition in one medium of display. After the ninth circuit held that its mounting process created derivative works, A.R.T. tried to obtain a copyright in one of its products; the Register of Copyrights sensibly informed A.R.T. that the card-on-a-tile could not be copyrighted independently of the note card itself. But Lee says that this is irrelevant—that a change in a work's appearance may infringe the exclusive right under §106(2) even if the alteration is too trivial to support an independent copyright. Pointing to the word "original" in the second sentence of the statutory definition, the district judge held that "originality" is essential to a derivative work. This understanding has the support of both cases and respected commentators. Pointing to the fact that the first sentence in the statutory definition omits any reference to originality, Lee insists that a work may be derivative despite the mechanical nature of the transformation. This view, too, has the support of both cases and respected commentators.

Fortunately, it is not necessary for us to choose sides. Assume for the moment that the first sentence recognizes a set of non-original derivative works. To prevail, then, Lee must show that A.R.T. altered her works in one of the ways mentioned in the first sentence. The tile is not an "art reproduction"; A.R.T. purchased and mounted Lee's original works. That leaves the residual clause: "any other form in which a work may be recast, transformed, or adapted." None of these words fits what A.R.T. did. Lee's works were not "recast" or "adapted." "Transformed" comes closer and gives the ninth circuit some purchase for its view that the permanence of the bond between art and base matters. Yet the copyrighted note cards and lithographs were not "transformed" in the slightest. The art was bonded to a slab of ceramic, but it was not changed in the process. It still depicts exactly what it depicted when it left Lee's studio. If mounting works is a "transformation," then changing a painting's frame or a photograph's mat equally produces a derivative work. Indeed, if Lee is right about the meaning of the definition's first sentence, then *any* alteration of a work, however slight, requires the author's permission. We asked at oral argument what would happen if a purchaser jotted a note on one of the note cards, or used it as a coaster for a drink, or cut it in half, or if a collector applied his seal (as is common in Japan); Lee's counsel replied that such changes prepare derivative works, but that as a practical matter artists would not file suit. A definition of derivative work that makes criminals out of art collectors and tourists is jarring despite Lee's gracious offer not to commence civil litigation.

If Lee (and the ninth circuit) are right about what counts as a derivative work, then the United States has established through the back door an extraordinarily broad version of authors' moral rights, under which artists may block any modification of their works of which they disapprove. No European version of *droit moral* goes this far. . . . We . . . decline to follow . . . *Mirage Editions*.

NOTES AND QUESTIONS

1. Do you agree with *Mirage Editions* or with *Lee*? Do the tiles represent a market that copyright law reserves to the owner of the underlying work, or have the artists already "captured the value" of their art? How should the law determine the answer to that question?

2. Recall what you learned in Chapter 2 about the requirements for copyright protection. Do the tiles in *Mirage Editions* and *Lee* satisfy the requirement of originality? Should that matter for the infringement analysis? Should originality be relevant to determining the copyrightability of a derivative work but not to deciding the issue of whether the derivative work infringes?

3. One scholar has suggested that protection for derivative works should depend on the nature of the use by the second comer. One type of use is "consumptive," that is, it incorporates a copy of the underlying work into the derivative work. In such cases, the derivative user could argue that the copyright owner of the underlying work has already been compensated by receiving the price on the first sale of the work. Because that kind of use does not necessarily create a "new" market, the copyright owner should not be able to preclude others from using the work in that way. A second type of use is a "productive" or "public goods use." Such uses create products related to the copyrighted work, effectively exploiting a single copy of the work in a new form and creating a new market for the derivative work. In such cases, the copyright owner of the underlying work should be able to claim the lost value of the use of the work because its price at first sale would not have compensated for the productive or public goods use. *See* Amy B. Cohen, *When Does a Work Infringe the Derivative Works Right of a Copyright Owner?*, 17 Cardozo Arts & Ent. L.J. 623 (1999).

Do you agree with that analysis? Was the use at issue in both *Mirage Editions* and *Lee* "consumptive" or "productive"? How significant to this question is the definition of the copyrighted work's market? In *Mirage* and *Lee* is the relevant market that for works of art or that for decorative tiles? What factors should be considered in defining the market(s) at issue?

PRACTICE EXERCISE: COUNSEL A CLIENT

Cesar is an artist who works in the medium of collage. He purchases magazines and newspapers and combines the cover images and headlines with other "found objects." For example, one of his most well-known works combines the cover of *People* magazine's annual "50 Most Beautiful People" issue with other materials that address issues of appearance, weight, diet, and self-image. The New York gallery that represents Cesar recently announced its upcoming exhibition of a new series of works by Cesar incorporating covers from *Cosmopolitan*. Cesar has received a cease-and-desist letter from *Cosmopolitan* asserting that the collages infringe its copyrights, and has requested your advice. Are the collages infringing derivative works?

Computer games are popular entertainment products and many users seek to enhance their experience when playing. This opens a market for products that make the user's experience of a game more rewarding. However, such enhancements often modify the game in some way. Do they therefore create infringing derivative works? Who should control the market for enhancements of computer games and other digital works? Should the answer depend on whether the enhancements meet the fixation requirement that applies to *copyrightable* derivative works, or on other considerations?

Micro Star v. FormGen Inc.
154 F.3d 1107 (9th Cir. 1998)

KOZINSKI, J.: Duke Nukem routinely vanquishes Octabrain and the Protozoid Slimer. But what about the dreaded Micro Star?

I

FormGen Inc., GT Interactive Software Corp. and Apogee Software, Ltd. (collectively FormGen) made, distributed and own the rights to Duke Nukem 3D (D/N-3D), an immensely popular (and very cool) computer game. D/N-3D is played from the first-person perspective; the player assumes the personality and point of view of the title character, who is seen on the screen only as a pair of hands and an occasional boot, much as one might see oneself in real life without the aid of a mirror. Players explore a futuristic city infested with evil aliens and other hazards. The goal is to zap them before they zap you, while searching for the hidden passage to the next level. The basic game comes with twenty-nine levels, each with a different combination of scenery, aliens, and other challenges. The game also includes a "Build Editor," a utility that enables players to create their own levels. With Form-Gen's encouragement, players frequently post levels they have created on the

Internet where others can download them. Micro Star, a computer software distributor, did just that: It downloaded 300 user-created levels and stamped them onto a CD, which it then sold commercially as Nuke It (N/I). N/I is packaged in a box decorated with numerous "screen shots," pictures of what the new levels look like when played.

Micro Star filed suit in district court, seeking a declaratory judgment that N/I did not infringe on any of FormGen's copyrights. FormGen counterclaimed, seeking a preliminary injunction barring further production and distribution of N/I. Relying on *Lewis Galoob Toys, Inc. v. Nintendo of Am., Inc.*, 964 F.2d 965 (9th Cir. 1992), the district court held that N/I was not a derivative work and therefore did not infringe FormGen's copyright. The district court did, however, grant a preliminary injunction as to the screen shots, finding that N/I's packaging violated FormGen's copyright by reproducing pictures of D/N-3D characters without a license. The court rejected Micro Star's fair use claims. Both sides appeal their losses. . . .

III . . .

FormGen alleges that its copyright is infringed by Micro Star's unauthorized commercial exploitation of user-created game levels. In order to understand FormGen's claims, one must first understand the way D/N-3D works. The game consists of three separate components: the game engine, the source art library and the MAP files.[2] The game engine is the heart of the computer program; in some sense, it *is* the program. It tells the computer when to read data, save and load games, play sounds and project images onto the screen. In order to create the audiovisual display for a particular level, the game engine invokes the MAP file that corresponds to that level. Each MAP file contains a series of instructions that tell the game engine (and, through it, the computer) what to put where. For instance, the MAP file might say scuba gear goes at the bottom of the screen. The game engine then goes to the source art library, finds the image of the scuba gear, and puts it in just the right place on the screen.[3] The MAP file describes the level in painstaking detail, but it does not actually contain any of the copyrighted art itself; everything that appears on the screen actually comes from the art library. Think of the game's audiovisual display as a paint-by-numbers kit. The MAP file might tell you to put blue paint in section number 565, but it doesn't contain any blue paint itself; the blue paint comes from your palette, which is the low-tech analog of the art library, while you play the role of the game engine. When the player selects one of the N/I levels, the game engine

2. So-called because the files all end with the extension ".MAP." Also, no doubt, because they contain the layout for the various levels.

3. Actually, this is all a bit metaphorical. Computer programs don't actually go anywhere or fetch anything. Rather, the game engine receives the player's instruction as to which game level to select and instructs the processor to access the MAP file corresponding to that level. The MAP file, in turn, consists of a series of instructions indicating which art images go where. When the MAP file calls for a particular art image, the game engine tells the processor to access the art library for instructions on how each pixel on the screen must be colored in order to paint that image.

references the N/I MAP files, but still uses the D/N-3D art library to generate the images that make up that level.

FormGen points out that a copyright holder enjoys the exclusive right to prepare derivative works based on D/N-3D. *See* 17 U.S.C. §106(2) (1994). According to FormGen, the audiovisual displays generated when D/N-3D is run in conjunction with the N/I CD MAP files are derivative works that infringe this exclusivity. . . .

. . . The statutory language [defining a derivative work] is hopelessly overbroad. . . . To narrow the statute to a manageable level, we have developed certain criteria a work must satisfy in order to qualify as a derivative work. One of these is that a derivative work must exist in a "concrete or permanent form," *Galoob*, 964 F.2d at 967 (internal quotation marks omitted), and must substantially incorporate protected material from the preexisting work. Micro Star argues that N/I is not a derivative work because the audiovisual displays generated when D/N-3D is run with N/I's MAP files are not incorporated in any concrete or permanent form, and the MAP files do not copy any of D/N-3D's protected expression. It is mistaken on both counts.

The requirement that a derivative work must assume a concrete or permanent form was recognized without much discussion in *Galoob*. There, we noted that all the Copyright Act's examples of derivative works took some definite, physical form and concluded that this was a requirement of the Act. *See Galoob*, 964 F.2d at 967-68; *see also* Edward G. Black & Michael H. Page, *Add-On Infringements*, 15 Hastings Comm/Ent. L.J. 615, 625 (1993) (noting that in *Galoob* the Ninth Circuit "re-examined the statutory definition of derivative works offered in section 101 and found an independent fixation requirement of sorts built into the statutory definition of derivative works"). Obviously, N/I's MAP files themselves exist in a concrete or permanent form; they are burned onto a CD-ROM. But what about the audiovisual displays generated when D/N-3D runs the N/I MAP files—i.e., the actual game level as displayed on the screen? Micro Star argues that, because the audiovisual displays in *Galoob* didn't meet the "concrete or permanent form" requirement, neither do N/I's.

In *Galoob*, we considered audiovisual displays created using a device called the Game Genie, which was sold for use with the Nintendo Entertainment System. The Game Genie allowed players to alter individual features of a game, such as a character's strength or speed, by selectively "blocking the value for a single data byte sent by the game cartridge to the [Nintendo console] and replacing it with a new value." *Galoob*, 964 F.2d at 967. Players chose which data value to replace by entering a code; over a billion different codes were possible. The Game Genie was dumb; it functioned only as a window into the computer program, allowing players to temporarily modify individual aspects of the game. *See Lewis Galoob Toys, Inc. v. Nintendo of Am., Inc.*, 780 F. Supp. 1283, 1289 (N.D. Cal. 1991).

Nintendo sued, claiming that when the Game Genie modified the game system's audiovisual display, it created an infringing derivative work. We rejected this claim because "[a] derivative work must incorporate a protected work in some concrete or permanent form." *Galoob*, 964 F.2d at 967 (internal quotation marks omitted). The audiovisual displays generated by combining the Nintendo System with the Game Genie were not incorporated in any permanent form; when the game was over, they were gone. Of course, they could be reconstructed, but only if the next player chose to reenter the same codes.[4]

Micro Star argues that the MAP files on N/I are a more advanced version of the Game Genie, replacing old values (the MAP files in the original game) with new values (N/I's MAP files). But, whereas the audiovisual displays created by Game Genie were never recorded in any permanent form, the audiovisual displays generated by D/N-3D from the N/I MAP files are in the MAP files themselves. In *Galoob,* the audiovisual display was defined by the original game cartridge, not by the Game Genie; no one could possibly say that the data values inserted by the Game Genie described the audiovisual display. In the present case the audiovisual display that appears on the computer monitor when a N/I level is played is described—in exact detail—by a N/I MAP file.

This raises the interesting question whether an exact, down to the last detail, description of an audiovisual display (and—by definition—we know that MAP files do describe audiovisual displays down to the last detail) counts as a permanent or concrete form for purposes of *Galoob.* We see no reason it shouldn't. What, after all, does sheet music do but describe in precise detail the way a copyrighted melody sounds? To be copyrighted, pantomimes and dances may be "described in sufficient detail to enable the work to be performed from that description." Similarly, the N/I MAP files describe the audiovisual display that is to be generated when the player chooses to play D/N-3D using the N/I levels. Because the audiovisual displays assume a concrete or permanent form in the MAP files, *Galoob* stands as no bar to finding that they are derivative works. . . .

Micro Star further argues that the MAP files are not derivative works because they do not, in fact, incorporate any of D/N-3D's protected expression. In particular, Micro Star makes much of the fact that the N/I MAP files reference the source art library, but do not actually contain any art files themselves. Therefore, it claims, nothing of D/N-3D's is reproduced in the MAP files. In making this argument, Micro Star misconstrues the protected work. The work that Micro Star infringes is the D/N-3D story itself—a beefy commando type named Duke who wanders around post-Apocalypse Los Angeles, shooting Pig Cops with a gun, lobbing hand grenades, searching for medkits and steroids, using a jetpack to leap over obstacles, blowing up gas tanks, avoiding radioactive slime. A copyright owner holds the right to create sequels, *see Trust Co. Bank v. MGM/UA Entertainment Co.,* 772 F.2d 740 (11th Cir. 1985), and the stories told in the N/I MAP files are surely sequels, telling new (though somewhat repetitive) tales of Duke's fabulous

---

4. A low-tech example might aid understanding. Imagine a product called the Pink Screener, which consists of a big piece of pink cellophane stretched over a frame. When put in front of a television, it makes everything on the screen look pinker. Someone who manages to record the programs with this pink cast (maybe by filming the screen) would have created an infringing derivative work. But the audiovisual display observed by a person watching television through the Pink Screener is not a derivative work because it does not incorporate the modified image in any permanent or concrete form. The Game Genie might be described as a fancy Pink Screener for video games, changing a value of the game as perceived by the current player, but never incorporating the new audiovisual display into a permanent or concrete form.

adventures. A book about Duke Nukem would infringe for the same reason, even if it contained no pictures.[5] . . .

NOTES AND QUESTIONS

1. What test did the *Micro Star* court apply to determine whether the defendants had prepared an unauthorized derivative work? (What, exactly, did the defendants prepare?) Does the *Micro Star* court's view of the derivative work right seem more similar to Professor Goldstein's or Professor Samuelson's?

2. Focus on the court's discussion of the "form" requirement recognized in *Lewis Galoob Toys*. The House Report accompanying the 1976 Act states:

> The exclusive right to prepare derivative works . . . overlaps the exclusive right of reproduction to some extent. It is broader than that right, however, in the sense that reproduction requires fixation in copies or phonorecords, whereas the preparation of a derivative work, such as a ballet, pantomime, or improvised performance, may be an infringement even though nothing is ever fixed in tangible form. . . .
>
> [T]o constitute a violation of section 106(2), the infringing work must incorporate a portion of the copyrighted work in some form; for example, a detailed commentary on a work or a programmatic musical composition inspired by a novel would not normally constitute infringements under this clause.

H.R. Rep. No. 94-1476, 94th Cong., 2d Sess. 62 (1976), *reprinted in* 1976 U.S.C.C.A.N. 5659, 5675. Does this legislative history support a "form" requirement for derivative works? Remember, if the statute is clear, the legislative history is not relevant to the question of statutory interpretation. No other circuit has adopted the Ninth Circuit's quasi-fixation requirement. Should the other circuits do so?

In what form did the N/I MAP files distributed by Micro Star incorporate the copyrighted work?

PRACTICE EXERCISE: COUNSEL A CLIENT

FamilyWeb, a Utah-based company that seeks to make browsing the Internet more "family friendly" by blocking images of nudity, consults you for legal advice. Its product, which a user must install as an Internet browser plug-in, scans incoming images to detect nudity and inserts a strategically placed black square or rectangle over the offending portion of the image. The plug-in doesn't change anything on the originating website; it only modifies the experience that the user has when viewing the site. Are the modified images derivative works?

---

5. We note that the N/I MAP files can only be used with D/N-3D. If another game could use the MAP files to tell the story of a mousy fellow who travels through a beige maze, killing vicious salt-shakers with paper-clips, then the MAP files would not incorporate the protected expression of D/N-3D because they would not be telling a D/N-3D story.

3. Should the right to prepare derivative works be construed differently when the allegedly "derivative" work is a by-product of new technology? Should the level of innovation achieved by the defendant, or efficiency considerations associated with a new technology, make a difference? If all rights to ancillary products are reserved to the owner of the underlying work, how do you think that will influence the development of new technologies? In *Lewis Galoob Toys*, the court observed:

> [i]n holding that the audiovisual displays created by the Game Genie are not derivative works, we recognize that technology often advances by improvement rather than replacement. Some time ago, for example, computer companies began marketing spell-checkers that operate within existing word processors by signalling the writer when a word is misspelled. These applications, as well as countless others, could not be produced and marketed if courts were to conclude that the word processor and spell-checker combination is a derivative work based on the word processor alone. The Game Genie is useless by itself. It can only enhance, and cannot duplicate or recast, a Nintendo game's output. It does not contain or produce a Nintendo game's output in some concrete or permanent form, nor does it supplant demand for Nintendo game cartridges. Such innovations rarely will constitute infringing derivative works under the Copyright Act.

Lewis Galoob Toys, 964 F.2d at 969. What do you think of this reasoning?

C. FICTIONAL CHARACTERS AND THE REPRODUCTION AND DERIVATIVE WORK RIGHTS

As you have seen in this chapter, the most difficult—and most interesting—copyright cases are those in which the defendant has taken some aspects of the plaintiff's work while also adding to it in some way. Such cases almost inevitably involve some overlap between the exclusive right of reproduction and the exclusive right to prepare derivative works, and often raise questions about the copyrightability of different elements.

Many copyrighted works contain fictional characters, and copyright disputes involving such characters present particularly interesting questions about the scope of the reproduction and derivative work rights. As the *Micro Star v. FormGen* case illustrates, courts tend to think that copyright owners should control works that are recognizable as sequels. One way in which the audience can perceive a new work as a sequel is if it contains a familiar character or characters from a previous work. Additionally, products portraying or featuring images of characters from popular movies, television shows, and cartoons are natural marketing tie-ins for fictional works and can be a significant source of revenue. For thousands of years, however, storytellers have been using the characters in stories they have heard to create new stories. Today's storytellers often use characters from television shows and movies as raw material for their expressive activity; in the modern era, such characters constitute a significant portion of our shared culture.

Should a character, by itself, ever be independently copyrightable? If so, what makes a character copyrightable? Consider the following case:

Warner Brothers Entertainment v. X One X Productions
644 F.3d 584 (8th Cir. 2011)

GRUENDER, J.: . . .

Warner Bros. asserts ownership of registered copyrights to the 1939 MetroGoldwyn-Mayer ("MGM") films *The Wizard of Oz* and *Gone with the Wind*. Before the films were completed and copyrighted, publicity materials featuring images of the actors in costume posed on the film sets were distributed to theaters and published in newspapers and magazines. The images in these publicity materials were not drawn from the film footage that was used in the films; rather, they were created independently by still photographers and artists before or during production of the films. The publicity materials, such as movie posters, lobby cards, still photographs, and press books . . . did not comply with the copyright notice requirements of the 1909 Copyright Act. Warner Bros. also asserts ownership of registered copyrights to various animated Tom & Jerry short films that debuted between 1940 and 1957. Movie posters and lobby cards for these short films also were distributed without the requisite copyright notice. As a result, Warner Bros. concedes that it has no registered federal copyrights in the publicity materials themselves.

[Defendant] AVELA has acquired restored versions of the movie posters and lobby cards for *The Wizard of Oz*, *Gone with the Wind*, and several Tom & Jerry short films. From these publicity materials, AVELA has extracted the images of famous characters from the films, including Dorothy, Tin Man, Cowardly Lion, and Scarecrow from *The Wizard of Oz*; Scarlett O'Hara and Rhett Butler from *Gone with the Wind*; and the eponymous Tom and Jerry. AVELA licenses the extracted images for use on items such as shirts, lunch boxes, music box lids, and playing cards, and as models for three-dimensional figurines such as statuettes, busts, figurines inside water globes, and action figures. In many cases, AVELA has modified the images, such as by adding a character's signature phrase from the movie to an image modeled on that character's publicity photograph. In other cases, AVELA has combined images extracted from different items of publicity material into a single product. In one example, a publicity photograph of Dorothy posed with Scarecrow serves as the model for a statuette and another publicity photograph of the "yellow brick road" serves as the model for the base of that same statuette. . . .

[The district court issued a permanent injunction finding that the extracted images infringed the copyrights in the films. AVELA appealed.]

Discussion . . .

C. *Copyright Infringement and the Right to Make Use of Public Domain Materials* . . .

Warner Bros. does not challenge the products that are exact reproductions of an entire item of publicity material. Instead, Warner Bros. contends that AVELA has extracted images from the public domain materials and used them in new ways that infringe the copyrights in the associated films. AVELA admits that it has used the images in new ways (and indeed has applied for its own copyrights for such derivative works), but it counters that there is no limitation on the public's right to modify or make new works from public domain materials.

AVELA is correct that, as a general proposition, the public is not limited solely to making exact replicas of public domain materials, but rather is free to use public domain materials in new ways (*i.e.*, to make derivative works by adding to and recombining elements of the public domain materials). . . . Nevertheless, this freedom to make new works based on public domain materials ends where the resulting derivative work comes into conflict with a valid copyright. . . .

. . . [I]f material related to certain characters is in the public domain, but later works covered by copyright add new aspects to those characters, a work developed from the public domain material infringes the copyrights in the later works to the extent that it incorporates aspects of the characters developed solely in those later works. Therefore, we must determine (1) the apparent scope of the copyrights in the later works (here, the films), (2) the scope of the material dedicated to the public in the publicity materials, which correspondingly limits the scope of the film copyrights, and (3) the scope into which each of AVELA's images falls. If an AVELA work falls solely within the scope of the material dedicated to the public, there can be no infringement liability under the film copyrights. On the other hand, if some portion of an AVELA work falls outside the scope of the material dedicated to the public, but within the scope of the film copyrights, AVELA is liable for infringement.

1. The Scope of the Film Copyrights

It is clear that when cartoons or movies are copyrighted, a component of that copyright protection extends to the characters themselves, to the extent that such characters are sufficiently distinctive. *See, e.g., Gaiman v. McFarlane*, 360 F.3d 644, 661 (7th Cir. 2004) ("[A] stock character, once he was drawn and named and given speech [in a comic book series] . . . became sufficiently distinctive to be copyrightable."); *Metro-Goldwyn-Mayer, Inc. v. Am. Honda Motor Co.*, 900 F. Supp. 1287, 1296 (C.D. Cal. 1995) (holding that plaintiffs' copyrighted James Bond films established a copyright in the character of James Bond). The district court thoroughly and accurately applied this principle to the instant case, and the parties do not contest the district court's analysis. We agree with the district court's conclusion that Dorothy, Tin Man, Cowardly Lion, and Scarecrow from *The Wizard of Oz*, Scarlett O'Hara and Rhett Butler from *Gone with the Wind*, and Tom and Jerry each exhibit "consistent, widely identifiable traits" in the films that are sufficiently distinctive to merit character protection under the respective film copyrights.

AVELA correctly points out that the scope of copyright protection for the characters in the films *The Wizard of Oz* and *Gone with the Wind* is limited to the increments of character expression in the films that go beyond the character expression in the books on which they were based. While true, this has little practical effect in the instant case, as a book's description of a character generally anticipates very little of the expression of the character in film:

> The reason is the difference between literary and graphic expression. The description of a character in prose leaves much to the imagination, even when the description is detailed—as in Dashiell Hammett's description of Sam Spade's physical appearance in the first paragraph of The Maltese Falcon. "Samuel Spade's jaw was long and bony, his chin a jutting v under the more flexible v of his mouth. His nostrils curved back to make another, smaller, v. His yellow-grey eyes were horizontal. The v motif was picked up again by thickish brows rising outward from twin creases above a hooked nose, and his pale brown hair grew down—from high flat temples—in a point on his forehead. He looked rather pleasantly like a blond satan." Even after all this, one hardly knows what Sam Spade looked like. But everyone knows what Humphrey Bogart looked like.

Gaiman, 360 F.3d at 660-61.

The film actors' portrayals of the characters at issue here appear to rely upon elements of expression far beyond the dialogue and descriptions in the books. AVELA has identified no instance in which the distinctive mannerisms, facial expressions, voice, or speech patterns of a film character are anticipated in the corresponding book by a literary description that evokes, to any significant extent, what the actor portrayed. Put more simply, there is no evidence that one would be able to visualize the distinctive details of, for example, Clark Gable's performance *before* watching the movie *Gone with the Wind*, even if one had read the book beforehand. At the very least, the scope of the film copyrights covers all visual depictions of the film characters at issue, except for any aspects of the characters that were injected into the public domain by the publicity materials.

2. The Scope of the Material Dedicated to the Public

AVELA contends that the injection of the publicity materials into the public domain simultaneously injected the film characters themselves into the public domain. To the extent that copyright-eligible aspects of a character are injected into the public domain, the character protection under the corresponding film copyrights must be limited accordingly.

As an initial matter, we reject AVELA's contention that the publicity materials placed the entirety of the film characters at issue into the public domain. The isolated still *images* included in the publicity materials cannot anticipate the full range of distinctive speech, movement, demeanor, and other personality traits that combine to establish a copyrightable character. *See, e.g., Gaiman*, 360 F.3d at 660 (holding that the character's "age, obviously phony title ('Count'), what he knows and says, [and] his name" combine with his visual appearance "to create a distinctive character"); *Metro-Goldwyn-Mayer*, 900 F. Supp. at 1296 (citing "various character traits that are specific to Bond—i.e. his cold-bloodedness; his overt sexuality; his love of martinis 'shaken, not stirred'; his marksmanship; his 'license to kill' and use of guns; his physical strength; [and] his sophistication," rather than his visual appearance alone, as establishing the copyrightability of the character). Nevertheless, the publicity materials could have placed some aspects of each character's visual appearance into the public domain. . . .

In the instant case, . . . the publicity materials here reveal nothing of each film character's signature traits or mannerisms. At most, the publicity materials could have injected some of the purely visual characteristics of each film character into the public domain. . . .

Because we must rely solely on visual characteristics, the individuals shown in the publicity materials establish "characters" for copyright purposes only if they display "consistent, widely identifiable" visual characteristics. [*Walker v. Viacom Int'l, Inc.*, 2008 WL 2050964, at *5-6 (N.D. Cal. May 13, 2008)] is instructive in this regard. There, the plaintiff asserted his copyright in a comic strip entitled "Mr. Bob Spongee, The Unemployed Sponge" against the producers of the animated television series "SpongeBob SquarePants." [*Id.*] at *1. The plaintiff had created sponge dolls based on his comic strip and placed advertisements in a newspaper. *Id.* Because these materials revealed "little to no information about Mr. Bob Spongee's personality or character traits," *id.* at *5, the court could look only to his visual appearance for distinctiveness. The court held that in such a situation, a consistent visual appearance throughout the materials was a prerequisite for character protection. *See id.* at *5-6. Because of variations in the sponge's clothing, color, eye and nose shape, and hair among the comic strip, dolls, and advertisements, the plaintiff's copyright did not create *any* character protection. *Id.* at *6.[8]

Therefore, we must determine if any individual is depicted with consistent, distinctive visual characteristics throughout the various publicity materials. If so, those consistent visual characteristics define the "copyrightable elements" of that film character, which were injected into the public domain by the publicity materials. If not, then there are no visual aspects of the film character in the public domain, apart from the publicity material images themselves.

With respect to the cartoon characters Tom and Jerry, we note that on the spectrum of character copyrightability, the category of cartoon characters often is cited as the paradigm of distinctiveness. . . . [T]he visual characteristics of Tom and Jerry in the first poster, for *Puss Gets the Boot* (released in 1940), are quite different from the characters popularly recognized as Tom and Jerry today. In addition, the first poster by itself reveals no distinctive character or visual traits, but only visual characteristics typical to cats and mice. As a result, the first poster is essentially a generic cat-and-mouse cartoon drawing that cannot establish independently copyrightable characters.

Meanwhile, the copyrighted short film that immediately followed the first poster revealed Tom and Jerry's character traits and signature antagonistic relationship. With the benefit of these strong character traits, the first short film *was* sufficient to establish the copyrightable elements of the Tom and Jerry characters as depicted therein. In such a situation, each subsequent movie poster could inject into the

---

8. Of course, the presence of distinctive qualities apart from visual appearance can diminish or even negate the need for consistent visual appearance. *See, e.g., Metro-Goldwyn-Mayer*, 900 F. Supp. at 1296 (holding that variations in the visual appearance of James Bond did not negate character protection in light of his many distinctive and consistently displayed character traits; the fact that "many actors can play Bond is a testament to the fact that Bond is a unique character whose specific qualities remain constant despite the change in actors").

public domain only the increments of expression, if any, that the movie poster itself added to the already-copyrighted characters from previously released Tom & Jerry films. *See Russell v. Price*, 612 F.2d 1123, 1128 (9th Cir. 1979) ("[A]lthough the derivative work may enter the public domain, the matter contained therein which derives from a work still covered by statutory copyright is not dedicated to the public."). Because they "derive[ ] from a work still covered by statutory copyright," the underlying characters of Tom and Jerry are not in the public domain until the copyrights in the Tom & Jerry short films begin to expire.

In contrast to Tom & Jerry, the record is clear that a veritable blitz of publicity materials for *Gone with the Wind* and *The Wizard of Oz* was distributed prior to the publication of each film. However, with respect to *Gone with the Wind,* the publicity material images are far from the cartoon-character end of the spectrum of character copyrightability. There is nothing consistent and distinctive about the publicity material images of Vivian Leigh as Scarlett O'Hara and Clark Gable as Rhett Butler. They certainly lack any cartoonishly unique physical attributes, and neither one is shown in a consistent, unique outfit and hairstyle. As a result, the district court correctly held that the publicity material images for *Gone with the Wind* are no more than "pictures of the actors in costume." Indeed, if the publicity material images from *Gone with the Wind* were sufficient to inject all visual depictions of the characters Scarlett O'Hara and Rhett Butler into the public domain, then almost *any* image of Vivian Leigh or Clark Gable would be sufficient to do so as well. Therefore, the only images in the public domain are the precise images in the publicity materials for *Gone with the Wind*.

The characters in *The Wizard of Oz* lie closer to the cartoon-character end of the spectrum. There are many stylized aspects to the visual appearances of Scarecrow, Tin Man, and Cowardly Lion, and they perhaps might be considered as live-action representations of cartoon characters. Dorothy, while not so thoroughly stylized, wears a somewhat distinctive costume and hairstyle. However, a close examination of the record reveals that these potentially distinctive visual features do not appear in a consistent fashion throughout the publicity materials. For example, in the publicity materials, Judy Garland as Dorothy sometimes wears a red dress and bow and black slippers, rather than the distinctive blue dress and bow and ruby slippers of the film, and her hairstyle also varies. From image to image, Scarecrow's costume color ranges from yellow to blue to black, Cowardly Lion's from light yellow to very dark brown, and Tin Man's from shiny silver to a dull blue-gray.[9] Moreover, there are publicity material images in which other stylized elements of the characters' costumes and faces are significantly different from the look used in the film. For example, in some images Tin Man's face appears metallic, and in others it appears flesh-colored. If the publicity material images

---

9. The record shows that these extreme color variations resulted from the practice of using artists to hand-color still photographs originally taken in black-and-white (because color photography was relatively new and expensive). The coloration artists often were left to their own discretion in choosing colors for each photograph.

for *The Wizard of Oz* were held to establish the visual elements of copyrightable characters, their scope would encompass almost any character who wears a scarecrow or lion costume, and a wide range of little girl and silver robotic costumes as well, creating an unacceptable result:

> If a drunken old bum were a copyrightable character, so would be a drunken suburban housewife, a gesticulating Frenchman, a fire-breathing dragon, a talking cat, a Prussian officer who wears a monocle and clicks his heels, a masked magician, and, in Learned Hand's memorable paraphrase of Twelfth Night, "a riotous knight who kept wassail to the discomfort of the household, or a vain and foppish steward who became amorous of his mistress." Nichols v. Universal Pictures Corp., 45 F.2d 119, 121 (2d Cir. 1930). It would be difficult to write successful works of fiction without negotiating for dozens or hundreds of copyright licenses, even though such stereotyped characters are the products not of the creative imagination but of simple observation of the human comedy.

Gaiman, 360 F.3d at 660. While the overly broad characters would be in the public domain rather than copyrighted in the instant case, the analysis of the copyrightability of a character must be the same in either case.

We conclude that the characters' visual appearances in the publicity materials for *The Wizard of Oz* do not present the requisite consistency to establish any "copyrightable elements" of the film characters' visual appearances. Therefore, once again, the only images in the public domain are the precise images in the publicity materials for *The Wizard of Oz*.

3. AVELA's Use of the Public Domain Images

We held above that no visual aspects of the film characters in *Gone with the Wind* and *The Wizard of Oz* are in the public domain, apart from the images in the publicity materials themselves. Therefore, any visual representation that is recognizable as a copyrightable character from one of these films, other than a faithful copy of a public domain image, has copied "original elements" from the corresponding film. We must examine the AVELA products based on *The Wizard of Oz* and *Gone with the Wind* to determine which ones display "increments of expression" of the film characters beyond the "pictures of the actors in costume" in the publicity materials. The AVELA products in the record can be analyzed in three categories.

The first category comprises AVELA products that each reproduce one image from an item of publicity material as an identical two-dimensional image. While Warner Bros. does not challenge the reproduction of movie "posters as posters (or lobby cards as lobby cards)," it does challenge the reproduction of a single image drawn from a movie poster or lobby card on T-shirts, lunch boxes, music box lids, or playing cards, for example. We read the district court's permanent injunction to follow Warner Bros.'s distinction, forbidding all uses except the reproduction of items of publicity material "in their entirety." However, no reasonable jury could find that merely printing a public domain image on a new type of surface (such as a T-shirt or playing card), instead of the original surface (movie poster paper or lobby card paper), adds an increment of expression of the film character to the image.[10] Similarly, Warner Bros. presents no reasoned argument as to why the reproduction of one smaller contiguous portion of an image from an item of publicity material, rather than the entirety of the image from that item, would add an increment of expression of the film character. As a result, products that reproduce in two dimensions any one portion of an image from any one item of publicity material, without more, do not infringe Warner Bros.'s copyright. For products in this category, we reverse the grant of summary judgment to Warner Bros. with respect to *The Wizard of Oz* and *Gone with the Wind* and direct the entry of summary judgment for AVELA. We also vacate the permanent injunction to the extent it applies to products in this category.

The second category comprises AVELA products that each juxtapose an image extracted from an item of publicity material with another image extracted from elsewhere in the publicity materials, or with a printed phrase from the book underlying the subject film, to create a new composite work. Even if we assume that each composite work is composed entirely of faithful extracts from public domain materials, the new arrangement of the extracts in the composite work is a new increment of expression that evokes the film character in a way the individual items of public domain material did not. For example, the printed phrase "There is no place like home" from the book *The Wizard of Oz* and a publicity material image of Judy Garland as Dorothy, viewed side by side in uncombined form, are still two separate works, one literary and one a picture of an actor in costume. In contrast, a T-shirt printed with the phrase "There's no place like home" along with the same image of Judy Garland as Dorothy is a new single work that evokes the film character of Dorothy much more strongly than the two separate works. Because "the increments of expression added [to the public domain materials] by the films are protectable," one making a new work from public domain materials infringes "if he copies these protectable increments." *Silverman* [*v. CBS Inc.*], 870 F.2d [40,] 50 [(2d Cir. 1989)]. Like the juxtaposition of an image and a phrase, a composite work combining two or more separate public-domain images (such as Judy Garland as Dorothy combined with an image of the Emerald City) also adds a new increment of expression of the film character that was not present in the separate images. Accordingly, products combining extracts from the public domain materials in a new arrangement infringe the copyright in the corresponding film. We affirm the district court's grant of summary judgment to Warner Bros. with respect to *The Wizard of Oz* and *Gone with the Wind* and the permanent injunction for this category of products.

The third category comprises AVELA products that each extend an image extracted from an item of publicity material into three dimensions (such as statuettes inside water globes, figurines, action figures, and busts). Many of these products also include a juxtaposition of multiple extracts from the public domain materials, and such composite works infringe for the reasons explained in the preceding paragraph. Even where the product extends a single two-dimensional public domain image into

10. This principle would not apply if the new surface itself is independently evocative of the film character. For example, reproducing a publicity image of Judy Garland as Dorothy on a ruby slipper might well infringe the film copyright for *The Wizard of Oz*.

three dimensions, a three-dimensional rendering must add new visual details regarding depth to the underlying two-dimensional image. (As a simple illustration, it is impossible to determine the length of someone's nose from a picture if they are looking directly at the camera.) Of course, even more visual details must be added if the two-dimensional image is transformed into a fully realized figure, as most three-dimensional AVELA products are. (Otherwise, for example, the back of each figurine character would be blank.) Much of this visual information is available in the feature-length films, where the characters are observable from a multitude of viewing angles.

In depositions, the AVELA licensees who developed the action figures, figurines, water globes, and busts made no pretense that they were not guided by their knowledge of the films. Instead, they indicated that, while each three dimensional design began with an image from the public domain photo stills and movie posters, the goal was to create a product recognizable as the film character. The only reasonable inference is that the details added to establish perspective and full realization were chosen to be consistent with the film characters. As a result, the addition of visual details to each two-dimensional public domain image to create the three-dimensional product makes impermissible use of the "further delineation of the characters contained in" the feature-length films. *See Silverman*, 870 F.2d at 50. Accordingly, we also affirm the district court's grant of summary judgment to Warner Bros. with respect to *The Wizard of Oz* and *Gone with the Wind* and the permanent injunction for this category of products. . . .

NOTES AND QUESTIONS

1. Most of the publicity materials at issue in *X One X Productions* were published prior to the release of the films. The Tom & Jerry publicity materials were different. Other than the first poster, the materials all were created and published after Tom and Jerry had appeared in films still subject to copyright protection. Noting that Warner Brothers had not challenged the reproduction of the later Tom & Jerry movie "posters as posters," the court concluded that AVELA was "authorized to make faithful reproductions, but not to reproduce those movie poster images on other products or to make derivative works based on Tom and Jerry." *X One X Prods.*, 644 F.3d at 604. Does the court's resolution make sense given the various copyright interests at stake? Had Warner Brothers challenged the reproduction of the movie posters as posters, how should the court have resolved that claim?

2. Into which §102 categories did the characters at issue in *X One X Productions* fall? Were they literary works? Pictorial or graphic works? Audiovisual works? Does it matter? Which right did AVELA infringe—the reproduction right? The derivative work right? Both?

3. How important is context to a character? Consider the court's statement in footnote 10 that if a public domain image of Dorothy were reproduced on a ruby slipper that might, in itself, infringe the copyright in the character as embodied in the film. Should it? If a James Bond-like character were hosting a cooking show, with no villains jumping out of helicopters to steal the filet mignon, would that infringe the copyright in the James Bond character? How would you know that it is James Bond hosting the show? Are a work's setting and minor characters, even ones so undelineated as to be just "bad guys," among the attributes that contribute to the copyrightability of literary characters? Should a court find infringement if those attributes are not present?

How about graphically depicted characters? If Mickey Mouse is speeding around in a spaceship with three unsightly one-eyed slimy alien creatures, will we still recognize Mickey and find Disney's copyright infringed? Does that mean graphically depicted characters do not need as much, or for that matter any, contextual support for the copyrights to be infringed?

> **LOOKING FORWARD**
>
> Many states recognize rights of publicity, which prohibit exploiting another's commercially valuable likeness or persona to sell a product or gain other advantages. When an actor portrays a character, the actor's personal attributes sometimes become intermingled with the character's. Who then owns the character? Usually this issue is handled by contract, but when it is not, litigation can result. We consider the intersection between state law rights of publicity and copyright law in Chapter 15.

4. In the late 1990s and early 2000s, online real-time interactive role-playing games such as Everquest and World of Warcraft became increasingly popular. In those games, individuals begin their life in a fantasy world by selecting a character type, for example, a sorcerer or a warrior, and as they play, their character takes on new attributes based on experiences and other actions in the fantasy world. Entrepreneurial gamers used online auction sites such as eBay to sell their characters, some of which they may have spent hundreds of hours developing. Sony Online Entertainment, the copyright owner of the Everquest game, asked eBay to halt those sales, asserting that the sale of the characters violated its copyrights, among other rights. eBay complied with the request. *See* Monty Phan, *Defining Their Own Reality*, Newsday, Feb. 13, 2001, at C08. Do you think Sony's copyright claim was a strong one? Why would eBay agree to halt those sales?

5. Many fans of particular movies, television shows, and popular novels write new scenes, stories, episodes, and even entire movie plots featuring the characters from their favorite shows. Those pieces of fan fiction are then shared with other fans, typically free of charge. Fan fiction writers often copy fully delineated characters but they typically do not copy the plots of existing stories or shows; instead, they create new story lines and plots. Many writers place copyright disclaimers on their fan fiction indicating that they created the works without permission from the copyright owners. They often assert that because they are not making any money, their works do not infringe. *See* Rebecca Tushnet, *Payment in Credit: Copyright Law and Subcultural Creativity*, 70 Law & Contemp. Probs. 135 (2007). As you know by now, that is incorrect. Should copyright owners be able to assert their reproduction and derivative work rights against fan fiction writers? If copyright law were to permit certain uses of shared cultural images without permission, would it effectively penalize the copyright owners of creative works that become the most successful and famous? Should it matter to an infringement analysis if a copyright owner has permitted some uses to occur then later changes its mind? Be sure to revisit the issue of fan fiction after you have read Chapter 10 on fair use.

6

The Rights of Distribution, Public Performance, and Public Display

In addition to the reproduction and derivative work rights, the Copyright Act gives copyright owners certain exclusive rights to disseminate their copyrighted works to the public. Copyrighted works may be distributed to the public in copies, or may be communicated to the public in nontangible form by performance or display. This chapter explores those rights.

The first copyright statute, the Act of 1790, granted copyright owners only the rights to "print, reprint, publish or vend" their works. Act of 1790, §1, 1 Stat. 124, 124 (1790). In the eighteenth and nineteenth centuries, means of access to copyrighted works were few. One might buy or borrow a printed copy of a book or sheet music, or attend an in-person performance of a play or a musical revue. As you learned in Chapter 1, over the course of the twentieth century, technologies and methods for communicating copyrighted content multiplied rapidly. Congress initially responded to these developments in piecemeal fashion, but in the 1976 Act, it formulated more generally applicable rights of distribution, public performance, and public display.

Networked information and communication technologies have fundamentally changed the copyright landscape yet again. In enacting the 1976 Act, Congress simply was not facing questions like whether making mp3 files available in the shared folder of a peer-to-peer application constitutes distribution of that file or whether hyperlinking to a file posted on another website implicates the rights of distribution and/or public display. As you read this chapter, consider how well the current statutory scheme responds to such situations.

A. DISTRIBUTION OF COPIES

We begin this chapter by discussing the various issues pertaining to the *distribution of copies* (whether physical or nonphysical) of works to the public, as opposed

345

to *communication of works by public performance or display.* We explore the latter topic in Section B, *infra.*

Section 106(3) of the Copyright Act gives copyright owners the exclusive right "to distribute copies or phonorecords of the copyrighted work to the public by sale or other transfer of ownership, or by rental, lease or lending." 17 U.S.C. §106(3). This right of public distribution has always gone hand in hand with the right to reproduce the work, and its scope and application have evolved in response to technological developments and consumer practices. Enumeration of the distribution right as a separate right gives the copyright owner the flexibility to pursue entities that are distributing (knowingly or not) unauthorized copies reproduced by others. Although the distribution right applies to any "copy" of a copyrighted work, it is most often invoked in cases involving exact copies.

1. What Constitutes a "Distribution"?

    Capitol Records, Inc. v. Thomas
579 F. Supp. 2d 1210 (D. Minn. 2008)

DAVIS, C.J.:

I. Introduction

. . . The Court has sua sponte raised the issue of whether it erred in instructing the jury that making sound recordings available for distribution on a peer-to-peer network, regardless of whether actual distribution was shown, qualified as distribution under the Copyright Act. . . .

II. Background

Plaintiffs are recording companies that owned or controlled exclusive rights to copyrights in sound recordings, including 24 at issue in this lawsuit. On April 19, 2006, Plaintiffs filed a Complaint against Defendant Jammie Thomas alleging that she infringed Plaintiffs' copyrighted sound recordings pursuant to the Copyright Act, 17 U.S.C. §§101, 106, 501–505, by illegally downloading and distributing the recordings via the online peer-to-peer file sharing application known as Kazaa. Plaintiffs sought injunctive relief, statutory damages, costs, and attorney fees. . . .

In Jury Instruction No. 15, the Court instructed: "The act of making copyrighted sound recordings available for electronic distribution on a peer-to-peer network, without license from the copyright owners, violates the copyright owners' exclusive right of distribution, regardless of whether actual distribution has been shown."

On October 4, 2007, the jury found that Thomas had willfully infringed on all 24 of Plaintiffs' sound recordings at issue, and awarded Plaintiffs statutory damages in the amount of $9,250 for each willful infringement. On October 5, the Court entered judgment on the jury's verdict. . . .

On May 15, 2008, the Court issued an Order stating that it was contemplating granting a new trial on the grounds that it had committed a manifest error of law in giving Jury Instruction No. 15. . . .

III. Discussion . . .

B. Prejudicial Effect of Any Error of Law . . .

2. Reproduction Right

Plaintiffs argue that regardless of the correctness of Jury Instruction No. 15, Plaintiffs had an indisputably valid reproduction claim, so even an erroneous instruction did not mislead the jury or prejudice Thomas.

The Special Verdict Form provides no insight as to whether the jurors found Thomas liable because of Jury Instruction No. 14, dealing with Plaintiffs' reproduction right, or because of Jury Instruction No. 15, dealing with Plaintiffs' distribution right. The Court cannot know whether the jury reached its verdict on permissible or impermissible grounds. Additionally, even if Thomas were liable under the reproduction right, there is no way for the Court to determine if the jury would have granted the same high statutory damage award based solely on violation of the reproduction right.

3. Distribution to MediaSentry[*]

The parties agree that the only evidence of actual dissemination of copyrighted works was that Plaintiffs' agent, MediaSentry, copied songs. Plaintiffs argue that even if distribution requires an actual transfer, the trial evidence established transfers of copyrighted works to MediaSentry. Thomas retorts that dissemination to an investigator acting as an agent for the copyright owner cannot constitute infringement.

"It is well-established that the lawful owner of a copyright cannot infringe its own copyright." *Olan Mills, Inc. v. Linn Photo Co.*, 23 F.3d 1345, 1348 (8th Cir.1994) (citation omitted). However, the Eighth Circuit holds that a copyright owner's authorization of an investigator to pursue infringement does "not authorize the investigator to validate [the third party's] unlawful conduct." *Id.* "Indeed, the investigator's assignment [i]s part of [the copyright owner's] attempt to stop . . . infringement." *Id. See also RCA/Ariola Int'l Inc. v. Thomas & Grayston Co.*, 845 F.2d 773, 781–82 (8th Cir. 1988) (holding retailer liable for actively assisting in reproduction of copyrighted works at request of authorized investigative agent of copyright owners). . . .

---

* MediaSentry was the private investigative firm hired by the plaintiffs to gather evidence for use at trial. The activities of MediaSentry are detailed in an earlier opinion in this litigation. *Capital Records v. Thomas-Rassett*, 79 Fed. R. Evid. Serv. 1203 (D. Minn. 2009). –Eds.

Plaintiffs further argue that even if the law required a defendant's active involvement in making distributions, Thomas is liable because she took the active steps of willfully reproducing copyrighted works without authorization and affirmatively choosing to place them in a shared folder making them available to anyone who wanted them on a computer network dedicated to the illegal distribution of copyrighted works. . . .

The Court holds that distribution to MediaSentry can form the basis of an infringement claim. Eighth Circuit precedent clearly approves of the use of investigators by copyright owners. While Thomas did not assist in the copying in the same manner as the retail defendant in *Olan Mills*—by actually completing the copying for the investigator—or as the retail defendants in *RCA/Ariola*—by assisting in selecting the correct tape on which to record and helping customers copy—she allegedly did assist in a different, but substantial manner. Plaintiffs presented evidence that Thomas, herself, provided the copyrighted works for copying and placed them on a network specifically designed for easy, unauthorized copying. These actions would constitute more substantial participation in the infringement than the actions of the defendants in the Eighth Circuit cases who merely assisted in copying works provided by the investigators.

Although the Court holds that distribution to an investigator, such as Media-Sentry, can constitute unauthorized distribution, in light of Jury Instruction No. 15, it is impossible to determine upon which basis the jury entered its verdict or how the erroneous jury instruction affected the jury's damage calculation. Therefore, if the Court determines that Jury Instruction No. 15 was incorrect, it will grant a new trial.

C. Statutory Framework

The Copyright Act provides that "the owner of copyright under this title has the exclusive rights to do and to authorize any of the following: . . . (3) to distribute copies or phonorecords of the copyrighted work to the public by sale or other transfer of ownership, or by rental, lease, or lending." 17 U.S.C. §106(3). The Act does not define the term "distribute."

Courts have split regarding whether making copyrighted materials available for distribution constitutes distribution under §106(3). The parties address four main arguments regarding the validity of the "making-available" interpretation: 1) whether the plain meaning of the term "distribution" requires actual dissemination of the copyrighted work; 2) whether the term "distribution" is synonymous with the term "publication," which, under the Copyright Act, does not require actual dissemination or transfer; 3) whether a defendant can be primarily liable for authorizing dissemination; and 4) whether U.S. treaty obligations and executive and legislative branch interpretations of the Copyright Act in relation to those obligations require a particular interpretation of the term "distribution."

D. Plain Meaning of the Term "Distribution"

. . . Each party asserts that the Court should adopt the plain meaning of the term "distribution"; however, they disagree on what that plain meaning is. Thomas and her supporters argue that the plain meaning of the statute compels the conclusion that merely making a work available to the public does not constitute a distribution. Instead, a distribution only occurs when a defendant actually transfers to the public the possession or ownership of copies or phonorecords of a work. Plaintiffs and their supporters assert that making a work available for distribution is sufficient.

1. Statutory Language

Starting with the language in §106(3), the Court notes that Congress explains the manners in which distribution can be effected: sale, transfer of ownership, rental, lease, or lending. The provision does not state that an offer to do any of these acts constitutes distribution. Nor does §106(3) provide that making a work available for any of these activities constitutes distribution. An initial reading of the provision at issue supports Thomas's interpretation.

2. Secondary Sources

The ordinary dictionary meaning of the word "distribute" necessarily entails a transfer of ownership or possession from one person to another. *See, e.g., Merriam–Webster's Collegiate Dictionary* (10th ed. 1999) (defining "distribute" as, among other things, "1: to divide among several or many: APPORTION . . . 2 . . . b: to give out or deliver esp. to members of a group").

Additionally, the leading copyright treatises conclude that making a work available is insufficient to establish distribution. *See, e.g.,* 2–8 *Nimmer on Copyright,* §8.11[A] (2008); 4 *William F. Patry, Patry on Copyright,* §13.11.50 (2008).

3. Opinion of the Register of Copyrights

Register of Copyrights, Marybeth Peters, has opined to Congress that making a copyrighted work available violates the distribution right. . . . However, opinion letters from the Copyright Office to Congress on matters of statutory interpretation are not binding. . . .

4. Use of the Term in Other Provisions of the U.S. Code

As Plaintiffs note, in other provisions of federal copyright law, Congress has explicitly defined "distribute" to include offers to distribute. *See* 17 U.S.C. §901(a)(4) (stating, in context of copyright protection of semiconductor chip products, that "to 'distribute' means to sell, or to lease, bail, or otherwise transfer, or to offer to sell, lease, bail, or otherwise transfer"); 17 U.S.C. §506(a)(1)(C) (imposing criminal penalties for "the distribution of a work being prepared for commercial distribution, by making it available on a computer network accessible to members of the public"). . . .

The differing definitions of "distribute" within copyright law demonstrate that there is not one uniform definition of the term throughout copyright law. . . . However, the Court notes that when Congress intends distribution to encompass making available or offering to transfer, it has demonstrated that it is quite capable of explicitly providing that definition within the statute. In this case, Congress provided the means by which a distribution occurs—"by sale or other transfer of ownership, or by rental, lease, or lending"—without also providing that a distribution occurs by an offer to do one of those actions, as it did in §901(a)(4). While the Copyright Act does not offer a uniform definition of "distribution," the Court concludes that, in light of the examined provisions, Congress's choice to not include offers to do the enumerated acts or the making available of the work indicates its intent that an actual distribution or dissemination is required in §106(3)....

The Court does not find the definitive interpretation of the term "distribute" in other titles of the U.S. Code. However, the Court does note that, while Congress has not added "offer to distribute" to §106(3) of the Copyright Act, it has added "offers to sell" in the related field of patent law. 35 U.S.C. §271(a). *See also Eldred v. Ashcroft,* 537 U.S. 186, 201–02 (2003) (citing patent practice as persuasive precedent in a copyright case). Before Congress amended the Patent Act to expressly include "offers to sell," courts strictly interpreted the statutory language, which expressly forbade sales but not offers to sell, as requiring proof of an actual sale. *Rotec Indus. v. Mitsubishi Corp.,* 215 F.3d 1246, 1251 (Fed. Cir. 2000). Court and congressional actions with regard to the Patent Act demonstrate two principles; 1) in the absence of a statutory definition that explicitly includes or excludes offers to sell or distribute, courts interpret liability narrowly to not include offers; and 2) Congress can and will amend a statute, when necessary, to explicitly include liability for an offer to do a prohibited act.

The Court's examination of the use of the term "distribution" in other provisions of the Copyright Act, as well as the evolution of liability for offers to sell in the analogous Patent Act, lead to the conclusion that the plain meaning of the term "distribution" does not includ[e] making available and, instead, requires actual dissemination....

E. Whether "Distribution" Is Synonymous with "Publication"

Plaintiffs advocate that, within the Copyright Act, the term "distribution" is synonymous with the term "publication."

> "Publication" is the distribution of copies or phonorecords of a work to the public by sale or other transfer of ownership, or by rental, lease, or lending. The offering to distribute copies or phonorecords to a group of persons for purposes of further distribution, public performance, or public display, constitutes publication. A public performance or display of a work does not of itself constitute publication.

17 U.S.C. §101. Under this definition, making sound recordings available on Kazaa could be considered distribution.

The first sentence of the definition of "publication" and §106(3) are substantially identical. However, there is additional language in the definition of "publication." Relying primarily on legislative history, Plaintiffs assert that the sentence defining publication as "[t]he offering to distribute copies or phonorecords to a group of persons for purposes of further distribution, public performance, or public display" should also apply to the definition of distribution.

Plaintiffs note that the text of §106 grants a copyright owner the following five exclusive rights: "(1) to reproduce the copyrighted work ... (2) to prepare derivative works . . . (3) to distribute copies of the work . . . (4) . . . to perform the copyrighted work publicly; and (5) . . . to display the work publicly." 17 U.S.C. §106. However, the House and Senate Committees evaluating the Copyright Act, described the following five rights: "the exclusive rights of reproduction, adaptation, *publication,* performance, and display." *Elektra Entm't Group, Inc. v. Barker,* 551 F. Supp. 2d 234, 241 (S.D.N.Y. 2008) (quoting H.R. Rep. No. 94–1476, at 61 (1976); S. Rep. No. 94–473, at 57 (1976)) (emphasis added in *Barker*). The Committee Reports identified the "Rights of Reproduction, Adaptation, and Publication" as "[t]he first three clauses of section 106." *Id.* (quoting H.R. Rep. at 61; S. Rep. at 57). Also, the House Committee Report stated that §106(3) " 'establishes the exclusive right of publication' and governs 'unauthorized public distribution'— using the words 'distribution' and 'publication' interchangeably within a single paragraph." *Id.* (citing H.R. Rep. at 62; S. Rep. at 58). The Court does not find these snippets of legislative history to be dispositive of the definition of distribution. Nowhere in this legislative history does Congress state that distribution should be given the same broad meaning as publication. In any case, even if the legislative history indicated that some members of Congress equated publications with distributions under §106(3), that fact cannot override the plain meaning of the statute. . . .

The Court concludes that simply because all distributions within the meaning of §106(3) are publications does not mean that all publications within the meaning of §101 are distributions. . . .

Congress's choice to use both terms within the Copyright Act demonstrates an intent that the terms have different meanings. . . .

F. Existence of a Protected Right to Authorize Distribution

Plaintiffs and their supporters also take the position that authorizing distribution is an exclusive right protected by the Copyright Act. They base this argument on the fact that §106 states "the owner of copyright under this title has the exclusive rights **to do** and **to authorize** any of the following . . . (3) to distribute . . . ." (emphasis added). Plaintiffs claim that the statute grants two separate rights—the right to "do" distribution and the right to "authorize" distribution. Therefore, making sound recordings available on Kazaa violates the copyright owner's exclusive right to authorize distribution.

The Court concludes that the authorization clause merely provides a statutory foundation for secondary liability, not a means of expanding the scope of direct infringement liability. . . .

I. Implications of International Law

1. U.S. Treaty Obligations Regarding the Making–Available Right

The United States is party to the World Intellectual Property Organization ("WIPO") Copyright Treaty ("WCT") and the WIPO Performances and Phonograms Treaty ("WPPT"). S. Rep. No. 105–190, 5, 9 (1998). It is undisputed that the WCT and the WPPT recognize a making-available right that is not dependent on proof that copies were actually transferred to particular individuals. WCT art. 6(1), art. 8; WPPT art. 12(1), art. 14. Additionally, by ratifying and adopting the treaties, the legislative and executive branches indicated that U.S. law complied with the treaties by protecting that making-available right.

Amici also note that the United States has entered various Free Trade Agreements ("FTA") that require the United States to provide a making-available right. *See, e.g.,* U.S.-Australia Free Trade Agreement, art. 17.5, May 18, 2004.

2. *Charming-Betsy* Doctrine . . .

Amici assert that under the *Charming Betsy* rule, the Court must adopt any reasonable interpretation of the Copyright Act that would grant Plaintiffs a making-available right to ensure that the U.S. complies with its treaty obligations. . . . *See Murray v. Schooner Charming Betsy,* 6 U.S. (2 Cranch) 64, 118 (1804) ("[A]n act of Congress ought never to be construed to violate the law of nations if any other possible construction remains."). . . .

The WIPO treaties are not self-executing and lack any binding legal authority separate from their implementation through the Copyright Act. . . . Therefore, the fact that the WIPO treaties protect a making-available right does not create an enforceable making-available right for Plaintiffs in this Court. *See, e.g., Guaylupo–Moya v. Gonzales,* 423 F.3d 121, 137 (2d Cir.2005). . . . Rather, the contents of the WIPO treaties are only relevant insofar as §106(3) is ambiguous and there is a reasonable interpretation of §106(3) that aligns with the United States' treaty obligations. . . .

The Court acknowledges that past Presidents, Congresses, and the Register of Copyrights have indicated their belief that the Copyright Act implements WIPO's make-available right. The Court also acknowledges that, given multiple reasonable constructions of U.S. law, the *Charming Betsy* doctrine directs the Court to adopt the reasonable construction that is consistent with the United States' international obligations. However, after reviewing the Copyright Act itself, legislative history, binding Supreme Court and Eighth Circuit precedent, and an extensive body of case law examining the Copyright Act, the Court concludes that Plaintiffs' interpretation of the distribution right is simply not reasonable. . . . Here, concern for U.S. compliance with the WIPO treaties and the FTAs cannot override the clear congressional intent in §106(3). . . .

NOTES AND QUESTIONS

1. Do you agree with the *Capitol Records* court's interpretation of §106(3)? *Capitol Records* reflects the majority position among courts that have considered what constitutes "distribution" in the digital context. Most courts have held that merely making files available for sharing via a peer-to-peer network does not violate the distribution right.

2. In part III.D.2 of its opinion, the *Capitol Records* court cites the leading copyright treatise, Nimmer on Copyright, for the proposition that making a work available is insufficient to establish distribution within the meaning of §106(3). After a detailed examination of the legislative history of the 1976 Copyright Act, Prof. David Nimmer subsequently reversed his previous position and revised his treatise to state that "the distribution right was formulated precisely so that it would extend to making copyrighted works available, rather than mandating proof of actual activities of distribution." *See* 2-8 *Nimmer on Copyright* §8.11[D][4][c]; *see also* Peter S. Menell, *In Search of Copyright's Lost Ark: Interpreting the Right to Distribute in the Internet Age,* 59 J. Copyright Soc'y U.S.A. 1, 30-63 (2011). What effect, if any, should a noted treatise writer's change of opinion have on the interpretation of the statute?

3. Neither the Berne Convention nor the TRIPS Agreement enumerates a separate right to distribute copies of copyrighted works. A general right of distribution was added to the international copyright framework in Article 6 of the WCT.

According to the *Capitol Records* court, "[i]t is undisputed that the WCT and the WPPT recognize a making-available right that is not dependent on proof that copies were actually transferred to particular individuals. WCT art. 6(1), art. 8; WPPT art. 12(1), art. 14." Article 6 directs that copyright owners be given "the exclusive right of authorizing the making available to the public of the original and copies of their works through sale or other transfer of ownership." According to the Agreed Statements Concerning the WIPO Copyright Treaty, adopted by the Diplomatic Conference on Dec. 20, 1996, WIPO CRNR/DC/96, the phrase "original and copies" applies to "fixed copies that can be put into circulation as tangible objects." Article 8 further directs that copyright owners be given "the exclusive right of authorizing any communication to the public of their works, by wire or wireless means, including the making available to the public of their works in such a way that members of the public may access these works from a place and at a time individually chosen by them." Are the rights afforded under §106(3) coextensive with these provisions? Should the court have relied on the *Charming Betsy* rule to reach a different interpretation of §106(3)? *See also* Restatement (Third) of Foreign Relations Law of the United States §114 ("Where fairly possible, a United States statute is to be construed so as not to conflict with international law or with an international agreement of the United States."). Why, or why not?

4. Does the ruling allowing Capitol Records to satisfy its burden of proving actual distribution of an unauthorized copy by showing distribution to plaintiff's investigator, MediaSentry, represent good policy? Why, or why not? If all circuits agreed, should this rule suffice to establish treaty compliance? On retrial, plaintiffs used the MediaSentry evidence to establish unauthorized distribution of copies of 24 songs.

> **LOOKING FORWARD**
>
> You will read the Eighth Circuit's decision in *Capitol Records* concerning the permissible range of statutory damages in Chapter 13.

2. The First Sale Doctrine and the Rental Rights Problem

The distribution right is subject to a number of important limitations. Prominent among these is the first sale doctrine, which has a lengthy pedigree and is rooted in the distinction between the ownership of copyright in a work and ownership of the physical object in which the work is embodied. Other limitations, developed more recently, reflect the concerns of industries affected by new consumer technologies that facilitate copying and distribution.

a. The First Sale Doctrine

The first sale doctrine is codified in §109(a) of the Act:

> Notwithstanding the provisions of section 106(3), the owner of a particular copy or phonorecord lawfully made under this title, or any person authorized by such owner, is entitled, without the authority of the copyright owner, to sell or otherwise dispose of the possession of that copy or phonorecord. . . .

17 U.S.C. §109(a). Its origins, however, lie not in the copyright law but in the common law right to control disposition of chattels in one's lawful possession.

 ### Bobbs-Merrill Co. v. Straus
210 U.S. 339 (1908)

DAY, J.:

The complainant in the Circuit Court, appellant here, the Bobbs-Merrill Company, brought suit against the respondents, appellees here, Isidor Straus and Nathan Straus, partners as R. H. Macy & Company, . . . to restrain the sale of a copyrighted novel, entitled "The Castaway," at retail at less than $1 for each copy. The Circuit Court dismissed the bill on final hearing. . . .

The appellant is the owner of the copyright upon "The Castaway," obtained on the 18th day of May, 1904, in conformity to the copyright statutes of the United States. Printed immediately below the copyright notice, on the page in the book following the title page, is inserted the following notice:

> The price of this book at retail is $1 net. No dealer is licensed to sell it at a less price, and a sale at a less price will be treated as an infringement of the copyright.
> The Bobbs-Merrill Company.

Macy & Company, before the commencement of the action, purchased copies of the book for the purpose of selling the same at retail. . . .

The wholesale dealers, from whom defendants purchased copies of the book, obtained the same either directly from the complainant or from other wholesale dealers at a discount from the net retail price, and, at the time of their purchase, knew that the book was a copyrighted book, and were familiar with the terms of the notice printed in each copy thereof, as described above, and such knowledge was in all wholesale dealers through whom the books passed from the complainants to defendants. But the wholesale dealers were under no agreement or obligation to enforce the observance of the terms of the notice by retail dealers, or to restrict their sales to retail dealers who would agree to observe the terms stated in the notice.

The defendants have sold copies of the book at retail at the uniform price of 89 cents a copy. . . .

. . . Recent cases in this court have affirmed the proposition that copyright property under the Federal law is wholly statutory, and depends upon the right created under the acts of Congress passed in pursuance of the authority conferred under article 1, §8, of the Federal Constitution. . . .

It is the contention of the appellant that the circuit court erred in failing to give effect to the provision of §4952 [of the Revised Statutes of the United States], protecting the owners of the copyright in the sole right of vending the copyrighted book or other article, and the argument is that the statute vested the whole field of the right of exclusive sale in the copyright owner; that he can part with it to another to the extent that he sees fit, and may withhold to himself, by proper reservations, so much of the right as he pleases.

What does the statute mean in granting "the sole right of vending the same?" Was it intended to create a right which would permit the holder of the copyright to fasten, by notice in a book or upon one of the articles mentioned within the statute, a restriction upon the subsequent alienation of the subject-matter of copyright after the owner had parted with the title to one who had acquired full dominion over it and had given a satisfactory price for it? It is not denied that one who has sold a copyrighted article, without restriction, has parted with all right to control the sale of it. The purchaser of a book, once sold by authority of the owner of the copyright, may sell it again, although he could not publish a new edition of it. . . .

The precise question, therefore, in this case is, Does the sole right to vend (named in §4952) secure to the owner of the copyright the right, after a sale of the book to a purchaser, to restrict future sales of the book at retail, to the right to sell it at a certain price per copy, because of a notice in the book that a sale at a different price will be treated as an infringement, which notice has been brought home to one undertaking to sell for less than the named sum? We do not think the statute can be given such a construction, and it is to be remembered that this is purely a question of statutory construction. There is no claim in this case of contract limitation, nor license agreement controlling the subsequent sales of the book.

In our view the copyright statutes, while protecting the owner of the copyright in his right to multiply and sell his production, do not create the right to impose, by notice, such as is disclosed in this case, a limitation at which the book shall be sold at retail by future purchasers, with whom there is no privity of contract. . . .

The common law principle underlying the first sale doctrine is easy to state. When you buy a copy of a book you become the owner of that copy, and as the owner you are empowered to engage in a wide variety of conduct. You can lend it to others to read or sell it at a flea market or via an online auction site. Stated differently, the copyright owner's exclusive rights with respect to a particular copy of a work become "exhausted" upon a lawful transfer of ownership of that copy. The first sale doctrine thus shields a wide variety of conduct from liability for infringement of the distribution right. For the last few decades, however, there has been significant dispute about the appropriate scope of the first sale doctrine, especially in relation to digital works. Review §109(a) and identify the elements that must be satisfied for the first sale doctrine to apply. Then consider the following case.

Capitol Records, LLC v. ReDigi Inc.
934 F. Supp. 2d 640 (S.D.N.Y. 2013)

SULLIVAN, J.: . . .

I. BACKGROUND

A. Facts

ReDigi markets itself as "the world's first and only online marketplace for digital used music." Launched on October 13, 2011, ReDigi's website invites users to "sell their legally acquired digital music files, and buy used digital music from others at a fraction of the price currently available on iTunes." Thus, much like used record stores, ReDigi permits its users to recoup value on their unwanted music. Unlike used record stores, however, ReDigi's sales take place entirely in the digital domain.

To sell music on ReDigi's website, a user must first download ReDigi's "Media Manager" to his computer. Once installed, Media Manager analyzes the user's computer to build a list of digital music files eligible for sale. A file is eligible only if it was purchased on iTunes or from another ReDigi user; music downloaded from a CD or other file-sharing website is ineligible for sale. After this validation process, Media Manager continually runs on the user's computer and attached devices to ensure that the user has not retained music that has been sold or uploaded for sale. However, Media Manager cannot detect copies stored in other locations. If a copy is detected, Media Manager prompts the user to delete the file. The file is not deleted automatically or involuntarily, though ReDigi's policy is to suspend the accounts of users who refuse to comply.

After the list is built, a user may upload any of his eligible files to ReDigi's "Cloud Locker," an ethereal moniker for what is, in fact, merely a remote server in Arizona. ReDigi's upload process is a source of contention between the parties. ReDigi asserts that the process involves "migrating" a user's file, packet by packet—"analogous to a train"—from the user's computer to the Cloud Locker so that data does not exist in two places at any one time. Capitol asserts that, semantics aside, ReDigi's upload process "necessarily involves copying" a file from the user's computer to the Cloud Locker. Regardless, at the end of the process, the digital music file is located in the Cloud Locker and not on the user's computer. Moreover, Media Manager deletes any additional copies of the file on the user's computer and connected devices.

Once uploaded, a digital music file undergoes a second analysis to verify eligibility. If ReDigi determines that the file has not been tampered with or offered for sale by another user, the file is stored in the Cloud Locker, and the user is given the option of simply storing and streaming the file for personal use or offering it for sale in ReDigi's marketplace. If a user chooses to sell his digital music file, his access to the file is terminated and transferred to the new owner at the time of purchase. Thereafter, the new owner can store the file in the Cloud Locker, stream it, sell it, or download it to her computer and other devices. No money changes hands in these transactions. Instead, users buy music with credits they either purchased from ReDigi or acquired from other sales. ReDigi credits, once acquired, cannot be exchanged for money. Instead, they can only be used to purchase additional music. . . .

Finally, ReDigi earns a fee for every transaction. ReDigi's website prices digital music files at fifty-nine to seventy-nine cents each. When users purchase a file, with credits, 20% of the sale price is allocated to the seller, 20% goes to an "escrow" fund for the artist, and 60% is retained by ReDigi.[3]

B. *Procedural History*

Capitol, which owns a number of the recordings sold on ReDigi's website . . . alleges multiple violations of the Copyright Act . . . .

On July 20, 2012, Capitol filed its motion for partial summary judgment on the claims that ReDigi directly and secondarily infringed Capitol's reproduction and distribution rights. . . .

III. DISCUSSION

. . . The novel question presented in this action is whether a digital music file, lawfully made and purchased, may be resold by its owner through ReDigi under the first sale doctrine. The Court determines that it cannot. . . .

1. Reproduction Rights . . .

. . . [T]he plain text of the Copyright Act makes clear that reproduction occurs when a copyrighted work is fixed in a new *material object*.

The legislative history of the Copyright Act bolsters this reading. . . .

Courts that have dealt with infringement on peer-to-peer ("P2P") file-sharing systems provide valuable guidance on the application of this right in the digital domain. For instance, in *London–Sire Records, Inc. v. John Doe 1*, the court addressed whether users of P2P software violated copyright owners' distribution rights. 542 F. Supp. 2d 153, 166 & n.16 (D. Mass. 2008). Citing the "material object" requirement, the court expressly differentiated between the copyrighted work—or digital music file—and the phonorecord—or "appropriate segment of the hard disk" that the file would be embodied in following its transfer. *Id.* at 171. . . .

---

3. On June 11, 2012, ReDigi launched ReDigi 2.0, new software that, when installed on a user's computer, purportedly directs the user's new iTunes purchases to upload from iTunes directly to the Cloud Locker. Accordingly, while access may transfer from user to user upon resale, the file is never moved from its initial location in the Cloud Locker. However, because ReDigi 2.0 launched after Capitol filed the Complaint and mere days before the close of discovery, the Court will not consider it in this action.

This understanding is, of course, confirmed by the laws of physics. It is simply impossible that the same "material object" can be transferred over the Internet. . . .

Given this finding, the Court concludes that ReDigi's service infringes Capitol's reproduction rights under any description of the technology. . . .

2. Distribution Rights

. . . Like the court in *London–Sire,* the Court agrees that "[a]n electronic file transfer is plainly within the sort of transaction that §106(3) was intended to reach [and] . . . fit[s] within the definition of 'distribution' of a phonorecord." *London–Sire,* 542 F. Supp. 2d at 173–74. For that reason, "courts have not hesitated to find copyright infringement by distribution in cases of file-sharing or electronic transmission of copyrighted works." *Arista Records LLC v. Greubel,* 453 F. Supp. 2d 961, 968 (N.D. Tex. 2006) (collecting cases). . . .

There is no dispute that sales occurred on ReDigi's website. Capitol has established that it was able to buy more than one-hundred of its own recordings on ReDigi's website, and ReDigi itself compiled a list of its completed sales of Capitol's recordings. . . .

Accordingly, the Court concludes that, absent the existence of an affirmative defense, the sale of digital music files on ReDigi's website infringes Capitol's exclusive right of distribution. . . .

B. Affirmative Defenses . . .

ReDigi asserts that its service, which involves the resale of digital music files lawfully purchased on iTunes, is protected by the first sale defense. The Court disagrees.

As an initial matter, it should be noted that the [first sale] defense is, by its own terms, limited to assertions of the *distribution right.* 17 U.S.C. §109 (referencing Section 106(3)). Because the Court has concluded that ReDigi's service violates Capitol's reproduction right, the first sale defense does not apply to ReDigi's infringement of those rights.

In addition, the first sale doctrine does not protect ReDigi's distribution of Capitol's copyrighted works. This is because, as an unlawful reproduction, a digital music file sold on ReDigi is not "lawfully made under this title." 17 U.S.C. §109(a). Moreover, the statute protects only distribution by "the owner of a *particular* copy or phonorecord . . . of *that* copy or phonorecord." *Id.* Here, a ReDigi user owns the phonorecord that was created when she purchased and downloaded a song from iTunes to her hard disk. But to sell that song on ReDigi, she must produce a new phonorecord on the ReDigi server. Because it is therefore impossible for the user to sell her "particular" phonorecord on ReDigi, the first sale statute cannot provide a defense. Put another way, the first sale defense is limited to material items, like records, that the copyright owner put into the stream of commerce. Here, ReDigi is not distributing such material items; rather, it is distributing *reproductions* of the copyrighted code embedded in new material objects, namely, the ReDigi server in Arizona and its users' hard drives. The first sale defense does not cover this any more than it covered the sale of cassette recordings of vinyl records in a bygone era.

. . . ReDigi asserts that refusal to apply the first sale doctrine to its service would grant Capitol "a Court sanctioned extension of rights under the [C]opyright [A]ct . . . which is against policy, and should not be endorsed by this Court."

The Court disagrees. ReDigi effectively requests that the Court amend the statute to achieve ReDigi's broader policy goals—goals that happen to advance ReDigi's economic interests. However, ReDigi's argument fails for two reasons. First, while technological change may have rendered Section 109(a) unsatisfactory to many contemporary observers and consumers, it has not rendered it ambiguous. The statute plainly applies to the lawful owner's "particular" phonorecord, a phonorecord that by definition cannot be uploaded and sold on ReDigi's website. Second, amendment of the Copyright Act in line with ReDigi's proposal is a legislative prerogative that courts are unauthorized and ill suited to attempt.

Nor are the policy arguments as straightforward or uncontested as ReDigi suggests. Indeed, . . . the United States Copyright Office (the "USCO") rejected extension of the first sale doctrine to the distribution of digital works, noting that the justifications for the first sale doctrine in the physical world could not be imported into the digital domain. *See* USCO, Library of Cong., DMCA Section 104 Report (2001) ("DMCA Report"). For instance, the USCO stated that "the impact of the [first sale] doctrine on copyright owners [is] limited in the off-line world by a number of factors, including geography and the gradual degradation of books and analog works." DMCA Report at xi. Specifically,

> [p]hysical copies of works degrade with time and use, making used copies less desirable than new ones. Digital information does not degrade, and can be reproduced perfectly on a recipient's computer. The "used" copy is just as desirable as (in fact, is indistinguishable from) a new copy of the same work. Time, space, effort and cost no longer act as barriers to the movement of copies, since digital copies can be transmitted nearly instantaneously anywhere in the world with minimal effort and negligible cost. The need to transport physical copies of works, which acts as a natural brake on the effect of resales on the copyright owner's market, no longer exists in the realm of digital transmissions. The ability of such "used" copies to compete for market share with new copies is thus far greater in the digital world.

Id. at 82–83 (footnotes omitted). Thus, while ReDigi mounts attractive policy arguments, they are not as one-sided as it contends.

Finally, ReDigi feebly argues that the Court's reading of Section 109(a) would in effect exclude digital works from the meaning of the statute. That is not the case. Section 109(a) still protects a lawful owner's sale of her "particular" phonorecord, be it a computer hard disk, iPod, or other memory device onto which the file was originally downloaded. While this limitation clearly presents obstacles to resale that are different from, and perhaps even more onerous than, those involved in the resale of CDs and cassettes, the limitation is hardly absurd—the first sale doctrine was enacted in a world where the ease and speed of data transfer could not have been imagined. There are many reasons, some discussed herein, for why such physical limitations may be desirable. It is left to Congress, and not this Court, to deem them outmoded. . . .

NOTES AND QUESTIONS

1. Did the *ReDigi* court reach the right decision on the applicability of the first sale doctrine in the digital context? Why, or why not?

2. Are the privileges enjoyed by owners of copies limited to those described in §109(a), or does *Bobbs-Merrill* suggest that such owners also may have other privileges that flow from their status as owners of chattel property? *See* Aaron Perzanowski & Jason Schultz, *Digital Exhaustion*, 58 UCLA L. Rev. 889 (2011) (arguing that courts should draw on a broader common law principle of exhaustion to preserve the benefits of the first sale doctrine to owners of digital copies).

3. In the digital era, copyright owners have made various efforts to restrict resale and other transfers of copies of works. Software manufacturers were the first to do so, employing so-called "shrinkwrap" restrictions—asserted license terms printed on the physical package containing the software, accompanied by notice to the purchaser that opening the package constituted consent to the restrictions. Many producers of software and other digital works now also convey the asserted license terms to consumers during the installation process, or if the work is purchased via the Internet, during the purchase process. How, if at all, do *Bobbs-Merrill* and *ReDigi* bear on the legitimacy of such efforts?

PRACTICE EXERCISE: ADVOCACY AND DRAFTING

You have been hired as a lobbyist by a coalition of digital media companies who specialize in on-line auctions of digital works. Your client has asked you to suggest language that could be proposed to amend §109(a) to permit transfers of copies of digital works. Draft the amendment and a short PowerPoint presentation of the arguments that you would present to congressional staffers to support its enactment.

---

b. Rental Restrictions

The protection that §109 confers on owners of copies is limited for some categories of works. In response to the introduction of new technological platforms such as the cassette deck, the videocassette recorder (VCR) and the personal computer, Congress enacted several exceptions to the first-sale doctrine to cope with perceived problems of market substitution by unauthorized copies. Recall that §109(a) applies not only to the resale of copies of copyrighted works and phonorecords, but also to other forms of distribution, including rental, lease, and lending. As new technologies have evolved, however, copyright owners have argued that such rental, lease, and lending simply facilitates unauthorized copying and thus creates market substitutes for the sale of authorized copies.

In the Record Rental Amendment of 1984, Congress enacted a new §109(b) of the Copyright Act, which banned owners of phonorecords from engaging in rental, lease, or lending "for direct or indirect commercial advantage." 17 U.S.C.

§109(b)(1)(A). This provision was expanded in the 1990s to include computer programs, "including any tape, disk, or other medium embodying such program."

Read §109(b) now. Note that Congress included some important exceptions to these restrictions. In particular, §109(b) does not apply to the lending, lease, or rental of phonorecords by nonprofit libraries and nonprofit educational institutions and also to computer programs that are "embodied in a machine or product and which cannot be copied during the ordinary operation or use of the machine or product." 17 U.S.C. §109(b)(1)(A)-(B). In addition, nonprofit libraries are permitted to engage in the lending of computer programs for nonprofit purposes, provided that "each copy of a computer program which is lent by such library has affixed to the packaging containing the program a warning of copyright. . . ." 17 U.S.C. §109(b)(2)(A).

At around the same time that it considered the Record Rental Amendment, Congress also considered amending §109 to prohibit the commercial rental of motion pictures. This amendment was supported both by the motion picture industry and the Register of Copyrights. However, due to a well-organized opposition, Congress abandoned the proposed restriction on movie rentals and limited §109(b) to phonorecords. The motion picture industry adjusted by pricing newly released videos at a level designed to compensate for losses in the rental markets. In addition, the industry has facilitated the adoption of new technologies, such as Macrovision (designed to prevent copying of prerecorded videotapes) and the Content Scramble System (CSS) (designed to prevent video playback on unauthorized devices).

> ### COMPARATIVE PERSPECTIVE
>
> Unlike the United States, the European Union has in place a framework that comprehensively regulates rental of all copyrightable works. The European Union first adopted a Rental Rights Directive in 1992. In 2006, the European Union repealed the 1992 Directive, replacing it with a new version that reflects changes in technology and methods of distribution. Directive 2006/115, of the European Parliament and of the Council of 12 December 2006 on Rental Right and Lending Right and on Certain Rights Related to Copyright in the Field of Intellectual Property, 2006 O.J. (L 376/28).
>
> The Directive requires EU Member States to provide authors, performers, phonogram producers, and film producers with the "exclusive right to authorize or prohibit rental and lending." Art. 3(1). In addition, authors and performers who have transferred or assigned their rental rights to a phonogram or film producer retain an unwaivable right "to obtain an equitable remuneration . . ." (Art. 5).

NOTES AND QUESTIONS

1. Do the exceptions enumerated in §109(b) strike you as sensible? Do the developments that followed the failure of the motion picture industry's effort to amend §109(b) indicate that the restrictions in §109(b) are unnecessary? Why, or why not?

2. In *Brilliance Audio, Inc. v. Haights Cross Communications, Inc.*, 474 F.3d 365 (6th Cir. 2007), the defendants purchased and repackaged retail editions of plaintiff's audiobooks and then distributed the works by, among other things, renting them in direct competition with the plaintiff. They argued that the phonogram rental exception in §109(b) does not apply to all sound recordings, but only to

sound recordings of musical works. After reviewing the legislative history of §109(b), the court agreed. Do you agree with that result? Do the concerns that motivated Congress to enact §109(b) also apply to audiobooks? If so, should Congress expand the scope of the phonogram rental exception? *See* Sean N. Kass, *Misinterpreting the Record Rental Amendment:* Brilliance Audio v. Haights Cross Communications, 21 Harv. J.L. & Tech. 297 (2007).

3. In the early 1990s, the differences between the European and U.S. positions on rental rights significantly complicated negotiations over the TRIPS Agreement. By then, the balance of interests in the United States had swung decisively in favor of allowing the commercial rental of movies to continue and U.S. negotiators insisted that the global trading community accommodate American practices. Article 11 of the TRIPS Agreement requires that Member States provide rental rights to authors of computer programs and cinematographic works. However, Member States are exempted from the obligation to grant rental rights in cinematographic works "unless such rental has led to widespread copying of such works which is materially impairing the exclusive right of reproduction."

c. Libraries and §108

The first sale doctrine allows libraries that have purchased copies of works to lend those copies, repeatedly, to members of the public. Nonprofit libraries and archives also enjoy some unique distribution privileges under copyright law. Section 108 authorizes certain acts of copying by these entities, and clearly allows some distribution of the resulting copies. Read §108 now.

The privileges established under §108 include reproduction in a single copy for the library itself or for library patrons for purposes of private study, scholarship, or research; reproduction and distribution for purposes of preservation, security, or research use by another library; reproduction to replace a damaged, deteriorating, or lost copy; and reproduction and distribution for patrons of other libraries within an interlibrary loan system. *See* 17 U.S.C. §108(a)-(e). Those provisions, however, include limitations designed to ensure that none of those activities can become a substitute for purchases of copyrighted works. Thus, for example, a library may not make copies for patrons if it has substantial reason to believe that it is facilitating "the related or concerted reproduction or distribution of multiple copies or phonorecords of the same material." *Id.* §108(g). In addition, it may not make copies of musical works, motion pictures, or pictorial, graphic, or sculptural works (other than

---

COMPARATIVE PERSPECTIVE

Article 6.1 of the EU Rental Rights Directive authorizes EU Member States to provide exceptions for public lending "provided that at least authors obtain a remuneration for such lending." A number of countries both within and outside the European Union have adopted a public lending right. In public lending right systems, the author of a copyrighted work receives a royalty each time a member of the public borrows the work. In some countries, payment to the author may be based on the number of titles in stock and available for public borrowing or use. The right to receive this royalty belongs to authors, not to subsequent assignees of the authors' copyright interests, although some countries also provide for separate payments to publishers. Unlike the exclusive rights afforded under 17 U.S.C. §106, in most countries the public lending right does not entitle an author to prohibit the public lending of a work; it entitles the author only to be paid.

illustrations) for purposes other than preservation, security, or replacement of a deteriorating or damaged copy—i.e., it may not make such copies for the personal use of library patrons. *Id.* §108(i). Finally, a library may not make replacement copies unless it has, "after a reasonable effort, determined that an unused replacement cannot be obtained at a fair price; . . ." *Id.* §108(c)(1).

Like §109(a), §108 has come under pressure in the digital environment. In 1998, Congress amended §108 to restrict libraries' ability to distribute copies of works in their collections to members of the public in digital format. As amended, §108 allows a library to reproduce copies or phonorecords in digital format, but prohibits them from making such copies available to the public outside the library's own premises. *Id.* §108(b)(2), (c)(2).

In 2008, the Copyright Office along with the National Digital Information Infrastructure and Preservation Program of the Library of Congress completed a study with the view of addressing the challenges faced by libraries in the digital age. The study, entitled *The Section 108 Study Group Report*, recommended a series of amendments designed to harmonize §108 with the library community's emerging consensus about "best practices" in the digital age. *See* The Section 108 Study Group Report, March 2008, *available at* http://www.section108.gov/; *see also* Savanna Nolan, Note, *Standing on the Shoulders of Giants: How a Drastic Remodeling of 17 U.S.C. §108 Could Help Save Academia*, 19 J. Intell. Prop. L. 457 (2012); Mary Rasenberger, *Copyright Issues and Section 108 Reform*, 34 Colum. J.L. & Arts 15 (2010). The recommended amendments include revisions to the definition of qualifying institutions to include museums, to require a public service mission, and to address the use of contractors for preservation activities. They also include a variety of changes to the portions of §108 establishing criteria for preservation and replacement copying. The study group was unable to reach consensus about amendments concerning distribution of digital copies to users.

PRACTICE EXERCISE: COUNSEL A CLIENT

You are counsel to the newly formed Digital Public Library of America, and have been asked to provide an opinion on the extent of the DPLA's freedom to digitize its holdings. Draft an opinion letter setting forth your conclusions. Based on your conclusions, what positions should the DPLA take on future revisions to §108?

NOTES AND QUESTIONS

1. Do the exceptions contained in §108 strike you as sensible or too complex to be useful? If the latter, what rules for libraries and archives would you propose?

2. Should Congress amend §108 to permit the distribution and/or display of digital works outside the physical premises of a library? If so, on what conditions?

3. Is the European "rental right plus public lending right" model superior to the all-or-nothing approach taken by U.S. copyright law? Why, or why not? Would

you recommend that the United States give all copyright owners the exclusive right to control rental or lending of their works? Would you recommend that the United States adopt a public lending right for noncommercial lending? How about a liability rule model for rentals of copyrighted works generally?

Bills to enact a public lending right in the United States were introduced several times during the 1970s and 1980s by a coalition led by the Authors Guild, but neither the House nor the Senate has ever approved such a bill. *See* Richard LeComte, *Writers Blocked: The Debate over Public Lending Right in the United States During the 1980s*, 44 Libr. & Cultural Rec. 395 (2009).

3. Importation and Exhaustion

An important adjunct of the §106(3) distribution right is the right to prevent the unauthorized importation of copies of a copyrighted work into the United States This right is set out in §602 of the Copyright Act:

> Importation into the United States, without the authority of the owner of copyright under this title, of copies or phonorecords of a work that have been acquired outside the United States is an infringement of the exclusive right to distribute copies or phonorecords under section 106. . . .

17 U.S.C. §602(a)(1).

As discussed in Chapter 1, copyright law has always been concerned with the territorial origin of copies of protected works. Modern copyright law is also concerned with whether the copies are infringing, and whether the importation is authorized by the copyright owner. Recall that §109(a) conditions the applicability of the first sale doctrine on whether the copies in question were "lawfully made under this title [i.e., under the U.S. copyright law]." Similarly, the importation of copies made without the authority of the copyright owner (U.S. or foreign) violates the §602(a) importation right.

Copyrights can be divided geographically, however. Sometimes, the foreign copyright holder is completely unrelated to, and unaffiliated with, the U.S. copyright owner of the same work. This might happen, for example, when the author of the work sells or licenses the U.S. rights and the foreign rights (or, more likely, the European rights, the Asian rights, etc.) to different publishers. It might also happen if a U.S. company owns the entire copyright but sells or licenses the rights to exploit the work outside the United States to a foreign company, or vice versa. In other cases, the U.S. and foreign copyright holders may have a parent-subsidiary relationship or may be sibling companies.

Foreign licensees or affiliates typically agree not to distribute the work within each other's territory, and also agree to impose these geographic restrictions on their distributors. However, the temptation to violate such restrictions is strong, since copyrighted products (like other products) can command substantially different prices in different countries. In an era of liberalized global trade and currency fluctuations, this presents an opportunity for arbitrage—i.e., buying in one country at a low price and then reselling in another country for a higher price. Under the first sale doctrine, resale of "lawfully made" copies is permissible. Just what is a "lawfully made" copy for the purposes of the importation right is an important question, involving difficult questions of statutory construction and policy.

Kirtsaeng v. John Wiley & Sons, Inc.
2013 WL 1104736, 113 S. Ct. 1351 (U.S. 2013)

BREYER, J.: . . .

Section 106 of the Copyright Act grants "the owner of copyright under this title" certain "exclusive rights," including the right "to distribute copies . . . of the copyrighted work to the public by sale or other transfer of ownership." 17 U. S. C. §106(3). These rights are qualified, however, by the application of various limitations set forth in the next several sections of the Act, §§107 through 122. Those sections, typically entitled "Limitations on exclusive rights," include . . . the doctrine at issue here, the "first sale" doctrine (§109).

Section 109(a) sets forth the "first sale" doctrine as follows:

> Notwithstanding the provisions of section 106(3) [the section that grants the owner exclusive distribution rights], the owner of a particular copy or phonorecord *lawfully made under this title* . . . is entitled, without the authority of the copyright owner, to sell or otherwise dispose of the possession of that copy or phonorecord. (Emphasis added.)

Thus, even though §106(3) forbids distribution of a copy of, say, the copyrighted novel *Herzog* without the copyright owner's permission, §109(a) adds that, once a copy of *Herzog* has been lawfully sold (or its ownership otherwise lawfully transferred), the buyer of *that copy* and subsequent owners are free to dispose of it as they wish. In copyright jargon, the "first sale" has "exhausted" the copyright owner's §106(3) exclusive distribution right.

What, however, if the copy of *Herzog* was printed abroad and then initially sold with the copyright owner's permission? Does the "first sale" doctrine still apply? Is the buyer, like the buyer of a domestically manufactured copy, free to bring the copy into the United States and dispose of it as he or she wishes?

To put the matter technically, an "importation" provision, §602(a)(1), says that

> [i]mportation into the United States, without the authority of the owner of copyright under this title, of copies . . . of a work that have been acquired outside the United States is an infringement of the exclusive right to distribute copies . . . *under section 106* . . . . 17 U. S. C. §602(a)(1) (2006 ed., Supp. V) (emphasis added).

Thus §602(a)(1) makes clear that importing a copy without permission violates the owner's exclusive distribution right. But in doing so, §602(a)(1) refers explicitly to the §106(3) exclusive distribution right. As we have just said, §106 is by its terms "[s]ubject to" the various doctrines and principles contained in §§107 through 122, including §109(a)'s "first sale" limitation. Do those same modifications apply—in particular, does the "first sale" modification apply—when considering whether §602(a)(1) prohibits importing a copy?

In *Quality King Distributors, Inc.* v. *L'anza Research Int'l, Inc.*, 523 U.S. 135, 145 (1998), we held that §602(a)(1)'s reference to §106(3)'s exclusive distribution right incorporates the later subsections' limitations, including, in particular, the "first sale" doctrine of §109. Thus, it might seem that, §602(a)(1) notwithstanding, one who buys a copy abroad can freely import that copy into the United States and dispose of it, just as he could had he bought the copy in the United States.

But *Quality King* considered an instance in which the copy, though purchased abroad, was initially manufactured in the United States (and then sent abroad and sold). This case is like *Quality King* but for one important fact. The copies at issue here were manufactured abroad. That fact is important because §109(a) says that the "first sale" doctrine applies to "a particular copy or phonorecord *lawfully made under this title*." And we must decide here whether the five words, "lawfully made under this title," make a critical legal difference. . . .

. . . We hold that the "first sale" doctrine applies to copies of a copyrighted work lawfully made abroad.

I

A

Respondent, John Wiley & Sons, Inc., publishes academic textbooks [and we will] refer to Wiley as the relevant American copyright owner. Wiley often assigns to its wholly owned foreign subsidiary, John Wiley & Sons (Asia) Pte Ltd., rights to publish, print, and sell Wiley's English language textbooks abroad. . . .

[A] copy of Wiley's American edition says, "Copyright © 2008 John Wiley & Sons, Inc. All rights reserved. . . . Printed in the United States of America." J. Walker, Fundamentals of Physics, p. vi (8th ed. 2008). A copy of Wiley Asia's Asian edition of that book says:

> Copyright © 2008 John Wiley & Sons (Asia) Pte Ltd[.] All rights reserved. This book is authorized for sale in Europe, Asia, Africa, and the Middle East only and may be not exported out of these territories. Exportation from or importation of this book to another region without the Publisher's authorization is illegal and is a violation of the Publisher's rights. The Publisher may take legal action to enforce its rights. . . . Printed in Asia. J. Walker, Fundamentals of Physics, p. vi (8th ed. 2008 Wiley Int'l Student ed.).

Both the foreign and the American copies say:

> No part of this publication may be reproduced, stored in a retrieval system, or transmitted in any form or by any means . . . except as permitted under Sections 107 or 108 of the 1976 United States Copyright Act. . . .

The upshot is that there are two essentially equivalent versions of a Wiley textbook . . .

Petitioner, Supap Kirtsaeng, a citizen of Thailand, moved to the United States in 1997 . . . completed [] undergraduate courses . . . successfully completed a Ph. D. program . . . and then . . . returned to Thailand. . . . While he was studying in the

United States, Kirtsaeng asked his friends and family in Thailand to buy copies of foreign edition English language textbooks at Thai book shops, where they sold at low prices, and mail them to him in the United States. Kirtsaeng would then sell them, reimburse his family and friends, and keep the profit.

B

In 2008 Wiley brought this federal lawsuit against Kirtsaeng for copyright infringement. Wiley claimed that Kirtsaeng's unauthorized importation of its books and his later resale of those books amounted to an infringement of Wiley's §106(3) exclusive right to distribute as well as §602's related import prohibition. Kirtsaeng replied that the books he had acquired were "'lawfully made'" and that he had acquired them legitimately. Thus, in his view, §109(a)'s "first sale" doctrine permitted him to resell or otherwise dispose of the books without the copyright owner's further permission.

The District Court held that Kirtsaeng could not assert the "first sale" defense because, in its view, that doctrine does not apply to "foreign-manufactured goods" (even if made abroad with the copyright owner's permission). The jury then found that Kirtsaeng had willfully infringed Wiley's American copyrights by selling and importing without authorization copies of eight of Wiley's copyrighted titles. And it assessed statutory damages of $600,000 ($75,000 per work).

On appeal, a split panel of the Second Circuit agreed with the District Court. It pointed out that §109(a)'s "first sale" doctrine applies only to "the owner of a particular copy . . . *lawfully made under this title*." And, in the majority's view, this language means that the "first sale" doctrine does not apply to copies of American copyrighted works manufactured abroad. . . .

We granted Kirtsaeng's petition for certiorari to consider this question in light of different views among the Circuits. . . .

II

We must decide whether the words "lawfully made under this title" restrict the scope of §109(a)'s "first sale" doctrine geographically. . . .

Under any of [the geographical interpretations advanced by the Second and Ninth Circuits, Wiley, and the Solicitor General], §109(a)'s "first sale" doctrine would not apply to the Wiley Asia books at issue here. And, despite an American copyright owner's permission to *make* copies abroad, one who *buys* a copy of any such book or other copyrighted work—whether at a retail store, over the Internet, or at a library sale—could not resell (or otherwise dispose of) that particular copy without further permission.

Kirtsaeng, however, reads the words "lawfully made under this title" as imposing a *non*-geographical limitation. He says that they mean made "in accordance with" or "in compliance with" the Copyright Act. In that case, §109(a)'s "first sale" doctrine would apply to copyrighted works as long as their manufacture met the requirements of American copyright law. In particular, the doctrine would apply where, as here, copies are manufactured abroad with the permission of the copyright owner. See §106 (referring to the owner's right to authorize).

In our view, §109(a)'s language, its context, and the common-law history of the "first sale" doctrine, taken together, favor a *non*-geographical interpretation. We also doubt that Congress would have intended to create the practical copyright-related harms with which a geographical interpretation would threaten ordinary scholarly, artistic, commercial, and consumer activities. We consequently conclude that Kirtsaeng's nongeographical reading is the better reading of the Act.

A

The language of §109(a) read literally favors Kirtsaeng's nongeographical interpretation . . . The language of §109(a) says nothing about geography. . . . And a nongeographical interpretation provides each word of the five-word phrase with a distinct purpose. The first two words of the phrase, "lawfully made," suggest an effort to distinguish those copies that were made lawfully from those that were not, and the last three words, "under this title," set forth the standard of "lawful[ness]." Thus, the nongeographical reading is simple, it promotes a traditional copyright objective (combatting piracy), and it makes word-by-word linguistic sense. . . .

To read the clause geographically, Wiley . . . must first emphasize the word "under." Indeed, Wiley reads "under this title" to mean "in conformance with the Copyright Act *where the Copyright Act is applicable*." Wiley must then take a second step, arguing that the Act "is applicable" only in the United States. . . .

One difficulty is that neither "under" nor any other word in the phrase means "where." . . . It might mean "subject to," but . . . the word ["under"] evades a uniform, consistent meaning. . . .

A far more serious difficulty arises out of the uncertainty and complexity surrounding the second step's effort to read the necessary geographical limitation into the word "applicable" (or the equivalent). Where, precisely, is the Copyright Act "applicable"? The Act does not instantly *protect* an American copyright holder from unauthorized piracy taking place abroad. But that fact does not mean the Act is *inapplicable* to copies made abroad. As a matter of ordinary English, one can say that a statute imposing, say, a tariff upon "any rhododendron grown in Nepal" applies to *all* Nepalese rhododendrons. And, similarly, one can say that the American Copyright Act is *applicable* to *all* pirated copies, including those printed overseas. Indeed, the Act itself makes clear that (in the Solicitor General's language) foreign-printed pirated copies are "subject to" the Act. §602(a)(2) (2006 ed., Supp. V) (referring to importation of copies "the making of which either constituted an infringement of copyright, or which would have constituted an infringement of copyright if this title had been applicable"). . . .

The appropriateness of this linguistic usage is underscored by the fact that §104 of the Act itself says that works "*subject to protection under this title*" include unpublished works "without regard to the nationality or domicile of the author," and works "first published" in any one of the nearly 180 nations that have signed a copyright treaty with the United States. . . . Thus, ordinary English permits us to say that the Act "applies" to an Irish manuscript lying in its author's Dublin desk drawer as well as to an original recording of a ballet performance first made in Japan and now on display in a Kyoto art gallery. Cf. 4 M. Nimmer & D. Nimmer, Copyright §17.02, pp. 17–18, 17–19 (2012) (hereinafter Nimmer on Copyright) (noting that the principle that "copyright laws do not have any extraterritorial operation" "requires some qualification").

The Ninth Circuit's geographical interpretation produces still greater linguistic difficulty. [T]hat Circuit interprets the "first sale" doctrine to cover both (1) copies manufactured in the United States and (2) copies manufactured abroad but first sold in the United States with the American copyright owner's permission. . . .

We can understand why the Ninth Circuit may have thought it necessary to add the second part of its definition. As we shall later describe, see Part II–D, *infra*, without some such qualification a copyright holder could prevent a buyer from domestically reselling or even giving away copies of a video game made in Japan, a film made in Germany, or a dress (with a design copyright) made in China, *even* if the copyright holder has granted permission for the foreign manufacture, importation, and an initial domestic sale of the copy. A publisher such as Wiley would be free to print its books abroad, allow their importation and sale within the United States, but prohibit students from later selling their used texts at a campus bookstore. We see no way, however, to reconcile this half geographical/half-nongeographical interpretation with the language of the phrase, "lawfully made under this title." As a matter of English, it would seem that those five words either do cover copies lawfully made abroad or they do not.

In sum, we believe that geographical interpretations create more linguistic problems than they resolve. And considerations of simplicity and coherence tip the purely linguistic balance in Kirtsaeng's, nongeographical, favor.

B

Both historical and contemporary statutory context indicate that Congress, when writing the present version of §109(a), did not have geography in mind. In respect to history, we compare §109(a)'s present language with the language of its immediate predecessor. That predecessor said: "[N]othing in this Act shall be deemed to forbid, prevent, or restrict the transfer of any copy of a copyrighted work *the possession of which has been lawfully obtained*." Copyright Act of 1909, §41, 35 Stat. 1084 (emphasis added).

See also Copyright Act of 1947, §27, 61 Stat. 660. The predecessor says nothing about geography (and Wiley does not argue that it does). So we ask whether Congress, in changing its language implicitly *introduced* a geographical limitation that previously was lacking. . . .

A comparison of language indicates that it did not. . . .

Other provisions of the present statute also support a nongeographical interpretation. For one thing, the statute phases out the "manufacturing clause," a clause that appeared in earlier statutes and had limited importation of many copies (of copyrighted works) printed outside the United States. §601, 90 Stat. 2588 ("Prior to July 1, 1982 . . . the importation into or public distribution in the United States of copies of a work consisting preponderantly of nondramatic literary material . . . is prohibited unless the portions consisting of such material have been manufactured in the United States or Canada"). The phasing out of this clause sought to equalize treatment of copies manufactured in America and copies manufactured abroad. See H. R. Rep. No. 94–1476, at 165–166.

The "equal treatment" principle, however, is difficult to square with a geographical interpretation of the "first sale" clause that would grant the holder of an American copyright (perhaps a foreign national . . . permanent control over the American distribution chain (sales, resales, gifts, and other distribution) in respect to copies printed abroad but not in respect to copies printed in America. And it is particularly difficult to believe that Congress would have sought this unequal treatment while saying nothing about it and while, in a related clause (the manufacturing phase-out), seeking the opposite kind of policy goal. . . .

C

A relevant canon of statutory interpretation favors a nongeographical reading. "[W]hen a statute covers an issue previously governed by the common law," we must presume that "Congress intended to retain the substance of the common law." *Samantar v. Yousuf*, 560 U. S. ___, ___, n.13 (2010) (slip op., at 14, n.13). . . .

The "first sale" doctrine is a common-law doctrine with an impeccable historic pedigree. In the early 17th century Lord Coke explained the common law's refusal to permit restraints on the alienation of chattels. . . .

. . . Coke emphasizes the importance of leaving buyers of goods free to compete with each other when reselling or otherwise disposing of those goods. American law too has generally thought that competition, including freedom to resell, can work to the advantage of the consumer. . . .

The "first sale" doctrine also frees courts from the administrative burden of trying to enforce restrictions upon difficult-to-trace, readily movable goods. And it avoids the selective enforcement inherent in any such effort. Thus, it is not surprising that for at least a century the "first sale" doctrine has played an important role in American copyright law. See *Bobbs-Merrill Co. v. Straus*, 210 U.S. 339 (1908); Copyright Act of 1909, §41, 35 Stat. 1084. . . .

The common-law doctrine makes no geographical distinctions; nor can we find any in *Bobbs-Merrill* (where this Court first applied the "first sale" doctrine) or in §109(a)'s predecessor provision, which Congress enacted a year later. . . . And we can find no language, context, purpose, or history that would rebut . . . application of that doctrine here. . . .

D

Associations of libraries, used-book dealers, technology companies, consumer-goods retailers, and museums point to various ways in which a geographical interpretation would fail to further basic constitutional copyright objectives, in particular "promot[ing] the Progress of Science and useful Arts." U. S. Const., Art. I, §8, cl. 8.

The American Library Association tells us that library collections contain at least 200 million books published abroad (presumably, many were first published in one of the nearly 180 copyright-treaty nations and enjoy American copyright protection under 17 U. S. C. §104); that many others were first published in the United States but printed abroad because of lower costs; and that a geographical interpretation will likely require the libraries to obtain permission (or at least create significant uncertainty) before circulating or otherwise distributing these books. . . .

Used-book dealers tell us that, from the time when Benjamin Franklin and Thomas Jefferson built commercial and personal libraries of foreign books, American readers have bought used books published and printed abroad. . . . But under a geographical interpretation a contemporary tourist who buys, say, at Shakespeare and Co. (in Paris), a dozen copies of a foreign book for American friends might find that she had violated the copyright law. The used book dealers cannot easily predict what the foreign copyright holder may think about a reader's effort to sell a used copy of a novel. And they believe that a geographical interpretation will injure a large portion of the used-book business.

Technology companies tell us that "automobiles, microwaves, calculators, mobile phones, tablets, and personal computers" contain copyrightable software programs or packaging. Many of these items are made abroad with the American copyright holder's permission and then sold and imported (with that permission) to the United States. A geographical interpretation would prevent the resale of, say, a car, without the permission of the holder of each copyright on each piece of copyrighted automobile software. . . .

Retailers tell us that over $2.3 trillion worth of foreign goods were imported in 2011. American retailers buy many of these goods after a first sale abroad. And, many of these items bear, carry, or contain copyrighted "packaging, logos, labels, and product inserts and instructions. . . ." The retailers add that American sales of more traditional copyrighted works, "such as books, recorded music, motion pictures, and magazines" likely amount to over $220 billion (electronic game industry is $16 billion). A geographical interpretation would subject many, if not all, of them to the disruptive impact of the threat of infringement suits.

Art museum directors ask us to consider their efforts to display foreign-produced works by, say, Cy Twombly, René Magritte, Henri Matisse, Pablo Picasso, and others. A geographical interpretation, they say, would require the museums to obtain permission from the copyright owners before they could display the work—even if the copyright owner has already sold or donated the work to a foreign museum. . . .

These examples, and others previously mentioned, help explain *why* Lord Coke considered the "first sale" doctrine necessary to protect "Trade and Traffi[c], and bargaining and contracting," and they help explain *why* American copyright law has long applied that doctrine.

Neither Wiley nor any of its many *amici* deny that a geographical interpretation could bring about these "horribles"—at least in principle. Rather, Wiley essentially says that the list is artificially invented. It points out that a federal court first adopted a geographical interpretation more than 30 years ago. *CBS, Inc.* v. *Scorpio Music Distributors, Inc.*, 569 F. Supp. 47, 49 (E.D. Pa. 1983), summarily aff'd, 738 F. 2d 424 (3d Cir. 1984) (table). Yet, it adds, these problems have not occurred. Why not? Because, says Wiley, the problems and threats are purely theoretical; they are unlikely to reflect reality.

We are less sanguine. For one thing, the law has not been settled for long in Wiley's favor. The Second Circuit, in its decision below, is the first Court of Appeals to adopt a purely geographical interpretation. . . . [O]ther courts have hesitated to adopt, and have cast doubt upon, the validity of the geographical interpretation. . . .

For another thing, reliance upon the "first sale" doctrine is deeply embedded in the practices of those, such as booksellers, libraries, museums, and retailers, who have long relied upon its protection. Museums, for example, are not in the habit of asking their foreign counterparts to check with the heirs of copyright owners before sending, *e.g.*, a Picasso on tour. . . . That inertia means a dramatic change is likely necessary before these institutions, instructed by their counsel, would begin to engage in the complex permission-verifying process that a geographical interpretation would demand. And this Court's adoption of the geographical interpretation could provide that dramatic change. . . .

Finally, the fact that harm has proved limited so far may simply reflect the reluctance of copyright holders so far to assert geographically based resale rights. They may decide differently if the law is clarified in their favor. Regardless, a copyright law that can work in practice only if unenforced is not a sound copyright law. It is a law that would create uncertainty, would bring about selective enforcement, and, if widely unenforced, would breed disrespect for copyright law itself.

Thus, we believe that the practical problems that petitioner and his *amici* have described are too serious, too extensive, and too likely to come about for us to dismiss them as insignificant—particularly in light of the ever growing importance of foreign trade to America. . . . The upshot is that copyright-related consequences along with language, context, and interpretive canons argue strongly against a geographical interpretation of §109(a).

III

Wiley and the dissent make several additional important arguments in favor of the geographical interpretation. *First*, they say that our *Quality King* decision strongly supports its geographical interpretation. In that case we asked whether the Act's "importation provision," now §602(a)(1) (then §602(a)), barred importation (without permission) of a copyrighted item (labels affixed to hair care products) where an American copyright owner authorized the first sale and export of hair care products with copyrighted labels made in the United States, and where a buyer sought to import them back into the United States without the copyright owner's permission. 523 U. S., at 138–139.

We held that the importation provision did *not* prohibit sending the products back into the United States (without the copyright owner's permission). That section says:

> Importation into the United States, without the authority of the owner of copyright under this title, of copies or phonorecords of a work that have been acquired outside the United States *is an infringement* of the exclusive right to distribute copies or phonorecords *under section 106.* 17 U. S. C. §602(a)(1) (2006 ed., Supp. V) (emphasis added). See also §602(a) (1994 ed.).

We pointed out that this section makes importation an infringement of the "exclusive right to distribute . . . *under 106*." We noted that §109(a)'s "first sale" doctrine limits the scope of the §106 exclusive distribution right. We took as given the fact that the products at issue had at least once been sold. And we held that consequently, importation of the copyrighted labels does not violate §602(a)(1). 523 U. S., at 145.

In reaching this conclusion we endorsed *Bobbs-Merrill* and its statement that the copyright laws were not "intended to create a right which would permit the holder of the copyright to fasten, by notice in a book . . . a restriction upon the subsequent alienation of the subject-matter of copyright after the owner had parted with the title to one who had acquired full dominion over it." 210 U.S., at 349-350.

We also explained why we rejected the claim that our interpretation would make §602(a)(1) pointless. Those advancing that claim had pointed out that the 1976 Copyright Act amendments retained a prior anti-piracy provision, prohibiting the importation of *pirated* copies. *Quality King, supra*, at 146. Thus, they said, §602(a)(1) must prohibit the importation of lawfully made copies, for to allow the importation of those lawfully made copies *after a first sale*, as *Quality King's* holding would do, would leave §602(a)(1) without much to prohibit. It would become superfluous, without any real work to do.

We do not believe that this argument is a strong one. Under *Quality King's* interpretation, §602(a)(1) would still forbid importing (without permission, and subject to the exceptions in §602(a)(3)) copies lawfully made abroad, for example, where (1) a foreign publisher operating as the licensee of an American publisher prints copies of a book overseas but, prior to any authorized sale, seeks to send them to the United States; (2) a foreign printer or other manufacturer (if not the "owner" for purposes of §109(a), e.g., before an authorized sale) sought to send copyrighted goods to the United States; (3) "a book publisher transports copies to a wholesaler" and the wholesaler (not yet the owner) sends them to the United States, see Copyright Law Revision, pt. 4, at 211 (giving this example); or (4) a foreign film distributor, having leased films for distribution, or any other licensee, consignee, or bailee sought to send them to the United States. . . . These examples show that §602(a)(1) retains significance. . . .

In *Quality King* we rejected the "superfluous" argument for similar reasons. But, when rejecting it, we said that, where an author gives exclusive American distribution rights to an American publisher and exclusive British distribution rights to a British publisher, "presumably *only those* [*copies*] *made by the publisher of the United States edition would be 'lawfully made under this title'* within the meaning of §109(a)." 523 U.S., at 148 (emphasis added). Wiley now argues that this phrase in the *Quality King* opinion means that books published abroad (under license) must fall outside the words "lawfully made under this title" and that we have consequently already given those words the geographical interpretation that it favors.

We cannot, however, give the *Quality King* statement the legal weight for which Wiley argues. The language "lawfully made under this title" was not at issue in *Quality King*; the point before us now was not then fully argued; we did not canvas the considerations we have here set forth; we there said nothing to suggest that the example assumes a "first sale"; and we there hedged our statement with the word "presumably." Most importantly, the statement is pure dictum. It is dictum contained in a rebuttal to a counterargument. And it is *unnecessary* dictum even in that respect. Is the Court having once written dicta calling a tomato a vegetable bound to deny that it is a fruit forever after? . . .

. . . Wiley and the dissent argue (to those who consider legislative history) that the Act's legislative history supports their interpretation. But the historical events to which it points took place more than a decade before the enactment of the Act and, at best, are inconclusive. . . .

[T]o ascertain the best reading of *§109(a)* . . . we would give greater weight to the congressional report accompanying §109(a), written a decade later when Congress passed the new law. That report says:

> Section 109(a) restates and confirms the principle that, where the *copyright* owner has transferred ownership of a particular copy or phonorecord of a work, the person to whom the copy or phonorecord is transferred is entitled to dispose of it by sale, rental, or any other means. Under this principle, which has been established by the court decisions and . . . the present law, the copyright owner's exclusive right of public distribution would have no effect upon anyone who owns "a particular copy or phonorecord lawfully made under this title" and who wishes to transfer it to someone else or to destroy it.
>
> . . . To come within the scope of section 109(a), a copy or phonorecord must have been "lawfully made under this title," though not necessarily with the copyright owner's authorization. For example, any resale of an illegally "pirated" phonorecord would be an infringement but the disposition of a phonorecord legally made under the compulsory licensing provisions of section 115 would not. H. R. Rep. No. 94–1476, at 79 (emphasis added). . . .

This history reiterates the importance of the "first sale" doctrine. . . . It explains, as we have explained, the nongeographical purposes of the words "lawfully made under this title." And it says nothing about geography. . . . We consequently believe that the legislative history, on balance, supports the nongeographical interpretation.

. . . Wiley and the dissent claim that a nongeographical interpretation will make it difficult, perhaps impossible, for publishers (and other copyright holders) to divide foreign and domestic markets. We concede that is so. A publisher may find it more difficult to charge different prices for the same book in different geographic markets. But we do not see how these facts help Wiley, for we can find no basic principle of copyright law that suggests that publishers are especially entitled to such rights. . . .

To the contrary, Congress enacted a copyright law that (through the "first sale" doctrine) limits copyright holders' ability to divide domestic markets. And that limitation is consistent with antitrust laws that ordinarily forbid market divisions. . . . Whether copyright owners should, or should not, have more than ordinary commercial power to divide international markets is a matter for Congress to decide. We do no more here than try to determine what decision Congress has taken.

. . . [T]he dissent and Wiley contend that our decision launches United States copyright law into an unprecedented regime of "international exhaustion." But they point to nothing indicative of congressional intent in 1976. The dissent also claims that it is clear that the United States now opposes adopting such a regime, but the Solicitor General as *amicus* has taken no such position in this case. . . .

Moreover, the exhaustion regime the dissent apparently favors would provide that "the sale in one country of a good" does not "exhaus[t] the intellectual-property owner's right to control the distribution of that good elsewhere." But our holding in *Quality King* that §109(a) is a defense in U.S. courts even when "the first sale occurred abroad," 523 U. S., at 145, n.14, has already significantly eroded such a principle.

NOTES AND QUESTIONS

1. Do you agree with the Court's reading of the relationship among §§602(a)(1), 106(3), and 109? In particular, could you read §602(a)(1) as not subject to §109(a)?

In a concurring opinion, Justice Kagan noted that the Court's prior decision in *Quality King* (discussed at some length by Justice Breyer in the excerpt above) forecloses such a reading:

> [*Quality King*] . . . is the decision holding that §109(a) limits §602(a)(1). Had we come out the opposite way in that case . . . [a] copyright owner [could] divide international markets in the way John Wiley claims Congress intended when enacting §602(a)(1). But it would do so without imposing downstream liability on those who purchase and resell in the United States copies that happen to have been manufactured abroad. In other words, that outcome would target unauthorized importers alone, and not the "libraries, used-book dealers, technology companies, consumer-goods retailers, and museums" with whom today the Court is rightly concerned. Assuming Congress adopted §602(a)(1) to permit market segmentation, I suspect that is how Congress thought the provision would work – not by removing first-sale protection from every copy manufactured abroad (as John Wiley urges us to do here), but by enabling the copyright holder to control imports even when the first-sale doctrine applies (as *Quality King* now prevents).

Kirtsaeng v. John Wiley & Sons, Inc., 133 S. Ct. 1351, 1372-73 (2013).

2. Read §602(b). Note that it authorizes the U.S. Customs and Border Protection service to prevent the importation of copies or phonorecords whose making "would have constituted an infringement of copyright *if this title had been applicable*." (emphasis added). Does this language help to shed light on how to interpret §602(a) (the question at issue in *Quality King*)? If the *Kirtsaeng* Court had reached a different conclusion about the proper interpretation of §109(a), could John Wiley & Sons have successfully asked U.S. Customs and Border Protection to seize the copies Kirtsaeng was importing? Why, or why not?

How else might the Court have interpreted the phrase "lawfully made under this title"? Are there interpretations besides the Court's that you find more convincing? If so, what are they?

3. Section 602(a) of the Copyright Act contains several important exceptions to the import prohibition of §602(a)(1). Read §602(a)(3) now. Can you think of any other exceptions that should be added to the list? If a fan of the *Harry Potter* series purchases copies of the British editions while visiting London and brings them back to the United States with her, has she committed copyright infringement? If after finishing the books, the fan decides to resell her copies on eBay, does §109(a) allow her to do so?

4. In dissent in *Kirtsaeng*, Justice Ginsburg noted that the omission of an exhaustion standard in TRIPS is no accident, but rather reflects the deep differences in opinion about the proper standard. In international trade negotiations, the United States has consistently argued against international exhaustion. *See Kirtsaeng*, 133 S. Ct. at 1383-85. Indeed, both the United States and European Union have worked to introduce provisions in free trade agreements (FTAs) that would allow a copyright owner to control importation in the way John Wiley & Sons sought. These efforts, if successful, would discourage the development of international exhaustion as a principle of customary international law, at least as between the member states of the FTAs. Should the stance taken by the United States in trade negotiations have influenced the Court?

5. As a policy matter, do you think that copyright owners should be able to divide markets, charging different prices in different areas and prohibiting importation of lower priced, "gray market" goods into a higher priced market as John Wiley & Sons attempted to do in *Kirtsaeng*? What types of questions would you ask and what empirical evidence would you like to have before deciding? How should copyright law respond to distribution of copies across national borders via the Internet? For scholarly discussion of issues pertaining to price discrimination and parallel imports, see, e.g., Glynn S. Lunney, Jr., *Copyright's Price Discrimination Panacea*, 21 Harv. J.L. & Tech. 387 (2008); Christine Ongchin, Note, *Price Dissemination in the Textbook Market: An Analysis of the Post-*Quality King *Proposals to Prevent and Disincentivize Reimportation and Arbitrage*, 15 Cardozo J. Int'l L. 223 (2007).

6. Gray market goods that involve trademarks receive a somewhat different treatment. The Tariff Act of 1930 (as amended) provides in relevant part: "[I]t shall be unlawful to import into the United States any merchandise of foreign manufacture if such merchandise . . . bears a trademark owned by a citizen of, or by a corporation or association organized within, the United States." 19 U.S.C. §1526(a). As interpreted in *K Mart Corp. v. Cartier, Inc.*, 486 U.S. 281 (1988), the Tariff Act prohibits unauthorized importation in cases where the U.S. trademark holder has licensed the use of the mark abroad by an independent foreign entity, or vice versa. It permits gray market imports if the goods are manufactured by an entity that shares common ownership or control with the U.S. trademark owner. The federal courts of appeals, however, have interpreted domestic trademark law to

---

LOOKING BACK – AND FORWARD

Recall discussion of the various "pie slices" of protection available to a copyright owner, which you read in Chapter 1. Some copyright industries have used technological protection measures (TPMs) to enforce region-based price discrimination. For example, the movie industry sells region-coded DVDs under a series of cooperative licensing agreements with manufacturers of home DVD players. DVDs manufactured in Europe will not work on DVD players sold in North America, and vice versa – and so on for other regions. Other types of digital content are sold via Internet downloads and accompanied by click-through user agreements. You will have the opportunity to consider these strategies in greater detail in Chapters 12 and 14 *infra*.

prohibit importation of goods that bear an identical trademark to the valid U.S. trademark if the goods are physically different from the U.S. trademark holder's goods, regardless of any affiliation or common ownership between the U.S. and foreign trademark holders. The rationale for this rule is that "[t]rademarks applied to physically different foreign goods are not genuine from the viewpoint of the American consumer." *Lever Bros. v. United States*, 981 F.2d 1330, 1338 (D.C. Cir. 1993). Are these rules more generous to trademark owners than the corresponding copyright rules are to copyright owners? Which rules do you prefer, and why?

PRACTICE EXERCISE: COUNSEL A CLIENT

Gabosky S.A. is a Belgian manufacturer of fine chocolates. Its chocolates are marketed in distinctively designed boxes. Gabosky S.A. markets its chocolates in the United States through its subsidiary, Gabosky USA, which has recorded the distinctive box design with the U.S. Copyright Office and obtained a valid registration copyright certificate. Balogun, a discount importer, lawfully obtained large quantities of Gabosky's fine chocolates abroad, imported them to the United States (still in their original, distinctive boxes), and resold them to Kooch. When Kooch began distributing the boxes of chocolates in the United States, Gabosky USA filed suit against Kooch. Kooch has consulted you for advice on defending the litigation. Advise Kooch.

B. COMMUNICATION TO THE PUBLIC BY PERFORMANCE OR DISPLAY

The Copyright Act grants the exclusive right of public performance to copyright owners of "literary, musical, dramatic and choreographic works, pantomimes, and motion pictures and other audiovisual works," 17 U.S.C. §106(4), and the exclusive right of public display to copyright owners of "literary, musical, dramatic and choreographic works, pantomimes, and pictorial, graphic, or sculptural works, including the individual images of a motion picture or other audiovisual work," *id.* §106(5). (Copyright owners of sound recordings enjoy a separate, narrower public performance right, which we discuss in Chapter 7, *infra*.)

Under the Copyright Act of 1909, public performance rights extended only to those performances engaged in for profit. However, determining what counted as for profit became more difficult as new business practices and new technologies for enjoying copyrighted works developed. Beginning in 1913, the newly formed American Society of Composers, Authors, and Publishers (ASCAP) attempted to convince businesses like restaurants and retail stores that they needed to pay royalties for the right to have musicians play copyrighted music as background entertainment in their establishments, but the businesses resisted and courts were divided on the question. In 1917, the Supreme Court decided a case brought by ASCAP and issued a unanimous opinion rejecting the argument that a performance is for profit only when tickets are sold at the door:

> If the rights under the copyright are infringed only by a performance where money is taken at the door they are very imperfectly protected. . . . The defendants' performances are not eleemosynary. They are part of a total for which the public pays, and the fact that the price of the whole is attributed to a particular item which those present are expected to order, is not important. It is true that the music is not the sole object, but neither is the food, which probably could be got cheaper elsewhere. The object is a repast in surroundings that to people having limited powers of conversation or disliking the rival noise give a luxurious pleasure not to be had from eating a silent meal. If music did not pay it would be given up. If it pays it pays out of the public's pocket. Whether it pays or not the purpose of employing it is profit, and that is enough.

Herbert v. Shanley, 242 U.S. 591, 594-95 (1917) (Holmes, J.).

Determining what counted as a performance also became less straightforward as technologies for enjoying copyrighted works developed. Courts struggled to decide whether playing music over the radio in a business open to the public constituted a public performance. Clearly, the radio station was engaged in a public performance for profit, but the conduct of the business was hard to characterize. The reasoning of *Herbert v. Shanley* seemed to apply, but if both the radio station and the business were engaged in a public performance for which the copyright owner was entitled to compensation, then arguably the copyright owner would be able to claim double compensation for a single performance. In 1975, the Supreme Court decided *Twentieth Century Music Corp. v. Aiken*, 422 U.S. 151 (1975), a case involving the owner of a small fast-food shop who played the radio over four speakers in the ceiling. The Court held that when Mr. Aiken turned on the radio, he was the audience, not the performer, for the performance engaged in by the radio station.

In another line of cases, courts considered whether so-called community antenna television (CATV) systems that had been formed to retransmit network television programming to remote and underserved areas were engaged in public performances for profit. Finally, in *Fortnightly Corp. v. United Artists Television, Inc.*, 392 U.S. 390 (1968), the Supreme Court ruled that a CATV provider that "neither edited the programs received nor originated any programs of its own," but instead amplified existing broadcast signals for the benefit of its subscribers, also was more like a viewer than a performer. The Court reaffirmed that conclusion in *Teleprompter Corp. v. Columbia Broadcasting System, Inc.*, 415 U.S. 394 (1974), ruling that a CATV provider that retransmitted broadcast programming over distances spanning hundreds of miles did not become a performer simply because it made an initial choice about which broadcast stations to retransmit.

The 1976 Act resolved these long-running disputes by removing the for-profit limitation and by defining "performance" broadly in a way that unambiguously covered not only a business like Mr. Aiken's that turns on a radio but also performances accomplished with use of new technologies:

> To "perform" a work means to recite, render, play, dance, or act it, either directly or by means of any device or process or, in the case of a motion picture or other audiovisual work, to show its images in any sequence or to make the sounds accompanying it audible.

17 U.S.C. §101. The 1976 Act defined "display" with equal breadth:

> To "display" a work means to show a copy of it, either directly or by means of a film, slide, television image, or any other device or process or, in the case of a motion picture or other audiovisual work, to show individual images nonsequentially.

Id.

While the definitions of "performance" and "display" cover a wide range of actions, only *public* performances and displays are subject to the control of the copyright owner. According to §101:

> To perform or display a work "publicly" means—
> (1) to perform or display it at a place open to the public or at any place where a substantial number of persons outside of a normal circle of a family and its social acquaintances is gathered; or
> (2) to transmit or otherwise communicate a performance or display of the work to a place specified by clause (1) or to the public, by means of any device or process, whether the members of the public capable of receiving the performance or display receive it in the same place or in separate places and at the same time or at different times.

Many applications of these definitions are straightforward. A radio or television station that broadcasts a copyrighted work is engaged in a public performance, but the person who turns on the radio or television in the privacy of her home is not. Other situations are more complicated, as the materials below illustrate.

1. Scope of the Exclusive Rights

The definitions of "performance," "display," and "publicly" in the 1976 Act were intended to cure perceived problems of underbreadth resulting from the application of the 1909 Act to new broadcast technologies. The new definitions, however, also have been tested by technological developments.

a. Once Publicly, Always Publicly?

Cartoon Network LP v. CSC Holdings, Inc.
536 F.3d 121 (2d Cir. 2008), cert. denied, 557 U.S. 946 (2009)

JOHN M. WALKER, JR., J.: . . .

In March 2006, Cablevision, an operator of cable television systems, announced the advent of its new "Remote Storage DVR System." As designed, the RS–DVR allows Cablevision customers who do not have a stand-alone DVR to record cable

---

LOOKING FORWARD

Under these definitions, turning on a radio or television or streaming an audio or video file constitutes a performance or display of any copyrighted work being broadcast or webcast, and doing so in a business like Mr. Aiken's constitutes a public performance. Congress also created exceptions allowing certain categories of nonprofit performances and displays. We will consider those exceptions, contained in §110 of the Act, in Section C.2 of this chapter.

programming on central hard drives housed and maintained by Cablevision at a "remote" location. RS–DVR customers may then receive playback of those programs through their home television sets, using only a remote control and a standard cable box equipped with the RS–DVR software. Cablevision notified its content providers, including plaintiffs, of its plans to offer RS–DVR, but it did not seek any license from them to operate or sell the RS–DVR.

Plaintiffs, which hold the copyrights to numerous movies and television programs, sued Cablevision for declaratory and injunctive relief. They alleged that Cablevision's proposed operation of the RS–DVR would directly infringe their exclusive rights to both reproduce and publicly perform their copyrighted works. Critically for our analysis here, plaintiffs alleged theories only of direct infringement, not contributory infringement, and defendants waived any defense based on fair use. . . .

I. Operation of the RS–DVR System . . .

[Review the facts of this case, Chapter 2, page 57, *supra.*]

As the district court observed, "the RS–DVR is not a single piece of equipment," but rather "a complex system requiring numerous computers, processes, networks of cables, and facilities staffed by personnel twenty-four hours a day and seven days a week." To the customer, however, the processes of recording and playback on the RS–DVR are similar to that of a standard set-top DVR. Using a remote control, the customer can record programming by selecting a program in advance from an on-screen guide, or by pressing the record button while viewing a given program. A customer cannot, however, record the earlier portion of a program once it has begun. To begin playback, the customer selects the show from an on-screen list of previously recorded programs. The principal difference in operation is that, instead of sending signals from the remote to an on-set box, the viewer sends signals from the remote, through the cable, to the Arroyo Server at Cablevision's central facility. In this respect, RS–DVR more closely resembles a [Video-on-demand (VOD)] service, whereby a cable subscriber uses his remote and cable box to request transmission of content, such as a movie, stored on computers at the cable company's facility. But unlike a VOD service, RS–DVR users can only play content that they previously requested to be recorded.

Cablevision has some control over the content available for recording: a customer can only record programs on the channels offered by Cablevision (assuming he subscribes to them). Cablevision can also modify the system to limit the number of channels available and considered doing so during development of the RS–DVR.

II. The District Court's Decision

In the district court, plaintiffs successfully argued that Cablevision's proposed system would directly infringe their copyrights . . . by transmitting the data from the Arroyo Server hard disks to its RS–DVR customers in response to a "playback" request, Cablevision would directly infringe plaintiffs' exclusive right of public performance. . . . [T]he district court awarded summary declaratory judgment to plaintiffs and enjoined Cablevision from operating the RS–DVR system without obtaining licenses from the plaintiff copyright holders. . . .

Discussion

We review a district court's grant of summary judgment de novo. . . .

III. Transmission of RS–DVR Playback

Plaintiffs' final theory is that Cablevision will violate the Copyright Act by engaging in unauthorized public performances of their works through the playback of the RS–DVR copies. The Act grants a copyright owner the exclusive right, "in the case of . . . motion pictures and other audiovisual works, to perform the copyrighted work publicly." 17 U.S.C. §106(4). . . .

The parties agree that this case does not implicate clause (1) [of §101's definition of what "to perform or display a work 'publicly' means"]. . . . Accordingly, we ask whether these facts satisfy the second, "transmit clause" of the public performance definition: Does Cablevision "transmit . . . a performance . . . of the work . . . to the public"? No one disputes that the RS–DVR playback results in the transmission of a performance of a work—the transmission from the Arroyo Server to the customer's television set. Cablevision contends that . . . the transmission is not "to the public" under the transmit clause. . . .

The statute itself does not expressly define the term "performance" or the phrase "to the public." It does explain that a transmission may be "to the public . . . whether the members of the public capable of receiving the performance . . . receive it in the same place or in separate places and at the same time or at different times." *Id*. This plain language instructs us that, in determining whether a transmission is "to the public," it is of no moment that the potential recipients of the transmission are in different places, or that they may receive the transmission at different times. The implication from this same language, however, is that it is relevant, in determining whether a transmission is made to the public, to discern who is "capable of receiving" the performance being transmitted. The fact that the statute says "capable of receiving the performance," instead of "capable of receiving the transmission," underscores the fact that a transmission of a performance is itself a performance.

The legislative history of the transmit clause supports this interpretation. The House Report on the 1976 Copyright Act states that

> [u]nder the bill, as under the present law, a performance made available *by transmission to the public at large* is "public" even though the recipients are not gathered in a single place, and even if there is no proof that any of the *potential recipients* was operating his receiving apparatus at the time of the transmission. The same principles apply whenever the *potential recipients of the transmission* represent a limited segment of the public, such as the occupants of hotel rooms or the subscribers of a cable television service.

H.R. Rep. No. 94–1476, at 64–65 (1976), *reprinted in* 1976 U.S.C.C.A.N. 5659, 5678 (emphases added).

Plaintiffs also reference a 1967 House Report, issued nearly a decade before the Act we are interpreting, stating that the same principles apply where the transmission is "*capable of reaching* different recipients at different times, as in the case of sounds or images stored in an information system and *capable of being performed or displayed* at the initiative of individual members of the public." H. R. Rep. No. 90–83, at 29 (1967) (emphases added). We question how much deference this report deserves. But we need not belabor the point here, as the 1967 report is consistent with both legislative history contemporaneous with the Act's passage and our own interpretation of the statute's plain meaning.

From the foregoing, it is evident that the transmit clause directs us to examine who precisely is "capable of receiving" a particular transmission of a performance. Cablevision argues that, because each RS–DVR transmission is made using a single unique copy of a work, made by an individual subscriber, one that can be decoded exclusively by that subscriber's cable box, only one subscriber is capable of receiving any given RS–DVR transmission. This argument accords with the language of the transmit clause, which, as described above, directs us to consider the potential audience of a given transmission. . . .

The district court, in deciding whether the RS–DVR playback of a program to a particular customer is "to the public," apparently considered all of Cablevision's customers who subscribe to the channel airing that program and all of Cablevision's RS–DVR subscribers who request a copy of that program. Thus, it concluded that the RS–DVR playbacks constituted public performances because "Cablevision would transmit the *same program* to members of the public, who may receive the performance at different times, depending on whether they view the program in real time or at a later time as an RS–DVR playback." In essence, the district court suggested that, in considering whether a transmission is "to the public," we consider not the potential audience of a particular transmission, but the potential audience of the underlying work (i.e., "the program") whose content is being transmitted.

We cannot reconcile the district court's approach with the language of the transmit clause. That clause speaks of people capable of receiving a particular "transmission" or "performance," and not of the potential audience of a particular "work." Indeed, such an approach would render the "to the public" language surplusage. Doubtless the *potential* audience for every copyrighted audiovisual work is the general public. As a result, any transmission of the content of a copyrighted work would constitute a public performance under the district court's interpretation. But the transmit clause obviously contemplates the existence of non-public transmissions; if it did not, Congress would have stopped drafting that clause after "performance."

On appeal, plaintiffs offer a slight variation of this interpretation. They argue that both in its real-time cablecast and via the RS–DVR playback, Cablevision is in fact transmitting the "same performance" of a given work: the performance of the work that occurs when the programming service supplying Cablevision's content transmits that content to Cablevision and the service's other licensees.

Thus, according to plaintiffs, when Congress says that to perform a work publicly means to transmit . . . a performance . . . to the public, they really meant "transmit . . . the 'original performance' . . . to the public." The implication of this theory is that to determine whether a given transmission of a performance is "to the public," we would consider not only the potential audience of that transmission, but also the potential audience of any transmission of the same under-lying "original" performance.

Like the district court's interpretation, this view obviates any possibility of a purely private transmission. Furthermore, it makes Cablevision's liability depend, in part, on the actions of legal strangers. Assume that HBO transmits a copyrighted work to both Cablevision and Comcast. Cablevision merely retransmits the work from one Cablevision facility to another, while Comcast retransmits the program to its subscribers. Under plaintiffs' interpretation, Cablevision would still be transmit-ting the performance to the public, solely because Comcast has transmitted the same underlying performance to the public. Similarly, a hapless customer who records a program in his den and later transmits the recording to a television in his bedroom would be liable for publicly performing the work simply because some other party had once transmitted the same underlying performance to the public.

We do not believe Congress intended such odd results. Although the transmit clause is not a model of clarity, we believe that when Congress speaks of transmitting a performance to the public, it refers to the performance created by the act of transmission. Thus, HBO transmits its own performance of a work when it transmits to Cablevision, and Cablevision transmits its own performance of the same work when it retransmits the feed from HBO.

Furthermore, we believe it would be inconsistent with our own transmit clause jurisprudence to consider the potential audience of an upstream transmission by a third party when determining whether a defendant's own subsequent transmission of a performance is "to the public." In *National Football League v. PrimeTime 24 Joint Venture* (NFL), 211 F.3d 10 (2000), we examined the transmit clause in the context of satellite television provider PrimeTime, which captured protected content in the United States from the NFL, transmitted it from the United States to a satellite ("the uplink"), and then transmitted it from the satellite to subscribers in both the United States and Canada ("the downlink"). PrimeTime . . . argued that the uplink transmission was not a public performance because it was a trans-mission to a single satellite.

The *NFL* court . . . flatly rejected th[is argument] . . . on a specific and germane ground:

> We believe the most logical interpretation of the Copyright Act is to hold that a public performance or display includes each step in the process by which a protected work wends its way to its audience. Under that analysis, it is clear that PrimeTime's uplink transmission of signals captured in the United States is a step in the process by which NFL's protected work wends its way *to a public audience.*

Id. at 13 (emphasis added) (internal quotation and citation omitted). . . . Notably, the *NFL* court did not base its decision on the fact that an upstream transmission by another party (the NFL) might have been to the public. Nor did the court base its decision on the fact that Primetime simultaneously transmitted a [licensed] perfor-mance of the work to the public in the United States. Because *NFL* directs us to look downstream, rather than upstream or laterally, to determine whether any link in a chain of transmissions made by a party constitutes a public performance, we reject plaintiffs' contention that we examine the potential recipients of the content provider's initial transmission to determine who is capable of receiving the RS–DVR playback transmission. . . .

In sum, none of the arguments advanced by plaintiffs or the district court alters our conclusion that, under the transmit clause, we must examine the potential audience of a given transmission by an alleged infringer to determine whether that transmission is "to the public." And because the RS–DVR system, as designed, only makes transmissions to one subscriber using a copy made by that subscriber, we believe that the universe of people capable of receiving an RS–DVR transmission is the single subscriber whose self-made copy is used to create that transmission.

Plaintiffs contend that it is "wholly irrelevant, in determining the existence of a public performance, whether 'unique' *copies* of the same work are used to make the transmissions." Fox Br. at 27. But plaintiffs cite no authority for this contention. And our analysis of the transmit clause suggests that, in general, any factor that limits the *potential* audience of a transmission is relevant.

Furthermore, no transmission of an audiovisual work can be made, we assume, without using a copy of that work: to transmit a performance of a movie, for example, the transmitter generally must obtain a copy of that movie. As a result, in the context of movies, television programs, and other audiovisual works, the right of reproduction can reinforce and protect the right of public performance. If the owner of a copyright believes he is injured by a particular transmission of a performance of his work, he may be able to seek redress not only for the infringing transmission, but also for the underlying copying that facilitated the transmission. Given this interplay between the various rights in this context, it seems quite consistent with the Act to treat a transmission made using Copy A as distinct from one made using Copy B, just as we would treat a transmission made by Cablevision as distinct from an otherwise identical transmission made by Comcast. Both factors—the identity of the transmitter and the source material of the transmission—limit the potential audience of a transmission in this case and are therefore germane in determining whether that transmission is made "to the public." . . .

In sum, we find that the transmit clause directs us to identify the potential audience of a given transmission, i.e., the persons "capable of receiving" it, to determine whether that transmission is made "to the public." Because each RS–DVR playback transmission is made to a single subscriber using a single unique copy produced by that subscriber, we conclude that such transmissions are not performances "to the public," and therefore do not infringe any exclusive right of public performance. We base this decision on the application of undisputed facts; thus, Cablevision is entitled to summary judgment on this point.

This holding, we must emphasize, does not generally permit content delivery networks to avoid all copyright liability by making copies of each item of content and associating one unique copy with each subscriber to the network, or by giving their subscribers the capacity to make their own individual copies. We do not address whether such a network operator would be able to escape any other form of copyright liability, such as liability for unauthorized reproductions or liability for contributory infringement. . . .

American Broadcasting Companies, Inc. v. Aereo, Inc.
134 S. Ct. 2498 (2014)

BREYER, J. :

I

A

For a monthly fee, Aereo offers subscribers broadcast television programming over the Internet, virtually as the programming is being broadcast. Much of this programming is made up of copyrighted works. Aereo neither owns the copyright in those works nor holds a license from the copyright owners to perform those works publicly.

Aereo's system is made up of servers, transcoders, and thousands of dime-sized antennas housed in a central warehouse. It works roughly as follows: First, when a subscriber wants to watch a show that is currently being broadcast, he visits Aereo's website and selects, from a list of the local programming, the show he wishes to see.

Second, one of Aereo's servers selects an antenna, which it dedicates to the use of that subscriber (and that subscriber alone) for the duration of the selected show. A server then tunes the antenna to the over-the-air broadcast carrying the show. The antenna begins to receive the broadcast, and an Aereo transcoder translates the signals received into data that can be transmitted over the Internet.

Third, rather than directly send the data to the subscriber, a server saves the data in a subscriber-specific folder on Aereo's hard drive. In other words, Aereo's system creates a subscriber-specific copy—that is, a "personal" copy—of the subscriber's program of choice.

Fourth, once several seconds of programming have been saved, Aereo's server begins to stream the saved copy of the show to the subscriber over the Internet. (The subscriber may instead direct Aereo to stream the program at a later time, but that aspect of Aereo's service is not before us.) The subscriber can watch the streamed program on the screen of his personal computer, tablet, smart phone, Internet-connected television, or other Internet-connected device. The streaming continues, a mere few seconds behind the over-the-air broadcast, until the subscriber has received the entire show.

Aereo emphasizes that the data that its system streams to each subscriber are the data from his own personal copy, made from the broadcast signals received by the particular antenna allotted to him. Its system does not transmit data saved in one subscriber's folder to any other subscriber. When two subscribers wish to watch the same program, Aereo's system activates two separate antennas and saves two separate copies of the program in two separate folders. It then streams the show to the subscribers through two separate transmissions—each from the subscriber's personal copy.

B

Petitioners are television producers, marketers, distributors, and broadcasters who own the copyrights in many of the programs that Aereo's system streams to its subscribers. They brought suit against Aereo for copyright infringement in Federal District Court. They sought a preliminary injunction, arguing that Aereo was infringing their right to "perform" their works "publicly," as the Transmit Clause defines those terms.

The District Court denied the preliminary injunction. Relying on prior Circuit precedent, a divided panel of the Second Circuit affirmed. . . .

II

This case requires us to answer two questions: First, in operating in the manner described above, does Aereo "perform" at all? And second, if so, does Aereo do so "publicly"? We address these distinct questions in turn.

. . . In Aereo's view, it does not perform. It does no more than supply equipment that "emulate[s] the operation of a home antenna and [digital video recorder (DVR)]." Brief for Respondent 41. Like a home antenna and DVR, Aereo's equipment simply responds to its subscribers' directives. So it is only the subscribers who "perform" when they use Aereo's equipment to stream television programs to themselves.

Considered alone, the language of the Act does not clearly indicate when an entity "perform[s]" (or "transmit[s]") and when it merely supplies equipment that allows others to do so. But when read in light of its purpose, the Act is unmistakable: An entity that engages in activities like Aereo's performs.

A

History makes plain that one of Congress' primary purposes in amending the Copyright Act in 1976 was to overturn this Court's determination that community antenna television (CATV) systems (the precursors of modern cable systems) fell outside the Act's scope. In *Fortnightly Corp. v. United Artists Television, Inc.*, 392 U.S. 390 (1968), the Court considered a CATV system that carried local television broadcasting, much of which was copyrighted, to its subscribers in two cities. The CATV provider placed antennas on hills above the cities and used coaxial cables to carry the signals received by the antennas to the home television sets of its subscribers. . . .

Asked to decide whether the CATV provider infringed copyright holders' exclusive right to perform their works publicly, the Court held that the provider did not "perform" at all. . . . The Court drew a line: "Broadcasters perform. Viewers do not perform." [*Fortnightly*,] 392 U.S., at 398 (footnote omitted). And a CATV provider "falls on the viewer's side of the line." *Id.*, at 399. . . .

In *Teleprompter Corp. v. Columbia Broadcasting System, Inc.*, 415 U.S. 394 (1974), the Court considered the copyright liability of a CATV provider that carried broadcast television programming into subscribers' homes from hundreds of miles away. Although the Court recognized that a viewer might not be able to afford amplifying equipment that would provide access to those distant signals, it nonetheless found that the CATV provider was more like a viewer than a broadcaster. *Id.*, at 408–409, 94 S. Ct. 1129. It explained: "The reception and rechanneling of [broadcast television signals] for simultaneous viewing is essentially a viewer function, irrespective of the distance between the broadcasting station and the ultimate viewer." *Id.*, at 408. . . .

B

In 1976, Congress amended the Copyright Act in large part to reject the Court's holdings in *Fortnightly* and *Teleprompter.* See H. R. Rep. No. 94–1476, pp. 86–87 (1976) (hereinafter H. R. Rep.) Congress enacted new language that erased the Court's line between broadcaster and viewer, in respect to "perform[ing]" a work. The amended statute clarifies that to "perform" an audiovisual work means "to show its images in any sequence or to make the sounds accompanying it audible." §101. Under this new language, *both* the broadcaster *and* the viewer of a television program "perform," because they both show the program's images and make audible the program's sounds.

Congress also enacted the Transmit Clause, which specifies that an entity performs publicly when it "transmit[s] . . . a performance . . . to the public." §101; see *ibid.* (defining "[t]o 'transmit' a performance" as "to communicate it by any device or process whereby images or sounds are received beyond the place from which they are sent"). Cable system activities, like those of the CATV systems in *Fortnightly* and *Teleprompter,* lie at the heart of the activities that Congress intended this language to cover. See H.R. Rep., at 63 (["A] cable television system is performing when it retransmits [a network] broadcast to its subscribers"). The Clause thus makes clear that an entity that acts like a CATV system itself performs, even if when doing so, it simply enhances viewers' ability to receive broadcast television signals. . . .

Congress further created a new section of the Act to regulate cable companies' public performances of copyrighted works. *See* §111. Section 111 creates a complex, highly detailed compulsory licensing scheme that sets out the conditions, including the payment of compulsory fees, under which cable systems may retransmit broadcasts. . . .

Congress made these three changes to achieve a similar end: to bring the activities of cable systems within the scope of the Copyright Act.

C

This history makes clear that Aereo is not simply an equipment provider. Rather, Aereo, and not just its subscribers, "perform[s]" (or "transmit[s]"). Aereo's activities are substantially similar to those of the CATV companies that Congress amended the Act to reach. . . . By means of its technology (antennas, transcoders, and servers), Aereo's system "receive[s] programs that have been released to the public and carr[ies] them by private channels to additional viewers." *Fortnightly,* 392 U.S., at 400. It "carr[ies] . . . whatever programs [it] receive[s]," and it offers "all the programming" of each over-the-air station it carries. *Id.,* at 392, 400.

Aereo's equipment may serve a "viewer function"; it may enhance the viewer's ability to receive a broadcaster's programs. It may even emulate equipment a viewer could use at home. But the same was true of the equipment that was before the Court, and ultimately before Congress, in *Fortnightly* and *Teleprompter*.

We recognize . . . one particular difference between Aereo's system and the cable systems at issue in *Fortnightly* and *Teleprompter*. The systems in those cases transmitted constantly; they sent continuous programming to each subscriber's television set. In contrast, Aereo's system remains inert until a subscriber indicates that she wants to watch a program. Only at that moment, in automatic response to the subscriber's request, does Aereo's system activate an antenna and begin to transmit the requested program. . . .

Given Aereo's overwhelming likeness to the cable companies targeted by the 1976 amendments, this sole technological difference between Aereo and traditional cable companies does not make a critical difference here. . . . Of course, in *Fortnightly* the television signals, in a sense, lurked behind the screen, ready to emerge when the subscriber turned the knob. Here the signals pursue their ordinary course of travel through the universe until today's "turn of the knob"—a click on a website—activates machinery that intercepts and reroutes them to Aereo's subscribers over the Internet. But this difference means nothing to the subscriber. It means nothing to the broadcaster. . . .

In other cases involving different kinds of service or technology providers, a user's involvement in the operation of the provider's equipment and selection of the content transmitted may well bear on whether the provider performs within the meaning of the Act. But the many similarities between Aereo and cable companies, considered in light of Congress' basic purposes in amending the Copyright Act, convince us that this difference is not critical here. We conclude that Aereo is not just an equipment supplier and that Aereo "perform[s]."

III

Next, we must consider whether Aereo performs petitioners' works "publicly," within the meaning of the Transmit Clause. Under the Clause, an entity performs a work publicly when it "transmit[s] . . . a performance . . . of the work . . . to the public." §101. . . .

Petitioners say Aereo transmits a *prior* performance of their works. Thus when Aereo retransmits a network's prior broadcast, the underlying broadcast (itself a performance) is the performance that Aereo transmits. Aereo . . . says the performance it transmits is the *new* performance created by its act of transmitting. That performance comes into existence when Aereo streams the sounds and images of a broadcast program to a subscriber's screen.

We assume *arguendo* that Aereo's first argument is correct. Thus, for present purposes, to transmit a performance of (at least) an audiovisual work means to communicate contemporaneously visible images and contemporaneously audible sounds of the work. . . . When an Aereo subscriber selects a program to watch, Aereo streams the program over the Internet to that subscriber. Aereo thereby "communicate[s]" to the subscriber, by means of a "device or process," the work's images and sounds. §101. And those images and sounds are contemporaneously visible and audible on the subscriber's computer (or other Internet-connected device). So under our assumed definition, Aereo transmits a performance whenever its subscribers watch a program.

But what about the Clause's further requirement that Aereo transmit a performance "to the public"? As we have said, an Aereo subscriber receives broadcast television signals with an antenna dedicated to him alone. Aereo's system makes from those signals a personal copy of the selected program. It streams the content of the copy to the same subscriber and to no one else. One and only one subscriber has the ability to see and hear each Aereo transmission. The fact that each transmission is to only one subscriber, in Aereo's view, means that it does not transmit a performance "to the public."

In terms of the Act's purposes, these differences do not distinguish Aereo's system from cable systems, which do perform "publicly." Viewed in terms of Congress' regulatory objectives, why should any of these technological differences matter? They concern the behind-the-scenes way in which Aereo delivers television programming to its viewers' screens. They do not render Aereo's commercial objective any different from that of cable companies. Nor do they significantly alter the viewing experience of Aereo's subscribers. . . . [W]hy, if Aereo is right, could not modern CATV systems simply continue the same commercial and consumer-oriented activities, free of copyright restrictions, provided they substitute such new technologies for old? . . .

The text of the Clause effectuates Congress' intent. . . . [T]he Clause suggests that an entity may transmit a performance through multiple, discrete transmissions. That is because one can "transmit" or "communicate" something through a *set* of actions. Thus one can transmit a message to one's friends, irrespective of whether one sends separate identical e-mails to each friend or a single e-mail to all at once. So can an elected official communicate an idea, slogan, or speech to her constituents, regardless of whether she communicates that idea, slogan, or speech during individual phone calls to each constituent or in a public square.

The fact that a singular noun ("a performance") follows the words "to transmit" does not suggest the contrary. One can sing a song to his family, whether he sings the same song one-on-one or in front of all together. . . . By the same principle, an entity may transmit a performance through one or several transmissions, where the performance is of the same work.

The Transmit Clause must permit this interpretation, for it provides that one may transmit a performance to the public "whether the members of the public capable of receiving the performance . . . receive it . . . at the same time or at different times." §101. Were the words "to transmit . . . a performance" limited to a single act of communication, members of the public could not receive the performance communicated "at different times." Therefore, in light of the purpose and text of the Clause, we conclude that when an entity communicates the same contemporaneously perceptible images and sounds to multiple people, it transmits a performance to them regardless of the number of discrete communications it makes.

COMPARATIVE PERSPECTIVE

Copyright regimes in many other countries define the scope of exclusive rights covering performance and display differently than the United States. Article 11 of the Berne Convention directs that authors of dramatic, dramatico-musical, and musical works shall enjoy the exclusive rights of "public performance of their works . . . by any means or process" and "communication to the public of their works." Authors of literary and visual works shall enjoy exclusive rights to authorize the communication of their works to the public by broadcasting or rebroadcasting, by wire or wireless means, and by "loudspeaker or any other analogous instrument." *Id.* art. 11*bis*. In addition, authors of literary works are to be granted exclusive rights of "public recitation of their works . . . by any means or process" and "communication to the public of the recitation of their works." *Id.* art. 11*ter*.

Pursuant to these provisions and to Article 8 of the WIPO Copyright Treaty, Article 3 of the European Copyright Directive instructs:

1. Member States shall provide authors with the exclusive right to authorise or prohibit any communication to the public of their works, by wire or wireless means, including the making available to the public of their works in such a way that members of the public may access them from a place and at a time individually chosen by them. . . .

3. The rights referred to in paragraphs 1 and 2 shall not be exhausted by any act of communication to the public or making available to the public as set out in this Article.

Directive 2001/29/, of the European Parliament and of the Council of 22 May 2001 on the harmonisation of certain aspects of copyright and related rights in the information society, 2001 O.J. (L 167/16).

We do not see how the fact that Aereo transmits via personal copies of programs could make a difference. The Act applies to transmissions "by means of any device or process." *Ibid.* And retransmitting a television program using user-specific copies is a "process" of transmitting a performance. . . .

Moreover, the subscribers to whom Aereo transmits television programs constitute "the public." . . .

Neither the record nor Aereo suggests that Aereo's subscribers receive performances in their capacities as owners or possessors of the underlying works. This is relevant because when an entity performs to a set of people, whether they constitute "the public" often depends upon their relationship to the underlying work. When, for example, a valet parking attendant returns cars to their drivers, we would not say that the parking service provides cars "to the public." We would say that it provides the cars to their owners. We would say that a car dealership, on the other hand, does provide cars to the public, for it sells cars to individuals who lack a pre-existing relationship to the cars. Similarly, an entity that transmits a performance to individuals in their capacities as owners or possessors does not perform to "the public," whereas an entity like Aereo that transmits to large numbers of paying subscribers who lack any prior relationship to the works does so perform. . . .

IV

Aereo and many of its supporting *amici* argue that to apply the Transmit Clause to Aereo's conduct will impose copyright liability on other technologies, including new technologies, that Congress could not possibly have wanted to reach. We agree that Congress, while intending the Transmit Clause to apply broadly to cable companies and their equivalents, did not intend to discourage or to control the emergence or use of different kinds of technologies. But we do not believe that our limited holding today will have that effect.

For one thing, the history of cable broadcast transmissions that led to the enactment of the Transmit Clause informs our conclusion that Aereo "perform[s]," but it does not determine whether different kinds of providers in different contexts also "perform." . . .

Further, we have interpreted the term "the public" to apply to a group of individuals acting as ordinary members of the public who pay primarily to watch broadcast television programs, many of which are copyrighted. We have said that it does not extend to those who act as owners or possessors of the relevant product. And we have not considered whether the public performance right is infringed when the user of a service pays primarily for something other than the transmission of copyrighted works, such as the remote storage of content. . . .

We also note that courts often apply a statute's highly general language in light of the statute's basic purposes. Finally, the doctrine of "fair use" can help to prevent inappropriate or inequitable applications of the Clause.

We cannot now answer more precisely how the Transmit Clause or other provisions of the Copyright Act will apply to technologies not before us. . . . And we note that, to the extent commercial actors or other interested entities may be concerned with the relationship between the development and use of such technologies and the Copyright Act, they are of course free to seek action from Congress. . . .

SCALIA, J., with whom THOMAS, J., and ALITO, J., join dissenting:

I. Legal Standard

There are two types of liability for copyright infringement: direct and secondary. As its name suggests, the former applies when an actor personally engages in infringing conduct. Secondary liability, by contrast, is a means of holding defendants responsible for infringement by third parties . . . .

The Networks' claim is governed by a simple but profoundly important rule: A defendant may be held directly liable only if it has engaged in volitional conduct that violates the Act. This requirement is firmly grounded in the Act's text, which defines "perform" in active, affirmative terms . . . . [T]he volitional-act requirement demands conduct directed to the plaintiff's copyrighted material. Every Court of Appeals to have considered an automated-service provider's direct liability for copyright infringement has adopted that rule. See *Fox Broadcasting Co.* v. *Dish Network LLC*, 747 F. 3d 1060, 1066–1068 (CA9 2014); *Cartoon Network, supra,* at 130–131 (CA2 2008); *CoStar Group, Inc.* v. *LoopNet, Inc.*, 373 F. 3d 544, 549–550 (CA4 2004). Although we have not opined on the issue, our cases are fully consistent with a volitional-conduct requirement. . . .

The distinction between direct and secondary liability would collapse if there were not a clear rule for determining whether *the defendant* committed the infringing act. The volitional-conduct requirement supplies that rule; its purpose is not to

> **LOOKING FORWARD**
>
> We will revisit *Aereo, Cartoon Network,* and the question of volitional conduct in Chapter 9, which considers the question of direct and secondary liability in more detail.

excuse defendants from accountability, but to channel the claims against them into the correct analytical track. See Brief for 36 Intellectual Property and Copyright Law Professors as *Amici Curiae* 7. . . .

II. Application to Aereo

. . . Unlike video-on-demand services, Aereo does not provide a prearranged assortment of movies and television shows. Rather, it assigns each subscriber an antenna that—like a library card—can be used to obtain whatever broadcasts are freely available. Some of those broadcasts are copyrighted; others are in the public domain. The key point is that subscribers call all the shots . . .

In sum, Aereo does not "perform" for the sole and simple reason that it does not make the choice of content. And because Aereo does not perform, it cannot be held directly liable for infringing the Networks' public-performance right. That conclusion does not necessarily mean that Aereo's service complies with the Copyright Act. Quite the contrary. The Networks' complaint alleges that Aereo is directly *and* secondarily liable for infringing their public-performance rights (§106(4)) *and also* their reproduction rights (§106(1)). . . . Affirming the judgment below would merely return this case to the lower courts for consideration of the Networks' remaining claims.

III. Guilt By Resemblance

The Court's conclusion that Aereo performs boils down to the following syllogism: (1) Congress amended the Act to overrule our decisions holding that cable systems do not perform when they retransmit over-the-air broadcasts; (2) Aereo looks a lot like a cable system; therefore (3) Aereo performs. That reasoning suffers from a trio of defects.

First, it is built on the shakiest of foundations. Perceiving the text to be ambiguous, the Court reaches out to decide the case based on a few isolated snippets of legislative history. . . .

Second, the Court's reasoning fails on its own terms because there are material differences between the cable systems at issue in *Teleprompter* and *Fortnightly*, on the one hand and Aereo on the other. The former . . . captured the full range of broadcast signals and forwarded them to all subscribers at all times, whereas Aereo transmits only specific programs selected by the user, at specific times selected by the user. . . . At the time of our *Teleprompter* decision, cable companies "perform[ed] the same functions as 'broadcasters' by deliberately selecting and importing distant signals, originating programs, [and] selling commercials," *id.,* at 20, thus making them curators of content—more akin to video-on-demand services than copy shops. So far as the record reveals, Aereo does none of those things.

Third, and most importantly, even accepting that the 1976 amendments had as their purpose the overruling of our cable-TV cases, what they were meant to do and how they did it are two different questions—and it is the latter that governs the case before us here. . . .

. . . [T]he Court provides no criteria for determining when its cable-TV-looka-like rule applies. . . .

That leaves as the criterion of cable-TV-resemblance nothing but th' ol' totality-of-the-circumstances test (which is not a test at all but merely assertion of an intent to perform test-free, ad hoc, case-by-case evaluation). It will take years, perhaps decades, to determine which automated systems now in existence are governed by the traditional volitional-conduct test and which get the *Aereo* treatment. . . .

* * *

I share the Court's evident feeling that what Aereo is doing (or enabling to be done) to the Networks' copyrighted programming ought not to be allowed. But perhaps we need not distort the Copyright Act to forbid it. . . . It is not the role of this Court to identify and plug loopholes. It is the role of good lawyers to identify and exploit them, and the role of Congress to eliminate them if it wishes. Congress can do that, I may add, in a much more targeted, better informed, and less disruptive fashion than the crude "looks-like-cable-TV" solution the Court invents today. . . .

NOTES AND QUESTIONS

1. Why do you think the plaintiffs in *Cartoon Network* and *Aereo* objected to the service that the defendant provided? From a practical standpoint, how might you predict that Cablevision's and Aereo's services would affect the market for plaintiffs' copyrighted works?

2. Why do you think Cablevision wanted to offer a remote DVR service to its subscribers? What considerations do you think motivated Aereo's entry into the Internet retransmission market?

3. Who has the better argument about whether Aereo "perform[s]" the plaintiffs' copyrighted works, the majority or Justice Scalia? Do you read the dissenting Justices to be arguing simply that there is a better/easier way to accomplish the goal of finding Aereo liable for copyright infringement, or that the interpretation put forth by the majority is inconsistent with the Copyright Act, or both?

4. Focus on the language of the Transmit Clause. According to the *Aereo* majority, to determine whether particular transmissions are made "publicly," a court may consider a set of actions that includes transmissions to other parties. Is that interpretation consistent with the portion of the Copyright Act's legislative history quoted by the *Cartoon Network* court?

After *Aereo*, is it ever appropriate to consider the group of recipients capable of receiving a transmission from a particular copy, as the *Cartoon Network* court did? Put differently, does *Aereo* overrule *Cartoon Network*? Are there legally relevant distinctions between the fact patterns in the two cases? Is the remote DVR service in Cartoon Network more like a valet parking service or a car dealership? (Is either comparison a good fit?) Which analogy better describes a provider of cloud storage?

5. How would the disputes in *Aereo* and *Cartoon Network* be decided under the approach prescribed by the European Directive? Do you prefer the European approach? Why, or why not?

PRACTICE EXERCISE: COUNSEL A CLIENT

You represent a startup company that wants to offer Internet-based cloud storage to paying subscribers. Users would be assigned dedicated server space according to a tiered pricing system, and would be able to upload their content to your client's servers and access it as needed. Video content would be accessed by streaming the content to any device registered to the user's account. What recommendations do you have for the company?

Now imagine that the company also plans to operate in jurisdictions governed by legislation implementing the European Copyright Directive. Does that change your advice? How?

---

b. Diving Deeper: Cable and Satellite Retransmission

Cable television originated as an attempt to address the problem of weak television signals in rural areas of the country. Cable operators erected large towers to receive broadcast television signals and retransmit them through wires to individual homes. As the *Aereo* Court recounts, copyright owners sought compensation for this activity, while cable system operators argued that their systems simply "enhance[d] the viewer's capacity to receive the broadcaster's signals" and therefore did not engage in a new public performance of the works. *Fortnightly Corp. v. United Artists Television, Inc.*, 392 U.S. 390, 399 (1968).

As you already know, the 1976 Act broadened the definition of "performance" to encompass rendering of copyrighted content by means of any device or process. At the same time, Congress balanced the competing interests of copyright owners and cable operators and viewers by subjecting cable retransmissions of broadcast television signals to a compulsory license. Pursuant to the license, codified in §111 of the Act, cable television operators are not liable for copyright infringement as long as they file periodic accountings of their broadcast operations and pay a license fee based on a formula in the statute. (As explained in Chapter 5, Section 1.A.c *supra*, the ephemeral copies generated in the course of retransmission are exempted from the scope of the §106(1) reproduction right by §112.)

In large measure, the details of the retransmission rules reflect concern for both the need for competition in the marketplace and the potential threat that cable systems posed to local broadcast stations. In the early years of cable television, it was the cable operators that needed assistance to enter the market for providing television signals to homes. Thus, retransmission of local signals and network programming does not require any fee. Cable retransmission of these signals and programs is thought not to invade the market for the underlying copyrighted work, because the rates charged for advertising take into account households that receive these broadcasts over cable as well. Additionally, cable systems are required by the Communications Act to carry local broadcast stations (this requirement is sometimes referred to as the "must carry" rule). *See* 47 U.S.C. §§534-535. The retransmission of distant non-network programs, however, is not required by FCC regulations, and may potentially harm the television market for those programs.

Thus, retransmission of distant non-networked programs requires payment of a license fee. Payments are made to the Copyright Office and subsequently divided among program suppliers, professional sports leagues, and individual copyright claimants. Additionally, FCC network nonduplication, syndicated exclusivity, and sports blackout rules limit the ability of a cable company to import a distant broadcast that duplicates certain local broadcasts. Finally, the statutory license contained in §111 cannot be used to authorize retransmission of most programming originating in Canada or Mexico.

The statutory license provided by the original 1976 Copyright Act only addressed cable television systems. An unintended consequence of that approach was that the next technological innovation, satellite systems, faced a clear disadvantage in the marketplace. In order to broadcast any stations, the provider of the satellite system had to negotiate licenses individually. In 1988, Congress enacted the Satellite Home Viewer Act, codifying a compulsory license scheme for satellite retransmissions in §119. Section 119 originally covered only delivery of broadcast programming to previously unserved households, but was amended in 1999 to cover all satellite retransmissions of local broadcasts. Such retransmissions are subject to a carry-one/carry all requirement: if a satellite provider retransmits any local broadcast station, it must carry them all. Like the must carry rule, this requirement is codified in the Communications Act. *See* 47 U.S.C. §338.

The amendments to the Satellite Home Viewer Act were to expire after 5 years; however, Congress has repeatedly renewed the provisions without allowing them to lapse. The Satellite Television Extension and Localism Act of 2010 (STELA), reauthorized the retransmission rules through December 31, 2014, and updated the law to reflect the transition to digital television. Recently, the retransmission rules were extended until December 31, 2019. See STELA Reauthorization Act of 2014, Pub. L. 113-200, 128 Stat 2059 (2014).

As *Aereo* illustrates, Internet retransmission of broadcast programming has once again upset the compromise reflected in the Copyright Act's statutory license provisions. Section 111(f)(3) defines a "cable system" as:

> a facility, located in any State, territory, trust territory, or possession of the United States, that in whole or in part receives signals transmitted or programs broadcast by one or more television broadcast stations licensed by the Federal Communications Commission, and makes secondary transmissions of such signals or programs by wires, cables, microwave, or other communications channels to subscribing members of the public who pay for such service.

Id. May an Internet-based service that captures broadcast programming and retransmits it to paying subscribers claim the benefit of the statutory license? Answering this question in the negative, the Second Circuit reasoned:

> The legislative history indicates that Congress enacted §111 with the intent to address the issue of poor television reception, or, more specifically, to mitigate the difficulties that certain communities and households faced in receiving over-the-air broadcast signals by enabling the expansion of cable systems.
>
> Through §111's compulsory license scheme, Congress intended to support localized—rather than nationwide—systems that use cable or optical fibers to transmit

signals through "a physical, point-to-point connection between a transmission facility and the television sets of individual subscribers." *Turner*, 512 U.S. at 627-28.[8]

Congress did not, however, intend for §111's compulsory license to extend to Internet transmissions. Indeed, the legislative history indicates that if Congress had intended to extend §111's compulsory license to Internet retransmissions, it would have done so expressly—either through the language of §111 as it did for microwave retransmissions or by codifying a separate statutory provision as it did for satellite carriers.

Extending §111's compulsory license to Internet retransmissions, moreover, would not fulfill or further Congress's statutory purpose. Internet retransmission services are not seeking to address issues of reception and remote access to over-the-air television signals. They provide not a local but a nationwide (arguably international) service. . . .

WPIX, Inc. v. ivi, Inc., 691 F.3d 275, 282 (2d Cir. 2012). The court noted, in addition, that the Copyright Office repeatedly had expressed the view that the statutory license in §111 did not encompass Internet retransmission. It opined that, absent clear legislative direction to the contrary, the reasonable views of the agency charged with administering the statutory regime were entitled to deference. *Id.* at 283-85 (citing *Chevron U.S.A., Inc. v. Natural Resources Defense Council, Inc.*, 467 U.S. 837, 843-44 (1984)).

PRACTICE EXERCISE: ADVOCACY

To date, Congress has not passed any legislation concerning Internet retransmission of broadcast programming. You are the legislative counsel to a member of the House Judiciary Committee. Your boss, who represents a district that is home to a large concentration of Internet companies, wants to propose that Congress adopt a compulsory licensing system for Internet retransmission of television broadcast programming. What arguments in support of such a provision would be most effective? What counter-arguments should you anticipate?

---

c. The Public Display Right and De Minimis Use

Until recently, very few cases discussed the public display right, and those few did so only in passing. One reason may be the rights reserved to an owner of a copy of a copyrighted work by §109. Recall that §109(a) codifies the first sale doctrine, which permits the owner of a copy to resell or rent it, notwithstanding the public distribution right of the copyright owner. Section 109(c), in turn, permits someone who owns a copy of a copyrighted work to publicly display that work,

---

8. The statute's reference to "contiguous communities," and a "headend" in defining a cable system also indicates that Congress intended to direct §111's license at localized—rather than national—retransmission services. *See* 17 U.S.C. §111(f).

notwithstanding the public display right of the copyright owner. Specifically, §109(c) provides:

> Notwithstanding the provisions of section 106(5), the owner of a particular copy lawfully made under this title, or any person authorized by such owner, is entitled, without the authority of the copyright owner, to display that copy publicly, either directly or by the projection of no more than one image at a time, to viewers present at the place where the copy is located.

Section 109(d) provides that the authorization in §109(c) does not "extend to any person who has acquired possession of the copy . . . from the copyright owner, by rental, lease, loan, or otherwise, without acquiring ownership of it." Thus, someone who rents or licenses a copy of the copyrighted work from the copyright owner does not have the right to publicly display that copy. Once the copyright owner has *sold* a copy of the work, the purchaser and others authorized by the purchaser may display the copy publicly. For example, if a museum buys a painting, it can display it in its gallery and loan it to other museums for them to display. If, however, the display is accomplished by projecting an image of the lawfully acquired copy to viewers located in a place other than where the copy is located, then §109(c) will not immunize the display from infringement liability. Thus, with the exception of unlawfully made copies, the §109(c) exemption effectively limits the reach of the public display right to those displays that are made either by transmission or by in-theater performance of a film incorporating images of copyrighted work.

When a displayed work is visible only briefly or partially within a transmission or in-theater performance of some other work, does that count as an infringing display? In *Ringgold v. Black Entertainment Television*, 126 F.3d 70 (2d Cir. 1997), the plaintiff, a visual artist, asserted that the use of an authorized poster depicting her work on the set of defendant's television program infringed her right of public display. The poster was visible in whole or in part on nine separate occasions, none lasting more than 4.20 seconds. Defendant BET argued that its use of the work should be excused as *de minimis*. The court agreed that the infringement analysis could consider whether the challenged act of reproduction or public display was too insubstantial to count:

> In cases involving visual works, like the pending one, the quantitative component of substantial similarity also concerns the observability of the copied work—the length of time the copied work is observable in the allegedly infringing work and such factors as focus, lighting, camera angles, and prominence. Thus, as in this case, a copyrighted work might be copied as a factual matter, yet a serious dispute might remain as to whether the copying that occurred was actionable. Since "substantial similarity," properly understood, includes a quantitative component, it becomes apparent why the concept of *de minimis* is relevant to a defendant's contention that an indisputably copied work has not been infringed.

Id. at 75. However, it rejected BET's argument that its use of the poster was quantitatively insubstantial, reasoning that the poster was recognizable with sufficient detail for the lay observer to discern its subject matter. It noted, as well, that Copyright Office regulations set royalty rates for qualifying displays of copyrighted works by public broadcasting entities, and that if the regulations had applied to BET, its use of the work would have qualified as a "background" display requiring payment. *Id.* at 77 (citing 37 C.F.R. §253.8).

For pictorial, graphic, or sculptural works reproduced in useful articles, §113(c) imposes additional limitations on the public display right:

> In the case of a work lawfully reproduced in useful articles that have been offered for sale or other distribution to the public, copyright does not include any right to prevent the making, distribution, or display of pictures or photographs of such articles in connection with advertisements or commentaries related to the distribution or display of such articles, or in connection with news reports.

Does this language permit display by transmission? Under what circumstances? Review *Gottlieb Development v. Paramount Pictures*, Chapter 5, Section A.2 *supra*. If the court had concluded that the case involved more than *de minimis* reproduction, would §113(c) allow display of the Silver Slugger pinball machine in the film?

PROBLEM: DRAFTING AND ADVOCACY

Should Congress amend the Copyright Act to privilege *de minimis* reproduction and display of copyrighted works? If so, what test should it choose, and why? Try your hand at drafting the new statutory language. Who do you think would support such an amendment, and who would oppose it?

---

d. Where Does a Display Occur?

Placing copyrighted material on a publicly accessible website constitutes a public display of that material. The same activity, however, may also implicate other exclusive rights of the copyright owner, such as the right of reproduction or the right to make derivative works. This may explain why, even in the last two decades, relatively few cases have been decided based on infringement of the public display right. One question that has been litigated has to do with responsibility for online infringement. In the Internet era, transmissions require the involvement of several parties. Who may be held liable for infringement of the public display right? Consider the following case.

Perfect 10, Inc. v. Amazon.com, Inc.
508 F.3d 1146 (9th Cir. 2007)

IKUTA, J.:

In this appeal, we consider a copyright owner's efforts to stop an Internet search engine from facilitating access to infringing images. Perfect 10, Inc. sued Google Inc., for infringing Perfect 10's copyrighted photographs of nude models, among other claims. . . . The district court preliminarily enjoined Google from creating and publicly displaying thumbnail versions of Perfect 10's images, but did not enjoin Google from linking to third-party websites that display infringing full-size versions of Perfect 10's images. . . .

I

Background

. . . Computer owners can provide information stored on their computers to other users connected to the Internet through a medium called a webpage. A webpage consists of text interspersed with instructions written in Hypertext Markup Language ("HTML") that is stored in a computer. No images are stored on a webpage; rather, the HTML instructions on the webpage provide an address for where the images are stored, whether in the webpage publisher's computer or some other computer. In general, webpages are publicly available and can be accessed by computers connected to the Internet through the use of a web browser.

Google operates a search engine, a software program that automatically accesses thousands of websites (collections of webpages) and indexes them within a database stored on Google's computers. When a Google user accesses the Google website and types in a search query, Google's software searches its database for websites responsive to that search query. Google then sends relevant information from its index of websites to the user's computer. Google's search engines can provide results in the form of text, images, or videos.

The Google search engine that provides responses in the form of images is called "Google Image Search." In response to a search query, Google Image Search identifies text in its database responsive to the query and then communicates to users the images associated with the relevant text. Google's software cannot recognize and index the images themselves. Google Image Search provides search results as a webpage of small images called "thumbnails," which are stored in Google's servers. The thumbnail images are reduced, lower-resolution versions of full-sized images stored on third-party computers.

When a user clicks on a thumbnail image, the user's browser program interprets HTML instructions on Google's webpage. These HTML instructions direct the user's browser to cause a rectangular area (a "window") to appear on the user's computer screen. The window has two separate areas of information. The browser fills the top section of the screen with information from the Google webpage, including the thumbnail image and text. The HTML instructions also give the user's browser the address of the website publisher's computer that stores the full-size version of the thumbnail. . . . By following the HTML instructions to access the third-party webpage, the user's browser connects to the website publisher's computer, downloads the full-size image, and makes the image appear at the bottom of the window on the user's screen. Google does not store the images that fill this lower part of the window and does not communicate the images to the user; Google simply provides HTML instructions directing a user's browser to access a third-party website. However, the top part of the window (containing the information from the

Google webpage) appears to frame and comment on the bottom part of the window. Thus, the user's window appears to be filled with a single integrated presentation of the full-size image, but it is actually an image from a third-party website framed by information from Google's website. The process by which the webpage directs a user's browser to incorporate content from different computers into a single window is referred to as "in-line linking." The term "framing" refers to the process by which information from one computer appears to frame and annotate the in-line linked content from another computer.

Google also stores webpage content in its cache. . . . For each cached webpage, Google's cache contains the text of the webpage as it appeared at the time Google indexed the page, but does not store images from the webpage. Google may provide a link to a cached webpage in response to a user's search query. However, Google's cache version of the webpage is not automatically updated when the webpage is revised by its owner. So if the webpage owner updates its webpage to remove the HTML instructions for finding an infringing image, a browser communicating directly with the webpage would not be able to access that image. However, Google's cache copy of the webpage would still have the old HTML instructions for the infringing image. Unless the owner of the computer changed the HTML address of the infringing image, or otherwise rendered the image unavailable, a browser accessing Google's cache copy of the website could still access the image where it is stored on the website publisher's computer. In other words, Google's cache copy could provide a user's browser with valid directions to an infringing image even though the updated webpage no longer includes that infringing image.

In addition to its search engine operations, Google generates revenue through a business program called "AdSense." Under this program, the owner of a website can register with Google to become an AdSense "partner." The website owner then places HTML instructions on its webpages that signal Google's server to place advertising on the webpages that is relevant to the webpages' content. Google's computer program selects the advertising automatically by means of an algorithm. AdSense participants agree to share the revenues that flow from such advertising with Google.

Google also generated revenues through an agreement with Amazon.com that allowed Amazon.com to in-line link to Google's search results. Amazon.com gave its users the impression that Amazon.com was providing search results, but Google communicated the search results directly to Amazon.com's users. Amazon.com routed users' search queries to Google and automatically transmitted Google's responses (i.e., HTML instructions for linking to Google's search results) back to its users.

Perfect 10 markets and sells copyrighted images of nude models. Among other enterprises, it operates a subscription website on the Internet. Subscribers pay a monthly fee to view Perfect 10 images in a "members' area" of the site. Subscribers must use a password to log into the members' area. Google does not include these password-protected images from the members' area in Google's index or database. Perfect 10 has also licensed Fonestarz Media Limited to sell and distribute Perfect 10's reduced-size copyrighted images for download and use on cell phones.

Some website publishers republish Perfect 10's images on the Internet without authorization. Once this occurs, Google's search engine may automatically index the webpages containing these images and provide thumbnail versions of images in response to user inquiries. When a user clicks on the thumbnail image returned by Google's search engine, the user's browser accesses the third-party webpage and in-line links to the full-sized infringing image stored on the website publisher's computer. This image appears, in its original context, on the lower portion of the window on the user's computer screen framed by information from Google's webpage. . . .

III

Direct Infringement

Perfect 10 claims that Google's search engine program directly infringes two exclusive rights granted to copyright holders: its display rights and its distribution rights. . . .

A. Display Right

In considering whether Perfect 10 made a prima facie case of violation of its display right, the district court reasoned that a computer owner that stores an image as electronic information and serves that electronic information directly to the user ("i.e., physically sending ones and zeroes over the [I]nternet to the user's browser") is displaying the electronic information in violation of a copyright holder's exclusive display right. Conversely, the owner of a computer that does not store and serve the electronic information to a user is not displaying that information, even if such owner in-line links to or frames the electronic information. The district court referred to this test as the "server test."

Applying the server test, the district court concluded that Perfect 10 was likely to succeed in its claim that Google's thumbnails constituted direct infringement but was unlikely to succeed in its claim that Google's in-line linking to full-size infringing images constituted a direct infringement. As explained below, because this analysis comports with the language of the Copyright Act, we agree with the district court's resolution of both these issues.

We have not previously addressed the question when a computer displays a copyrighted work for purposes of section 106(5). . . . The Copyright Act explains that "display" means "to show a copy of it, either directly or by means of a film, slide, television image, or any other device or process. . . ." 17 U.S.C. §101. Section 101 defines "copies" as "material objects, other than phonorecords, in which a work is fixed by any method now known or later developed, and from which the work can be perceived, reproduced, or otherwise communicated, either directly or with the aid of a machine or device." *Id.* Finally, the Copyright Act provides that "[a] work is 'fixed' in a tangible medium of expression when its embodiment in a copy or phonorecord, by or under the authority of the author, is sufficiently permanent or stable to permit it to be perceived, reproduced, or otherwise communicated for a period of more than transitory duration." *Id.*

We must now apply these definitions to the facts of this case. A photographic image is a work that is "'fixed' in a tangible medium of expression," for purposes of the Copyright Act, when embodied (i.e., stored) in a computer's server (or hard disk, or other storage device). The image stored in the computer is the "copy" of the work for purposes of copyright law. The computer owner shows a copy "by means of a . . . device or process" when the owner uses the computer to fill the computer screen with the photographic image stored on that computer, or by communicating the stored image electronically to another person's computer. In sum, based on the plain language of the statute, a person displays a photographic image by using a computer to fill a computer screen with a copy of the photographic image fixed in the computer's memory. There is no dispute that Google's computers store thumbnail versions of Perfect 10's copyrighted images and communicate copies of those thumbnails to Google's users. . . . Therefore, Perfect 10 has made a prima facie case that Google's communication of its stored thumbnail images directly infringes Perfect 10's display right.

Google does not, however, display a copy of full-size infringing photographic images for purposes of the Copyright Act when Google frames in-line linked images that appear on a user's computer screen. Because Google's computers do not store the photographic images, Google does not have a copy of the images for purposes of the Copyright Act. In other words, Google does not have any "material objects . . . in which a work is fixed . . . and from which the work can be perceived, reproduced, or otherwise communicated" and thus cannot communicate a copy.

Instead of communicating a copy of the image, Google provides HTML instructions that direct a user's browser to a website publisher's computer that stores the full-size photographic image. Providing these HTML instructions is not equivalent to showing a copy. First, the HTML instructions are lines of text, not a photographic image. Second, HTML instructions do not themselves cause infringing images to appear on the user's computer screen. The HTML merely gives the address of the image to the user's browser. The browser then interacts with the computer that stores the infringing image. It is this interaction that causes an infringing image to appear on the user's computer screen. Google may facilitate the user's access to infringing images. However, such assistance raises only contributory liability issues, and does not constitute direct infringement of the copyright owner's display rights.

Perfect 10 argues that Google displays a copy of the full-size images by framing the full-size images, which gives the impression that Google is showing the image within a single Google webpage. While in-line linking and framing may cause some computer users to believe they are viewing a single Google webpage, the Copyright Act, unlike the Trademark Act, does not protect a copyright holder against acts that cause consumer confusion. . . .

Nor does our ruling that a computer owner does not display a copy of an image when it communicates only the HTML address of the copy erroneously collapse the display right in section 106(5) into the reproduction right set forth in section 106(1). Nothing in the Copyright Act prevents the various rights protected in section 106 from overlapping. Indeed, under some circumstances, more than one right must be infringed in order for an infringement claim to arise. For example, a "Game Genie" device that allowed a player to alter features of a Nintendo computer game did not infringe Nintendo's right to prepare derivative works because the

Game Genie did not incorporate any portion of the game itself. *See Lewis Galoob Toys, Inc. v. Nintendo of Am., Inc.*, 964 F.2d 965, 967 (9th Cir.1992). We held that a copyright holder's right to create derivative works is not infringed unless the alleged derivative work "incorporate[s] a protected work in some concrete or permanent 'form.'" In other words, in some contexts, the claimant must be able to claim infringement of its reproduction right in order to claim infringement of its right to prepare derivative works.

Because Google's cache merely stores the text of webpages, our analysis of whether Google's search engine program potentially infringes Perfect 10's display and distribution rights is equally applicable to Google's cache. Perfect 10 is not likely to succeed in showing that a cached webpage that in-line links to full-size infringing images violates such rights. For purposes of this analysis, it is irrelevant whether cache copies direct a user's browser to third-party images that are no longer available on the third party's website, because it is the website publisher's computer, rather than Google's computer, that stores and displays the infringing image. . . .

[As to the thumbnail images, the court ruled that Google would likely succeed in establishing fair use. *See* Chapter 10, Section B.2 *infra*.]

NOTES AND QUESTIONS

1. Do you agree that the plain language of the Act mandates rejection of Perfect 10's claims for direct infringement with respect to the full-size images? If not, is the district court's "server test" a good one? The district court rejected an alternative approach, which it called the "incorporation test," that would define "'display' as the mere act of incorporating content into a webpage that is then pulled up by the browser." *Perfect 10 v. Google, Inc.*, 416 F. Supp. 2d 828, 839 (C.D. Cal. 2006). The court thought the server test preferable because it "is based on what happens at the technological level . . . [and] neither invites copyright infringing activity by a search engine . . . nor flatly precludes liability for such activity." *Id.* at 843-44. Do you agree?

> ## COMPARATIVE PERSPECTIVE
>
> Review the language of Article 3 of the European Copyright Directive, page 386 *supra*. In *Svensson v. Retriever Sverige* AB, Case C-466/12 (13 February 2014), the European Court of Justice held that a search engine that searched the contents of news sites and provided hyperlinked results did not infringe the exclusive rights of the copyright holders. In analyzing whether hyperlinking was "communication to the public," the Court reasoned:
>
> [I]n order to be covered by the concept of "communication to the public," within the meaning of Article 3(1) of Directive 2001/29, a communication . . . made, as in the case of the initial communication, on the Internet, and therefore by the same technical means, must also be directed at a new public, that is to say, at a public that was not taken into account by the copyright holders when they authorised the initial communication to the public.
>
> *Id.* at ¶ 24; *see also Paperboy*, Case I ZR 259/00 (17 July 2003) [2005] ECDR (7) 67 (German Supreme Court), at ¶¶ 42-43 ("A person who sets a hyperlink to a website with a work protected under copyright law which has been made available to the public by the copyright owner, does not commit an act of exploitation under copyright law by doing so but only refers to the work in a manner which facilitates the access already provided. . . . Access to the work is only made possible through the hyperlink and therefore the work literally is made available to a user, who does not already know the URL as the precise name of the source of the webpage on the internet. This is however no different to a reference to a print or to a website in the footnote of a publication.").

2. Review *Capitol Records v. Thomas*, Section A.1 *supra*. Perfect 10 also asserted a claim against Google for direct infringement of its distribution right. It argued that, like users of peer-to-peer file-sharing services, Google made the infringing full-size images "available" to its users. The court rejected that argument, reasoning that "Google does not own a collection of Perfect 10's full-size images and does not communicate these images to the computers of people using Google's search engine." It concluded that therefore "the 'deemed distribution' rule does not apply to Google." *Perfect 10, Inc. v. Amazon.com, Inc.,* 508 F.3d 1146, 1162 (9th Cir. 2007). If copyright law were to adopt a "deemed distribution" rule, how broadly should such a rule extend? Would you agree that a "deemed distribution" rule should not extend to search engines? Why, or why not? Should such a rule extend to platforms like Facebook and YouTube?

3. Linking and framing occur in many contexts other than search. Are there contexts in which courts should scrutinize linking and framing more closely? Would any of the tests described by the Ninth Circuit and the district court in *Perfect 10* facilitate such scrutiny?

COMPARATIVE PERSPECTIVE

Many of the exceptions to copyright owners' exclusive rights set out in §110 of the U.S. Copyright Act are mirrored in the copyright legislation of other countries, although significant variations persist due to differing legal traditions and domestic policy priorities. In Europe, article 5 of Directive 2001/29/EC sets out an indicative list of exceptions and limitations (E&Ls) that EU Member States are allowed to include in their domestic legislation. EU countries may retain some other E&Ls already included in their domestic legislation.

Article 5.5 of the Directive, however, mandates that all E&Ls allowed under Article 5.1-5.4 be applied by Member States only "in certain special cases which do not conflict with a normal exploitation of the work or other subject-matter and do not unreasonably prejudice the legitimate interests of the rightholder." *Id.,* art. 5.5. This three-pronged "limit on limitations" is known as the three-step test (TST). Under the Berne Convention, the TST only applies to limitations on the reproduction right. Article 13 of the TRIPS Agreement extends the TST to all of the copyright exclusive rights. Several EU countries have transposed the TST directly into their domestic copyright legislation. Other countries, such as China, have taken a similar approach.

---

2. Limitations: Section 110

The Copyright Act contains a set of public interest exceptions pertaining specifically to the public dissemination rights. These exceptions, which are available to users in addition to the limitations of §107 and §109, are enumerated in 17 U.S.C §110. As you will see, many of these provisions are intricate and technical. In addition, there are unresolved issues concerning the interaction of §110 with the international copyright regime.

a. Section 110

Recall that the 1909 Act granted copyright owners the right to control only for-profit performances of their works. When the 1976 Act removed that qualification, exceptions were considered necessary for certain nonprofit uses. Those exceptions were codified in §110. Currently, §110 contains 11 subsections, each of which is extremely specific. Sometimes an exception applies only to certain types of works, sometimes it applies only to certain establishments, and sometimes it applies only to certain kinds of individuals.

As you might suspect, many of the provisions in §110 are the direct result of lobbying groups' efforts to protect their interests. *See* Jessica Litman, *Copyright, Compromise, and Legislative History*, 72 Cornell L. Rev. 857 (1987). Section 110 also became a convenient place for Congress to insert new exceptions, or to threaten to do so. For example, when industry groups tried to require the Girl Scouts to agree to licenses for popular campfire songs, legislators indicated that if they continued to press their demand, a new exception would be added.

The newest addition to §110 is §110(11), added in 2005, which shields technologies designed to permit individuals to skip objectionable content while watching authorized copies of movies on DVDs.

Read §110 carefully now, and then consider the following hypotheticals. Remember that a performance or display must be done "publicly" to trigger an infringement claim, and that the limitations in §109(c) may also apply.

PROBLEMS

1. Molly purchases a copy of *Frozen* for her daughter's eighth birthday. She shows the movie at her daughter's birthday party, to which she has invited all 27 students in the third-grade class.
2. The student ACLU group at your law school rents a copy of *Dead Man Walking* and shows it for movie night in the student lounge.
3. Jack Jackson clips a political cartoon from the newspaper and tapes it to the outside of his office cubicle for his co-workers to see.
4. Jack Jackson copies a political cartoon from his favorite news website and posts the copy on his Facebook page.
5. A rural radio station makes unlicensed broadcasts of copyrighted religious music every Sunday morning for local churches, which tune in to the broadcasts during their religious services.
6. A band plays copyrighted songs during a charitable event at a local bar. The bar owner provides the premises free of charge but keeps the proceeds from liquor sales made during the event.
7. A large apparel chain plays radio broadcasts in its stores during regular business hours. The chain has 855 stores across the United States and combined annual revenues of 15 billion dollars. Each store has one radio receiver of a kind frequently purchased by consumers for home use. The broadcasts cannot be heard beyond the premises of each store and no charge is assessed to any person to hear the broadcasts.
8. Sally brings portable speakers to the beach and uses her iPhone to stream music via Spotify loud enough for those around her to hear.
9. A wireless communication provider offers its customers ringtones featuring copyrighted songs. The customers download the ringtones and then use them to receive calls.

> 10. A wireless communication provider makes ringtones available for preview on its website. A customer can play the preview files by clicking on an icon. The preview file is streamed to the customer's computer and is not stored after playback.

NOTES AND QUESTIONS

1. Do you find the list of privileged uses included in 17 U.S.C §110 sensible and sufficient? Would you recommend the addition of others? Why, or why not?

2. In hearings on the bill that became §110(11), copyright owners had asserted that content-skipping technologies infringed their derivative work rights. The Register of Copyrights, meanwhile, had testified that the exemption was unnecessary because infringement of the derivative work right requires creation of a fixed copy. The title of §110 indicates that it provides exemptions from infringement liability for "certain performances and displays." The exemption in §110(11) does not mention the term "derivative work." Does the addition of §110(11) support the Register's argument or undermine it? Remember that to infringe the public performance right, a performance must be *public*. Does the exemption in §110(11) target public performances or private performances (or both)?

3. As the debate about content-skipping technologies illustrates, there is some uncertainty about the relationship of the derivative work right to the other exclusive rights. In rejecting Perfect 10's claim for infringement of the public display right, the court observed: "Nothing in the Copyright Act prevents the various rights protected in section 106 from overlapping. Indeed, under some circumstances, more than one right *must* be infringed in order for an infringement claim to arise. . . . [I]n some contexts, the claimant must be able to claim infringement of its reproduction right in order to claim infringement of its right to prepare derivative works." *Perfect 10, Inc. v. Amazon.com, Inc.*, 508 F.3d 1146, 1161 (9th Cir. 2007) (emphasis added). What is the extent of the overlap between the derivative work right and the public performance right? One scholar has suggested that:

> the exclusive right to prepare derivative works is not independent of the other four exclusive rights, but is infringed *only* in conjunction with at least one of the other four exclusive rights. The right to derivative works is infringed only when a modified version of a copyrighted work is reproduced, distributed to the public, or publicly performed or displayed; if the allegedly infringing activity is the private performance of a derivative work, without any fixation of that derivative work, the exclusive right to prepare derivative works is not violated.

Tyler Ochoa, *Copyright, Derivative Works and Fixation: Is* Galoob *a Mirage, or Does the Form (Gen) of the Alleged Derivative Work Matter?* 20 Santa Clara Comp. & High Tech. L.J. 991, 1020 (2004). So if someone creates a new set of lyrics sung to a popular song and sings them at a public concert venue, should that performance constitute infringement of the copyright in the underlying work? If so, which right has been infringed – the derivative work right or the public performance right? Or both?

b. Diving Deeper: Education and Distance Learning

Section 110 contains two exceptions for public performances and public displays relating to teaching activities. The first exempts:

> performance or display of a work by instructors or pupils in the course of face-to-face teaching activities of a nonprofit educational institution, in a classroom or similar place devoted to instruction, unless, in the case of a motion picture or other audiovisual work, the performance, or the display of individual images, is given by means of a copy that was not lawfully made under this title, and that the person responsible for the performance knew or had reason to believe was not lawfully made; . . .

17 U.S.C. §110(1). Note that the requirement of a lawfully made copy applies only to motion pictures or audiovisual works. Thus, teachers can explore infringing paintings by displaying them in their classrooms, but §110(1) does not immunize performing infringing movies or even infringing television commercials during class. It is possible that other exemptions, specifically fair use (which you will study in Chapter 10), might apply. Note also that the requirement in §110(1) that the performance or display occur in the course of face-to-face teaching in a classroom or similar place excludes transmission that might be used in distance learning activities.

Section 110(2) addresses distance learning activities that occur via transmission. The exemption applies to transmission of "nondramatic literary or musical works," as well as "reasonable and limited portions of any other works." To qualify for the §110(2) exemption, the transmission of a performance or display of a work must be limited to "students officially enrolled" in a course offered by "an accredited nonprofit educational institution," or to "officers or employees of governmental bodies as a part of their official duties or employment." The use of the copyrighted works must be an integral part of the class experience and be controlled by or under the actual supervision of the instructor. Not eligible for the exemption are works that are "produced or marketed primarily for performance or display as part of mediated instructional activities transmitted via digital networks," a limitation argued to be essential by the publishing industry.

An important part of making the distance learning exception acceptable to publishers was the requirement that the transmitting body apply technological measures that reasonably prevent retention of the work in accessible form by the recipients of the transmission after the class session has ended, and prevent unauthorized further dissemination of the work in accessible form by the recipients to others. *See id.* §110(2)(D). Additionally, institutions must not interfere with technological measures used by copyright owners to prevent such retention and further dissemination. We discuss technological protections for copyrighted works and legal protections granted to them by the Digital Millennium Copyright Act in Chapter 14.

Section 110(2) also provides that if temporary copies ("ephemeral" copies) are necessary to make the exempt transmissions, such reproductions may be made without infringing the reproduction right of the copyright owner. This exemption for ephemeral copies is codified in §112, which contains exemptions for other kinds of ephemeral copies and which we discussed in more detail in Chapter 5, Section A.1.c. *supra*. It expressly allows conversion of print or other analog versions of works into digital formats if no digital version of the work is available to the institution, or if the digital version that is available contains technological protections that prevent its use. *See id.*

Since its enactment, §110(2) has not been widely utilized. Eligible institutions cite the vague and expensive requirement to make "reasonable efforts" to prevent unauthorized dissemination or retention, the complexity of complying with the Act's requirements, potential liability for student misuse, and the availability of simpler, if less comprehensive, alternatives as reasons for declining to implement §110(2) policies. *See* Stephana Colbert & Oren Griffin, *The TEACH Act: Recognizing Its Challenges and Overcoming Its Limitations*, 33 J.C. & U.L. 499 (2007).

PRACTICE EXERCISE: COUNSEL A CLIENT

You are in-house counsel for a private university that wishes to participate in the emerging market for Massively Open Online Courses (MOOCs). You have been asked for your opinion on whether, as part of such courses, the university may make copyrighted course materials available online. As you already know, §110 contains two exemptions for public performances and displays relating to teaching activities. Review those exemptions now, and then draft a short opinion letter.

7

Copyright in Musical Works and Sound Recordings

Copyright in the music industry is both particularly complex and particularly important. The complexity arises because there are two copyrights in any recorded piece of music: the copyright in the musical work, which can involve both musical notes and lyrics, and the copyright in the sound recording. In the music industry, this sound recording copyright creates an important second layer of protection, even though that protection is limited in various ways that we discuss below.

This chapter is designed to help you appreciate how the different §106 rights in musical works and sound recordings are utilized by the various industry players and to introduce limits on those rights that are specific to musical works and sound recordings. It also explores some of the ways that Congress has responded to the needs of existing market players whose business models, established around the then-existing copyright law, have been threatened by new technologies. Sometimes, Congress has established new licensing models to facilitate market entry; sometimes, however, new business models have been subjected to new obligations that do not apply to established entities. As new copyright arrangements have proliferated, market entry increasingly requires clearance of multiple rights, each administered by a different entity. Partly for this reason, the music industry has had difficulty adapting to the digital era.

A. INTRODUCTION TO THE "PLAYERS" IN THE MUSIC INDUSTRY

Understanding copyright issues in the music industry requires keeping straight both the layers of copyright protection involved and various interested parties.

Almost everyone understands the role of the songwriter and also the role of the recording artist who performs and records a musical work. But in between these two known players are several other important entities. Below is a chart depicting the various rights in musical works and sound recordings and the entities that administer each right. It may be helpful to refer back to this chart as you read through the following materials.

	Reproduction and Distribution in Phonorecords	Other Reproduction/ Creation of Derivative Works	Public Performance
Musical Works	**Statutory right:** §§106(1) & (3) **Specific limitations on §106 rights:** §115 — compulsory license §§1001-1008 — Audio Home Recording Act (AHRA) **Rights Administered by:** — Music Publishers — Copyright Office (§115; AHRA) — Harry Fox Agency	**Statutory right:** §§106(1) & (2) **Rights Administered by:** — Music Publishers	**Statutory right:** §106(4) **Specific limitations on §106 rights:** §110 – various limitations **Rights Administered by:** — ASCAP, BMI, or SESAC
Sound Recordings	**Statutory right:** §§106(1) & (3) **Specific limitations on §106 rights:** §114(b) — "sound alikes" not covered §§1001-1008 — AHRA **Rights Administered by:** — Record Labels — Copyright Office (AHRA)	**Statutory right:** §§106(1) & (2) **Specific limitations on §106 rights:** §114(b) — actual sounds must be reproduced **Rights Administered by:** — Record Labels	**Statutory right:** §106(6) **Specific limitations on §106 rights:** §§106(6) & 114(a) — digital audio transmission only §§114(d)-(j) — exemptions and statutory license **Rights Administered by:** — Record Labels — SoundExchange (§114 statutory license)

The music publisher is the "middleman" between the songwriter and other industry players, including not only performing artists but also record companies, collective rights organizations, and any other entities that might license a songwriter's compositions. While a songwriter is not required to engage a music publisher, she often does so because the music publisher knows the business and can therefore be a significant asset to the songwriter. To a large extent, the genre of music determines how active a role the publisher plays. In country music, it is common for recording artists to perform and record musical works written by others, and thus a role of the music publisher is to promote a songwriter's songs. In rock music, it is more common for the artist to write most, if not all, of her songs. In that case, the publishing company's role is to administer the catalog of that artist's musical works, including licensing the use of the musical works by others. In general, music publishing companies require that the copyright in the musical work be assigned to them, but agree to split royalties earned on the musical work 50/50 with the songwriter.

Record companies play the middleman role for performing artists. When a performing artist creates a sound recording, often there is a record company that works with the artist to produce, distribute, and promote the recorded songs, whether through sales of copies or through licensing of the recording for audio streaming. Typically, the recording artist will assign all copyright interest in the sound recording to the recording company in exchange for royalties or other compensation. The contract often specifies that the sound recording is created as a work made for hire and that, to the extent that it is not a work made for hire, the artist assigns "all right, title, and interest" to the recording company.

If the recording artist is recording a musical work written by someone else, she will need permission. The songwriter will be the proper person from whom to obtain permission only if the songwriter has not contracted with a music publisher. Even the music publisher may not be the proper entity from whom to obtain authorization, however, because a majority of music publishers contract with the Harry Fox Agency. Harry Fox licenses the right to record and reproduce in phonorecords millions of musical works, as well as the right to publicly distribute those phonorecords. As explained in more detail in Section 7.B.1 below, such licenses are referred to in the industry as "mechanicals" because they originally involved the mechanical reproduction of musical works.

At this point, distributors of recorded music enter the music industry picture. A record company may distribute CDs to brick and mortar stores, or it may make sound recordings available to digital distributors, such as Apple's iTunes and Amazon.com, which will offer them to consumers via "digital phonorecord delivery" or DPD. The statutory duties surrounding DPDs are discussed in more detail in Sections 7.B.1 and 7.B.2.

Radio stations broadcasting over the Internet or over the airwaves, and concert venues, nightclub owners, and other businesses that "play" music also are part of the music industry. As you know from Chapter 6, these entities are all engaging in "public performances." Because musical work copyright owners have a public performance right, permission will be needed, assuming no specific exemption applies (e.g., §110). In many cases, obtaining authorization from each copyright owner (generally, the music publisher) would involve insurmountable transaction costs. However, collective rights organizations (CROs) exist that have licensed the public performance rights from the music publishers, and that administer blanket licenses for millions of copyrighted works. The American Society of Composers, Authors, and Publishers (ASCAP), Broadcast Music, Inc. (BMI), and the Society of European Stage Authors and Composers (SESAC) are the three main CROs. The creation and evolution of these CROs are explored in Section 7.D.1 below.

Radio stations and nightclubs also are engaged in public performances of sound recordings. As discussed in Section 7.D.2 below, the Copyright Act does not grant copyright owners of sound recordings a general public performance right. However, when the public performance is by means of a digital audio transmission—for example, streamed from an online site—the online site will need authorization to publicly perform the sound recording. *See* 17 U.S.C. §106(6). The statute exempts certain digital public performances of sound recordings and provides a statutory license covering certain other performances. The statutory license is administered by SoundExchange, an entity created by the trade organization for the record companies, the Recording Industry Association of America (RIAA). If neither the exemption nor the statutory license applies, an entity engaged in a public performance of sound recordings via digital audio transmission will need the permission of the copyright owners of the sound recordings being performed, as well as, of course, authorization to perform the musical works.

Finally, a number of other entities, such as film and television producers and video game companies, license musical works and sound recordings for inclusion in their own works. Such uses, which we discuss in more detail in Section 7.B.3, can implicate the reproduction right, the public performance right, and/or the derivative work right as well.

NOTES AND QUESTIONS

1. Where, at the end of the day, are the creative individuals who write the songs and perform the music? How big a role do these individuals play in the operation of the music industry?

2. Of course, there are individuals who listen to music, play music, make their own creative works using other people's recordings, and upload the resulting works to blogs and websites like Facebook and YouTube. The music landscape has shifted dramatically in the last decade, challenging the legal structure that was mostly established for a different technological reality. As you continue through this section, consider whether the structure as a whole is well designed for the digital world in which individuals can play a far more direct and integral role in the creation, dissemination and use of recorded music.

B. REPRODUCTION, PUBLIC DISTRIBUTION, AND DERIVATIVE WORKS

Like all of the other categories of works, musical works and sound recordings are protected by the exclusive rights granted to copyright owners in §106. In music, however, each of the exclusive rights seems to take at least one special twist or turn.

1. Musical Works and Section 115

The mechanical license dates back to the turn of the last century, when player pianos and phonograph record players gained popularity. Previously, sales of sheet music had been the primary revenue source for musical work copyright owners. Initially, the makers of player piano rolls and phonograph records did not pay royalties for embodying musical works in the rolls and records. After an unsuccessful challenge to this practice in the Supreme Court, Congress amended the statute, granting musical work copyright owners the right to control the "mechanical reproduction" of their works. Congress, however, was suspicious of the market power of one piano roll company, the Aeolian Company, and so, for the first time in the history of the Copyright Act, Congress adopted a compulsory license system. Any manufacturer of piano rolls could use any musical composition without negotiating with the copyright owner for permission, so long as the musical work had been previously licensed to someone else for mechanical reproduction and the manufacturer paid a statutory royalty. The statutory royalty rate was set at two cents per mechanical copy distributed.

Today the compulsory license for mechanical reproductions of musical works continues to allow recording artists to record what are commonly known in the industry as "covers"—musical works written by someone else and previously released by a different recording artist. Codified in §115, the compulsory license applies not just to player piano rolls, but also to CDs, cassettes, and any other "phonorecord" that mechanically reproduces sounds embodying the musical work. The international copyright system expressly contemplates this sort of compulsory licensing. Article 13 of the Berne Convention allows countries to permit the recording of musical works that have already been recorded with permission of the copyright owner, subject to the requirement that such permission not be "prejudicial to the rights of these authors to obtain equitable remuneration which, in the absence of agreement, shall be fixed by competent authority." Berne Conv., art. 13(3).

In 1998, Congress amended §115 to make clear that it applied to distribution of phonorecords by means of digital downloads. The Act uses the term "digital phonorecord delivery" (DPD) and defines it as "each individual delivery of a phonorecord by a digital transmission of a sound recording which results in a specifically identifiable reproduction." 17 U.S.C. §115(d). The definition of a DPD specifically excludes web streaming—i.e., real-time transmissions "where no reproduction of the sound recording or the musical work embodied therein is made from the inception of the transmission through to its receipt by the transmission recipient in order to make the sound recording audible." *Id.*

Section 115 retains the requirement that, to be subject to the compulsory license, the musical work must have been previously distributed to the public, embodied in a phonorecord created under the authority of the copyright owner. The recording artist may make a new arrangement of the work to conform it to his or her own style, but may not change

> ### LOOKING FORWARD
>
> Web streaming implicates rights of public performance for both musical works and sound recordings. We discuss those rights in Section D *infra*.

the "basic melody or fundamental character of the work." *Id.* §115(a)(2). The new arrangement is expressly excluded from obtaining protection as a derivative work, however, unless the copyright owner consents. *See id.* The statutory royalty rate for phonorecords made and distributed after March 2009 is 9.1 cents or 1.75 cents per minute of playing time or fraction thereof, whichever is greater. The responsibility for setting rates lies with the Copyright Royalty Judges.

The compulsory license in §115 is not, however, the way in which many creators of sound recordings obtain permission to use musical works. If one recording artist desires to record a performance of a musical work that has already been the subject of an authorized recording, instead of complying with the requirements of §115, a representative for the later recording artist typically contacts the Harry Fox Agency. Established in New York City in 1927 as a wholly owned subsidiary of the National Music Publishing Company, Harry Fox serves as an agent for many musical work copyright owners (but not all), licensing musical works for reproduction and distribution in phonorecords—i.e., granting "mechanical" licenses. Songwriters who have not contracted with a music publisher may utilize Songtrust, an entity that has arrangements with Harry Fox as well.

The availability of the compulsory mechanical license does affect the rates paid to music publishers via Harry Fox. In effect, the parties to the licenses administered by Harry Fox are negotiating in the shadow of a compulsory license that they know could be used instead. Thus, it is rare that the agreed license rate exceeds the rate set by the Copyright Royalty Judges. The number of copyright owners that have entered into licensing agreements with Harry Fox is staggering: Harry Fox represents over 48,000 music publishers, who collectively own millions of copyrighted musical works.

NOTES AND QUESTIONS

1. The Copyright Office has ruled that cellular phone ringtones that are excerpts of preexisting sound recordings "fall squarely within the scope of the statutory license" under §115 and constitute DPDs. *In the Matter of Mechanical & Digital Phonorecord Delivery Rate Adjustment Proceeding,* U.S. Copyright Office, No. RF 2006-1 (Oct. 16, 2006). If additional material is added, the ringtone may be a derivative work and thus ineligible for the §115 mechanical license. *Id.* Songwriters, represented by the National Music Publishers Association, the Songwriters Guild of America, and the Nashville Songwriters Association International, had argued that all ringtones are derivative works. Why do you think the Copyright Office ruled as it did?

2. The mechanical royalty rate for distribution of ringtones, regardless of the duration of the ring tone, is 24 cents. Does it make sense that the royalty rate for a five minute song would be 9.4 cents, but a 20-second snippet of that same song as a ringtone would carry a rate of 24 cents?

PROBLEMS

Rod Stewart and Martin Quittenton wrote the song "Maggie May," and Stewart recorded the song in 1971 for his album *Every Picture Tells a Story.* The song was covered by a standard music publishing agreement with music publisher EMI, which has agreements with Harry Fox and ASCAP. The song has been covered by several different recording artists, including Matthew Sweet, Garth Brooks, and 2013 *The Voice* finalist Cole Vosbury.

1. What rights did each of the subsequent artists need to obtain to record the song? What were their options for obtaining those rights?
2. Could Stewart, Quittenton, or EMI have stopped any of the subsequent artists from recording and releasing the song?
3. If 15-year-old Don Dronner records his version of "Maggie May" in his basement and makes it available for free via his personal website, does he need a license? Will he be eligible for a §115 license after he has uploaded the song? (Examine §§115(a)-(b) carefully before answering.)

---

2. Sound Recordings and Section 114

The sound recording copyright protects the elements of original authorship that inhere in a fixed recording of sounds, whether it is a recording of a musical performance, a dramatic reading, or a sequence of railroad whistles. Whereas most copyrighted works are fixed in "copies," sound recordings are fixed in "phonorecords," which the Copyright Act defines as

> material objects in which sounds, other than those accompanying a motion picture or other audiovisual work, are fixed by any method now known or later developed, and from which the sounds can be perceived, reproduced, or otherwise communicated, either directly or with the aid of a machine or device.

17 U.S.C. §101. Thus, phonorecords include vinyl albums, cassettes, and CDs, as well as digital files.

When phonorecords are created and distributed to the public, it is important to remember that the compulsory mechanical license only authorizes reproduction and distribution of the musical work, not the sound recording. Sales of CDs at brick and mortar stores rely on the first sale doctrine, which permits stores to purchase authorized copies of those CDs from the record companies and resell the CDs without further concern for copyright rights. When a DPD is made, however, the distributor must pay the royalty negotiated with the record company for the sound recording.

Section 114 sets forth some additional limits on sound recording copyrights. It indicates that the §106(1) right "is limited to the right to duplicate the sound recording in the form of phonorecords or copies that directly or indirectly recapture the actual sounds fixed in the recording." *Id.* §114(b). Put differently, the Act does not protect the sound recording copyright owner against imitation of the sounds in a sound recording, but only against direct duplication of the recorded sounds. While one might expect the derivative work right to cover sound alikes, it is subject to the same limit as the reproduction right. A derivative work is created only when "the actual sounds fixed in the sound recording are rearranged, remixed, or otherwise altered in sequence or quality." *Id.* To further clarify both of these limitations, §114 provides that neither the reproduction nor the derivative work right "extends to the making of an independent fixation of other sounds, even though such sounds imitate or simulate those in the copyrighted sound recording." *Id.*

NOTES AND QUESTIONS

1. Other copyrighted works are protected against imitation as well as exact duplication. What is different about sound recordings? At least two considerations may have influenced Congress. First, Congress was focusing primarily on stopping record piracy, not imitations. Second, there is some indication in the legislative history that Congress was concerned about safeguarding our musical heritage. How does permitting sound-alike recordings help to do this?

3. Synchronization Licenses

The compulsory license codified in §115 and the licenses that the Harry Fox Agency grants only authorize mechanical reproductions in "phonorecords." Licenses for other types of reproductions of musical works must be negotiated directly with the music publisher. Most notably, this includes synchronization ("synch") licenses, which allow the musical work to be included in the soundtrack to an audiovisual work such as a video game, television commercial, or movie. Of course, to use a previously recorded version of a song (as opposed to hiring musicians to record a new version strictly for the audiovisual work at issue) permission to reproduce the sound recording will also be necessary.

While use in a soundtrack clearly requires a synch license, new product offerings sometimes can be difficult to classify. Imagine that you are a manufacturer of a karaoke product, which you hope to sell for use in restaurants and bars. What kinds of licenses do you need, and from whom? Does it make a difference whether you put the recordings on cassettes or compact discs or embed them in a microchip, which, when plugged into a television, displays the lyrics of the song on the television screen in real time? Courts have reached different answers to these questions. *Compare Leadsinger Inc. v. BMG Music Publ'g,* 512 F.3d 522 (9th Cir. 2008) (holding that a karaoke device that displays lyrics is not a phonorecord but is an audiovisual work excluded from §115's compulsory licensing scheme), *with EMI Entm't World, Inc. v. Priddis Music, Inc.,* 505 F. Supp. 2d 1217 (D. Utah 2007) (finding that mere display of lyrics as a song is played does not amount to an audiovisual work and does not require a synch license).

PROBLEMS

Review your answers to the Problems in Section 7.B.1 *supra*, and then consider the following:

1. What types of licenses would be needed to use Garth Brooks' version of the song "Maggie May" in a movie? From whom can the movie studio obtain those licenses? Would additional licenses be needed to release "Maggie May" as part of a soundtrack album?
2. What types of licenses would be needed to include "Maggie May" in the video games Rock Band or Guitar Hero?

---

4. Diving Deeper: The Audio Home Recording Act and Personal Copying

Today, individuals can easily make playlists of hundreds of their favorite songs, share those lists with others, add music to videos and share the videos online, and use music to enhance other content such as websites and school projects. Prior to the advent of digital technology, individuals who engaged in similar activities did so on a much smaller scale, making mixtapes for friends or playing a cassette tape during a school presentation. Copyright owners typically did not bother objecting to such uses and many users assumed that the Copyright Act did not define such actions as infringement. Today, however, individuals can reach millions of other users with the click of a button. And today, copyright owners care about capturing the potential value that their works add to individuals' online activities.

Initially, copyright owners enlisted Congress in the regulation of digital copying technologies. The Audio Home Recording Act (AHRA) of 1992 established ground rules for the manufacture and sale of digital audio tape (DAT) technology. Because DAT technology was quickly superseded by the personal computer, today the AHRA is interesting largely for historical purposes.

The AHRA contains three key elements. First, manufacturers of digital audio recorders and tapes must embed Serial Copy Management System (SCMS) technology that allows first-generation copies to be created but prevents subsequent generation copying. The AHRA includes prohibitions on circumventing the SCMS and on marketing technology designed to circumvent the SCMS.

The second key element of the AHRA is a royalty pooling scheme. DAT manufacturers must pay royalties on both recording devices and recording media. The royalties are then pooled and subsequently divided among copyright owners of musical works, copyright owners of sound recordings, and featured recording artists, with a small percentage of the fund paid to nonfeatured musicians and vocalists.

> **COMPARATIVE PERSPECTIVE**
>
> Many countries, including France and Germany, have imposed royalty levies on sales of blank recording media. The funds collected as a result of such levies are divided among authors, producers, and performers, and in some cases a portion also is allotted to a cultural fund meant to sponsor creative activities.

The final key element of the AHRA is an exemption from copyright infringement liability for consumers engaged in certain activities, as well as for manufacturers of certain devices and media. Section 1008 provides:

> No action may be brought under this title alleging infringement of copyright based on the manufacture, importation, or distribution of a digital audio recording device, a digital audio recording medium, an analog recording device, or an analog recording medium, or based on the noncommercial use by a consumer of such a device or medium for making digital musical recordings or analog musical recordings.

17 U.S.C. §1008. Prior to the AHRA, the recording industry took the public position that copies made for personal use were infringing, while others asserted that fair use permitted such personal noncommercial copying. When Congress extended copyright protection to sound recordings, it indicated that such protection was not intended "to restrain the home recording, from broadcast or from tapes or records, of recorded performances, where home recording is for private use and with no purpose of reproducing or otherwise capitalizing commercially on it." H.R. Rep. No. 487, 92d Cong., 1st Sess. 7 (1971), *reprinted in* 1971 U.S.C.C.A.N. 1566, 1572. No case had ever directly addressed the issue. Section 1008 made an exemption explicit.

The AHRA, however, specifically exempted general purpose computers from its coverage. During the negotiations leading up to the AHRA, the computer industry made clear that it would not agree to a law that would require computers to incorporate the SCMS technology or manufacturers to pay royalties on computers and blank disks. The other interested parties knew that if the computer industry opposed the law, passage was unlikely. The quickest route to passage of the AHRA was to exempt the entire computer industry from its coverage. Congress drafted a set of nested definitions for the terms "digital music recording" and "digital audio recording device" that had the effect of excluding computers from the definitions of the devices covered by the AHRA. Relying on these definitions, the Ninth Circuit has held that the AHRA does not apply to the downloading of MP3 files. *A&M Records, Inc. v. Napster, Inc.,* 239 F.3d 1004, 1024-25 (9th Cir. 2001).

While there is no specific "personal use" exemption in the Copyright Act, millions of individuals continue to use music in their daily lives in ways that produce copies, cause distributions of copies, create derivative works, and constitute public performances. Congress has provided no guidance about the treatment of such uses. Instead, significant industry players have sought to shape the rights and abilities of individuals through private market arrangements. For example, YouTube's "Content ID" system allows copyright owners to capture advertising revenue associated with user videos that employ their works. We discuss private market arrangements that respond to user-generated content in more detail in Chapter 9 which considers the liability of online service providers for infringement by users.

NOTES AND QUESTIONS

1. Compulsory licensing is one approach to balancing the competing interests of copyright owners and those who desire to use copyrighted works in certain ways.

With compulsory licensing, individual copyright owners are compensated directly for the use of their works, albeit at a rate set either by statute or by some statutorily defined method. Royalty pooling, on the other hand, is not a direct payment of royalties to the copyright owners of the works used. Rather, as the name implies, the pool of royalty payments is divided in an attempt at a rough estimate of the level of use of any particular copyrighted work. Consider online distribution of music. Does either a compulsory license or a royalty pooling scheme seem appropriate? How would such a license fee or royalty payment be computed, and on whom (or what) would it be levied? Personal computers? Cell phones? CD burners and recording media? Internet service contracts?

2. Should the AHRA's exemption from infringement liability be expressly extended to cover digital file formats created using computers? Does your answer depend on the establishment of a royalty pool?

C. SAMPLING

In certain musical genres, such as rap, hip hop, and dubstep, "sampling" is a common practice. Sampling involves digitally copying and remixing sounds from previously recorded albums. As you now know, this practice may implicate two copyrights. When should sampling require the permission of the musical work copyright owner? When should it require the permission of the sound recording copyright owner?

Newton v. Diamond
388 F.3d 1189 (9th Cir. 2004), cert. denied, 545 U.S. 1114 (2005)

SCHROEDER, J.: . . .

Background and Procedural History

The plaintiff and appellant in this case, James W. Newton, is an accomplished avant-garde jazz flutist and composer. In 1978, he composed the song "Choir," a piece for flute and voice intended to incorporate elements of African-American gospel music, Japanese ceremonial court music, traditional African music, and classical music, among others. According to Newton, the song was inspired by his earliest memory of music, watching four women singing in a church in rural Arkansas. In 1981, Newton performed and recorded "Choir" and licensed all rights in the sound recording to ECM Records for $5000. The license covered only the sound recording, and it is undisputed that Newton retained all rights to the composition of "Choir." . . .

The defendants and appellees include the members of the rap and hip-hop group Beastie Boys, and their business associates. In 1992, Beastie Boys obtained a license from ECM Records to use portions of the sound recording of "Choir" in various renditions of their song "Pass the Mic" in exchange for a one-time fee of $1000. Beastie Boys did not obtain a license from Newton to use the underlying composition.

The portion of the composition at issue consists of three notes, C—D flat—C, sung over a background C note played on the flute. The score to "Choir" also indicates that the entire song should be played in a "largo/senza-misura" tempo, meaning "slowly/without-measure." The parties disagree about whether two additional elements appear in the score. First, Newton argues that the score contains an instruction that requires overblowing the background C note that is played on the flute. Second, Newton argues that multiphonics are part of the composition because they are necessarily created when a performer follows the instructions on the score to simultaneously play the flute note and sing the vocal notes. Because we review the district court's grant of summary judgment to the Beastie Boys, we must construe the evidence in Newton's favor. We therefore assume that these two elements are part of the "Choir" composition. . . .

The dispute between Newton and Beastie Boys centers around the copyright implications of the practice of sampling, a practice now common to many types of popular music. Sampling entails the incorporation of short segments of prior sound recordings into new recordings. The practice originated in Jamaica in the 1960s, when disc jockeys (DJs) used portable sound systems to mix segments of prior recordings into new mixes, which they would overlay with chanted or "scatted" vocals. *See* Robert M. Szymanski, *Audio Pastiche: Digital Sampling, Intermediate Copying, Fair Use*, 3 U.C.L.A. Ent. L. Rev. 271, 277 (Spring 1996). Sampling migrated to the United States and developed throughout the 1970s, using the analog technologies of the time. *Id.* The digital sampling involved here developed in the early 1980s with the advent of digital synthesizers having MIDI (Musical Instrument Digital Interface) keyboard controls. These digital instruments allowed artists digitally to manipulate and combine sampled sounds, expanding the range of possibilities for the use of pre-recorded music. Whereas analog devices limited artists to "scratching" vinyl records and "cutting" back and forth between different sound recordings, digital technology allowed artists to slow down, speed up, combine, and otherwise alter the samples. *See id.*

Pursuant to their license from ECM Records, Beastie Boys digitally sampled the opening six seconds of Newton's sound recording of "Choir." Beastie Boys repeated or "looped" this six-second sample as a background element throughout "Pass the Mic," so that it appears over forty times in various renditions of the song. In addition to the version of "Pass the Mic" released on their 1992 album, "Check Your Head," Beastie Boys included the "Choir" sample in two remixes, "Dub the Mic" and "Pass the Mic (Pt. 2, Skills to Pay the Bills)." It is unclear whether the sample was altered or manipulated, though Beastie Boys' sound engineer stated that alterations of tone, pitch, and rhythm are commonplace, and Newton maintains that the pitch was lowered slightly.

Newton filed the instant action in federal court on May 9, 2000, alleging violations of his copyright in the underlying composition. . . . The district court . . . granted summary judgment in favor of Beastie Boys . . . . The district court held that the three-note segment of the "Choir" composition could not be copyrighted because, as a matter of law, it lacked the requisite originality. The court also concluded that even if the segment were copyrightable, Beastie Boys' use of the work was de minimis and therefore not actionable. . . .

Whether Defendants' Use Was De Minimis

. . . Assuming that the sampled segment of the composition was sufficiently original to merit copyright protection, we nevertheless affirm on the ground that Beastie Boys' use was de minimis and therefore not actionable.

For an unauthorized use of a copyrighted work to be actionable, the use must be significant enough to constitute infringement. This means that even where the fact of copying is conceded, no legal consequences will follow from that fact unless the copying is substantial. The principle that trivial copying does not constitute actionable infringement has long been a part of copyright law. . . .

A leading case on de minimis infringement in our circuit is *Fisher v. Dees*, 794 F.2d 432 (9th Cir. 1986), where we observed that a use is de minimis only if the average audience would not recognize the appropriation. *See id.* at 434 n.2. This observation reflects the relationship between the de minimis maxim and the general test for substantial similarity, which also looks to the response of the average audience, or ordinary observer, to determine whether a use is infringing. To say that a use is de minimis because no audience would recognize the appropriation is thus to say that the use is not sufficiently significant. . . .

This case involves not only use of a composition, . . . but also use of a sound recording of a particular performance of that composition. Because the defendants were authorized to use the sound recording, our inquiry is confined to whether the unauthorized use of the composition itself was substantial enough to sustain an infringement claim. Therefore, we may consider only Beastie Boys' appropriation of the song's compositional elements and must remove from consideration all the elements unique to Newton's performance. Stated another way, we must "filter out" the licensed elements of the sound recording to get down to the unlicensed elements of the composition, as the composition is the sole basis for Newton's infringement claim. *See Cavalier* [*v. Random House, Inc.*, 297 F.3d 815, 822 (9th Cir. 2002)]; *Apple Computer, Inc. v. Microsoft Corp.*, 35 F.3d 1435, 1446 (9th Cir. 1994).

In filtering out the unique performance elements from consideration, and separating them from those found in the composition, we find substantial assistance in the testimony of Newton's own experts. . . . Newton's experts . . . reveal the extent to which the sound recording of "Choir" is the product of Newton's highly developed performance techniques, rather than the result of a generic rendition of the composition. As a general matter, according to Newton's expert Dr. Christopher Dobrian, "[t]he contribution of the performer is often so great that s/he in fact provides as much musical content as the composer." This is particularly true with works like "Choir," given the improvisational nature of jazz performance and the minimal scoring of the composition. Indeed, as Newton's expert Dr. Oliver Wilson explained:

> [T]he copyrighted score of "Choir," as is the custom in scores written in the jazz tradition, does not contain indications for all of the musical subtleties that it is assumed the performer-composer of the work will make in the work's performance. The function of the score is more mnemonic in intention than prescriptive.

And it is clear that Newton goes beyond the score in his performance. For example, Dr. Dobrian declared that "Mr. Newton blows and sings in such a way as to emphasize the upper partials of the flute's complex harmonic tone, [although] such a modification of tone color is not explicitly requested in the score." Dr. Dobrian also concludes that Newton "uses breath control to modify the timbre of the sustained flute note rather extremely" and "uses portamento to glide expressively from one pitch to another in the vocal part." Dr. Dobrian concedes that these elements do not appear in the score, and that they are part of Newton's performance of the piece. . . .

. . . [R]egardless of whether the average audience might recognize the "Newton technique" at work in the sampled sound recording, those performance elements are beyond consideration in Newton's claim for infringement of his copyright in the underlying composition.

Once we have isolated the basis of Newton's infringement action—the "Choir" composition, devoid of the unique performance elements found only in the sound recording—we turn to the nub of our inquiry: whether Beastie Boys' unauthorized use of the composition, as opposed to their authorized use of the sound recording, was substantial enough to sustain an infringement action. . . . The practice of music sampling will often present cases where the degree of similarity is high. Indeed, unless the sample has been altered or digitally manipulated, it will be identical to the sampled portion of the original recording. Yet as Nimmer explains, "[if] the similarity is only as to nonessential matters, then a finding of no substantial similarity should result." 4 Nimmer §13.03[A][2], at 13-48; *cf. Warner Bros. v. Am. Broad. Cos.*, 720 F.2d 231, 242 (2d Cir. 1983). This reflects the principle that the substantiality requirement applies throughout the law of copyright, including cases of music sampling, even where there is a high degree of similarity.

The high degree of similarity between the works here (i.e., "Pass the Mic" and "Choir"), but the limited scope of the copying, place Newton's claim for infringement into the class of cases that allege what Nimmer refers to as "fragmented literal similarity." 4 Nimmer §13.03[A][2], at 13-45. Fragmented literal similarity exists where the defendant copies a portion of the plaintiff's work exactly or nearly exactly, without appropriating the work's overall essence or structure. *Id.* Because the degree of similarity is high in such cases, the dispositive question is whether the copying goes to trivial or substantial elements. Substantiality is measured by considering the qualitative and quantitative significance of the copied portion in relation to the plaintiff's work as a whole. This focus on the sample's relation to the plaintiff's work as a whole embodies the fundamental question in any infringement action . . . . Courts also focus on the relationship to the plaintiff's work because a contrary rule that measured the significance of the copied segment in the defendant's work would allow an unscrupulous defendant to copy large or qualitatively significant portions of another's work and escape liability by burying them beneath noninfringing material in the defendant's own work, even where the average audience might recognize the appropriation. . . .

On the undisputed facts of this record, no reasonable juror could find the sampled portion of the composition to be a quantitatively or qualitatively significant portion of the composition as a whole. Quantitatively, the three-note sequence appears only once in Newton's composition. It is difficult to measure the precise relationship between this segment and the composition as a whole, because the score calls for between 180 and 270 seconds of improvisation. When played, however, the segment lasts six seconds and is roughly two percent of the four-and-a-half-minute "Choir" sound recording licensed by Beastie Boys. Qualitatively, this section of the composition is no more significant than any other section. Indeed, with the exception of two notes, the entirety of the scored portions of "Choir" consist of notes separated by whole and half-steps from their neighbors and is played with the same technique of singing and playing the flute simultaneously; the remainder of the composition calls for sections of improvisation that range between 90 and 180 seconds in length.

The Beastie Boys' expert, Dr. Lawrence Ferrara, concludes that the compositional elements of the sampled section do not represent the heart or the hook of the "Choir" composition, but rather are "simple, minimal and insignificant." . . . Newton has failed to offer any evidence . . . to rebut Dr. Ferrara's testimony and to create a triable issue of fact on the key question, which is whether the sampled section is a qualitatively significant portion of the "Choir" composition as a whole. Instead, Newton's experts emphasize the uniqueness of the "Newton technique," which is found throughout the "Choir" composition and in Newton's other work. . . .

Because Newton conceded that "Choir" and "Pass the Mic" "are substantially dissimilar in concept and feel, that is, in [their] overall thrust and meaning" and failed to offer any evidence to rebut Dr. Ferrara's testimony that the sampled section is not a quantitatively or qualitatively significant portion of the "Choir" composition, the Beastie Boys are entitled to prevail on summary judgment. . . . [A]n average audience would not discern Newton's hand as a composer, apart from his talent as a performer, from Beastie Boys' use of the sample. The copying was not significant enough to constitute infringement. Beastie Boys' use of the "Choir" composition was de minimis. . . .

GRABER, J., dissenting: . . . As the majority observes, a use is de minimis only if an average audience would not recognize the appropriation. *Fisher v. Dees*, 794 F.2d 432, 434 n.2 (9th Cir. 1986). The majority is correct that James Newton's considerable skill adds many recognizable features to the performance sampled by Beastie Boys. Even after those features are "filtered out," however, the composition, standing alone, is distinctive enough for a fact-finder reasonably to conclude that an average audience would recognize the appropriation of the sampled segment and that Beastie Boys' use was therefore not de minimis.

Newton has presented evidence that the compositional elements of "Choir" are so compositionally distinct that a reasonable listener would recognize the sampled segment even if it were performed by the featured flautist of a middle school orchestra. It is useful to begin by observing that the majority's references to the sampled segment of "Choir" as a "3 note-sequence" are overly simplified. The sampled segment is actually a three-note sequence sung above a fingered held C note, for a total of four separate tones. Even passages with relatively few notes may be qualitatively significant. The opening melody of Beethoven's Fifth Symphony is relatively simple and features only four notes, but it certainly is compositionally distinctive and recognizable.

The majority, while citing the correct standard of review, fails fully to apply it. First, the majority usurps the function of the fact-finder by weighing the opinions of the various experts and emphasizing some parts of their testimony over others. The majority also fails to interpret the evidence in Newton's favor when, for example, it asserts that Newton's experts failed to distinguish between the sound recording and the composition. To the contrary, Newton presented expert evidence that the composition *alone* is distinctive and recognizable.

. . . Professor Wilson acknowledges that much of the distinctiveness of the sampled material is due to Newton's performance and that the copyrighted score does not fully convey the quality of the piece as performed. Nevertheless, Professor Wilson concludes that the score

> clearly indicates that the performer will simultaneously sing and finger specific pitches, gives a sense of the rhythm of the piece, and also provides the general structure of this section of the piece. Hence, in my opinion, the digital sample of the performance . . . is clearly a realization of the musical score filed with the copyright office.

. . . [The letter from Professor Christopher Dobrian] concludes:

> Applying traditional analysis to this brief excerpt from Newton's "Choir"—i.e., focusing solely on the notated pitches—a theorist could conclude (erroneously, in my opinion) that the excerpt contains an insignificant amount of information because it contains a simple "neighboring-tone" figure: C to D-flat and back to C. . . . If, on the other hand, one considers the special playing technique *described in* the score (holding one fingered note constant while singing the other pitches) and the resultant complex, expressive effect that results, it is clear that the "unique expression" of this excerpt is not solely in the pitch choices, but is actually in those particular pitches performed in that particular way on that instrument. These components in this particular combination are not found anywhere else in the notated music literature, and they are *unique and distinctive* in their sonic/musical result.

(Emphasis added.)

Professor Dobrian is not talking about Newton's performance of the sampled portion. Rather, he is speaking of the distinctiveness of the underlying composition. The "playing technique" is not a matter of personal performance, but is a built-in feature of the score itself. In essence, Dobrian is stating that *any* flautist's performance of the sampled segment would be distinctive and recognizable, because the score itself is distinctive and recognizable. . . .

The majority also asserts that Newton failed to offer evidence to rebut Beastie Boys' expert on the question whether the sampled section of "Choir" is qualitatively significant. Again, the majority improperly discounts, or improperly interprets, Dr. Dobrian's unequivocal description of the sampled passage: "These components in this particular combination are not found anywhere else in the notated music literature, and they are unique and distinctive in their sonic/musical result." A fact-finder would be entitled to find either that the sampled passage is trivial and trite (Beastie Boys' expert) or, instead, that it is "unique and distinctive" in the musical literature (Newton's expert).

Because Newton has presented evidence establishing that reasonable ears differ over the qualitative significance of the composition of the sampled material, summary judgment is inappropriate in this case. . . .

Bridgeport Music, Inc. v. Dimension Films
410 F.3d 792 (6th Cir. 2005)

GUY, J.: . . . This action arises out of the use of a sample from the composition and sound recording "Get Off Your Ass and Jam" ("Get Off") in the rap song "100 Miles and Runnin" ("100 Miles"), which was included in the sound track of the movie *I Got the Hook Up* (*Hook Up*). Specifically, [plaintiff] Westbound [Records, Inc.] appeals from the district court's decision to grant summary judgment to defendant on the grounds that the alleged infringement was *de minimis* . . . .

I. . . .

Bridgeport and Westbound claim to own the musical composition and sound recording copyrights in "Get Off Your Ass and Jam" by George Clinton, Jr. and the Funkadelics. We assume, as did the district court, that plaintiffs would be able to establish ownership in the copyrights they claim. There seems to be no dispute either that "Get Off" was digitally sampled or that the recording "100 Miles" was included on the sound track of *I Got the Hook Up*. Defendant No Limit Films, in conjunction with Priority Records, released the movie to theaters on May 27, 1998. The movie was apparently also released on VHS, DVD, and cable television. Fatal to Bridgeport's claims of infringement [of the musical work copyright] was the Release and Agreement it entered into with two of the original owners of the composition "100 Miles," . . . granting a sample use license . . . . Finding that No Limit Films had previously been granted an oral synchronization license to use the composition "100 Miles" in the sound track of *Hook Up,* the district court concluded Bridgeport's claims against No Limit Films were barred by the unambiguous terms of the Release and Agreement. . . .

Westbound's claims are for infringement of the sound recording "Get Off." Because defendant does not deny it, we assume that the sound track of *Hook Up* used portions of "100 Miles" that included the allegedly infringing sample from "Get Off." The recording "Get Off" opens with a three-note combination solo guitar "riff" that lasts four seconds. According to one of plaintiffs' experts, Randy Kling, the recording "100 Miles" contains a sample from that guitar solo. Specifically, a two-second sample from the guitar solo was copied, the pitch was lowered, and the copied piece was "looped" and extended to 16 beats. Kling states that this sample appears in the sound recording "100 Miles" in five places; specifically, at 0:49, 1:52, 2:29, 3:20 and 3:46. By the district court's estimation, each looped segment lasted approximately 7 seconds. As for the segment copied from "Get Off," the district court described it as follows:

> The portion of the song at issue here is an arpeggiated chord—that is, three notes that, if struck together, comprise a chord but instead are played one at a time in very quick succession—that is repeated several times at the opening of "Get Off." The arpeggiated chord is played on an unaccompanied electric guitar. The rapidity of the notes and the way they are played produce a high-pitched, whirling sound that captures the listener's attention and creates anticipation of what is to follow.

Bridgeport, 230 F. Supp. 2d at 839. . . .

II. . . .

. . . After listening to the copied segment, the sample, and both songs, the district court found that no reasonable juror, even one familiar with the works of George Clinton, would recognize the source of the sample without having been told of its source. This finding, coupled with findings concerning the quantitatively small amount of copying involved and the lack of qualitative similarity between the works, led the district court to conclude that Westbound could not prevail on its claims for copyright infringement of the sound recording.

Westbound does not challenge the district court's characterization of either the segment copied from "Get Off" or the sample that appears in "100 Miles." . . . The heart of Westbound's arguments is the claim that no substantial similarity or *de minimis* inquiry should be undertaken at all when the defendant has not disputed that it digitally sampled a copyrighted sound recording. We agree . . . .

B. Analysis . . .

Before discussing what we believe to be the import of [the relevant statutory language], a little history is necessary. The copyright laws attempt to strike a balance between protecting original works and stifling further creativity. The provisions, for example, for compulsory licensing make it possible for "creators" to enjoy the fruits of their creations, but not to fence them off from the world at large. 17 U.S.C. §115. Although musical compositions have always enjoyed copyright protection, it was not until 1971 that sound recordings were subject to a separate copyright. . . . The balance that was struck was to give sound recording copyright holders the exclusive right "to duplicate the sound recording in the form of phonorecords or copies that directly or indirectly recapture the actual sounds fixed in the recording." 17 U.S.C. §114(b). This means that the world at large is free to imitate or simulate the creative work fixed in the recording so long as an actual copy of the sound recording itself is not made. . . .

Section 114(b) provides that "[t]he exclusive right of the owner of copyright in a sound recording under clause (2) of section 106 is limited to the right to prepare a derivative work in which the actual sounds fixed in the sound recording are rearranged, remixed, or otherwise altered in sequence or quality." Further, the rights of sound recording copyright holders under clauses (1) and (2) of section 106 "do not extend to the making or duplication of another sound recording that consists *entirely* of an independent fixation of other sounds, even though such sounds imitate or simulate those in the copyrighted sounds recording." 17 U.S.C. §114(b) (emphasis added). The significance of this provision is amplified by the fact that the Copyright Act of 1976 added the word "entirely" to this language. In other words, a sound recording owner has the exclusive right to "sample" his own recording. We find much to recommend this interpretation.

To begin with, there is ease of enforcement. Get a license or do not sample. We do not see this as stifling creativity in any significant way. It must be remembered that if an artist wants to incorporate a "riff" from another work in his or her recording, he is free to duplicate the sound of that "riff" in the studio. Second, the market will control the license price and keep it within bounds. The sound recording copyright holder cannot exact a license fee greater than what it would cost the person seeking the license to just duplicate the sample in the course of making the new recording. Third, sampling is never accidental. It is not like the case of a composer who has a melody in his head, perhaps not even realizing that the reason he hears this melody is that it is the work of another which he had heard before. When you sample a sound recording you know you are taking another's work product.

This analysis admittedly raises the question of why one should, without infringing, be able to take three notes from a musical composition, for example, but not three notes by way of sampling from a sound recording. . . . Our first answer to this question is what we have earlier indicated. We think this result is dictated by the applicable statute. Second, even when a small part of a sound recording is sampled, the part taken is something of value. No further proof of that is necessary than the fact that the producer of the record or the artist on the record intentionally sampled because it would (1) save costs, or (2) add something to the new recording, or (3) both. For the sound recording copyright holder, it is not the "song" but the sounds that are fixed in the medium of his choice. When those sounds are sampled they are taken directly from that fixed medium. It is a physical taking rather than an intellectual one.

This case also illustrates the kind of mental, musicological, and technological gymnastics that would have to be employed if one were to adopt a *de minimis* or substantial similarity analysis. . . . We would want to emphasize, however, that considerations of judicial economy are not what drives this opinion. If any consideration of economy is involved it is that of the music industry. As this case and other companion cases make clear, it would appear to be cheaper to license than to litigate.

. . . The record companies and performing artists are not all of one mind, however, since in many instances, today's sampler is tomorrow's samplee. The incidence of "live and let live" has been relatively high, which explains why so many instances of sampling go unprotested and why so many sampling controversies have been settled.

. . . [T]o pursue further the subject of stifling creativity, many artists and record companies have sought licenses as a matter of course. Since there is no record of those instances of sampling that either go unnoticed or are ignored, one cannot come up with precise figures, but it is clear that a significant number of persons and companies have elected to go the licensing route. Also there is a large body of pre-1972 sound recordings that is not subject to federal copyright protection. Additionally, just as many artists and companies choose to sample and take their chances, it is likely that will continue to be the case.

> ### LOOKING FORWARD
>
> The suggestion that pre-1972 sound recordings are available for sampling may be incorrect. Section 301(c) of the Act, which we discuss in more detail in Chapter 15, expressly preserves state law protection for sound recordings fixed prior to February 15, 1972.

... [T]he record industry, including the recording artists, has the ability and know-how to work out guidelines, including a fixed schedule of license fees, if they so choose. ...

... Since the district judge found no infringement, there was no necessity to consider the affirmative defense of "fair use." On remand, the trial judge is free to consider this defense and we express no opinion on its applicability to these facts. ...

NOTES AND QUESTIONS

1. Is explicit recognition of a "*de minimis* use" shelter for sampling a good idea? Why, or why not? How well does the *Newton* court's opinion define the line between permissible copying and improper appropriation?

2. Arguably, the problem in *Newton* was that it was impossible to use the licensed sound recording without also using the composition. Does the *de minimis* use rule in effect allow a royalty-free license for underlying musical works under limited circumstances? If so, why shouldn't the same rule apply when the underlying musical work is licensed but the sound recording is not, as in *Bridgeport*?

3. Do you agree with the *Bridgeport* court's reading of the statute? Is §114 meant to limit or expand the rights granted in §106? *Bridgeport's* bright-line rule has not been adopted by other circuit courts, and at least one district court has expressly rejected the Sixth Circuit's approach, finding the statutory interpretation flawed. *Saregama India Ltd. v. Mosley*, 687 F. Supp. 2d 1325 (S.D. Fla. 2009), *aff'd on other grounds*, 635 F.3d 1284 (11th Cir. 2011).

4. The *Bridgeport* court concluded that its bright-line rule, "[g]et a license or do not sample," was also sound policy. Do you agree? In deciding this question, would it be important to understand why recording artists sample when, as the court notes, they are free to make sound-alike recordings? Consider the following excerpt:

> Cultural judgments about borrowing, repetition and originality are central to understanding legal evaluations of both sampling and hip hop. Repetition expressed through sampling and looping has been, for much of the history of hip hop, an inherent part of what makes hip hop music identifiably hip hop. Consequently, the question of whether and how sampling should be permitted is in some measure an inquiry about how and to what extent hip hop can and should continue to exist as a

musical form. Copyright standards, particularly in the music area, must have greater flexibility to accommodate varying styles and types of musical production, whether based on an African American aesthetic of repetition and revision, a postmodern style, transformative imitation and borrowing in the manner of Handel, allusion as practiced by Brahms or another aesthetic that fails to conform to the Romantic author ideal that has to this point been integral to copyright.

Musical borrowing is not necessarily antithetical to originality or creativity. The conceptions of creativity and originality that pervade copyright discussions are incomplete or inaccurate models of actual musical production, particularly the collaborative aspects of musical practice evident in borrowing. Similarly, views of past musical composition should be tempered with a recognition of the operation of invented traditions and cultural ideals that play a powerful role in shaping both representations and contemporary beliefs and attitudes.

Olufunmilayo B. Arewa, *From J.C. Bach to Hip Hop: Musical Borrowing, Copyright, and Cultural Context*, 84 N.C. L. Rev. 547, 630-31 (2006); *see also* K. J. Greene, *Copyright, Culture & Black Music: A Legacy of Unequal Protection*, 21 Hastings Comm. & Ent. L.J. 339 (1999) (exploring how copyright rules functioned to routinely deny protection to African American music artists). Should Professor Arewa's analysis inform the legal treatment of sampling? If so, in what way?

D. PUBLIC PERFORMANCE

As you know from Chapter 6, §106 grants copyright owners not only the right to reproduce the work in copies, but also the right to publicly perform that work. Musical work copyright owners are granted a general public performance right under §106(4) while sound recording copyright owners are granted a narrower right to control only public performance "by means of a digital audio transmission." 17 U.S.C. §106(6).

1. Musical Works and Performing Rights Organizations

Although copyright owners of musical works were first granted a public performance right in 1897, it was not until almost 20 years later that this right began to have significant revenue potential. The problem concerned transaction costs: How were all of the different copyright owners realistically going to be able to detect and collect royalties for each public performance of their works in restaurants, dance halls, and theaters? To solve the transaction cost problem, a group of nine music business luminaries, headed by attorney Nathan Burkan, established ASCAP in 1913. After its successful litigation of *Herbert v. Shanley*, 242 U.S. 591 (1917), *see supra* Chapter 6.B, which established that licenses were needed for live performances of musical works in for-profit establishments, ASCAP began the business of collective licensing, bringing together thousands of musical works and offering to license them under a blanket license agreement.

Next, as radio increased in popularity during the 1930s, ASCAP brought litigation to establish that music performed on the radio was for profit and required authorization. In 1939, after ASCAP began raising its fees considerably, radio broadcasters formed their own performing rights organization (PRO), BMI. Some of ASCAP's members had developed a general sense that ASCAP's distribution of royalty payments was unjust, and agreed to join the new organization. However, BMI managed to lure away only one major music publisher, and its signing of new and less established artists was accomplished mainly through the use of advance payments against future royalties. Nonetheless, on January 1, 1941, radio stations began a boycott of ASCAP music, instead broadcasting almost exclusively Latin music, which ASCAP had thus far ignored. ASCAP was forced to the bargaining table, and signed a new deal with the radio broadcasters in October 1941. After establishing a foothold in Latin music, BMI expanded its catalog to include musical works of all kinds. (The third PRO, SESAC, was established in 1930 in Nashville, Tennessee, with an initial foothold in country music, and now also has a varied catalog of works).

Today, a license from ASCAP, BMI, or SESAC will allow a business to publicly perform all of the musical works in the PRO's catalog. Different licenses are available depending on the nature of the business. For example, ASCAP has license agreements for restaurants, dance schools, bowling alleys, festivals, private clubs, funeral establishments, and music on hold. As discussed in Section 7.B.1 above, streaming music over the Internet does not constitute a DPD and thus is not covered by the §115 mechanical license. Web streaming is, instead, a public performance. ASCAP, BMI, and SESAC all offer webcasting licenses for the musical works in their respective catalogs.

Public performance royalties paid to the PROs are divided among rightholders (typically, music publishers) according to formulas determined by each PRO. To make that process more accurate, the PROs use a variety of sampling procedures to determine how often different songs are being played. Payments to music publishers typically are then split 50/50 with the songwriters.

Over the years, ASCAP's and BMI's practice of pooling thousands of copyrights and then offering blanket licenses to publicly perform those works on an all-or-nothing basis has raised claims of antitrust violations. Cases filed in the 1940s and 1950s by the Justice Department's Antitrust Division resulted in consent decrees that continue to govern aspects of the operations of both ASCAP and BMI. The federal district court for the Southern District of New York administers the ASCAP and BMI consent decrees. One of the requirements of those consent decrees is that a potential licensee may apply to the court for a binding determination of "reasonable fees" in the event that the licensee and the PRO cannot come to an agreement on the fee to be paid.

NOTES AND QUESTIONS

1. Should something that qualifies as a DPD also qualify as a performance? Recall that a public performance includes one transmitted "to the public, by means of any device or process, whether the members of the public capable of receiving the performance or display receive it in the same place or in separate places and at the same time or at different times." 17 U.S.C. §101. Does it matter if the receiving computer is set up to automatically play the downloaded song? In *United States v. ASCAP*, 485 F. Supp. 2d 438 (S.D.N.Y. 2008), the court rejected ASCAP's argument that downloading constitutes a public performance, concluding that "in light of the distinct classification and treatment of performances and reproductions under the Act . . . Congress did not intend the two uses to overlap to the extent proposed by ASCAP . . . ." *Id.* at 447.

2. Should the result change if the DPD is a ringtone delivered to a mobile phone and the individual then programs the phone to play the ringtone whenever a call is received? *See* In re *Application of Cellco Partnership*, 663 F. Supp. 2d 363 (S.D.N.Y. 2009) (holding that use of a copyrighted ringtone by a mobile phone subscriber is not a public performance and that in any event, such a performance would be covered by the §110(4) limitation for certain nonprofit performances).

3. Unlike compulsory licenses and royalty pooling, PROs are not the result of any congressional action. Which is the better approach? Compulsory licenses reduce transaction costs by setting the terms of the agreement and by providing administrative support in the form of record keeping, royalty collection, and distribution. Collective rights organizations such as PROs also reduce transaction costs, but do so in a different way.

> In a [collective rights organization ("CRO")], knowledgeable industry participants set the rules of exchange. These rules are not likely to be uniform, one-size-fits-all terms as in a statutory compulsory license; they often vary according to the broad features of the rights. Individual works covered by discrete [intellectual property rights] are assigned to categories based on the members' knowledge and experience. Through this expert tailoring, CROs produce an intermediate level of contract detail, reflecting not only collective industry expertise but also the need for efficiency in carrying out a high volume of transactions.
>
> An important component of expert tailoring, then, is the use of royalty rates as set by experts. But the statutory compulsory licenses often begin with rational royalty rates as well. What separates private CROs from compulsory licensing schemes is that the former have proven to be more flexible over time. ASCAP, for example, frequently adjusts the rates it charges radio and television stations. Statutes, on the other hand, are difficult to change. Because interested parties can often spend enough to veto a change in legislation, compulsory licenses in the [intellectual property rights] field are subject to "legislative lock-in." CROs avoid this problem.

Robert P. Merges, *Contracting into Liability Rules: Intellectual Property Rights and Collective Rights Organizations*, 84 Cal. L. Rev. 1293, 1295-96 (1996). While legislative lock-in is certainly a problem for statutorily established rights, the lock-in associated with licensing rates has been tempered through the use of panels of Copyright Royalty Judges to periodically revise rates. In addition, the antitrust decrees that govern the two main PROs for the public performance rights of musical work copyright owners restrict the extent of permissible tailoring. How do these considerations affect your evaluation of which is a better approach, PROs or compulsory licenses? Do these rate revisions affect your evaluation of Professor Merges's argument?

2. Public Performance of Sound Recordings by Digital Audio Transmission

Following the recognition of a sound recording copyright in 1971, copyright owners lobbied for a public performance right, but strong opposition from broadcasters thwarted any attempted legislation. The potential for digital audio transmissions to supplant purchases of CDs and DPDs finally outweighed objections by the broadcast industry, and Congress added subsection (6) to §106 in 1995. While §106(4) grants copyright owners of musical works the right to publicly perform their works, §106(6) grants sound recording copyright owners a more limited public performance right covering only public performances that occur "by means of a digital audio transmission." Because sound recordings are not protected by a general public performance right, no license is required to publicly perform those sound recordings in most cases, whether the performance is by a DJ playing music in a nightclub, piped-in music in an elevator, or jukeboxes blasting out the latest hits. The §106(6) right is further qualified by a number of exemptions and statutory licenses, which are codified in §114.

Understanding the exemptions from the §106(6) right and the types of activities for which a statutory license is available is easier if one keeps the policy behind the law in mind. First, the amendment represents Congress' attempt to address the concerns of the recording industry without "upsetting the longstanding business and contractual relationships among record producers and performers, music composers and publishers and broadcasters that have served all of these industries well for decades." S. Rep. No. 104-128, at 17 (1995). To that end, Congress exempted "nonsubscription broadcast transmission[s]." 17 U.S.C. §114(d)(1)(A)-(B). Pursuant to rules issued by the Copyright Office and subsequently upheld in court, this exemption covers only free, over-the-air digital broadcasts by FCC-licensed broadcasters. *See* Public Performance of Sound Recordings: Definition of a Service, Final Rule, 65 Fed. Reg. 77292 (Dec. 11, 2000); *see also Bonneville Int'l Corp. v. Peters,* 347 F.3d 485 (3d Cir. 2003). Such broadcasts only require authorization from the musical work copyright owners. Internet transmission, even of the same broadcasts, is not covered by the exemption, and requires either a statutory license or a negotiated license.

Second, Congress' purpose in granting sound recording copyright owners a limited public performance right was to guard against harm to the market for sales of phonorecords. If an individual can hear the songs she wants at any time she wants, she will be unlikely to purchase phonorecords of those songs. Thus, those digital transmissions that are "interactive"—i.e., that "enable[] a member of the public to receive a transmission of a program specially created for the recipient, or on request, a transmission of a particular sound recording, whether or not as part of a program, which is selected by or on behalf of the recipient," 17 U.S.C. §114(j)(7)— are not exempt, nor are they eligible for statutory licensing; the webcaster must negotiate a license directly with the sound recording copyright owner. *See id.* §114(d)(2). (Remember, authorization from the musical work copyright owner will also be necessary.) Archived programs that allow individuals to effectively rewind and fast forward through the program also are considered "interactive."

The third category of digital audio transmissions consists of those covered by the statutory license. Services that digitally perform sound recordings but are not interactive can utilize the statutory license codified in §114(d) if they (1) do not use a signal that causes the receiver to change from one program channel to another; (2) do not pre-announce the broadcast of particular songs; (3) include various information about the recording being transmitted if feasible; and (4) do not violate the "sound recording performance complement." *See id.* The sound recording performance complement is defined as

> the transmission during any 3-hour period, on a particular channel used by a transmitting entity, of no more than—
> (A) 3 different selections of sound recordings from any one phonorecord lawfully distributed for public performance or sale in the United States, if no more than 2 such selections are transmitted consecutively; or
> (B) 4 different selections of sound recordings—
>> (i) by the same featured—recording artist; or
>> (ii) from any set or compilation of phonorecords lawfully distributed together as
> a unit for public performance or sale in the United States, if no more than three such selections are transmitted consecutively . . .

Id. §114(j)(13). A webcaster that exceeds the numerical limits may still qualify if the programming transmitted "was not willfully intended to avoid the numerical limitations prescribed." *Id.* The vast majority of webcasting stations attempt to stay within the definition so that they can use the statutory license scheme.

Reconciling user demand for tailored programming with the complicated requirements for remaining on the noninteractive side of the line requires careful system design. Webcasters have developed sophisticated algorithms for creating personalized stations based on user feedback and, inevitably, such efforts have led to litigation. The statutory definition of "interactive" refers to programs "specially created" for users but does not define that term. The House Conference Report indicates that a transmission would be considered interactive "if a transmission recipient is permitted to select particular sound recordings in a prerecorded or predetermined program," or "if a transmission recipient has the ability to move forward and backward between songs in a program." H.R. Rep. No. 105-796, at 88 (Conf. Rep.). In litigation over the LAUNCHcast digital music service (which eventually became Yahoo! Music), the court described the defendant's process for creating personalized radio stations as follows:

> . . . First, the user is prompted to select artists whose music the user prefers. The user is then asked which music genres the user enjoys and asked to rate the genres on a scale. The user is also asked the percentage of new music - songs the user has not previously rated - the user would like to incorporate into the user's station (the "unrated quota") and whether the user permits playing songs with profane lyrics. The minimum unrated quota is 20%, meaning no less than 20% of the songs played can be unrated.
> Once LAUNCHcast begins playing music based on the user's preferred artists and genres, the user rates the songs, artists, or albums LAUNCHcast plays between zero and 100, with 100 being the best rating. . . . While a song is playing, the user has the ability to pause the song, skip the song, or delete the song from the station by rating the song zero. Notably, the user may not go back to restart the song that is playing, or repeat any of the previously played songs in the playlist.

Whenever the user logs into LAUNCHcast and selects a station, LAUNCHcast generates a playlist of fifty songs based on several variables. LAUNCHcast does not provide a list of the pool of songs or of the songs in the generated playlist, and therefore, the user does not know what songs might be played. LAUNCHcast selects the songs by first looking to the unrated quota and whether to exclude songs with profane lyrics or songs that cannot be transmitted over the user's bandwidth. Next LAUNCHcast creates a list of all the potential songs that can be put in the playlist (called a "hashtable"). LAUNCHcast then generates a list of all songs played for the user within the last thirty days, a list of all DJs, genres, and radio stations to which the user subscribes, and a list of all the ratings of all the songs, artists, and albums rated by either the user or any DJ to which the user subscribes. Songs that the user has rated are "explicitly rated" songs. LAUNCHcast "implicitly rates" songs that appear in an album that the user or a subscribed-to DJ has rated and songs that appear in the same album as another song the user has already rated. All of these songs are initially added to the hashtable. LAUNCHcast then excludes: (1) all songs that the user, or a DJ to which the user subscribes, requests be skipped permanently (rated as zero) and (2) songs played within the last three hours for the user on any LAUNCHcast station. This yields approximately 4,000 songs.

LAUNCHcast then adds to the hashtable the 1,000 most popular songs—songs most highly rated by all LAUNCHcast users—in the bandwidth specified by the user, provided those songs are not already on the hashtable. [The court describes in detail the creation of the hashtable, which eventually contains approximately 10,000 songs. To create a playlist of 50 songs LAUNCHcast randomly selects songs from the hashtable and tests each song to determine if it should be discarded based on a set of rules.] . . .

. . . .LAUNCHcast does not play the same song twice in a playlist [and] LAUNCHcast excludes a song from a playlist if three other songs by that artist have already been selected for the playlist. . . . LAUNCHcast excludes a song from a playlist if two other songs from the same album have already been selected for the playlist. . . .

Finally, once all fifty songs are selected for the playlist, LAUNCHcast orders the playlist. The ordering of the songs is random, provided LAUNCHcast does not play more than two songs in the same album or three songs by the same artist consecutively. . . .

Arista Records, LLC v. Launch Media, Inc., 578 F.3d 148, 157-160 (2d Cir. 2009).

The court held that even though any playlist generated through this process was "unique to that user at that particular time," that did not necessarily make it "specially created" for purposes of the statutory definition of "interactive." *Id.* at 162. Rather, according to the court, the statutory touchstone for interactivity is predictability. LAUNCHcast was noninteractive because it did "not provide sufficient control to users such that playlists are so predictable that users will choose to listen to the webcast in lieu of purchasing music, thereby—in the aggregate—diminishing record sales." *Id.*

The royalty rates for the §114 statutory license are to be determined by voluntary industry negotiation, with referral to the Copyright Royalty Judges (CRJs) if no agreement can be achieved. 17 U.S.C. §§114(j), 804(a). After a panel of CRJs established a per-performance, per-listener escalating royalty rate for all stations that exceeded a monthly aggregate tuning-hours threshold, webcasters protested that rates computed in that manner would drive them out of business. In response, Congress passed additional legislation authorizing SoundExchange to enter into webcasting licenses on behalf of all sound recording copyright owners and performers. In 2009, the Copyright Office announced a series of agreements that SoundExchange had reached with various webcasting entities and indicated that the rates and terms in the agreements are "available to any webcasters meeting the respective eligibility conditions of the agreements as an alternative to the rates and terms of any determination by the Copyright Royalty Judges." *See* U.S. Copyright Office, *Notification of Agreements Under the Webcaster Settlement Act of 2008*, 74 Fed. Reg. 9293 (Mar. 3, 2009); U.S. Copyright Office, *Notification of Agreements Under the Webcaster Settlement Act of 2009*, 74 Fed. Reg. 34796 (July 17, 2009) and 74 Fed. Reg. 40614 (August 12, 2009). In 2013, SoundExchange reported licensing revenue of $650 million.

The §114 statutory license also mandates direct payments to the performing artists. Statutory license royalties collected by SoundExchange are split between featured artists (45%) and sound recording copyright owners (50%), with the remaining 5% divided between a fund for nonfeatured artists, typically session musicians, and a fund for background singers. 17 U.S.C. §114(g)(2).

NOTES AND QUESTIONS

1. Should Congress have drafted the exemption in §114(d)(1) broadly enough to cover free, over-the-air radio stations that simultaneously transmit their broadcasts via the Web? Why, or why not? How would that affect competition in the webcasting market?

2. Why did the *Arista Records* court need to give such a detailed description of the manner in which LAUNCHcast selected the music to be played for a listener? Do you agree with the court's determination that LAUNCHcast was not an interactive service? Recognize what is at stake in the determination: The defendant must pay a license fee; the question is whether it will be able to use the statutory license or whether it will need to obtain individually negotiated licenses.

3. Note that SoundExchange became a PRO by accident; as originally drafted, the amendment adding the §106(6) public performance right for sound recordings did not give SoundExchange the authority to negotiate rates. What do you think of the SoundExchange model? How does it compare with the musical work PROs that you read about in Section 7.D.1, above?

PROBLEMS

Review your answers to the Problems in Section 7.B.1 *supra*, and then consider the following:

1. If Cole Vosbury wants permission to publicly perform his version of "Maggie May" from whom must he get permission?
2. If a college radio station wants permission to publicly perform Vosbury's recording of "Maggie May," from whom must it get permission? What if it wants to stream the recording over the Internet?

PRACTICE EXERCISE: ADVOCACY

Legislation to give sound recording copyright owners broader public performance rights has been pending in Congress for the past several years. As amended §106(6) of the Copyright Act would read as follows: "in the case of sound recordings, to perform the copyrighted work publicly by means of an audio transmission." Noncommercial radio stations, including public, educational, and religious stations would have the option of paying a nominal, annual flat fee, and the legislation would provide similar relief for commercial stations with annual revenue under $1.25 million, which currently comprise approximately 75 percent of all music radio stations. Most other industrialized countries already provide similar protection for performance rights for sound recordings. The bill has broad support, including from quarters traditionally resistant to the expansion of copyright rights, but the National Association of Broadcasters has opposed it. If you were a lobbyist for the Recording Industry Association of America, how would you convince a congressperson to vote for the bill?

---

3. Technological Disruption and the Future of Music

The options for experiencing music continue to evolve with technological change, yet the complicated layers of copyright rights that must be cleared create obstacles for new market entrants involved in digital music transmissions. Each of the major rightholder groups, meanwhile, has found reasons to be unhappy with its own share of the revenues resulting from current licensing arrangements. The resulting disputes suggest that more fundamental change may be brewing.

Like the LAUNCHcast service described in Section 7.D.2 above, the webcasting service Pandora uses complicated algorithms in an effort to stay within the §114 statutory license for the sound recordings that it performs. To clear the musical work public performance rights, Pandora obtained blanket licenses from the three PROs (ASCAP, BMI, and SESAC). The rates Pandora paid to the musical work PROs, combined, totaled approximately 4 percent of its revenue. The rate it paid for clearing the sound recording performance rights was much higher, approximately 48 percent.[*] Citing the stark difference in royalty rates, the major music publishers attempted to withdraw the authorization for the PROs to license "new media" public performances. Pandora instituted rate court proceedings against both ASCAP and BMI to challenge the attempted partial withdrawal and to obtain a rate for its blanket licenses. Below is an excerpt from the rate court's decision:

---

[*] Pandora's 10-K filing from February 2014 (covering a later time period) stated that: "For the eleven months ended December 31, 2013 we incurred SoundExchange related content acquisition costs representing 48% of our total revenue for that period."

≣ *In Re Pandora Media, Inc.*
   6 F. Supp. 3d 317 (S.D.N.Y. 2014)

COTE, J.: . . . .

B. The ASCAP Consent Decree

Since 1941, ASCAP has operated under a consent decree stemming from a Department of Justice antitrust lawsuit. This consent decree has been modified from time to time. The most recent version of the consent decree was issued in 2001 and is known as "AFJ2." AFJ2 governs here.

In an attempt to ameliorate the anti-competitive concerns raised by ASCAP's consolidation of music licenses, AFJ2 restricts how ASCAP may issue licenses in a variety of ways. . . . AFJ2 requires ASCAP to grant a license to perform all of the musical compositions in ASCAP's repertoire to any entity that requests such a license. . . . AFJ2 [also] prevents ASCAP from discriminating in pricing or with respect to other terms or conditions between "similarly situated" licensees. ASCAP members agree to be bound in the exercise of their copyright rights by the terms of AFJ2. . . .

In addition to operating under a consent decree, ASCAP is governed by a series of internal rules and contracts. The most important internal rule set for purposes of this litigation is the ASCAP Compendium. The ASCAP Compendium can be modified by the ASCAP Board and reflects many of the important rules that govern ASCAP's obligations to its copyright holder members and vice versa. . . .

IV. Pandora

Pandora is the most successful internet radio service operating in the United States today. It is estimated to have approximately 200 million registered users worldwide and an approximately 70% share of the internet radio market in the United States. Pandora launched its internet radio service in 2005. Roughly eight years later, it had achieved great popularity, streaming an average of 17.7 billion songs per month in the fiscal year 2013.

A. Pandora's Music Genome Project

Pandora's exponential growth and popularity can be directly attributed to its substantial investment in its proprietary Music Genome Project ("MGP") database and associated algorithms. Pandora uses the MGP database to create customized internet radio stations for each of its customers. A Pandora customer creates a station by "seeding" it with a song, artist, genre, or composer. That seed serves as a starting point to which Pandora then applies the information in its MGP database to match that seed with other songs that Pandora's algorithms predict that the listener is likely to enjoy. The listener continues to give feedback by giving a thumbs-up or thumbs-down when a composition is played, or by signaling that a song should be skipped. . . .

Pandora has a catalog of between approximately 1,000,000 to 2,000,000 songs, somewhat less than half of which are licensed through ASCAP. This number is considerably lower than the catalog size of an on-demand service like Spotify, which must have the ability to play virtually any composition any customer might select. Successful on-demand services have catalogs in the range of 20 million songs. . . .

VI. *The April 2011 ASCAP Compendium Modification*

A. *Overview and Context*

In 2011, ASCAP modified its Compendium to permit its members to selectively withdraw from ASCAP the right to license works to new media entities. This was an unprecedented event. Never before had ASCAP granted partial withdrawal rights to its members. . . . In the year and a half that followed the adoption of the modification of the Compendium, three of the four largest music publishers withdrew their new media rights from ASCAP. . . .

To place the Compendium modification in broader context, it was simply one of the many ripple effects that have followed the onset of the digital age in the music business, and the industry's attempt to recover from the concomitant decline in some types of music sales. The modification of the Compendium came in response to pressure from ASCAP's largest music publishers. These publishers were focused principally on the disparity between the enormous fees paid by Pandora to record companies for sound recording rights and the significantly lower amount it paid to the PROs for public performance rights to compositions. The modification was enacted despite significant concern about the impact of this change on ASCAP, its writers and its independent publishers. . . .

VIII. *Pandora Negotiates Direct Licenses with EMI, Sony, and UMPG [, i.e., Universal Music Publishing Group,] and Fails to Negotiate an Agreement with ASCAP.*

A. *The Pandora–EMI License Negotiations*

Upon learning in May 2011 of EMI's withdrawal of its new media licensing rights from ASCAP, Pandora immediately began to negotiate with EMI for a license to its catalog. The negotiations were not contentious and the contours of the license were quickly settled. . . .

B. *The Pandora–ASCAP License Negotiations*

. . . [In October 2010, Pandora had applied] for a new license for the calendar years 2011 through 2015. It remained an applicant for such a license throughout 2011 and 2012, as ASCAP adopted its modification to the Compendium and as EMI withdrew new media rights from ASCAP. . . .

. . . [O]n September 28, 2012, Pandora learned that Sony was also withdrawing its new media rights from ASCAP. With its discussions with ASCAP "languish[ing]," and with Sony's withdrawal from ASCAP due to take effect at year end, which was just weeks away, Pandora filed this rate court petition on November 5.

Pandora's filing in rate court angered some in the ASCAP community, particularly the major publishers. They expressed their outrage not only to Pandora, but also to its outside counsel . . . . The day after the rate court filing, UMPG's [Chairman and CEO, Zach] Horowitz called one of Pandora's attorneys at Greenberg Traurig. As Horowitz promptly memorialized in an email to ASCAP's [CEO] LoFrumento, Horowitz

> told [Pandora's outside counsel], as a "friend" of the firm, that I thought both the firm and Pandora are completely tone deaf. That whether his firm has the legal right to rep Pandora in litigation, the firm has lost huge goodwill with writers and artists by doing so. And that filing now for a rate court proceeding against ASCAP . . . had the effect of unifying artists, writers, and PROs against Pandora.

Horowitz also gave some advice to LoFrumento regarding ASCAP's negotiating stance with Pandora. His advice boiled down to two words: be strong. Horowitz wrote:

> My take: [Pandora's outside counsel] and Pandora are scared. They just want to settle with ASCAP and settle fast. Be strong. Time is on your side. Pandora is now under intense pressure to settle with ASCAP. They have to put this behind them. You can really push Pandora and get a much better settlement as a result. They are reeling. They will pay more, a lot more than they originally intended, to do that.

. . . LoFrumento assured Horowitz that he was approaching Pandora with the mindset Horowitz advocated. . . .

Not surprisingly, given the fallout from Pandora's filing of the rate court petition, and with the deadline for Sony's withdrawal from ASCAP approaching, the negotiations between Pandora and ASCAP intensified. Had those negotiations succeeded, of course, this rate court action would have become moot.

By the end of November, Pandora believed that it had reached an agreement on terms with ASCAP, although it understood that the agreement needed final approval from ASCAP. . . . ASCAP had assured Pandora that if they finalized their agreement before the end of 2012, the license would cover the Sony repertoire since the Sony withdrawal from ASCAP was only effective as of January 1, 2013.

LoFrumento decided to reject the license that his team had negotiated with Pandora. He knew that either way he faced litigation. He knew that if he executed the license, Sony would sue ASCAP. Sony had threatened to sue ASCAP in the event any license agreement with Pandora that encompassed the Sony repertoire was executed before the end of 2012. Sony had also notified ASCAP that it might not use ASCAP for administration services if ASCAP issued a license to Pandora. LoFrumento was already facing rate court litigation with Pandora. . . .

Thus, in mid-December 2012, ASCAP set itself on a course to have its rate for licensing Pandora set in this rate court proceeding, despite the cost associated with that litigation. The decision was made in the midst of great turmoil, uncertainty and pressure. The partial withdrawals of new media rights by major publishers, who collectively controlled about 50% of ASCAP's music, threatened to make ASCAP a weaker organization. Sony and UMPG had also made clear to LoFrumento that they wanted to negotiate direct licenses with Pandora and opposed ASCAP entering into a final license with Pandora. There was, of course, a chance that by placating the major publishers, they might later exercise their option to rejoin ASCAP for all purposes. . . . In the midst of all of this, LoFrumento cast the lot of ASCAP with the withdrawing major publishers and chose to let the rate court decide the dispute between Pandora and ASCAP. On December 14, ASCAP surprised Pandora and rejected the terms they had negotiated.

C. The Pandora–Sony License Negotiations . . .

As of the Fall of 2012, Sony was the world's largest music publisher. It owned or controlled between 25% and 30% of the market. It had taken this frontrunner position in the summer of 2012, when it became responsible for licensing EMI's catalog. Combined, the Sony and EMI catalogs contain roughly 3 million songs.

While the effective date of the withdrawal came as a surprise to Pandora, Pandora had been aware that the withdrawal was a possibility ever since ASCAP adopted the Compendium modification. Indeed, in the Spring of 2012, Pandora wrote to the Federal Trade Commission in opposition to Sony's acquisition of EMI and referred to this very possibility. Noting that a Sony withdrawal from the PROs would require Pandora to negotiate directly with Sony and that Pandora would be faced with a choice of either paying higher rates "or continuing to operate without Sony's songs," Pandora's [former CEO Joseph] Kennedy expressed concern that the combination of the Sony and EMI catalogs would give Pandora "no choice" but to enter into a direct license for the content. While Pandora "could survive without access to Sony's musical content," it "could not survive without access to the combined Sony and EMI catalogues."

The first substantive discussion between Pandora and Sony occurred in a telephone call on October 25 between Sony's [Executive Vice President of Business and Legal Affairs, Peter] Brodsky and Pandora's [lawyer, Robert] Rosenbloum. Sony promptly set the tenor for the negotiations with a not-too-veiled threat. Brodsky stated "[i]t's not our intention to shut down Pandora." In his many years of negotiating music licenses, Rosenbloum testified that [he] had never before heard such a threat. In some ways, this threat put on the table no more than what was obvious. Sony's works were already being played on Pandora; they were incorporated in the MGP. Unless Pandora could do without those works and remove them from its repertoire by January 1, Pandora had to obtain a license from Sony or face crippling copyright infringement claims. Sony was in the driver's seat and the clock was ticking.

The remainder of the conversation was largely devoted to Sony's statement of the reasons why it needed Pandora to pay for the public performance of music at a substantially higher rate. The principal reason was the "massive unfair disparity" between what Pandora was paying the record labels for sound recording rights and what it was paying the music publishers for composition rights. Brodsky explained that if the labels were getting 50% of Pandora's revenue, then it would be "fair" for music publishers to get 12% of the revenue, although Brodsky acknowledged that Pandora could not afford to pay that much. As Brodsky emphasized, it was the "differential" between the rates paid to the labels and the publishers that was the problem, and that Pandora was really just caught in the middle of a tug of war between the labels and publishers. Brodsky admitted that if the labels were getting only 25% of Pandora's revenue, then Pandora's current industry-wide rate of 4% for the licensing of rights to publicly perform compositions would probably be alright and there wouldn't be any need to increase it. . . .

Following this conversation, Pandora decided on a two-prong strategy. It would intensify its efforts to get an ASCAP license before the end of the year. To bring ASCAP to the negotiating table it filed its petition in this rate court for an ASCAP license on November 5. Secondly, Pandora attempted to obtain leverage in its negotiations with Sony. It requested a list of the Sony catalog so that it could take the Sony works off, or at least threaten to take them off, of the Pandora service if no deal could be reached. In his years of negotiating licenses, this was the first time that Rosenbloum had ever requested a list of works from a publisher.

Pandora's first request for the list came on November 1, 2012, in an email from Rosenbloum to Brodsky. . . .

Brodsky received this request for a list of the Sony works, but never responded. In their telephone conversations during the month of November, Rosenbloum reiterated the request for a list of works on several occasions but never got any response. Rosenbloum repeated the request once more at a breakfast meeting . . . on November 30. Again, Sony did not respond.

The list of Sony works was potentially important for several purposes, and Pandora referred to those several purposes in its discussions with Sony. In addition to wanting to be able to remove the Sony works from its service if Pandora and Sony could not come to terms, Pandora needed the list so that it could understand how to apportion any payments between the EMI and Sony catalogues since the payments would apparently be made at two different rates. Pandora also wanted the list so it could evaluate whether the substantial, non-refundable advance that Sony was demanding would likely be recouped.

Sony had a list readily at hand, since the Compendium required that a publisher and ASCAP work together during the 90-day period before the effective withdrawal date to confirm precisely which works were being withdrawn. Sony understood that it would lose an advantage in its negotiations with Pandora if it provided the list of works and deliberately chose not to do so. Brodsky's explanation at trial that he did not provide the list because he believed that negotiations were proceeding smoothly and did not want to impose an unnecessary "burden" on Sony's staff is not credible. The negotiations were not going smoothly; the list had already been prepared and its production imposed no burden. As Brodsky recognized in his testimony, the list was "necessary" to Pandora in the event the parties did not reach a deal. Sony decided quite deliberately to withhold from Pandora the information Pandora needed to strengthen its hand in its negotiations with Sony.

Ultimately, Sony made an offer to Pandora in early December. Still hoping to reach an agreement with ASCAP which would obviate the need for license from Sony, Pandora did not respond to the offer or to a follow-up email of December 6.

On Friday, December 14, with two weeks left in the year, and one week remaining before the music industry took its annual holiday break, ASCAP notified Pandora that it would not execute the agreement they had negotiated. The following Monday, Pandora urgently made two renewed written requests for the list of Sony's works, one to Sony and another to ASCAP.

. . . Not wishing to empower Pandora, Sony never responded.

. . . It would have taken ASCAP about a day to respond to Pandora's request with an accurate list of the Sony works. But, ASCAP, like Sony, stonewalled Pandora and refused to provide the list. . . .

If either Sony or ASCAP had provided Pandora with a list of the Sony works, Pandora would have been able to remove Sony's compositions from its service within about a week. Although ASCAP attempted at trial to show that Pandora could have used public sources of information to identify the Sony catalog, it failed to show that such an effort would have produced a reliable, comprehensive list, even if Pandora had made the extraordinary commitment necessary to try to compile such a list from public data.

The terms of the Pandora license with Sony were negotiated in four business days during the single week that ran between ASCAP's rejection of the Pandora term sheet and the start of the holiday break. On December 18, Brodsky sent Rosenbloom a term sheet. As proposed in that document, the license term would be one year, starting January 1, 2013. It required Pandora to pay a non-refundable but recoupable advance of [REDACTED] and a non-refundable [REDACTED] advance as an administrative fee. The royalty rate was set at Sony's pro-rata share of an industry-wide rate of 5%. Sony understood this to be a 25% increase over the then prevailing industry rate of approximately 4%. In his March 2013 report to his Board of Directors, Sony's Bandier bragged that Sony had leveraged its size to get this 25% increase in rate. . . .

. . . The parties executed a Binding Heads of Agreement on December 21, 2012. . . .

D. The Pandora–UMPG License Negotiations

Pandora did not have to wait long for the next publisher to leave ASCAP and demand a yet higher rate for a direct license. In February 2013, Pandora learned that UMPG was scheduled to withdraw its new media licensing rights from ASCAP effective July 1, 2013. [The court recounted the licensing negotiations with UMPG—Eds.]. . . .

IX. *September 17 Partial Summary Judgment Opinion*

On September 17, 2013, [this court] held, *inter alia,* that AFJ2 prohibited ASCAP from withdrawing from Pandora the rights to perform any compositions over which ASCAP retained any licensing rights. Consequently, the publishers' purported withdrawals of only new media rights under the Compendium modification were held inoperative. The Court found that AFJ2 prohibited a regime in which publishers allowed ASCAP to license a composition to some music users but not others. AFJ2 required each work that was in the ASCAP repertoire to be available to any user who requested a blanket license. The publishers, of course, remained free to withhold works from ASCAP entirely. . . .

Conclusions of Law . . .

II. ASCAP's Rate Proposal . . .

ASCAP's Theoretical Arguments and Motivations . . .

3. Disparity Between Sound Recording and Composition Fees . . .

ASCAP has not offered any theoretical support for raising the rate for public performance of a composition by a comparison to the rate set for sound recording rights. There may be several reasons for this, but first and foremost is the statutory prohibition on considering sound recording rates in setting a rate for a license for public performance of a musical work. *See* 17 U.S.C. §114(i) ("License fees payable for the public performance of sound recordings . . . shall not be taken into account in any . . . proceeding to set or adjust the royalties payable to copyright owners of musical works for the public performance of their works."). Thus, this Court may not take the rates set [for sound recording licenses paid to SoundExchange] into account in determining the fair market rate for a public performance license from ASCAP to Pandora.

Despite this statutory prohibition, one observation may be safely made. Unhappiness about the gap between what Pandora pays record companies and what it pays the PROs drove the modification to the ASCAP Compendium, the publishers' withdrawals from ASCAP, and the Sony and UMPG negotiations with Pandora. The corporate rivalries over digital age revenues explain a great deal of this history. In any event, the record is devoid of any principled explanation given by either Sony or UMPG to Pandora why the rate for sound recording rights should dictate any change in the rate for composition rights.

4. Cannibalization of Music Sales

There is agreement between the parties that it is appropriate to require a higher licensing fee from a music service that acts as a substitute for the sale of a musical work, when compared to one that does not. To the extent that a music service is a replacement for sales, it is said to cannibalize the sales; to the extent it encourages sales, it is said to be promotional. . . .

The parties have argued about the extent to which Pandora and services like it are promotional or cannibalistic. There is apparently no industry consensus on this question. It is worth noting, however, that what evidence was presented at trial suggests that Pandora is promotional.

To begin with, radio has traditionally been considered promotional. The record industry has long sought to have its music played on radio stations.[83] Pandora is no exception. Record labels have taken advantage of Pandora Premieres to feature new work in advance of release, with the hope that that exposure will engender sales. Pandora itself has buy buttons that permit listeners to buy digital downloads from Amazon and Apple, and they use them with some frequency.[84] There is no evidence that artists have taken steps to prevent Pandora from playing the artist's work. As significantly, one of Pandora's principal competitors—iTunes Radio—was created to complement Apple's iTunes Store and promote sales in that digital store.

In contrast, on-demand streaming services like Spotify are widely considered cannibalistic and are licensed at a higher rate accordingly. After all, a listener has no need to purchase a digital download when the listener has any song that she wants to hear instantaneously available through Spotify. For this very reason, some prominent performers have acted to prevent Spotify from playing their recordings. In sum, while this metric—whether a service is promotional or cannibalistic—could justify a differentiation of rates between services, ASCAP failed to show that Pandora is anything other than promotional of sales.[86]

[The court went on to set a rate for the ASCAP license based on an industry-wide rate of 4% of revenue for every year of the license term.]

NOTES AND QUESTIONS

1. Sony/ATV Music Publishing is co-owned by the Sony Corporation, which also owns Sony Music Entertainment, one of the world's largest record companies. Sony therefore controls vast catalogs of both musical works and sound recordings. Why do you think Sony objected to the disparity in licensing revenues paid by Pandora for musical works versus sound recordings?

2. The statutory license for noninteractive digital performances was meant to facilitate licensing, but some services that would qualify for the statutory license have chosen to negotiate private agreements with the major labels instead. Nothing in the statute prohibits such private arrangements. Spotify, iTunes Radio, and iHeartRadio are services that have negotiated private licensing arrangements with the major record labels. Such arrangements can offer advantages to both parties. For example,

---

83. There is a well-documented history of record promoters going so far as to use bribes, or "payola," to increase the number of times songs are played on a radio station.

84. Pandora's "buy button" resulted in over $3 million per month in music sales on Amazon and the iTunes Store during 2013.

86. ASCAP relies on an annual 2012 study by a firm called NPD which showed that Pandora users tend to purchase less music than do users of on-demand services like Spotify. But this does not show that Pandora is more cannibalistic of music sales than on-demand services (or that it is cannibalistic at all). Correlation does not equal causation, and the disparity may be fully explained by the self-selection of music users into on-demand services versus customized or programmed radio services. Users of on-demand services tend to be music "super fans" who know what they want to listen to and use on-demand services as supplements to purchased music collections. Users of customized radio services like Pandora tend to be more casual, or "lean back" music listeners, who are less likely to purchase music for their own collections.

iHeartRadio agreed to pay public performance royalties for sound recordings for its terrestrial radio station broadcasts. Remember, the default rule is that terrestrial radio stations do not need to pay for public performances of sound recordings because of the limited scope of the §106(6) public performance right. Why might iHeartRadio have agreed to that arrangement? One notable advantage of private licenses is that they can extend beyond the geographic region of the United States, something that the §114 statutory license cannot offer.

3. Spotify offers an advertising-supported free service that allows users to set up custom designed playlists. As you now know, this service is interactive and does not qualify for the §114 statutory license. To clear the sound recording copyrights, Spotify entered into a private arrangement with the major record labels, offering large up-front advances and a reported 18 percent equity stake in the company in exchange for authority to use the vast catalog of sound recordings owned by the labels. Of course, like Pandora, Spotify must pay for blanket licenses from the musical work CROs (ASCAP, BMI, and SESAC).

Pandora's service does not involve any DPDs and thus does not trigger a requirement for clearance of reproduction rights. In contrast, Spotify's monthly subscription premium service allows users to load their customized playlists onto personal devices. This means that Spotify also must pay the mechanical license for reproducing and distributing the musical works. Recall that no comparable arrangement exists to clear the reproduction and distribution of sound recordings. Spotify's private deal with the record labels solves this problem as well.

The advantages of this transaction for Spotify are obvious. Why do you think the record labels agreed to the deal?

4. Privately negotiated deals do not need to be disclosed. Many have become concerned that Spotify's private deal was structured, in part, to avoid the direct payments to performing artists required under the §114 statutory license. Some preliminary evidence suggests that royalty payments to performing artists from Spotify are much lower than the corresponding payments received by those artists from SoundExchange. In contrast, §114 and the subsequent amendments authorizing SoundExchange to negotiate webcasting rates require transparency, and the antitrust consent decrees that govern ASCAP and BMI also impose certain transparency requirements. (Note, however, that facts relating to certain aspects of ASCAP's business were redacted from the rate court's opinion). Would it be appropriate to require public disclosure of the terms of private agreements relating to musical work and/or sound recording copyrights? Under what circumstances?

PRACTICE EXERCISE: COUNSEL A CLIENT

You are staff counsel to the Register of Copyrights. The House Judiciary Committee's Subcommittee on Courts, Intellectual Property, and the Internet has asked the Register to testify on the question of copyright reform in the music industry. The Register has asked you to prepare a preliminary draft of her remarks. What should the Register say to the subcommittee, and why?

4. Diving Deeper: Section 110 Limitations, Revisited

As you learned in Chapter 6, §110 contains many different exemptions to the public performance rights of copyright owners, several of which apply to music. Some exemptions are directed at specific activities or specific actors, for example public performances of musical works that occur in religious gatherings, §110(3), at annual agricultural or horticultural fairs or exhibitions, §110(6), or at social functions of nonprofit veterans groups, §110(10). Note that none of these exemptions apply to sound recordings, which, given the limited nature of the public performance right (digital audio transmissions only) makes sense.

Another important exemption applies to public performances that occur when someone turns on a transmission, such as a radio or television broadcast. This exemption, found in §110(5)(A) and sometimes referred to as the "homestyle" exemption, permits anyone to turn on the radio or television in a public place so long as three conditions are met: (1) the public reception of the transmission is "on a single receiving apparatus of a kind commonly used in private homes"; (2) no direct charge is made to see or hear the transmission; and (3) the transmission is not further transmitted to the public. This exemption ostensibly applies to all categories of works and all types of public transmissions. Prior to 1998, courts addressing this exemption often focused not only on the type of equipment used, but also on the number of speakers and the physical size of the establishment, despite no mention of these factors in the statute.

In 1998, Congress passed the Fairness in Music Licensing Act (FIMLA), Pub. L. No. 105-298, 112 Stat. 2830, title II. The FIMLA created, for the first time, bright-line requirements concerning square footage and equipment type for businesses to be able to play nondramatic musical works by turning on the radio or television without having to pay license fees to the PROs. The National Restaurant Association and the National Federation of Independent Businesses strongly supported the passage of this Act. Not surprisingly, ASCAP and BMI vehemently opposed what they viewed as a significant expansion of the homestyle exemption. The exemption created by the FIMLA, codified in §110(5)(B), only applies to broadcasts of musical works "originated by a radio or television station licensed as such by the FCC, or, if an audiovisual transmission, by a cable system or satellite carrier." This limitation effectively narrows the exemption to apply only to broadcasts for which a royalty already has been paid to the copyright owner by the broadcaster.

The §110(5)(B) exemption applies only to nondramatic musical works. Small business establishments—those of less than 2,000 square feet (or less than 3,750 square feet if the business is a food service or drinking establishment)—can use any kind of equipment to receive and play the radio or television broadcast. Establishments that exceed these square footage limits face restrictions on the type of equipment they use (including the number of speakers and the screen size of any television) in order to stay within the bounds of the exemption.

Shortly after the passage of the FIMLA, the European Union commenced proceedings against the United States before the World Trade Organization (WTO), asserting that both exemptions in §110(5) violated the TRIPS Agreement. This was the first time that the United States had been accused of violating its TRIPS obligations. The United States argued that Article 13 of TRIPS permitted the §110(5) exemptions. Article 13 allows countries to adopt exceptions to the rights of copyright owners so long as the exceptions are limited to "certain special cases which do not conflict with a normal exploitation of the work and do not unreasonably prejudice the legitimate interests of the right holder"—the so-called "three-step test." In July 2000, the WTO dispute settlement body (DSB) held that the §110(5)(B) exemption did not meet the three-step test and thus violated the TRIPS Agreement.

The decision found that the §110(5)(A) homestyle exemption, however, was limited enough not to violate the TRIPS Agreement. The panel decision found that the homestyle exemption was narrowed by the FIMLA:

> [T]he homestyle exemption was originally intended to apply to performances of all types of works. However, given that the present subparagraph (B) applies to "a performance or display of a nondramatic musical work," the parties agree, by way of an *a contrario* interpretation, that the effect of the introductory phrase "except as provided in subparagraph (B)," that was added to the text in subparagraph (A), is that it narrows down the application of subparagraph (A) to works other than "nondramatic musical works."

United States—Section 110(5) of the US Copyright Act, WT/DS160/R (15 June 2000) ¶ 2.7.

While the WTO found that §110(5)(B) violates the U.S. obligations under TRIPS, the United States has not repealed or amended §110(5)(B).

NOTES AND QUESTIONS

1. In determining that the "homestyle" exemption of §110(5)(A) was consistent with the TRIPS Agreement, the panel noted that the United States had agreed that after the passage of the FIMLA, subsection (5)(A) did not apply to "nondramatic musical works." In proceedings before the WTO, the United States is represented by the U.S. Trade Representative (USTR). The USTR's interpretation of the scope of the homestyle exemption does not bind U.S. courts. Does it matter that the WTO panel expressly relied on the USTR's narrow interpretation? If this interpretation of the homestyle exemption is correct, turning on the radio in a public place—e.g., a boombox at the beach—would not be exempted from liability by §110(5)(A). Is there another provision of §110 that might exempt that activity?

2. How likely is Congress to change the §110(5) exemption? On the one hand, many members of Congress opposed the FIMLA, and it only passed after procedural maneuvering tied its fate to legislation that increased the duration of copyright by 20 years (a change in the law that is discussed in Chapter 11), an extension that a solid majority of Congress favored. On the other hand, some members of Congress have a certain disdain for altering domestic legislation solely because the WTO requires it.

3. Assuming the USTR's view of §110(5)(A) is not correct and it does apply to all works, does §110(5)(A) apply to Internet radio transmissions? If a business uses equipment commonly found in the home to play an Internet radio station in its establishment, must it also have ASCAP, BMI, and SESAC licenses?

8

Moral Rights and Performers' Rights

In Chapters 5-6, you learned about the exclusive rights granted in §106 of the Copyright Act and some of their limitations. This chapter considers rights recognized within the international copyright system for which the U.S. Copyright Act does not provide direct counterparts. These rights originate within the continental European copyright tradition, and reflect the strong authors' rights approach to copyright you first read about in Chapter 1. In this chapter, we also consider the concept of "performers' rights" introduced into U.S. law by the TRIPS Agreement. As you will learn, these new categories of rights continue to present implementation challenges for the United States.

A. MORAL RIGHTS IN THE UNITED STATES

Moral rights originated in French law, and are commonly viewed as a central and distinguishing feature of the continental European copyright tradition. Today, most other countries also afford protection for moral rights pursuant to the requirements of Article 6*bis* of the Berne Convention:

> (1) Independently of the author's economic rights, and even after the transfer of the said rights, the author shall have the right to claim authorship of the work and to object to any distortion, mutilation or other modification of, or other derogatory action in relation to, the said work, which would be prejudicial to his honor or reputation.

Two principal rights flow from the provisions of Article 6*bis*: (1) the right to claim paternity of the work (known in the United States as the right of attribution) and (2) the right to protect the work's integrity. The Berne Convention directs that these rights should last at least as long as the author's economic rights; however, member states may choose to provide protection for moral rights only during the author's life. *See* Berne Conv. art. 6*bis*(2). Article 9 of the TRIPS Agreement, in contrast, provides

KEEP IN MIND	that "Members shall not have rights or obligations . . . in respect of the rights conferred under Article 6*bis* of [the Berne] Convention."

<table>
<tr><td>

KEEP IN MIND

The United States was the last major industrialized country to join the Berne Convention. Accordingly, the utilitarian emphasis of U.S. copyright law was less influential in the first century of international copyright lawmaking. The TRIPS Agreement, on the other hand, reflects the strong influence of the U.S. approach.
</td></tr>
</table>

that "Members shall not have rights or obligations . . . in respect of the rights conferred under Article 6*bis* of [the Berne] Convention."

1. An Early Approach to Moral Rights

The scope and sufficiency of moral rights protection under U.S. law are subjects of considerable debate. In the Berne Convention Implementation Act (BCIA), Congress made no new provision for moral rights, declaring that the BCIA, "together with [other] law satisf[ies] the obligations of the United States in adhering to the Berne Convention and no further rights or interests shall be recognized or created for that purpose." BCIA of 1988 §2(3). According to the legislative history, "existing U.S. law [that provides sufficient protection for moral rights to comply with the Berne Convention] includes various provisions of the Copyright Act and the Lanham Act, various state statutes, and common law principles such as libel, defamation, misrepresentation, and unfair competition. . . ." S. Rep. No. 352, 100th Cong., 2d Sess. 9-10 (1988), *reprinted in* 1988 U.S.C.C.A.N. 3706, 3714-15. Consider whether the following case provides support for Congress's statement.

≡ *Gilliam v. American Broadcasting Companies, Inc.*
   538 F.2d 14 (2d Cir. 1976)

LUMBARD, J.: Plaintiffs, a group of British writers and performers known as "Monty Python,"[2] appeal from a denial by Judge Lasker in the Southern District of a preliminary injunction to restrain the American Broadcasting Company (ABC) from broadcasting edited versions of three separate programs originally written and performed by Monty Python for broadcast by the British Broadcasting Corporation (BBC). We agree with Judge Lasker that the appellants have demonstrated that the excising done for ABC impairs the integrity of the original work. We further find that the countervailing injuries that Judge Lasker found might have accrued to ABC as a result of an injunction at a prior date no longer exist. We therefore direct the issuance of a preliminary injunction by the district court.

Since its formation in 1969, the Monty Python group has gained popularity primarily through its thirty-minute television programs created for BBC as part of a comedy series entitled "Monty Python's Flying Circus." In accordance with an agreement between Monty Python and BBC, the group writes and delivers to BBC scripts for use in the television series. This scriptwriters' agreement recites in great detail the procedure to be followed when any alterations are to be made in the script prior to recording of the program. The essence of this section of the agreement is that, while BBC retains final authority to make changes, appellants or

---

2. Appellant Gilliam is an American citizen residing in England.

their representatives exercise optimum control over the scripts consistent with BBC's authority and only minor changes may be made without prior consultation with the writers. Nothing in the scriptwriters' agreement entitles BBC to alter a program once it has been recorded. The agreement further provides that, subject to the terms therein, the group retains all rights in the script.

Under the agreement, BBC may license the transmission of recordings of the television programs in any overseas territory. The series has been broadcast in this country primarily on non-commercial public broadcasting television stations, although several of the programs have been broadcast on commercial stations in Texas and Nevada. In each instance, the thirty-minute programs have been broadcast as originally recorded and broadcast in England in their entirety and without commercial interruption.

In October 1973, Time-Life Films acquired the right to distribute in the United States certain BBC television programs, including the Monty Python series. Time-Life was permitted to edit the programs only "for insertion of commercials, applicable censorship or governmental . . . rules and regulations, and National Association of Broadcasters and time segment requirements." No similar clause was included in the scriptwriters' agreement between appellants and BBC. Prior to this time, ABC had sought to acquire the right to broadcast excerpts from various Monty Python programs in the spring of 1975, but the group rejected the proposal for such a disjointed format. Thereafter, in July 1975, ABC agreed with Time-Life to broadcast two ninety-minute specials each comprising three thirty-minute Monty Python programs that had not previously been shown in this country.

Correspondence between representatives of BBC and Monty Python reveals that these parties assumed that ABC would broadcast each of the Monty Python programs "in its entirety." On September 5, 1975, however, the group's British representative inquired of BBC how ABC planned to show the programs in their entirety if approximately 24 minutes of each 90 minute program were to be devoted to commercials. BBC replied on September 12, "we can only reassure you that ABC have decided to run the programmes 'back to back,' and that there is a firm undertaking not to segment them."

ABC broadcast the first of the specials on October 3, 1975. Appellants did not see a tape of the program until late November and were allegedly "appalled" at the discontinuity and "mutilation" that had resulted from the editing done by Time-Life for ABC. Twenty-four minutes of the original 90 minutes of recording had been omitted. Some of the editing had been done in order to make time for commercials; other material had been edited, according to ABC, because the original programs contained offensive or obscene matter.

In early December, Monty Python learned that ABC planned to broadcast the second special on December 26, 1975. The parties began negotiations concerning editing of that program and a delay of the broadcast until Monty Python could view it. These negotiations were futile, however, and on December 15 the group filed this action to enjoin the broadcast and for damages. Following an evidentiary hearing, Judge Lasker found that "the plaintiffs have established an impairment of the integrity of their work" which "caused the film or program . . . to lose its iconoclastic verve." According to Judge Lasker, "the damage that has been caused to the plaintiffs is irreparable by its nature." Nevertheless, the judge denied the motion for the preliminary injunction on the grounds that it was unclear who owned the copyright in the programs produced by BBC from the scripts written by Monty Python;. . . .

Judge Lasker granted Monty Python's request for more limited relief by requiring ABC to broadcast a disclaimer during the December 26 special to the effect that the group dissociated itself from the program because of the editing. A panel of this court, however, granted a stay of that order until this appeal could be heard and permitted ABC to broadcast, at the beginning of the special, only the legend that the program had been edited by ABC. . . .

I

Judge Lasker denied the preliminary injunction in part because he was unsure of the ownership of the copyright in the recorded program. Appellants first contend that the question of ownership is irrelevant because the recorded program was merely a derivative work taken from the script in which they hold the uncontested copyright. Thus, even if BBC owned the copyright in the recorded program, its use of that work would be limited by the license granted to BBC by Monty Python for use of the underlying script. We agree.

Section 7 of the Copyright Law, 17 U.S.C. §7, provides in part that "adaptations, arrangements, dramatizations . . . or other versions of . . . copyrighted works when produced with the consent of the proprietor of the copyright in such works . . . shall be regarded as new works subject to copyright. . . . " Manifestly, the recorded program falls into this category as a dramatization of the script, and thus the program was itself entitled to copyright protection. However, section 7 limits the copyright protection of the derivative work, as works adapted from previously existing scripts have become known, to the novel additions made to the underlying work, and the derivative work does not affect the "force or validity" of the copyright in the matter from which it is derived. Thus, any ownership by BBC of the copyright in the recorded program would not affect the scope or ownership of the copyright in the underlying script.

Since the copyright in the underlying script survives intact despite the incorporation of that work into a derivative work, one who uses the script, even with the permission of the proprietor of the derivative work, may infringe the underlying copyright.

If the proprietor of the derivative work is licensed by the proprietor of the copyright in the underlying work to vend or distribute the derivative work to third parties, those parties will, of course, suffer no liability for their use of the underlying work consistent with the license to the proprietor of the derivative work. Obviously, it was just this type of arrangement that was contemplated in this instance. The scriptwriters' agreement between Monty Python and BBC specifically permitted the latter to license the transmission of the recordings made by BBC to distributors such as Time-Life for broadcast in overseas territories.

One who obtains permission to use a copyrighted script in the production of a derivative work, however, may not exceed the specific purpose for which permission was granted. Most of the decisions that have reached this conclusion have dealt with the improper extension of the underlying work into media or time, i.e., duration of the license, not covered by the grant of permission to the derivative work proprietor. Appellants herein do not claim that the broadcast by ABC violated media or time restrictions contained in the license of the script to BBC. Rather, they claim that revisions in the script, and ultimately in the program, could be made only after consultation with Monty Python, and that ABC's broadcast of a program edited after recording and without consultation with Monty Python exceeded the scope of any license that BBC was entitled to grant.

. . . Whether intended to allow greater economic exploitation of the work, as in the media and time cases, or to ensure that the copyright proprietor retains a veto power over revisions desired for the derivative work, the ability of the copyright holder to control his work remains paramount in our copyright law. We find, therefore, that unauthorized editing of the underlying work, if proven, would constitute an infringement of the copyright in that work similar to any other use of a work that exceeded the license granted by the proprietor of the copyright. . . .

II

It also seems likely that appellants will succeed on the theory that, regardless of the right ABC had to broadcast an edited program, the cuts made constituted an actionable mutilation of Monty Python's work. This cause of action, which seeks redress for deformation of an artist's work, finds its roots in the continental concept of droit moral, or moral right, which may generally be summarized as including the right of the artist to have his work attributed to him in the form in which he created it.

American copyright law, as presently written, does not recognize moral rights or provide a cause of action for their violation, since the law seeks to vindicate the economic, rather than the personal, rights of authors. Nevertheless, the economic incentive for artistic and intellectual creation that serves as the foundation for American copyright law cannot be reconciled with the inability of artists to obtain relief for mutilation or misrepresentation of their work to the public on which the artists are financially dependent. Thus courts have long granted relief for misrepresentation of an artist's work by relying on theories outside the statutory law of copyright, such as contract law or the tort of unfair competition. Although such decisions are clothed in terms of proprietary right in one's creation, they also properly vindicate the author's personal right to prevent the presentation of his work to the public in a distorted form.

Here, the appellants claim that the editing done for ABC mutilated the original work and that consequently the broadcast of those programs as the creation of Monty Python violated the Lanham Act §43(a), 15 U.S.C. §1125(a). This statute, the federal counterpart to state unfair competition laws, has been invoked to prevent misrepresentations that may injure plaintiff's business or personal reputation, even where no registered trademark is concerned. It is sufficient to violate the Act that a representation of a product, although technically true, creates a false impression of the product's origin.

These cases cannot be distinguished from the situation in which a television network broadcasts a program properly designated as having been written and performed by a group, but which has been edited, without the writer's consent, into a form that departs substantially from the original work. "To deform his work is to present him to the public as the creator of a work not his own, and thus makes him subject to criticism for work he has not done." [Martin A.] Roeder, [*The Doctrine of Moral Rights*, 53 Harv. L. Rev. 554, 569 (1940)]. In such a case, it is the writer or performer, rather than the network, who suffers the consequences of the mutilation, for the public will have only the final product by which to evaluate the work. Thus, an allegation that a defendant has presented to the public a "garbled," distorted version of plaintiff's work seeks to redress the very rights sought to be protected by the Lanham Act, 15 U.S.C. §1125(a), and should be recognized as stating a cause of action under that statute. . . .

. . . We find that the truncated version at times omitted the climax of the skits to which appellants' rare brand of humor was leading and at other times deleted essential elements in the schematic development of a story line. We therefore agree with Judge Lasker's conclusion that the edited version broadcast by ABC impaired the integrity of appellants' work and represented to the public as the product of appellants what was actually a mere caricature of their talents. We believe that a valid cause of action for such distortion exists and that therefore a preliminary injunction may issue to prevent repetition of the broadcast prior to final determination of the issues. . . .

NOTES AND QUESTIONS

1. How effective were the alternative theories of protection posited by the plaintiffs in *Gilliam*? Would the reasoning used by the court to find a likely violation of the derivative work right apply in a case in which the parties lacked a preexisting contractual relationship? Is there a way for a defendant to cure an alleged Lanham Act violation?

2. *Gilliam* suggests that the right to prepare derivative works may also provide some protection for the noneconomic interests of authors. Should derivative rights be construed this way? Recall the economic rationale for derivative rights articulated by Professor Goldstein in Chapter 5.B.2, *supra*. Are derivative rights an appropriate vehicle for complying with the Berne Convention's requirements for the protection of moral rights?

3. Recall the various justifications for copyright protection that you studied in Chapter 1. Are any of those theories fundamentally incompatible with moral rights protection? Consider this critique:

. . . A perspective grounded in economic and conventionally understood utilitarian rationales for legal protection emphasizes the commodification and dissemination of intellectual works. This perspective fails to take into account that human enterprise also embodies inspirational or spiritual motivations for creativity. This failure creates turmoil for many authors because it fosters a dominant market exchange reality that ignores the importance of noneconomically-based motivations for innovation. . . . As the twenty-first century progresses, the world will likely continue toward an orientation that is based on information processing rather than pure knowledge. Creative thinking is particularly essential in this environment, and our legal structure must reflect a fuller comprehension of the creative being so that it can respond more effectively to all aspects of authors' needs. . . .

Roberta Rosenthal Kwall, *Inspiration and Innovation: The Intrinsic Dimension of the Artistic Soul*, 81 Notre Dame L. Rev. 1945, 1946-47 (2006). Do you agree with Professor Kwall that copyright law currently does not fully respond to the full spectrum of authorial needs and that it should? Why do you think the United States has been reluctant to embrace robust moral rights protection?

2. The Lanham Act and Attribution

In *Gilliam*, the Second Circuit considered the question of attribution under §43(a) of the Lanham Act. The next case sets forth the Supreme Court's view of the relationship between that section and the Copyright Act.

Dastar Corp. v. Twentieth Century Fox Film Corp.
539 U.S. 23 (2003)

SCALIA, J.: In this case, we are asked to decide whether §43(a) of the Lanham Act, 15 U.S.C. §1125(a), prevents the unaccredited copying of a work. . . .

I

In 1948, three and a half years after the German surrender at Reims, General Dwight D. Eisenhower completed Crusade in Europe, his written account of the allied campaign in Europe during World War II. Doubleday published the book, registered it with the Copyright Office in 1948, and granted exclusive television rights to an affiliate of respondent Twentieth Century Fox Film Corporation (Fox). Fox, in turn, arranged for Time, Inc., to produce a television series, also called Crusade in Europe, based on the book, and Time assigned its copyright in the series to Fox. The television series, consisting of 26 episodes, was first broadcast in 1949. . . . In 1975, Doubleday renewed the copyright on the book as the "proprietor of copyright in a work made for hire." Fox, however, did not renew the copyright on the Crusade television series, which expired in 1977, leaving the television series in the public domain. . . .

. . . In 1995, Dastar decided to expand its product line from music compact discs to videos. Anticipating renewed interest in World War II on the 50th anniversary of the war's end, Dastar released a video set entitled World War II Campaigns in Europe. To make Campaigns, Dastar purchased eight beta cam tapes of the *original* version of the Crusade television series, which is in the public domain, copied them, and then edited the series. . . . Dastar substituted a new opening sequence, credit page, and final closing for those of the Crusade television series; inserted new chapter-title sequences and narrated chapter introductions; moved the "recap" in the Crusade television series to the beginning and retitled it as a "preview"; and removed references to and images of the book. Dastar created new packaging for its Campaigns series and . . . a new title.

Dastar manufactured and sold the Campaigns video set as its own product. The advertising states: "Produced and Distributed by: *Entertainment Distributing*" (which is owned by Dastar), and makes no reference to the Crusade television series. Similarly, the screen credits state "DASTAR CORP presents" and "an ENTERTAINMENT DISTRIBUTING Production," and list as executive producer, producer, and associate producer, employees of Dastar. The Campaigns videos themselves also make no reference to the Crusade television series, New Line's Crusade videotapes, or the book. . . .

In 1998, respondents Fox, SFM, and New Line brought this action alleging that Dastar's sale of its Campaigns video set infringes Doubleday's copyright in General Eisenhower's book and, thus, their exclusive television rights in the book. Respondents later amended their complaint to add claims that Dastar's sale of Campaigns "without proper credit" to the Crusade television series constitutes "reverse passing off" in violation of §43(a) of the Lanham Act . . . and in violation of state unfair-competition law. . . . [T]he District Court found for respondents on all three counts, . . . awarded Dastar's profits to respondents and doubled them pursuant to §35 of the Lanham Act. . . .

. . . [T]he Ninth Circuit affirmed the judgment for respondents on the Lanham Act claim, but reversed as to the copyright claim. . . .

II

The Lanham Act was intended to make "actionable the deceptive and misleading use of marks," and "to protect persons engaged in . . . commerce against unfair competition." While much of the Lanham Act addresses the registration, use, and infringement of trademarks and related marks, §43(a), 15 U.S.C. §1125(a) is one of the few provisions that goes beyond trademark protection. As originally enacted, §43(a) created a federal remedy against a person who used in commerce either "a false designation of origin, or any false description or representation" in connection with "any goods or services." . . .

. . . [A]s it comes to us, the gravamen of respondents' claim is that, in marketing and selling *Campaigns* as its own product without acknowledging its nearly wholesale reliance on the *Crusade* television series, Dastar has made a "false designation of origin, false or misleading description of fact, or false or misleading representation of fact, which . . . is likely to cause confusion . . . as to the origin . . . of his or her goods." That claim would undoubtedly be sustained if Dastar had bought some of New Line's *Crusade* videotapes and merely repackaged them as its own. Dastar's alleged wrongdoing, however, is vastly different: it took a creative work in the public domain—the *Crusade* television series—copied it, made modifications (arguably minor), and produced its very own series of videotapes. If "origin" refers only to the manufacturer or producer of the physical "goods" that are made available to the public (in this case the videotapes), Dastar was the origin. If, however, "origin" includes the creator of the underlying work that Dastar copied, then someone else (perhaps Fox) was the origin of Dastar's product. At bottom, we must decide what §43(a)(1)(A) of the Lanham Act means by the "origin" of "goods."

III

. . . We think the most natural understanding of the "origin" of "goods"—the source of wares—is the producer of the tangible product sold in the marketplace, in this case the physical Campaigns videotape sold by Dastar. The concept might be stretched . . . to include not only the actual producer, but also the trademark owner who commissioned or assumed responsibility for ("stood behind") production of the physical product. But as used in the Lanham Act, the phrase "origin of goods" is in our view incapable of connoting the person or entity that originated the ideas or communications that "goods" embody or contain. Such an extension would not only stretch the text, but it would be out of accord with the history and purpose of the Lanham Act and inconsistent with precedent. . . .

. . . The right to copy, and to copy without attribution, once a copyright has expired, like "the right to make [an article whose patent has expired]—including the right to make it in precisely the shape it carried when patented—passes to the public." The rights of a patentee or copyright holder are part of a "carefully crafted bargain," under which, once the patent or copyright monopoly has expired, the public may use the invention or work at will and without attribution. Thus, in construing the Lanham Act, we have been "careful to caution against misuse or over-extension" of trademark and related protections into areas traditionally occupied by patent or copyright. . . . Assuming for the sake of argument that Dastar's representation of itself as the "Producer" of its videos amounted to a representation that it originated the creative work conveyed by the videos, allowing a cause of action under §43(a) for that representation would create a species of mutant copyright law that limits the public's "federal right to 'copy and to use'" expired copyrights.

When Congress has wished to create such an addition to the law of copyright, it has done so with much more specificity than the Lanham Act's ambiguous use of "origin." The Visual Artists Rights Act of 1990 provides that the author of an artistic work "shall have the right . . . to claim authorship of that work." That express right of attribution is carefully limited and focused: It attaches only to specified "work[s] of visual art," is personal to the artist, and endures only for "the life of the author." Recognizing in §43(a) a cause of action for misrepresentation of authorship of noncopyrighted works (visual or otherwise) would render these limitations superfluous. . . .

In sum, reading the phrase "origin of goods" in the Lanham Act in accordance with the Act's common-law foundations (which were *not* designed to protect originality or creativity), and in light of the copyright and patent laws (which *were*), we conclude that the phrase refers to the producer of the tangible goods that are offered for sale, and not to the author of any idea, concept, or communication embodied in those goods. To hold otherwise would be akin to finding that §43(a) created a species of perpetual patent and copyright, which Congress may not do.

. . . For merely saying it is the producer of the video . . . no Lanham Act liability attaches to Dastar. . . .

AFTERMATH

On remand, the district court found Dastar liable for infringement of Doubleday's copyright in the Eisenhower book and the Ninth Circuit affirmed. *See Twentieth Century Fox Film Corp. v. Ent. Distrib.*, 429 F.3d 869 (9th Cir. 2005), *cert. denied sub nom. Dastar Corp. v. Random House, Inc.*, 548 U.S. 919 (2006).

NOTES AND QUESTIONS

1. Consider the changes made by Dastar to the original *Crusade* television series. Are these changes sufficient to give Dastar copyright in *World War II Campaigns*? If so, then didn't Dastar accurately credit itself? If Dastar had credited Fox, would that have given Fox different grounds for complaint under the Lanham Act?

2. In *Gilliam*, the court recognized a right of relief under §43(a) of the Lanham Act for artists whose works have been mutilated before presentation to the public. How did the claims by the plaintiffs in *Dastar* differ from the claims made by the plaintiffs in *Gilliam*?

3. *Dastar* dealt with a work in which copyright had expired. Does its holding about the availability of Lanham Act claims also apply to works still within their copyright terms? Several courts have said yes. *See, e.g., General Universal Sys. v. Lee,* 379 F.3d 131 (5th Cir. 2004) (software); *Zyla v. Wadsworth,* 360 F.3d 243 (1st Cir. 2004) (textbook). If so, does *Dastar* overrule *Gilliam*?

3. The Visual Artists Rights Act

Dastar, unlike *Gilliam*, construed the Lanham Act against the backdrop of the Visual Artists Rights Act of 1990, Pub. L. No. 101-650, tit. VI, 104 Stat. 5089, 5128-33 (1990) (codified at 17 U.S.C. §106A) ("VARA"). Congress enacted VARA just two years after the BCIA. VARA grants the author of a "work of visual art" a limited and unique set of moral rights protections: the right of attribution, including both the right to claim authorship of her own works and the right to prevent attribution of works that she did not create; the right to prevent any intentional distortion, mutilation or other modification of the work that would be prejudicial to her reputation; and, in the case of works of art of "recognized stature," the right to prevent their destruction. *See* 17 U.S.C. §106A(a). The rights generally endure for the life of the author unless waived. *See id.* (d)-(e). VARA also provides for damages and addresses the moral rights concerns associated with removing works of visual art from buildings. *See generally id.* §§113(d), 501, 504.

a. Covered Works

Section 106A grants rights only to the author of a "work of visual art." Section 101 defines that term as:

(1) a painting, drawing, print, or sculpture, existing in a single copy, in a limited edition of 200 copies or fewer that are signed and consecutively numbered by the author, or, in the case of a sculpture, in multiple cast, carved, or fabricated sculptures of 200 or fewer that are consecutively numbered by the author and bear the signature or other identifying mark of the author; or

(2) a still photographic image produced for exhibition purposes only, existing in a single copy that is signed by the author, or in a limited edition of 200 copies or fewer that are signed and consecutively numbered by the author.

A work of visual art does not include—

(A)

   (i) any poster, map, globe, chart, technical drawing, diagram, model, applied art, motion picture or other audiovisual work, book, magazine, newspaper, periodical, data base, electronic information service, electronic publication, or similar publication;

   (ii) any merchandising item or advertising, promotional, descriptive, covering, or packaging material or container;

   (iii) any portion or part of any item described in clause (i) or (ii);

(B) any work made for hire; or

(C) any work not subject to copyright protection under this title.

17 U.S.C. §101.

The case law interpreting VARA is sparse, but courts have interpreted the statute's coverage narrowly. Note, for example, that to qualify for protection, photographs must be "produced for exhibition purposes only." At least one court has concluded that this language requires examining the intent of the author at the time the photographic print was created. *Lilley v. Stout*, 384 F. Supp. 2d 83 (D.D.C. 2005) (rejecting claim because the photographer's intent at time of printing photograph was that it was not *only* for exhibition). Other cases take a similarly narrow stance toward the question whether artwork is promotional in character. *See e.g., Pollara v. Seymour*, 344 F.3d 265 (2d Cir. 2003) (rejecting claim to 10' x 30' painting because it was meant to draw attention and promote a lobbying message). Note, finally, that the definition excludes any work created as a work made for hire, even if the work would otherwise qualify for protection. *See* 17 U.S.C. §101 (definition of "work of visual art"); *Carter v. Helmsley-Spear, Inc.*, 71 F.3d 77 (2d Cir. 1995), *cert. denied*, 517 U.S. 1208 (1996) (rejecting claim).

NOTES AND QUESTIONS

1. Why do you think courts have interpreted the definition of "work of visual art" narrowly?

2. Why do you think Congress excluded works made for hire from the definition of "work of visual art"?

b. Distortions and Modifications Harmful to Honor or Reputation

LOOKING FORWARD

Note that all of the rights granted by VARA are subject to the general limiting doctrine of fair use codified in §107 of the Copyright Act. You will learn about the fair use doctrine in Chapter 10.

Section 106A(a)(3) grants authors of works of visual art the right "to prevent any intentional distortion, mutilation, or other modification of that work which would be prejudicial to his or her honor or reputation, and any intentional distortion, mutilation, or modification of that work is a violation of that right." Consider the following case:

Massachusetts Museum of Contemporary Art Foundation, Inc. v. Büchel
593 F.3d 38 (1st Cir. 2010)

LIPEZ, J.:

. . . Artist Christoph Büchel conceived of an ambitious, football-field-sized art installation entitled "Training Ground for Democracy," which was to be exhibited at the Massachusetts Museum of Contemporary Art ("MASS MoCA," or "the Museum"). Unfortunately, the parties never memorialized the terms of their relationship or their understanding of the intellectual property issues involved in the installation in a written agreement. Even more unfortunately, the project was never completed. Numerous conflicts and a steadily deteriorating relationship between the artist and the Museum prevented the completion of "Training Ground for Democracy" in its final form. . . .

I.

A. *The Parties*

MASS MoCA opened in 1999 as a center for the creation and display of contemporary art. . . . MASS MoCA prides itself on exposing its audiences to "all stages of art production: rehearsals, sculptural fabrication, and developmental workshops are frequently on view, as are finished works of art."

Christoph Büchel is a Swiss visual artist who lives and works in Basel, Switzerland. He is "known for building elaborate, politically provocative environments for viewers to wander, and sometimes to crawl, through." Randy Kennedy, *The Show Will Go On, but the Art Will Be Shielded*, N.Y. Times, May 22, 2007, at E1 ("*The Show Will Go On* "). . . .

B. *Factual Background* . . .

Büchel conceived of the exhibit as "essentially a village, . . . contain[ing] several major architectural and structural elements integrated into a whole, through which a visitor could walk (and climb)." According to an affidavit submitted to the district court, Büchel envisioned the work in the following way:

> It was to adopt the role-play of U.S. military training for its visitors, who would be given the opportunity to "virtually" change their own various identities in relation to the collective project called "democracy": training to be an immigrant, training to vote, protest, and revolt, training to loot, training iconoclasm, training to join a political rally, training to be the objects of propaganda, training to be interrogated and detained and to be tried or to judge, training to reconstruct a disaster, training to be in conditions of suspended law, and training various other social and political behavior.

In August 2006, Büchel spent ten days in residence at MASS MoCA. During this time, he and a partner prepared a basic schematic model of the proposed installation. MASS MoCA agreed to acquire, at Büchel's direction but its own expense, the materials and items necessary for the project. . . .

. . . [F]or our purposes, the key conflict between MASS MoCA and the artist involved Büchel's dissatisfaction with the way in which the Museum was implementing his instructions and procuring the items necessary for the installation. Büchel himself was not present in North Adams for the first several months of work on the project. Instead, he conducted much of his work on the installation throughout the fall of 2006 remotely, by providing Museum personnel with detailed instructions as to the particular materials he required and their placement within the exhibition space.

. . . [P]roblems soon arose, especially between [Museum Director Joseph] Thompson and Büchel, as to the progress of the project, particularly when, as Thompson explained in an internal Museum email dated October 28, 2006, he had tried to "move the project along" by "making a few decisions in [Büchel's] stead." Thompson noted that Büchel, whom he described as having "clear vision" and "rock solid integrity," had taken "extreme, mortal[ ] offense" to Thompson's efforts.

On October 29, 2006, Büchel returned to North Adams to complete [the work to be entitled] "Training Ground for Democracy," and three of his assistants from Switzerland arrived shortly thereafter. Unhappy with some of the work that had been done by the Museum in his absence, Büchel felt that certain logistical and organizational failures by the Museum had endangered the timely opening of the show. . . . By early December 2006, Büchel insisted that the Museum postpone the opening of the show and asserted that he would not "accept an opening of a work in progress or other compromise." . . .

Büchel remained onsite at the Museum working on "Training Ground" until December 17, 2006, when he left for the holidays. In Büchel's estimation, "Training Ground" was then only about 40% complete. At the time, he planned to return on January 8, 2007, in order to finish the work in time for a March 3 opening. When he left North Adams, the artist was obviously disappointed with the progress of "Training Ground." . . . . He felt that Museum employees, by failing to precisely carry out his detailed instructions and making artistic decisions in his stead, had generated even more work for his crew, as numerous components of the installation had to be reworked to Büchel's specifications. In general, he felt that the Museum was trying to scale back his artistic vision without consulting him.

Meanwhile, the Museum was running out of money for the project. In an attempt to secure further funding, it disregarded Büchel's express wishes and, in late December 2006, asked for money from his galleries. . . . By mid-January 2007, tensions had escalated to the point where Büchel informed the Museum that he would not return to continue work on "Training Ground" unless certain conditions, both financial and artistic, were met.

In Büchel's absence, MASS MoCA staff continued to work on the installation. The parties disagree as to whether the employees were merely executing instructions left by the artist or whether their actions represented independent artistic judgment, exercised in direct contravention of Büchel's express wishes. The parties also disagree as to whether, in the spring of 2007, while negotiations had stalled but work on the installation was ongoing, the Museum promoted—and even showed—the unfinished work to numerous visitors without Büchel's consent, in one form or another.

. . . On May 22, 2007, MASS MoCA announced the cancellation of "Training Ground," and contemporaneously publicized the opening of a new exhibit entitled "Made at MASS MoCA," which was to be "a documentary project exploring the issues raised in the course of complex collaborative projects between artists and institutions." The press release noted that this lawsuit had been filed the previous day; it also highlighted the Museum's desire to use its "other experiences working with artists" to "provide [its] audience with thought-provoking insights into the complexities of the art-making process." The release further explained that, due to "space constraints imposed by the materials assembled for *Training Ground for Democracy*," the exhibition would be presented in the Museum's "only remaining available gallery space"; therefore, in order to enter the exhibit, visitors would have to pass through Building 5, "housing the materials and unfinished fabrications that were to have comprised elements of *Training Ground for Democracy*." The Museum represented that "[r]easonable steps [had] been taken to control and restrict the view of these materials, pending a court ruling."

When "Made at MASS MoCA" opened, many in the art world disagreed with the Museum's handling of its dispute with Büchel, though the parties have different views on whether the Museum's actions ultimately tarnished the artist's reputation. Moreover, the parties differ on whether the "reasonable steps . . . taken to control and restrict the view of the[ ] materials"—the placement of yellow tarpaulins over the unfinished work—actually concealed all of the individual components and vital design elements of "Training Ground," or whether the tarpaulins simply "hid[ ] an elephant behind a napkin," effectively inviting individuals to peek behind the cloth coverings and view the unfinished work. *See* Charles Giuliano, *Christoph Buchel's Tarp Art at Mass MoCA: Crap Under Wrap* (July 31, 2007) ("*Crap Under Wrap*"), *available at* http://www. berkshirefinearts.com/show_article.php?article_id=368 & category=finearts.

C. *Procedural Background*

The Museum . . . sought a declaration that it was "entitled to present to the public the materials and partial constructions assembled in connection with an exhibit planned with the Swiss artist Büchel." [Büchel counterclaimed, *inter alia*, for damages and injunctive relief under VARA. The district court granted summary judgment in favor of the Museum.]

However, several days after obtaining the ruling in its favor, MASS MoCA . . . posted an announcement on its website stating that it had "begun removing materials gathered for *Training Ground for Democracy* and [would] not permit the public to enter the planned installation." MASS MoCA Blog, "We'll Remove *Training Ground*," http://blog.massmoca.org/2007/09/28/well-remove-training-ground/ (Sept. 28, 2007) (last visited Jan. 13, 2010). . . .

II. . . .

C. *Does VARA Apply to Unfinished Works of Art?*

Büchel argues that the district court erred by failing to recognize that VARA applies with equal force to incomplete artistic endeavors that would otherwise be subject to VARA protection. . . .

The text of VARA itself does not state when an artistic project becomes a work of visual art subject to its protections. However, VARA is part of the Copyright Act, and that Act's definition section, which defines "work of visual art," specifies that its definitions, unless otherwise provided, control throughout Title 17. *See* 17 U.S.C. §101. That general definitional section of the Copyright Act states that a work is "created" when it "is fixed in a copy . . . for the first time." Further, "where a work is prepared over a period of time, *the portion of it that has been fixed at any particular time constitutes the work as of that time*." 17 U.S.C. §101 (emphasis added). A work is "fixed" when it has been formed, "by or under the authority of the author," in a way that is "sufficiently permanent or stable to permit it to be perceived, reproduced, or otherwise communicated for a period of more than transitory duration." *Id.*

Not surprisingly, based on section 101's general definitions, courts have held that the Copyright Act's protections extend to unfinished works.

Reading VARA in accordance with the definitions in section 101, it too must be read to protect unfinished, but "fixed," works of art that, if completed, would qualify for protection under the statute.. . . .

III. . . .

A. *The Scope of VARA's Integrity and Attribution Rights*

1. The Right of Integrity

VARA's right of integrity, codified at 17 U.S.C. §106A(a)(3)(A), provides that an artist shall have the right "to prevent any intentional distortion, mutilation, or other modification of [his or her] work which would be prejudicial to his or her honor or reputation, and [that] any intentional distortion, mutilation, or modification of that work is a violation of that right." . . .

There is arguably some uncertainty about the plaintiff's burden of proof in a case such as this because the second part of section (a)(3)(A)—stating that "any intentional distortion, mutilation, or modification of th[e] work is a violation" of the right of integrity—does not explicitly require a showing of prejudice when the alteration already has occurred and damages, rather than injunctive relief, would be the appropriate remedy. Because those VARA cases that make it to court are "generally . . . decided on threshold questions such as whether the artist's work is a work of visual art within the scope of the Act," courts have had little occasion to give content to the rights that VARA guarantees. . . .

. . . Given the stated purpose of the legislation and the similar depiction of the integrity right in the Berne Convention, we conclude that Congress intended the prejudice requirement to apply to the right of integrity whether the remedy sought is injunctive relief or damages. . . .

2. The Right of Attribution

VARA's right of attribution grants the author of a work of visual art the right, in part, (1) "to claim authorship of that work"; (2) "to prevent the use of his or her name as the author of any work of visual art which he or she did not create"; and (3) "to prevent the use of his or her name as the author of the work of visual art in the event of a distortion, mutilation, or other modification of the work which would be prejudicial to his or her honor or reputation." . . .

The right of attribution under VARA thus gives an artist a claim for injunctive relief to, inter alia, assert or disclaim authorship of a work. Whether VARA entitles an artist to damages for violation of the right of attribution is a separate question. We find the answer in the difference between the statutory language on the right of integrity and the language on the right of attribution. Subsection (a)(3) of section 106A, which codifies the right of integrity, is further divided into two subsections: (A) confers the right to protect the work against intentional alterations that would be prejudicial to honor or reputation, and (B) confers the right to protect a work of "recognized stature" from destruction. Although both subsections are framed as rights "to prevent" certain conduct, they both also contain an additional clause stating that the occurrence of that conduct is, at least in certain circumstances, "a violation of th[e] right" to prevent the conduct from happening. *See* 17 U.S.C. §106A(a)(3)(A) ("any intentional distortion, mutilation, or modification of that work is a violation of that right"); *id.* at §106(a)(3)(B) ("any intentional or grossly negligent destruction of that work is a violation of that right").

No such "violation" clause is included in the sections codifying the right of attribution. *See* [Melville B. Nimmer, 3-8D Nimmer on Copyright] §8D.06[B][1]. . . . Nimmer speculates as follows:

> Perhaps the implication is that whereas an integrity violation could give rise to a monetary recovery, failure to attribute is remediable solely through injunction. If

that conclusion were intended, Congress certainly could have expressed its intent less obliquely.

Id. We agree with Nimmer's surmise that VARA does not provide a damages remedy for an attribution violation. Where the statutory language is framed as a right "to prevent" conduct, it does not necessarily follow that a plaintiff is entitled to damages once the conduct occurs. . . .

B. Büchel's VARA Claims

With this legal framework in mind, we turn to the record before the district court. By dismantling "Training Ground," the Museum prevented the further use of Büchel's name in connection with the work, eliminating any basis for injunctive relief, and we therefore do not address the attribution claim in our VARA analysis. We thus consider the evidence in the light most favorable to Büchel in determining whether there are genuine issues of material fact regarding the alleged violations of his right of integrity. . . .

It cannot be disputed that, at least by the time Büchel left North Adams in December 2006, "Training Ground" was "fixed" within the meaning of the Copyright Act. . . . Büchel thus had rights in the work that were protected under VARA, notwithstanding its unfinished state. . . .

1. Continuing Work on "Training Ground"

Büchel asserts that, in the months following his departure from North Adams in December 2006, the Museum encroached on his artistic vision by making modifications to the installation that in some instances were directly contrary to his instructions. In rejecting Büchel's VARA claims, the district court described the Museum's actions as perhaps "occasionally misguided" attempts "to implement Büchel's long-distance instructions." . . .

Although a jury might agree with the court's assessment, the evidence viewed in the light most favorable to Büchel would allow a finding that at least some of the Museum's actions violated VARA. The record permits the inference that, even during his time as an artist-in-residence at MASS MoCA, Museum staff members were disregarding his instructions and intentionally modifying "Training Ground" in a manner that he did not approve. . . .

The record also contains evidence from which a jury could conclude that the Museum's alterations had a detrimental impact on Büchel's honor or reputation. An article in the Boston Globe reported that, in February, Museum officials had shown the unfinished project to a group of Museum directors and curators who were attending an arts conference in the area. . . .

Although the commentary generated by these visits is not all negative, there was sufficient evidence for a jury to find that the changes to "Training Ground" caused prejudice to Büchel. The New York Times noted that the exhibition would "certainly give people unfamiliar with his obsessive, history-driven aesthetic an inaccurate sense of his art, and this is indeed a form of damage." A critic for the Boston Globe similarly observed that "many people are going to judge [Büchel] and his work on the basis of this experience." Ken Johnson, *No admittance: MASS MoCA has mishandled disputed art installation,* Boston Globe, July 1, 2007, at 1N. . . .

The record thus shows that some viewers of the installation reacted unfavorably to the work in its allegedly modified and distorted form. A factfinder might conclude, of course, that it was Büchel's underlying concept (notwithstanding its unfinished state) rather than MASS MoCA's actions that elicited the negative reactions. . . .

. . . Our holding that the summary judgment record precludes an affirmance of the district court on this claim may serve as a cautionary tale to museums contemplating similar installations in the future—guiding them to document the terms of their relationship and obtain VARA waivers where necessary . . . .

2. Showing "Training Ground" Covered with Tarpaulins

Büchel also claims that MASS MoCA improperly modified and distorted "Training Ground" when it partially covered it with the yellow tarpaulins and displayed it in that condition. . . .

. . . [A]lthough the installation unquestionably looked different with the tarpaulins partially covering it, we agree with the district court that the mere covering of the artwork by the Museum, its host, cannot reasonably be deemed an intentional act of distortion or modification of Büchel's creation. To conclude otherwise would be to say that, even if all had gone well, the Museum would have been subject to a right-of-integrity claim if it had partially covered the work before its formal opening to prevent visitors from seeing it prematurely. . . .

3. Exhibiting "Training Ground" in Its Unfinished State

Büchel maintains that, even aside from the alleged modifications to "Training Ground," merely exhibiting the work of art in its unfinished state, without the artist's consent, constitutes a distortion. We reject this claim. A separate moral right of disclosure (also known as the right of divulgation) protects an author's authority to "prevent third parties from disclosing [his or her] work to the public without the author's consent," and is not covered by VARA. *See* Cyrill P. Rigamonti, *Deconstructing Moral Rights,* 47 Harv. Int'l L.J. 353, 373, 405 (2006) "([T]he VARA ignores the rights of disclosure and withdrawal and instead focuses on the rights of attribution and integrity. . . .").

Although Büchel proffered an expert who opined that showing an unfinished work without the artist's permission is inherently a distortion, we decline to interpret VARA to include such a claim where a separate moral right of disclosure is widely recognized in other jurisdictions and Congress explicitly limited the statute's coverage to the rights of attribution and integrity. . . .

NOTES AND QUESTIONS

1. Do you agree with the court's conclusion that damages are unavailable for violations of the attribution rights provided by VARA? Assume that MASS

MoCA had not dismantled "Training Ground for Democracy." The *Büchel* district court determined that the museum could display the work under certain conditions: (1) it must post a disclaimer informing patrons that the exhibit was an unfinished work that did not reflect the artist's original intent and; (2) it could not make mention of Büchel's name in association with the exhibit. The court also allowed Büchel to suggest his own language for the disclaimer, including disavowal of any responsibility for it. *Massachusetts Museum of Contemporary Art Found., Inc. v. Büchel*, 565 F. Supp. 2d 245, 248 (D. Mass. 2008), *aff'd in part, vacated in part, Massachusetts Museum of Contemporary Art Found., Inc.v. Büchel*, 593 F.3d 38 (1st Cir. 2010). Did those conditions effectively preserve Büchel's right of attribution under VARA?

2. As the court notes, in addition to the rights of paternity (attribution) and integrity secured by the Berne Convention, many countries recognize a moral right of divulgation, which includes the right to control the terms under which a work is first disclosed to the public, and a moral right to withdraw the work from circulation if it no longer represents the author's views. Can you think of any existing laws in the United States that might provide comparable protections to authors? Should U.S. law provide such protections?

3. Was the court right to allow Büchel's integrity claim to move forward based on unauthorized actions taken by MASS MoCA staff? How should the museum protect itself in future collaborations?

4. VARA provides that the rights granted by §106A apply to works created before the effective date of the Act only if title to those works is transferred by the author *after* the effective date of the Act. Pub. L. No. 101-650, 104 Stat. 5089, §610 (1990). Does this limitation on the effect of VARA for previously created works make sense? For works created after the effective date of VARA (June 1, 1991), the rights granted to the author of a work of visual art under §106A last for the life of the author, no matter how many times the artwork is sold or transferred.

LOOKING FORWARD

Unlike a copyright plaintiff, a VARA plaintiff need not register the work prior to suit, nor to preserve eligibility for statutory damages and attorneys' fees. We discuss copyright formalities and remedies in more detail in Chapters 11 and 13.

PRACTICE EXERCISE: ADVOCACY

The owner of the copyright to a black-and-white film directed by Randy Stone colorized the film, added Spanish subtitles, and licensed it for broadcast on Spanish television. Stone, an American citizen, successfully sued in Spain and obtained an injunction against the broadcasting organization, arguing that the colorized Spanish version infringed his right of integrity. Stone also brought a claim under U.S. law seeking to enjoin the broadcast of the film in the United States, but died prior to the commencement of the lawsuit. Your firm has been retained by his heirs to represent Stone's interests in court. You have been asked by a senior partner to research whether the moral right of integrity should prevent the broadcast of the colorized movie in the United States. Write the memorandum. Would your answer be different if Stone were still alive?

c. Destruction of Works of Recognized Stature

One of the rights granted to the author of a work of visual art under §106A(a)(3) is the right to prevent the destruction of the work, and to be compensated in certain cases of destruction. That right, however, only applies to works of recognized stature. Read the following case.

Martin v. City of Indianapolis
192 F.3d 608 (7th Cir. 1999)

WOOD, J.: We are not art critics, do not pretend to be and do not need to be to decide this case. A large outdoor stainless steel sculpture by plaintiff Jan Martin, an artist, was demolished by the defendant as part of an urban renewal project. Plaintiff brought a one-count suit against the City of Indianapolis (the "City") under the Visual Artists Rights Act of 1990 ("VARA"), 17 U.S.C. §101 *et seq.* . . .

I. Background

Plaintiff is an artist, but in this instance more with a welding torch than with a brush. He offered evidence to show, not all of it admitted, that his works have been displayed in museums, and other works created for private commissions, including a time capsule for the Indianapolis Museum of Art Centennial. He has also done sculptured jewelry for the Indiana Arts Commission. In 1979, at the Annual Hoosier Salem Art Show, plaintiff was awarded the prize for best of show in any medium. He holds various arts degrees from Purdue University, the Art Institute of Chicago and Bowling Green State University in Ohio. Plaintiff had been employed as production coordinator for Tarpenning-LaFollette Co. (the "Company"), a metal contracting firm in Indianapolis. It was in this position that he turned his artistic talents to metal sculpture fabrication.

In 1984, plaintiff received permission from the Indianapolis Metropolitan Development Commission to erect a twenty-by-forty-foot metal sculpture on land owned by John LaFollette, chairman of the Company. The Company also agreed to furnish the materials. . . .

Plaintiff went to work on the project and in a little over two years it was completed. He named it "Symphony #1," but as it turns out in view of this controversy, a more suitable musical name might have been "1812 Overture." Because of the possibility that the sculpture might someday have to be removed, as provided for in the Project Agreement, Symphony #1 was engineered and built by plaintiff so that it could be disassembled for removal and later reassembled. The sculpture did not go unnoticed by the press, public or art community. . . .

[The City subsequently acquired the land on which Symphony #1 was located. During the negotiations that led to the sale the City was repeatedly told that the sculpture could be moved if the City did not want it. The City promised to notify the plaintiff if it planned to remove the sculpture. Despite these assurances, shortly after the City acquired the land, it had the sculpture demolished without notice to the plaintiff.] . . . This lawsuit resulted in which summary judgment was allowed for plaintiff. However, his victory was not entirely satisfactory to him, nor was the City satisfied. The City appealed, and plaintiff cross-appealed.

II. Analysis

Although recognized under the Berne Convention, the legal protection of an artist's so-called "moral rights" was controversial in this country. The United States did not join the Berne Convention until 1988 when it did so in a very limited way. Then Congress followed up by enacting VARA in 1990, with this explanation found in the House Reports:

> An artist's professional and personal identity is embodied in each work created by that artist. Each work is a part of his or her reputation. Each work is a form of personal expression (oftentimes painstakingly and earnestly recorded). It is a rebuke to the dignity of the visual artist that our copyright law allows distortion, modification and even outright permanent destruction of such efforts.

H.R. Rep. No. 101-514, at 15 (1990), *reprinted in* 1990 U.S.C.C.A.N. 6915, 6925.

. . . VARA provides: "[T]he author of a work of visual art . . . shall have the right . . . to prevent any destruction of a work of *recognized stature,* and any intentional or grossly negligent destruction of that work is a violation of that right." 17 U.S.C. §106A(a)(3)(B) (emphasis added). The district court considered Symphony #1 to be of "recognized stature" under the evidence presented and thus concluded that the City had violated plaintiff's rights under VARA. That finding is contested by the City.

. . . The only case found undertaking to define and apply "recognized stature" is *Carter v. Helmsley-Spear, Inc.*, 861 F. Supp. 303 (S.D.N.Y. 1994), *aff'd in part, vacated in part, rev'd in part,* 71 F.3d 77 (2d Cir. 1995). . . . Although the Second Circuit reversed the district court and held that the work was not a work of visual art protected by VARA, *id.* at 88, the district court presented an informative discussion in determining whether a work of visual art may qualify as one of "recognized stature." *See Carter I*, 861 F. Supp. at 324-26. That determination is based greatly on the testimony of experts on both sides of the issue, as would ordinarily be expected.

The stature test formulated by the New York district court required:

> (1) that the visual art in question has "stature," i.e. is viewed as meritorious, and (2) that this stature is "recognized" by art experts, other members of the artistic community, or by some cross-section of society. In making this showing, plaintiffs generally, but not inevitably, will need to call expert witnesses to testify before the trier of fact.

Carter I, 861 F. Supp. at 325.

Even though the district court in this present case found that test was satisfied by the plaintiff's evidence, plaintiff argues that the *Carter v. Helmsley-Spear* test may be more rigorous than Congress intended. That may be, but we see no need for the

Symphony #1
Original artwork © Jan Martin. Reprinted by Permission.

purposes of this case to endeavor to refine that rule. Plaintiff's evidence, however, is not as complete as in *Carter v. Helmsley-Spear,* possibly because Symphony #1 was destroyed by the City without the opportunity for experts to appraise the sculpture in place.

The City objects to the "stature" testimony that was offered by plaintiff as inadmissible hearsay. If not admitted, it would result in plaintiff's failure to sustain his burden of proof. . . . Plaintiff's evidence of "stature" consisted of certain newspaper and magazine articles, and various letters, including a letter from an art gallery director and a letter to the editor of *The Indianapolis News,* all in support of the sculpture, as well as a program from the show at which a model of the sculpture won "Best of Show." After reviewing the City's objection, the district court excluded plaintiff's "programs and awards" evidence as lacking adequate foundation . . . but nevertheless found Martin had met his "stature" burden of proof with his other evidence.

Included in the admitted evidence, for example, was a letter dated October 25, 1982 from the Director of the Herron School of Art, Indiana University, Indianapolis. It was written to the Company and says in part, "The proposed sculpture is, in my opinion, an interesting and aesthetically stimulating configuration of forms and structures." *The Indianapolis Star,* in a four-column article by its visual arts editor, discussed public sculpture in Indianapolis. This article included a photograph of Symphony #1. The article lamented that the City had "been graced by only five pieces of note," but that two more had been added that particular year, one being plaintiff's sculpture. It noted, among other things, that Symphony #1 had been erected without the aid of "federal grants" and without the help of any committee of concerned citizens. Other public sculptures came in for some criticism in the article. However, in discussing Symphony #1, the author wrote: "Gleaming clean and abstract, yet domestic in scale and reference, irregularly but securely cabled together, the sculpture shows the site what it might be. It unites the area, providing a nexus, a marker, a designation, an identity and, presumably, a point of pride."

The district judge commented on the City's hearsay objection to plaintiff's admitted evidence as follows:

> The statements contained within the proffered newspaper and magazine articles and letters are offered by Martin to show that respected members of the art community and members of the public at large consider Martin's work to be socially valuable and to have artistic merit, and to show the newsworthiness of Symphony #1 and Martin's work. *These statements are offered by Martin to show that the declarants said them,* not that the statements are, in fact, true. . . . The statements contained within the exhibits show how art critics and the public viewed Martin's work, particularly Symphony #1, and show that the sculpture was a matter worth reporting to the public. Therefore, the statements contained within these challenged exhibits are not hearsay because they are not being offered for the truth of the matters asserted therein.

Martin I, 982 F. Supp. at 630 (emphasis added).

We agree with the assessment made by the district court. . . .

MANION, J., concurring in part and dissenting in part: . . . I begin with the well-worn adage that one man's junk is another man's treasure. . . . For the Martin sculpture to receive protection under the Visual Artists Rights Act (VARA), it has to rise to the statutory level of "recognized stature." Because at this summary judgment stage, at least, it has clearly not merited the protection that goes with that description, I respectfully dissent. . . .

. . . VARA was . . . designed . . . to protect great works of art from destruction and mutilation, among other things. 17 U.S.C. §106A(a). In order to restrict VARA's reach, the Act was limited to preventing destruction of works of art that had attained a "recognized stature." 17 U.S.C. §106A(a)(3)(B). . . . As the district court in *Carter v. Helmsley-Spear, Inc.* stated: "the recognized stature requirement is best viewed as a gate-keeping mechanism—protection is afforded only to those works of art that art experts, the art community, or society in general views as possessing stature." 861 F. Supp. 303, 325 (S.D.N.Y. 1994), *rev'd in part and aff'd in part*, 71 F.3d 77 (2d Cir. 1995). . . .

I dissent . . . because summary judgment is not appropriate here. A plaintiff cannot satisfy his burden of demonstrating recognized stature through old newspaper articles and unverified letters, some of which do not even address the artwork in question. Rather, as the district court stated in *Carter*, in "making this showing [of recognized stature] plaintiffs generally, but not inevitably, will need to call expert witnesses to testify before the trier of fact." 861 F. Supp. at 325. Instances where expert testimony on this point is not necessary will be rare, and this is not one of those exceptional cases where something of unquestioned recognition and stature was destroyed. . . . The newspaper articles are hearsay and not admitted for the truth of the matter asserted in them. Construed in the light most favorable to the defendant, they cannot demonstrate by a preponderance of the evidence that the plaintiff's art was of a recognized stature, and that no reasonable jury could find otherwise. Experts need to weigh in here, and the trial court and perhaps this court need to come up with a clearer definition of when works of art achieve "recognized stature."

For now, however, those who are purchasers or donees of art had best beware. To avoid being the perpetual curator of a piece of visual art that has lost (or perhaps never had) its luster, the recipient must obtain at the outset a waiver of the artist's rights under VARA. Before awarding building permits for erection of sculptures, municipalities might be well advised to obtain a written waiver of the artist's rights too. If not, once destroyed, art of questionable value may acquire a minimum worth of $20,000.00 under VARA.

NOTES AND QUESTIONS

1. What justifies the requirement in §106A(a)(3)(B) that a work be of "recognized stature" to be protected against destruction? Should experts be required to determine whether a work is of "recognized stature," as the *Martin* dissent suggests? For discussion of the "recognized stature" requirement, see Christopher J. Robinson, Note, *The "Recognized Stature" Standard in the Visual Artists Rights Act*, 68 Fordham L. Rev. 1935 (2000).

2. Section 106(A)(a)(3) is subject to §113(d). Read that section now. What is its purpose?

3. Section 106A creates a third category of rights that may exist in certain works of visual art. First, there is the right in the intangible work (the copyright); second, there is the right in the physical object (personal property); and third, under §106A, there is the right of the artist to protect against certain actions related to the physical object (VARA entitlement). The artist's VARA rights exist even if the copyright belongs to someone else (except in the case of a work made for hire) and even if the physical object belongs to someone else. Are rights in physical embodiments of the work the only sort of moral rights contemplated by Article 6*bis*?

COMPARATIVE PERSPECTIVE

A number of countries provide visual artists with a right called the *droit de suite*. Generally, the *droit de suite* gives an artist the right to receive a part of the proceeds from a resale of the artist's work. The right is particularly useful to painters and graphic artists, whose income generally comes from sales of their original artwork, and whose works may appreciate significantly over time. The United States has not implemented the *droit de suite* at the federal level, although one state, California, recognizes it. The California Resale Royalties Act, enacted in 1976, provides for payment to the artist on the resale of a "work of fine art," and applies to sellers who reside in California as well as sales taking place there. The artist is entitled to a royalty of 5 percent of the gross sale price. *See* Cal. Civ. Code §986 (2005).

PRACTICE EXERCISE: COUNSEL A CLIENT

Chris is an artist who has exhibited work at museums in New York, San Francisco, Paris, and Tokyo. Over a 25-year period, he also painted a large number of murals on the walls of a juvenile detention facility in San Francisco. Over time, most of the murals were destroyed. Two remain. The city would like to tear down the facility (destroying the murals) and build a new detention center. Chris wants the city to remove the remaining murals and then redisplay them at the new facility when it is completed. You work in the San Francisco City Attorney's Office. Please advise the city whether Chris can invoke VARA to stop the destruction. (Don't forget to consult §113(d).) Based on your conclusions, what might you suggest be included in contracts for works that the city commissions in the future?

B. PERFORMERS' RIGHTS AND RELATED TREATY OBLIGATIONS

Article 14 of the TRIPS Agreement specifies various rights to be afforded to performers, producers of phonograms (i.e., sound recordings), and broadcasters. Reflecting the continental European approach to copyright, these entities are not considered authors in the strict sense. For that reason, some countries formally designate the rights held by these entities as "neighboring rights"—rights owing their inception to the rise of new technologies for propagating authorial expression. As Paul Goldstein and Bernt Hugenholtz explain:

> At the same time that philosophies of authorial personality and case law on moral right were forging a doctrine of author's right, technologies were beginning to emerge that would challenge the doctrine's assumptions respecting authorship. Photographs, it might be thought, were the products of a mechanical process, not an artist's creative vision; motion pictures were the product of corporate organizations, not the labors of individual authors. After some agonizing, civil law countries brought photographs and films within author's right, but they drew the line there and rejected author's right protection for performances, sound recordings or phonograms, and broadcasts. Instead, they created for these and other new productions a regime of neighboring rights. . . .
>
> The main consequential difference between the systems of author's right and neighboring rights, on the one side, and copyright systems, on the other, lies in the international obligations the two approaches entail. If Country A defines a form of creative production . . . as being something other than a "literary" or "artistic work," the subject matter will fall outside the country's obligation under the Berne Convention to extend the Convention's minimum standards and national treatment requirement to productions coming from Country B. . . .

Paul Goldstein & P. Bernt Hugenholtz, International Copyright: Principles, Law, and Practice 21-22 (3d ed. 2012).

Although Berne Convention's national treatment obligations do not extend directly to subject matter covered by neighboring rights, TRIPS Article 14 makes some of those obligations relevant. Read it now. The remaining subsections of this chapter are designed to give you an overview of the principal issues for U.S. copyright law raised by Article 14's requirements.

1. Anti-Bootlegging Protection in U.S. Law

LOOKING BACK

Recall from Chapter 2 that a contemporaneous recording of a live public performance can satisfy the fixation requirement for copyright protection if it is (1) prepared by or under the authority of the author and (2) simultaneously being transmitted.

Article 14(1) of the TRIPS Agreement requires that "performers shall have the possibility of preventing . . . the fixation of their unfixed performance and the reproduction of such fixation . . . [and] the communication to the public of their live performance." In 1994, Congress amended the Copyright Act by adding §1101, which prohibits the fixation or transmission of a live musical performance without the consent of the performers, and also prohibits the reproduction or distribution of copies or phonorecords of an unauthorized fixation of a live musical performance. Congress also enacted a criminal version of these prohibitions, which is codified at 18 U.S.C. §2319A. The constitutionality of that provision is the subject of the next case.

United States v. Martignon
492 F.3d 140 (2d Cir. 2007)

POOLER, J.:

This appeal presents a recurring issue in constitutional law: the extent to which Congress can use one of its powers to enact a statute that it could not enact under another of its arguably relevant powers. *See, e.g., Ry. Labor Executives' Ass'n v. Gibbons,* 455 U.S. 457 (1982); *Heart of Atlanta Motel, Inc. v. United States,* 379 U.S. 241 (1964); *In re Trade-Mark Cases,* 100 U.S. 82 (1879). Here the statute involved is Section 2319A of Title 18, which prohibits the unauthorized recording of performances as well as the copying, distribution, sale, rental, and trafficking of these bootlegged phonorecords. The constitutional grants of congressional power at issue are the Commerce Clause . . . and the Copyright Clause . . . .

Background . . .

On October 27, 2004, a grand jury charged Martignon, the proprietor of Midnight Records in Manhattan, with one count of violating Section 2319A by reproducing an unauthorized phonorecord and by distributing and selling and offering to distribute and sell phonorecords of performances which had been recorded or fixed without the consent of the performer or performers. Martignon moved to dismiss the indictment, arguing that Section 2319A violated the Copyright Clause because live performances are not "Writings" within the meaning of the clause and because live performances were given protection for perpetuity rather than for a "limited Time[ ]". . . . The government responded that Congress had authority to enact Section 2319A under the Commerce and Necessary and Proper Clauses.

The district court granted the motion to dismiss. *Martignon,* 346 F. Supp. 2d at 429. The court began its analysis with an examination of whether Section 2319A was copyright or commercial regulation. Although the court acknowledged that if Congress had the power to enact Section 2319A under the Commerce Clause, its belief that it was acting under the Copyright Clause would not be dispositive, it held that "it is still essential to determine how to classify a statute in order to ensure that it does not run afoul of any express limitations imposed on Congress when regulating in the respective arena," *id.* at 420. For four separate but related reasons, Judge Baer concluded that Section 2319A was more closely tied to the Copyright than to the Commerce Clause. First, the agreement that it implemented, TRIPS, was intended to protect intellectual property. Second, the words of the statute were consistent with the purpose of the Copyright Clause, encouraging authors and inventors to create by granting them exclusive rights in their writings and discoveries. Third, the Committee on the Judiciary's report describes the legislation in terms of copyright and contains no mention of commerce. Fourth, Section 2319A follows the criminal copyright provision and refers to the definitions in Title 17, the copyright title of the United States Code.

Despite the copyright-like appearance of Section 2319A, the district court held that it could not be sustained under the Copyright Clause because it "provides seemingly *perpetual protection* for *unfixed* musical performances." *Id.* at 423. . . .

Finally, the court held that Congress could not do indirectly, under the Commerce Clause or the Necessary and Proper Clause, what it is forbidden to do directly under the Copyright Clause. . . . As an alternative to finding an absolute ban against enacting copyright-like legislation under any clause other than the Copyright Clause, Judge Baer held that "even if Congress may enact copyright-like legislation under grants other than the Copyright Clause, . . . such legislation may not be 'fundamentally inconsistent' with the fixation and durational limitations imposed by the Copyright Clause." *Id.* He then found fundamental inconsistency between the "limited Times" provision and Section 2319A's failure to impose a time limit for violations.[3] . . .

Discussion . . .

Scope and Limits of the Copyright Clause

In *Graham v. John Deere Co.,* the Court described the Copyright Clause as "both a grant of power and a limitation." 383 U.S. 1, 5 (1966). . . .

---

3. The only other court to assess the constitutionality of Section 2319A concluded that it was properly enacted pursuant to the Commerce Clause. *See United States v. Moghadam,* 175 F.3d 1269 (11th Cir.1999). Moghadam, unlike Martignon, did not argue that Section 2319A violated the "limited Times" provision of the Copyright Clause, and the Eleventh Circuit carefully noted that it did not reach this issue.

It is not clear from the wording of the Copyright Clause where the grant of power ends and where the limitation(s) begin(s). This clause allows Congress "[t]o promote the Progress of Science and useful Arts, by securing for limited Times to Authors and Inventors the exclusive Right to their respective Writings and Discoveries." One could draw the line between grant and limitation(s) almost anywhere in this sentence. For example, the grant of power could be to pass legislation to promote the useful arts and sciences, limited, however, to the realm of the original, to the method of granting exclusive rights, and to a period of limited duration. Conversely, the Clause can be construed to allow Congress to pass legislation giving creators of original work an exclusive right in their fixed work, limited only by the requirement that the grant be of limited duration. We find no useful punctuation or structural clues in the text of the clause. Indeed, the "limited Times" language, which both parties agree is a limitation rather than part of a grant of power, is squarely in the middle of the Clause. Further, the *Graham* Court read the creativity requirement, "[t]o promote the . . . useful Arts," as a limitation on Congress's power, thus suggesting that the power granted and the limitations are virtually coterminous. . . .

The Supreme Court has indicated that Congress can sometimes enact legislation under one constitutional provision that it could not have enacted under another. . . . However, this power is not unlimited. . . .

We turn . . . to *Gibbons,* which is at the heart of Martignon's claim that Congress could not enact Section 2319A under the Commerce Clause because of limitations contained in the Copyright Clause. In 1975, The Chicago, Rock Island, and Pacific Railroad Co. ("Rock Island") petitioned for reorganization under the bankruptcy laws. . . . In June 1980, the bankruptcy court concluded that employee-labor-protection claims could not be paid out of Rock Island's assets. Congress responded by enacting the Rock Island Railroad Transition and Employee Assistance Act ("RITA"). RITA provided that the trustee must pay up to $75 million to Rock Island employees who were not hired by other carriers. These payments were to be made as administrative expenses, which would give them priority over other creditors' claims.

When the matter reached the Supreme Court, it invalidated the pertinent RITA provisions as "repugnant to Art. I, §8, cl. 4, the Bankruptcy Clause, of the Constitution." *Id*. at 465. First, the Court analyzed whether RITA was an exercise of Congress's Bankruptcy Clause or Commerce Clause power. It acknowledged that "[d]istinguishing a congressional exercise of power under the Commerce Clause from an exercise under the Bankruptcy Clause is . . . not an easy task, for the two Clauses are closely related." *Id*. Nevertheless, and for several reasons, the Court found that Congress exercised its power under the Bankruptcy Clause. First, RITA contained specific directives to the bankruptcy court concerning the distribution of the property of a particular estate. Second, it rearranged the priorities of various payments from the estate, giving the employees priority over other creditors. Third, the events surrounding the enactment of the legislation indicated that Congress knew it was exercising its powers under the Bankruptcy Clause. Finally, RITA was passed almost five years after Rock Island sought the protection of the bankruptcy laws.

The Court then turned its attention briefly to the Commerce Clause, saying, "[w]e do not understand either appellant or the United States to argue that Congress may enact bankruptcy laws pursuant to its power under the Commerce Clause." *Id*. at 468. The Court also noted that the Bankruptcy Clause "contain[ed] an affirmative limitation or restriction upon Congress' power"—that bankruptcy laws must be uniform throughout the United States—that was not contained in the Commerce Clause. *Id*. The Court therefore reasoned that "if we were to hold that Congress had the power to enact nonuniform bankruptcy laws pursuant to the Commerce Clause, we would eradicate from the Constitution a limitation on the power of Congress to enact bankruptcy laws." *Id*. at 468-69. The Court then examined the uniformity requirement, found that RITA violated this requirement, and declared it unconstitutional.

Gibbons' analysis . . . considers whether RITA was really a bankruptcy or a commercial regulation. Read too broadly, this aspect of *Gibbons* would conflict with clear Supreme Court precedent holding that it does not matter that Congress believes it is legislating under a clause which would not give it the power it seeks as long as it actually has the power to legislate under another. A careful reading of *Gibbons* avoids any such conflict. The *Gibbons* Court considered primarily what RITA did, not Congress's belief as to which clause authorized its action. RITA mandated that an existing bankruptcy proceeding be handled differently from any other bankruptcy in the United States. It also altered the statutory priorities for paying debts and the administrative scheme contemplated by the Bankruptcy Code. It was a bankruptcy law.

We believe that the Supreme Court's cases allow the regulation of matters that could not be regulated under the Copyright Clause in a manner arguably inconsistent with that clause unless the statute at issue is a copyright law. . . . [W]e conclude that Congress exceeds its power under the Commerce Clause by transgressing limitations of the Copyright Clause only when (1) the law it enacts is an exercise of the power granted Congress by the Copyright Clause and (2) the resulting law violates one or more specific limits of the Copyright Clause. For reasons that follow, though, to resolve this appeal, we need not identify the full scope of the power granted by the Copyright Clause.

With these principles in mind we consider whether Section 2319A is a copyright law in the sense that RITA was a bankruptcy law. . . .

. . . Unlike the Bankruptcy Clause analyzed in *Gibbons*, the Copyright Clause does not identify the type of law Congress may pass pursuant to it—indeed, the word "copyright" does not appear in it at all. . . .

The second way to identify the controlling characteristic of the power granted Congress by Article I, Section 8, cl. 8 is to rely on its history and context. Although the clause does not mention the word "copyright," the framers did. *See The Federalist*, No. 43 (quoting the clause and arguing for its utility by referencing the "copyright of authors" in England). If the clause is meant to give Congress the power to pass copyright laws, we can fashion a working definition of a "copyright law" by looking for characteristics common to statutes, not governed by the grant of power embodied in the Copyright Clause, that are concededly copyright laws. Copyright laws adopted by the colonies prior to ratification, colonial-era British copyright laws, and state copyright laws are helpful. They all seem to share a common feature: They allocate property rights in expression. . . .

Section 2319A does not create and bestow property rights upon authors or inventors, or allocate those rights among claimants to them. It is a criminal statute, falling in its codification (along with Section 2319B about bootlegged films) between the law criminalizing certain copyright infringement and the law criminalizing "trafficking in counterfeit goods or services." It is, perhaps, analogous to the law of criminal trespass. Rather than creating a right in the performer him- or herself, it creates a power in the government to protect the interest of performers from commercial predations. Section 2319A does not grant the performer the right to exclude others from the performance—only the government can do that. Neither may the performer transfer his or her interests under Section 2319A to another. Section 2319A only prevents others from doing something without the authorization of the protected person. It may therefore protect the property interests an individual holds by virtue of other laws, but it does not itself allocate those interests. Section 2319A is not a law "secur[ing] . . . rights," nor is it a copyright law. . . .

. . . We therefore conclude that it was not enacted under the Copyright Clause. We have no need to examine whether it violates limits of the Copyright Clause and proceed instead to an examination of its sustainability under the Commerce Clause.

Commerce Clause Authority

"It is by now well established that legislative Acts adjusting the burdens and benefits of economic life come to the Court with a presumption of constitutionality." *Usery v. Turner Elkhorn Mining Co.,* 428 U.S. 1, 15 (1976). "A court may invalidate legislation enacted under the Commerce Clause only if it is clear that there is no rational basis for a congressional finding that the regulated activity affects interstate commerce, or that there is no reasonable connection between the regulatory means selected and the asserted ends." *Fed. Energy Regulatory Comm'n v. Mississippi,* 456 U.S. 742, 754 (1982). Section 2319A has substantial commercial and economic aspects. Indeed, regulation of bootlegging is necessary at the federal level because of its interstate and international commercial aspects. . . . Further, Section 2319A regulates only fixing, selling, distributing, and copying with a commercial motive, activities at the core of the Commerce Clause.[8] It would have been eminently reasonable for Congress to conclude that the sale and distribution of bootleg phonorecords will have a substantial interstate effect on the sale and distribution of legitimate phonorecords. Because Section 2319A is not a copyright law and its enactment was well within the scope of Congress's Commerce Clause authority, it is constitutionally permissible unless some other constitutional provision prevents its enforcement. . . .

---

8. This commercial purpose distinguishes Section 2319A from Section 1101. A person who recorded a concert for her personal enjoyment would not violate Section 2319A. Further, because no commercial motive is required for a Section 1101 violation, we specifically limit today's holding to Section 2319A and express no opinion on Section 1101's constitutionality.

NOTES AND QUESTIONS

1. Do you agree with the court that §2319A is not a copyright law, or are you relatively more persuaded by the district court's approach?

2. If a civil suit under §1101 were to come before the court, how should the issue reserved in footnote 8 be decided?

3. The WIPO Performances and Phonograms Treaty (WPPT) goes beyond the requirements of TRIPS Article 14(1), directing that performers be granted moral rights as well as economic rights. *See* WPPT, art. 5(1). The United States ratified the WPPT in 1998. The implementing legislation, however, stated: "no works other than sound recordings shall be eligible for protection under this title solely by virtue of the adherence of the United States to the . . . WIPO Performances and Phonograms Treaty." Digital Millennium Copyright Act, Pub. L. No. 105-304, §102(b)(2), 112 Stat. 2860 (1998), *codified as amended a*t 17 U.S.C. §104(d).

2. Diving Deeper: Treaty Obligations Regarding Sound Recordings and Broadcasting Organizations

Article 14 of the TRIPS Agreement includes several requirements that pertain to phonograms (sound recordings). Paragraph (2) mandates rights to control "direct or indirect reproduction"; paragraph (4) mandates rental rights but subjects those rights to preexisting systems of equitable remuneration; and paragraph (5) provides for a minimum term of protection. Review those paragraphs now.

The United States also has acceded to the WPPT's requirements covering sound recordings. Article 14 of the WPPT provides: "Producers of phonograms shall enjoy the exclusive right of authorizing the making available to the public of their phonograms, by wire or wireless means, in such a way that members of the public may access them from a place and at a time individually chosen by them." Article 15 indicates that this right may be made subject, in full or in part, to a system of equitable remuneration. Under Article 16(2), member states must "confine any limitations of or exceptions to rights provided for in this Treaty to certain special cases which do not conflict with a normal exploitation of the . . . phonogram and do not unreasonably prejudice the legitimate interests of the . . . producer of the phonogram."

Paragraph 3 of Article 14 of the WPPT pertains to broadcasting organizations. It allows member states to choose between granting separate, neighboring rights to such organizations and granting copyright rights to "owners of copyright in the subject matter of broadcasts." The latter option appears to have been included to accommodate the United States. As you learned in Chapter 2, *supra*, the United States permits broadcasters who fix copies of their broadcasts as they are being transmitted to claim copyright protection. Other common law nations choosing to protect broadcasts within their copyright law include Canada and the United Kingdom. However, many countries have adopted *sui generis* neighboring rights protection that is arguably broader than the protection for performer's rights as recognized in U.S. law. Many of these countries are party to an international treaty, the Rome Convention, which establishes international minimum standards for the protection of neighboring rights. These include minimum protection for performers (Article 7), a right of reproduction for producers of phonograms (Article 10), and minimum rights for broadcasting organizations (Article 13). There are currently 92 countries that are members of the Rome Convention. The United States is not a member.

NOTES AND QUESTIONS

1. Recall what you learned in Chapter 7 about protection for sound recordings. Does U.S. law concerning copyright in sound recordings comply with the requirements of Article 14 of the WPPT?

2. In 2012, the international framework for neighboring rights came full circle with the successful conclusion of a new WIPO treaty establishing minimum standards of protection for performers. The Beijing Treaty for Audiovisual Performances fills a gap left by the Rome Convention and the WPPT, namely protection for audiovisual performers. The Beijing Treaty requires member states to provide protection in fixed and unfixed audiovisual performances, including moral rights (Article 5); economic rights in unfixed performances (Article 6); the rights of reproduction, distribution, rental, making available of fixed copies, and broadcasting and communication to the public (Articles 7-11). The Beijing Treaty will enter into force once it has been ratified by 30 countries. By the end of 2014, only Botswana, China, Japan, Slovakia Syria, and the United Arab Emirates had ratified it. Read the text of the Beijing Treaty. Should the United States ratify it? Why, or why not?

IV

INDIRECT INFRINGEMENT AND LAWFUL USE

9

The Different Faces of Infringement

The materials in Part II focused primarily on identifying what activities constitute infringement rather than on the equally important questions of who is an infringer and what is the nature of her liability. In many cases, the infringer's identity seems obvious. For example, if you were to perform a copyrighted song in concert, you would be liable for infringement unless you had paid the required license fee or unless you had some other defense. In this example, however, it is necessary to consider whether the operator of the concert venue also is liable. Indeed, that potential liability leads venues to be the ones that typically secure the necessary licenses. More advanced technology introduces additional complications. If you record your performance and distribute it online, either by posting a copy to a website for others to access and download or by using file-sharing software to make it available to others, the question then arises whether the Internet access provider, the website operator, and/or the provider of file-sharing software might be liable for copyright infringement.

Copyright law has developed doctrines of direct and secondary liability to address who should be liable when infringement occurs. This chapter begins by considering the nature of the liability of those who commit the act that violates one of the copyright owner's §106 rights—so-called direct infringers. It then moves to questions of secondary liability: Under what circumstances should one who is not a direct infringer but who somehow participates in the infringing conduct be liable? As you read the material in this chapter, consider whether Congress and the courts have assigned liability in ways that are likely to further copyright law's underlying goals.

A. DIRECT INFRINGEMENT

1. Volition

Religious Technology Center v. Netcom On-Line Communication Services, Inc.
907 F. Supp. 1361 (N.D. Cal. 1995)

WHYTE, J.: This case concerns an issue of first impression regarding intellectual property rights in cyberspace. Specifically, this order addresses whether the operator of a computer bulletin board service ("BBS"), and the large Internet access provider that allows that BBS to reach the Internet, should be liable for copyright infringement committed by a subscriber of the BBS.

Plaintiffs Religious Technology Center ("RTC") and Bridge Publications, Inc. ("BPI") hold copyrights in the unpublished and published works of L. Ron Hubbard, the late founder of the Church of Scientology ("the Church"). Defendant Dennis Erlich ("Erlich") is a former minister of Scientology turned vocal critic of the Church, whose pulpit is now the Usenet newsgroup alt.religion.scientology ("a.r.s."), an online forum for discussion and criticism of Scientology. Plaintiffs maintain that Erlich infringed their copyrights when he posted portions of their works on a.r.s. Erlich gained his access to the Internet through defendant Thomas Klemesrud's ("Klemesrud's") BBS "support.com." Klemesrud is the operator of the BBS, which is run out of his home and has approximately 500 paying users. Klemesrud's BBS is not directly linked to the Internet, but gains its connection through the facilities of defendant Netcom On-Line Communications, Inc. ("Netcom"), one of the largest providers of Internet access in the United States.

After failing to convince Erlich to stop his postings, plaintiffs contacted defendants Klemesrud and Netcom. Klemesrud responded to plaintiffs' demands that Erlich be kept off his system by asking plaintiffs to prove that they owned the copyrights to the works posted by Erlich. However, plaintiffs refused Klemesrud's request as unreasonable. Netcom similarly refused plaintiffs' request that Erlich not be allowed to gain access to the Internet through its system. Netcom contended that it would be impossible to prescreen Erlich's postings and that to kick Erlich off the Internet meant kicking off the hundreds of users of Klemesrud's BBS. Consequently, plaintiffs named Klemesrud and Netcom in their suit against Erlich. . . .

1. Direct Infringement

Infringement consists of the unauthorized exercise of one of the exclusive rights of the copyright holder delineated in section 106. 17 U.S.C. §501. Direct infringement does not require intent or any particular state of mind, although willfulness is relevant to the award of statutory damages. 17 U.S.C. §504(c). . . .

a. Undisputed Facts

The parties do not dispute the basic processes that occur when Erlich posts his allegedly infringing messages to a.r.s. Erlich connects to Klemesrud's BBS using a telephone and a modem. Erlich then transmits his messages to Klemesrud's computer, where they are automatically briefly stored. According to a prearranged pattern established by Netcom's software, Erlich's initial act of posting a message to the Usenet results in the automatic copying of Erlich's message from Klemesrud's computer onto Netcom's computer and onto other computers on the Usenet. In order to ease transmission and for the convenience of Usenet users, Usenet servers maintain postings from newsgroups for a short period of time—eleven days for Netcom's system and three days for Klemesrud's system. Once on Netcom's computers, messages are available to Netcom's customers and Usenet neighbors, who may then download the messages to their own computers. Netcom's local server makes available its postings to a group of Usenet servers, which do the same for other servers until all Usenet sites worldwide have obtained access to the postings, which takes a matter of hours.

Unlike some other large on-line service providers, such as CompuServe, America Online, and Prodigy, Netcom does not create or control the content of the information available to its subscribers. It also does not monitor messages as they are posted. It has, however, suspended the accounts of subscribers who violated its terms and conditions, such as where they had commercial software in their posted files. Netcom admits that, although not currently configured to do this, it may be possible to reprogram its system to screen postings containing particular words or coming from particular individuals. Netcom, however, took no action after it was told by plaintiffs that Erlich had posted messages through Netcom's system that violated plaintiffs' copyrights, instead claiming that it could not shut out Erlich without shutting out all of the users of Klemesrud's BBS.

b. Creation of Fixed Copies

. . . In the present case, there is no question after *MAI* [*Systems Corp. v. Peak Computer, Inc.*] that "copies" were created, as Erlich's act of sending a message to a.r.s. caused reproductions of portions of plaintiffs' works on both Klemesrud's and Netcom's storage devices. Even though the messages remained on their systems for at most eleven days, they were sufficiently "fixed" to constitute recognizable copies under the Copyright Act.

c. Is Netcom Directly Liable for Making the Copies?

Accepting that copies were made, Netcom argues that Erlich, and not Netcom, is directly liable for the copying. *MAI* did not address the question raised in this case: whether possessors of computers are liable for incidental copies automatically made on their computers using their software as part of a process initiated by a third party. . . . Netcom's actions, to the extent that they created a copy of plaintiffs' works, were necessary to having a working system for transmitting Usenet postings to and from the Internet. Unlike the defendants in *MAI*, neither Netcom nor

Klemesrud initiated the copying. . . . Thus, unlike *MAI*, the mere fact that Netcom's system incidentally makes temporary copies of plaintiffs' works does not mean Netcom has caused the copying. The court believes that Netcom's act of designing or implementing a system that automatically and uniformly creates temporary copies of all data sent through it is not unlike that of the owner of a copying machine who lets the public make copies with it. Although some of the people using the machine may directly infringe copyrights, courts analyze the machine owner's liability under the rubric of contributory infringement, not direct infringement. Plaintiffs' theory would create many separate acts of infringement and, carried to its natural extreme, would lead to unreasonable liability. It is not difficult to conclude that Erlich infringes by copying a protected work onto his computer and by posting a message to a newsgroup. However, plaintiffs' theory further implicates a Usenet server that carries Erlich's message to other servers regardless of whether that server acts without any human intervention beyond the initial setting up of the system. It would also result in liability for every single Usenet server in the worldwide link of computers transmitting Erlich's message to every other computer. These parties, who are liable under plaintiffs' theory, do no more than operate or implement a system that is essential if Usenet messages are to be widely distributed. There is no need to construe the Act to make all of these parties infringers. Although copyright is a strict liability statute, there should still be some element of volition or causation which is lacking where a defendant's system is merely used to create a copy by a third party.

Plaintiffs point out that the infringing copies resided for eleven days on Netcom's computer and were sent out from it onto the "Information Superhighway." However, under plaintiffs' theory, any storage of a copy that occurs in the process of sending a message to the Usenet is an infringement. While it is possible that less "damage" would have been done if Netcom had heeded plaintiffs' warnings and acted to prevent Erlich's message from being forwarded, this is not relevant to its *direct* liability for copying. The same argument is true of Klemesrud and any Usenet server. Whether a defendant makes a direct copy that constitutes infringement cannot depend on whether it received a warning to delete the message. . . .

Playboy Enterprises, Inc. v. Frena involved a suit against the operator of a small BBS whose system contained files of erotic pictures. 839 F. Supp. 1552, 1554 (M.D. Fla. 1993). A subscriber of the defendant's BBS had uploaded files containing digitized pictures copied from the plaintiff's copyrighted magazine, which files remained on the BBS for other subscribers to download. *Id.* The court did not conclude, as plaintiffs suggest in this case, that the BBS is itself liable for the unauthorized *reproduction* of plaintiffs' work; instead, the court concluded that the BBS operator was liable for violating the plaintiff's right to publicly *distribute and display* copies of its work. *Id.* at 1556-57. . . .

[T]his court holds that the storage on a defendant's system of infringing copies and retransmission to other servers is not a direct infringement by the BBS operator of the exclusive right to *reproduce* the work where such copies are uploaded by an infringing user. *Playboy* does not hold otherwise. . . .

Playboy concluded that the defendant infringed the plaintiff's exclusive rights to publicly distribute and display copies of its works. . . . Such a holding suffers from the same problem of causation as the reproduction argument. Only the subscriber should be liable for causing the distribution of plaintiffs' work, as the contributing actions of the BBS provider are automatic and indiscriminate. Erlich could have posted his messages through countless access providers and the outcome would be the same: anyone with access to Usenet newsgroups would be able to read his messages. There is no logical reason to draw a line around Netcom and Klemesrud and say that they are uniquely responsible for distributing Erlich's messages. . . . Every Usenet server has a role in the distribution, so plaintiffs' argument would create unreasonable liability. Where the BBS merely stores and passes along all messages sent by its subscribers and others, the BBS should not be seen as causing these works to be publicly distributed or displayed.

Even accepting the *Playboy* court's holding, the case is factually distinguishable. Unlike the BBS in that case, Netcom does not maintain an archive of files for its users. Thus, it cannot be said to be "suppl[ying] a product." . . . Netcom does not create or control the content of the information available to its subscribers; it merely provides *access* to the Internet, whose content is controlled by no single entity. Although the Internet consists of many different computers networked together, some of which may contain infringing files, it does not make sense to hold the operator of each computer liable as an infringer merely because his or her computer is linked to a computer with an infringing file. It would be especially inappropriate to hold liable a service that acts more like a conduit, in other words, one that does not itself keep an archive of files for more than a short duration. Finding such a service liable would involve an unreasonably broad construction of public distribution and display rights. No purpose would be served by holding liable those who have no ability to control the information to which their subscribers have access, even though they might be in some sense helping to achieve the Internet's automatic "public distribution" and the users' "public" display of files. . . .

Cartoon Network LP v. CSC Holdings, Inc.
536 F.3d 121 (2d Cir. 2008)

[Review the facts of this case, *supra*, Chapter 2.A.]

WALKER, J.: . . . After an RS–DVR subscriber selects a program to record, and that program airs, a copy of the program—a copyrighted work—resides on the hard disks of Cablevision's Arroyo Server, its creation unauthorized by the copyright holder. The question is *who* made this copy. If it is Cablevision, plaintiffs' theory of direct infringement succeeds; if it is the customer, plaintiffs' theory fails because Cablevision would then face, at most, secondary liability, a theory of liability expressly disavowed by plaintiffs.

Few cases examine the line between direct and contributory liability. Both parties cite a line of cases beginning with *Religious Technology Center v. Netcom On–Line Communication Services,* 907 F. Supp. 1361 (N.D. Cal. 1995). . . . Recently, the Fourth Circuit endorsed the *Netcom* decision, noting that

> to establish *direct* liability under . . . the Act, something more must be shown than mere ownership of a machine used by others to make illegal copies. There must be

actual infringing conduct with a nexus sufficiently close and causal to the illegal copying that one could conclude that the machine owner himself trespassed on the exclusive domain of the copyright owner.

CoStar Group, Inc. v. LoopNet, Inc., 373 F.3d 544, 550 (4th Cir.2004).

Here, the district court pigeon-holed the conclusions reached in *Netcom* and its progeny as "premised on the unique attributes of the Internet." *Cablevision I,* 478 F. Supp. 2d at 620. While the *Netcom* court was plainly concerned with a theory of direct liability that would effectively "hold the entire Internet liable" for the conduct of a single user, 907 F. Supp. at 1372, its reasoning and conclusions, consistent with precedents of this court and the Supreme Court, and with the text of the Copyright Act, transcend the Internet. Like the Fourth Circuit, we reject the contention that "the *Netcom* decision was driven by expedience and that its holding is inconsistent with the established law of copyright," *CoStar,* 373 F.3d at 549, and we find it "a particularly rational interpretation of §106," *id.* at 551, rather than a special-purpose rule applicable only to ISPs.

When there is a dispute as to the author of an allegedly infringing instance of reproduction, *Netcom* and its progeny direct our attention to the volitional conduct that causes the copy to be made. There are only two instances of volitional conduct in this case: Cablevision's conduct in designing, housing, and maintaining a system that exists only to produce a copy, and a customer's conduct in ordering that system to produce a copy of a specific program. In the case of a VCR, it seems clear—and we know of no case holding otherwise—that the operator of the VCR, the person who actually presses the button to make the recording, supplies the necessary element of volition, not the person who manufactures, maintains, or, if distinct from the operator, owns the machine. We do not believe that an RS–DVR customer is sufficiently distinguishable from a VCR user to impose liability as a direct infringer on a different party for copies that are made automatically upon that customer's command.

The district court emphasized the fact that copying is "instrumental" rather than "incidental" to the function of the RS–DVR system. *Cablevision I,* 478 F. Supp. 2d at 620. While that may distinguish the RS–DVR from the ISPs in *Netcom* and *CoStar,* it does not distinguish the RS–DVR from a VCR, a photocopier, or even a typical copy shop. And the parties do not seem to contest that a company that merely makes photocopiers available to the public on its premises, without more, is not subject to liability for direct infringement for reproductions made by customers using those copiers. They only dispute whether Cablevision is similarly situated to such a proprietor. . . .

. . . In determining who actually "makes" a copy, a significant difference exists between making a request to a human employee, who then volitionally operates the copying system to make the copy, and issuing a command directly to a system, which automatically obeys commands and engages in no volitional conduct. . . . Here, by selling access to a system that automatically produces copies on command, Cablevision more closely resembles a store proprietor who charges customers to use a photocopier on his premises, and it seems incorrect to say, without more, that such a proprietor "makes" any copies when his machines are actually operated by his customers. *See Netcom,* 907 F. Supp. at 1369.

The district court also emphasized Cablevision's "unfettered discretion in selecting the programming that it would make available for recording." *Cablevision I,* 478 F. Supp. 2d at 620. This conduct is indeed more proximate to the creation of illegal copying than, say, operating an ISP or opening a copy shop, where all copied content was supplied by the customers themselves or other third parties. Nonetheless, we do not think it sufficiently proximate to the copying to displace the customer as the person who "makes" the copies when determining liability under the Copyright Act. Cablevision, we note, also has subscribers who use home VCRs or DVRs (like TiVo), and has significant control over the content recorded by these customers. But this control is limited to the channels of programming available to a customer and not to the programs themselves. Cablevision has no control over what programs are made available on individual channels or when those programs will air, if at all. In this respect, Cablevision possesses far less control over recordable content than it does in the [video-on-demand] context, where it actively selects and makes available beforehand the individual programs available for viewing. For these reasons, we are not inclined to say that Cablevision, rather than the user, "does" the copying produced by the RS–DVR system. As a result, we find that the district court erred in concluding that Cablevision, rather than its RS–DVR customers, makes the copies carried out by the RS–DVR system. . . .

NOTES AND QUESTIONS

1. Does the *Netcom* court's holding on Netcom's liability for direct infringement of the reproduction right apply equally to Klemesrud? Who is (are) the direct infringer(s) in *Netcom* and *Cartoon Network?* Why do you think the plaintiffs are not satisfied with recovering against the direct infringer(s)?

2. The *Netcom* court also holds that Netcom is not a direct infringer of either the plaintiff's exclusive right of public display or its exclusive right of public distribution. Do you agree? What do you think of the way that the court distinguishes the BBS in *Netcom* from the one in *Playboy v. Frena?* How do you think the *Netcom* court would resolve the direct infringement claim in *Cartoon Network?*

Review *American Broadcasting Cos. v. Aereo,* Chapter 6.B.1, *supra,* noting particularly Justice Scalia's dissent. Does *Aereo* implicitly overrule the holdings of *Netcom* and *Cartoon Network* about the requirements for direct infringement? If not, what is different about the fact pattern in *Aereo?* According to Justice Scalia, the majority opinion in *Aereo* "will sow confusion for years to come." *American Broadcasting Cos. v. Aereo,* 134 S. Ct. 2498, 2512 (2014) (Scalia, J., dissenting). Do you agree?

3. The *Netcom* court notes that "copyright is a strict liability statute." What does that mean? Consider the following hypothetical: A book publisher infringes an author's copyright by publishing it without authorization. It markets the infringing book through major retail chains that stock tens of thousands of titles. The chains sell the books to their customers. Are the chains liable for direct infringement? Which exclusive right(s) of the copyright owner are implicated? Does the chains' likely lack of both knowledge of the infringement and an intent to infringe insulate them from liability? Would it be fair to hold them liable for infringement? How are *Netcom* and *Cartoon Network* different from this hypothetical?

4. While direct infringement essentially reflects a strict liability approach, the decisions in *Netcom* and *Cartoon Network* suggest the need for a more nuanced approach to assessing the liability of certain parties. The secondary liability cases discussed in the remainder of this chapter involve intermediaries for whom the courts and/or Congress have concluded that strict liability would be inappropriate for a variety of reasons. As you read the material, identify and evaluate those reasons and consider why they may not shelter the retail chains in Question 3's hypothetical.

PRACTICE EXERCISE: COUNSEL A CLIENT

Coolfile.com operates a website that is a virtual storage locker. When users upload files for storage on its servers, the servers automatically make five additional copies of the uploaded files and assign each a unique link. Coolfile itself does not index the files or provide a search function, but it encourages users to share the links. Some do so by setting up their own searchable websites. Third parties can download the content at regular speed for free and at a higher speed if they pay subscription fees to Coolfile. Coolfile has the ability to prevent uploading and to remove uploaded files. It also retains the right to block anyone's access to its site. Coolfile pays some users to upload popular content and asks those users to promote its services to others. Independent video makers use Coolfile to promote their own work, but most files uploaded and downloaded infringe copyright. You represent a movie studio that is upset by the amount of its content moving through Coolfile. The studio has asked you whether it is likely to succeed on a claim of direct infringement against Coolfile. What do you advise?

---

2. Diving Deeper: Infringement by Authorization

A brief reading of §§501 and 106 of the Copyright Act might lead one to conclude that a person who authorizes another to infringe is herself a direct infringer. Section 501 defines an infringer as "[a]nyone who violates any of the exclusive rights of the copyright owner as provided by section[] 106. . . ." 17 U.S.C. §501(a). In turn, §106 states, "the owner of copyright . . . has the *exclusive rights to do and to authorize* . . . ." *Id.* §106 (emphasis added). Thus, one might argue that among the copyright owner's exclusive rights is the right to authorize one of the acts (such as reproduction) enumerated in subsections (1)-(6) of §106. One who violates this right is therefore a direct infringer under §501.

The House Report accompanying the 1976 Act, however, indicates that Congress added the words "to authorize" to confirm its intent that contributory infringers be liable under the Act. The Report states, "[u]se of the phrase 'to authorize' [in §106] is intended to avoid any questions as to the liability of contributory infringers."

H.R. Rep. No. 94-1476, 94th Cong., 2d Sess. 61 (1976), *reprinted in* 1976 U.S.C.C.A.N. 5659, 5674.

In many cases, the question whether authorization of an infringing act constitutes direct infringement is irrelevant. The court will hold the defendant liable for contributory infringement. Harder cases, however, arise when the authorization occurs in the United States but the infringing act is committed abroad. For example, the defendant may enter into a license agreement in the United States under which it authorizes another to make infringing copies of a work, but the actual copying takes place in another country.

Copyright laws are territorial in nature. An action in the United States based on contributory infringement must be based on an act of direct infringement that is cognizable under U.S. law. If the copyright owner may not sue the U.S.-based "authorizer" as a direct infringer, it will have to journey to the country where the act occurred, hope that country's law prohibits the conduct, and seek a remedy there.

Courts are divided on whether a plaintiff may successfully sue for direct infringement based on the authorization to commit acts abroad. In *Subafilms, Ltd. v. MGM-Pathe Communications Co.*, 24 F.3d 1088 (9th Cir.) (en banc), *cert. denied*, 513 U.S. 1001 (1994), the court stated:

> Because the copyright laws do not apply extraterritorially, each of the rights conferred under the five section 106 categories must be read as extending "no farther than the [U.S.] borders." In light of our . . . conclusion that the "authorization" right refers to the doctrine of contributory infringement, which requires that the authorized act *itself* could violate one of the exclusive rights listed in section 106(1)-(5) [now (1)-(6)— EDs.], we believe that "[i]t is simply not possible to draw a principled distinction" between an act that does not violate a copyright because it is not the type of conduct proscribed by section 106, and one that does not violate section 106 because the illicit act occurs overseas. In both cases, the authorized conduct could not violate the exclusive rights guaranteed by section 106. In both cases, therefore, there can be no liability for "authorizing" such conduct.
>
> To hold otherwise would produce the untenable anomaly, inconsistent with the general principles of third party liability, that a party could be held liable as an infringer for violating the "authorization" right when the party that it authorized could not be considered an infringer under the Copyright Act. Put otherwise, we do not think Congress intended to hold a party liable for *merely* "authorizing" conduct that, had the *authorizing* party chosen to engage in itself, would have resulted in no liability under the Act. . . .
>
> We are not persuaded by Appellees' parade of horribles.[10]

Id. at 1094-95.

10. As Appellants note, breach of contract remedies (such as those pursued in this case) remain available. Moreover, at least one court has recognized that actions under the copyright laws of other nations may be brought in United States courts. *See London Film Prods. Ltd. v. Intercontinental Communications, Inc.*, 580 F. Supp. 47, 48-50 (S.D.N.Y. 1984). . . . Finally, although we note that the difficulty of protecting American films abroad is a significant international trade problem, . . . the United States Congress, in acceding to the Berne Convention, has expressed the view that it is through increasing the protection afforded by *foreign* copyright laws that domestic industries that depend on copyright can best secure adequate protection. . . .

A number of courts have taken issue with *Subafilms.* For example, in *Curb v. MCA Records, Inc.*, 898 F. Supp. 586 (M.D. Tenn. 1995), the court stated:

Subafilms . . . reads the authorization right out of the Act in cases of foreign infringement.

But piracy has changed since the Barbary days. Today, the raider need not grab the bounty with his own hands; he need only transmit his go-ahead by wire or telefax to start the presses in a distant land. *Subafilms* ignores this economic reality, and the economic incentives underpinning the Copyright Clause designed to encourage creation of new works, and transforms infringement of the authorization right into a requirement of domestic presence by a primary infringer. Under this view, a phone call to Nebraska results in liability; the same phone call to France results in riches. In a global marketplace, it is literally a distinction without a difference.

A better view, one supported by the text, the precedents, and, ironically enough, the legislative history to which the *Subafilms* court cited, would be to hold that domestic violation of the authorization right is an infringement, sanctionable under the Copyright Act, whenever the authorizee has committed an act that would violate the copyright owner's §106 rights.

Id. at 595.

NOTES AND QUESTIONS

1. Do you find *Subafilms* or *Curb* more persuasive, and why? Does an interpretation of §§501 and 106 that finds authorization not to constitute direct infringement comport with typical canons of statutory construction? Why should the legislative history be relevant if the statutory language is clear?

2. The *Curb* court analogizes to phone calls, arguing that the *Subafilms* rule results in liability attaching for a call made to Nebraska but not one to France. How would you respond to this argument? Why do you think the plaintiffs are concerned about being able to bring suit in the United States?

B. VICARIOUS LIABILITY AND CONTRIBUTORY INFRINGEMENT

Review the introductory material to this chapter. There we raised the question of liability of parties other than the direct infringer—so-called secondary liability. What policies do you think should guide the liability of those who are not direct infringers but who nonetheless somehow participate in the infringing activity?

1. The History of Secondary Liability

Courts rather than Congress have been at the forefront of considering the relevant policies and developing theories of secondary liability (sometimes also called "indirect liability"). The 1909 Act did not mention liability for acts committed by one other than the direct infringer. As discussed above, the legislative history of the 1976 Act indicates that the addition of the words "to authorize" in §106 was intended to confirm congressional intent that secondary participants could be liable for copyright infringement under appropriate circumstances. Yet Congress still did not believe it necessary to codify those circumstances.

A line of cases decided under the 1909 Act developed two theories of secondary liability—vicarious liability and contributory infringement. Vicarious liability finds its theoretical basis in the *respondeat superior* doctrine developed under agency law. Under that doctrine, in certain circumstances, a principal may be held liable for an agent's acts. Courts looked to *respondeat superior* principles when addressing secondary liability cases in the employer/employee and landlord/tenant contexts and in cases against owners of venues for infringement by performers. A leading case stating the test for vicarious liability in copyright infringement cases is *Shapiro, Bernstein & Co. v. H. L. Green Co.*, 316 F.2d 304 (2d Cir. 1963). There, the court held a chain store owner vicariously liable for infringement by a record concessionaire operating on the store's premises. The court stated,

> When the *right and ability to supervise* coalesce with an obvious and *direct financial interest* in the exploitation of copyrighted materials—even in the absence of actual knowledge that the copyright monopoly is being impaired the purposes of copyright law may be best effectuated by the imposition of liability upon the beneficiary of that exploitation.

Id. at 307 (emphasis added). The store owner's retention of "the ultimate right of supervision" over the concessionaire and the right to "a proportionate share of the gross receipts from [record] sales" satisfied both prongs of the court's test. *Id.* at 308.

Contributory copyright infringement finds its theoretical basis in tort law, particularly principles of joint and several liability. In *Gershwin Publishing Corp. v. Columbia Artists Management, Inc.* (CAMI), 443 F.2d 1159 (2d Cir. 1971), the court addressed a claim of indirect infringement against CAMI. CAMI helped set up local associations that sponsored community concerts at which copyrighted works were performed without a license. The performing artists were sometimes managed by CAMI and sometimes not. Regardless, artists would pay CAMI a portion of their fee to compensate it for its services in forming the local association. Artists managed by CAMI would pay an additional management fee. The court held that "one who, with *knowledge of the infringing activity, induces, causes or materially contributes* to the infringing conduct of another, may be held liable as a 'contributory' infringer," and found the facts of the case sufficient to support contributory liability. *Id.* at 1162 (emphasis added).

Although the elements of the two types of secondary liability differ, the dividing line between them can be blurry. Indeed, in many cases, a defendant may be held both vicariously and contributorily liable. *See id.* Also, the traditional categories were developed in a different era.

> **KEEP IN MIND**
>
> There can be no secondary liability in the absence of primary liability. Thus, there must be a direct infringer for there to be a possibility of a secondary infringer.

It is sometimes unclear how the tests should apply to someone who markets equipment that is not itself infringing but provides the means for others to infringe, or how the test should apply to providers of online services. Courts have also been asked to address whether those who finance or otherwise enable secondary infringers to conduct their businesses should be liable for infringement themselves.

2. Contemporary Approaches to Secondary Liability

As you read the material that follows, try to identify the tests that courts are using in different factual situations and think about whether you can reconcile the results in the cases.

≡ ***Fonovisa, Inc. v. Cherry Auction, Inc.***
76 F.3d 259 (9th Cir. 1996)

SCHROEDER, J.: This is a copyright and trademark enforcement action against the operators of a swap meet, sometimes called a flea market, where third-party vendors routinely sell counterfeit recordings that infringe on the plaintiff's copyrights and trademarks. The district court dismissed on the pleadings, holding that the plaintiffs, as a matter of law, could not maintain any cause of action against the swap meet for sales by vendors who leased its premises. . . .

Background

The plaintiff and appellant is Fonovisa, Inc., a California corporation that owns copyrights and trademarks to Latin/Hispanic music recordings. Fonovisa filed this action in district court against defendant-appellee, Cherry Auction, Inc., and its individual operators (collectively "Cherry Auction"). For purposes of this appeal, it is undisputed that Cherry Auction operates a swap meet in Fresno, California, similar to many other swap meets in this country where customers come to purchase various merchandise from individual vendors. The vendors pay a daily rental fee to the swap meet operators in exchange for booth space. Cherry Auction supplies parking, conducts advertising and retains the right to exclude any vendor for any reason, at any time, and thus can exclude vendors for [copyright] and trademark infringement. In addition, Cherry Auction receives an entrance fee from each customer who attends the swap meet.

There is also no dispute for purposes of this appeal that Cherry Auction and its operators were aware that vendors in their swap meet were selling counterfeit recordings in violation of Fonovisa's trademarks and copyrights. . . .

. . . In this appeal, Fonovisa [challenges] the dismissal of its claims for contributory copyright infringement, vicarious copyright infringement and contributory trademark infringement.

The copyright claims are brought pursuant to 17 U.S.C. §§101 *et seq.* Although the Copyright Act does not expressly impose liability on anyone other than direct infringers, courts have long recognized that in certain circumstances, vicarious or contributory liability will be imposed. *See Sony Corp. of America v. Universal City Studios, Inc.,* 464 U.S. 417, 435 (1984) (explaining that "vicarious liability is imposed in virtually all areas of the law, and the concept of contributory infringement is merely a species of the broader problem of identifying circumstances in which it is just to hold one individually accountable for the actions of another"). . . .

Vicarious Copyright Infringement

The concept of vicarious copyright liability was developed in the Second Circuit as an outgrowth of the agency principles of respondeat superior. The landmark case on vicarious liability for sales of counterfeit recordings is *Shapiro, Bernstein and Co. v. H.L. Green Co.,* 316 F.2d 304 (2d Cir. 1963). In *Shapiro,* the court was faced with a copyright infringement suit against the owner of a chain of department stores where a concessionaire was selling counterfeit recordings. . . .

The *Shapiro* court looked at the two lines of cases it perceived as most clearly relevant. In one line of cases, the landlord-tenant cases, the courts had held that a landlord who lacked knowledge of the infringing acts of its tenant and who exercised no control over the leased premises was not liable for infringing sales by its tenant. In the other line of cases, the so-called "dance hall cases," the operator of an entertainment venue was held liable for infringing performances when the operator (1) could control the premises and (2) obtained a direct financial benefit from the audience, who paid to enjoy the infringing performance.

From those two lines of cases, the *Shapiro* court determined that the relationship between the store owner and the concessionaire in the case before it was closer to the dance-hall model than to the landlord-tenant model. It imposed liability even though the defendant was unaware of the infringement. *Shapiro* deemed the imposition of vicarious liability neither unduly harsh nor unfair because the store proprietor had the power to cease the conduct of the concessionaire, and because the proprietor derived an obvious and direct financial benefit from the infringement. 316 F.2d at 307. The test was more clearly articulated in a later Second Circuit case as follows: "even in the absence of an employer-employee relationship one may be vicariously liable if he has the right and ability to supervise the infringing activity and also has a direct financial interest in such activities." *Gershwin Publishing Corp. v. Columbia Artists Management, Inc.,* 443 F.2d 1159, 1162 (2d Cir. 1971). . . .

The district court in this case agreed with defendant Cherry Auction that Fonovisa did not, as a matter of law, meet either the control or the financial benefit prong of the vicarious copyright infringement test articulated in *Gershwin, supra.* . . . In the district court's view, with respect to both control and financial benefit, Cherry Auction was in the same position as an absentee landlord who has surrendered its exclusive right of occupancy in its leased property to its tenants.

This analogy to [an] absentee landlord is not in accord with the facts as alleged in the district court and which we, for purposes of appeal, must accept. The allegations below were that vendors occupied small booths within premises that Cherry Auction controlled and patrolled. According to the complaint, Cherry Auction had the right to terminate vendors for any reason whatsoever and through that right had the ability to control the activities of vendors on the premises. In addition, Cherry Auction promoted the swap meet and controlled the access of customers to the swap meet area. In terms of control, the allegations before us are strikingly similar to those in *Shapiro*. . . .

In *Shapiro* . . . the concessionaire selling the bootleg recordings had a licensing agreement with the department store (H.L. Green Company) that required the concessionaire and its employees to "abide by, observe and obey all regulations promulgated from time to time by the H.L. Green Company," and H.L. Green Company had the "unreviewable discretion" to discharge the concessionaires' employees. 316 F.2d at 306. In practice, H.L. Green Company was not actively involved in the sale of records and the concessionaire controlled and supervised the individual employees. *Id.* Nevertheless, H.L. Green's ability to police its concessionaire—which parallels Cherry Auction's ability to police its vendors under Cherry Auction's similarly broad contract with its vendors—was sufficient to satisfy the control requirement. *Id.* at 308. . . .

We next consider the issue of financial benefit. The plaintiff's allegations encompass many substantive benefits to Cherry Auction from the infringing sales. These include the payment of a daily rental fee by each of the infringing vendors; a direct payment to Cherry Auction by each customer in the form of an admission fee, and incidental payments for parking, food and other services by customers seeking to purchase infringing recordings.

Cherry Auction nevertheless contends that these benefits cannot satisfy the financial benefit prong of vicarious liability because a commission, directly tied to the sale of particular infringing items, is required. They ask that we restrict the financial benefit prong to the precise facts presented in *Shapiro*, where defendant H.L. Green Company received a 10 or 12 percent commission from the direct infringers' gross receipts. Cherry Auction points to the low daily rental fee paid by each vendor, discounting all other financial benefits flowing to the swap meet, and asks that we hold that the swap meet is materially similar to a mere landlord. The facts alleged by Fonovisa, however, reflect that the defendants reap substantial financial benefits from admission fees, concession stand sales and parking fees, all of which flow directly from customers who want to buy the counterfeit recordings at bargain basement prices. The plaintiff has sufficiently alleged direct financial benefit.

Our conclusion is fortified by the continuing line of cases, starting with the dance hall cases, imposing vicarious liability on the operator of a business where infringing performances enhance the attractiveness of the venue to potential customers. . . . In this case, the sale of pirated recordings at the Cherry Auction swap meet is a "draw" for customers, as was the performance of pirated music in the dance hall cases and their progeny.

Plaintiffs have stated a claim for vicarious copyright infringement.

Contributory Copyright Infringement

Contributory infringement originates in tort law and stems from the notion that one who directly contributes to another's infringement should be held accountable. Contributory infringement has been described as an outgrowth of enterprise liability and imposes liability where one person knowingly contributes to the infringing conduct of another. The classic statement of the doctrine is in *Gershwin*: "[O]ne who, with knowledge of the infringing activity, induces, causes or materially contributes to the infringing conduct of another, may be held liable as a 'contributory' infringer." . . .

There is no question that plaintiff adequately alleged the element of knowledge in this case. The disputed issue is whether plaintiff adequately alleged that Cherry Auction materially contributed to the infringing activity. We have little difficulty in holding that the allegations in this case are sufficient to show material contribution to the infringing activity. Indeed, it would be difficult for the infringing activity to take place in the massive quantities alleged without the support services provided by the swap meet. These services include, *inter alia,* the provision of space, utilities, parking, advertising, plumbing, and customers.

Here again Cherry Auction asks us to ignore all aspects of the enterprise described by the plaintiffs, to concentrate solely on the rental of space, and to hold that the swap meet provides nothing more. Yet Cherry Auction actively strives to provide the environment and the market for counterfeit recording sales to thrive. Its participation in the sales cannot be termed "passive," as Cherry Auction would prefer. . . .

. . . [W]e agree with the Third Circuit's analysis in *Columbia Pictures Industries, Inc. v. Aveco, Inc.*, 800 F.2d 59 (3rd Cir. 1986) that providing the site and facilities for known infringing activity is sufficient to establish contributory liability. . . .

Perfect 10, Inc. v. Amazon.com, Inc.
508 F.3d 1146 (9th Cir. 2007), cert. denied, 553 U.S. 1079 (2008)

IKUTA, J.: [Review the facts of this case, *supra*, Chapter 6.B.] . . .

Secondary Liability for Copyright Infringement

. . . [W]e must assess Perfect 10's arguments that Google is secondarily liable in light of the direct infringement that is undisputed by the parties: third-party websites' reproducing, displaying, and distributing unauthorized copies of Perfect 10's images on the Internet. . . .

A. *Contributory Infringement*

. . . We have adopted the general rule set forth in *Gershwin Publishing Corp. v. Columbia Artists Management, Inc.*, namely: "one who, with knowledge of the infringing activity, induces, causes or materially contributes to the infringing conduct of another, may be held liable as a 'contributory' infringer," 443 F.2d 1159, 1162 (2d Cir.1971).

We have further refined this test in the context of cyberspace to determine when contributory liability can be imposed on a provider of Internet access or services. *See* [*A & M Records, Inc. v. Napster, Inc.*, 239 F.3d 1004, 1019-20 (9th Cir.2001)]. In *Napster,* we considered claims that the operator of an electronic file sharing system was contributorily liable for assisting individual users to swap copyrighted music files stored on their home computers with other users of the system. *Napster,* 239 F.3d at 1011-13, 1019-22. We stated that "if a computer system operator learns of specific infringing material available on his system and fails to purge such material from the system, the operator knows of and contributes to direct infringement." *Id.* at 1021. Because Napster knew of the availability of infringing music files, assisted users in accessing such files, and failed to block access to such files, we concluded that Napster materially contributed to infringement. *Id.* at 1022.

The *Napster* test for contributory liability was modeled on the influential district court decision in *Religious Technology Center v. Netcom On-Line Communication Services, Inc. (Netcom),* 907 F. Supp. 1361, 1365-66 (N.D.Cal.1995). *See Napster,* 239 F.3d at 1021. In *Netcom,* a disgruntled former Scientology minister posted allegedly infringing copies of Scientological works on an electronic bulletin board service. *Netcom,* 907 F. Supp. at 1365-66. The messages were stored on the bulletin board operator's computer, then automatically copied onto Netcom's computer, and from there copied onto other computers comprising "a worldwide community" of electronic bulletin board systems. *Id.* at 1366-67 & n.4 (internal quotation omitted). *Netcom* held that if plaintiffs could prove that Netcom knew or should have known that the minister infringed plaintiffs' copyrights, "Netcom [would] be liable for contributory infringement since its failure to simply cancel [the former minister's] infringing message and thereby stop an infringing copy from being distributed worldwide constitute[d] substantial participation in [the former minister's] public distribution of the message." *Id.* at 1374.

. . . [B]oth decisions ruled that a service provider's knowing failure to prevent infringing actions could be the basis for imposing contributory liability. Under such circumstances, intent may be imputed. In addition, *Napster* and *Netcom* are consistent with the longstanding requirement that an actor's contribution to infringement must be material to warrant the imposition of contributory liability. *Gershwin,* 443 F.2d at 1162. Both *Napster* and *Netcom* acknowledge that services or products that facilitate access to websites throughout the world can significantly magnify the effects of otherwise immaterial infringing activities. *See Napster,* 239 F.3d at 1022; *Netcom,* 907 F. Supp. at 1375. . . . Moreover, copyright holders cannot protect their rights in a meaningful way unless they can hold providers of such services or products accountable for their actions pursuant to a test such as that enunciated in *Napster. See* [*Metro–Goldwyn–Mayer Studios, Inc. v. Grokster, Ltd.*, 545 U.S. 913, 929-30 (2005)] ("When a widely shared service or product is used to commit infringement, it may be impossible to enforce rights in the protected work effectively against all direct infringers, the only practical alternative being to go against the distributor of the copying device for secondary liability on a theory of contributory or vicarious infringement."). Accordingly, we hold that a computer system operator can be held contributorily liable if it "has *actual* knowledge that *specific* infringing material is available using its system," *Napster*, 239 F.3d at 1022, and can "take simple measures to prevent further damage" to copyrighted works, *Netcom*, 907 F. Supp. at 1375, yet continues to provide access to infringing works.

Here, the district court held that even assuming Google had actual knowledge of infringing material available on its system, Google did not materially contribute to infringing conduct because it did not undertake any substantial promotional or advertising efforts to encourage visits to infringing websites, nor provide a significant revenue stream to the infringing websites. *Perfect 10*, 416 F. Supp. 2d at 854-56. This analysis is erroneous. There is no dispute that Google substantially assists websites to distribute their infringing copies to a worldwide market and assists a worldwide audience of users to access infringing materials. We cannot discount the effect of such a service on copyright owners, even though Google's assistance is available to all websites, not just infringing ones. Applying our test, Google could be held contributorily liable if it had knowledge that infringing Perfect 10 images were available using its search engine, could take simple measures to prevent further damage to Perfect 10's copyrighted works, and failed to take such steps.

The district court did not resolve the factual disputes over the adequacy of Perfect 10's notices to Google and Google's responses to these notices. Moreover, there are factual disputes over whether there are reasonable and feasible means for Google to refrain from providing access to infringing images. Therefore, we must remand this claim to the district court for further consideration . . .

B. Vicarious Infringement

Perfect 10 also challenges the district court's conclusion that it is not likely to prevail on a theory of vicarious liability against Google. *Perfect 10*, 416 F. Supp. 2d at 856-58. . . . [T]o succeed in imposing vicarious liability, a plaintiff must establish that the defendant exercises the requisite control over the direct infringer and that the defendant derives a direct financial benefit from the direct infringement. . . . [A] defendant exercises control over a direct infringer when he has both a legal right to stop or limit the directly infringing conduct, as well as the practical ability to do so.

. . . In order to prevail at this preliminary injunction stage, Perfect 10 must demonstrate a likelihood of success [on these issues]. . . . Perfect 10 has not met this burden.

With respect to the "control" element . . . Perfect 10 has not demonstrated a likelihood of showing that Google has the legal right to stop or limit the direct infringement of third-party websites. Unlike *Fonovisa*, where by virtue of a "broad contract" with its vendors the defendant swap meet operators had the right to stop the vendors from selling counterfeit recordings on its premises, *Fonovisa*, 76 F.3d at 263, Perfect 10 has not shown that Google has contracts with third-party websites that empower Google to stop or limit them from reproducing, displaying, and distributing infringing copies of Perfect 10's images on the Internet. Perfect 10 does point to Google's AdSense agreement, which states that Google reserves "the right to monitor and terminate partnerships with entities that violate others' copyright[s]." *Perfect 10*, 416 F. Supp. 2d at 858. However, Google's right to terminate an AdSense partnership does not give Google the right to stop direct infringement by third-party websites. An infringing third-party website can continue to reproduce, display, and distribute its infringing copies of Perfect 10 images after its participation in the AdSense program has ended. . . .

Moreover, the district court found that Google lacks the practical ability to police the third-party websites' infringing conduct. *Id.* at 857-58. Specifically, the court found that Google's supervisory power is limited because "Google's software lacks the ability to analyze every image on the [I]nternet, compare each image to all the other copyrighted images that exist in the world . . . and determine whether a certain image on the web infringes someone's copyright." *Id.* at 858. The district court also concluded that Perfect 10's suggestions regarding measures Google could implement to prevent its web crawler from indexing infringing websites and to block access to infringing images were not workable. *Id.* at 858 n.25. Rather, the suggestions suffered from both "imprecision and overbreadth." *Id.* We hold that these findings are not clearly erroneous. Without image-recognition technology, Google lacks the practical ability to police the infringing activities of third-party websites. This distinguishes Google from the defendants held liable in *Napster* and *Fonovisa*. *See Napster*, 239 F.3d at 1023-24 (Napster had the ability to identify and police infringing conduct by searching its index for song titles); *Fonovisa*, 76 F.3d at 262 (swap meet operator had the ability to identify and police infringing activity by patrolling its premises).

Perfect 10 argues that Google could manage its own operations to avoid indexing websites with infringing content and linking to third-party infringing sites. . . . Google's failure to change its operations to avoid assisting websites to distribute their infringing content may constitute contributory liability. However, this failure is not the same as declining to exercise a right and ability to make third-party websites stop their direct infringement. We reject Perfect 10's efforts to blur this distinction.

Because we conclude that Perfect 10 has not shown a likelihood of establishing Google's right and ability to stop or limit the directly infringing conduct of third-party websites, we agree with the district court's conclusion that Perfect 10 "has not established a likelihood of proving the [control] prong necessary for vicarious liability." *Perfect 10*, 416 F. Supp. 2d at 858.[15] . . .

NOTES AND QUESTIONS

1. How does each court: (1) define the elements of contributory and vicarious liability; and (2) apply the tests it defines to the facts before it? Are the cases consistent?

2. Are contributory infringement and vicarious liability truly distinct concepts? Do the courts implement them in that way? Are knowledge and right to control synonymous? If one exists, must the other necessarily also exist?

---

15. Having so concluded, we need not reach Perfect 10's argument that Google received a direct financial benefit.

In the *Netcom* case, *supra* Section A, the court concluded that triable issues of fact remained as to both knowledge and ability to control:

> [T]he evidence reveals a question of fact as to whether Netcom knew or should have known that Erlich had infringed plaintiffs' copyrights following receipt of plaintiffs' letter. Because Netcom was arguably participating in Erlich's public distribution of plaintiffs' works, there is a genuine issue as to whether Netcom knew of any infringement by Erlich before it was too late to do anything about it. If plaintiffs can prove the knowledge element, Netcom will be liable for contributory infringement since its failure to simply cancel Erlich's infringing message and thereby stop an infringing copy from being distributed worldwide constitutes substantial participation in Erlich's public distribution of the message. . . .
>
> The first element of vicarious liability will be met if plaintiffs can show that Netcom has the right and ability to supervise the conduct of its subscribers. . . .
>
> Netcom argues that it could not possibly screen messages before they are posted given the speed and volume of the data that goes through its system. Netcom further argues that it has never exercised control over the content of its users' postings. Plaintiffs' expert opines otherwise, stating that with an easy software modification Netcom could identify postings that contain particular words or come from particular individuals. . . . Plaintiffs further dispute Netcom's claim that it could not limit Erlich's access to Usenet without kicking off all 500 subscribers of Klemesrud's BBS. . . . Further evidence shows that Netcom can delete specific postings. . . . Whether such sanctions occurred before or after the abusive conduct is not material to whether Netcom can exercise control.

Religious Tech. Ctr. v. Netcom On-Line Commc'n Servs., Inc., 907 F. Supp. 1361, 1374-76 (N.D. Cal. 1995). Do you agree with the court's reasoning? How would you evaluate knowledge (for contributory infringement) and right and ability to control (for vicarious liability) in the case of a web-hosting service such as YouTube or Facebook?

3. Are the cases in this section consistent in their statements of what constitutes material contribution to the infringement for purposes of supporting a contributory infringement claim? Under the *Amazon.com* court's reasoning, does every online service inevitably materially contribute to infringement? If so, then contributory infringement cases involving online conduct would focus only on knowledge. Would that be appropriate?

4. When might a factfinder reasonably conclude that the availability of infringing material constitutes a "draw" for customers? For example, America On-Line (AOL) offers its subscribers a variety of services including Internet access, email, and access to chat rooms and Usenet groups. Subscribers occasionally upload infringing materials to Usenet groups. Does the availability of this material constitute a "draw" sufficient to meet the requirements of vicarious liability? In *Ellison v. Robertson*, the court stated:

> AOL offers access to USENET groups as part of its service for a reason: it helps to encourage overall subscription to its services. Here, AOL's future revenue is directly dependent upon increases in its userbase. Certainly, the fact that AOL provides its subscribers access to certain USENET groups constitutes a small "draw" in proportion to its overall profits, but AOL's status as a behemoth online service

provider, by itself, does not insulate it categorically from vicarious liability. Regardless of what fraction of AOL's earnings are considered a direct result of providing its subscribers access to the USENET groups that contained infringing material . . . they would be earnings nonetheless. The essential aspect of the "direct financial benefit" inquiry is whether there is a causal relationship between the infringing activity and any financial benefit a defendant reaps, regardless of *how substantial* the benefit is in proportion to a defendant's overall profits. . . .

357 F.3d 1072, 1079 (9th Cir. 2004). Because the "record lack[ed] evidence that AOL attracted or retained subscriptions because of the infringement or lost subscriptions because of AOL's eventual obstruction of the infringement," the court affirmed a grant of summary judgment to AOL on the plaintiff's vicarious liability claim. *Id.* What do you think of this test as a practical matter? Suppose the plaintiff had produced evidence of two subscriptions attracted by the availability of infringing material on USENET groups accessible via AOL. Would summary judgment for AOL be improper? Doctrinally, does the court's formulation of the "direct financial benefit" inquiry make sense? (What kind of "causal relationship" is the court describing?)

PRACTICE EXERCISE: COUNSEL A CLIENT

Review the Practice Exercise involving Coolfile in section A.1, *supra*. The studio head asks you whether Coolfile is likely to be secondarily liable for infringement. What do you advise and why?

---

3. Diving Deeper: Secondary Liability for Those Assisting Secondary Infringers?*

There are many types of intermediaries who may play roles in enabling infringement. For example, venture capitalists provide startup and other financing for Internet companies; advertisers pay to market on websites; and service firms help sites remain in existence by processing the payments they receive. Should any of these entities be liable for the role they play in enabling OSPs, ISPs, and websites to come into and remain in existence? Particularly in high-technology settings, such seemingly remote parties may have the deepest pockets, making them attractive defendants. Consider the following case.

---

* Litigants sometimes refer to liability for assisting a secondary party as "tertiary liability," perhaps as a rhetorical tactic to convey the remoteness of the defendant from the infringement. We do not use that term because there is no legal doctrine of tertiary liability; rather, usual doctrines of secondary liability apply.—Eds

Perfect 10, Inc. v. Visa International Service Association
494 F.3d 788 (9th Cir. 2007)

SMITH, J.: Perfect 10, Inc. (Perfect 10) sued Visa International Service Association, MasterCard International Inc., and several affiliated banks and data processing services (collectively, the Defendants), alleging secondary liability under federal copyright . . . law. . . . It sued because Defendants continue to process credit card payments to websites that infringe Perfect 10's intellectual property rights after being notified by Perfect 10 of infringement by those websites. The district court dismissed . . . under Federal Rule of Civil Procedure 12(b)(6) for failure to state a claim upon which relief can be granted. We affirm . . . .

Facts and Prior Proceedings

Perfect 10 publishes the magazine "PERFECT10" and operates the subscription website www.perfect 10.com., both of which "feature tasteful copyrighted images of the world's most beautiful natural models." Appellant's Opening Brief at 1. Perfect 10 claims copyrights in the photographs published in its magazine and on its website . . . . Perfect 10 alleges that numerous websites based in several countries have stolen its proprietary images, altered them, and illegally offered them for sale online.

Instead of suing the direct infringers in this case, Perfect 10 sued Defendants, financial institutions that process certain credit card payments to the allegedly infringing websites. . . . Defendants collect fees for their services in these transactions. Perfect 10 alleges that it sent Defendants repeated notices specifically identifying infringing websites and informing Defendants that some of their consumers use their payment cards to purchase infringing images. Defendants admit receiving some of these notices, but they took no action in response to the notices after receiving them. . . .

Discussion

Secondary Liability Under Federal Copyright . . . Law

A. Secondary Liability for Copyright Infringement

. . . We evaluate Perfect 10's claims with an awareness that credit cards serve as the primary engine of electronic commerce and that Congress has determined it to be the "policy of the United States—(1) to promote the continued development of the Internet and other interactive computer services and other interactive media [and] (2) to preserve the vibrant and competitive free market that presently exists for the Internet and other interactive computer services, unfettered by Federal or State regulation." 47 U.S.C. §§230(b)(1), (2).

1. Contributory Copyright Infringement

... We have found that a defendant is a contributory infringer if it (1) has knowledge of a third party's infringing activity, and (2) "induces, causes, or materially contributes to the infringing conduct." *Ellison v. Robertson*, 357 F.3d 1072, 1076 (9th Cir. 2004) (citing *Gershwin Publ'g Corp. v. Columbia Artists Mgmt., Inc.*, 443 F.2d 1159, 1162 (2d Cir.1971)). In an Internet context, we have found contributory liability when the defendant "engages in personal conduct that encourages or assists the infringement." *A & M Records, Inc. v. Napster, Inc.*, 239 F.3d 1004, 1019 (9th Cir.2001) (internal citations omitted). ...

We understand these several criteria to be non-contradictory variations on the same basic test, i.e., that one contributorily infringes when he (1) has knowledge of another's infringement and (2) ... materially contributes to [it]. ...

a. Knowledge of the Infringing Activity

Because we find that Perfect 10 has not pled facts sufficient to establish that Defendants ... materially contribute to the infringing activity, Perfect 10's contributory copyright infringement claim fails and we need not address the Defendants' knowledge of the infringing activity.

b. Material Contribution, Inducement, or Causation

To state a claim of contributory infringement, Perfect 10 must allege facts showing that Defendants induce, cause, or materially contribute to the infringing conduct. ... Perfect 10 argues that by continuing to process credit card payments to the infringing websites despite having knowledge of ongoing infringement, Defendants induce, enable and contribute to the infringing activity. ... We disagree. ...

The credit card companies cannot be said to materially contribute to the infringement in this case because they have no direct connection to that infringement. Here, the infringement rests on the reproduction, alteration, display and distribution of Perfect 10's images over the Internet. Perfect 10 has not alleged that any infringing material passes over Defendants' payment networks or through their payment processing systems, or that Defendants' systems are used to alter or display the infringing images. In *Fonovisa*, the infringing material was physically located in and traded at the defendant's market. Here, it is not. Nor are Defendants' systems used to locate the infringing images. The search engines in *Amazon.com* provided links to specific infringing images, and the service[ ] in *Napster* ... allowed users to locate and obtain infringing material. Here, in contrast, the services provided by the credit card companies do not help locate and are not used to distribute the infringing images. While Perfect 10 has alleged that Defendants make it easier for websites to profit from this infringing activity, the issue here is reproduction, alteration, display and distribution, which can occur without payment. Even if infringing images were not paid for, there would still be infringement. *See Napster*, 239 F.3d at 1014 (Napster users infringed the distribution right by uploading file names to the search index for others to copy, despite the fact that no money changed hands in the transaction).

Our analysis is fully consistent with this court's recent decision in *Perfect 10 v. Amazon.com*. . . . The salient distinction is that Google's search engine itself assists in the distribution of infringing content to Internet users, while Defendants' payment systems do not. . . . [Defendants] in no way assist or enable Internet users to locate infringing material, and they do not distribute it. They do, as alleged, make infringement more profitable, and people are generally more inclined to engage in an activity when it is financially profitable. However, there is an additional step in the causal chain: Google may materially contribute to infringement by making it fast and easy for third parties to locate and distribute infringing material, whereas Defendants make it easier for infringement to be *profitable,* which tends to increase financial incentives to infringe, which in turn tends to increase infringement.

. . . Helping users to locate an image might substantially assist users to download infringing images, but processing payments does not. If users couldn't pay for images with credit cards, infringement could continue on a large scale because other viable funding mechanisms are available. For example, a website might decide to allow users to download some images for free and to make its profits from advertising, or it might develop other payment mechanisms that do not depend on the credit card companies. . . .

2. Vicarious Copyright Infringement

. . . To state a claim for vicarious copyright infringement, a plaintiff must allege that the defendant has (1) the right and ability to supervise the infringing conduct and (2) a direct financial interest in the infringing activity. *Ellison,* 357 F.3d at 1078; *Napster,* 239 F.3d at 1022 (citations omitted). . . .

a. Right and Ability to Supervise the Infringing Activity

In order to join a Defendant's payment network, merchants and member banks must agree to follow that Defendant's rules and regulations. These rules, among other things, prohibit member banks from providing services to merchants engaging in certain illegal activities and require the members and member banks to investigate merchants suspected of engaging in such illegal activity and to terminate their participation in the payment network if certain illegal activity is found. Perfect 10 has alleged that certain websites are infringing Perfect 10's copyrights and that Perfect 10 sent notices of this alleged infringement to Defendants. Accordingly, Perfect 10 has adequately pled that (1) infringement of Perfect 10's copyrights was occurring, (2) Defendants were aware of the infringement, and (3) on this basis, Defendants could have stopped processing credit card payments to the infringing websites. These allegations are not, however, sufficient to establish vicarious liability because even with all reasonable inferences drawn in Perfect 10's favor, Perfect 10's allegations of fact cannot support a finding that Defendants have the right and ability to control the infringing activity.

In reasoning closely analogous to the present case, the *Amazon.com* court held that Google was not vicariously liable for third-party infringement that its search engine facilitates. In so holding, the court found that Google's ability to control its own index, search results, and webpages does not give Google the right to control the infringing acts of third parties even though that ability would allow Google to affect those infringing acts to some degree. *Amazon.com*, 487 F.3d at 730-32. Moreover, and even more importantly, the *Amazon.com* court rejected a vicarious liability claim based on Google's policies with sponsored advertisers, which state that it reserves "the right to monitor and terminate partnerships with entities that violate others' copyright[s]." *Id*. at 730 (alteration in original). The court found that

> Google's right to terminate an AdSense partnership does not give Google the right to stop direct infringement by third-party websites. An infringing third-party website can continue to reproduce, display, and distribute its infringing copies of Perfect 10 images after its participation in the AdSense program has ended.

Id. This reasoning is equally applicable to the Defendants in this case. Just like Google, Defendants could likely take certain steps that may have the indirect effect of reducing infringing activity on the Internet at large. However, neither Google nor Defendants has any ability to directly control that activity, and the mere ability to withdraw a financial "carrot" does not create the "stick" of "right and ability to control" that vicarious infringement requires. A finding of vicarious liability here, under the theories advocated by the dissent, would also require a finding that Google is vicariously liable for infringement—a conflict we need not create, and radical step we do not take. . . .

b. Obvious and Direct Financial Interest in the Infringing Activity

Because Perfect 10 has failed to show that Defendants have the right and ability to control the alleged infringing conduct, it has not pled a viable claim of vicarious liability. Accordingly, we need not reach the issue of direct financial interest. . . .

KOZINSKI, J., dissenting . . . :

. . . Accepting the truth of plaintiff's allegations, as we must on a motion to dismiss, the credit cards are easily liable for indirect copyright infringement: They knowingly provide a financial bridge between buyers and sellers of pirated works, enabling them to consummate infringing transactions, while making a profit on every sale. If such active participation in infringing conduct does not amount to indirect infringement, it's hard to imagine what would. By straining to absolve defendants of liability, the majority leaves our law in disarray.

Contributory Infringement

. . . Our recent opinion in *Perfect 10, Inc. v. Amazon.com, Inc.*, 487 F.3d 701 (9th Cir.2007), canvasses the caselaw in this area and concludes that Google "could be held contributorily liable if it had knowledge that infringing Perfect 10 images were available using its search engine, could take simple measures to prevent further damage to Perfect 10's copyrighted works, and failed to take such steps." *Amazon*, 487 F.3d at 729. Substitute "payment systems" for "search engine" in this sentence, and it describes defendants here: If a consumer wishes to buy an infringing image from one of the Stolen Content Websites, he can do so by using Visa or MasterCard, just as he can use Google to find the infringing images in the first place. . . .

The majority struggles to distinguish *Amazon* by positing an "additional step in the causal chain" between defendants' activities and the infringing conduct. *Id.* at 797. . . . The majority is mistaken; there is no "additional step." Defendants participate in every credit card sale of pirated images; the images are delivered to the buyer only after defendants approve the transaction and process the payment. This is not just an economic incentive for infringement; it's an essential step in the infringement process.

In any event, I don't see why it matters whether there is an "additional step." Materiality turns on how significantly the activity helps infringement, not on whether it's characterized as one step or two steps removed from it. . . . Taking the majority at its word, it sounds like defendants are providing very significant help to the direct infringers.

My colleagues recognize, as they must, that helping consumers locate infringing content can constitute contributory infringement, but they consign the means of payment to secondary status. But why is *locating* infringing images more central to infringement than *paying* for them? If infringing images can't be found, there can be no infringement; but if infringing images can't be paid for, there can be no infringement either. Location services and payment services are equally central to infringement. . . .

The majority dismisses the significance of credit cards by arguing that "infringement could continue on a large scale [without them] because other viable funding mechanisms are available." Of course, the same could be said about Google. . . . [I]f Google were unwilling or unable to serve up infringing images, consumers could use Yahoo!, Ask.com, Microsoft Live Search, A9.com or AltaVista instead. Even if none of these were available, consumers could still locate websites with infringing images through e-mails from friends, messages on discussion forums, . . . peer-to-peer networking using BitTorrent or eDonkey, offline and online advertisements . . . , disreputable search engines hosted on servers in far-off jurisdictions or even old-fashioned word of mouth. . . .

Vicarious Infringement

. . . There is no doubt that defendants profit from the infringing activity of the Stolen Content Websites; after all, they take a cut of virtually every sale of pirated material. First Am. Compl. at 4 ¶ 13, 7 ¶ 25. The majority does not dispute this point so I need not belabor it.

Defendants here also have a right to stop or limit the infringing activity, a right they have refused to exercise. As the majority recognizes, "Perfect 10 . . . claims that Defendants' rules and regulations permit them to require member merchants to cease illegal activity—presumably including copyright infringement—as a condition to their continuing right to receive credit card payments from the relevant Defendant entities." Maj. op. at 804. Assuming the truth of this allegation, the cards have the authority, given to them by contract, to force the Stolen Content Websites to remove infringing images from their inventory as a condition for using defendants' payment systems. If the merchants comply, their websites stop peddling stolen content and so infringement is stopped or limited. If they don't comply, defendants have the right—and under copyright law the duty—to kick the pirates off their payment networks, forcing them to find other means of getting paid or go out of business. In that case, too, infringement is stopped or limited. The swap meet in *Fonovisa* was held vicariously liable precisely because it did not force the pirates to stop infringing or leave; there is no reason to treat defendants here differently.

That the pirates might find some other way of doing business is of no consequence; our cases make this perfectly clear. It didn't matter in *Fonovisa* that the infringers there could have continued their illegal sales by mail order or by hawking their unlawful merchandise on street corners. . . . Indeed, there is no case involving secondary infringement, going back to the dance hall cases of the last century, where the secondary infringer's refusal to do business with the direct infringer could have stopped infringement altogether and forever. Yet, courts have presumed that removing the particular means of infringement challenged in each case would make direct infringement more difficult and thereby diminish the scale of infringing activity. . . .

. . . [I]t makes no difference that defendants control only the means of payment, not the mechanics of transferring the material. Maj. op. at 802, 805, 806. In a commercial environment, distribution and payment are (to use a quaint anachronism) like love and marriage—you can't have one without the other. If cards don't process payment, pirates don't deliver booty. The credit cards, in fact, control distribution of the infringing material. . . .

NOTES AND QUESTIONS

1. Do you agree with the majority in the *Visa* case that its decision is consistent with *Amazon.com*? Does the majority offer a desirable way of limiting the material contribution doctrine in the case of OSPs, or do you agree with Judge Kozinski that the majority's analysis is deficient?

2. What is the disagreement between the majority and the dissent in *Visa* regarding the right to control? Which approach do you find more persuasive?

3. From a policy standpoint, would extending indirect liability to entities that provide financial services to alleged infringers be a good idea? Why, or why not?

4. Are venture capitalists (VCs) more like OSPs or Visa? In *UMG Recordings, Inc. v. Shelter Capital Partners, LLC*, 718 F.3d 1006 (2013), the court addressed the question whether the investors in Veoh Networks, the operator of a website with infringing content, were liable for indirect infringement. The court said:

> UMG acknowledges that funding alone cannot satisfy the material assistance requirement [of contributory infringement]. It thus argues that the Investor Defendants "provided Veoh's necessary funding *and* directed its spending" on "basic operations including . . . hardware, software, and employees"—"elements" [that] UMG argues "form 'the site and facilities' for Veoh's direct infringement." UMG thus attempts to liken its case to *UMG Recordings, Inc. v. Bertelsmann AG, et al.*, 222 F.R.D. 408 (N.D.Cal.2004), where the district court denied an investor's motion to dismiss claims of contributory infringement. In *Bertelsmann*, however, the investor was Napster's "only available source of funding," and thus "held significant power and

control over Napster's operations." *Id.* at 412. Here, by contrast, there were multiple investors, and none of the Investor Defendants could individually control Veoh. Accordingly, UMG hinges its novel theory of secondary liability on the contention that the three Investor Defendants *together* took control of Veoh's operations by "obtain[ing] three of the five seats on Veoh's Board of Directors," and effectively provided the "site and facilities" for direct infringement by wielding their majority power to direct spending.

Even assuming that such joint control, not typically an element of contributory infringement, could satisfy *Fonovisa's* site and facilities requirement, UMG's argument fails on its own terms, because the complaint nowhere alleged that the Investor Defendants agreed to work in concert to this end. . . . [T]hree investors individually acquiring one seat apiece is not the same as agreeing to operate as a unified entity to obtain and leverage majority control. Unless the three independent investors were on some level working in concert, then none of them actually had sufficient control over the Board to direct Veoh in the way UMG contends. This missing allegation is critical because finding secondary liability without it would allow plaintiffs to sue any collection of directors making up 51 percent of the board on the theory that they constitute a majority, and therefore together they control the company. . . . We therefore affirm the dismissal of UMG's contributory infringement claim.

This missing allegation likewise requires us to affirm the district court's dismissal of UMG's vicarious liability . . . claim[]. . . . UMG's arguments that the Investor Defendants "distribute[d]" Veoh's services and had the right and ability to supervise the infringing users are premised on the unalleged contention that the Investor Defendants agreed to act in concert, and thus *together* they held a majority of seats on the Board and "maintained operational control over the company." We therefore affirm the dismissal of the complaint against the Investor Defendants.

Id. at 1032-33. Should VCs be liable for secondary infringement committed by the companies they finance?

C. ONLINE SERVICE PROVIDER LIABILITY

In the 1990s, as Internet technologies came into more widespread use and traditional theories of indirect liability began to come under pressure, companies offering online services to the public became increasingly concerned about incurring liability for material exchanged and posted by users. In any litigation, the online service provider (OSP) usually would be a deeper pocket than the direct infringer, making the OSP an attractive target. Because the infringing material could be distributed across the Internet, there existed the potential for large liability. Contractual solutions, like requiring subscribers to indemnify the OSP for infringement, were of little practical comfort because even if the OSP could enforce the contract against the subscriber, the subscriber would be unlikely to have the funds to indemnify it.

Against this background, Congress considered a number of proposals to provide OSPs, including both Internet access providers and providers of other online services, with greater legal certainty. Strong lobbies represented each side, with telecommunications companies arguing for a broad exemption from infringement liability and copyright owners arguing for no—or at least a narrow—exemption. The eventual compromise is reflected in §512 of the Copyright Act, enacted in 1998 as Title II (Online Copyright Infringement Liability Limitation) of the Digital Millennium Copyright Act. Once again, because the legislation resulted from bargaining between interest groups, it is quite complex. Read §512 from the perspective of an OSP and consider how it would affect the manner in which you conduct your business. Then read the following materials.

1. Section 512 Overview

Generally, §512 establishes "safe harbors" that provide immunity from infringement liability under certain circumstances for a "service provider" that engages in any of the following activities: (1) transitory digital network communications; (2) system caching; (3) storing information on its systems at the direction of users; or (4) providing information location tools like hypertext links. The definition of "service provider," set forth in §512(k)(1), varies depending on which safe harbor is invoked.

An OSP must comply with certain threshold requirements to take advantage of any of the safe harbors. To qualify for *any* exemption, the OSP must not interfere with "standard technical measures" applied by copyright owners to protect their works, and must adopt and reasonably implement a policy providing for termination of repeat infringers' accounts and must inform subscribers of this policy. 17 U.S.C. §512(i). In addition, each safe harbor has its own requirements that the OSP must meet to qualify for immunity from liability.

The first safe harbor exempts an OSP from liability for transmitting or transiently storing infringing material. For it to apply, the transmission must be initiated by someone other than the OSP and must be carried out through an automatic process; the OSP must not select the recipient except through an automatic process; the OSP must not maintain a copy accessible to anyone other than the recipients; and the OSP must transmit the material without modifying its content. *Id.* §512(a).

KEEP IN MIND

Compliance with §512 is voluntary. An OSP may choose not to rely on the pertinent safe harbor and take its chances in the courts with any and all of the defenses otherwise available. *Id.* §512(1). Note also that §512 does not shelter an OSP from injunctive and other equitable relief *See id.* §512(j).

The second safe harbor exempts an OSP from liability for caching copies of copyrighted material if the material is made available by someone else, transmitted from that person to the recipient at the recipient's direction, and the storage is automatic. *Id.* §512(b). The caching OSP must further comply with "conditions" imposed by the copyright owner (including password protection and deadlines for refreshing or updating the cached copy), and must disable access to cached material upon notice that a court has ordered the cached material removed from the originating website. *Id.* §512(b)(2).

The third and fourth safe harbors may be the most important to OSPs. The third safe harbor exempts an OSP from liability for infringing material "hosted" on its servers on behalf of subscribers, such as blog entries and photos shared online, and for infringing material downloaded by its servers and retained for limited periods, such as USENET postings. This exemption also covers the provision of server space for chatrooms and other fora in which users may post material. *Id.* §512(c). The fourth safe harbor shelters OSPs that provide links, indices, or other directories referencing infringing material. *Id.* §512(d). To qualify for either of these safe harbors, the OSP must designate an agent to receive notification of claimed infringement from copyright owners, file that designation with the Copyright Office, and make it publicly available. *Id.* §512(c)(2). The OSP must not have "actual knowledge" that the material is infringing or "aware[ness] of facts or circumstances from which infringing activity is apparent." If it does, it must "act[] expeditiously to remove, or disable access to, the material." *Id.* §512(c)(1)(A). Finally, the OSP must not obtain a "financial benefit directly attributable to the infringing activity, in a case in which the service provider has the right and ability to control such activity." *Id.* §512(c)(1)(B).

Under the "notice and takedown" regime established by the third and fourth safe harbors, a copyright owner may send a notice of alleged infringement to the OSP's designated agent. *Id.* §512(c)(3). Section 512(c)(3) provides detailed rules about the content and form of this notice and the OSP's obligations on its receipt. Among other things, the notice must provide contact information for the complaining party; must identify the allegedly infringing material with information sufficient to permit the OSP to locate it; and must state that the complaining party "has a good faith belief" that the material is unauthorized. The complaining party must state under penalty of perjury that he or she is authorized to act on behalf of the copyright owner, but none of the other required statements need be made under penalty of perjury. *See id.* However, if the complaining party "knowingly materially misrepresents . . . that material or activity is infringing," a court may award damages to the alleged infringer or the affected OSP. *Id.* §512(f).

To maintain the protection of the safe harbor, when an OSP receives a proper takedown notice, the OSP must respond "expeditiously to remove, or disable access to, the material that is claimed to be infringing. . . ." *Id.* §512(c)(1)(C).

Section 512 also provides the OSP with an exemption from liability for "any claim based on" the OSP's good faith removal. *Id.* §512(g)(1). To maintain this further exemption from claims of liability by the users whose material is removed, the OSP must "take[] reasonable steps promptly to notify the subscriber" of the removal. *Id.* §512(g)(2)(A). If the subscriber wishes, he or she may furnish a counter notification that identifies the material; states

> **COMPARATIVE PERSPECTIVE**
>
> In its directive on electronic commerce, the European Union adopted safe harbors for transmission, caching, and hosting services that are similar to those in §512. *See* Directive 2000/31/EC of the European Parliament and of the Council of 8 June 2000 on certain legal aspects of information society services, in particular electronic commerce, in the Internal Market, 2000 O.J. (L 178) 1, arts. 12-15. Member countries may determine the specific procedures for removing or disabling access to material that has been identified as infringing. *Id.*, arts. 12(3), 13(2), 14(3).

under penalty of perjury that the subscriber has a good faith belief that it was removed by mistake; and consents to the jurisdiction of the federal district court where the subscriber's contact address is located or, for subscribers who reside outside the United States, where the OSP is located. *Id.* §512(g)(3). Upon receipt of the counter notification, the OSP must notify the complainant, and must restore the material within 10 business days unless it first receives notice that a lawsuit has been filed. *Id.* §512(g)(2). A subscriber who "knowingly materially misrepresents" that material was removed by mistake will be liable for damages incurred by the copyright owner or its authorized licensee, or by the OSP. *Id.* §512(f).

Finally, §512(h) authorizes federal district court clerks, upon a copyright owner's request, to issue subpoenas for identification of subscribers who have posted allegedly infringing material, and OSPs receiving such subpoenas must "expeditiously disclose" the information. *Id.* §512(h).

NOTES AND QUESTIONS

1. Consider first whether the idea of a "safe harbor" regime for OSPs makes sense. Would it make more sense simply to exempt OSPs from liability by analogizing them to common carriers like phone companies? No court has held a phone company liable for engaging in conduct like transmitting an infringing fax or storing an infringing recording on a voicemail service. *See also* §111(a)(3) of the Copyright Act (exempting a passive carrier from infringement liability when it engages in a secondary transmission by providing solely "wires, cables, or other communications channels for the use of others"). Are there relevant distinctions between phone companies and OSPs?

2. Focus now on §512(a) and (b). What are the differences between them? Does either adopt a common carrier model?

3. Why would the §512(c) safe harbor be the most important to an OSP? Assume that your client, an OSP that provides hosting services, seeks your advice on avoiding copyright infringement liability. Would you advise your client to ignore the requirements of §512(c) and rely solely on other defenses afforded by the Copyright Act? Why, or why not?

4. Note that nonprofit educational institutions that offer Internet services may rely on a safe harbor with a slightly different set of requirements, set forth in §512(e).

2. Safe Harbor Versus Secondary Liability

The eligibility requirements for the third and fourth safe harbors refer to some now-familiar concepts. An OSP must show that it did not have knowledge of the infringing activity and that it did not receive "financial benefit directly attributable to the infringing activity" in a case in which it had the "right and ability to control" the infringing activity. 17 U.S.C. §512(c)(1). What is the relationship between the statutory eligibility requirements and the traditional, judge-made theories of secondary liability? Consider the following case.

Viacom International, Inc. v. YouTube, Inc.
676 F.3d 19 (2d Cir. 2012)

CABRANES, J.:

This appeal requires us to clarify the contours of the "safe harbor" provision of the Digital Millennium Copyright Act (DMCA) that limits the liability of online service providers for copyright infringement that occurs "by reason of the storage at the direction of a user of material that resides on a system or network controlled or operated by or for the service provider." 17 U.S.C. §512(c). . . .

Background . . .

YouTube was founded in February 2005 by Chad Hurley ("Hurley"), Steve Chen ("Chen"), and Jawed Karim ("Karim"), three former employees of the internet company Paypal. When YouTube announced the "official launch" of the website in December 2005, a press release described YouTube as a "consumer media company" that "allows people to watch, upload, and share personal video clips at www.YouTube.com." Under the slogan "Broadcast yourself," YouTube achieved rapid prominence and profitability, eclipsing competitors such as Google Video and Yahoo Video by wide margins. In November 2006, Google acquired YouTube in a stock-for-stock transaction valued at $1.65 billion. By March 2010, at the time of summary judgment briefing in this litigation, site traffic on YouTube had soared to more than 1 billion daily video views, with more than 24 hours of new video uploaded to the site every minute.

The basic function of the YouTube website permits users to "upload" and view video clips free of charge. Before uploading a video to YouTube, a user must register and create an account with the website. The registration process requires the user to accept YouTube's Terms of Use agreement, which provides, *inter alia,* that the user "will not submit material that is copyrighted . . . unless [he is] the owner of such rights or ha[s] permission from their rightful owner to post the material and to grant YouTube all of the license rights granted herein." When the registration process is complete, the user can sign in to his account, select a video to upload from the user's personal computer, mobile phone, or other device, and instruct the YouTube system to upload the video by clicking on a virtual upload "button."

Uploading a video to the YouTube website triggers a series of automated software functions. During the upload process, YouTube makes one or more exact copies of the video in its original file format. YouTube also makes one or more additional copies of the video in "Flash" format,[4] a process known as "transcoding." The transcoding process ensures that YouTube videos are available for viewing by most users at their request. The YouTube system allows users to gain access to video content by "streaming" the video to the user's computer in response to a playback request. YouTube uses a computer algorithm to identify clips that are "related" to a video the user watches and display links to the "related" clips. . . .

Plaintiff Viacom, an American media conglomerate, and various Viacom affiliates filed suit against YouTube on March 13, 2007, alleging direct and secondary copyright infringement based on the public performance, display, and reproduction of their audiovisual works on the YouTube website. Plaintiff Premier League, an English soccer league, and Plaintiff Bourne Co. filed a putative class action against YouTube on May 4, 2007, alleging direct and secondary copyright infringement on behalf of all copyright owners whose material was copied, stored, displayed, or performed on YouTube without authorization. Specifically at issue were some 63,497 video clips identified by Viacom, as well as 13,500 additional clips (jointly, the "clips-in-suit") identified by the putative class plaintiffs.

The plaintiffs in both actions principally demanded statutory damages pursuant to 17 U.S.C. §504(c) or, in the alternative, actual damages plus the defendants' profits from the alleged infringement, as well as declaratory and injunctive relief. Judge Stanton, to whom the *Viacom* action was assigned, accepted the *Premier League* class action as related. At the close of discovery, the parties in both actions cross-moved for partial summary judgment with respect to the applicability of the DMCA safe harbor defense.[7]

. . . [T]he District Court denied the plaintiffs' motions and granted summary judgment to the defendants, finding that YouTube qualified for DMCA safe harbor protection with respect to all claims of direct and secondary copyright infringement. *Viacom Int'l*, 718 F. Supp. 2d at 529. The District Court prefaced its analysis of the DMCA safe harbor by holding that, based on the plaintiffs' summary judgment submissions, "a jury could find that the defendants not only were generally aware of, but welcomed, copyright-infringing material being placed on their website." *Id.* at 518. However, the District Court also noted that the defendants had properly designated an agent pursuant to §512(c)(2), and "when they received specific notice that a particular item infringed a copyright, they swiftly removed it." *Id.* at 519. . . .

4. The "Flash" format "is a highly compressed streaming format that begins to play instantly. Unlike other delivery methods, it does not require the viewer to download the entire video file before viewing."

7. It is undisputed that all clips-in-suit had been removed from the YouTube website by the time of summary judgment, mostly in response to DMCA takedown notices.

Discussion . . .

A. *Actual and "Red Flag" Knowledge: §512(c)(1)(A)* . . .

1. The Specificity Requirement

. . . Under §512(c)(1)(A), safe harbor protection is available only if the service provider:

> (i) does not have actual knowledge that the material or an activity using the material on the system or network is infringing;
> (ii) in the absence of such actual knowledge, is not aware of facts or circumstances from which infringing activity is apparent; or
> (iii) upon obtaining such knowledge or awareness, acts expeditiously to remove, or disable access to, the material. . . .

17 U.S.C. §512(c)(1)(A). . . . [T]he District Court held that the statutory phrases "actual knowledge that the material . . . is infringing" and "facts or circumstances from which infringing activity is apparent" refer to "knowledge of specific and identifiable infringements." *Viacom*, 718 F. Supp. 2d at 523. For the reasons that follow, we substantially affirm that holding.

Although the parties marshal a battery of other arguments on appeal, it is the text of the statute that compels our conclusion. In particular, we are persuaded that the basic operation of §512(c) requires knowledge or awareness of specific infringing activity. Under §512(c)(1)(A), knowledge or awareness alone does not disqualify the service provider; rather, the provider that gains knowledge or awareness of infringing activity retains safe-harbor protection if it "acts expeditiously to remove, or disable access to, the material." 17 U.S.C. §512(c)(1)(A)(iii). Thus, the nature of the removal obligation itself contemplates knowledge or awareness of specific infringing material, because expeditious removal is possible only if the service provider knows with particularity which items to remove. Indeed, to require expeditious removal in the absence of specific knowledge or awareness would be to mandate an amorphous obligation to "take commercially reasonable steps" in response to a generalized awareness of infringement. Such a view cannot be reconciled with the language of the statute, which requires "expeditious[]" action to remove or disable "*the material*" at issue. 17 U.S.C. §512(c)(1)(A)(iii) (emphasis added).

On appeal, the plaintiffs dispute this conclusion by drawing our attention to §512(c)(1)(A)(ii), the so-called "red flag" knowledge provision. In their view, the use of the phrase "facts or circumstances" demonstrates that Congress did not intend to limit the red flag provision to a particular type of knowledge. The plaintiffs contend that requiring awareness of specific infringements in order to establish "aware[ness] of facts or circumstances from which infringing activity is apparent," 17 U.S.C. §512(c)(1)(A)(ii), renders the red flag provision superfluous, because that provision would be satisfied only when the "actual knowledge" provision is also satisfied. For that reason, the plaintiffs urge the Court to hold that the red flag provision "requires less specificity" than the actual knowledge provision.

This argument misconstrues the relationship between "actual" knowledge and "red flag" knowledge. . . . The phrase "actual knowledge," which appears in §512(c)(1)(A)(i), is frequently used to denote subjective belief. *See, e.g., United States v. Quinones*, 635 F.3d 590, 602 (2d Cir. 2011) ("[T]he belief held by the defendant need not be reasonable in order for it to defeat . . . actual knowledge."). By contrast, courts often invoke the language of "facts or circumstances," which appears in §512(c)(1)(A)(ii), in discussing an objective reasonableness standard. *See, e.g., Maxwell v. City of New York*, 380 F.3d 106, 108 (2d Cir. 2004) ("Police officers' application of force is excessive . . . if it is objectively unreasonable in light of the facts and circumstances confronting them, without regard to their underlying intent or motivation." (internal quotation marks omitted)).

The difference between actual and red flag knowledge is thus not between specific and generalized knowledge, but instead between a subjective and an objective standard. In other words, the actual knowledge provision turns on whether the provider actually or "subjectively" knew of specific infringement, while the red flag provision turns on whether the provider was subjectively aware of facts that would have made the specific infringement "objectively" obvious to a reasonable person. The red flag provision, because it incorporates an objective standard, is not swallowed up by the actual knowledge provision under our construction of the §512(c) safe harbor. Both provisions do independent work, and both apply only to specific instances of infringement.

The limited body of case law interpreting the knowledge provisions of the §512(c) safe harbor comports with our view of the specificity requirement. Most recently, a panel of the Ninth Circuit addressed the scope of §512(c) in *UMG Recordings, Inc. v. Shelter Capital Partners LLC*, 667 F.3d 1022 (9th Cir. 2011), a copyright infringement case against Veoh Networks, a video-hosting service similar to YouTube.[*] As in this case, various music publishers brought suit against the service provider, claiming direct and secondary copyright infringement based on the presence of unauthorized content on the website, and the website operator sought refuge in the §512(c) safe harbor. The Court of Appeals affirmed the district court's determination on summary judgment that the website operator was entitled to safe harbor protection. With respect to the actual knowledge provision, the panel declined to "adopt[] a broad conception of the knowledge requirement," *id.* at 1038, holding instead that the safe harbor "[r]equir[es] specific knowledge of particular infringing activity," *id.* at 1037. The Court of Appeals "reach[ed] the same conclusion" with respect to the red flag provision, noting that "[w]e do not place the burden of determining whether [materials] are actually illegal on a service provider." *Id.* at 1038.

Although *Shelter Capital* contains the most explicit discussion of the §512(c) knowledge provisions, other cases are generally in accord. . . . [W]e note that no court has embraced the contrary proposition—urged by the plaintiffs—that the red flag provision "requires less specificity" than the actual knowledge provision. . . .

---

* [The Ninth Circuit subsequently granted a rehearing on other grounds and issued a superseding opinion. *UMG Recordings., Inc. v. Shelter Capital Partners LLC*, 718 F.3d 1006 (9th Cir. 2013)—Eds.]

2. The Grant of Summary Judgment

The corollary question on appeal is whether, under the foregoing construction of §512(c)(1)(A), the District Court erred in granting summary judgment to You-Tube on the record presented. . . .

i. Specific Knowledge or Awareness

The plaintiffs argue that, even under the District Court's construction of the safe harbor, the record raises material issues of fact regarding YouTube's actual knowledge or "red flag" awareness of specific instances of infringement. To that end, the plaintiffs draw our attention to various estimates regarding the percentage of infringing content on the YouTube website. For example, Viacom cites evidence that YouTube employees conducted website surveys and estimated that 75-80% of all YouTube streams contained copyrighted material. The class plaintiffs similarly claim that Credit Suisse, acting as financial advisor to Google, estimated that more than 60% of YouTube's content was "premium" copyrighted content—and that only 10% of the premium content was authorized. These approximations suggest that the defendants were conscious that significant quantities of material on the YouTube website were infringing. But such estimates are insufficient, standing alone, to create a triable issue of fact as to whether YouTube actually knew, or was aware of facts or circumstances that would indicate, the existence of particular instances of infringement.

Beyond the survey results, the plaintiffs rely upon internal YouTube communications that do refer to particular clips or groups of clips. The class plaintiffs argue that YouTube was aware of specific infringing material because, *inter alia*, YouTube attempted to search for specific Premier League videos on the site in order to gauge their "value based on video usage." In particular, the class plaintiffs cite a February 7, 2007 e-mail from Patrick Walker, director of video partnerships for Google and YouTube, requesting that his colleagues calculate the number of daily searches for the terms "soccer," "football," and "Premier League" in preparation for a bid on the global rights to Premier League content. On another occasion, Walker requested that any "clearly infringing, official broadcast footage" from a list of top Premier League clubs . . . be taken down in advance of a meeting with the heads of "several major sports teams and leagues." YouTube ultimately decided not to make a bid for the Premier League rights—but the infringing content allegedly remained on the website.

The record in the *Viacom* action includes additional examples. For instance, YouTube founder Jawed Karim prepared a report in March 2006 which stated that, "[a]s of today[,] episodes and clips of the following well-known shows can still be found [on YouTube]: Family Guy, South Park, MTV Cribs, Daily Show, Reno 911, [and] Dave Chapelle [sic]." Karim further opined that, "although You-Tube is not legally required to monitor content . . . and complies with DMCA takedown requests, we would benefit from *preemptively* removing content that is blatantly illegal and likely to attract criticism." He also noted that "a more thorough analysis" of the issue would be required. At least some of the TV shows to which Karim referred are owned by Viacom. A reasonable juror could conclude from the

March 2006 report that Karim knew of the presence of Viacom-owned material on YouTube, since he presumably located specific clips of the shows in question before he could announce that YouTube hosted the content "[a]s of today." A reasonable juror could also conclude that Karim believed the clips he located to be infringing (since he refers to them as "blatantly illegal"), and that YouTube did not remove the content from the website until conducting "a more thorough analysis," thus exposing the company to liability in the interim.

Furthermore, in a July 4, 2005 e-mail exchange, YouTube founder Chad Hurley sent an e-mail to his co-founders with the subject line "budlight commercials," and stated, "we need to reject these too." Steve Chen responded, "can we please leave these in a bit longer? another week or two can't hurt." Karim also replied, indicating that he "added back in all 28 bud videos." Similarly, in an August 9, 2005 e-mail exchange, Hurley urged his colleagues "to start being *diligent* about rejecting copyrighted/inappropriate content," noting that "there is a cnn clip of the shuttle clip on the site today, if the boys from Turner would come to the site, they might be pissed?" Again, Chen resisted:

> but we should just keep that stuff on the site. i really don't see what will happen. what? someone from cnn sees it? he happens to be someone with power? he happens to want to take it down right away. he gets in touch with cnn legal. 2 weeks later, we get a cease & desist letter. we take the video down.

And again, Karim agreed, indicating that "the CNN space shuttle clip, I like. we can remove it once we're bigger and better known, but for now that clip is fine."

Upon a review of the record, we are persuaded that the plaintiffs may have raised a material issue of fact regarding YouTube's knowledge or awareness of specific instances of infringement. The foregoing Premier League e-mails request the identification and removal of "clearly infringing, official broadcast footage." The March 2006 report indicates Karim's awareness of specific clips that he perceived to be "blatantly illegal." Similarly, the Bud Light and space shuttle e-mails refer to particular clips in the context of correspondence about whether to remove infringing material from the website. On these facts, a reasonable juror could conclude that YouTube had actual knowledge of specific infringing activity, or was at least aware of facts or circumstances from which specific infringing activity was apparent. *See* §512(c)(1)(A)(i)-(ii). Accordingly, we hold that summary judgment to YouTube on all clips-in-suit, especially in the absence of any detailed examination of the extensive record on summary judgment, was premature.[9]

We hasten to note, however, that although the foregoing e-mails were annexed as exhibits to the summary judgment papers, it is unclear whether the clips

---

9. We express no opinion as to whether the evidence discussed above will prove sufficient to withstand a renewed motion for summary judgment by YouTube on remand. In particular, we note that there is at least some evidence that the search requested by Walker in his February 7, 2007, e-mail was never carried out. *See* Joint App'x III:256. We also note that the class plaintiffs have failed to identify evidence indicating that any infringing content discovered as a result of Walker's request in fact remained on the YouTube website. The class plaintiffs, drawing on the voluminous record in this case, may be able to remedy these deficiencies in their briefing to the District Court on remand.

referenced therein are among the current clips-in-suit. By definition, only the current clips-in-suit are at issue in this litigation. Accordingly, we vacate the order granting summary judgment and instruct the District Court to determine on remand whether any specific infringements of which YouTube had knowledge or awareness correspond to the clips-in-suit in these actions.

ii. "Willful Blindness"

The plaintiffs further argue that the District Court erred in granting summary judgment to the defendants despite evidence that YouTube was "willfully blind" to specific infringing activity. On this issue of first impression, we consider the application of the common law willful blindness doctrine in the DMCA context.

"The principle that willful blindness is tantamount to knowledge is hardly novel." *Tiffany (NJ) Inc. v. eBay, Inc.*, 600 F.3d 93, 110 n.16 (2d Cir. 2010) (collecting cases); *see In re Aimster Copyright Litig.*, 334 F.3d 643, 650 (7th Cir. 2003) ("Willful blindness is knowledge, in copyright law . . . as it is in the law generally."). A person is "willfully blind" or engages in "conscious avoidance" amounting to knowledge where the person "'was aware of a high probability of the fact in dispute and consciously avoided confirming that fact.'" *United States v. Aina-Marshall*, 336 F.3d 167, 170 (2d Cir. 2003). Writing in the trademark infringement context, we have held that "[a] service provider is not . . . permitted willful blindness. When it has reason to suspect that users of its service are infringing a protected mark, it may not shield itself from learning of the particular infringing transactions by looking the other way." *Tiffany*, 600 F.3d at 109.

The DMCA does not mention willful blindness. As a general matter, we interpret a statute to abrogate a common law principle only if the statute "speak[s] directly to the question addressed by the common law." *Matar v. Dichter*, 563 F.3d 9, 14 (2d Cir. 2009). . . . The DMCA provision most relevant to the abrogation inquiry is §512(m), which provides that safe harbor protection shall not be conditioned on "a service provider monitoring its service or affirmatively seeking facts indicating infringing activity, except to the extent consistent with a standard technical measure complying with the provisions of subsection (i)." 17 U.S.C. §512(m)(1). Section 512(m) is explicit: DMCA safe harbor protection cannot be conditioned on affirmative monitoring by a service provider. For that reason, §512(m) is incompatible with a broad common law duty to monitor or otherwise seek out infringing activity based on general awareness that infringement may be occurring. That fact does not, however, dispose of the abrogation inquiry; as previously noted, willful blindness cannot be defined as an affirmative duty to monitor. Because the statute does not "speak[ ] directly" to the willful blindness doctrine, §512(m) limits—but does not abrogate—the doctrine. Accordingly, we hold that the willful blindness doctrine may be applied, in appropriate circumstances, to demonstrate knowledge or awareness of specific instances of infringement under the DMCA.

The District Court cited §512(m) for the proposition that safe harbor protection does not require affirmative monitoring, but did not expressly address the principle of willful blindness or its relationship to the DMCA safe harbors.

As a result, whether the defendants made a "deliberate effort to avoid guilty knowledge," *In re Aimster*, 334 F.3d at 650, remains a fact question for the District Court to consider in the first instance on remand.

B. Control and Benefit: §512(c)(1)(B)

Apart from the foregoing knowledge provisions, the §512(c) safe harbor provides that an eligible service provider must "not receive a financial benefit directly attributable to the infringing activity, in a case in which the service provider has the right and ability to control such activity." 17 U.S.C. §512(c)(1)(B). . . .

On appeal, the parties advocate two competing constructions of the "right and ability to control" infringing activity. 17 U.S.C. §512(c)(1)(B). . . .

The first construction, pressed by the defendants, is the one adopted by the District Court, which held that "the provider must know of the particular case before he can control it." *Viacom*, 718 F. Supp. 2d at 527. . . . The trouble with this construction is that importing a specific knowledge requirement into §512(c)(1)(B) renders the control provision duplicative of §512(c)(1)(A). Any service provider that has item-specific knowledge of infringing activity and thereby obtains financial benefit would already be excluded from the safe harbor under §512(c)(1)(A) for having specific knowledge of infringing material and failing to effect expeditious removal. No additional service provider would be excluded by §512(c)(1)(B) that was not already excluded by §512(c)(1)(A). Because statutory interpretations that render language superfluous are disfavored, we reject the District Court's interpretation of the control provision.

The second construction, urged by the plaintiffs, is that the control provision codifies the common law doctrine of vicarious copyright liability. The common law imposes liability for vicarious copyright infringement "[w]hen the right and ability to supervise coalesce with an obvious and direct financial interest in the exploitation of copyrighted materials—even in the absence of actual knowledge that the copyright mono[poly] is being impaired." *Shapiro, Bernstein & Co. v. H.L. Green Co.*, 316 F.2d 304, 407 (2d Cir. 1963). To support their codification argument, the plaintiffs rely on a House Report relating to a preliminary version of the DMCA: "The 'right and ability to control' language . . . codifies the second element of vicarious liability. . . . Subparagraph (B) is intended to preserve existing case law that examines all relevant aspects of the relationship between the primary and secondary infringer." H.R. Rep. No. 105-551(I), at 26 (1998). In response, YouTube notes that the codification reference was omitted from the committee reports describing the final legislation, and that Congress ultimately abandoned any attempt to "embark[ ] upon a wholesale clarification" of vicarious liability, electing instead "to create a series of 'safe harbors' for certain common activities of service providers." S. Rep. No. 105-190, at 19.

Happily, the future of digital copyright law does not turn on the confused legislative history of the control provision. The general rule with respect to common law codification is that when "Congress uses terms that have accumulated settled meaning under the common law, a court must infer, unless the statute otherwise dictates, that Congress means to incorporate the established meaning of those terms." *Neder v. United States*, 527 U.S. 1, 21 (1999). Under the common law vicarious liability standard, "'[t]he ability to block infringers' access to a particular environment for any reason whatsoever is evidence of the right and ability to supervise.'" *Arista Records LLC v. Usenet.com, Inc.*, 633 F. Supp. 2d 124, 157 (S.D.N.Y. 2009). To adopt that principle in the DMCA context, however, would render the statute internally inconsistent. Section 512(c) actually presumes that service providers have the ability to "block . . . access" to infringing material. *Id*. at 157; *see Shelter Capital*, 667 F.3d at 1042-43. Indeed, a service provider who has knowledge or awareness of infringing material or who receives a takedown notice from a copyright holder is *required* to "remove, or disable access to, the material" in order to claim the benefit of the safe harbor. 17 U.S.C. §§512(c)(1)(A)(iii) & (C). But in taking such action, the service provider would—in the plaintiffs' analysis—be admitting the "right and ability to control" the infringing material. Thus, the prerequisite to safe harbor protection under §§512(c)(1)(A)(iii) & (C) would at the same time be a disqualifier under §512(c)(1)(B).

Moreover, if Congress had intended §512(c)(1)(B) to be coextensive with vicarious liability, "the statute could have accomplished that result in a more direct manner." *Shelter Capital*, 667 F.3d at 1045. . . .

In any event, the foregoing tension . . . is sufficient to establish that the control provision "dictates" a departure from the common law vicarious liability standard, *Neder*, 527 U.S. at 21. Accordingly, we conclude that the "right and ability to control" infringing activity under §512(c)(1)(B) "requires something more than the ability to remove or block access to materials posted on a service provider's website." The remaining—and more difficult—question is how to define the "something more" that is required.

To date, only one court has found that a service provider had the right and ability to control infringing activity under §512(c)(1)(B). In *Perfect 10, Inc. v. Cybernet Ventures, Inc.*, 213 F. Supp. 2d 1146 (C.D. Cal. 2002), the court found control where the service provider instituted a monitoring program by which user websites received "detailed instructions regard[ing] issues of layout, appearance, and content." *Id*. at 1173. The service provider also forbade certain types of content and refused access to users who failed to comply with its instructions. Similarly, inducement of copyright infringement under *Metro-Goldwyn-Mayer Studios Inc. v. Grokster, Ltd.*, 545 U.S. 913 (2005), which "premises liability on purposeful, culpable expression and conduct," *id*. at 937, might also rise to the level of control under §512(c)(1)(B). Both of these examples involve a service provider exerting substantial influence on the activities of users, without necessarily—or even frequently—acquiring knowledge of specific infringing activity.

In light of our holding that §512(c)(1)(B) does not include a specific knowledge requirement, we think it prudent to remand to the District Court to consider in the first instance whether the plaintiffs have adduced sufficient evidence to allow a reasonable jury to conclude that YouTube had the right and ability to control the infringing activity and received a financial benefit directly attributable to that activity.

C. "By Reason of" Storage: §512(c)(1)

The §512(c) safe harbor is only available when the infringement occurs "by reason of the storage at the direction of a user of material that resides on a system or network controlled or operated by or for the service provider." 17 U.S.C. §512(c)(1). In this case, the District Court held that YouTube's software functions fell within the safe harbor for infringements that occur "by reason of" user storage. *Viacom*, 718 F. Supp. 2d at 526 (noting that a contrary holding would "confine[ ] the word 'storage' too narrowly to meet the statute's purpose"). For the reasons that follow, we affirm that holding with respect to three of the challenged software functions—the conversion (or "transcoding") of videos into a standard display format, the playback of videos on "watch" pages, and the "related videos" function. We remand for further fact-finding with respect to a fourth software function, involving the third-party syndication of videos uploaded to YouTube.

As a preliminary matter, we note that . . . [t]he structure of the statute distinguishes between so-called "conduit only" functions under §512(a) and the functions addressed by §512(c) and the other subsections. Most notably, [§512] contains two definitions of "service provider." 17 U.S.C. §512(k)(1)(A)-(B). The narrower definition, which applies only to service providers falling under §512(a), is limited to entities that "offer[ ] the transmission, routing or providing of connections for digital online communications, between or among points specified by a user, of material of the user's choosing, *without modification to the content of the material* as sent or received." *Id.* §512(k)(1)(A) (emphasis added). No such limitation appears in the broader definition, which applies to service providers—including YouTube—falling under §512(c). Under the broader definition, "the term 'service provider' means a provider of online services or network access, or the operator of facilities therefor, and includes an entity described in subparagraph (A)." *Id.* §512(k)(1)(B). In the absence of a parallel limitation on the ability of a service provider to modify user-submitted material, we conclude that §512(c) "is clearly meant to cover more than mere electronic storage lockers." *UMG Recordings, Inc. v. Veoh Networks, Inc.*, 620 F. Supp. 2d 1081, 1088 (C.D. Cal. 2008) ("*UMG I*").

The relevant case law makes clear that the §512(c) safe harbor extends to software functions performed "for the purpose of facilitating access to user-stored material." *Id.*; *see Shelter Capital*, 667 F.3d at 1031-35. Two of the software functions challenged here—transcoding and playback—were expressly considered by our sister Circuit in *Shelter Capital*, which held that liability arising from these functions occurred "by reason of the storage at the direction of a user." 17 U.S.C. §512(c); *see Shelter Capital*, 667 F.3d at 1027-28, 1031. Transcoding involves "[m]aking copies of a video in a different encoding scheme" in order to render the video "viewable over the Internet to most users." The playback process involves "deliver[ing] copies of YouTube videos to a user's browser cache" in response to a user request. The District Court correctly found that to exclude these automated functions from the safe harbor would eviscerate the protection afforded to service providers by §512(c).

A similar analysis applies to the "related videos" function, by which a YouTube computer algorithm identifies and displays "thumbnails" of clips that are "related" to the video selected by the user. The plaintiffs claim that this practice constitutes content promotion, not "access" to stored content, and therefore falls beyond the scope of the safe harbor. Citing similar language in the Racketeer Influenced and Corrupt Organizations Act ("RICO"), 18 U.S.C. §§1961-68, and the Clayton Act, 15 U.S.C. §§12 *et seq.*, the plaintiffs argue that the statutory phrase "by reason of" requires a finding of proximate causation between the act of storage and the infringing activity. But even if the plaintiffs are correct that §512(c) incorporates a principle of proximate causation—a question we need not resolve here—the indexing and display of related videos retain a sufficient causal link to the prior storage of those videos. The record makes clear that the related videos algorithm "is fully automated and operates solely in response to user input without the active involvement of YouTube employees." Furthermore, the related videos function serves to help YouTube users locate and gain access to material stored at the direction of other users. Because the algorithm "is closely related to, and follows from, the storage itself," and is "narrowly directed toward providing access to material stored at the direction of users," *UMG I*, 620 F. Supp. 2d at 1092, we conclude that the related videos function is also protected by the §512(c) safe harbor.

The final software function at issue here—third-party syndication—is the closest case. In or around March 2007, YouTube transcoded a select number of videos into a format compatible with mobile devices and "syndicated" or licensed the videos to Verizon Wireless and other companies. The plaintiffs argue—with some force—that business transactions do not occur at the "direction of a user" within the meaning of §512(c)(1) when they involve the manual selection of copyrighted material for licensing to a third party. The parties do not dispute, however, that none of the clips-in-suit were among the approximately 2,000 videos provided to Verizon Wireless. In order to avoid rendering an advisory opinion on the outer boundaries of the storage provision, we remand for factfinding on the question of whether any of the clips-in-suit were in fact syndicated to any other third party.

D. *Other Arguments*

1. Repeat Infringer Policy

The class plaintiffs briefly argue that YouTube failed to comply with the requirements of §512(i), which conditions safe harbor eligibility on the service provider having "adopted and reasonably implemented . . . a policy that provides for the termination in appropriate circumstances of subscribers and account holders of the service provider's system or network who are repeat infringers." 17 U.S.C. §512(i)(1)(A). Specifically, the class plaintiffs allege that YouTube "deliberately set up its identification tools to try to avoid identifying infringements of class plaintiffs' works." This allegation rests primarily on the assertion that YouTube permitted only designated "partners" to gain access to content identification tools by which YouTube would conduct network searches and identify infringing material.

Because the class plaintiffs challenge YouTube's deployment of search technology, we must consider their §512(i) argument in conjunction with §512(m). As previously noted, §512(m) provides that safe harbor protection cannot be conditioned on "a service provider monitoring its service or affirmatively seeking facts indicating infringing activity, *except to the extent consistent with a standard technical measure complying with the provisions of subsection (i)*." 17 U.S.C. §512(m)(1) (emphasis added). In other words, the safe harbor expressly disclaims any affirmative monitoring requirement—except to the extent that such monitoring comprises a "standard technical measure" within the meaning of §512(i). . . . In this case, the class plaintiffs make no argument that the content identification tools implemented by YouTube constitute "standard technical measures," such that YouTube would be exposed to liability under §512(i). For that reason, YouTube cannot be excluded from the safe harbor by dint of a decision to restrict access to its proprietary search mechanisms.

2. Affirmative Claims

Finally, the plaintiffs argue that the District Court erred in denying summary judgment to the plaintiffs on their claims for direct infringement, vicarious liability, and contributory liability under *Metro-Goldwyn-Mayer Studios Inc. v. Grokster, Ltd.*, 545 U.S. 913 (2005). . . .

The District Court correctly determined that a finding of safe harbor application necessarily protects a defendant from all affirmative claims for monetary relief. For the reasons previously stated, further fact-finding is required to determine whether YouTube is ultimately entitled to safe harbor protection in this case. Accordingly, we vacate the order denying summary judgment to the plaintiffs and remand the cause without expressing a view on the merits of the plaintiffs' affirmative claims. . . .

NOTES AND QUESTIONS

1. A threshold question in the *Viacom* case is whether the §512(c) safe harbor is available to a platform like YouTube's. Does the court's interpretation of the statutory reference to infringement "by reason of" storage make sense? In terms of simple chronology, plaintiffs' attempted distinction between mere storage and the sorts of activities performed by YouTube has some merit. Web platforms offering functionality such as transcoding, playback, and search did not exist when the DMCA was being drafted. Should that fact influence interpretation of the statutory language? What facts would support a conclusion that third-party syndication of videos falls outside the scope of the safe harbor?

2. Should YouTube's manipulation of the files uploaded by users be deemed "volitional" and therefore subject to a claim of direct infringement under *Netcom*'s reasoning? In *CoStar Group, Inc. v. LoopNet, Inc.*, 373 F.3d 544 (4th Cir.

2004), defendant LoopNet operated a commercial real estate listing system. All photographs uploaded to the system were reviewed by a LoopNet employee "for two purposes: (1) to block photographs that do not depict commercial real estate, and (2) to block photographs with obvious signs that they are copyrighted by a third party." *Id.* at 556. The court ruled that such conduct could not supply the basis for a direct infringement claim: "LoopNet can be compared to an owner of a copy machine who has stationed a guard by the door to turn away customers who are attempting to duplicate clearly copyrighted works. LoopNet has not by this screening process become engaged as a 'copier' of copyrighted works." *Id.* at 556. What do you think of that reasoning? Does it translate to the context of services like YouTube's? As a policy matter, is direct infringement liability for OSPs desirable?

3. Consider the *Viacom* court's interpretation of the "actual knowledge" and "red flag" provisions of §512(c). According to the court, the provisions describe different types of ways to know about specific infringing acts, not different degrees of specificity regarding what is known. Does the court's reasoning make sense as a matter of statutory interpretation? Does it make sense as a matter of policy?

In *Viacom*, what type(s) of evidence should be sufficient to support a conclusion that YouTube had "red flag" awareness of specific infringing acts? Would media coverage of YouTube referring specifically to any of the clips-in-suit suffice? What about a personal email from Viacom's CEO to one of YouTube's founders? *See UMG Recordings Inc. v. Shelter Capital Partners LLC*, 718 F.3d 1006, 1025-26 (9th Cir. 2013) (on rehearing) (content owners seeking to establish knowledge must use the statutory notification procedure).

4. What do you make of the *Viacom* court's holding that §512 does not abrogate the common law principle that willful blindness amounts to knowledge? Is that conclusion consistent with the policies underlying §512? Why, or why not?

5. Consider the *Viacom* court's interpretation of the statutory reference to "right and ability to control" the infringing activity. Does that interpretation make sense? Based on the *Viacom* court's summary of the facts, did YouTube's conduct evidence "something more" or "substantial influence" that should negate the protection of the safe harbor?

AFTERMATH

On remand, the district court granted summary judgment for YouTube on all remaining issues. Notably, it ruled that the scope of the willful blindness doctrine is limited by the requirement that knowledge or "red flag" awareness must relate to specific instances of infringement: "Under appropriate circumstances the imputed knowledge of the willfully avoided fact may impose a duty to make further inquiries that a reasonable person would make—but that depends on the law governing the factual situation." *Viacom Int'l v. YouTube*, 940 F. Supp. 2d 110, 116 (S.D.N.Y. 2013).

PRACTICE EXERCISE: COUNSEL A CLIENT

An OSP cannot claim the §512(c) safe harbor if it has received knowledge of specific acts of alleged infringement via notification. The notification must identify the allegedly infringing material and provide "information reasonably sufficient to permit the service provider to locate the material." 17 U.S.C. §512(c)(3)(A)(iii). You are in-house counsel to an online auction company that has received the following notices. How should your client respond? If you conclude that any of the notices is sufficient, for how long should your client monitor its system for the infringing material?

   a. A letter stating that counterfeit copies of a particular work are being traded on your client's site, but not providing the relevant item numbers.
   b. A letter identifying "all *Man of Steel* DVDs" as infringing.
   c. A letter identifying "all *Man of Steel* DVDs offered by MovieMan43" as infringing.

PRACTICE EXERCISE: DRAFTING AND ADVOCACY

You are legislative counsel to the chair of the House Judiciary Committee's Subcommittee on Courts, Intellectual Property, and the Internet. Your boss has asked you to draft proposed language for a safe harbor for Web platforms such as YouTube's, and to do so in a way that anticipates and responds to likely objections from copyright industry lobbyists. Draft some statutory language, along with a short memo explaining your drafting choices.

---

3. Section 512 and Internet Users

Section 512 contains several subsections that directly affect the rights and obligations of users.

a. Suits by Users: Knowing Material Misrepresentation

Review §512(g), which specifies the procedure by which a user objecting to a takedown notice may furnish a counternotification. According to the statute, a user whose materials are removed pursuant to a takedown notice cannot sue the OSP if the OSP followed the §512(g) procedures as prescribed. The user may, however, be able to sue the party that issued the takedown notice. Read §512(f) and then consider the following case.

≣ *Lenz v. Universal Music Corp.*
   572 F. Supp. 2d 1150 (N.D. Cal. 2008)

FOGEL, J.: . . .

Plaintiff Stephanie Lenz ("Lenz") videotaped her young children dancing in her family's kitchen. The song "Let's Go Crazy" by the artist professionally known as Prince ("Prince") played in the background. The video is twenty-nine seconds in length, and "Let's Go Crazy" can be heard for approximately twenty seconds, albeit with difficulty given the poor sound quality of the video. . . . On February 8, 2007, Lenz titled the video "Let's Go Crazy # 1" and uploaded it to YouTube.com . . . for the alleged purpose of sharing her son's dancing with friends and family. . . . The video was available to the public at http://www.youtube.com/watch?v=N1KfJHFW1hQ.

Universal owns the copyright to "Let's Go Crazy." On June 4, 2007, Universal sent YouTube a takedown notice pursuant to Title II of the Digital Millennium Copyright Act ("DMCA"). . . . YouTube removed the video the following day and sent Lenz an email notifying her that it had done so in response to Universal's accusation of copyright infringement. YouTube's email also advised Lenz of the DMCA's counter-notification procedures and warned her that any repeated incidents of copyright infringement could lead to the deletion of her account and all of her videos. After conducting research and consulting counsel, Lenz sent YouTube a DMCA counter-notification pursuant to 17 U.S.C. §512(g) on June 27, 2007. Lenz asserted that her video constituted fair use of "Let's Go Crazy" and thus did not infringe Universal's copyrights. Lenz demanded that the video be reposted. YouTube re-posted the video on its website about six weeks later. As of the date of this order, the "Let's Go Crazy #1" video has been viewed on YouTube more than 593,000 times. . . .

[Lenz sued Universal alleging violation of §512(f), which provides a cause of action against one who "knowingly materially misrepresents . . . that material or activity is infringing." Universal moved to dismiss pursuant to Fed. R. Civ. P. 12(b)(6).]

III. Discussion . . .

. . . [T]he question in this case is whether 17 U.S.C. §512(c)(3)(A)(v) requires a copyright owner to consider the fair use doctrine in formulating a good faith belief that "use of the material in the manner complained of is not authorized by the copyright owner, its agent, or the law."

Universal contends that copyright owners cannot be required to evaluate the question of fair use prior to sending a takedown notice because fair use is merely an *excused* infringement of a copyright rather than a use *authorized* by the copyright owner or by law. Universal emphasizes that Section 512(c)(3)(A) does not even mention fair use, let alone require a good faith belief that a given use of copyrighted material is not fair use. Universal also contends that even if a copyright owner were required by the DMCA to evaluate fair use with respect to allegedly infringing material, any such duty would arise only *after* a copyright owner receives a counter-notice and considers filing suit. *See* 17 U.S.C. §512(g)(2)(C). . . .

. . . [T]he Court concludes that the plain meaning of "authorized by law" is unambiguous. An activity or behavior "authorized by law" is one permitted by law or not contrary to law. Though Congress did not expressly mention the fair use doctrine in the DMCA, the Copyright Act provides explicitly that "the fair use of a copyrighted work . . . is not an infringement of copyright." 17 U.S.C. §107. Even if Universal is correct that fair use only *excuses* infringement, the fact remains that fair use is a lawful use of a copyright. Accordingly, in order for a copyright owner to proceed under the DMCA with "a good faith belief that use of the material in the manner complained of is not authorized by the copyright owner, its agent, or the law," the owner must evaluate whether the material makes fair use of the copyright. 17 U.S.C. §512(c)(3)(A)(v). An allegation that a copyright owner acted in bad faith by issuing a takedown notice without proper consideration of the fair use doctrine thus is sufficient to state a misrepresentation claim pursuant to Section 512(f) of the DMCA. Such an interpretation of the DMCA furthers both the purposes of the DMCA itself and copyright law in general. In enacting the DMCA, Congress noted that the "provisions in the bill balance the need for rapid response to potential infringement with the end-users [sic] legitimate interests in not having material removed without recourse." Sen. Rep. No. 105-190 at 21 (1998).

Universal suggests that copyright owners may lose the ability to respond rapidly to potential infringements if they are required to evaluate fair use prior to issuing takedown notices. Universal also points out that the question of whether a particular use of copyrighted material constitutes fair use is a fact-intensive inquiry, and that it is difficult for copyright owners to predict whether a court eventually may rule in their favor. However, while these concerns are understandable, their actual impact likely is overstated. Although there may be cases in which such considerations will arise, there are likely to be few in which a copyright owner's determination that a particular use is not fair use will meet the requisite standard of subjective bad faith required to prevail in an action for misrepresentation under 17 U.S.C. §512(f). *See Rossi v. Motion Picture Ass'n of America, Inc.*, 391 F.3d 1000, 1004 (9th Cir. 2004) (holding that "the 'good faith belief' requirement in §512(c)(3)(A)(v) encompasses a subjective, rather than objective, standard").

. . . Undoubtedly, some evaluations of fair use will be more complicated than others. But in the majority of cases, a consideration of fair use prior to issuing a takedown notice will not be so complicated as to jeopardize a copyright owner's ability to respond rapidly to potential infringements. . . . As the Ninth Circuit observed in *Rossi*, a full *investigation* to verify the accuracy of a claim of infringement is not required. *Rossi*, 391 F.3d at 1003-04.

The purpose of Section 512(f) is to prevent the abuse of takedown notices. If copyright owners are immune from liability by virtue of ownership alone, then to a large extent Section 512(f) is superfluous. As Lenz points out, the unnecessary removal of non-infringing material causes significant injury to the public where time-sensitive or controversial subjects are involved and the counter-notification remedy does not sufficiently address these harms. A good faith consideration of whether a particular use is fair use is consistent with the purpose of the statute.

Requiring owners to consider fair use will help "ensure[ ] that the efficiency of the Internet will continue to improve and that the variety and quality of services on the Internet will expand" without compromising "the movies, music, software and literary works that are the fruit of American creative genius." Sen. Rep. No. 105-190 at 2 (1998). . . .

The [complaint] contains sufficient allegations of bad faith and deliberate ignorance of fair use to survive the instant motion to dismiss. Lenz alleges that Universal is a sophisticated corporation familiar with copyright actions, and that rather than acting in good faith, Universal acted solely to satisfy Prince. Lenz alleges that Prince has been outspoken on matters of copyright infringement on the Internet and has threatened multiple suits against internet service providers to protect his music. . . . Although the Court has considerable doubt that Lenz will be able to prove that Universal acted with the subjective bad faith required by *Rossi*, and following discovery her claims well may be appropriate for summary judgment, Lenz's allegations are sufficient at the pleading stage. . . .

NOTES AND QUESTIONS

1. *Lenz* involves the intersection of §512(c)(3)(A)(v)'s requirement of "good faith belief" that material is infringing with §512(f)'s requirement that a user seeking damages must show that the copyright owner "knowingly materially misrepresent[ed]" the material's infringing status. The court indicates that the standard for "good faith belief" is a subjective one. Does §512(f) similarly indicate a subjective standard of knowledge? In *Online Policy Group v. Diebold, Inc.*, 337 F. Supp. 2d 1195 (N.D. Cal. 2004), the court assessed a notification sent by Diebold, a manufacturer of electronic voting machines, demanding removal from the Internet of copied portions of an archive of email exchanged among Diebold employees that revealed serious technical problems with Diebold's machines. In concluding that Diebold had violated §512(f), the court reasoned:

> "Knowingly" means that a party actually knew, should have known if it acted with reasonable care or diligence, or would have had no substantial doubt had it been acting in good faith, that it was making misrepresentations. . . . "Material" means that the misrepresentation affected the ISP's response to a DMCA letter. . . .
>
> . . . No reasonable copyright holder could have believed that [the material] was protected by copyright, and there is no genuine issue of fact that Diebold knew—and indeed that it specifically intended . . . that its [notifications] would result in prevention of publication of that content. . . . Diebold sought to use [§512] . . . as a sword to suppress publication of embarrassing content rather than as a shield to protect its intellectual property.

Id. at 1204-05. Is this interpretation of §512(f) consistent with the interpretation of §512(c)(3)(A)(v) as requiring a subjective standard of good faith belief?

2. In cases like *Lenz* that involve disputes about so-called user-generated content (UGC), what type of evidence would show lack of good faith belief on the part of the copyright holder? How would you craft discovery requests to elicit the required

evidence? Following the rejection of Universal's Rule 12(b)(6) motion, the parties in Lenz engaged in a number of discovery battles and then filed cross-motions for summary judgment on the question of subjective good faith. Lenz argued that Universal's procedures for evaluating UGC for copyright infringement evidenced willful blindness to the possibility of fair use. The court rejected that argument, reasoning that the evidence did not show that Universal "subjectively believed either that there was a high probability that any given video might make fair use of a Prince composition or that her own video in particular made fair use of Prince's song." *Lenz v. Universal Music Corp.*, 2013 WL 271673 (Jan 24, 2013), at *7, *appeal granted*, No. 13-80056 (9th Cir. May 30, 2013). It also concluded, however, that Universal had not shown as a matter of undisputed fact that it lacked such a belief.

The summary judgment motions focused principally on deposition testimony by the Universal employee assigned to review YouTube videos for violation of Prince's copyrights. A video would be excluded from the removal list "if it had only 'a second or less of a Prince song, literally a one line, half line of a Prince song,' or if it was shot in a noisy environment like a bar where the song was playing 'deep in the background.'" Lenz's video was placed on the removal list because "it was titled 'Let's Go Crazy # 1'; [the employee] recognized the song in the background 'right off the bat'; the song was loud and played through the entire video; and the audio track included a voice asking the children whether they liked the music." *Id.* at *5. If the case proceeds to trial, where a preponderance-of-the-evidence standard applies, who should prevail on the question of subjective bad faith?

3. Note that YouTube took six weeks to restore Lenz's video, rather than the statutorily provided 10 to 14 business days. What do you think explains the delay? From the perspective of an Internet user, what do you make of the notification and counternotification procedures established by §512? Do they reflect an appropriate balancing of the various interests affected? If not, what changes would you recommend?

b. Suits Against Users: Identifying the Defendant

If an OSP cannot be sued for infringement, a copyright owner's remaining option for monetary redress is to sue the direct infringer. Software tools for studying file-sharing activities on peer-to-peer networks can identify the Internet Protocol (IP) addresses used by individuals who are sharing files. Because IP addresses are assigned in blocks to the OSPs that provide Internet access, one can identify the OSP whose services are being used. However, linking a particular IP address to a particular user requires access to the OSP's internal usage records.

Pursuant to §512(h), a copyright owner may obtain a subpoena requiring an OSP to reveal a subscriber's identity. The copyright owner need not file a lawsuit before seeking this information. Instead, it simply must file three items with a federal district court: (1) a proposed subpoena; (2) a copy of the takedown notice described in §512(c)(3), *see* Section C.1 *supra*; and (3) a sworn declaration that the information is being sought solely to pursue "rights protected under this title." No judge reviews the requested subpoena; rather, §512(h) directs that the clerk "shall expeditiously issue" the subpoena if the required items are in proper form.

In 2003, the Recording Industry Association of America (RIAA) began a coordinated campaign to identify and sue individual music sharers. When the RIAA served Verizon with a §512(h) subpoena, Verizon refused to identify the subscriber and instead sought to quash the subpoena, arguing that §512(h) did not apply in situations where the OSP was a mere conduit for arguably infringing transmissions. Ultimately, the D.C. Circuit agreed with Verizon's interpretation of the statute. It reasoned that §512(h) refers to documentation required under §512(c), and that "the cross-references to §512(c)(3) in §§512(b)-(d) demonstrate that §512(h) applies to an ISP storing infringing material on its servers in any capacity. . . ." *RIAA v. Verizon Internet Servs., Inc.*, 351 F.3d 1229, 1237 (D.C. Cir. 2003), *cert. denied*, 543 U.S. 924 (2004); *see also In re: Charter Commc'ns, Inc. Subpoena Enforcement Matter*, 393 F.3d 771 (8th Cir. 2005) (same).

Without the ability to use the §512(h) subpoena to identify individuals engaged in file sharing, the RIAA turned to a mechanism available to any civil litigant desiring to sue an individual whose identity is unknown—a lawsuit filed against "John Doe." In the context of a John Doe lawsuit, the plaintiff may seek the court's assistance in determining the defendant's identity. It may do so by filing an ex parte request for a subpoena to a nonparty. In *Sony Music Entertainment, Inc. v. Does 1-40*, 326 F. Supp. 2d 556 (S.D.N.Y. 2004), the court granted an ex parte request for access to an OSP's subscriber records, but required that the OSP notify the subscribers whose identities would be disclosed with sufficient time to permit them to move to quash the subpoena. In addressing the subscribers' motion to quash, the court identified five considerations relevant in balancing First Amendment, privacy, and copyright interests: (i) whether the plaintiffs had established a prima facie case of copyright infringement; (ii) the specificity of the discovery request; (iii) the availability of alternative means of obtaining the information; (iv) the extent of the plaintiffs' need for the information; and (v) the defendants' expectation of privacy. *Id.* at 564-67. It concluded that the first four considerations weighed strongly in favor of disclosure, and outweighed any privacy interest that the defendants might have. Courts across the country generally have agreed with this analysis.

Over time, the RIAA filed over 30,000 infringement lawsuits against individuals suspected of exchanging infringing files via peer-to-peer networks. *See* Steve Karnowski, *Facing the Music*, USA Today (June 19, 2009), http://www.usatoday.com/tech/news/2009-06-18-music-downloading_N.htm. The RIAA did not attempt to proceed to judgment against most of these defendants, but instead encouraged settlement. In 2009, USA Today's on-line edition reported that "[t]he vast majority . . . settled for about $3,500 each." *Id.* The strategy of suing individuals, however, was expensive for the RIAA and resulted in some negative press. Moreover, according to most accounts, peer-to-peer file sharing continued to increase both in the United States and elsewhere. *See* http://www.eff.org/wp/riaa-v-people-years-later#3. Ultimately, the RIAA announced that it would halt its litigation campaign against individual users. The Motion Picture Association of America (MPAA) also briefly used and then abandoned the John Doe litigation strategy.

More recently, lawyers operating on behalf of various independent and adult filmmakers also have experimented with mass litigation against defendants identified only by their IP addresses. At the same time, federal courts have begun to push back against the John Doe litigation strategy for a variety of procedural reasons. Some courts have dismissed the lawsuits, and others have sharply limited access to early discovery. *See, e.g., AF Holdings, LLC v. Does 1-1058*, 752 F.3d 990 (D.C. Cir. May 27, 2014) (no evidence of personal jurisdiction over the OSP's subscribers, and joinder improper absent proof that all Does were involved in same transaction); *Elf-Man, LLC v. Cariveau*, No. C13–0507RSL, 2014 WL 202096 (W.D. Wash. Jan. 17, 2014) (IP address alone does not necessarily identify a single individual); In re *BitTorrent Adult Film Copyright Infringement Cases*, 296 F.R.D. 80 (E.D.N.Y. 2012) (IP address does not necessarily identify a single individual, joinder improper absent proof that all Does were involved in the same transaction, and record contained evidence of abusive litigation tactics).

NOTES AND QUESTIONS

1. With the availability of a John Doe lawsuit, do copyright owners need the §512(h) subpoena authority? How do the two procedural options compare?

2. In challenging the §512(h) subpoenas, Verizon argued that the federal district courts lack Article III jurisdiction to issue subpoenas when there is no underlying "case or controversy," and that the First Amendment requires greater safeguards than §512(h) provides to protect an Internet user's ability to speak and associate with others anonymously. Because the court held that §512(h) could not be used in the case, it did not reach the constitutional challenges. What should happen if constitutional challenges to §512(h) are raised by an OSP that *does* store the disputed material on its servers? Should a copyright owner be able to obtain a subpoena from a federal court without having to file a complaint? Should a copyright owner be able to obtain a subscriber's identity solely based on the information contained in the notice described in §512(c)(3)?

3. According to the conventional wisdom when the RIAA began its litigation campaign, suing individual users was economically irrational. The average cost of filing each lawsuit was approximately $250, and the cost (including filing) of reaching a resolution likely totaled about $2,500. Justin Hughes, *On the Logic of Suing One's Customers and the Dilemma of Infringement-Based Business Models*, 22 Cardozo Arts & Ent. L.J. 725, 750 (2005). An average settlement of $3,500- $4,500 covers those costs. *See id.* at 749 & n.89 (giving the $4,500 figure as the 2004 average); Steve Karnowski, *Facing the Music*, USA Today (June 19, 2009), http://www.usatoday.com/tech/news/2009-06-18-music-downloading_N.htm (stating an average of $3,500). Was the conventional wisdom wrong? Does suing users create other disadvantages for copyright owners? For discussion of these questions, see Hughes, *supra*.

4. How do the advantages and disadvantages of suing direct infringers compare to the advantages and disadvantages of expanding the traditional theories of indirect liability? *Compare* Marybeth Peters, *Copyright Enters the Public Domain*, 51 J. Copyright Soc'y 701 (2004) (arguing that indirect infringement liability should be expanded so that the copyright industries would not need to resort to suing individual consumers), *with* Mark A. Lemley & R. Anthony Reese, *Reducing Digital Copyright Infringement Without Restricting Innovation*, 56 Stan. L. Rev. 1345 (2004) (advocating the creation of a relatively inexpensive, quasi-administrative procedure for suing direct infringers to take the pressure off third-party providers of multipurpose technologies).

COMPARATIVE PERSPECTIVE

The European Union's 2004 enforcement directive establishes a "right of information" for intellectual property owners. A court may issue a disclosure order to the alleged infringer or to any person who, on a commercial scale, is in possession of infringing goods, using infringing services, or providing services used in infringing activities. Corrigendum to Directive 2004/48/EC of the European Parliament and of the Council of 29 April 2004 on the enforcement of intellectual property rights, art. 8, ¶ 1, 2004 O.J. (L 195) 16. The information to be disclosed includes names, addresses, quantities, and prices. *Id.* ¶ 2.

In *Scarlet Extended SA v. Société belge des auteurs, compositeurs et éditeurs SCRL (SABAM)*, [2012] E.C.D.R. 4, a Belgian ISP challenged a court order directing it to implement a system to monitor its subscribers' peer-to-peer downloads and filter out all works in the catalog of the Belgian collective rights organization SABAM. The Court of Justice of the European Union ruled that the order violated the EU directive mandating certain OSP safe harbors, which specifies that OSPs should not be subjected to a general monitoring requirement. *See* Directive 2000/31/EC of the European Parliament and of the Council of June 8, 2000, on certain legal aspects of information society services, in particular electronic commerce, in the Internal Market, 2000 O.J. (L 178) 1, art. 15. It further ruled that user IP addresses were "protected personal information" and that their routine monitoring would violate rights to the protection of personal information and to freedom of information secured by the Charter of Fundamental Rights of the European Union, arts. 8 and 11. It cautioned that courts "must strike a fair balance between the protection of copyright and the protection of the fundamental rights of individuals who are affected by such measures," and also between the protection of copyright and protection of "the freedom to conduct a business enjoyed by operators such as ISPs." *SABAM*, [2012] E.C.D.R. 4, ¶¶ 45-46. Can this ruling be reconciled with the "right of information"?

---

4. Diving Deeper: New Enforcement Procedures

From the copyright owner's perspective, one persistent drawback of the regime established by §512 is that once infringing content becomes available online, it is virtually impossible to recapture even if takedown occurs fairly quickly. For this reason, copyright owners have continued to pursue additional enforcement strategies both before Congress and in negotiations with OSPs. In addition, as *Perfect 10 v. Visa International Service Association*, Section B.3 *supra*, illustrates, other third parties may play a role in enabling infringement. Copyright owners have pursued additional enforcement strategies against those third parties as well.

a. Automated Enforcement

As *Lenz* illustrates, many users rely on the Internet to distribute content that they have created. Web platforms like YouTube and Flickr, which did not exist when Congress enacted §512, were designed specifically as venues for such user-generated content (UGC). Today, those sites and many others receive millions of visitors daily. Those visits translate into substantial advertising revenues for the OSPs that operate the sites. Often, UGC includes material drawn from preexisting copyright works. The uses of preexisting materials are so diverse as to defy description, and include everything from mashups and fan fiction to snippets of video material reproduced for commentary to videos of users dancing or singing (or simply going about their daily activities) to a soundtrack consisting of copyrighted music.

Shortly after the *Viacom v. YouTube* litigation was filed, the major copyright industries attempted to engage the OSP industry in negotiations that would yield a privately agreed, standardized approach to automated enforcement. In October 2007, a group of major copyright owners including Disney, Fox, Microsoft, NBC Universal, and Viacom released a document titled "Copyright Principles for UGC Services," http://www.ugcprinciples.com. According to the proposed principles, Web platforms for UGC should implement "effective content identification technology." *Id.* ¶3. The proposed principles define "effective content identification technology" as any technology that is both "commercially reasonable" and "highly effective, in relation to other technologies commercially available at the time of implementation." *Id.* The technology should automatically block user uploads for which a copyright owner has provided "reference data for content required to establish a match with user-uploaded content" unless the copyright owner has instructed that matches should be handled in some other way. *Id.* ¶3(a)-(c). A UGC service may undertake "manual (human) review of all user-uploaded audio and video content in lieu of, or in addition to, use of identification technology, if feasible and if such review is as effective as identification technology in achieving the goal of eliminating infringing content." *Id.* ¶3(f). UGC services also must give copyright owners that register with them access to "commercially reasonable enhanced searching and identification means" to locate infringing content themselves. *Id.* ¶5.

As of this writing, only a handful of OSPs have endorsed the proposed Copyright Principles for UGC services. During the course of the litigation with *Viacom*, however, YouTube did institute a "content verification program" through which copyright owners with an "ongoing need to remove allegedly infringing content" can register to expedite the notification process, and a "content ID" program through which copyright owners who "own exclusive rights to a substantial body of original material that is frequently uploaded by the YouTube user community" can submit reference data for identification of their copyrighted content. *See* https://support.google.com/youtube/answer/2797370. Copyright owners can request removal of content so identified or can seek to monetize the content through advertising associated with that video and/or track the video's viewership statistics. Any of these actions can be country-specific; for example, a video may be monetized in one country and blocked or tracked in another. *See id.*

Peer-to-peer file-sharing technologies that enable users to share material maintained on their own computers present different challenges for automated enforcement. Automated enforcement is feasible from a technical standpoint. Internet access providers can use "deep packet inspection" technologies to analyze traffic passing through their networks. Deep packet inspection examines bits of digital information to determine which application generated the information, and can also be used to identify digital watermarks. Once identified, traffic generated by particular applications can be blocked or slowed.

The extent of a provider's legal authority to discriminate against particular types of network traffic is the subject of considerable controversy, however. In 2007, Comcast's interference with subscribers' use of the popular BitTorrent file-sharing protocol triggered an investigation by the Federal Communications Commission (FCC). Comcast appealed the FCC's order directing it to explore other methods for managing network traffic, and prevailed in the D.C. Circuit on jurisdictional grounds. *See Comcast Corp. v. Federal Communications Comm'n*, 600 F.3d 642 (D.C. Cir. 2010). Subsequently, after the FCC conducted a rulemaking on network nondiscrimination, or "net neutrality," the D.C. Circuit ruled that the FCC had established jurisdiction to regulate the conditions of broadband access to Internet services, but vacated the particular nondiscrimination rule the FCC had drafted because it was inconsistent with the basis on which the FCC asserted jurisdiction. *See Verizon v. Federal Communications Comm'n*, 740 F.3d 623 (D.C. Cir. 2014). As of this writing, the FCC is conducting a second rulemaking, and legislation relating to net neutrality also has been introduced in Congress. *See* In the Matter of Protecting and Promoting the Open Internet, FCC No. 14-61, 79 Fed. Reg. 37448-01 (July 1, 2014); Online Competition and Consumer Choice Act, H.R. 4880 and S. 2476, 113th Cong., 2d Sess. (June 17, 2014). Questions relating to the FCC's regulatory authority are beyond the scope of this book. For a useful introduction to the issues, see Justin Fox, *Understanding the New Battle over Net Neutrality*, Harvard Business Review Blog (May 12, 2014), http://blogs.hbr .org/2014/05/understanding-the-new-battle-over-net-neutrality/.

NOTES AND QUESTIONS

1. What do you think of copyright owners' options under the content ID system developed by YouTube? Should it be available to all copyright owners? If an individual creates a video and uses copyrighted music as the sound track, should the copyright owner of the music be able to monetize the video? Should there be any kind of sharing of that advertising revenue with the creator of the video? Given its size, YouTube can afford the expense of developing and operating the content ID system. Should smaller OSPs have to implement a similar system?

> ### LOOKING FORWARD
>
> In response to the proposed Copyright Principles for UGC Services, a group of nonprofit organizations offered a competing proposal, titled "Fair Use Principles for User Generated Video Content." We will consider that proposal in Chapter 10, which addresses fair use.

2. If you represented an OSP that provides hosting services, would you favor adoption of the proposed Copyright Principles for UGC Services? Why, or why not? If you were a member of Congress, would you favor amending §512 to include some version of the principles? In making that decision, would it matter whether automated filtering would result in the blocking of Stephanie Lenz's video?

3. Is deep packet inspection by Internet access providers a good solution to the problem of online copyright infringement via peer-to-peer file-sharing? Why, or why not? Review §512(a) again. If an OSP engages in deep packet inspection, will it lose eligibility to claim the safe harbor? If so, is that result appropriate?

4. Pursuant to the Higher Education Opportunity Act (HEOA), Pub. L. No. 110-315, as a condition for obtaining federal financial aid for students, colleges and universities must develop plans to block peer-to-peer file sharing and must offer students an alternative to illegal downloading. *See* 20 U.S.C. §1094(a)(29). If you were a member of Congress, would you have voted for the provision? Would deep packet inspection be an appropriate measure for colleges and universities to implement?

b. Graduated Sanctions

In 2008, when the RIAA announced that it would de-emphasize suits against individuals, it stated that it would focus instead on negotiating so-called three strikes agreements with OSPs. Under these agreements as envisioned by the RIAA, OSPs would implement a program of graduated sanctions to be triggered following receipt of a notice of infringement, culminating in loss of service following the third notice. *See Music Industry to Drop Mass Suits,* Wall St. J., Dec. 27, 2008, *available at* 2008 WLNR 24774194. Initially, the RIAA had only limited success in convincing OSPs to enter such agreements, although some OSPs did appear to be taking a more aggressive stance toward the issuance of subscriber warning letters under their existing repeat-infringer policies. However, partly as a result of the requirement in the Higher Education Opportunity Act mentioned above, some colleges and universities did adopt "three strikes" policies.

In July 2011, the RIAA announced that it had reached a "six strikes" agreement with five major providers of Internet access. The agreement provides for a Copyright Alert System that issues a graduated series of warnings to subscribers whose activities are identified as infringing. Alerts at the first two stages are informational; those at the next two stages require subscriber acknowledgment of receipt; and those at the final two stages may involve sanctions such as referral to a copyright education program, reductions in transmission speed, or temporary suspension of service. Cessation of service is not mandated. *See* Memorandum of Understanding, July 6, 2011, http://www.copyrightinformation.org/wp-content/uploads/2013/02/Memorandum-of-Understanding.pdf. The system is administered by a new entity, the Center for Copyright Information (CCI). As of this writing, the CCI has declared the system a success, but has released no statistics. For a detailed evaluation of the system in light of due process, free speech, and privacy norms, see Annemarie Bridy, *Graduated Response American Style: "Six Strikes" Measured Against Five Norms,* 23 Fordham Intell. Prop., Media & Ent. L.J. 1 (2012).

COMPARATIVE PERSPECTIVE

In 2009, France enacted "three strikes" legislation after lengthy discussion. The first version of the law called for the establishment of a High Authority for Diffusion of Works and Protection of Rights ("HADOPI"), and empowered the HADOPI to issue fines and to block Internet access after two warnings. The French Constitutional Council, however, ruled that "only a court can authorize such action, because depriving a citizen of internet access could violate his or her fundamental right to communicate." *French Constitutional Panel OKs Piracy Law, Cutting Internet Access After "Three-Strikes,"* 78 Pat. Trademark & Copyright J. (BNA), Oct. 30, 2009 at 804. The next version of the legislation, HADOPI 2, cured this defect by providing for judicial review of termination orders, and was upheld in virtually its entirety by the Constitutional Council. *Id.* The law remained extremely controversial, however, and ultimately the provisions for disconnection of service were repealed and replaced with a system of escalating fines.

c. Interdiction Orders

Section 512(j)(B)(ii) permits a court to order an OSP to refuse access to an infringing subscriber or to block access to an online location outside the United States even if the OSP qualifies for §512(a)'s limitations on monetary remedies. In the years since §512 was enacted, however, the copyright industries have continued to press Congress for expanded interdiction authority.

In 2011, the Senate considered the Preventing Real Online Threats to Economic Creativity and Theft of Intellectual Property Act ("PROTECT IP Act" or "PIPA"). S. 968, 112th Cong., 1st Sess. The House debated a similar bill entitled the Stop Online Piracy Act ("SOPA"), H.R. 3261, 112th Cong., 1st Sess. Both bills would have permitted the U.S. Attorney General or "qualifying plaintiffs" to bring *in rem* proceedings against a nondomestic Internet domain name that was hosting infringing materials if the individual infringer could not be located and sued within the United States. Proceeding ex parte, courts could issue orders requiring operators of domain name servers that translate the domain name into its Internet protocol address to sever the translation, making it impossible for users to locate the website using the domain name. The orders could require other intermediaries, including payment providers, Internet advertising services, search engines, and other information location tools to prevent their services from dealing with or being used to access the infringing site. As originally drafted, SOPA would have permitted plaintiffs to send written notifications of infringing activity directly to payment providers and Internet advertising services, triggering a requirement for those entities to cease dealing with an infringing site within five days after delivery of a notification naming it.

Both bills proved enormously controversial. Critics argued that the provisions requiring domain blocking would pose technical problems that could affect the Internet's reliability and security. They also questioned the wisdom of

LOOKING BACK

In Chapter 1 you learned about the new role that plurilateral free trade agreements have begun to play in international copyright lawmaking. Some industry observers expect to see provisions resembling SOPA and PIPA emerging in those agreements.

allowing a court to determine whether a site is dedicated to infringing activity based solely on ex parte submissions. A number of sites, including Wikipedia, went dark for a day to protest the legislation. In part as a result of the unprecedented public outcry, the bills were tabled. The question of how to address large-scale infringements on sites hosted offshore is unlikely to decline in importance, however.

NOTES AND QUESTIONS

1. Did the SOPA and PIPA proposals appropriately balance copyright owners' desires to stop infringement and concerns about permitting potentially lawful uses? Is there a way to accommodate both the goal of protecting copyright owners from large-scale electronic infringements and that of upholding traditional Internet values of freedom of expression and the largely unfettered flow of information? In light of §512(j), is additional legislation necessary?

2. Recall that §512 does not shelter an OSP that fails to adopt and reasonably implement a policy for terminating repeat infringers. Read §512(i) and identify its requirements. Why do you think the RIAA has sought private agreements with OSPs? What are the pros and cons of that approach from the RIAA's perspective? From an OSP's perspective? Why do you think OSPs initially were reluctant to adopt a graduated sanctions approach?

3. Should the United States legislate a graduated sanctions procedure for OSPs?

D. DEVICE MANUFACTURERS AND LIABILITY FOR INDUCING INFRINGEMENT

Many entities market devices that can be used to infringe copyrights, including photocopying machines, CD burners, MP3 recorders, and DVRs. Practically, those entities know that at least some people will use their devices to commit copyright infringement. Some uses, however, will be lawful. Under what circumstances should a device manufacturer incur indirect liability? The materials in this section address that question.

1. *Sony* and the Staple Article of Commerce Doctrine

In *Sony Corp. of America v. Universal City Studios, Inc.*, 464 U.S. 417 (1984), owners of copyrights in television programs sued a manufacturer of home video-cassette recorders (VCRs) for contributory copyright infringement. Noting the "historic kinship between patent law and copyright law," the Court turned to the Patent Act for guidance in formulating a test for contributory copyright infringement suitable for device manufacturers. *Id.* at 439. Unlike the Copyright

Act, the Patent Act defines the scope of contributory infringement liability. Section 271 of the Patent Act provides that one who sells a "staple article or commodity of commerce suitable for substantial noninfringing use" is not liable for contributory infringement. 35 U.S.C. §271(c). The *Sony* Court observed that this rule reflects a balancing of the "public interest in access to [an] article of commerce" and the interest in providing appropriate incentives to the patentee. *Sony*, 464 U.S. at 440. Applying the same reasoning to copyright law, the Court stated:

> We recognize that there are substantial differences between the patent and copyright laws. But in both areas the contributory infringement doctrine is grounded on the recognition that adequate protection of a monopoly may require the courts to look beyond actual duplication of a device or publication to the products or activities that make such duplication possible. The staple article of commerce doctrine must strike a balance between a copyright holder's legitimate demand for effective—not merely symbolic—protection of the statutory monopoly, and the rights of others freely to engage in substantially unrelated areas of commerce. Accordingly, the sale of copying equipment, like the sale of other articles of commerce, does not constitute contributory infringement if the product is widely used for legitimate, unobjectionable purposes. Indeed, it need merely be capable of substantial noninfringing uses.

Id. at 442.

The Court then found that the Betamax VCR at issue was capable of "commercially significant noninfringing uses." *Id.* at 442. First, many copyright owners did not object to the taping of their programs for purposes of time-shifting (enabling the taper to view the show at her convenience rather than at its scheduled time). Whether or not a particular copyright owner consented, however, the Court held that individuals taping TV programs off the air for time-shifting purposes were sheltered by the fair use doctrine. (We excerpt that part of the opinion in Chapter 10.) Because the VCR was capable of being used in a noninfringing way, the Court rejected the contributory infringement claim. That result allowed Sony to continue marketing its VCRs to the public without licenses from the copyright owners of the television programs that many VCR purchasers taped.

The *Sony* standard—"capable of substantial noninfringing uses"—has presented interpretive difficulties for the courts, particularly in the context of digital technologies that permit reproduction and distribution of perfect copies of copyrighted works. The development of peer-to-peer file-sharing technology has posed especially thorny problems. Peer-to-peer technology enables Internet users to communicate directly with other users and access the files stored on each other's hard drives. This technology avoids the expense of maintaining a centralized server to store all of the files in which one might be interested, and opens up the hard drives of everyone using the same peer-to-peer networking program to each other. From the perspective of an Internet user, therefore, peer-to-peer technology vastly increases the Internet's potential as a tool for finding and sharing information. From the perspective of a copyright owner, however, centralized servers and the entities that operate them perform a valuable gatekeeping function: They provide a vantage point from which to guard against infringement. Copyright's secondary liability doctrines, in turn, supply third-party gatekeepers who meet certain threshold criteria of involvement with incentives to minimize infringing activity. The development of peer-to-peer file-sharing technology thus raises two important questions: (1) when do secondary liability doctrines apply to developers of technologies that enable users to copy and share digital copyrighted content directly with one another; and (2) exactly what must be shown, and by whom, for a technology developer to claim the protection of the *Sony* rule?

The first round of copyright infringement litigation over peer-to-peer technology involved the file-sharing service known as Napster. Napster's MusicShare software allowed users to search for MP3 music files stored on each others' computers and exchange the files directly with one another. The software maintained a dynamic directory of the files available from users currently logged on to the system. Each time a user logged on, the software would add that user's IP address and list of available files to the directory. A logged-on user could then search the directory for desired files or recording artists, click on a file name in the list of search results, and download that file directly from whoever had offered it.

The Ninth Circuit held that once Napster had been notified of specific infringing files being traded on its system, it could be held contributorily liable for infringing the copyrights in those works. *A & M Records, Inc. v. Napster, Inc.*, 239 F.3d 1004, 1021-22 (9th Cir. 2001). Regarding *Sony*, it observed: "We are compelled to make a clear distinction between the architecture of the Napster system and Napster's conduct in relation to the operational capacity of the system. . . . [A]bsent specific information which identifies infringing activity, a computer system operator cannot be liable for contributory infringement merely because the structure of the system allows for the exchange of copyrighted material." *Id*. at 1020-21. Napster, however, had both specific knowledge and the ability to "purge" the infringing files. *Id*. The court ruled that Napster also could be held vicariously liable for infringement, because it received a direct financial benefit from advertising sales and had both the right and ability to control the infringement by filtering or otherwise blocking the exchange of files specifically identified as infringing. *Id*. at 1023-24.

The second round of copyright infringement litigation over peer-to-peer technology was *In re Aimster Copyright Litigation*, 334 F.3d 643 (7th Cir. 2003), *cert. denied*, 540 U.S. 1107 (2004), which involved a system designed to piggyback on America Online's Instant Messenger network. Unlike Napster, the Aimster system did not create a central directory of files offered for sharing by logged-in users, but simply created a dynamic listing of all users currently logged on to the system. An individual user could conduct file searches that would display to that user a list of all logged-on users who had the designated files available. In addition, the Aimster system automatically encrypted all communications between users.

The Seventh Circuit ruled that Aimster's encryption-based strategy amounted to willful blindness, and could not be used to avoid contributory infringement liability. In light of other facts, particularly an Aimster software tutorial that the court characterized as an "invitation to infringement," 334 F.3d at 651, the court held that Aimster had the burden to show that its service in fact currently had substantial noninfringing uses, and to provide "evidence concerning the frequency of such uses." *Id*. at 652-53. Because Aimster had produced no evidence of any actual noninfringing uses, it upheld a preliminary injunction shutting Aimster down.

The court opined, however, that even if Aimster had produced sufficient evidence of noninfringing uses, to avoid liability it also would need to "show that it would have been disproportionately costly . . . to eliminate or at least reduce substantially the infringing uses." *Id.* at 653. The court expressed doubt about the applicability of vicarious liability to Aimster's conduct. It observed that vicarious liability is a theory that allows liability in "cases in which the only effective relief is obtainable from someone who bears a relation to the direct infringers that is analogous to the relation of a principal to an agent." *Id.* at 654. Ultimately, the court declined to rule on that question.

NOTES AND QUESTIONS

1. In *Sony*, the Court borrowed a secondary liability doctrine developed largely in the patent context. Is it appropriate to look to patent law to inform copyright law's content? Recall Chapter 2.A.2's discussion of some of the doctrinal differences between patent and copyright law, *supra*. Might it be misleading to view patent law's secondary liability rules apart from its entire doctrinal system? Put differently, patent law may be forgiving toward manufacturers of staple articles of commerce because the patentee is adequately protected by the broad rights it otherwise has. Alternatively, Congress may have codified the inducement doctrine in the patent context because the monopoly granted by the Patent Act lasts for a shorter duration. Should a court simply transplant doctrine from one system to another?

2. Although the decision in *Sony* may seem obvious 30 years after the fact, it was a 5-4 ruling. Four members of the Court would have held Sony liable for contributory infringement. If Sony had been liable as a copyright infringer, those who owned the copyrights in the programs that VCR owners could record would essentially have the power to direct the VCR market. Between that group and Sony, who would be more likely to exploit the technology efficiently? Consider the following quote from *Sony*:

> It seems extraordinary to suggest that the Copyright Act confers upon all copyright owners collectively, much less the two respondents in this case, the exclusive right to distribute V[C]R's simply because they may be used to infringe copyrights. That, however, is the logical implication of their claim. The request for an injunction below indicates that respondents seek, in effect, to declare V[C]R's contraband.

Sony, 464 U.S. at 470 n.21. If you were a copyright owner and your rights entitled you to control the distribution of VCRs, would you permit their distribution and, if so, under what terms? Why shouldn't you have control over that market?

3. Should the *Sony* rule ever shield a defendant that exercises ongoing control over a service related to its technology? Does the *Napster* court or the *Aimster* court offer a better answer to this question? Does the *Aimster* court's reliance on the willful blindness doctrine amount to premising liability on a system's architecture?

4. If you were constructing a black-letter outline of secondary liability doctrine, where would you put the *Sony* rule? Which element(s) of contributory liability doctrine does it modify?

2. *Grokster* and Inducement Liability

Both the *Napster* and *Aimster* disputes involved software-based systems whose providers played ongoing roles in their use. In a true peer-to-peer network, once the software is downloaded, there is no support at all from a central server. In that sense, it is similar to a VCR – once the VCR is sold, the manufacturer or seller has no control over its use. The third round of copyright infringement litigation over peer-to-peer file-sharing involved two such systems, developed and distributed by Grokster and StreamCast after Napster's legal battles had begun. This litigation thus seemed to present both the secondary liability question and the *Sony* question in their purest forms: Should an entity that creates and releases true peer-to-peer software and exercises no ongoing control over its use, and that knows the software will be used on a widespread basis to infringe copyrights, be held secondarily liable for acts of copyright infringement committed by users of the software?

Metro-Goldwyn-Mayer Studios, Inc. v. Grokster, Ltd.
545 U.S. 913 (2005)

SOUTER, J.: . . .

I

A

Respondents, Grokster, Ltd., and StreamCast Networks, Inc. . . . distribute free software products that allow computer users to share electronic files through peer-to-peer networks, so called because users' computers communicate directly with each other, not through central servers. . . .

. . . A group of copyright holders (MGM for short, but including motion picture studios, recording companies, songwriters, and music publishers) sued Grokster and StreamCast for their users' copyright infringements, alleging that they knowingly and intentionally distributed their software to enable their users to reproduce and distribute the copyrighted works. . . .

. . . Grokster and StreamCast use no servers to intercept the content of the search requests or to mediate the file transfers conducted by users of the software, there being no central point through which the substance of the communications passes in either direction. . . .

Although Grokster and StreamCast do not therefore know when particular files are copied, a few searches using their software would show what is available on the networks the software reaches. MGM commissioned a statistician to conduct a systematic search, and his study showed that nearly 90% of the files available for download on [Grokster's] FastTrack system were copyrighted works. Grokster and StreamCast dispute this figure, raising methodological problems and arguing that free copying even of copyrighted works may be authorized by the rightholders.

They also argue that potential noninfringing uses of their software are significant in kind, even if infrequent in practice. . . .

. . . [T]he parties' anecdotal and statistical evidence entered thus far to show the content available on the . . . networks does not say much about which files are actually downloaded by users, and no one can say how often the software is used to obtain copies of unprotected material. But MGM's evidence gives reason to think that the vast majority of users' downloads are acts of infringement, and because well over 100 million copies of the software in question are known to have been downloaded, and billions of files are shared across the . . . networks each month, the probable scope of copyright infringement is staggering.

Grokster and StreamCast concede the infringement in most downloads, and it is uncontested that they are aware that users employ their software primarily to download copyrighted files. . . . From time to time, moreover, the companies have learned about their users' infringement directly, as from users who have sent e-mail to each company with questions about playing copyrighted movies they had downloaded, to whom the companies have responded with guidance. . . .

Grokster and StreamCast are not, however, merely passive recipients of information about infringing use. The record is replete with evidence that from the moment Grokster and StreamCast began to distribute their free software, each one clearly voiced the objective that recipients use it to download copyrighted works, and each took active steps to encourage infringement.

After the notorious file-sharing service, Napster, was sued by copyright holders for facilitation of copyright infringement, StreamCast gave away a software program known as OpenNap, designed as compatible with the Napster program and open to Napster users for downloading files from other Napster and OpenNap users' computers. Evidence indicates that "[i]t was always [StreamCast's] intent to use [its OpenNap network] to be able to capture email addresses of [its] initial target market so that [it] could promote [its] StreamCast Morpheus interface to them," . . .

StreamCast monitored both the number of users downloading its OpenNap program and the number of music files they downloaded. It also used the resulting OpenNap network to distribute copies of the Morpheus software and to encourage users to adopt it. Internal company documents indicate that StreamCast hoped to attract large numbers of former Napster users if that company was shut down by court order or otherwise. . . . [I]t introduced itself to some potential advertisers as a company "which is similar to what Napster was." . . .

The evidence that Grokster sought to capture the market of former Napster users is sparser but revealing, for Grokster launched its own OpenNap system called Swaptor and inserted digital codes into its Web site so that computer users using Web search engines to look for "Napster" or "[f]ree file sharing" would be directed to the Grokster Web site, where they could download the Grokster software. And Grokster's name is an apparent derivative of Napster.

StreamCast's executives monitored the number of songs by certain commercial artists available on their networks, and an internal communication indicates they aimed to have a larger number of copyrighted songs available on their networks than other file-sharing networks. . . . Morpheus in fact allowed users to search specifically for "Top 40" songs. . . . Similarly, Grokster sent users a newsletter promoting its ability to provide particular, popular copyrighted materials. . . .

In addition to this evidence of express promotion, marketing, and intent to promote further, the business models employed by Grokster and StreamCast confirm that their principal object was use of their software to download copyrighted works. Grokster and StreamCast receive no revenue from users, who obtain the software itself for nothing. Instead both companies generate revenue by selling advertising space, and they stream the advertising to Grokster and Morpheus users while they are employing the programs. As the number of users of each program increases, advertising opportunities become worth more. . . . Users seeking Top 40 songs, for example, or the latest release by Modest Mouse, are certain to be far more numerous than those seeking a free Decameron. . . .

Finally, there is no evidence that either company made an effort to filter copyrighted material from users' downloads or otherwise impede the sharing of copyrighted files. . . .

B

After discovery, the parties on each side of the case cross-moved for summary judgment. . . . The District Court held that those who used the Grokster and Morpheus software to download copyrighted media files directly infringed MGM's copyrights, a conclusion not contested on appeal, but the court nonetheless granted summary judgment in favor of Grokster and StreamCast as to any liability arising from distribution of the then current versions of their software. Distributing that software gave rise to no liability in the court's view, because its use did not provide the distributors with actual knowledge of specific acts of infringement.

The Court of Appeal affirmed. . . . [T]he court read *Sony Corp. of America v. Universal City Studios, Inc.*, 464 U.S. 417 (1984), as holding that distribution of a commercial product capable of substantial noninfringing uses could not give rise to contributory liability for infringement unless the distributor has actual knowledge of specific instances of infringement and failed to act on that knowledge. The fact that the software was capable of substantial noninfringing uses in the Ninth Circuit's view meant that Grokster and StreamCast were not liable, because they had no such actual knowledge, owing to the decentralized architecture of their software. The court also held that Grokster and StreamCast did not materially contribute to their users' infringement because . . . [there was] no involvement by the defendants beyond providing the software in the first place. . . .

[The Ninth Circuit also rejected MGM's vicarious liability argument because Grokster and StreamCast had "no agreed-upon right or current ability to supervise" the use of their software.]

II

A . . .

The argument for imposing indirect liability in this case is . . . a powerful one, given the number of infringing downloads that occur every day using StreamCast's and Grokster's software. When a widely shared service or product is used to commit infringement, it may be impossible to enforce rights in the protected work effectively against all direct infringers. . . .

One infringes contributorily by intentionally inducing or encouraging direct infringement, and infringes vicariously by profiting from direct infringement by declining to exercise a right to stop or limit it.[9] Although "[t]he Copyright Act does not expressly render anyone liable for infringement committed by another," *Sony*, 464 U.S., at 434, these doctrines of secondary liability emerged from common law principles and are well established in the law. . . .

B

. . . [T]his Court has dealt with secondary copyright infringement in only one recent case, and because MGM has tailored its principal claim to our opinion there, a look at our earlier holding is in order. . . . At the trial on the merits [in *Sony*], the evidence showed that the principal use of the VCR was for "'time-shifting,'" or taping a program for later viewing at a more convenient time, which the Court found to be a fair, not an infringing, use. There was no evidence that Sony had expressed an object of bringing about taping in violation of copyright or had taken active steps to increase its profits from unlawful taping. Although Sony's advertisements urged consumers to buy the VCR to "'record favorite shows'" or "'build a library'" of recorded programs, neither of these uses was necessarily infringing.

On those facts . . . the only conceivable basis for imposing liability was on a theory of contributory infringement arising from its sale of VCRs to consumers with knowledge that some would use them to infringe. But, because the VCR was "capable of substantial noninfringing uses," we held the manufacturer could not be faulted solely on the basis of its distribution. . . .

. . . [W]here an article is "good for nothing else" but infringement, there is no legitimate public interest in its unlicensed availability and there is no injustice in presuming or imputing an intent to infringe. Conversely, the [staple article of commerce] doctrine absolves the equivocal conduct of selling an item with substantial lawful as well as unlawful uses, and limits liability to instances of more acute fault than the mere understanding that some of one's products will be misused. It leaves breathing room for innovation and a vigorous commerce.

The parties and many of the *amici* in this case think the key to resolving it is the *Sony* rule and, in particular, what it means for a product to be "capable of commercially significant noninfringing uses." MGM advances the argument that granting summary judgment to Grokster and StreamCast as to their current activities gave too much weight to the value of innovative technology, and too little to the copyrights infringed by users of their software, given that 90% of works available on one of the networks was shown to be copyrighted. Assuming the remaining 10% to be its noninfringing use, MGM says this should not qualify as "substantial," and the Court should quantify *Sony* to the extent of holding that a product used "principally" for infringement does not qualify. . . .

9. We stated in *Sony* . . . that "'the lines between direct infringement, contributory infringement and vicarious liability are not clearly drawn' . . . ," *id*. at 435, n.17. . . . Because we resolve th[is] case based on an inducement theory, there is no need to analyze separately MGM's vicarious liability theory.

We agree with MGM that the Court of Appeals misapplied *Sony*, which it read as limiting secondary liability quite beyond the circumstances to which the case applied. *Sony* barred secondary liability based on presuming or imputing intent to cause infringement solely from the design or distribution of a product capable of substantial lawful use, which the distributor knows is in fact used for infringement. The Ninth Circuit has read *Sony*'s limitation to mean that whenever a product is capable of substantial lawful use, the producer can never be held contributorily liable for third parties' infringing use of it . . . even when an actual purpose to cause infringing use is shown by evidence independent of design and distribution of the product. . . .

This view of *Sony*, however, was error, converting the case from one about liability resting on imputed intent to one about liability on any theory. Because *Sony* did not displace other theories of secondary liability . . . we do not revisit *Sony* further, as MGM requests, to add a more quantified description of the point of balance between protection and commerce when liability rests solely on distribution with knowledge that unlawful use will occur. . . .

C

Sony's rule limits imputing culpable intent as a matter of law from the characteristics or uses of a distributed product. But nothing in *Sony* requires courts to ignore evidence of intent if there is such evidence, and the case was never meant to foreclose rules of fault-based liability derived from the common law.[10] . . .

The classic case of direct evidence of unlawful purpose occurs when one induces commission of infringement by another, or "entic[es] or persuad[es] another" to infringe, Black's Law Dictionary 790 (8th ed. 2004), as by advertising. Thus at common law a copyright or patent defendant who "not only expected but invoked [infringing use] by advertisement" was liable for infringement. . . .

The rule on inducement of infringement as developed in the early cases is no different today. . . . [A]dvertising an infringing use or instructing how to engage in an infringing use, show[s] an affirmative intent that the product be used to infringe, and a showing that infringement was encouraged overcomes the law's reluctance to find liability when a defendant merely sells a commercial product suitable for some lawful use, see, *e.g.*, *Fromberg, Inc. v. Thornhill*, 315 F.2d 407, 412-13 (5th Cir. 1963) (demonstrations by sales staff of infringing uses supported liability for inducement); *Haworth Inc. v. Herman Miller Inc.*, 37 U.S.P.Q. 2d 1080, 1090 (W.D. Mich. 1994) (evidence that defendant "demonstrated and recommend[ed] infringing configurations" of its product could support inducement liability); *Sims v. Mack Trucks, Inc.*, 459 F. Supp. 1198, 1215 (E.D. Pa. 1978) (finding inducement where the use "depicted by the defendant in its promotional film and brochures infringes the . . . patent").

For the same reasons that *Sony* took the staple-article doctrine of patent law as a model for its copyright safe-harbor rule, the inducement rule, too, is a sensible one

---

10. Nor does the Patent Act's exemption from liability for those who distribute a staple article of commerce, 35 U.S.C. §271(c), extend to those who induce patent infringement, §271(b).

for copyright. We adopt it here, holding that one who distributes a device with the object of promoting its use to infringe copyright, as shown by clear expression or other affirmative steps taken to foster infringement, is liable for the resulting acts of infringement by third parties. We are, of course, mindful of the need to keep from trenching on regular commerce or discouraging the development of technologies with lawful and unlawful potential. Accordingly . . . mere knowledge of infringing potential or of actual infringing uses would not be enough here to subject a distributor to liability. Nor would ordinary acts incident to product distribution, such as offering customers technical support or product updates, support liability in themselves. The inducement rule, instead, premises liability on purposeful, culpable expression and conduct, and thus does nothing to compromise legitimate commerce or discourage innovation having a lawful promise.

III

A

The only apparent question about treating MGM's evidence as sufficient to withstand summary judgment under the theory of inducement goes to the need on MGM's part to adduce evidence that StreamCast and Grokster communicated an inducing message to their software users. . . . It is undisputed that StreamCast beamed onto the computer screens of users of Napster-compatible programs ads urging the adoption of its OpenNap program. . . . Those who accepted Stream-Cast's OpenNap program were offered software to perform the same services, which a factfinder could conclude would readily have been understood in the Napster market as the ability to download copyrighted music files. Grokster distributed an electronic newsletter containing links to articles promoting its software's ability to access popular copyrighted music. And anyone whose Napster or free file-sharing searches turned up a link to Grokster would have understood Grokster to be offering the same file-sharing ability as Napster . . . ; that would also have been the understanding of anyone offered Grokster's suggestively named Swaptor software, its version of OpenNap. And both companies communicated a clear message by responding affirmatively to requests for help in locating and playing copyrighted materials.

In StreamCast's case, of course, the evidence just described was supplemented by other unequivocal indications of unlawful purpose in . . . internal communications. . . . Whether the messages were communicated is not to the point on this record. . . .

Three features of this evidence of intent are particularly notable. First, each company showed itself to be aiming to satisfy a known source of demand for copyright infringement, the market comprising former Napster users. . . .

Second, this evidence of unlawful objective is given added significance by MGM's showing that neither company attempted to develop filtering tools or other mechanisms to diminish the infringing activity using their software. While the Ninth Circuit treated the defendants' failure to develop such tools as irrelevant because they lacked an independent duty to monitor their users' activity, we think this evidence underscores Grokster's and StreamCast's intentional facilitation of their users' infringement.[12]

Third, there is a further complement to the direct evidence of unlawful objective. . . . StreamCast and Grokster make money by selling advertising space, by directing ads to the screens of computers employing their software. . . . [T]he more the software is used, the more ads are sent out and the greater the advertising revenue becomes. . . . This evidence alone would not justify an inference of unlawful intent, but viewed in the context of the entire record its import is clear.

The unlawful objective is unmistakable.

B

In addition to intent to bring about infringement and distribution of a device suitable for infringing use, the inducement theory of course requires evidence of actual infringement by recipients of the device. . . . [T]here is no serious issue of the adequacy of MGM's showing on this point in order to survive the companies' summary judgment requests. . . .

GINSBURG, J., with whom REHNQUIST, C.J., and KENNEDY, J., join, concurring: . . . There is here at least a "genuine issue as to [a] material fact" on the liability of Grokster or StreamCast, not only for actively inducing infringement, but also, or alternatively, based on the distribution of their software products, for contributory copyright infringement. . . .

This case differs markedly from *Sony*. Here, there has been no finding of fair use and little beyond anecdotal evidence of noninfringing uses. . . . [T]he District Court and the Court of Appeals appear to have relied largely on declarations submitted by the defendants. These declarations include assertions (some of them hearsay) that a number of copyright owners authorize distribution of their works on the Internet and that some public domain material is available through peer-to-peer networks including those accessed through Grokster's and StreamCast's software.

. . . Review of these declarations reveals mostly anecdotal evidence, sometimes obtained second-hand, of authorized copyrighted works or public domain works available online . . . and general statements about the benefits of peer-to-peer technology. These declarations do not support summary judgment in the face of evidence, proffered by MGM, of overwhelming use of Grokster's and StreamCast's software for infringement.[3]

---

12. Of course, in the absence of other evidence of intent, a court would be unable to find contributory infringement liability merely based on a failure to take affirmative steps to prevent infringement, if the device otherwise was capable of substantial noninfringing uses. Such a holding would tread too close to the *Sony* safe harbor.

3. Justice Breyer finds support for summary judgment in this motley collection of declarations and in a survey conducted by an expert retained by MGM. . . . Even assuming, as Justice Breyer does, that the *Sony* Court would have absolved Sony of contributory liability solely on the basis of the use of the Betamax for authorized time-shifting, summary judgment is not inevitably appropriate here. *Sony* stressed that the plaintiffs there owned "well below 10%" of copyrighted television programming, and found, based on trial testimony from representatives of the four major sports leagues and other individuals authorized to consent to home-recording of their copyrighted broadcasts, that a similar

. . . [T]he District Court and the Court of Appeals did not sharply distinguish between uses of Grokster's and StreamCast's software products (which this case is about) and uses of peer-to-peer technology generally (which this case is not about).

. . . On this record, the District Court should not have ruled dispositively on the contributory infringement charge by granting summary judgment to Grokster and StreamCast. . . .

BREYER, J., with whom STEVENS, J., and O'CONNOR, J., join, concurring: . . . The [*Sony*] Court had before it a survey . . . showing that roughly 9% of all VCR recordings were of the type—namely, religious, educational, and sports programming—owned by producers and distributors testifying on Sony's behalf who did not object to time-shifting. A much higher percentage of VCR *users* had at one point taped an authorized program, in addition to taping unauthorized programs. And the plaintiffs—not a large class of content producers as in this case—owned only a small percentage of the total available *un*authorized programming. But of all the taping actually done by Sony's customers, only around 9% was of the sort the Court referred to as authorized.

The Court found that the magnitude of authorized programming was "significant," and it also noted the "significant potential for future authorized copying." The Court supported this conclusion by referencing the trial testimony of professional sports league officials and a religious broadcasting representative. It also discussed (1) a Los Angeles educational station affiliated with the Public Broadcasting Service that made many of its programs available for home taping, and (2) Mr. Rogers' Neighborhood, a widely watched children's program. On the basis of this testimony and other similar evidence, the Court determined that producers of this kind had authorized duplication of their copyrighted programs "in significant enough numbers to create a *substantial* market for a noninfringing use of the" VCR.

The Court, in using the key word "substantial," indicated that these circumstances alone constituted a sufficient basis for rejecting the imposition of secondary liability. . . .

As in *Sony*, witnesses here explained the nature of the noninfringing files on Grokster's network without detailed quantification. Those files include:

—Authorized copies of music by artists such as Wilco, Janis Ian, Pearl Jam, Dave Mathews, John Mayer, and others.

—Free electronic books and other works from various online publishers, including Project Gutenberg.

—Public domain and authorized software, such as WinZip.

—Licensed music videos and television and movie segments distributed via digital video packaging with the permission of the copyright holder.

---

percentage of program copying was authorized. Here, the plaintiffs allegedly control copyrights for 70% or 75% of the material exchanged through the Grokster and StreamCast software, and the District Court does not appear to have relied on comparable testimony about authorized copying from copyright holders.

The nature of these and other lawfully swapped files is such that it is reasonable to infer quantities of current lawful use roughly approximate to those at issue in *Sony*. . . .

Importantly, *Sony* also used the word "capable," asking whether the product is "*capable of*" substantial noninfringing uses. Its language and analysis suggest that a figure like 10%, if fixed for all time, might well prove insufficient, but that such a figure serves as an adequate foundation where there is a reasonable prospect of expanded legitimate uses over time. . . .

And that is just what is happening. Such legitimate noninfringing uses are coming to include the swapping of *research information* . . . ; *public domain films* . . . ; *historical recordings and digital educational materials* . . . ; *digital photos* . . . ; "*shareware*" *and* "*freeware*" . . . ; *secure licensed music and movie files* . . . ; *news broadcasts past and present* . . . ; *user-created audio and video files* . . . ; *and all manner of free "open content" works collected by Creative Commons*. . . .

The real question here, I believe, is not whether the record evidence satisfies *Sony*. . . .

Instead, the real question is whether we should modify the *Sony* standard, as MGM requests, or interpret *Sony* more strictly, as I believe Justice Ginsburg's approach would do in practice.

. . . [T]o determine whether modification, or a strict interpretation, of *Sony* is needed, I would ask whether MGM has shown that *Sony* incorrectly balanced copyright and new-technology interests. In particular: (1) Has *Sony* (as I interpret it) worked to protect new technology? (2) If so, would modification or strict interpretation significantly weaken that protection? (3) If so, would new or necessary copyright-related benefits outweigh any such weakening? . . .

The first question is the easiest to answer. . . .

Sony's rule is clear. That clarity allows those who develop new products that are capable of substantial noninfringing uses to know, *ex ante*, that distribution of their product will not yield massive monetary liability. At the same time, it helps deter them from distributing products that have no other real function than—or that are specifically intended for—copyright infringement, deterrence that the Court's holding today reinforces. . . .

Sony's rule is strongly technology protecting. The rule deliberately makes it difficult for courts to find secondary liability where new technology is at issue. . . .

Sony's rule is forward looking. It does not confine its scope to a static snapshot of a product's current uses (thereby threatening technologies that have underdeveloped future markets). . . .

Sony's rule is mindful of the limitations facing judges where matters of technology are concerned. Judges have no specialized technical ability to answer questions about present or future technological feasibility or commercial viability where technology professionals, engineers, and venture capitalists themselves may radically disagree and where answers may differ depending upon whether one focuses upon the time of product development or the time of distribution. Consider, for example, the question whether devices can be added to Grokster's software that will filter out infringing files. . . .

[With respect to the second question,] [t]o require defendants to provide, for example, detailed evidence—say business plans, profitability estimates, projected technological modifications, and so forth—would doubtless make life easier for copyrightholder plaintiffs. But it would simultaneously increase the legal uncertainty that surrounds the creation or development of a new technology capable of being put to infringing uses. Inventors and entrepreneurs (in the garage, the dorm room, the corporate lab, or the boardroom) would have to fear (and in many cases endure) costly and extensive trials when they create, produce, or distribute the sort of information technology that can be used for copyright infringement. . . . The price of a wrong guess—even if it involves a good-faith effort to assess technical and commercial viability—could be large statutory damages (not less than $750 and up to $30,000 *per infringed work*). 17 U.S.C. §504(c)(1). . . .

The third question . . . I find the most difficult of the three. I do not doubt that a more intrusive *Sony* test would generally provide greater revenue security for copyright holders. But it is harder to conclude that the gains on the copyright swings would exceed the losses on the technology roundabouts. . . .

Unauthorized copying likely diminishes industry revenues, though it is not clear by how much. . . .

The extent to which related production has actually and resultingly declined remains uncertain, though there is good reason to believe that the decline, if any, is not substantial. *See, e.g.*, M. Madden, Pew Internet & American Life Project, Artists, Musicians, and the Internet, p. 21, http://www.pewinternet.org/pdfs/PIP_Artists. Musicians_Report.pdf (nearly 70% of musicians believe that file sharing is a minor threat or no threat at all to creative industries); Benkler, *Sharing Nicely: On Shareable Goods and the Emergence of Sharing as a Modality of Economic Production*, 114 Yale L.J. 273, 351-52 (2004) ("Much of the actual flow of revenue to artists—from performances and other sources—is stable even assuming a complete displacement of the CD market by peer-to-peer distribution. . . . [I]t would be silly to think that music, a cultural form without which no human society has existed, will cease to be in our world [because of illegal file swapping]").

More importantly, copyright holders at least potentially have other tools available to reduce piracy and to abate whatever threat it poses to creative production. As today's opinion makes clear, a copyright holder may proceed against a technology provider where a provable specific intent to infringe (of the kind the Court describes) is present. . . .

. . . [S]ince September 2003, the Recording Industry of America has filed "thousands of suits against people for sharing copyrighted material." These suits . . . apparently have had a real and significant deterrent effect. . . .

Further, copyright holders may develop new technological devices that will help curb unlawful infringement. . . .

At the same time, advances in lawful technology have discouraged unlawful copying by making *lawful* copying (*e.g.*, downloading music with the copyright holder's permission) cheaper and easier to achieve. . . .

Finally, as *Sony* recognized, the legislative option remains available. . . .

AFTERMATH

On remand in *Grokster*, the district court granted summary judgment against StreamCast on the question of liability. Plaintiffs then requested a permanent injunction requiring StreamCast to "'use all technologically feasible means to prevent or inhibit' infringement" by users of existing versions of the Morpheus software. *Metro-Goldwyn-Mayer Studios, Inc. v. Grokster, Ltd.*, 518 F. Supp. 2d 1197 (C.D. Cal. 2007). In response, StreamCast asserted that plaintiffs' proposal effectively would require enjoining it from continued distribution of its software. It argued, further, that requiring filtering would be inconsistent with a line of patent cases in which, although defendants had been found liable for inducing infringement, courts refused to *enjoin* the sale of products that were staple articles of commerce suitable for substantial noninfringing use. *Id*. at 1231-32.

The court rejected StreamCast's argument, reasoning that StreamCast's own actions had so closely associated the Morpheus software with copyright infringement that "continued distribution of Morpheus alone[, without filtering,] constitutes infringement." *Id*. at 1235. It ordered "StreamCast to reduce Morpheus' infringing capabilities, while preserving its core noninfringing functionality, as effectively as possible." *Id*. at 1236. It also ruled, however, that StreamCast had no duty to filter out particular works until it had been given sufficient notice of those works' presence on its network. The court appointed a special master to oversee implementation of the injunction. What do you think of the court's solution?

NOTES AND QUESTIONS

1. What is the reach of the inducement doctrine as outlined by *Grokster*? First, does the Court's opinion clearly separate the issues of intent and design? May design properly be considered in an inducement case? For what purpose? Second, what sort of advertising conduct constitutes evidence of inducement? Would Apple Computer's famous 2001 slogan advertising the introduction of iTunes with CD burning capability—"Rip. Mix. Burn."—establish a violation? If Apple had been sued for contributory infringement of music and movie copyrights, would its use of the slogan preclude a grant of summary judgment based on the *Sony* rule?

2. Would it be appropriate to apply the approach in *Grokster* to claims of inducement to infringe in the *Perfect 10, Inc. v. Amazon.com, Inc.*, *Perfect 10, Inc. v. Visa Int'l Serv. Ass'n*, and *Viacom Int'l, Inc. v. YouTube, Inc.* cases? How do you think each court would hold and why?

3. Both the petition for certiorari in *Grokster* and the respondents' opposition framed the case as presenting questions related to the *Sony* doctrine. Why do you think the Court decided the case on an inducement theory instead? Absent sufficient evidence of intent to induce infringement, how should the *Sony* test apply to software like Grokster's and StreamCast's? Do you prefer Justice Ginsburg's approach, or Justice Breyer's, or some other approach?

4. After *Grokster*, where does *Sony*'s test fit within the scheme of secondary liability? Where does *Grokster*'s inducement theory of liability fit?

5. Review footnote 9 of the court's opinion. Would the *Sony* rule shield a technology developer against a vicarious liability claim? Should it? Is vicarious liability an appropriate theory of liability to use in device cases?

6. If the law does not mandate that digital technologies be designed to minimize infringement, will technology developers do so anyway, to reduce the risk of secondary liability? Consider digital video recorders (DVRs), which allow users to record digital copies of television and cable programming. Although DVRs, like VCRs, generally allow fast forwarding through recorded commercials during playback, one DVR, the RePlayTV, originally could be programmed to skip commercials entirely while recording. A service offered by the RePlayTV's manufacturer, SONICblue, could be used to send copied programs to other RePlayTV owners via the Internet. A group of movie and television studios sued SONICblue for contributory copyright infringement. While the litigation was in its discovery phase, SONICblue filed for bankruptcy and sold its RePlayTV business to a large consumer electronics company. After the purchaser agreed to remove the features to which the copyright plaintiffs objected, the secondary liability claims were settled. More recently, satellite television provider Dish Network successfully defended its Hopper DVR, which includes commercial-skipping functionality, against direct and indirect infringement claims in the Ninth Circuit, but litigation in the Second Circuit is ongoing. *See Fox Broadcasting Co., Inc. v. Dish Network, L.L.C.*, 747 F.3d 1060 (9th Cir. 2014), In re AutoHop Litigation, 2013 Copr. L. Dec. ¶ 30,498 (S.D.N.Y. 2013); Jonathan Stempel & Dan Levine, "Fox Loses U.S. Copyright Claims Over Dish Ad-Skipper," Reuters, Jan. 20, 2015, http://www.reuters.com/article/2015/01/21/dish-network-twenty-first-ruling-idUSL1N0V002320150121.

PRACTICE EXERCISE: ADVOCACY

GoodVids, a social bookmarking platform, enables its members to tag videos hosted elsewhere on the Internet and recommend those videos to others with similar tastes. When a user bookmarks a video, the GoodVids platform contacts the server where the video is stored and requests an "embed code" consisting of the video's URL and any display instructions. It then generates a web page that includes a thumbnail of the video's opening shot, along with GoodVids' content framing the thumbnail and advertising. Users who click on a member's bookmark are directed to this page. Clicking on the thumbnail activates the link to the originating site, causing the video to play. Many of the videos tagged and recommended by Good-Vids' members are probably infringing. A television production company has sued GoodVids for contributory copyright infringement and inducing infringement, and GoodVids has retained you to represent it. Draft an outline for a summary judgment motion.

3. Diving Deeper: Inducement Liability for OSPs?

In its initial order granting summary judgment in the *Viacom* litigation, the district court rejected Viacom's argument that YouTube had induced infringement by designing its service to enable infringement on a massive scale:

> The *Grokster* model does not comport with that of a service provider who furnishes a platform on which its users post and access all sorts of materials as they wish, while the provider is unaware of its content, but identifies an agent to receive complains of infringement, and removes identified material when he learns it infringes. To such a provider, the DMCA gives a safe harbor, even if otherwise he would be held as a contributory infringer under the general law.

Viacom Int'l, Inc. v. YouTube, Inc., 718 F. Supp. 2d 514, 526 (S.D.N.Y. 2010), *aff'd in part, vacated in part, and rev'd in part*, 676 F.3d 19 (2d Cir. 2012). According to the court, YouTube was exactly the sort of entity that Congress intended §512 to protect, and allowing inducement liability to nullify the safe harbor would make no sense. Does that reasoning extend to all types of OSPs? Consider the following case.

Columbia Pictures Industries v. Fung
710 F.3d 1020 (9th Cir. 2013)

BERZON, J.: . . . Various film studios alleged that the services offered and websites maintained by Appellants Gary Fung and his company, isoHunt Web Technologies, Inc. (isohunt.com, torrentbox.com, podtropolis.com, and ed2k-it.com, collectively referred to in this opinion as "Fung" or the "Fung sites") induced third parties to download infringing copies of the studios' copyrighted works. The district court agreed, holding that the undisputed facts establish that Fung is liable for contributory copyright infringement. The district court also held as a matter of law that Fung is not entitled to protection from damages liability under any of the "safe harbor" provisions of the Digital Millennium Copyright Act. . . .

Technological Background

This case concerns a peer-to-peer file sharing protocol known as BitTorrent. We begin by providing basic background information useful to understanding the role the Fung sites play in copyright infringement. . . .

III. BitTorrent protocol

The BitTorrent protocol, first released in 2001, is a further variant on the P2P theme. . . .

A. BitTorrent file transfers

Traditionally, if a user wanted to download a file on a P2P network, he would locate another peer with the desired file and download the entire file from that peer. . . .

With the BitTorrent protocol, however, the file is broken up into lots of smaller "pieces," each of which is usually around 256 kilobytes (one-fourth of one megabyte) in size. Whereas under the older protocols the user would download the entire file in one large chunk from a single peer at a time, BitTorrent permits users to download lots of different pieces at the same time from different peers. Once a user has downloaded all the pieces, the file is automatically reassembled into its original form.

BitTorrent has several advantages over the traditional downloading method. Because a user can download different pieces of the file from many different peers at the same time, downloading is much faster. Additionally, even before the entire download is complete, a user can begin sharing the pieces he has already downloaded with other peers, making the process faster for others. . . . [T]he collection of peers swapping pieces with each other is known as a "swarm."

B. BitTorrent architecture

To describe the structure of BitTorrent further, an example is helpful. Let us suppose that an individual (the "publisher") decides to share via BitTorrent her copy of a particular movie. The movie file, we shall assume, is quite large, and is already on the publisher's computer; the publisher has also already downloaded and installed a BitTorrent "client" program on her computer.[4]

To share her copy of the movie file, the publisher first creates a very small file called a "torrent" or "dot-torrent" file, which has the file extension ".torrent." The torrent file is quite small, as it contains none of the actual content that may be copyrighted but, instead, a minimal amount of vital information: the size of the (separate) movie file being shared; the number of "pieces" the movie file is broken into; a cryptographic "hash" that peers will use to authenticate the downloaded file as a true and complete copy of the original; and the address of one or more "trackers." Trackers, discussed more below, serve many of the functions of an indexing server; there are many different trackers, and they typically are not connected or related to each other.

Second, the publisher makes the torrent file available by uploading it to one or more websites ("torrent sites") that collect, organize, index, and host torrent files. . . . There is no central repository of torrent files, but torrent sites strive to have the most comprehensive torrent collection possible.

The Fung sites have two primary methods of acquiring torrent files: soliciting them from users, who then upload the files; and using several automated processes

---

4. . . . BitTorrent is an "open" system, permitting the use of any number of client programs, nearly all of which are free. The Fung sites do not supply any of the client programs necessary to use dot-torrent files to download the copies of movies or other content files; users of the Fung sites have to download such a program from elsewhere.

(called "bots," "crawlers," or "spiders") that collect torrent files from *other* torrent sites. . . . Because the torrent sites typically contain only torrent files, no copyrighted material resides on these sites.

Lastly, the publisher leaves her computer on and connected to the Internet, with her BitTorrent program running. The publisher's job is essentially done; her computer will continue to communicate with the tracker assigned to the torrent file she uploaded, standing ready to distribute the movie file (or, more accurately, parts thereof) to others upon request.

A user seeking the uploaded movie now goes to the torrent site to which the torrent file was uploaded and runs a search for the movie. The search results then provide the torrent file for the user to download. Once the user downloads the torrent file and opens it with his BitTorrent program, the program reads the torrent file, learns the address of the tracker, and contacts it. The program then informs the tracker that it is looking for the movie associated with the downloaded torrent file and asks if there are any peers online that have the movie available for download. Assuming that publishers of that movie are online, the tracker will communicate their address to the user's BitTorrent program. The user's BitTorrent program will then contact the publishers' computers directly and begin downloading the pieces of the movie. . . .

IV. *Fung's role*

Three of Fung's websites—isohunt.com ("isoHunt"); torrentbox.com ("Torrentbox"), and podtropolis.com ("Podtropolis")—are torrent sites. As described above, they collect and organize torrent files and permit users to browse in and search their collections. Searching is done via keyword; users can also browse by category (movies, television shows, music, etc.).

IsoHunt, however, which appears to be Fung's "flagship" site, goes a step beyond merely collecting and organizing torrent files. Each time a torrent file is added to isoHunt, the website automatically modifies the torrent file by adding additional backup trackers to it. That way, if the primary tracker is down, the users' BitTorrent client program will contact the backup trackers, making it more likely that the user will be successful in downloading the content sought. . . .

Torrentbox and Podtropolis, in addition to being torrent sites, run associated trackers. Their collections of torrent files appear to be fairly small. Every torrent file available on Torrentbox and Podtropolis is tracked by the Torrentbox and Podtropolis trackers, respectively, but the Torrentbox and Podtropolis trackers are *much* busier than the Torrentbox and Podtropolis websites. For example, a torrent file for the movie "Casino Royale" was downloaded from Torrentbox.com 50,000 times, but the Torrentbox tracker registered approximately 1.5 million downloads of the movie. This disparity indicates that users obtain the torrent files tracked by Torrentbox and Podtropolis from torrent sites other than Torrentbox.com and Podtropolis.com. The Torrentbox and Podtropolis websites both have continually updated lists of, *inter alia,* the "Top 20 TV Shows," the "Top 20 Movies," and the "Top 20 Most Active Torrents." . . . IsoHunt does not run a tracker, so it cannot measure how frequently the content associated with each torrent file is downloaded; instead, it keeps a continually updated list of the "Top Searches."

IsoHunt also hosts an electronic message board, or "forum," where users can post comments, queries, and the like. In addition to posting to the forum himself, Fung also had some role in moderating posts to the forum. . . .

Discussion

As always, we review the district court's grant of summary judgment de novo . . . .

I. *Liability*

A. Inducement Liability under *Grokster III* . . .

. . . Th[e] inducement principle, as enunciated in *Grokster III,* has four elements: (1) the distribution of a device or product, (2) acts of infringement, (3) an object of promoting its use to infringe copyright, and (4) causation.

i. Distribution of a "device" or "product " . . .

The analogy between *Grokster III* and this case is not perfect. Here, Fung did not develop and does not provide the client programs used to download media products, nor did he develop the BitTorrent protocol (which is maintained by nonparty BitTorrent, Inc., a privately-held company founded by the creators of the protocol). Fung argues that because he did not develop or distribute any "device"—that is, the software or technology used for downloading—he is not liable under the inducement rule enunciated in *Grokster III.*

We cannot agree. Unlike patents, copyrights protect expression, not products or devices. Inducement liability is not limited, either logically or as articulated in *Grokster III,* to those who distribute a "device." As a result, one can infringe a copyright through culpable actions resulting in the impermissible reproduction of copyrighted expression, whether those actions involve making available a device or product or providing some service used in accomplishing the infringement. . . .

ii. Acts of infringement

To prove copyright infringement on an inducement theory, Columbia also had to adduce "evidence of actual infringement by" users of Fung's services. *Grokster III,* 545 U.S. at 940. This they have done. . . .

. . . Based on statistical sampling, Columbia's expert averred that between 90 and 96% of the content associated with the torrent files available on Fung's websites are for "confirmed or highly likely copyright infringing" material. . . . [E]ven giving Fung the benefit of all doubts by tripling the margins of error in the expert's reports, Columbia would still have such overwhelming evidence that any reasonable jury would have to conclude that the vastly predominant use of Fung's services has been to infringe copyrights. . . .

iii. With the object of promoting its use to infringe copyright

The third, usually dispositive, requirement for inducement liability is that the "device" or service be distributed "with the object of promoting its use to infringe copyright, as shown by clear expression or other affirmative steps taken to foster infringement." *Id.* at 936–37. . . .

. . . [T]here is more than enough unrebutted evidence in the summary judgment record to prove that Fung offered his services with the object of promoting their use to infringe copyrighted material. No reasonable jury could find otherwise.

. . . [T] he most important [evidence] is Fung's active encouragement of the uploading of torrent files concerning copyrighted content. For a time, for example, isoHunt prominently featured a list of "Box Office Movies," containing the 20 highest-grossing movies then playing in U.S. theaters. When a user clicked on a listed title, she would be invited to "upload [a] torrent" file for that movie. In other words, she would be asked to upload a file that, once downloaded by other users, would lead directly to their obtaining infringing content. Fung also posted numerous messages to the isoHunt forum requesting that users upload torrents for specific copyrighted films; in other posts, he provided links to torrent files for copyrighted movies, urging users to download them. . . .

As in *Grokster,* moreover, Fung "communicated a clear message by responding affirmatively to requests for help in locating and playing copyrighted materials." *Id.* at 938. The record is replete with instances of Fung responding personally to queries for assistance in: uploading torrent files corresponding to obviously copyrighted material, finding particular copyrighted movies and television shows, getting pirated material to play properly, and burning the infringing content onto DVDs for playback on televisions.

Two types of supporting evidence, insufficient in themselves—like the similar evidence in *Grokster III*—corroborate the conclusion that Fung "acted with a purpose to cause copyright violations by use of" their services. *Id.* at 938. First, Fung took no steps "to develop filtering tools or other mechanisms to diminish the infringing activity" by those using his services.[15] *Id.* at 939. Second, Fung generates revenue almost exclusively by selling advertising space on his websites. The more users who visit Fung's websites and view the advertisements supplied by Fung's business partners, the greater the revenues to Fung. . . .

iv. Causation

Grokster III mentions causation only indirectly, by speaking of "*resulting* acts of infringement by third parties." *Id.* at 937 (emphasis added). The parties here advance competing interpretations of the causation requirement adopted through that locution: Fung and amicus curiae Google argue that the acts of infringement must be caused by the manifestations of the distributor's improper object—that is,

---

15. Fung did attempt to keep certain types of torrents off his websites. First, because Fung is personally opposed to pornography, he took steps to keep torrent files related to pornography out of his sites' collections. Second, Fung attempted to remove torrent files that led to downloads of fake or corrupted content files. . . .

by the inducing messages themselves. Columbia, on the other hand, maintains that it need only prove that the "acts of infringement by third parties" were caused by the product distributed or services provided.

We think Columbia's interpretation of *Grokster III* is the better one. On that view, if one provides a service that could be used to infringe copyrights, with the manifested intent that the service actually be used in that manner, that person is liable for the infringement that occurs through the use of the service. . . .

We are mindful, however, of the potential severity of a loose causation theory for inducement liability. Under this theory of liability, the only causation requirement is that the product or service at issue was used to infringe the plaintiff's copyrights. The possible reach of liability is enormous, particularly in the digital age.

Copyright law attempts to strike a balance amongst three competing interests: those of the copyright holders in benefitting from their labor; those of entrepreneurs in having the latitude to invent new technologies without fear of being held liable if their innovations are used by others in unintended infringing ways; and those of the public in having access both to entertainment options protected by copyright and to new technologies that enhance productivity and quality of life. . . . [I]t is important that we not permit inducement liability's relatively lax causation requirement to "enlarge the scope of [copyright's] statutory monopolies to encompass control over an article of commerce"—such as technology capable of substantial non-infringing uses—"that is not the subject of copyright protection." *Sony*, 464 U.S. at 421.

We emphasize a few points in this regard. First, as previously discussed, proper proof of the defendant's intent that its product or service be used to infringe copyrights is paramount. . . .

Moreover, proving that an entity had an unlawful purpose at a particular time in providing a product or service does not infinitely expand its liability in either temporal direction. If an entity begins providing a service with infringing potential at time *A,* but does not appreciate that potential until later and so does not develop and exhibit the requisite intent to support inducement liability until time *B,* it would not be held liable for the infringement that occurred between time *A* and *B.* Relatedly, an individual or entity's unlawful objective at time *B* is not a virus that infects all future actions. People, companies, and technologies must be allowed to rehabilitate, so to speak, through actions actively discouraging the infringing use of their product, lest the public be deprived of the useful good or service they are still capable of producing.

We also note, as Fung points out, that *Grokster III* seemingly presupposes a condition that is absent in this case: that there is but a single producer of the "device" in question. Only Sony sold the Betamax, and only Grokster and Stream-Cast distributed their respective software applications. Assessing causation was thus a straightforward task. In *Sony,* for example, there was no question that some customers would purchase and use the Betamax in ways that infringed copyright. Thus, in a "but-for" sense, there was no question that Sony *caused* whatever infringement resulted from the use of Betamax sets; the Court nonetheless held Sony not liable on the ground that even if Sony caused the infringement, it was not at *fault,* with fault measured by Sony's intent. But as *Grokster III* explained, "nothing in *Sony* requires courts to ignore evidence of intent if there is such evidence, and the case was never meant to foreclose rules of fault-based liability." 545 U.S. at 934. *Grokster III thus* held that where there is sufficient evidence of fault—that is, an unlawful objective—distributors are liable for causing the infringement that resulted from use of their products. In other words, *Grokster III* and *Sony* were able to assume causation and assess liability (or not) based on fault. In the present case, however, where other individuals and entities provide services identical to those offered by Fung, causation, even in the relatively loose sense we have delineated, cannot be assumed, even though fault is unquestionably present.

Fung argues, on this basis, that some of the acts of infringement by third parties relied upon by the district court may not have involved his websites at all. He points out, for example, that by far the largest number of torrents tracked by the Torrentbox tracker are obtained from somewhere *other* than Torrentbox.com. If a user obtained a torrent from a source other than his websites, Fung maintains, he cannot be held liable for the infringement that resulted. *Cf. Perfect 10, Inc. v. Google, Inc.*, 653 F.3d 976, 982 (9th Cir.2011) (affirming the district court's denial of a preliminary injunction based on Google's alleged direct copyright infringement because the plaintiff, Perfect 10, failed to show "a sufficient causal connection between irreparable harm to [its] business and Google's operation of its search engine"); *Visa*, 494 F.3d at 796–802 (affirming the district court's dismissal under Federal Rule of Civil Procedure 12(b)(6) in part because the "causal chain" between defendant credit card companies' services and infringing activity by Internet users was too attenuated).

On the other hand, Fung's services encompass more than the provision of torrent files. . . . If Plaintiffs can show a sufficient casual connection between users' infringing activity and the use of Fung's trackers, the fact that torrent files were obtained from elsewhere may not relieve Fung of liability.

We do not decide the degree to which Fung can be held liable for having caused infringements by users of his sites or trackers. The only issue presently before us is the permanent injunction, which, as in *Grokster III*, does not in this case depend on the "exact calculation of infringing use[ ] as a basis for a claim of damages." 545 U.S. at 941. We therefore need not further entertain Fung's causation arguments at this time, but leave it to the district court to consider them, in light of the observations we have made, when it calculates damages. . . .

B. DMCA Safe Harbors . . .

Columbia argues, and the district court agreed, that inducement liability is inherently incompatible with protection under the DMCA safe harbors. . . .

. . . [The court disagreed.] For example, a prerequisite for the safe harbors is that the service provider implement a policy of removing repeat infringers. Although at first glance that requirement that might seem impossible to establish where the requisites for inducing infringement are met, on closer examination the appearance of *inherent* incompatibility dissipates. In some instances, for example, the *Grokster* standard for inducement might be met even where a service provider has a policy of removing proven repeat infringers. It is therefore *conceivable* that a service provider liable for inducement could be entitled to protection under the safe harbors.

In light of these considerations, we are not clairvoyant enough to be sure that there are no instances in which a defendant otherwise liable for contributory copyright infringement could meet the prerequisites for one or more of the DMCA safe harbors. We therefore think it best to conduct the two inquiries independently—although, as will appear, aspects of the inducing behavior that give rise to liability are relevant to the operation of some of the DMCA safe harbors and can, in some circumstances, preclude their application. . . .

[The court ruled that Fung could not invoke the protection of either §512(c) or §512(d) because he had "'red flag' knowledge of a broad range of infringing activity for reasons independent of any notifications from Columbia." Additionally, it ruled that "Fung's revenue stream is predicated on the broad availability of infringing materials for his users, thereby attracting advertisers," and that "Fung's ability to control infringing activity on his websites went well beyond merely locating and terminating users' access to infringing material." Therefore, the circumstances established a financial benefit directly attributable to the infringing activity and the right and ability to control that activity.]

NOTES AND QUESTIONS

1. Does it make sense to conclude that an inducement claim can be maintained against an entity that provides a service rather than a product or device?

2. Focus in particular on the court's discussion of causation. As you may recall from your torts class, when confronted with pharmaceutical products liability cases in which the plaintiffs could not prove which company manufactured the drugs they had taken, courts developed a theory of enterprise liability to allow the claims to proceed. Is the *Fung* court articulating the beginnings of a theory of enterprise liability for OSPs? If so, is that appropriate?

3. Is the court's application of the "red flag" knowledge provision to Fung consistent with the "specific infringing acts" standard articulated by the *Viacom* court (and by the Ninth Circuit itself in its earlier decision in *UMG Recordings, Inc. v. Shelter Capital Partners LLC*, 667 F.3d 1022 (9th Cir. 2011), *superseded*, 718 F.3d 1006, 1023-26 (9th Cir. 2013))? Would the "willful blindness" doctrine provide a better resolution of Fung's §512(c) and (d) defenses? Why, or why not?

> ### LOOKING FORWARD
>
> As you will learn in Chapter 13, a successful infringement plaintiff may recover actual damages suffered as a result of the infringement. For purposes of calculating damages, should Fung's liability extend to every infringement committed with the assistance of files hosted by his sites? If not, how would you calculate damages?

4. What are the salient differences between Fung's revenue model and You-Tube's? What are the salient differences between Fung's conduct in relation to the infringing activity and that of YouTube's founders in *Viacom*?

5. Should §512 be amended to provide safe harbor protection against a claim for inducing infringement? If so, under what circumstances? If not, why not? Should §512 be amended to foreclose invocation of the safe harbors by a defendant otherwise liable for inducing infringement?

10

Fair Use

In this chapter, we turn to the most well-known limit to the rights granted to a copyright owner, namely, the fair use doctrine. The fair use doctrine is a *general* limit that applies to all copyright rights, including those rights that also are subject to more specific exceptions.

The fair use doctrine began as a judge-made limitation to the rights of copyright owners. In England, the "fair abridgement" doctrine had permitted certain abridgements of the copyrighted works of others without liability for infringement. *See, e.g., Cary v. Kearsley*, 170 Eng. Rep. 679, 680 (K.B. 1803) (recognizing a right to "fairly adopt part of the work of another" and noting that the court must not "put manacles upon science"). The first American case to consider the applicability of the fair abridgement doctrine was *Folsom v. Marsh*, 9 F. Cas. 342 (C.C.D. Mass. 1841). The plaintiff in that case had written a 12-volume, 7,000-page biography of President George Washington. The defendant copied 353 pages from the plaintiff's work to create a two-volume work. Writing for the court, Justice Story rejected the argument that the defendant's work was a fair abridgement:

> [A] reviewer may fairly cite largely from the original work, if his design be really and truly to use the passages for the purposes of fair and reasonable criticism. On the other hand, it is as clear, that if he thus cites the most important parts of the work, with a view, not to criticise, but to supersede the use of the original work, and substitute the review for it, such a use will be deemed in law a piracy.

Id. at 344-45. In what has become the most cited passage in the history of fair use, Justice Story listed the criteria a court should examine to evaluate whether the use was a fair abridgement:

> In short, we must often, in deciding questions of this sort, look to the nature and objects of the selections made, the quantity and value of the materials used, and the degree in which the use may prejudice the sale, or diminish the profits, or supersede the objects, of the original work.

Id. at 348.

Justice Story's opinion in *Folsom* never used the phrase "fair use." That term did not appear in the case law until 28 years later. *See Lawrence v. Dana*, 15 F. Cas. 26, 60 (C.C.D. Mass. 1869). For the next hundred years, however, courts continued to look to the factors identified by Justice Story as most relevant in resolving fair use cases.

During the extensive revision process that led to enactment of the 1976 Act, Congress determined that codification of the fair use doctrine was necessary. Unlike other, more specific exceptions to copyright set forth in other sections of the Act, however, §107 simply enumerates factors for courts to consider in making fair use determinations:

> §107. **Limitations on exclusive rights: Fair use**
> Notwithstanding the provisions of sections 106 and 106A, the fair use of a copyrighted work, including such use by reproduction in copies or phonorecords or by any other means specified by that section, for purposes such as criticism, comment, news reporting, teaching (including multiple copies for classroom use), scholarship, or research, is not an infringement of copyright. In determining whether the use made of a work in any particular case is a fair use the factors to be considered shall include—
>
> (1) the purpose and character of the use, including whether such use is of a commercial nature or is for nonprofit educational purposes;
> (2) the nature of the copyrighted work;
> (3) the amount and substantiality of the portion used in relation to the copyrighted work as a whole; and
> (4) the effect of the use upon the potential market for or value of the copyrighted work.
>
> The fact that a work is unpublished shall not itself bar a finding of fair use if such finding is made upon consideration of all the above factors.

Beyond the factors set forth in the statute, the legislative history provides little to guide courts in applying §107. "Although the courts have considered and ruled upon the fair use doctrine over and over again, no real definition of the concept has ever emerged. Indeed, since the doctrine is an equitable rule of reason, no generally applicable definition is possible, and each case raising the question must be decided on its own facts." H.R. Rep. No. 94-1476, 94th Cong., 2d Sess. 65 (1976), *reprinted in* 1976 U.S.C.C.A.N. 5659, 5679.

In practice, whether a particular use is deemed fair depends not only on the particular circumstances, but also on underlying normative theories relied on by the court. Here we present common fact patterns that arise in fair use cases and leading theories that one might employ to understand the results.

A. CULTURAL INTERCHANGE

Many of the illustrative uses listed in the preamble to §107 are those that further the development of a common culture. "[C]riticism, comment, news reporting, teaching . . . scholarship, [and] research" all promote the progress of learning and the arts. Such uses help to produce a public that is educated and informed not only about current events, but also about shared values, interests, and debates. How far, though, should fair use privileges extend in the name of cultural progress and dissemination of knowledge? At one end of the spectrum, it is reasonably clear that if you copy your neighbor's recent book on modern American politics and sell thousands of copies to the public at a discount below the retail price simply because you think everyone ought to read it, the fair use doctrine will not shield your conduct. At the other end, it is equally clear that if you publish a review of the book, whether flattering or harshly critical, and quote from it to illustrate your points, the quotations are fair use. For cases falling somewhere between these two extremes, however, determining the right outcome can be much harder.

1. The Classic Cases

Two of the Supreme Court's three post-1976 Act fair use decisions fall into the category of "cultural interchange" cases. As you read the decisions, identify the guidelines that the Court develops to interpret, and to supplement, the §107 fair use factors and ask yourself whether those guidelines seem to strike the right balance.

Harper & Row, Publishers, Inc. v. Nation Enterprises
471 U.S. 539 (1985)

O'CONNOR, J.: . . . In February 1977, shortly after leaving the White House, former President Gerald R. Ford contracted with petitioners Harper & Row and Reader's Digest, to publish his as yet unwritten memoirs. The memoirs were to contain "significant hitherto unpublished material" concerning the Watergate crisis, Mr. Ford's pardon of former President Nixon and "Mr. Ford's reflections on this period of history, and the morality and personalities involved." In addition to the right to publish the Ford memoirs in book form, the agreement gave petitioners the exclusive right to license prepublication excerpts, known in the trade as "first serial rights." Two years later, as the memoirs were nearing completion, petitioners negotiated a prepublication licensing agreement with Time, a weekly news magazine. Time agreed to pay $25,000, $12,500 in advance and an additional $12,500 at publication, in exchange for the right to excerpt 7,500 words from Mr. Ford's account of the Nixon pardon. The issue featuring the excerpts was timed to appear approximately one week before shipment of the full length book version to bookstores. Exclusivity was an important consideration; Harper & Row instituted procedures designed to maintain the confidentiality of the manuscript, and Time retained the right to renegotiate the second payment should the material appear in print prior to its release of the excerpts.

Two to three weeks before the Time article's scheduled release, an unidentified person secretly brought a copy of the Ford manuscript [A Time to Heal: The Autobiography of Gerald R. Ford] to Victor Navasky, editor of The Nation, a political commentary magazine. Mr. Navasky knew that his possession of the manuscript was not authorized and that the manuscript must be returned quickly to his "source" to avoid discovery. He hastily put together what he believed was "a real hot news story" composed of quotes, paraphrases, and facts drawn exclusively from the manuscript. Mr. Navasky attempted no independent commentary, research or criticism, in part because of the need for speed if he was to "make news" by "publish[ing] in advance of publication of the Ford book." App. 416-417. The 2,250-word article . . . appeared on April 3, 1979. As a result of The Nation's article, Time canceled its piece and refused to pay the remaining $12,500. . . .

[The district court found that The Nation's actions constituted copyright infringement. The Court of Appeals for the Second Circuit reversed.]

. . . [T]here is no dispute that the unpublished manuscript of "A Time to Heal," as a whole, was protected by §106 from unauthorized reproduction. Nor do respondents dispute that verbatim copying of excerpts of the manuscript's original form of expression would constitute infringement unless excused as fair use. . . .

III.

A.

Fair use was traditionally defined as "a privilege in others than the owner of the copyright to use the copyrighted material in a reasonable manner without his consent." H. Ball, Law of Copyright and Literary Property 260 (1944) (hereinafter Ball). . . . "[T]he author's consent to a reasonable use of his copyrighted works ha[d] always been implied by the courts as a necessary incident of the constitutional policy of promoting the progress of science and the useful arts, since a prohibition of such use would inhibit subsequent writers from attempting to improve upon prior works and thus . . . frustrate the very ends sought to be attained." Ball 260. Professor Latman, in a study of the doctrine of fair use commissioned by Congress for the revision effort, summarized prior law as turning on the "importance of the material copied or performed from the point of view of the reasonable copyright owner. In other words, would the reasonable copyright owner have consented to the use?" [A. Latman, Fair Use of Copyrighted Works 15 (1958), reprinted as Study No. 14 in Copyright Law Revision Studies Nos. 14-16, prepared for the Senate Committee on the Judiciary, 86th Cong., 2d Sess. 7 (1960)]. . . .

Perhaps because the fair use doctrine was predicated on the author's implied consent to "reasonable and customary" use when he released his work for public consumption, fair use traditionally was not recognized as a defense to charges of copying from an author's as yet unpublished works. Under common-law copyright, "the property of the author . . . in his intellectual creation [was] absolute until he voluntarily part[ed] with the same." *American Tobacco Co. v. Werckmeister*, 207 U.S. 284 (1907). This absolute rule, however, was tempered in practice by the equitable nature of the fair use doctrine. In a given case, factors such as implied consent through *de facto* publication on performance or dissemination of a work may tip the balance of equities in favor of prepublication use. . . . But it has never been seriously disputed that "the fact that the plaintiff's work is unpublished . . . is a factor tending to negate the defense of fair use." [3 M. Nimmer, Copyright 13.05, at 13-62, n.2] . . . Publication of an author's expression before he has authorized its dissemination seriously infringes the author's right to decide when and whether it will be made public, a factor not present in fair use of published works. . . .

We also find unpersuasive respondents' argument that fair use may be made of a soon-to-be-published manuscript on the ground that the author has demonstrated he has no interest in nonpublication. This argument assumes that the unpublished nature of copyrighted material is only relevant to letters or other confidential writings not intended for dissemination. It is true that common-law copyright was often enlisted in the service of personal privacy. *See* Brandeis & Warren, *The Right to Privacy*, 4 Harv. L. Rev. 193, 198-199 (1890). In its commercial guise, however, an author's right to choose when he will publish is no less deserving of protection. . . .

B.

Respondents, however, contend that First Amendment values require a different rule under the circumstances of this case. . . . Respondents advance the substantial public import of the subject matter of the Ford memoirs as grounds for excusing a use that would ordinarily not pass muster as a fair use—the piracy of verbatim quotations for the purpose of "scooping" the authorized first serialization. Respondents explain their copying of Mr. Ford's expression as essential to reporting the news story it claims the book itself represents. In respondents' view, not only the facts contained in Mr. Ford's memoirs, but "the precise manner in which [he] expressed himself [were] as newsworthy as what he had to say." Respondents argue that the public's interest in learning this news as fast as possible outweighs the right of the author to control its first publication. . . .

Respondents' theory, however, would expand fair use to effectively destroy any expectation of copyright protection in the work of a public figure. Absent such protection, there would be little incentive to create or profit in financing such memoirs, and the public would be denied an important source of significant historical information. The promise of copyright would be an empty one if it could be avoided merely by dubbing the infringement a fair use "news report" of the book. . . .

In our haste to disseminate news, it should not be forgotten that the Framers intended copyright itself to be the engine of free expression. By establishing a marketable right to the use of one's expression, copyright supplies the economic incentive to create and disseminate ideas. . . .

In view of the First Amendment protections already embodied in the Copyright Act's distinction between copyrightable expression and uncopyrightable facts and ideas, and the latitude for scholarship and comment traditionally afforded by fair use, we see no warrant for expanding the doctrine of fair use to create what amounts to a public figure exception to copyright. Whether verbatim copying from a public figure's manuscript in a given case is or is not fair must be judged according to the traditional equities of fair use.

IV.

Fair use is a mixed question of law and fact. *Pacific & Southern Co. v. Duncan*, 744 F.2d 1490, 1495, n.8 (CA11 1984). Where the district court has found facts sufficient to evaluate each of the statutory factors, an appellate court "need not remand for further factfinding . . . [but] may conclude as a matter of law that [the challenged use] do[es] not qualify as a fair use of the copyrighted work." *Id.*, at 1495. . . .

Purpose of the Use. The Second Circuit correctly identified news reporting as the general purpose of The Nation's use. News reporting is one of the examples enumerated in §107 to "give some idea of the sort of activities the courts might regard as fair use under the circumstances." Senate Report, at 61. This listing was not intended to be exhaustive, see *ibid.*; §101 (definition of "including" and "such as"), or to single out any particular use as presumptively a "fair" use. . . . The fact that an article arguably is "news" and therefore a productive use is simply one factor in a fair use analysis.

We agree with the Second Circuit that the trial court erred in fixing on whether the information contained in the memoirs was actually new to the public. As Judge Meskill wisely noted, "[c]ourts should be chary of deciding what is and what is not news." 723 F.2d, at 215 (dissenting). "The issue is not what constitutes 'news,' but whether a claim of news reporting is a valid fair use defense to an infringement of *copyrightable expression*." [W. Patry, The Fair Use Privilege in Copyright Law 119 (1985).] The Nation has every right to seek to be the first to publish information. But The Nation went beyond simply reporting uncopyrightable information and actively sought to exploit the headline value of its infringement, making a "news event" out of its unauthorized first publication of a noted figure's copyrighted expression.

The fact that a publication was commercial as opposed to nonprofit is a separate factor that tends to weigh against a finding of fair use. . . . In arguing that the purpose of news reporting is not purely commercial, The Nation misses the point entirely. The crux of the profit/nonprofit distinction is not whether the sole motive of the use is monetary gain but whether the user stands to profit from exploitation of the copyrighted material without paying the customary price.

In evaluating character and purpose we cannot ignore The Nation's stated purpose of scooping the forthcoming hardcover and Time abstracts. The Nation's use had not merely the incidental effect but the *intended purpose* of supplanting the copyright holder's commercially valuable right of first publication. Also relevant to the "character" of the use is "the propriety of the defendant's conduct." 3 Nimmer §13.05[A], at 13-72. "Fair use presupposes 'good faith' and 'fair dealing.' " *Time Inc. v. Bernard Geis Associates*, 293 F. Supp. 130, 146 (SDNY 1968). The trial court found that The Nation knowingly exploited a purloined manuscript. . . .

Nature of the Copyrighted Work. Second, the Act directs attention to the nature of the copyrighted work. "A Time to Heal" may be characterized as an unpublished historical narrative or autobiography. The law generally recognizes a greater need to disseminate factual works than works of fiction or fantasy. *See* Gorman, *Fact or Fancy? The Implications for Copyright*, 29 J. Copyright Soc. 560, 561 (1982).

"[E]ven within the field of fact works, there are gradations as to the relative proportion of fact and fancy. One may move from sparsely embellished maps and directories to elegantly written biography. The extent to which one must permit expressive language to be copied, in order to assure dissemination of the underlying facts, will thus vary from case to case." *Id.,* at 563.

Some of the briefer quotes from the memoirs are arguably necessary adequately to convey the facts; for example, Mr. Ford's characterization of the White House tapes as the "smoking gun" is perhaps so integral to the idea expressed as to be inseparable from it. . . . But The Nation did not stop at isolated phrases and instead excerpted subjective descriptions and portraits of public figures whose power lies in the author's individualized expression. Such use, focusing on the most expressive elements of the work, exceeds that necessary to disseminate the facts.

The fact that a work is unpublished is a critical element of its "nature." Our prior discussion establishes that the scope of fair use is narrower with respect to unpublished works. While even substantial quotations might qualify as fair use in a review of a published work or a news account of a speech that had been delivered to the public or disseminated to the press, *see* House Report, at 65, the author's right to control the first public appearance of his expression weighs against such use of the work before its release. The right of first publication encompasses not only the choice whether to publish at all, but also the choices of when, where, and in what form first to publish a work. . . .

Amount and Substantiality of the Portion Used. Next, the Act directs us to examine the amount and substantiality of the portion used in relation to the copyrighted work as a whole. In absolute terms, the words actually quoted were an insubstantial portion of "A Time to Heal." The District Court, however, found that "[T]he Nation took what was essentially the heart of the book." 557 F. Supp., at 1072. We believe the Court of Appeals erred in overruling the District Judge's evaluation of the qualitative nature of the taking. A Time editor described the chapters on the pardon as "the most interesting and moving parts of the entire manuscript." The portions actually quoted were selected by Mr. Navasky as among the most powerful passages in those chapters. He testified that he used verbatim excerpts because simply reciting the information could not adequately convey the "absolute certainty with which [Ford] expressed himself," or show that "this comes from President Ford," or carry the "definitive quality" of the original. In short, he quoted these passages precisely because they qualitatively embodied Ford's distinctive expression.

As the statutory language indicates, a taking may not be excused merely because it is insubstantial with respect to the *infringing* work. As Judge Learned Hand cogently remarked, "no plagiarist can excuse the wrong by showing how much of his work he did not pirate." *Sheldon v. Metro-Goldwyn Pictures Corp.*, 81 F.2d 49, 56 (CA2), *cert. denied*, 298 U.S. 669 (1936). Conversely, the fact that a substantial portion of the infringing work was copied verbatim is evidence of the qualitative value of the copied material, both to the originator and to the plagiarist who seeks to profit from marketing someone else's copyrighted expression.

Stripped to the verbatim quotes, the direct takings from the unpublished manuscript constitute at least 13% of the infringing article. The Nation article is structured around the quoted excerpts which serve as its dramatic focal points. . . . In view of the expressive value of the excerpts and their key role in the infringing work, we cannot agree with the Second Circuit that the "magazine took a meager, indeed an infinitesimal amount of Ford's original language." 723 F.2d, at 209.

Effect on the Market. Finally, the Act focuses on "the effect of the use upon the potential market for or value of the copyrighted work." This last factor is undoubtedly the single most important element of fair use. "Fair use, when properly applied, is limited to copying by others which does not materially impair the marketability of the work which is copied." 1 Nimmer §1.10[D], at 1-87. The trial court found not merely a potential but an actual effect on the market. Time's cancellation of its projected serialization and its refusal to pay the $12,500 were the direct effect of the infringement. . . .

More important, to negate fair use one need only show that if the challenged use "should become widespread, it would adversely affect the *potential* market for the copyrighted work." *Sony Corp. of America v. Universal City Studios, Inc.*, 464 U.S., at 451 (emphasis added); *id.*, at 484, and n.36 (collecting cases) (dissenting opinion). This inquiry must take account not only of harm to the original but also of harm to the market for derivative works. . . .

It is undisputed that the factual material in the balance of The Nation's article, besides the verbatim quotes at issue here, was drawn exclusively from the chapters on the pardon. The excerpts were employed as featured episodes in a story about the Nixon pardon—precisely the use petitioners had licensed to Time. The borrowing of these verbatim quotes from the unpublished manuscript lent The Nation's piece a special air of authenticity—as Navasky expressed it, the reader would know it was Ford speaking and not The Nation. Thus it directly competed for a share of the market for prepublication excerpts. The Senate Report states:

> With certain special exceptions . . . a use that supplants any part of the normal market for a copyrighted work would ordinarily be considered an infringement. Senate Report, at 65.

Placed in a broader perspective, a fair use doctrine that permits extensive prepublication quotations from an unreleased manuscript without the copyright owner's consent poses substantial potential for damage to the marketability of first serialization rights in general. "Isolated instances of minor infringements, when multiplied many times, become in the aggregate a major inroad on copyright that must be prevented." *Ibid.* . . .

BRENNAN, J., with whom WHITE, J., and MARSHALL, J., join, dissenting: The Court holds that The Nation's quotation of 300 words from the unpublished 200,000-word manuscript of President Gerald R. Ford infringed the copyright in that manuscript, even though the quotations related to a historical event of undoubted significance—the resignation and pardon of President Richard M. Nixon. Although the Court pursues the laudable goal of protecting "the economic incentive to create and disseminate ideas," this zealous defense of the copyright owner's prerogative will, I fear, stifle the broad dissemination of ideas and information copyright is intended to nurture. Protection of the copyright owner's economic interest is achieved in this case through an exceedingly narrow definition of the scope of fair use. The progress of arts and sciences and the robust public debate essential to an enlightened citizenry are ill served by this constricted reading of the fair use doctrine. I therefore respectfully dissent. . . .

. . . Th[e] limitation of protection to literary form precludes any claim of copyright in facts, including historical narrative.

The "promotion of science and the useful arts" requires this limit on the scope of an author's control. Were an author able to prevent subsequent authors from using concepts, ideas, or facts contained in his or her work, the creative process would wither and scholars would be forced into unproductive replication of the research of their predecessors. This limitation on copyright also ensures consonance with our most important First Amendment values. Our "profound national commitment to the principle that debate on public issues should be uninhibited, robust, and wide-open," *New York Times Co. v. Sullivan*, 376 U.S. 254, 270 (1964), leaves no room for a statutory monopoly over information and ideas. "The arena of public debate would be quiet, indeed, if a politician could copyright his speeches or a philosopher his treatises and thus obtain a monopoly on the ideas they contained." *Lee v. Runge*, 404 U.S. 887, 893 (1971) (Douglas, J., dissenting from denial of certiorari). A broad dissemination of principles, ideas, and factual information is crucial to the robust public debate and informed citizenry that are "the essence of self-government." *Garrison v. Louisiana*, 379 U.S. 64, 74-75 (1964). And every citizen must be permitted freely to marshal ideas and facts in the advocacy of particular political choices.[4] . . .

NOTES AND QUESTIONS

1. Focus first on the majority's analysis of the first and fourth statutory fair use factors. Does the majority treat these factors as distinct from one another, or as related?

2. Now focus on the interrelationship between the third and fourth statutory factors. As Justice Brennan's dissent notes, in total *The Nation* quoted only 300 words from the forthcoming book. Quotations in a book review have long been considered a paradigmatic example of fair use. Why was this case different? What rules seem to be relevant to determining the "substantiality" of the quoted excerpts?

3. In its analysis of the second statutory factor, the majority acknowledges that the fair use doctrine generally affords more latitude to uses of works that are predominantly factual, but then downplays the importance of this consideration with

---

4. It would be perverse to prohibit government from limiting the financial resources upon which a political speaker may draw, see *FEC v. National Conservative Political Action Committee*, 470 U.S. 480 (1985), but to permit government to limit the intellectual resources upon which that speaker may draw.

respect to President Ford's manuscript. The dissenters, in contrast, view this attribute of the manuscript as extremely important. Who has the better argument? Does your conclusion depend at all on your view of the first factor, the purpose and character of *The Nation*'s use?

4. The majority begins its fair use discussion by noting that fair use was "traditionally defined" as being based on a theory of implied consent. If fair use is indeed based on implied consent, then wouldn't the plaintiff, who clearly has not consented to the use at issue, have a leg up going into the fair use analysis? Many times in its opinion the Court refers to the "purloined" or "stolen" nature of the copy *The Nation* received. The Court also discusses the unpublished nature of the plaintiff's work. Was consideration of those factors appropriate?

5. Slightly different from an implied consent theory of fair use is a customary use theory. Under this theory, a use should be found to be fair if it is "within . . . accepted norms and customary practice." Lloyd L. Weinreb, *Fair's Fair: A Comment on the Fair Use Doctrine*, 103 Harv. L. Rev. 1137, 1159-60 (1990) (characterizing this inquiry as "the most relevant inquiry"). Do you agree with Professor Weinreb?

What factors should guide a court in deciding that a use is "customary practice"? Professor Michael Madison argues that the fair use doctrine implicitly validates certain favored patterns and practices and that these practices should be more explicitly acknowledged in fair use analysis. *See* Michael J. Madison, *A Pattern-Oriented Approach to Fair Use*, 45 Wm. & Mary L. Rev. 1525 (2004). Should the fair use doctrine be used to endorse or reject particular social practices? How should courts decide which practices to endorse?

6. In 1992, Congress enacted legislation to clarify that the unpublished nature of a copyrighted work does not bar a finding of fair use. The legislation added the final sentence of §107: "The fact that a work is unpublished shall not itself bar a finding of fair use if such finding is made upon consideration of all the above factors."

PRACTICE EXERCISE: COUNSEL A CLIENT

Your client, the general counsel of a publishing company, has just asked for your advice. The company is planning to publish an unauthorized biography of the reclusive author Bill Watterson, best known for his famous comic strip, "Calvin and Hobbes." The biographer, Sarah Jarrett, discovered an old manuscript in an antique desk that she purchased at an estate sale. She determined that the manuscript was an unpublished work by Watterson containing the first and only known account of how he came to create "Calvin and Hobbes" and why he decided to retire it and withdraw completely from the public eye. Jarrett's biography of Watterson contains many excerpts from the manuscript. Can the company safely publish the biography?

Campbell v. Acuff-Rose Music, Inc.
510 U.S. 569 (1994)

SOUTER, J.: . . . In 1964, Roy Orbison and William Dees wrote a rock ballad called "Oh, Pretty Woman" and assigned their rights in it to respondent Acuff-Rose Music, Inc. Acuff-Rose registered the song for copyright protection.

Petitioners Luther R. Campbell, Christopher Wongwon, Mark Ross, and David Hobbs, are collectively known as 2 Live Crew, a popular rap music group. In 1989, Campbell wrote a song entitled "Pretty Woman," which he later described in an affidavit as intended, "through comical lyrics, to satirize the original work. . . ."

. . . On July 5, 1989, 2 Live Crew's manager informed Acuff-Rose that 2 Live Crew had written a parody of "Oh, Pretty Woman," that they would afford all credit for ownership and authorship of the original song to Acuff-Rose, Dees, and Orbison, and that they were willing to pay a fee for the use they wished to make of it. Enclosed with the letter were a copy of the lyrics and a recording of 2 Live Crew's song. . . . Acuff-Rose's agent refused permission, stating that "I am aware of the success enjoyed by 'The 2 Live Crews,' but I must inform you that we cannot permit the use of a parody of 'Oh, Pretty Woman.'" . . . Nonetheless, in June or July 1989, 2 Live Crew released records, cassette tapes, and compact discs of "Pretty Woman" in a collection of songs entitled "As Clean As They Wanna Be." The albums and compact discs identify the authors of "Pretty Woman" as Orbison and Dees and its publisher as Acuff-Rose.

Almost a year later, after nearly a quarter of a million copies of the recording had been sold, Acuff-Rose sued 2 Live Crew and its record company, Luke Skyywalker Records, for copyright infringement. The District Court granted summary judgment for 2 Live Crew. . . .

The Court of Appeals for the Sixth Circuit reversed and remanded. . . .

II . . .

Congress meant §107 "to restate the present judicial doctrine of fair use, not to change, narrow, or enlarge it in any way" and intended that courts continue the common law tradition of fair use adjudication. H. R. Rep. No. 94-1476, p. 66 (1976) (hereinafter House Report); S. Rep. No. 94-473, p. 62 (1975) (hereinafter Senate Report). The fair use doctrine thus "permits [and requires] courts to avoid rigid application of the copyright statute when, on occasion, it would stifle the very creativity which that law is designed to foster." *Stewart v. Abend*, 495 U.S. 207, 236 (1990). . . .

. . . [T]he four statutory factors [may not] be treated in isolation, one from another. All are to be explored, and the results weighed together, in light of the purposes of copyright. *See* Leval[, *Toward a Fair Use Standard*, 103 Harv. L. Rev. 1105,] 1110-1111 [(1990) (hereinafter Leval)]; Patry & Perlmutter, *Fair Use Misconstrued: Profit, Presumptions, and Parody*, 11 Cardozo Arts & Ent. L.J. 667, 685-687 (1993) (hereinafter Patry & Perlmutter).

A

The first factor in a fair use enquiry is "the purpose and character of the use, including whether such use is of a commercial nature or is for nonprofit educational purposes." §107(1). . . . The central purpose of this investigation is to see, in Justice Story's words, whether the new work merely "supersede[s] the objects" of the original creation, *Folsom v. Marsh, supra*, at 348; accord, *Harper & Row, supra*, at 562 ("supplanting" the original), or instead adds something new, with a further purpose or different character, altering the first with new expression, meaning, or message; it asks, in other words, whether and to what extent the new work is "transformative." Leval 1111. Although such transformative use is not absolutely necessary for a finding of fair use, *Sony [Corp. of America v. Universal City Studios, Inc.*, 464 U.S. 417 (1984)], *supra*, at 455, n.40,[11] the goal of copyright, to promote science and the arts, is generally furthered by the creation of transformative works. Such works thus lie at the heart of the fair use doctrine's guarantee of breathing space within the confines of copyright, see, e.g., *Sony, supra*, at 478-80 (Blackmun, J., dissenting), and the more transformative the new work, the less will be the significance of other factors, like commercialism, that may weigh against a finding of fair use.

. . . Suffice it to say now that parody has an obvious claim to transformative value, as Acuff-Rose itself does not deny. Like less ostensibly humorous forms of criticism, it can provide social benefit, by shedding light on an earlier work, and, in the process, creating a new one. . . .

The germ of parody lies in the definition of the Greek *parodeia*, quoted in Judge Nelson's Court of Appeals dissent, as "a song sung alongside another." 972 F.2d, at 1440, quoting 7 Encyclopedia Britannica 768 (15th ed. 1975). Modern dictionaries accordingly describe a parody as a "literary or artistic work that imitates the characteristic style of an author or a work for comic effect or ridicule," or as a "composition in prose or verse in which the characteristic turns of thought and phrase in an author or class of authors are imitated in such a way as to make them appear ridiculous." For the purposes of copyright law, the nub of the definitions, and the heart of any parodist's claim to quote from existing material, is the use of some elements of a prior author's composition to create a new one that, at least in part, comments on that author's works. . . . If, on the contrary, the commentary has no critical bearing on the substance or style of the original composition, which the alleged infringer merely uses to get attention or to avoid the drudgery in working up something fresh, the claim to fairness in borrowing from another's work diminishes accordingly (if it does not vanish), and other factors, like the extent of its commerciality, loom larger.[14] Parody needs to mimic an original to make its point, and so has

11. The obvious statutory exception to this focus on transformative uses is the straight reproduction of multiple copies for classroom distribution.

14. A parody that more loosely targets an original than the parody presented here may still be sufficiently aimed at an original work to come within our analysis of parody. If a parody whose wide dissemination in the market runs the risk of serving as a substitute for the original or licensed derivatives (see *infra*, . . . discussing factor four), it is more incumbent on one claiming fair use to establish the extent of transformation and the parody's critical relationship to the original. . . .

some claim to use the creation of its victim's (or collective victims') imagination, whereas satire can stand on its own two feet and so requires justification for the very act of borrowing.[15] . . .

The fact that parody can claim legitimacy for some appropriation does not, of course, tell either parodist or judge much about where to draw the line. . . . [P]arody, like any other use, has to work its way through the relevant factors, and be judged case by case, in light of the ends of the copyright law.

Here, the District Court held, and the Court of Appeals assumed, that 2 Live Crew's "Pretty Woman" contains parody, commenting on and criticizing the original work, whatever it may have to say about society at large. As the District Court remarked, the words of 2 Live Crew's song copy the original's first line, but then "quickly degenerat[e] into a play on words, substituting predictable lyrics with shocking ones . . . [that] derisively demonstrat[e] how bland and banal the Orbison song seems to them." 754 F. Supp., at 1155 (footnote omitted). . . .

We have less difficulty in finding that critical element in 2 Live Crew's song than the Court of Appeals did, although having found it we will not take the further step of evaluating its quality. The threshold question when fair use is raised in defense of parody is whether a parodic character may reasonably be perceived. Whether, going beyond that, parody is in good taste or bad does not and should not matter to fair use. As Justice Holmes explained, "[i]t would be a dangerous undertaking for persons trained only to the law to constitute themselves final judges of the worth of [a work], outside of the narrowest and most obvious limits. At the one extreme some works of genius would be sure to miss appreciation. Their very novelty would make them repulsive until the public had learned the new language in which their author spoke." *Bleistein v. Donaldson Lithographing Co.*, 188 U.S. 239, 251 (1903) (circus posters have copyright protection); cf. *Yankee Publishing Inc. v. News America Publishing, Inc.*, 809 F. Supp. 267, 280 (SDNY 1992) (Leval, J.) ("First Amendment protections do not apply only to those who speak clearly, whose jokes are funny, and whose parodies succeed.") (trademark case).

While we might not assign a high rank to the parodic element here, we think it fair to say that 2 Live Crew's song reasonably could be perceived as commenting on the original or criticizing it, to some degree. 2 Live Crew juxtaposes the romantic musings of a man whose fantasy comes true, with degrading taunts, a bawdy demand for sex, and a sigh of relief from paternal responsibility. The later words can be taken as a comment on the naivete of the original of an earlier day, as a rejection of its sentiment that ignores the ugliness of street life and the debasement that it signifies. It is this joinder of reference and ridicule that marks off the author's choice of parody from the other types of comment and criticism that traditionally have had a claim to fair use protection as transformative works.[17]

15. Satire has been defined as a work "in which prevalent follies or vices are assailed with ridicule," 14 Oxford English Dictionary [2d ed. 1989], at 500, or are "attacked through irony, derision, or wit," American Heritage Dictionary[3d ed. 1992], at 1604.

17. We note in passing that 2 Live Crew need not label its whole album, or even this song, a parody in order to claim fair use protection, nor should 2 Live Crew be penalized for this being its first parodic essay. Parody serves its goals whether labeled or not, and there is no reason to require parody to state the obvious (or even the reasonably perceived). *See* Patry & Perlmutter 716-717.

The Court of Appeals, however, immediately cut short the enquiry into 2 Live Crew's fair use claim by confining its treatment of the first factor essentially to one relevant fact, the commercial nature of the use. The court then inflated the significance of this fact by applying a presumption ostensibly culled from *Sony*, that "every commercial use of copyrighted material is presumptively . . . unfair. . . ." *Sony*, 464 U.S., at 451. In giving virtually dispositive weight to the commercial nature of the parody, the Court of Appeals erred.

The language of the statute makes clear that the commercial or nonprofit educational purpose of a work is only one element of the first factor enquiry into its purpose and character. Section 107(1) uses the term "including" to begin the dependent clause referring to commercial use, and the main clause speaks of a broader investigation into "purpose and character." As we explained in *Harper & Row*, Congress resisted attempts to narrow the ambit of this traditional enquiry by adopting categories of presumptively fair use, and it urged courts to preserve the breadth of their traditionally ample view of the universe of relevant evidence. . . . Accordingly, the mere fact that a use is educational and not for profit does not insulate it from a finding of infringement, any more than the commercial character of a use bars a finding of fairness. If, indeed, commerciality carried presumptive force against a finding of fairness, the presumption would swallow nearly all of the illustrative uses listed in the preamble paragraph of §107, including news reporting, comment, criticism, teaching, scholarship, and research, since these activities "are generally conducted for profit in this country." *Harper & Row, supra*, at 592 (Brennan, J., dissenting). Congress could not have intended such a rule, which certainly is not inferable from the common-law cases, arising as they did from the world of letters in which Samuel Johnson could pronounce that "[n]o man but a blockhead ever wrote, except for money." 3 Boswell's Life of Johnson 19 (G. Hill ed. 1934).

Sony itself called for no hard evidentiary presumption. There, we emphasized the need for a "sensitive balancing of interests," 464 U.S., at 455 n.40, noted that Congress had "eschewed a rigid, bright-line approach to fair use," *id.*, at 449, n.31, and stated that the commercial or nonprofit educational character of a work is "not conclusive," *id.*, at 448-49, but rather a fact to be "weighed along with other[s] in fair use decisions." *Id.*, at 449, n.32, (quoting House Report, p. 66). The Court of Appeals's elevation of one sentence from *Sony* to a *per se* rule thus runs as much counter to *Sony* itself as to the long common-law tradition of fair use adjudication. Rather, as we explained in *Harper & Row*, *Sony* stands for the proposition that the "fact that a publication was commercial as opposed to nonprofit is a separate factor that tends to weigh against a finding of fair use." 471 U.S., at 562. But that is all, and the fact that even the force of that tendency will vary with the context is a further reason against elevating commerciality to hard presumptive significance. The use, for example, of a copyrighted work to advertise a product, even in a parody, will be entitled to less indulgence under the first factor of the fair use enquiry, than the sale of a parody for its own sake, let alone one performed a single time by students in school. . . .[18]

---

18. Finally, regardless of the weight one might place on the alleged infringer's state of mind, compare *Harper & Row*, 471 U.S., at 562 (fair use presupposes good faith and fair dealing) (quotation marks omitted), with *Folsom v. Marsh*, 9 F. Cas. 342, 349 (No. 4,901) (CCD Mass. 1841) (good faith

B

The second statutory factor, "the nature of the copyrighted work," §107(2), draws on Justice Story's expression, the "value of the materials used." *Folsom v. Marsh*, 9 F. Cas., at 348. This factor calls for recognition that some works are closer to the core of intended copyright protection than others, with the consequence that fair use is more difficult to establish when the former works are copied. . . . [T]he Orbison original's creative expression for public dissemination falls within the core of the copyright's protective purposes. This fact, however, is not much help in this case, or ever likely to help much in separating the fair use sheep from the infringing goats in a parody case, since parodies almost invariably copy publicly known, expressive works.

C

The third factor asks whether "the amount and substantiality of the portion used in relation to the copyrighted work as a whole," §107(3) (or, in Justice Story's words, "the quantity and value of the materials used," *Folsom v. Marsh, supra*, at 348) are reasonable in relation to the purpose of the copying. Here, attention turns to the persuasiveness of a parodist's justification for the particular copying done, and the enquiry will harken back to the first of the statutory factors, for, as in prior cases, we recognize that the extent of permissible copying varies with the purpose and character of the use. . . . The facts bearing on this factor will also tend to address the fourth, by revealing the degree to which the parody may serve as a market substitute for the original or potentially licensed derivatives. *See* Leval 1123.

The District Court considered the song's parodic purpose in finding that 2 Live Crew had not helped themselves overmuch. 754 F. Supp., at 1156-1157. The Court of Appeals disagreed, stating that "[w]hile it may not be inappropriate to find that no more was taken than necessary, the copying was qualitatively substantial. . . . We conclude that taking the heart of the original and making it the heart of a new work was to purloin a substantial portion of the essence of the original." 972 F.2d, at 1438.

The Court of Appeals is of course correct that this factor calls for thought not only about the quantity of the materials used, but about their quality and importance, too. . . .

Where we part company with the court below is in applying these guides to parody, and in particular to parody in the song before us. Parody presents a difficult case. Parody's humor, or in any event its comment, necessarily springs from recognizable allusion to its object through distorted imitation. Its art lies in the tension between a known original and its parodic twin. When parody takes aim at a particular

---

does not bar a finding of infringement); Leval 1126-1127 (good faith irrelevant to fair use analysis), we reject Acuff-Rose's argument that 2 Live Crew's request for permission to use the original should be weighed against a finding of fair use. Even if good faith were central to fair use, 2 Live Crew's actions do not necessarily suggest that they believed their version was not fair use; the offer may simply have been made in a good faith effort to avoid this litigation. If the use is otherwise fair, then no permission need be sought or granted. Thus, being denied permission to use a work does not weigh against a finding of fair use. *See Fisher v. Dees*, 794 F.2d 432, 437 (CA9 1986).

original work, the parody must be able to "conjure up" at least enough of that original to make the object of its critical wit recognizable. . . .

We think the Court of Appeals was insufficiently appreciative of parody's need for the recognizable sight or sound when it ruled 2 Live Crew's use unreasonable as a matter of law. It is true, of course, that 2 Live Crew copied the characteristic opening bass riff (or musical phrase) of the original, and true that the words of the first line copy the Orbison lyrics. But if quotation of the opening riff and the first line may be said to go to the "heart" of the original, the heart is also what most readily conjures up the song for parody, and it is the heart at which parody takes aim. Copying does not become excessive in relation to parodic purpose merely because the portion taken was the original's heart. If 2 Live Crew had copied a significantly less memorable part of the original, it is difficult to see how its parodic character would have come through. . . .

This is not, of course, to say that anyone who calls himself a parodist can skim the cream and get away scot free. In parody, as in news reporting, see *Harper & Row, supra*, context is everything, and the question of fairness asks what else the parodist did besides go to the heart of the original. It is significant that 2 Live Crew not only copied the first line of the original, but thereafter departed markedly from the Orbison lyrics for its own ends. 2 Live Crew not only copied the bass riff and repeated it,[19] but also produced otherwise distinctive sounds, interposing "scraper" noise, overlaying the music with solos in different keys, and altering the drum beat. *See* 754 F. Supp., at 1155. This is not a case, then, where "a substantial portion" of the parody itself is composed of a "verbatim" copying of the original. It is not, that is, a case where the parody is so insubstantial, as compared to the copying, that the third factor must be resolved as a matter of law against the parodists.

Suffice it to say here that, as to the lyrics, we think the Court of Appeals correctly suggested that "no more was taken than necessary," 972 F.2d, at 1438, but just for that reason, we fail to see how the copying can be excessive in relation to its parodic purpose, even if the portion taken is the original's "heart." As to the music, we express no opinion whether repetition of the bass riff is excessive copying, and we remand to permit evaluation of the amount taken, in light of the song's parodic purpose and character, its transformative elements, and considerations of the potential for market substitution sketched more fully below.

D

The fourth fair use factor is "the effect of the use upon the potential market for or value of the copyrighted work." §107(4). . . . The enquiry "must take account not only of harm to the original but also of harm to the market for derivative works." *Harper & Row, supra*, at 568.

Since fair use is an affirmative defense, its proponent would have difficulty carrying the burden of demonstrating fair use without favorable evidence about

---

19. This may serve to heighten the comic effect of the parody, as one witness stated . . . or serve to dazzle with the original's music, as Acuff-Rose now contends.

relevant markets.[21] In moving for summary judgment, 2 Live Crew left themselves at just such a disadvantage when they failed to address the effect on the market for rap derivatives, and confined themselves to uncontroverted submissions that there was no likely effect on the market for the original. They did not, however, thereby subject themselves to the evidentiary presumption applied by the Court of Appeals. . . . [T]he court resolved the fourth factor against 2 Live Crew, just as it had the first, by applying a presumption about the effect of commercial use, a presumption which as applied here we hold to be error.

No "presumption" or inference of market harm that might find support in *Sony* is applicable to a case involving something beyond mere duplication for commercial purposes. *Sony*'s discussion of a presumption contrasts a context of verbatim copying of the original in its entirety for commercial purposes, with the non-commercial context of *Sony* itself (home copying of television programming). In the former circumstances, what *Sony* said simply makes common sense: when a commercial use amounts to mere duplication of the entirety of an original, it clearly "supersede[s] the objects," *Folsom v. Marsh, supra,* at 348, of the original and serves as a market replacement for it, making it likely that cognizable market harm to the original will occur. *Sony, supra,* at 451. But when, on the contrary, the second use is transformative, market substitution is at least less certain, and market harm may not be so readily inferred. Indeed, as to parody pure and simple, it is more likely that the new work will not affect the market for the original in a way cognizable under this factor, that is, by acting as a substitute for it ("supersed[ing] [its] objects"). *See* Leval 1125; Patry & Perlmutter 692, 697-698. This is so because the parody and the original usually serve different market functions. . . .

We do not, of course, suggest that a parody may not harm the market at all, but when a lethal parody, like a scathing theater review, kills demand for the original, it does not produce a harm cognizable under the Copyright Act. Because "parody may quite legitimately aim at garroting the original, destroying it commercially as well as artistically," B. Kaplan, An Unhurried View of Copyright 69 (1967), the role of the courts is to distinguish between "[b]iting criticism [that merely] suppresses demand [and] copyright infringement[, which] usurps it." *Fisher v. Dees*, 794 F.2d, at 438.

This distinction between potentially remediable displacement and unremediable disparagement is reflected in the rule that there is no protectible derivative market for criticism. The market for potential derivative uses includes only those that creators of original works would in general develop or license others to develop. Yet the unlikelihood that creators of imaginative works will license critical reviews or lampoons of their own productions removes such uses from the very notion of a potential licensing market. "People ask . . . for criticism, but they only want praise." S. Maugham, Of Human Bondage 241 (Penguin ed. 1992). Thus, to the extent that

---

21. Even favorable evidence, without more, is no guarantee of fairness. Judge Leval gives the example of the film producer's appropriation of a composer's previously unknown song that turns the song into a commercial success; the boon to the song does not make the film's simple copying fair. Leval 1124, n.84. This factor, no less than the other three, may be addressed only through a "sensitive balancing of interests." *Sony* . . . [at] 455, n.40. . . . Market harm is a matter of degree, and the importance of this factor will vary, not only with the amount of harm, but also with the relative strength of the showing on the other factors.

the opinion below may be read to have considered harm to the market for parodies of "Oh, Pretty Woman," the court erred.[22] . . .

. . . 2 Live Crew's song comprises not only parody but also rap music, and the derivative market for rap music is a proper focus of enquiry, see *Harper & Row, supra*, at 568. . . . Evidence of substantial harm to it would weigh against a finding of fair use, because the licensing of derivatives is an important economic incentive to the creation of originals. *See* 17 U.S.C. §106(2) (copyright owner has rights to derivative works). Of course, the only harm to derivatives that need concern us, as discussed above, is the harm of market substitution. The fact that a parody may impair the market for derivative uses by the very effectiveness of its critical commentary is no more relevant under copyright than the like threat to the original market.[24]

Although 2 Live Crew submitted uncontroverted affidavits on the question of market harm to the original, neither they, nor Acuff-Rose, introduced evidence or affidavits addressing the likely effect of 2 Live Crew's parodic rap song on the market for a non-parody, rap version of "Oh, Pretty Woman." And while Acuff-Rose would have us find evidence of a rap market in the very facts that 2 Live Crew recorded a rap parody of "Oh, Pretty Woman" and another rap group sought a license to record a rap derivative, there was no evidence that a potential rap market was harmed in any way by 2 Live Crew's parody, rap version. . . . The evidentiary hole will doubtless be plugged on remand. . . .

NOTES AND QUESTIONS

1. How does the Court's analysis of the first and fourth statutory factors compare to that in *Harper & Row*? Are the two decisions consistent? Why not require 2 Live Crew to pay the "customary price" before profiting from its treatment of the song?

2. Does the Court's distinction between parody and satire make sense? If the fair use doctrine prizes "transformative" uses, why bother to make such a distinction?

Justice Kennedy's concurring opinion expressed doubt about whether 2 Live Crew's song was "legitimate parody," and noted that the Court's opinion left the issue open for the District Court on remand. Do you share Justice Kennedy's concern? How does one prove that the "parodic nature" of a work "may reasonably be perceived"? Whose perception matters? If it is the trier of fact's perception that matters, how does one apply the test laid out by the Court while remaining true to the aesthetic nondiscrimination principle?

---

22. We express no opinion as to the derivative markets for works using elements of an original as vehicles for satire or amusement, making no comment on the original or criticism of it.

24. In some cases it may be difficult to determine whence the harm flows. In such cases, the other fair use factors may provide some indicia of the likely source of the harm. A work whose overriding purpose and character is parodic and whose borrowing is slight in relation to its parody will be far less likely to cause cognizable harm than a work with little parodic content and much copying.

3. How persuaded are you by the Court's analysis of the third statutory factor? Does this analysis seem to be informed by the analysis of the fourth factor, as in *Harper & Row*? By any other factor?

4. The Court indicates that a defendant will have difficulty proving that the fourth fair use factor supports a finding of fair use without "favorable evidence about relevant markets." For the defendant, favorable evidence means evidence of little or no harm to the market for the plaintiff's work or to protectible derivative markets. How is the defendant to prove this? For example, how is 2 Live Crew to prove no harm to "the market for [non-parodic] rap derivatives"?

5. The *Campbell* Court states that fair use is an affirmative defense, and that the burden is on the defendant to prove facts that support the defense. Section 106 states that the rights granted to copyright owners are "subject to" §107, while §107 states that a use that qualifies as fair "is not an infringement of copyright." Does this statutory language support the characterization of fair use as an affirmative defense? Do the policies underlying copyright law support placing the burden of proving fair use on the defendant? For discussion of the evolution of fair use see Ned Snow, *The Forgotten Right of Fair Use*, 62 Case West. Res. L. Rev. 135 (2011).

6. Note that *Campbell* was decided on defendants' motion for summary judgment. Fair use is a mixed question of law and fact. In many cases, the underlying facts—how much of the plaintiff's work has been copied, how many copies of defendant's work were sold, etc.—are not in dispute. The dispute involves how to characterize those activities and how to weigh them using the fair use factors. When is summary judgment on the issue of fair use appropriate? The Court has held that the Seventh Amendment right to jury trial applies to copyright infringement cases. *Feltner v. Columbia Pictures Television*, 523 U.S. 340 (1998). In tort law, application of the law to undisputed facts is often reserved for the jury. *See, e.g., Sioux City & Pacific R.R. v. Stout*, 84 U.S. 657 (1873). Is determination of whether the defendant's use was fair similar to determination of whether the defendant's conduct was reasonable in tort law?

AFTERMATH

On remand, the parties in *Campbell* agreed to a settlement that gave 2 Live Crew a license to use "Oh, Pretty Woman." *See* Stan Soocher, They Fought the Law: Rock Music Goes to Court 189-91 (1999).

PROBLEM: ADVOCACY

In 2004 Gregg Spiridellis, co-founder of JibJab, a digital entertainment studio, wrote and designed a video titled "This Land" that featured animated versions of presidential candidates George W. Bush and John Kerry singing a parody of Woody Guthrie's song "This Land Is Your Land." (You may view the video at http://www.jibjab.com/originals/this_land.) After a music publishing company claiming to own the Guthrie copyright threatened to sue, JibJab filed a declaratory judgment action asserting that its use of the song was fair. JibJab also asserted that the song had passed into the public domain as a result of failure to renew the copyright. Likely as a result of the latter allegation, the publisher withdrew its objection to JibJab's use of the song and the litigation settled. Imagine that no settlement occurred, and that you represent JibJab. Prepare an outline of a summary judgment motion on the fair use issue.

2. Transformative Use Beyond Parody

Reconciling fair use with the rights of copyright owners to prepare derivative works can be difficult. What other kinds of uses of copyrighted content qualify as "transformative" enough to be fair? Consider the following cases.

 Castle Rock Entertainment, Inc. v. Carol Publishing Group, Inc.
150 F.3d 132 (2d Cir. 1998)

WALKER, JR., J.: . . .

Background

The material facts in this case are undisputed. Plaintiff Castle Rock is the producer and copyright owner of each episode of the *Seinfeld* television series. The series revolves around the petty tribulations in the lives of four single, adult friends in New York: Jerry Seinfeld, George Costanza, Elaine Benes, and Cosmo Kramer. Defendants are Beth Golub, the author, and Carol Publishing Group, Inc., the publisher, of *The SAT*, a 132-page book containing 643 trivia questions and answers about the events and characters depicted in *Seinfeld*. These include 211 multiple choice questions, in which only one out of three to five answers is correct; 93 matching questions; and a number of short-answer questions. The questions are divided into five levels of difficulty, labeled (in increasing order of difficulty) "Wuss Questions," "This, That, and the Other Questions," "Tough Monkey Questions," "Atomic Wedgie Questions," and "Master of Your Domain Questions." Selected examples from level 1 are indicative of the questions throughout *The SAT*:

   1. To impress a woman, George passes himself off as
     a) a gynecologist
     b) a geologist
     c) a marine biologist
     d) a meteorologist
  11. What candy does Kramer snack on while observing a surgical procedure from an operating-room balcony?

12. Who said, "I don't go for those nonrefundable deals . . . I can't commit to a woman . . . I'm not committing to an airline."?
    a) Jerry
    b) George
    c) Kramer

The book draws from 84 of the 86 *Seinfeld* episodes that had been broadcast as of the time *The SAT* was published. Although Golub created the incorrect answers to the multiple choice questions, every question and correct answer has as its source a fictional moment in a *Seinfeld* episode. Forty-one questions and/or answers contain dialogue from *Seinfeld*. The single episode most drawn upon by *The SAT*, "The Cigar Store Indian," is the source of 20 questions that directly quote between 3.6% and 5.6% of that episode (defendants' and plaintiff's calculations, respectively).

The name "Seinfeld" appears prominently on the front and back covers of *The SAT*, and pictures of the principal actors in *Seinfeld* appear on the cover and on several pages of the book. On the back cover, a disclaimer states that "This book has not been approved or licensed by any entity involved in creating or producing *Seinfeld*." The front cover bears the title "The Seinfeld Aptitude Test" and describes the book as containing "[h]undreds of spectacular questions of minute details from TV's greatest show about absolutely nothing." . . .

Golub has described *The SAT* as a "natural outgrowth" of *Seinfeld* which, "like the *Seinfeld* show, is devoted to the trifling, picayune and petty annoyances encountered by the show's characters on a daily basis." According to Golub, she created *The SAT* by taking notes from *Seinfeld* programs at the time they were aired on television and subsequently reviewing videotapes of several of the episodes, as recorded by her or various friends.

The SAT's publication did not immediately provoke a challenge. The National Broadcasting Corporation, which broadcasted *Seinfeld*, requested free copies of *The SAT* from defendants and distributed them together with promotions for the program. *Seinfeld*'s executive producer characterized *The SAT* as "a fun little book." There is no evidence that *The SAT*'s publication diminished *Seinfeld*'s profitability, and in fact *Seinfeld*'s audience grew after *The SAT* was first published.

Castle Rock has nevertheless been highly selective in marketing products associated with *Seinfeld*, rejecting numerous proposals from publishers seeking approval for a variety of projects related to the show. Castle Rock licensed one *Seinfeld* book, *The Entertainment Weekly Seinfeld Companion*, and has licensed the production of a CD-ROM product that includes discussions of *Seinfeld* episodes; the CD-ROM allegedly might ultimately include a trivia bank. Castle Rock claims in this litigation that it plans to pursue a more aggressive marketing strategy for *Seinfeld*-related products, including "publication of books relating to *Seinfeld*."

In November 1994, Castle Rock notified defendants of its copyright and trademark infringement claims. In February 1995, after defendants continued to distribute *The SAT*, Castle Rock filed this action alleging federal copyright and trademark infringement and state law unfair competition. . . . [The district court granted summary judgment to plaintiffs and enjoined publication of *The SAT*; defendants appealed.]

Discussion . . .

III. *Fair Use*

Defendants claim that, even if *The SAT*'s copying of *Seinfeld* constitutes *prima facie* infringement, *The SAT* is nevertheless a fair use of *Seinfeld*. . . .

A. **Purpose/Character of Use . . .**

. . . That *The SAT*'s use is commercial, at most, "tends to weigh against a finding of fair use." *Campbell*, 510 U.S. at 585. . . . But we do not make too much of this point. . . .

The more critical inquiry under the first factor and in fair use analysis generally is whether the allegedly infringing work "merely supersedes" the original work "or instead adds something new, with a further purpose or different character, altering the first with new . . . meaning [ ] or message," in other words "whether and to what extent the new work is 'transformative.' " *Id*. at 579 . . . (quoting Leval at 1111). . . .

. . . [T]he fact that the subject matter of the quiz is plebeian, banal, or ordinary stuff does not alter the fair use analysis. Criticism, comment, scholarship, research, and other potential fair uses are no less protectable because their subject is the ordinary.

. . . [D]efendants style *The SAT* as a work "decod[ing] the obsession with . . . and mystique that surround[s] 'Seinfeld,' " by "critically restructur[ing] [*Seinfeld*'s mystique] into a system complete with varying levels of 'mastery' that relate the reader's control of the show's trivia to knowledge of and identification with their hero, Jerry Seinfeld." Citing one of their own experts for the proposition that "[t]he television environment cannot speak for itself but must be spoken for and about," defendants argue that "*The SAT* is a quintessential example of critical text of the TV environment . . . expos[ing] all of the show's nothingness to articulate its true motive forces and its social and moral dimensions." Castle Rock dismisses these arguments as post hoc rationalizations, claiming that had defendants been half as creative in creating *The SAT* as were their lawyers in crafting these arguments about transformation, defendants might have a colorable fair use claim.

Any transformative purpose possessed by *The SAT* is slight to non-existent. We reject the argument that *The SAT* was created to educate *Seinfeld* viewers or to criticize, "expose," or otherwise comment upon *Seinfeld*. *The SAT*'s purpose, as evidenced definitively by the statements of the book's creators and by the book itself, is to repackage *Seinfeld* to entertain *Seinfeld* viewers. *The SAT*'s back cover makes no mention of exposing *Seinfeld* to its readers, for example, as a pitiably vacuous reflection of a puerile and pervasive television culture, but rather urges *SAT* readers to "open this book to satisfy [their] between-episode [*Seinfeld*] cravings." Golub, *The SAT*'s author, described the trivia quiz book not as a commentary or a *Seinfeld* research tool, but as an effort to "capture Seinfeld's flavor in quiz book fashion." Finally, even viewing *The SAT* in the light most favorable to defendants, we find scant reason to conclude that this trivia quiz book seeks to educate, criticize, parody, comment, report upon, or research *Seinfeld,* or otherwise serve a transformative purpose.[7] The book does not contain commentary or analysis about *Seinfeld*, nor does it suggest how *The SAT* can be used to research *Seinfeld*; rather, the book simply poses trivia questions. *The SAT*'s plain purpose, therefore, is not to expose *Seinfeld*'s "nothingness," but to satiate *Seinfeld* fans' passion for the "nothingness" that *Seinfeld* has elevated into the realm of protectable creative expression.

Although a secondary work need not necessarily transform the original work's expression to have a transformative purpose . . . the fact that *The SAT* so minimally alters *Seinfeld*'s original expression in this case is further evidence of *The SAT*'s lack of transformative purpose. To be sure, the act of testing trivia about a creative work, in question and answer form, involves some creative expression. While still minimal, it does require posing the questions and hiding the correct answer among three or four incorrect ones.[8] Also, dividing the trivia questions into increasing levels of difficulty is somewhat more original than arranging names in a telephone book in alphabetical order. *See Feist*, 499 U.S. at 362-63. *The SAT*'s incorrect multiple choice answers are also original. However, the work as a whole, drawn directly from the *Seinfeld* episodes without substantial alteration, is far less transformative than other works we have held not to constitute fair use. . . .

B. Nature of the Copyrighted Work

. . . Defendants concede that the scope of fair use is somewhat narrower with respect to fictional works, such as *Seinfeld*, than to factual works. Although this factor may be of less (or even of no) importance when assessed in the context of certain transformative uses the fictional nature of the copyrighted work remains significant in the instant case, where the secondary use is at best minimally transformative. Thus, the second statutory factor favors the plaintiff.

C. Amount and Substantiality of the Portion Used in Relation to the Copyrighted Work as a Whole . . .

In *Campbell* . . . the Supreme Court clarified that the third factor . . . must be examined in context. The inquiry must focus upon whether "[t]he extent of . . . copying" is consistent with or more than necessary to further "the purpose and character of the use." 510 U.S. at 586-87. . . .

In the instant case, it could be argued that *The SAT* could not expose *Seinfeld*'s "nothingness" without repeated, indeed exhaustive examples deconstructing *Seinfeld*'s humor, thereby emphasizing *Seinfeld*'s meaninglessness to *The SAT*'s readers. That *The SAT* posed as many as 643 trivia questions to make this rather straightforward point, however, suggests that *The SAT*'s purpose was entertainment, not commentary. Such an argument has not been advanced on appeal, but

7. Had *The SAT*'s incorrect answer choices attempted to parody *Seinfeld*, for example, defendants would have a stronger case for fair use. . . .

8. In the time it took to write this last sentence, for example, one could have easily created the following trivia question about the film trilogy *Star Wars:* "Luke Skywalker was aghast to learn that Darth Vader was Luke's (a) father (b) father-in-law (c) best friend (d) Jerry Seinfeld," and innumerable other such trivia questions about original creative works.

if it had been, it would not disturb our conclusion that, under any fair reading, *The SAT* does not serve a critical or otherwise transformative purpose. Accordingly, the third factor weighs against fair use.

D. Effect of Use Upon Potential Market for or Value of Copyrighted Work . . .

In considering the fourth factor, our concern is not whether the secondary use suppresses or even destroys the market for the original work or its potential derivatives, but whether the secondary use usurps or substitutes for the market of the original work. [*Campbell*, 510 U.S.] at 593. . . .

Unlike parody, criticism, scholarship, news reporting, or other transformative uses, *The SAT* substitutes for a derivative market that a television program copyright owner such as Castle Rock "would in general develop or license others to develop." *Campbell*, 510 U.S. at 592.[11] Because *The SAT* borrows exclusively from *Seinfeld* and not from any other television or entertainment programs, *The SAT* is likely to fill a market niche that Castle Rock would in general develop. Moreover, as noted by the district court, this "*Seinfeld* trivia game is not critical of the program, nor does it parody the program; if anything, *SAT* pays homage to *Seinfeld*." Although Castle Rock has evidenced little if any interest in exploiting this market for derivative works based on *Seinfeld,* such as by creating and publishing *Seinfeld* trivia books (or at least trivia books that endeavor to "satisfy" the "between-episode cravings" of *Seinfeld* lovers), the copyright law must respect that creative and economic choice. . . . The fourth statutory factor therefore favors Castle Rock. . . .

Bill Graham Archives v. Dorling Kindersley, Ltd.
448 F.3d 605 (2d Cir. 2006)

RESTANI, J.: . . .

In October of 2003, [Dorling Kindersley ("DK")] published *Grateful Dead: The Illustrated Trip* ("Illustrated Trip"), in collaboration with Grateful Dead Productions, intended as a cultural history of the Grateful Dead. The resulting 480-page coffee table book tells the story of the Grateful Dead along a timeline running continuously through the book, chronologically combining over 2,000 images representing dates in the Grateful Dead's history with explanatory text. A typical page of the book features a collage of images, text, and graphic art designed to

---

11. Just as secondary users may not exploit markets that original copyright owners would "in general develop or license others to develop" even if those owners had not actually done so, copyright owners may not preempt exploitation of transformative markets, which they would not "*in general* develop or license others to develop," by actually developing or licensing others to develop those markets. Thus, by developing or licensing a market for parody, news reporting, educational or other transformative uses of its own creative work, a copyright owner plainly cannot prevent others from entering those fair use markets. *See* 4 Nimmer §13.05[A][4], at 13-181-13-182 (recognizing "danger of circularity" where original copyright owner redefines "potential market" by developing or licensing others to develop that market). . . .

simultaneously capture the eye and inform the reader. Plaintiff [Bill Graham Archives ("BGA" or "Appellant")] claims to own the copyright to seven images displayed in *Illustrated Trip*, which DK reproduced without BGA's permission.

Initially, DK sought permission from BGA to reproduce the images. In May of 2003, the CEO of Grateful Dead Productions sent a letter to BGA seeking permission. . . . BGA responded by offering permission in exchange for Grateful Dead Productions' grant of permission to BGA to make CDs and DVDs out of concert footage in BGA's archives. Next, DK directly contacted BGA seeking to negotiate a license agreement, but the parties disagreed as to an appropriate license fee. Nevertheless, DK proceeded with publication of *Illustrated Trip* without entering a license fee agreement with BGA. Specifically, DK reproduced seven artistic images originally depicted on Grateful Dead event posters and tickets. BGA's seven images are displayed in significantly reduced form and are accompanied by captions describing the concerts they represent.

When DK refused to meet BGA's post-publication license fee demands, BGA filed suit for copyright infringement. . . . [T]he district court determined that DK's reproduction of the images was fair use and granted DK's motion for summary judgment.

Discussion

I. *Purpose and Character of Use . . .*

[W]e agree with the district court that DK's actual use of each image is transformatively different from the original expressive purpose. Preliminarily, we recognize, as the district court did, that *Illustrated Trip* is a biographical work documenting the 30-year history of the Grateful Dead. While there are no categories of presumptively fair use, *see Campbell v. Acuff-Rose Music, Inc.*, 510 U.S. at 584 . . . courts have frequently afforded fair use protection to the use of copyrighted material in biographies, recognizing such works as forms of historic scholarship, criticism, and comment that require incorporation of original source material for optimum treatment of their subjects. . . . No less a recognition of biographical value is warranted in this case simply because the subject made a mark in pop culture rather than some other area of human endeavor. . . .

In the instant case, DK's purpose in using the copyrighted images at issue in its biography of the Grateful Dead is plainly different from the original purpose for which they were created. Originally, each of BGA's images fulfilled the dual purposes of artistic expression and promotion. The posters were apparently widely distributed to generate public interest in the Grateful Dead and to convey information to a large number [of] people about the band's forthcoming concerts. In contrast, DK used each of BGA's images as historical artifacts to document and represent the actual occurrence of Grateful Dead concert events featured on *Illustrated Trip*'s timeline.

In some instances, it is readily apparent that DK's image display enhances the reader's understanding of the biographical text. In other instances, the link between image and text is less obvious; nevertheless, the images still serve as historical artifacts graphically representing the fact of significant Grateful Dead concert events selected by the *Illustrated Trip*'s author for inclusion in the book's timeline. We conclude that both types of uses fulfill DK's transformative purpose of enhancing the biographical information in *Illustrated Trip,* a purpose separate and distinct from the original artistic and promotional purpose for which the images were created. . . . [B]ecause DK's use of the disputed images is transformative both when accompanied by referencing commentary and when standing alone, we agree with the district court that DK was not required to discuss the artistic merits of the images to satisfy this first factor of fair use analysis.

This conclusion is strengthened by the manner in which DK displayed the images. First, DK significantly reduced the size of the reproductions. . . . While the small size is sufficient to permit readers to recognize the historical significance of the posters, it is inadequate to offer more than a glimpse of their expressive value. In short, DK used the minimal image size necessary to accomplish its transformative purpose.

Second, DK minimized the expressive value of the reproduced images by combining them with a prominent timeline, textual material, and original graphical artwork, to create a collage of text and images on each page of the book. To further this collage effect, the images are displayed at angles and the original graphical artwork is designed to blend with the images and text. Overall, DK's layout ensures that the images at issue are employed only to enrich the presentation of the cultural history of the Grateful Dead, not to exploit copyrighted artwork for commercial gain. . . .

Third, BGA's images constitute an inconsequential portion of *Illustrated Trip.* The extent to which unlicensed material is used in the challenged work can be a factor in determining whether a biographer's use of original materials has been sufficiently transformative to constitute fair use. . . . Although our circuit has counseled against considering the percentage the allegedly infringing work comprises of the copyrighted work in conducting *third-factor* fair use analysis, . . . several courts have done so, *see, e.g., Harper,* 471 U.S. at 565-66 . . . (finding the fact that quotes from President Ford's unpublished memoirs played a central role in the allegedly infringing magazine article, constituting 13% of that article, weighed against a finding of fair use). . . . We find this inquiry more relevant in the context of *first-factor* fair use analysis.

In the instant case, the book is 480 pages long, while the BGA images appear on only seven pages. Although the original posters range in size from 13"×19" to more than 19"×27", the largest reproduction of a BGA image in *Illustrated Trip* is less than 3"×4½", less than 1/20 the size of the original. And no BGA image takes up more than one-eighth of a page in a book or is given more prominence than any other image on the page. In total, the images account for less than one-fifth of one percent of the book. . . . [W]e are aware of no case where such an insignificant taking was found to be an unfair use of original materials.

Finally, as to this first factor, we briefly address the commercial nature of *Illustrated Trip.* . . . Even though *Illustrated Trip* is a commercial venture, we recognize that "nearly all of the illustrative uses listed in the preamble paragraph of §107 . . . are generally conducted for profit. . . ." *Campbell,* 510 U.S. at 584. . . . Moreover, "[t]he crux of the profit/nonprofit distinction is not whether the sole motive of the use is monetary gain but whether the user stands to profit from exploitation of the copyrighted material without paying the customary price." *Harper,* 471 U.S. at 562. . . . Here, *Illustrated Trip* does not exploit the use of BGA's images as such for commercial gain. Significantly, DK has not used any of BGA's images in its commercial advertising or in any other way to promote the sale of the book. *Illustrated Trip* merely uses pictures and text to describe the life of the Grateful Dead. By design, the use of BGA's images is incidental to the commercial biographical value of the book. . . .

II. Nature of the Copyrighted Work . . .

We agree with the district court that the creative nature of artistic images typically weighs in favor of the copyright holder. We recognize, however, that the second factor may be of limited usefulness where the creative work of art is being used for a transformative purpose. . . . Here, we conclude that DK is using BGA's images for the transformative purpose of enhancing the biographical information provided in *Illustrated Trip.* Accordingly, we hold that even though BGA's images are creative works, which are a core concern of copyright protection, the second factor has limited weight in our analysis because the purpose of DK's use was to emphasize the images' historical rather than creative value.

III. Amount and Substantiality of the Portion Used . . .

The district court determined that even though the images are reproduced in their entirety, the third fair use factor weighs in favor of DK because the images are displayed in reduced size and scattered among many other images and texts. In faulting this conclusion, Appellant contends that the amount used is substantial because the images are copied in their entirety. Neither our court nor any of our sister circuits has ever ruled that the copying of an entire work *favors* fair use. At the same time, however, courts have concluded that such copying does not necessarily weigh against fair use because copying the entirety of a work is sometimes necessary to make a fair use of the image.

Here, DK used BGA's images because the posters and tickets were historical artifacts that could document Grateful Dead concert events and provide a visual context for the accompanying text. To accomplish this use, DK displayed reduced versions of the original images and intermingled these visuals with text and original graphic art. As a consequence, even though the copyrighted images are copied in their entirety, the visual impact of their artistic expression is significantly limited because of their reduced size. . . .

IV. Effect of the Use Upon the Market for or Value of the Original . . .

In the instant case, the parties agree that DK's use of the images did not impact BGA's primary market for the sale of the poster images. Instead, we look to whether

DK's unauthorized use usurps BGA's potential to develop a derivative market. Appellant argues that DK interfered with the market for licensing its images for use in books. Appellant contends that there is an established market for licensing its images and it suffered both the loss of royalty revenue directly from DK and the opportunity to obtain royalties from others. . . .

[W]e look at the impact on potential licensing revenues for "traditional, reasonable, or likely to be developed markets." [*American Geophysical Union v.*] *Texaco,* [*Inc.*] 60 F.3d [913,] at 930 [(2d Cir. 1995)]. In order to establish a traditional license market, Appellant points to the fees paid to other copyright owners for the reproduction of their images in *Illustrated Trip*. Moreover, Appellant asserts that it established a market for licensing its images, and in this case expressed a willingness to license images to DK. Neither of these arguments shows impairment to a traditional, as opposed to a transformative market. . . .

Here . . . we hold that DK's use of BGA's images is transformatively different from their original expressive purpose. In a case such as this, a copyright holder cannot prevent others from entering fair use markets merely "by developing or licensing a market for parody, news reporting, educational or other transformative uses of its own creative work." *Castle Rock,* 150 F.3d at 146 n. 11. "[C]opyright owners may not preempt exploitation of transformative markets. . . ." *Id*. Moreover, a publisher's willingness to pay license fees for reproduction of images does not establish that the publisher may not, in the alternative, make fair use of those images. *Campbell,* 510 U.S. at 585, n.18 . . . (stating that "being denied permission to use [or pay license fees for] a work does not weigh against a finding of fair use"). Since DK's use of BGA's images falls within a transformative market, BGA does not suffer market harm due to the loss of license fees. . . .

NOTES AND QUESTIONS

1. Are *Castle Rock* and *Bill Graham Archives* consistent with one another? Are they consistent with *Harper & Row* and *Campbell*? *Campbell* notwithstanding, do these courts appear to be applying a standard based on aesthetic merit to determine which arguably "derivative" uses warrant protection under the fair use doctrine?

2. Do you agree that DK's use of BGA's images was transformative? Should courts treat the inclusion of images in a biographical account differently from the inclusion of text? Note the *BGA* court's conclusion that DK minimized its use of the expressive aspect of the images by reducing their size. Should that matter? If DK had reproduced full-page versions of the images, should the fair use analysis be different?

3. In *Ty, Inc. v. Publications International Ltd.*, 292 F.3d 512 (7th Cir. 2002), *cert. denied*, 537 U.S. 1110 (2003), the manufacturer of "Beanie Babies" brought a copyright infringement action against a publisher of Beanie Babies collectors' guides. The court distinguished "copying that is complementary to the copyrighted work (in the sense that nails are complements of hammers)" from "copying that is a substitute for the copyrighted work (in the sense that nails are substitutes for pegs or screws), or for derivative works from the copyrighted work." *Id*. at 517. It held that complementary copying is fair use while substitutional copying is not. *Id*. at 517-18.

Do you think this is a helpful way to distinguish between uses that are fair and uses that infringe on the copyright owner's right to prepare derivative works? How would the complements-substitutes distinction apply to *The SAT*?

Cariou v. Prince
714 F.3d 694 (2d. Cir. 2013)

PARKER, J.: . . .

Background

. . . Cariou is a professional photographer who, over the course of six years in the mid–1990s, lived and worked among Rastafarians in Jamaica. The relationships that Cariou developed with them allowed him to take a series of portraits and landscape photographs that Cariou published in 2000 in a book titled *Yes Rasta*. As Cariou testified, *Yes Rasta* is "extreme classical photography [and] portraiture," and he did not "want that book to look pop culture at all." Cariou Dep. 187:8–15, Jan. 12, 2010.

Cariou's publisher, PowerHouse Books, Inc., printed 7,000 copies of *Yes Rasta*, in a single printing. Like many, if not most, such works, the book enjoyed limited commercial success. The book is currently out of print. As of January 2010, Power-House had sold 5,791 copies, over sixty percent of which sold below the suggested retail price of sixty dollars. PowerHouse has paid Cariou, who holds the copyrights to the *Yes Rasta* photographs, just over $8,000 from sales of the book. Except for a handful of private sales to personal acquaintants, he has never sold or licensed the individual photographs.

Prince is a well-known appropriation artist. The Tate Gallery has defined appropriation art as "the more or less direct taking over into a work of art a real object or even an existing work of art." J.A. 446. Prince's work, going back to the mid–1970s, has involved taking photographs and other images that others have produced and incorporating them into paintings and collages that he then presents, in a different context, as his own. He is a leading exponent of this genre and his work has been displayed in museums around the world, including New York's Solomon R. Guggenheim Museum and Whitney Museum, San Francisco's Museum of Modern Art, Rotterdam's Museum Boijmans van Beuningen, and Basel's Museum fur Gegenwartskunst. As Prince has described his work, he "completely tr[ies] to change [another artist's work] into something that's completely different." Prince Dep. 338:4–8, Oct. 6, 2009.

> **LOOKING BACK**
>
> Recall from Chapter 8 that the Berne Convention requires member states to grant authors the right to protect the integrity of their works. As described by Article 6*bis*, the right of integrity includes the right to object to modifications of the copyrighted work, and also to any "distortion" or "mutilation" of the work. Under U.S. copyright law, such modifications, distortion, or mutilation may be excused by the fair use doctrine.

Prince first came across a copy of *Yes Rasta* in a bookstore in St. Barth's in 2005. Between December 2007 and February 2008, Prince had a show at the Eden Rock hotel in St. Barth's that included a collage, titled *Canal Zone (2007)*, comprising 35 photographs torn out of *Yes Rasta* and pinned to a piece of plywood. Prince altered those photographs significantly, by among other things painting "lozenges" over their subjects' facial features and using only portions of some of the images. In June 2008, Prince purchased three additional copies of *Yes Rasta*. He went on to create thirty additional artworks in the *Canal Zone* series, twenty-nine of which incorporated partial or whole images from *Yes Rasta*. The portions of *Yes Rasta* photographs used, and the amount of each artwork that they constitute, vary significantly from piece to piece. In certain works, such as *James Brown Disco Ball*, Prince affixed headshots from *Yes Rasta* onto other appropriated images, all of which Prince placed on a canvas that he had painted. In these, Cariou's work is almost entirely obscured. The Prince artworks also incorporate photographs that have been enlarged or tinted, and incorporate photographs appropriated from artists other than Cariou as well. *Yes Rasta* is a book of photographs measuring approximately 9.5″ x 12″. Prince's artworks, in contrast, comprise inkjet printing and acrylic paint, as well as pasted-on elements, and are several times that size. For instance, *Graduation* measures 72 3/4″ x 52 1/2″ and *James Brown Disco Ball* 100 1/2″ x 104 1/2″. The smallest of the Prince artworks measures 40″ x 30″, or approximately ten times as large as each page of *Yes Rasta*.

Patrick Cariou, photographs from *Yes Rasta*, pp. 11, 59

Richard Prince, James Brown Disco Ball

In other works, such as *Graduation*, Cariou's original work is readily apparent: Prince did little more than paint blue lozenges over the subject's eyes and mouth, and paste a picture of a guitar over the subject's body.

Between November 8 and December 20, 2008, the [Tate] Gallery put on a show featuring twenty-two of Prince's *Canal Zone* artworks, and also published and sold an exhibition catalog from the show. The catalog included all of the *Canal Zone* artworks (including those not in the Gagosian show) except for one, as well as, among other things, photographs showing *Yes Rasta* photographs in Prince's studio. Prince never sought or received permission from Cariou to use his photographs.

Prior to the Gagosian show, in late August, 2008, a gallery owner named Cristiane Celle contacted Cariou and asked if he would be interested in discussing the

Patrick Cariou, photographs from *Yes Rasta*, pp. 118

Richard Prince, Graduation

possibility of an exhibit in New York City. . . . The two subsequently met and discussed Cariou's exhibiting work in Celle's gallery, including prints from *Yes Rasta*. They did not select a date or photographs to exhibit, nor did they finalize any other details about the possible future show.

At some point during the *Canal Zone* show at Gagosian, Celle learned that Cariou's photographs were "in the show with Richard Prince." Celle then phoned Cariou and, when he did not respond, Celle mistakenly concluded that he was "doing something with Richard Prince. . . ." At that point, Celle decided that she would not put on a "Rasta show" because it had been "done already." . . .

According to Cariou, he learned about the Gagosian *Canal Zone* show from Celle in December 2008. On December 30, 2008, he sued Prince, the Gagosian Gallery, and Lawrence Gagosian, raising claims of copyright infringement. The defendants asserted a fair use defense, arguing that Prince's artworks are transformative of Cariou's photographs and, accordingly, do not violate Cariou's copyrights. . . . Ruling on the parties' subsequently filed cross-motions for summary judgment, the district court . . . "impose[d] a requirement that the new work in some way comment on, relate to the historical context of, or critically refer back to the original works" in order to be qualify as fair use, and stated that "Prince's Paintings are transformative only to the extent that they comment on the Photos." *Cariou v. Prince*, 784 F. Supp. 2d 337, 348-49 (S.D.N.Y. 2011). The court concluded that "Prince did not intend to comment on Cariou, on Cariou's Photos, or on aspects of popular culture closely associated with Cariou or the Photos when he appropriated the Photos," . . . and for that reason rejected the defendants' fair use defense. . . .

Discussion . . .

II

The purpose of the copyright law is "[t]o promote the Progress of Science and useful Arts. . . ." U.S. Const., Art. I, §8, cl. 8. As Judge Pierre Leval of this court has explained, "[t]he copyright is not an inevitable, divine, or natural right that confers on authors the absolute ownership of their creations. It is designed rather to stimulate activity and progress in the arts for the intellectual enrichment of the public." Pierre N. Leval, *Toward a Fair Use Standard*, 103 Harv. L. Rev. 1105, 1107 (1990) (hereinafter "Leval"). Fair use is "necessary to fulfill [that] very purpose." Because "'excessively broad protection would stifle, rather than advance, the law's objective,'" fair use doctrine "mediates between" "the property rights [copyright law] establishes in creative works, which must be protected up to a point, and the ability of authors, artists, and the rest of us to express them—or ourselves by reference to the works of others, which must be protected up to a point." *Blanch* [*v. Koons*], 467 F.3d, [244] at 250 [2nd Cir. 2006] (brackets omitted) (quoting Leval at 1109). . . .

The first statutory factor to consider, which addresses the manner in which the copied work is used, is "[t]he heart of the fair use inquiry." *Blanch*, 467 F.3d at 251. We ask

> whether the new work merely "supersedes the objects" of the original creation, or instead adds something new, with a further purpose or different character, altering the first with new expression, meaning, or message [,] . . . in other words, whether and to what extent the new work is transformative. . . . [T]ransformative works . . . lie at the heart of the fair use doctrine's guarantee of breathing space. . . .

Campbell [*v. Acuff–Rose Music, Inc.*, 510 U.S. 569,] 579 (1994). . . .

The district court imposed a requirement that, to qualify for a fair use defense, a secondary use must "comment on, relate to the historical context of, or critically refer back to the original works." *Cariou*, 784 F. Supp. 2d at 348. Certainly, many types of fair use, such as satire and parody, invariably comment on an original work and/or on popular culture. . . . Much of Andy Warhol's work, including work incorporating appropriated images of Campbell's soup cans or of Marilyn Monroe, comments on consumer culture and explores the relationship between celebrity culture and advertising. As even Cariou concedes, however, the district court's legal premise was not correct. The law imposes no requirement that a work comment on the original or its author in order to be considered transformative, and a secondary work may constitute a fair use even if it serves some purpose other than those . . . identified in the preamble to the statute. . . . Instead, as the Supreme Court as well as decisions from our court have emphasized, to qualify as a fair use, a new work generally must alter the original with "new expression, meaning, or message." *Campbell*, 510 U.S. at 579. . . .

Here, our observation of Prince's artworks themselves convinces us of the transformative nature of all but five, which we discuss separately below. These twenty-five of Prince's artworks manifest an entirely different aesthetic from Cariou's photographs. Where Cariou's serene and deliberately composed portraits and landscape photographs depict the natural beauty of Rastafarians and their surrounding environs, Prince's crude and jarring works, on the other hand, are hectic and provocative. Cariou's black-and-white photographs were printed in a 9 1/2″ x 12″ book. Prince has created collages on canvas that incorporate color, feature distorted human and other forms and settings, and measure between ten and nearly a hundred times the size of the photographs. Prince's composition, presentation, scale, color palette, and media are fundamentally different and new compared to the photographs, as is the expressive nature of Prince's work.

Prince's deposition testimony further demonstrates his drastically different approach and aesthetic from Cariou's. Prince testified that he "[doesn't] have any really interest in what [another artist's] original intent is because . . . what I do is I completely try to change it into something that's completely different. . . . I'm trying to make a kind of fantastic, absolutely hip, up to date, contemporary take on the music scene." Prince Dep. 338:4–339:3, Oct. 6, 2009.

The district court based its conclusion that Prince's work is not transformative in large part on Prince's deposition testimony that he "do[es]n't really have a message," that he was not "trying to create anything with a new meaning or a new message," and that he "do[es]n't have any . . . interest in [Cariou's] original intent." *Cariou*, 784 F. Supp. 2d at 349; *see* Prince Dep. 45:25–46:2, 338:5–6, 360:18–20, Oct. 6, 2009. On appeal, Cariou argues that we must hold Prince to his testimony and that we are not to consider how Prince's works may reasonably be perceived unless Prince claims that they were satire or parody. No such rule exists, and we do not analyze satire or parody differently from any other transformative use.

It is not surprising that, when transformative use is at issue, the alleged infringer would go to great lengths to explain and defend his use as transformative. Prince did not do so here. However, the fact that Prince did not provide those sorts of explanations in his deposition—which might have lent strong support to his defense—is not dispositive. What is critical is how the work in question appears to the reasonable observer, not simply what an artist might say about a particular piece or body of work. Prince's work could be transformative even without commenting on Cariou's work or on culture, and even without Prince's stated intention to do so. Rather than confining our inquiry to Prince's explanations of his artworks, we instead examine how the artworks may "reasonably be perceived" in order to assess their transformative nature. *Campbell*, 510 U.S. at 582. The focus of our infringement analysis is primarily on the Prince artworks themselves, and we see twenty-five of them as transformative as a matter of law. . . .

We turn next to the fourth statutory factor, the effect of the secondary use upon the potential market for the value of the copyrighted work, because such discussion further demonstrates the significant differences between Prince's work, generally, and Cariou's. Much of the district court's conclusion that Prince and Gagosian infringed on Cariou's copyrights was apparently driven by the fact that Celle decided not to host a *Yes Rasta* show at her gallery once she learned of the Gagosian *Canal Zone* show. The district court determined that this factor weighs against Prince because he "has unfairly damaged both the actual and potential markets for Cariou's original work and the potential market for derivative use licenses for Cariou's original work." *Cariou,* 784 F. Supp. 2d at 353.

Contrary to the district court's conclusion, the application of this factor does not focus principally on the question of damage to Cariou's derivative market. We have made clear that "our concern is not whether the secondary use suppresses or even destroys the market for the original work or its potential derivatives, but whether the secondary use *usurps* the market of the original work." *Blanch,* 467 F.3d at 258 (quotation marks omitted) (emphasis added). "The market for potential derivative uses includes only those that creators of original works would in general develop or license others to develop." *Campbell,* 510 U.S. at 592. Our court has concluded that an accused infringer has usurped the market for copyrighted works, including the derivative market, where the infringer's target audience and the nature of the infringing content is the same as the original. For instance, a book of trivia about the television show *Seinfeld* usurped the show's market because the trivia book "substitute[d] for a derivative market that a television program copyright owner . . . would in general develop or license others to develop." *Castle Rock,* 150 F.3d at 145 (quotation marks omitted). Conducting this analysis, we are mindful that "[t]he more transformative the secondary use, the less likelihood that the secondary use substitutes for the original," even though "the fair use, being transformative, might well harm, or even destroy, the market for the original." *Id.*

As discussed above, Celle did not decide against putting on a *Yes Rasta* show because it had already been done at Gagosian, but rather because she mistakenly believed that Cariou had collaborated with Prince on the Gagosian show. Although certain of Prince's artworks contain significant portions of certain of Cariou's photographs, neither Prince nor the *Canal Zone* show usurped the market for those photographs. Prince's audience is very different from Cariou's, and there is no evidence that Prince's work ever touched—much less usurped—either the primary or derivative market for Cariou's work. There is nothing in the record to suggest that Cariou would ever develop or license secondary uses of his work in the vein of Prince's artworks. . . . Indeed, Cariou has not aggressively marketed his work, and has earned just over $8,000 in royalties from *Yes Rasta* since its publication. . . .

Prince's work appeals to an entirely different sort of collector than Cariou's. Certain of the *Canal Zone* artworks have sold for two million or more dollars. The invitation list for a dinner that Gagosian hosted in conjunction with the opening of the *Canal Zone* show included a number of the wealthy and famous such as the musicians Jay–Z and Beyonce Knowles, artists Damien Hirst and Jeff Koons, professional football player Tom Brady, model Gisele Bundchen, *Vanity Fair* editor Graydon Carter, *Vogue* editor Anna Wintour, authors Jonathan Franzen and Candace Bushnell, and actors Robert DeNiro, Angelina Jolie, and Brad Pitt. Prince sold eight artworks for a total of $10,480,000, and exchanged seven others for works by painter Larry Rivers and by sculptor Richard Serra. Cariou on the other hand has not actively marketed his work or sold work for significant sums, and nothing in the record suggests that anyone will not now purchase Cariou's work, or derivative non-transformative works (whether Cariou's own or licensed by him) as a result of the market space that Prince's work has taken up. This fair use factor therefore weighs in Prince's favor.

The next statutory factor that we consider, the nature of the copyrighted work, "calls for recognition that some works are closer to the core of intended copyright protection than others, with the consequence that fair use is more difficult to establish when the former works are copied." *Campbell,* 510 U.S. at 586. . . .

Here, there is no dispute that Cariou's work is creative and published. Accordingly, this factor weighs against a fair use determination. However, just as with the commercial character of Prince's work, this factor "may be of limited usefulness where," as here, "the creative work of art is being used for a transformative purpose." *Bill Graham Archives v. Dorling Kindersley Ltd.,* 448 F.3d 605, 612 (2d Cir. 2006).

The final factor that we consider in our fair use inquiry is "the amount and substantiality of the portion used in relation to the copyrighted work as a whole." 17 U.S.C. §107(3). We ask "whether the quantity and value of the materials used[ ] are reasonable in relation to the purpose of the copying." *Blanch,* 467 F.3d at 257 (quotation marks omitted). In other words, we consider the proportion of the original work used, and not how much of the secondary work comprises the original. . . .

The district court determined that Prince's "taking was substantially greater than necessary." *Cariou,* 784 F. Supp. 2d at 352. We are not clear as to how the district court could arrive at such a conclusion. In any event, the law does not require that the secondary artist may take no more than is necessary. *See Campbell,* 510 U.S. at 588. We consider not only the quantity of the materials taken but also "their quality and importance" to the original work. *Campbell,* 510 U.S. at 587. The secondary use "must be [permitted] to 'conjure up' *at least* enough of the original" to fulfill its transformative purpose. *Id.* at 588 (emphasis added). Prince used key portions of certain of Cariou's photographs. In doing that, however, we determine that in twenty-five of his artworks, Prince transformed those photographs into something new and different and, as a result, this factor weighs heavily in Prince's favor.

As indicated above, there are five artworks that, upon our review, present closer questions. Specifically, *Graduation, Meditation, Canal Zone (2008), Canal Zone (2007),* and *Charlie Company* do not sufficiently differ from the photographs of Cariou's that they incorporate for us confidently to make a determination about their transformative nature as a matter of law. Although the minimal alterations that Prince made in those instances moved the work in a different direction from Cariou's classical portraiture and landscape photos, we can not say with certainty at this point whether those artworks present a "new expression, meaning, or message." *Campbell,* 510 U.S. at 579.

Certainly, there are key differences in those artworks compared to the photographs they incorporate. *Graduation,* for instance, is tinted blue, and the jungle background is in softer focus than in Cariou's original. Lozenges painted over the subject's eyes and mouth—an alteration that appears frequently throughout the *Canal Zone* artworks—make the subject appear anonymous, rather than as the strong individual who appears in the original. Along with the enlarged hands and electric guitar that Prince pasted onto his canvas, those alterations create the impression that the subject is not quite human. Cariou's photograph, on the other hand, presents a human being in his natural habitat, looking intently ahead. Where the photograph presents someone comfortably at home in nature, *Graduation* combines divergent elements to create a sense of discomfort. However, we cannot say for sure whether *Graduation* constitutes fair use or whether Prince has transformed Cariou's work enough to render it transformative.

We have the same concerns with *Meditation, Canal Zone (2007), Canal Zone (2008),* and *Charlie Company. . . .*

We believe the district court is best situated to determine, in the first instance, whether such relatively minimal alterations render *Graduation, Meditation, Canal Zone (2007), Canal Zone (2008),* and *Charlie Company* fair uses (including whether the artworks are transformative) or whether any impermissibly infringes on Cariou's copyrights in his original photographs. We remand for that determination. . . .

Conclusion

For the reasons discussed, we hold that all except five (*Graduation, Meditation, Canal Zone (2007), Canal Zone (2008),* and *Charlie Company*) of Prince's artworks make fair use of Cariou's photographs. . . .

NOTES AND QUESTIONS

1. What do you make of the court's determination that the author of an allegedly infringing work who asserts the fair use defense need not have intended to create a transformative work? If Prince had in fact testified that his purpose was to create new meaning, should such testimony carry any significant weight? Absent such testimony, is it appropriate for an appellate court to undertake its own determination of whether a transformative character may reasonably be perceived?

2. The *Cariou* court cites *Campbell* to support its conclusion that a transformative work is one that "alter[s] the original with 'new expression, meaning or message'"? Is that a fair reading of *Campbell*? Does the standard provide sufficient clarity? Does it effectively distinguish fair uses and uses covered by the copyright holder's derivative work right?

3. Should either Mr. Prince's celebrity status or Mr. Cariou's relative obscurity be relevant to the analysis of the fourth factor? Why, or why not?

4. Finally, focus on the court's discussion of the third fair use factor. Do you think a court can objectively determine whether a defendant has taken "enough" or "more than enough" or "substantially greater than necessary" of the plaintiff's work? According to the court, it could not "confidently" evaluate the substantiality of the taking in the case of five of the Prince artworks. How confident are you about the court's evaluation of the other 25 works? Test your judgment against the court's: the opinion includes an appendix with images of all of the works at issue: http://www.ca2.uscourts.gov/11-1197apx.htm.

> **AFTERMATH**
>
> Shortly after the Second Circuit's decision, the parties in *Cariou* settled their dispute. The settlement obviated the need for the district court to analyze the remaining five images.

Note on "Best Practices" Guidelines

The approach Congress adopted to codifying fair use enables courts to balance competing interests in a flexible and context-sensitive manner. It also allows fair use jurisprudence to change over time to accommodate changing sensibilities. At the same time, fair use is an ex post ordering tool. Both businesses and individuals sometimes may prefer ex ante clarity about the applicable law, particularly in light of the costly nature of copyright litigation.

In recent years, various groups have sought to establish voluntary, industry-specific fair use guidelines. For example, American University's Center for Social Media has worked actively to develop and publicize codes of best practices that address the most common situations faced by a variety of groups, including documentary filmmakers, journalists, and media literacy educators. *See* http://www.centerforsocialmedia.org/resources/fair_use/. Development of the codes typically has not involved significant participation by the content-owning industries. Instead, each code of best practices reflects efforts to describe what those working in the field see as appropriate behavior.

The Center for Social Media's best known product, the "Documentary Filmmakers' Statement of Best Practices in Fair Use," identifies four types of use that are generally permissible:

1. Documentarians may "employ[] copyrighted material as the object of social, political, or cultural critique," subject to the limitation that "[t]he use should not be so extensive or pervasive that it ceases to function as critique and becomes, instead, a way of satisfying the audience's taste for the thing (or the kind of thing) critiqued";
2. Documentarians may "quot[e] copyrighted works of popular culture to illustrate an argument or point," subject to the limitations that the material be properly attributed, that "to the extent possible and appropriate, quotations are drawn from a range of different sources," that each quotation "is no longer than is necessary to achieve the intended effect," and that "the quoted material is not employed merely to avoid the cost or inconvenience of shooting equivalent footage;"
3. Documentarians may "captur[e] copyrighted media content in the process of filming something else," subject to the limitations that the captured content "was not requested or directed," is properly attributed, is "integral to the scene/action" but is not "the scene's primary focus of interest," and in the case of music "does not function as a substitute for a synch track"; and
4. Documentarians may "us[e] copyrighted material in a historical sequence," subject to the limitations that "the film project was not specifically designed around the

material in question," "the material serves a critical illustrative function and no suitable substitute exists," "the material cannot be licensed, or the material can be licensed only on terms that are excessive relative to a reasonable budget for the film in question," "the use is no more extensive than is necessary to make the point for which the material has been selected," "the film project does not rely predominantly or disproportionately on any single source for illustrative clips," and "the copyright owner of the material used is properly identified."

It remains unclear whether and to what extent courts will be willing to rely on these more recently developed guidelines to aid in a determination in any particular case. Such guidelines can, however, shape norms and practices in particular industries. For example, after publication of the Best Practices guideline related to documentary filmmakers, insurance and production companies "became more willing to insure, produce, and distribute documentary films that had not licensed all copyrighted material included within the films. If a filmmaker claimed that the uses were fair and that he or she had complied with the terms of the [Best Practices], then . . . insurers were willing to issue insurance." Jennifer E. Rothman, *Best Intentions: Reconsidering Best Practices Statements in the Context of Fair Use and Copyright Law,* 57 J. Copyright Soc'y 371 (2010).

NOTES AND QUESTIONS

1. What probative value, if any, should courts accord private efforts to define the scope of fair use on an industry-specific basis? What facts might make a "best practices" document useful in litigation? Under what fair use factor would a defendant's compliance with a particular set of "best practices" be relevant?

2. The "Documentary Filmmakers Statement of Best Practices in Fair Use" represents a "customary practice" approach to fair use. In the particular context of documentary filmmaking, is such an approach preferable to one that would articulate which sorts of uses are transformative?

3. What other types of activities might benefit from developing guidelines for best practices? Who should be involved in promulgating such instruments?

PRACTICE EXERCISE: ADVOCACY

Your client, a documentary filmmaker, has created a 90-minute documentary about the legendary boxer Cassius Clay, a.k.a. Muhammad Ali. The film includes several excerpts totaling 41 seconds from television footage of the widely watched 1974 heavyweight title match between Ali and George Foreman, including the deciding knockout punch by Ali in the eighth round. The copyright owner of the footage sent a letter to your client threatening to sue for copyright infringement. Draft a response to the letter.

3. Fair Use and the First Amendment

Cultural interchange cases also implicate freedom of expression concerns. Recall that in *Harper & Row*, the Court rejected *The Nation*'s argument that the First Amendment should afford it a separate defense to copyright infringement. It did so in part because of the unpublished nature of the work. The Court noted that "freedom of thought and expression 'includes both the right to speak freely and the right to refrain from speaking at all.'" *Harper & Row*, 471 U.S 539, 559 (quoting *Wooley v. Maynard*, 430 U.S. 705, 714 (1977)). Copyright law and the right of first publication in particular, the Court observed, serve "this countervailing First Amendment value." *Id.* at 560. The Court further noted that both the idea-expression distinction and the fair use doctrine "embod[y]" First Amendment protections. *Id.*

Should the First Amendment ever provide a separate defense to a copyright infringement claim? One interpretation of *Harper & Row* is that existing fair use doctrine sufficiently accommodates First Amendment values. On this view, there is no need for courts evaluating fair use cases expressly to consider First Amendment principles or doctrine.

A different view of the First Amendment's role in the fair use inquiry emerged in *Suntrust Bank v. Houghton Mifflin Co.*, 268 F.3d 1257 (11th Cir. 2001), which vacated a preliminary injunction barring publication of Alice Randall's book, *The Wind Done Gone*. Relying on *Campbell v. Acuff-Rose Music, Inc.*, Section A.1 *supra*, the court held that the book was a highly transformative parody of *Gone With the Wind*, and that Suntrust, Margaret Mitchell's trustee, had not shown any likelihood of harm to the market for authorized derivative works. It further held that the issuance of the preliminary injunction "was at odds with the shared principles of the First Amendment and the copyright law, acting as a prior restraint on speech because the public had not had access to Randall's ideas or viewpoint in the form of expression that she chose." *Id.* at 1277. The *Suntrust Bank* court characterized copyright and the First Amendment as working toward the shared goal of preventing censorship. *Id.* at 1263. Citing *Harper & Row*, it noted that "courts often need not entertain related First Amendment arguments in a copyright case," but that courts "must remain cognizant of the First Amendment protections interwoven into copyright law." *Id.* at 1265. What do you make of this approach? How would "remain[ing] cognizant" of the First Amendment affect the fair use analysis? For a useful discussion of this question, see Neil Weinstock Netanel, *Locating Copyright Within the First Amendment Skein*, 54 Stan. L. Rev. 1, 81-85 (2001).

Suntrust Bank, however, remains an unusual case. In particular, defendants in fair use cases have repeatedly raised First Amendment arguments to justify uses claimed to be in the public interest because of the "newsworthy" nature of the copied work. In these cases, courts generally have declined to give First Amendment considerations separate and independent weight. *See, e.g., Los Angeles News Serv. v. Tullo*, 973 F.2d 791 (9th Cir. 1992). *But see Swatch Grp. Mgmt. Servs. Ltd. v. Bloomberg L.P.*, 756 F.3d 73, 83-84 (2d Cir. 2014) (observing that the purpose of "deliver[ing] news-worthy financial information to investors and analysts . . . lies at the core of the First Amendment, [and] would be crippled if the news media and similar organizations were limited to sources of information that authorize disclosure").

B. TRANSFORMATIVE USE REVISITED

So far, our exploration of fair use has identified at least two underlying theories of fair use. First, a court is more likely to take a favorable view of uses that are reasonable and customary, whether under an implied consent theory or under a more general theory of socially acceptable conduct. Second, a court is more likely to excuse a use as fair if it is transformative, altering the original to add new expression or a new message. Uses of copyrighted content enabled by new technologies test the boundaries of both approaches. Such uses are not the subjects of established custom, and often do not align with accepted understandings of what makes a use transformative in nature. The cases in this section consider fair use disputes arising from the development of computer software and networked communications technologies.

1. Technical Interchange

As you know from Chapter 4.C., computer programs exhibit a high degree of interdependence. In order to accomplish the tasks for which they were designed, computer programs typically must interoperate with (or "talk to") one another, and must do so according to precise technical specifications. As a practical matter, achieving interoperability with a preexisting computer program often requires copying elements of that program. If the program is distributed in object code only, with no source code accessible, programmers will engage in a process called decompilation—converting the program from the zeros and ones representing machine-readable object code into human-readable commands—so that they can understand and reverse engineer the program's technical requirements. The eventual new program that results may be one that works with the copyrighted work (as Apache OpenOffice works with the Microsoft Windows operating system) or one that substitutes for the copyrighted work (as Apache OpenOffice for Windows substitutes for Microsoft's own Office for Windows). The process of decompilation necessarily involves making copies of large portions of the copyrighted work. How should copyright law treat those copies? Should it matter whether the defendant has designed a complementary or competing product?

≡ *Sega Enterprises, Ltd. v. Accolade, Inc.*
≡ *977 F.2d 1510 (9th Cir. 1992)*

REINHARDT, J.: . . . Plaintiff-appellee Sega Enterprises, Ltd. ("Sega") . . . develop[s] and market[s] video entertainment systems, including the "Genesis" console . . . and video game cartridges. Defendant-appellant Accolade, Inc., is an independent developer, manufacturer, and marketer of computer entertainment software, including game cartridges that are compatible with the Genesis console, as well as game cartridges that are compatible with other computer systems.

Sega licenses its copyrighted computer code and its "SEGA" trademark to a number of independent developers of computer game software. . . . Accolade is not and never has been a licensee of Sega. Prior to rendering its own games compatible with the Genesis console, Accolade explored the possibility of entering into a licensing agreement with Sega, but abandoned the effort because the agreement would have required that Sega be the exclusive manufacturer of all games produced by Accolade.

Accolade used a two-step process to render its video games compatible with the Genesis console. First, it "reverse engineered" Sega's video game programs in order to discover the requirements for compatibility with the Genesis console. As part of the reverse engineering process, Accolade transformed the machine-readable object code contained in commercially available copies of Sega's game cartridges into human-readable source code using a process called "disassembly" or "decompilation." Accolade purchased a Genesis console and three Sega game cartridges, wired a decompiler into the console circuitry, and generated printouts of the resulting source code. Accolade engineers studied and annotated the printouts in order to identify areas of commonality among the three game programs. They then loaded the disassembled code back into a computer, and experimented to discover the interface specifications for the Genesis console by modifying the programs and studying the results. At the end of the reverse engineering process, Accolade created a development manual that incorporated the information it had discovered about the requirements for a Genesis-compatible game. According to the Accolade employees who created the manual, the manual contained only functional descriptions of the interface requirements and did not include any of Sega's code.

In the second stage, Accolade created its own games for the Genesis. According to Accolade, at this stage it did not copy Sega's programs, but relied only on the information concerning interface specifications for the Genesis that was contained in its development manual. Accolade maintains that with the exception of the interface specifications, none of the code in its own games is derived in any way from its examination of Sega's code. In 1990, Accolade released "Ishido," a game which it had originally developed and released for use with the Macintosh and IBM personal computer systems, for use with the Genesis console. . . .

In 1991, Accolade released five more games for use with . . . Genesis. . . . With the exception of "Mike Ditka Power Football," all of those games, like "Ishido," had originally been developed and marketed for use with other hardware systems. . . .

[Sega brought a number of claims against Accolade, including a claim alleging that Accolade's disassembling of Sega's code constituted copyright infringement. The district court, holding that Sega would likely succeed on the merits of this claim, entered a preliminary injunction enjoining Accolade from disassembling Sega's code and from distributing any games developed through disassembly. The district court rejected Accolade's argument that the copying involved in its disassembly was sheltered by the fair use doctrine. The Ninth Circuit agreed that the disassembly process had reproduced Sega's code in copies for purposes of §106(1). The court then went on to consider Accolade's fair use argument.]

(a)

With respect to the first statutory factor, we observe initially that the fact that copying is for a commercial purpose weighs against a finding of fair use. *Harper & Row*, 471 U.S. at 562. . . .

. . . We must consider other aspects of "the purpose and character of the use" as well. As we have noted, the use at issue was an intermediate one only and thus any commercial "exploitation" was indirect or derivative.

The declarations of Accolade's employees indicate, and the district court found, that Accolade copied Sega's software solely in order to discover the functional requirements for compatibility with the Genesis console—aspects of Sega's programs that are not protected by copyright. 17 U.S.C. §102(b). With respect to the video game programs contained in Accolade's game cartridges, there is no evidence in the record that Accolade sought to avoid performing its own creative work. Indeed, most of the games that Accolade released for use with the Genesis console were originally developed for other hardware systems. Moreover, with respect to the interface procedures for the Genesis console, Accolade did not seek to avoid paying a customarily charged fee for use of those procedures, nor did it simply copy Sega's code; rather, it wrote its own procedures based on what it had learned through disassembly. Taken together, these facts indicate that although Accolade's ultimate purpose was the release of Genesis-compatible games for sale, its direct purpose in copying Sega's code, and thus its direct use of the copyrighted material, was simply to study the functional requirements for Genesis compatibility so that it could modify existing games and make them usable with the Genesis console. Moreover, as we discuss below, no other method of studying those requirements was available to Accolade. On these facts, we conclude that Accolade copied Sega's code for a legitimate, essentially non-exploitative purpose, and that the commercial aspect of its use can best be described as of minimal significance.

We further note that we are free to consider the public benefit resulting from a particular use notwithstanding the fact that the alleged infringer may gain commercially. . . . Public benefit need not be direct or tangible, but may arise because the challenged use serves a public interest. . . . In the case before us, Accolade's identification of the functional requirements for Genesis compatibility has led to an increase in the number of independently designed video game programs offered for use with the Genesis console. It is precisely this growth in creative expression, based on the dissemination of other creative works and the unprotected ideas contained in those works, that the Copyright Act was intended to promote. *See Feist Publications, Inc. v. Rural Tel. Serv. Co.*, [499] U.S. [340, 348] (1991) (citing *Harper & Row*, 471 U.S. at 556-57). The fact that Genesis-compatible video games are not scholarly works, but works offered for sale on the market, does not alter our judgment in this regard. We conclude that given the purpose and character of Accolade's use of Sega's video game programs, the presumption of unfairness has been overcome and the first statutory factor weighs in favor of Accolade.

(b)

As applied, the fourth statutory factor, effect on the potential market for the copyrighted work, bears a close relationship to the "purpose and character" inquiry in that it, too, accommodates the distinction between the copying of works in order to make independent creative expression possible and the simple exploitation of another's creative efforts. We must, of course, inquire whether, "if [the challenged use] should become widespread, it would adversely affect the potential market for the copyrighted work," *Sony Corp. v. Universal City Studios*, 464 U.S. 417, 451 . . . by diminishing potential sales, interfering with marketability, or usurping the market. . . . If the copying resulted in the latter effect, all other considerations might be irrelevant. The *Harper & Row* Court found a use that effectively usurped the market for the copyrighted work by supplanting that work to be dispositive. 471 U.S. at 567-69. However, the same consequences do not and could not attach to a use which simply enables the copier to enter the market for works of the same type as the copied work.

Unlike the defendant in *Harper & Row* . . . Accolade did not attempt to "scoop" Sega's release of any particular game or games, but sought only to become a legitimate competitor in the field of Genesis-compatible video games. Within that market, it is the characteristics of the game program as experienced by the user that determine the program's commercial success. As we have noted, there is nothing in the record that suggests that Accolade copied any of those elements.

By facilitating the entry of a new competitor, the first lawful one that is not a Sega licensee, Accolade's disassembly of Sega's software undoubtedly "affected" the market for Genesis-compatible games in an indirect fashion. We note, however, that while no consumer except the most avid devotee of President Ford's regime might be expected to buy more than one version of the President's memoirs, video game users typically purchase more than one game. There is no basis for assuming that Accolade's "Ishido" has significantly affected the market for Sega's "Altered Beast," since a consumer might easily purchase both; nor does it seem unlikely that a consumer particularly interested in sports might purchase both Accolade's "Mike Ditka Power Football" and Sega's "Joe Montana Football," particularly if the games are, as Accolade contends, not substantially similar. In any event, an attempt to monopolize the market by making it impossible for others to compete runs counter to the statutory purpose of promoting creative expression and cannot constitute a strong equitable basis for resisting the invocation of the fair use doctrine. Thus, we conclude that the fourth statutory factor weighs in Accolade's, not Sega's, favor, notwithstanding the minor economic loss Sega may suffer.

(c)

The second statutory factor, the nature of the copyrighted work, reflects the fact that not all copyrighted works are entitled to the same level of protection. . . . Works of fiction receive greater protection than works that have strong factual elements, such as historical or biographical works . . . or works that have strong functional elements, such as accounting textbooks, *Baker*, 101 U.S. at 104. Works that are merely compilations of fact are copyrightable, but the copyright in such a work is "thin." *Feist Publications*, [499] U.S. at [349]. . . .

Sega argues that even if many elements of its video game programs are properly characterized as functional and therefore not protected by copyright, Accolade copied protected expression. Sega is correct. The record makes clear that disassembly is wholesale copying. Because computer programs are also unique among copyrighted works in the form in which they are distributed for public use, however, Sega's observation does not bring us much closer to a resolution of the dispute.

The unprotected aspects of most functional works are readily accessible to the human eye. The systems described in accounting textbooks or the basic structural concepts embodied in architectural plans, to give two examples, can be easily copied without also copying any of the protected, expressive aspects of the original works. Computer programs, however, are typically distributed for public use in object code form, embedded in a silicon chip or on a floppy disk. For that reason, humans often cannot gain access to the unprotected ideas and functional concepts contained in object code without disassembling that code—i.e., making copies. . . .

. . . [T]he record clearly establishes that disassembly of the object code in Sega's video game cartridges was necessary in order to understand the functional requirements for Genesis compatibility. The interface procedures for the Genesis console are distributed for public use only in object code form, and are not visible to the user during operation of the video game program. Because object code cannot be read by humans, it must be disassembled, either by hand or by machine. Disassembly of object code necessarily entails copying. Those facts dictate our analysis of the second statutory fair use factor. If disassembly of copyrighted object code is *per se* an unfair use, the owner of the copyright gains a *de facto* monopoly over the functional aspects of his work—aspects that were expressly denied copyright protection by Congress. 17 U.S.C. §102(b). In order to enjoy a lawful monopoly over the idea or functional principle underlying a work, the creator of the work must satisfy the more stringent standards imposed by the patent laws. *Bonito Boats, Inc. v. Thunder Craft Boats, Inc.*, 489 U.S. 141 (1989). Sega does not hold a patent on the Genesis console.

Because Sega's video game programs contain unprotected aspects that cannot be examined without copying, we afford them a lower degree of protection than more traditional literary works. . . . In light of all the considerations discussed above, we conclude that the second statutory factor also weighs in favor of Accolade.

(d)

As to the third statutory factor, Accolade disassembled entire programs written by Sega. Accordingly, the third factor weighs against Accolade. The fact that an entire work was copied does not, however, preclude a finding of fair use. *Sony Corp.*, 464 U.S. at 449-50. . . . In fact, where the ultimate (as opposed to direct) use is as limited as it was here, the factor is of very little weight. . . .

(e)

In summary, careful analysis of the purpose and characteristics of Accolade's use of Sega's video game programs, the nature of the computer programs involved, and the nature of the market for video game cartridges yields the conclusion that the first, second, and fourth statutory fair use factors weigh in favor of Accolade, while only the third weighs in favor of Sega, and even then only slightly. Accordingly, Accolade clearly has by far the better case on the fair use issue.

We are not unaware of the fact that to those used to considering copyright issues in more traditional contexts, our result may seem incongruous at first blush. To oversimplify, the record establishes that Accolade, a commercial competitor of Sega, engaged in wholesale copying of Sega's copyrighted code as a preliminary step in the development of a competing product. However, the key to this case is that we are dealing with computer software, a relatively unexplored area in the world of copyright law. We must avoid the temptation of trying to force "the proverbial square peg in[to] a round hole." [*Computer Assocs. Int'l, Inc. v. Altai, Inc.*], 23 U.S.P.Q.2d at 1257.

In determining whether a challenged use of copyrighted material is fair, a court must keep in mind the public policy underlying the Copyright Act. . . . As discussed above, the fact that computer programs are distributed for public use in object code form often precludes public access to the ideas and functional concepts contained in those programs, and thus confers on the copyright owner a *de facto* monopoly over those ideas and functional concepts. That result defeats the fundamental purpose of the Copyright Act—to encourage the production of original works by protecting the expressive elements of those works while leaving the ideas, facts, and functional concepts in the public domain for others to build on. *Feist Publications*, [499] U.S. at [349-50]. . . .

Sega argues that the considerable time, effort, and money that went into development of the Genesis and Genesis-compatible video games militate against a finding of fair use. Borrowing from antitrust principles, Sega attempts to label Accolade a "free rider" on its product development efforts. In *Feist Publications*, however, the Court unequivocally rejected the "sweat of the brow" rationale for copyright protection. [499] U.S. at [353-54]. . . . Under the Copyright Act, if a work is largely functional, it receives only weak protection. "This result is neither unfair nor unfortunate. It is the means by which copyright advances the progress of science and art." *Id.* at [350]. . . . Here, while the work may not be largely functional, it incorporates functional elements which do not merit protection. The equitable considerations involved weigh on the side of public access. Accordingly, we reject Sega's argument.

(f)

We conclude that where disassembly is the only way to gain access to the ideas and functional

---

LOOKING FORWARD

Some software companies have responded to the reverse engineering of their products by employing license agreements, including mass-market "clickwrap" agreements, that prohibit reverse engineering. We address the enforceability of such provisions in Chapter 15.

elements embodied in a copyrighted computer program and where there is a legitimate reason for seeking such access, disassembly is a fair use of the copyrighted work, as a matter of law. Our conclusion does not, of course, insulate Accolade from a claim of copyright infringement with respect to its finished products. Sega has reserved the right to raise such a claim, and it may do so on remand. . . .

NOTES AND QUESTIONS

1. Do you agree with the court's conclusion that §107 may sometimes operate to privilege research by private-sector, commercial entities? What would be an "illegitimate" reason for seeking access to functional elements of computer software?

2. Why shouldn't Accolade be required to enter a license agreement with Sega if it wishes to create games that can be played on the Sega consoles? Do you think that customers are likely to buy both Joe Montana Football and Mike Ditka Power Football? Should that decision be left to Sega, or to the market? Note that gaming companies often have adopted a "razor and blades" pricing strategy, selling consoles at a low price to generate an installed base of users and reaping their profits on the sale of games. Should that fact matter to the fair use analysis?

3. Recall that in analyzing the fourth statutory fair use factor, the *Campbell* Court drew a "distinction between potentially remediable displacement and unremediable disparagement." *Campbell v. Acuff-Rose Music, Inc.*, 510 U.S. at 592. Where on this spectrum do Accolade's products lie? Does either end of the *Campbell* spectrum adequately capture the sort of competition at issue in *Sega*?

4. As you saw in Section A of this chapter, the second fair use factor doesn't seem to drive the results in cases that reflect a concern for cultural interchange. In *Sega*, in contrast, the second fair use factor was enormously important. Does it make sense to give special consideration to the nature of computer software, as the Ninth Circuit did? Do you agree with the court's conclusion that denying fair use would threaten the boundary between copyright law and patent law?

5. In *Sega* the defendant created new games that could be played on the plaintiff's gaming platform, a special use gaming console. In a subsequent case Sony sued Connectix Corp. for using decompilation to create a piece of software called a "Virtual Game Station" that allowed consumers to play Sony PlayStation games on personal computers. The court reasoned that

> because the Virtual Game Station is transformative, and does not merely supplant the PlayStation console, the Virtual Game Station is a legitimate competitor in the market for platforms on which Sony and Sony-licensed games can be played. For this reason, some economic loss by Sony as a result of this competition does not compel a finding of no fair use. Sony understandably seeks control over the market for devices that play

games Sony produces or licenses. The copyright law, however, does not confer such a monopoly. . . .

Sony Computer Entertainment, Inc. v. Connectix Corp., 203 F.3d 596, 608 (9th Cir.), *cert. denied*, 531 U.S. 871 (2000). Is *Connectix* a necessary extension of the *Sega* holding? Against which of the plaintiffs' products did the defendants in each case compete? Does anything about the *Connectix* facts change the analysis of the second factor?

6. Does a rule allowing decompilation and reverse engineering of computer software represent good policy? Professors Pamela Samuelson and Suzanne Scotchmer argue that licensing can be beneficial because it enables innovators to recoup their research and development costs, and that reducing a second comer's costs of entry too far may harm innovation. They note, however that reverse engineering also costs money, and that the expense of reverse engineering can be a factor influencing a company's decision whether to take a license instead. Pamela Samuelson & Suzanne Scotchmer, *The Law and Economics of Reverse Engineering*, 111 Yale L.J. 1575 (2002).

> ## COMPARATIVE PERSPECTIVE
>
> Article 6 of the EU Council Directive of 14 May 1991 on the legal protection of computer programs, 1991 O.J. (L 122) 42, permits reproduction of portions of computer programs "where reproduction of the code and translation of its form . . . are indispensable to obtain the information necessary to achieve the interoperability of an independently created computer program with other programs." The directive provides that "[a]ny contractual provisions contrary to Article 6 . . . shall be null and void." *Id.* art. 9(1).

PRACTICE EXERCISE: ADVOCACY

Review the facts of *Oracle v. Google* from Chapter 4.C. After reversing the district court's ruling that the Java API's were not copyrightable, the Federal Circuit remanded the case for further consideration of Google's fair use defense. You represent Google. Under each of the four factors, prepare a list of facts you should highlight for the district court on remand.

---

2. Online Search

Displaying certain kinds of search results to Internet users also can entail both infringing copying and infringing public display. The following case explores the application of the traditional fair use factors to this new use.

≡ *Perfect 10, Inc. v. Amazon, Inc.*
  508 F.3d 1146 (9th Cir. 2007)

[Review the facts of this case, Chapter 6.B.1.d *supra*. The court found that the inclusion in search results of small, "thumbnail" images residing on Google's servers infringed the plaintiff's public display right. It then turned to defendant's fair use argument.]

IKUTA, J.: . . .

. . . Google contends that its use of thumbnails is a fair use of the images and therefore does not constitute an infringement of Perfect 10's copyright. . . .

In applying the fair use analysis in this case, we are guided by *Kelly v. Arriba Soft Corp.,* which considered substantially the same use of copyrighted photographic images as is at issue here. *See* 336 F.3d 811 [(9th Cir. 2003)]. In *Kelly,* a photographer brought a direct infringement claim against Arriba, the operator of an Internet search engine. The search engine provided thumbnail versions of the photographer's images in response to search queries. *Id.* at 815-16. We held that Arriba's use of thumbnail images was a fair use primarily based on the transformative nature of a search engine and its benefit to the public. *Id.* at 818-22. We also concluded that Arriba's use of the thumbnail images did not harm the photographer's market for his image. *Id.* at 821-22.

In this case, the district court determined that Google's use of thumbnails was not a fair use and distinguished *Kelly.* We consider these distinctions in the context of the four-factor fair use analysis.

Purpose and character of the use. . . . As noted in *Campbell,* a "transformative work" is one that alters the original work "with new expression, meaning, or message." *Campbell* [*v. Acuff-Rose Music, Inc.*], 510 U.S. [569, 579 (1994)]. . . .

Google's use of thumbnails is highly transformative. In *Kelly,* we concluded that Arriba's use of thumbnails was transformative because "Arriba's use of the images serve[d] a different function than Kelly's use—improving access to information on the [I]nternet versus artistic expression." *Kelly,* 336 F.3d at 819. Although an image may have been created originally to serve an entertainment, aesthetic, or informative function, a search engine transforms the image into a pointer directing a user to a source of information. Just as a "parody has an obvious claim to transformative value" because "it can provide social benefit, by shedding light on an earlier work, and, in the process, creating a new one," *Campbell,* 510 U.S. at 579, a search engine provides social benefit by incorporating an original work into a new work, namely, an electronic reference tool. Indeed, a search engine may be more transformative than a parody because a search engine provides an entirely new use for the original work, while a parody typically has the same entertainment purpose as the original work. . . . In other words, a search engine puts images "in a different context" so that they are "transformed into a new creation."

The fact that Google incorporates the entire Perfect 10 image into the search engine results does not diminish the transformative nature of Google's use. As the district court correctly noted, we determined in *Kelly* that even making an exact copy of a work may be transformative so long as the copy serves a different function than the original work. . . . Here, Google uses Perfect 10's images in a new context to serve a different purpose.

The district court nevertheless determined that Google's use of thumbnail images was less transformative than Arriba's use of thumbnails in *Kelly* because Google's use of thumbnails superseded Perfect 10's right to sell its reduced-size images for use on cell phones. . . .

Additionally, the district court determined that the commercial nature of Google's use weighed against its transformative nature. . . . The district court held that because Google's thumbnails "lead users to sites that directly benefit Google's bottom line," the AdSense program increased the commercial nature of Google's use of Perfect 10's images. *Id.* at 847. . . .

We note that the superseding use in this case is not significant at present: the district court did not find that any downloads for mobile phone use had taken place. Moreover, while Google's use of thumbnails to direct users to AdSense partners containing infringing content adds a commercial dimension that did not exist in *Kelly*, the district court did not determine that this commercial element was significant. . . .

We conclude that the significantly transformative nature of Google's search engine, particularly in light of its public benefit, outweighs Google's superseding and commercial uses of the thumbnails in this case. . . .

Therefore, this factor weighs heavily in favor of Google.

The nature of the copyrighted work. With respect to the second factor, "the nature of the copyrighted work," . . . our decision in *Kelly* is directly on point. There we held that the photographer's images were "creative in nature" and thus "closer to the core of intended copyright protection than are more fact-based works." *Kelly,* 336 F.3d at 820 (internal quotation omitted). However, because the photos appeared on the Internet before Arriba used thumbnail versions in its search engine results, this factor weighed only slightly in favor of the photographer. *Id.*

Here, the district court found that Perfect 10's images were creative but also previously published. *Perfect 10,* 416 F. Supp. 2d at 850. The right of first publication is "the author's right to control the first public appearance of his expression." *Harper & Row* [*Publishers v. Nation Enters.,* 471 U.S. 539, 564 (1985)]. Because this right encompasses "the choices of when, where, and in what form first to publish a work," *id.,* an author exercises and exhausts this one-time right by publishing the work in any medium. . . . Once Perfect 10 has exploited this commercially valuable right of first publication by putting its images on the Internet for paid subscribers, Perfect 10 is no longer entitled to the enhanced protection available for an unpublished work. Accordingly the district court did not err in holding that this factor weighed only slightly in favor of Perfect 10.

The amount and substantiality of the portion used. . . . In *Kelly,* we held Arriba's use of the entire photographic image was reasonable in light of the purpose of a search engine. *Kelly,* 336 F.3d at 821. Specifically, we noted, "[i]t was necessary for Arriba to copy the entire image to allow users to recognize the image and decide whether to pursue more information about the image or the originating [website]. If Arriba only copied part of the image, it would be more difficult to identify it, thereby reducing the usefulness of the visual search engine." *Id.* Accordingly, we concluded that this factor did not weigh in favor of either party. *Id.* Because the same analysis applies to Google's use of Perfect 10's image, the district court did not err in finding that this factor favored neither party.

Effect of use on the market. . . . In *Kelly,* we concluded that Arriba's use of the thumbnail images did not harm the market for the photographer's full-size images. We reasoned that because thumbnails were not a substitute for the full-sized images, they did not harm the photographer's ability to sell or license his full-sized images. *Id.* The district court here followed *Kelly's* reasoning, holding that Google's use of thumbnails did not hurt Perfect 10's market for full-size images. We agree.

Perfect 10 argues that the district court erred because the likelihood of market harm may be presumed if the intended use of an image is for commercial gain. However, this presumption does not arise when a work is transformative because "market substitution is at least less certain, and market harm may not be so readily inferred." *Campbell*, 510 U.S. at 591. As previously discussed, Google's use of thumbnails for search engine purposes is highly transformative, and so market harm cannot be presumed.

Perfect 10 also has a market for reduced-size images, an issue not considered in *Kelly*. The district court held that "Google's use of thumbnails likely does harm the potential market for the downloading of [Perfect 10's] reduced-size images onto cell phones." *Perfect 10*, 416 F. Supp. 2d at 851 (emphasis omitted). . . . [T]he district court did not make a finding that Google users have downloaded thumbnail images for cell phone use. This potential harm to Perfect 10's market remains hypothetical. We conclude that this factor favors neither party.

Having undertaken a case-specific analysis of all four factors, we now weigh these factors together "in light of the purposes of copyright." *Campbell*, 510 U.S. at 578. . . . In this case, Google has put Perfect 10's thumbnail images (along with millions of other thumbnail images) to a use fundamentally different than the use intended by Perfect 10. In doing so, Google has provided a significant benefit to the public. Weighing this significant transformative use against the unproven use of Google's thumbnails for cell phone downloads, and considering the other fair use factors, all in light of the purpose of copyright, we conclude that Google's use of Perfect 10's thumbnails is a fair use. . . . [W]e vacate the preliminary injunction regarding Google's use of thumbnail images.

NOTES AND QUESTIONS

1. Did Arriba or Google transform the plaintiffs' works or simply their context? Should the answer to this question affect the fair use analysis?

2. After *Perfect 10*, what arguments can a copyright owner make about a visual search engine's effects on the potential market for or value of its works? What evidence might demonstrate such effects? Should such evidence change the result of the fair use analysis?

3. If Google had not succeeded in its fair use defense, what steps would Google have had to take to offer an image search database?

3. Access to Knowledge

The development of search technologies has continued to progress. As any user of LEXIS-NEXIS or Westlaw knows, the ability to perform full-text searches of stored content can yield highly useful results. For such searches to be possible, however, it generally is necessary to create a copy of the content that can be stored close at hand and accessed readily. Consider the following case:

≡ ***The Authors Guild, Inc. v. HathiTrust***
755 F.3d 87 (2d Cir. 2014)

PARKER, J.: Beginning in 2004, several research universities including the University of Michigan, the University of California at Berkeley, Cornell University, and the University of Indiana agreed to allow Google to electronically scan the books in their collections. In October 2008, thirteen universities announced plans to create a repository for the digital copies and founded an organization called HathiTrust to set up and operate the HathiTrust Digital Library (or "HDL"). Colleges, universities, and other nonprofit institutions became members of HathiTrust and made the books in their collections available for inclusion in the HDL. HathiTrust currently has 80 member institutions and the HDL contains digital copies of more than ten million works, published over many centuries, written in a multitude of languages, covering almost every subject imaginable. . . .

HathiTrust permits three uses of the copyrighted works in the HDL repository. First, HathiTrust allows the general public to search for particular terms across all digital copies in the repository. Unless the copyright holder authorizes broader use, the search results show only the page numbers on which the search term is found within the work and the number of times the term appears on each page. The HDL does not display to the user any text from the underlying copyrighted work (either in "snippet" form or otherwise). Consequently, the user is not able to view either the page on which the term appears or any other portion of the book.

Below is an example of the results a user might see after running an HDL full-text search:

Second, the HDL allows member libraries to provide patrons with certified print disabilities access to the full text of copyrighted works. A "print disability" is any disability that prevents a person from effectively reading printed material. Blindness is one example, but print disabilities also include those that prevent a person from physically holding a book or turning pages. To use this service, a patron must obtain certification of his disability from a qualified expert. Through the HDL, a print-disabled user can obtain access to the contents of works in the digital library using adaptive technologies such as software that converts the text into spoken words, or that magnifies the text. . . .

Third, by preserving the copyrighted books in digital form, the HDL permits members to create a replacement copy of the work, if the member already owned an original copy, the member's original copy is lost, destroyed, or stolen, and a replacement copy is unobtainable at a "fair" price elsewhere.

The HDL stores digital copies of the works in four different locations. One copy is stored on its primary server in Michigan, one on its secondary server in Indiana, and two on separate backup tapes at the University of Michigan.[3] Each copy contains the full text of the work, in a machine readable format, as well as the *images* of each page in the work as they appear in the print version. . . .

This case began when twenty authors and authors' associations (collectively, the "Authors") sued HathiTrust, one of its member universities, and the presidents of four other member universities (collectively, the "Libraries") for copyright infringement seeking declaratory and injunctive relief. . . .

The District Court's Opinion

The district court granted the Libraries' . . . motions for summary judgment on the infringement claims on the basis that the three uses permitted by the HDL were fair uses. In this assessment, the district court gave considerable weight to what it found to be the "transformative" nature of the three uses and to what it described as the HDL's "invaluable" contribution to the advancement of knowledge. The district court explained:

> Although I recognize that the facts here may on some levels be without precedent, I am convinced that they fall safely within the protection of fair use such that there is no genuine issue of material fact. I cannot imagine a definition of fair use that would not encompass the transformative uses made by [the HDL] and would require that I terminate this invaluable contribution to the progress of science and cultivation of the arts that at the same time effectuates the ideals espoused by the [Americans With Disabilities Act of 1990, Pub. L. No. 101–336, 104 Stat. 327 (codified as amended at 42 U.S.C. §§12101, et seq.)].

[*Authors Guild, Inc. v. HathiTrust,* 902 F. Supp. 2d 445, 464 (S.D.N.Y.2012).] . . .

---

3. Separate from the HDL, one copy is also kept by Google. Google's use of its copy is the subject of a separate lawsuit currently pending in this Court. *See Authors Guild, Inc. v. Google, Inc.,* 721 F.3d 132 (2d Cir. 2013), *on remand,* 954 F. Supp. 2d 282 (S.D.N.Y. 2013), *appeal docketed,* No. 13–4829 (2d Cir. Dec. 23, 2013).

I. Fair Use...

. . . Section 107 requires a court to consider four nonexclusive factors which are to be weighed together to assess whether a particular use is fair. . . .

An important focus of the first factor is whether the use is "transformative." A use is transformative if it does something more than repackage or republish the original copyrighted work. The inquiry is whether the work "adds something new, with a further purpose or different character, altering the first with new expression, meaning or message. . . ." *Campbell*, 510 U.S. at 579. "[T]he more transformative the new work, the less will be the significance of other factors . . . that may weigh against a finding of fair use." *Id*. Contrary to what the district court implied, a use does not become transformative by making an "invaluable contribution to the progress of science and cultivation of the arts." *HathiTrust*, 902 F. Supp. 2d at 464. Added value or utility is not the test: a transformative work is one that serves a new and different function from the original work and is not a substitute for it. . . .

1. Full-Text Search

It is not disputed that, in order to perform a full-text search of books, the Libraries must first create digital copies of the entire books. Importantly, as we have seen, the HDL does not allow users to view any portion of the books they are searching. Consequently, in providing this service, the HDL does not add into circulation any new, human-readable copies of any books. Instead, the HDL simply permits users to "word search"—that is, to locate where specific words or phrases appear in the digitized books. Applying the relevant factors, we conclude that this use is a fair use.

i.

Turning to the first factor, we conclude that the creation of a full-text searchable database is a quintessentially transformative use. As the example . . . *supra*, demonstrates, the result of a word search is different in purpose, character, expression, meaning, and message from the page (and the book) from which it is drawn. Indeed, we can discern little or no resemblance between the original text and the results of the HDL full-text search.

There is no evidence that the Authors write with the purpose of enabling text searches of their books. Consequently, the full-text search function does not "supersede[ ] the objects [or purposes] of the original creation," *Campbell*, 510 U.S. at 579. The HDL does not "merely repackage[ ] or republish[ ] the original[s]," Leval, 103 Harv. L. Rev. at 1111, or merely recast "an original work into a new mode of presentation," *Castle Rock Entm't, Inc. v. Carol Publ'g Grp., Inc.*, 150 F.3d 132, 143 (2d Cir. 1998). Instead, by enabling full-text search, the HDL adds to the original something new with a different purpose and a different character.

Full-text search adds a great deal more to the copyrighted works at issue than did the transformative uses we approved in several other cases. For example, in *Cariou v. Prince*, we found that certain photograph collages were transformative, even though the collages were cast in the same medium as the copyrighted photographs. 714

F.3d at 706. Similarly, in *Bill Graham Archives v. Dorling Kindersley Ltd.*, we held that it was a transformative use to include in a biography copyrighted concert photos, even though the photos were unaltered (except for being reduced in size). 448 F.3d 605, 609-11 (2d Cir. 2006).

Cases from other Circuits reinforce this conclusion. In *Perfect 10, Inc.*, the Ninth Circuit held that the use of copyrighted thumbnail images in internet search results was transformative because the thumbnail copies served a different function from the original copyrighted images. 508 F.3d at 1165. And in *A.V. ex rel. Vanderhye v. iParadigms, LLC*, a company created electronic copies of unaltered student papers for use in connection with a computer program that detects plagiarism. Even though the electronic copies made no "substantive alteration to" the copyrighted student essays, the Fourth Circuit held that plagiarism detection constituted a transformative use of the copyrighted works. 562 F.3d 630, 639–40.

ii.

The second fair-use factor—the nature of the copyrighted work—is not dispositive. The HDL permits the full-text search of every type of work imaginable. Consequently, there is no dispute that the works at issue are of the type that the copyright laws value and seek to protect. However, "this factor 'may be of limited usefulness where,' as here, 'the creative work . . . is being used for a transformative purpose." *Cariou*, 714 F.3d at 710 (quoting *Bill Graham Archives*, 448 F.3d at 612). Accordingly, our fair-use analysis hinges on the other three factors.

iii.

The third factor asks whether the copying used more of the copyrighted work than necessary and whether the copying was excessive. As we have noted, "[t]here are no absolute rules as to how much of a copyrighted work may be copied and still be considered a fair use." *Maxtone-Graham v. Burtchaell*, 803 F.2d 1253, 1263 (2d Cir. 1986). "[T]he extent of permissible copying varies with the purpose and character of the use." *Campbell*, 510 U.S. at 586-87. The crux of the inquiry is whether "no more was taken than necessary." *Id*. at 589. For some purposes, it may be necessary to copy the entire copyrighted work, in which case Factor Three does not weigh against a finding of fair use.

In order to enable the full-text search function, the Libraries, as we have seen, created digital copies of all the books in their collections.[5] Because it was reasonably necessary for the HDL to make use of the entirety of the works in order to enable the full-text search function, we do not believe the copying was excessive.

The Authors also contend that the copying is excessive because the HDL creates and maintains copies of the works at four different locations. But the record demonstrates that these copies are also reasonably necessary in order to facilitate the HDL's legitimate uses. In particular, the HDL's services are offered to patrons through two

---

5. The HDL also creates digital copies of the images of each page of the books. As the Libraries acknowledge, the HDL does not need to retain these copies to enable the full-text search use. We discuss the fair-use justification for these copies in the context of the disability-access use, ...

servers, one at the University of Michigan (the primary server) and an identical one at the University of Indiana (the "mirror" server). Both servers contain copies of the digital works at issue. According to the HDL executive director, the "existence of a[n] [identical] mirror site allows for balancing the load of user web traffic to avoid overburdening a single site, and each site acts as a back-up of the HDL collection in the event that one site were to cease operation (for example, due to failure caused by a disaster, or even as a result of routine maintenance)." (Wilkin Decl.). To further guard against the risk of data loss, the HDL stores copies of the works on two encrypted backup tapes, which are disconnected from the internet and are placed in separate secure locations on the University of Michigan campus. *Id.* The HDL creates these backup tapes so that the data could be restored in "the event of a disaster causing large-scale data loss" to the primary and mirror servers. *Id.*

We have no reason to think that these copies are excessive or unreasonable in relation to the purposes identified by the Libraries and permitted by the law of copyright. In sum, even viewing the evidence in the light most favorable to the Authors, the record demonstrates that these copies are reasonably necessary to facilitate the services HDL provides to the public and to mitigate the risk of disaster or data loss. Accordingly, we conclude that this factor favors the Libraries.

iv.

The fourth factor requires us to consider "the effect of the use upon the potential market for or value of the copyrighted work," 17 U.S.C. §107(4), and, in particular, whether the secondary use "usurps the market of the original work," *NXIVM Corp.*, 364 F.3d at 482.

The Libraries contend that the full-text-search use poses no harm to any existing or potential traditional market and point to the fact that, in discovery, the Authors admitted that they were unable to identify "any specific, quantifiable past harm, or any documents relating to any such past harm," resulting from any of the Libraries' uses of their works (including full-text search). Defs.-Appellees' Br. 38 (citing Pls.' Resps. to Interrogs.). The district court agreed with this contention, as do we.

At the outset, it is important to recall that the Factor Four analysis is concerned with only one type of economic injury to a copyright holder: the harm that results because the secondary use serves as a substitute for the original work. *See Campbell*, 510 U.S. at 591 ("cognizable market harm" is limited to "market substitution"). In other words, under Factor Four, any economic "harm" caused by transformative uses does not count because such uses, by definition, do not serve as substitutes for the original work. *See Bill Graham Archives*, 448 F.3d at 614.

To illustrate why this is so, consider how copyright law treats book reviews. Book reviews often contain quotations of copyrighted material to illustrate the reviewer's points and substantiate his criticisms; this is a paradigmatic fair use. And a negative book review can cause a degree of economic injury to the author by dissuading readers from purchasing copies of her book, even when the review does not serve as a substitute for the original. But, obviously, in that case, the author has no cause for complaint under Factor Four: The only market harms that count are the ones that are caused because the secondary use serves as a substitute for the original, not when the secondary use is transformative (as in quotations in a book review). *See Campbell,* 510 U.S. at 591-92 ("[W]hen a lethal parody, like a scathing theater review, kills demand for the original, it does not produce a harm cognizable under the Copyright Act.").

The Authors assert two reasons why the full-text-search function harms their traditional markets. The first is a "lost sale" theory which posits that a market for licensing books for digital search could possibly develop in the future, and the HDL impairs the emergence of such a market because it allows patrons to search books without any need for a license. Thus, according to the Authors, every copy employed by the HDL in generating full-text searches represents a lost opportunity to license the book for search.

This theory of market harm does not work under Factor Four, because the full-text search function does not serve as a substitute for the books that are being searched. Thus, it is irrelevant that the Libraries might be willing to purchase licenses in order to engage in this transformative use (if the use were deemed unfair). Lost licensing revenue counts under Factor Four only when the use serves as a substitute for the original and the full-text-search use does not.

Next, the Authors assert that the HDL creates the risk of a security breach which might impose irreparable damage on the Authors and their works. In particular, the Authors speculate that, if hackers were able to obtain unauthorized access to the books stored at the HDL, the full text of these tens of millions of books might be distributed worldwide without restriction, "decimat[ing]" the traditional market for those works.

The record before us documents the extensive security measures the Libraries have undertaken to safeguard against the risk of a data breach. . . .

This showing of the security measures taken by the Libraries is essentially unrebutted. Consequently, we see no basis in the record on which to conclude that a security breach is likely to occur, much less one that would result in the public release of the specific copyrighted works belonging to any of the plaintiffs in this case. *Cf. Sony Corp.,* 464 U.S. at 453-54 (concluding that time-shifting using a Betamax is fair use because the copyright owners' "prediction that live television or movie audiences will decrease" was merely "speculative"). Factor Four thus favors a finding of fair use.

Without foreclosing a future claim based on circumstances not now predictable, and based on a different record, we hold that the balance of relevant factors in this case favors the Libraries. In sum, we conclude that the doctrine of fair use allows the Libraries to digitize copyrighted works for the purpose of permitting full-text searches.

2. Access to the Print-Disabled

The HDL also provides print-disabled patrons with versions of all of the works contained in its digital archive in formats accessible to them. . . .

i.

In applying the Factor One analysis, the district court concluded that "[t]he use of digital copies to facilitate access for print-disabled persons is [a] transformative" use. *HathiTrust*, 902 F. Supp. 2d at 461. This is a misapprehension; providing expanded access to the print disabled is not "transformative."

As discussed above, a transformative use adds something new to the copyrighted work and does not merely supersede the purposes of the original creation. *See Campbell*, 510 U.S. at 579. The Authors state that they "write books to be read (or listened to)." By making copyrighted works available in formats accessible to the disabled, the HDL enables a larger audience to read those works, but the underlying purpose of the HDL's use is the same as the author's original purpose.

Indeed, when the HDL recasts copyrighted works into new formats to be read by the disabled, it appears, at first glance, to be creating derivative works over which the author ordinarily maintains control. *See* 17 U.S.C. §106(2). . . . [P]aradigmatic examples of derivative works include translations of the original into a different language, or adaptations of the original into different forms or media. *See id.* §101 (defining "derivative work"). The Authors contend that by converting their works into a different, accessible format, the HDL is simply creating a derivative work.

It is true that, oftentimes, the print-disabled audience has no means of obtaining access to the copyrighted works included in the HDL. But, similarly, the non-English-speaking audience cannot gain access to untranslated books written in English and an unauthorized translation is not transformative simply because it enables a new audience to read a work.

This observation does not end the analysis. "While a transformative use generally is more likely to qualify as fair use, 'transformative use is not absolutely necessary for a finding of fair use.'" *Swatch Grp. Mgmt. Servs. Ltd. v. Bloomberg L.P.*, ___ F.3d ___, ___, 2014 WL 2219162, at *7 (2d Cir.2014) (quoting *Campbell*, 510 U.S. at 579). We conclude that providing access to the print-disabled is still a valid purpose under Factor One even though it is not transformative. We reach that conclusion for several reasons.

First, the Supreme Court has already said so. As Justice Stevens wrote for the Court: "Making a copy of a copyrighted work for the convenience of a blind person is expressly identified by the House Committee Report as an example of fair use, with no suggestion that anything more than a purpose to entertain or to inform need motivate the copying." *Sony Corp. of Am.*, 464 U.S. at 455 n.40.

Our conclusion is reinforced by the legislative history on which he relied. The House Committee Report that accompanied codification of the fair use doctrine in the Copyright Act of 1976 expressly stated that making copies accessible "for the use of blind persons" posed a "special instance illustrating the application of the fair use doctrine. . . ." H.R. Rep. No. 94-1476, at 73 (1976), *reprinted in* 1976 U.S.C.C.A.N. 5659, 5686. The Committee noted that "special [blind-accessible formats] . . . are not usually made by the publishers for commercial distribution." *Id.* In light of its understanding of the market (or lack thereof) for books accessible to the blind, the Committee explained that "the making of a single copy or phonorecord by an individual as a free service for a blind persons [*sic*] would properly be considered a fair use under section 107." *Id.* We believe this guidance supports a finding of fair use in the unique circumstances presented by print-disabled readers.

Since the passage of the 1976 Copyright Act, Congress has reaffirmed its commitment to ameliorating the hardships faced by the blind and the print disabled. In the Americans with Disabilities Act, Congress declared that our "Nation's proper goals regarding individuals with disabilities are to assure equality of opportunity, full participation, independent living, and economic self-sufficiency for such individuals." 42 U.S.C. §12101(7). . . .

ii.

Through the HDL, the disabled can obtain access to copyrighted works of all kinds, and there is no dispute that those works are of the sort that merit protection under the Copyright Act. As a result, Factor Two weighs against fair use. This does not preclude a finding of fair use, however, given our analysis of the other factors.

iii.

Regarding Factor Three, as previously noted, the HDL retains copies as digital image files and as text-only files, which are then stored in four separate locations. The Authors contend that this amount of copying is excessive because the Libraries have not demonstrated their need to retain the digital *image* files in addition to the text files.

We are unconvinced. The text files are required for text searching and to create text-to-speech capabilities for the blind and disabled. But the image files will provide an additional and often more useful method by which many disabled patrons, especially students and scholars, can obtain access to these works. These image files contain information, such as pictures, charts, diagrams, and the layout of the text on the printed page that cannot be converted to text or speech. None of this is captured by the HDL's text-only copies. Many legally blind patrons are capable of viewing these images if they are sufficiently magnified or if the color contrasts are increased. And other disabled patrons, whose physical impairments prevent them from turning pages or from holding books, may also be able to use assistive devices to view all of the content contained in the image files for a book. For those individuals, gaining access to the HDL's image files—in addition to the text-only files— is necessary to perceive the books fully. Consequently, it is reasonable for the Libraries to retain both the text and image copies.

iv.

The fourth factor also weighs in favor of a finding of fair use. It is undisputed that the present-day market for books accessible to the handicapped is so insignificant that "it is common practice in the publishing industry for authors to forgo royalties that are generated through the sale of books manufactured in specialized formats for the blind. . . ." Appellants' Br. 34. "[T]he number of accessible books currently available to the blind for borrowing is a mere few hundred thousand titles, a minute percentage of the world's books. In contrast, the HDL contains more than ten million accessible volumes." J.A. 173 ¶ 10 (Maurer Decl.). When considering the 1976 Act, Congress was well aware of this problem. The House Committee

Report observed that publishers did not "usually ma[ke]" their books available in specialized formats for the blind. H.R. Rep. No. 94-1476, at 73, 1976 U.S.C.C.A.N. at 5686. That observation remains true today.

Weighing the factors together, we conclude that the doctrine of fair use allows the Libraries to provide full digital access to copyrighted works to their print-disabled patrons.

3. Preservation

By storing digital copies of the books, the HDL preserves them for generations to come, and ensures that they will still exist when their copyright terms lapse. Under certain circumstances, the HDL also proposes to make one additional use of the digitized works while they remain under copyright: The HDL will permit member libraries to create a replacement copy of a book, to be read and consumed by patrons, if (1) the member already owned an original copy, (2) the member's original copy is lost, destroyed, or stolen, and (3) a replacement copy is unobtainable at a fair price. The Authors claim that this use infringes their copyrights.

Even though the parties assume that this issue is appropriate for our determination, we are not convinced that this is so. The record before the district court does not reflect whether the plaintiffs own copyrights in any works that would be effectively irreplaceable at a fair price by the Libraries and, thus, would be potentially subject to being copied by the Libraries in case of the loss or destruction of an original. The Authors are not entitled to make this argument on behalf of others, because §501 of "the Copyright Act does not permit copyright holders to choose third parties to bring suits on their behalf." *ABKCO Music,* 944 F.2d at 980.

Because the record before us does not reflect the existence of a non-speculative risk that the HDL might create replacement copies of the *plaintiffs'* copyrighted work, we do not believe plaintiffs have standing to bring this claim, and this concern does not present a live controversy for adjudication. . . .

NOTES AND QUESTIONS

1. Do you agree with the court's conclusion that "the creation of a full-text searchable database is a quintessentially transformative use"? Do you think the *Campbell* Court would agree with that characterization of the HDL database? Would courts be better served by employing terms such as "productive use" or even "socially valuable" use in cases such as this one?

2. Given the court's characterization of the HDL database as transformative, do you agree with its conclusion that providing access to the print-disabled is not a transformative use? Is that conclusion consistent with the *Perfect 10* court's interpretation of the transformative use standard?

In *Swatch Grp. Mgmt. Servs. Ltd. v. Bloomberg L.P.,* 756 F.3d 73 (2d Cir. 2014), cited by the *HathiTrust* court, the plaintiff hosted an earnings conference call with group of securities analysts. One of the analysts made an audio recording of the call without authorization and then circulated a transcript. The defendant asserted that it was reporting important news. In discussing the first factor, after noting that a transformative use was not "absolutely necessary," the court observed:

> In the context of news reporting and analogous activities, moreover, the need to convey information to the public accurately may in some instances make it desirable and consonant with copyright law for a defendant to faithfully reproduce an original work without alteration. Courts often find such uses transformative by emphasizing the altered purpose or context of the work, as evidenced by surrounding commentary or criticism."

Id. at 84. Does this analysis support a different characterization of the accessible versions created and made available by the HathiTrust?

3. What do you make of the Second Circuit's refusal to consider lost licensing revenues resulting from the HDL unless the "use serves as a substitute for the original"? Is the court's treatment of the fourth factor consistent with the Supreme Court's guidance in *Campbell* and *Harper & Row*?

4. In 2013, 51 countries, including the United States, signed the Marrakesh Treaty to Facilitate Access to Published Works by Visually Impaired Persons and Persons with Print Disabilities that requires member countries to provide a limitation on the reproduction right "to facilitate the availability of works in accessible format copies" for those who are blind or have other disabilities or visual impairments. Twenty countries must ratify this treaty for it to take effect. As of this writing, 3 countries have ratified the treaty but over 75 countries signed it, suggesting that more ratifications will be forthcoming. Some countries, like Israel, implemented the treaty without ratifying it.

5. As part of the program described in the HathiTrust opinion, Google scanned more than 20 million books and created its own publicly available, searchable database, Google Books. The Authors Guild filed a class action against Google in 2004. Initially, the parties proposed a settlement that would have involved Google paying millions of dollars into a fund to compensate copyright owners, but the district court rejected the settlement. Subsequently, after a protracted battle over class certification, the district court ruled that Google's use of the copied books was fair. As this edition of this book was going to press, The Authors Guild's appeal was pending in the Second Circuit. In light of the *HathiTrust* ruling, do you think Google will prevail? How would you expect the Second Circuit's fair use analysis to differ in the *Google* case?

C. OTHER PRODUCTIVE USES

As you have learned in this chapter, over the past several decades the courts have adopted a flexible, generous approach to determining what sorts of uses qualify as sufficiently transformative. Courts have disagreed, however, about how to treat certain acts of simple copying, such as copying for personal use or for research or classroom use, under these theories. Under the "reasonable and customary use" theory, should the fact that certain kinds of copying are widespread and customary be enough to insulate them, even as technological developments make such copying much easier? The cases in this section consider what kinds of uses are sufficiently productive that they should be regarded as fair.

1. The Classic Case

The leading fair use case involving copying entire works for personal use is the Supreme Court's decision in *Sony Corp. of America v. Universal City Studios, Inc.*, reproduced below. As you read the case, ask yourself whether the Court seems to adopt a "reasonable and customary use" theory of fair use or some other theory.

Sony Corporation of America v. Universal City Studios, Inc.
464 U.S. 417 (1984)

STEVENS, J.: Petitioners manufacture and sell home video tape recorders [called "Betamax" or "VTRs"]. Respondents own the copyrights on some of the television programs that are broadcast on the public airwaves. Some members of the general public use video tape recorders sold by petitioners to record some of these broadcasts, as well as a large number of other broadcasts. The question presented is whether the sale of petitioners' copying equipment to the general public violates any of the rights conferred upon respondents by the Copyright Act. . . .

The respondents and Sony both conducted surveys of the way the Betamax machine was used by several hundred owners during a sample period in 1978. Although there were some differences in the surveys, they both showed that the primary use of the machine for most owners was "time-shifting,"—the practice of recording a program to view it once at a later time, and thereafter erasing it. Time-shifting enables viewers to see programs they otherwise would miss because they are not at home, are occupied with other tasks, or are viewing a program on another station at the time of a broadcast that they desire to watch. Both surveys also showed, however, that a substantial number of interviewees had accumulated libraries of tapes. Sony's survey indicated that over 80% of the interviewees watched at least as much regular television as they had before owning a Betamax. Respondents offered no evidence of decreased television viewing by Betamax owners.

Sony introduced considerable evidence describing television programs that could be copied without objection from any copyright holder, with special emphasis on sports, religious, and educational programming. For example, their survey indicated that 7.3% of all Betamax use is to record sports events, and representatives of professional baseball, football, basketball, and hockey testified that they had no objection to the recording of their televised events for home use. . . .

[As discussed in Chapter 9.D.1 *supra*, the Court looked to the Patent Act in formulating a standard for contributory liability of equipment manufacturers and distributors, and concluded that "the sale of copying equipment, like the sale of other articles of commerce, does not constitute contributory infringement if the product is widely used for legitimate, unobjectionable purposes. Indeed, it need merely be capable of substantial noninfringing uses."]

The question is thus whether the Betamax is capable of commercially significant noninfringing uses. In order to resolve that question, we need not explore *all* the different potential uses of the machine and determine whether or not they would constitute infringement. Rather, we need only consider whether on the basis of the facts as found by the district court a significant number of them would be noninfringing. Moreover, in order to resolve this case we need not give precise content to the question of how much use is commercially significant. For one potential use of the Betamax plainly satisfies this standard, however it is understood: private, noncommercial time-shifting in the home. It does so both (A) because respondents have no right to prevent other copyright holders from authorizing it for their programs, and (B) because the District Court's factual findings reveal that even the unauthorized home time-shifting of respondents' programs is legitimate fair use.

A. Authorized Time-Shifting

. . . [T]he findings of the District Court make it clear that time-shifting may enlarge the total viewing audience and that many producers are willing to allow private time-shifting to continue, at least for an experimental time period. . . .

. . . [T]wo items in the record deserve specific mention.

First is the testimony of John Kenaston, the station manager of Channel 58, an educational station in Los Angeles affiliated with the Public Broadcasting Service. He explained and authenticated the station's published guide to its programs. For each program, the guide tells whether unlimited home taping is authorized, home taping is authorized subject to certain restrictions (such as erasure within seven days), or home taping is not authorized at all. The Spring 1978 edition of the guide described 107 programs. Sixty-two of those programs or 58% authorize some home taping. Twenty-one of them or almost 20% authorize unrestricted home taping.

Second is the testimony of Fred Rogers, president of the corporation that produces and owns the copyright on *Mister Rogers' Neighborhood*. The program is carried by more public television stations than any other program. Its audience numbers over 3,000,000 families a day. He testified that he had absolutely no objection to home taping for noncommercial use and expressed the opinion that it is a real service to families to be able to record children's programs and to show them at appropriate times.

If there are millions of owners of VTR's who make copies of televised sports events, religious broadcasts, and educational programs such as *Mister Rogers' Neighborhood*, and if the proprietors of those programs welcome the practice, the business of supplying the equipment that makes such copying feasible should not be stifled simply because the equipment is used by some individuals to make unauthorized reproductions of respondents' works. The respondents do not represent a class composed of all copyright holders. . . .

Of course, the fact that other copyright holders may welcome the practice of time-shifting does not mean that respondents should be deemed to have granted a license to copy their programs. Third-party conduct would be wholly irrelevant in an action for direct infringement of respondents' copyrights. But in an action for *contributory* infringement against the seller of copying equipment, the copyright holder may not prevail unless the relief that he seeks affects only his programs, or unless he speaks for virtually all copyright holders with an interest in the outcome. . . .

B. Unauthorized Time-Shifting

Even unauthorized uses of a copyrighted work are not necessarily infringing. An unlicensed use of the copyright is not an infringement unless it conflicts with one of the specific exclusive rights conferred by the copyright statute. *Twentieth Century Music Corp. v. Aiken*, 422 U.S. 151, 154-155. Moreover, the definition of exclusive rights in §106 of the present Act is prefaced by the words "subject to sections 107 through 118." Those sections describe a variety of uses of copyrighted material that "are not infringements of copyright notwithstanding the provisions of §106." The most pertinent in this case is §107, the legislative endorsement of the doctrine of "fair use."

That section identifies various factors that enable a Court to apply an "equitable rule of reason" analysis to particular claims of infringement. Although not conclusive, the first factor requires that "the commercial or nonprofit character of an activity" be weighed in any fair use decision. If the Betamax were used to make copies for a commercial or profit-making purpose, such use would presumptively be unfair. The contrary presumption is appropriate here, however, because the District Court's findings plainly establish that time-shifting for private home use must be characterized as a noncommercial, nonprofit activity. Moreover, when one considers the nature of a televised copyrighted audiovisual work, see 17 U.S.C. §107(2) . . . and that time-shifting merely enables a viewer to see such a work which he had been invited to witness in its entirety free of charge, the fact that the entire work is reproduced, see §107(3), does not have its ordinary effect of militating against a finding of fair use.[33]

---

33. It has been suggested that "consumptive uses of copyrights by home VTR users are commercial even if the consumer does not sell the homemade tape because the consumer will not buy tapes separately sold by the copyright holder." Home Recording of Copyrighted Works: Hearing before Subcommittee on Courts, Civil Liberties and the Administration of Justice of the House Committee on the Judiciary, 97th Congress, 2d Session, pt. 2, p. 1250 (1982) (memorandum of Prof. Laurence H. Tribe). Furthermore, "[t]he error in excusing such theft as noncommercial," we are told, "can be seen by simple analogy: jewel theft is not converted into a noncommercial veniality if stolen jewels are simply worn rather than sold." *Ibid*. The premise and the analogy are indeed simple, but they add nothing to the argument. The use to which stolen jewelry is put is quite irrelevant in determining whether depriving its true owner of his present possessory interest in it is venial; because of the nature of the item and the true owner's interests in physical possession of it, the law finds the taking objectionable even if the thief does not use the item at all. Theft of a particular item of personal property of course may have commercial significance, for the thief deprives the owner of his right to sell that particular item to any individual. Time-shifting does not even remotely entail comparable

This is not, however, the end of the inquiry because Congress has also directed us to consider "the effect of the use upon the potential market for or value of the copyrighted work." §107(4). The purpose of copyright is to create incentives for creative effort. Even copying for noncommercial purposes may impair the copyright holder's ability to obtain the rewards that Congress intended him to have. But a use that has no demonstrable effect upon the potential market for, or the value of, the copyrighted work need not be prohibited in order to protect the author's incentive to create. The prohibition of such noncommercial uses would merely inhibit access to ideas without any countervailing benefit.

Thus, although every commercial use of copyrighted material is presumptively an unfair exploitation of the monopoly privilege that belongs to the owner of the copyright, noncommercial uses are a different matter. A challenge to a noncommercial use of a copyrighted work requires proof either that the particular use is harmful, or that if it should become widespread, it would adversely affect the potential market for the copyrighted work. Actual present harm need not be shown; such a requirement would leave the copyright holder with no defense against predictable damage. Nor is it necessary to show with certainty that future harm will result. What is necessary is a showing by a preponderance of the evidence that *some* meaningful likelihood of future harm exists. If the intended use is for commercial gain, that likelihood may be presumed. But if it is for a noncommercial purpose, the likelihood must be demonstrated.

In this case, respondents failed to carry their burden with regard to home time-shifting. . . .

[The District Court] rejected respondents' "fear that persons 'watching' the original telecast of a program will not be measured in the live audience and the ratings and revenues will decrease," by observing that current measurement technology allows the Betamax audience to be reflected. *Id.*, at 466. It rejected respondents' prediction "that live television or movie audiences will decrease as more people watch Betamax tapes as an alternative," with the observation that "[t]here is no factual basis for [the underlying] assumption." *Ibid.* It rejected respondents' "fear that time-shifting will reduce audiences for telecast reruns," and concluded instead that "given current market practices, this should aid plaintiffs rather than harm them." *Ibid.* And it declared that respondents' suggestion that "theater or film rental exhibition of a program will suffer because of time-shift recording of that program" "lacks merit." *Id.*, at 467. . . .

The District Court's conclusions are buttressed by the fact that to the extent time-shifting expands public access to freely broadcast television programs, it yields societal benefits. In *Community Television of Southern California v. Gottfried*, 459 U.S. 458, 508 n.12 (1983), we acknowledged the public interest in making television broadcasting more available. Concededly, that interest is not unlimited. But it supports an interpretation of the concept of "fair use" that requires the copyright

---

consequences to the copyright owner. Moreover, the time-shifter no more steals the program by watching it once than does the live viewer, and the live viewer is no more likely to buy prerecorded videotapes than is the time-shifter. Indeed, no live viewer would buy a prerecorded videotape if he did not have access to a VTR.

holder to demonstrate some likelihood of harm before he may condemn a private act of time-shifting as a violation of federal law.

When these factors are all weighed in the "equitable rule of reason" balance, we must conclude that this record amply supports the District Court's conclusion that home time-shifting is fair use. In light of the findings of the District Court regarding the state of the empirical data, it is clear that the Court of Appeals erred in holding that the statute as presently written bars such conduct.[40]. . .

BLACKMUN, J., with whom MARSHALL, J., POWELL, J., and REHNQUIST, J., join, dissenting: . . . *Two* kinds of Betamax usage are at issue here.[2] The first is "time-shifting," whereby the user records a program in order to watch it at a later time, and then records over it, and thereby erases the program, after a single viewing. The second is "library-building," in which the user records a program in order to keep it for repeated viewing over a longer term. Sony's advertisements, at various times, have suggested that Betamax users "record favorite shows" or "build a library." Sony's Betamax advertising has never contained warnings about copyright infringement, although a warning does appear in the Betamax operating instructions. . . .

There are situations . . . in which strict enforcement of th[e copyright] monopoly would inhibit the very "Progress of Science and useful Arts" that copyright is intended to promote. An obvious example is the researcher or scholar whose own work depends on the ability to refer to and to quote the work of prior scholars. Obviously, no author

40. The Court of Appeals chose not to engage in any "equitable rule of reason" analysis in this case. Instead, it assumed that the category of "fair use" is rigidly circumscribed by a requirement that every such use must be "productive." . . . That understanding of "fair use" was erroneous.

Congress has plainly instructed us that fair use analysis calls for a sensitive balancing of interests. The distinction between "productive" and "unproductive" uses may be helpful in calibrating the balance, but it cannot be wholly determinative. Although copying to promote a scholarly endeavor certainly has a stronger claim to fair use than copying to avoid interrupting a poker game, the question is not simply two-dimensional. For one thing, it is not true that all copyrights are fungible. Some copyrights govern material with broad potential secondary markets. Such material may well have a broader claim to protection because of the greater potential for commercial harm. Copying a news broadcast may have a stronger claim to fair use than copying a motion picture. And, of course, not all uses are fungible. Copying for commercial gain has a much weaker claim to fair use than copying for personal enrichment. But the notion of social "productivity" cannot be a complete answer to this analysis. A teacher who copies to prepare lecture notes is clearly productive. But so is a teacher who copies for the sake of broadening his personal understanding of his specialty. Or a legislator who copies for the sake of broadening her understanding of what her constituents are watching; or a constituent who copies a news program to help make a decision on how to vote.

Making a copy of a copyrighted work for the convenience of a blind person is expressly identified by the House Committee Report as an example of fair use, with no suggestion that anything more than a purpose to entertain or to inform need motivate the copying. In a hospital setting, using a VTR to enable a patient to see programs he would otherwise miss has no productive purpose other than contributing to the psychological well-being of the patient. Virtually any time-shifting that increases viewer access to television programming may result in a comparable benefit. The statutory language does not identify any dichotomy between productive and nonproductive time-shifting, but does require consideration of the economic consequences of copying.

2. This case involves only the home recording for home use of television programs broadcast free over the airwaves. No issue is raised concerning cable or pay television, or the sharing or trading of tapes.

could create a new work if he were first required to repeat the research of every author who had gone before him. The scholar, like the ordinary user, of course could be left to bargain with each copyright owner for permission to quote from or refer to prior works. But there is a crucial difference between the scholar and the ordinary user. When the ordinary user decides that the owner's price is too high, and forgoes use of the work, only the individual is the loser. When the scholar forgoes the use of a prior work, not only does his own work suffer, but the public is deprived of his contribution to knowledge. The scholar's work, in other words, produces external benefits from which everyone profits. In such a case, the fair use doctrine acts as a form of subsidy— albeit at the first author's expense—to permit the second author to make limited use of the first author's work for the public good. See Latman Fair Use Study 31; Gordon, Fair Use as Market Failure: A Structural Analysis of the *Betamax* Case and its Predecessors, 82 Colum. L. Rev. 1600, 1630 (1982).

A similar subsidy may be appropriate in a range of areas other than pure scholarship. The situations in which fair use is most commonly recognized are listed in §107 itself; fair use may be found when a work is used "for purposes such as criticism, comment, news reporting, teaching . . . scholarship, or research." The House and Senate Reports expand on this list somewhat, and other examples may be found in the case law. Each of these uses, however, reflects a common theme: each is a *productive* use, resulting in some added benefit to the public beyond that produced by the first author's work. The fair use doctrine, in other words, permits works to be used for "socially laudable purposes." See Copyright Office, Briefing Papers on Current Issues, reprinted in 1975 House Hearings 2051, 2055. I am aware of no case in which the reproduction of a copyrighted work for the sole benefit of the user has been held to be fair use. . . .

The making of a videotape recording for home viewing is an ordinary rather than a productive use of the Studios' copyrighted works. The District Court found that "Betamax owners use the copy for the same purpose as the original. They add nothing of their own." 480 F. Supp., at 453. Although applying the fair use doctrine to home VTR recording, as Sony argues, may increase public access to material broadcast free over the public airwaves, I think Sony's argument misconceives the nature of copyright. Copyright gives the author a right to limit or even to cut off access to his work. *Fox Film Corp. v. Doyal*, 286 U.S. 123, 127 (1932). A VTR recording creates no public benefit sufficient to justify limiting this right. Nor is this right extinguished by the copyright owner's choice to make the work available over the airwaves. Section 106 of the 1976 Act grants the copyright owner the exclusive right to control the performance and the reproduction of his work, and the fact that he has licensed a single television performance is really irrelevant to the existence of his right to control its reproduction. Although a television broadcast may be free to the viewer, this fact is equally irrelevant; a book borrowed from the public library may not be copied any more freely than a book that is purchased.

It may be tempting, as, in my view, the Court today is tempted, to stretch the doctrine of fair use so as to permit unfettered use of this new technology in order to increase access to television programming. But such an extension risks eroding the very basis of copyright law, by depriving authors of control over their works and consequently of their incentive to create. . . .

"NO MORE PACKING IN THE MIDDLE OF THE NIGHT! NO MORE RUNNING FROM THE BETAMAX PATROL! HERBERT, DARLING, WE'RE CLEAN!"

© 1984 King Features. Reprinted with special permission of King Features Syndicate.

Note on Fair Use as Market Failure

The *Sony* dissenters cited a well-known article by Professor Wendy Gordon, who articulated an economic perspective on fair use that has become enormously influential. Wendy J. Gordon, *Fair Use as Market Failure: A Structural and Economic Analysis of the* Betamax *Case and Its Predecessors*, 82 Colum. L. Rev. 1600 (1982). The article begins with the assumption that in a perfectly competitive market, consensual transactions would result in the movement of resources to those who value them the most. Market failures of various sorts, however, may prevent consensual transactions in copyright rights from occurring. In such cases, the fair use doctrine allows the use to proceed.

Professor Gordon describes three types of market failure that may exist in markets for copyrighted works:

> Copyright markets will not . . . always function adequately. . . . [A]t times bargaining may be exceedingly expensive or it may be impractical to obtain enforcement against nonpurchasers, or other market flaws might preclude achievement of desirable consensual exchanges. In those cases, the market cannot be relied on to mediate public interests in dissemination and private interests in remuneration. . . .

1. *Market Barriers.* . . . A particular type of market barrier is transaction costs. As long as the cost of reaching and enforcing bargains is lower than anticipated benefits from the bargains, markets will form. If transaction costs exceed anticipated benefits, however, no transactions will occur. . . . This may help explain why the "personal," "individual" nature of copying has been held relevant to fair use, and why "home use" may be relevant to the reach of copyright law. . . .

2. *Externalities.* . . . An analysis of the limitations of markets can also illuminate the special status that certain uses, such as scholarship, have in fair use tradition. The costs and benefits of the parties contracting for the uses often differ from the social costs and benefits at stake, so that transactions leading to an increase in social benefit may not occur. Thus, for example, a critic of the Warren Commission's investigation of the Kennedy assassination might write a "serious, thoughtful and impressive" book that will further public interest more than the revenues of his book alone would indicate. One might say that publication of his book gives an "external benefit" to persons who gain knowledge from the public debate sparked by the book without having purchased the book itself. . . .

In cases of externalities, then, the potential user may wish to produce socially meritorious new works by using some of the copyright owner's material, yet be unable to purchase permission because the market structure prevents him from being able to capitalize on the benefits to be realized. . . .

Distrust of the market may also be triggered when defendant's activities involve social values that are not easily monetized. . . . If the defendant's interest impinges on a first amendment interest, relying upon the market may become particularly inappropriate; constitutional values are rarely well paid in the marketplace. . . .

3. *Anti-Dissemination Motives.* . . . The case law has tended to grant fair use treatment where copyright owners seemed to be using their property right not for economic gain but to control the flow of information. . . .

. . . Even if money were offered, the owner of a play is unlikely to license a hostile review or a parody. . . .

Id. at 1613, 1627-33.

In the decades since *Sony* was decided, digital technologies have enabled the creation of automated systems that charge for access to and use of copyrighted works. In some copyright markets, such systems have significantly reduced the transaction costs associated with locating copyright owners and reaching bargained-for exchanges. Such systems, then, alleviate the first type of market failure that Professor Gordon described.

At the same time, the idea that market failure supplies a unifying explanation for the results in fair use cases has generated controversy. In particular, critics charge that focusing too narrowly on the problem of transaction costs can cause one to miss other types of market failure that might also be at play. "A permission system can cure the market failure that results from high transaction costs. . . . [It] does not cure the market failure that exists when there are diffuse external benefits that cannot be efficiently internalized in any bargained-for exchange." Lydia Pallas Loren, *Redefining the Market Failure Approach to Fair Use in an Era of Copyright Permission Systems*, 5 J. Intell. Prop. L. 1, 33 (1997); *see also* Brett M. Frischmann & Mark A. Lemley, *Spillovers*, 107 Colum. L. Rev. 257 (2007) (arguing that external benefits are an intended consequence of the copyright system); Paul Goldstein, Copyright's Highway: From Gutenberg to the Celestial Jukebox, 207-08 (rev. ed. 2003) ("[S]ome of the 1976 Act's exemptions—indeed, some aspects of fair use itself—are there, not because of transaction costs, but because certain uses and users serve socially valuable ends. . . ."). It would be difficult, for example, for a historian to charge all of those who might benefit from her research. In some contexts, society might decide that it is preferable for those external benefits to flow freely, and that a legal rule favoring internalization—i.e., allowing authors to extract remuneration for such benefits—would be ill-advised.

NOTES AND QUESTIONS

1. In part, the disagreement between the majority and the dissent in Sony can be characterized as a disagreement about which types of market failure should result in a finding of fair use. Justice Blackmun argues that the fair use doctrine should permit copying only for socially valuable purposes that generate "external benefits" for everyone, and not for personal copying by ordinary users. Review footnote 40 of the majority opinion, which responds to Justice Blackmun's argument. Who has the better argument about what makes a use productive?

2. Is the *Sony* majority correct in describing the use of VCRs for time-shifting as noncommercial? In an era in which many episodes of popular television series can be purchased or rented, would the fair use determination be the same? Would the fair use determination change if the plaintiff copyright owners could produce evidence that VCRs (or, today, DVRs) are primarily used to create libraries of programs for repeat viewing?

> **LOOKING BACK**
>
> As you saw in Chapter 9, copyright owners sometimes assert theories of indirect infringement liability against the manufacturers and distributors of consumer electronic equipment and software. To minimize the risk of such litigation, a manufacturer might consider designing its technology to foreclose certain types of uses, thereby "baking in" the boundaries of fair use as a practical matter.

3. Would the fair use analysis in *Sony* have differed if technology embedded in the VCRs either caused the VCRs not to record commercial advertisements in television broadcasts or allowed users automatically to skip over any commercials that were recorded? Should it differ?

4. Should the fair use analysis shield personal uses or uses that occur in the privacy of the home? Why, or why not?

2. Copying by Institutional Users

Many cases of simple copying for research or classroom use involve institutional users. Mechanisms for licensing such copying, essentially nonexistent when Congress enacted the 1976 Act, now are much more widespread. Should either fact affect the fair use analysis? Consider the following case.

Cambridge University Press v. Patton
769 F.3d 1232 (11th Cir. 2014)

TJOFLAT, J.:

Three publishing houses, Cambridge University Press, Oxford University Press, and Sage Publications, Inc. (collectively, "Plaintiffs") allege that members of the

Board of Regents of the University System of Georgia and officials at Georgia State University ("GSU") (collectively, "Defendants") infringed Plaintiffs' copyrights by maintaining a policy which allows GSU professors to make digital copies of excerpts of Plaintiffs' books available to students without paying Plaintiffs. . . .

I.

A. . . .

. . . Plaintiffs publish advanced scholarly works, which might be used in upper-level undergraduate and graduate courses. Cambridge and Oxford publish scholarly books and journals on niche subject areas. . . . Sage primarily publishes books on the social sciences. . . .

Plaintiffs market their books to professors who teach at universities and colleges. Cambridge and Oxford regularly send complimentary copies of their publications to professors. Sage provides trial copies upon request. Plaintiffs intend that professors use Plaintiffs' publications in their work and assign them as required reading so that students will purchase them.

Rather than assigning whole books, some professors assign or suggest excerpts from Plaintiffs' books as part of the curriculum for their courses. Professors . . . might prepare a bound, photocopied, paper "coursepack" containing excerpts from several works for a particular course. . . . In recent years, however, universities—following the trend with regard to distribution of many forms of media the world over—have increasingly abandoned paper coursepacks in favor of digital distribution of excerpts over the Internet.

GSU is a public university in Atlanta, Georgia. It is part of the University System of Georgia, and is overseen by the Board of Regents of the University System of Georgia. GSU maintains two on-campus systems known as "ERes" and "uLearn" for digital distribution of course materials to students. . . .

There exists a well-established system for the licensing of excerpts of copyrighted works. Copyright Clearance Center ("CCC") is a not-for-profit corporation with headquarters in Danvers, Massachusetts. CCC licenses excerpts from copyrighted works for a fee, acting on behalf of publishers who choose to make their works available through CCC. These licenses are called "permissions." All three Plaintiffs offer excerpt-specific permissions to photocopy or digitally reproduce portions of their works, which may be obtained directly from Plaintiffs or through CCC. Permissions are not, however, available for licensed copying of excerpts from all of Plaintiffs' works.

CCC offers a variety of permissions services to various categories of users, including corporate, educational, and institutional users. One such service, the Academic Permissions Service ("APS"), licenses educational users to make print copies on a per-use basis. CCC also offers an electronic course content service ("ECCS") for licensing of digital excerpts by educational users on a per-use basis, that—in 2008, the year for which evidence on the question was presented—offered only a small percentage of the works that were available through APS. ECCS is designed for electronic reserve systems such as ERes and uLearn.

Software is available that would allow GSU library personnel to place an order with CCC for a permission to provide students with a digital copy of an excerpt via ERes. CCC also offers an Academic Repertory License Service ("ARLS") which affords subscribers access to excerpts from a set group of about nine million titles, approximately 17 percent of which are available in digital format. Sage participates in ARLS and did so in 2009, Oxford participated in 2009 with regard to journals but not books, and Cambridge does not participate. GSU did not and does not subscribe to this program.

When the GSU bookstore assembles and sells a paper coursepack containing excerpts from copyrighted works, GSU pays permissions fees for use of the excerpts. The central issue in this case is under what circumstances GSU must pay permissions fees to post a digital copy of an excerpt of Plaintiffs' works to ERes or uLearn.

B.

On April 15, 2008, Plaintiffs filed their original complaint in the United States District Court for the Northern District of Georgia. Plaintiffs alleged that hundreds of GSU professors have made thousands of copyrighted works—including works owned or controlled by Plaintiffs—available on GSU's electronic reserve systems without obtaining permissions from copyright holders, and that GSU's administration facilitated, encouraged, and induced this practice. . . .

In late December 2008, the University System of Georgia convened a Select Committee on Copyright to review GSU's then-existing copyright policy, which was called the "Regents' Guide to Understanding Copyright & Educational Fair use." On February 17, 2009, the Select Committee announced a new copyright policy for GSU (the "2009 Policy"), which went into effect the same day. Under the 2009 Policy, a revised version of which remains in effect today, GSU professors who wish to post an excerpt of a copyrighted work on ERes or uLearn for distribution to their students must first determine whether they believe that doing so would be fair use. In order to make this determination, professors must fill out a "Fair use Checklist" for each excerpt.[9]

. . . For each [statutory] factor, the Checklist provides several criteria that purportedly weigh either for or against a finding of fair use, each with a corresponding checkbox. The Checklist instructs professors to check each criterion that applies, and then add up the checks to determine whether the factor weighs in favor of or against a finding of fair use. After making this tally, the Checklist explains that "[w]here the factors favoring fair use outnumber those against it, reliance on fair use is justified.

---

9. GSU's 2009 Policy was modeled on the copyright policy of Columbia University, which employs a similar approach, including use of a four-factor fair use checklist. The 2009 Policy is also similar to a policy jointly drafted in 2006 by Cornell University and the Association of American Publishers (the "AAP") for the use of materials in Cornell's electronic review system, after publishers represented by the AAP threatened to sue Cornell for copyright infringement. Many other universities incorporate a fair use checklist as part of their copyright policy to assist instructors with making fair use determinations, including Duke University, Florida State University, University of Tennessee–Knoxville, and Louisiana State University.

Where fewer than half the factors favor fair use, instructors should seek permission from the rights holder." . . .

. . . Plaintiffs' proposed injunction would essentially limit GSU to copying that fell within the parameters set forth in the Agreement on Guidelines for Classroom Copying in Not–For–Profit Educational Institutions with Respect to Books and Periodicals (the "Classroom Guidelines").[12] . . .

[Following a bench trial, t]he District Court found that "Plaintiffs earn considerable annual rights and permissions income through CCC. CCC made rights and permissions payments to Cambridge, Oxford, and Sage totaling $4,722,686.24 in FY 2009 and $5,165,445.10 in FY 2010," amounting to an average of $1,574,228.74 per-Plaintiff in FY 2009. *Id.* at 1216. However, these totals involve payments through services which have "no demonstrated relevance to this case." *Id.*

Considering only payments for permissions under the academic permissions services—the APS, ECCS, and [ARLS] programs—in FY 2009 Cambridge earned $404,494.90, Oxford earned $480,622.47, and Sage earned $352,759.84. APS income, which "is dominated by payments for printed coursepacks," accounted for the majority of these totals. Thus, in FY 2009, through ECCS—CCC's academic permissions service for individual licensing of *digital* copies of excerpts—Cambridge earned $81,671.35, Oxford earned $70,485.81, and Sage earned $85,660.91. The figures for FY 2010 are similar.

12. The Classroom Guidelines are the result of independent meetings that took place prior to passage of the Copyright Act of 1976 between "representatives of the Ad Hoc Committee of Educational Institutions and Organizations on Copyright Law Revision, and of the Authors League of America, Inc., and the Association of American Publishers, Inc.," groups representing, respectively, educators, authors, and publishers. *See* H.R. Rep. No. 94–1476 at 67 (1976), *reprinted in* 1976 U.S.C.C.A.N. 5659, 5680–81. . . .

In a letter dated March 8, 1976, the three groups delivered to Congress an "Agreement on Guidelines for Classroom Copying in Not–For–Profit Educational Institutions with Respect to Books and Periodicals," which came be known as the Classroom Guidelines. *Id., reprinted in* 1976 U.S.C.C.A.N. 5659, 5681. The Classroom Guidelines, which are reproduced in the legislative history of the 1976 Act, begin by stating that their "purpose . . . is to state the minimum and not the maximum standards of educational fair use under Section 107." *Id.* at 68, *reprinted in* 1976 U.S.C.C.A.N. 5659, 5681.

Under the terms of the Classroom Guidelines, teachers may make individual copies of excerpts of certain works for use in teaching, research, and class preparation, and may make multiple copies of works for classroom use so long as the copying meets the conditions of "brevity," "spontaneity," and "cumulative effect." *Id., reprinted in* 1976 U.S.C.C.A.N. 5659, 5682. "Brevity" places strict word count limits on allowable copying, such as "an excerpt from any prose work of not more than 1,000 words or 10 percent of the work." *Id.* "Spontaneity" provides that "[t]he inspiration and decision to use the work and the moment of its use for maximum teaching effectiveness are so close in time that it would be unreasonable to expect a timely reply to a request for permission." *Id.* at 69, *reprinted in* 1976 U.S.C.C.A.N. 5659, 5682. "Cumulative effect" places caps on the total amount of copying permissible under the Classroom Guidelines. *Id., reprinted in* 1976 U.S.C.C.A.N. 5659, 5683. The Classroom Guidelines also contain other provisions, including prohibitions on charging students for copied materials beyond the cost of copying, copying that substitutes for the purchase of books and other publications, copying the same material in multiple terms, and copying that "substitute[s] for anthologies, compilations or collective works." *Id.* at 69–70, *reprinted in* 1976 U.S.C.C.A.N. 5659, 5683. . . .

The District Court calculated the percentage of Plaintiffs' total revenues that these figures represent and determined that

> on average, APS and ECCS permissions represent .0024 (one-quarter of one percent) of net revenue in FY 2009 for each of the Plaintiffs. If the calculation is limited to ECCS income [for licensing of digital excerpts] (an average of $79,272 per Plaintiff), the percentage would be .00046 (five one-hundredths of one percent) of average net revenues. Even if all of the types of permissions payments reflected in Plaintiffs' referenced exhibits are included, this income would represent an average of .0093 (nine-tenths of one percent) of net revenues per Plaintiff for FY 2009.

[*Cambridge Univ. Press v. Becker*, 863 F. Supp. 2d 1190, 1216 (N.D. Ga. 2012).]

The District Court noted that Plaintiffs offered no testimony or evidence demonstrating that they lost book sales on account of Defendants' actions, and accordingly found that no book sales were lost. . . .

[The district court held that the first and second fair use factors favored the Defendants in all instances. As to the third factor, it held that:]

> [w]here a book is not divided into chapters or contains fewer than ten chapters, unpaid copying of no more than 10 percent of the pages in the book is permissible under factor three. . . . Where a book contains ten or more chapters, the unpaid copying of up to but no more than one chapter (or its equivalent) will be permissible under fair use factor three. . . . The chapter or other excerpt must fill a demonstrated, legitimate purpose in the course curriculum and must be narrowly tailored to accomplish that purpose. Where the foregoing limitations are met factor three will favor fair use, i.e., will favor Defendants. Otherwise factor three will favor Plaintiffs.

Id. at 1243.

[The district court held that the fourth factor weighed heavily in favor of Plaintiffs where digital permissions were readily available and in favor of Defendants where digital permissions were not readily available.] . . .

In weighing the fair use factors to assess each of the forty-eight instances of alleged infringement for which the District Court found that Plaintiffs had established a prima facie case, the District Court held that fair use applied whenever at least three of the four factors favored Defendants. Because the District Court found that factors one and two favored Defendants in all cases, the District Court essentially held that fair use applied each time a professor posted an excerpt that fell within the 10 percent-or-one-chapter limit on allowable copying the District Court had set (such that factor three favored Defendants) and each time there was no evidence that digital permissions were available for excerpts of the work in question (such that factor four favored Defendants). . . .

When the District Court's weighing of the factors resulted in a tie—factors one and two favored Defendants and factors three and four favored Plaintiffs—the District Court revisited its analysis of the factors, reviewing and reweighing the importance of the factors for the specific work in question. The District Court performed this reweighing for seven claims of infringement. In two instances, the District Court held that fair use applied because Plaintiffs' revenues from digital permissions were sufficiently small as a proportion of total revenues to render factor four of less importance. The District Court held that fair use did not apply in the remaining five instances. . . .

III. . . .

C. . . .

Plaintiffs contend that the District Court erred by performing a work-by-work analysis that focused on whether the use of each individual work was fair use rather than on the broader context of ongoing practices at GSU. We disagree. Fair use must be determined on a case-by-case basis, by applying the four factors to each work at issue. *See Campbell,* 510 U.S. at 577. Were we to accept Plaintiffs' argument, the District Court would have no principled method of determining whether a nebulous cloud of infringements purportedly caused by GSU's "ongoing practices" should be excused by the defense of fair use. . . .

Plaintiffs also argue that the District Court erred in giving each of the four factors equal weight, essentially taking a mechanical "add up the factors" approach, finding fair use if three factors weighed in favor of fair use and one against and vice versa, and only performing further analysis in case of a "tie." We agree that the District Court's arithmetic approach was improper. . . .

D. . . .

Plaintiffs argue that the District Court erred in its application of each of the four fair use factors. Plaintiffs' argument centers on a comparison of the circumstances of the instant case to those of the so-called "coursepack cases," in which courts rejected a defense of fair use for commercial copyshops that assembled paper coursepacks containing unlicensed excerpts of copyrighted works for use in university courses.

In *Basic Books, Inc. v. Kinko's Graphics Corp.,* publishing houses sued Kinko's, a commercial copyshop, alleging that Kinko's infringed the publishers' copyrights when it copied excerpts from the publishers' books, without permission and without payment of a license fee, and sold the copies for profit in bound, paper coursepacks to students for use in college courses. 758 F. Supp. 1522, 1526 (S.D.N.Y. 1991). The District Court rejected Kinko's claim that its use of the excerpts was fair use, and granted injunctive relief to the publishers. *Id.*

Similarly, in *Princeton University Press v. Michigan Document Services, Inc.,* the Sixth Circuit upheld the District Court's ruling that Michigan Document Services, a commercial copyshop, was not entitled to a fair use defense when it reproduced substantial portions of copyrighted academic works and sold the copies in bound, paper coursepacks to students for use in courses at the University of Michigan, without obtaining permission from the copyright holder. 99 F.3d 1381, 1383 (6th Cir.1996) (en banc). The Sixth Circuit held that injunctive relief was therefore warranted. *Id.* at 1392. . . .

. . . [B]ecause the fair use analysis is highly fact-specific and must be performed on a work-by-work basis, *see Cariou,* 714 F.3d at 694, the coursepack cases provide guidance but do not dictate the results here, which must be based upon a careful consideration of the circumstances of the individual instances of alleged infringement involved in this case.

1.

. . . The inquiry under the first factor has several facets, including (1) the extent to which the use is a "transformative" rather than merely superseding use of the original work and (2) whether the use is for a nonprofit educational purpose, as opposed to a commercial purpose. . . .

Here, Defendants' use of excerpts of Plaintiffs' works is not transformative. The excerpts of Plaintiffs' works posted on GSU's electronic reserve system are verbatim copies of portions of the original books which have merely been converted into a digital format. Although a professor may arrange these excerpts into a particular order or combination for use in a college course, this does not imbue the excerpts themselves with any more than a *de minimis* amount of new meaning. *See Princeton University Press,* 99 F.3d at 1389 ("[I]f you make verbatim copies of 95 pages of a 316–page book, you have not transformed the 95 pages very much—even if you juxtapose them to excerpts from other works."). . . .

However, we must also consider under the first factor whether Defendants' use is for a nonprofit educational purpose, as opposed to a commercial purpose. . . .

In the coursepack cases, *Princeton University Press,* 99 F.3d at 1389, and *Basic Books,* 758 F. Supp. at 1531-32, the first factor weighed against a finding of fair use when the nontransformative, educational use in question was performed by a for-profit copyshop, and was therefore commercial. . . . [T]he court[s] refused to allow the defendants, who were engaged in commercial operations, to stand in the shoes of students and professors in claiming that their making of multiple copies of scholarly works was for nonprofit educational purposes.

However, in both of the coursepack cases, the courts expressly declined to conclude that the copying would fall outside the boundaries of fair use if conducted by professors, students, or academic institutions. . . .

Defendants' use of Plaintiffs' works in the teaching of university courses is clearly for educational purposes. Nevertheless, it is not entirely clear that use by a nonprofit entity for educational purposes is always a "nonprofit" use as contemplated by §107(1). The Supreme Court has explained that "[t]he crux of the profit/nonprofit distinction is not whether the sole motive of the use is monetary gain but whether the user stands to profit from exploitation of the copyrighted material without paying the customary price." *Harper & Row,* 471 U.S. at 562. . . .

. . . [Plaintiffs argue that] Defendants "exploited" Plaintiffs' copyrighted material for use in university courses without "paying the customary price"—a licensing fee. Defendants profited from the use of excerpts of Plaintiffs' works—however indirectly—because GSU collects money from students in the form of tuition and fees (which students pay in part for access to ERes and uLearn) and reduces its costs by avoiding fees it might have otherwise paid for the excerpts.

However, this reasoning is somewhat circular, and hence of limited usefulness to our fair use inquiry. Of course, any unlicensed use of copyrighted material profits the user in the sense that the user does not pay a potential licensing fee, allowing the user to keep his or her money. If this analysis were persuasive, no use could qualify as "nonprofit" under the first factor. Moreover, if the use is a fair use, then the copyright owner is not entitled to charge for the use, and there is no "customary price" to be paid in the first place.

Accordingly, evaluating the indirect profit GSU gained by refusing to pay to license Plaintiffs' works provides little useful guidance under the first factor. Simply put, the greater the amount of a work taken by the secondary user (or the more valuable the portion taken), the more the user "profits" by not paying for the use. Thus, the concern we have identified with profit in this sense is better dealt with under the third factor . . . .

Although GSU certainly benefits from its use of Plaintiffs' works by being able to provide the works conveniently to students, and profits in the sense that it avoids paying licensing fees, Defendants' use is not fairly characterized as "commercial exploitation." . . . At the same time, the use provides a broader public benefit—furthering the education of students at a public university. . . .

Notably, early drafts of §107 did not include the parenthetical "including multiple copies for classroom use" or the specific direction to consider "whether [the] use is of a commercial nature or is for nonprofit educational purposes." *See* S. 3008, H.R. 11947, H.R. 12354, 88th Cong. (1st Sess. 1964); S. 1006, H.R. 4347, H.R. 5680, H.R. 6831, H.R. 6835, 89th Cong. (1st Sess. 1965); S. 597, H.R. 2512, H.R. 5650, 90th Cong. (1st Sess. 1967). This language was not inserted until one month before the passage of the Copyright Act of 1976. *See* S. 22, 94th Cong. (2d Sess. 1976).

In sum, Congress devoted extensive effort to ensure that fair use would allow for educational copying under the proper circumstances and was sufficiently determined to achieve this goal that it amended the text of the statute at the eleventh hour in order to expressly state it. Furthermore, as described above, allowing latitude for educational fair use promotes the goals of copyright. Thus, we are persuaded that, despite the recent focus on transformativeness under the first factor, use for teaching purposes by a nonprofit, educational institution such as Defendants' favors a finding of fair use under the first factor, despite the nontransformative nature of the use. . . .

2. . . .

The coursepack cases—which involved copying of academic works similar to those involved here—reached opposite conclusions as to the effect of the second factor. *Compare Princeton Univ. Press,* 99 F.3d at 1389 ("[T]he excerpts copied for the coursepacks contained creative material, or 'expression;' it was certainly not telephone book listings that the defendants were reproducing. This factor . . . cuts against a finding of fair use."), *with Basic Books,* 758 F. Supp. at 1533 ("The books infringed in suit were factual in nature. This factor weighs in favor of defendant.").

Nevertheless, relevant precedent indicates the proper approach. In *Harper & Row,* a publisher holding exclusive rights to President Ford's unpublished memoirs sued The Nation magazine after The Nation published portions of the memoirs. 471 U.S. at 543. Although it focused on the unpublished nature of the memoir, the

Court held that the second factor disfavored fair use in part because "The Nation did not stop at isolated phrases and instead excerpted subjective descriptions and portraits of public figures whose power lies in the author's individualized expression. Such use, focusing on the most expressive elements of the work, exceeds that necessary to disseminate the facts." *Id.* at 563-64. . . .

Defendants argue that GSU professors chose the excerpts of Plaintiffs' works for their factual content, not for any expressive content the works may contain, noting that several professors testified that if the use of a particular excerpt was not a fair use, they would have found another source. Of course, other professors testified that they chose particular excerpts because of the author's interpretative originality and significance. Regardless of whether GSU faculty chose the excerpts for their expressive or factual content, the excerpts were copied wholesale—facts, ideas, and original expression alike. Which aspect the secondary user was interested in is irrelevant to the disposition of the second factor.

Accordingly, we find that the District Court erred in holding that the second factor favored fair use in every instance. . . . That being said, the second fair use factor is of relatively little importance in this case.

3.

The third fair use factor . . . ["]examines whether defendants have 'helped themselves overmuch' of the copyrighted work in light of the purpose and character of the use." *Peter Letterese & Assocs.*, 533 F.3d at 1314 (quoting *Campbell*, 510 U.S. at 587). Thus, this factor is intertwined with the first factor.

"[T]his factor is [also] intertwined with the fourth factor and partly functions as a heuristic to determine the impact on the market for the original." *Id.* (footnote omitted). . . .

. . . Plaintiffs argue that the copying permitted by the District Court exceeds the amounts outlined in the Classroom Guidelines. We note that the Classroom Guidelines, although part of the legislative history of the Copyright Act, do not carry force of law. In any case, to treat the Classroom Guidelines as indicative of what is allowable would be to create the type of "hard evidentiary presumption" that the Supreme Court has cautioned against, because fair use must operate as a "'sensitive balancing of interests.'" *Campbell*, 510 U.S. at 584 (quoting *Sony*, 464 U.S. at 455, n.40). . . .

Furthermore, although Plaintiffs characterize the amounts set forth in the Classroom Guidelines as "limits," the Classroom Guidelines were intended to suggest a minimum, not maximum, amount of allowable educational copying that might be fair use. . . .

. . . The District Court should have analyzed each instance of alleged copying individually, considering the quantity and the quality of the material taken—including whether the material taken constituted the heart of the work—and whether that taking was excessive in light of the educational purpose of the use and the threat of market substitution.

4. . . .

The central question under the fourth factor is not whether Defendants' use of Plaintiffs' works caused Plaintiffs to lose *some* potential revenue. Rather, it is whether

Defendants' use—taking into account the damage that might occur if "everybody did it"—would cause *substantial* economic harm such that allowing it would frustrate the purposes of copyright by materially impairing Defendants' incentive to publish the work. *See Harper & Row*, 471 U.S. at 566-67 ("Fair use, when properly applied, is limited to copying by others which does not *materially* impair the marketability of the work which is copied." (emphasis added) (quotation marks omitted)).

We agree with the District Court that the small excerpts Defendants used do not substitute for the full books from which they were drawn. . . .

However, CCC's various programs for academic permissions—and Plaintiffs' own permissions programs—constitute a workable market through which universities like GSU may purchase licenses to use excerpts of Plaintiffs' works. . . .

We note that it is not determinative that programs exist through which universities may license excerpts of Plaintiffs' works. In other words, the fact that Plaintiffs have made paying easier does not automatically dictate a right to payment. . . . The goal of copyright is to stimulate the creation of new works, not to furnish copyright holders with control over all markets. Accordingly, the ability to license does not demand a finding against fair use.

Nevertheless, . . . absent evidence to the contrary, if a copyright holder has not made a license available to use a particular work in a particular manner, the inference is that the author or publisher did not think that there would be enough such use to bother making a license available. In such a case, there is little damage to the publisher's market when someone makes use of the work in that way without obtaining a license, and hence the fourth factor should generally weigh in favor of fair use. This is true of Plaintiffs' works for which no license for a digital excerpt was available. . . .

An analogy is helpful. A publisher acts like a securities underwriter. A publisher determines the value of a work, which is set by the anticipated demand for the work. Thus, the greater the demand for the work—the greater the market—the more the publisher will pay the author of the work up front, and the more the publisher will endeavor to make the work widely available. If a publisher makes licenses available for some uses but not for others, this indicates that the publisher has likely made a reasoned decision not to enter the licensing market for those uses, which implies that the value of that market is minimal.

With regard to the works for which digital permissions were unavailable, Plaintiffs choose to enter those works into some markets—print copies of the whole work, or perhaps licenses for paper copies of excerpts—but not the digital permission market. This tells us that Plaintiffs likely anticipated that there would be little to no demand for digital excerpts of the excluded works and thus saw the value of that market as de minimis or zero. If the market for digital excerpts were in fact de minimis or zero, then neither Defendants' particular use nor a widespread use of similar kind would be likely to cause significant market harm. Of course, if publishers choose to participate in the market the calculation will change.

. . . We find that . . . the District Court properly took license availability into account in determining whether the fourth factor weighted for or against fair use.

Plaintiffs argue that the District Court erred by placing the burden on Plaintiffs to show that digital licenses for the particular works in question were reasonably available through CCC in 2009. . . . Plaintiffs argue that this amounted to relieving the Defendants of their burden of proof on the fourth factor.

We disagree. . . . Plaintiffs—as publishers—can reasonably be expected to have the evidence as to availability of licenses for their own works. It is therefore reasonable to place on Plaintiffs the burden of going forward with the evidence on this question.

In effect, this creates a presumption that no market for digital permissions exists for a particular work. This is reasonable, because if a license was available during the relevant time period, Plaintiffs can rebut the presumption of no market by going forward with evidence of license availability. . . . Then, Defendants—retaining the overall burden of persuasion on the fourth factor—must demonstrate that their use does not materially impair the existing or potential market in order to prevail.

Although the District Court did not articulate its approach to the evidentiary burden on license availability in exactly this manner, the District Court did essentially what we have described. . . .

. . . Accordingly, we find that the District Court did not err in its application of the fourth factor. However, because Defendants' copying was nontransformative and the threat of market substitution was therefore serious, the District Court erred by not affording the fourth factor additional weight in its overall fair use calculus. . . .

E.

In sum, we hold that the District Court did not err in performing a work-by-work analysis of individual instances of alleged infringement in order to determine the need for injunctive relief. However, the District Court did err by giving each of the four fair use factors equal weight, and by treating the four factors mechanistically. The District Court should have undertaken a holistic analysis which carefully balanced the four factors in the manner we have explained. . . .

[The court remanded for further proceedings consistent with its opinion.]

VINSON, J., concurring specially: It seems to me that the District Court's error was broader and more serious than the majority's analysis concludes, and I write separately to highlight some of those differences. . . .

This case does not involve an individual using a single copyrighted work, nor does it involve a single course, a single professor, or even a one-time use of "multiple copies for classroom distribution." *See Campbell, supra,* 510 U.S. at 579 n.11. Nor, in my opinion, should it be confined to the seventy-four specific instances of infringement that were the focus during trial. Rather, this case arises out of a university-wide practice to substitute "paper coursepacks" (the functional equivalent of textbooks) that contained *licensed* copyrighted works with "digital coursepacks" that contained *unlicensed* copyrighted works. This was done for the vast majority of courses offered at GSU and . . . it was done primarily to save money.[3] . . .

---

3. . . . Plaintiffs contend on appeal that the District Court erred by performing a work-by-work analysis which focused on each individual work rather than analyzing fair use in the context of this broad ongoing practice at GSU. The majority opinion rejects this argument, concluding that "[c]ourts

... The Sixth Circuit undertook a proper market-harm analysis in one of the Coursepack Cases when it assessed the potential impact on publishers if unauthorized reproduction of scholarly works for paper coursepacks was replicated nationwide:

> If copyshops across the nation were to start doing what the defendants have been doing here, this revenue stream would shrivel and the potential value of the copyrighted works of scholarship published by the plaintiffs would be diminished accordingly.

Princeton Univ. Press, supra, 99 F.3d at 1387. One could substitute "universities" for "copyshops" in the above quoted passage . . . and would have to reach the same conclusion. . . .

NOTES AND QUESTIONS

1. Do you agree with the majority's conclusion that the first statutory fair use factor weighed in favor of the Georgia State defendants? Do you think the *Sony* Court would have agreed?

2. Should the Classroom Guidelines have carried more weight in the analysis of the third statutory factor? As is inevitably the case in any such effort, not all affected parties were included in the discussions that led to the Guidelines. Although some higher education groups were represented, neither the Association of American Law Schools (AALS) nor the American Association of University Professors (AAUP) participated. Both the AALS and the AAUP objected strongly to the Guidelines as too restrictive and not reflective of then-existing higher education practice. Their objections are expressly noted in the legislative history. H.R. Rep. No. 94-1476, at 72 (1976), reprinted in 1976 U.S.C.C.A.N. 5659, 5685.

3. The first circuit court opinion in a case involving large-scale copying by an institutional user was *American Geophysical Union v. Texaco, Inc.,* 60 F.3d 913 (2d Cir. 1994), in which publishers of scientific journal articles sued a petrochemical company whose research scientists had been making personal archival copies. Texaco had paid for subscriptions to the journals, but plaintiffs asserted that Texaco could, and should, obtain a blanket license from the Copyright Clearance Center (CCC) that would authorize archival photocopying. A majority of the panel agreed, endorsing a view of fair use informed by the market failure theory: "[I]t is sensible that a particular unauthorized use should be considered 'more fair' when there is no

---

must apply the fair use factors to each work at issue. Otherwise, courts would have no principled method of determining whether a nebulous cloud of alleged infringements purportedly caused by a secondary user should be excused by the defense of fair use." If we were writing on a blank slate in the normal case, I would agree that the court should focus on the details. But, we are not writing on a blank slate in a normal case. . . . The fact that GSU previously paid the permissions fees is strong, if not conclusive, evidence that the underlying use at issue was *not* "fair use;" indeed, it is practically an admission that it was not. Thus, in my view, there is no "nebulous cloud" surrounding what happened here that would otherwise require a work-by-work analysis. Rather, it seems clear that the challenged use (replacing paper coursepacks comprised of licensed copyrighted works with digital versions comprised of unlicensed works) is an aggregated one that should be viewed in the "big picture." . . .

ready market or means to pay for the use, while such an unauthorized use should be considered 'less fair' when there is a ready market or means to pay for the use." *Id*. at 930-31. The "coursepack cases" adopted a similar approach, as did the *Cambridge University Press* court.

Dissenting in *American Geophysical Union*, Judge Jacobs charged that the majority's reasoning was circular: "[T]he market will not crystallize unless courts reject the fair use argument that Texaco presents; but, under the statutory test, we cannot declare a use to be an infringement unless (assuming other factors also weigh in favor of the secondary user) there is a market to be harmed." 60 F.3d at 937 (Jacobs, J., dissenting). The *Cambridge University Press* court noted that a similar circularity problem complicates the determination of whether the defendant is engaged in "nonprofit" use for purposes of the first factor. Is there a way out of these circularity problems? With regard to the fourth factor, the majority in *American Geophysical Union* stated that "[t]he vice of circular reasoning arises only if the availability of payment is conclusive against fair use." *Id*. at 931. Do you agree? How else might the fourth factor be analyzed?

4. What do you make of the concurring judge's view that the defendants' copying should be evaluated in aggregate rather than on a case-by-case basis? Does the statute authorize such an approach? How would such an analysis be conducted?

5. Operationally, how should a university or other nonprofit institutional user implement safeguards designed to keep copying within the bounds of fair use? What do you make of the "checklist" approach adopted by Georgia State and a number of other universities (see footnote 9 in the majority opinion)? Would you expect such an approach to produce good—or "good enough"—results? How should other universities that have adopted the checklist approach respond to the Eleventh Circuit's opinion?

In articulating its "one chapter or ten percent" rule, the district court appears to have been attempting to develop a set of guidelines that was more flexible than the Classroom Guidelines but more constraining than the checklist. Why was that inappropriate? Is it realistic to expect actors in an institutional setting to analyze fair use as a court would?

3. Personal Use Revisited

Consider, again, whether the result in *Sony* would have been different if then-available technology allowed Sony to give users more control over playback of recorded works. The capabilities of networked digital technologies have made questions about design and control more pressing. Such technologies enable ordinary users of copyrighted works to interact with those works in ways that formerly required specialized knowledge and equipment, but also enable equipment and service providers to exercise more fine-grained control over what types of uses to allow.

Many personal uses occur in the privacy of the home or in other offline settings; others occur online and may be shared with large numbers of people. In either case, however, personal use of copyrighted works in digital form generally involves a variety of intermediaries including equipment providers, Internet service providers, web-hosting providers, and others. For the most part, copyright owners that object to particular uses have preferred to sue intermediaries rather than end users themselves. As you learned in Chapter 9, there are a variety of reasons for this. One is that equipment and service providers have deeper pockets than most ordinary individuals. Another is that successful litigation may result in changes to the technical design of equipment and services. Judges may craft injunctive relief ordering defendants to do things differently (as was the ultimate result in *Grokster*, Chapter 9.D.2), or industry players may attempt to manage litigation risk by providing users with certain capabilities but not others.

> ### COMPARATIVE PERSPECTIVE
>
> Exceptions to copyright for private or personal use have long been part of the copyright laws of many European countries. In particular, prior to the EU's 2001 directive on copyright harmonization, the copyright laws of France, Germany, the Netherlands, and Spain included broad private use exceptions. More recently, Canada has adopted an exception specifically for qualifying user generated content. *See* Canadian Copyright Act (R.S.C. 1985, c C-42), s 29.21 (as amended).

As you learned in Chapter 9.C, following the enactment of §512, online service providers have looked for ways to manage the flood of take-down notices, thereby preserving their eligibility for safe-harbor protection, while still facilitating the activities valued by their users. One increasingly widespread approach involves automated filtering and blocking based on content-matching algorithms. In 2007, a group of major copyright owners including Disney, Fox, Microsoft, NBC Universal, and Viacom released a statement of "Principles for User Generated Content Services," http://ugcprinciples.com/, that sought to encourage automated filtering of infringing content. Review the description of those principles in Chapter 9.E.4.a *supra*, now. In response, a group of nonprofit organizations issued a counterproposal titled "Fair Use Principles for User Generated Video Content," http://www.eff.org/files/UGC_Fair_Use_Best_Practices_0.pdf. According to the latter proposal, automated content filters should be designed to incorporate protections for fair use, removing user generated video content only if:

(1) the video track matches the video track of a copyrighted work submitted by a content owner;

(2) the audio track matches the audio track of that *same* copyrighted work; and

(3) nearly the entirety (e.g., 90% or more) of the challenged content is comprised of a single copyrighted work (i.e., a "ratio test").

If filtering technologies cannot establish these three facts, the document recommends manual review by the content owner before a video is taken down or blocked.

NOTES AND QUESTIONS

1. Consider, again, whether fair use should protect uses that occur in the privacy of the home. If you think it should, is that because market failures make licensing infeasible, or for other reasons?

2. Should fair use protect personal uses that occur online? Why, or why not? How should the statutory fair use factors be evaluated in the case of a user-generated mashup that combines the video track from one work with the audio track from another? How should they be evaluated in the case of a video that simply shows a person lip-synching or dancing to a popular song? In addition to the statutory factors, what other factors should a fair use analysis of user generated content consider?

3. Should automated content filters be understood as a type of reasonable and customary best practices, imposed via technological means but otherwise similar to the "Documentary Filmmakers Statement of Best Practices in Fair Use" discussed in section A.2 of this chapter? Why, or why not? Who should be involved in setting the parameters for automated content filters?

PRACTICE EXERCISE: COUNSEL A CLIENT

You are in-house counsel to a company that operates a video-hosting website. You need to decide whether the site should adopt either the industry-sponsored "Principles for UGC Services" or the nonprofit-sponsored "UGC Guidelines," or whether it should manually review videos that trigger takedown notices. What approach do you recommend, and why?

D. FAIR USE IN COMPARATIVE PERSPECTIVE

Most countries recognize a need for limitations on copyright owners' exclusive rights. However, most other countries historically have not used a doctrine like fair use to help define those limits. Instead, they designate specific types of uses that are permitted. The divergence between the U.S. fair use doctrine and other approaches to defining privileged uses of copyrighted works has become both increasingly apparent and increasingly problematic in a world where multilateral intellectual property treaties seek increasing harmonization of copyright norms.

In the United Kingdom, courts initially developed common law principles for limiting copyright owners' rights. In 1911, the British Parliament codified certain of these limits, primarily by reference to the concept of "fair dealing." These included uses of copyrighted works for educational purposes, review, private study, research or news commentary, and public recitation. The British copyright acts of 1956 and 1988 continued these exceptions. Today, most common law countries (many of them former British colonies) use the concept of fair dealing, which at least in some jurisdictions has proved to be considerably narrower than the U.S. concept of fair use. For a summary of different countries' practices regarding copyright limitations and exceptions, see Paul Goldstein & Bernt Hugenholtz, International Copyright: Principles, Law, and Practice 371-403 (2013).

Continental European countries such as France, Germany, and Belgium, on the other hand, provide only narrow, specific limitations. Brazil follows this Continental

European model of specifying exceptions and limitations in the statute, as does Japan, which, in addition to a list, also has a reference to "fair practice" as a copyright limitation. *See* Japanese Copyright Act art. 32(1). In this Continental European approach, courts rarely, if ever, depart from these statutes to find limitations of their own for other types of conduct not envisioned ex ante by the legislature. The enumerated exceptions often include permission for private noncommercial use, quotation, parody, news reporting, and educational and research uses and so there is rarely any question about what uses are beyond the copyright owner's scope of control.

Historically, the diverse approaches to limitations on the exclusive rights of copyright owners made it difficult for negotiators of multilateral treaties to settle on an approach acceptable to all signatories. The Berne Convention, which was drafted in the late 1800s by the major European powers without U.S. participation, generally follows a mixture of traditional Continental and British approaches to delineating permissible limitations and exceptions. For example, Article 10 permits quotations from published works "compatible with fair practice." Berne Conv., art. 10(1). Other provisions in Articles 10 and 10*bis* allow national legislation to permit specific uses, including uses for news reporting. Article 9(2), however, contains the "three-step test," which permits member countries to place additional limitations on the reproduction right: "It shall be a matter for legislation in the countries of the Union to permit the reproduction of such works in [1] certain special cases, provided that [2] such reproduction does not conflict with a normal exploitation of the work and [3] does not unreasonably prejudice the legitimate interests of the author." *Id.* art. 9(2).

The negotiators of the TRIPS Agreement used the language of Article 9(2) of the Berne Convention as the basis for Article 13 of TRIPS: "Members shall confine limitations or exceptions to exclusive rights to certain special cases which do not conflict with a normal exploitation of the work and do not unreasonably prejudice the legitimate interests of the right holder." TRIPS Agreement, art. 13.

Guided by the language of TRIPS Article 13, the European Union allows member states to provide exceptions or limitations to copyright, national discretion is limited by language that very closely tracks the three-step test. Exceptions "shall only be applied in certain special cases which do not conflict with a normal exploitation of the work or other subject-matter and do not unreasonably prejudice the legitimate interests of the rightholder." Directive 2001/29/EC of the European Parliament and of the Council of 22 May 2001 on the harmonisation of certain aspects of copyright and related rights in the information society, 2001 O.J. (L 167) 10, art. 5(5).

Because Article 13 applies to limitations on *any* of the exclusive copyright rights, some commentators view it as more restrictive than Article 9(2) of the Berne Convention, which applies only to limitations on the reproduction right. In particular, some commentators argue that the three steps should be applied cumulatively, first limiting the scope of permissible exceptions to narrow, discrete issues (step 1) and then requiring an assessment of the impact on existing (step 2) and prospective (step 3) interests of a copyright owner.

Others argue, however, that courts should not interpret the TRIPS Agreement's version of the three-step test restrictively. The Max Planck Institute for Intellectual

Property, Competition and Tax Law has issued a declaration that calls for a balanced interpretation of the test. *See* http://www.ip.mpg.de/en/pub/news/declaration_threesteptest.cfm. The Declaration emphasizes, *inter alia*, that the three steps do not require limitations to be interpreted narrowly, nor do they prevent either courts or legislatures from adopting open-ended limitations of reasonably foreseeable scope. *Id.* Many leading copyright scholars have signed the declaration. *See id.* Despite ongoing disagreement over the meaning and application of the three-step test, it continues to be included in the text proposals for multilateral and plurilateral intellectual property negotiations in a number of fora including those you read about in Chapter 1.C.4.

NOTES AND QUESTIONS

1. Which approach to defining privileged uses of copyrighted works seems to make more sense, the U.S. fair use doctrine, the Continental European approach, or a mixture?

2. Some commentators argue that the U.S. fair use doctrine does not comply with TRIPS Article 13. If Congress added language modeled on TRIPS Article 13 to the end of §107, would that assure U.S. compliance? Would such a sentence change the nature of the fair use inquiry?

3. Recall from Chapter 5 that the Berne Convention allows countries to impose limitations on the rights of copyright owners of musical works, so long as the limitation is linked to a system of equitable compensation. *See* Berne Conv., art. 13(1). Article 11*bis*(2) imposes a similar requirement for equitable remuneration with respect to limitations on the broadcast right. Would a rule subjecting all limitations to payment of reasonable compensation be consistent with U.S. copyright policy?

4. Negotiations over the WIPO Copyright Treaty ("WCT") included proposals (made, interestingly, by the United States) to limit allowable exceptions in a way that would appear to contract the permissible sphere of U.S.-style fair use. However, the version of the WCT eventually signed contains language essentially similar to Article 13 of the TRIPS Agreement. *See* WCT, art. 10. The Agreed Statement for Article 10 indicates that the treaty is intended to permit signatories to "carry forward and appropriately extend into the digital environment limitations and exceptions in their national laws which have been considered acceptable under the Berne Convention. Similarly, these provisions should be understood to permit [signatory countries] to devise new exceptions and limitations that are appropriate in the digital network environment."

V

PRACTICAL CONSIDERATIONS IN LICENSING AND ENFORCING COPYRIGHTS

H

Copyright Due Diligence

Parts III and IV of this book addressed the doctrines that establish liability for copyright infringement and limitations on liability. The chapters in this part address a variety of practical considerations that relate to licensing and enforcing copyrights. We begin in this chapter with an examination of the rules that bear on the integrity of the copyright title and on the duration of copyright protection. As you know, copyright law has changed significantly since the enactment of the first Copyright Act. While the 1976 Act's rules apply to newer works, many of the rules contained in the 1909 Act still shape copyright law and practice for older works. Those rules primarily concern how copyright is obtained and maintained, and how to determine when copyright protection has lapsed. In copyright practice, due diligence requires ascertaining which rules apply and determining their effect.

A. FORMALITIES

Recall from Chapter 1 that until relatively recently, the United States did not play a significant role in the evolution of international copyright law. American isolationism from the international copyright system was most evident in statutory provisions, dating back to the Copyright Act of 1790, that required compliance with certain formalities as a quid quo pro for federal copyright protection. These formalities were: (1) publication; (2) notice; (3) registration; and (4) deposit of a copy of the copyrighted work with a designated entity.

The Berne Convention expressly prohibits member countries from subjecting "the enjoyment and exercise of . . . rights" to any formality. Berne Conv., art. 5(2). Accordingly, when it joined the Berne Convention in 1989, the United States amended its statutory provisions relating to formalities. Today, failure to comply with copyright formalities no longer results in loss of copyright protection.

Nevertheless, the four formalities listed above continue to complicate contemporary copyright analysis. First, the changes only apply prospectively, so some older works continue to be affected by the prior rules. Second, while failure to comply with formalities no longer affects any substantive rights, there are practical reasons that the formalities remain important and should be observed.

1. An Overview

In 1790, Congress enacted the first Copyright Act to provide statutory protection to authors of maps, charts, and books. As a condition of protection, the Act prescribed certain requirements. First, the Act required that the author or proprietor deposit a copy of the title page of the work, but not the work itself, with the clerk's office in the district court of the place where the author or proprietor resided. The clerk was required to maintain a book of record in which the titles of protected works would be entered. Second, the Act required the author or proprietor to give notice of copyright to the public by publishing a copy of the record of copyright received from the clerk in at least one domestic newspaper within two months from the date of the record, and to maintain this newspaper notice for a period of four weeks. Third, the author or proprietor had to deposit a copy of the work in the office of the U.S. secretary of state within six months of its publication. Each of these three formalities was essential to perfecting the title of the copyright owner under the 1790 Act. *See Wheaton v. Peters,* 33 U.S. (8 Pet.) 591 (1834). In 1802, Congress added the requirement that the copy of record published in the newspapers also be inserted in the title page or in the page immediately following the title of *every* book.

The basic copyright framework established by the 1790 Act was amended many times throughout the nineteenth century, but the first significant changes to the required formalities occurred with passage of the Copyright Act of 1909. This Act abandoned the requirement of notice in a newspaper. Instead, proper notice of copyright was required on each copy of the work published or offered for sale in the United States. Proper notice consisted of the word "Copyright" or "Copr.," and the name of the copyright proprietor. Printed literary, musical, and dramatic works also had to include the year copyright was secured by publication, and notice had to appear on the title page or the page immediately following. For all other works eligible for protection under the Act (maps, works of art such as models or designs and their reproductions, scientific or technical drawings, photographs and prints/pictorial illustrations), proper notice consisted of the symbol "©" accompanied by an identifying mark, symbol, or initials of the copyright owner. Further, the owner's full name had to appear on some accessible part of the work. The Act demanded strict compliance with the notice requirements in order to preserve copyright protection. It also required prompt deposit of "two complete copies of the best [published] edition" of the work with the Copyright Office and authorized the Copyright Office to demand deposit. Failure to comply with such a demand in a timely manner resulted not only in a fine but also in forfeiture of the copyright.

Under the 1909 Act a copyright owner was entitled to register his or her claim with the Copyright Office and obtain a certificate of registration. Registration was optional during the first term of the copyright, but failure to register and deposit copies of the work barred any action for copyright infringement. In addition, the owner was required to register in order to receive a renewal term. (We discuss copyright duration

> **KEEP IN MIND**
>
> Prior to January 1, 1978 (the effective date of the 1976 Act), if a work did not qualify for federal statutory protection, it may have been eligible for state protection (either statutory or common law), although certain activities would result in the loss of that protection as well.

and renewal in Sections B and C, *infra*.) Finally, under the 1909 Act, certain unpublished works that were "not reproduced for sale" could be registered, thus bringing such works under federal statutory protection. Section 12 of the 1909 Act indicated that the types of unpublished works eligible for statutory protection through registration were lectures and similar productions, dramatic compositions, musical compositions, dramatico-musical compositions, motion picture photoplays, motion pictures other than photoplays, photographs, works of art, and plastic works and drawings.

Like its predecessor acts, the 1909 Act did not provide a definition of "publication." Yet, unless a work was eligible for registration as an unpublished work "not reproduced for sale," this concept was now central to determining whether or not an author or proprietor was entitled to statutory protection. The absence of a statutory definition meant that it was up to the courts to determine when exactly publication occurred.[*] Over time, judicial construction yielded several different rules about what might constitute publication and, even more important, what kinds of actions did *not* result in a publication for copyright purposes. For example, it became settled case law that the public nature of a particular use of a copyrighted work, such as a public performance or public delivery of a lecture or speech, did not necessarily constitute a publication of the work. *See, e.g., Ferris v. Frohman*, 223 U.S. 424 (1912); *Nutt v. National Inst. Inc. for the Improvement of Memory*, 31 F.2d 236 (2d Cir. 1929); *McCarthy & Fischer, Inc. v. White*, 259 F.364 (S.D.N.Y. 1919). Instead, "publication" seemed to turn on the degree to which a large number of people had both access to and control over multiple tangible copies of the work, or whether the public was given unrestricted access to copy the work. *See Burke v. National Broad. Co.*, 598 F.2d 688, 693 (1st Cir. 1979); *Patterson v. Century Prods.*, 93 F.2d 489, 492 (2d Cir. 1937). With the advent of the new broadcast technologies of radio and television, however, the focus on access to and control over physical copies began to seem more and more artificial.

When Congress enacted a new copyright statute in 1976, the United States did not wish to wholly abandon formalities as a prerequisite for copyright protection.

---

[*] The Act did provide guidelines to determine the precise moment that publication occurred for the purpose of calculating the term of copyright protection. Section 62 stated that the date of publication for a work "of which copies are reproduced for sale or distribution . . . shall be held to be the earliest date when copies of the first authorized edition were placed on sale, sold, or publicly distributed by the proprietor of the copyright or under his authority." However, at least one case held that this provision should not be construed to provide a general definition of "publication." *See Cardinal Film Corp. v. Beck*, 248 F. 368 (S.D.N.Y. 1918).

Nonetheless, the legislative history of the 1976 Act indicates that Congress was sensitive to the hardship placed on authors and proprietors who failed to comply with the formalities required by the 1909 Act. In addition, other issues, such as the difficulty of defining the threshold concept of "publication," signaled the need for a general revision of these requirements.

The 1976 Act abandoned the requirement of publication as a condition of statutory protection and replaced it with the requirement of "fixation" in a tangible medium of expression. The change effectively abolished a dual system of protection, under which unpublished works were protected by state common law and published works by federal statutory copyright. The House Report asserted the following rationale for this fundamental shift:

> "Publication," perhaps the most important single concept under the . . . [1909 Act] also represents its most serious defect. Although at one time, when works were disseminated almost exclusively through printed copies, "publication" could serve as a practical dividing line between common law and statutory protection, this is no longer true. With the development of the 20th-century communications revolution, the concept of publication has become increasingly artificial and obscure. To cope with the legal consequences of an established concept that has lost much of its meaning and justification, the courts have given "publication" a number of diverse interpretations, some of them radically different. Not unexpectedly, the results in individual cases have become unpredictable and often unfair.

H.R. Rep. No. 94-1476, 94th Cong., 2d Sess., 129-30 (1976), *reprinted in* 1976 U.S.C.C.A.N. 5659, 5741-43. Further, the House Report stated that abolishing the publication requirement would facilitate fidelity to the constitutional provision stating that protection should be afforded to authors only for "limited Times." According to the Report, "[c]ommon law protection in 'unpublished' works is now perpetual, no matter how widely they may be disseminated by means other than 'publication'; the bill would place a time limit on the duration of exclusive rights in them. The provision would also aid scholarship and the dissemination of historical materials by making unpublished, undisseminated manuscripts available for publication after a reasonable period." *Id.* at 130. Finally, the House Report noted that having a uniform copyright system would facilitate U.S. adherence to international copyright treaties because "[n]o other country has anything like our present dual system." *Id.*

The 1976 Act retained a notice requirement, but here too it mitigated the harshness of the 1909 Act. In explaining Congress' decision to retain the requirement, the House Report identified four principal functions of the notice formality: (1) it had the effect of placing in the public domain a substantial body of published material that no one was interested in copyrighting, because the authors of such material could simply omit the required notice; (2) it informed the public whether a particular work was copyrighted; (3) it identified the copyright owner; and (4) it showed the date of publication. Accordingly, the Act required that notice of copyright be included on works published by authority of the copyright owner. Congress retained the basic form of notice: (1) the word "Copyright" or its abbreviated version, "Copr.," or the symbol "©"; (2) the year of first publication; and

(3) the name of the copyright owner. Errors in the name or date could be corrected without forfeiting copyright protection. Further, the requirement regarding the location of notice on a copyrighted work was relaxed to allow notice to be placed on copies "in such manner and location as to give reasonable notice of the claim of copyright." 17 U.S.C. §401(c). In addition, the 1976 Act provided that protection would not be lost by omission of copyright notice, whether intentional or not, if "no more than a relatively small number" of copies or phonorecords were distributed without notice, or if registration of the work occurred within five years of publication and a reasonable effort was made to cure the earlier omission. *Id*. §405.

Like the 1909 Act, the 1976 Act required deposit of published works with the Copyright Office and authorized the Register of Copyright to demand that an author comply with the deposit requirements. Failure to comply within three months of the demand no longer resulted in forfeiture but rather only in a civil fine.

The 1976 Act made registration of copyright voluntary and provided that registration could take place at any time during the copyright term. Like the 1909 Act before it, however, the 1976 Act required the copyright owner to register and deposit copies of the work before filing an infringement lawsuit. Registration under the 1976 Act was effected by depositing two complete copies or phonorecords of the best edition of a published work or one complete copy or phonorecord of an unpublished work, along with a registration form and the required fee. A deposit for registration purposes also could be used to satisfy the deposit requirement, but an author could choose to satisfy the deposit requirement without registering the copyrighted work. *See id*. §§407-408.

In 1988, when the United States joined the Berne Convention, Congress modified both the notice and the registration requirements. Consistent with the requirements of the Berne Convention, notice is no longer a condition of protection for works published after March 1, 1989, the effective date of the Berne Convention Implementation Act (BCIA). Instead, notice "may" be placed on publicly distributed copies of the copyrighted work. *See id*.§401(a). Note, however, that there still remains an important reason for copyright owners to satisfy the "optional" notice provisions in a post-Berne environment: The presence of a copyright notice will defeat a defendant's assertion of "innocent infringement," which affects the damages that may be recovered. *See id*. §401(d). In addition, the pre-1989 notice rules (and the concept of "publication") continue to have significance because the BCIA only applies prospectively to copies of works publicly distributed after March 1, 1989. The notice requirements of the 1909 and 1976 Copyright Acts remain in effect for copies publicly distributed before January 1, 1978, and March 1, 1989, respectively.

The BCIA also modified the rule that made registration of copyright a precondition of commencing an infringement suit. Here, Congress drew a distinction between works of U.S. origin and works originating from countries that belonged to the Berne Convention. For works originating from a Berne Convention country, an infringement action may be initiated without registering the work with the Copyright Office. However, for U.S. works, the copyright owner still must register before filing suit. *See id*. §411.

As in the case of notice, there are good reasons to register a copyright. First, a copyright owner cannot elect to recover statutory damages, and is not eligible to receive an award of attorneys' fees, unless registration occurs prior to the start of the infringing activity or within three months of first publication. *See id.* §412. In addition, the certificate of registration of a work issued before or within five years of first publication will serve as presumptive, albeit rebuttable, proof of the dates of creation and publication, the identity of the copyright owner, and the validity of the copyright. *See id.* §410(c).

Finally, in 1993 under implementing legislation for the North American Free Trade Agreement (NAFTA), and in 1994 under the implementing legislation for the TRIPS Agreement, Congress remedied the loss of U.S. copyright protection for certain works of foreign origin due to failure to comply with the notice requirement and/or the registration and deposit requirements under the 1909 and 1976 Acts. The restoration provisions are discussed in section A.6, *infra*.

Having reviewed the history of formalities in U.S. law, we turn now to the current rules regarding each of them.

2. What Is Publication?

Prior to the effective date of the 1976 Copyright Act, unpublished creative works of authorship were protected by state common law copyright. Publication of a work destroyed the common law rights, and at the same time marked the point at which federal statutory protection became available. An author who chose to receive protection under the statutory regime received the benefit of federal copyright so long as she complied with the formalities. However, an author who, upon publication, failed to comply with the statutory formalities, or whose attempts at compliance were defective in some way, lost both state common law protection and federal statutory protection. As the case below explains, courts developed strategies for countering the harshness of this rule.

Estate of Martin Luther King, Jr., Inc. v. CBS, Inc.
194 F.3d 1211 (11th Cir. 1999)

ANDERSON, C.J.: . . . The facts underlying this case form part of our national heritage and are well-known to many Americans. On the afternoon of August 28, 1963, the Southern Christian Leadership Conference ("SCLC") held the March on Washington ("March") to promote the growing civil rights movement. The events of the day were seen and heard by some 200,000 people gathered at the March, and were broadcast live via radio and television to a nationwide audience of millions of viewers. The highlight of the March was a rousing speech that Dr. Martin Luther King, Jr., the SCLC's founder and president, gave in front of the Lincoln Memorial ("Speech"). The Speech contained the famous utterance, "I have a dream . . . ," which became symbolic of the civil rights movement. The SCLC had sought out wide press coverage of the March and the Speech, and these efforts were successful; the Speech was reported in daily newspapers across the country, was broadcast live on radio and television, and was extensively covered on television and radio subsequent to the live broadcast.

On September 30, 1963, approximately one month after the delivery of the Speech, Dr. King took steps to secure federal copyright protection for the Speech under the Copyright Act of 1909, and a certificate of registration of his claim to copyright was issued by the Copyright Office on October 2, 1963. Almost immediately thereafter, Dr. King filed suit in the Southern District of New York to enjoin the unauthorized sale of recordings of the Speech and won a preliminary injunction on December 13, 1963.

For the next twenty years, Dr. King and the Estate enjoyed copyright protection in the Speech and licensed it for a variety of uses, and renewed the copyright when necessary. In 1994, CBS entered into a contract with the Arts & Entertainment Network to produce a historical documentary series entitled "The 20th Century with Mike Wallace." One segment was devoted to "Martin Luther King, Jr. and The March on Washington." That episode contained material filmed by CBS during the March and extensive footage of the Speech (amounting to about 60% of its total content). CBS, however, did not seek the Estate's permission to use the Speech in this manner and refused to pay royalties to the Estate. The instant litigation ensued.

On summary judgment, the district court framed the issue as "whether the public delivery of Dr. King's speech . . . constituted a general publication of the speech so as to place it in the public domain." 13 F. Supp. 2d at 1351. After discussing the relevant case law, the District Court held that Dr. King's "performance coupled with such wide and unlimited reproduction and dissemination as occurred concomitant to Dr. King's speech during the March on Washington can be seen only as a general publication which thrust the speech into the public domain." *Id.* at 1354.[1] Thus, the

> **KEEP IN MIND**
>
> The timing of the alleged publication, not the timing of the alleged infringement, determines which notice rules apply.

District Court granted CBS's motion for summary judgment. The Estate now appeals to this Court. . . .

Because of the dates of the critical events, the determinative issues in this case are properly analyzed under the Copyright Act of 1909 ("1909 Act"), rather than the Copyright Act of 1976 ("1976 Act") that is currently in effect. The question is whether Dr. King's attempt to obtain statutory copyright protection on September 30, 1963 was effective, or whether it was a nullity because the Speech had already been forfeited to the public domain via a general publication.

Under the regime created by the 1909 Act, an author received state common law protection automatically at the time of creation of a work. This state common law protection persisted until the moment of a general publication. When a general

---

1. The district court noted that there potentially was some additional evidence of general publication. First, the SCLC published a newsletter of wide circulation containing the full text of the Speech. Second, an advance text of the Speech may have been freely available to the public in a press tent at the March. However, the district court disregarded both of these items of evidence because the procedural posture of the case was one of summary judgment, and "material facts [were] in dispute as to whether the use of Dr. King's speech in the newsletter was authorized and also as to the actual availability of the advance text." 13 F. Supp. 2d at 1353 n.5.

publication occurred, the author either forfeited his work to the public domain, or, if he had therebefore complied with federal statutory requirements, converted his common law copyright into a federal statutory copyright.

In order to soften the hardship of the rule that publication destroys common law rights, courts developed a distinction between a "general publication" and a "limited publication." Only a general publication divested a common law copyright. A general publication occurred "when a work was made available to members of the public at large without regard to their identity or what they intended to do with the work." Conversely, a non-divesting limited publication was one that communicated the contents of a work to a select group and for a limited purpose, and without the right of diffusion, reproduction, distribution or sale. The issue before us is whether Dr. King's delivery of the Speech was a general publication.

Numerous cases stand for the proposition that the performance of a work is not a general publication.

It appears from the case law that a general publication occurs only in two situations. First, a general publication occurs if tangible copies of the work are distributed to the general public in such a manner as allows the public to exercise dominion and control over the work. Second, a general publication may occur if the work is exhibited or displayed in such a manner as to permit unrestricted copying by the general public. However, the case law indicates that restrictions on copying may be implied, and that express limitations in that regard are deemed unnecessary.

The case law indicates that distribution to the news media, as opposed to the general public, for the purpose of enabling the reporting of a contemporary news-worthy event, is only a limited publication. For example, in *Public Affairs Assoc., Inc. v. Rickover*, 284 F.2d 262 (D.C. Cir. 1960), *vacated on other grounds*, 369 U.S. 111 (1962), the court said that general publication occurs only when there is "a studied effort not only to secure publicity for the contents of the addresses through the channels of information, but to *go beyond customary sources of press or broadcasting* in distributing the addresses to any interested individual." Although the *Rickover* court ultimately held that a general publication had occurred, it contrasted the "limited use of the addresses by the press for fair comment," i.e., limited publication, with "the unlimited distribution to anyone who was interested," i.e., general publication. This rule comports with common sense; it does not force an author whose message happens to be newsworthy to choose between obtaining news coverage for his work and preserving his common-law copyright. As the dissenting judge in the *Rickover* case remarked "[t]here is nothing in the law which would compel this court to deprive the creator of the right to reap financial benefits from these efforts because, at the time of their creation, they had the added virtue of being newsworthy events of immediate public concern." *Rickover*, 284 F.2d at 273 (Washington J., dissenting).

With the above principles in mind, in the summary judgment posture of this case and on the current state of this record, we are unable to conclude that CBS has demonstrated beyond any genuine issue of material fact that Dr. King, simply through his oral delivery of the Speech, engaged in a general publication making the Speech "available to members of the public at large without regard to their identity or what they intended to do with the work." A performance, no matter how broad the audience, is not a publication; to hold otherwise would be to upset a long line of precedent. This conclusion is not altered by the fact that the Speech was broadcast live to a broad radio and television audience and was the subject of extensive contemporaneous news coverage. We follow . . . case law indicating that release to the news media for contemporary coverage of a newsworthy event is only a limited publication. . . .

The district court held that "the circumstances in this case take the work in question outside the parameters of the 'performance is not a publication' doctrine." These circumstances included "the overwhelmingly public nature of the speech and the fervent intentions of the March organizers to draw press attention." Certainly, the Speech was one of a kind—a unique event in history. However, the features that make the Speech unique—e.g., the huge audience and the Speech's significance in terms of newsworthiness and history—are features that, according to the case law, are not significant in the general versus limited publication analysis. . . .

Because there exist genuine issues of material fact as to whether a general publication occurred, we must reverse the district court's grant of summary judgment for CBS. . . .

NOTES AND QUESTIONS

1. While the *Estate of Martin Luther King, Jr.* court notes that distribution to the news media may qualify as a limited publication, in some circumstances such distribution may be used to bolster proof of a general publication. For example, in Chapter 5 you read *Warner Bros. Entm't v. X One X Prods.*, 644 F.3d 584 (8th Cir. 2011), which involved promotional materials for upcoming films that were sent to movie theaters. Courts have held that "distribution of promotional photographs to theaters, even under an effective condition that the photographs be returned, is not sufficient to demonstrate a limited publication where the photographs are also distributed for use by newspapers and magazines." *Id.* at 594. Is this reasoning consistent with that in *Estate of Martin Luther King, Jr.*, or are the two situations distinguishable?

2. Section 101 of the 1976 Act defines publication as follows:

> "Publication" is the distribution of copies or phonorecords of a work to the public by sale or other transfer of ownership, or by rental, lease, or lending. The offering to distribute copies or phonorecords to a group of persons for purposes of further distribution, public performance, or public display, constitutes publication. A public performance or display of a work does not of itself constitute publication.

LOOKING AHEAD
Under the 1976 Act, the concept of publication continues to have some importance for determining copyright duration and the proper time window for termination of certain transfers. We discuss those issues later in this chapter.

Does this language clarify the definition of "publication" that subsisted prior to the passage of the 1976 Act? What are the reasons for the rule that public performance or display does not, alone, constitute publication?

3. Generally, courts have held that posting material to a website, such as photographs, music files, and computer software, constitutes publication. In *Getaped.com Inc. v. Cangemi*, 188 F. Supp. 2d 398 (S.D.N.Y 2002), the court held that a web page itself is also published when it "goes live" because at that time an Internet user can make a copy of the web page. Does this view of publication comport with the statutory definition? Why, or why not?

4. Recall the discussion of the fixation requirement in Chapter 2.A.1. Does the fixation requirement accomplish the goals of copyright more effectively than the concept of publication?

3. Notice of Copyright

As discussed above, under the Copyright Act of 1909, works published in the United States without strict compliance with the notice requirements prescribed by the Act lost copyright protection. The 1976 Act kept the form of notice prescribed by the 1909 Act, but afforded opportunities to cure inadequate notice. After accession to the Berne Convention, Congress amended the 1976 Act to make notice optional rather than mandatory.

The notice requirement that existed in U.S. law prior to 1989 facilitated public knowledge of the copyright status of a work in several ways. First, prior to 1989, if notice was not included on copies of the work, the work was not protected by copyright (although remember that from 1978 through 1989, there were some possibilities for "curing" defective notice). Second, prior to 1978, the notice was required to include the work's first publication date, which enabled the public to determine the duration of the copyright. Today, the absence of notice does not mean that the work is in the public domain. Also, without proper notice, the public cannot easily determine the date of first publication.

An additional consequence of elimination of the notice requirement relates to abandonment of copyright. The default status of a work lacking a copyright notice has flipped: Before 1989, the lack of a copyright notice indicated no copyright in the work, sometimes referred to as a forfeiture or "abandonment" of copyright. Today, lack of a copyright notice does not result in abandonment. Abandonment can only occur as the result of an "intentional relinquishment of a known right" by the copyright owner. *See, e.g., A&M Records, Inc. v. Napster, Inc.*, 239 F.3d 1004 (9th Cir. 2001). Certainly, including a statement such as "I dedicate this work to the public domain" on the work in place of a copyright notice would suffice. Mere failure to enforce one's rights does not result in an abandonment.

PROBLEMS

Read §§401-406 of the 1976 Act, which contain the current optional notice provisions for the different categories of copyrightable works. Keeping in mind that prior to March 1, 1989, these requirements were mandatory, consider the following problems. You can find the answers on this book's companion website, http://www.coolcopyright.com:

a. In 1985, Tom published his first novel. What should the copyright notice contain?

b. Assume that notice was omitted from the first edition of Tom's novel. What are the consequences of that error? What if, in 1986, Tom's publisher alerted bookstores that had purchased copies of the novel, and asked the bookstores to paste a proper notice of copyright inside all the copies that still remained on their shelves?

c. Janice is a freelance writer. In 1991, she wrote an op-ed article for the *Sun Times*, a weekly periodical. The *Sun Times* affixed notice to the periodical. Did Janice also need to affix notice to her article?

d. What result if neither Janice nor the *Sun Times* affixed notice to their respective works?

4. Deposit Requirements

The 1976 Copyright Act requires copyright owners to deposit two complete copies of the "best edition" of their published works with the Copyright Office. *See* 17 U.S.C. §407. There are special deposit requirements for works first published outside the United States, as well as for particular categories of works such as collective works, sound recordings, and recordings of transmission programs. *See id.* §§407-408. In addition, the registration requirement (which we examine next) requires a deposit of copies of the work. Thus, a work is not properly registered unless the deposit requirement is met.

The deposit requirement serves two important policy objectives. First, it enriches the resources of the Library of Congress, the largest library in the world. In keeping with the evolution of digital media for storing and locating works of authorship, the Copyright Office now encourages deposits of digital copies in place of physical copies. Second, and important for practical reasons, the deposit requirement facilitates the ongoing development of a comprehensive record of copyright claims through the optional registration system codified in §408 of the 1976 Act.

Despite these objectives, the Copyright Act also provides that the Register of Copyrights may issue regulations modifying the deposit requirements for any category of copyrightable works. The Register is authorized to consider the nature of the work and, in the case of individual authors of pictorial, graphic, or sculptural works produced in limited editions, the copyright owner's financial condition. *See id.* §407; 37 C.F.R. §§202.19-202.24 (2014). One type of work for which the Copyright Office has issued special deposit rules is computer programs. For published or unpublished computer programs, the first 25 pages and the last 25 pages of the source code must be deposited either on paper or in microform. *See* 37 C.F.R. §202.20. For a program that is less than 50 pages, the entire source code must be deposited. *Id.* If a computer program contains a trade secret, the owner should write a letter stating this fact, and may block out portions of the code that contain the trade secret. Some commentators have argued that the ability to register a copyrighted work while retaining trade secret protection is inconsistent with the copyright system's goal of promoting progress in knowledge and learning. Do you agree?

5. Registration

As discussed above, registration is no longer mandatory to maintain copyright protection. However, registration, or at least attempted registration, for U.S. works is required in order to commence an infringement action. *See* 17 U.S.C. §411(a). To preserve the ability to elect statutory damages as opposed to actual damages (which must be proved) and eligibility to receive an award of attorneys' fees, registration must have been made before the infringement commences. *Id.* at §412. For newly published works, copyright owners have three months in which to register their work and remain eligible for statutory damages and attorneys' fees even if the infringement commences prior to registration. *Id.* Additionally, registration permits a copyright owner to seek the assistance of U.S. Customs and Border Protection agents in seizing infringing items at the border. Finally, registration within five years of publication constitutes prima facie evidence of the validity of the copyright and of the facts stated in the certificate. *Id.* at §410.

Registration can be effected either electronically via the Electronic Copyright Office (eCO) online portal or by mail. In either case, the registration must be accompanied by the required fee and deposit copies. For a list of fees associated with the different types of filings, see http://www.copyright.gov/docs/fees.html. Printable registration forms can be obtained through the Copyright Office website: http://www.loc.gov/copyright/forms/. These forms are relatively simple to complete, and many individuals complete and file them without the assistance of an attorney.

In some instances, the Copyright Office may deny registration even though all the requirements, such as deposit, application, and fee, have been met. An author in this situation may nevertheless institute an infringement lawsuit, but will not have the benefit of the evidentiary presumptions that accompany registration. Additionally, a copy of the complaint must be served on the Register of Copyrights, and the Register may choose to join the case with regard to the issue of registrability. Alternatively, a party whose registration has been denied can file suit against the Register of Copyrights to compel issuance of the registration. The Copyright Act indicates that "all actions taken by the Register of Copyrights under this title are subject to the provisions of the Administrative Procedure Act" (APA). 17 U.S.C. §701(e). As provided in the APA, an agency action may be set aside only if "arbitrary, capricious, an abuse of discretion, or otherwise not in accordance with law." 5 U.S.C. §706(2)(A); s*ee, e.g., Darden v. Peters,* 488 F.3d 277 (4th Cir. 2007) (rejecting argument that a *de novo* standard should be applied to review of Copyright Office decisions). Unlike the Patent Act and the Lanham Act (trademark), the Copyright Act does not contain any formal mechanism for cancelling a registration once issued.

The registration process for individual works is straightforward in most cases, but registering large numbers of works can be more complicated. Consider, for example, an issue of a newspaper or magazine containing dozens of articles, or a portfolio of photographs or digital images. Must every article or image be described separately? For decades, the Copyright Office has allowed registration of a collective work to effect registration of independently copyrightable works included within the collective work. 37 C.F.R. §202.3(b)(4). More recently, it approved a procedure by which stock photography agencies can register portfolios containing hundreds of images by multiple authors in a single, abbreviated registration. Under the procedure, the photographers temporarily assign their copyrights to the agency for purposes of registration only.

In 2005, Congress modified the registration requirements for certain categories of works thought to need additional protection prior to their release for commercial distribution. *See* 17 U.S.C. §408(f). One impetus for these amendments was the regular availability of first-run, not-yet-released, movies for download via Internet swarming distribution software such as BitTorrent. In addition to making it a felony to make such works available for distribution on a publicly accessible computer network, see Chapter 13, *infra*, §408(f)(2) directs the Copyright Office to establish abbreviated procedures for "preregistration" for any class of works determined to have "a history of infringement prior to authorized commercial distribution." The Copyright Office currently permits preregistration of motion pictures, sound recordings, and software. Preregistration requires only a form and a fee; no deposit copy is required.

Preregistration provides the copyright owner with the ability to bring an infringement lawsuit as though full registration had been made. *See id.* §411(a). Preregistration, however, should be followed by a full registration within three months of first publication or within one month of learning of the infringement (whichever is *earlier*). Failure to file the full registration within that time frame has two consequences. First, such a failure will result in dismissal of any action for an infringement that commenced less than two months after publication. *See id.* §408(f)(4). Second, it will render the copyright owner ineligible to receive statutory damages and attorneys' fees for infringements commenced before the eventual registration has been made. *See id.* §412.

NOTES AND QUESTIONS

1. The deposit requirement can pose difficulties for registration of copyright in works that are updated frequently, such as computer programs and websites. Submitting a later-revised version of the work sought to be registered can invalidate the registration. *See, e.g., Geoscan, Inc. v. Geotrace Techs., Inc.,* 226 F.3d 387, 393 (5th Cir. 2000) (dismissing lawsuit for failure to submit deposit copies of the source code of the original program).

2. Review §409 of the Act, which describes the requirements for a valid application for copyright registration. Do the registration practices for collective works meet the statutory requirements? Every circuit to consider this question has held that the Copyright Office's administrative practices concerning registration are entitled to deference. *See Alaska Stock v. Houghton Mifflin Harcourt Publishing Co.,* 747 F.3d 673, 683-86 (9th Cir. 2014) (collecting cases).

3. In light of the Berne Convention's prohibition on formalities as a condition of copyright protection, most countries have eliminated registration systems entirely, while others retain nonmandatory registration systems. The United States is one of a few countries that impose some measure of mandatory registration on their own nationals, but not on foreign authors. As an international matter, such bifurcated treatment is permissible; the nondiscrimination requirements of the Berne Convention and the TRIPS Agreement prohibit treating foreign authors worse than national authors, not vice versa. Why might a nation elect such discriminatory treatment of its own authors?

4. Recall from Chapter 1 that continental European countries approach copyright law from an authors' rights perspective. As you have learned, this view of copyright often results in a broader scope of protection for authors. Given that the Berne Convention was conceived and negotiated by continental European countries as an instrument to strengthen authors' rights, it is no surprise that the treaty forbids conditioning copyright protection on compliance with any formalities. Read Article 5(2) of the Berne Convention again. Is there a difference between formalities that affect the vesting of copyright and formalities that affect the ability to enforce copyright? Recall that §412 limits all authors' eligibility to recover statutory damages and attorneys' fees when infringement occurs prior to registration. Is the United States in compliance with Article 5(2)?

5. Does the prohibition on formalities as a condition of copyright protection make sense as a policy matter? Is it appropriate to have a system for intangible property that allows individuals to assert claims of ownership without any registration or public notice of ownership claims? Recordation rules are a common feature of real property systems, where they facilitate identification of owners and resolution of competing claims. Are there characteristics of copyright that justify the difference? Might a modernized system of copyright formalities perform a useful function? For discussion of this issue, see Christopher Sprigman, *Reform(aliz)ing Copyright*, 57 Stan. L. Rev. 484 (2004).

PRACTICE EXERCISE: COUNSEL A CLIENT

Bartolini Designs, a high-end jeweler, recently released a line of jewelry consisting of flattened triangular shapes linked together with oblong links. Bartolini attempted to register the pieces as pictorial, graphic, or sculptural works, but the Copyright Office denied registration. Caravan, a mail-order jeweler that specializes in designer knock-offs, has begun advertising a new jewelry line that appears identical to Bartolini's. Bartolini has consulted you for advice on how to proceed. Should Bartolini pursue an action against the Register or file an infringement lawsuit against Caravan?

---

6. Diving Deeper: Restoration of Copyright Protection for Certain Works of Foreign Authors

Recall that prior to Berne accession, failure to comply with copyright formalities led to loss of U.S. copyright protection for a number of works. Both foreign and domestic authors were affected. Although Article 18 of the Berne Convention requires retroactive protection of foreign works that have lost copyright for failure to satisfy formalities imposed by domestic laws, the United States did not comply with this requirement immediately. The North American Free Trade Agreement Implementation Act of 1993 added §104A to the Copyright Act to restore copyright protection in Canadian and Mexican motion picture works that had lost protection for failure to comply with copyright formalities. In 1994, the Uruguay Round Agreements Act (URAA), which implemented the TRIPS Agreement in U.S. law, amended §104A to extend restoration to all types of works by authors from all WTO countries.

Under the URAA amendments to §104A, the effective date of restoration was January 1, 1996, for works whose source countries (defined in 17 U.S.C. §104A(h)(8)) were members of the Berne Convention or the WTO on that date. *See id.* §104A(h)(2). The Act defines a "restored work" to include foreign works that lost copyright protection because of: (1) failure to include a copyright notice; (2) noncompliance with other formalities imposed at any time by U.S. copyright law; (3) lack of subject matter protection in the case of sound recordings fixed before February 15, 1972; or (4) lack of national eligibility.[*] *See id.* §104A(h)(6)(C). To be eligible for restoration in the United States, the work's copyright must not have expired in the source country before the date of restoration in the United States. It is important to note that §104A vests ownership of a restored work "initially in the author or initial rightholder in the work as determined by the law in the source country of the work." *See id.* §104A(b). The length of protection for a restored copyright is the remainder of the term of copyright that the work would have been granted had it not lost protection. The owner of a restored copyright is entitled to full remedies for any infringing act that occurs on or after the date of restoration. *See id.* §104A(d)(1).

As you might imagine, restoration of lapsed copyright protection had serious consequences for individuals who had invested in restored works in reliance on their public domain status. Section 104A provides special rules for these "reliance parties" including a period of immunity to wind down otherwise infringing activity. Before the owner of a restored copyright can bring an infringement action against a reliance party, the owner must give a notice of intent to enforce the restored copyright. The notice requirements are complicated and require attention to the detailed requirements spelled out in the statute.

> ### COMPARATIVE PERSPECTIVE
>
> Under Chinese copyright law, works that fail to satisfy "content review" are ineligible for copyright protection. Are content restrictions "formalities" proscribed under Article 5(2) of the Berne Convention? Ruling on a complaint initiated by the United States, a WTO Panel elected not to reach that question, and ruled instead that Chinese law effectively denies protection to certain classes of works in violation of Article 5(1) of the Berne Convention as incorporated by Article 9(1) of the TRIPS Agreement. *See China—Measures Affecting the Protection and Enforcement of Intellectual Property Rights,* WT/DS362/R ¶¶ 7.50, 7.60 (Jan. 26, 2009).

---

[*] If an author was a national of a country with which the United States had no treaty related to copyright, that author's work would not have been protected by U.S. copyright law at all.

B. DURATION

This section describes the complicated rules governing the duration of copyright. After we explain the rules, we explore the policy impetus for, and the implications of, the ever-increasing duration of copyright protection.

1. The Basics of Duration

> **KEEP IN MIND**
>
> Regardless of which set of rules is applicable, all copyright durations run until the end of the calendar year. *See* 17 U.S.C. §305.

It would be nice if we could simply say that copyright lasts for the life of the author plus 70 years. Unfortunately, a more complex set of rules governs the duration of copyright. To assist in understanding these rules and keeping them straight, it will help if you remember that they stem from two different regimes, one under the 1909 Act and one under the 1976 Act. Additionally, in 1998 Congress passed the Sonny Bono Copyright Term Extension Act (CTEA), which amended the 1976 Act. To understand some of the rules discussed later in this section and in the cases that you will read, it is important to know that as a result of the CTEA, the current duration of copyright protection is 20 years longer than that initially adopted in the 1976 Act. The 1976 Act originally provided for a basic term of protection of the life of the author plus 50 years, and for works made for hire and anonymous or pseudonymous works, a term of either 100 years from creation or 75 years from publication, whichever is shorter.

a. Works Created on or After January 1, 1978

The easiest duration rules to understand are for those works first fixed on or after January 1, 1978 (recall that this is the effective date of the 1976 Act). For these works, the duration rules of the 1976 Act, as modified by the CTEA, apply:

(1) The copyright in a work created by a single author endures for the life of the author plus 70 years.
(2) The copyright in a work created by joint authors who did not create the work as a work made for hire endures for the life of the last surviving author plus 70 years.
(3) The copyright in a work that is an anonymous work, a pseudonymous work, or a work made for hire endures for a term of 120 years from the year of creation or 95 years from the year of publication, *whichever expires first*. *See* 17 U.S.C. §302.

b. Works First Published Before January 1, 1978

The more complicated durations are for those works published prior to January 1, 1978. As you learned in the first section of this chapter, under the 1909 Act, publication with proper notice marked the moment at which federal copyright protection began. Published works displaying the proper copyright notice were granted a 28-year term of copyright protection. Additionally, a copyright owner could extend copyright protection for a renewal term of 28 years, for a total of 56 years, by filing a renewal certificate with the Copyright Office (and by registering the copyright if it had not previously been registered). The renewal certificate had to be filed during the final year of the initial term of protection. If the author had assigned the copyright in its first term, copyright would revert to the author once the second term began. If the copyright owner failed to file the renewal, copyright protection ended after 28 years.

Under this dual term scheme of protection, the date of death of the author was irrelevant for purposes of copyright duration. What mattered was the date of publication, the use of proper notice, and the filing of a renewal certificate.

It is not, however, accurate to say that copyrights in all works published prior to 1978 had a maximum duration of 56 years. The 1976 Act extended protection for these works by an additional 19 years so that the duration would be more comparable to the life plus 50 being adopted for works created after January 1, 1978. The way that the 1976 Act accomplishes this extension is by adding 19 years to the renewal term. Thus, if the copyright owner secured a renewal term by the timely filing of a renewal certificate, the owner ultimately received an additional 47 years of protection (28 renewal + 19 extension) beyond the initial 28-year term. This led to a total possible term of protection of 75 years.

In 1998, Congress once again extended the duration of protection, this time by 20 more years. As in the 1976 Act, Congress accomplished this extension by adding these additional years to the renewal term. Thus, the longest duration possible for works *published* prior to 1978 is now 95 years (28 initial + 28 renewal + 19 extension + 20 extension).

You might be tempted to think that this is not all that complicated; after all, the bottom line is that copyright duration in works published prior to 1978 is 95 years from publication. Under this rationale, works published in 1920 would remain subject to protection until the year 2015. But as a result of the timing of the CTEA, adopted in 1998, there were works that had already entered the public domain because of the expiration of the 75-year term in or before 1997. The CTEA did not grant new protection for these works. This means that works published prior to 1923 are in the public domain (1997 − 75 = 1922). Beginning with works first published with proper copyright notice in 1923, copyright in works published before January 1, 1978, will have a potential total duration of 95 years.

There is one further complicating matter related to the renewal requirement under the 1909 Act. As stated above, if a renewal certificate was not filed in the final year of the first term of copyright protection (i.e., the 28th year), copyright protection ceased at the end of the initial term. This requirement caught more than a few authors off guard and resulted in the loss of copyright protection for some rather famous works, including, among others, the holiday classic *It's a Wonderful Life* and the movie *Pygmalion*. In 1992, Congress decided to eliminate the requirement of the renewal certificate, making all renewals automatic. However, Congress did not revive protection for works that had passed into the public domain due to a failure to file the renewal certificate. Thus, in 1992, Congress could only reach back 28 years to make renewals automatic for those works published in or after 1964 (1992 − 28 = 1964). For works published prior to 1964, actual filing of a renewal certificate with the Copyright Office was required to obtain protection for the renewal term.

Below is a graphic depiction of these rules.

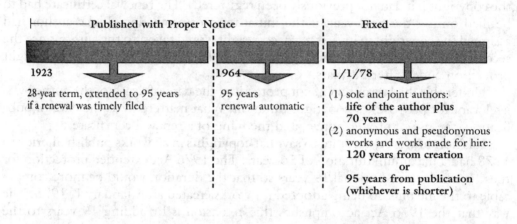

┝─────Published with Proper Notice─────┤	├─────Fixed─────┤

1923 — 28-year term, extended to 95 years if a renewal was timely filed

1964 — 95 years renewal automatic

1/1/78 —
(1) sole and joint authors: **life of the author plus 70 years**
(2) anonymous and pseudonymous works and works made for hire: **120 years from creation** or **95 years from publication** (whichever is shorter)

c. Works Created but Unpublished Before January 1, 1978

As the above chart indicates and as discussed in an earlier portion of this chapter, the 1909 Act only protected *published* works,* yet the 1976 Act protects both published and unpublished works so long as they are fixed. Works created but not published prior to January 1, 1978 (the effective date of the 1976 Act) were subject to common law or state statutory copyright protection. Not all of these sources of law provided for a finite term of protection. In adopting the 1976 Act, Congress decided to grant previously unpublished works federal copyright protection. These works were, after all, *fixed*; they just had not yet been published. Granting previously unpublished works federal copyright protection, coupled with broad preemption provisions barring all state laws that granted copyright-like protection, would bring all fixed works under one system of protection. On the issue of duration for these previously unpublished works, Congress determined that the same duration rules used for works created after January 1, 1978, should apply—i.e., life of the author plus 50 (now 70) years.

There was a problem in applying the same duration rules to unpublished works, however. Calculating the duration of copyright based on the date of death of the authors would divest some works of federal copyright protection at the same moment that all state law protection was extinguished. For example, a work created

---

* As noted earlier in this chapter, under the 1909 Act unpublished works that were "not reproduced for sale" could be registered, thus bringing the unpublished work under federal statutory protection. The statute indicated that the types of unpublished works eligible to elect statutory protection through registration were: "lectures and similar productions, dramatic compositions, musical compositions, dramatico-musical compositions, motion picture photoplays, motion pictures other than photoplays, photographs, works of art and plastic works and drawings." Section 12, 1909 Act. The discussion here assumes that no registration took place.

in 1920 by an author who died in 1925, and never published, would be granted federal copyright protection under the 1976 Act, but such protection only lasted until 1975 (life + 50, the original duration under the 1976 Act). Some commentators expressed concern about the unfairness of this treatment as well as the potential "takings" arguments that might be raised.

Congress solved this problem by providing a minimum term of federal copyright protection for previously unpublished works. Federal copyright protection for works created prior to 1978 but not yet published as of January 1, 1978, endures for the term otherwise provided for newly created works, except that in no event would copyright expire before December 31, 2002. Congress also provided an additional incentive to publish those unpublished works by granting an additional 25 (now 45) years of protection if the work was published before December 31, 2002.

Below is a graphic representation of these rules.

Unpublished before 1/1/1978 and not published before 12/31/2002	Unpublished before 1/1/1978 and published before 12/31/2002

(1) sole and joint authors:
life of the author plus 70 years
BUT no earlier than 12/31/2002

(2) anonymous/pseudonymous works
and works made for hire:
120 years from creation,
or
95 years from publication
(whichever is shorter)
BUT
no earlier than 12/31/2002

(1) sole and joint authors:
life of the author plus 70 years
BUT no earlier than 12/31/2047

(2) anonymous/pseudonymous works
and works made for hire:
120 years from creation,
Or
95 years from publication
(whichever is shorter)
BUT
no earlier than 12/31/2047

NOTES AND QUESTIONS

1. The explanation of the rules governing copyright duration shows that for works published prior to January 1, 1978, the date of first publication is the important date for determining the expiration of copyright. At first blush, for works created after January 1, 1978, the date of first publication is not relevant to determining duration; what matters for these works is the date of death of the author of the work, and copyright in those works will last for 70 years after the date of death. However, the Copyright Act provides that 95 years after the year of first publication, there is a presumption that the death of the author occurred at least 70 years earlier. *See* 17 U.S.C. §302(e). This presumption can be applied if the Copyright Office records contain no indication of the life status of the author. Additionally, for works that are made for hire or published anonymously or under a pseudonym, the date of first publication remains an important date: As described above, copyright in those works will last for 95 years from publication (or 120 years from creation if that date results in a shorter copyright duration). Thus, the year of first publication also can be relevant for works created after January 1, 1978.

2. If there is no copyright notice indicating a publication date, examining the records of the Copyright Office may help because the registration form requires the date of first publication. For those copyrights whose duration is measured based on the life of the author, the registration form also requires information that would assist future researchers in determining the date of death of an author, such as the place and year of birth of the author.

But remember, registration is not required for copyright protection. Thus, despite someone's best intentions, it may be impossible to obtain the information necessary to determine whether a work remains under copyright protection. In such cases, a would-be user of a work may need to seek that information from the copyright owner directly. Of course, the copyright owner may have an interest in not being entirely forthcoming about facts relating to the copyright status of a work.

PROBLEMS

To test your understanding of these rules, determine the date on which the following works entered, or will enter, the public domain. You can find the answers on this book's companion website, http://www.coolcopyright.com:

1. A novel, written by Alice Author, first published with proper copyright notice on July 1, 1930. Alice Author died December 1, 1931.
2. A novel, written by Benjamin Author, never published. Benjamin Author died in 1900. Would the answer be different if the work were first published in 1980? Would it matter whether the published copies bore proper copyright notice?
3. A computer software program written by Patience Programmer, an employee of DataSystems, Inc., in 1988. Copies of the program were sold to the public, with no copyright notice, from November 1989 through January 1992. Patience Programmer died in 1990.
4. A song written in 2001 by the mother/daughter team of Mamma Moore and Cindy Moore, copies of which were distributed beginning on January 1, 2010. Mamma Moore died in 2002, Cindy Moore dies in 2040.
5. A novel by the German novelist Hans Schmidt, first published in Germany in 1927 and republished in the United States without proper notice of copyright in 1935. Schmidt died in 1955. (Review the materials on restoration of lapsed foreign copyrights, section A.6 *supra*, before you answer.)

---

d. Diving Deeper: Duration of Copyright in Foreign Works

Foreign works created on or after January 1, 1978, are subject to the 1976 Act's ordinary duration rules, as modified by the CTEA. For foreign works created before January 1, 1978, the determination of duration may sometimes be more complicated, particularly since important consideration must be given to events that took place outside the United States. For example, in *Societe Civile Succession v. Renoir*, 549 F.3d 1182 (9th Cir. 2008), the plaintiff, a French trust, sued for copyright infringement of sculptures co-authored by the famous French artist Pierre-Auguste Renoir and one of his assistants, Richard Guino. Societe Civile Succession (SCS) obtained the copyrights pursuant to a settlement agreement between Renoir's family and Guino's family. However, Renoir's great-grandson, a defendant in this case, was not part of the settlement agreement. The sculptures were first published in France no later than 1917 in Renoir's name, but there was no American-style notice affixed to the works. In 1984, SCS obtained U.S. copyright registrations for the sculptures and indicated that they were either first published in England in 1983 or unpublished.

The court held that publication without copyright notice in a foreign country does not place a work in the public domain in the United States. Further, because the sculptures were never published with a copyright notice, they did not fall under the 1909 Act. Consequently, "the sculptures were neither protected by copyright nor injected into the public domain." *Id.* at 1187. Ultimately, the court held that U.S. copyright protection for the sculptures began upon registration in 1984 and therefore was governed by the rules of the 1976 Act. Thus, the sculptures are protected for the life of the last surviving author, Guino, who died in 1973, plus 70 years (i.e., until 2043).

As a practical matter, then, the court treated works first published abroad without notice of copyright as analogous to works created but unpublished prior to January 1, 1978 (without needing to reach the question of a guaranteed minimum term of protection). Does that result make sense?

2. The Policies Behind Copyright Duration

The Constitution requires that the exclusive rights granted to authors be "for limited Times." The first Copyright Act provided for a duration of 14 years with the possibility of an additional 14-year term, a total of 28 years. That duration was doubled in 1909 to a total possible term of protection of 56 years. Today, as you have just learned, copyright lasts far longer.

In large measure, the shift in duration from a dual term to a unitary term resulted from an increased desire to harmonize U.S. law with copyright protection schemes in other countries. The Berne Convention requires a minimum term of protection of life plus 50 years. Berne Conv., art. 7. While the United States was not prepared to become a member of the Berne Convention at the time of the 1976 Act, adopting a term consistent with that treaty helped pave the way for U.S. ratification of it. Supporters of the further term extensions granted by the CTEA also pointed to international harmonization as a justification for increasing the term of protection in the United States. Copyright protection in many European countries lasts for life plus 70 years, exceeding the Berne Convention's minimum requirement.

Supporters of the 1976 Act and the CTEA also cited other justifications for term extension. As you read the materials in this section, identify those justifications and consider whether Congress and the courts have accorded them too much, too little, or appropriate significance.

At the same time, however, the elimination of required formalities, the lengthening duration of copyright, and the shift to a unitary term have resulted in the slower entry of works into the public domain. Under a system requiring affirmative steps on the part of the copyright owner to extend the duration of copyright (i.e., registration and the filing of a renewal certificate), many works entered the public domain after a mere 14 or 28 years. Today, no affirmative steps are needed to obtain or maintain copyright protection for the full, much longer duration. As a result of the CTEA, moreover, no additional works of authorship will enter the public domain as the result of the expiration of copyright protection until January 1, 2019. As you read the materials in this section, consider also the extent to which enrichment of the public domain should affect copyright law and policy.

a. Extension of Subsisting Copyrights

In the United States, the various extensions of copyright duration have applied not only to new works created after the passage of each new duration extension, but also to works already created. In fact, the copyright industries lobby Congress hard to get these extensions in order to protect works already in existence. For example, the first film in which Mickey Mouse appears, *Steamboat Willy*, was copyrighted in 1928 and was facing the expiration of copyright protection in 2003.[*] Disney executives testified before Congress in support of the CTEA.

Since 1995, Eric Eldred had maintained a website, http://www.eldritchpress.org, devoted to literary works that are in the public domain. In 1997, the National Endowment for the Humanities recognized Eldritch Press as one of the 20 best humanities sites on the Web. Prior to enactment of the CTEA, an entire year's worth of new material would enter the public domain on December 31 each year, and Eldred would begin the process of making those works freely available through his website. The passage of the CTEA, however, meant that Eldred would have to wait 20 years for any new works to enter the public domain. Eldred alleged that the CTEA violated the First Amendment and the originality and "limited Times" requirements of the Intellectual Property Clause. Below is an excerpt from the Supreme Court's opinion in that case.

≡ **Eldred v. Ashcroft**
≡ *537 U.S. 186 (2003)*

GINSBURG, J.: . . . Petitioners . . . seek a determination that the [Copyright Term Extension Act (CTEA), Pub. L. 105-298, §102(b) and (d), 112 Stat. 2827-2828] fails constitutional review under both the Copyright Clause's "limited Times" prescription and the First Amendment's free speech guarantee. . . .

---

[*] *But see* Douglas A. Hedenkamp, *Free Mickey Mouse: Copyright Notice, Derivative Works, and the Copyright Act of 1909*, 2 Va. Sports & Ent. L.J. 254 (2003) (arguing that defect in the required notices of copyright for the earliest Mickey Mouse films placed Mickey in the public domain in 1929).

I

A

. . . The Nation's first copyright statute, enacted in 1790, provided a federal copyright term of 14 years from the date of publication, renewable for an additional 14 years if the author survived the first term. The 1790 Act's renewable 14-year term applied to existing works (i.e., works already published and works created but not yet published) and future works alike. Congress expanded the federal copyright term to 42 years in 1831 (28 years from publication, renewable for an additional 14 years), and to 56 years in 1909 (28 years from publication, renewable for an additional 28 years). . . . Both times, Congress applied the new copyright term to existing and future works . . . ; to qualify for the 1831 extension, an existing work had to be in its initial copyright term at the time the Act became effective.

In 1976, Congress altered the method for computing federal copyright terms. 1976 Act §§302-304. For works created by identified natural persons, the 1976 Act provided that federal copyright protection would run from the work's creation, not—as in the 1790, 1831, and 1909 Acts—its publication; protection would last until 50 years after the author's death. §302(a). In these respects, the 1976 Act aligned United States copyright terms with the then-dominant international standard adopted under the Berne Convention for the Protection of Literary and Artistic Works. . . .

These new copyright terms, the 1976 Act instructed, governed all works not published by its effective date of January 1, 1978, regardless of when the works were created. §§302-303. For published works with existing copyrights as of that date, the 1976 Act granted a copyright term of 75 years from the date of publication, §304(a) and (b), a 19-year increase over the 56-year term applicable under the 1909 Act.

The measure at issue here, the CTEA, installed the fourth major duration extension of federal copyrights. Retaining the general structure of the 1976 Act, the CTEA enlarges the terms of all existing and future copyrights by 20 years. For works created by identified natural persons, the term now lasts from creation until 70 years after the author's death. 17 U.S.C. §302(a). This standard harmonizes the baseline United States copyright term with the term adopted by the European Union in 1993. . . .

. . . [I]n common with the 1831, 1909, and 1976 Acts, the CTEA's new terms apply to both future and existing copyrights. . . .

II

A

We address first the determination of the courts below that Congress has authority under the Copyright Clause to extend the terms of existing copyrights. Text, history, and precedent, we conclude, confirm that the Copyright Clause empowers Congress to prescribe "limited Times" for copyright protection and to secure the same level and duration of protection for all copyright holders, present and future.

The CTEA's baseline term of life plus 70 years, petitioners concede, qualifies as a "limited Tim[e]" as applied to future copyrights. Petitioners contend, however, that existing copyrights extended to endure for that same term are not "limited." Petitioners' argument essentially reads into the text of the Copyright Clause the command that a time prescription, once set, becomes forever "fixed" or "inalterable." The word "limited," however, does not convey a meaning so constricted. At the time of the Framing, that word meant what it means today: "confine[d] within certain bounds," "restrain[ed]," or "circumscribe[d]." S. Johnson, A Dictionary of the English Language (7th ed. 1785). Thus understood, a time span appropriately "limited" as applied to future copyrights does not automatically cease to be "limited" when applied to existing copyrights. And as we observe, *infra*, there is no cause to suspect that a purpose to evade the "limited Times" prescription prompted Congress to adopt the CTEA.

. . . History reveals an unbroken congressional practice of granting to authors of works with existing copyrights the benefit of term extensions so that all under copyright protection will be governed evenhandedly under the same regime. . . .

Because the Clause empowering Congress to confer copyrights also authorizes patents, congressional practice with respect to patents informs our inquiry. We count it significant that early Congresses extended the duration of numerous individual patents as well as copyrights. The courts saw no "limited Times" impediment to such extensions; renewed or extended terms were upheld in the early days. . . .

Satisfied that the CTEA complies with the "limited Times" prescription, we turn now to whether it is a rational exercise of the legislative authority conferred by the Copyright Clause. On that point, we defer substantially to Congress. . . .

The CTEA reflects judgments of a kind Congress typically makes, judgments we cannot dismiss as outside the Legislature's domain. . . . [A] key factor in the CTEA's passage was a 1993 European Union (EU) directive instructing EU members to establish a copyright term of life plus 70 years. Consistent with the Berne Convention, the EU directed its members to deny this longer term to the works of any non-EU country whose laws did not secure the same extended term. By extending the base-line United States copyright term to life plus 70 years, Congress sought to ensure that American authors would receive the same copyright protection in Europe as their European counterparts. The CTEA may also provide greater incentive for American and other authors to create and disseminate their work in the United States.

In addition to international concerns, Congress passed the CTEA in light of demographic, economic, and technological changes,[14] and rationally credited

---

14. Members of Congress expressed the view that, as a result of increases in human longevity and in parents' average age when their children are born, the pre-CTEA term did not adequately secure "the right to profit from licensing one's work during one's lifetime and to take pride and comfort in knowing that one's children—and perhaps their children—might also benefit from one's posthumous popularity." 141 Cong. Rec. 6553 (1995) (statement of Sen. Feinstein) . . .

projections that longer terms would encourage copyright holders to invest in the restoration and public distribution of their works.[15]

In sum, we find that the CTEA is a rational enactment; we are not at liberty to second-guess congressional determinations and policy judgments of this order, however debatable or arguably unwise they may be. . . .

B . . .

Petitioners dominantly advance a series of arguments all premised on the proposition that Congress may not extend an existing copyright absent new consideration from the author. . . .

. . . [P]etitioners contend that the CTEA's extension of existing copyrights does not "promote the Progress of Science" as contemplated by the preambular language of the Copyright Clause. Art. I, §8, cl. 8. . . . [Petitioners] maintain that the preambular language identifies the sole end to which Congress may legislate. . . . The CTEA's extension of existing copyrights categorically fails to "promote the Progress of Science," petitioners argue, because it does not stimulate the creation of new works but merely adds value to works already created.

As petitioners point out, we have described the Copyright Clause as "both a grant of power and a limitation," *Graham v. John Deere Co. of Kansas City*, 383 U.S. 1, 5 (1966), and have said that "[t]he primary objective of copyright" is "[t]o promote the Progress of Science," *Feist*, 499 U.S., at 349. The "constitutional command," we have recognized, is that Congress, to the extent it enacts copyright laws at all, create a "system" that "promote[s] the Progress of Science." *Graham*, 383 U.S., at 6.

We have also stressed, however, that it is generally for Congress, not the courts, to decide how best to pursue the Copyright Clause's objectives. The justifications we earlier set out for Congress' enactment of the CTEA provide a rational basis for the conclusion that the CTEA "promote[s] the Progress of Science."

On the issue of copyright duration, Congress, from the start, has routinely applied new definitions or adjustments of the copyright term to both future works and existing works not yet in the public domain. . . . Congress' unbroken practice since the founding generation thus overwhelms petitioners' argument that the CTEA's extension of existing copyrights fails *per se* to "promote the Progress of Science."

---

15. Justice Breyer urges that the economic incentives accompanying copyright term extension are too insignificant to "mov[e]" any author with a "rational economic perspective." Calibrating rational economic incentives, however, like "fashion[ing] . . . new rules [in light of] new technology," *Sony*, 464 U.S., at 431, is a task primarily for Congress, not the courts. Congress heard testimony from a number of prominent artists; each expressed the belief that the copyright system's assurance of fair compensation for themselves and their heirs was an incentive to create. *See, e.g.*, House Hearings 233-239 (statement of Quincy Jones); Copyright Term Extension Act of 1995: Hearings before the Senate Committee on the Judiciary, 104th Cong., 1st Sess., 55-56 (1995) (statement of Bob Dylan); *id.*, at 56-57 (statement of Don Henley); *id.*, at 57 (statement of Carlos Santana). We would not take Congress to task for crediting this evidence which, as Justice Breyer acknowledges, reflects general "propositions about the value of incentives" that are "undeniably true." . . .

Closely related to petitioners' preambular argument, or a variant of it, is their assertion that the Copyright Clause "imbeds a quid pro quo." They contend, in this regard, that Congress may grant to an "Autho[r]" an "exclusive Right" for a "limited Tim[e]," but only in exchange for a "Writin[g]." Congress' power to confer copyright protection, petitioners argue, is thus contingent upon an exchange: The author of an original work receives an "exclusive Right" for a "limited Tim[e]" in exchange for a dedication to the public thereafter. Extending an existing copyright without demanding additional consideration, petitioners maintain, bestows an unpaid-for benefit on copyright holders and their heirs, in violation of the *quid pro quo* requirement.

We can demur to petitioners' description of the Copyright Clause as a grant of legislative authority empowering Congress "to secure a bargain—this for that." But the legislative evolution earlier recalled demonstrates what the bargain entails. Given the consistent placement of existing copyright holders in parity with future holders, the author of a work created in the last 170 years would reasonably comprehend, as the "this" offered her, a copyright not only for the time in place when protection is gained, but also for any renewal or extension legislated during that time. Congress could rationally seek to "promote . . . Progress" by including in every copyright statute an express guarantee that authors would receive the benefit of any later legislative extension of the copyright term. Nothing in the Copyright Clause bars Congress from creating the same incentive by adopting the same position as a matter of unbroken practice. . . .

We note, furthermore, that patents and copyrights do not entail the same exchange, and that our references to a *quid pro quo* typically appear in the patent context. This is understandable, given that immediate disclosure is not the objective of, but is *exacted from*, the patentee. It is the price paid for the exclusivity secured. For the author seeking copyright protection, in contrast, disclosure is the desired objective, not something exacted from the author in exchange for the copyright. Indeed, since the 1976 Act, copyright has run from creation, not publication.

Further distinguishing the two kinds of intellectual property, copyright gives the holder no monopoly on any knowledge. A reader of an author's writing may make full use of any fact or idea she acquires from her reading. The grant of a patent, on the other hand, does prevent full use by others of the inventor's knowledge. In light of these distinctions, one cannot extract from language in our patent decisions—language not trained on a grant's duration—genuine support for petitioners' bold view. Accordingly, we reject the proposition that a quid pro quo requirement stops Congress from expanding copyright's term in a manner that puts existing and future copyrights in parity.[22] . . .

---

22. The fact that patent and copyright involve different exchanges does not, of course, mean that we may not be guided in our "limited Times" analysis by Congress' repeated extensions of existing patents. If patent's *quid pro quo* is more exacting than copyright's, then Congress' repeated extensions of existing patents without constitutional objection suggests even more strongly that similar legislation with respect to copyrights is constitutionally permissible.

III

Petitioners separately argue that the CTEA is a content-neutral regulation of speech that fails heightened judicial review under the First Amendment. We reject petitioners' plea for imposition of uncommonly strict scrutiny on a copyright scheme that incorporates its own speech-protective purposes and safeguards. The Copyright Clause and First Amendment were adopted close in time. This proximity indicates that, in the Framers' view, copyright's limited monopolies are compatible with free speech principles. Indeed, copyright's purpose is to *promote* the creation and publication of free expression. . . .

In addition to spurring the creation and publication of new expression, copyright law contains built-in First Amendment accommodations. See [*Harper & Row, Publishers Inc. v. Nation Enterprises,* 471 U.S. 539, 560 (1985)]. First, it distinguishes between ideas and expression and makes only the latter eligible for copyright protection. . . . Due to this distinction, every idea, theory, and fact in a copyrighted work becomes instantly available for public exploitation at the moment of publication.

Second, the "fair use" defense allows the public to use not only facts and ideas contained in a copyrighted work, but also expression itself in certain circumstances. . . . The fair use defense affords considerable "latitude for scholarship and comment," . . . and even for parody.

The CTEA itself supplements these traditional First Amendment safeguards. First, it allows libraries, archives, and similar institutions to "reproduce" and "distribute, display, or perform in facsimile or digital form" copies of certain published works "during the last 20 years of any term of copyright . . . for purposes of preservation, scholarship, or research" if the work is not already being exploited commercially and further copies are unavailable at a reasonable price. 17 U.S.C. §108(h). Second, Title II of the CTEA, known as the Fairness in Music Licensing Act of 1998, exempts small businesses, restaurants, and like entities from having to pay performance royalties on music played from licensed radio, television, and similar facilities. 17 U.S.C. §110(5)(B). . . .

. . . [The CTEA] protects authors' original expression from unrestricted exploitation. Protection of that order does not raise the free speech concerns present when the government compels or burdens the communication of particular facts or ideas. The First Amendment securely protects the freedom to make—or decline to make—one's own speech; it bears less heavily when speakers assert the right to make other people's speeches. To the extent such assertions raise First Amendment concerns, copyright's built-in free speech safeguards are generally adequate to address them. . . . [W]hen, as in this case, Congress has not altered the traditional contours of copyright protection, further First Amendment scrutiny is unnecessary. . . .

STEVENS, J., dissenting: . . . [In the Copyright Act of 1790,] Congress set in place a federal structure governing certain types of intellectual property for the new Republic. That Congress exercised its unquestionable constitutional authority to *create* a new federal system securing rights for authors and inventors in 1790 does not provide support for the proposition that Congress can *extend pre-existing* federal protections retroactively. . . .

[Justice Stevens summarized the individual patents that were extended by acts of Congress during the 1800s. He concluded that these incidents were "patently unconstitutional."]

. . . [A]s our decision in *INS v. Chadha*, 462 U.S. 919 (1983), demonstrates, the fact that Congress has repeatedly acted on a mistaken interpretation of the Constitution does not qualify our duty to invalidate an unconstitutional practice when it is finally challenged in an appropriate case. . . .

It would be particularly unwise to attach constitutional significance to the 1831 amendment because of the very different legal landscape against which it was enacted. Congress based its authority to pass the amendment on grounds shortly thereafter declared improper by the Court. The Judiciary Committee Report prepared for the House of Representatives asserted that "an author has an exclusive and perpetual right, in preference to any other, to the fruits of his labor." 7 Gales & Seaton, Register of Debates in Congress CXX (1831). The floor debate echoed this same sentiment. *See, e.g., id.,* at 423 (statement of Mr. Verplanck (rejecting the idea that copyright involved "an implied contract existing between an author and the public" for "[t]here was no contract; the work of an author was the result of his own labor" and copyright was "merely a legal provision for the protection of a natural right")). This sweat-of-the-brow view of copyright, however, was emphatically rejected by this Court in 1834 in *Wheaton v. Peters,* 8 Pet., at 661 ("Congress, then, by this act, instead of sanctioning an existing right, as contended for, created it"). No presumption of validity should attach to a statutory enactment that relied on a shortly thereafter discredited interpretation of the basis for congressional power. . . .

Respondent also argues that the Act promotes the useful arts by providing incentives to restore old movies. For at least three reasons, the interest in preserving perishable copies of old copyrighted films does not justify a wholesale extension of existing copyrights. First, such restoration and preservation will not even arguably promote any new works by authors or inventors. And, of course, any original expression in the restoration and preservation of movies will receive new copyright protection. Second, however strong the justification for preserving such works may be, that justification applies equally to works whose copyrights have already expired. Yet no one seriously contends that the Copyright/Patent Clause would authorize the grant of monopoly privileges for works already in the public domain solely to encourage their restoration. Finally, even if this concern with aging movies would permit congressional protection, the remedy offered—a blanket extension of all copyrights—simply bears no relationship to the alleged harm. . . .

By failing to protect the public interest in free access to the products of inventive and artistic genius—indeed, by virtually ignoring the central purpose of the Copyright/Patent Clause—the Court has quitclaimed to Congress its principal responsibility in this area of the law. Fairly read, the Court has stated that Congress' actions under the Copyright/Patent Clause are, for all intents and purposes, judicially unreviewable. That result cannot be squared with the basic tenets of our constitutional structure. . . .

BREYER, J., dissenting: . . . The Copyright Clause and the First Amendment seek related objectives—the creation and dissemination of information. When working in tandem, these provisions mutually reinforce each other, the first serving as an "engine of free expression," *Harper & Row, Publishers, Inc. v. Nation Enterprises,* 471 U.S. 539, 558 (1985), the second assuring that government throws up no obstacle to its dissemination. At the same time, a particular statute that exceeds proper Copyright Clause bounds may set Clause and Amendment at cross-purposes, thereby depriving the public of the speech-related benefits that the Founders, through both, have promised.

Consequently, I would review plausible claims that a copyright statute seriously, and unjustifiably, restricts the dissemination of speech somewhat more carefully than reference to this Court's traditional Commerce Clause jurisprudence might suggest. . . .

Thus, I would find that the statute lacks the constitutionally necessary rational support (1) if the significant benefits that it bestows are private, not public; (2) if it threatens seriously to undermine the expressive values that the Copyright Clause embodies; and (3) if it cannot find justification in any significant Clause-related objective. Where, after examination of the statute, it becomes difficult, if not impossible, even to dispute these characterizations, Congress' "choice is clearly wrong." *Helvering v. Davis,* 301 U.S. 619, 640 (1937). . . .

First, the present statute primarily benefits the holders of existing copyrights, i.e., copyrights on works already created. And a Congressional Research Service (CRS) study prepared for Congress indicates that the added royalty-related sum that the law will transfer to existing copyright holders is large. E. Rappaport, CRS Report for Congress, Copyright Term Extension: Estimating the Economic Values (1998) (hereinafter CRS Report). In conjunction with official figures on copyright renewals, the CRS Report indicates that only about 2% of copyrights between 55 and 75 years old retain commercial value—i.e., still generate royalties after that time. But books, songs, and movies of that vintage still earn about $400 million per year in royalties. CRS Report 8, 12, 15. Hence, (despite declining consumer interest in any given work over time) one might conservatively estimate that 20 extra years of copyright protection will mean the transfer of several billion extra royalty dollars to holders of existing copyrights—copyrights that, together, already will have earned many billions of dollars in royalty "reward." See *id.,* at 16.

The extra royalty payments will not come from thin air. Rather, they ultimately come from those who wish to read or see or hear those classic books or films or recordings that have survived. . . .

A second, equally important, cause for concern arises out of the fact that copyright extension imposes a "permissions" requirement—not only upon potential users of "classic" works that still retain commercial value, but also upon potential users of any other work still in copyright. Again using CRS estimates, one can estimate that, by 2018, the number of such works 75 years of age or older will be about 350,000. Because the Copyright Act of 1976 abolished the requirement that an owner must renew a copyright, such still-in-copyright works (of little or no commercial value) will eventually number in the millions. . . .

... [T]he permissions requirement can inhibit or prevent the use of old works (particularly those without commercial value): (1) because it may prove expensive to track down or to contract with the copyright holder, (2) because the holder may prove impossible to find, or (3) because the holder when found may deny permission either outright or through misinformed efforts to bargain. The CRS, for example, has found that the cost of seeking permission "can be prohibitive." CRS Report 4. . . .

... The costs to the users of nonprofit databases, now numbering in the low millions, will multiply as the use of those computer-assisted databases becomes more prevalent. And the qualitative costs to education, learning, and research will multiply as our children become ever more dependent for the content of their knowledge upon computer-accessible databases—thereby condemning that which is not so accessible, say, the cultural content of early 20th-century history, to a kind of intellectual purgatory from which it will not easily emerge. . . .

The majority also invokes the "fair use" exception, and it notes that copyright law itself is restricted to protection of a work's expression, not its substantive content. Neither the exception nor the restriction, however, would necessarily help those who wish to obtain from electronic databases material that is not there . . .

What copyright-related benefits might justify the statute's extension of copyright protection? First, no one could reasonably conclude that copyright's traditional economic rationale applies here. . . . Using assumptions about the time value of money provided us by a group of economists (including five Nobel prize winners), Brief for George A. Akerlof et al. as *Amici Curiae* 5-7, it seems fair to say that, for example, a 1% likelihood of earning $100 annually for 20 years, starting *75 years into the future,* is worth less than seven cents today.

What potential Shakespeare, Wharton, or Hemingway would be moved by such a sum? What monetarily motivated Melville would not realize that he could do better for his grandchildren by putting a few dollars into an interest-bearing bank account? . . .

. . . Of course Congress did not intend to act unconstitutionally. But it may have sought to test the Constitution's limits. After all, the statute was named after a Member of Congress, who, the legislative history records, "wanted the term of copyright protection to last forever." 144 Cong. Rec. H9952 (daily ed. Oct. 7, 1998) (statement of Rep. Mary Bono). See also Copyright Term, Film Labeling, and Film Preservation Legislation: Hearings on H.R. 989 et al. before the Subcommittee on Courts and Intellectual Property of the House Judiciary Committee, 104th Cong., 1st Sess., 94 (1995) (hereinafter House Hearings) (statement of Rep. Sonny Bono) (questioning why copyrights should ever expire); *ibid.* (statement of Rep. Berman) ("I guess we could . . . just make a permanent moratorium on the expiration of copyrights"); *id.,* at 230 (statement of Rep. Hoke) ("Why 70 years? Why not forever? Why not 150 years?"); *id.,* at 234 (statement of Quincy Jones) ("I'm particularly fascinated with Representative Hoke's statement. . . . [W]hy not forever?"); *id.,* at 277 (statement of Quincy Jones) ("If we can start with 70, add 20, it would be a good start"). . . .

Second, the Court relies heavily for justification upon international uniformity of terms. . . . [I]n this case the justification based upon foreign rules is surprisingly weak. . . .

Despite appearances, the statute does *not* create a uniform American-European term with respect to the lion's share of the economically significant works that it affects—*all* works made "for hire" and *all* existing works created prior to 1978. With respect to those works the American statute produces an extended term of 95 years while comparable European rights in "for hire" works last for periods that vary from 50 years to 70 years to life plus 70 years. Neither does the statute create uniformity with respect to anonymous or pseudonymous works. . . .

Third, several publishers and filmmakers argue that the statute provides incentives to *those who act as publishers* to republish and to redistribute older copyrighted works. This claim cannot justify this statute, however, because the rationale is inconsistent with the basic purpose of the Copyright Clause—as understood by the Framers and by this Court. The Clause assumes an initial grant of monopoly, designed primarily to encourage creation, followed by termination of the monopoly grant in order to promote dissemination of already-created works. It assumes that it is the *disappearance* of the monopoly grant, not its *perpetuation,* that will, on balance, promote the dissemination of works already in existence. . . .

I share the Court's initial concern, about intrusion upon the decisionmaking authority of Congress. But I do not believe it intrudes upon that authority to find the statute unconstitutional on the basis of (1) a legal analysis of the Copyright Clause's objectives; (2) the total implausibility of any incentive effect; and (3) the statute's apparent failure to provide significant international uniformity Nor does it intrude upon congressional authority to consider rationality in light of the expressive values underlying the Copyright Clause, related as it is to the First Amendment, and given the constitutional importance of correctly drawing the relevant Clause/ Amendment boundary. . . .

. . . Even if it is difficult to draw a single clear bright line, the Court could easily decide (as I would decide) that this particular statute simply goes too far. . . .

NOTES AND QUESTIONS

1. Who has the better argument about the significance of past copyright and patent extensions, the majority or Justice Stevens?

2. The majority and Justice Stevens also disagreed about the level of deference owed to Congress under Art. I, §8, cl. 8. Who has the better argument there? The majority pointed to international uniformity in copyright duration as a permissible policy choice supporting passage of the CTEA. Did you find the majority's reasoning on this point persuasive?

3. In upholding the CTEA as a rational exercise of Congress' copyright power, the Court noted the incentive effects of the extra 20 years in light of "demographic, economic, and technological" changes. Was the majority or

> ### COMPARATIVE PERSPECTIVE
>
> Atricle 7 of the Berne Convention mandates a minimum term of copyright protection of life plus 50 years. However, both the United States and the European Union separately have concluded numerous bilateral and regional trade agreements that require parties to protect copyright for life plus 70 years. As a practical matter, then, this may become the *de facto* international rule of copyright duration.

Justice Breyer more persuasive on this point? Do you think the majority agreed or disagreed with Congress' conclusion that the CTEA represented sound policy? Do you think the Court would have reached a different decision about the rationality of the CTEA if petitioners had also challenged the constitutionality of prospective term extension?

4. Do Justice Breyer's arguments about the economic rationality of the CTEA concern the deference owed to Congress under Art. I, §8, cl. 8, or under the First Amendment? Are his concerns well founded? Did the majority adequately answer these concerns?

5. The Court rejected the plaintiff's argument that the Constitution requires a quid pro quo for the grant of a copyright and that giving existing works 20 additional years of protection violated this requirement. Do you agree with the majority's reasoning? Is Congress' decision to omit the quid pro quo of publication from the 1976 Act relevant to determination of the constitutional question? Why, or why not?

b. Restoration of Lapsed Copyrights

If Congress can extend the copyright term, can it also restore copyright protection to works that have passed into the public domain? In 2012, the Supreme Court considered a constitutional challenge to §104A of the Copyright Act, which restores copyright to eligible foreign works. The lead plaintiff, Lawrence Golan, conducted a small college orchestra that, following the enactment of §104A, had to pay royalties to perform works by Shostakovich, Prokofiev, and others. Like the plaintiffs in *Eldred*, the *Golan* plaintiffs argued that the restoration provision unlawfully impinged upon the public domain, and invoked both Art. I, §8, cl. 8 and the First Amendment. By a 6–2 majority, the Court rejected both arguments.

In an opinion by Justice Ginsburg, the Court first observed that *Eldred* defeated Golan's argument based on the constitutional reference to "limited Times," Art. I, §8, cl. 8, because the copyright terms made available to restored foreign works had definite endpoints and thus remained limited. It rejected Golan's argument that this construction of "limited Times" opened the door to abuse by Congress, reasoning that "[i]n aligning the United States with other nations bound by the Berne Convention, and thereby according equitable treatment to once disfavored foreign authors, Congress can hardly be charged with a design to move stealthily toward a regime of perpetual copyrights." *Golan v. Holder*, 132 S. Ct. 873, 885 (2012). The Court noted that Congress had removed works from the public domain both in 1790, when it created the federal copyright system, and on subsequent occasions to restore protection to works that had lost it during the two world wars. "Installing a federal copyright system and ameliorating the interruptions of global war, it is true, presented Congress with extraordinary situations. Yet the TRIPS accord, leading the United States to comply in full measure with Berne, was also a signal event. Given the authority we hold Congress has, we will not second-guess the political choice Congress made between leaving the public domain untouched and embracing Berne unstintingly." *Id.* at 887.

The Court next rejected the argument that the term "progress of Science," as used in Art. I, §8, cl. 8, concerns only the provision of incentives to create works initially. In the Court's view, the grant of legislative authority also encompasses dissemination incentives, and Congress could reasonably have expected §104A to supply such incentives. "Full compliance with Berne, Congress had reason to believe, would expand the foreign markets available to U.S. authors and invigorate protection against piracy of U.S. works abroad, S. Rep. No. 103-412, pp. 224, 225 (1994); URAA Joint Hearing 291 (statement of Berman, RIAA); *id.*, at 244, 247 (statement of Smith, IIPA), thereby benefitting copyright-intensive industries stateside and inducing greater investment in the creative process." *Golan*, 132 S. Ct. at 889.

Finally, as it had in *Eldred*, the Court rejected the First Amendment challenge:

> Given the "speech-protective purposes and safeguards" embraced by copyright law, we concluded in *Eldred* that there was no call for the heightened review petitioners sought in that case. We reach the same conclusion here. Section 514 [of the Uruguay Round Agreements Act, codified as 17 U.S.C. §104A] leaves undisturbed the "idea/ expression" distinction and the "fair use" defense. Moreover, Congress adopted measures to ease the transition from a national scheme to an international copyright regime: It deferred the date from which enforcement runs, and it cushioned the impact of restoration on "reliance parties" who exploited foreign works denied protection before §514 took effect. . . .

> Petitioners attempt to distinguish their challenge from the one turned away in *Eldred*. First Amendment interests of a higher order are at stake here, petitioners say, because they—unlike their counterparts in *Eldred*—enjoyed "vested rights" in works that had already entered the public domain. The limited rights they retain under copyright law's "built-in safeguards" are, in their view, no substitute for the unlimited use they enjoyed before §514's enactment. . . .

> However spun, these contentions depend on an argument we considered and rejected . . . namely, that the Constitution renders the public domain largely untouchable by Congress. . . . [N]othing in the historical record, congressional practice, or our own jurisprudence warrants exceptional First Amendment solicitude for copyrighted works that were once in the public domain. Neither this challenge nor that raised in *Eldred*, we stress, allege Congress transgressed a generally applicable First Amendment prohibition; we are not faced, for example, with copyright protection that hinges on the author's viewpoint. . . .

> To copyright lawyers, the "vested rights" formulation might sound exactly backwards: Rights typically vest at the *outset* of copyright protection, in an author or rightholder. Once the term of protection ends, the works do not revest in any rightholder. Instead, the works simply lapse into the public domain. Anyone has free access to the public domain, but no one, after the copyright term has expired, acquires ownership rights in the once-protected works.

> Congress recurrently adjusts copyright law to protect categories of works once outside the law's compass. For example, Congress broke new ground when it extended copyright protection to foreign works in 1891; to dramatic works in 1856; to photographs and photographic negatives in 1865; to motion pictures in 1912; to fixed sound recordings in 1972; and to architectural works in 1990. . . . If Congress could grant protection to these works without hazarding heightened First Amendment scrutiny,

then what free speech principle disarms it from protecting works prematurely cast into the public domain for reasons antithetical to the Berne Convention?

Section 514, we add, does not impose a blanket prohibition on public access. Petitioners protest that fair use and the idea/expression dichotomy "are plainly inadequate to protect the speech and expression rights that Section 514 took from petitioners, or . . . the public"—that is, "the unrestricted right to perform, copy, teach and distribute the *entire* work, for any reason." . . .

But Congress has not put petitioners in this bind. The question here, as in *Eldred,* is whether would-be users must pay for their desired use of the author's expression, or else limit their exploitation to "fair use" of that work. Prokofiev's *Peter and the Wolf* could once be performed free of charge; after §514 the right to perform it must be obtained in the marketplace. This is the same marketplace, of course, that exists for the music of Prokofiev's U.S. contemporaries: works of Copland and Bernstein, for example, that enjoy copyright protection, but nevertheless appear regularly in the programs of U.S. concertgoers.

Id. at 889-93.

In dissent, Justice Breyer characterized the question to be decided as "whether the Copyright Clause permits Congress seriously to exacerbate . . . [the 'dissemination-restricting harms of copyright'] by taking works out of the public domain without a countervailing benefit." *Id.* at 906. He concluded that the question was one appropriate for judicial resolution: "[U]nlike *Eldred* where the Court had to decide a complicated line-drawing question—when is a copyright term too long?—here an easily administrable standard is available—a standard that would require works that have already fallen into the public domain to stay there." *Id.* Because the speech harms entailed in removing material from the public domain were significant, and because the evidence before Congress consisted principally of testimony "from the representatives of existing copyright holders, who hoped that passage of the statute would enable them to benefit from reciprocal treatment of American authors abroad," in Justice Breyer's view §104A merited some degree of heightened scrutiny. *Id.* at 907. He then argued that the asserted justifications for §104A were insufficient, and that careful attention to the historical record—including the legislative history of the Berne Convention Implementation Act of 1988—revealed "a virtually unbroken string of legislation preventing the withdrawal of works from the public domain." *Id.* at 909. According to Justice Breyer, the majority's argument about the importance of dissemination incentives

is the kind of argument that the Stationers' Company might well have made and which the British Parliament rejected. It is the kind of argument that could justify a legislature's withdrawing from the public domain the works, say, of Hawthorne or of Swift or for that matter the King James Bible in order to encourage further publication of those works; and, it could even more easily justify similar action in the case of lesser known early works, perhaps those of the Venerable Bede. The Court has not, to my knowledge, previously accepted such a rationale—a rationale well removed from the special economic circumstances that surround the nonrepeatable costs of the initial creation of a "Writing." And I fear that doing so would read the Copyright Clause as if it were a blank check made out in favor of those who are not themselves creators.

Id. at 910.

Justice Breyer was "willing to speculate, for argument's sake, that the statute might indirectly encourage production of new works by making the United States' place in the international copyright regime more secure." Ultimately, however, he concluded that

> I cannot find this argument sufficient to save the statute. For one thing, this is a dilemma of the Government's own making. The United States obtained the benefits of Berne for many years despite its failure to enact a statute implementing Article 18. But in 1994, the United States and other nations signed the Agreement on Trade-Related Aspects of Intellectual Property Rights, which enabled signatories to use World Trade Organization dispute resolution mechanisms to complain about other members' Berne Convention violations. But at that time the Government, although it successfully secured reservations protecting other special features of American copyright law, made no effort to secure a reservation permitting the United States to keep some or all restored works in the American public domain. And it made no effort to do so despite the fact that Article 18 explicitly authorizes countries to negotiate exceptions to the Article's retroactivity principle.

Id. at 911. In Justice Breyer's view, the constitutional values attached to the public domain required the U.S. government to do more to preserve it.

NOTES AND QUESTIONS

1. Justice Ginsburg's majority opinion in *Golan* observes: "Neither the Copyright and Patent Clause nor the First Amendment, we hold, makes the public domain, in any and all cases, a territory that works may never exit." 132 S. Ct. at 878. Does this reasoning have any limiting principle? Could Congress restore the copyrights in U.S. works that still would be copyrighted if their authors had satisfied then-applicable formalities? Could Congress restore the copyright in "The Star-Spangled Banner," whose author, Francis Scott Key, died in 1843?

2. In rejecting petitioners' requests for heightened First Amendment scrutiny, *Eldred* and *Golan* observed that the idea/expression distinction and the fair use doctrine safeguard First Amendment values. Should copyright legislation be exempted from heightened scrutiny so long as Congress leaves the idea/expression distinction and the fair use doctrine in place?

3. Article 18 of the Berne Convention provides:

> (1) This Convention shall apply to all works which, at the moment of its coming into force, have not yet fallen into the public domain in the country of origin through the expiry of the term of protection.
>
> (2) If, however, through the expiry of the term of protection which was previously granted, a work has fallen into the public domain of the country where protection is claimed, that work shall not be protected anew.
>
> (3) The application of this principle shall be subject to any provisions contained in special conventions to that effect existing or to be concluded between countries of the Union. In the absence of such provisions, the respective countries shall determine, each in so far as it is concerned, the conditions of application of this principle.

(4) The preceding provisions shall also apply in the case of new accessions to the Union. . . .

The *Golan* majority argued that this language required restoration; the dissent argued that it preserved latitude for Congress to withhold restoration and extend copyright without regard to formalities on a prospective basis only. What do you read the treaty language to require? What do you think the drafting parties saw as the purpose of Art. 18(3)? How do you think the United States formulated its negotiating position with respect to Article 18?

C. RENEWALS AND TERMINATIONS OF TRANSFERS

Since its inception, the U.S. copyright regime has included provisions meant to give the author and her family a chance to recapture the value of a previously assigned copyright. The practical import of these provisions is that under certain circumstances, title to a subsisting copyright can revert back to the author or her heirs. Determining whether the conditions for reversion have been met is another important aspect of copyright due diligence.

> **KEEP IN MIND**
>
> Although the 1976 Act uses a unitary term, the 1909 Act's duration scheme applies to works created before the effective date of the 1976 Act (January 1, 1978). The last of the renewal terms for such works will not expire until the year 2072 (1977 + 95)!

1. Renewals

As discussed earlier in this chapter, the 1909 Act granted copyright protection for an initial 28-year term with the possibility for a renewal term of 28 years. To obtain protection for that renewal term, the author had to file a renewal certificate with the Copyright Office. The Supreme Court's decision in *Stewart v. Abend*, excerpted below, addresses the reasons for and effects of this dual term system.

 Stewart v. Abend
495 U.S. 207 (1990)

O'CONNOR, J.: The author of a pre-existing work may assign to another the right to use it in a derivative work. In this case the author of a pre-existing work agreed to assign the rights in his renewal copyright term to the owner of a derivative work, but died before the commencement of the renewal period. The question presented is whether the owner of the derivative work infringed the rights of the successor owner of the pre-existing work by continued distribution and publication of the derivative work during the renewal term of the pre-existing work.

I

Cornell Woolrich authored the story "It Had to Be Murder," which was first published in February 1942 in Dime Detective Magazine. . . . In 1945, Woolrich agreed to assign the rights to make motion picture versions of six of his stories, including "It Had to Be Murder," to B. G. De Sylva Productions for $9,250. He also agreed to renew the copyrights in the stories at the appropriate time and to assign the same motion picture rights to De Sylva Productions for the 28-year renewal term. In 1953, actor Jimmy Stewart and director Alfred Hitchcock formed a production company, Patron, Inc., which obtained the motion picture rights in "It Had to Be Murder" from De Sylva's successors in interest for $10,000.

. . . In 1954, Patron, Inc., along with Paramount Pictures, produced and distributed "Rear Window," the motion picture version of Woolrich's story "It Had to Be Murder." Woolrich died in 1968 before he could obtain the rights in the renewal term for petitioners as promised and without a surviving spouse or child. He left his property to a trust administered by his executor, Chase Manhattan Bank, for the benefit of Columbia University. On December 29, 1969, Chase Manhattan Bank renewed the copyright in the "It Had to Be Murder" story pursuant to 17 U.S.C. §24 (1976 ed.). Chase Manhattan assigned the renewal rights to respondent Abend for $650 plus 10% of all proceeds from exploitation of the story.

"Rear Window" was broadcast on the ABC television network in 1971. Respondent then notified petitioners Hitchcock (now represented by cotrustees of his will), Stewart, and MCA Inc., the owners of the "Rear Window" motion picture and renewal rights in the motion picture, that he owned the renewal rights in the copyright and that their distribution of the motion picture without his permission infringed his copyright in the story. Hitchcock, Stewart, and MCA nonetheless entered into a second license with ABC to rebroadcast the motion picture. In 1974, respondent filed suit against these same petitioners, and others, in the United States District Court for the Southern District of New York, alleging copyright infringement. Respondent dismissed his complaint in return for $25,000.

Three years later, the United States Court of Appeals for the Second Circuit decided *Rohauer v. Killiam Shows, Inc.*, 551 F.2d 484, *cert. denied*, 431 U.S. 949 (1977), in which it held that the owner of the copyright in a derivative work may continue to use the existing derivative work according to the original grant from the author of the pre-existing work even if the grant of rights in the pre-existing work lapsed. Several years later, apparently in reliance on *Rohauer*, petitioners re-released the motion picture in a variety of media, including new 35 and 16 millimeter prints for theatrical exhibition in the United States, videocassettes, and videodiscs. They also publicly exhibited the motion picture in theaters, over cable television, and through videodisc and videocassette rentals and sales.

Respondent then brought the instant suit in the United States District Court for the Central District of California against Hitchcock, Stewart, MCA, and Universal Film Exchanges, a subsidiary of MCA and the distributor of the motion picture. Respondent's complaint alleges that the re-release of the motion picture infringes his copyright in the story because petitioners' right to use the story during the renewal term lapsed when Woolrich died before he could register for the renewal term and transfer his renewal rights to them. Respondent also contends that petitioners have interfered with his rights in the renewal term of the story in other ways. He alleges that he sought to contract with Home Box Office (HBO) to produce a play and television version of the story, but that petitioners wrote to him and HBO stating that neither he nor HBO could use either the title, "Rear Window" or "It Had to Be Murder." Respondent also alleges that petitioners further interfered with the renewal copyright in the story by attempting to sell the right to make a television sequel and that the re-release of the original motion picture itself interfered with his ability to produce other derivative works. . . .

II

A . . .

Since the earliest copyright statute in this country, the copyright term of ownership has been split between an original term and a renewal term. Originally, the renewal was intended merely to serve as an extension of the original term; at the end of the original term, the renewal could be effected and claimed by the author, if living, or by the author's executors, administrators, or assigns. In 1831, Congress altered the provision so that the author could assign his contingent interest in the renewal term, but could not, through his assignment, divest the rights of his widow or children in the renewal term. . . . In this way, Congress attempted to give the author a second chance to control and benefit from his work. Congress also intended to secure to the author's family the opportunity to exploit the work if the author died before he could register for the renewal term. "The evident purpose of [the renewal provision] is to provide for the family of the author after his death. Since the author cannot assign his family's renewal rights, [it] takes the form of a compulsory bequest of the copyright to the designated persons." *De Sylva v. Ballentine*, 351 U.S. 570, 582 (1956).

> **KEEP IN MIND**
>
> The order of succession to the renewal interest is prescribed by statute. The renewal term of the copyright in "It Had to Be Murder" vested in the executor of Woolrich's estate, Chase Manhattan Bank, because Woolrich died without any widow or children to claim an interest in his copyrights.

In its debates leading up to the Copyright Act of 1909, Congress elaborated upon the policy underlying a system comprised of an original term and a completely separate renewal term. "It not infrequently happens that the author sells his copyright outright to a publisher for a comparatively small sum." H.R. Rep. No. 2222, 60th Cong., 2d Sess., 14 (1909). The renewal term permits the author, originally in a poor bargaining position, to renegotiate the terms of the grant once the value of the work has been tested. "[U]nlike real property and other forms of personal property, [a copyright] is by its very nature incapable of accurate monetary evaluation prior to its exploitation." 2 M. Nimmer & D. Nimmer, Nimmer on Copyright §9.02, p. 9-23 (1989) (hereinafter Nimmer). "If the work proves to be a great success and lives beyond the term of twenty-eight years, . . . it should be the exclusive right of the author to take the renewal term, and the law should be framed . . . so that [the author] could not be deprived of that right." H.R. Rep. No. 2222, *supra*, at 14. With these purposes in mind, Congress enacted the renewal provision of the Copyright Act of 1909, 17 U.S.C. §24 (1976 ed.). With respect to works in their original or renewal term as of January 1, 1978, Congress retained the two-term system of copyright protection in the 1976 Act.

Applying these principles in *Miller Music Corp. v. Charles N. Daniels, Inc.*, 362 U.S. 373 (1960), this Court held that when an author dies before the renewal period arrives, his executor is entitled to the renewal rights, even though the author previously assigned his renewal rights to another party. "An assignment by an author of his renewal rights made before the original copyright expires is valid against the world, if the author is alive at the commencement of the renewal period. [*Fred*] *Fisher Co. v.* [*M.*] *Witmark & Sons*, 318 U.S. 643, [1943] so holds." *Id.*, at 375. If the author dies before that time, the "next of kin obtain the renewal copyright free of any claim founded upon an assignment made by the author in his lifetime. These results follow not because the author's assignment is invalid but because he had only an expectancy to assign; and his death, prior to the renewal period, terminates his interest in the renewal which by §24 vests in the named classes." *Ibid.* . . . Thus, the renewal provisions were intended to give the author a second chance to obtain fair remuneration for his creative efforts and to provide the author's family a "new estate" if the author died before the renewal period arrived.

. . . If the assignee of all of the renewal rights holds nothing upon the death of the assignor before arrival of the renewal period, then, *a fortiori*, the assignee of a portion of the renewal rights, e.g., the right to produce a derivative work, must also hold nothing. Therefore, if the author dies before the renewal period, then the assignee may continue to use the original work only if the author's successor transfers the renewal rights to the assignee. This is the rule adopted by the Court of Appeals below and advocated by the Register of Copyrights. Application of this rule to this case should end the inquiry. Woolrich died before the commencement of the renewal period in the story, and, therefore, petitioners hold only an unfulfilled expectancy. Petitioners have been "deprived of nothing. Like all purchasers of contingent interests, [they took] subject to the possibility that the contingency may not occur." *Miller Music, supra*, at 378.

B

The reason that our inquiry does not end here, and that we granted certiorari, is that the Court of Appeals for the Second Circuit reached a contrary result in *Rohauer v. Killiam Shows, Inc.*, 551 F.2d 484 (1977). Petitioners' theory is drawn largely from *Rohauer*. The Court of Appeals in *Rohauer* attempted to craft a "proper reconciliation" between the owner of the pre-existing work, who held the right to the work pursuant to *Miller Music*, and the owner of the derivative work, who had a great deal to lose if the work could not be published or distributed. 551 F.2d, at 490. Addressing a case factually similar to this case, the court concluded that even if the death of the author caused the renewal rights in the pre-existing work to revert to the statutory successor, the owner of the derivative work could continue to exploit that work. The court reasoned that the 1976 Act and the relevant precedents did not preclude such a result and that it was necessitated by a balancing of the equities:

> [T]he equities lie preponderantly in favor of the proprietor of the derivative copyright. In contrast to the situation where an assignee or licensee has done nothing more than print, publicize and distribute a copyrighted story or novel, a person who with the consent of the author has created an opera or a motion picture film will often have made contributions literary, musical and economic, as great as or greater than the original author. . . . [T]he purchaser of derivative rights has no truly effective way to protect himself against the eventuality of the author's death before the renewal period since there is no way of telling who will be the surviving widow, children or next of kin or the executor until that date arrives. *Id.*, at 493. . . .

Though petitioners do not, indeed could not, argue that its language expressly supports the theory they draw from *Rohauer*, they implicitly rely on §6 of the 1909 Act, 17 U.S.C. §7 (1976 ed.), which states that "dramatizations . . . of copyrighted works when produced with the consent of the proprietor of the copyright in such works . . . shall be regarded as new works subject to copyright under the provisions of this title." Petitioners maintain that the creation of the "new," i.e., derivative, work extinguishes any right the owner of rights in the pre-existing work might have had to sue for infringement that occurs during the renewal term.

We think, as stated in Nimmer, that "[t]his conclusion is neither warranted by any express provision of the Copyright Act, nor by the rationale as to the scope of protection achieved in a derivative work. It is moreover contrary to the axiomatic copyright principle that a person may exploit only such copyrighted literary material as he either owns or is licensed to use." 1 Nimmer §3.07[A], pp. 3-23 to 3-24 (footnotes omitted). The aspects of a derivative work added by the derivative author are that author's property, but the element drawn from the pre-existing work remains on grant from the owner of the pre-existing work. So long as the pre-existing work remains out of the public domain, its use is infringing if one who employs the work does not have a valid license or assignment for use of the pre-existing work. It is irrelevant whether the pre-existing work is inseparably intertwined with the derivative work. Indeed, the plain language of [§7 of the 1909 Act] supports the view that the full force of the copyright in the pre-existing work is preserved despite incorporation into the derivative work. This well-settled rule also was made explicit in the 1976 Act:

> The copyright in a compilation or derivative work extends only to the material contributed by the author of such work, as distinguished from the preexisting material employed in the work, and does not imply any exclusive right in the preexisting material. The copyright in such work is independent of, and does not affect or enlarge the scope, duration, ownership, or subsistence of, any copyright protection in the preexisting material. 17 U.S.C. §103(b) [1988 ed.].

Properly conceding there is no explicit support for their theory in the 1909 Act, its legislative history, or the case law, petitioners contend, as did the court in *Rohauer*, that the termination provisions of the 1976 Act, while not controlling, support their theory of the case. For works existing in their original or renewal terms as of January 1, 1978, the 1976 Act added 19 years to the 1909 Act's provision of 28 years of initial copyright protection and 28 years of renewal protection. See 17 U.S.C. §§304(a) and (b) [1988 ed.]. For those works, the author has the power to terminate the grant of rights at the end of the renewal term and, therefore, to gain the benefit of that additional 19 years of protection. *See* §304(c). In effect, the 1976 Act provides a third opportunity for the author to benefit from a work in its original or renewal term as of January 1, 1978. Congress, however, created one exception to the author's right to terminate: The author may not, at the end of the renewal term, terminate the right to use a derivative work for which the owner of the derivative work has held valid rights in the original and renewal terms. *See* §304(c)(6)(A). The author, however, may terminate the right to create new derivative works. *Ibid.* For example, if petitioners held a valid copyright in the story throughout the original and renewal terms, and the renewal term in "Rear Window" were about to expire, petitioners could continue to distribute the motion picture even if respondent terminated the grant of rights, but could not create a new motion picture version of the story. Both the court in *Rohauer* and petitioners infer from this exception to the right to terminate an intent by Congress to prevent authors of pre-existing works from blocking distribution of derivative works. In other words, because Congress decided not to permit authors to exercise a third opportunity to benefit from a work incorporated into a derivative work, the Act expresses a general policy of undermining the author's second opportunity. We disagree.

The process of compromise between competing special interests leading to the enactment of the 1976 Act undermines any such attempt to draw an overarching policy out of §304(c)(6)(A), which only prevents termination with respect to works in their original or renewal copyright terms as of January 1, 1978, and only at the end of the renewal period. . . .

In fact, if the 1976 Act's termination provisions provide any guidance at all in this case, they tilt against petitioners' theory. The plain language of the termination provision itself indicates that Congress assumed that the owner of the pre-existing work possessed the right to sue for infringement even after incorporation of the preexisting work in the derivative work.

> A derivative work *prepared* under authority of the grant before its termination may continue to be utilized under the terms of the grant after its termination, but this privilege does not extend to the preparation after the termination of other derivative works based upon the copyrighted work covered by the terminated grant. §304(c)(6)(A) (emphasis added).

Congress would not have stated explicitly in §304(c)(6)(A) that, at the end of the renewal term, the owner of the rights in the pre-existing work may not terminate use rights in existing derivative works unless Congress had assumed that the owner continued to hold the right to sue for infringement even after incorporation of the preexisting work into the derivative work.

Accordingly, we conclude that neither the 1909 Act nor the 1976 Act provides support for the theory set forth in *Rohauer*. . . .

Finally, petitioners urge us to consider the policies underlying the Copyright Act. They argue that the rule announced by the Court of Appeals will undermine one of the policies of the Act—the dissemination of creative works—by leading to many fewer works reaching the public. *Amicus* Columbia Pictures asserts that "[s]ome owners of underlying work renewal copyrights may refuse to negotiate, preferring instead to retire their copyrighted works, and all derivative works based thereon, from public use. Others may make demands—like respondent's demand for 50% of petitioners' future gross proceeds in excess of advertising expenses . . . —which are so exorbitant that a negotiated economic accommodation will be impossible." Brief for Columbia Pictures et al. as *Amici Curiae* 21. These arguments are better addressed by Congress than the courts.

> **LOOKING FORWARD**
>
> This reasoning suggests that absent such a bargain, Abend could seek to enjoin continuing distribution and public performance of the film. In fact, the Ninth Circuit had denied Abend's request for injunctive relief, ruling instead that royalties should be awarded. The Supreme Court did not grant certiorari on the remedy issue. We discuss the remedies available to a copyright owner in Chapter 13.

In any event, the complaint that respondent's monetary request in this case is so high as to preclude agreement fails to acknowledge that an initially high asking price does not preclude bargaining. Presumably, respondent is asking for a share in the proceeds because he wants to profit from the distribution of the work, not because he seeks suppression of it.

Moreover, although dissemination of creative works is a goal of the Copyright Act, the Act creates a balance between the artist's right to control the work during the term of the copyright protection and the public's need for access to creative works. The copyright term is limited so that the public will not be permanently deprived of the fruits of an artist's labors. But nothing in the copyright statutes would prevent an author from hoarding all of his works during the term of the copyright. In fact, this Court has held that a copyright owner has the capacity arbitrarily to refuse to license one who seeks to exploit the work. *See Fox Film Corp. v. Doyal*, 286 U.S. 123, 127 (1932).

The limited monopoly granted to the artist is intended to provide the necessary bargaining capital to garner a fair price for the value of the works passing into public use. When an author produces a work which later commands a higher price in the market than the original bargain provided, the copyright statute is designed to provide the author the power to negotiate for the realized value of the work. That is how the separate renewal term was intended to operate. At heart, petitioners' true complaint is that they will have to pay more for the use of works they have employed in creating their own works. But such a result was contemplated by Congress and is consistent with the goals of the Copyright Act. . . .

NOTES AND QUESTIONS

1. As the *Stewart* Court explains, the vesting of the renewal term may not be varied by the author's will or state laws of intestate succession. Thus, if an author died before the vesting of the renewal term, it was irrelevant that her will left all of her copyrights to her best friend and not her husband or children because at that point she had no interest to pass on, only a mere expectancy that was extinguished upon her death. The best friend may have owned the copyrights temporarily, but only until their first terms of protection expired; the statutory beneficiaries took the renewal terms. This aspect of renewal term vesting has caused some commentators to describe the renewal rules as forced inheritance rules. What considerations justify those rules? Are the justifications convincing?

If the author survived long enough to have the renewal term vest in her, then her will (or the laws of intestate succession) determines who owns any remaining years of copyright protection.

2. The *Stewart* Court's interpretation of the right to a second bite at the apple given to authors and their families was not entirely protective because the Court reaffirmed its earlier decisions permitting the renewal right to be assigned in advance. Indeed, it became standard practice in many form agreements not only for the author to assign the initial and renewal terms of copyright, but also for the author's spouse to sign the agreement as well, thereby assigning any rights the spouse might have in the renewal term. Do you think that judicial enforcement of such agreements was faithful to the policies underlying the renewal rules? Note that the transfer of rights in the renewal period had to be explicitly stated. Generally, transfers of "all rights, title and interests" during the initial copyright term did not transfer such rights for the renewal term.

2. Diving Deeper: Inheritance and Vesting of Renewal Rights

Section 304 of the Copyright Act dictates the succeeding claimants to the renewal term in the event of an author's death. The first class of successor claimants is the widow, widower, or children of the author. The statute does not specify how the interest is to be divided among members of this class. One court has held that if both a widow or widower and children survive the author, 50 percent of the interest belongs to the widow or widower and the remaining 50 percent is divided among the children. *BMI, Inc. v. Roger Miller Music, Inc.*, 396 F.3d 762 (6th Cir.) *cert. denied*, 546 U.S. 871 (2005). If no widow, widower, or children are living, the next class of claimants is the author's executor as fiduciary to the beneficiaries under the author's will. If the author fails to leave a will, the final class of claimants is the author's next of kin, as determined by state intestacy rules. *See DeSylva v. Ballentine*, 351 U.S. 570 (1956).

As originally enacted, the 1976 Act also did not address the issue of when the right to the renewal term vests. Because the renewal certificate could be filed at any point during the final year of the first term of protection, an issue arose as to the timing of the vesting of the renewal term, with three possible options: the beginning of the final year of protection, the date of the filing of the renewal certificate, or the first day of the renewal term. *Compare Marascalco v. Fantasy, Inc.*, 953 F.2d 469 (9th Cir. 1991) (vesting occurred upon commencement of the renewal term), with *Frederick Music Co. v. Sickler*, 708 F. Supp. 587 (S.D.N.Y. 1989) (vesting occurred upon registration of the renewal certificate). If an author died during the final year of the first term, the timing of the vesting of the renewal right had important implications.

Congress addressed this previously complicated question in the Copyright Renewal Act of 1992, which abolished the renewal certificate requirement. As described earlier in this chapter, works first covered by federal copyright protection in or after 1964 obtained protection for the full 75 (now 95) years without the requirement of filing a renewal certificate. However, Congress encouraged renewal certificates to be filed by providing certain benefits in exchange for filing. One of those benefits is certainty of vesting. If a renewal certificate was timely filed in the final year of the first term, the renewal term interest vested in the appropriate person(s) measured as of the date of the filing of the renewal certificate. If the renewal certificate was not filed, then the renewal vested in the appropriate person(s) measured as of the first day of the renewal term. *See* 17 U.S.C. §304(a)(2).

Another incentive to file the renewal relates to the ability to bring the kind of infringement claim like the one at issue in *Stewart*. Section 304(a)(4)(A) provides that if the renewal application was not filed, then a derivative work prepared under authority of a grant or license from the copyright owner may continue to be used "under the terms of the grant." This effectively changes the result of *Stewart* in situations where the renewal was not filed. The section provides that while new derivative works may not be prepared during the renewal term, the copyright owner cannot stop the exploitation of authorized derivative works that were created prior to end of the first term. Requiring that the exploitation of the derivative work be "under the terms of the grant" may mean that royalties will need to be paid, if the transfer or license requires such payments.

3. Terminations of Transfers

As the Court in *Stewart* describes, the 1976 Act includes provisions for terminating transfers of copyright interests. Specifically, the Act speaks of terminating a "grant of a transfer or license of a copyright." In this section we will use the traditional phrase "termination of transfers" to encompass terminations of both transfers and licenses. The Act contains two different provisions concerning terminations of transfers: (1) transfers made prior to January 1, 1978, that convey an interest in the renewal term, and (2) transfers made after January 1, 1978. These two types of termination provisions are motivated by different policy concerns. The latter termination provisions, codified in §203, have a policy rationale similar to that for the renewal term: Congress wanted to provide authors with a second opportunity to obtain remuneration for their creative endeavors. The former set of termination provisions relating to transfers of interests in the renewal term, codified in §304(c)-(d), reflect a different policy decision concerning who should benefit from the lengthening of the renewal term by 19 years under the 1976 Act and by 20 additional years under the CTEA. Should these added years of protection benefit creators and their families, or assignees of the renewal term? The termination provisions favor creators and their families, if they are interested in recapturing the value of the copyright by following the procedure set forth in the Act for terminating transfers.

The termination provisions contain complex rules about what kinds of transfers may be terminated and the procedures and timing that must be followed in order to effect a termination. Keeping in mind the underlying policy rationales assists in understanding these rules. Note also that, while courts had enforced assignments of contingent interests in renewal terms executed by authors, spouses, and even children, Congress expressly prohibited any assignment or waiver of termination rights. Under both sections, the statute provides that termination "may be effected notwithstanding any agreement to the contrary, including an agreement to make a will or to make any future grant." 17 U.S.C. §§203(a)(5), 304(c)(5). Therefore, an author may exercise the right to terminate even when she has agreed by contract not to do so.

a. Terminations of Transfers Made After January 1, 1978: Section 203

Types of Transfers That Can Be Terminated.   The provisions that allow for the termination of transfers executed on or after January 1, 1978, are meant to allow an author, who may have been in a poor bargaining position initially, an opportunity to recapture the value of her work. Thus, these termination provisions do not apply to works made for hire, and they apply only to transfers made by the author, not any subsequent transfer of copyright interests by those in the chain of title (although subsquent transfers will be affected if the initial transfer from the author is terminated). Both exclusive and nonexclusive licenses, as well as outright transfers of copyright interest, can be terminated. Transfers by will are not subject to termination.

Who May Exercise the Termination Right.   In the case of a grant executed by one author, termination may be exercised by the author, or if the author is dead, by those who own at least 51 percent of the author's termination interest. In the case of grants executed by more than one author, a majority of the authors must act together to terminate the grant, with each author's interest being exercised as a unit. If the author is dead, his or her termination interest is owned first by the widow or widower. If in addition to the widow or widower there are surviving children or grandchildren, then the widow or widower owns one half of the termination interest and the children and grandchildren divide the other half on a *per stirpes*[1] basis. If only children or grandchildren remain, with no widow or widower surviving, then the children or grandchildren divide the termination interest based on the number of children represented on a *per stirpes* basis. The share of a deceased child represented by grandchildren (the children of that deceased child) may only be exercised by the action of the majority of those grandchildren. In the event that there is no widow, widower, children, or grandchildren, the author's executor, administrator, personal representative, or trustee owns the author's entire termination interest.

---

1. *Per stirpes* denotes a method of dividing interests in an estate. Under this method, a class or group of distributees takes the share to which their deceased ancestor would have been entitled. For example, if author *A* had two children, *B* and *C*, now deceased, and *B* had two children and *C* had four children, the termination interest will not be divided equally among the six grandchildren. Instead, two will exercise their parent *B*'s one-half interest, and four will exercise their parent *C*'s one-half interest. The opposite of a *per stirpes* distribution is a *per capita* distribution.

When Termination May Be Effected.   The termination may be effected at any time during a five-year window, which begins at the end of 35 years from the date of execution of the grant. For example, a grant executed on February 1, 2000, could be terminated anytime between February 1, 2035, and January 31, 2040. The only exception to this rule is where the grant covers the right of publication of the work, in which case the five-year window begins 35 years from the date of publication or 40 years from the date of execution, whichever is earlier.

How Termination Is Effected.   Notice of termination must be given by serving advance notice on the grantee or the grantee's successor in title. The notice must state the effective date of termination (which must fall within the five-year window described above) and must be served not less than two or more than ten years prior to that effective date. The statute further provides that a copy of the notice shall be recorded with the Copyright Office before the effective date of termination as a condition to its taking effect.

The Effect of Termination.   Upon the effective date of a properly exercised termination, all rights that were covered by the grant revert to the author or the person(s) owning termination interests. Those ownership rights vest as of the date the notice of termination was served and vest in the same proportionate shares as the termination right was divided (i.e., on a *per stirpes* basis). Further grants of the terminated rights, or agreements to make a further grant, are only valid if they are made after the effective date of termination. However, further valid grants to the grantees whose rights are being terminated may be made after notice of termination has been served.

The Act does provide that derivative works prepared under authority of the grant before its termination may continue to be utilized after the termination, but that use remains subject to the terms of the grant. For example, if the grant required annual royalty payments based on gross sales of the derivative work, termination would not extinguish the obligation to make those royalty payments. This exception for derivative works applies only to derivative works prepared prior to the termination date. It does not extend to permit preparation of other derivative works after such termination date.

b. Terminations of Transfers Made Before January 1, 1978: Section 304(c)-(d)

Types of Transfers That Can Be Terminated.   For transfers made prior to January 1, 1978, only those transfers that convey any interest in the renewal term can be terminated. Thus, a transfer made in 1975 of "all right title and interest during the initial term of copyright" is not terminable. As with the termination provision under §203, the termination provisions of §304 apply to exclusive and nonexclusive licenses as well as outright transfers. Because these termination provisions focus on allowing recapture of the extended renewal term by the statutorily designated beneficiaries of the original renewal term, transfers that can be terminated include not only those made by the author but those made by a widow, widower, children, executor or next of kin. Also, given the underlying policy reasons for these termination provisions, transfers concerning works made for hire are not terminable, nor are transfers made by will.

Who May Exercise the Termination Right.   When the transfer sought to be terminated is a grant by someone other than the author, termination can only be exercised by the surviving person or persons that executed that grant. Thus, a transfer executed by a widow who dies before timely notice of termination can be sent is no longer terminable. Termination of transfer by the author, on the other hand, can be exercised by the author, or, if the author is deceased, by a majority of those owning termination interests. The ownership of termination interests and the majority requirements under the §304 termination provisions are identical to those under the §203 termination provision.

When Termination May Be Effected.   The termination right granted under §304(c) concerns the additional 19 years added to the renewal term by the 1976 Act. Termination can be effected during a five-year window that begins 56 years from the date copyright protection was originally secured (typically upon publication with proper notice). The termination provisions under §304(d) concern the additional 20 years provided by the CTEA. Termination can be effected during the five-year window that begins at the end of 75 years from the date copyright was originally secured. Note, however, that the provisions of §304(d) can be used only if the termination right under §304(c) expired prior to the effective date of the CTEA (which was October 27, 1998), and if the termination right provided in §304(c) had not previously been exercised.

How the Termination Is Effected.   Similar to terminations under §203, notice of termination must be given by serving advance notice on the grantee or the grantee's successor in title. The notice must state the effective date of termination (which must fall within the five-year windows described above) and must be served not less than two or more than ten years prior to that effective date. As with terminations under §203, a copy of the notice must be recorded with the Copyright Office before the effective date of termination as a condition to its taking effect.

The Effect of Termination.   The effect of termination under §304(c) or (d) is similar to the effect of termination under §203, including the requirements for valid subsequent grants and for ongoing use of derivative works prepared prior to termination.

NOTES AND QUESTIONS

1. Are authors better off under the 1976 Act's termination of transfer provisions than under the 1909 Act's dual-term scheme? Recall that under the Supreme Court's interpretation of the renewal term rules, both authors and statutory heirs were permitted to assign their contingent interests in the renewal term at any time. The termination of transfer provisions, on the other hand, make the right to terminate a transfer inalienable. Is this a sensible policy?

2. The termination provisions in §203, for transfers executed on or after January 1, 1978, and §304, for transfers executed before that date, create an interesting problem in coverage: For transfers executed before January 1, 1978, but under which the subject works are not created until after that date, which set of termination rules should apply? The duration of copyright in such works is measured using the unitary term of the 1976 Copyright Act, not the dual term of the 1909 Act, making application of the §304 termination rules problematic. Should these transfers therefore be subject to §203 terminations after 35 years? Did the transferees have notice of that possibility? In 2011, the Copyright Office amended the relevant regulations to permit recordation of a §203 termination notice in these situations. 37 C.F.R. §201.10(f)(5) (2012). At the same time, the Office acknowledged that the availability of recordation was not meant to prejudice the question that ultimately would need to be decided by a court of competent jurisdiction. *See* U.S. Copyright Office, *Gap in Termination Provision*, 74 Fed. Reg. 32316, 32317 (June 6, 2011).

PROBLEMS

For each hypothetical below, consider the question of termination rights. You can find the answers on this book's companion website, http://www.coolcopyright.com:

1. Arthur created a work in 1950 and first published it with proper copyright notice on July 10, 1955. In 1954, Arthur assigned "all right title and interest" to the copyright in the work, including "any and all rights in the renewal term," to Bob. Arthur died on December 1, 1982, leaving his widow, Carol. Arthur's will bequeathed all his copyrights to Denise, his secretary. Assume a renewal registration was properly filed. Who owns copyright in the work today? Can any rights be terminated by anyone? By whom and when?

2. Same facts as in 1, except Arthur lived until December 1, 1985. Who owns copyright in the work today? Can any rights be terminated by anyone? By whom and when?

3. Flora comes to your office to talk to you about an upcoming merger of her company. Before the meeting starts, Flora tells you that she wrote and recorded a song back in 1975 that went platinum in 1990 but she received only $2,000 because she had assigned the copyright to a company, Giga, Inc., in 1979. She tells you that this song recently has been included in a blockbuster hit movie and is on the soundtrack that is a hot-selling album. She is quite proud of her big hit and that's why she told you the story. Is there anything to which you should alert her?

4. Henry created a play, titled *Georgia's Garden,* in 2001. Henry died in 2002, leaving two sons, Leo and Mike. His will leaves all his literary property including all his copyrights to his long-time companion, Orin. Leo and Mike would like to regain control over the play—can they?

c. Diving Deeper: "Agreements to the Contrary"

Recall that the renewal term provided by the 1909 Act was meant to provide authors with an opportunity to renegotiate assignments made before the full value of a work was known. However, the ability to transfer the contingent interest in the renewal term meant that such transfers became standard in industry contracts and significantly undermined the purpose of the renewal term as a second bite at the apple. With the termination provisions, Congress provided a stronger right for authors and their statutory heirs. Both §203 and §304 provide that "termination of the grant may be effected notwithstanding any agreement to the contrary, including any agreement to make a will or to make any future grant." 17 U.S.C. §§203(a)(5), 304(c)(5), 304(d)(1). The Supreme Court has characterized the termination right as inalienable. *Stewart v. Abend*, 495 U.S. 207, 230 (1990).

Just what constitutes an "agreement to the contrary"? It seems clear that an agreement that the author will not seek to exercise her termination rights would qualify. What if the parties to an oral agreement dispute copyright ownership many years later and, in settling that dispute, agree that the work was created as a "work made for hire"? Recall that work-made-for-hire agreements are not subject to termination rights. Should the settlement agreement characterizing the work as a work made for hire be considered "an agreement to the contrary"? *See Marvel Characters Inc. v. Simon*, 310 F.3d 280, 290-91 (2d Cir. 2002) (yes, because a different construction would vitiate the statutory purpose of protecting authors in light of publishers' superior bargaining power).

Questions about what constitutes an "agreement to the contrary" also arise when the parties to a transfer of copyright renegotiate their agreement without using the formal statutory process for terminating the initial transfer. If the purpose of the statute is to permit authors and their heirs an opportunity to renegotiate the terms once the full value of the work is known, would it be appropriate to characterize a newly renegotiated agreement as "an agreement to the contrary" because it effectively cuts off the statutory termination right? Should it matter how many years had passed since the time of the first agreement or whether the terms of the new agreement are more favorable to the author? According to both the Second and Ninth Circuits, Congress could not have intended to prevent an author's heirs from negotiating a regrant on more favorable terms. *See Penguin Group v. Steinbeck*, 537 F.3d 193 (2d Cir. 2008); *Milne ex rel. Coyne v. Stephen Slesinger, Inc.*, 430 F.3d 1036 (9th Cir. 2005), *cert. denied*, 548 U.S. 904 (2006). For discussion of this issue, see Lydia Pallas Loren, *Renegotiating the Copyright Deal in the Shadow of the "Inalienable" Right to Terminate*, 62 Fla. L. Rev. 1329 (2010).

PRACTICE EXERCISE: COUNSEL A CLIENT

Jake Turner, a bass player, worked as a session musician on a number of recordings produced by Ventura Records in the 1970s and 1980s. Each time he participated in a recording session, he executed a form agreement assigning his rights in the recording to Ventura in exchange for a flat fee of $250. (Ventura also paid Turner his regular hourly wage.) Some of the recordings on which Turner worked have become quite valuable. In 2010, Turner's widow, Melanie, contacted Ventura to inquire about negotiating increased compensation. After protracted discussions, she and Ventura signed an agreement that provided for an ongoing stream of royalties. The agreement stated: "Turner agrees that the decedent was Ventura's employee and that the Works were works made for hire. In the alternative, Turner assigns the Works to Ventura in perpetuity." Turner's children by his first marriage are unhappy with the deal (and have not been paid any of the money). They have consulted you to inquire about the possibility of recapturing the rights and renegotiating the compensation. What is your advice? (Be sure to review the material in Chapter 3.D, *supra*, on works made for hire before preparing your answer.)

D. THE ORPHAN WORKS PROBLEM

As you learned earlier in this chapter, when Congress adopted the first federal Copyright Act in 1790, it selected a regime that required affirmative steps on the copyright owner's part to obtain a federal copyright—publication with proper notice and registration. This meant that authors of works eligible for federal protection had to "opt in" in order to obtain protection. Over time, Congress progressively reduced the magnitude of the required affirmative steps. Today, protection is automatic on fixation of an original work of authorship. A copyright owner must take affirmative steps to "opt out" of such protection. This significant change in the copyright system results in many more works being subject to protection. At the same time, changes in the duration rules mean that federal copyright protection lasts for much longer.

The current system of automatic, lengthy protection without notice and registration requirements can lead to difficulties in locating copyright owners. Works published after Berne Convention implementation may contain no identifying information, and older works published with proper notice and properly renewed may be difficult to trace to a current owner. Works whose owners cannot be located are referred to as "orphan works." As you already know, the 1976 Copyright Act includes a number of exceptions and limitations, so some uses of orphan works may be made without locating the current copyright owner. In other cases, however, inability to locate the owner may result in a decision not to use the work at all.

1. Private Solutions

Review Note 5 after the *The Authors Guild, Inc. v. HathiTrust* case you read in Chapter 10.B.3, which describes the Google Book Search (GBS) project. When it announced the project, Google stated that it would accommodate copyright interests by designing its system to return full-text search results only for public domain works. For books still under copyright, searches would return only small excerpts unless the copyright owner entered an agreement with Google permitting Google to return additional text. In addition, Google offered any copyright owner that objected to inclusion of its works the opportunity to have them excluded entirely from search results. After the Authors Guild sued Google for copyright infringement, the parties eventually proposed a complex settlement under which Google would pay 63 percent of its GBS-related revenues into a fund that would be administered by a Book Rights Registry.

The settlement agreement would have required the Registry to use "commercially reasonable efforts" to locate copyright owners of digitized books, but also contemplated that some owners would not be found. It provided for the creation of an Unclaimed Works Fiduciary to represent the interests of those owners, and obligated the Registry to hold funds collected for them for ten years. After the first five years, unclaimed funds could be used to help cover the expense of locating copyright owners of orphan works. At the end of the ten years, funds remaining unclaimed could be distributed to literary charities.

In addition to creating a database of orphan works, the Registry would have provided procedures for copyright owners of works in the Google Book Search corpus to document their claims of ownership. Under the proposed settlement agreement, the Registry also would have been responsible for allocating GBS-related revenues among the registered rightholders. Rightholders who so chose could remove their works from the Registry entirely.

The court rejected the proposed settlement agreement, and in light of subsequent developments the Registry was never created. As of this writing, Google has announced no new initiatives either with respect to orphan works or more generally with respect to a rights registry.

Many of the books that Google scanned for the GBS project were obtained through agreements with major research libraries. In return for access to the physical copies, Google provided the libraries with digital copies of those books once the scans were completed. As you learned in Chapter 10.B.3, *supra*, several of those libraries then formed HathiTrust to create and manage a comprehensive archive of their digitized materials.

In September 2011, while the Google Book Search litigation was bogged down in a dispute about the validity of the proposed settlement agreement, HathiTrust announced its own Orphan Works Project. Under that project, HathiTrust attempted to locate copyright holders by following a protocol it had established. If HathiTrust determined a work to be an "orphan," it would list the work as such on its website for 90 days. If at the end of that time the copyright owner had not come forward, HathiTrust would allow patrons of its member libraries to access the work online. After the Authors Guild sued HathiTrust for digitizing the copyrighted works of its members without permission, HathiTrust suspended its Orphan Works Project. For that reason, the district court dismissed the claims pertaining to orphan works as not yet ripe for adjudication. *See Authors Guild, Inc. v. HathiTrust*, 902 F. Supp. 2d 445, 455-56 (S.D.N.Y. 2012), *aff'd*, 755 F.3d 97 (2d Cir. 2014). As of this writing, HathiTrust has not announced plans to resume the project.

2. Legislative Solutions

In January 2005, several members of Congress requested that the Copyright Office undertake a review of potential problems posed by orphan works. In January 2006, the Copyright Office submitted a final report to Congress in which it urged a "meaningful legislative solution" to the orphan works problem. The Report recommended that would-be users of orphan works be required to conduct a "reasonably diligent search" for the copyright owner and "provide attribution to the author and copyright owner of the work if such attribution is possible and as is reasonably appropriate under the circumstances." Report on Orphan Works 10 (2006), http://copyright.gov/orphan/orphan-report-full.pdf. In addition, it recommended that Congress limit the scope of monetary relief to a requirement of "reasonable compensation," withhold monetary relief for certain noncommercial uses, withhold injunctive relief in cases involving the preparation of derivative works reflecting "significant expression of the user," and limit injunctive relief in other cases to protect reliance parties. *Id.* at 11-13. It declined to recommend adoption of an escrow system for royalties payable to orphan work owners, and also declined to recommend a requirement of public notice of intent to use orphan works.

Proposed legislation generally tracking these recommendations has been introduced twice, but both times failed to move forward after some constituencies expressed strong opposition. In particular, associations representing photographers, illustrators, and textile manufacturers argued that the proposed legislation would effectively create a presumption in favor of orphan status that would work to their members' disadvantage.

Meanwhile, the European Union has adopted a directive addressing the orphan works issue. *See* Directive 2012/28/EU of the European Parliament and of the Council of 25 October 2012 on certain permitted uses of orphan works, L 299/5. The directive applies only to literary and audiovisual works and phonograms, and works embedded in them, that are "contained in the collections of publicly accessible libraries, educational establishments or museums as well as in the collections of archives or of film or audio heritage institutions." *Id.* art 1(2). A work may be deemed an orphan only after a "diligent search is carried out in good faith." *Id.* art. 3(1). Permitted uses of orphan works include communication to the public and reproduction for purposes of digitization, indexing, making available, and preservation. Additionally member states must provide for reasonable compensation to be paid to rightholders who come forward. *Id.* art. 6(1), (5).

In the wake of the district court's fair use ruling in the *Authors Guild v. HathiTrust* litigation, the Copyright Office initiated a new process intended to generate recommendations for a legislative solution to the orphan works problem. *See* Orphan Works and Mass Digitization, 77 Fed. Reg. 64,555 (Oct. 22, 2012); *see also* Orphan Works and Mass Digitization: Request for Additional Comments and Announcement of Public Roundtables, 79 Fed. Reg. 7706 (Feb. 10, 2014) (revising the original notice and extending the comment period following the Second Circuit's affirmance in *HathiTrust* and the district court's fair use ruling in the Google Book Search case).

NOTES AND QUESTIONS

1. What do you think of the orphan works processes devised by HathiTrust and by the parties to the proposed GBS settlement agreement? Recall that Google required copyright owners to opt-out of inclusion in its database, and that this proved enormously controversial. Would moving to an opt-in system be feasible in the case of orphan works? How else might workable private arrangements for orphan works evolve? HathiTrust, in contrast, allows copyright owners of works in its archive of digital scans to opt out of all uses except those permitted under §§107-108 of the Copyright Act. Is that system preferable to Google's?

2. Is a legislated solution to the orphan works problem preferable? Why, or why not? What should such legislation contain? In particular, how does the approach proposed by the Copyright Office compare with the European approach in terms of coverage, permitted uses, and limitations on remedies. Which approach to you prefer? Do you think that either approach effectively addresses disincentives to use orphan works? If not, what modifications would you propose?

3. In general, private solutions to the orphan works problem have focused first on developing registries of works and owners, while legislated solutions have focused on remedial limitations and requirements of diligence. What do you make of this pattern? Which approach do you think is better, and why? Could legislation address the registry issues? How? Keep in mind that any domestic solution requires consideration of the interests of foreign authors.

4. Would enactment of orphan works legislation sufficiently ameliorate the concerns associated with long copyright terms and optional formalities? As it embarks on the copyright reform process, should Congress consider other changes? Under patent law, a patentee must pay periodic maintenance fees. 35 U.S.C. §41(b) (providing for fees to be paid at four-year intervals, beginning three years and six months after the patent grant and ending with the payment eleven years and six months after the grant). Failure to do so results in expiration of the patent. Would you favor adoption of an analogous requirement for copyrights? Why, or why not? Would such a requirement be consistent with U.S. obligations under international treaties? For discussion of a different proposal that would involve conditioning eligibility for enhanced remedies on a reinvigorated set of formalities, see Christopher Jon Sprigman, *Berne's Vanishing Ban on Formalities*, 28 Berkeley Tech. L.J. 1565 (2013).

12

Copyright and Contract

In Chapter 1, you learned about the significant economic role of industries that depend heavily on copyright to sustain their business models. Those industries rely on the existence and enforcement of contractual arrangements to order their affairs. As an initial matter, contracts are necessary to transfer title or interests in the intangible asset of a copyright. Contracts also can embody licenses that authorize licensees to engage in activities that otherwise would constitute infringement. Many contract issues relating to formation and interpretation are governed by state law. Other issues are governed by copyright-specific rules, some arising from the statute and others developed by courts. This chapter considers those rules.

A. MODES OF TRANSFER

Section 106 of the Act grants a "bundle of rights" to the author of a copyrighted work. Each right in the bundle may be transferred and owned separately and each right also is divisible. For example, the copyright owner may grant (and, indeed, is likely to grant) the right to reproduce the work to more than one person or entity. The owner of any particular right is entitled to the full protection and remedies afforded copyright owners under the Act. *See* 17 U.S.C. §201(d)(2). An author may transfer an interest in the copyrighted work in a number of ways.

1. Writing and Recording "Transfers" of Copyright

The Copyright Act defines a "transfer of ownership" as "an assignment, mortgage, exclusive license, or any other conveyance, alienation, or hypothecation of a copyright or of any of the exclusive rights comprised in a copyright, whether or not it is limited in time or place of effect, but not including a nonexclusive license." 17 U.S.C. §101. Section 204 of the Act prescribes a particular form for the effective transfer of copyright ownership rights:

§204. Execution of transfers and other documents

(a) A transfer of copyright ownership, other than by operation of law, is not valid unless an instrument of conveyance, or a note or memorandum of the transfer, is in writing and signed by the owner of the rights conveyed or such owner's duly authorized agent.

In essence, §204 is a statute of frauds requirement, providing that any purported transfer of a copyright interest must be stated in a writing signed by the owner of the right being transferred. Because of the broad definition of "transfer of ownership" contained in §101, the Copyright Act's writing requirement applies not only to complete transfers of copyright ownership, but also to exclusive licenses of some or all of the §106 rights. As the Ninth Circuit has noted:

Section 204's writing requirement is not unduly burdensome; it necessitates neither protracted negotiations nor substantial expense. The rule is really quite simple: If the copyright holder agrees to transfer ownership to another party, that party must get the copyright holder to sign a piece of paper saying so. It doesn't have to be the Magna Charta; a one-line pro forma statement will do.

Effects Assocs., Inc. v. Cohen, 908 F.2d 555, 557 (9th Cir. 1990) (rejecting defendant's "argument that . . . Moviemakers do lunch, not contracts").

When a copyright is transferred, §205 of the Act authorizes recordation of the transfer with the Copyright Office and specifies procedures for recordation. Although recording a transfer with the Copyright Office is not required, important benefits flow from proper and timely recording. Recordation provides constructive notice of the facts stated in the document so long as the document or attached materials identify the work in question and the copyright has been registered. Not only will such recordation provide information to potential licensees seeking to use a work, but recordation also establishes priority of ownership in the event of conflicting claims.

Section 205(d) sets forth the order for determining which claim prevails between two conflicting transferees. As a preliminary matter, the transfer first executed and properly recorded within one month of its execution (or within two months if executed outside the United States) prevails. The first transfer will still prevail if, notwithstanding expiration of the time frame, it is recorded before a later transfer. However, the later transfer will prevail if the recipient (1) properly recorded it before the earlier transfer was recorded, (2) took the transfer in good faith, for valuable consideration or on the basis of a promise to pay a royalty, and (3) had no notice of the earlier transfer. Finally, §205 provides that whether recorded or not, a nonexclusive license prevails over a conflicting transfer of copyright ownership if the license is in writing and signed by the owner of the rights or her duly authorized agent, so long as the license was taken (1) in good faith before the conflicting transfer was recorded and (2) without notice of the conflicting transfer.

NOTES AND QUESTIONS

1. In addition to §204's provisions requiring transfers to be written, a copyright also may be transferred by "operation of law." Section 201(d)(1) recognizes transfers by will (which would satisfy the writing requirement) as well as by intestate succession, which is governed by state law. Note, however, that intestate succession to the copyright is distinct from intestate succession to the termination interest, which is governed by §§203 and 304 and discussed in Chapter 11, *supra*.

2. Read §205(d) carefully. Do the rules that govern priority between conflicting transferees make sense in light of the ostensibly reduced role of formalities in U.S. copyright law?

3. As noted in Section A, *supra*, a copyright owner may grant more than one person or entity the same right, such as the right to reproduce the copyrighted work. Such rights typically are called nonexclusive licenses. If a copyright owner grants a license to one party that purports to be exclusive, what stops the copyright owner from granting a license to another party? Should an exclusive licensee simply trust that the copyright owner will not engage in subsequent transfers? The ability to record a transfer of ownership, including an exclusive license, with the Copyright Office is an important mechanism for policing grants of exclusivity.

4. Copyrights can be valuable assets. When seeking financing, a borrower may offer a copyright itself or an interest in it as collateral for a loan. If the borrower fails to repay, the lender may foreclose on the copyright. Generally, notice of such a transaction is filed in the Copyright Office if the copyright is registered and in the relevant state office specified by the state's implementation of the Uniform Commercial Code (UCC) if the copyright is unregistered. The law is unclear, however, and so the best advice is to file in both locations in all cases, and also to file in both places when the collateral is royalties owed under the license. *See In re National Peregrine, Inc.* 116 B.R. 194 (C.D. Cal. 1990).

PRACTICE EXERCISE: DRAFTING

Creative Images (CI) designs custom graphics for companies. Two years ago, CI agreed to create a series of graphic designs for Reading Commons (RC), a nonprofit organization that provides supplementary reading instruction to underprivileged children. When the designs were finished, CI submitted the original files to RC. RC and CI did not sign a written agreement. Recently, RC has been approached by another nonprofit organization that wants to license RC's designs for use in a similar reading program, but wants evidence that RC owns the copyright in the designs. RC has asked CI to sign an agreement granting RC the copyright in the designs, and CI has agreed to do so. Draft language that transfers copyright in the designs to RC. What other kinds of provisions do you think might be needed in this contract?

2. Implied Licenses

What happens if the writing requirement is not satisfied? Section 101's definition of "transfer of ownership" does not include nonexclusive licenses; therefore, no writing is required for such a license. When should a court imply a nonexclusive license? Other than being nonexclusive, what should the terms of such a license be?

≣ *Asset Marketing Systems, Inc. v. Gagnon*
542 F.3d 748 (9th Cir. 2008), cert. denied, 129 S. Ct. 2442 (2009)

SMITH, J.: . . . From May 1999 to September 2003, Gagnon [doing business as "Mister Computer"] was an at-will, independent contractor for [Asset Marketing Systems, Inc. (AMS)], hired to assist with its information technology needs. . . . Gagnon was asked to develop custom software for AMS. AMS was Gagnon's largest client, accounting for 98% of his business. Jay Akerstein, a partner at AMS who later became the Chief Operating Officer, was Gagnon's primary contact. Over the course of their four-year relationship, AMS paid Gagnon over $2 million, $250,000 of which was for custom software development and computer classes. Gagnon developed six computer programs for AMS.

In May 2000, AMS and Gagnon entered a Technical Services Agreement (TSA), which was scheduled to expire on April 30, 2001. The TSA, printed on Mister Computer letterhead, set forth Gagnon's fees and the services to be provided. The services included "Custom Application Programming—Consultant will provide Contractor with specific add-on products to enhance Contractor's current in-house database application," and mentioned nothing about a license. The TSA was not renewed, though the relationship continued.

AMS claims that on June 12, 2002, Gagnon signed a Vendor Nondisclosure Agreement (NDA).[1] The NDA would have given AMS ownership of all intellectual property developed for AMS by Gagnon. Gagnon claims that the document is a forgery and that his signature cannot be authenticated.

In June 2003, Gagnon proposed that AMS execute an Outside Vendor Agreement (OVA). The OVA included a Proprietary Rights clause providing:

> Client agrees that all designs, plans, specifications, drawings, inventions, processes, and other information or items produced by Contractor while performing services under this agreement will be the property of Contractor and will be licensed to Client on a non-exclusive basis as will any copyrights, patents, or trademarks obtained by Contractor while performing services under this agreement. On request and at Contractor's expense, Client agrees to help Contractor obtain patents and copyrights for any new developments. This includes providing data, plans, specifications, descriptions, documentation, and other information, as well as assisting Contractor in completing any required application or registration. Any source code or intellectual property will remain the property of Contractor. Trademarks, service marks, or any items identifying said Company shall remain the Company's said property. Contractor

---

1. The NDA was located and produced six months into the litigation.

will allow Company non exclusive, unlimited licensing of software developed for Company.

Akerstein declined to execute the OVA, but countered with a redlined version of the OVA, which substantially rewrote the Proprietary Rights clause to read:

> Contractor agrees that all designs, plans, specifications, drawings, inventions, processes, and other information or items produced by Contractor while performing services under this agreement will be the sole property of Client. Any source code or intellectual property agreed to and documented as Contractor's will remain the property of Contractor.

By the end of June 2003, AMS had decided to terminate Gagnon's services. AMS extended an employment offer to Gagnon, but he declined to accept the offer. AMS and Gagnon then discussed an exit strategy, and by late July, the parties had set a target exit date of September 15, 2003.

In August 2003, Gagnon responded to Akerstein's redlined OVA draft with a letter asserting that his "position has always been that Asset Marketing Systems shall be entitled to unlimited software licensing as long as my company had a business relationship with Asset Marketing Systems." The parties never executed the OVA.

In a letter to AMS dated September 18, 2003, Gagnon demanded $1.75 million for AMS to have the right to continue to use the programs and $2 million for Gagnon's agreement not to sell or disclose the programs to AMS's competitors.

In a letter dated September 23, 2003, AMS terminated its relationship with Gagnon. According to AMS, a consultant identified numerous problems with Gagnon's work. It also stated:

> Recently, we had discussed employee and intellectual property issues which have yet to be resolved. Despite the foregoing, I learned that we did not have copies of the source code for the software we developed and that copies of our SalesLogix software and our entire database may be maintained by you and your agents offsite.

The letter then demanded:

> In connection with that separation, you must immediately provide any and all copies of the source code for all software developed by and on behalf of Asset Marketing Systems immediately. You are not authorized to utilize that software which we believe is owned and all copyrights belong to Asset Marketing Systems. Furthermore, despite your claimed ownership in that copyright, we believe that Asset Marketing Systems' trade secrets are embedded and utilized throughout that software which would preclude use by you as well.
>
> We also demand that you return to us any copies of the SalesLogix software or Asset Marketing databases, programs or other materials that may have come into your possession during our relationship. . . .

In October 2003, Gagnon sent AMS a cease and desist letter, asserting that the use of the programs was unauthorized. . . . Gagnon demanded that AMS certify that it had undertaken to remove "all original and derivative source code" and all related files for the programs from AMS computers.

AMS responded by asserting that Gagnon could not unilaterally stop AMS from continuing to use and update the programs because it had an irrevocable license to use, copy, and modify the programs based on the course of conduct of the parties over the past two-and-a-half years. . . .

Gagnon alleges that AMS's continued use of the six programs constitutes copyright infringement because the programs were used by AMS without its obtaining a license or Gagnon's permission. AMS asserts three defenses to Gagnon's copyright infringement claim: an implied license, a transfer of copyright ownership via the NDA, and 17 U.S.C. §117. We hold that AMS has an implied unlimited license for the programs, and we do not reach the other defenses asserted by AMS.

Though exclusive licenses must be in writing, 17 U.S.C. §204, grants of non-exclusive licenses need not be in writing, and may be granted orally or by implication. *Foad Consulting Group, Inc. v. Azzalino*, 270 F.3d 821, 825-26 (9th Cir. 2001). We have previously considered the grant of an implied license in the context of movie footage and architectural drawings. *Id.; Effects Assocs., Inc. v. Cohen*, 908 F.2d 555, 558 (9th Cir. 1990).

In *Effects Associates*, a movie producer hired Effects Associates to create certain special effects for a movie. Though the film footage containing the special effects was used without the producer's obtaining a written license from Effects Associates, we found that an implied license had been granted because the footage was created at the producer's request with the intent that it be used in the film with no warning that use of the footage would constitute infringement. We determined that "[t]o hold that Effects did not at the same time convey a license to use the footage . . . would mean that plaintiff's contribution to the film was 'of minimal value,' a conclusion that can't be squared with the fact that Cohen paid Effects almost $56,000 for this footage." *Id.* at 559.

Thus, we have held that an implied license is granted when "(1) a person (the licensee) requests the creation of a work, (2) the creator (the licensor) makes that particular work and delivers it to the licensee who requested it,[4] and (3) the licensor intends that the licensee-requestor copy and distribute his work." *I.A.E., Inc. v. Shaver*, 74 F.3d 768, 776 (7th Cir. 1996) (citing *Effects*, 908 F.2d at 558- 59) (footnote added). We apply the same analysis we did in *Effects* to implied licenses for computer programs. The last prong of the *Effects* test, however, is not limited to copying and distribution; instead we look at the protected right at issue—here, whether Gagnon intended that AMS use, retain, and modify the programs.

1. AMS Requested the Creation of the Programs

Gagnon argues that AMS never specifically requested that he create the programs, but "rather relayed its needs to Mr. Gagnon and he satisfied them by providing either computer hardware or computer software at his discretion." We

---

4. Though delivery of a copy of software does not compel the conclusion that Gagnon granted AMS a license, it is a relevant factor that we may consider. *See* 17 U.S.C. §202; *Effects*, 908 F.2d at 558 n.6 (recognizing that delivery is not dispositive, but "one factor that may be relied upon in determining that an implied license has been granted").

find this interpretation of "request" to be strained. Gagnon did not create the programs on his own initiative and market them to AMS; rather, he created them in response to AMS's requests. Moreover, after prototype software was developed, he made changes to the programs in response to Akerstein and other AMS employees' requests. No genuine issue of material fact remains as to whether AMS requested the programs.

2. Gagnon Created the Software for AMS and Delivered It

Though Gagnon argues that the programs could be converted for use by another company, Gagnon admitted that the programs were created specifically for AMS and that AMS paid for the work related to drafting of the programs as well as some related costs. It is, therefore, undisputed that Gagnon created these programs for AMS.

The remaining question is whether Gagnon delivered the programs to AMS. We agree with the district court that Gagnon delivered them when he installed them onto the AMS computers and stored the source code on-site at AMS. Gagnon argues that even if he had installed the programs onto the AMS computers, he never delivered the source code so that AMS could modify the code. If AMS did not have the right to modify the code, it may have infringed Gagnon's copyright by exceeding the scope of its license. Gagnon primarily points to AMS's inability to locate the code on its own computer systems after his services were terminated to show that AMS did not possess the code. But, as we explain below, Gagnon's conduct manifested an objective intent to give AMS an unlimited license at the time of creation; thus, when he stored the source code at AMS, the code was delivered.

3. Gagnon's Intent as Manifested by His Conduct

Gagnon argues that he never intended that AMS would retain and modify the programs he delivered. Gagnon misunderstands the inquiry into intent, and we conclude that his conduct did manifest an intent to grant a license. The relevant intent is the licensor's objective intent at the time of the creation and delivery of the software as manifested by the parties' conduct. *See Effects*, 908 F.2d at 559 n.6 (noting that "every objective fact concerning the transaction" supported the finding that an implied license existed). The First and Fourth Circuits consider the following factors to determine such an intent:

> (1) whether the parties were engaged in a short-term discrete transaction as opposed to an ongoing relationship; (2) whether the creator utilized written contracts . . . providing that copyrighted materials could only be used with the creator's future involvement or express permission; and (3) whether the creator's conduct during the creation or delivery of the copyrighted material indicated that use of the material without the creator's involvement or consent was permissible.

[*John G. Danielson, Inc. v. Winchester–Conant Props. Inc.*, 322 F.3d 26, 41 (1st Cir. 2003).] We find this approach to be persuasive.

Gagnon and AMS had an ongoing service relationship in which Gagnon provided technical support for all computer-related problems at AMS; he also created certain custom software applications at AMS's request. The relationship of the parties indicates neither an intent to grant nor deny a license without Gagnon's future involvement.

Several documents exist, however, that reflect the parties' objective intent: the TSA, signed by both parties, the OVA submitted by Gagnon, and Gagnon's letter objecting to Akerstein's proposed changes to the OVA.[6] Courts have looked to contracts, even if unexecuted, as evidence of the intent of the party submitting the contract. *See Johnson v. Jones*, 149 F.3d 494, 501 (6th Cir. 1998) (finding no license where architect submitted contracts containing express provision that drawings could not be used by others except with agreement and compensation).

The TSA, signed by both parties in 2000 and printed on Mister Computer letterhead, stated only that Gagnon "will provide" AMS "specific add-on products." Nothing in the TSA indicates Gagnon's understanding or intent that continued use of the custom application programming undertaken by Gagnon would be prohibited after the TSA terminated. . . . Like the special effects creators in *Effects Associates*, Gagnon was well paid for his services. Under the circumstances, it defies logic that AMS would have paid Gagnon for his programming services if AMS could not have used the programs without further payment pursuant to a separate licensing arrangement that was never mentioned in the TSA, and never otherwise requested at the time. This is especially so because custom software is far less valuable without the ability to modify it and because the TSA was set to expire in one year; one would expect some indication of the need for future licensing if the custom programs were to become unusable after the TSA expired.

The OVA submitted by Gagnon, but never executed, did not evidence any intent by Gagnon to limit AMS's use of the programs. Gagnon argues that the clause, "Client agrees that [intellectual property] produced by Contractor while performing services under this agreement will be the property of Contractor and will be licensed to Client on a non-exclusive basis as will any copyrights, patents, or trademarks obtained by Contractor while performing services under this agreement . . . ," means that his license was conditioned on a continuing relationship with AMS. We disagree. The clause "while performing services under this agreement" modifies the production of the intellectual property and the obtainment of copyrights. Furthermore, the contract then expressly stated, "Contractor will allow Company non-exclusive, unlimited licensing of software developed for Company," eliminating any ambiguity.

Moreover, Gagnon and AMS did not discuss a licensing agreement until their relationship was ending. Gagnon delivered the software without any caveats or limitations on AMS's use of the programs. Even if Gagnon and his employees maintained the software and had primary control over the code, they programmed on-site at AMS on AMS computers to which key AMS personnel had

---

6. We do not consider the NDA, allegedly signed by Gagnon, because Gagnon contests its validity and argues that his signature was forged, creating a factual dispute inappropriate for resolution on summary judgment.

access—conduct that does not demonstrate an intent to retain sole control. The first time Gagnon expressed a contrary intent was in his letter to Aker[stein] sent after AMS had decided to terminate Gagnon's services. . . .

4. Scope and Irrevocability of Implied License

For the reasons outlined, we hold that Gagnon granted AMS an unlimited, nonexclusive license to retain, use, and modify the software. Furthermore, because AMS paid consideration, this license is irrevocable. *See Lulirama Ltd., Inc. v. Axcess Broad. Servs., Inc.*, 128 F.3d 872, 882 (5th Cir. 1997). "[A] nonexclusive license supported by consideration is a contract." *Lulirama*, 128 F.3d at 882; *see also Effects*, 908 F.2d at 559 n.7 (an implied license is a "creature of law, much like any other implied-in-fact contract"). If an implied license accompanied by consideration were revocable at will, the contract would be illusory. . . .

NOTES AND QUESTIONS

1. As *AMS* shows, parties do not always put their arrangements in writing. Is it good policy for courts to imply nonexclusive licenses? Under what circumstances?

2. If a court determines that a license should be implied, how should it determine the scope of the license? Could an implied license encompass all of the §106 rights? What role, if any, should contract doctrines such as promissory estoppel play?

3. Review *Aalmuhammed v. Lee*, 202 F.3d 1227 (9th Cir. 1999), excerpted in Chapter 3.B, *supra*. In that case, it was clear that Aalmuhammed had contributed copyrightable expression to the film *Malcolm X*. It was also clear that the film's producers had neglected to secure a work made for hire agreement from Aalmuhammed as authorized by §101(2). Should a court imply a license in such a situation? If so, what should the scope of the license be?

4. Sometimes even when there is a written contract courts must imply some terms of the contract. Silence on the issue of whether sublicensing is permitted is one example. A sublicense is a grant by a licensee to a third party, permitting that third party (the sublicensee) to engage in acts authorized by the initial grant from the copyright owner. Although an exclusive license constitutes a transfer of ownership, at least one court has ruled that an exclusive licensee is not equivalent to a copyright owner. *Gardner v. Nike, Inc.*, 279 F.3d 774 (9th Cir. 2002). In that case the Ninth Circuit held that an exclusive licensee may not transfer the licensed rights without the consent of the original licensor because "§201(d)(2) only conferred the 'protections and remedies' afforded a copyright owner under the 1976 Act, not the rights." *Id.* at 779. A logical implication from *Gardner* is that rights obtained pursuant to any license, including an exclusive license, may not be sublicensed without authorization from the copyright owner. Would such a rule be good policy?

PRACTICE EXERCISE: ADVOCACY

In 2011, Zeno Corp (ZC) a web design company, entered into negotiations with TechDigi concerning a website framework that TechDigi could use to market advertising services. The negotiations ultimately resulted in a written agreement that stated "To be valid, this agreement must be countersigned within 45 days of the date signed by ZC, and be accompanied by an initial deposit of $10,000 (ten thousand dollars)." ZC signed the agreement on August 23, 2012. TechDigi never countersigned the agreement, although the parties both continued to work together as set forth in the contract. The parties' relationship later broke down, and ZC demanded that TechDigi stop using the parts of the website framework already delivered by ZC. TechDigi refused and sued ZC for breach of contract. ZC consults you to determine whether it can sue TechDigi for copyright infringement. Evaluate ZC's potential claims and defenses.

---

3. The Revision Privilege for Collective Works

Section 201(c) of the Copyright Act contains a provision that affords the creators of collective works an automatic, royalty-free license to republish copyrighted contributions to those works in certain circumstances. The scope of that privilege is the subject of the next case.

New York Times Company v. Tasini
533 U.S. 483 (2001)

[Six freelance authors ("Authors") contributed 21 articles ("Articles") to three different periodicals, the *New York Times, Newsday*, and *Sports Illustrated*, each published by different companies. The publishing companies ("Publishers") contracted with two different electronic database providers to include their periodicals in certain databases ("Databases"): LEXIS/NEXIS, the operator of the computerized database NEXIS, and University Microfilms, Inc. (UMI), the provider of the New York Times OnDisc (NYTO) and General Periodicals OnDisc (GPO), both CD-ROM products. Computer programs allow users to search the different databases using search criteria such as the author, headline, or date. The programs display lists of results matching the search criteria. The user may then view each article and download or print a copy if the user desires.]

GINSBURG, J..: . . . The freelance authors' complaint alleged that their copyrights had been infringed by the inclusion of their articles in the databases. The publishers, in response, relied on the privilege of reproduction and distribution accorded them by §201(c) of the Copyright Act. . . .

. . . When, as in this case, a freelance author has contributed an article to a "collective work" such as a newspaper or magazine, the statute recognizes two distinct copyrighted works: "Copyright in *each separate contribution to a collective work* is distinct from copyright in *the collective work as a whole. . . .*" §201(c) (emphasis added). Copyright in the separate contribution "vests initially in the author of the contribution" (here, the freelancer). *Ibid.* Copyright in the collective work vests in the collective author (here, the newspaper or magazine publisher) and extends only to the creative material contributed by that author, not to "the preexisting material employed in the work," §103(b). . . .

Section 201(c) both describes and circumscribes the "privilege" a publisher acquires regarding an author's contribution to a collective work:

> In the absence of an express transfer of the copyright or of any rights under it, the owner of copyright in the collective work is presumed to have acquired *only* the privilege of reproducing and distributing the contribution as part of that particular collective work, any revision of that collective work, and any later collective work in the same series. (Emphasis added.)

A newspaper or magazine publisher is thus privileged to reproduce or distribute an article contributed by a freelance author, absent a contract otherwise providing, only "as part of" any (or all) of three categories of collective works: (a) "that collective work" to which the author contributed her work, (b) "any revision of that collective work," or (c) "any later collective work in the same series." In accord with Congress' prescription, a "publishing company could reprint a contribution from one issue in a later issue of its magazine, and could reprint an article from a 1980 edition of an encyclopedia in a 1990 revision of it; the publisher could not revise the contribution itself or include it in a new anthology or an entirely different magazine or other collective work." H.R. Rep. 122-123, U.S. Code Cong. & Admin. News 1976, pp. 5659, 5738.

Essentially, §201(c) adjusts a publisher's copyright in its collective work to accommodate a freelancer's copyright in her contribution. If there is demand for a freelance article standing alone or in a new collection, the Copyright Act allows the freelancer to benefit from that demand; after authorizing initial publication, the freelancer may also sell the article to others. It would scarcely "preserve the author's copyright in a contribution" as contemplated by Congress, H.R. Rep. 122, U.S. Code Cong. & Admin. News 1976, pp. 5659, 5738, if a newspaper or magazine publisher were permitted to reproduce or distribute copies of the author's contribution in isolation or within new collective works. . . .

. . . When the user conducts a search, each article appears as a separate item within the search result. In NEXIS and NYTO, an article appears to a user without the graphics, formatting, or other articles with which the article was initially published. In GPO, the article appears with the other materials published on the same page or pages, but without any material published on other pages of the original periodical. In either circumstance, we cannot see how the Database perceptibly reproduces and distributes the article "as part of" either the original edition or a "revision" of that edition.

One might view the articles as parts of a new compendium—namely, the entirety of works in the Database. In that compendium, each edition of each periodical represents only a minuscule fraction of the ever-expanding Database. The Database no more constitutes a "revision" of each constituent edition than a 400-page novel quoting a sonnet in passing would represent a "revision" of that poem. "Revision" denotes a new "version," and a version is, in this setting, a "distinct form of something regarded by its creators or others as one work." Webster's Third New International Dictionary 1944, 2545 (1976). The massive whole of the Database is not recognizable as a new version of its every small part.

Alternatively, one could view the Articles in the Databases "as part of" no larger work at all, but simply as individual articles presented individually. That each article bears marks of its origin in a particular periodical (less vivid marks in NEXIS and NYTO, more vivid marks in GPO) suggests the article was *previously* part of that periodical. But the markings do not mean the article is *currently* reproduced or distributed as part of the periodical. The Databases' reproduction and distribution of individual Articles — simply *as individual Articles* — would invade the core of the Authors' exclusive rights under §106.

The Publishers press an analogy between the Databases, on the one hand, and microfilm and microfiche, on the other. We find the analogy wanting. Microforms typically contain continuous photographic reproductions of a periodical in the medium of miniaturized film. Accordingly, articles appear on the microforms, writ very small, in precisely the position in which the articles appeared in the newspaper. . . .

Invoking the concept of "media neutrality," the Publishers urge that the "transfer of a work between media" does not "alte[r] the character of" that work for copyright purposes. That is indeed true. But unlike the conversion of newsprint to microfilm, the transfer of articles to the Databases does not represent a mere conversion of intact periodicals (or revisions of periodicals) from one medium to another. The Databases offer users individual articles, not intact periodicals. In this case, media neutrality should protect the Authors' rights in the individual Articles to the extent those Articles are now presented individually, outside the collective work context, within the Databases' new media.[11] . . .

For the purpose at hand — determining whether the Authors' copyrights have been infringed — an analogy to an imaginary library may be instructive. Rather than maintaining intact editions of periodicals, the library would contain separate copies of each article. . . . The library would store the folders containing the articles in a file room, indexed based on diverse criteria, and containing articles from vast numbers of editions. In response to patron requests, an inhumanly speedy librarian would search the room and provide copies of the articles matching patron-specified criteria.

Viewing this strange library, one could not, consistent with ordinary English usage, characterize the articles "as part of" a "revision" of the editions in which the

---

11. The dissenting opinion apparently concludes that, under the banner of "media-neutrality," a copy of a collective work, even when considerably changed, must constitute a "revision" of that collective work so long as the changes were "necessitated by . . . the medium." We lack the dissent's confidence that the current form of the Databases is entirely attributable to the nature of the electronic media, rather than the nature of the economic market served by the Databases. In any case, we see no grounding in §201(c) for a "medium driven" necessity defense to the Authors' infringement claims. Furthermore, it bears reminder here and throughout that these Publishers and all others can protect their interests by private contractual arrangement.

articles first appeared. In substance, however, the Databases differ from the file room only to the extent they aggregate articles in electronic packages (the LEXIS/ NEXIS central discs or UMI CD-ROMs), while the file room stores articles in spatially separate files. The crucial fact is that the Databases, like the hypothetical library, store and retrieve articles separately within a vast domain of diverse texts. Such a storage and retrieval system effectively overrides the Authors' exclusive right to control the individual reproduction and distribution of each Article, 17 U.S.C. §§106(1), (3). . . .

The Publishers warn that a ruling for the Authors will have "devastating" consequences. The Databases, the Publishers note, provide easy access to complete newspaper texts going back decades. A ruling for the Authors, the Publishers suggest, will punch gaping holes in the electronic record of history. The Publishers' concerns are echoed by several historians, see Brief for Ken Burns et al. as *Amici Curiae*, but discounted by several other historians, see Brief for Ellen Schrecker et al. as *Amici Curiae*; Brief for Authors' Guild, Jacques Barzun et al. as *Amici Curiae*.

Notwithstanding the dire predictions from some quarters, see also *post*, at 520 (STEVENS, J., dissenting), it hardly follows from today's decision that an injunction against the inclusion of these Articles in the Databases (much less all freelance articles in any databases) must issue. *See* 17 U.S.C. §502(a) (court "may" enjoin infringement); *Campbell v. Acuff-Rose Music, Inc.*, 510 U.S. 569, 578, n.10 (1994) (goals of copyright law are "not always best served by automatically granting injunctive relief"). The parties (Authors and Publishers) may enter into an agreement allowing continued electronic reproduction of the Authors' works; they, and if necessary the courts and Congress, may draw on numerous models for distributing copyrighted works and remunerating authors for their distribution. *See, e.g.*, 17 U.S.C. §118(b); *Broadcast Music, Inc. v. Columbia Broadcasting System, Inc.*, 441 U.S. 1, 4-6, 10-12 (1979) (recounting history of blanket music licensing regimes and consent decrees governing their operation).[13] In any event, speculation about future harms is no basis for this Court to shrink authorial rights Congress established in §201(c). Agreeing with the Court of Appeals that the Publishers are liable for infringement, we leave remedial issues open for initial airing and decision in the District Court. . . .

STEVENS, J., with whom BREYER, J. joins, dissenting: . . . I see no compelling reason why a collection of files corresponding to a single edition of the New York Times, standing alone, cannot constitute a "revision" of that day's New York Times. It might be argued, as respondents appear to do, that the presentation of each article

---

13. Courts in other nations, applying their domestic copyright laws, have also concluded that Internet or CD-ROM reproduction and distribution of freelancers' works violate the copyrights of freelancers. *See, e.g., Union Syndicale des Journalistes Français v. SDV Plurimedia* (T.G.I., Strasbourg, Fr., Feb. 3, 1998); *S.C.R.L. Central Station v. Association Generale des Journalistes Professionnels de Belgique* (CA, Brussels, Belg., 9e ch., Oct. 28, 1997), transl. and ed. in 22 Colum.-VLA J.L. & Arts 195 (1998); *Heg v. De Volskrant B.V.* (Dist. Ct., Amsterdam, Neth., Sept. 24, 1997), transl. and ed. in 22 Colum.-VLA J.L. & Arts, at 181. After the French *Plurimedia* decision, the journalists' union and the newspaper-defendant entered into an agreement compensating authors for the continued electronic reproduction of their works. *See FR3 v. Syndicats de Journalistes* (CA, Colmar, Sept. 15, 1998). . . .

within its own electronic file makes it impossible to claim that the collection of files as a whole amounts to a "revision." But the conversion of the text of the overall collective work into separate electronic files should not, by itself, decide the question. After all, one of the hallmarks of copyright policy, as the majority recognizes, is the principle of media neutrality.

No one doubts that the New York Times has the right to reprint its issues in Braille, in a foreign language, or in microform, even though such revisions might look and feel quite different from the original. Such differences, however, would largely result from the different medium being employed. Similarly, the decision to convert the single collective work newspaper into a collection of individual ASCII files can be explained as little more than a decision that reflects the different nature of the electronic medium. Just as the paper version of the New York Times is divided into "sections" and "pages" in order to facilitate the reader's navigation and manipulation of large batches of newsprint, so too the decision to subdivide the electronic version of that collective work into individual article files facilitates the reader's use of the electronic information. The bare-bones nature of ASCII text would make trying to wade through a single ASCII file containing the entire content of a single edition of the New York Times an exercise in frustration.[9]

. . . I think that a proper respect for media neutrality suggests that the New York Times, reproduced as a collection of individual ASCII files, should be treated as a "revision" of the original edition, as long as each article explicitly refers to the original collective work and as long as substantially the rest of the collective work is, at the same time, readily accessible to the reader of the individual file. . . .

To see why an electronic version of the New York Times made up of a group of individual ASCII article-files, standing alone, may be considered a §201(c) revision, suppose that, instead of transmitting to NEXIS the articles making up a particular day's edition, the New York Times saves all of the individual files on a single floppy disk, labels that disk "New York Times, October 31, 2000," and sells copies of the disk to users as the electronic version of that day's New York Times. The disk reproduces the creative, editorial selection of that edition of the New York Times. The reader, after all, has at his fingertips substantially all of the relevant content of the October 31 edition of the collective work. Moreover, each individual article makes explicit reference to that selection by including tags that remind the reader that it is a part of the New York Times for October 31, 2000. Such a disk might well constitute "that particular collective work"; it would surely qualify as a "revision" of the original collective work. Yet all the features identified as essential by the majority and by the respondents would still be lacking. An individual looking at one of the articles contained on the disk would still see none of the original formatting context and would still be unable to flip the page.

---

9. An ASCII version of the October 31, 2000, New York Times, which contains 287 articles, would fill over 500 printed pages. Conversely, in the case of graphical products like GPO, the demands that memory-intensive graphics files can place on underpowered computers make it appropriate for electronic publishers to divide the larger collective work into manageably sized subfiles. The individual article is the logical unit. The GPO version of the April 7, 1996, New York Times Magazine, for example, would demand in the neighborhood of 200 megabytes of memory if stored as a single file, whereas individual article files range from 4 to 22 megabytes, depending on the length of the article.

Once one accepts the premise that a disk containing all the files from the October 31, 2000, New York Times can constitute a "revision," there is no reason to treat any differently the same set of files, stored in a folder on the hard disk of a computer at the New York Times. . . .

If my hypothetical October 31, 2000, floppy disk can be a revision, I do not see why the inclusion of other editions and other periodicals is any more significant than the placement of a single edition of the New York Times in a large public library or in a book store. Each individual file still reminds the reader that he is viewing "part of" a particular collective work. And the *entire* editorial content of that work still exists at the reader's fingertips. . . .

My reading of "revision," as encompassing products like the Electronic Databases, is not the only possible answer to the complex questions presented by this case. It is, nevertheless, one that is consistent with the statutory text and entirely faithful to the statute's purposes. . . .

The majority discounts the effect its decision will have on the availability of comprehensive digital databases, but I am not as confident. As petitioners' *amici* have persuasively argued, the difficulties of locating individual freelance authors and the potential of exposure to statutory damages may well have the effect of forcing electronic archives to purge freelance pieces from their databases. "The omission of these materials from electronic collections, for any reason on a large scale or even an occasional basis, undermines the principal benefits that electronic archives offer historians—efficiency, accuracy and comprehensiveness." Brief for Ken Burns et al. as *Amici Curiae* 13.

Moreover, it is far from clear that my position even deprives authors of much of anything (with the exception of perhaps the retrospective statutory damages that may well result from their victory today).[19] . . . The ready availability of that edition, both at the time of its first publication and subsequently in libraries and electronic databases, would be a benefit, not an injury, to most authors. . . .

NOTES AND QUESTIONS

1. In *Tasini*, does the majority or the dissent have the better argument concerning the likely consequences of the Court's decision? Should projected effects on current industry practice influence the Court's interpretation of the statute?

2. Under the 1909 Act copyrights were "indivisible"; in order to assign the right to publish a work, the entire copyright had to be assigned. That rule was especially harsh for authors of contributions to collective works. Additionally, in order to retain copyright in a separate contribution to a collective work, a separate notice in the copyright owner's name was required. Publishers declined to print such notices, leaving authors with a choice between assigning their entire copyrights and having their works pass into the public domain upon publication of the collective work. The 1976 Act expressly rejected the indivisibility rule, allowing the different rights of a copyright

---

19. It is important to remember that the prospect of payment by the Print Publishers was sufficient to stimulate each petitioner to create his or her part of the collective works, presumably with full awareness of its intended inclusion in the Electronic Databases.

owner to be transferred separately. The 1976 Act also adopted the rule that a single copyright notice on the collective work as a whole protected the individual contributions as well. *See* 17 U.S.C. §404(c). The *Tasini* majority points to this history as evidencing the importance of preserving the author's copyright in a contribution, while the dissent argues that a finding in favor of the publishers would not jeopardize the independent copyright in the contribution. Which side has the better argument?

3. In light of §201(c), an agreement by an author to publish her work in a collective work creates a default royalty-free license to include the work in revisions of that collective work. After *Tasini*, what factors are relevant in determining the scope of the collective work publisher's revision privilege?

4. In *Tasini*, the majority indicates that an injunction might not be an appropriate remedy. If the court fashions a remedy that permits the inclusion of articles in the databases without the consent of the copyright owners of the articles, but requires the publishers to pay a set amount to them, that amounts to a compulsory license. As the majority indicates, Congress has enacted certain compulsory license schemes in the Copyright Act. Would you advocate adoption of a compulsory license scheme for the inclusion of news articles in electronic databases such as those in the *Tasini* litigation?

AFTERMATH

Following the *Tasini* decision, the *New York Times* posted a notice on its website stating that any freelance writer's work affected by the *Tasini* decision would be removed from the electronic databases unless the writer executed a release of all claims arising out of the *New York Times*'s infringement in connection with that work. Jonathan Tasini again filed suit, this time alleging that the release agreement was unlawful and unenforceable. The court, however, dismissed that complaint, finding that Tasini lacked standing because he had not signed the release agreement. *Tasini v. New York Times Co., Inc.,* 184 F. Supp. 2d 350 (S.D.N.Y. 2002).

PRACTICE EXERCISE: COUNSEL A CLIENT

NDS is a nonprofit organization that publishes a monthly magazine featuring articles about environmental hazards worldwide. NDS has recently compiled all its magazine issues in a single digital compilation and has made the compilation available for purchase as a downloadable file. In addition to the original contributions, the new product contains never-before-seen pictures, highlights of particular environmental disasters, and interviews with activists. Purchasers can interact with the content using digital tools that allow short text excerpts to be highlighted and copied for reposting elsewhere. Dr. Ted Grunge, an expert on climate change and environmental policy, authored numerous articles for NDS over the years but never signed any agreement with NDS. He is outraged that he was not asked permission nor offered any payment for the inclusion of his articles in the new compilation. He contacted NDS to demand that his articles be removed from the digital compilation, but NDS flatly refused, claiming that the compilation is within the §201(c) privilege. Dr. Grunge has come to you for advice. What advice should you give him?

B. NEW USES AND OLD LANGUAGE

The dispute in *Tasini* arose in part because of technological change. CD-ROMs and massive networked databases did not exist when the 1976 Act was enacted. Understanding what constituted a "revision" in the new technological landscape challenged the parties and the Court. Interpreting the scope of a privilege can be equally difficult when that privilege is granted by contract. Unless the contract transfers "all right, title, and interest," selecting the language to memorialize the parties' intentions is a task to be undertaken with great care. The goal in contract drafting is to avoid ambiguity because ambiguity can foster litigation. If the contract is clear concerning the parties' respective rights and obligations, it is less likely that a dispute will arise and, if it does, that resort to the courts will be necessary. Avoiding ambiguity may be simple enough for the particular uses contemplated by the parties, but, as you now know, copyrights can last for a very long time. What happens when the relevant technologies and distribution methods change? The two cases that follow illustrate this problem and explore the various contract interpretation methods employed by the courts.

Boosey & Hawkes Music Publishers, Ltd. v. The Walt Disney Company
145 F.3d 481 (2d Cir. 1998)

LEVAL, J.: Boosey & Hawkes Music Publishers Ltd., an English corporation and the assignee of Igor Stravinsky's copyrights for "The Rite of Spring," brought this action alleging that the Walt Disney Company's foreign distribution in video cassette and laser disc format ("video format") of the film "Fantasia," featuring Stravinsky's work, infringed Boosey's rights. . . .

I. Background

During 1938, Disney sought Stravinsky's authorization to use The Rite of Spring (sometimes referred to as the "work" or the "composition") throughout the world in a motion picture. Because under United States law the work was in the public domain, Disney needed no authorization to record or distribute it in this country, but permission was required for distribution in countries where Stravinsky enjoyed copyright protection. In January 1939 the parties executed an agreement (the "1939 Agreement") giving Disney rights to use the work in a motion picture in consideration of a fee to Stravinsky of $6,000.

The 1939 Agreement provided that

In consideration of the sum of Six Thousand ($6,000.) Dollars, receipt of which is hereby acknowledged, [Stravinsky] does hereby give and grant unto Walt

Disney Enterprises, a California corporation . . . the nonexclusive, irrevocable right, license, privilege and authority to record in any manner, medium or form, and to license the performance of, the musical composition hereinbelow set out. . . .

Under "type of use" in ¶ 3, the Agreement specified that

The music of said musical composition may be used in one motion picture throughout the length thereof or through such portion or portions thereof as the Purchaser shall desire. The said music may be used in whole or in part and may be adapted, changed, added to or subtracted from, all as shall appear desirable to the Purchaser in its uncontrolled discretion. . . . The title "Rites of Spring" or "Le Sacre de Printemps," or any other title, may be used as the title of said motion picture and the name of [Stravinsky] may be announced in or in connection with said motion picture.

The Agreement went on to specify in ¶ 4 that Disney's license to the work "is limited to the use of the musical composition in synchronism or timed-relation with the motion picture." . . .

Finally, ¶ 7 of the Agreement provided that "the licensor reserves to himself all rights and uses in and to the said musical composition not herein specifically granted" (the "reservation clause").

Disney released Fantasia, starring Mickey Mouse, in 1940. The film contains no dialogue. It matches a pantomime of animated beasts and fantastic creatures to passages of great classical music, creating what critics celebrated as a "partnership between fine music and animated film." The soundtrack uses compositions of Bach, Beethoven, Dukas, Schubert, Tchaikovsky, and Stravinsky, all performed by the Philadelphia Orchestra under the direction of Leopold Stokowski. As it appears in the film soundtrack, The Rite of Spring was shortened from its original 34 minutes to about 22.5; sections of the score were cut, while other sections were reordered. For more than five decades Disney exhibited The Rite of Spring in Fantasia under the 1939 license. The film has been re-released for theatrical distribution at least seven times since 1940, and although Fantasia has never appeared on television in its entirety, excerpts including portions of The Rite of Spring have been televised occasionally over the years. Neither Stravinsky nor Boosey has ever previously objected to any of the distributions.

In 1991 Disney first released Fantasia in video format. The video has been sold in foreign countries, as well as in the United States. To date, the Fantasia video release has generated more than $360 million in gross revenue for Disney.

Boosey brought this action in February 1993. The complaint sought (1) a declaration that the 1939 Agreement did not include a grant of rights to Disney to use the Stravinsky work in video format; (2) damages for copyright infringement in at least 18 foreign countries. . . .

II. Discussion . . .

1. Whether the "motion picture" license covers video format.   Boosey contends that the license to use Stravinsky's work in a "motion picture" did not authorize distribution of the motion picture in video format, especially in view of the absence of an express provision for "future technologies" and Stravinsky's reservation of all rights not granted in the Agreement. Disputes about whether licensees may exploit licensed works through new marketing channels made possible by technologies developed after the licensing contract—often called "new-use" problems—have vexed courts since at least the advent of the motion picture.

In *Bartsch v. Metro-Goldwyn-Mayer, Inc.,* we held that "licensee[s] may properly pursue any uses which may reasonably be said to fall within the medium as described in the license." 391 F.2d 150, 155 (2d Cir. 1968) (Friendly, J.). We held in Bartsch that a license of motion picture rights to a play included the right to telecast the motion picture. We observed that "[i]f the words are broad enough to cover the new use, it seems fairer that the burden of framing and negotiating an exception should fall on the grantor," at least when the new medium is not completely unknown at the time of contracting. *Id.* at 154, 155.

The 1939 Agreement conveys the right "to record [the composition] in any manner, medium or form" for use "in [a] motion picture." We believe this language is broad enough to include distribution of the motion picture in video format. At a minimum, *Bartsch* holds that when a license includes a grant of rights that is reasonably read to cover a new use (at least where the new use was foreseeable at the time of contracting), the burden of excluding the right to the new use will rest on the grantor. The license "to record in any manner, medium or form" doubtless extends to videocassette recording and we can see no reason why the grant of "motion picture" reproduction rights should not include the video format, absent any indication in the Agreement to the contrary. If a new-use license hinges on the foreseeability of the new channels of distribution at the time of contracting—a question left open in *Bartsch*—Disney has proffered unrefuted evidence that a nascent market for home viewing of feature films existed by 1939. The *Bartsch* analysis thus compels the conclusion that the license for motion picture rights extends to video format distribution.

We recognize that courts and scholars are not in complete accord on the capacity of a broad license to cover future developed markets resulting from new technologies. The Nimmer treatise describes two principal approaches to the problem. According to the first view, advocated here by Boosey, "a license of rights in a given medium (*e.g.,* 'motion picture rights') includes only such uses as fall within the unambiguous core meaning of the term (*e.g.,* exhibition of motion picture film in motion picture theaters) and excludes any uses that lie within the ambiguous penumbra (*e.g.,* exhibition of motion picture on television)." Nimmer, §10.10[B] at 10-90; *see also Cohen v. Paramount Pictures Corp.,* 845 F.2d 851, 853-54 (9th Cir. 1988) (holding that license to use musical score in television production does not extend to use in videocassette release); *Rey v. Lafferty,* 990 F.2d 1379, 1390-91 (1st Cir. 1993) (holding that license to portray Curious George in animations for "television viewing" does not extend to videocassette release). Under this approach, a license given in 1939 to "motion picture" rights would include only the core uses of "motion picture" as understood in 1939—presumably theatrical distribution—and would not include subsequently developed methods of distribution of a motion picture such as television videocassettes or laser discs. *See* Nimmer §10.10[B] at 10-90.

The second position described by Nimmer is "that the licensee may properly pursue any uses that may reasonably be said to fall within the medium as described in the license." *Id.* at 10-91. Nimmer expresses clear preferences for the latter approach on the ground that it is "less likely to prove unjust." *Id.* As Judge Friendly noted in *Bartsch,* "[S]o do we." 391 F.2d at 155.

We acknowledge that a result which deprives the author-licensor of participation in the profits of new unforeseen channels of distribution is not an altogether happy solution. Nonetheless, we think it more fair and sensible than a result that would deprive a contracting party of the rights reasonably found in the terms of the contract it negotiates. This issue is too often, and improperly, framed as one of favoritism as between licensors and licensees. Because licensors are often authors—whose creativity the copyright laws intend to nurture—and are often impecunious, while licensees are often large business organizations, there is sometimes a tendency in copyright scholarship and adjudication to seek solutions that favor licensors over licensees. . . .

In our view, new-use analysis should rely on neutral principles of contract interpretation rather than solicitude for either party. Although *Bartsch* speaks of placing the "burden of framing and negotiating an exception . . . on the grantor," 391 F.2d at 155, it should not be understood to adopt a default rule in favor of copyright licensees or any default rule whatsoever. What governs under *Bartsch* is the language of the contract. If the contract is more reasonably read to convey one meaning, the party benefitted by that reading should be able to rely on it; the party seeking exception or deviation from the meaning reasonably conveyed by the words of the contract should bear the burden of negotiating for language that would express the limitation or deviation. This principle favors neither licensors nor licensees. It follows simply from the words of the contract.

The words of Disney's license are more reasonably read to include than to exclude a motion picture distributed in video format. Thus, we conclude that the burden fell on Stravinsky, if he wished to exclude new markets arising from subsequently developed motion picture technology, to insert such language of limitation in the license, rather than on Disney to add language that reiterated what the license already stated.

Other significant jurisprudential and policy considerations confirm our approach to new-use problems. We think that our view is more consistent with the law of contract than the view that would exclude new technologies even when they reasonably fall within the description of what is licensed. Although contract interpretation normally requires inquiry into the intent of the contracting parties, intent is not likely to be helpful when the subject of the inquiry is something the parties were not thinking about. . . . Especially where, as here, evidence probative of intent is likely to be both scant and unreliable, the burden of justifying a departure from the most reasonable reading of the contract should fall on the party advocating the departure.[4]

Neither the absence of a future technologies clause in the Agreement nor the presence of the reservation clause alters that analysis. The reservation clause stands for no more than the truism that Stravinsky retained whatever he had not granted. . . .

≡ ### *Random House v. Rosetta Books, LLC*
*150 F. Supp. 2d 613 (S.D.N.Y. 2001), aff'd, 283 F.3d 490
(2d Cir. 2002)*

STEIN, J.: . . . In the year 2000 and the beginning of 2001, Rosetta Books contracted with several authors to publish certain of their works—including *The Confessions of Nat Turner* and *Sophie's Choice* by William Styron; *Slaughterhouse-Five, Breakfast of Champions, The Sirens of Titan, Cat's Cradle,* and *Player Piano* by Kurt Vonnegut; and *Promised Land* by Robert B. Parker—in digital format over the internet. On February 26, 2001 Rosetta Books launched its ebook business, offering those titles and others for sale in digital format. The next day, Random House filed this complaint accusing Rosetta Books of committing copyright infringement and tortiously interfering with the contracts Random House had with Messrs. Parker, Styron and Vonnegut by selling its ebooks. It simultaneously moved for a preliminary injunction prohibiting Rosetta from infringing plaintiff's copyrights.

A. Ebooks

Ebooks are "digital book[s] that you can read on a computer screen or an electronic device." Ebooks are created by converting digitized text into a format readable by computer software. The text can be viewed on a desktop or laptop computer, personal digital assistant or handheld dedicated ebook reading device.

Included in a Rosetta ebook is a book cover, title page, copyright page and "eforward" all created by Rosetta Books. Although the text of the ebook is exactly the same as the text of the original work, the ebook contains various features that take advantage of its digital format. . . .

---

4. We note also that an approach to new-use problems that tilts against licensees gives rise to antiprogressive incentives. Motion picture producers would be reluctant to explore and utilize innovative technologies for the exhibition of movies if the consequence would be that they would lose the right to exhibit pictures containing licensed works. *See Bartsch,* 391 F.2d at 155.

Nor do we believe that our approach disadvantages licensors. By holding contracting parties accountable to the reasonable interpretation of their agreements, we encourage licensors and licensees to anticipate and bargain for the full value of potential future uses. Licensors reluctant to anticipate future developments remain free to negotiate language that clearly reserves the rights to future uses. But the creation of exceptional principles of contract construction that places doubt on the capacity of a license to transfer new technologies is likely to harm licensors together with licensees, by placing a significant percentage of the profits they might have shared in the hands of lawyers instead.

B. Random House's licensing agreements

While each agreement between the author and Random House differs in some respects, each uses the phrase "print, publish and sell the work in book form" to convey rights from the author to the publisher.

1. Styron Agreements

Forty years ago, in 1961, William Styron granted Random House the right to publish *The Confessions of Nat Turner*. Besides granting Random House an exclusive license to "print, publish and sell the work in book form," Styron also gave it the right to "license publication of the work by book clubs," "license publication of a reprint edition," "license after book publication the publication of the work, in whole or in part, in anthologies, school books," and other shortened forms, "license without charge publication of the work in Braille, or photographing, recording, and micro-filming the work for the physically handicapped," and "publish or permit others to publish or broadcast by radio or television . . . selections from the work, for publicity purposes. . . ." Styron demonstrated that he was not granting Random House the rights to license publication in the British Commonwealth or in foreign languages by crossing out these clauses on the form contract supplied by Random House.

The publisher agreed in the contract to "publish the work at its own expense and in such style and manner and at such a price as it deems suitable." The contract also contains a non-compete clause that provides, in relevant part, that "[t]he Author agrees that during the term of this agreement he will not, without the written permission of the Publisher, publish or permit to be published any material in book or pamphlet form, based on the material in the work, or which is reasonably likely to injure its sale." Styron's contract with Random House for the right to publish *Sophie's Choice,* executed in 1977, is virtually identical to his 1961 contract to publish *The Confessions of Nat Turner.*

2. Vonnegut Agreements

Kurt Vonnegut's 1967 contract granting Random House's predecessor-in-interest Dell Publishing Co., Inc. the license to publish *Slaughterhouse-Five* and *Breakfast of Champions* follows a similar structure to the Styron agreements. Paragraph #1 is captioned "grant of rights" and contains those rights the author is granting to the book publisher. Certain rights on the publisher's form contract are crossed out, indicating that the author reserved them for himself. One of the rights granted by the author includes the "[e]xclusive right to publish and to license the Work for publication, after book publication . . . in anthologies, selections, digests, abridgements, magazine condensations, serialization, newspaper syndication, picture book versions, microfilming, Xerox and other forms of copying, either now in use or hereafter developed."

Vonnegut specifically reserved for himself the "dramatic . . . motion picture (silent and sound) . . . radio broadcasting (including mechanical renditions and/or recordings of the text) . . . [and] television" rights. Unlike the Styron agreements, this contract does not contain a non-compete clause.

Vonnegut's 1970 contract granting Dell the license to publish *The Sirens of Titan, Cat's Cradle,* and *Player Piano* contains virtually identical grants and reservations of rights as his 1967 contract. However, it does contain a non-compete clause, which provides that "the Author . . . will not publish or permit to be published any edition, adaptation or abridgment of the Work by any party other than Dell without Dell's prior written consent." . . .

[The court then described the Parker Agreements, which are similar to the Styron and Vonnegut Agreements.]

DISCUSSION . . .

B. Ownership of a Valid Copyright

Two elements must be proven in order to establish a prima facie case of infringement: "(1) ownership of a valid copyright, and (2) copying of constituent elements of the work that are original." *Feist Publications, Inc. v. Rural Tel. Serv. Co.,* 499 U.S. 340 (1991). In this case, only the first element—ownership of a valid copyright—is at issue, since all parties concede that the text of the ebook is identical to the text of the book published by Random House. . . .

1. Contract Interpretation of Licensing Agreements—Legal Standards

Random House claims to own the rights in question through its licensing agreements with the authors. Interpretation of an agreement purporting to grant a copyright license is a matter of state contract law. All of the agreements state that they "shall be interpreted according to the law of the State of New York."

In New York, a written contract is to be interpreted so as to give effect to the intention of the parties as expressed in the contract's language. The court must consider the entire contract and reconcile all parts, if possible, to avoid an inconsistency.

These principles are in accord with the approach the U.S. Court of Appeals for the Second Circuit uses in analyzing contractual language in disputes, such as this one, "about whether licensees may exploit licensed works through new marketing channels made possible by technologies developed after the licensing contract—often called 'new use' problems." *Boosey & Hawkes Music Publishers, Ltd. v. Walt Disney Co.,* 145 F.3d 481, 486 (2d Cir. 1998). The two leading cases in this Circuit on how to determine whether "new uses" come within prior grants of rights are *Boosey* and *Bartsch v. Metro-Goldwyn-Mayer, Inc.,* 391 F.2d 150 (2d Cir. 1968), decided three decades apart. . . .

2. Application of Legal Standards

Relying on "the language of the license contract and basic principles of interpretation," *Boosey,* 145 F.3d at 487 n.3, as instructed to do so by *Boosey* and *Bartsch,* this Court finds that the most reasonable interpretation of the grant in the contracts at issue to "print, publish and sell the work in book form" does not include the right to publish the work as an ebook. At the outset, the phrase itself distinguishes between the pure content—*i.e.* "the work"—and the format of display—"in book form." The *Random House Webster's Unabridged Dictionary* defines a "book" as "a written or printed work of fiction or nonfiction, usually on sheets of paper fastened or bound together within covers" and defines "form" as "external appearance of a clearly defined area, as distinguished from color or material; the shape of a thing or person." *Random House Webster's Unabridged Dictionary* (2001), available in searchable form at *http://www.allwords.com*.

Manifestly, paragraph # 1 of each contract—entitled either "grant of rights" or "exclusive publication right"—conveys certain rights from the author to the publisher. In that paragraph, separate grant language is used to convey the rights to publish book club editions, reprint editions, abridged forms, and editions in Braille. This language would not be necessary if the phrase "in book form" encompassed all types of books. That paragraph specifies exactly which rights were being granted by the author to the publisher. Indeed, many of the rights set forth in the publisher's form contracts were in fact not granted to the publisher, but rather were reserved by the authors to themselves. For example, each of the authors specifically reserved certain rights for themselves by striking out phrases, sentences, and paragraphs of the publisher's form contract. This evidences an intent by these authors not to grant the publisher the broadest rights in their works.

Random House contends that the phrase "in book form" means to faithfully reproduce the author's text in its complete form as a reading experience and that, since ebooks concededly contain the complete text of the work, Rosetta cannot also possess those rights. While Random House's definition distinguishes "book form" from other formats that require separate contractual language—such as audio books and serialization rights—it does not distinguish other formats specifically mentioned in paragraph # 1 of the contracts, such as book club editions and reprint editions. Because the Court must, if possible, give effect to all contractual language in order to "safeguard against adopting an interpretation that would render any individual provision superfluous," *Sayers,* 7 F.3d at 1095, Random House's definition cannot be adopted. . . .

Random House also cites the non-compete clauses as evidence that the authors granted it broad, exclusive rights in their work. Random House reasons that because the authors could not permit any material that would injure the sale of the work to be published without Random House's consent, the authors must have granted the right to publish ebooks to Random House. This reasoning turns the analysis on its head. First, the grant of rights follows from the grant language alone. Second, non-compete clauses must be limited in scope in order to be enforceable in New York. Third, even if the authors did violate this provision of their Random House agreements by contracting with Rosetta Books—a point on which this Court does not opine—the remedy is a breach of contract action against the authors, not a copyright infringement action against Rosetta Books. . . .

Not only does the language of the contract itself lead almost ineluctably to the conclusion that Random House does not own the right to publish the works as ebooks, but also a reasonable person "cognizant of the customs, practices, usages and terminology as generally understood in the particular trade or business," *Sayers,*

7 F.3d at 1095, would conclude that the grant language does not include ebooks. "To print, publish and sell the work in book form" is understood in the publishing industry to be a "limited" grant. *See Field v. True Comics,* 89 F. Supp. 611, 613-14 (S.D.N.Y. 1950); *see also* Melville B. Nimmer & David Nimmer, *Nimmer on Copyright,* §10.14[C] (2001) (citing *Field*).

In *Field v. True Comics,* the court held that "the sole and exclusive right to publish, print and market *in book form*"—especially when the author had specifically reserved rights for himself—was "much more limited" than "the sole and exclusive right to publish, print and market *the book*." 89 F. Supp. at 612 (emphasis added). In fact, the publishing industry generally interprets the phrase "in book form" as granting the publisher "the exclusive right to publish a hardcover trade book in English for distribution in North America." 1 *Lindey on Entertainment, Publishing and the Arts* Form 1.01-1 (2d ed. 2000) (using the Random House form contract to explain the meaning of each clause).

3. Comparison to Prior "New Use" Caselaw

The finding that the five licensing agreements at issue do not convey the right to publish the works as ebooks accords with Second Circuit and New York case law. Indeed, the two leading cases . . . that found that a particular new use was included within the grant language—*Boosey,* 145 F.3d 481 (2d Cir. 1998), and *Bartsch,* 391 F.2d 150 (2d Cir. 1968)—can be distinguished from this case on four grounds.

First, the language conveying the rights in *Boosey* and *Bartsch* was far broader than here. Second, the "new use" in those cases—*i.e.* display of a motion picture on television or videocassette—fell squarely within the same medium as the original grant. *See Boosey,* 145 F.3d at 486 (describing videocassettes and laser discs as "subsequently developed methods of distribution of a motion picture").

In this case, the "new use"—electronic digital signals sent over the internet—is a separate medium from the original use—printed words on paper. Random House's own expert concludes that the media are distinct because information stored digitally can be manipulated in ways that analog information cannot. Ebooks take advantage of the digital medium's ability to manipulate data by allowing ebook users to electronically search the text for specific words and phrases, change the font size and style, type notes into the text and electronically organize them, highlight and bookmark, hyperlink to specific parts of the text, and, in the future, to other sites on related topics as well, and access a dictionary that pronounces words in the ebook aloud. The need for a software program to interact with the data in order to make it usable, as well as the need for a piece of hardware to enable the reader to view the text, also distinguishes analog formats from digital formats. . . .

The third significant difference between the licensee in the motion picture cases cited above and the book publisher in this action is that the licensees in the motion picture cases have actually created a new work based on the material from the licensor. Therefore, the right to display that new work—whether on television or video—is derivative of the right to create that work. In the book publishing context, the publishers, although they participate in the editorial process, display the words written by the author, not themselves.

Fourth, the courts in *Boosey* and *Bartsch* were concerned that any approach to new use problems that "tilts against licensees [here, Random House] gives rise to antiprogressive incentives" insofar as licensees "would be reluctant to explore and utilize innovative technologies." *Boosey*, 145 F.3d at 488, n.4; *see also Bartsch*, 391 F.2d at 155. However, in this action, the policy rationale of encouraging development in new technology is at least as well served by finding that the licensors—*i.e.*, the authors—retain these rights to their works. In the 21st century, it cannot be said that licensees such as book publishers and movie producers are ipso facto more likely to make advances in digital technology than start-up companies. . . .

NOTES AND QUESTIONS

1. Which of these two cases has the better reasoning? Are the cases inconsistent, or does each case simply turn on the language of the contract at issue? If you had represented Random House in drafting and negotiating the author agreements, would you have drafted the grant of rights provision differently? Remember, at the time those agreements were negotiated the computer industry was in its infancy.

2. As you know, a copyright owner is granted a number of different rights under §106, including the right to reproduce the work, the right to prepare derivative works, the right to distribute copies of the work to the public, and the rights to publicly perform and display the work. The exact bundle of rights granted to a licensee can be extremely important, particularly as technology changes. If a licensee is granted the right to publicly perform the work, what happens when a technologically enhanced means of rendering that performance also results in copies being made? Should a license to make such copies ever be implied? Is that what the *Boosey & Hawke*s court did?

3. The contract interpretation problems associated with changing technologies create a strong incentive on the part of the transferee simply to obtain the entire copyright. That way, there can be no dispute concerning what rights the transferee possesses. Subject only to termination rights, the transferee of "all right, title, and interest" in a particular copyright can exercise all of the rights of a copyright owner. Under what circumstances might a transferee be willing to accept less than the entire copyright?

> ### LOOKING BACK
>
> Recall that in *CCNV v. Reid*, 490 U.S. 730 (1989), Chapter 3.C.1.a, *supra*, the Supreme Court held that a federal common law of agency, as opposed to the principles of agency law applied in each of the separate states, should be used to determine if the creator of a work is an employee.

4. Contract interpretation is typically, although not always, governed by state law. There are many canons of construction that you learned in your first-year Contracts class. For example, in certain situations the contract is said to be construed against the drafter. Should state law rules of contract interpretation apply to copyright contracts, or should courts develop federal common law canons of copyright contract interpretation?

PRACTICE EXERCISE: DRAFTING

Anna Lee, a novelist, has just completed the manuscript for a novel titled *A Time for Everything*. Anna has never published her novels in electronic formats and her publishing contracts explicitly reserve nonprint publication rights. Recently, she orally agreed to assign her electronic publishing rights to the publisher. The publisher is a client of your firm and has asked you to draft the new provision assigning Anna's electronic rights. Draft the language you would propose.

C. NEW LICENSING MODELS AND THE CONTRACT/LICENSE DISTINCTION

Historically, negotiated contracts have been an important piece of the contract and copyright puzzle. In recent decades, different types of contracting practices have emerged for mass market distribution of copyrighted works. We consider the most well-known of these approaches below.

> **KEEP IN MIND**
>
> There is a conceptual difference between a contract and a license. A contract must be supported by consideration to be enforceable. A license, on the other hand, need not involve consideration. When a license is not supported by consideration it is sometimes referred to as a "bare license." Such a license is simply authorization to engage in an activity that requires permission from another person. In the copyright context, a license permits someone to engage in activity that, without the authorization of the copyright owner, would constitute infringement. Many times consideration is given to obtain that permission, making the license a contract.

1. End User Licenses

As you learned in Chapter 4, software is easily copied, and initially software providers were uncertain whether they could successfully claim intellectual property protection for the information embodied in mass-marketed software products. They began to distribute their software with "end user license agreements" (EULAs) that prohibited end users from engaging in a variety of practices, some of which would be permissible under the Copyright Act.

Providers of other types of digital content also have adopted the practice of using EULAs. These take a variety of forms, including agreements printed on physical packages (shrinkwraps), electronic agreements to be "accepted" by the user's clicking "I agree" (clickwraps), and electronic agreements to be "accepted" by some act like downloading without having to click on a separate "I agree" button or box (browsewraps). Some early cases labeled shrinkwraps contracts of adhesion and held them unenforceable in the absence of a state statute permitting enforcement. Subsequently, however, courts have generally held shrinkwrap and clickwrap agreements enforceable contracts under the common law of contract or the Uniform Commercial Code (UCC). What are the implications of this contracting practice? Consider the following case.

Vernor v. Autodesk, Inc.
621 F.3d 1102 (9th Cir. 2010)

CALLAHAN, J.: . . .

I.

A. *Autodesk's Release 14 Software and Licensing Practices*

The material facts are not in dispute. Autodesk makes computer-aided design software used by architects, engineers, and manufacturers. It has more than nine million customers. It first released its AutoCAD software in 1982. It holds registered copyrights in all versions of the software including the discontinued Release 14 version, which is at issue in this case. It provided Release 14 to customers on CD-ROMs.

Since at least 1986, Autodesk has offered AutoCAD to customers pursuant to an accompanying software license agreement ("SLA"), which customers must accept before installing the software. A customer who does not accept the SLA can return the software for a full refund. Autodesk offers SLAs with different terms for commercial, educational institution, and student users. The commercial license, which is the most expensive, imposes the fewest restrictions on users and allows them software upgrades at discounted prices.

The SLA for Release 14 first recites that Autodesk retains title to all copies. Second, it states that the customer has a nonexclusive and nontransferable license to use Release 14. Third, it imposes transfer restrictions, prohibiting customers from renting, leasing, or transferring the software without Autodesk's prior consent and from electronically or physically transferring the software out of the Western Hemisphere. Fourth, it imposes significant use restrictions:

> YOU MAY NOT: (1) modify, translate, reverse-engineer, decompile, or disassemble the Software . . . (3) remove any proprietary notices, labels, or marks from the Software or Documentation; (4) use . . . the Software outside of the Western Hemisphere; (5) utilize any computer software or hardware designed to defeat any hardware copy-protection device, should the software you have licensed be equipped with such protection; or (6) use the Software for commercial or other revenue-generating purposes if the Software has been licensed or labeled for educational use only.

Fifth, the SLA provides for license termination if the user copies the software without authorization or does not comply with the SLA's restrictions. Finally, the SLA provides that if the software is an upgrade of a previous version [the licensee must destroy the software within 60 days and furnish proof of destruction on Autodesk's request.] . . . Autodesk takes measures to enforce these license requirements. It assigns a serial number to each copy of AutoCAD and tracks registered licensees. It requires customers to input "activation codes" within one month after installation to continue using the software. The customer obtains the code by providing the product's serial number to Autodesk. Autodesk issues the activation code after confirming that the serial number is authentic, the copy is not registered to a different customer, and the product has not been upgraded. Once a customer has an activation code, he or she may use it to activate the software on additional computers without notifying Autodesk.

B. Autodesk's Provision of Release 14 Software to CTA

In March 1999, Autodesk reached a settlement agreement with its customer Cardwell/Thomas & Associates, Inc. ("CTA"), which Autodesk had accused of unauthorized use of its software. As part of the settlement, Autodesk licensed ten copies of Release 14 to CTA. CTA agreed to the SLA, which appeared (1) on each Release 14 package that Autodesk provided to CTA; (2) in the settlement agreement; and (3) on-screen, while the software is being installed.

CTA later upgraded to the newer, fifteenth version of the AutoCAD program, AutoCAD 2000. It paid $495 per upgrade license, compared to $3,750 for each new license. The SLA for AutoCAD 2000, like the SLA for Release 14, required destruction of copies of previous versions of the software, with proof to be furnished to Autodesk on request. However, rather than destroying its Release 14 copies, CTA sold them to Vernor at an office sale with the handwritten activation codes necessary to use the software.

C. Vernor's eBay Business and Sales of Release 14

Vernor has sold more than 10,000 items on eBay. In May 2005, he purchased an authentic used copy of Release 14 at a garage sale from an unspecified seller. He never agreed to the SLA's terms, opened a sealed software packet, or installed the Release 14 software. Though he was aware of the SLA's existence, he believed that he was not bound by its terms. He posted the software copy for sale on eBay.

Autodesk filed a Digital Millennium Copyright Act ("DMCA") take-down notice with eBay claiming that Vernor's sale infringed its copyright, and eBay terminated Vernor's auction. Autodesk advised Vernor that it conveyed its software copies pursuant to non-transferable licenses, and resale of its software was copyright infringement. Vernor filed a DMCA counter-notice with eBay contesting the validity of Autodesk's copyright claim. Autodesk did not respond to the counter-notice. eBay reinstated the auction, and Vernor sold the software to another eBay user.

In April 2007, Vernor purchased four authentic used copies of Release 14 at CTA's office sale. The authorization codes were handwritten on the outside of the box. He listed the four copies on eBay sequentially, representing, "This software is not currently installed on any computer." On each of the first three occasions, the same DMCA process [as discussed above] ensued. Autodesk filed a DMCA takedown notice with eBay, and eBay removed Vernor's auction. Vernor submitted a counter-notice to which Autodesk did not respond, and eBay reinstated the auction.

When Vernor listed his fourth, final copy of Release 14, Autodesk again filed a DMCA take-down notice with eBay. This time, eBay suspended Vernor's account because of Autodesk's repeated charges of infringement. Vernor also wrote to Autodesk, claiming that he was entitled to sell his Release 14 copies pursuant to the first sale doctrine, because he never installed the software or agreed to the SLA.

In response, Autodesk's counsel directed Vernor to stop selling the software. Vernor filed a final counter-notice with eBay. When Autodesk again did not respond to Vernor's counter-notice, eBay reinstated Vernor's account. At that point, Vernor's eBay account had been suspended for one month, during which he was unable to earn income on eBay.

Vernor currently has two additional copies of Release 14 that he wishes to sell on eBay. Although the record is not clear, it appears that Vernor sold two of the software packages that he purchased from CTA, for roughly $600 each, but did not sell the final two to avoid risking further suspension of his eBay account.

II.

In August 2007, Vernor brought a declaratory action against Autodesk to establish that his resales of used Release 14 software are protected by the first sale doctrine and do not infringe Autodesk's copyright. . . . On January 15, 2008, Autodesk moved to dismiss Vernor's complaint, or in the alternative, for summary judgment. The district court denied the motion, holding that Vernor's sales were non-infringing under the first sale doctrine and the essential step defense. *See Vernor v. Autodesk, Inc.*, 555 F. Supp. 2d 1164, 1170-71, 1175 (W.D. Wash. 2008).

Following discovery, the parties filed cross-motions for summary judgment. The district court granted summary judgment to Vernor as to copyright infringement in an unpublished decision. . . .

III. . . .

. . . The [Copyright Act's] exclusive distribution right is limited by the **first sale doctrine**, an affirmative defense to copyright infringement that allows owners of copies of copyrighted works to resell those copies. The exclusive reproduction right is limited within the software context by the **essential step defense**, another affirmative defense to copyright infringement that is discussed further *infra*. Both of these affirmative defenses are unavailable to those who are only licensed to use their copies of copyrighted works. . . .

B. Owners vs. licensees

We turn to our precedents governing whether a transferee of a copy of a copyrighted work is an owner or licensee of that copy. . . .

1. United States v. Wise, 550 F.2d 1180 (9th Cir. 1977)

In *Wise*, a criminal copyright infringement case, we considered whether copyright owners who transferred copies of their motion pictures pursuant to written distribution agreements had executed first sales. The defendant was found guilty of copyright infringement based on his for-profit sales of motion picture prints. The copyright owners distributed their films to third parties pursuant to written agreements that restricted their use and transfer. On appeal, the defendant argued that the government failed to prove the absence of a first sale for each film. If the copyright owners' initial transfers of the films were first sales, then the defendant's resales were protected by the first sale doctrine and thus were not copyright infringement.

To determine whether a first sale occurred, we considered multiple factors pertaining to each film distribution agreement. Specifically, we considered whether the agreement (a) was labeled a license, (b) provided that the copyright owner retained title to the prints, (c) required the return or destruction of the prints, (d) forbade duplication of prints, or (e) required the transferee to maintain possession of the prints for the agreement's duration. *Id*. at 1190-92. Our use of these several considerations, none dispositive, may be seen in our treatment of each film print.

For example, we reversed the defendant's conviction with respect to *Camelot*. It was unclear whether the *Camelot* print sold by the defendant had been subject to a first sale. Copyright owner Warner Brothers distributed *Camelot* prints pursuant to multiple agreements, and the government did not prove the absence of a first sale with respect to each agreement. We noted that, in one agreement, Warner Brothers had retained title to the prints, required possessor National Broadcasting Company ("NBC") to return the prints if the parties could select a mutual agreeable price, and if not, required NBC's certification that the prints were destroyed. We held that these factors created a license rather than a first sale.

We further noted, however, that Warner Brothers had also furnished another *Camelot* print to actress Vanessa Redgrave. The print was provided to Redgrave at cost, and her use of the print was subject to several restrictions. She had to retain possession of the print and was not allowed to sell, license, reproduce, or publicly exhibit the print. She had no obligation to return the print to Warner Brothers. We concluded, "While the provision for payment for the cost of the film, standing alone, does not establish a sale, when taken with the rest of the language of the agreement, it reveals a transaction strongly resembling a sale with restrictions on the use of the print." *Id*. [at 1192]. There was no evidence of the print's whereabouts, and we held that "[i]n the absence of such proof," the government failed to prove the absence of a first sale with respect to this Redgrave print. *Id*. at 1191-92. Since it was unclear which copy the defendant had obtained and resold, his conviction for sale of *Camelot* had to be reversed.

Thus, under *Wise*, where a transferee receives a particular copy of a copyrighted work pursuant to a written agreement, we consider all of the provisions of the agreement to determine whether the transferee became an owner of the copy or received a license. We may consider (1) whether the agreement was labeled a license and (2) whether the copyright owner retained title to the copy, required its return or destruction, forbade its duplication, or required the transferee to maintain possession of the copy for the agreement's duration. We did not find any one factor dispositive in *Wise*: we did not hold that the copyright owner's retention of title itself established the absence of a first sale or that a transferee's right to indefinite possession itself established a first sale.

2. The "MAI trio" of cases

Over fifteen years after *Wise*, we again considered the distinction between owners and licensees of copies of copyrighted works in three software copyright cases, the "*MAI* trio." *See MAI Sys. Corp. v. Peak Computer, Inc.*, 991 F.2d 511 (9th Cir. 1993); *Triad Sys. Corp. v. Se. Express Co.*, 64 F.3d 1330 (9th Cir. 1995); *Wall Data, Inc. v. Los Angeles County Sheriff's Dep't*, 447 F.3d 769 (9th Cir. 2006). In the *MAI* trio, we considered which software purchasers were owners of copies of copyrighted works for purposes of a second affirmative defense to infringement, the essential step defense.

The enforcement of copyright owners' exclusive right to reproduce their work under the Copyright Act, 17 U.S.C. §106(1), has posed special challenges in the software context. In order to use a software program, a user's computer will automatically copy the software into the computer's random access memory ("RAM"), which is a form of computer data storage. Congress enacted the **essential step defense** to codify that a software user who is the "owner of a copy" of a copyrighted software program does not infringe by making a copy of the computer program, if the new copy is "created as an essential step in the utilization of the computer program in conjunction with a machine and . . . is used in no other manner." 17 U.S.C. §117(a)(1). . . .

In *MAI* and *Triad*, the defendants maintained computers that ran the plaintiffs' operating system software. When the defendants ran the computers, the computers automatically loaded plaintiffs' software into RAM. The plaintiffs in both cases sold their software pursuant to restrictive license agreements, and we held that their customers were licensees who were therefore not entitled to claim the essential step defense. We found that the defendants infringed plaintiffs' software copyrights by their unauthorized loading of copyrighted software into RAM. In *Triad*, the plaintiff had earlier sold software outright to some customers. We noted that these customers were owners who were entitled to the essential step defense, and the defendant did not infringe by making RAM copies in servicing their computers.

In *Wall Data*, plaintiff sold 3,663 software licenses to the defendant. The licenses (1) were non-exclusive; (2) permitted use of the software on a single computer; and (3) permitted transfer of the software once per month, if the software was removed from the original computer. The defendant installed the software onto 6,007 computers via hard drive imaging, which saved it from installing the software manually on each computer. It made an unverified claim that only 3,663 users could simultaneously access the software.

The plaintiff sued for copyright infringement, contending that the defendant violated the license by "over-installing" the software. The defendant raised an essential step defense, contending that its hard drive imaging was a necessary step of installation. On appeal, we held that the district court did not abuse its discretion in denying the defendant's request for a jury instruction on the essential step defense. Citing *MAI*, we held that the essential step defense does not apply where the copyright owner grants the user a license and significantly restricts the user's ability to transfer the software. Since the plaintiff's license imposed "significant restrictions" on the defendant's software rights, the defendant was a licensee and was not entitled to the essential step defense. . . .

We read *Wise* and the *MAI* trio to prescribe three considerations that we may use to determine whether a software user is a licensee, rather than an owner of a copy. First, we consider whether the copyright owner specifies that a user is granted a license. Second, we consider whether the copyright owner significantly restricts the user's ability to transfer the software. Finally, we consider whether the copyright owner imposes notable use restrictions. Our holding reconciles the *MAI* trio and *Wise*, even though the *MAI* trio did not cite *Wise*.

In response to *MAI*, Congress amended §117 to permit a *computer owner* to copy software for maintenance or repair purposes. *See* 17 U.S.C. §117(c); *see also* H.R. Rep. No. 105-551, pt. 1, at 27 (1998). However, Congress did not disturb *MAI*'s holding that licensees are not entitled to the essential step defense.

IV . . .

The district court interpreted *Wise* to hold that a first sale occurs whenever the transferee is entitled to keep the copy of the work. Since Autodesk does not require its customers to return their copies of Release 14, the district court found that Autodesk had sold Release 14 to CTA. . . .

The district court acknowledged that were it to follow the *MAI* trio, it would conclude that Autodesk had licensed Release 14 copies to CTA, rather than sold them. However, it viewed *Wise* and the *MAI* trio as irreconcilable, and it followed *Wise* as the first-decided case. . . .

We hold today that a software user is a licensee rather than an owner of a copy where the copyright owner (1) specifies that the user is granted a license; (2) significantly restricts the user's ability to transfer the software; and (3) imposes notable use restrictions. Applying our holding to Autodesk's SLA, we conclude that CTA was a licensee rather than an owner of copies of Release 14 and thus was not entitled to invoke the first sale doctrine or the essential step defense.

Autodesk retained title to the software and imposed significant transfer restrictions: it stated that the license is nontransferable, the software could not be transferred or leased without Autodesk's written consent, and the software could not be transferred outside the Western Hemisphere. The SLA also imposed use restrictions against the use of the software outside the Western Hemisphere and against modifying, translating, or reverse-engineering the software, removing any proprietary marks from the software or documentation, or defeating any copy protection device. Furthermore, the SLA provided for termination of the license upon the licensee's unauthorized copying or failure to comply with other license restrictions. Thus, because Autodesk reserved title to Release 14 copies and imposed significant transfer and use restrictions, we conclude that its customers are licensees of their copies of Release 14 rather than owners.

CTA was a licensee rather than an "owner of a particular copy" of Release 14, and it was not entitled to resell its Release 14 copies to Vernor under the first sale doctrine. 17 U.S.C. §109(a). Therefore, Vernor did not receive title to the copies from CTA and accordingly could not pass ownership on to others. Both CTA's and Vernor's sales infringed Autodesk's exclusive right to distribute copies of its work. *Id*. §106(3).

Because Vernor was not an owner, his customers are also not owners of Release 14 copies. Therefore, when they install Release 14 on their computers, the copies of the software that they make during installation infringe Autodesk's exclusive reproduction right because they too are not entitled to the benefit of the essential step defense.[13] 17 U.S.C. §§106(1), 117(a)(1). . . .

Vernor contends that *Bobbs-Merrill* establishes his entitlement to a first sale defense. *See Bobbs-Merrill Co. v. Straus*, 210 U.S. 339 (1908). However, *Bobbs-Merrill* stands only for the proposition that a copyright owner's exclusive distribution right does not allow it to control sales of copies of its work after the first sale. Decided in 1908, *Bobbs-Merrill* did not and could not address the question of whether the right to use software is distinct from the ownership of copies of software. Moreover, the Supreme Court in *Bobbs-Merrill* made explicit that its decision did not address the use of restrictions to create a license. *Id*. [at 350]. ("There is no claim in this case of contract limitation, nor license agreement controlling the subsequent sales of the book.") . . .

V.

Although our holding today is controlled by our precedent, we recognize the significant policy considerations raised by the parties and amici on both sides of this appeal.

Autodesk, the Software & Information Industry Association ("SIIA"), and the Motion Picture Association of America ("MPAA") have presented policy arguments that favor our result. For instance, Autodesk argues in favor of judicial enforcement of software license agreements that restrict transfers of copies of the work. Autodesk contends that this (1) allows for tiered pricing for different software markets, such as reduced pricing for students or educational institutions; (2) increases software companies' sales; (3) lowers prices for all consumers by spreading costs among a large number of purchasers; and (4) reduces the incidence of piracy by allowing copyright owners to bring infringement actions against unauthorized resellers. SIIA argues that a license can exist even where a customer (1) receives his copy of the work after making a single payment and (2) can indefinitely possess a software copy, because it is the software code and associated rights that are valuable rather than the inexpensive discs on which the code may be stored. Also, the MPAA argues that a customer's ability to possess a copyrighted work

---

13. It may seem intuitive that every lawful user of a copyrighted software program, whether they own their copies or are merely licensed to use them, should be entitled to an "essential step defense" that provides that they do not infringe simply by using a computer program that they lawfully acquired. However, the Copyright Act confers this defense only on owners of software copies. *See* 17 U.S.C. §117. In contrast, a licensee's right to use the software, including the right to copy the software into RAM, is conferred by the terms of its license agreement.

indefinitely should not compel a finding of a first sale, because there is often no practically feasible way for a consumer to return a copy to the copyright owner.

Vernor, eBay, and the American Library Association ("ALA") have presented policy arguments against our decision. Vernor contends that our decision (1) does not vindicate the law's aversion to restraints on alienation of personal property; (2) may force everyone purchasing copyrighted property to trace the chain of title to ensure that a first sale occurred; and (3) ignores the economic realities of the relevant transactions, in which the copyright owner permanently released software copies into the stream of commerce without expectation of return in exchange for upfront payment of the full software price. eBay contends that a broad view of the first sale doctrine is necessary to facilitate the creation of secondary markets for copyrighted works, which contributes to the public good by (1) giving consumers additional opportunities to purchase and sell copyrighted works, often at below-retail prices; (2) allowing consumers to obtain copies of works after a copyright owner has ceased distribution; and (3) allowing the proliferation of businesses.

The ALA contends that the first sale doctrine facilitates the availability of copyrighted works after their commercial lifespan, by *inter alia* enabling the existence of libraries, used bookstores, and hand-to-hand exchanges of copyrighted materials. The ALA further contends that judicial enforcement of software license agreements, which are often contracts of adhesion, could eliminate the software resale market, require used computer sellers to delete legitimate software prior to sale, and increase prices for consumers by reducing price competition for software vendors. It contends that Autodesk's position (1) undermines 17 U.S.C. §109(b)(2), which permits non-profit libraries to lend software for non-commercial purposes, and (2) would hamper efforts by non-profits to collect and preserve out-of-print software. The ALA fears that the software industry's licensing practices could be adopted by other copyright owners, including book publishers, record labels, and movie studios.

These are serious contentions on both sides, but they do not alter our conclusion that our precedent from *Wise* through the *MAI* trio requires the result we reach. Congress is free, of course, to modify the first sale doctrine and the essential step defense if it deems these or other policy considerations to require a different approach. . . .

We vacate the district court's grant of summary judgment in Vernor's favor and remand. We hold that because CTA is a licensee, not an owner, the "sale" of its Release 14 copies to Vernor did not convey ownership. Vernor is accordingly not entitled to invoke the first sale doctrine or the essential step defense, on behalf of his customers. . . .

NOTES AND QUESTIONS

1. There can be a lot at stake in determining who is an owner of a copy and who is a mere licensee. If copyright owners can control the subsequent transfer of copies of software, they will not need to compete with aftermarket copies of their own products. Should copyright owners be protected against such competition? Are markets for used software the same as markets for new software? Are there other ways software producers can effectively maintain a competitive edge without relying on copyright law?

2. In *Vernor* the court had to determine whether the transaction was properly characterized as a sale or a license in order to decide whether an infringement claim would be permissible. The court confronted a similar issue in *UMG Recordings, Inc. v. Augusto*, 628 F.3d 1175 (9th Cir. 2011). The plaintiff had sent promotional CDs to music industry insiders. The CDs contained a label that stated:

> This CD is the property of the record company and is licensed to the intended recipient for personal use only. Acceptance of this CD shall constitute an agreement to comply with the terms of the license. Resale or transfer of possession is not allowed and may be punishable under federal and state laws.

Id. at 1177-78. The defendant had obtained copies of the CDs and, as in *Vernor*, was selling them on eBay, advertising them as "'rare . . . industry editions' and . . . 'Promo CDs.'" *Id.* at 1178. Nothing required the recipient to return the promotional CDs to UMG and there were no consequences if the CDs were lost or destroyed.

The same judges that decided *Vernor* held that a first sale had occurred. The court stated:

> [The *Vernor*] formulation . . . applies in terms to software users, and software users who order and pay to acquire copies are in a very different position from that held by the recipients of UMG's promotional CDs. . . . UMG has virtually no control over the unordered CDs it issues because of its means of distribution, and it has no assurance that any recipient has assented or will assent to the creation of any license or accept its limitations. UMG also does not require the ultimate return of the promotional CDs to its possession . . . [,] one more indication that UMG had no control over the promotional CDs once it dispatched them. UMG thus did not retain "sufficient incidents of ownership" over the promotional copies "to be sensibly considered the owner of the cop[ies]." . . .

Id. at 1183.

Are *Augusto* and *Vernor* consistent? Under the standard announced in *Vernor*, had a first sale of the CDs occurred? Should there be a different rule for software than for other copyrighted works? Does the statute permit courts to treat different types of works differently?

3. *Vernor* and *UMG* both involved the transfer of physical objects that contained copies of the work. Physical copies often can be resold before the defendants confront a EULA with its "I agree" button. When copyrighted works are downloaded from the Internet, there is no tangible physical object. Are contractual restrictions on resale more or less troubling in such circumstances?

4. Companies attempting to use contracts to restrict resale of copies of their software may be able to maintain actions for breach of contract against distributors who breach their distribution agreements. The company from which Vernor purchased the copies, CTA, had entered into a settlement agreement binding itself to the EULA. In addition to its infringement lawsuit against Vernor, should Autodesk also be able to sue CTA for breach of contract? Would it matter how the settlement agreement was worded?

5. As the ALA predicted in its amicus brief in *Vernor*, some major publishers have begun experimenting with restrictions for libraries. In March 2011, for example, Harper-Collins announced a shift in its policy and now requires that ebooks purchased by public libraries be checked out only 26 times before the book expires. *See* Julie Bosman, *Library E-Books Live Longer, So Publisher Limits Shelf Life*, N.Y. Times, Mar. 15, 2011, at A1. In defense of its policy, HarperCollins stated that "selling e-books to libraries in perpetuity, if left unchanged, would undermine the emerging e-book ecosystem, hurt the growing e-book channel, place additional pressure on physical bookstores, and in the end lead to a decrease in book sales and royalties paid to authors." *Id.* Who has the better policy argument, HarperCollins or the ALA?

2. Open Licensing Models

In the late twentieth century, some authors began experimenting with mass license agreements designed to ensure ongoing public availability of a rich supply of works. One way to attempt to ensure public availability of a work of authorship and to permit re-use of the expression the work embodies would be to abandon the work to the public domain. However, abandonment results in a complete loss of control. Others may freely use the work's expression as the basis for derivative works and may exercise their exclusive rights as copyright owners of those derivative works. If, rather than abandoning the underlying work, the author were to retain copyright ownership and merely license the creation of derivative works, the license could insist on certain conditions.

The use of mass licenses designed to ensure ongoing public availability began with what is known as the open source or free software movement. The most well-known open source license is the GNU General Public License (GNU GPL), under which the GNU/Linux computer operating system is distributed. The GNU GPL authorizes others to copy, modify, and redistribute covered software programs and to create and distribute new programs based on the initial ones. The license requires that if those new derivative programs are publicly distributed, they must be distributed subject to the same GNU GPL. The GNU GPL also requires that the program's source code be distributed along with the object code. As you know, access to the source code is critically important to understanding how a program functions and building interoperable programs. Thus, the open source movement uses copyright ownership and licenses to enforce social norms of sharing and openness. Open source licenses like the GNU GPL are also called "copyleft" licenses. The GNU GPL and other open source licenses are available at http://www.fsf.org/licensing/licenses/. The use of mass market licenses presents a host of challenging questions. Consider the following case.

≣≣   *Jacobsen v. Katzer*
     535 F.3d 1373 (Fed. Cir. 2008)

HOCHBERG, J.: . . . Jacobsen manages an open source software group called Java Model Railroad Interface ("JMRI"). Through the collective work of many participants, JMRI created a computer programming application called DecoderPro, which allows model railroad enthusiasts to use their computers to program the decoder chips that control model trains. DecoderPro files are available for download and use by the public free of charge from an open source incubator website called SourceForge. . . . The downloadable files contain copyright notices and refer the user to a "COPYING" file, which clearly sets forth the terms of the Artistic License.

[Matthew Katzer and Kamind Associates, Inc. (collectively "Katzer/Kamind") offer] a competing software product, Decoder Commander, which is also used to program decoder chips. During development of Decoder Commander, one of Katzer/Kamind's predecessors or employees is alleged to have downloaded the decoder definition files from DecoderPro and used portions of these files as part of the Decoder Commander software. The Decoder Commander software files that used DecoderPro definition files did not comply with the terms of the Artistic License. Specifically, the Decoder Commander software did not include (1) the authors' names, (2) JMRI copyright notices, (3) references to the COPYING file, (4) an identification of SourceForge or JMRI as the original source of the definition files, and (5) a description of how the files or computer code had been changed from the original source code. The Decoder Commander software also changed various computer file names of DecoderPro files without providing a reference to the original JMRI files or information on where to get the Standard Version.

Jacobsen moved for a preliminary injunction, arguing that the violation of the terms of the Artistic License constituted copyright infringement. . . . The District Court found that Jacobsen had a cause of action only for breach of contract, rather than an action for copyright infringement based on a breach of the conditions of the Artistic License. . . .

II. . . .

A. . . .

Open Source software projects invite computer programmers from around the world to view software code and make changes and improvements to it. Through such collaboration, software programs can often be written and debugged faster and at lower cost than if the copyright holder were required to do all of the work independently. In exchange and in consideration for this collaborative work, the copyright holder permits users to copy, modify and distribute the software code subject to conditions that serve to protect downstream users and to keep the code accessible. By requiring that users copy and restate the license and attribution information, a copyright holder can ensure that recipients of the redistributed computer code know the identity of the owner as well as the scope of the license granted by the original owner. The Artistic License in this case also requires that changes to the computer code be tracked so that downstream users know what part of the computer code is the original code created by the copyright holder and what part has been newly added or altered by another collaborator.

Traditionally, copyright owners sold their copyrighted material in exchange for money. The lack of money changing hands in open source licensing should not be presumed to mean that there is no economic consideration, however. There are substantial benefits, including economic benefits, to the creation and distribution of copyrighted works under public licenses that range far beyond traditional license royalties. For example, program creators may generate market share for their programs by providing certain components free of charge. Similarly, a programmer or company may increase its national or international reputation by incubating open source projects. Improvement to a product can come rapidly and free of charge from an expert not even known to the copyright holder. . . .

B.

The parties do not dispute that Jacobsen is the holder of a copyright for certain materials distributed through his website. Katzer/Kamind also admits that portions of the DecoderPro software were copied, modified, and distributed as part of the Decoder Commander software. Accordingly, Jacobsen has made out a prima facie case of copyright infringement. Katzer/Kamind argues that they cannot be liable for copyright infringement because they had a license to use the material. Thus, the Court must evaluate whether the use by Katzer/Kamind was outside the scope of the license. The copyrighted materials in this case are downloadable by any user and are labeled to include a copyright notification and a COPYING file that includes the text of the Artistic License. The Artistic License grants users the right to copy, modify, and distribute the software:

> provided that [the user] insert a prominent notice in each changed file stating how and when [the user] changed that file, and provided that [the user] do at least ONE of the following:
>
> a) place [the user's] modifications in the Public Domain or otherwise make them Freely Available . . .
> b) use the modified Package only within [the user's] corporation or organization.
> c) rename any non-standard executables so the names do not conflict with the standard executables, which must also be provided, and provide a separate manual page for each nonstandard executable that clearly documents how it differs from the Standard Version, or
> d) make other distribution arrangements with the Copyright Holder.

The heart of the argument on appeal concerns whether the terms of the Artistic License are conditions of, or merely covenants to, the copyright license. Generally, a "copyright owner who grants a nonexclusive license to use his copyrighted material waives his right to sue the licensee for copyright infringement" and can sue only for breach of contract. *Sun Microsystems, Inc., v. Microsoft Corp.,* 188 F.3d 1115, 1121

(9th Cir.1999). If, however, a license is limited in scope and the licensee acts outside the scope, the licensor can bring an action for copyright infringement.

Thus, if the terms of the Artistic License allegedly violated are both covenants and conditions, they may serve to limit the scope of the license and are governed by copyright law. If they are merely covenants, by contrast, they are governed by contract law. . . .

III.

The Artistic License states on its face that the document creates conditions: "The intent of this document is to state the *conditions* under which a Package may be copied." (Emphasis added.) The Artistic License also uses the traditional language of conditions by noting that the rights to copy, modify, and distribute are granted "*provided that*" the conditions are met. Under California contract law, "provided that" typically denotes a condition.

The conditions set forth in the Artistic License are vital to enable the copyright holder to retain the ability to benefit from the work of downstream users. By requiring that users who modify or distribute the copyrighted material retain the reference to the original source files, downstream users are directed to Jacobsen's website. Thus, downstream users know about the collaborative effort to improve and expand the SourceForge project once they learn of the "upstream" project from a "downstream" distribution, and they may join in that effort.

The District Court interpreted the Artistic License to permit a user to "modify the material in any way" and did not find that any of the "provided that" limitations in the Artistic License served to limit this grant. The District Court's interpretation of the conditions of the Artistic License does not credit the explicit restrictions in the license that govern a downloader's right to modify and distribute the copyrighted work. The copyright holder here expressly stated the terms upon which the right to modify and distribute the material depended and invited direct contact if a downloader wished to negotiate other terms. These restrictions were both clear and necessary to accomplish the objectives of the open source licensing collaboration, including economic benefit. . . .

Copyright holders who engage in open source licensing have the right to control the modification and distribution of copyrighted material. As the Second Circuit explained in *Gilliam v. ABC*, 538 F.2d 14, 21 (2d Cir.1976), the "unauthorized editing of the underlying work, if proven, would constitute an infringement of the copyright in that work similar to any other use of a work that exceeded the license granted by the proprietor of the copyright." Copyright licenses are designed to support the right to exclude; money damages alone do not support or enforce that right. The choice to exact consideration in the form of compliance with the open source requirements of disclosure and explanation of changes, rather than as a dollar-denominated fee, is entitled to no less legal recognition. Indeed, because a calculation of damages is inherently speculative, these types of license restrictions might well be rendered meaningless absent the ability to enforce through injunctive relief.

In this case, a user who downloads the JMRI copyrighted materials is authorized to make modifications and to distribute the materials "provided that" the user follows the restrictive terms of the Artistic License. A copyright holder can grant the right to make certain modifications, yet retain his right to prevent other modifications. Indeed, such a goal is exactly the purpose of adding conditions to a license grant. . . .

It is outside the scope of the Artistic License to modify and distribute the copyrighted materials without copyright notices and a tracking of modifications from the original computer files. If a downloader does not assent to these conditions stated in the COPYING file, he is instructed to "make other arrangements with the Copyright Holder." Katzer/Kamind did not make any such "other arrangements." The clear language of the Artistic License creates conditions to protect the economic rights at issue in the granting of a public license. These conditions govern the rights to modify and distribute the computer programs and files included in the downloadable software package. The attribution and modification transparency requirements directly serve to drive traffic to the open source incubation page and to inform downstream users of the project, which is a significant economic goal of the copyright holder that the law will enforce. Through this controlled spread of information, the copyright holder gains creative collaborators to the open source project; by requiring that changes made by downstream users be visible to the copyright holder and others, the copyright holder learns about the uses for his software and gains others' knowledge that can be used to advance future software releases.

IV.

. . . Having determined that the terms of the Artistic License are enforceable copyright conditions, we remand to enable the District Court to determine whether Jacobsen [is entitled to a preliminary injunction.] . . .

NOTES AND QUESTIONS

1. The requirement that publicly distributed works based on code available under the GPL also must be licensed under the GPL, thus allowing others to use the new works, has been characterized as "viral licensing": Once you "catch" the "virus" you can't get rid of it. Is the "viral" label an accurate and/or fair one?

2. In what ways is *Jacobsen* similar to *Vernor*? In what ways are they different? Should a license authorizing activities that otherwise would be infringing be analyzed differently than a license prohibiting activities that otherwise would be authorized under the Copyright Act?

3. One way to think about open source licenses is as defenses to claims of infringement: The copyright owner could assert that a user of the work has engaged in an activity that constitutes infringement, but the user can point to the license as authorizing the activity. When the activity is outside of the scope of the license, the defense of "licensed use" fails and the user is left to defend against the infringement claim.

According to the *Jacobsen* court, Katzer/Kamind did not simply receive a mere license – i.e., a grant of permission to use the copyrighted material – but instead had entered into an exchange for consideration. Why did the court so conclude? Do you agree with the court's reasoning? If the court had not found consideration, are there provisions of the license that Jacobson would not have been able to enforce? Which ones? Recall that a mere license allows a plaintiff to enforce only those rights conferred in §106.

LOOKING FORWARD

Determining whether the appropriate claim is one for copyright infringement, breach of contract, or both affects the remedies available. The usual remedy for breach of contract is an award of expectation damages. The remedial provisions of the Copyright Act permit recovery of either actual damages or statutory damages. Further, injunctive relief is common in copyright cases and rare in contract cases. Claim characterization also affects subject matter jurisdiction. As you know, a lawsuit for breach of contract can be heard in federal court only if some other basis for subject matter jurisdiction exists. Chapter 13 considers remedies and jurisdictional issues in more detail.

---

4. Do you agree with the court's conclusion that the disputed terms were conditions rather than covenants? If a transaction subject to an open source license is viewed as a mere license, should that affect the analysis of whether the license terms impose conditions or covenants?

In *MDY Industries LLC v. Blizzard Entertainment, Inc.*, 629 F.3d 928 (9th Cir. 2010), the Ninth Circuit considered what the appropriate cause of action is when an end user violates a use restriction in a license agreement. Blizzard licensed the online game World of Warcraft (WoW) under terms that limited use in a number of ways, including by prohibiting users from combining WoW with third-party software and from using automated tools called "bots" to play the game. MDY marketed a product called Glider that allowed users to play early levels of the game by using a bot. The court held that the license limitations were covenants rather than conditions, stating:

> . . . [W]e have held that the potential for infringement exists only where the licensee's action (1) exceeds the license's scope (2) in a manner that implicates one of the licensor's exclusive statutory rights.
>
> Here, [the license] contains certain restrictions that are grounded in Blizzard's exclusive rights of copyright and other restrictions that are not. For instance, . . . §4(D) [of the license] forbids creation of derivative works based on WoW without Blizzard's consent. A player who violates this prohibition would exceed the scope of her license and violate one of Blizzard's exclusive rights under the Copyright Act. . . . The antibot provisions at issue in this case . . . [are] covenants rather than conditions. A Glider user violates the covenants with Blizzard, but does not thereby commit copyright infringement because Glider does not infringe any of Blizzard's exclusive rights. For instance, the use does not alter or copy WoW software.
>
> Were we to hold otherwise, Blizzard—or any software copyright holder—could designate any disfavored conduct during software use as copyright infringement, by purporting to condition the license on the player's abstention from the disfavored conduct. The rationale would be that because the conduct occurs while the player's computer is copying the software code into RAM in order for it to run, the violation is copyright infringement. This would allow software copyright owners far greater rights than Congress has generally conferred on copyright owners.

Id. at 940–41. Do you agree with this approach? Is it consistent with *Jacobsen*?

5. The court in *Jacobsen* seems to divide cases neatly into two categories— those involving conditions (governed by copyright law) and those involving covenants (governed by contract law). But the *Jacobsen* case involved breach of contract as well as copyright infringement, and a plaintiff often can assert both causes of action.

AFTERMATH

On remand, the district court addressed both the contract claim and the copyright infringement claim. The court dismissed the contract claim because Jacobsen failed to plead damages proximately caused by the breach and because it overlapped too greatly with the infringement claim and was therefore preempted. *Jacobsen v. Katzer*, 609 F. Supp. 2d 925 (N.D. Cal. 2009). We address preemption of breach of contract claims in Chapter 15.

Note on Creative Commons

Inspired in part by the success of the open source software movement, an organization called Creative Commons developed licensing tools with the similar aim of using "private rights to create public goods." *See* http://creativecommons.org/about/history. The Creative Commons licenses allow authors of all types of works to place notices on their works that declare, with reference to specific licenses made available by Creative Commons, what rights are reserved and what rights users may exercise. Specifically, there are three different attributes that a copyright owner can select, each with a corresponding symbol that can be placed on the work:

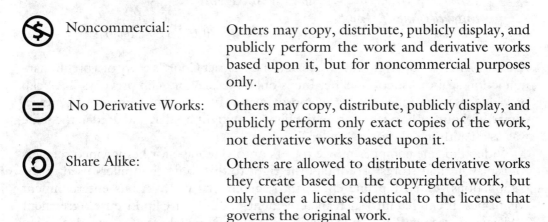

Noncommercial:	Others may copy, distribute, publicly display, and publicly perform the work and derivative works based upon it, but for noncommercial purposes only.
No Derivative Works:	Others may copy, distribute, publicly display, and publicly perform only exact copies of the work, not derivative works based upon it.
Share Alike:	Others are allowed to distribute derivative works they create based on the copyrighted work, but only under a license identical to the license that governs the original work.

A copyright owner can pick and choose among the different attributes, but cannot select both the Share Alike and No Derivative Works options. Moreover, in all Creative Commons licenses, the creator of the work must be given credit in any subsequent use of the work. The following symbol is used to notify users of the attribution requirement:

 When Creative Commons first began, its licenses allowed authors to select whether they desired attribution as a condition of granting the permissions in the license. It found that 98 percent of individuals selected the attribution requirement. Creative Commons now includes the attribution provision as a standard element of all the licenses it provides for copyright owners to employ. Many open source licenses employ a similar provision.

If you were an author, musician, or composer, would you distribute your works under a Creative Commons license? Since its inception in 2001, the Creative Commons movement has spread to many other countries. To search for works available on the Web under a Creative Commons license you can use the search engines linked by Creative Commons: http://search.creativecommons.org/.

D. MISUSE

The previous section raised questions about what terms a copyright owner can include in mass market licenses, and about how far those terms can reach. One potential limit on the contracting behavior of copyright owners is a doctrine known as copyright misuse.

Video Pipeline, Inc. v. Buena Vista Home Entertainment, Inc.,
342 F.3d 191, 203 (3d Cir. 2003), cert. denied, 540 U.S. 1178 (2004)

AMBRO, J.: In this copyright case we review the District Court's entry of a preliminary injunction against Video Pipeline, Inc.'s online display of "clip previews." A "clip preview," as we use the term, is an approximately two-minute segment of a movie, copied without authorization from the film's copyright holder, and used in the same way as an authorized movie "trailer.". . . .

Video Pipeline compiles movie trailers onto videotape for home video retailers to display in their stores. To obtain the right to distribute the trailers used in the compilations, Video Pipeline enters into agreements with various entertainment companies. It entered into such an agreement, the Master Clip License Agreement ("License Agreement"), with Disney in 1988, and Disney thereafter provided Video Pipeline with over 500 trailers for its movies.

In 1997, Video Pipeline took its business to the web, where it operates Video-Pipeline.net and VideoDetective.com. The company maintains a database accessible from VideoPipeline.net, which contains movie trailers Video Pipeline has received throughout the years. Video Pipeline's internet clients—retail websites selling home videos—use VideoPipeline.net to display trailers to site visitors. . . .

Video Pipeline included in its online database trailers it received under the License Agreement from Disney. Because the License Agreement did not permit this use, Disney requested that Video Pipeline remove the trailers from the database. It complied with that request.

On October 24, 2000, however, Video Pipeline filed a complaint in the District Court for the District of New Jersey seeking a declaratory judgment that its online use of the trailers did not violate federal copyright law. Disney shortly thereafter terminated the License Agreement.

Video Pipeline decided to replace some of the trailers it had removed at Disney's request from its database. In order to do so, it copied approximately two minutes from each of at least 62 Disney movies to create its own clip previews of the movies. . . .

[The District Court granted Disney's request for a preliminary injunction and Video Pipeline appealed. After rejecting Video Pipeline's fair use argument, the court turned to its next defense.]

Video Pipeline further contends that Disney has misused its copyright and, as a result, should not receive the protection of copyright law. Video Pipeline points to certain licensing agreements that Disney has entered into with three companies and sought to enter into with a number of other companies operating web sites. Each of these licensing agreements provides that Disney, the licensor, will deliver trailers by way of hyperlinks for display on the licensee's web site. The Agreements further state:

> The Website in which the Trailers are used may not be derogatory to or critical of the entertainment industry or of [Disney] (and its officers, directors, agents, employees, affiliates, divisions and subsidiaries) or of any motion picture produced or distributed by [Disney] . . . [or] of the materials from which the Trailers were taken or of any person involved with the production of the Underlying Works. Any breach of this paragraph will render this license null and void and Licensee will be liable to all parties concerned for defamation and copyright infringement, as well as breach of contract. . . .

As Video Pipeline sees it, such licensing agreements seek to use copyright law to suppress criticism and, in so doing, misuse those laws, triggering the copyright misuse doctrine. . . .

Neither the Supreme Court nor this Court has affirmatively recognized the copyright misuse doctrine. There is, however, a well-established patent misuse doctrine, *see, e.g., Morton Salt Co. v. G.S. Suppiger Co.,* 314 U.S. 488 (1942), and, as noted below, other courts of appeals have extended the doctrine to the copyright context.

The misuse doctrine extends from the equitable principle that courts "may appropriately withhold their aid where the plaintiff is using the right asserted contrary to the public interest." *Morton Salt,* 314 U.S. at 492. Misuse is not cause to invalidate the copyright or patent, but instead "precludes its enforcement during the period of misuse." *Practice Management Info. Corp. v. American Med. Assoc.,* 121 F.3d 516, 520 n.9 (9th Cir.1997) (citing *Lasercomb America, Inc. v.*

Reynolds, 911 F.2d 970, 979 n.22 (4th Cir.1990)). To defend on misuse grounds, the alleged infringer need not be subject to the purported misuse. *Morton Salt,* 314 U.S. at 494 ("It is the adverse effect upon the public interest of a successful infringement suit in conjunction with the patentee's course of conduct which disqualifies him to maintain the suit, regardless of whether the particular defendant has suffered from the misuse of the patent."); *Lasercomb,* 911 F.2d at 979 ("[T]he fact that appellants here were not parties to one of Lasercomb's standard license agreements is inapposite to their copyright misuse defense. The question is whether Lasercomb is using its copyright in a manner contrary to public policy, which question we have answered in the affirmative.").

Misuse often exists where the patent or copyright holder has engaged in some form of anti-competitive behavior. More on point, however, is the underlying policy rationale for the misuse doctrine set out in the Constitution's Copyright and Patent Clause: "to promote the Progress of Science and useful Arts." Const. Art. I, §8, cl. 8; *see also Morton Salt,* 314 U.S. at 494, ("The patentee, like these other holders of an exclusive privilege granted in furtherance of a public policy [trademark and copyright holders], may not claim protection of his grant by the courts where it is being used to subvert that policy."); *Lasercomb,* 911 F.2d at 978 ("The question is . . . whether the copyright is being used in a manner violative of the public policy embodied in the grant of a copyright."). The "ultimate aim" of copyright law is "to stimulate artistic creativity for the general public good." *Sony Corp.,* 464 U.S. at 432; *see also Eldred v. Ashcroft,* 537 U.S. 186 (2003) ("[C]opyright's purpose is to *promote* the creation and publication of free expression.") (emphasis in original). Put simply, our Constitution emphasizes the purpose and value of copyrights and patents. Harm caused by their misuse undermines their usefulness.

Anti-competitive licensing agreements may conflict with the purpose behind a copyright's protection by depriving the public of the would-be competitor's creativity. The fair use doctrine and the refusal to copyright facts and ideas also address applications of copyright protection that would otherwise conflict with a copyright's constitutional goal. But it is possible that a copyright holder could leverage its copyright to restrain the creative expression of another without engaging in anti-competitive behavior or implicating the fair use and idea/expression doctrines.[13]

For instance, the concurring opinion, written for a majority of the judges, in *Rosemont Enters., Inc. v. Random House, Inc.,* 366 F.2d 303 (2d Cir.1966),

---

13. *See* Note, *Clarifying the Copyright Misuse Defense: The Role of Antitrust Standards and First Amendment Values,* 104 Harv. L. Rev. 1289, 1304-06 (1991) (advocating application of the copyright misuse defense where "the plaintiff has improperly used its copyright power to restrain free trade in ideas," and explaining: "The copyright misuse defense provides a necessary complement to the idea/ expression dichotomy [under which an author's expression may be copyrighted, but an idea may not] and fair use doctrine in vindicating the public interest in the dissemination of ideas. The idea/expression limitation merely restricts the scope of the particular copyright being sued upon, and absent a claim of misuse, it cannot be brought to bear on improper licensing restrictions or other misconduct. As with the misuse defense, fair use doctrine excuses copying that would otherwise be infringement in order to vindicate the copyright policy promoting the diffusion of ideas. Unlike misuse doctrine, however, the fair use inquiry directs courts' attention to the social value of the defendant's conduct rather than the social harm caused by the plaintiff's use of its copyright.").

concluded that pursuant to the unclean hands doctrine the District Court should not have entered a preliminary injunction against an alleged copyright infringer where the copyright holder sought to use his copyright "to restrict the dissemination of information." *Id.* at 311 (Lumbard, C.J., concurring). In *Rosemont Enters.,* a corporation acting for the publicity-shy Howard Hughes purchased the copyright to an article about Hughes solely to bring an infringement suit to enjoin the publication of a forthcoming biography on Hughes. *Id.* at 313. The concurring opinion reasoned:

> The spirit of the First Amendment applies to the copyright laws at least to the extent that the courts should not tolerate any attempted interference with the public's right to be informed regarding matters of general interest when anyone seeks to use the copyright statute which was designed to protect interests of quite a different nature.

Id. at 311.

Although *Rosemont Enters.* did not concern an anti-competitive licensing agreement as in the typical misuse case, it focused—as do the misuse cases—on the copyright holder's attempt to disrupt a copyright's goal to increase the store of creative expression for the public good. 366 F.2d at 311. A copyright holder's attempt to restrict expression that is critical of it (or of its copyrighted good, or the industry in which it operates, *etc.*) may, in context, subvert—as do anti-competitive restrictions—a copyright's policy goal to encourage the creation and dissemination to the public of creative activity.

The licensing agreements in this case do seek to restrict expression by licensing the Disney trailers for use on the internet only so long as the web sites on which the trailers will appear do not derogate Disney, the entertainment industry, *etc.* But we nonetheless cannot conclude on this record that the agreements are likely to interfere with creative expression to such a degree that they affect in any significant way the policy interest in increasing the public store of creative activity. The licensing agreements do not, for instance, interfere with the licensee's opportunity to express such criticism on other web sites or elsewhere. There is no evidence that the public will find it any more difficult to obtain criticism of Disney and its interests, or even that the public is considerably less likely to come across this criticism, if it is not displayed on the same site as the trailers. Moreover, if a critic wishes to comment on Disney's works, the fair use doctrine may be implicated regardless of the existence of the licensing agreements. Finally, copyright law, and the misuse doctrine in particular, should not be interpreted to require Disney, if it licenses its trailers for display on any web sites but its own, to do so willy-nilly regardless of the content displayed with its copyrighted works. Indeed such an application of the misuse doctrine would likely decrease the public's access to Disney's works because it might as a result refuse to license at all online display of its works.

Thus, while we extend the patent misuse doctrine to copyright, and recognize that it might operate beyond its traditional anti-competition context, we hold it inapplicable here. On this record Disney's licensing agreements do not interfere significantly with copyright policy (while holding to the contrary might, in fact, do so). The District Court therefore correctly held that Video Pipeline will not likely succeed on its copyright misuse defense. . . .

In re Napster, Inc. Copyright Litigation
191 F. Supp. 2d 1087 (N.D. Cal. 2002)

[Reread the description of the *Napster* system and litigation, *supra* Chapter 9.D.1. This part of the litigation addresses Napster's claim that the record labels' licensing practices constituted misuse, and thus that the court should deny the labels relief until they purged themselves of the misuse.]

PATEL, C.J.: . . . The court is also asked to permit discovery to determine whether plaintiffs have misused their copyrights by attempting to control the market for the digital distribution of music. Having considered the arguments presented, and for the reasons set forth below, the court rules as follows. . . .

B. Plaintiffs' Entry into the Digital Distribution Market

. . . In mid-2001, plaintiffs announced the formation of two joint ventures, MusicNet and press*play*. The aim of these joint ventures is to provide platforms for the digital distribution of music. MusicNet is a joint venture between three of the five record company plaintiffs—EMI, BMG, and Warner. MusicNet is also owned in part by RealNetworks (and possibly another entity). Press*play* is a venture between the other two plaintiffs—Sony and Universal.

In June 2001, Napster signed a licensing agreement with MusicNet, allowing Napster access to all of the copyrighted works licensed to MusicNet. Prior to signing the MusicNet agreement, Napster was unable to obtain individual licenses from any of the recording company plaintiffs. The MusicNet agreement explicitly limits Napster's ability to obtain individual licenses from any of the five plaintiffs, including the non-MusicNet plaintiffs—Sony and Universal—until March 2002. The agreement also allows MusicNet to terminate the agreement within ninety days, even after March 2002, if Napster licenses content from any of the five recording companies other than through MusicNet. Additionally, the agreement mandates a separate pricing structure for any content that Napster licenses from anyone other than MusicNet. Napster has only provided the court with the MusicNet agreement and the court has no other information as to how MusicNet operates or exactly what content it will offer and to whom. . . .

II. Copyright Misuse

Napster argues that the court should deny summary judgment or stay the matter to allow for further discovery because plaintiffs are engaged in copyright misuse. . . . This court and the Ninth Circuit dismissed Napster's misuse defense at the preliminary injunction stage, noting that copyright misuse is rarely a defense to injunctive relief and that there was not enough evidence at that stage to support a finding of misuse. Since those rulings, the factual and procedural landscape has changed significantly. The motion now before the court is for summary judgment, not preliminary injunctive relief. Additionally, the prior inapplicability of copyright misuse rested on the fact that none of the plaintiffs had granted licenses to Napster, let alone impermissibly restrictive ones. The evidence now shows that plaintiffs have licensed their catalogs of works for digital distribution in what could be an over-reaching manner. . . .

A. The Development of the Copyright Misuse Defense

. . . . Recently, courts have displayed a greater willingness to find copyright misuse, employing two different, though interrelated approaches. The first approach requires a finding that plaintiff engaged in antitrust violations before the court will apply the doctrine of copyright misuse. *See, e.g., Saturday Evening Post v. Rumbleseat Press, Inc.,* 816 F.2d 1191, 1200 (7th Cir. 1987).[10] The second approach, adopted by the Ninth Circuit, focuses on public policy and has been applied to a greater range of conduct than the antitrust approach. *See Practice Mgmt. Info. Corp. v. American Med. Assoc.,* 121 F.3d 516 (9th Cir. 1997). Under the "public policy" approach, copyright misuse exists when plaintiff expands the statutory copyright monopoly in order to gain control over areas outside the scope of the monopoly. The test is whether plaintiff's use of his or her copyright violates the public policy embodied in the grant of a copyright, not whether the use is anti-competitive. However, as a practical matter, this test is often difficult to apply and inevitably requires courts to rely on antitrust principles or language to some degree.

The scope of the defense of copyright misuse has not been significantly tested in the Ninth Circuit. . . . As a result, the doctrine of copyright misuse remains largely undeveloped, with little case law to aid this court in its inquiry.

1. Lasercomb America, Inc. v. Reynolds

The Fourth Circuit was the first to explicitly recognize a copyright misuse defense, *Lasercomb America, Inc. v. Reynolds,* 911 F.2d 970 (4th Cir. 1990). . . . Lasercomb's [software license] agreement forbade a licensee from developing any kind of computer assisted die-making software. The court held that Lasercomb's licensing agreement attempted to control any expression by [defendant] of the underlying idea embodied in Lasercomb's software. Because the idea was outside the scope of the copyright monopoly, the court found that Lasercomb's licensing agreement constituted copyright misuse. . . .

2. Practice Management

In 1997, the Ninth Circuit followed the reasoning of the Fourth Circuit and explicitly adopted a defense of copyright misuse. *Practice Mgmt. Info. Corp. v. American Med. Assoc.,* 121 F.3d 516 (9th Cir. 1997). The American Medical Association ("AMA") licensed a copyrighted coding system to the Health Care Financing Administration ("HCFA"). The agreement granted HCFA a royalty-free, non-

---

10. This approach labels certain activities as *per se* copyright misuse and uses a rule of reason approach for others. For those activities that fall within the rule of reason test, the court first asks whether the restraint is within the scope of the copyright monopoly. If it is, then the conduct is *per se* legal. If not, the court then asks whether the activity as a whole promotes or restricts competition. If the particular activity (e.g., licensing provision) restricts competition, then it is copyright misuse.

exclusive license to use the AMA's coding system. In return, HCFA promised not to use any other coding system and also promised to use its powers as a regulatory agency to require use of the AMA's system in programs administered by its agents.

A separate dispute arose between Practice Management, the largest reseller of books of the AMA's coding system, and the AMA. Practice Management argued in its action for declaratory relief that the AMA was misusing its copyrights because the licensing agreement between HCFA and the AMA was unduly restrictive. The Ninth Circuit looked closely at the licensing agreement and sided with Practice Management. In particular, the court held that the requirement that HCFA not use competing coding systems represented an expansion of the monopoly power of the AMA's copyright. The court labeled this exclusivity clause the "controlling fact." *Id.* [at 521] (copyright misuse is implicated by "the limitation imposed by the AMA licensing agreement on HCFA's rights to decide whether or not to use other forms as well").

The court did not investigate the extent of the AMA's market power or the actual effects on competition as it would have done in an antitrust analysis. Instead, considering only the text of the agreement, the court merely noted the "apparent" adverse effects of the licensing agreement which "gave the AMA a substantial and unfair advantage over its competitors." *Id.* The court reasoned that this use of a copyright to gain competitive advantage violates the public policy embodied in the grant of a copyright.

3. The Current State of Copyright Misuse

Lasercomb and *Practice Management*, along with other "public policy" cases, hold that copyright misuse exists when plaintiffs commit antitrust violations or enter unduly restrictive copyright licensing agreements. . . . However, no courts [sic] has thus far articulated the boundaries of "unduly restrictive licensing" or when licensing or other conduct would violate the amorphous concept of public policy.

Additional confusion arises because while courts have repeatedly stated that misuse is different from antitrust, they still rely on antitrust-like inquiries in determining what licensing agreements violate public policy. Of the cases reviewed by the court, all mimic the *per se* rules of antitrust in holding that the relevant licensing agreements constitute copyright misuse because they are unduly restrictive on their face. *See, e.g., Practice Mgmt.*, 121 F.3d at 521. No court has yet found it necessary to investigate the effects of a licensing provisions [sic] by adopting an analysis similar to the antitrust rule-of-reason approach but focusing instead on public policy. As a result, the "public policy" misuse case law only helps to identify the egregious cases of misuse—when it is obvious that the particular licensing provision is overreaching. Currently, there is no guidance as to how to approach the more sophisticated cases where the text of the licensing provision itself is not dispositive.

Fortunately, this court need not answer these questions today. Instead, the court focuses on these issues to guide the parties in the evidentiary development of the scope of plaintiffs' alleged misuse.

B. Napster's Allegations of Misuse

Napster alleges two bases for misuse. First, Napster contends that the licensing clauses in Napster's agreement with plaintiffs' joint venture, MusicNet, are unduly restrictive. In the alternative, Napster argues that even if that particular agreement is not unduly restrictive, plaintiffs' practices as they enter the market for the digital distribution of music are so anti-competitive as to give rise to a misuse defense.

1. The MusicNet Agreement

Napster contends that licensing requirements of plaintiffs' online venture, MusicNet, are unduly restrictive. MusicNet is a joint venture between three of the five record company plaintiffs (EMI, BMG, and Warner) to distribute digital music. This joint venture anticipates obtaining licenses from the other two major labels (Sony and Universal) to distribute their catalogs of copyrighted music. While Napster was unable to secure licenses from any of the individual plaintiffs, Napster reached an agreement with MusicNet that allows Napster to distribute the music from the catalogs of the three participating MusicNet plaintiffs and any other label that licenses its catalog to MusicNet.

Section 19.1 of the MusicNet agreement prevents Napster from entering into any licensing agreement with any individual plaintiffs until March 1, 2002. . . . The agreement also provides that even after March 2002 if Napster enters into any individual license with any of the major labels—i.e., the plaintiffs—including the MusicNet plaintiffs, MusicNet may terminate the agreement with ninety-day notice. Additionally, section 6.3(a) lays out a pricing structure under which Napster will be charged higher fees if it fails to use MusicNet as its exclusive licensor for content.

It is unclear from the text of the agreement if the exclusivity provision operates to impermissibly extend plaintiffs' control beyond the scope of their copyright monopoly. In other misuse cases, the offending provision was exclusive and the "adverse effects of the licensing agreement [were] apparent." *Practice Mgmt.*, 121 F.3d at 521 (provision prevented defendant from using any competitor's coding system); *Lasercomb*, 911 F.2d at 978 (defendant prohibited from producing any die-making software); *Alcatel* [*USA, Inc. v. DGI Technologies, Inc.*], 166 F.3d [772,] 793-4 [(5th Cir. 1999)] (software licensing provision effectively gave plaintiff control over uncopyrighted microprocessor cards). In contrast, the MusicNet provision is non-exclusive. Napster may obtain licenses from any of the record label plaintiffs, but may only do it through its agreement with MusicNet. Despite this theoretical non-exclusivity, the provision effectively grants MusicNet control over which content Napster licenses. Napster's use of other music catalogs is predicated on MusicNet's securing an individual license to those catalogs. For example, under the MusicNet agreement, Napster no longer has the ability to obtain an individual license from Sony (a non-MusicNet plaintiff). Instead, Napster must rely on MusicNet to obtain a license to Sony's catalog. And, if MusicNet chooses not to obtain such a license, Napster is effectively prevented from using Sony's catalog. The result is an expansion of the powers of the three MusicNet plaintiffs' copyrights to cover the catalogs of the two non-MusicNet plaintiffs.

The MusicNet plaintiffs argue that this restriction is unimportant because they fully expect to obtain licenses from the other two majors [sic] recording companies. That the restriction only applies until MusicNet obtains licenses from Sony and Universal (non-MusicNet plaintiffs) or until March 2002 is irrelevant. *See Practice Mgmt.*, 121 F.3d 516, 521 ("The controlling fact is that HCFA is prohibited from using any other coding system by virtue of the binding commitment . . . to use the AMA's copyrighted material exclusively."). The critical issue is that the agreement binds Napster to obtain licenses from MusicNet and not its competitors. Napster was caught in a position where its only options were to sign the agreement to gain access to the catalogs of the major record companies and thereby incur these restrictions in all their murkiness or to refuse to sign the agreement and have virtually no access to most commercially available music.

Though the agreement is troubling on its face, too many questions remain unanswered for the court to effectively rule on the issue. It is unclear to what extent it is appropriate to impute the actions of MusicNet to plaintiffs as MusicNet is a joint venture and technically remains a separate entity from plaintiffs. However, plaintiffs cannot hide behind the shell of a joint venture to protect themselves from misuse claims. The court views with great suspicion plaintiffs' claims of ignorance as to MusicNet's activities. Surely the three parties to MusicNet discussed their joint venture before embarking on it. MusicNet did not suddenly appear full blown from the head of a fictitious entity. The evidence suggests that plaintiffs formed a joint venture to distribute digital music and simultaneously refused to enter into individual licenses with competitors, effectively requiring competitors to use MusicNet as their source for digital licensing. If this proves to be the case, the propriety of treating MusicNet as a separate entity is in question.

A few of plaintiffs' arguments can be disposed of summarily. First, plaintiffs argue that Napster, as a party to the MusicNet agreement, cannot now challenge an agreement that it negotiated and subsequently signed. *Practice Management* explicitly holds that it is irrelevant who includes an exclusivity provision in an agreement. That Napster is both the party alleging misuse and a party to the offending agreement does not affect the court's analysis.[16]

Second, plaintiffs contend that because MusicNet is not yet in operation, there is no ongoing misuse. This argument fails. The issue is not whether MusicNet is yet in operation, but whether the exclusivity provision in the agreement is active. Because Napster is already bound by the agreement, the restriction on Napster's ability to negotiate for licenses with individual plaintiffs is *currently* restricted.

Third, plaintiffs contend that even if they are engaged in misuse, be it through restrictive licensing or antitrust violations, they should still be able to recover for infringement that occurred prior to the MusicNet agreement. Plaintiffs

---

16. Plaintiffs' argument would have merit if there was any evidence that Napster introduced and negotiated for the exclusivity provision. In that scenario, it would be unseemly to allow Napster to use the same provision as protection against infringement actions. Such a rule would create perverse incentives to artificially manufacture overreaching clauses as liability shields under the misuse doctrine. However, the evidence thus far shows that the relevant provisions were inserted at MusicNet's urging and not as an end-run around copyright laws by Napster.

misunderstand the misuse doctrine. Misuse limits enforcement of rights, not remedies. If plaintiffs are engaged in misuse, they cannot bring suit based on their rights until the misuse ends. The doctrine does not prevent plaintiffs from ultimately recovering for acts of infringement that occur during the period of misuse. The issue focuses on when plaintiffs can bring or pursue an action for infringement, not for which acts of infringement they can recover.

2. Antitrust Violations as Copyright Misuse . . .

Antitrust violations can give rise to copyright misuse if those violations offend the public policy behind the copyright grant. *See Lasercomb*, 911 F.2d at 977 ("[A]ntitrust law is the statutory embodiment of that public policy."). However, generalized antitrust violations will not suffice. Napster must establish a "nexus between . . . alleged anti-competitive actions and [plaintiffs'] power over copyrighted material." *Orth-O-Vision, Inc. v. Home Box Office*, 474 F. Supp. 672, 686 (S.D.N.Y. 1979).

Napster's arguments are based primarily on the declaration of Roger Noll, a Stanford professor who specializes in antitrust economics and the recording industry. Based on Dr. Noll's review of the MusicNet agreement and facts in the public record, Napster alleges that there are a host of anti-competitive behaviors by the plaintiffs that violate antitrust laws. Dr. Noll concludes that plaintiffs' joint ventures, MusicNet and press*play*, have anti-competitive features and facilitate collusive activity between plaintiffs. Dr. Noll further asserts that plaintiffs engage in vertical foreclosure of the digital distribution market through retail price squeezes, raising costs through licensing provisions, refusals to deal, and exclusive dealing. Dr. Noll also discusses myriad other behaviors that Napster alleges provide a sufficient nexus to the copyright monopoly to invoke the doctrine of copyright misuse.

For example, Dr. Noll alleges that plaintiffs' joint ventures, MusicNet (Warner, EMI and BMG) and press*play* (Sony and Universal), allow plaintiffs to engage in retail price-coordination. Plaintiffs hotly dispute this allegation and noted at oral argument that both MusicNet and press*play* were designed with numerous protections (none of which are in the record) to avoid implicating antitrust concerns. The current record on the licensing practices of these joint ventures and their operations is negligible. However, even a naif must realize that in forming and operating a joint venture, plaintiffs' representatives must necessarily meet and discuss pricing and licensing, raising the specter of possible antitrust violations. These joint ventures bear the indicia of entities designed to allow plaintiffs to use their copyrights and extensive market-power to dominate the market for digital music distribution. Even on the undeveloped record before the court, these joint ventures look bad, sound bad and smell bad.

Of course, plaintiffs object strenuously to the Noll Declaration and have filed a lengthy separate evidentiary objection accusing Dr. Noll of everything from speculation to mistake to deliberate misrepresentation. Plaintiffs argue that much of Dr. Noll's declaration refers to activities that have no relationship to plaintiffs' ownership of copyrights. For example, plaintiffs contend that it should not matter for the purposes of copyright misuse if plaintiffs engage in price fixing because the behavior is unrelated to the manner in which plaintiffs use their copyright monopoly. *See Orth-O-Vision*, 474 F. Supp. at 686. However, there can be no doubt that price-fixing carries antitrust and public policy considerations that may be relevant to misuse. While further evidentiary development may sustain plaintiffs' argument, on the current record defendants have demonstrated a sufficient nexus to allow for further discovery. . . .

NOTES AND QUESTIONS

1. In *Video Pipeline*, the court noted that if Disney were required to license its trailers "willy-nilly regardless of the content displayed with its copyrighted works," public access to Disney works likely would decrease because Disney might "refuse to license at all online display of its works." Given the court's stated concern about allowing a copyright owner to restrict criticism, what kinds of licensing behavior should tip the balance in favor of finding misuse? Are there other ways for Disney to control the context in which its trailers are made available without openly restricting licensees from engaging in critical speech?

2. The *Napster* court ruled that despite Napster's own "unclean hands," it could still raise the equitable defense of misuse against the plaintiffs. Do you agree with that ruling? What public policy interests are furthered by allowing an infringing party to raise an equitable defense? If both parties have engaged in behavior that constitutes an abuse of the copyright interest, what should be the appropriate outcome or remedy?

3. As both *Video Pipeline* and *Napster* indicate, some courts may be willing to find copyright misuse in the absence of an antitrust violation. Other courts, however, are not. *See, e.g., Antioch Co. v. Scrapbook Borders, Inc.*, 291 F. Supp. 2d 980 (D. Minn. 2003). Which approach makes more sense? *See* Brett Frischmann & Dan Moylan, *The Evolving Common Law Doctrine of Copyright Misuse: A Unified Theory and Its Application to Software*, 15 Berkeley Tech. L.J. 865 (2000) (arguing that the misuse doctrine serves a valuable gap-filling function). What areas do you think constitute the "areas outside the scope of the [copyright] monopoly" that the *Napster* court identifies as a key element in determining misuse under the public policy approach?

In *Omega S.A. v. Costco Wholesale Corp.*, 541 F.3d 982 (9th Cir. 2008), *aff'd by an equally divided court*, 562 U.S. 40 (2010), Omega sold its watches, which have a tiny copyrighted "Omega Globe" design engraved on the underside, to authorized dealers overseas. When some of those watches made their way to Costco in the United States, Omega sued for violation of its distribution right. The Ninth Circuit rejected Costco's first sale defense. On remand, the district court held that Omega had misused its copyright: "Omega used the defensive shield of copyright law as an offensive sword . . . and misused its copyright . . . by leveraging its limited monopoly in being able to control the importation of that design to control the importation of its . . . watches." *Omega S.A. v. Costco Wholesale Corp.*, 2011 WL 8492716 *1-2 (C.D. Cal. 2011), *aff'd on other grounds*, ___ F.3d ___, 2015 WL 235479 (9th Cir. Jan. 20, 2015). Omega argued that the copyrighted design had other purposes besides controlling importation of the watches, including "promot[ing] the creativity and aesthetics of the [design] and [increasing] the value that the design gives to a watch." *Id.* at *2. The court rejected that argument, reasoning that "[w]hile the [design] might have its own independent creative and aesthetic values, those aspects of the design are protected by its copyright and are not a defense to copyright misuse." *Id.* Do you agree with that reasoning?

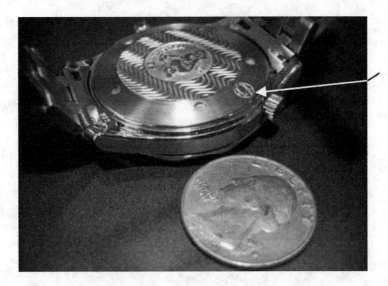

Omega Globe

4. Note that copyright misuse is not a recognized defense to a breach of contract claim, but only to a copyright infringement claim. There is no consensus on whether copyright misuse can be brought as an independent claim (distinct from an affirmative defense) and district courts come down on both sides of the issue. *See Amaretto Ranch Breedables, LLC v. Ozimals, Inc.*, 790 F. Supp. 2d 1024 (N.D. Cal. 2011) (collecting cases). Should copyright misuse be an affirmative claim? What would be an appropriate remedy if misuse were found?

5. Under the traditional misuse doctrine as defined in patent cases, the party engaging in misuse may not enforce the patent until it purges itself of the misuse. Do you agree with that rule or do you think it is too harsh? Note the *Napster* court's suggestion that after misuse is purged, the copyright owner may be able to reach back to collect damages for infringements that occurred during the period of misuse.

Under the TRIPS Agreement an abuse of intellectual property rights is considered sufficient justification for a country to grant a compulsory license. TRIPS Art. 31(k). That license may remain in place until the anticompetitive behavior is purged. *Id.*

13 Copyright Litigation

Like other kinds of litigation, copyright infringement lawsuits raise many procedural issues. Before a lawsuit is even filed, lawyers must consider the strategy to be employed. In addition to the substantive viability of the lawsuit, they must evaluate a variety of other issues ranging from timing and forum selection to likely recovery. These issues also can significantly affect the possibility of settlement. This chapter examines a number of litigation-related issues specific to copyright law. It also explores the remedies available in civil litigation and the scope of criminal infringement liability.

A. PROPER COURT

As provided in 28 U.S.C. §1338, the federal courts have exclusive subject matter jurisdiction over copyright infringement actions:

> (a) The district courts shall have original jurisdiction of any civil action arising under any Act of Congress relating to . . . copyrights. . . . Such jurisdiction shall be exclusive of the courts of the states in . . . copyright cases.

Thus, when copyright infringement is alleged, the proper court in which to sue will be a federal district court. In the vast majority of cases the question whether the asserted cause of action arises under copyright law will be clear and undisputed. Sometimes, however, the interplay between copyright and state law claims makes subject matter jurisdiction more difficult to determine. For example, as the case that follows illustrates, is the action one for breach of contract, arising under state law, or rather one for copyright infringement?

Bassett v. Mashantucket Pequot Tribe
204 F.3d 343 (2d Cir. 2000)

LEVAL, J.: . . . According to the allegations of the complaint: Plaintiff Debra Bassett operates a business, Bassett Productions, that produces films and television programs. Defendant Mashantucket Pequot Tribe is a federally recognized Indian tribe with a reservation located within the geographical boundaries of the State of Connecticut. Defendant Mashantucket Pequot Museum is a Connecticut corporation located on the Pequot Reservation.

In October 1994, Bassett met with representatives of the Tribe to discuss the possibility of producing a film for the Museum about the Pequot War of 1636-38. . . .

In August 1995, Bassett Productions entered into a letter agreement with the Tribe (the "Letter Agreement") for the development and production of a film about the 1636-38 Pequot War. The Letter Agreement identified Bassett Productions as the "Producer" and the Tribe as the "Owner," but did not define these terms. It stipulated that Bassett Productions would "hire and supervise the development and writing of a screenplay by Keith Merrill and George Burdeau," and that the Tribe would "compensate" Bassett Productions for development costs according to an agreed schedule. It also stipulated that "at such time" that the Tribe approved the final draft of the screenplay, Bassett Productions would have exclusive rights to produce the film for exhibition at the Pequot Museum.

Some time before October 30, 1995, Bassett had delivered to the Tribe a script that she herself had written, based on a "script scenario" she had developed with assistance from her associate Allan Eckert. . . .

On October 30, 1995, Bassett received a notice from the Tribe terminating the Letter Agreement. The notice asserted that Bassett had not "perform[ed] the contract as the parties anticipated."

Following the termination of the Letter Agreement, the Tribe continued to pursue the development and production of a film on the 1636-38 Pequot War for exhibition at the Museum. In October 1996, filming was completed on a motion picture entitled, "The Witness." Bassett asserts the Tribe intends to screen the film at the Museum "in the near future" as part of "an interstate-driven tourist attraction." . . .

In September 1996, Bassett commenced this lawsuit in the United States District Court for the District of Connecticut. The complaint sought an injunction as well as other copyright remedies on the ground that the Tribe and the Museum used Bassett's copyrighted script without her consent or license in order to produce their own film; it further alleged that they breached the Letter Agreement, and that they committed various state-law torts resulting in injury to Bassett. . . .

In March 1997, Defendants moved to dismiss Bassett's complaint for lack of subject matter jurisdiction and for failure to exhaust tribal remedies. In their motion papers, Defendants argued (*inter alia*) that the court lacked federal question jurisdiction because Bassett's sole federal claim—her claim for copyright infringement—was "incidental to" her contract claims, and therefore did not "arise under" federal law.

The district court granted Defendants' motion to dismiss the complaint, and Bassett appealed.

Discussion . . .

Prior to our landmark decision in *T.B. Harms* [*Co. v. Eliscu*, 339 F.2d 823 (2d Cir. 1964)], several district courts in the Second Circuit resolved the issue of jurisdiction under Section 1338 for "hybrid" claims raising both copyright and contract issues by attempting to discern whether the copyright issues constituted the "essence" of the dispute, or whether instead the copyright issues were "incidental to" the contract dispute. . . .

That approach, however, left a class of plaintiffs who suffered copyright infringement bereft of copyright remedies. Plaintiffs whose federal lawsuits were dismissed for lack of subject matter jurisdiction on the ground that their copyright claims were "incidental to" their contract claims had no way either to obtain an adjudication of infringement or to obtain relief provided by the Copyright Act, because the Act confers exclusive jurisdiction over copyright claims on federal courts. . . . That approach had the added defect of requiring a court to make findings at the outset of the litigation that could not be discerned from the complaint but instead required a deep understanding of the dispute not usually gained until the case had been heard at trial.

In *T.B. Harms*, Judge Friendly . . . established a test for this circuit that focused on whether and how a complaint implicates the Copyright Act. . . . At issue [in *T.B. Harms*] was whether one of the defendants had previously assigned his interest in the copyrights to the plaintiff's agent, or whether this defendant had retained his interest and had validly assigned it at a later date to a second defendant. No claim of infringement was asserted and no relief provided by the Copyright Act was sought. . . .

Synthesizing the Supreme Court authorities, Judge Friendly concluded that a suit "arises under" the Copyright Act if:

(1) "[T]he complaint is for a remedy expressly granted by the Act, e.g., a suit for infringement or for the statutory royalties for record reproduction . . ."; or,

(2) "[T]he complaint . . . asserts a claim requiring construction of the Act. . . ."

Id. at 828.[3] As the suit in *T.B. Harms* did not fall within any of these enumerated categories, the court found that it did not "arise under" the copyright laws for purposes of Section 1338 and that jurisdiction was therefore lacking. . . .

Nearly thirty years after the *T.B. Harms* decision, a panel of this court in *Schoenberg* [*v. Shapolsky Publishers, Inc.*, 971 F.2d 926 (2d Cir. 1992)] undertook in dictum to state the test for determining the existence of Section 1338 jurisdiction in cases alleging violations of the Copyright Act resulting from breach of contract.

3. . . . Judge Friendly speculated that jurisdiction might also exist, "perhaps more doubtfully," in a third category of cases "where a distinctive policy of the Act requires that federal principles control the disposition of the claim." *T.B. Harms*, 339 F.2d at 828.

The plaintiff, an author, alleged that he had licensed the defendant, a publisher, to publish plaintiff's work. The license obligated the defendant to publish within six months of plaintiff's delivery of the manuscript, to promote and market the work, and to license foreign language editions. According to plaintiff's allegations, the publisher breached numerous obligations of the license. As a result of these failures, plaintiff claimed that the license was terminated and that defendant's further publication of the work constituted an infringement. Although the appeal related to a different issue, the opinion undertook to state "the appropriate test under the *T.B. Harms* paradigm. . . ." *Schoenberg*, 971 F.2d at 932.

The opinion . . . observed . . . that notwithstanding the *T.B. Harms* formulation, some district courts had "looked beyond the complaint in order to determine whether the plaintiff was really concerned with the infringement of his copyright, or, alternatively, was, in fact, more interested in" free enjoyment of his property or other non-copyright issues. *Id.* at 932. Other courts, it noted, had adopted the even "broader proposition that no claim arises under the Copyright Act whenever an infringement would necessarily result from the breach of a contract that licensed or assigned a copyright." *Id.* at 931.

In undertaking to reconcile the varying approaches of those district court opinions (and perhaps concluding that the authority of *T.B. Harms* extended only to disputes over copyright ownership and not to hybrid copyright/contract claims), *Schoenberg* created a new, complex three-step test; the first step of the test was precisely that which *T.B. Harms* had rejected—whether the claim for copyright remedies is "'merely incidental'" to a determination of contract rights. The opinion declared that in hybrid copyright and contract cases Section 1338 jurisdiction should be analyzed in the following manner:

> A district court must first ascertain whether the plaintiff's infringement claim is only "incidental" to the plaintiff's claim seeking a determination of ownership or contractual rights under the copyright. . . . If it is determined that the claim is not merely incidental, then a district court must next determine whether the complaint alleges a breach of a condition to, or a covenant of, the contract licensing or assigning the copyright. . . . [I]f a breach of a condition is alleged, then the district court has subject matter jurisdiction. . . . But if the complaint merely alleges a breach of a contractual covenant in the agreement that licenses or assigns the copyright, then the court must undertake a third step and analyze whether the breach is so material as to create a right of rescission in the grantor. If the breach would create a right of rescission, then the asserted claim arises under the Copyright Act.

Id. at 932-33 (citations omitted).

We believe for a number of reasons that the *Schoenberg* test is unworkable. At the outset, it overlooks that, because the Copyright Act gives federal courts *exclusive* jurisdiction to enforce its provisions, *see* 28 U.S.C. §1338, a plaintiff who is denied access to a federal forum on the theory that his copyright claims are incidental to a contract dispute is thereby absolutely denied the benefit of copyright remedies. Such a denial of copyright remedies undermines the Act's capacity to protect copyright interests. A plaintiff with meritorious copyright claims and entitlement to the special remedies provided by the Act is deprived of these remedies merely because the first hurdle of proving entitlement is a show-ing of a contractual right.[9]

A second problem with the *Schoenberg* test is that it is vague. *Schoenberg* char-acterizes the first part of its test in two ways: whether "the 'essence' of the plaintiff's claim" is in contract or copyright, or whether the "infringement claim is only 'inci-dental' to the plaintiff's claim seeking determination of ownership or contractual rights under the copyright." The meaning of either of these phrases is difficult to discern. . . .

[E]ven if the complaint sets forth in full the allegations relating to the license, and the defendant promptly moves to dismiss, the *Schoenberg* test requires the court to make complex factual determinations relating to the merits at the outset of the litigation—before the court has any familiarity with the case. Ascertaining what are a plaintiff's principal motives in bringing suit, and what issues will loom largest in the case, may well require extensive hearings and fact finding. The need for such fact finding recurs at each stage of *Schoenberg's* three-step formula. Thus, if a court finds that a copyright claim is not "merely incidental to" a contract claim (step one), it must still determine whether the contractual term alleged to have been breached was in the nature of a covenant or a condition (step two). And if it finds that the alleged breach was of a covenant, the court must next determine "whether the breach is so material as to create a right of rescission," 971 F.2d at 933, failing which the case must be dismissed (step three). This third inquiry in particular, which entails an assessment of the importance of the particular covenant, as well as the seriousness of the breach, raises questions that are not appropriately, easily or reliably answered at the start of litigation.

Finally, *Schoenberg* failed to recognize that in deviating from the test explained in *T.B. Harms*, it was failing to follow the governing Supreme Court authority on which *T.B. Harms* relied. *Schoenberg's* reliance on whether the disputed issues focus on matters of contract ownership rather than copyright cannot be reconciled with Justice Holmes' formulation in *American Well Works* that a "suit arises under the law that creates the cause of action." 241 U.S. at 260. The test, furthermore, is at odds with the well-established approach to federal question jurisdiction, pursuant to

---

9. Ironically, under the *Schoenberg* test, the more clear it is that plaintiff is entitled to copyright remedies (assuming plaintiff prevails on the disputed contract issues), the less likely it is that plaintiff will be accorded those remedies. This can be seen by considering two hypothetical cases, identical in that each defendant claims entitlement to exploit the copyright under a license, and each plaintiff claims the defendant forfeited the license by breaching the contract terms. In the first case, the defendant has no defense other than its contractual right; it concedes that, if plaintiff prevails on the contract issue, plaintiff is entitled to the copyright remedies sought in the complaint. In the second case, the defendant asserts, in addition to its contract defense, (a) that the work is not original as required by the Copyright Act; (b) that the author's assignment to plaintiff was void for failure to conform to the requirements of the Copyright Act; (c) that Defendant's work is not "substantially similar" to plaintiff's work; and (d) that defendant's work should be considered "fair use."

In the first case, because the only disputed issue is contractual, the court might conclude that the copyright claims are merely "incidental" and dismiss the case. In the second case, because issues of copyright law are in dispute, the court will not dismiss. Thus, the greater the likelihood that plaintiff will be found entitled to the copyright remedies sought in the complaint, the less likely it is that he will receive them.

which jurisdiction is determined by ascertaining whether the plaintiff's complaint asserts a right under federal law. *See, e.g., The Fair v. Kohler Die & Specialty Co.*, 228 U.S. 22, 25 (1913) (Holmes, J.) ("[T]he party who brings a suit is master to decide what law he will rely upon, and therefore does determine whether he will bring a 'suit arising under' the patent or other law of the United States by his declaration or bill.").

For the reasons discussed above, we conclude that, for claims of infringement arising from, or in the context of, an alleged contractual breach, this circuit's standard for determining jurisdiction under Section 1338 is furnished by *T.B. Harms*, and not by *Schoenberg*. When a complaint alleges a claim or seeks a remedy provided by the Copyright Act, federal jurisdiction is properly invoked.

Applying the *T.B. Harms* standard to this case leads us to conclude that Bassett's copyright claims "arise under" the Copyright Act for purposes of Section 1338. Unlike the complaint in *T.B. Harms*, the complaint in this case alleges that the defendants, without authority, used plaintiff's copyrighted script to produce a new film intended and advertised for imminent exhibition. The amended complaint alleged copyright infringement and sought "a remedy expressly granted by the Act," *T.B. Harms*, 339 F.2d at 828, specifically, an injunction against further infringement of Bassett's copyrighted script. Because the complaint alleges the defendants violated the Copyright Act and seeks the injunctive remedy provided by the Act, under the rule of *T.B. Harms*, the action falls within the jurisdictional grant of Section 1338. The district court's contrary holding was in error.[14] . . .

NOTES AND QUESTIONS

1. Compare the *T.B. Harms/Bassett* test with the *Schoenberg* test. Is the *Schoenberg* test really as unworkable as the Second Circuit suggests? Or is the real concern that as a result of denying federal court access to plaintiffs whose copyright claims are judged "incidental" to contract claims, state courts may end up indirectly influencing copyright policy in their treatment of the contract claims? Would that necessarily be a bad result? Is the import of §1338 that the integrity of federal power over copyright matters must not in any way be compromised?

14. Indeed this case serves as an excellent example of the shortcomings of the *Schoenberg* test. Plaintiff alleges entitlement to an injunction provided by the Copyright Act. If the case is dismissed because of the court's perception that the copyright claim is "incidental to" a dispute about contractual rights, plaintiff will have no opportunity to receive either an adjudication of infringement or copyright remedies from the state courts.

The scenario most often analyzed under the *Schoenberg* test is one in which a plaintiff owns a copyright and undisputedly assigns or licenses defendant who allegedly breaches the terms of the contract by, for example, failing to pay royalties. Plaintiff then claims the license is terminated and that the defendant infringed plaintiff's copyright through unauthorized, continued use of the protected material after the breach. *See, e.g., Living Music Records, Inc.*, 827 F. Supp. at 980-81 (declining jurisdiction over copyright infringement claim based on allegations that defendant failed to pay royalties under a license agreement permitting it to make and sell copies of plaintiff's musical recordings). Here, however, plaintiff disputes that the Letter Agreement constituted any type of transfer, license or assignment of her copyrighted script. . . .

2. Consider the scenario described by the court in footnote 14. How will the subject matter jurisdiction question in those types of cases be resolved under the *T.B. Harms* test? If the court finds a valid assignment, will there be an occasion to consider any aspect of the Copyright Act? In such a case, should the federal court have exclusive subject matter jurisdiction?

3. When a plaintiff files a breach of contract claim in state court and the defendant asserts a counterclaim for copyright infringement, may the state court resolve the copyright claim? Until recently, the answer appeared to be yes. In 2011, Congress amended the second sentence of 28 U.S.C. §1338(a) to clarify that "[n]o State court shall have jurisdiction over any claim for relief arising from any Act of Congress relating to patents, plant variety protection, or copyrights." Congress also amended the removal provisions to permit removal of a "civil action in which *any party* asserts a claim for relief arising under any Act of Congress relating to patents, plant variety protection, or copyrights." 28 U.S.C. §1454 (emphasis added).

> **LOOKING BACK – AND FORWARD**
>
> Chapter 12 explored how to distinguish between copyright and contract claims and explained how claim categorization might affect the remedies to be awarded. Claim categorization also affects the choice of forum. A contract claim cannot be filed in federal court unless an independent basis for subject matter jurisdiction exists. We explore the possibility that state law claims, including breach of contract claims, may be preempted by federal copyright law in Chapter 15.

B. STANDING TO SUE & IMMUNITY FROM SUIT

There are different kinds of lawsuits involving copyrights that can be brought under the Copyright Act. This section considers who can bring both copyright infringement actions and declaratory judgment actions, as well as limits on the ability to sue certain types of defendants.

1. Standing to Sue for Copyright Infringement

Recall from Chapter 3 that copyright vests initially in the author of the copyrighted work. Recall also that copyright ownership may change hands many times before copyright in the work expires. The rules governing ownership and transfer are important in the litigation context because they determine who has standing to file a copyright infringement lawsuit.

Section 501(b) provides:

> The legal or beneficial owner of an exclusive right under a copyright is entitled, subject to the requirements of section 411, to institute an action for any infringement of that particular right committed while he or she is the owner of it. The court may require such owner to serve written notice of the action with a copy of the complaint upon any person shown, by the records of the Copyright Office or otherwise, to have or claim an interest in the copyright, and shall require that such notice be served upon any person

whose interest is likely to be affected by a decision in the case. The court may require joinder, and shall permit the intervention, of any person having or claiming an interest in the copyright.

Section 501(b) is intended to supplement the Federal Rules of Civil Procedure by enabling "the owner of a particular right to bring an infringement action in that owner's name alone, while at the same time insuring to the extent possible that the other owners whose rights may be affected are notified and given a chance to join the action." H.R. Rep. No. 94-1476, 94th Cong., 2d Sess. 159 (1976), *reprinted in* 1976 U.S.C.C.A.N. 5659, 5739. The ability of others who have an interest in the copyright to join in the lawsuit is particularly important if the validity of the copyright is at issue. For further discussion, see Roger D. Blair & Thomas F. Cotter, *The Elusive Logic of Standing Doctrine in Intellectual Property Law*, 74 Tul. L. Rev. 1323, 1365-73 (2000).

A "legal" owner of copyright may be the author or someone to whom the copyright has been assigned or subsequent assignees in the chain of title. When will something short of assignment of the copyright be sufficient to confer standing? Consider the following case.

Eden Toys, Inc. v. Florelee Undergarment Co.
697 F.2d 27 (2d Cir. 1982)

MANSFIELD, J.: . . . The subject of this case is the alleged copying of a drawing of the copyrighted fictional character Paddington Bear, the central figure in a series of children's books written by Michael Bond. Paddington and Company, Limited ("Paddington"), a British corporation, holds all rights to these books, and to the characters therein. In 1975 Paddington entered into an agreement with [Eden Toys, Inc. ("Eden")], an American corporation, granting Eden exclusive North American rights to produce and sell, and to sublicense the production and sale of, a number of Paddington products.[2] This agreement was amended in 1980

---

2. The relevant portions of the 1975 Eden/Paddington exclusive licensing agreement are as follows:

> 1. *Grant of License*
>   (a) Paddington hereby grants to Eden, for the term of this agreement and all renewals thereof, subject to the terms and conditions and for the territory hereinafter set forth [North America], the exclusive right and license to use the Michael Bond books, characters, names, copyrights and trademarks in the manufacture and sale of all Licensed Products in both Schedules B and C, and to license others to use the Michael Bond books, characters, names, copyrights and trademarks in the manufacture and sale of all Licensed Products listed in Schedule C alone. . . .
>   *SCHEDULE B*
>   Stuffed animals, also described as dolls, and puppets, all of various sizes.
>   *SCHEDULE C*
>   1. Ready-to-wear sold in the children's division of department and specialty stores, including, without limitations, infants, babette, toddler, and 2-4 sizes for boys and girls; 4-7, 8-20, and 27-30 sizes for boys; and 3-6X, 7-14, pre-teen and junior sizes for girls.

to grant Eden the exclusive North American rights to produce and sublicense *all* Paddington products except books, tapes and records, stage plays, motion pictures, and radio and television productions.

At some point between 1975 and 1977 Ivor Wood, the illustrator of the Paddington Bear books, drew a series of sketches ("the Ivor Wood sketches") for the use of Eden and its sublicensees. . . . Using the Ivor Wood sketches as a point of departure, the C.R. Gibson Company ("Gibson"), pursuant to a sublicense from Eden, produced a design for gift wrap that included seven drawings of Paddington Bear ("the Eden/ Gibson drawings"). . . .

In November 1979, Eden discovered that [Florelee Undergarment Co., Inc. ("Florelee")] was selling a nightshirt featuring a print of a bear later found by the district court to be "identical in almost all respects" to one of the Eden/Gibson drawings of Paddington Bear. . . . After discovering a second nightshirt with the same apparent "knockoff" of the Eden/Gibson drawing Eden filed suit against Florelee in April 1980, alleging . . . that Florelee had violated Eden's rights under the Copyright Act. . . .

Eden's Claim as Exclusive Licensee

Eden . . . sues for infringement as exclusive North American licensee for certain Paddington Bear products. An exclusive licensee of a right under a copyright is entitled to bring suits for infringement "of that particular right," without being required to join his licensor. The question, then, is whether Eden was the exclusive licensee of the right allegedly infringed by Florelee, i.e., the right to produce images of Paddington Bear on adult clothing. Florelee argues correctly that adult clothing was clearly not among the "licensed products" listed in the 1975 agreement between Eden and Paddington, see note 2, *supra,* and concludes from this fact that Eden was not the exclusive licensee of this right at the time the allegedly infringing garments were sold in 1979. Eden responds that at that time Eden was operating under an informal understanding with Paddington, later formalized in the 1980 amendment to the 1975 agreement, that gave Eden the exclusive North

---

2. All accessories normally sold in the children's divisions of department and specialty stores.

3. Infants, juvenile and youth domestics and textiles.

4. Juvenile and youth furniture and accessories normally sold in the juvenile furniture department of department and specialty stores.

5. Toys, games, crafts and other articles normally sold in the toy department of department stores, toy stores and specialty stores.

Excluded from this Schedule are the items of Schedule B and:

  a. Books

  b. Tapes and Records

  c. Stage Plays

  d. Motion Pictures

  e. Radio and Television Productions.

American rights to produce any Paddington Bear product except books, records, and a few other items not relevant here.

Under the pre-1978 copyright law, exclusive licenses could be granted orally or by conduct. Under the new Copyright Act, however, Eden's claim of an informal grant of an exclusive license seemingly must fail in light of the statute of frauds provision of the new Act, which states that an exclusive license "is not valid unless an instrument of conveyance, or a note or memorandum of the transfer, is in writing and signed by the owner of the rights conveyed. . . ." 17 U.S.C. §204(a) (Supp. IV 1980). However, since the purpose of the provision is to protect copyright holders from persons mistakenly or fraudulently claiming oral licenses, the "note or memorandum of the transfer" need not be made at the time when the license is initiated; the requirement is satisfied by the copyright owner's later execution of a writing which confirms the agreement. In this case, in which the copyright holder appears to have no dispute with its licensee on this matter, it would be anomalous to permit a third party infringer to invoke this provision against the licensee. . . .

If Paddington granted Eden an informal exclusive license to sell Paddington Bear products in the market in which Florelee sold—adult clothing—and that informal license was later confirmed in a writing signed by Paddington, Eden may sue in its own name, without joining Paddington, for infringement of any Paddington-owned copyrights in that market. . . .

If the district court finds that no such informal understanding existed, or that such an understanding was never memorialized, Paddington, which has expressed a willingness to be made a co-plaintiff in this lawsuit, should be joined as a plaintiff. The district court has the power to order the joinder of "any person having or claiming an interest in the copyright [at issue]." 17 U.S.C. §501(b) (Supp. IV 1980). In this case, the exercise of that power would clearly be appropriate if Paddington in fact owns some of the rights apparently infringed by Florelee. The equities in this case lie heavily in favor of Eden, and it would be unjust to deny redress to Eden because of an easily remediable procedural defect. . . .

NOTES AND QUESTIONS

1. The *Eden Toys* court construes the Copyright Act's statute of frauds requirement to support its holding that the plaintiff has standing as an exclusive licensee. The court concludes that the lack of a dispute between Paddington and Eden Toys regarding the exclusivity of the license satisfies the purpose of §204(a). As a matter of statutory interpretation, do you agree with the court's approach? What about as a matter of policy?

What if the licensor (Paddington) *did* have a dispute with Eden Toys and claimed that the license did not convey the exclusive right to market adult garments with the copyrighted images? In that case, should a court rule differently on Eden Toys' standing?

2. Section 501(b) also grants standing to "beneficial" owners of copyright. A beneficial owner includes "an author who ha[s] parted with legal title to the copyright in exchange for percentage royalties based on sales or license fees."

H.R. Rep. No. 94-1476, 94th Cong., 2d Sess. 159 (1976), *reprinted in* 1976 U.S.C.C.A.N. 5659, 5739.

If an author has assigned her copyright for a lump sum, not a percentage royalty, may she assert that her right to terminate that agreement under §203 confers standing? *See, e.g.,* Hearn v. Meyer, 664 F. Supp. 832, 843-44 (S.D.N.Y. 1987) (no). Read §203. Does §203 mandate that result? Can you envision situations in which the argument in favor of allowing standing for an author with a reversionary interest would be strong?

3. A nonexclusive licensee does not have standing. Nor does an agent who has been granted the exclusive right to negotiate licenses. Associations also do not have standing under the Copyright Act to sue on behalf of their members. *Authors Guild, Inc. v. HathiTrust,* 755 F.3d 87, 94 (2d Cir. 2014).

4. In recent years, courts have focused increased attention on the ability of nonpracticing entities, sometimes referred to as "trolls," to enforce intellectual property rights. In the copyright context, courts have read the requirements of §501(b) strictly, requiring would-be plaintiffs to demonstrate an assignment of an exclusive right, not merely an assignment of a right to sue for infringement. *See, e.g., Righthaven LLC v. Hoehn,* 716 F.3d 1166, 1169 (9th Cir. 2013); *see also Silvers v. Sony Pictures Entm't, Inc.,* 402 F.3d 881 (9th Cir.) (en banc) (rejecting assertion of beneficial ownership based on assignment of accrued infringement claim without assignment of underlying rights in the copyrighted work), *cert. denied,* 546 U.S. 827 (2005).

> **COMPARATIVE PERSPECTIVE**
>
> Under some foreign copyright laws, associations are authorized to administer their members' rights and thus have standing to assert those rights in U.S. courts. *See*; *Itar–Tass Russian News Agency v. Russian Kurier, Inc.,* 153 F.3d 82, 92 (2d Cir. 1998).

2. Standing to Seek Declaratory Judgment

Sometimes it is not the copyright owner that initiates litigation. Potential defendants may decide to go to court first, seeking a declaration that their activities do not constitute infringement. The next case addresses when such actions are permissible.

Shloss v. Sweeney
515 F.Supp.2d 1068 (N.D. Cal. 2007)

WARE, J.: . . . . Plaintiff Carol Loeb Shloss ("Plaintiff") . . . seeks a declaratory judgment that the use of certain written works in an electronic supplement to her book, if published, will not infringe any copyrights controlled or owned by the Estate of James Joyce ("Estate") and Seán Sweeney, in his capacity as the trustee of the Estate (collectively, "Defendants").

Presently before the Court is Defendants' Motion to Dismiss. . . .

Plaintiff alleges as follows:

Plaintiff is the author of the book *Lucia Joyce: To Dance in the Wake,* a work about Lucia Joyce and the creative impact of Lucia's relationship with her father, the Irish expatriate author James Joyce, on James Joyce's literary works. Between 1988 and 2003, she conducted research on the book throughout the United States and Europe and wrote her manuscript. The work "describes the extraordinary influence that James Joyce's daughter Lucia exercised on her father's emotions and work and challenges Lucia's conventional portrayal as a troublesome blight on the Joyce family."

Defendants became aware of Plaintiff's research on Lucia Joyce around 1994. Defendants did not contact Plaintiff to discuss her work. *Id.* When Plaintiff contacted Stephen Joyce to request help on her book, he responded with a "definitive no" in 1996. He purported specifically to prohibit Plaintiff from using letters or papers written by Lucia Joyce. . . .

In August 2002, Stephen Joyce wrote to Plaintiff. . . . He threatened Plaintiff by referring to the Estate's recent copyright litigation. . . .

On November 4, 2002, Stephen Joyce called Farrar, Straus & Giroux ("Publisher"), the publisher for Plaintiff's book. He informed the Publisher that he had heard about the book, was opposed to any publication, and had never lost a lawsuit. *Id.* The same day, he sent a letter to Jonathon Galassi ("Galassi"), the Publisher's President, to the same effect.

On November 5, 2002, Stephen Joyce again wrote to Galassi. Joyce claimed that as of March 31, 2002, he was the "sole beneficiary owner" of James Joyce's rights and the sole owner of the rights to Lucia Joyce's works. . . . On November 6, 2002, Leon Friedman ("Friedman"), the Publisher's attorney, wrote to Stephen Joyce, informing him that the Publisher believed Plaintiff's work to be protected by the fair use doctrine of copyright law.

On November 21, 2002, Stephen Joyce wrote to Friedman, stating that Friedman "should be aware of the fact that over the past decade the Estate's 'record,' in legal terms, is crystal clear and we have proven on a number of occasions that we are prepared to put our money where our mouth is." Stephen Joyce further wrote that the Publisher's fair use claim "sounds like a bad joke or wishful thinking." . . .

On January 23, 2003, the Publisher wrote to Plaintiff, describing the edits that it thought necessary to avoid a suit from Defendants, including all unpublished writings of James Joyce and Lucia Joyce. Plaintiff voiced concerns to the Publisher that "the proposed cuts eliminate[d] almost all of the evidence in the book," undermined the book's "scholarly integrity," and excluded the evidence it took her twelve years to assemble. Ultimately, more than thirty pages were cut from a manuscript of four hundred pages. The book was published in edited form in December 2003. *Id.* Many reviews . . . remarked on Plaintiff's lack of documentary support for her theories.

In 2005, Plaintiff created an electronic supplement to her book ("Electronic Supplement"), which she placed on a website ("Website") The website is presently password protected and is not available to the public. *Id.* Plaintiff plans to provide the Electronic Supplement as a resource to scholars, researchers, and the general public who have United States Internet Protocol ("IP") addresses. *Id.* The Electronic Supplement will contain material that the Publisher removed from the book as a result of Defendants' threats, material that Plaintiff removed for fear of attracting Defendants' negative attention, and other material related to Plaintiff's analysis of her research.

On March 9, 2005, Plaintiff's counsel wrote to Defendants to describe the planned Electronic Supplement. The letter explained Plaintiff's belief that the copyrighted material in the Electronic Supplement was protected by the fair use doctrine and thus did not require Defendants' permission. Plaintiff's counsel nonetheless offered Defendants the opportunity to review the material before its publication. . . . Defendants' responses reiterated the Estate's denial of permission for Plaintiff to use its copyrighted materials and "reserve[d] all rights if [Plaintiff] persevere[d] with her proposed activities." Based on Defendants' numerous threats, Plaintiff fears "that Defendants will sue if she makes the Electronic Supplement on the Website publicly available in its present form."

Plaintiff filed this lawsuit in June 2006 alleging . . . : (1) Count 1, for a declaratory judgment that the Electronic Supplement does not infringe any of Defendants' copyrights; (2) Count 2, for a declaratory judgment that Plaintiff's use of Defendants' copyrighted material in her planned Electronic Supplement is presumptively fair use. . . .

IV. DISCUSSION

A. *Motion to Dismiss*

1. **Subject Matter Jurisdiction**

Plaintiff bases the Court's subject matter jurisdiction on the Declaratory Judgment Act. A federal district court has jurisdiction to render a declaratory judgment pursuant to the Declaratory Judgment Act, 28 U.S.C. §2201, if an "actual controversy" exists. The "actual controversy" requirement under the Declaratory Judgment Act is coextensive with the "case or controversy" requirement of Article III of the United States Constitution. The Act, then, permits suit "once the adverse positions [of the parties] have crystallized and the conflict of interests is real and immediate." *Societe de Conditionnement En Aluminium v. Hunter Engineering Co.*, 655 F.2d 938, 943 (9th Cir.1981) (internal quotations omitted). For a copyright action in the Ninth Circuit, a declaratory judgment plaintiff must (1) demonstrate a "real and reasonable" apprehension that she will be subject to liability if she continues to manufacture her product that (2) the defendant caused by its actions. A court applies these principles "with a flexibility that is oriented to the reasonable perceptions of the plaintiff." *Chesebrough-Pond's, Inc. v. Faberge, Inc.*, 666 F.2d 393, 396 (9th Cir.1982).

Defendants contend that (1) Plaintiff has not proved that she had a reasonable apprehension of being subject to liability for copyright infringement at the time she filed her complaint; (2) their covenant not to sue eliminates any possible reasonable apprehension of liability; and (3) any ruling by the Court would be an advisory opinion, as Plaintiff has not yet published her electronic supplement. . . .

. . . [T]he Court finds that Plaintiff has a real and reasonable apprehension of copyright liability that Defendants caused by their actions. First, Defendants repeatedly wrote to Plaintiff and her Publisher, purportedly denying Plaintiff permission to use materials that she planned to include in her book and reiterating the clear, if implicit, threats of litigation previously described. These communications occurred regularly over a period of nine years, from 1996 to 2005, and easily left Plaintiff with a reasonable apprehension of copyright liability when she filed this suit in 2006.

Second, Defendants propose a covenant not to sue based on the Electronic Supplement as it existed in 2005. A court should dismiss an intellectual property suit for a declaratory judgment as moot when the defendant releases the plaintiff from all liability based on plaintiff's allegedly infringing activities (for instance, pursuant to a settlement agreement.) *See, e.g. Gator.com Corp. v. L.L. Bean, Inc.,* 398 F.3d 1125, 1130–31 (9th Cir.2005). On the other hand, when a defendant represents to a court that it will not sue the plaintiff for *some* of the potentially infringing activities in which the plaintiff is engaged, the plaintiff retains a reasonable apprehension of suit as to the remaining potentially infringing activities. *Sierra Applied Sciences, Inc. v. Advanced Energy Indus., Inc.,* 363 F.3d 1361, 1375 (Fed.Cir.2004). Since Plaintiff filed suit, she has undisputedly amended her Electronic Supplement once and has amended her complaint to reflect the change. Thus, if the Court dismissed this action, Defendants could sue Plaintiff on the first day on which her website in its current form was made available to the public, notwithstanding their covenant not to sue. The Court finds that Defendants' putative covenant not to sue based on the Electronic Supplement as it existed in 2005 is inadequate to moot the actual controversy between the parties.

Third, the Court may rule in this case without rendering an advisory opinion. A plaintiff does not have to begin distribution of the potentially infringing product in order to have a controversy ripe for declaratory judgment adjudication, so long as the plaintiff has completed all preparatory work. In other words, the plaintiff "must establish that the product presented to the court is the same product which will be produced if a declaration of noninfringement is obtained." *Sierra,* 363 F.3d at 1378. Here, Plaintiff has represented to the Court under penalty of perjury that the contents of the Electronic Supplement on the Website will not change again absent the Court's explicit leave to amend the Website. Based on Plaintiff's representation, the Court finds that the copyright controversy between the parties over the Electronic Supplement is sufficiently definite to proceed.

Since Plaintiff has a real and reasonable apprehension of copyright liability, the Court finds that this action satisfies the "case or controversy" requirement for a declaratory judgment. The Court has subject matter jurisdiction over Plaintiff's First Cause of Action for a declaratory judgment of copyright noninfringement. . . .

AFTERMATH

Following the court's refusal to dismiss, the parties settled their dispute with the Defendants covenanting "not to sue Shloss for infringement of any copyrights resulting from Shloss's publication, in either electronic or printed form, of the Supplement. . . ." *Shloss v. Sweeney,* 515 F. Supp. 2d 1083 (N.D. Cal. 2007). Subsequently, the court granted Shloss her costs and attorneys' fees. *Id.* Ultimately, the Joyce Estate paid $240,000 in attorneys' fees. *See* http://cyberlaw.stanford .edu/our-work/cases/shloss-v-estate-joyce.

NOTES AND QUESTIONS

1. If the Joyce estate had not responded to Shloss's final letter concerning plans for the Electronic Supplement, would Shloss have been able to bring a declaratory judgment action? What would Shloss's options have been at that point?

2. From the defendant's perspective, what are the advantages to filing first? Note that Shloss's publisher, Farrar, Straus & Giroux, is headquartered in New York, but Shloss filed suit in California. Why might she have preferred the latter venue?

3. Should sending a cease-and-desist letter automatically give the recipient standing to seek a declaratory judgment? Why, or why not? Articulate the competing policies at stake. Are there ways to word a cease-and-desist letter without creating the predicate for a declaratory judgment action?

4. Should receipt of a take-down notice under §512 trigger the right to seek declaratory relief?

5. If an equipment manufacturer or service provider is sued for indirect infringement, do its customers have standing to seek a declaratory judgment that their activities are noninfringing? *See Newmark v. Turner Broadcasting Network*, 226 F. Supp. 2d 1215 (C.D. Cal. 2002) (denying defendant's motion to dismiss such a lawsuit and observing that "no explicit threat of litigation is required to meet the 'case or controversy' requirement").

3. Sovereign Immunity

In Chapter 9, you learned that direct, contributory, and vicarious infringers are all proper defendants. Some potential defendants, however, may be immune from suit. The immunity relevant here is sovereign immunity, which stems from the Eleventh Amendment:

> In *Chisholm v. Georgia*, 2 Dall. 419 (1793), we asserted jurisdiction over an action in assumpsit brought by a South Carolina citizen against the State of Georgia. In so doing, we reasoned that Georgia's sovereign immunity was qualified by the general jurisdictional provisions of Article III, and, most specifically, by the provision extending the federal judicial power to controversies "between a State and Citizens of another State." U.S. Const., Art. III, §2, cl. 1. The "shock of surprise" created by this decision, *Principality of Monaco v. Mississippi*, 292 U.S. 313, 325 (1934), prompted the immediate adoption of the Eleventh Amendment, which provides:
>
> > The Judicial power of the United States shall not be construed to extend to any suit in law or equity, commenced or prosecuted against one of the United States by Citizens of another State, or by Citizens or Subjects of any Foreign State.
>
> Though its precise terms bar only federal jurisdiction over suits brought against one State by citizens of another State or foreign state, we have long recognized that the Eleventh Amendment accomplished much more: It repudiated the central premise of

Chisholm that the jurisdictional heads of Article III superseded the sovereign immunity that the States possessed before entering the Union. This has been our understanding of the Amendment since the landmark case of *Hans v. Louisiana*, 134 U.S. 1 (1890).

While this immunity from suit is not absolute, we have recognized only two circumstances in which an individual may sue a State. First, Congress may authorize such a suit in the exercise of its power to enforce the Fourteenth Amendment—an Amendment enacted after the Eleventh Amendment and specifically designed to alter the federal-state balance. Second, a State may waive its sovereign immunity by consenting to suit.

Coll. Sav. Bank v. Fla. Prepaid Postsecondary Educ. Expense Bd., 527 U.S. 666, 669-70 (1999).

In 1990, Congress amended the Copyright Act to provide for suits against states. Copyright Remedy Clarification Act (CRCA), Pub. L. No. 101-553, 104 Stat. 2749 (1990) (*codified at* 17 U.S.C. §§501(a), 511). The Supreme Court has not decided whether the CRCA was a valid authorization of suits against states in federal court (characterized as an "abrogation" of sovereign immunity), but recent developments leave the distinct impression that the Court, if presented with the issue, would decide that it was not.

First, in 1996, the Court decided *Seminole Tribe of Florida v. Florida*, 517 U.S. 44 (1996), a turning point in Eleventh Amendment jurisprudence. *Seminole Tribe* makes clear that Congress may not abrogate state sovereign immunity pursuant to its Article I powers. Therefore, Congress may not rely on the Intellectual Property Clause or the Commerce Clause as the source of authority for abrogation. However, because intellectual property can be conceptualized as a "property" right, some believed that Congress might be able to abrogate sovereign immunity pursuant to the Fourteenth Amendment.

In 1999, the Supreme Court addressed the issue of sovereign immunity when a state is sued for patent infringement, *Fla. Prepaid Postsecondary Educ. Expense Bd. v. Coll. Sav. Bank*, 527 U.S. 627 (1999), and when a state is sued for trademark infringement, *Coll. Sav. Bank v. Fla. Prepaid Postsecondary Educ. Expense Bd.*, 527 U.S. 666 (1999). The two 5-4 decisions (issued on the same day) held that states are immune from suits in federal court for violations of the patent and trademark laws, respectively. The Court held that in order to rely on the Fourteenth Amendment to abrogate sovereign immunity, Congress would need to "identify conduct transgressing the Fourteenth Amendment's substantive provisions, and must tailor its legislative scheme to remedying or preventing such conduct." *Fla. Prepaid*, 527 U.S. at 639. The Court determined that neither the Patent Act nor the Lanham Act met those requirements.

Following those decisions, the Court was invited to review a case from the Fifth Circuit concerning the CRCA. The Court declined that invitation but remanded the case for reconsideration in light of its recent decisions. The following is the Fifth Circuit's decision after remand.

Chavez v. Arte Publico Press
204 F.3d 601 (5th Cir. 2000)

JONES, J.: . . . Plaintiff Chavez asserts that the University of Houston infringed her copyright by continuing to publish her book without her consent. . . . The University of Houston contends that because it enjoys immunity from unconsented-to suit in federal court under the Eleventh Amendment, the case must be dismissed. . . . [W]e agree with the University.

Abrogation of a state's Eleventh Amendment immunity turns on an express statement of intent by Congress and a constitutionally valid exercise of power. *See Seminole Tribe of Fla. v. Florida*, 517 U.S. 44, 55 (1996). Congress amended . . . the Copyright Act and explicitly required states to submit to suit in federal court for violation of [its] provisions; thus, the express statement requirement is fulfilled. The remaining question, to be considered in the light of *College Savings, Florida Prepaid*, and *Kimel v. Fla. Bd. of Regents*, 528 U.S. 62 (2000), is whether Congress had authority to abrogate state sovereign immunity in the Act[]. . . .

Chavez and *amici* justify the CRCA abrogation of state Eleventh Amendment immunity under section 5 of the Fourteenth Amendment, because Congress acted to prevent states from depriving copyright holders of their property without due process of law. They contend that the legislative history demonstrates that the waiver effected by the CRCA is proportional to its remedial object. . . .

Congress can abrogate the states' sovereign immunity when acting to enforce constitutional rights pursuant to section 5 of the Fourteenth Amendment. *See Seminole*, 116 S. Ct. at 1128. *City of Boerne*[*v. Flores*, 521 U.S. 507 (1997)], however, states that when Congress legislates pursuant to section 5, "there must be a congruence and proportionality between the injury to be prevented or remedied and the means adopted to that end." . . . The analytical framework that *Florida Prepaid* sets forth requires examination of three aspects of the legislation: 1) the nature of the injury to be remedied; 2) Congress's consideration of the adequacy of state remedies to redress the injury; and 3) the coverage of the legislation. . . .

The first consideration is the nature of the injury to be remedied and whether the state's conduct evinced a pattern of constitutional violations. *See Florida Prepaid*, 119 S. Ct. at 2207. The underlying conduct at issue here is state infringement of copyrights, rather than patents, and the "constitutional injury" consists of possibly unremedied, or uncompensated, violation of copyrights by states. *See* H.R. Rep. No. 101-282, pt. 1, at 3 (1989), *reprinted in* 1990 U.S.C.C.A.N. 3949, 3951 [hereinafter H.R. Rep.]. Such infringements, it is contended, would "take" the copyright owners' property without due process of law.[6]

The Supreme Court concluded in *Florida Prepaid* that "Congress identified no pattern of patent infringement by the States, let alone a pattern of constitutional

---

6. . . . The Supreme Court held in *Florida Prepaid* that patents are considered property within the meaning of the due process clause. *See Florida Prepaid*, 119 S. Ct. at 2208. Since patent and copyright are of a similar nature, and patent is a form of property protectable against the states, copyright would seem to be so too.

violations." *Florida Prepaid*, 119 S. Ct. at 2207. Although the legislative history for the CRCA documents a few more instances of copyright infringement than the [Patent Remedy Act's (PRCA's)] legislative history did of patent violations, the CRCA's history exhibits similar deficiencies. For example, testimony before the House Subcommittee in favor of the CRCA acknowledged that "the States are not going to get involved in wholesale violation of the copyright laws." Copyright Remedy Clarification Act and Copyright Office Report on Copyright Liability of States: Hearings Before the Subcomm. on Courts, Intellectual Property, and the Administration of Justice of the House Comm. on the Judiciary, 101st Cong. 53 (1989) [hereinafter House Hearings] (statement of Ralph Oman, Register of Copyrights, Library of Congress).[7] In addition, the bill's sponsor stated that "thus far there have not been any significant number of wholesale takings of copyright rights by States or State entities." *Id.*, at 48 (statement of Rep. Kastenmeier).

At the request of Congress, the Copyright Office reported on the relation between the states' copyright liability and the Eleventh Amendment; in that report, no more than seven incidents of State copyright infringement enabled by the Eleventh Amendment were documented. Register of Copyrights, Copyright Liability of States and the Eleventh Amendment 5-9 (1988) [hereinafter Copyright Office Report]. Nor did the Senate hear evidence of a pattern of unremedied copyright infringement by the States. Rather than expose a current epidemic of unconstitutional deprivations, the testimony before Congress worried principally about the *potential* for future abuse, see House Hearings, at 7 (statement of Ralph Oman), and the concerns of copyright owners about that potential, see Copyright Office Report, at 5-17.

Second, we consider whether Congress studied the existence and adequacy of state remedies for injured copyright owners when a state infringes their copyrights. *See Florida Prepaid*, 119 S. Ct. at 2208. The legislative histories of the PRCA and CRCA are again parallel. In each case, Congress barely considered the availability of state remedies for infringement. With regard to the CRCA, one witness testified that his company's attorneys told him that state and local courts were unavailable because only federal courts can hear copyright infringement cases. *See* House Hearings, at 51 (statement of James Healy, Vice President of Enterprise Media). In addition, the Copyright Office provided a survey of state waivers of Eleventh Amendment immunity as an appendix to its report. These are the only two allusions to state remedies in the legislative history. While Congress referred briefly to the Copyright Office's report in the House Report on the bill, Appendix C was mentioned neither in the House Report nor in any of the congressional hearings. Furthermore, as pointed out in a statement submitted to Congress, the survey failed to include information on state remedies for the unlawful taking of private property by the state government. *See* The Copyright Remedy Clarification Act: Hearing Before the Subcomm. on Patents, Copyrights and Trademarks of the Senate Comm. on the Judiciary, 101st Cong. 123 (1989) [hereinafter Senate Hearing] (statement on behalf of the Educators' Ad Hoc Committee on Copyright Law). . . . [T]here are other

---

7. Mr. Oman also stated that "[the States] are all respectful of the copyright laws." House Hearings, at 8.

possible remedies in state courts—breach of contract claims, for example—that Congress also never considered.[8]

As if to emphasize its lack of interest in state remedies, Congress rejected the idea of granting state courts concurrent jurisdiction over copyright cases, an alternative solution that would have avoided any Eleventh Amendment problems. Congress rejected this solution not because it was an inadequate remedy, but because Congress believed concurrent jurisdiction would undermine the uniformity of copyright law. *See* H.R. Rep., at 9. Although uniformity is undoubtedly an important goal, "that is a factor which belongs to the Article I patent-power calculus, rather than to any determination of whether a state plea of sovereign immunity deprives a patentee of property without due process of law." *Florida Prepaid*, 119 S. Ct. at 2209. The same is true here.

Finally, *Florida Prepaid* examined the breadth of coverage of the legislation. *See id.* at 2210. In enacting legislation pursuant to section 5 of the Fourteenth Amendment, Congress should ensure that there is "a congruence and proportionality between the injury to be prevented or remedied and the means adopted to that end." *City of Boerne*, 521 U.S. at 520; *see also id.* at 533 ("Where, however, a congressional enactment pervasively prohibits constitutional state action in an effort to remedy or to prevent unconstitutional state action, limitations . . . tend to ensure Congress' [sic] means are proportionate to ends legitimate under §5."). As the Court noted in *Florida Prepaid*, Supreme Court jurisprudence indicates that a deprivation, to fit the meaning of the due process clause, must be intentional; a negligent act that causes unintended injury is not sufficient. *See Florida Prepaid*, 119 S. Ct. at 2209. Copyright infringement actions, like those for patent infringement, ordinarily require no showing of intent to infringe. Instead, knowledge and intent are relevant in regard to damages. In addition, Mr. Oman, the Register of Copyrights, acknowledged that most copyright infringement by states is unintentional, stating that "[the States] would want [immunity] only as a shield for the State treasury from the occasional error or misunderstanding or innocent infringement." House Hearings, at 8. In enacting the CRCA, however, Congress did nothing "to confine the reach of the Act by limiting the remedy to certain types of infringement, . . . or providing for suits only against States with questionable remedies or a high incidence of infringement." *Florida Prepaid*, 119 S. Ct. at 2210. Its "indiscriminate scope" cannot be reconciled with the principle that legislation pursuant to the due process clause of the Fourteenth Amendment must be proportionate to legitimate section 5 ends. *See id.*

Since the record does not indicate that Congress was responding to the kind of massive constitutional violations that have prompted proper remedial legislation, that it considered the adequacy of state remedies that might have provided the required due process of law, or that it sought to limit the coverage to arguably constitutional violations, we conclude that the CRCA is, like the PRCA, an improper exercise of Congressional legislative power. . . .

---

8. Instead of considering the adequacy of possible state remedies, Congress focused on the adequacy of injunctive relief, stating that injunctive relief was not adequate protection for copyright owners. *See* H.R. Rep, at 8.

NOTES AND QUESTIONS

1. How serious do you think the problem of state governments' infringing copyrighted works really is? Before you answer, consider the multitude of state agencies, departments, and public institutions (such as state universities) that are protected by sovereign immunity. What congressional findings would be sufficient to justify remedial legislation abrogating sovereign immunity? What should such legislation require?

2. If an infringing state wanted to provide remedies for infringements, how would it implement such a system? An example of such a remedy might be royalty payments based on use of copyrighted works. Another example would be for states to negotiate contracts with authors. Are there reasons that states should *not* implement a system that compensates authors for state uses of copyrighted works? What kind of remedy and what kind of system would be appropriate?

LOOKING BACK

Recall the *Cambridge University Press v. Patton* litigation concerning electronic course reserves at Georgia State University, which you read about in Chapter 10.C.2, *supra*. Because of the sovereign immunity issue, the plaintiff filed the case as an *Ex parte Young* action, naming as defendants Carl Patton, the President of the University, along with several members of the Board of Regents.

---

3. Despite the sweeping nature of Eleventh Amendment immunity, the Supreme Court has long permitted suits for injunctive and declaratory relief against state officers in their official capacities. *See Ex parte Young*, 209 U.S. 123 (1908). This rule applies to copyright infringement litigation as well.

4. If states can infringe the rights of copyright owners, the United States may be in violation of its international treaty obligations. At least one scholar has argued that those obligations may provide valid authority for congressional abrogation of sovereign immunity. *See* Peter S. Menell, *Economic Implications of State Sovereign Immunity from Infringement of Federal Intellectual Property Rights*, 33 Loy. L.A. L. Rev. 1399, 1460-64 (2000).

5. The *Chavez* and *Florida Prepaid* cases address state sovereign immunity. Other court decisions have established that the United States is not subject to suit without its consent. Congress, however, may choose to waive the sovereign immunity of the United States and has done so in copyright infringement cases. *See* 28 U.S.C. §1498(b) (permitting claims against the United States in the Court of Federal Claims and specifying recovery of "reasonable and entire compensation as damages for such infringement, including the minimum statutory damages as set forth in section 504(c) of title 17, United States Code"). Why do you think the United States has waived sovereign immunity in copyright cases?

The waiver of sovereign immunity does not extend to cases in which the copyright owner is (or was) a government employee and "was in a position to order, influence, or induce use of the copyrighted work by the Government . . ." *Id*. Also, a copyright owner has no cause of action against the government when the copyrighted work was "prepared as part of the official functions of the employee, or in the preparation of which Government time, material, or facilities were used . . ." *Id*. In light of the rules of copyright ownership for works made for hire, is this last exception necessary?

C. PROPER TIMING

Determining whether and when to bring a copyright infringement action is partly a matter of litigation strategy, but some mandatory timing rules must be observed.

1. Filing Too Early

Subject to certain exceptions, §411 requires copyright owners to register their works before filing an infringement lawsuit. Is registration therefore a prerequisite for federal subject matter jurisdiction? The next case addresses that question.

Reed Elsevier, Inc. v. Muchnick
559 U.S. 154 (2010)

THOMAS, J.: . . . "Anyone who violates any of the exclusive rights of the copyright owner as provided" in the Act "is an infringer of the copyright." §501(a). When such infringement occurs, a copyright owner "is entitled, *subject to the requirements of section 411,* to institute an action" for copyright infringement. §501(b) (emphasis added).

This case concerns "the requirements of section 411" to which §501(b) refers. Section 411(a) provides, *inter alia* and with certain exceptions, that "no civil action for infringement of the copyright in any United States work shall be instituted until preregistration or registration of the copyright claim has been made in accordance with this title." This provision is part of the Act's remedial scheme. It establishes a condition—copyright registration—that plaintiffs ordinarily must satisfy before filing an infringement claim and invoking the Act's remedial provisions. We address whether §411(a) also deprives federal courts of subject-matter jurisdiction to adjudicate infringement claims involving unregistered works.

[I.] B

The relevant proceedings in this case began after we issued our opinion in *New York Times Co. v. Tasini*, 533 U.S. 483 (2001). In *Tasini,* we agreed with the Court of Appeals for the Second Circuit that several owners of online databases and print publishers had infringed the copyrights of six freelance authors by reproducing the authors' works electronically without first securing their permission. See *id.,* at 493. In so holding, we affirmed the principal theory of liability underlying copyright infringement suits that other freelance authors had filed after the Court of Appeals had issued its opinion in *Tasini.* These other suits, which were stayed pending our decision in *Tasini,* resumed after we issued our opinion and were consolidated in the United States District Court for the Southern District of New York by the Judicial Panel on Multidistrict Litigation.

The consolidated complaint alleged that the named plaintiffs each own at least one copyright, typically in a freelance article written for a newspaper or a magazine, that they had registered in accordance with §411(a). The class, however, included both authors who had registered their copyrighted works and authors who had not. . . .

The parties moved the District Court to certify a class for settlement and to approve the settlement agreement [reached after more than three years of negotiation]. Ten freelance authors, including Irvin Muchnick (hereinafter Muchnick respondents), objected. The District Court overruled the objections; certified a settlement class . . . ; approved the settlement . . . ; and entered final judgment. . . .

The Muchnick respondents appealed . . . . Shortly before oral argument, the Court of Appeals *sua sponte* ordered briefing on the question whether §411(a) deprives federal courts of subject-matter jurisdiction over infringement claims involving unregistered copyrights. . . .

. . . . [T]he Court of Appeals concluded that the District Court lacked jurisdiction to certify a class of claims arising from the infringement of unregistered works, and also lacked jurisdiction to approve a settlement with respect to those claims, [In re *Literary Works in Elec. Databases Copyright Litig.*, 509 F.3d 116, 121 (2d Cir. 2007)] (citing "widespread agreement among the circuits that section 411(a) is jurisdictional").[2] . . .

We granted the owners' and publishers' petition for a writ of certiorari, and formulated the question presented to ask whether §411(a) restricts the subject-matter jurisdiction of the federal courts over copyright infringement actions. 555 U.S. ___, 129 S. Ct. 1523 (2009). Because no party supports the Court of Appeals' jurisdictional holding, we appointed an *amicus curiae* to defend the Court of Appeals' judgment. We now reverse.

II.

A . . .

While perhaps clear in theory, the distinction between jurisdictional conditions and claim-processing rules can be confusing in practice. Courts—including this Court—have sometimes mischaracterized claim-processing rules or elements of a cause of action as jurisdictional limitations, particularly when that characterization was not central to the case, and thus did not require close analysis. . . .

. . . . In *Arbaugh* [*v. Y & H Corp.*, 546 U.S. 500 (2006)], we described the general approach to distinguish "jurisdictional" conditions from claim-processing requirements or elements of a claim:

---

2. See *La Resolana Architects, PA v. Clay Realtors Angel Fire,* 416 F.3d 1195, 1200-1201 (C.A. 10 2005); *Positive Black Talk Inc. v. Cash Money Records Inc.,* 394 F.3d 357, 365 (C.A. 5 2004); *Xoom, Inc. v. Imageline, Inc.,* 323 F.3d 279, 283 (C.A. 4 2003); *Murray Hill Publications, Inc. v. ABC Communications, Inc.,* 264 F.3d 622, 630, and n. 1 (C.A. 6 2001); *Brewer-Giorgio v. Producers Video, Inc.,* 216 F.3d 1281, 1285 (C.A. 11 2000); *Data Gen. Corp. v. Grumman Systems Support Corp.,* 36 F.3d 1147, 1163 (C.A. 1 1994).

"If the Legislature clearly states that a threshold limitation on a statute's scope shall count as jurisdictional, then courts and litigants will be duly instructed and will not be left to wrestle with the issue. But when Congress does not rank a statutory limitation on coverage as jurisdictional, courts should treat the restriction as nonjurisdictional in character." 546 U.S. at 515-516 (citation and footnote omitted) . . . .

B

Section 411(a) provides:

"Except for an action brought for a violation of the rights of the author under section 106A(a), and subject to the provisions of subsection (b), no civil action for infringement of the copyright in any United States work shall be instituted until preregistration or registration of the copyright claim has been made in accordance with this title. In any case, however, where the deposit, application, and fee required for registration have been delivered to the Copyright Office in proper form and registration has been refused, the applicant is entitled to institute a civil action for infringement if notice thereof, with a copy of the complaint, is served on the Register of Copyrights. The Register may, at his or her option, become a party to the action with respect to the issue of registrability of the copyright claim by entering an appearance within sixty days after such service, but the Register's failure to become a party shall not deprive the court of jurisdiction to determine that issue."

KEEP IN MIND
Section 411 references "any United States work." This term is defined in §101 of the Act. Be sure to read that definition.

We must consider whether §411(a) "clearly states" that its registration requirement is "jurisdictional." *Arbaugh, supra,* at 515. It does not. *Amicus* disagrees, pointing to the presence of the word "jurisdiction" in the last sentence of §411(a) and contending that the use of the term there indicates the jurisdictional cast of §411(a)'s first sentence as well. But this reference to "jurisdiction" cannot bear the weight that *amicus* places upon it. The sentence upon which *amicus* relies states:

"The Register [of Copyrights] may, at his or her option, become a party to the [copyright infringement] action with respect to *the issue of registrability of the copyright claim* by entering an appearance within sixty days after such service, but the Register's failure to become a party shall not deprive the court of jurisdiction to determine *that issue.*" §411(a) (emphasis added).

Congress added this sentence to the Act in 1976, 90 Stat. 2583, to clarify that a federal court can determine "the issue of registrability of the copyright claim" even if the Register does not appear in the infringement suit. That clarification was necessary because courts had interpreted §411(a)'s precursor provision, which imposed a similar registration requirement, as prohibiting copyright owners who had been *refused* registration by the Register of Copyrights from suing for infringement until the owners *first* sought mandamus against the Register. See *Vacheron & Constantin-Le Coultre Watches, Inc. v. Benrus Watch Co.,* 260 F.2d 637, 640-641 (C.A.2 1958) (construing §411(a)'s precursor). The 1976 amendment made it clear that a federal court plainly has adjudicatory authority to determine "*that* issue,"

§411(a) (emphasis added)-*i.e.*, the issue of *registrability*—regardless of whether the Register is a party to the *infringement* suit. The word "jurisdiction," as used here, thus says nothing about whether a federal court has subject-matter jurisdiction to adjudicate claims for infringement of unregistered works.

Moreover, §411(a)'s registration requirement . . . is located in a provision "separate" from those granting federal courts subject-matter jurisdiction over those respective claims. Federal district courts have subject-matter jurisdiction over copyright infringement actions based on 28 U.S.C. §§1331 and 1338. But neither §1331, which confers subject-matter jurisdiction over questions of federal law, nor §1338(a), which is specific to copyright claims, conditions its jurisdictional grant on whether copyright holders have registered their works before suing for infringement.

Nor does any other factor suggest that 17 U.S.C.A. §411(a)'s registration requirement can be read to "'speak in jurisdictional terms or refer in any way to the jurisdiction of the district courts.'" *Arbaugh*, 546 U.S., at 515 (quoting *Zipes v. Trans World Airlines, Inc.*, 455 U.S. 385, 394 (1982)). First, and most significantly, §411(a) expressly *allows* courts to adjudicate infringement claims involving unregistered works in three circumstances: where the work is not a U.S. work, where the infringement claim concerns rights of attribution and integrity under §106A, or where the holder attempted to register the work and registration was refused. Separately, §411(c) permits courts to adjudicate infringement actions over certain kinds of unregistered works where the author "declare[s] an intention to secure copyright in the work" and "makes registration for the work, if required by subsection (a), within three months after [the work's] first transmission." 17 U.S.C. §§411(c)(1)-(2). It would be at least unusual to ascribe jurisdictional significance to a condition subject to these sorts of exceptions.

. . . We similarly have treated as nonjurisdictional other types of threshold requirements that claimants must complete, or exhaust, before filing a lawsuit.

The registration requirement in 17 U.S.C.A. §411(a) fits in this mold. Section 411(a) imposes a precondition to filing a claim that is not clearly labeled jurisdictional, is not located in a jurisdiction-granting provision, and admits of congressionally authorized exceptions. Section 411(a) thus imposes a type of precondition to suit that supports nonjurisdictional treatment under our precedents.

C

Amicus insists that our decision in *Bowles* [*v. Russell*], 551 U.S. 205 [(2007)], compels a conclusion contrary to the one we reach today. *Amicus* cites *Bowles* for the proposition that where Congress did not explicitly label a statutory condition as jurisdictional, a court nevertheless should treat it as such if that is how the condition consistently has been interpreted and if Congress has not disturbed that interpretation. . . .

Bowles did not hold that any statutory condition devoid of an express jurisdictional label should be treated as jurisdictional simply because courts have long treated it as such. Nor did it hold that all statutory conditions imposing a time limit should be considered jurisdictional. Rather, *Bowles* stands for the proposition that context, including this Court's interpretation of similar provisions in many years past, is relevant to whether a statute ranks a requirement as jurisdictional. . . .

. . . Although §411(a)'s historical treatment as "jurisdictional" is a factor in the analysis, it is not dispositive. The other factors discussed above demonstrate that §411(a)'s registration requirement is more analogous to the nonjurisdictional conditions we considered in *Zipes* and *Arbaugh* than to the statutory time limit at issue in *Bowles*. We thus conclude that §411(a)'s registration requirement is nonjurisdictional, notwithstanding its prior jurisdictional treatment. . . .

NOTES AND QUESTIONS

1. In *Reed Elsevier* the question about the nature of the registration requirement arose in the context of approval of a class action settlement involving both registered and unregistered works. How will the Court's holding affect non-class action lawsuits? If a plaintiff files an infringement lawsuit but has not yet registered the copyright that she claims has been infringed, should the case be dismissed for failure to meet a "precondition to suit"? Does the court have the authority to stay the action pending registration? Does the defendant in such a case have to file a motion to dismiss or can the court dismiss the case *sua sponte*?

2. Focus on the exemptions to the registration requirement that the Court identifies. What policy might animate exempting claims under §106A from the registration requirement? Why are non–U.S. works exempted?

3. Before *Reed Elsevier* a circuit split had developed concerning whether a copyright owner could sue upon filing an application for registration (the "application approach") or had to wait until receiving the Copyright Office's decision on the application (the "registration approach"). After *Reed Elsevier* courts continue to confront the same issue. *See, e.g., Cosmetic Ideas, Inc. v. IAC/ Interactive Corp.*, 606 F.3d 612, 615-21 (9th Cir.), *cert. denied*, 131 S. Ct. 686 (2010), (concluding that "the application approach better fulfills Congress' purpose of providing broad copyright protection while maintaining a robust federal register"). Should *Reed Elsevier* affect how courts interpret the timing aspects of the registration requirement?

4. Timing can be critically important in infringement lawsuits. In 2014, the Copyright Office reported that the processing time for electronically filed applications was 3 to 5 months, with paper applications taking 7 to 13 months. If the plaintiff must wait for the Copyright Office to issue the registration before filing suit, the suit may be barred by the statute of limitations. Other times, a plaintiff desires prompt injunctive relief. If the plaintiff must wait for the registration certificate before filing suit, the delay in obtaining injunctive relief may be devastating. The Copyright Office allows registrants to request special expedited handling in cases of pending or prospective litigation. The fee is $800 as of this writing, and every attempt is made to process the claim within five working days. Should the existence of this process influence courts' interpretations of the timing requirements for §411?

2. Filing Too Late

Like other causes of action, claims of copyright infringement are subject to a statute of limitations that establishes the time frame in which legal proceedings must be filed. The next case addresses the interplay between the statute of limitations and equitable doctrines such as laches and estoppel.

Petrella v. Metro-Goldwyn-Mayer, Inc.
134 S. Ct. 1962 (2014)

GINSBURG, J.: The Copyright Act provides that "[n]o civil action shall be maintained under the [Act] unless it is commenced within three years after the claim accrued." 17 U.S.C. §507(b). This case presents the question whether the equitable defense of laches (unreasonable, prejudicial delay in commencing suit) may bar relief on a copyright infringement claim brought within §507(b)'s three-year limitations period. . . .

I . . .

The federal limitations prescription governing copyright suits serves two purposes: (1) to render uniform and certain the time within which copyright claims could be pursued; and (2) to prevent the forum shopping invited by disparate state limitations periods, which ranged from one to eight years. To comprehend how the Copyright Act's limitations period works, one must understand when a copyright infringement claim accrues.

> **LOOKING FORWARD**
>
> Section 507 also provides a five-year statute of limitation for criminal actions. We address criminal proceedings later in this chapter.

A claim ordinarily accrues "when [a] plaintiff has a complete and present cause of action." *Bay Area Laundry and Dry Cleaning Pension Trust Fund v. Ferbar Corp. of Cal.*, 522 U.S. 192, 201 (1997) (internal quotation marks omitted). In other words, the limitations period generally begins to run at the point when "the plaintiff can file suit and obtain relief." *Ibid.* A copyright claim thus arises or "accrue[s]" when an infringing act occurs.[4]

It is widely recognized that the separate-accrual rule attends the copyright statute of limitations. Under that rule, when a defendant commits successive violations, the statute of limitations runs separately from each violation. Each time an infringing work is reproduced or distributed, the infringer commits a new wrong. Each wrong

---

4. Although we have not passed on the question, nine Courts of Appeals have adopted, as an alternative to the incident of injury rule, a "discovery rule," which starts the limitations period when "the plaintiff discovers, or with due diligence should have discovered, the injury that forms the basis for the claim." *William A. Graham Co. v. Haughey*, 568 F.3d 425, 433 (C.A. 3 2009) (internal quotation marks omitted). See also 6 W. Patry, Copyright §20:19, p. 20-28 (2013) (hereinafter Patry) ("The overwhelming majority of courts use discovery accrual in copyright cases.").

gives rise to a discrete "claim" that "accrue[s]" at the time the wrong occurs. In short, each infringing act starts a new limitations period.

Under the Act's three-year provision, an infringement is actionable within three years, and only three years, of its occurrence. And the infringer is insulated from liability for earlier infringements of the same work. Thus, when a defendant has engaged (or is alleged to have engaged) in a series of discrete infringing acts, the copyright holder's suit ordinarily will be timely under §507(b) with respect to more recent acts of infringement (*i.e.,* acts within the three-year window), but untimely with respect to prior acts of the same or similar kind. . . .

II. A

The allegedly infringing work in this case is the critically acclaimed motion picture Raging Bull, based on the life of boxing champion Jake LaMotta. After retiring from the ring, LaMotta worked with his longtime friend, Frank Petrella, to tell the story of the boxer's career. Their venture resulted in three copyrighted works: two screenplays, one registered in 1963, the other in 1973, and a book, registered in 1970. This case centers on the screenplay registered in 1963. The registration identified Frank Petrella as sole author, but also stated that the screenplay was written "in collaboration with" LaMotta.

In 1976, Frank Petrella and LaMotta assigned their rights in the three works, including renewal rights, to Chartoff-Winkler Productions, Inc. Two years later, respondent United Artists Corporation, a subsidiary of respondent Metro-Goldwyn-Mayer, Inc. (collectively, MGM), acquired the motion picture rights to the book and both screenplays, rights stated by the parties to be "exclusiv[e] and forever, including all periods of copyright and renewals and extensions thereof." In 1980, MGM released, and registered a copyright in, the film Raging Bull, directed by Martin Scorsese and starring Robert De Niro, who won a Best Actor Academy Award for his portrayal of LaMotta. MGM continues to market the film, and has converted it into formats unimagined in 1980, including DVD and Blu-ray.

Frank Petrella died in 1981, during the initial terms of the copyrights in the screenplays and book. As this Court's decision in *Stewart* [*v. Abend,* 495 U.S. 207 (1990)] confirmed, Frank Petrella's renewal rights reverted to his heirs, who could renew the copyrights unburdened by any assignment previously made by the author. See 495 U.S., at 220–221.

Plaintiff below, petitioner here, Paula Petrella (Petrella) is Frank Petrella's daughter. Learning of this Court's decision in *Stewart,* Petrella engaged an attorney who, in 1991, renewed the copyright in the 1963 screenplay. Because the copyrights in the 1973 screenplay and the 1970 book were not timely renewed, the infringement claims in this case rest exclusively on the screenplay registered in 1963. Petrella is now sole owner of the copyright in that work.

In 1998, seven years after filing for renewal of the copyright in the 1963 screenplay, Petrella's attorney informed MGM that Petrella had obtained the copyright to that screenplay. Exploitation of any derivative work, including Raging Bull, the attorney asserted, infringed on the copyright now vested in Petrella. During the next two years, counsel for Petrella and MGM exchanged letters in which MGM denied the validity of the infringement claims, and Petrella repeatedly threatened to take legal action.

B

Some nine years later, on January 6, 2009, Petrella filed a copyright infringement suit in the United States District Court for the Central District of California. She alleged that MGM violated and continued to violate her copyright in the 1963 screenplay by using, producing, and distributing Raging Bull, a work she described as derivative of the 1963 screenplay. Petrella's complaint sought monetary and injunctive relief. Because the statute of limitations for copyright claims requires commencement of suit "within three years after the claim accrued," §507(b), Petrella sought relief only for acts of infringement occurring on or after January 6, 2006. No relief, she recognizes, can be awarded for infringing acts prior to that date.

MGM moved for summary judgment on several grounds, among them, the equitable doctrine of laches. Petrella's 18-year delay, from the 1991 renewal of the copyright on which she relied, until 2009, when she commenced suit, MGM maintained, was unreasonable and prejudicial to MGM.

The District Court granted MGM's motion . . . [holding] laches barred Petrella's complaint. . . . In particular, the court stated, MGM had shown "expectations-based prejudice," because the company had "made significant investments in exploiting the film"; in addition, the court accepted that MGM would encounter "evidentiary prejudice," because Frank Petrella had died and LaMotta, then aged 88, appeared to have sustained a loss of memory.

The U.S. Court of Appeals for the Ninth Circuit affirmed the laches-based dismissal. . . . "[T]he true cause of Petrella's delay," the court suggested, "was, as [Petrella] admits, that 'the film hadn't made money' [in years she deferred suit]." . . .

We granted certiorari to resolve a conflict among the Circuits on the application of the equitable defense of laches to copyright infringement claims brought within the three-year look-back period prescribed by Congress.

III

We consider first whether, as the Ninth Circuit held, laches may be invoked as a bar to Petrella's pursuit of legal remedies under 17 U.S.C. §504(b). The Ninth Circuit erred, we hold, in failing to recognize that the copyright statute of limitations, §507(b), itself takes account of delay. As earlier observed, a successful plaintiff can gain retrospective relief only three years back from the time of suit. No recovery may be had for infringement in earlier years. Profits made in those years remain the defendant's to keep. Brought to bear here, §507(b) directs that MGM's returns on its investment in Raging Bull in years outside the three-year window (years before 2006) cannot be reached by Petrella. Only by disregarding that feature of the statute, and the separate-accrual rule attending §507(b), could the Court of Appeals presume that infringing acts occurring before January 6, 2006 bar all relief, monetary and injunctive, for infringement occurring on and after that date.[13] . . .

IV . . .

A . . .

The expansive role for laches MGM envisions careens away from understandings, past and present, of the essentially gap-filling, not legislation-overriding, office of laches. Nothing in this Court's precedent suggests a doctrine of such sweep. Quite the contrary, we have never applied laches to bar in their entirety claims for discrete wrongs occurring within a federally prescribed limitations period. Inviting individual judges to set a time limit other than the one Congress prescribed, we note, would tug against the uniformity Congress sought to achieve when it enacted §507(b). . . .

C

MGM insists that the defense of laches must be available to prevent a copyright owner from sitting still, doing nothing, waiting to see what the outcome of an alleged infringer's investment will be. In this case, MGM stresses, "[Petrella] *conceded* that she waited to file because 'the film was deeply in debt and in the red and would probably never recoup.'" The Ninth Circuit similarly faulted Petrella for waiting to sue until the film Raging Bull "made money."

It is hardly incumbent on copyright owners, however, to challenge each and every actionable infringement. And there is nothing untoward about waiting to see whether an infringer's exploitation undercuts the value of the copyrighted work, has no effect on the original work, or even complements it. Fan sites prompted by a book or film, for example, may benefit the copyright owner. See Wu, Tolerated Use, 31 Colum. J.L. & Arts 617, 619–620 (2008). Even if an infringement is harmful, the harm may be too small to justify the cost of litigation.

If the rule were, as MGM urges, "sue soon, or forever hold your peace," copyright owners would have to mount a federal case fast to stop seemingly innocuous infringements, lest those infringements eventually grow in magnitude. Section 507(b)'s three-year limitations period, however, coupled to the separate-accrual rule, avoids such litigation profusion. It allows a copyright owner to defer suit until she can estimate whether litigation is worth the candle. She will miss out on damages for periods prior to the three-year look-back, but her right to prospective injunctive relief should, in most cases, remain unaltered.[19] . . .

---

13. Assuming Petrella had a winning case on the merits, the Court of Appeals' ruling on laches would effectively give MGM a cost-free license to exploit Raging Bull throughout the long term of the copyright. The value to MGM of such a free, compulsory license could exceed by far MGM's expenditures on the film.

19. The dissent worries that a plaintiff might sue for profits "every three years . . . until the copyright expires." That suggestion neglects to note that a plaintiff who proves infringement will likely gain forward-looking injunctive relief stopping the defendant's repetition of infringing acts.

E

Finally, when a copyright owner engages in intentionally misleading representations concerning his abstention from suit, and the alleged infringer detrimentally relies on the copyright owner's deception, the doctrine of estoppel may bar the copyright owner's claims completely, eliminating all potential remedies. The test for estoppel is more exacting than the test for laches, and the two defenses are differently oriented. The gravamen of estoppel, a defense long recognized as available in actions at law, see *Wehrman v. Conklin*, 155 U.S. 314, 327 (1894), is misleading and consequent loss. Delay may be involved, but is not an element of the defense. For laches, timeliness is the essential element. In contrast to laches, urged by MGM entirely to override the statute of limitations Congress prescribed, estoppel does not undermine Congress' prescription, for it rests on misleading, whether engaged in early on, or later in time. . . .

V

. . . Congress' time provisions secured to authors a copyright term of long duration, and a right to sue for infringement occurring no more than three years back from the time of suit. That regime leaves "little place" for a doctrine that would further limit the timeliness of a copyright owner's suit. In extraordinary circumstances, however, the consequences of a delay in commencing suit may be of sufficient magnitude to warrant, at the very outset of the litigation, curtailment of the relief equitably awardable.

Chirco v. Crosswinds Communities, Inc., 474 F.3d 227 (C.A.6 2007), is illustrative. In that case, the defendants were alleged to have used without permission, in planning and building a housing development, the plaintiffs' copyrighted architectural design. Long aware of the defendants' project, the plaintiffs took no steps to halt the housing development until more than 168 units were built, 109 of which were occupied. *Id.*, at 230. Although the action was filed within §507(b)'s three-year statute of limitations, the District Court granted summary judgment to the defendants, dismissing the entire case on grounds of laches. The trial court's rejection of the entire suit could not stand, the Court of Appeals explained, for it was not within the Judiciary's ken to debate the wisdom of §507(b)'s three-year look-back prescription. *Id.*, at 235. Nevertheless, the Court of Appeals affirmed the District Court's judgment to this extent: The plaintiffs, even if they might succeed in proving infringement of their copyrighted design, would not be entitled to an order mandating destruction of the housing project. That relief would be inequitable, the Sixth Circuit held, for two reasons: the plaintiffs knew of the defendants' construction plans before the defendants broke ground, yet failed to take readily available measures to stop the project; and the requested relief would "work an *unjust* hardship" upon the defendants and innocent third parties. *Id.*, at 236.

In sum, the courts below erred in treating laches as a complete bar to Petrella's copyright infringement suit. The action was commenced within the bounds of §507(b), the Act's time-to-sue prescription, and does not present extraordinary circumstances of the kind involved in *Chirco* . . . . Petrella notified MGM of her copyright claims *before* MGM invested millions of dollars in creating a new edition of Raging Bull. . . . MGM released Raging Bull more than three decades ago and has marketed it continuously since then. Allowing Petrella's suit to go forward will put at risk only a fraction of the income MGM has earned during that period and will work no unjust hardship on innocent third parties, such as consumers who have purchased copies of Raging Bull. Cf. *Chirco*, 474 F.3d, at 235–236 (destruction remedy would have ousted families from recently purchased homes). The circumstances here may or may not (we need not decide) warrant limiting relief at the remedial stage, but they are not sufficiently extraordinary to justify threshold dismissal.

Should Petrella ultimately prevail on the merits, the District Court, in determining appropriate injunctive relief and assessing profits, may take account of her delay in commencing suit. In doing so, however, that court should closely examine MGM's alleged reliance on Petrella's delay.[22] This examination should take account of MGM's early knowledge of Petrella's claims, the protection MGM might have achieved through pursuit of a declaratory judgment action, the extent to which MGM's investment was protected by the separate-accrual rule, the court's authority to order injunctive relief "on such terms as it may deem reasonable," §502(a), and any other considerations that would justify adjusting injunctive relief or profits. . . .

NOTES AND QUESTIONS

1. After *Petrella* is there any role left for laches in copyright cases?

2. Does the rolling statute of limitations make sense? If each new infringement begins a new three-year clock, what is the purpose of the statute of limitations?

3. While the three-year statute of limitations may be brief, the "rolling" nature of its application creates situations in which a defendant can be infringing for decades, with the full knowledge of the copyright owner, and the copyright owner can still bring an action and not be time-barred. Justice Breyer, joined by Chief Justice Roberts and Justice Kennedy, dissented. He argued that "it may well be 'inequitable for the owner of a copyright, with full notice of an intended infringement, to stand inactive while the proposed infringer spends large sums of money in its exploitation, and to intervene only when his speculation has proved a success.'" *Petrella v. Metro-Goldwyn-Mayer, Inc.*, 134 S. Ct. 1962, 1979 (2014) (Breyer, J., dissenting) (quoting *Haas v. Leo Feist, Inc.*, 234 F. 105, 108 (S.D.N.Y. 1916)). The dissenters were concerned, *inter alia*, that in some cases, long delay by the copyright owner could be prejudicial to the defendant either because witnesses had died or evidence was lost. In those cases should equity be able to ameliorate the consequences of delay?

4. Sometimes the plaintiff's delay in filing suit is due to a lack of awareness of the infringing activity. Review footnote 4 of the Court's opinion in *Petrella*. The rule that the statute of limitations does not begin to run until the plaintiff discovers the alleged wrongful act is often described as "tolling" the statute of limitations.

---

22. While reliance or its absence may figure importantly in this case, we do not suggest that reliance is in all cases a *sine qua non* for adjustment of injunctive relief or profits.

According to current practice in the majority of circuits, one must consider both rolling and tolling when analyzing statute of limitations concerns.

D. JURY TRIAL

As you now know, federal courts have exclusive subject matter jurisdiction over copyright infringement actions. In the federal courts, the Seventh Amendment guarantees a right to a jury trial in certain kinds of litigation. For infringement actions seeking actual damages, either party is entitled to a jury trial. Actions for injunctive relief, however, do not give rise to a right to demand a jury trial. In the case that follows, the Supreme Court addresses the right to a jury trial when the remedy sought is statutory damages.

Feltner v. Columbia Pictures Television, Inc.
523 U.S. 340 (1998)

THOMAS, J.: . . . Petitioner C. Elvin Feltner owns Krypton International Corporation, which in 1990 acquired three television stations in the southeastern United States. Respondent Columbia Pictures Television, Inc., had licensed several television series to these stations, including "Who's the Boss," "Silver Spoons," "Hart to Hart," and "T. J. Hooker." After the stations became delinquent in making their royalty payments to Columbia, Krypton and Columbia entered into negotiations to restructure the stations' debt. These discussions were unavailing, and Columbia terminated the stations' license agreements in October 1991. Despite Columbia's termination, the stations continued broadcasting the programs.

Columbia sued Feltner, Krypton, the stations, various Krypton subsidiaries, and certain Krypton officers in Federal District Court alleging, *inter alia*, copyright infringement arising from the stations' unauthorized broadcasting of the programs. . . . On Columbia's motion, the District Court entered partial summary judgment as to liability for Columbia on its copyright infringement claims.

Columbia exercised the option afforded by §504(c) of the Copyright Act to recover "Statutory Damages" in lieu of actual damages. . . .

The District Court denied Feltner's request for a jury trial on statutory damages, ruling instead that such issues would be determined at a bench trial. After two days of trial . . . the trial judge determined that Columbia was entitled to $8,800,000 in statutory damages, plus costs and attorney's fees.

The Court of Appeals for the Ninth Circuit affirmed in all relevant respects. . . . The Court of Appeals . . . concluded that the "Seventh Amendment does not provide a right to a jury trial on the issue of statutory damages because an award of such damages is equitable in nature." . . .

II . . .

The language of §504(c) does not grant a right to have a jury assess statutory damages. Statutory damages are to be assessed in an amount that "the court considers just." §504(c)(1). Further, in the event that "the court finds" the infringement was willful or innocent, "the court in its discretion" may, within limits, increase or decrease the amount of statutory damages. §504(c)(2). These phrases, like the entire statutory provision, make no mention of a right to a jury trial or, for that matter, to juries at all. . . .

III

The Seventh Amendment provides that "[i]n Suits at common law, where the value in controversy shall exceed twenty dollars, the right of trial by jury shall be preserved. . . ." U.S. Const., Amdt. 7. Since Justice Story's time, the Court has understood "Suits at common law" to refer "not merely [to] suits, which the *common* law recognized among its old and settled proceedings, but [to] suits in which *legal* rights were to be ascertained and determined, in contradistinction to those where equitable rights alone were recognized, and equitable remedies were administered." *Parsons v. Bedford*, 3 Pet. 433, 447 (1830) (emphasis in original). The Seventh Amendment thus applies not only to common-law causes of action, but also to "actions brought to enforce statutory rights that are analogous to common-law causes of action ordinarily decided in English law courts in the late 18th century, as opposed to those customarily heard by courts of equity or admiralty." *Granfinanciera, S.A. v. Nordberg*, 492 U.S. 33, 42 (1989) (citing *Curtis v. Loether*, 415 U.S. [189, 193 (1974)]). . . .

. . . [I]n this case there are close analogues to actions seeking statutory damages under §504(c). Before the adoption of the Seventh Amendment, the common law and statutes in England and this country granted copyright owners causes of action for infringement. More importantly, copyright suits for monetary damages were tried in courts of law, and thus before juries.

By the middle of the 17th century, the common law recognized an author's right to prevent the unauthorized publication of his manuscript. This protection derived from the principle that the manuscript was the product of intellectual labor and was as much the author's property as the material on which it was written. See *Millar v. Taylor*, 4 Burr. 2303, 2398, 98 Eng. Rep. 201, 252 (K.B. 1769) (opinion of Mansfield, C.J.) (common-law copyright derived from principle that "it is just, that an Author should reap the pecuniary Profits of his own ingenuity and Labour"). Actions seeking damages for infringement of common-law copyright, like actions seeking damages for invasions of other property rights, were tried in courts of law in actions on the case. Actions on the case, like other actions at law, were tried before juries.

In 1710, the first English copyright statute, the Statute of Anne, was enacted to protect published books. . . . Like the earlier practice with regard to common-law copyright claims for damages, actions seeking damages under the Statute of Anne were tried in courts of law.

The practice of trying copyright damages actions at law before juries was followed in this country, where statutory copyright protections were enacted even before adoption of the Constitution. In 1783, the Continental Congress passed a resolution recommending that the States secure copyright protections for authors. Twelve States (all except Delaware) responded by enacting copyright statutes, each of which provided a cause of action for damages, and none of which made any reference to equity jurisdiction. At least three of these state statutes expressly stated that damages were to be recovered through actions at law, while four others provided that damages would be recovered in an "action of debt," a prototypical action brought in a court of law before a jury. Although these statutes were short-lived, and hence few courts had occasion to interpret them, the available evidence suggests that the practice was for copyright actions seeking damages to be tried to a jury.

Moreover, three of the state statutes specifically authorized an award of damages from a statutory range, just as §504(c) does today. . . .

There is no evidence that the Copyright Act of 1790 changed the practice of trying copyright actions for damages in courts of law before juries. As we have noted, actions on the case and actions of debt were actions at law for which a jury was required. Moreover, actions to recover damages under the Copyright Act of 1831— which differed from the Copyright Act of 1790 only in the amount (increased to $1 from 50 cents) authorized to be recovered for certain infringing sheets—were consistently tried to juries.

Columbia does not dispute this historical evidence. . . . Rather, Columbia merely contends that statutory damages are clearly equitable in nature.

We are not persuaded. We have recognized the "general rule" that monetary relief is legal and an award of statutory damages may serve purposes traditionally associated with legal relief, such as compensation and punishment. Nor, as we have previously stated, is a monetary remedy rendered equitable simply because it is "not fixed or readily calculable from a fixed formula." And there is historical evidence that cases involving discretionary monetary relief were tried before juries. Accordingly, we must conclude that the Seventh Amendment provides a right to a jury trial where the copyright owner elects to recover statutory damages.

The right to a jury trial includes the right to have a jury determine the *amount* of statutory damages, if any, awarded to the copyright owner. . . . [T]here is overwhelming evidence that the consistent practice at common law was for juries to award damages.

More specifically, this was the consistent practice in copyright cases. In *Hudson v. Patten*, 1 Root, at 134, for example, a jury awarded a copyright owner £100 under the Connecticut copyright statute, which permitted damages in an amount double the value of the infringed copy. In addition, juries assessed the amount of damages under the Copyright Act of 1831, even though that statute, like the Copyright Act of 1790, fixed damages at a set amount per infringing sheet. . . .

AFTERMATH

Following remand from the Supreme Court, the district court held a jury trial on the issue of statutory damages, and the jury awarded plaintiffs $31.68 million. The Ninth Circuit affirmed the award. *See Columbia Pictures Television, Inc. v. Krypton Broad. of Birmingham, Inc.,* 259 F.3d 1186 (9th Cir. 2001), *cert. denied sub nom., Feltner v. Columbia Pictures Television, Inc.,* 534 U.S. 1127 (2002).

NOTES AND QUESTIONS

1. Review the practice exercise in Chapter 5.A.3.b, *supra,* concerning the Persian carpets. If you represented the plaintiff in that case, would you seek a jury trial? Why, or why not?

2. What are the advantages and disadvantages of having a jury trial? For what kinds of subject matter would a jury trial be more or less appropriate? Would your answer depend on the type of evidence likely to be offered at trial? Would your answer also depend on the particular infringement test that a circuit applies?

3. It is an open question whether the Seventh Amendment affords a jury trial right in suits brought under the Visual Artists Rights Act because such claims appear to lack any analog in common law. *See Pollara v. Seymour,* 344 F.3d 265, 268 (2d Cir. 2003). Would you seek a jury trial if you represented a sculptor in a case involving the destruction of her work?

E. FOREIGN COPYRIGHT LAW IN U.S. COURTS

1. Choice of Law

As you have learned, international copyright treaties do not have any direct effect in the United States; rather, Congress must adopt implementing legislation. However, the copyright laws of other countries sometimes do have direct effect in domestic litigation. Courts sometimes must consider claims of infringement by foreign plaintiffs who assert copyright interests based upon their own countries' laws. How does a court decide which law to apply to determine whether the work is protectable in the United States, who owns rights in the work, and whether the copyright has been infringed? Neither the Berne Convention nor the TRIPS Agreement supplies a choice of law rule. Thus, countries may differ in their approaches to these questions. The following cases illustrate how U.S. courts have determined the applicable law.

≣   *Itar-Tass Russian News Agency v. Russian Kurier, Inc.*
≣   *153 F.3d 82 (2d Cir. 1998)*

NEWMAN, J.: This appeal primarily presents issues concerning the choice of law in international copyright cases and the substantive meaning of Russian copyright law as to the respective rights of newspaper reporters and newspaper publishers. The conflicts issue is which country's law applies to issues of copyright ownership and to issues of infringement. . . .

On the conflicts issue, we conclude that, with respect to the Russian plaintiffs, Russian law determines the ownership and essential nature of the copyrights alleged to have been infringed and that United States law determines whether those copyrights have been infringed in the United States and, if so, what remedies are available. . . .

The lawsuit concerns *Kurier*, a Russian language weekly newspaper with a circulation in the New York area of about 20,000. It is published in New York City by defendant Kurier. Defendant Pogrebnoy is president and sole shareholder of *Kurier* and editor-in-chief of *Kurier*. The plaintiffs include corporations that publish, daily or weekly, major Russian language newspapers in Russia and Russian language magazines in Russia or Israel; Itar-Tass Russian News Agency ("Itar-Tass"), formerly known as the Telegraph Agency of the Soviet Union (TASS), a wire service and news gathering company centered in Moscow, functioning similarly to the Associated Press; and the Union of Journalists of Russia ("UJR"), the professional writers union of accredited print and broadcast journalists of the Russian Federation.

The Kurier defendants do not dispute that *Kurier* has copied about 500 articles that first appeared in the plaintiffs' publications or were distributed by Itar-Tass. The copied material, though extensive, was a small percentage of the total number of articles published in *Kurier*. The Kurier defendants also do not dispute how the copying occurred: articles from the plaintiffs' publications, sometimes containing headlines, pictures, bylines, and graphics, in addition to text, were cut out, pasted on layout sheets, and sent to *Kurier*'s printer for photographic reproduction and printing in the pages of *Kurier*.

Most significantly, the Kurier defendants also do not dispute that, with one exception, they had not obtained permission from any of the plaintiffs to copy the articles that appeared in *Kurier*. . . .

[At issue on appeal was the interpretation of Article 11 of the Russian Copyright law, which provides for the rights of compilers of works excluded from the Russian work-for-hire doctrine (i.e., newspapers). There was conflicting expert testimony regarding the rights of publishers in the work as a whole. The district court accepted the interpretation of plaintiffs' expert, who opined that Article 11 vests publishers with the right to redress copying. The Kurier defendants appealed from the district court's judgment enjoining them from copying the articles appearing in the plaintiffs' publications and awarding damages for infringement.]

I. Choice of Law

The threshold issue concerns the choice of law for resolution of this dispute. That issue was not initially considered by the parties, all of whom turned directly to Russian law for resolution of the case. . . .

Choice of law issues in international copyright cases have been largely ignored in the reported decisions and dealt with rather cursorily by most commentators. Examples pertinent to the pending appeal are those decisions involving a work created by the employee of a foreign corporation. Several courts have applied the United States work-for-hire doctrine, without explicit consideration of the conflicts issue. . . .

The Nimmer treatise briefly (and perhaps optimistically) suggests that conflicts issues "have rarely proved troublesome in the law of copyright." *Nimmer on Copyright* §17.05 (1998) ("*Nimmer*"). Relying on the "national treatment" principle of the Berne Convention and the Universal Copyright Convention ("U.C.C."), *Nimmer* asserts, correctly in our view, that "an author who is a national of one of the member states of either Berne or the U.C.C., or one who first publishes his work in any such member state, is entitled to the same copyright protection in each other member state as such other state accords to its own nationals." *Id.* *Nimmer* then somewhat overstates the national treatment principle: "The applicable law is the copyright law of the state in which the infringement occurred, not that of the state of which the author is a national, or in which the work is first published." *Id.* The difficulty with this broad statement is that it subsumes under the phrase "applicable law" the law concerning two distinct issues—ownership and substantive rights, *i.e.*, scope of protection.[8] Another commentator has also broadly stated the principle of national treatment, but described its application in a way that does not necessarily cover issues of ownership. "The principle of national treatment also means that both the question of whether the right exists and the question of the scope of the right are to be answered in accordance with the law of the country where the protection is claimed." S.M. Stewart, International Copyright and Neighboring Rights §3.17 (2d ed. 1989). We agree with the view of the Amicus that the Convention's principle of national treatment simply assures that if the law of the country of infringement applies to the scope of substantive copyright protection, that law will be applied uniformly to foreign and domestic authors.

Source of conflicts rules. Our analysis of the conflicts issue begins with consideration of the source of law for selecting a conflicts rule. Though *Nimmer* turns directly to the Berne Convention and the U.C.C., we think that step moves too quickly past the Berne Convention Implementation Act of 1988. Section 4(a)(3) of the Act amends Title 17 to provide: "No right or interest in a work eligible for protection under this title may be claimed by virtue of . . . the

---

8. Prof. Patry's brief, as Amicus Curiae, helpfully points out that the principle of national treatment is really not a conflicts rule at all; it does not direct application of the law of any country. It simply requires that the country in which protection is claimed must treat foreign and domestic authors alike. Whether U.S. copyright law directs U.S. courts to look to foreign or domestic law as to certain issues is irrelevant to national treatment, so long as the scope of protection would be extended equally to foreign and domestic authors.

provisions of the Berne Convention. . . . Any rights in a work eligible for protection under this title that derive from this title . . . shall not be expanded or reduced by virtue of . . . the provisions of the Berne Convention." 17 U.S.C. §104(c).

We start our analysis with the Copyrights [sic] Act itself, which contains no provision relevant to the pending case concerning conflicts issues. We therefore fill the interstices of the Act by developing federal common law on the conflicts issue. In doing so, we are entitled to consider and apply principles of private international law, which are "'part of our law.'"

The choice of law applicable to the pending case is not necessarily the same for all issues. *See* Restatement (Second) of Conflict of Laws §222 ("The courts have long recognized that they are not bound to decide all issues under the local law of a single state."). We consider first the law applicable to the issue of copyright ownership.

Conflicts rule for issues of ownership.   Copyright is a form of property, and the usual rule is that the interests of the parties in property are determined by the law of the state with "the most significant relationship" to the property and the parties. *See id.* The Restatement recognizes the applicability of this principle to intangibles such as "a literary idea." *Id.* Since the works at issue were created by Russian nationals and first published in Russia, Russian law is the appropriate source of law to determine issues of ownership of rights. . . . In terms of the United States Copyrights [sic] Act and its reference to the Berne Convention, Russia is the "country of origin" of these works, *see* 17 U.S.C. §101 (definition of "country of origin" of Berne Convention work); Berne Convention, Art. 5(4), although "country of origin" might not always be the appropriate country for purposes of choice of law concerning ownership.[11]

To whatever extent we look to the Berne Convention itself as guidance in the development of federal common law on the conflicts issue, we find nothing to alter our conclusion. The Convention does not purport to settle issues of ownership. . . .

Conflicts rule for infringement issues.   On infringement issues, the governing conflicts principle is usually *lex loci delicti*, the doctrine generally applicable to torts. We have implicitly adopted that approach to infringement claims, applying United States copyright law to a work that was unprotected in its country of origin. In the pending case, the place of the tort is plainly the United States. To whatever extent *lex loci delicti* is to be considered only one part of a broader "interest" approach, United States law would still apply to infringement issues, since not only is this country the place of the tort, but also the defendant is a United States corporation.

The division of issues, for conflicts purposes, between ownership and infringement issues will not always be as easily made as the above discussion implies. If the issue is the relatively straightforward one of which of two contending parties owns a

---

11. In deciding that the law of the country of origin determines the ownership of copyright, we consider only initial ownership, and have no occasion to consider choice of law issues concerning assignments of rights.

copyright, the issue is unquestionably an ownership issue, and the law of the country with the closest relationship to the work will apply to settle the ownership dispute. . . .

Bridgeman Art Library, Ltd. v. Corel Corp.
36 F. Supp. 2d 191 (S.D.N.Y. 1999)

KAPLAN, J.: On November 13, 1998, this Court granted defendant's motion for summary judgment dismissing plaintiff's copyright infringement claim on the alternative grounds that the allegedly infringed works—color transparencies of paintings which themselves are in the public domain—were not original and therefore not permissible subjects of valid copyright and, in any case, were not infringed. It applied United Kingdom law in determining whether plaintiff's transparencies were copyrightable. The Court noted, however, that it would have reached the same result under United States law. . . .

[The plaintiff filed a postjudgment motion for reconsideration.]

Choice of Law . . .

. . . Bridgeman claims that the infringed works are protected by United Kingdom copyrights and that the United States, by acceding to the . . . Berne Convention, and the Universal Copyright Convention and by enacting the Berne Convention Implementation Act of 1988 (the "BCIA"), agreed to give effect to its United Kingdom copyrights.

The fact that plaintiff's rights allegedly derive from its claimed British copyrights arguably is material. Granting . . . that Congress, in light of the originality requirement of the Copyright Clause, in ordinary circumstances may not extend copyright protection to works that are not original, the questions remain whether (1) the United States constitutionally may obligate itself by treaty to permit enforcement of a foreign copyright where that copyright originates under the law of a signatory nation which does not limit copyright protection to works that are original in the sense required by the United States Constitution and, if so, (2) the United States in fact has done so. . . .

. . . [I]t cannot seriously be denied that international copyright protection is "properly the subject of negotiation with" foreign countries.

Decades ago, the Supreme Court held in *Missouri v. Holland*[, 252 U.S. 416 (1920),] that Congress could enact legislation necessary and proper to the implementation of a treaty which, absent the treaty, would have been beyond its powers. Although the case arose in a different context, it suggests that the Conventions, if their purported effect actually is to permit enforcement in the United States of foreign copyrights which do not meet U.S. standards of originality . . . would not be obviously invalid.

In view of these considerations, the proposition advanced . . . that the Copyright Clause forecloses any choice of law issue with respect to the validity of a foreign Berne Convention work, is not free from doubt. It is necessary to decide that question, however, only if the Conventions require application of foreign law in determining the existence of copyright and, if so, whether there is any true conflict of law in this case on that point.

In most circumstances, choice of law issues do not arise under the Berne and Universal Copyright Conventions. Each adopts a rule of national treatment. Article 5 of the Berne Convention, for example, provides that "[a]uthors shall enjoy, in respect of works for which they are protected under this Convention, in countries of the Union other than the country of origin, the rights which their respective laws do now or may hereafter grant to their nationals, as well as the rights specially granted by this convention" and that "the extent of protection, as well as the means of redress afforded to the author to protect his rights, shall be governed exclusively by the laws of the country where protection is claimed." Hence, the Conventions make clear that the holder of, for example, a British copyright who sues for infringement in a United States court is entitled to the same remedies as holders of United States copyrights and, as this Court previously held, to the determination of infringement under the same rule of law.

While the nature of the protection accorded to foreign copyrights in signatory countries thus is spelled out in the Conventions, the position of the subject matter of copyright thereunder is less certain. Do the Conventions purport to require signatory nations to extend national treatment with respect to such enforcement-related subjects as remedies for infringement only where the copyright for which protection is sought would be valid under the law of the nation in which enforcement is sought? Or do they purport to require also that a signatory nation in which enforcement is sought enforce a foreign copyright even if that copyright would not be valid under its own law? But there is an even more fundamental issue, viz. whether United States courts may give effect to any provisions of the Conventions which might require or suggest that the existence of copyright be determined under the law of another nation.

. . . 17 U.S.C. §104(c), states in relevant part that "[n]o right or interest in a work eligible for protection under this title may be claimed by virtue of, or in reliance upon, the provisions of the Berne Convention or the adherence of the United States thereto." Thus, while the Copyright Act, as amended by the BCIA, extends certain protection to the holders of copyright in Berne Convention works as there defined, the Copyright Act is the exclusive source of that protection.

. . . Section 102(a) limits copyright protection in relevant part to "original works of authorship. . . ." Accordingly, there is no need to decide whether the Berne Convention adopts any rule regarding the law governing copyrightability or whether the treaty power constitutionally might be used to extend copyright protection to foreign works which are not "original" within the meaning of the Copyright Clause. Congress has made it quite clear that the United States' adherence to the Berne Convention has no such effect in the courts of this country. . . .

NOTES AND QUESTIONS

1. Do you agree with the *Itar-Tass* court that Russian law should apply to the question of copyright ownership? If so, should British law have applied to the question of copyrightability in *Bridgeman Art Library*? Why, or why not?

2. The *Bridgeman Art Library* court concluded that even if principles of international law might be construed to require a country to extend protection to a work that would not be protected by its own domestic law, Congress explicitly eschewed that result in the BCIA. Is the United States in compliance with its treaty obligations?

2. Enforcement of Judgments

Quite apart from deciding which law should apply to a foreign copyrighted work, the Internet has raised some difficult questions about jurisdiction in copyright cases. If an infringing work is hosted on a server located in country A, and is accessed in country B, do courts in country B have jurisdiction over a lawsuit filed against the foreign website owner? Some courts have indicated a willingness to assert jurisdiction over foreign parties for activity occurring online. *See CYBERsitter, LLC v. People's Republic of China*, 805 F. Supp. 2d 958, 968-74 (C.D. Cal. 2011) (discussing decisions). Copyright owners have repeatedly sought legislation granting courts additional authority, including the ability to grant relief "*in rem*" against nondomestic domain names. The failed SOPA and PIPA bills, *see* Chapter 9.C.4.c, *supra*, would have authorized courts to issue orders against domain names. Such orders then could have been served on operators of domain name servers and other third-party facilitators of the infringement (such as advertisers and credit card companies), requiring those entities to assist in blocking access to the named domain and cease dealing with its owner. What are the pros and cons of such an approach to the problem of cross-border infringement?

If the foreign infringer can be located, but the U.S. courts would not have personal jurisdiction over that infringer, an alternative is to sue the infringer in her home country and then seek to enforce the foreign judgment against assets in the United States. *See, e.g., Sarl Louis Feraud Int'l v. Viewfinder, Inc.*, 489 F.3d 474 (2d Cir. 2007) (addressing whether a French judgment against a website operator should be enforced under New York's Uniform Foreign Money Judgment Recognition Act). Domestic statutes typically provide that a "foreign country judgment need not be recognized if . . . *the cause of action* on which the judgment is based is repugnant to the public policy of this state." N.Y. C.P.L.R. §5304(b)(4) (emphasis added). Application of that rule to intellectual property cases can be complicated. The Second Circuit has articulated a two-part test:

> In deciding whether the French Judgments are repugnant to the public policy of New York, the district court should first determine the level of First Amendment protection required by New York public policy when a news entity engages in the

unauthorized use of intellectual property [like that] at issue here. Then, it should determine whether the French intellectual property regime provides comparable protections.

Viewfinder, 489 F.3d at 481-82. Should a U.S. court enforce a foreign judgment if it finds that the underlying use would be fair under U.S. copyright law? What if the work at issue would not be copyrightable under U.S. law?

Even beyond the online environment, the question of jurisdiction is important in an era in which many transactions cross national borders. To reduce legal uncertainty, parties to such transactions often include jurisdictional provisions in their contracts, and similar provisions may appear in end user shrinkwrap and clickwrap licenses. The American Law Institute's *Intellectual Property: Principles Governing Jurisdiction, Choice of Law, and Judgments in Transnational Disputes* (ALI 2008) [hereinafter "Principles"] seeks to establish standards for the enforcement of choice of forum and choice of law agreements, with special safeguards in the case of mass-market agreements. In such agreements, the clause at issue must be "reasonable and readily accessible to the nondrafting party at the time the agreement was concluded. . . ." Principles §§202, 302. The Principles provide a list of factors for a court to consider in determining reasonableness. *See id*. According to the Principles, a court should enforce a judgment rendered by a foreign court if the foreign court applied the Principles to the case. *Id*. §401(1)(a). Otherwise, the court should determine enforceability based on its ordinary rules regarding enforcement of foreign judgments, but should reject application of "particular rules of foreign law . . . if such application leads to a result in the forum State that is repugnant to the public policy in that State." *Id*. §§322, 401(1)(b). Courts have begun referring to the Principles as support for their decisions. *See, e.g,. Fairchild Semiconductor Corp. v. Third Dimension (3D) Semiconductor, Inc*., 589 F. Supp. 2d 84 (D. Maine 2008).

F. CIVIL REMEDIES

The Copyright Act provides a range of civil remedies for infringement. These are: (1) temporary and final injunctions necessary to prevent or restrain infringement (§502); (2) impoundment of all copies or phonorecords that allegedly infringe the copyright owner's rights (§503(a)); (3) upon a final adjudication of infringement, destruction or disposition of all infringing copies or phonorecords (§503(b)); and (4) monetary damages (§504). The TRIPS Agreement requires member countries to provide for these remedies in their domestic legislation. *See* TRIPS Agreement, art. 44 (injunctions), art. 45 (damages), art. 46 (destruction of infringing goods and the materials and implements used to create them). The Copyright Act also provides that a court may, in its discretion, award costs and attorneys' fees to a prevailing party (§505). In this section, we explore the nature and scope of each remedy. We begin with an examination of the injunctive remedy.

1. Injunctive Relief

The Copyright Act provides that "[a]ny court having jurisdiction of a civil action arising under this title may . . . grant temporary and final injunctions on such terms as it may deem reasonable to prevent or restrain infringement of a copyright." 17 U.S.C. §502. As with other types of litigation in federal court, a copyright infringement plaintiff can seek a preliminary injunction at the beginning of the litigation, as well as a permanent injunction upon successful conclusion of the suit.

a. Permanent Injunctions

In the United States, courts traditionally have considered four factors in determining whether to grant an injunction. Although the precise formulation of the factors varies, a plaintiff generally must show

> (1) that it has suffered an irreparable injury; (2) that remedies available at law, such as monetary damages, are inadequate to compensate for that injury; (3) that, considering the balance of hardships between the plaintiff and defendant, a remedy in equity is warranted; and (4) that the public interest would not be disserved by a permanent injunction.

eBay Inc. v. MercExchange, L.L.C., 547 U.S. 388, 391 (2006).

Historically, courts were willing to grant injunctions in copyright cases without engaging in a detailed analysis of each of the traditional four factors. *See, e.g., Walt Disney Co. v. Powell*, 897 F.2d 565, 567 (D.C. Cir. 1990) ("When a copyright plaintiff has established a threat of continuing infringement, he is *entitled* to an injunction."). This practice can be traced back to the English Courts of Equity, where injunctions were readily granted in copyright cases. *See* H. Tomas Gomez-Arostegui, *What History Teaches Us About Copyright Injunctions and the Inadequate-Remedy-at-Law Requirement*, 81 S. Cal. L. Rev. 1197 (2008). The authority to grant final injunctions was understood as very broad, extending to unregistered works and, sometimes to future works and works not in suit. *See Olan Mills, Inc. v. Linn Photo Co.*, 23 F.3d 1345 (8th Cir. 1994).

In *eBay Inc. v. MercExchange, L.L.C.*, 547 U.S. 388 (2006), the Supreme Court ruled that courts must evaluate the traditional four factors before granting a final injunction in a patent infringement case. The Patent Act provides that courts may "grant injunctions in accordance with the principles of equity to prevent the violation of any right secured by patent, on such terms as the court deems reasonable." 35 U.S.C. §283. The Court rejected the asserted "'general rule,' unique to patent disputes, 'that a permanent injunction will issue once infringement and validity have been adjudged.'" *eBay*, 547 U.S. at 393-94. It held that an injunction should be granted only after a court considers the four factors and also noted that the "decision to grant or deny permanent injunctive relief is an act of equitable discretion by the . . . court." *Id.* at 391.

The *eBay* Court observed that the rule it announced for patent cases was

> consistent with our treatment of injunctions under the Copyright Act. Like a patent owner, a copyright holder possesses "the right to exclude others from using his

property." Like the Patent Act, the Copyright Act provides that courts "may" grant injunctive relief "on such terms as it may deem reasonable to prevent or restrain infringement of a copyright." 17 U.S.C. §502(a). And as in our decision today, this Court has consistently rejected invitations to replace traditional equitable considerations with a rule that an injunction automatically follows a determination that a copyright has been infringed. *See, e.g., New York Times Co. v. Tasini,* 533 U.S. 483, 505 (2001) (citing *Campbell v. Acuff-Rose Music, Inc.,* 510 U.S. 569, 578 n. 10 (1994))....

Id. at 392. The following cases illustrate courts' efforts to apply the four-factor standard in the context of copyright litigation.

Christopher Phelps & Associates, LLC v. Galloway
492 F.3d 532 (4th Cir. 2007)

NIEMEYER, J.: After R. Wayne Galloway began construction of his retirement home on Lake Wylie, near Charlotte, North Carolina, using architectural plans designed and copyrighted by Christopher Phelps & Associates, LLC ("Phelps & Associates"), without permission, Phelps & Associates commenced this action against Galloway for copyright infringement. Phelps & Associates sought damages . . . and injunctive relief. A jury found that Galloway infringed Phelps & Associates' copyright and awarded it $20,000 in damages . . . . The district court thereafter declined to enter an injunction, finding that the jury verdict had made Phelps & Associates "whole". . . . Phelps & Associates appeals, requesting a new trial on damages and the entry of an injunction prohibiting the future lease or sale of the infringing house and mandating the destruction or return of the infringing plans. . . .

Insofar as Phelps & Associates suggests that it is *entitled* to injunctive relief, we reject the argument. *See eBay Inc. v. MercExchange, L.L.C.,*—U.S.—, 126 S. Ct. 1837, 1839 (2006). . . .

We agree with Phelps & Associates that Galloway will inevitably sell or transfer his house within the period during which Phelps & Associates still holds the copyright—*i.e.* 95 years, *see* 17 U.S.C. §302(c)—and that such a sale could, absent this action, expose Galloway to further relief, *see id.* §106(3); *id.* §501(a); *cf. id.* §109(a) (permitting resale of "lawfully made" copies). But Phelps & Associates has requested relief for that inevitable transaction now *in this action,* as part of the panoply of remedies available under the Copyright Act, and therefore entitlement to that relief can be and is resolved in this action under the principles of *eBay,* 126 S. Ct. at 1839.

The first two *eBay* criteria for injunctive relief—irreparable injury and the inadequacy of monetary damages—have most likely been demonstrated. Irreparable injury often derives from the nature of copyright violations, which deprive the copyright holder of intangible exclusive rights. Damages at law will not remedy the continuing existence of Phelps & Associates' design in the Galloway house. Moreover, while the calculation of future damages and profits for each future sale might be possible, any such effort would entail a substantial amount of speculation and guesswork that renders the effort difficult or impossible in this case.

Accordingly, we conclude that Phelps & Associates most likely has satisfied the first two *eBay* factors.

When considering the third and fourth factors, however—the balance of hardships and the public interest—Phelps & Associates' showing has fallen short.

First, Phelps & Associates has been fully and adequately compensated for the copying and use of its design as manifested in the single Galloway house. . . . A sale of the house would not be a second copy or manifestation of the design, but merely a transfer of the structure in which the design was first copied. An injunction against sale would but slightly benefit Phelps & Associates' legitimate entitlements because the infringing house would retain the same form and location, remaining a permanent nuisance to the copyright regardless of whether there is an injunction. An injunction against sale would neither undo the prior infringement, nor diminish the chances of future copying. At the same time, a permanent injunction would impose a draconian burden on Galloway, effectively creating a *lis pendens* on the house and subjecting him to contempt proceedings simply for selling his own property.

Second, a house or building, as an expression of the architect's copyrighted plans, usually has a predominantly functional character. . . . This is the same reason that Congress manifested an expectation that injunctions will not be routinely issued against substantially completed houses whose designs violated architectural copyrights. H.R. Rep. No. 101-735, at 13-14 (1990), *reprinted in* 1990 U.S.C.C.A.N. 6935, 6944 (explaining that buildings "are the only form of copyrightable subject matter that is habitable"). Those considerations are at their strongest when the architectural structure is completed and inhabited by the infringer, as here. While Galloway infringed the copyright, he now is living in a "copy" of the architectural work. His interest in remaining there, with the same rights as other homeowners to alienate his property, is substantial and, in this case, trumps Phelps & Associates' interests in any injunction prohibiting a lease or sale of the house.

Third, an injunction against sale of the house would be overbroad, as it would encumber a great deal of property unrelated to the infringement. The materials and labor that went into the Galloway house, in addition to the swimming pool, the fence, and other non-infringing features, as well as the land underneath the house, would be restrained by the requested injunction. As such, the injunction would take on a fundamentally punitive character, which has not been countenanced in the Copyright Act's remedies. In a similar vein, the requested injunction would undermine an ancient reluctance by the courts to restrain the alienability of real property. For these reasons, the public interest would be disserved by the entry of an injunction.

Finally, ultimate discretion to grant any such injunctive relief rests with the district court, and for the reasons enumerated, we conclude that deference to the district court's refusal is appropriate in the absence of any showing that such refusal was otherwise an abuse of discretion. *See eBay*, 126 S. Ct. at 1839. . . .

Phelps & Associates relies upon *Sony Corporation of America v. Universal City Studios, Inc.*, 464 U.S. 417, 446 n.28 (1984), to argue that the refusal to issue an injunction against future leases and sales of the Galloway house amounts to a judicially created compulsory license, which is disfavored. The reliance on *Sony*, however, is misplaced. The remedies under the Copyright Act do not resemble a license because the Copyright Act remedies are far broader than simply requiring a defendant to make license payments. Under the Copyright Act, a copyright holder is entitled to both actual damages—the market price of the license— *and* disgorgement of the infringer's profits, which might be immensely greater than the price of a license. *See* 17 U.S.C. §504. Moreover, the infringer takes the risk that the district court will order, in its discretion, the destruction or other disposition of the infringing article. *See id*. §503(b). In the garden-variety piracy case, such orders are routinely issued. Given the risks attendant to infringement, denying an injunction is not equivalent to a compulsory license. *See Walker v. Forbes, Inc.,* 28 F.3d 409, 412 (4th Cir.1994) ("By stripping the infringer not only of the licensing fee but also of the profit generated as a result of the use of the infringed item, the law makes clear that there is no gain to be made from taking someone else's intellectual property without their consent"). While granting an injunction to destroy an infringing article might be usual with respect to personal property, especially in the garden-variety music or movie piracy case, refusing to order destruction or the inalienability of property is also consistent with the Copyright Act's remedial scheme and does not amount to a compelled license.

For all of these reasons, we affirm the district court's order denying an injunction against the future lease or sale of Galloway's house.

[The court remanded to the district court to consider whether, in light of the *eBay* factors, it should grant an injunction ordering the destruction of copies of the plans.] . . .

Metro-Goldwyn-Mayer Studios, Inc. v. Grokster, Ltd.
518 F. Supp. 2d 1197 (N.D. Cal. 2007)

[Review the facts of this case in Chapter 9.C.2, *supra*. After articulating a theory of liability for inducement of infringement, the Supreme Court remanded the case to the district court, which found defendants liable on that theory. In this opinion, the district court addresses whether the plaintiffs are entitled to injunctive relief.]

WILSON, J.: . . . The first question to address is whether Plaintiffs "ha[ve] suffered an irreparable injury." *eBay* [*Inc. v. MercExchange, L.L.C.*], 126 S. Ct. [1837, 1839 (2006)]. . . . [T]he Tenth Circuit has observed that "irreparable harm is often suffered when the injury can[not] be adequately atoned for in money, or when the district court cannot remedy [the injury] following a final determination on the merits." *Prairie Band* [*of Potawatomi Indians v. Pierce*], 253 F.3d [1234, 1250 (10th Cir. 2001)]. . . .

The parties dispute whether, in light of *eBay*, irreparable harm can be presumed.
. . . Other courts have in the past presumed the existence of irreparable injury upon the establishment of liability in copyright cases. . . .

Yet, these cases were all decided prior to the Supreme Court's decision in *eBay*. The *eBay* Court held that it is Plaintiffs who "must demonstrate" (meaning, have the burden of proof) that the traditional factors favor a permanent injunction. 126 S. Ct. at 1839. The Supreme Court also highlighted that it has "consistently rejected" the rule that "an injunction automatically follows" an infringement holding. *Id*. at 1840. Given Plaintiffs' burden of proof and the inability of a district court to "automatically" issue injunctions, it is perhaps unclear in *eBay*'s wake whether a permanent injunction can be granted based on a rebuttable presumption of irreparable harm. . . .

. . . [T]he *eBay* district court has subsequently decided that there can be no presumption of irreparable harm in the permanent injunction context. *See MercExchange, L.L.C. v. eBay, Inc.*, 500 F. Supp. 2d 556, 568 (E.D. Va. 2007) ("[A] review of relevant caselaw, as well as the language of the Supreme Court's decision, supports defendants' position that such presumption no longer exists."). This view appears to have been followed by perhaps every court expressly considering *eBay*.

This Court agrees with StreamCast, and these district courts, that the presumption of irreparable harm no longer inures to the benefit of Plaintiffs. The *eBay* Court plainly stated that Plaintiffs "must demonstrate" the presence of the traditional factors, and therefore have the burden of proof with regard to irreparable harm. . . .

Irreparable harm cannot be established solely on the fact of past infringement. Additionally, it must also be true that the mere likelihood of future infringement by a defendant does not by itself allow for an inference of irreparable harm. As to the latter, future copyright infringement can always be redressed via damages, whether actual or statutory. *See* 17 U.S.C. §504. . . .

"[I]rreparable harm may not be presumed[, but] [i]n run-of-the-mill copyright litigation, such proof should not be difficult to establish. . . ." 6 [William F.] Patry, [*Patry on Copyrights,*] §22:74. Thus, Plaintiffs may establish an irreparable harm stemming from the infringement (*e.g.*, loss of market share, reputational harm). It is also possible that some qualitative feature about the infringement itself, such as its peculiar nature, could elevate its status into the realm of "irreparable harm."

StreamCast accepts that certain harms caused by infringement, such as loss of brand recognition and market share, can amount to irreparable harm. However, StreamCast rejects the argument that copyright infringement can itself ever represent irreparable harm. StreamCast asserts that "[i]f damages can be calculated, the injury is **not** irreparable . . . —the Copyright Act specifically provides for statutory damages, which are calculable assuming Plaintiffs can prove direct infringement of their works, and a basis for the range requested." This Court has doubts regarding StreamCast's position. In *eBay*, Chief Justice Roberts indicated that irreparable harm can result from the infringement itself, depending upon the circumstances of the case:

> From at least the early 19th century, courts have granted injunctive relief upon a finding of infringement in the vast majority of patent cases. This "long tradition of equity practice" is not surprising, given the difficulty of protecting a right to exclude through monetary remedies that allow an infringer to use an invention against the patentee's wishes—a difficulty that often implicates the first two factors of the traditional four-factor test.

126 S. Ct. at 1841 (Roberts, C.J., concurring)[.] And "[l]ike a patent owner, a copyright holder possesses 'the right to exclude others from using his property.'" [*Id*.] at 1840.

This Court also recognizes that a competing *eBay* concurrence took issue with Chief Justice Roberts's "right to exclude" language. Justice Kennedy explained his view that "the existence of a right to exclude does not dictate the remedy for a violation of that right." *eBay*, 126 S. Ct. at 1842 (Kennedy, J., concurring). This Court agrees, since a contrary conclusion would come close to permitting a presumption of irreparable harm. This Court also observes that Justice Kennedy's statement was made primarily in the context of certain recent developments in the patent field that are wholly inapplicable to this lawsuit. For example, this is simply not a case in which the copyright infringement represents "but a small component of the product the companies seek to produce," such that "legal damages may well be sufficient to compensate for the infringement." *Id.* As this Court previously held, StreamCast's entire business was built around the fundamental premise that Morpheus would be utilized to infringe copyrights, including those owned by Plaintiffs. Furthermore, Justice Kennedy emphasized that "[t]he equitable discretion over injunctions . . . is well suited to allow courts to adapt to the rapid technological and legal developments. . . ." *Id.* Given the technological aspects of the infringement induced by StreamCast, and the flexibility conferred by the Copyright Act, this Court is persuaded that its bases for finding irreparable harm, *infra*, are supported by both Chief Justice Roberts's and Justice Kennedy's concurrences.

In light of this authority, the Court concludes that certain qualities pertaining to the nature of StreamCast's inducement of infringement are relevant to a finding of irreparable harm. . . .

The irreparable harm analysis centers on two basic themes: (1) StreamCast has and will continue to induce far more infringement than it could ever possibly redress with damages; and (2) Plaintiffs' copyrights (especially those of popular works) have and will be rendered particularly vulnerable to continuing infringement on an enormous scale due to StreamCast's inducement. The Court agrees with both arguments, and each is independently sufficient to support [a] finding of irreparable harm in this case.

First, the Court must ask whether a particular defendant's probable inability to pay damage constitutes irreparable harm. In the ordinary case, "merely alleging an opponent's inability to pay damages does not constitute irreparable harm." *Rosewood Apartments Corp. v. Perpignano*, 200 F. Supp. 2d 269, 278 (S.D.N.Y. 2002). But "[i]n some limited circumstances, parties have demonstrated such a strong likelihood that their opponent will be unable to pay that courts have awarded them equitable relief." *Id.* . . . The rationale in such cases must be that an award of monetary damages will be meaningless, and the plaintiff will have no substantive relief, where it will be impossible to collect an award for past and/or future infringements perpetrated by a defendant.

Plaintiffs have not yet sought an award of statutory damages. Additionally, Plaintiffs have not provided this Court with specific evidence as part of this motion demonstrating that StreamCast would be unable to pay damages for the infringements it has induced in the past, and could continue to induce in the future. But such evidence is not necessary here. Based on the undisputed evidence at summary judgment of massive end-user infringement, it is highly likely that the award of statutory damages that ultimately befalls StreamCast in this case will be enormous (especially considering the potential relationship between inducement and a finding of willfulness), and would far outstrip the amount of revenue the company has garnered in recent years. This Court's conclusion would also be the same even if Plaintiffs chose to forgo a damages award as part of this lawsuit. This is because the amount of infringement that StreamCast could induce in the future is so staggering that the recoverable statutory damages would very probably be well beyond Stream-Cast's anticipated resources. Because it is extremely unlikely that StreamCast will be able to compensate Plaintiffs monetarily for the infringements it has induced in the past, or the infringements it could induce in the future through Morpheus, Plaintiffs have and will continue to suffer irreparable harm.

Second, the Court agrees with Plaintiffs' claim that a substantial number of their copyrighted works have and would continue to become irreparably exposed to infringement on a tremendous scale due to StreamCast's inducement. This inducement greatly erodes Plaintiffs' ability to enforce their exclusive rights. *See A & M Records, Inc. v. Napster, Inc.*, 239 F.3d 1004, 1029 (9th Cir.2001) (rejecting Napster's request for compulsory royalties as opposed to injunctive relief because "Plaintiffs would lose the power to control their intellectual property"). It also promises no realistic mechanism through which statutory damages can be collected for all of the inevitable subsequent infringements occurring outside of the Morpheus System and Software. . . .

The Court is aware that Plaintiffs can seek an award of statutory damages from StreamCast for infringements occurring through the Morpheus System and Software (ignoring for now the likely reality regarding StreamCast's ability to pay). However, Plaintiffs cannot recover damages from StreamCast for the inevitable derivative infringements that will occur outside of Morpheus, with copyrighted content originally acquired within it, as a consequence [of] StreamCast's inducement. Even numerous lawsuits against direct infringers will necessarily prove to be insufficient under these conditions. *Cf.* [*Metro-Goldwyn-Mayer Studios Inc. v. Grokster, Ltd.*, 545 U.S. 913, 929-30 (2005)] ("When a widely shared service or product is used to commit infringement, it may be impossible to enforce rights in the protected work effectively against all direct infringers. . . ."). Indeed, the very need to file multiple lawsuits as a consequence of StreamCast's inducement is itself supportive of an irreparable harm finding.

In sum, Plaintiffs have offered two independently sufficient grounds for a finding of irreparable harm. . . .

[The court found the other three *eBay* factors also favored the plaintiffs and concluded that a permanent injunction should issue.]

NOTES AND QUESTIONS

1. What advantages are there to the four-factor test? Would a presumption in favor of injunctive relief in cases of copyright infringement be preferable? Do you think that either *Phelps* or *Grokster* would have been decided differently pre-*eBay*? Why, or why not?

2. Are you persuaded by the *Grokster* court's analysis of the irreparable harm factor? Isn't part of the value of the exclusive copyright rights just that—the right to *exclude*? Are there other kinds of harm from infringing activity that would not be remedied adequately by an award of monetary damages? Is that harm the kind of harm that copyright law is meant to protect? In *Phelps*, while the third and fourth factors were paramount, did the court apply a presumption of irreparable harm upon a showing of infringement? If so, is such a presumption appropriate?

3. The *Phelps* court expressed concern that an injunction would encumber other contributions to the houses beyond the plaintiff's copyrighted designs. In the litigation leading to *Stewart v. Abend,* the case concerning renewal terms that you read in Chapter 11.C.1, the Ninth Circuit expressed a similar concern:

> . . . We are mindful that this case presents compelling equitable considerations which should be taken into account by the district court in fashioning an appropriate remedy . . . . Defendants invested substantial money, effort, and talent in creating the "Rear Window" film. Clearly the tremendous success of that venture initially and upon re-release is attributable in significant measure to, inter alia, the outstanding performances of its stars—Grace Kelly and James Stewart—and the brilliant directing of Alfred Hitchcock. The district court must recognize this contribution in determining Abend's remedy.

> The district court may choose from several available remedies for the infringement. Abend seeks first an injunction against the continued exploitation of the "Rear Window" film. . . . However, . . . "where great public injury would be worked by an injunction, the courts might . . . award damages or a continuing royalty instead of an injunction in such special circumstances." [3 M. Nimmer, Nimmer on Copyright §14.06[B] at 14-56.2 (1988).]

> We believe such special circumstances exist here. The "Rear Window" film resulted from the collaborative efforts of many talented individuals other than Cornell Woolrich, the author of the underlying story. The success of the movie resulted in large part from factors completely unrelated to the underlying story, "It Had To Be Murder." It would cause a great injustice for the owners of the film if the court enjoined them from further exhibition of the movie. An injunction would also effectively foreclose defendants from enjoying legitimate profits derived from exploitation of the "new matter" comprising the derivative work, which is given express copyright protection by section 7 of the 1909 Act. Since defendants could not possibly separate out the "new matter" from the underlying work, their right to enjoy the renewal copyright *in the derivative work* would be rendered meaningless by the grant of an injunction. We also note that an injunction could cause public injury by denying the public the opportunity to view a classic film for many years to come.

> This is not the first time we have recognized that an injunction may be an inappropriate remedy for copyright infringement. In *Universal City Studios v. Sony Corp. of America,* 659 F.2d 963, 976 (9th Cir. 1981), *rev'd on other grounds,* 464 U.S. 417 (1984), we stated that Professor Nimmer's suggestion of damages or a continuing royalty would constitute an acceptable resolution for infringement caused by in-home taping of television programs by VCR—"time-shifting." *See also Sony Corp. v. Universal City Studios,* 464 U.S. 417, 499-500 (1984) (Blackmun, J., dissenting).

Abend v. MCA, Inc., 863 F.2d 1465, 1478-79 (9th Cir. 1988) *aff'd sub nom., Stewart v. Abend,* 495 U.S. 207 (1990). On *certiorari,* the Supreme Court did not address the question of appropriate remedies. Evaluate the reasoning in *Phelps* and *Abend* – do you find the courts' analysis of the third and fourth factors persuasive?

4. Did the courts' decisions in *Phelps* and *Abend* effectively create compulsory licenses? Do you find the *Phelps* court's rejection of the "compulsory license" characterization convincing? Why, or why not? Since Congress has instituted compulsory licenses elsewhere in the Copyright Act, would it be appropriate for a court to impose such a license without prior congressional authorization?

In economic terms, a compulsory license scheme is described as a liability regime. Liability rules allow use by third parties but require compensation for such use. In contrast, property rules allow the property owner to preclude unauthorized uses by third parties and to receive both injunctive and monetary relief. Recall the goals of copyright, which you studied in Chapter 1. Which model—a property regime or a liability regime—is more consistent with copyright objectives? Would you argue, along with Chief Justice Roberts, that the nature of the right protected by a patent or copyright regime is the right to exclude, or are you persuaded by Justice Kennedy's distinction between rights and remedies? Is either model mandated by the language of the Intellectual Property Clause?

5. Review the Supreme Court's decision in *Petrella* concerning the applicability of laches in copyright infringement cases. The Court indicated that the district court could consider the plaintiff's delay in bringing suit when crafting appropriate relief. If you were the district judge in *Petrella*, how would you weigh the *eBay* factors on remand?

b. Preliminary Injunctions

Copyright plaintiffs often seek preliminary injunctive relief. As had been the case with permanent injunctions, courts were willing to grant preliminary injunctions in copyright cases without engaging in a detailed analysis of each of the traditional four factors. The Second Circuit's view in the following quote exemplifies this approach:

> . . . [A] preliminary injunction can be granted if [the] plaintiff shows irreparable injury, combined with either a probability of success on the merits, or a fair ground for litigation and a balance of the hardships in his favor. In copyright cases, however, if probable success—a prima facie case of copyright infringement—can be shown, the allegations of irreparable injury need not be very detailed, because such injury can normally be presumed when a copyright is infringed.

Wainwright Sec., Inc. v. Wall St. Transcript Corp., 558 F.2d 91, 94 (2d Cir. 1977), *cert. denied*, 434 U.S. 1014 (1978). The next case exemplifies how the Supreme Court's *eBay* decision affects preliminary injunctions.

Perfect 10, Inc. v. Google, Inc.
653 F.3d 976 (9th Cir. 2011), cert. denied, 132 S. Ct. 1713 (2012)

IKUTA, J.: In this appeal, we once again consider a request by Perfect 10, Inc. for a preliminary injunction against Google, Inc. *See Perfect 10, Inc. v. Amazon.com, Inc.*

(*Perfect 10 II*), 508 F.3d 1146 (9th Cir.2007). Because Perfect 10 has not demonstrated that it would likely suffer irreparable harm in the absence of a preliminary injunction, we affirm the district court's denial of that relief.

I

This appeal is the latest installment in a legal saga of several years' duration. That history is recounted elsewhere, *see Perfect 10 II,* 508 F.3d 1146, so we focus here on only those facts material to the questions before us now. . . . [Perfect 10 alleged that Google's image search activities, including links to infringing copies and thumbnails of infringing copies, infringed Perfect 10's copyrights. Portions of the earlier opinions are included in Chapters 6.B.1.d and 10.B.2, *supra*].

. . . Under Google's notification policies, the take-down notice must include, among other things, the URL for the infringing material. Google forwards the takedown notices it receives to the website "chillingeffects.org," a nonprofit, educational project run jointly by the Electronic Frontier Foundation and various law schools, which posts such notices on the Internet. As a result, even if Google removes Perfect 10's images from its search results, a person can still find the URL for the allegedly infringing images on chillingeffects.org.

Following our remand in *Perfect 10 II,* Perfect 10 once again moved for a preliminary injunction against Google. Perfect 10 argued that it was entitled to an injunction because Google's web and image search and related caching feature, its Blogger service, and its practice of forwarding Perfect 10's takedown notices to chillingeffects.org constituted copyright infringement. . . .

The district court rejected each of these arguments and denied Perfect 10's motion for preliminary injunctive relief. In doing so, the court held that Perfect 10 had not shown that it was likely to suffer irreparable harm in the absence of such relief, and that it had failed to satisfy any of the other requirements for a preliminary injunction. . . . On appeal, Perfect 10 claims that the district court erred in denying its motion for a preliminary injunction . . . .

II

We begin by considering whether the district court erred in denying Perfect 10's request for preliminary injunctive relief. "A plaintiff seeking a preliminary injunction must establish [(1)] that he is likely to succeed on the merits, [(2)] that he is likely to suffer irreparable harm in the absence of preliminary relief, [(3)] that the balance of equities tips in his favor, and [(4)] that an injunction is in the public interest." *Winter v. Natural Res. Def. Council, Inc.,* 555 U.S. 7 (2008). We review the district court's determination that the plaintiff satisfied each of these four factors for abuse of discretion. In doing so, our review is "limited and deferential." *Am. Trucking Ass'ns v. City of Los Angeles,* 559 F.3d 1046, 1052 (9th Cir.2009).

In explaining how it meets the four-factor test for preliminary injunctive relief, Perfect 10 argues primarily that because it has made a strong showing of likely success on the merits of its copyright claims, a court must presume it will suffer irreparable harm. In making this argument, Perfect 10 relies on a long line of cases, beginning with *Apple Computer, Inc. v. Formula International, Inc.*, 725 F.2d 521 (9th Cir.1984), where we held that "[a] showing of a reasonable likelihood of success on the merits in a copyright infringement claim raises a presumption of irreparable harm" for purposes of a preliminary injunction. *Id*. at 525. We have repeated and relied on this rule numerous times in the nearly three decades since *Apple Computer*.

These cases, however, all predate *eBay Inc. v. MercExchange, L.L.C.*, 547 U.S. 388 (2006), which indicated that an injunction in a patent infringement case may issue only in accordance with "traditional equitable principles" and warned against reliance on presumptions or categorical rules. *Id*. at 393. . . .

Although *eBay* dealt with a permanent injunction, the rule enunciated in that case is equally applicable to preliminary injunctive relief. This conclusion is compelled by Supreme Court precedent, cited in *eBay*, holding that "[t]he standard for a preliminary injunction is essentially the same as for a permanent injunction with the exception that the plaintiff must show a likelihood of success on the merits rather than actual success." *Amoco Prod. Co. v. Vill. of Gambell*, 480 U.S. 531, 546 n.12 (1987).

In sum, we conclude that our longstanding rule that "[a] showing of a reasonable likelihood of success on the merits in a copyright infringement claim raises a presumption of irreparable harm," *Apple Computer, Inc.*, 725 F.2d at 525, "is clearly irreconcilable with the reasoning" of the Court's decision in *eBay* and has therefore been "effectively overruled." *Miller v. Gammie*, 335 F.3d 889, 893 (9th Cir.2003) (en banc).

III

Having disposed of Perfect 10's argument that the district court should have presumed that it would suffer irreparable harm, we now turn to whether the district court abused its discretion in holding that Perfect 10 had not established this factor. Perfect 10's theory of irreparable harm is that Google's various services provide free access to Perfect 10's proprietary images, and this access has both destroyed its business model and threatened it with financial ruin, since no one would be willing to pay a subscription fee for material that is available without charge. To support this theory, Perfect 10 relies on several declarations by Dr. Norman Zada, Perfect 10's founder, president, and major financial backer. In these declarations, Dr. Zada stated that the number of thumbnail versions of Perfect 10 images available via Google's Image Search had increased significantly between 2005 and 2010. Further, Dr. Zada stated that the company's "revenues have declined from close to $2,000,000 a year to less than $150,000 a year," resulting in over $50 million in losses from 1996 to 2007, and an annual loss of at least $3 million since then, pushing the company "very close to bankruptcy."

Given the limited nature of this evidence, the district court did not abuse its discretion in concluding that Perfect 10 failed to establish that Google's operations would cause it irreparable harm. While being forced into bankruptcy qualifies as a form of irreparable harm, *Doran v. Salem Inn, Inc.*, 422 U.S. 922, 932 (1975),

Perfect 10 has not established that the requested injunction would forestall that fate. To begin with, Perfect 10 has not alleged that it was ever in sound financial shape. Indeed, Dr. Zada acknowledges that the company "los[t] money at the beginning" and has never made up that ground during its 15 years of operation. Dr. Zada also acknowledges that search engines other than Google contribute to making Perfect 10 images freely available. In one of his declarations, he states that, in addition to spending "at least 2,000 hours using Google's search engine to locate infringements of Perfect 10's copyrighted works," he has also "spent thousands of hours viewing [infringing] websites and search results of other search engines, including Yahoo! and MSN." Moreover, notwithstanding Perfect 10's theory of irreparable harm, it failed to submit a statement from even a single former subscriber who ceased paying for Perfect 10's service because of the content freely available via Google. . . .

In sum, Perfect 10 has not shown a sufficient causal connection between irreparable harm to Perfect 10's business and Google's operation of its search engine. Because Perfect 10 has failed to satisfy this necessary requirement for obtaining preliminary injunctive relief, the district court's ruling was not an abuse of discretion. *See Winter*, 129 S. Ct. at 374.

NOTES AND QUESTIONS

1. Other circuit courts have begun requiring the same type of causal connection or "nexus." *See e.g., Apple, Inc. v. Samsung Elecs. Co.*, 735 F.3d 1352 (Fed. Cir. 2013). Is a causal connection requirement a good idea? What evidence would demonstrate the required causal connection? Should a causal connection also be required when a copyright owner seeks a permanent injunction after a finding of infringement?

2. Of what value is a preliminary injunction to a plaintiff in a copyright infringement case? Is there any reason that a court should address irreparable harm differently in the copyright context than other contexts? How does your view of the theoretical justification(s) for copyright law affect your answers to these questions?

3. Before the *eBay* case, some scholars had argued that preliminary injunctions in copyright infringement cases could violate the First Amendment:

> . . . [W]hen a court concludes that the defendant's expression is probably not substantially similar to the plaintiff's expression, or is probably a fair use, the court should never issue a preliminary injunction, even if the balance of hardships tilts in the plaintiff's favor. Likewise when the court concludes that the case is genuinely close: erroneously failing to enjoin speech is better than erroneously enjoining speech, especially when erroneous failure to enjoin speech is remediable by a damages award. . . .
>
> . . . Thus, a court should not enter a preliminary injunction unless it is clearly convinced that the speech falls within the copyright exception (i.e., that it's substantially similar to the plaintiff's expression and is not a fair use). . . .

Mark A. Lemley & Eugene Volokh, *Freedom of Speech and Injunctions in Intellectual Property Cases*, 48 Duke L.J. 147, 215-16 (1998). Does *eBay* resolve this objection?

To avoid tension with First Amendment principles, why not refuse preliminary injunctions as a matter of course and simply order monetary compensation? In *Suntrust Bank v. Houghton Mifflin Co.*, 252 F.3d 1165 (11th Cir. 2001), discussed in Chapter 10.A.3, *supra,* the court vacated a preliminary injunction on First Amendment grounds, stating that the injunction was an unconstitutional prior restraint. In a subsequent opinion clarifying that First Amendment protections for the defendant's parody were preserved via the fair use doctrine, the court ruled that any injury resulting from the alleged infringement could be adequately remedied by money damages. *Suntrust Bank v. Houghton Mifflin Co.*, 268 F.3d 1257, 1277 (11th Cir. 2001). Should courts do this more often in fair use cases? In other types of infringement cases?

2. Seizure and Impoundment

Section 503 of the Copyright Act provides that while an infringement action is pending, the court may impound all copies or phonorecords claimed to have been made or used in violation of the copyright owner's rights. All the means by which the allegedly infringing copies or phonorecords were reproduced also are subject to impoundment. Upon a final judgment or decree of infringement, a court may order the disposition of all infringing copies or phonorecords and of the means by which the infringing copies were made. In cases of criminal liability for infringement, all infringing copies or phonorecords and all the means by which they were made may be seized and forfeited to the United States. *See* 18 U.S.C. §2319. Section 603(c) of the Copyright Act provides that infringing goods imported into the United States are subject to seizure and forfeiture as property imported in violation of customs laws. Forfeited articles are to be destroyed under the direction of the Secretary of the Treasury or the court.

3. Actual Damages and Profits

Section 504(b) of the Copyright Act provides that an infringer of copyright is liable for the copyright owner's "actual damages suffered . . . as a result of the infringement, and any profits of the infringer that are attributable to the infringement and are not taken into account in computing the actual damages."

As the cases below illustrate, the exact amount of damages and profits may be difficult to prove. Cases in which the protected work is incorporated into a new work along with creative contributions by the alleged infringer are particularly difficult. In such circumstances, courts dissect the infringing work to determine what portion of the defendant's profits is attributable to the infringement. Generally, the goal is to award damages proportionate to the contribution of the copyright owner and no more. Read §§504(a) and (b) and consider the next two cases.

a. Attribution of Profits

Bouchat v. Baltimore Ravens Football Club, Inc.
346 F.3d 514 (4th Cir. 2003), cert. denied, 541 U.S. 1042 (2004).

KING, J.: This appeal arises from the damages phase of a protracted copyright dispute involving the Baltimore Ravens football team. Frederick Bouchat, the holder of the infringed copyright, . . . asserts that the court erroneously failed to accord him the benefit of a statutory presumption that an infringer's revenues are entirely attributable to the infringement. For the reasons explained below, we affirm.

I.

On November 6, 1995, the National Football League ("NFL") announced that one of its teams, the Cleveland Browns, would shortly be moving to Baltimore. The team was to leave its entire Browns identity in Cleveland, and thus would need a new name and logo when it moved to its new Maryland home. Bouchat, a Baltimore security guard and amateur artist, became interested in the new team, and he began drawing logo designs based on the various names that the team was considering, including the name "Ravens." On or about December 5, 1995, Bouchat created a drawing of a winged shield (the "Shield Drawing") as a "Ravens" logo.

In March of 1996, the Baltimore team adopted the name "Ravens." In early April, Bouchat sent the Shield Drawing via fax to the Maryland Stadium Authority. Beside the Shield Drawing, Bouchat penned a note asking the Chairman of the Authority to send the sketch to the Ravens' president. Bouchat also requested that if the Ravens used the Shield Drawing, they send him a letter of recognition and an autographed helmet.

In a jury trial on the issue of liability, Bouchat's Shield Drawing was found to have been mistakenly used by National Football League Properties, Inc. ("NFLP"), the Raven's licensing agent, in NFLP's production of the Ravens' new logo, the "Flying B." The Ravens had no knowledge that the NFLP had infringed anyone's work and assumed that the Flying B was an original work owned by NFLP. The Ravens used the Flying B as their primary identifying symbol, and the logo appeared in every aspect of the Ravens' activities, including uniforms, stationery, tickets, banners, on-field insignia, and merchandise.

II. . . .

Bouchat sought damages from the Ravens and NFLP pursuant to 17 U.S.C. §504(a)(1), which renders an infringer liable for "the copyright owner's actual damages and any additional profits of the infringer, as provided by [17 U.S.C. §504(b)]." Section 504(b), in turn, entitles the copyright owner to recover both "the actual damages suffered by him or her as a result of the infringement, and any profits of the infringer that are attributable to the infringement and are not taken into account in computing the actual damages." 17 U.S.C. §504(b). . . .

In his complaint, Bouchat contended that some portion of essentially *all* of the Defendants' revenues was attributable to the infringing use of Bouchat's artwork.[3] To satisfy his initial burden under §504(b), Bouchat presented evidence of the gross receipts from all NFLP and Ravens activities. The district court, however, awarded partial summary judgment to the Defendants with respect to all revenues derived from sources other than (1) sales of merchandise bearing the Flying B logo, and (2) royalties obtained from licensees who sold such merchandise (collectively, the "Merchandise Revenues"). *Bouchat v. Baltimore Ravens, Inc.,* 215 F. Supp. 2d 611, 619, 621 (D. Md. 2002). The court reasoned that "[i]f the use of the Flying B logo to designate the Ravens could not reasonably be found to have affected the amount of revenue obtained from an activity, the revenue from that activity could not reasonably be found attributable to the infringement." *Id.* at 617-18. Concluding that only the Merchandise Revenues could reasonably be found to have been affected by the Defendants' unlawful use of the Flying B, the court excluded, as a matter of law, the remainder of the Defendants' revenues (collectively, the "Non-Merchandise Revenues") from the pool of income that the jury could consider in awarding §504 damages.[4]

At the close of discovery, the district court further narrowed the scope of the Defendants' revenues from which the jury would be permitted to award §504 damages, when it excluded certain portions of the Merchandise Revenues. Specifically, the court awarded partial summary judgment to the Defendants as to Bouchat's claims for profits from "minimum guarantee shortfalls,"[5] "free merchandise,"[6] trading cards, video games, and game programs (collectively, the "Excluded Merchandise Revenues"). Though it recognized that the Defendants "ha[ve] the burden of proof," the court nonetheless ruled that, with respect to the minimum guarantee shortfalls and the free merchandise, there could be no rational connection between the particular source of revenue and the act of infringement; and that, with respect to the trading cards, video games, and game program

---

3. Bouchat conceded in the district court that there are a few categories of the Defendants' revenues that could not, in any part, be attributable to the infringement. So, for example, Bouchat did not seek to recover interest earned on Ravens' checking accounts, even though the checks bore the Flying B logo; nor did he seek to recover the revenues obtained from stadium rentals, even though the Flying B logo was prominently featured on the playing field. *See Bouchat v. Baltimore Ravens, Inc.,* 215 F. Supp. 2d 611, 616 (D.Md.2002).

4. The Non–Merchandise Revenues would include, for instance, revenues from the sale of game tickets, stadium parking, food, drinks (with the exception of those sold in special logo-bearing cups), broadcast rights, and sponsorships.

5. Under NFLP's retail licensing agreements, licensed vendors of official, logo-bearing merchandise are required to pay a certain sum each year, regardless of whether any sales of licensed products actually occur. Thus, if actual sales fall short of what would be required to generate the guaranteed minimum royalty, a vendor must tender payment in the amount needed to make up the difference. This sum is a "minimum guarantee shortfall" payment.

6. Under NFLP's retail licensing agreements, a licensed vendor of official, logo-bearing merchandise must provide to NFLP, at no cost, a certain quantity of its licensed products each year. These products are referred to as "free merchandise."

sales, the Defendants had produced unrebutted evidence establishing that the revenues received from those sources were not attributable to the infringement. . . . Both the Non-Merchandise Revenues and a substantial portion of the Merchandise Revenues having thus been excluded, only those revenues derived from the sale of t-shirts, caps, souvenir cups, and other items bearing the Flying B logo (collectively, the "Non-Excluded Merchandise Revenues") would go to the jury for a finding on attributability.

. . . [T]he jury was asked to decide whether the Defendants had proven, by a preponderance of the evidence, that the Non-Excluded Merchandise Revenues were attributable entirely to factors other than the Defendants' infringement of Bouchat's copyright. If the jury found that they were not, then it was charged to decide the percentage of the Non-Excluded Merchandise Revenues attributable to factors other than the infringement.

After a full day of deliberations, the jury answered the first question in the affirmative, thereby denying Bouchat any monetary recovery. . . . Bouchat filed a timely notice of appeal. . . .

III.

A.

. . . Bouchat asserts that the court failed to give him the benefit of the §504 statutory presumption that an infringer's revenues are entirely attributable to the infringement. That presumption, he maintains, creates a question of material fact that cannot be resolved on summary judgment. Thus, he asserts, whether any portion of an infringer's revenues are attributable to some source other than the infringement is a question that can be resolved *only* by a jury. As explained below, we disagree. . . .

2.

. . . Section 504(b) entitles a successful copyright plaintiff to recover "any profits of the infringer that are attributable to the infringement." 17 U.S.C. §504(b). The statute goes on to specify that,

> [i]n establishing the infringer's profits, the copyright owner is required to present proof only of the infringer's gross revenue, and the infringer is required to prove his or her deductible expenses and the elements of profit attributable to factors other than the copyrighted work.

Id. Thus, §504(b) creates an initial presumption that the infringer's "profits . . . attributable to the infringement" are equal to the infringer's gross revenue. Once the copyright owner has established the amount of the infringer's gross revenues, the burden shifts to the infringer to prove either that part or all of those revenues are "deductible expenses" (i.e., are not profits), or that they are "attributable to factors other than the copyrighted work." *Id.* Although §504(b) places the burden on the infringer to demonstrate that certain portions of its revenues were due to factors other than the infringement, the infringer need not prove these amounts with mathematical precision.

3.

Despite the existence of §504(b)'s burden-shifting provision, summary judgment in favor of an infringer with respect to some portion of the infringer's gross revenues may, in the proper circumstances, be appropriate. . . .

. . . [T]he Defendants could properly be awarded summary judgment with respect to any given revenue stream if either (1) there exists no conceivable connection between the infringement and those revenues; or (2) despite the existence of a conceivable connection, Bouchat offered only speculation as to the existence of a causal link between the infringement and the revenues. It is to these inquiries that we turn next.

4.

The Defendants derive revenues from six major sources: (1) sponsorships; (2) broadcast and other media licenses; (3) sale of tickets; (4) miscellaneous business activities, which appear to include provision of game-day stadium parking; (5) sale of official team merchandise; and (6) royalties from licensees who sell official team merchandise. The first four of these sources we characterize as the "Non-Merchandise Revenues," while the fifth and sixth are the "Merchandise Revenues." . . .

Bouchat contends that, because of the Defendants' widespread use of the Flying B as the primary logo—and as an integral marketing tool—for the Baltimore Ravens, some portion of the revenues that the Defendants earned from both the Non-Merchandise Revenues and the Excluded Merchandise Revenues is attributable to the Defendants' infringement of his copyright. When the district court awarded summary judgment to the Defendants as to large segments of their revenues, however, it denied Bouchat the opportunity to prove this contention to the jury. Despite the fact that §504(b) places on the infringer the burden of proving that revenues are not attributable to the infringement, summary judgment was appropriate with respect to both the Non-Merchandise Revenues and the Excluded Merchandise Revenues. . . .

a.

Of all the excluded revenues, only the revenues from minimum guarantee shortfalls and free merchandise lack all conceivable connection to the Defendants' infringement of Bouchat's copyright. Because no rational trier of fact could find that these two subcategories of the Excluded Merchandise Revenues were affected by the Defendants' adoption of the infringing Flying B logo, the court properly removed them from the pool of Defendants' revenues submitted to the jury for consideration under §504(b).

The levels of each licensee's minimum guarantee and free merchandise obligation were established, *ex ante*, by the terms of the licensee's contract with NFLP; neither figure could fluctuate in response to consumer behavior. As a consequence, the amount of revenue that the Defendants received in the form of minimum guarantee shortfalls and free merchandise was necessarily independent of any reaction that any individual might have had to the Flying B logo. Whereas it is at least hypothetically possible (albeit highly unlikely) that an individual became so enamored of the infringing aspects of the Flying B logo that he was thus inspired to purchase tickets for the Ravens' games, to pay for parking, to buy non-logo-bearing concessions, and thus to boost the Defendants' revenues from these sources, a similar scenario cannot be conjured with respect to revenues whose levels were fixed and immutable before licensees had an opportunity to stock their shelves with logo-bearing goods. . . .

b.

Having concluded that summary judgment in favor of the Defendants was proper with respect to both the minimum guarantee short-falls and the free merchandise, we turn now to the Non-Merchandise Revenues and the remaining subcategories of the Excluded Merchandise Revenues (i.e., the revenues from trading cards, video games, and game programs). Our inquiry on this point is whether, despite the existence of a conceivable connection between the infringement and the level of revenue that the Defendants earned from these sources, the court was correct in excluding them through summary judgment. Because Bouchat offered only speculative evidence of a causal link between the infringement and the level of the revenues that the Defendants earned from these sources, and because the Defendants' request for summary judgment was supported by unrebutted evidence demonstrating that these revenues were not, in fact, in any way attributable to the infringement, there was no issue of material fact for consideration by the jury. As a result, the court did not err in awarding summary judgment to the Defendants with respect to these remaining categories of revenue. . . .

B.

Finally, Bouchat contends that the district court, in its instructions to the jury, failed to accord him the full benefit of the statutory presumption contained in §504(b). Specifically, Bouchat maintains that the court abused its discretion by failing to make clear to the jury that the Ravens bore the burden of proof in the damages trial. To the contrary, the court made it eminently clear in its instructions that the Ravens were obliged to shoulder the burden of proof. . . .

WIDENER, J., dissenting: . . . I am of [the] opinion that the district court erred by refusing to instruct the jury that the defendants' profits are deemed attributable to the alleged copyright infringement unless the defendants prove otherwise. . . . [1]

At the close of evidence in the damages trial, Bouchat asked the district court to give the jury instruction approved by this court in *Walker v. Forbes,* 28 F.3d 409 (4th

---

1. . . . Bouchat is entitled to defendants' profits attributable to the infringement because the award of profits is intended to "prevent the infringer from unfairly benefiting from a wrongful act" and not to compensate the copyright owner. H.R. Rep. No. 94-1476, at 161 (1976), *reprinted in* 1976 U.S.C.C.A.N. 5659, 5777.

Cir.1994). In *Walker*, we affirmed the district court's instruction on the award of profits in a copyright infringement case. Bouchat asked for the instruction by name and also read the relevant language into the record. . . .

I agree with the majority's conclusion that the district court correctly instructed the jury on the burden of proof. Under *Walker*, however, merely stating that the defendant bears the burden of proof is not enough. The *Walker* instruction also informs the jury that profits should be deemed attributable to the alleged infringement unless the defendant proves otherwise. *Walker*, 28 F.3d at 414. Indeed, our opinion emphasized the following portion of the district court's instruction: "*amounts or elements of profits should be deemed attributable to the alleged infringement unless [the defendant] proves by a preponderance of the evidence that they are not.*" *Walker*, 28 F.3d at 414 (emphasis in original). The importance of this portion of the instruction is evident from our analysis following the emphasized language:

> This instruction correctly stated the law concerning the shifted burden of proof that the defendant bears to show the portion of revenues and profits that are not attributable to the infringement, and, *in the emphasized language, explained the impact of this shifted burden upon the apportionment calculation.*

Walker, 28 F.3d at 414 (emphasis added). The emphasized language in *Walker* is the basic thought around which the decision is based, and its conscious omission here is, I think, reversible error. . . .

Other courts similarly acknowledge that §504(b) creates a presumption in favor of the copyright owner. In *Data General Corp. v. Grumman Systems Support Corp.*, 36 F.3d 1147, 1173 (1st Cir.1994), the First Circuit held that "the plaintiff must meet only a minimal burden of proof in order to trigger a rebuttable presumption that the defendant's revenues are entirely attributable to the infringement." The rebuttable presumption language in *Data General* has been used by a number of district courts.

In addition to refusing to give the *Walker* instruction, the district court limited its instructions on the award of profits under §504(b) to an explanation of the special verdict form. The court read each question from the verdict form and then gave a brief explanation of what the question meant. The first question asked "have the defendants proven by a preponderance of the evidence that income derived by the defendants from the sale of products bearing the Flying B logo was attributable completely to factors other than the artwork of the Flying B logo[?]" The jury answered "yes" to question one and ended their deliberations. . . .

In this case, the lack of a clear, or any, instruction relating to the presumption of award of profits, together with the limited scope of the verdict form questions, can only have discouraged the jury from awarding damages to the plaintiff, even if the facts and the law supported such an award. This result runs counter to the fundamental purposes of trial by jury. . . .

[In a subsequent opinion, this district included images of Bouchat's drawing, the Flying B logo, and the logo that Ravens adopted in 1999. *Bouchat v. Baltimore Ravens Ltd. Partnership*, 2012 WL 6738321, at *1 n.1 (D. Md. 2012). –Eds.]

NOTES AND QUESTIONS

1. Do you agree with the *Bouchat* court that summary disposition of most of Bouchat's claims to a portion of the Ravens' profits was proper?

2. In light of the jury's rejection of Bouchat's claim to a portion of the Non-Excluded Merchandise Revenues, would the jury instruction that Judge Widener describes have made any difference? If you had represented Bouchat, how would you have sought to prove a nonspeculative link between the various revenue categories and the infringement? What kind of evidence would you need? Do you think you could have succeeded?

3. Although *Bouchat* is in some respects an unusual case, many established visual artists confront similar problems of proof when their work is copied in the course of a much larger enterprise. In *Mackie v. Rieser*, 296 F.3d 909 (9th Cir. 2002), *cert. denied*, 537 U.S. 1226 (2003), a sculptor's work had been depicted, without his authorization, in a promotional brochure distributed by the local symphony orchestra. The Ninth Circuit emphasized the importance of the causation requirement for an award of indirect profits, noting that the threshold inquiry is whether there is a legally sufficient causal link between the infringement and subsequent indirect profits. The court observed that "[s]uch an approach dovetails with common sense—there must first be a demonstration that the infringing acts had an effect on profits before the parties can wrangle about apportionment." *Id.* at 915. Accordingly, it held that the sculptor was entitled only to the royalty that he could have charged for inclusion of the image, and not to a share of the symphony's profits. *Id.* at 916. Do the results in *Bouchat* and *Mackie* serve either the purpose of deterrence or that of compensation?

4. Article 45 of the TRIPS Agreement requires the availability of monetary damages "adequate to compensate for the injury the right holder has suffered" as a result of infringement by a party that knew or had reason to know that the conduct was infringing. Article 45(2) of the TRIPS Agreement provides that in "appropriate" cases, members *may* "authorize the judicial authorities to order recovery of profits and/or payment of pre-established damages even where the infringer did not knowingly, or with reasonable grounds to know, engage in infringing activity." Section 504 of the Copyright Act does not authorize any adjustment of actual damages and profits in cases of innocent infringement.

Do you think that the *Bouchat* jury's conclusion that defendants "mistakenly" infringed influenced its decision that Bouchat was not entitled to any profits? If so, was that appropriate given the statutory language? What effect do you think Bouchat's initial "payment" request (a letter of acknowledgment and an autographed helmet) had on the jury's decision?

5. Section 504(b) also entitles a successful copyright infringement plaintiff to recover actual damages. How would you compute such damages in *Bouchat*? The Patent Act provides for "damages adequate to compensate for the infringement, but in no event less than a reasonable royalty." 35 U.S.C. §284. Is an award of a reasonable royalty permissible for copyright infringement given the language of the statute? *Compare OnDavis v. The Gap, Inc.*, 246 F.3d 152 (2d Cir. 2001) (awarding a reasonable license fee), *with Dash v. Mayweather*, 731 F.3d 303, 333 n.6 (4th Cir. 2013), *cert. denied*, 134 S. Ct. 1761 (2014) (refusing to award a license fee because plaintiff had failed to present "sufficient nonspeculative evidence to show that [plaintiff's infringed work] had a fair market value").

AFTERMATH

Bouchat continued to pursue infringement claims against the Ravens and a variety of others for use of the old Flying B logo. *Bouchat v. Baltimore Ravens Ltd. Partnership*, 2012 WL 6738321, at *1 n.1 (D. Md. 2012) (noting seven different reported decisions). Bouchat did eventually receive an award of damages in one of those cases: $721 for the logo's use in highlight films sold by the NFL that included the 1996-98 seasons. *Id.* at *5. The court also set a royalty of $100 for each use of highlight footage played in the stadium during the Ravens home games. *Id.*

---

b. Apportionment of Profits

Frank Music Corp. v. Metro-Goldwyn-Mayer, Inc.
886 F.2d 1545 (9th Cir. 1989)

FLETCHER, J.: In *Frank Music Corp. v. Metro-Goldwyn-Mayer, Inc.*, 772 F.2d 505 (9th Cir. 1985) (*Frank Music I*), we affirmed the district court's holding that defendants infringed plaintiffs' copyright in the dramatico-musical play *Kismet*, but remanded for reconsideration of the amount of profits attributable to the infringement . . . .

I. Facts

. . . Plaintiffs are the copyright owners and authors of *Kismet*, a dramatico-musical work. MGM, Inc. under license produced a musical motion picture version of *Kismet*. Beginning April 26, 1974, MGM Grand presented a musical revue entitled *Hallelujah Hollywood* in the hotel's Ziegfeld Theatre. *Hallelujah Hollywood* was largely created by an employee of MGM Grand, Donn Arden, who also staged, produced and directed the show. The show comprised ten acts, four billed as "tributes" to MGM motion pictures. Act IV was entitled "Kismet," and was a tribute to the MGM movie of that name. It was based almost entirely on music from *Kismet*, and used characters and settings from that musical. Act IV "Kismet" was performed approximately 1700 times, until July 16, 1976, when, under pressure resulting from this litigation, MGM Grand substituted a new Act IV. . . .

II. Discussion

A. *Apportionment of Profits*

1. **Direct Profits**

In *Frank Music I,* 772 F.2d at 524, we upheld the district court's conclusion that the plaintiffs failed to prove actual damages arising from the infringement, but vacated the district court's award of $22,000 in apportioned profits as "grossly inadequate," *id.* at 518, and remanded to the district court for reconsideration.

On remand, the district court calculated MGM Grand's net profit from *Hallelujah Hollywood* at $6,131,606, by deducting from its gross revenues the direct costs MGM Grand proved it had incurred. Neither party challenges this calculation.

In apportioning the profits between Act IV and the other acts in the show, the district court made the following finding:

> Act IV of "Hallelujah Hollywood" was one of ten acts, approximately a ten minute segment of a 100 minute revue. On this basis, the Court concludes that ten percent of the profits of "Hallelujah Hollywood" are attributable to Act IV.

Memorandum of Decision and Order (Decision II) at 4.

Plaintiffs assert that this finding is in error in several respects. First, they point out that on Saturdays *Hallelujah Hollywood* contained only eight acts, not ten, and that on Saturdays the show ran only 75 minutes, not 100. Second, Act IV was approximately eleven and a half minutes long, not ten. Because the show was performed three times on Saturdays, and twice a night on the other evenings of the week, the district court substantially underestimated the running time of Act IV in relation to the rest of the show.[2]

If the district court relied exclusively on a quantitative comparison and failed to consider the relative quality or drawing power of the show's various component parts, it erred. However, the district court's apportionment based on comparative durations would be appropriate if the district court implicitly concluded that all the acts of the show were of roughly equal value. *Cf. Frank Music I,* 772 F.2d at 518 ("Each element contributed significantly to the show's success, but no one element

---

2. There were twelve shows weekly which ran for 100 minutes, plus three on Saturday which ran 75, totaling 1425 minutes per week. Act IV remained constant throughout the week, for a total of approximately 173 minutes. Accordingly, Act IV comprised 12% of the total weekly running time of *Hallelujah Hollywood.* Because the district court's findings differ from those previously found and affirmed in *Frank Music I,* we substitute 12% as the appropriate figure on which we base our subsequent calculations.

was the sole or overriding reason for that success."). While a more precise statement of the district court's reasons would have been desirable, we find support in the record for the conclusion that all the acts in the show were of substantially equal value.

The district court went on to apportion the parties' relative contributions to Act IV itself:

> The infringing musical material was only one of several elements contributing to the segment. A portion of the profits attributable to Act IV must be allocated to other elements, including the creative talent of the producer and director, the talents of performers, composers, choreographers, costume designers and others who participated in creating Act IV, and the attraction of the unique Ziegfeld Theatre with its elaborate stage effects. . . . While no precise mathematical formula can be applied, the Court concludes that . . . a fair approximation of the value of the infringing work to Act IV is twenty-five percent.

Decision II at 4-5.

The district court was correct in probing into the parties' relative contributions to Act IV. Where a defendant alters infringing material to suit its own unique purposes, those alterations and the creativity behind them should be taken into account in apportioning the profits of the infringing work. However, the district court appears to have ignored its finding in its previous decision that defendants used not only the plaintiffs' music, but also their lyrics, characters, settings, and costume designs, recreating to a substantial extent the look and sound of the licensed movie version of *Kismet*.

While it was not inappropriate to consider the creativity of producers, performers and others involved in staging and adapting excerpts from *Kismet* for use in *Hallelujah Hollywood,* the district court erred in weighing these contributions so heavily. In performing the apportionment, the benefit of the doubt must always be given to the plaintiff, not the defendant. And while the apportionment may take into account the role of uncopyrightable elements of a work in generating that work's profits, the apportionment should not place too high a value on the defendants' staging of the work, at the expense of undervaluing the plaintiffs' more substantive creative contributions. Production contributions involving expensive costumes and lavish sets will largely be taken into account when deducting the defendants' costs. . . .

The district court found that defendants' staging of the *Kismet* excerpts was highly significant to Act IV's success. While we believe that a defendant's efforts in staging an infringing production will generally not support more than a *de minimis* deduction from the plaintiff's share of the profits, we cannot say the district court's conclusion that the defendants' contributions were substantial in this case is clearly erroneous. We recognize that there will be shows in which the attraction of the costumes, scenery or performers outweighs the attraction of the music or dialogue. On the other hand, a producer's ability to stage a lavish presentation, or a performer's ability to fill a hall from the drawing power of her name alone, is not a license to use freely the copyrighted works of others.

We conclude that apportioning 75% of Act IV to the defendants grossly undervalues the importance of the plaintiffs' contributions. Act IV was essentially *Kismet*, with contributions by the defendants; it was not essentially a new work incidentally plagiarizing elements of *Kismet*. A fairer apportionment, giving due regard to the district court's findings, attributes 75% of Act IV to elements taken from the plaintiffs and 25% to the defendants' contributions.

2. Indirect Profits

In *Frank Music I*, we held that the plaintiffs were entitled to recover, in addition to direct profits, a proportion of ascertainable indirect profits from defendants' hotel and gaming operations attributable to the promotional value of *Hallelujah Hollywood*. The district court considered the relative contributions of *Hallelujah Hollywood* and other factors contributing to the hotel's profits, including the hotel's guest accommodations, restaurants, cocktail lounges, star entertainment in the "Celebrity" room, the movie theater, Jai Alai, the casino itself, convention and banquet facilities, tennis courts, swimming pools, gym and sauna, and also the role of advertising and general promotional activities in bringing customers to the hotel. The district court concluded that two percent of MGM Grand's indirect profit was attributable to *Hallelujah Hollywood*. In light of the general promotion and the wide variety of attractions available at MGM Grand, this conclusion is not clearly erroneous.

B. *Prejudgment Interest*

The district court, without comment, declined to award prejudgment interest. The availability of prejudgment interest under the Copyright Act of 1909 is an issue of first impression in this circuit.

The 1909 Act does not mention prejudgment interest. Nevertheless, courts may allow prejudgment interest even though the governing statute is silent. . . . The goal of compensating the injured party fairly for the loss caused by the defendant's breach of the statutory obligation should be kept in mind. Prejudgment interest compensates the injured party for the loss of the use of money he would otherwise have had. . . .

Because the 1909 Act allows plaintiffs to recover only the greater of the defendant's profits *or* the plaintiff's actual damages, an award of profits or damages under the 1909 Act will not necessarily be adequate to compensate a prevailing copyright owner. Accordingly, we conclude prejudgment interest ordinarily should be awarded.

Awarding prejudgment interest on the apportioned share of defendant's profits is consistent with the purposes underlying the profits remedy. Profits are awarded to the plaintiff not only to compensate for the plaintiff's injury, but also and primarily to prevent the defendant from being unjustly enriched by its infringing use of the plaintiff's property. For the restitutionary purpose of this remedy to be served fully, the defendant generally should be required to turn over to the plaintiff not only the profits made from the use of his property, but also the interest on these profits, which can well exceed the profits themselves. Indeed, one way to view this interest is as another form of indirect profit accruing from the infringement, which should be turned over to the copyright owner along with other forms of indirect profit. It would be anomalous to hold that a plaintiff can recover, for example, profits derived from the promotional use of its copyrighted material, but not for the value of the use of the revenue generated by the infringement.[10]

We accordingly remand to the district court to enter an award of prejudgment interest. . . .

NOTES AND QUESTIONS

1. In *Frank Music*, the court considered a variety of elements in determining the infringers' profits. Profits included both direct profits reflected in the commercial revenues earned from the infringing work and indirect profits reflecting the value that the infringement added to the defendant's enterprise. Why is an award of indirect profits justified? Should indirect profits be awarded in cases such as *Frank Music* where the infringing work also includes independent contributions by the defendant?

2. Assume that incorporation of a copyrighted work into a second work (as in *Frank Music*) reduces the value of the second work, instead of enhancing it. Should the damages award be reduced accordingly? If there are no ascertainable profits, how should a court determine whether the infringement was a "value-adding" contribution to the infringing work?

3. What should be the principal goal of apportionment: to prevent unjust enrichment of either party or to deter the infringing creation of derivative works? Is there a real distinction between these two goals? Which goal is likely to engender larger damage awards? What apportionment formula would you have suggested if you had represented the plaintiffs in *Frank Music*? If you had represented the defendants?

4. Why should a defendant be allowed to deduct the cost of producing the infringing work from the calculation of damages? In *Hamil America, Inc. v. GFI*, 193 F.3d 92 (2d Cir. 1999), *cert. denied*, 528 U.S. 1160 (2000), the district court had limited the defendant's deductible expenses to the actual costs of producing the infringing items. In remanding for a recalculation of damages, the Second Circuit held that overhead expense categories are deductible once a sufficient nexus has been shown between the category of overhead and the production or sale of the infringing product. The infringer has the burden of offering a reasonable formula for allocating a portion of the overhead expenses to the infringing products. *See id.* at 105. Further, where there has been a finding of willful infringement, the district court should give "extra scrutiny" to the categories of overhead expenses to determine whether there is a "strong nexus" between each category and the sale and production of the infringing product. *Id.* at 107. All presumptions are drawn against the infringer. *Id.* Do the standards for deducting overhead expenses articulated by

---

10. Prejudgment interest will, of course, be available on both the direct and indirect profits earned by MGM Grand, since both forms of profit are equally attributable to the infringement. *Frank Music I*, 772 F.2d at 517.

the court in *Hamil* sufficiently balance the competing interests? Does a presumption against the infringer in this context make sense?"

PRACTICE EXERCISE: COUNSEL A CLIENT

Defendant Storm Entertainment (SE) produced a rap album called *Ready to Rain* that contained 17 tracks. Bayspan Music, Inc., sued for infringement, alleging that the title track included a 23-second sample from its copyrighted sound recording "Yelling in the Evening." The court bifurcated the trial into liability and damages phases. In the liability phase it ruled in favor of Bayspan. The title track from *Ready to Rain is* 2:52 minutes long and repeats the sample twice. Bayspan is able to prove that SE's profits from the album totaled $1.5 million. You represent SE. Outline the arguments you will make about how the court should reduce that figure to arrive at a final award.

---

c.   *Attribution Across National Borders*

The calculation of damages may sometimes involve issues of territoriality. Should U.S. courts include infringements that take place abroad in their calculation of damages? Review the material on Infringement by Authorization, Chapter 9.A.2, *supra*, and then consider the following case.

Los Angeles News Service v. Reuters Television International, Ltd.
340 F.3d 926 (9th Cir. 2003), *cert. denied,* 541 U.S. 1041 (2004)

O'SCANNLAIN, J.: We must decide whether a news organization may recover actual damages under the Copyright Act for acts of infringement that mostly occurred outside the United States.

I

The copyright works at issue here ("the works") are two video recordings, "The Beating of Reginald Denny" and "Beating of Man in White Panel Truck," which depict the infamous events at Florence Ave. and Normandie Blvd. during the 1992 Los Angeles riots. Los Angeles News Services ("LANS"), an independent news organization which produces video and audio tape recordings of newsworthy events and licenses them for profit, produced the works . . . while filming the riots from its helicopter. LANS copyrighted the works and sold a license to rebroadcast them to, among others, . . . [NBC], which used them on the *Today Show*.

Visnews International (USA), Ltd. ("Visinews") is a joint venture among NBC, Reuters Television Ltd., and the British Broadcasting Company ("BBC"). Pursuant to a news supply agreement between NBC and Visnews, NBC transmitted the *Today*

Show broadcast by fiber link to Visnews in New York; Visnews made a videotape copy of the works, which it then transmitted via satellite to its subscribers in Europe and Africa and via fiber link to the New York Office of the European Broadcast Union ("EBU"), a joint venture of Visnews and Reuters. The EBU subsequently made another videotape copy of the works, and transmitted it to Reuters in London, which in turn distributed the works via video "feed" to its own subscribers.

LANS sued Reuters . . . and Visnews for copyright infringement . . . . The district court subsequently granted Reuters and Visnews partial summary judgment on the issue of extraterritorial infringement, holding that no liability could arise under the Copyright Act for acts of infringement that occurred outside the United States. However, the district court held that Visnews's act of copying the works in New York was a domestic act of infringement . . . .

The district court further concluded that LANS had failed to prove any actual damages arising domestically and that damages arising extraterritorially were unavailable under the Act, which meant that LANS was limited to statutory damages. . . .

LANS appealed the district court's ruling on actual damages. . . . We subsequently reversed the district court's actual damages ruling, disagreeing with its interpretation of the Copyright Act's extraterritorial application. We concluded that although the district court was correct to hold that the Copyright Act does not apply extraterritorially, an exception may apply where an act of infringement is completed entirely within the United States and that such infringing act enabled further exploitation abroad. Relying on *Sheldon v. Metro-Goldwyn Pictures Corp.*, 106 F.3d 45 (2d Cir. 1939), *aff'd*, 309 U.S. 390 (1940), which held that profits from overseas infringement can be recovered on the theory that the infringer holds them in a constructive trust for the copyright owner, we reversed the grant of summary judgment. We held that "LANS [was] entitled to recover damages flowing from exploitation abroad of the domestic acts of infringement committed by defendants." [*L.A. News Serv. v. Reuters Television Int'l, Ltd.*, 149 F.3d 987, 992 (9th Cir. 1998) ("*Reuters III*")]. . . .

. . . The [district] court concluded that *Reuters III* had held only that LANS could recover any profits or unjust enrichment from domestic infringers, on the theory that the infringers held such profits in a constructive trust for LANS. "To permit [LANS] to recover damages other than Defendants' profits or unjust enrichment," the court stated, "would . . . effectively permit [LANS] to recover damages for extraterritorial acts of infringement."

. . . [T]he district court concluded that Reuters and Visnews had reaped no such profits from their infringement. . . . [T]he district court stated that LANS could elect to take the $60,000 in statutory damages awarded [previously] . . . .

II . . .

A

Both parties engage in detailed exegesis of our opinion in *Reuters III*. On LANS's reading, the *Reuters III* court's use of the terms "damages" is dispositive.

The statute uses "actual damages" and "profits" separately and distinctly, and provides that an infringer may recover both (in the ordinary case). LANS asserts therefore that the *Reuters III* court should be read as having meant what it said: "damages" means actual damages.

But LANS's interpretation does not fit with the context in which the *Reuters III* court discussed the recoverability of "damages." There, we relied on Judge Learned Hand's opinion in *Sheldon* and discussed damages entirely in the context of that case, which dealt exclusively with the recovery of the defendants' profits. . . .

B

Of course, *Sheldon* did not explicitly deal with the issue of actual damages. But as LANS points out, there is some support in the Second Circuit's post-*Sheldon* case law for the recovery of actual damages once an act of domestic infringement is proven.

The most direct support for such a position comes from *Update Art, Inc. v. Modiin Publ'g, Ltd.*, 843 F.2d 67 (2d Cir. 1988), in which the Second Circuit considered an Israeli newspaper's unauthorized reproduction of a poster copyrighted in the United States. . . .

Update Art, however, is distinguishable from LANS's claim in a couple of important respects. First, several issues of the newspaper in which the infringing reproduction appeared were circulated in the United States. *Id.* at 73 & n.6. Second, and more importantly, the amount of damages awarded by the district court was based on defendants' profits. *Id.* at 70 & n.4. Finally, the panel did not even discuss the distinction between damages and profits, much less cite *Sheldon*. Rather, it merely concluded that the damages award could stand despite the extraterritoriality issue, which the magistrate judge had not considered in calculating the amount. *Id.* at 70. . . .

C

On the whole, we conclude that *Reuters III* adhered very closely to our decision in *Subafilms, Ltd. v. MGM-Pathe Communications Co.*, 24 F.3d 1088 (9th Cir. 1994) (en banc) [discussed in Chapter 9.A.2, *supra*— Eds.]. *Subafilms* reaffirmed that the copyright laws have no application beyond the U.S. border, and expressly took no position on the merits of the *Update Art* court's apparent willingness to award damages. LANS's appeal thus presents the precise question that *Subafilms* reserved and as the prior panel recognized, such question should be resolved in light of the principles the en banc court laid down.

The import of such principles counsel a narrow application of the adoption in *Reuters III* of the *Sheldon* exception to the general rule. In particular, the *Sheldon* constructive trust rationale preserves a territorial connection . . . . Moreover, no rational deterrent function is served by making an infringer whose domestic act of infringement—from which he earns no profit—leads to widespread extraterritorial infringement, liable for the copyright owner's entire loss of value or profit from that overseas infringement, particularly if the overseas infringement is legal where it takes place. *See Subafilms*, 24 F.3d at 1097-98 (warning of the disruption to

American foreign policy interests and to the policy of domestic enforcement expressed in the Berne Convention that extraterritorial enforcement would cause). Moreover, the resulting over-deterrence might chill the fair use of copyrighted works in close cases. . . .

III

Accordingly, we read *Reuters III* to allow only a narrow exception for the recovery of the infringer's profits to *Subafilms*'s general rule against extraterritorial application. . . .

NOTES AND QUESTIONS

1. Do you agree with the court's interpretation of its own prior ruling in this case? With its interpretation of Second Circuit law?

2. Under the rule articulated by the *Reuters IV* court, a claim for profits from infringement abroad will be allowed if a predicate act of infringement took place in the United States. Does that rule make sense? Does it make any more sense than a rule allowing LANS to recover actual damages?

3. How might the *Reuters IV* rule affect domestic affiliates of foreign corporations who use allegedly infringing materials sent to them from the corporate main office? Should the Ninth Circuit's rule apply if the works are not subject to protection in the originating foreign country? What would you think if a foreign court allowed a plaintiff to recover profits flowing from exploitation within the United States of works that are in the public domain here?

4. Is *Reuters IV* consistent with *Subafilms*? Is *Subafilms* relevant to the proper resolution of disputes like this one?

5. Does the court's concern regarding extraterritorial application of the Copyright Act seem as relevant today in light of strengthened multilateral obligations regarding enforcement of copyright? Recall from Chapter 1 that all the members of the WTO (currently 160 countries) are obligated to comply with the minimum requirements of the TRIPS Agreement, including provisions on damages. To what extent should treaty membership be considered by a U.S. court in determining whether profits from infringement occurring in a particular country can be recovered by a U.S. plaintiff?

4. Statutory Damages

In lieu of actual damages and profits, §504(c) provides that a plaintiff may elect statutory damages. Recall, however, that timely registration of copyright is a prerequisite for eligibility to take advantage of this option. *See* 17 U.S.C. §412. In cases where actual damages and attributable profits are difficult to prove, statutory damages may be the more feasible and more rewarding remedial option from the plaintiff's perspective. The calculation of actual damages is especially challenging when the defendant has distributed the copyrighted material online without requiring payment.

From the defendant's perspective, the amount of statutory damages available can be staggering, especially as compared to actual damages. As you read the material in this section, consider whether the application of the statutory damages rules produces results that seem appropriate and fair. Most other countries do not provide for statutory damages, and such remedies are not required by the TRIPS Agreement.

a. The Basics of Statutory Damages

Zomba Enterprises, Inc. v. Panorama Records, Inc.
491 F. 3d 574 (6th Cir. 2007)

MOORE, J.: . . .

I. FACTS AND PROCEDURE . . .

B. Factual Background

Since 1998, Panorama has been in the business of manufacturing and selling karaoke compact discs. It issues a new disc monthly in each of a variety of musical genres, including country, pop, rock, and R & B. Each installment (or "karaoke package") contains the top hits in that genre for the relevant month. . . .

The individual discs that Panorama makes and sells are in the CD + G format – shorthand for "compact disc plus graphics." As Panorama explains, "[t]hese are compact discs on which musicians that are hired by Panorama record a musical composition of a work which at some time may have been made popular by another artist. The CD + G contains a graphic element and is designed to be viewed when played on a karaoke machine." The graphic element consists of the text of each song's lyrics, and it scrolls across a screen as the music (sans vocals) plays, permitting karaoke participants to read the lyrics as they sing along. Each of Panorama's karaoke packages contained nine or ten songs, with two tracks for each song, one track released with audible lyrics and one without.

Zomba Enterprises, Inc. and Zomba Songs, Inc. (collectively, "Zomba") are music publishing corporations . . . . [A]t all times relevant to this case, Zomba held and administered the copyrights to a variety of musical compositions, including songs performed by pop music performers such as 98 Degrees, Backstreet Boys, *NSYNC, and Britney Spears. . . .

. . . Zomba . . . discovered that Panorama's karaoke packages contained copies of songs it owned. Zomba . . . [sent a] cease-and-desist letter [and] specified the terms upon which [it] would be willing to grant a license: a $250 fixing fee for each Zomba-owned song on each package, plus royalties of $0.16 per song per CD + G sold for the first half of the five-year license term, and $0.19 per song per CD + G sold for the second-half of the term. [Panorama] contacted [Zomba's attorney] in response to this letter, but [it] did not stop selling CD + Gs with Zomba's songs on them, nor did it obtain any licenses. . . .

C. Procedural History

On January 13, 2003, Zomba filed its complaint, asserting thirty counts of copyright infringement – one count for each Zomba-owned musical composition that Panorama recorded and sold in its karaoke packages. . . . On April 22, 2003, the parties entered into a consent order in which Panorama agreed "to be restrained from distributing, releasing or otherwise exploiting any karaoke package containing compositions owned or administered by" Zomba. Within a week of entering this consent order, Panorama breached its agreement and resumed selling CD + Gs containing Zomba's copyrighted work. This conduct continued, and a year later, Zomba moved for sanctions on this basis. . . .

. . . On November 5, 2005, the district court held a hearing to determine the amount of damages. . . . The district court concluded that Panorama's infringement was willful, and accordingly awarded Zomba $31,000 for each of the twenty-six infringements at issue, for a total of $806,000. . . .

III. ANALYSIS

. . . Panorama . . . disputes the district court's statutory-damage calculation, arguing both that any infringement was not willful and that the $806,000 damage award is unconstitutionally high. . . .

B. Willfulness

. . . Panorama argues that even if it infringed Zomba's copyrights, the district court erred by concluding that the infringement was willful and thus was subject to enhanced statutory damages. According to Panorama, any infringement was innocent, and certainly not willful. We disagree.

For infringement to be "willful," it must be done "with knowledge that [one's] conduct constitutes copyright infringement." *Princeton Univ. Press v. Mich. Doc. Servs., Inc.*, 99 F.3d 1381, 1392 (6th Cir. 1996), *cert. denied*, 520 U.S. 1156 (1997) (quoting Melville B. Nimmer & David Nimmer, 3 NIMMER ON COPYRIGHT §14.04[B][3] (1996)). Accordingly, "one who has been notified that his conduct constitutes copyright infringement, but who reasonably and in good faith believes the contrary, is not 'willful' for these purposes." *Id.* This belief must be both (1) reasonable and (2) held in good faith. *See id.*

Panorama argues that it held a good-faith belief that the copying here at issue was a fair use, and contends that even if ultimately erroneous, this belief precludes a finding of willfulness. . . . [T]he issue is not so much whether Panorama held in good faith its belief that its copying was fair use (although we have serious misgivings on this matter), but whether Panorama reasonably believed that its conduct did not amount to copyright infringement. To decide this issue, we must determine "whether the copyright law supported the plaintiffs' position so clearly that the defendants must be deemed as a matter of law to have exhibited a reckless disregard of the plaintiffs' property rights." . . .

Here, we conclude that Panorama exhibited a reckless disregard for Zomba's rights, and accordingly, that Panorama's reliance on its fair-use defense was objectively unreasonable. The fact most crucial to this inquiry is that Panorama continued to sell karaoke packages containing copies of each of the relevant compositions after the district court entered its April 22, 2003, consent order forbidding Panorama to do so. . . .

. . . By entering into the consent decree, Panorama agreed to cease infringing Zomba's copyrights. Thus, it implicitly agreed to suspend its reliance on the fair-use defense at least temporarily, and this agreement was reduced to an order of the court. Because an order entered by a court of competent jurisdiction must be obeyed even if it is erroneously issued, Panorama lacked any legal justification for continuing to distribute copies of Zomba's copyrighted works after April 22, 2003. . . .

C. Amount of Statutory-Damage Award . . .

1. Abuse of Discretion

Panorama contends that the district court believed that, after making a finding of willfulness, it lacked discretion to award statutory damages of less than $30,000 per infringement. On this basis, Panorama maintains that the district court abused its discretion. The record does not support this argument.

In its conclusions of law, the district court recognized that it had "wide discretion in determining the amount of statutory damages to be awarded, constrained only by the maximum and minimum amounts." It found "that the maximum statutory amount of $30,000 per work for 'innocent' infringement is not sufficient in this case because of the clearly willful nature of Defendant's conduct," but that the maximum award of $150,000 per infringement was excessive, given the dollar amounts involved in the case.

> **KEEP IN MIND**
>
> Under current practice, a plaintiff may elect statutory damages even after a jury has returned a verdict on liability and an award of actual damages. *Feltner v. Columbia Pictures Television, Inc.*, 523 U.S. 340, 347 n.5 (1998).

Nowhere did the district court indicate that it believed that it lacked discretion to award statutory damages of less than $30,000 per infringement. To the contrary, Panorama's willfulness prompted the district court to conclude that the maximum penalty for nonwillful infringement was *not sufficient* given Panorama's conduct. We therefore conclude that Panorama has not shown that the district court abused its discretion by setting the statutory damage award at $31,000 per infringement. . . .

NOTES AND QUESTIONS

1. Read §504(c)(1). Could the district court have set the statutory damage award for each infringement at less than $30,000? Based on the court's analysis in *Zomba*, what factors do you think should be most significant in the court's determination of statutory damages? If the scope of discretion is as wide as the *Zomba* court intimates, can any amount within the prescribed statutory parameters ever reflect an abuse of discretion? Under what circumstances?

2. The *Zomba* court notes with suspicion Panorama's claim that it held a good faith belief that its actions constituted fair use. Section 504(c)(2) gives the court discretion to reduce a statutory damages award "to a sum of not less than $200" where the infringer proves that she "was not aware and had no reason to believe that . . . her acts constituted an infringement of copyright." Is a good faith belief that one's conduct is lawful sufficient? Or, must that good faith belief also be reasonable? *See Bryant v. Media Right Prods., Inc.*, 603 F.3d 135 (2d Cir.), *cert. denied*, 131 S. Ct. 656

> **LOOKING BACK**
>
> Recall from Chapter 11 that a court's ability to lower the minimum amount of statutory damages to $200 is cabined by §§401(d) and 402(d), which provide that no weight should be given to an assertion of innocent infringement if notice "appears on the published copies to which a defendant in a copyright infringement suit had access. . . ."

(2010) (affirming a reduced statutory damages award where the district court found it was "reasonable for [defendant] to believe" that its conduct was lawful).

3. An award of statutory damages is made "with respect to any one work, for which any one infringer is liable" regardless of the number of "infringements involved in the action." 17 U.S.C. §504(c). What constitutes "one work"? The only guidance the statute provides is that "parts of a compilation or derivative work constitute one work." *Id.*

PRACTICE PROBLEM: COUNSEL A CLIENT

Your client Jack Lane seeks advice about his line of greeting cards. To create the cards, Jack scours Goodwill stores, flea markets, and garage sales for old family photos. Sometimes the cards are collages of multiple pictures; sometimes a card contains just one photo. Once he has settled on a design, the cards are mass-produced and sold to retail stores throughout the United States. He also offers ecards that can be personalized and sent electronically. Jack has been creating these cards for the past five years and business is good. He has never tried to locate a copyright owner of any of the photographs. Recently he has become concerned that what he is doing might land him in some copyright trouble. Advise Jack concerning his potential liability for copyright infringement.

---

b. Policies Underlying Statutory Damages

Capitol Records, Inc. v. Thomas-Rasset
692 F.3d 899 (8th Cir. 2012), cert denied, 133 S. Ct. 1584 (2013)

COLLOTON, J.: This appeal arises from a dispute between several recording companies and Jammie Thomas–Rasset. . . . [F]or purposes of appeal, it is undisputed that

Thomas-Rasset willfully infringed copyrights of twenty-four sound recordings by engaging in file-sharing on the Internet. After a first jury found Thomas-Rasset liable and awarded damages of $222,000, the district court granted a new trial on the ground that the jury instructions incorrectly provided that the Copyright Act forbids making sound recordings available for distribution on a peer-to-peer network, regardless of whether there is proof of "actual distribution." A second jury found Thomas-Rasset liable for willful copyright infringement under a different instruction, and awarded statutory damages of $1,920,000. The district court remitted the award to $54,000, and the companies opted for a new trial on damages. A third jury awarded statutory damages of $1,500,000, but the district court ultimately ruled that the maximum amount permitted by the Due Process Clause of the Fifth Amendment was $54,000 and reduced the verdict accordingly. The court also enjoined Thomas-Rasset from taking certain actions with respect to copyrighted recordings owned by the recording companies.

The companies appeal two aspects of the remedy . . . . They object to the district court's ruling on damages, and they seek an award of $222,000, which was the amount awarded by the jury in the first trial. . . . For tactical reasons, the companies do not seek reinstatement of the third jury's award of $1,500,000. They urge instead that this court should reverse the district court's order granting a new trial, rule that the Copyright Act does protect a right to "making available" sound recordings, reinstate the first jury's award of $222,000, and direct entry of a broader injunction. In a cross-appeal, Thomas-Rasset argues that *any* award of statutory damages is unconstitutional, and urges us to vacate the award of damages altogether. . . .

II. . . .

. . . [T]his court reviews judgments, not decisions on issues. . . . The entitlement of the companies to these remedies—damages of $222,000 and an injunction against making copyrighted works available to the public—are the matters in controversy. . . . Once the requested remedies are ordered, the desire of the companies for an opinion on the meaning of the Copyright Act, or for a statement that Thomas-Rasset violated the law by making works available, is not sufficient to maintain an Article III case or controversy.

For the reasons set forth below, we conclude . . . that statutory damages of at least $222,000 were constitutional, and that the district court erred in holding that the Due Process Clause allowed statutory damages of only $54,000. . . .

B. . . .

The Supreme Court long ago declared that damages awarded pursuant to a statute violate due process only if they are "so severe and oppressive as to be wholly disproportioned to the offense and obviously unreasonable." *St. Louis, I. M. & S. Ry. Co. v. Williams*, 251 U.S. 63, 67, (1919). Under this standard, Congress possesses a "wide latitude of discretion" in setting statutory damages. . . .

Thomas-Rasset urges us to consider . . . the "guideposts" announced by the Supreme Court for the review of punitive damages awards under the Due Process

Clause. When a party challenges an award of punitive damages, a reviewing court is directed to consider three factors in determining whether the award is excessive and unconstitutional: "(1) the degree of reprehensibility of the defendant's misconduct; (2) the disparity between the actual or potential harm suffered by the plaintiff and the punitive damages award; and (3) the difference between the punitive damages awarded by the jury and the civil penalties authorized or imposed in comparable cases." *State Farm Mut. Auto. Ins. Co. v. Campbell*, 538 U.S. 408, 418, (2003); *see also BMW of N. Am., Inc. v. Gore*, 517 U.S. 559, 574-75 (1996).

The Supreme Court never has held that the punitive damages guideposts are applicable in the context of statutory damages. Due process prohibits excessive punitive damages because "'[e]lementary notions of fairness enshrined in our constitutional jurisprudence dictate that a person receive fair notice not only of the conduct that will subject him to punishment, but also of the severity of the penalty that a State may impose.'" *Campbell*, 538 U.S. 408 at 417 (2003), (quoting *Gore*, 517 U.S. at 574). This concern about fair notice does not apply to statutory damages, because those damages are identified and constrained by the authorizing statute. The guideposts themselves, moreover, would be nonsensical if applied to statutory damages. It makes no sense to consider the disparity between "actual harm" and an award of statutory damages when statutory damages are designed precisely for instances where actual harm is difficult or impossible to calculate. Nor could a reviewing court consider the difference between an award of statutory damages and the "civil penalties authorized," because statutory damages *are* the civil penalties authorized.

Applying the *Williams* standard, we conclude that an award of $9,250 per each of twenty-four works is not "so severe and oppressive as to be wholly disproportioned to the offense and obviously unreasonable." 251 U.S. at 67. Congress, exercising its "wide latitude of discretion," set a statutory damages range for willful copyright infringement of $750 to $150,000 per infringed work. The award here is toward the lower end of this broad range. As in *Williams*, "the interests of the public, the numberless opportunities for committing the offense, and the need for securing uniform adherence to [federal law]" support the constitutionality of the award. *Id*. . . .

Congress's protection of copyrights is not a "special private benefit," but is meant to achieve an important public interest: "to motivate the creative activity of authors and inventors by the provision of a special reward, and to allow the public access to the products of their genius after the limited period of exclusive control has expired." *Sony Corp. of Am. v. Universal City Studios, Inc.*, 464 U.S. 417, 429 (1984). With the rapid advancement of technology, copyright infringement through online file-sharing has become a serious problem in the recording industry. Evidence at trial showed that revenues across the industry decreased by fifty percent between 1999 and 2006, a decline that the record companies attributed to piracy. This decline in revenue caused a corresponding drop in industry jobs and a reduction in the number of artists represented and albums released. *See Sony BMG Music Entm't v. Tenenbaum*, 660 F.3d 487, 492 (1st Cir. 2011).

Congress no doubt was aware of the serious problem posed by online copyright infringement, and the "numberless opportunities for committing the offense," when it last revisited the Copyright Act in 1999. To provide a deterrent against such infringement, Congress amended §504(c) to increase the minimum per-work award from $500 to $750, the maximum per-work award from $20,000 to $30,000, and the maximum per-work award for willful infringement from $100,000 to $150,000.

Thomas-Rasset contends that the range of statutory damages established by §504(c) reflects only a congressional judgment "at a very general level," but that courts have authority to declare it "severe and oppressive" and "wholly disproportioned" in particular cases. The district court similarly emphasized that Thomas-Rasset was "not a business acting for profit, but rather an individual consumer illegally seeking free access to music for her own use." By its terms, however, the statute plainly encompasses infringers who act without a profit motive, and the statute already provides for a broad range of damages that allows courts and juries to calibrate the award based on the nature of the violation. For those who favor resort to legislative history, the record also suggests that Congress was well aware of the threat of noncommercial copyright infringement when it established the lower end of the range. *See* H.R. Rep. 106–216, at 3 (1999), 1999 WL 446444, at *3. Congressional amendments to the criminal provisions of the Copyright Act in 1997 also reflect an awareness that the statute would apply to noncommercial infringement. *See* No Electronic Theft (NET) Act, Pub. L. No. 105-147, §2(a), 111 Stat. 2678 (1997).

In holding that any award over $2,250 per work would violate the Constitution, the district court effectively imposed a treble damages limit on the $750 minimum statutory damages award. The district court based this holding on a "broad legal practice of establishing a treble award as the upper limit permitted to address willful or particularly damaging behavior." Any "broad legal practice" of treble damages for statutory violations, however, does not control whether an award of statutory damages is within the limits prescribed by the Constitution. The limits of treble damages to which the district court referred, such as in the antitrust laws or other intellectual property laws, represent congressional judgments about the appropriate maximum in a given context. They do not establish a *constitutional* rule that can be substituted for a different congressional judgment in the area of copyright infringement. Although the United States seems to think that the district court's ruling did not question the constitutionality of the statutory damages statute, the district court's approach in our view would make the statute unconstitutional as applied to a significant category of copyright infringers. The evidence against Thomas-Rasset demonstrated an aggravated case of willful infringement by an individual consumer who acted to download and distribute copyrighted recordings without profit motive. If an award near the bottom of the statutory range is unconstitutional as applied to her infringement of twenty-four works, then it would be the rare case of noncommercial infringement to which the statute could be applied.

. . . The Supreme Court in *Williams* . . . disagreed that the constitutional inquiry calls for a comparison of an award of statutory damages to actual damages caused by the violation. 251 U.S. at 66. Because the damages award "is imposed as a punishment for the violation of a public law, the Legislature may adjust its amount to the public wrong rather than the private injury, just as if it were going to the state." *Id.* The protection of copyrights is a vindication of the public interest and statutory damages are "by definition a substitute for unproven or unprovable actual damages." *Cass Cnty. Music Co.* [*v. C.H.L.R., Inc.*, 88 F.3d 635], 643 [(8th Cir.1996)]. For copyright infringement, moreover, statutory damages are "designed to discourage wrongful conduct," in addition to providing "restitution of profit and reparation for injury." *F.W. Woolworth Co. v. Contemporary Arts*, 344 U.S. 228, 233 (1952). . . .

. . . The judgment of the district court is vacated, and the case is remanded with directions to enter a judgment for damages in the amount of $222,000 . . . .

NOTES AND QUESTIONS

1. Do you agree with the *Capitol Records* court that imposing a treble damages limit on the maximum statutory damages award for due process reasons would amount to holding the statutory damages provision of the Copyright Act unconstitutional as applied to many small scale infringers like Thomas-Rasset? As a policy matter, why do you think Congress chose not to impose a treble damages rule for willful infringement, given that it chose such an approach in both antitrust law and patent law?

2. What do you make of the Eighth Circuit's conclusion that the size of a statutory damages award raises no due process concerns because Congress has prescribed the outer limits for such awards in the Copyright Act? Review §504(c) once again. Do you agree that it provides sufficient "fair notice" of the severity of the penalty that could be imposed on an infringer? Should the three factors the Supreme Court directs courts to employ in reviewing punitive damages awards play no role in assessing the constitutionality of statutory damages?

3. Which defendant seems more culpable to you, Thomas-Rasset or Zomba? During the first trial, the jury heard evidence that Thomas-Rasset had removed and replaced the hard drive on her computer after she was notified of potential infringement. *Capitol Records*, 692 F. 3d at 903. At the second trial, Thomas-Rasset tried to conceal her actions by suggesting that either her boyfriend or daughter had engaged in the file-sharing. Do these facts alter your relative culpability assessment? Should the degree of a defendant's culpability affect how statutory damages are assessed? Should courts apply a different rule for assessing statutory damages awards against individual defendants than against business defendants? Should Congress create such a rule? *See* Pamela Samuelson & Tara Wheatland, *Statutory Damages in Copyright Law: A Remedy in Need of Reform*, 51 Wm. & Mary L. Rev. 439, 495 (2009).

4. If deterrence is a goal of a damages award, can courts award punitive damages? In *TVT Records v. Island Def Jam Music Group*, 262 F. Supp. 2d 185 (S.D.N.Y. 2003), the court held that punitive damages are not categorically barred in copyright infringement cases where the plaintiff is seeking actual damages, and allowed a jury instruction authorizing a punitive damages award if plaintiffs proved willful infringement. Is there any reason that punitive damages would *not* be consistent with the goals of copyright law? The court also noted that "many cases" hold that a copyright plaintiff may not seek punitive damages if it has elected to recover the statutory damages authorized under §504(c). *Id.* at 186.

PRACTICE EXERCISE: DRAFTING

Draft an amendment to §504(c) to modify the statutory damages rules in a way you believe to be appropriate. Create a one- to two-page "talking points" memorandum to support your proposed legislative change.

---

5. Attorneys' Fees

Section 505 of the Copyright Act provides that a court may, in its discretion, allow the prevailing party to recover its costs (except when the other party is the United States or an officer thereof). The court also may award reasonable attorneys' fees to the prevailing party. An award of attorneys' fees is reviewable for abuse of discretion. Read §505 now, and then consider the following cases.

Fantasy, Inc. v. Fogerty
94 F.3d 553 (9th Cir. 1996)

RYMER, J.: This appeal requires us to consider the scope of a district court's discretion to award a reasonable attorney's fee to a prevailing defendant in a copyright infringement action, and in particular, to decide whether a court must find some "culpability" on the part of the plaintiff in pursuing the suit before it can award a fee to a prevailing defendant whose victory on the merits furthers the purposes of the Copyright Act.

John Fogerty, former lead singer and songwriter for "Creedence Clearwater Revival," recognized as one of the greatest American rock and roll bands, successfully defended a copyright infringement action in which Fantasy, Inc., alleged that Fogerty had copied the music from one of his earlier songs which Fantasy now owned, changed the lyrics, and released it as a new song. After concluding that Fogerty's victory on the merits vindicated his right (and the right of others) to continue composing music in the distinctive "Swamp Rock" style and genre and therefore furthered the purposes of the Copyright Act, the district court awarded Fogerty $1,347,519.15 in attorney's fees. Fantasy appeals the award mainly on the ground that the court had no discretion to award Fogerty *any* attorney's fees inasmuch as its conduct in bringing and maintaining the lawsuit was "faultless."

We hold that, after *Fogerty v. Fantasy, Inc.*, 510 U.S. 517 (1994), an award of attorney's fees to a prevailing defendant that furthers the underlying purposes of the Copyright Act is reposed in the sound discretion of the district courts, and that such discretion is not cabined by a requirement of culpability on the part of the losing party. As we agree with the district court that Fogerty's victory on the merits furthered the purposes of the Copyright Act, and as we cannot say that the district court abused its discretion by awarding fees under the circumstances of this case, we affirm the award. We also uphold the district court's exercise of discretion not to award interest on Fogerty's fee award.

I

This action began July 26, 1985, when Fantasy sued Fogerty for copyright infringement, alleging that Fogerty's song "The Old Man Down the Road" infringed the copyright on another of his songs, "Run Through the Jungle," which Fantasy owned. About three years later, on November 7, 1988, the jury disagreed, returning a verdict in favor of Fogerty.

Fogerty moved for a reasonable attorney's fee pursuant to 17 U.S.C. §505. The district court denied the request on the ground that Fantasy's lawsuit was neither frivolous nor prosecuted in bad faith and our then-existing precedent precluded an award of fees in the absence of one or the other. We affirmed for the same reason, *Fantasy, Inc. v. Fogerty*, 984 F.2d 1524, 1533 (9th Cir. 1993) [*Fogerty I*], but the Supreme Court reversed and remanded in *Fogerty v. Fantasy, Inc.*, 510 U.S. 517 (1994) [*Fogerty II*]. We then remanded to the district court for further proceedings consistent with *Fogerty II. Fantasy, Inc. v. Fogerty*, 21 F.3d 354 (9th Cir. 1994) [*Fogerty III*].

On remand, the district court granted Fogerty's motion and, after reviewing extensive billing records, awarded $1,347,519.15. Its decision was based on several factors. First, Fogerty's vindication of his copyright in "The Old Man Down the Road" secured the public's access to an original work of authorship and paved the way for future original compositions—by Fogerty and others—in the same distinctive "Swamp Rock" style and genre. Thus, the district court reasoned, Fogerty's defense was the type of defense that furthers the purposes underlying the Copyright Act and therefore should be encouraged through a fee award. Further, the district court found that a fee award was appropriate to help restore to Fogerty some of the lost value of the copyright he was forced to defend. In addition, Fogerty was a defendant author and prevailed on the merits rather than on a technical defense, such as the statute of limitations, laches, or the copyright registration requirements. Finally, the benefit conferred by Fogerty's successful defense was not slight or insubstantial relative to the costs of litigation, nor would the fee award have too great a chilling effect or impose an inequitable burden on Fantasy, which was not an impecunious plaintiff.

Fogerty also sought interest to account for the lost use of the money paid to his lawyers over the years. While the district court awarded Fogerty almost all of what he asked for in fees, it declined to award interest. Fantasy timely appeals the fee award; Fogerty timely cross-appeals the refusal to award interest. . . .

III

Fantasy contends that the district court had no discretion to award fees to Fogerty because Fantasy conducted a "good faith" and "faultless" lawsuit upon reasonable factual and legal grounds, or to put it somewhat differently, because Fantasy was "blameless." According to Fantasy, once the district court could find no fault in the way Fantasy conducted this case, that should have been the end of the matter. . . .

Fogerty, on the other hand, contends that *Fogerty II* focuses a district court's discretion on whether the prevailing party has furthered the purposes of the Copyright Act in litigating the action to a successful conclusion; under that standard, the district court was well within its discretion in finding that his successful defense of this action served important copyright policies. He also argues that the evenhanded approach does not mean that only "neutral" factors may be considered in the exercise of the court's discretion since, contrary to Fantasy's view, the Court itself recognized that somewhat different policies of the Copyright Act may be furthered when either plaintiffs or defendants prevail. Fogerty points out that the Court specifically observed that his successful defense of this action "increased public exposure to a musical work that could, as a result, lead to further creative pieces," *Fogerty II*, 510 U.S. at 527, and maintains that the fact that this factor happened to tip in Fogerty's favor as a prevailing defendant in this case should not prevent it from being considered at all.

A

In *Fogerty II*, the Supreme Court granted certiorari to resolve a conflict among the circuits concerning "what standards should inform a court's decision to award attorney's fees to a prevailing defendant in a copyright infringement action. . . ." The Court rejected both the "dual" standard that we had followed and applied in *Fogerty I*— whereby prevailing plaintiffs generally were awarded attorney's fees as a matter of course, while prevailing defendants had to show that the original lawsuit was frivolous or brought in bad faith—and the "British Rule" for which Fogerty argued—whereby the prevailing party (whether plaintiff or defendant) automatically receives fees. The Court instead adopted the "evenhanded" approach exemplified by the Third Circuit's opinion in *Lieb v. Topstone Indus., Inc.*, 788 F.2d 151 (3d Cir. 1986). The Court held that:

> Prevailing plaintiffs and prevailing defendants are to be treated alike, but attorney's fees are to be awarded to prevailing parties only as a matter of the court's discretion. "There is no precise rule or formula for making these determinations," but instead equitable discretion should be exercised "in light of the considerations we have identified."

Fogerty II, 510 U.S. at 534 (quoting *Hensley v. Eckerhart*, 461 U.S. 424, 436-37 (1983)). Considerations discussed by the Court include the Copyright Act's primary objective, "to encourage the production of original literary, artistic, and musical expression for the good of the public," *id.* at 524; the fact that defendants as well as plaintiffs may hold copyrights, *id.* at 525-527, and "run the gamut from corporate behemoths to starving artists," *id.* at 524; the need to encourage "defendants who seek to advance a variety of meritorious copyright defenses . . . to litigate them to the same extent that plaintiffs are encouraged to litigate meritorious claims of infringement," *id.* at 527; and the fact that "a successful defense of a copyright infringement action may further the policies of the Copyright Act every bit as much as a successful prosecution of an infringement claim by the holder of a copyright," *id.*

The district court's decision was informed by these considerations, but Fantasy argues that it failed to appreciate the culpability underpinnings of the evenhanded rule and to apply the *Lieb* factors, which Fantasy contends are fault-based and were embraced by the Supreme Court in *Fogerty II.* However, neither *Lieb* nor the Court's discussion of the evenhanded rule and the *Lieb* factors in *Fogerty II* suggests that discretion to award fees to prevailing defendants is constrained by the plaintiff's culpability, or is limited to the specific factors identified in *Lieb.* . . . [W]hile courts may take the *Lieb* factors into account, they are "nonexclusive." Even so, courts may not rely on the *Lieb* factors if they are not "faithful to the purposes of the Copyright Act." Faithfulness to the purposes of the Copyright Act is, therefore, the pivotal criterion.

By the same token, a court's discretion may be influenced by the plaintiff's culpability in bringing or pursuing the action, but blameworthiness is not a prerequisite to awarding fees to a prevailing defendant. . . .

Although we have not squarely addressed this question before, our post-*Fogerty II* opinions have recognized that a plaintiff's culpability is no longer required, that the *Lieb* factors may be considered but are not exclusive and need not all be met, and that attorney's fee awards to prevailing defendants are within the district court's discretion if they further the purposes of the Copyright Act and are evenhandedly applied. . . . We have been careful to indicate that such factors are only "some" of the factors to consider, and that courts are not limited to considering them. And in *Historical Research v. Cabral*, 80 F.3d 377 (9th Cir. 1996), we concluded that, under *Fogerty II*, "'exceptional circumstances' are not a prerequisite to an award of attorney's fees; district courts may freely award fees, as long as they treat prevailing plaintiffs and prevailing defendants alike and seek to promote the Copyright Act's objectives." *Id.* at 378.

We also have not previously been asked to decide whether the factors relied upon by a district court in awarding fees to a prevailing copyright defendant must be exactly capable of being applied to a prevailing plaintiff in order to satisfy the evenhanded rule. However, *Fogerty II* has already answered this question. Fantasy argues that the point of evenhandedness is to eliminate as the premise for any fee award any factor which cannot occur on both sides of the litigation equation. But we believe this asks more of "evenhandedness" than *Fogerty II* expects. . . . [T]he Court states: . . .

> More importantly, the policies served by the Copyright Act are more complex, more measured, than simply maximizing the number of meritorious suits for copyright infringement.

Fogerty II, 510 U.S. at 526. . . . [T]he Court says, speaking directly to this case:

> In the case before us, the successful defense of "The Old Man Down the Road" increased public exposure to a musical work that could, as a result, lead to further creative pieces. Thus a successful defense of a copyright infringement action may

further the policies of the Copyright Act every bit as much as a successful prosecution of an infringement claim by the holder of a copyright.

Id. at 527. We cannot, therefore, say that the district court erred by relying on factors identified by the Supreme Court which in this case led it to conclude that Fogerty's defense sufficiently furthered the purposes of the Copyright Act to warrant an award of attorney's fees. . . .

In sum, evenhandedness means that courts should begin their consideration of attorney's fees in a copyright action with an evenly balanced scale, without regard to whether the plaintiff or defendant prevails, and thereafter determine entitlement without weighting the scales in advance one way or the other. Courts may look to the nonexclusive *Lieb* factors as guides and may apply them so long as they are consistent with the purposes of the Copyright Act and are applied evenly to prevailing plaintiffs and defendants; a finding of bad faith, frivolous or vexatious conduct is no longer required; and awarding attorney's fees to a prevailing defendant is within the sound discretion of the district court informed by the policies of the Copyright Act.

Since the reasons given by the district court in this case are well-founded in the record and are in keeping with the purposes of the Copyright Act, the court acted within its discretion in awarding a reasonable attorney's fee to Fogerty. . . .

V

Fogerty requests attorney's fees for this appeal pursuant to 17 U.S.C. §505 . . . . [W]e conclude that fees are warranted under §505 inasmuch as it served the purposes of the Copyright Act for Fogerty to defend an appeal so that the district court's fee award would not be taken away from him. We therefore award Fogerty the attorney's fees he incurred in defending this appeal and we remand to the district court for calculation of the amount. . . .

Positive Black Talk, Inc. v. Cash Money Records, Inc.
394 F.3d 357 (5th Cir. 2004)

KING, J.: . . . In 1997, two rap artists based in New Orleans, Louisiana—Terius Gray, professionally known as Juvenile ("Juvenile"), and Jerome Temple, professionally known as D.J. Jubilee ("Jubilee")—each recorded a song that included the poetic four-word phrase "back that ass up." Specifically, with respect to Jubilee, he recorded his song in November 1997 and entitled it *Back That Ass Up*. In the Spring of 1998, Positive Black Talk, Inc. ("PBT"), a recording company, released Jubilee's *Back That Ass Up* on the album TAKE IT TO THE ST. THOMAS. Jubilee subsequently performed the song at a number of live shows, including the New Orleans Jazzfest on April 26, 1998.

Turning to Juvenile, at some point during the fall of 1997, Juvenile recorded his song and entitled it *Back That Azz Up*. In May 1998, Cash Money Records, Inc. ("CMR"), the recording company that produced Juvenile's album 400 DEGREEZ, signed a national distribution contract with Universal Records. Consequently, 400 DEGREEZ, which contained Juvenile's song *Back That Azz Up,* was released in November 1998. 400 DEGREEZ quickly garnered national acclaim, selling over four million albums and grossing more than $40 million. . . .

[PBT sued CMR, Juvenile, and Universal for copyright infringement, and] the defendants filed counterclaims, alleging copyright infringement, violation of [the Louisiana Unfair Trade Practices Act ("LUPTA")], and negligent misrepresentation. . . .

In May 2003, the case proceeded to a jury trial. Although the jury found that PBT proved by a preponderance of the evidence that it owned a copyright interest in the lyrics and music of Jubilee's song *Back That Ass Up*, it nevertheless found in favor of the defendants on PBT's copyright infringement claim. Specifically, the jury found that: (1) PBT failed to prove that Juvenile or CMR factually copied *Back That Ass Up*; (2) the defendants proved that CMR and Juvenile independently created *Back That Azz Up*; and (3) PBT failed to prove that *Back That Azz Up* is substantially similar to *Back That Ass Up*. . . . In addition, the jury found in favor of the defendants on their LUPTA and negligent misrepresentation counterclaims. . . . The court awarded the defendants attorney's fees in relation to their LUPTA counterclaim but not for their successful defense of PBT's copyright infringement claim. . . .

V. Attorney's Fees

The defendants . . . appeal the denial of their requests for attorney's fees. Universal requested $323,121.25 in fees, and CMR and Juvenile requested $263,040. Of those, CMR and Juvenile traced $39,456 of their fees to their successful LUPTA counterclaim . . . . The district court denied the fee requests for the successful copyright defense and granted CMR and Juvenile's request for the LUPTA fees at the markedly reduced sum of $2,500.

This court reviews the district court's refusal to award attorney's fees in a copyright infringement case for an abuse of discretion. *Creations Unlimited, Inc.* [*v. McCain*, 112 F.3d 814, 817 (5th Cir. 1997)]. A trial court abuses its discretion in awarding or refusing to award attorney's fees when its ruling is based on an erroneous view of the law or a clearly erroneous assessment of the evidence. *Sanmina Corp. v. BancTec USA, Inc.*, 94 Fed. Appx. 194, 196 n.10 (5th Cir. 2004).

. . . As the district court below explicitly recognized, an award of attorney's fees to the prevailing party in a copyright action, although left to the trial court's discretion, "is the rule rather than the exception and should be awarded routinely." *McGaughey v. Twentieth Century Fox Film Corp.*, 12 F.3d 62, 65 (5th Cir.1994) (quoting *Micromanipulator Co. v. Bough*, 779 F.2d 255, 259 (5th Cir.1985)). . . . [T]he district court nevertheless exercised its discretion not to award such fees in this case.

After *McGaughey* was decided, the Supreme Court decided *Fogerty v. Fantasy, Inc.*, 510 U.S. 517 (1994). . . . *Fogerty* adopted the Third Circuit's "'evenhanded' approach in which no distinction is made between prevailing plaintiffs and prevailing defendants." *Id.* at 521. . . . However, the Court made clear that it was not adopting the British Rule, under which prevailing parties—whether plaintiffs or defendants—are *always* granted attorney's fees. *See id.* at 533. . . .

The *Fogerty* Court . . . agreed that a non-exclusive list of factors may be used to guide the district court's discretion; this list includes "frivolousness, motivation, objective unreasonableness (both in the factual and in the legal components of the case) and the need in particular circumstances to advance considerations of compensation and deterrence."[22] *Id.* at 534 n.19 (internal quotation marks omitted). The Fifth Circuit previously applied these factors to deny a successful copyright defendant's request for attorney's fees. *Creations Unlimited, Inc.*, 112 F.3d at 817.

Here, the district court set forth the standard described above, noting the text of §505, the principle that fee awards—although discretionary—are the rule rather than the exception and should be awarded routinely, and that under *Fogerty* the court's discretion is guided by the non-exclusive list of *Lieb* factors. The court then determined that in this case, those factors suggested that attorney's fees should not be awarded to the defendants. Specifically, the court stated:

> In addition to presiding over the [five] day trial of this matter, the [c]ourt considered several complex and potentially dispositive pre-trial motions. Having gained an understanding of the applicable law and a thorough appreciation of PBT's claims, the [c]ourt does not feel that this litigation was frivolous, objectively unreasonable, or without proper motive. PBT had a renowned music expert to support its position even though the jury gave greater weight to the testimony of Defendants' expert. The [c]ourt is convinced that PBT's claims were brought in good faith. Therefore, an award of attorney's fees would not serve to deter future meritless litigation brought by other parties.

The defendants' claim that the district court applied the wrong legal standard is incorrect. The Supreme Court has explicitly approved of a district court considering frivolity and motivation as two of the multiple factors in a non-exclusive list [that] may guide the court's discretion over attorney's fees in copyright cases. *Fogerty,* 510 U.S. at 535 n. 19. Thus, to the extent that the defendants argue that the district court erred in considering these factors at all, they are unquestionably wrong. Second, to the extent that the defendants argue that the district court erred because it considered *only* frivolity and bad faith, they are equally wrong. The district court did not focus solely on whether the lawsuit was frivolous or brought in bad faith; rather, the court expressly found that the claims were "not objectively unreasonable," and it provided a reasonable explanation for this finding. Furthermore, the district court considered the possible effect, or lack thereof, that awarding fees would have on deterring future meritless lawsuits, and it determined that this is a rare case in which awarding fees is not appropriate. Finally, the defendants' assertion that the district court improperly "might have been motivated by sympathy for a small, locally owned, family company" simply has no support in the record.

---

22. The Third Circuit set forth these factors in *Lieb v. Topstone Indus., Inc.,* 788 F.2d 151, 156 (3d Cir.1986).

Therefore, the district court did not abuse its discretion in concluding that the defendants were not entitled to attorney's fees under §505 in this instance. . . .

NOTES AND QUESTIONS

1. Given the court's insistence on a unitary standard for awards to both prevailing plaintiffs and prevailing defendants, how much guidance do the *Lieb* factors really provide? Which rule seems best calculated to encourage creative investment: supporting good faith claims of infringement by awarding attorneys' fees to the prevailing plaintiff; refusing to award attorneys' fees to either party when there is a bona fide dispute about the legitimacy of the defendant's conduct; or supporting good faith defenses by awarding attorneys' fees to the prevailing defendant? Should lack of good faith also play a role in the decision whether to award attorneys' fees?

2. As *Fogerty* and *Positive Black Talk* illustrate, it is possible to apply the *Lieb* factors in different ways. *Fogerty* considers in detail whether a fee award would serve the purposes of the Copyright Act, while *Positive Black Talk* approves a more narrowly targeted evaluation of the factors. Which approach do you prefer, and why? As in *Fogerty*, the defendants' win in *Positive Black Talk* increased public access to songs within a particular musical genre. Was the district court wrong to deny a fee award?

3. In a series of recent cases, the Seventh Circuit has attempted to craft a set of presumptive rules to structure disposition of claims for attorneys' fees. *See Gonzales v. Transfer Techs., Inc.*, 301 F.3d 608, 610 (7th Cir. 2002) ("[T]he smaller the damages, provided there is a real, and especially a willful, infringement, the stronger the case for an award of attorneys' fees. . . . [T]he prevailing party in a copyright case in which the monetary stakes are small should have a presumptive entitlement of an award of attorneys' fees."); *See also Assessment Techs. of WI, LLC v. WIREdata, Inc.*, 361 F.3d 434, 436-37 (7th Cir. 2004) ("If the case was a toss-up and the prevailing party obtained generous damages, or injunctive relief of substantial monetary value, there is no urgent need to add an award of attorneys' fees. . . . But if at the other extreme the claim or defense was frivolous and the prevailing party obtained no relief at all, the case for awarding him attorneys' fees is compelling.").

The Second Circuit, meanwhile, has indicated that in ruling on claims for attorneys' fees, district courts should give "substantial weight" to the third *Lieb* factor, which concerns the objective reasonableness of the losing party's position. *Matthew Bender & Co. v. West Publ'g Co.*, 240 F.3d 116, 121-22 (2d Cir. 2001).

What do you think of these approaches? Is either one more likely to further the purposes of the Copyright Act?

4. The TRIPS Agreement requires judicial authorities in Member States to have the authority to indemnify a defendant wrongfully enjoined or restrained by a plaintiff "who has abused enforcement procedures." TRIPS Agreement, art. 48 (1). Indemnification in this setting means that the plaintiff is ordered to pay "adequate compensation" for the injury suffered because of the abuse of process. Article 48 (1) also requires judicial authorities to have the authority to order payment of the defendant's expenses, which may include attorneys' fees.

G. CRIMINAL INFRINGEMENT

From the first Copyright Act of 1790 until 1897, copyright law did not contain criminal penalties. In 1897, Congress authorized misdemeanor punishment for infringing public performances of dramatic and musical compositions conducted willfully and for profit. The 1909 Act extended misdemeanor liability to any infringement committed "willfully and for profit." The 1976 Act reworded the *mens rea* element slightly, authorizing criminal liability for infringement done "willfully and for purposes of commercial advantage or private financial gain."

Criminal copyright infringement remained a misdemeanor offense until 1982 when, under pressure from the motion picture and recording industries, Congress designated certain categories of infringements of sound recordings and motion pictures as felonies. Just one decade later, in 1992, Congress expanded felony penalties to qualifying infringements for all categories of copyrighted works. Subsequent amendments to the 1976 Act have increased penalties, expanded the categories of infringements that may incur prosecution, and lowered the standards that conduct must meet to give rise to criminal liability. Often, those amendments have responded to arguments made by economically important industries like the software, recording, and motion picture industries about the losses caused by digital distribution of unauthorized copies and the need for strong deterrence. Additionally, the TRIPS Agreement requires member countries to provide criminal penalties in "cases of willful . . . copyright piracy on a commercial scale." TRIPS Agreement, art. 61.

Read §506 now. Today, criminal copyright liability under the Copyright Act involves two main requirements: First, the infringement must be willful. Second, the infringement must be economically motivated or sufficiently economically harmful to the copyright owner.

1. Willfulness

First we examine the *mens rea* requirement and what "willfulness" means in the context of a criminal copyright prosecution.

  United States v. Liu
731 F.3d 982 (9th Cir. 2013)

Nguyen, J.: Julius Liu appeals his convictions and sentence for criminal copyright infringement . . . . Liu's company, Super DVD, commercially replicated CDs and DVDs for various clients on a scale that subjects him to substantial criminal liability if a client—and, by extension, Liu—lacked permission from the copyright holder to make the copies. . . .

BACKGROUND

I. *The Replication of CDs and DVDs*

Commercial CD and DVD replication differs from the process of recording content onto CDs and DVDs in that prerecorded discs have their content stamped onto them—requiring a molding machine and a stamper—rather than burned. To create a CD stamper, a process known as "mastering," some source material containing digital content is necessary, such as a tape, recordable CD, or music file. Counterfeiters making a "straight counterfeit," i.e., an exact copy of an existing CD, can start with either a legitimate or counterfeit version of the CD. Counterfeiters making a previously nonexistent compilation of tracks take multiple legitimate disks and burn the relevant tracks onto a recordable CD, which then serves as the source material for the stamper.

Replication plants process orders for customers, who are typically the publishers (or persons purporting to be the publishers) who own the reproduction rights to the works in question. While a few plants specialize in mastering, most deal exclusively with replicating. Plants offering both types of services are rare because of the higher cost associated with mastering, which requires more expensive equipment, larger premises, a clean room environment, and greater expertise to operate. A replication plant that does not create stampers in-house will outsource the work to a mastering plant.

II. *The Investigation of Liu and Super DVD*

[Defendant] Liu . . . founded, and became the CEO of, a DVD-manufacturing company called Super DVD. By 2001, Super DVD employed about 65 people and operated four replication machines at its Hayward, California warehouse. . . .

. . . In May 2003, Immigration and Customs Enforcement agents raided the warehouse of Vertex International Trading . . . where agents recovered counterfeit copies of the Symantec software "Norton Anti-Virus 2003" and related documentation. The documentation included purchase orders, handwritten notes, and FedEx shipping labels from more than 50 vendors, including Super DVD. . . .

At the end of July 2003, agents executed a search warrant on the Super DVD warehouse and recovered thousands of DVDs and CDs. One room stored CDs and DVDs, and another held stampers, artwork, and masters. The CDs included a compilation of rap tracks, *Rap Masters Vol. 2*; three compilations of Latin music tracks, *Los Tucanes de Tijuana: Romanticas, Lo Mejor de la Mafia,* and *3 Reyars*[sic] *del Tex Mex: Romanticas;* and a greatest hits album, *Beatles 1.* The agents also recovered DVD copies of the film *Crouching Tiger, Hidden Dragon.* Liu did not have authorization from the copyright holders to replicate any of these works.

During an interview and at trial, Liu admitted that Super DVD manufactured the *Crouching Tiger* DVDs in 2001 for a company called R & E Trading. R & E gave Super DVD a stamper with the name "Tiger" on it but not the full title of the film. The DVDs were still in Super DVD's warehouse at the time the search warrant was executed because R & E had rejected them, claiming that the movies would freeze.

Liu stated that when R & E refused to pay for the order, he became personally involved and realized that R & E did not have the rights to duplicate such a famous movie. Super DVD filed a lawsuit against R & E alleging that R & E deceived it about the copyrights. The lawsuit sought payment from R & E on about 40 invoices totaling approximately $85,000, including work done on the *Crouching Tiger* movie. Super DVD obtained a jury verdict for approximately $600.

Liu generally denied any knowledge of or involvement in replicating the other works. Liu explained that he became involved with the Latin music compilations when one of the former Super DVD engineers introduced Liu to his uncle, Juan Valdez, a famous mariachi singer. Liu and Valdez got together and played music—Liu on the guitar, Valdez singing. Valdez expressed interest in publishing CDs, and Liu told him that he didn't have the facility to do it but suggested companies that could take care of the mastering, printing, and even the sleeve. Liu volunteered to do the overwrapping for Valdez because it only cost him "pennies." Valdez told Liu that he created the tracks by mixing his voice with music from a Karaoke machine and that he had paid for the license. Liu listened to some of the tracks and, believing that it was Valdez's voice, thought that the music "belong[ed] to him."

III. Liu's Convictions and Sentence

The government charged Liu with three counts of criminal copyright infringement under 17 U.S.C. §506(a)(1)(A) and 18 U.S.C. §2319(b)(1) based on the music CDs, the *Crouching Tiger* DVD, and the Norton Anti-Virus software. . . . Following a three-day jury trial, Liu was convicted on all counts. The district court sentenced Liu to four years in prison followed by three years of supervised release. . . .

ANALYSIS

I. The District Court Erred in Instructing the Jury on the "Willfulness" . . . Element[] . . .

Liu requested an instruction parroting 17 U.S.C. §506(a)(2)—that "[e]vidence of reproduction or distribution of a copyrighted work, by itself, shall not be sufficient to establish willful infringement of a copyright." . . . The government informed the court that it had no problem with Liu's requested instruction. . . .

. . . [T]he district court did not include in the final version the instruction regarding proof of willful copyright infringement requested by Liu and acquiesced to by the government. Instead, it added its own explanation of willful infringement that incorporated the government's requested instruction defining infringement generally, without a mens rea element. The court instructed the jury that Liu "willfully infringed" if he "without authorization duplicated, reproduced or sold the copyright belonging to the owners of the works." The court further adopted the government's requested definition of willfully—that "[a]n act is done 'willfully' if the act is done knowingly and intentionally, not through ignorance, mistake or accident." . . .

B. The "Willfulness" Element of Criminal Copyright Infringement Requires Knowledge that the Conduct Was Unlawful . . .

. . . The general approach to criminal copyright enforcement . . . has been to punish only those violations that are both willful and economically motivated.

Of the two factors that distinguish criminal from noncriminal copyright violations, willfulness and commerciality, the latter is of little practical importance. The Copyright Act defines "financial gain" broadly to include "receipt, or expectation of receipt, of anything of value, including the receipt of other copyrighted works." 17 U.S.C. §101. The commerciality requirement thus "does not meaningfully winnow down the population of copyright defendants potentially liable to incarceration. . . . [T]he only bar against an overzealous prosecutor criminalizing nearly every copyright infringement case lies in the other prerequisite to criminal liability: willfulness." 4 [Melville B. Nimmer & David Nimmer, Nimmer on Copyright] §15.01[A][2] [(Matthew Bender rev. ed. 2011)].

But the term "willfully" is ambiguous.[2] *See Ratzlaf v. United States,* 510 U.S. 135, 141 (1994). To infringe willfully could simply mean to intentionally commit the act that constitutes infringement. Alternatively, it could mean that the defendant must act with a "'bad purpose' or 'evil motive' in the sense that there was an 'intentional violation of a known legal duty.'" *United States v. Moran,* 757 F. Supp. 1046, 1048 (D. Neb. 1991) (quoting *Cheek v. United States,* 498 U.S. 192, 200 (1991)). The 1976 Copyright Act does not define "willfully," and its legislative history offers little guidance.

When faced with a criminal statute containing an ambiguous "willfulness" element, courts normally resolve any doubt in favor of the defendant. *Ratzlaf,* 510 U.S. at 148. Although the general rule is that "ignorance of the law or a mistake of law is no defense to criminal prosecution," the modern proliferation of statutes and regulations "sometimes ma[kes] it difficult for the average citizen to know and comprehend the extent of the duties and obligations imposed by the . . . laws." *Cheek,* 498 U.S. at 199-200. Thus, the government must prove that the defendant acted "willfully"—that is, with "specific intent to violate the law"—to be convicted of certain federal criminal offenses. *Id.* at 200.

In reviewing a conviction for criminal copyright infringement, we, and numerous other circuits, have assumed that proof of the defendant's specific intent to violate someone's copyright is required. We now explicitly hold that "willfully" as used in 17 U.S.C. §506(a) connotes a "voluntary, intentional violation of a known legal duty." *Cheek,* 498 U.S. at 201.

The Copyright Act's legislative history supports our interpretation. In 1997, Congress updated the statutory provision governing criminal copyright infringement by inserting the language that Liu requested: "evidence of reproduction or distribution of a copyrighted work, by itself, shall not be sufficient to establish willful infringement." No Electronic Theft (NET) Act, Pub. L. 105-147, §2(b), 111 Stat

---

2. Even within the context of *civil* copyright infringement, we have defined "willful" to mean different things in different contexts. *See Barboza v. New Form, Inc. (In re Barboza),* 545 F.3d 702, 707-08 (9th Cir.2008) ("The term 'willful' as used in copyright infringement cases is not equivalent to 'willful' as used in determining whether a debt is nondischargeable under the bankruptcy code.").

2678, 2678 (1997) (codified as amended at 17 U.S.C. §506(c)). This language was in response to the "on-going debate about what precisely is the 'willfulness' standard in the Copyright Act." 143 Cong. Rec. S12,689 (daily ed. Nov. 13, 1997) (statement of Sen. Orrin Hatch). . . .

As a practical matter, requiring only a general intent to copy as a basis for a criminal conviction would not shield any appreciable amount of infringing conduct from the threat of prosecution. Civil liability will not lie if an author fortuitously creates a work that is substantially similar to another author's copyrighted work. To infringe a copyright, one must *copy* the protected work. Copying is of necessity an intentional act. If we were to read 17 U.S.C. §506(a)'s willfulness requirement to mean only an intent to copy, there would be no meaningful distinction between civil and criminal liability in the vast majority of cases. That cannot be the result that Congress sought.

In the present case . . . the district court exacerbated the omission [of the requested instruction] by defining willful infringement without the crucial knowledge component:

> In order for the defendant to be found guilty of [copyright infringement], the government must prove each of the following elements beyond a reasonable doubt:
>
> First, that on a date beginning in 2001 and continuing to on or about July 31, 2003, in the Northern District of California, defendant willfully infringed, that is, without authorization, duplicated, reproduced, or sold compact disks that infringed the copyright belonging to the owners of the works. . . .

By defining "willfully infringed" without any requirement that the defendant knew he was committing copyright infringement, the district court instructed the jury to apply a civil liability standard.

The district court further compounded this error a short time later, instructing the jury that "[a]n act is done 'willfully' if the act is done knowingly and intentionally, not through ignorance, mistake, or accident." . . .

We conclude that the district court in this case erred by defining willfulness such that the jury could have convicted Liu without finding that he knew that his actions were unlawful.

C. The Instructional Error Was Not Harmless

Liu's convictions on the copyright infringement counts cannot stand unless the instructional error was harmless. . . .

The conclusion was irresistible that the infringing CDs and DVDs were replicated in the Super DVD warehouse. The discs all were found there with the exception of the Norton Anti-Virus software, which was discovered at the Vertex warehouse along with purchase orders and shipping labels linking it to Liu and Super DVD. Almost all of the music CDs bore Liu's initials, "JL." Liu admitted to reproducing the *Crouching Tiger* DVDs for R & E Trading, and there was a written agreement from early 2001 between Super DVD and R & E to press 2,000 copies of the *Beatles* CD. Although Liu claimed to have no knowledge of how the other discs were made, suggesting that the orders may have been handled by his sales staff, it is unclear whether the jury disbelieved him, thought he had forgotten, or found his employees' acts attributable to him.

Whatever the case, Liu's state of mind was critical. Liu was aware of copyright laws and admittedly had been sued for copyright infringement in the past. His guilt thus hinged on whether he knew that his clients did not have authorization to replicate the disks at issue.

Liu presented evidence that his customers signed agreements stating that they had the copyright to the works in question and promising "to be responsible for all copyright related legal responsibilities." His expert witness testified that other replicators also rely on such agreements rather than carefully investigate each customer. Liu testified that he attempted to verify that there were no copyright violations on the Latin music compilations by listening to the some of the tracks and satisfying himself that it was Valdez's voice. He further claimed that he did not realize R & E's order for *Crouching Tiger* DVDs was unauthorized until he became embroiled in the payment dispute, at which time he filed a lawsuit against R & E. The fact that he initiated a lawsuit over a dispute involving thousands of infringing copies of *Crouching Tiger, Hidden Dragon* that he created is arguably compelling evidence that he did not understand his conduct to have been wrongful.

We cannot say that the jury would not have credited some or all of this evidence had the jury appreciated its relevance. The evidence may have supported a finding that Liu did not know that he was illegally copying copyrighted material and thus he did not willfully infringe the copyrights. Therefore, the failure to provide a proper willfulness instruction was not harmless beyond a reasonable doubt. . . .

Accordingly, we vacate Liu's convictions and sentence for criminal copyright infringement . . .

NOTES AND QUESTIONS

1. Given that the *mens rea* requirement involves an evaluation of the defendant's subjective state of mind, what evidence could the prosecution have offered to meet its burden? If the jury had been properly instructed in the *Liu* case would there have been sufficient evidence to find Liu guilty?

2. If a defendant chooses to testify and swears he did not know his conduct was unlawful, would an acquittal be required? The Ninth Circuit is clear that the standard to be employed for determining willfulness is a subjective one. However, the more objectively unreasonable a person's belief is, "the more likely it is that the finder of fact will consider the asserted belief or misunderstanding to be nothing more than simple disagreement with known legal duties imposed by the law, and will find that the government has carried its burden of proving knowledge." *U.S. v. Moran*, 757 F. Supp. 1046, 1051 (D. Neb. 1991).

3. The district court sentenced Mr. Liu to four years in prison. The range of allowable sentences for criminal copyright infringement is set forth in 18 U.S.C. §2319.

4. Criminal copyright prosecutions have a five-year statute of limitations. As you learned in section C.2, a three-year statute

> ### LOOKING AHEAD
>
> The anticircumvention provisions of the Digital Millennium Copyright Act (DMCA) covered in Chapter 14, provide separately for criminal liability.

of limitations applies to civil infringement lawsuits. Why do you think the criminal statute of limitations is longer?

2. Economic Motivation or Significance

In addition to proving that the infringement was willful, to obtain a conviction for criminal copyright infringement the government also must show that the infringement was either (1) committed "for purposes of commercial advantage or private financial gain," or (2) exceeded a threshold quantity. 17 U.S.C. §506(a)(1)(A)-(C).

The second alternative arose in response to widespread, commercially harmful infringement conducted over computer networks by those not necessarily motivated by financial gain. In a 1994 prosecution that became the impetuous for the 1997 No Electronic Theft (NET) Act, the government charged a 21-year-old Massachusetts Institute of Technology student, David LaMacchia, with wire fraud. *U.S. v. LaMacchia*, 871 F. Supp. 535 (D. Mass 1994). LaMacchia had set up a system for sharing copyrighted computer software files over the Internet, encouraging users to upload popular software applications and computer games in return for a password to an encrypted address from which all of the uploaded programs could then be downloaded. The court ruled that the attempt to prosecute LaMacchia for wire fraud was an impermissible end run around the then-existing "for profit" requirement for criminal copyright infringement. *See generally id.* at 540-45.

The *LaMacchia* court relied on *Dowling v. United States*, 473 U.S. 207 (1985), in which the Supreme Court had similarly rejected the government's attempt to resort to a more general criminal statute when the defendant's infringing activity failed to meet the elements for copyright infringement. In *Dowling* the government had sought to convict the defendant of interstate transportation of stolen property for selling bootleg Elvis Presley recordings via mail order. The Supreme Court ruled that the "copyright owner . . . holds no ordinary chattel" and that a musical composition impressed on a bootleg phonograph is not property that is "stolen, converted, or taken by fraud" within the meaning of the crime charged. *Id.* at 216.

The *LaMacchia* court emphasized both its disapproval of LaMacchia's conduct and the risks of an overly lax approach to the statutory requirements for criminal infringement liability:

> While the government's objective is a laudable one, particularly when the facts alleged in this case are considered, its interpretation of the wire fraud statute would serve to criminalize the conduct of not only persons like LaMacchia, but also the myriad of home computer users who succumb to the temptation to copy even a single software program for private use. It is not clear that making criminals of a large number of consumers of computer software is a result that even the software industry would consider desirable. . . .
>
> This is not, of course, to suggest that there is anything edifying about what LaMacchia is alleged to have done. If the indictment is to be believed, one might at best describe his actions as heedlessly irresponsible, and at worst as nihilistic, self-indulgent, and lacking in any fundamental sense of values. Criminal as well as civil penalties should

probably attach to willful, multiple infringements of copyrighted software even absent a commercial motive on the part of the infringer. One can envision ways that the copyright law could be modified to permit such prosecution. But, " '[i]t is the legislature, not the Court which is to define a crime, and ordain its punishment.' " . . .

LaMacchia, 871 F. Supp. at 544-45.

Congress responded to the *LaMacchia* case with the 1997 enactment of the No Electronic Theft (NET) Act. The legislative history states that the purpose of the NET Act is "to reverse the practical consequences of *United States v. LaMacchia* . . . by criminaliz[ing] computer theft of copyrighted works, whether or not the defendant derives a direct financial benefit from the act(s) of misappropriation, thereby preventing such willful conduct from destroying businesses, especially small businesses, that depend on licensing agreements and royalties for survival." H.R. Rep. 105-339, 105th Cong., 1st Sess. 1997. To that end, the NET Act added a definition: "The term 'financial gain' includes receipt, or expectation of receipt, of anything of value, including the receipt of other copyrighted works." 17 U.S.C. §101. In addition, it amended §506(a) to provide for criminal liability even in the absence of private financial gain, in cases involving the "reproduction or distribution, including by electronic means, during any 180-day period, of 1 or more copies or phonorecords of 1 or more copyrighted works with a total retail value of more than $1,000. . . ." *Id.* §506(a)(1)(B). Two years later, Congress enacted the Digital Theft Deterrence and Copyright Damages Improvement Act of 1999, Pub. L. No. 106-160, 113 Stat. 1774, which authorized enhanced prison sentences based on the retail price of the items embodying the work and the number of infringing copies in certain circumstances.

Neither the NET Act nor the penalty enhancements proved effective to address a phenomenon that the motion picture industry perceived as particularly damaging - the availability of movies on the Internet before they are available for purchase on DVD and sometimes even before they are released to theaters. In 2005, Congress added two new criminal prohibitions. The first prohibition makes it a felony to knowingly use an audiovisual device to make a copy of a copyrighted movie "from a performance of such work in a motion picture exhibition facility," a practice sometimes referred to as "camcording" a movie. 18 U.S.C. §2319B. The second prohibition specifies another way in which willful infringement of a copyright rises to the level of criminal infringement: "by the distribution of a work being prepared for commercial distribution, by making it available on a computer network accessible to members of the public, if such person knew or should have known that the work was intended for commercial distribution." 17 U.S.C. §506(a)(1)(C). Although this legislation clearly was aimed at Internet availability of prerelease motion pictures, it defines "work being prepared for commercial distribution" to include computer programs, musical works, and sound recordings, as well as motion pictures and other audiovisual works, that have not been commercially distributed. *Id.* §506(a)(3). It also expressly includes motion pictures that have "been made available for viewing in a motion picture exhibition facility" but have not yet been "made available in copies for sale to the general public in the United States in a format intended to permit viewing outside a motion picture exhibition facility." *Id.* §506(a)(3)(B).

NOTES AND QUESTIONS

1. With private financial gain defined broadly, and two additional ways to satisfy the second element of criminal infringement, prosecutorial discretion plays a critical role. What are the factors that should guide a prosecutor in deciding whether to prosecute a defendant for criminal copyright infringement?

2. Pursuant to §404 of the Prioritizing Resources and Organization for Intellectual Property Act of 2008 ("PRO IP Act"), Pub. L. No. 110-403, 122 Stat. 4256, both the FBI and the Department of Justice (DOJ) are required to submit "a summary of the efforts, activities, and resources the [Department] has allocated to the enforcement, investigation, and prosecution of intellectual property crimes." In its 2013 report, the DOJ indicated that:

> Through its IP Task Force, the Department identified three enforcement priorities for IP investigations and prosecutions, including offenses that involve (1) health and safety, (2) trade secret theft or economic espionage, and (3) large-scale commercial counterfeiting and piracy. The Department has also increased its focus on IP crimes that are committed or facilitated by use of the Internet or perpetrated by organized criminal networks.

U.S. Dep't of Justice, PRO IP Act Annual Report FY2013, at 14 (2013).

3. The "retail value" of copies is relevant for meeting the threshold requirement for the alternative to the element of private financial gain added by the NET Act. Retail value is also important to determining the level of the offense—i.e., felony or misdemeanor—and the sentence to impose. How should the court set the retail value? Consider the conviction of David Armstead who sold 100 bootleg DVDs to an undercover federal agent for $500 and then, more than six months later, sold 200 DVDs to the agent for $1,000. The Fourth Circuit rejected defendant's argument that the value of the DVDs was the amount paid by the agent. *United States v. Armstead*, 524 F.3d 442, 443 (4th Cir. 2008). Instead the court held that "'value' is measured not only by actual transactions that define a market, but also by face or par values assigned to commodities or goods before reaching the market." *Id.* at 445.

Whether unauthorized distributions have a one-for-one correspondence to lost retail sales is another contested issue. While courts generally calculate the "retail value" for purposes of criminal liability based on the price of legitimate copies, they sometimes use different valuations in other contexts. For example, the Federal Mandatory Victims Restitution Act requires proof of the actual loss suffered. One court reasoned:

> It is a basic principle of economics that as price increases, demand decreases. Customers who download music and movies for free would not necessarily spend money to acquire the same product. . . . I am skeptical that customers would pay $7.22 or $19 for something they got for free. Certainly 100% of the illegal downloads . . . did not result in the loss of a sale. . . .

United States v. Dove, 585 F. Supp. 2d 865, 870 (W.D. Va. 2008).

4. The Patent Act contains no criminal sanctions for infringement. Why are some types of copyright infringement subject to criminal sanctions? Should they be?

PRACTICE EXERCISE: COUNSEL A CLIENT

Sam Smith set up a network among a dozen friends for sharing their favorite music. In each of the first six months, each friend shared between 2 and 10 albums. The albums each contain, on average, 10 songs. Thelma Tran is one of the friends in Sam's sharing network. Thelma shared 10 albums each month. Thelma writes a blog on which she comments about music. Her blog also contains commentary concerning her disagreements with the major labels' approach to dealing with copyright infringement. You are an Assistant U.S. Attorney, and your supervisor asks your recommendation on whether to charge Sam or Thelma with criminal copyright infringement. What do you advise, and why?

VI

NEW ENFORCEMENT STRATEGIES AND PUBLIC POLICY LIMITS

14

Technological Protections

Throughout this book you have learned how technological developments have challenged the balance between the rights of copyright owners and the rights and privileges of users of copyrighted works, typically by enabling new methods of copying and distributing protected works. Usually, Congress has responded to new technological developments by legislating more rights for copyright holders and/or by extending copyright law to cover new subject matter. Recall from Chapter 12 that copyright owners can supplement copyright protection by using contracts to bind users to specified terms of use. In the digital age, copyright owners also can use technological measures that regulate access to, restrict uses of, and/or monitor uses of the protected work.

Resort to technological protection as a general model for protecting creative works in the digital environment raises an entirely new set of policy concerns. As with contracts, technological protections may be used to obtain greater (or simply different) protection than copyright law affords. Alternatively, one might see the additional protection afforded by those measures as encroaching on the rights or interests that copyright law reserves to the public. For example, a copyright owner might attempt to use technological protection or contract, or both, to prevent access to or use of material that is in the public domain. It might also seek to control all copying, including copying permitted under the fair use doctrine.

Technological protection also raises the possibility of a "technological arms race" between copyright owners and those who seek to defeat technological locks applied to copyrighted works. What one should think about the latter depends substantially on whether one thinks that reasons for seeking to access or copy technologically protected works are legitimate or illegitimate. For the copyright industries, the answer is clear: There are no, or hardly any, legitimate reasons for defeating technological protection measures applied to a work by the copyright owner. More important, they argue, if users of copyrighted works can defeat technological protections with impunity, the security afforded by those measures will be wholly illusory; therefore, the law should penalize such conduct. Others, however, contend that legitimate reasons for seeking to defeat technological protections do exist, and that the law should penalize only acts of circumvention undertaken for illegitimate purposes.

This chapter focuses on the use of technological protection measures by copyright owners and on provisions of the Copyright Act that grant additional legal protections to copyright owners who employ such measures. As you read this chapter, ask yourself how new technologies designed to control access and/or copying, and laws enacted to protect those technologies, affect the copyright balance.

A. EARLY EXAMPLES OF TECHNOLOGICAL PROTECTION

Although current debates about technological protection focus on general purpose restrictions capable of application to any kind of digital content, both technological protection devices and legislative provisions relating to them originally were medium-specific. A trio of experiments in the 1980s, followed by the Audio Home Recording Act of 1992, explored a variety of restrictions designed to erect technical "fences" against certain unauthorized uses of copyrighted material.

> **LOOKING BACK**
>
> The adoption of Macrovision was a response to the Supreme Court's *Sony* decision, which you read about in Chapter 9.D.1 and Chapter 10.C.1, and to Congress' subsequent refusal to enact a rental right for audiovisual works, which you read about in Chapter 6.A.2. The video rental industry, which had opposed the creation of a video rental right, does not appear to have objected to the implementation of Macrovision, since the technology did not threaten, and indeed more likely strengthened, its own market.

In the early 1980s, the motion picture industry adopted a patented technology, Macrovision, to prevent unauthorized copying of pre-recorded videocassettes containing copyrighted motion pictures. For the Macrovision standard to work as intended, both recording media and home video recording equipment needed to continue to function in a particular way. *See* Nicholas E. Sciorra, *Self-Help and Contributory Infringement: The Law and Legal Thought Behind a Little "Black-Box,"* 11 Cardozo Arts & Ent. L.J. 905, 925 (1993) (describing how Macrovision works). Thus, cooperation by the home electronics industry, which had prevailed in the *Sony* litigation, was essential to the Macrovision venture. Notably, however, the motion picture industry did not attempt to implement Macrovision in blank video recording media, or otherwise to address uses of video recording technology such as the home taping of broadcast programs that the *Sony* Court had ruled to be a fair use. While hackers developed "black boxes" capable of defeating the restrictions imposed by Macrovision, those devices did not achieve wide penetration among ordinary consumers, *id.* at 928-29, and the motion picture industry's efforts to obtain legal protection against the devices were unsuccessful.

Also in the 1980s, satellite and cable broadcasters began to encrypt their signals to prevent unauthorized reception by viewers who had not paid for cable subscription service. Once again, hackers quickly developed devices to circumvent the encryption. In this case, however, Congress added a provision to the Communications Act to prohibit the manufacture or distribution of devices that can be used to decrypt satellite and cable broadcast transmissions. Pub. L. No. 100-667, §204, 102 Stat. 3935 (codified as amended at U.S.C. §605(e)(4) (1988)). The amendment seems to have occasioned very little public debate. The satellite and cable industries urged that people who had not paid to receive the subscription broadcasts should not have access to them. Because the legislation targeted special purpose devices that had no other uses, there were few dissenters.

The third experiment with technological protection during the 1980s involved computer software. Alarmed by the ease with which software could be copied and redistributed, software manufacturers began experimenting with various devices designed to prevent copying. Unlike either Macrovision or encryption of broadcast cable subscription signals, both of which operated in a manner largely invisible to users, these devices often caused system crashes and peripheral device failures. In addition, they prevented users from making backup copies, and sometimes even from loading legitimately purchased software onto hard disk storage—practices that, as you have learned, §117 of the Copyright Act permits. Customers protested loudly, and popular software magazines published harsh critiques. Almost as quickly as the software companies developed new copy protection technologies, other programmers developed and distributed methods of defeating them. Both individual and business customers enthusiastically participated in this software "arms race." Finally, several major institutional software users, including the U.S. Department of Defense, informed software vendors that they would not purchase copy-protected software. *See* Julie E. Cohen, Lochner *in Cyberspace: The New Economic Orthodoxy of "Rights Management,"* 97 Mich. L. Rev. 462, 524-25 (1998). In the face of this widespread resistance, software companies abandoned their efforts at copy protection. Throughout the debate, Congress remained silent.

As personal computers spread more extensively to businesses and homes, and digital formats were developed to store and distribute increasingly diverse works, the concept of technological protection became more important to all of the industries that produce and distribute copyrighted works. The medium-specific model for technological protection began to disintegrate. In its place came a focus on general-purpose copy protection techniques suitable for the digital age.

The first harbinger of these developments was the invention, in Japan, of the digital audiotape (DAT) recording format—the first copying format capable of producing, and reproducing, perfect copies of recorded sounds. As had been the case in the *Sony* litigation, manufacturers of home recording equipment sought to import the new devices and recording media and distribute them to consumers. This time, rather than filing suit, members of the music and recording industries sought protection from Congress, which sought to broker a compromise among the affected industries. That compromise became the Audio Home Recording Act (AHRA) of 1992.

The AHRA is significant for the hybrid copy-protection model that it adopted: First, it required that all digital audio recording devices incorporate the Serial Copy Management System (SCMS)—a technical protocol for DAT that allows the making of first-generation copies without significant degradation in quality but prevents the making of subsequent generations of copies. 17 U.S.C. §1002. The AHRA also made it unlawful to manufacture or distribute any device or provide any service that would circumvent the SCMS. *Id*. Second, it required manufacturers to pay royalties on covered digital audio recording media and equipment: These royalties were then pooled and subsequently divided among copyright owners of sound recordings and musical works, and featured recording artists, with a small percentage paid to non-featured musicians and vocalists. *Id*. §§1003-1007. Finally, it barred infringement actions against consumers for personal, noncommercial copying, and also barred actions against manufacturers and distributors of digital audio recording devices and media. *Id*. §1008. This three-pronged model, which incorporated "permeable" or incomplete copy protection as part of a package of features, was an entirely different approach to the question of copy protection from any of those that industry or Congress had previously tried. Unfortunately, because the market so quickly bypassed the narrow definitions of "digital audio recording device" and "digital audio recording medium" supplied by the statute, it is impossible to say how well this hybrid model would have worked.

NOTES AND QUESTIONS

1. Why do you think the affected industries received legal protection against devices for decrypting satellite signals, but not against devices for circumventing Macrovision? Why do you think Congress chose to intervene in the case of DAT, but not in the software copy-protection debate?

2. To what extent is law necessary to buttress technological restrictions? What considerations should affect the enactment of such laws?

B. THE DIGITAL MILLENNIUM COPYRIGHT ACT AND CIRCUMVENTION OF TECHNOLOGICAL PROTECTIONS

As digital technologies for reproduction and distribution of copyrighted works continued to evolve, so too did copy protection technologies. By the mid-1990s, the most sophisticated of the technologies under development did far more than simply prevent copying. At high technology research centers such as the Xerox Palo Alto Research Center, researchers had developed prototypes for "trusted systems" that could exercise extremely fine-grained control over the functionality of digital copies. For example, the system might be programmed to detect, permit, and charge different fees for accessing different portions of a work, for printing those portions, or for creating digital copies of all or part of the work. Alternatively, the system might be designed to forbid digital copying, but not printing, or to forbid both digital copying and printing. *See generally* Mark Stefik, *Shifting the Possible: How Digital Property Rights Challenge Us to Rethink Digital Publishing*, 12 Berkeley Tech. L.J. 138 (1997).

After the software "arms race" of the 1980s, however, the copyright industries were keenly aware that technological protections for digital works could be circumvented. They argued that the threat of uncontrolled copying and distribution via the Internet was so great that copyright owners needed additional, legal protection against the circumvention of any copy-control measures that they might choose to implement. As originally introduced in Congress, the proposed anticircumvention legislation would have prohibited the manufacture or distribution of any device, product, or service with the "primary purpose or effect" of deactivating or circumventing a technological protection measure designed to protect a copyright owner's copyright rights.

Almost immediately, the proposed legislation encountered strong opposition from a diverse group of interests, including educators, librarians, scientists, computer software companies, online service providers, and manufacturers of home recording equipment. Some of these groups feared that the legislation would effectively result in the elimination of fair use and other copyright limitations and would enable content producers to "lock up" public domain works and uncopyrightable ideas. Others feared that the proposed legislation would usher in an era of unprecedented infringement liability for equipment manufacturers and communications providers.

Meanwhile, notwithstanding the significant resistance to domestic legislation, the United States sought to have protections against circumvention incorporated into international treaties. At the 1996 Diplomatic Conference to draft the WIPO Copyright Treaty (WCT), however, delegates declined to adopt the proposed text for anticircumvention protection advanced by the United States, which had closely tracked the language of the proposed domestic legislation, and instead agreed on a more open-ended statement. Article 11 of the WCT directs:

> Contracting Parties shall provide adequate legal protection and effective legal remedies against the circumvention of effective technological measures that are used by authors in connection with the exercise of their rights under this Treaty or the Berne Convention and that restrict acts, in respect of their works, which are not authorized by the authors concerned or permitted by law.

When the 105th Congress opened in January 1997, shortly after finalization of the WCT, the battle over domestic anticircumvention legislation resumed. As before, the proposal encountered strong opposition. This time, however, the newly concluded WCT lent additional momentum to supporters, who argued that the legislation would be necessary for U.S. compliance once the treaty entered into force. Over the next 21 months, the original proposal was gradually modified and made subject to a series of exceptions. For a detailed description of that bargaining process, see Pamela Samuelson, *Intellectual Property and the Digital Economy: Why the Anti-Circumvention Regulations Need to Be Revised*, 14 Berkeley Tech. L.J. 519 (1999). Congress enacted anticircumvention legislation as part of the Digital Millennium Copyright Act of 1998 (DMCA).

1. Section 1201 Overview

As a result of the interest group bargaining process, the anticircumvention provision of the DMCA, now codified at §1201 of Title 17, is complex, lengthy, and highly technical. Fundamentally, however, §1201 makes two important distinctions. The first is a distinction between technological controls that restrict *access* to a copyrighted work and technological controls designed to prevent violation of an *exclusive right* of the copyright owner. The second distinction is between individual *acts of circumvention* and the manufacture and distribution of *technologies designed to circumvent* technological protection measures. Opponents of the legislation had argued that the law should not prohibit or frustrate circumvention undertaken by those who wished to take advantage of limitations imposed on an owner's exclusive rights by copyright law. The copyright industries, meanwhile, had argued that the conduct targeted by anticircumvention provisions was no different than breaking into a locked building to steal a work for which one had not paid. Congress used the two distinctions described above in an attempt to address both groups' concerns.

The prohibition against manufacture and distribution of technologies designed to circumvent technological protection measures (the "device ban") applies to both access controls, §1201(a)(2), and controls directed at exclusive copyright rights, §1201(b). Individual acts of circumvention, on the other hand, are treated differently depending on the type of technological protection measure being circumvented. Section 1201 prohibits the act of circumventing access controls, §1201(a)(1), but does not prohibit circumvention of controls designed to protect a copyright owner's exclusive rights. In theory, therefore, a user who has paid the required price for access to the work would remain free to circumvent technological controls that prevented the exercise of fair use and other user privileges. The following chart depicts these prohibitions:

	Access protection measures	Rights protection measures
Individual acts of circumvention	Prohibition: §1201(a)(1)	Prohibition: None
Manufacturing or offering devices that circumvent	Prohibition: §1201(a)(2)	Prohibition: §1201(b)

Consider this example: An individual purchases a digital copy of an article from an online publisher. The digital copy downloaded by the purchaser to her computer can be accessed from the computer's memory and displayed on the screen for 12 months, but coding within the file prevents the article from being printed. Section 1201 would not prohibit the purchaser's bypassing the code to enable printing (the upper right-hand box in the chart above). Distributing a utility designed to bypass the no-print code, however, would violate §1201(b) (the lower right-hand box). After 12 months have passed, if the purchaser bypasses the code that makes the file inaccessible, the purchaser's activity would violate §1201(a)(1) (the upper left-hand box). Distributing the means used to bypass this latter code and access the file would violate §1201(a)(2) (the lower left-hand box).

In addition to the two important distinctions identified above, §1201 contains a number of different exemptions targeted at specific types of circumvention activities. Read §1201 in full now, noting in particular the subsection headings that describe the various exemptions.

2. Access Protection Versus Copy Protection

We turn now to exploring the interplay among the different prohibitions and exceptions contained in §1201.

Universal City Studios, Inc. v. Reimerdes
111 F. Supp. 2d 294 (S.D.N.Y. 2000), aff'd sub nom. Universal City Studios, Inc. v. Corley, 273 F.3d 429 (2d Cir. 2001)

KAPLAN, J.: Plaintiffs, eight major United States motion picture studios, distribute many of their copyrighted motion pictures for home use on digital versatile disks ("DVDs"), which contain copies of the motion pictures in digital form. They protect those motion pictures from copying by using an encryption system called CSS. CSS-protected motion pictures on DVDs may be viewed only on players and computer drives equipped with licensed technology that permits the devices to decrypt and play—but not to copy—the films.

Late last year, computer hackers devised a computer program called DeCSS that circumvents the CSS protection system and allows CSS-protected motion pictures to be copied and played on devices that lack the licensed decryption technology. Defendants quickly posted DeCSS on their Internet web site, thus making it readily available to much of the world. Plaintiffs promptly brought this action under the Digital Millennium Copyright Act (the "DMCA") to enjoin defendants from posting DeCSS and to prevent them from electronically "linking" their site to others that post DeCSS. Defendants responded with what they termed "electronic civil disobedience"—increasing their efforts to link their web site to a large number of others that continue to make DeCSS available.

Defendants contend that their actions do not violate the DMCA and, in any case, that the DMCA, as applied to computer programs, or code, violates the First Amendment. This is the Court's decision after trial . . . .

I. The Genesis of the Controversy . . .

Defendant Eric Corley is viewed as a leader of the computer hacker community and goes by the name Emmanuel Goldstein, after the leader of the underground in George Orwell's classic, *1984*. He and his company, defendant 2600 Enterprises, Inc., together publish a magazine called *2600: The Hacker Quarterly*, which Corley founded in 1984, and which is something of a bible to the hacker community. . . . *2600: The Hacker Quarterly* has included articles on such topics as how to steal an Internet domain name, access other people's e-mail, intercept cellular phone calls, and break into the computer systems at Costco stores and Federal Express. . . .

As the motion picture companies did not themselves develop CSS and, in any case, are not in the business of making DVD players and drives, the technology for making compliant devices, i.e., devices with CSS keys, had to be licensed to consumer electronics manufacturers.[60] In order to ensure that the decryption technology did not become generally available and that compliant devices could not be used to copy as well as merely to play CSS-protected movies, the technology is licensed subject to strict security requirements. Moreover, manufacturers may not, consistent with their licenses, make equipment that would supply digital output that could be used in copying protected DVDs. Licenses to manufacture compliant devices are granted on a royalty-free basis subject only to an administrative fee.[63] At the time of trial, licenses had been issued to numerous hardware and software manufacturers, including two companies that plan to release DVD players for computers running the Linux operating system. . . .

In late September 1999, Jon Johansen, a Norwegian subject then fifteen years of age, and two individuals he "met" under pseudonyms over the Internet, reverse engineered a licensed DVD player and discovered the CSS encryption algorithm and keys. They used this information to create DeCSS, a program capable of decrypting or "ripping" encrypted DVDs, thereby allowing playback on non-compliant computers as well as the copying of decrypted files to computer hard drives. Mr. Johansen then posted the executable code on his personal Internet web site and informed members of an Internet mailing list that he had done so. . . .

Although Mr. Johansen testified at trial that he created DeCSS in order to make a DVD player that would operate on a computer running the Linux operating system, DeCSS is a Windows executable file; that is, it can be executed only on computers running the Windows operating system. Mr. Johansen explained the fact that he created a Windows rather than a Linux program by asserting that Linux, at the time he created DeCSS, did not support the file system used on DVDs. Hence, it was necessary, he said, to decrypt the DVD on a Windows computer in order subsequently to play the decrypted files on a Linux machine. Assuming that to be true, however, the fact remains that Mr. Johansen created DeCSS in the full knowledge that it could be used on computers running Windows rather than Linux. Moreover, he was well aware that the files, once decrypted, could be copied like any other computer files. . . .

In the months following its initial appearance on Mr. Johansen's web site, DeCSS has become widely available on the Internet, where hundreds of sites now purport to offer the software for download. . . .

The movie studios, through the Internet investigations division of the Motion Picture Association of America ("MPAA"), became aware of the availability of DeCSS on the Internet in October 1999. The industry responded by sending

---

60. The licensing function initially was performed by [Matsushita Electric Industrial Co., i.e.,] MEI[,] and Toshiba. Subsequently, MEI and Toshiba granted a royalty free license to the DVD Copy Control Association ("DVD CCA"), which now handles the licensing function. . . .

63. The administrative fee is one million yen, now about $9,200. . . .

out a number of cease and desist letters to web site operators who posted the software, some of which removed it from their sites. In January 2000, the studios filed this lawsuit against defendant Eric Corley and two others.[91] . . .

Following the issuance of the preliminary injunction, defendants removed DeCSS from the 2600.com web site. In what they termed an act of "electronic civil disobedience," however, they continued to support links to other web sites purporting to offer DeCSS for download, a list which had grown to nearly five hundred by July 2000. Indeed, they carried a banner saying "Stop the MPAA" and, in a reference to this lawsuit, proclaimed:

> "We have to face the possibility that we could be forced into submission. For that reason it's especially important that as many of you as possible, all throughout the world, take a stand and mirror these files."

Thus, defendants obviously hoped to frustrate plaintiffs' recourse to the judicial system by making effective relief difficult or impossible. . . .

These circumstances have two major implications for plaintiffs. First, the availability of DeCSS on the Internet has effectively compromised plaintiffs' system of copyright protection for DVDs . . . . It is analogous to the publication of a bank vault combination in a national newspaper. Even if no one uses the combination to open the vault, its mere publication has the effect of defeating the bank's security system, forcing the bank to reprogram the lock. Development and implementation of a new DVD copy protection system, however, is far more difficult and costly than reprogramming a combination lock and may carry with it the added problem of rendering the existing installed base of compliant DVD players obsolete.

Second, the application of DeCSS to copy and distribute motion pictures on DVD, both on CD-ROMs and via the Internet, threatens to reduce the studios' revenue from the sale and rental of DVDs. It threatens also to impede new, potentially lucrative initiatives for the distribution of motion pictures in digital form, such as video-on-demand via the Internet. . . .

II. The Digital Millennium Copyright Act . . .

B. Posting of DeCSS

1. Violation of Anti-Trafficking Provision

Section 1201(a)(2) of the Copyright Act, part of the DMCA, provides that:

> "No person shall . . . offer to the public, or otherwise traffic in any technology . . . that—
>> "(A) is primarily designed or produced for the purpose of circumventing a technological measure that effectively controls access to a work protected under [the Copyright Act];

---

91. The other two defendants entered into consent decrees with plaintiffs. Plaintiffs subsequently amended the complaint to add 2600 Enterprises, Inc. as a defendant.

"(B) has only limited commercially significant purpose or use other than to circumvent a technological measure that effectively controls access to a work protected under [the Copyright Act]; or

"(C) is marketed by that person or another acting in concert with that person with that person's knowledge for use in circumventing a technological measure that effectively controls access to a work protected under [the Copyright Act]."

In this case, defendants concededly offered and provided and, absent a court order, would continue to offer and provide DeCSS to the public by making it available for download on the 2600.com web site. DeCSS, a computer program, unquestionably is "technology" within the meaning of the statute. "[C]ircumvent a technological measure" is defined to mean descrambling a scrambled work, decrypting an encrypted work, or "otherwise to avoid, bypass, remove, deactivate, or impair a technological measure, without the authority of the copyright owner," so DeCSS clearly is a means of circumventing a technological access control measure. In consequence, if [De]CSS otherwise falls within paragraphs (A), (B) or (C) of Section 1201(a)(2), and if none of the statutory exceptions applies to their actions, defendants have violated and, unless enjoined, will continue to violate the DMCA by posting DeCSS. . . .

During pretrial proceedings and at trial, defendants attacked plaintiffs' Section 1201(a)(2)(A) claim, arguing that CSS, which is based on a 40-bit encryption key, is a weak cipher that does not "effectively control" access to plaintiffs' copyrighted works. They reasoned from this premise that CSS is not protected under this branch of the statute at all. . . .

. . . [T]he statute expressly provides that "a technological measure 'effectively controls access to a work' if the measure, in the ordinary course of its operation, requires the application of information or a process or a treatment, with the authority of the copyright owner, to gain access to a work." One cannot gain access to a CSS-protected work on a DVD without application of the three keys that are required by the software. One cannot lawfully gain access to the keys except by entering into a license with the DVD CCA [(DVD Copy Control Association)] under authority granted by the copyright owners or by purchasing a DVD player or drive containing the keys pursuant to such a license. In consequence, under the express terms of the statute, CSS "effectively controls access" to copyrighted DVD movies. It does so, within the meaning of the statute, whether or not it is a strong means of protection. . . .

. . . [T]he interpretation of the phrase "effectively controls access" offered by defendants at trial—viz., that the use of the word "effectively" means that the statute protects only successful or efficacious technological means of controlling access— would gut the statute if it were adopted. . . .

As CSS effectively controls access to plaintiffs' copyrighted works, the only remaining question under Section 1201(a)(2)(A) is whether DeCSS was designed primarily to circumvent CSS. The answer is perfectly obvious. By the admission of both Jon Johansen, the programmer who principally wrote DeCSS, and defendant Corley, DeCSS was created solely for the purpose of decrypting CSS—that is all it does. . . .

As the only purpose or use of DeCSS is to circumvent CSS, the foregoing is sufficient to establish a *prima facie* violation of Section 1201(a)(2)(B) as well.

c. The Linux Argument

Perhaps the centerpiece of defendants' statutory position is the contention that DeCSS was not created for the purpose of pirating copyrighted motion pictures. Rather, they argue, it was written to further the development of a DVD player that would run under the Linux operating system, as there allegedly were no Linux compatible players on the market at the time. . . .

. . . [T]he question whether the development of a Linux DVD player motivated those who wrote DeCSS is immaterial to the question whether the defendants now before the Court violated the anti-trafficking provision of the DMCA. The inescapable facts are that (1) CSS is a technological means that effectively controls access to plaintiffs' copyrighted works, (2) the one and only function of DeCSS is to circumvent CSS, and (3) defendants offered and provided DeCSS by posting it on their web site. Whether defendants did so in order to infringe, or to permit or encourage others to infringe, copyrighted works in violation of other provisions of the Copyright Act simply does not matter for purposes of Section 1201(a)(2). The offering or provision of the program is the prohibited conduct—and it is prohibited irrespective of why the program was written, except to whatever extent motive may be germane to determining whether their conduct falls within one of the statutory exceptions.

2. Statutory Exceptions . . .

a. Reverse engineering

Defendants claim to fall under Section 1201(f) of the statute, which provides in substance that one may circumvent, or develop and employ technological means to circumvent, access control measures in order to achieve interoperability with another computer program provided that doing so does not infringe another's copyright and, in addition, that one may make information acquired through such efforts "available to others, if the person . . . provides such information solely for the purpose of enabling interoperability of an independently created computer program with other programs, and to the extent that doing so does not constitute infringement. . . ." They contend that DeCSS is necessary to achieve interoperability between computers running the Linux operating system and DVDs and that this exception therefore is satisfied. This contention fails.

First, Section 1201(f)(3) permits information acquired through reverse engineering to be made available to others only by the person who acquired the information. But these defendants did not do any reverse engineering. They simply took DeCSS off someone else's web site and posted it on their own.

Defendants would be in no stronger position even if they had authored DeCSS. The right to make the information available extends only to dissemination "solely for the purpose" of achieving interoperability as defined in the statute. It does not apply to public dissemination of means of circumvention, as the legislative history confirms. These defendants, however, did not post DeCSS "solely" to achieve interoperability with Linux or anything else.

Finally, it is important to recognize that even the creators of DeCSS cannot credibly maintain that the "sole" purpose of DeCSS was to create a Linux DVD player. . . .

b. Encryption research

. . . In determining whether one is engaged in good faith encryption research [for purposes of the statutory exception in §1201(g)], the Court is instructed to consider factors including whether the results of the putative encryption research are disseminated in a manner designed to advance the state of knowledge of encryption technology versus facilitation of copyright infringement, whether the person in question is engaged in legitimate study of or work in encryption, and whether the results of the research are communicated in a timely fashion to the copyright owner.

Neither of the defendants remaining in this case was or is involved in good faith encryption research. They posted DeCSS for all the world to see. There is no evidence that they made any effort to provide the results of the DeCSS effort to the copyright owners. Surely there is no suggestion that either of them made a good faith effort to obtain authorization from the copyright owners. . . .

c. Security testing

[The court ruled that DeCSS also did not fall within the statutory exception for "security testing," §1201(j).]

d. Fair use . . .

The use of technological means of controlling access to a copyrighted work may affect the ability to make fair uses of the work.[159] Focusing specifically on the facts of this case, the application of CSS to encrypt a copyrighted motion picture requires the use of a compliant DVD player to view or listen to the movie. Perhaps more significantly, it prevents exact copying of either the video or the audio portion of all or any part of the film. This latter point means that certain uses that might qualify as "fair" for purposes of copyright infringement—for example, the preparation by a film studies professor of a single CD-ROM or tape containing two scenes from different movies in order to illustrate a point in a lecture on cinematography, as opposed to showing relevant parts of two different DVDs—would be difficult or impossible absent circumvention of the CSS encryption. Defendants therefore argue that the DMCA cannot properly be construed to make it difficult or impossible to make any fair use of plaintiffs' copyrighted works and that the statute therefore does not reach their activities, which are simply a means to enable users of DeCSS to make such fair uses.

Defendants have focused on a significant point. Access control measures such as CSS do involve some risk of preventing lawful as well as unlawful uses of copyrighted

---

159. Indeed, as many have pointed out, technological means of controlling access to works create a risk, depending upon future technological and commercial developments, of limiting access to works that are not protected by copyright such as works upon which copyright has expired. . . .

material. Congress, however, clearly faced up to and dealt with this question in enacting the DMCA.

. . . Section 107 of the Copyright Act provides in critical part that certain uses of copyrighted works that otherwise would be wrongful are "not . . . infringement[s] of copyright." Defendants . . . are not here sued for copyright infringement. They are sued for offering and providing technology designed to circumvent technological measures that control access to copyrighted works and otherwise violating Section 1201(a)(2) of the Act. If Congress had meant the fair use defense to apply to such actions, it would have said so. . . .

Defendants claim also that the possibility that DeCSS might be used for the purpose of gaining access to copyrighted works in order to make fair use of those works saves them under *Sony Corp. v. Universal City Studios, Inc.* [, 464 U.S. 417 (1984)]. But they are mistaken. *Sony* does not apply to the activities with which defendants here are charged. Even if it did, it would not govern here. *Sony* involved a construction of the Copyright Act that has been overruled by the later enactment of the DMCA to the extent of any inconsistency between *Sony* and the new statute. . . .

The policy concerns raised by defendants were considered by Congress. Having considered them, Congress crafted a statute that, so far as the applicability of the fair use defense to Section 1201(a) claims is concerned, is crystal clear. In such circumstances, courts may not undo what Congress so plainly has done by "construing" the words of a statute to accomplish a result that Congress rejected. The fact that Congress elected to leave technologically unsophisticated persons who wish to make fair use of encrypted copyrighted works without the technical means of doing so is a matter for Congress unless Congress' decision contravenes the Constitution, a matter to which the Court turns below. . . .

C. Linking to Sites Offering DeCSS

Plaintiffs seek also to enjoin defendants from "linking" their 2600.com web site to other sites that make DeCSS available to users. . . .

The statute makes it unlawful to offer, provide or otherwise traffic in described technology. To "traffic" in something is to engage in dealings in it, conduct that necessarily involves awareness of the nature of the subject of the trafficking. To "provide" something, in the sense used in the statute, is to make it available or furnish it. To "offer" is to present or hold it out for consideration. . . .

To the extent that defendants have linked to sites that automatically commence the process of downloading DeCSS upon a user being transferred by defendants' hyperlinks, there can be no serious question. Defendants are engaged in the functional equivalent of transferring the DeCSS code to the users themselves.

Substantially the same is true of defendants' hyperlinks to web pages that display nothing more than the DeCSS code or present the user only with the choice of commencing a download of DeCSS and no other content. . . .

Potentially more troublesome might be links to pages that offer a good deal of content other than DeCSS . . . . If one assumed, for the purposes of argument, that the *Los Angeles Times* web site somewhere contained the DeCSS code, it would be wrong to say that anyone who linked to the *Los Angeles Times* web site, regardless of purpose or the manner in which the link was described, thereby offered, provided or otherwise trafficked in DeCSS . . . . But that is not this case. Defendants urged others to . . . disseminate DeCSS and to inform defendants that they were doing so. Defendants then linked their site to those "mirror" sites . . . and proclaimed on their own site that DeCSS could be had by clicking on the hyperlinks on defendants' site. . . .

III. The First Amendment . . .

[The court determined that computer code is a form of expression protected by the First Amendment. After deciding that the antitrafficking provision of the DMCA is content neutral, it held that the provision survived the intermediate scrutiny that applies to content-neutral restrictions on speech. The court next addressed defendants' argument that §1201(a)(2) is unconstitutionally overbroad. This argument was based largely on the statute's implications for the fair use doctrine; defendants argued that this doctrine is constitutionally mandated. The court did not reach this latter argument, however, because it concluded that it was not possible to determine whether §1201(a)(2) substantially affected the interests of parties not before the court.]

. . . [Fair uses] now are affected by the anti-trafficking provision of the DMCA, but probably only to a trivial degree. To begin with, all or substantially all motion pictures available on DVD are available also on videotape. In consequence, anyone wishing to make lawful use of a particular movie may buy or rent a videotape, play it, and even copy all or part of it with readily available equipment. But even if movies were available only on DVD, as someday may be the case, the impact on lawful use would be limited. Compliant DVD players permit one to view or listen to a DVD movie without circumventing CSS in any prohibited sense. The technology permitting manufacture of compliant DVD players is available to anyone on a royalty-free basis and at modest cost, so CSS raises no technological barrier to their manufacture. Hence, those wishing to make lawful use of copyrighted movies by viewing or listening to them are not hindered in doing so in any material way by the anti-trafficking provision of the DMCA[243]. . . .

The DMCA does have a notable potential impact on uses that copy portions of a DVD movie because compliant DVD players are designed so as to prevent copying. . . . It is the interests of these individuals upon which defendants rely most heavily in contending that the DMCA violates the First Amendment . . . .[245]

---

243. Defendants argue that the right of third parties to view DVD movies on computers running the Linux operating system will be materially impaired if DeCSS is not available to them. However, the technology to build a Linux-based DVD player has been licensed by the DVD CCA to at least two companies, and there is no reason to think that others wishing to develop Linux players could not obtain licenses if they so chose. . . . Further, it is not evident that the constitutional protection of free expression extends to the type of device on which one plays copyrighted material. . . .

245. The same point might be made with respect to copying of works upon which copyright has expired. . . . As the DMCA is not yet two years old, this does not yet appear to be a problem, although it may emerge as one in the future.

. . . [T]he interests of persons wishing to circumvent CSS in order to make lawful uses of the copyrighted movies it protects are remarkably varied. . . . [T]he prudential concern with ensuring that constitutional questions be decided only when the facts before the Court so require counsels against permitting defendants to mount an overbreadth challenge here. . . .

[Finally, the court considered whether enjoining defendants from linking to sites that offered DeCSS would violate the First Amendment.]

. . . [T]he real significance of an anti-linking injunction would not be with U.S. web sites subject to the DMCA, but with foreign sites that arguably are not subject to it and not subject to suit here. An anti-linking injunction to that extent would have a significant impact and thus materially advance a substantial governmental purpose. . . .

The possible chilling effect of a rule permitting liability for or injunctions against Internet hyperlinks is a genuine concern. But it is not unique to the issue of linking. The constitutional law of defamation provides a highly relevant analogy. . . .

Accordingly, there may be no injunction against, nor liability for, linking to a site containing circumvention technology, the offering of which is unlawful under the DMCA, absent clear and convincing evidence that those responsible for the link (a) know at the relevant time that the offending material is on the linked-to site, (b) know that it is circumvention technology that may not lawfully be offered, and (c) create or maintain the link for the purpose of disseminating that technology. . . .

IV. Relief . . .

. . . [T]he likelihood is that this decision will serve notice on others that "the strong right arm of equity" may be brought to bear against them absent a change in their conduct and thus contribute to a climate of appropriate respect for intellectual property rights in an age in which the excitement of ready access to untold quantities of information has blurred in some minds the fact that taking what is not yours and not freely offered to you is stealing. Appropriate injunctive and declaratory relief will issue simultaneously with this opinion. . . .

NOTES AND QUESTIONS

1. Recall the distinctions made by §1201 between access protection measures and rights protection measures. Characterizing a technological protection as one or the other sometimes can be difficult. *See* R. Anthony Reese, *Will Merging Access Controls and Rights Controls Undermine the Structure of Anticircumvention Law?*, 18 Berkeley Tech. L.J. 619 (2003). Why was *Reimerdes* cast as a case about §1201(a) and not §1201(b)? Examine the table at the beginning of this subsection before you answer.

Note that under the CSS licensing regime, CSS protection also varies by geographic zone. DVDs marketed in the United States will not play on DVD players marketed in Europe, Africa, or Asia, and vice versa. This arrangement was designed to thwart high-volume, cross-border piracy operations, but it also enables copyright owners to implement geographic price discrimination. Users in relatively affluent regions—e.g., North America and Europe—can be charged higher prices than those in less affluent regions—e.g., Southeast Asia and Africa. Gray marketers cannot exploit these price differences by shipping lawful DVDs sold in Africa to the United States, even though the Supreme Court's cases interpreting the Act's importation and first sale provisions (*see* Chapter 6.A.3, *supra*) would allow this, because U.S. consumers will not be able to play them. Disabling the region coding would enable users to play DVDs lawfully purchased in other countries. Would this violate §1201?

2. Examine the definitions in §1201(a)(3). If you purchase a copy of a password protected program on a CD-ROM and let a friend use your password to access the program, has your friend circumvented a technological measure that "effectively controls access to" the work? Have you trafficked in a device or service covered by §1201(a)(2)? *See I.M.S. Inquiry Mgmt. Sys. v. Berkshire Info. Sys.*, 307 F. Supp. 2d 521 (S.D.N.Y. 2004) (no).

Some programs require users to provide certain personal identifying information when they install the program, and use that information to monitor use of the program and any affiliated programs (such as programs for word processing, photo editing, playing music, and so on). Is such functionality a technological measure that "effectively controls access to" such programs, within the meaning of §1201? Would defeating the functionality, so that one could use the programs without providing the personal information, violate §1201(a)(2)? Examine §1201(i) before you answer.

3. Examine §1201(f). Should the court have accepted defendants' argument that DeCSS was created to achieve interoperability between CSS-protected DVDs and the Linux operating system? Under the court's interpretation of this subsection, what is the difference between circumvention and enabling interoperability?

Recall the discussion of open source software in Chapter 12.C.2. Linux is an open source operating system—i.e., all of the program code that makes up the Linux system is distributed with its source code and may be freely modified by users. The court noted that two licenses to develop Linux-compatible DVD players had been issued at the time of trial. No such licenses had been issued before plaintiffs filed their complaint. Why do you think that was the case?

4. Now examine §1201(a)(2). Should the court have concluded that potential use with the Linux operating system was a commercially significant use of DeCSS? Under the *Sony* standard, such a finding would have excused defendants from liability for contributory copyright infringement. Would such evidence have been sufficient to support a ruling that distribution of DeCSS did not violate §1201(a)(2)?

5. At the time the plaintiff instituted the litigation there were hundreds, if not thousands, of sites on the Web where one could obtain a copy of DeCSS. Why do you think plaintiffs chose to name Eric Corley as one of the defendants in this litigation? For a current list of DMCA-related disputes and warnings, visit the Electronic Frontier Foundation's website at http://www.eff.org and search for "DMCA consequences."

6. Examine §1201(c) carefully. Why do you think that Congress included this provision in the statute? During trial, the *Reimerdes* defendants urged the court to construe §1201(c)(1) to require a limited, judicially created exception to §1201(a)(2)'s device ban, but the court declined. On appeal, the Second Circuit was equally unpersuaded: "We disagree that subsection 1201(c)(1) permits such a reading. Instead, it simply clarifies that the DMCA targets the *circumvention* of digital walls guarding copyrighted material (and trafficking in circumvention tools), but does not concern itself with the *use* of those materials after circumvention has occurred." *Universal City Studios, Inc. v. Corley*, 273 F.3d 429, 443 (2d Cir. 2001). Do you agree with the court's reading of the statute? In a situation in which individual acts of circumvention are not prohibited (i.e., circumventing protection measures involving rights controls as opposed to access controls) how does an individual obtain the tools to engage in the circumvention?

Note on Section 1201 and Computer Science Research

A declaratory judgment action brought by Princeton University computer science professor Edward Felten sought interpretation of §1201 in a different context. Professor Felten and his research team accepted a public challenge issued by the recording industry to crack its prototype technological protection specifications for digital music files. Professor Felten and his team decided not to claim the cash prize offered by the recording industry, however, because they would have been required not to disclose the results of their research, and to agree that those results were now the intellectual property of the Secure Digital Music Initiative (SDMI). As Professor Felten was preparing to present his findings at a prominent research conference, representatives of the Recording Industry Association of America (RIAA) contacted the conference organizers and the legal counsel for Princeton University and warned that publication of the paper would violate the DMCA. Shortly thereafter, one of the conference organizers informed Professor Felten that his paper could not be presented unless the RIAA and SDMI agreed in writing.

The Felten incident sparked an uproar in the computer science community. Two days before the paper was scheduled to be presented, the conference organizers reversed their decision, but Professor Felten and his fellow researchers ultimately decided to withdraw the paper. The RIAA immediately issued a press release stating that it had never seriously intended to sue.

Professor Felten then sued the RIAA, asserting that publication of the paper would not violate §1201(a)(2), and, in the alternative, that §1201(a)(2) could not be enforced because Congress lacked the constitutional authority to enact it. The court granted the RIAA's motion to dismiss, finding that the dispute had not ripened into an actual controversy since Professor Felten was able to present his research at a different conference. *Felten v. Recording Indus. Ass'n of Am., Inc.*, Case No. CV-01-2669 (GEB) (D.N.J. Nov. 28, 2001). Professor Felten chose not to appeal the decision.

NOTES AND QUESTIONS

1. Is an academic research paper a "device"? If it is a device, did Professor Felten's conduct fall within any of the statutory exceptions to the DMCA's device ban provisions? Does anything in the language of §1201 support an argument that its provisions did not apply to Professor Felten's actions? If not, why do you think the RIAA disclaimed any intention to sue? Why do you think the RIAA moved to dismiss the *Felten* lawsuit?

2. Examine §§1201(g) and (j) carefully. Could Professor Felten have invoked either of these exemptions? What would one need to do to qualify? Do the exemptions in §§1201(f), (g) and (j) provide sufficient leeway for computer science research? Why, or why not?

3. Section 1201 and the First Amendment

The appeal of the *Reimerdes* decision focused primarily on the defendants' constitutional challenges to §1201(a)(2). The Second Circuit agreed with the district court's conclusions that instructions in computer code qualify as speech protected under the First Amendment, and that the regulation imposed by §1201(a)(2) is content neutral and permissible. In determining that the statutory provision is content neutral, it reasoned:

> . . . The[] realities of what code is and what its normal functions are require a First Amendment analysis that treats code as combining nonspeech and speech elements; i.e., functional and expressive elements. . . .
>
> In considering the scope of First Amendment protection for a decryption program like DeCSS, we must recognize that the essential purpose of encryption code is to prevent unauthorized access. Owners of all property rights are entitled to prohibit access to their property by unauthorized persons. . . .
>
> . . . In its basic function, [DeCSS] is like a skeleton key that can open a locked door, a combination that can open a safe, or a device that can neutralize the security device attached to a store's products . . . .

Universal City Studios, Inc. v. Corley, 273 F.3d 429, 451-53 (2d Cir. 2001).

To survive constitutional scrutiny, a content neutral speech restriction must further a substantial government interest unrelated to the suppression of free expression, and must not "burden substantially more speech than is necessary to further the government's legitimate interests." *Ward v. Rock Against Racism*, 491 U.S. 781, 799 (1989). The Second Circuit concluded that §1201(a)(2), as applied by the district court to prohibit defendants from posting DeCSS, met this standard:

> . . . The Government's interest in preventing unauthorized access to encrypted copy-righted material is unquestionably substantial, and the regulation of DeCSS by the posting prohibition plainly serves that interest. Moreover, the interest is unrelated to the suppression of free expression. The injunction regulates the posting of DeCSS,

regardless of whether DeCSS code contains any information comprehensible by human beings that would qualify as speech. . . .

. . . Although the prohibition on posting prevents the Appellants from conveying to others the speech component of DeCSS, the Appellants have not suggested, much less shown, any technique for barring them from making this instantaneous worldwide distribution of a decryption code that makes a lesser restriction on the code's speech component. . . . [A] content-neutral regulation need not employ the least restrictive means of accomplishing the governmental objective. . . .

Corley, 273 F.3d at 454-55. The court also affirmed the district court's prohibition against linking to DeCSS. It rejected an analogy to an injunction prohibiting a newspaper from publishing the addresses of bookstores carrying obscene materials:

. . . If a bookstore proprietor is knowingly selling obscene materials, the evil of distributing such materials can be prevented by injunctive relief against the unlawful distribution. . . . And if others publish the location of the bookstore, preventive relief against a distributor can be effective before any significant distribution of the prohibited materials has occurred. The digital world, however, creates a very different problem. If obscene materials are posted on one web site and other sites post hyperlinks to the first site, the materials are available for worldwide distribution before any preventive measures can be effectively taken. . . .

Id. at 457.

Finally, the Second Circuit rejected the defendants' overbreadth challenge based on the failure of §1201, as interpreted by the district court, to accommodate the fair use doctrine. The court expressed doubt that any part of the Constitution requires recognition of a fair use doctrine: "[W]e note that the Supreme Court has never held that fair use is constitutionally required, although some isolated statements in its opinions might arguably be enlisted for such a requirement." *Id.* at 458. Like the district court, however, the court of appeals concluded that it need not reach the question whether the fair use doctrine is constitutionally required. It indicated that it would consider constitutional challenges based on §1201(a)(2)'s implications for fair use on a case-by-case, or "as-applied," basis when presented by defendants entitled to raise them. In closing, the court noted:

. . . We know of no authority for the proposition that fair use, as protected by the Copyright Act, much less the Constitution, guarantees copying by the optimum method or in the identical format of the original. Although the Appellants insisted at oral argument that they should not be relegated to a "horse and buggy" technique in making fair use of DVD movies, the DMCA does not impose even an arguable limitation on the opportunity to make a variety of traditional fair uses of DVD movies, such as commenting on their content, quoting excerpts from their screenplays, and even recording portions of the video images and sounds on film or tape by pointing a camera, a camcorder, or a microphone at a monitor as it displays the DVD movie. . . . Fair use has never been held to be a guarantee of access to copyrighted material in order to copy it by the fair user's preferred technique or in the format of the original. . . .

Id. at 459.

NOTES AND QUESTIONS

1. The *Corley* court's reasoning about whether §1201 is content neutral echoes the "breaking and entering" argument advanced by the copyright industries to support their request for a ban on circumvention and circumvention tools. In the words of Allan Adler, a lobbyist for the Association of American Publishers, "Fair use doesn't allow you to break into a locked library in order to make 'fair use' copies of the books in it, or steal newspapers from a vending machine in order to copy articles and share them with a friend." WIPO Copyright Treaties Implementation Act; and Online Copyright Liability Limitation Act: Hearing on H.R. 2281 and H.R. 2280 Before the Subcomm. on Courts and Intellectual Property of the House Comm. on the Judiciary, 105th Cong. 208 (1997) (statement of Allan Adler). Is this metaphor sufficient to capture all of the implications of circumvention? Why, or why not? Do you agree with the court's conclusion that a law that targets decryption devices is content neutral?

2. Was the *Corley* court correct to conclude that no less restrictive means exists by which Congress might prevent or deter unauthorized copying of copyrighted works? Can you think of any less restrictive measures that Congress might have enacted?

Legislation introduced in the 109th Congress, titled the "Digital Media Consumers' Rights Act" (H.R. 1201), sought to amend §1201(c)(1) by adding at the end: "and it is not a violation of this section to circumvent a technological measure in connection with access to, or the use of, a work if such circumvention does not result in an infringement of copyright in the work." A proposed new §1201(c)(5) would have provided: "It shall not be a violation of this title to manufacture, distribute, or make noninfringing use of a hardware or software product capable of enabling significant noninfringing use of a copyrighted work." Finally, the bill would have amended §1201's device-related provisions by adding to §1201(a)(2)(A) and (b)(1)(A) a narrow exception for persons "acting solely in furtherance of scientific research into technological protection measures." If you had been a member of Congress, would you have supported passage of such legislation? Why, or why not?

3. In *Eldred v. Ashcroft,* 537 U.S. 186 (2003), which you read in Chapter 11.B.2, the Supreme Court rejected the plaintiff's First Amendment challenge to the Copyright Term Extension Act, emphasizing the importance of copyright law's "built-in First Amendment accommodations" and expressly identifying the idea/expression distinction and the fair use doctrine. *Id.* at 219-20. The Court held that when "Congress has not altered the traditional contours of copyright protection, further First Amendment scrutiny is unnecessary." *Id.* at 221. *Eldred* was decided after the Second Circuit's decision in *Corley.* Does §1201 alter the "traditional contours of copyright protection"? If *Corley* had been decided after *Eldred,* would the Second Circuit have ruled differently?

4. Can you think of any fair or otherwise privileged uses of DVD movies that might require the ability to make copies directly in the digital format?

5. Sections 1203 and 1204 establish separate civil and criminal penalties for violations of §1201. Violations of §1201 are subject to criminal sanctions if done willfully and for purposes of commercial advantage or private financial gain. *See* 17 U.S.C. §1204. Is that provision consistent with the First Amendment? Why, or why not?

4. Library of Congress Rulemakings Under §1201

Section 1201(a)'s ban on the circumvention of access controls is subject to a grant of rulemaking authority that allows the Librarian of Congress, in consultation with the Copyright Office and the Department of Commerce, to declare exemptions if the Librarian finds that particular users are "adversely affected by the prohibition under [§1201(a)(1)(A)] in their ability to make noninfringing uses of a particular class of copyrighted works." 17 U.S.C. §1201(a)(1)(C). Any exemption granted pursuant to this procedure does not supply a defense to an action for violation of any other provision of Title 17—including the device bans set forth in §1201(a)(2) and (b)(1). Thus, one who is granted an exemption may circumvent access controls, but apparently may not manufacture or distribute circumvention technologies. The statute directs that the rulemaking be conducted every three years.

In the first rulemaking, the Librarian of Congress rejected arguments that the language of the statute permitted an exemption to the circumvention ban whenever the underlying use would be considered fair, and ruled that the statutory reference to "a particular class of copyrighted works" required any exemptions to be narrowly drawn. The Librarian further ruled that any exemption must be based on a showing of a "substantial adverse effect." U.S. Copyright Office, Exemption to Prohibition on Circumvention of Copyright Protection Systems for Access Control Technologies: Final Rule, 65 Fed. Reg. 64,556, 64,558 (Oct. 27, 2000).

In later rulemakings, the Librarian of Congress has clarified the proponent's burden of proof, ruling that the requirement to show the likelihood of a "substantial adverse effect" does not impose a burden higher than the statute requires, but "simply means that [one's proof] must have a substance." U.S. Copyright Office: Exemption to Prohibition on Circumvention of Copyright Protection Systems for Access Control Technologies: Final Rule, 68 Fed. Reg. 62,011, 62,013 (Oct. 31, 2003) (codified at 37 C.F.R. §201.40). In addition, the Librarian has ruled that in some circumstances "a particular class of copyrighted works" may be defined "by reference to the type of user who may take advantage of the exemption or by reference to the type of use of the work that may be made pursuant to the exemption." U.S. Copyright Office, Exemption to Prohibition on Circumvention of Copyright Protection Systems for Access Control Technologies: Final Rule, 71 Fed. Reg. 68,472, 68,473 (Nov. 27, 2006) (codified at 37 C.F.R. §201.40).

The following table summarizes the exemptions granted as of this writing. Note that exemptions are granted for three years only, and must be justified again to be renewed in the next rulemaking.

Year	Exemptions Granted
2000	Literary works in malfunctioning/obsolete formats; Lists of criteria used by Internet filtering software.
2003	Software in malfunctioning/obsolete formats; Software and video games in obsolete formats requiring original media/hardware for access; Literary works when all ebook editions prevent enabling of accessibility for blind/visually-impaired users; Lists of criteria used by spam filters and antivirus software.
2006	Software in malfunctioning/obsolete formats; Software and video games in obsolete formats requiring original media/hardware for access, but only for libraries and archives; Literary works when all ebook editions prevent enabling of accessibility for visually-impaired users; Audiovisual works in university film/media studies libraries, for the purpose of making compilations of clips for classroom use; Computer programs that enable mobile phones to connect to wireless telephone networks, for the sole purpose of lawfully connecting to a network other than the one for which the phone was originally programmed; Audio and audiovisual works on CDs, for the sole purpose of investigating and correcting security flaws.
2010	Audiovisual works on DVDs, by university film/media studies professors for the purpose of making compilations of clips for classroom use, by the professors or their students for purposes of criticism and commentary, or by filmmakers to excerpt short clips for use in documentary filmmaking and noncommercial videos; Computer programs on mobile phones for the sole purpose of enabling interoperability with third-party software applications; Computer programs that enable mobile phones to connect to wireless telephone networks, for the sole purpose of lawfully connecting to a network other than the one for which the phone was originally programmed; Video games accessible on personal computers, for the sole purpose of investigating and correcting security flaws; Computer programs whose protections are malfunctioning, damaged, or obsolete; Literary works when all ebook editions prevent enabling of accessibility for visually impaired users.
2012	Audiovisual works on DVDs, by university film/media studies professors for the purpose of making compilations of clips for classroom use, by the professors or their students for purposes of criticism and commentary, or by filmmakers to excerpt short clips for use in documentary filmmaking and noncommercial videos; Computer programs on mobile phones *but not tablets*, for the sole purpose of enabling interoperability with third-party software applications; Computer programs that enable mobile phones to connect to wireless telephone networks, *for legacy phones only*, for the sole purpose of lawfully connecting to a network other than the one for which the phone was originally programmed; Literary works when all ebook editions prevent enabling of accessibility for visually-impaired users; Audiovisual works to facilitate captioning for hearing-impaired users and provision of descriptive audio for visually impaired users.

NOTES AND QUESTIONS

1. Is the §1201 rulemaking process a good substitute for the comparatively unconstrained equitable standard that applies in fair use cases? Why, or why not? Would it be appropriate to give the Librarian of Congress and the Copyright Office broad equitable discretion in rulemaking? For discussion of these issues in the context of a proposed exemption for noncommercial remix video, see Rebecca Tushnet, *I Put You There: User-Generated Content and Anti-Circumvention*, 12 Vand. J. Ent. & Tech. L. 889 (2010).

2. What do you think of the conclusion that exemptions may be defined in part by classes of users? Is that approach supported by the statutory language? How does it affect the scope of approved exemptions?

3. Would you advocate expanding the grant of rulemaking authority under §1201 to include exemptions to the device bans? Why, or why not? If in your view expanded rulemaking authority is warranted, under what circumstances should exemptions to the device bans be granted?

4. The discontinuation of the 2010 exemption for mobile phone unlocking became highly controversial. In 2014, Congress enacted the Unlocking Consumer Choice and Wireless Competition Act, Pub. L. 113-144, 128 Stat. 1751 (2014), which reinstated the 2010 exemption and directed the Librarian of Congress to consider whether to extend it to additional devices.

Note on International Approaches to WCT Implementation

The language of the WCT and the accompanying Agreed Statements preserves flexibility for member countries to implement its requirements. Indeed, national implementation of the WCT does vary because countries engage in the process of domestic implementation in a way that responds to the various interests at stake.

The European Union's 2001 directive on copyright harmonization expressly incorporates the language of the WCT. Thus, member countries are required to provide "adequate legal protection" against both the act of circumvention of "effective technological measures" and the manufacture and distribution of technologies that can be used to accomplish the circumvention. Directive 2001/29/EC of the European Parliament and of the Council of 22 May 2001 on the harmonisation of certain aspects of copyright and related rights in the information society, 2001 O.J. (L 167) 10, art. 6(1)-(2). The language of the provision regarding circumvention technologies substantially tracks the language of §§1201(a)(2) and (b)(1). Overall, however, the directive contemplates a different approach to the design and implementation of technological protections for copyrighted works. Article 6 provides:

> . . . [I]n the absence of voluntary measures taken by rightholders, including agreements between rightholders and other parties concerned, Member States shall take appropriate measures to ensure that rightholders make available to the beneficiary of an exception or limitation provided for in national law . . . [under certain other provisions of the directive] the means of benefiting from that exception or limitation, to the

extent necessary to benefit from that exception or limitation and where that beneficiary has legal access to the protected work or subject-matter concerned.

Id. art. 6(4). The exceptions and limitations for which accommodation is mandated do not include exceptions for private noncommercial copying; as to such exceptions, Article 6 provides that member states "may" take measures to ensure their survival if rightholders have not already enabled such private copying. *Id.*

These provisions require policymakers, copyright owners, and technologists to determine whether it might be possible to design technological protection systems that respect underlying copyright rules. The evidence suggests that the answer to this question is a qualified yes. On the one hand, it probably is impossible to design an automated system that internalizes the complex norms of the U.S. fair use doctrine. On the other, it plainly is possible to design systems that enable more specifically defined conduct. Accordingly, some commentators, both in Europe and in the United States, have advocated a "fair use by design" approach, which would require rightholders to design technological measures that are programmed to allow users to use the work consistent with existing exemptions and limitations. They argue that if an owner fails to make such accommodation for legitimate uses, then the law should permit circumvention for such uses, or require the owner to make a nonencrypted version of the work available. *See* Dan L. Burk & Julie E. Cohen, *Fair Use Infrastructure for Rights Management Systems*, 15 Harv. J.L. & Tech. 41, 55-70 (2001); Séverine Dusollier, *Exceptions and Technological Measures in the European Copyright Directive of 2001—An Empty Promise*, 34 Int'l Rev. Indus. Prop. & Copyright 62, 70 (2003). The United Kingdom has adopted a version of this approach; it provides an administrative remedy in cases where a technological protection system prevents a user from engaging in activity permitted by the copyright law. *See* Copyright, Designs and Patents Act, 1988, ch. 48, P 296ZE, *amended by* Copyright and Related Rights Regulations (2003 SI 2003/2498).

The United States, meanwhile, has sought to encourage other countries to adopt the approach reflected in the DMCA. The United States Trade Representative has negotiated a series of bilateral and regional free trade agreements (FTAs) that include accession to the WCT among their terms. Some of these agreements incorporate DMCA-style language requiring prohibition of anticircumvention measures in the domestic legislation of countries that are party to the FTA. *See, e.g.*, United States-South Korea Free Trade Agreement, June 30, 2007 (Art. 18.4); United States-Panama Trade Promotion Agreement, June 28, 2007 (Art. 15.5);United States-Columbia Free Trade Agreement, Feb. 27, 2006 (Art. 16.7).

NOTES AND QUESTIONS

1. If you were a European copyright holder, what sorts of "voluntary measures" might you undertake to stave off government regulation? If you were a legislator in one of the EU member countries, what sorts of legislative measures would you recommend?

2. What do you think of the "fair use by design" approach? Recall the *Corley* court's conclusion that no means less restrictive than §1201(a)(2) were available to prevent unauthorized copying and distribution of copyrighted works. Do the EU approaches represent viable "less restrictive alternatives" for preventing unauthorized copying? Should that affect the way that U.S. courts evaluate the constitutionality of §1201?

3. As of this writing, 93 countries have ratified the WCT since its entry into force on March 6, 2002. Many of them are developing and least-developed countries. In May 2001, the British government established a Commission on Intellectual Property Rights (CIPR) to study the effects of intellectual property rights in developing countries. The CIPR's report concluded that developing countries should not endorse the WCT and should not adopt the DMCA model for regulation of technological measures. Why do you think the CIPR reached those conclusions? If you were representing a developing country in FTA negotiations with the United States, would you recommend acceptance of language requiring WCT accession and enactment of legislation mirroring §1201?

C. AUTHORIZED VERSUS UNAUTHORIZED ACCESS AND INTEROPERABLE PRODUCTS

As you saw in Chapter 10.B.1, courts have interpreted the fair use doctrine to permit reverse engineering of computer software as a step in the process of developing interoperable products. This section addresses how §1201 may affect the practice of creating interoperable products.

Chamberlain Group, Inc. v. Skylink Tech., Inc.
381 F.3d 1178 (Fed. Cir. 2004), cert. denied, 544 U.S. 923 (2005)

GAJARSA, J.: . . . The technology at issue involves Garage Door Openers (GDOs). A GDO typically consists of a hand-held portable transmitter and a garage door opening device mounted in a homeowner's garage. . . .

When a homeowner purchases a GDO system, the manufacturer provides both an opener and a transmitter. Homeowners who desire replacement or spare transmitters can purchase them in the aftermarket. Aftermarket consumers have long been able to purchase "universal transmitters" that they can program to interoperate with their GDO system regardless of make or model. Skylink and Chamberlain are the only significant distributors of universal GDO transmitters. Chamberlain places no explicit restrictions on the types of transmitter that the homeowner may use with its system at the time of purchase. Chamberlain's customers therefore assume that they enjoy all of the rights associated with the use of their GDOs and any software embedded therein that the copyright laws and other laws of commerce provide.

This dispute involves Chamberlain's Security+ line of GDOs and Skylink's Model 39 universal transmitter. Chamberlain's Security+ GDOs incorporate a copyrighted "rolling code" computer program that constantly changes the transmitter signal needed to open the garage door. Skylink's Model 39 transmitter, which does not incorporate rolling code, nevertheless allows users to operate Security+

openers. Chamberlain alleges that Skylink's transmitter renders the Security+ insecure by allowing unauthorized users to circumvent the security inherent in rolling codes. . . .

These facts frame the dispute now before us on appeal. Though only Chamberlain's DMCA claim is before us, and though the parties dispute whether or not Skylink developed the Model 39 independent of Chamberlain's copyrighted products, it is nevertheless noteworthy that Chamberlain *has not* alleged either that Skylink infringed its copyright or that Skylink is liable for contributory copyright infringement. What Chamberlain *has* alleged is that because its opener and transmitter both incorporate computer programs "protected by copyright" and because rolling codes are a "technological measure" that "controls access" to those programs, Skylink is prima facie liable for violating §1201(a)(2). In the District Court's words, "Chamberlain claims that the rolling code computer program has a protective measure that protects itself. Thus, only one computer program is at work here, but it has two functions: (1) to verify the rolling code; and (2) once the rolling code is verified, to activate the GDO motor, by sending instructions to a microprocessor in the GDO." *Chamberlain I,* 292 F. Supp. 2d at 1028.

C. The Summary Judgment Motions . . .

According to undisputed facts, a homeowner who purchases a Chamberlain GDO owns it and has a right to use it to access his or her own garage. At the time of sale, Chamberlain does not place any explicit terms or condition on use to limit the ways that a purchaser may use its products. A homeowner who wishes to use a Model 39 must first program it into the GDO. Skylink characterizes this action as the home-owner's authorization of the Model 39 to interoperate with the GDO. In other words, according to Skylink, Chamberlain GDO consumers who purchase a Skylink transmitter have Chamberlain's implicit permission to purchase and to use any brand of transmitter that will open their GDO. The District Court agreed that Chamberlain's unconditioned sale implied authorization. *Id.* . . .

The District Court further noted that under Chamberlain's proposed construction of the DMCA, not only would Skylink be in violation of §1201(a)(2) (prohibiting trafficking in circumvention devices), but Chamberlain's own customers who used a Model 39 would be in violation of §1201(a)(1) (prohibiting circumvention). The District Court declined to adopt a construction with such dire implications. . . .

Discussion . . .

D. The Statute and Liability under the DMCA

The essence of the DMCA's anticircumvention provisions is that §§1201(a), (b) establish causes of action for liability. They do not establish a new property right. The DMCA's text indicates that circumvention is not infringement, 17 U.S.C. §1201(c)(1), and the statute's structure makes the point even clearer. This distinction between property and liability is critical. Whereas copyrights, like patents, are property, liability protection from unauthorized circumvention merely creates a new cause of action under which a defendant may be liable. The distinction between property and liability goes straight to the issue of authorization, the issue upon which the District Court both denied Chamberlain's and granted Skylink's motion for summary judgment.

A plaintiff alleging copyright infringement need prove *only* "(1) ownership of a valid copyright, and (2) copying of constituent elements of the work that are original." *Feist Pub., Inc. v. Rural Tel. Serv. Co.*, 499 U.S. 340, 361 (1991). "[T]he existence of a license, exclusive or nonexclusive, creates an affirmative defense to a claim of copyright infringement." *I.A.E., Inc. v. Shaver*, 74 F.3d 768, 775 (7th Cir. 1996). In other words, . . . a plaintiff only needs to show that the defendant has used her property; the burden of proving that the use was authorized falls squarely on the defendant. *Id.* The DMCA, however, *defines* circumvention as an activity undertaken "without the authority of the copyright owner." 17 U.S.C. §1201(a)(3)(A). The plain language of the statute therefore requires a plaintiff alleging circumvention (or trafficking) to prove that the defendant's access was unauthorized—a significant burden where, as here, the copyright laws authorize consumers to use the copy of Chamberlain's software embedded in the GDOs that they purchased. . . .

. . . [Chamberlain] claim[s] that the DMCA overrode all pre-existing consumer expectations about the legitimate uses of products containing copyrighted embedded software. Chamberlain contends that Congress empowered manufacturers to prohibit consumers from using embedded software products in conjunction with competing products when it passed §1201(a)(1). According to Chamberlain, *all* such uses of products containing copyrighted software to which a technological measure controlled access are now per se illegal under the DMCA unless the manufacturer provided consumers with *explicit* authorization. . . .

Such [a construction], however, is only plausible if the anticircumvention provisions established a new property right capable of conflicting with the copyright owner's other legal responsibilities—which as we have already explained, they do not. The anticircumvention provisions convey no additional property rights in and of themselves; they simply provide property owners with new ways to secure their property. Like all property owners taking legitimate steps to protect their property, however, copyright owners relying on the anticircumvention provisions remain bound by all other relevant bodies of law. Contrary to Chamberlain's assertion, the DMCA emphatically *did not* "fundamentally alter" the legal landscape governing the reasonable expectations of consumers or competitors; *did not* "fundamentally alter" the ways that courts analyze industry practices; and *did not* render the pre-DMCA history of the GDO industry irrelevant.

What the DMCA did was introduce new grounds for liability in the context of the unauthorized access of copyrighted material. The statute's plain language requires plaintiffs to prove that those circumventing their technological measures controlling access did so "without the authority of the copyright owner." 17 U.S.C. §1201(3)(A). Our inquiry ends with that clear language. We note, however, that the statute's structure, legislative history, and context within the Copyright Act all support our construction. They also help to explain why Chamberlain's warranty conditions and website postings cannot render users of Skylink's Model 39 "unauthorized" users for the purposes of establishing trafficking liability under the DMCA.

E. Statutory Structure and Legislative History . . .

. . . Statutory structure and legislative history both make it clear that §1201 applies only to circumventions reasonably related to protected rights. Defendants who traffic in devices that circumvent access controls in ways that facilitate infringement may be subject to liability under §1201(a)(2). Defendants who use such devices may be subject to liability under §1201(a)(1) whether they infringe or not. Because all defendants who traffic in devices that circumvent rights controls necessarily facilitate infringement, they may be subject to liability under §1201(b). Defendants who use such devices may be subject to liability for copyright infringement. And finally, defendants whose circumvention devices do not facilitate infringement are not subject to §1201 liability.

The key to understanding this relationship lies in §1201(b), which prohibits trafficking in devices that circumvent technological measures tailored narrowly to protect an individual right of the copyright owner while nevertheless allowing access to the protected work. Though §1201 (b) parallels the anti-trafficking ban of §1201(a)(2), there is no narrowly tailored ban on direct circumvention to parallel §1201(a)(1). This omission was intentional.

> The prohibition in 1201(a)(1) [was] necessary because prior to [the DMCA], the conduct of circumvention was never before made unlawful. The device limitation in 1201(a)(2) enforces this new prohibition in conduct. The copyright law has long forbidden copyright infringements, so no new prohibition was necessary. The device limitation in 1201(b) enforces the longstanding prohibitions on infringements.

S. Rep. No. 105-90 at 12 (1998).

Prior to the DMCA, a copyright owner would have had no cause of action against anyone who circumvented any sort of technological control, but did not infringe. The DMCA rebalanced these interests to favor the copyright owner; the DMCA created circumvention liability for "digital trespass" under §1201(a)(1). It also created trafficking liability under §1201(a)(2) for facilitating such circumvention and under §1201(b) for facilitating infringement (both subject to the numerous limitations and exceptions outlined throughout the DMCA).[13] . . .

The most significant and consistent theme running through the entire legislative history of the anticircumvention and anti-trafficking provisions of the DMCA, §§1201(a)(1), (2), is that Congress attempted to balance competing interests, and "endeavored to specify, with as much clarity as possible, how the right against anti-circumvention would be qualified to maintain balance between the interests of content creators and information users." H.R. Rep. No. 105-551, at 26 (1998). The Report of the House Commerce Committee concluded that §1201 "fully respects and extends into the digital environment the bedrock principle of 'balance' in American intellectual property law for the benefit of both copyright owners and users." *Id*. . . .

. . . We must understand that balance to resolve this dispute.

---

13. For obvious reasons, §1201(a)(2) trafficking liability cannot exist in the absence of §1201(a)(1) violations. . . .

F. Access and Protection . . .

. . . [I]t is significant that virtually every clause of §1201 that mentions "access" links "access" to "protection." The import of that linkage may be less than obvious. Perhaps the best way to appreciate the necessity of this linkage—and the disposition of this case—is to consider three interrelated questions inherent in the DMCA's structure: What does §1201(a)(2) prohibit above and beyond the prohibitions of §1201(b)? What is the relationship between the sorts of "access" prohibited under §1201(a) and the rights "protected" under the Copyright Act? and What is the relationship between anticircumvention liability under §1201(a)(1) and anti-trafficking liability under §1201(a)(2)? The relationships among the new liabilities that these three provisions, §§1201(a)(1), (a)(2), (b), create circumscribe the DMCA's scope—and therefore allow us to determine whether or not Chamberlain's claim falls within its purview. And the key to disentangling these relationships lies in understanding the linkage between access and protection.

Chamberlain urges us to read the DMCA as if Congress simply created a new protection for copyrighted works without any reference at all either to the protections that copyright owners already possess or to the rights that the Copyright Act grants to the public. Chamberlain has not alleged that Skylink's Model 39 infringes its copyrights, nor has it alleged that the Model 39 contributes to third-party infringement of its copyrights. Chamberlain's allegation is considerably more straightforward: The only way for the Model 39 to interoperate with a Security+ GDO is by "accessing" copyrighted software. Skylink has therefore committed a per se violation of the DMCA. Chamberlain urges us to conclude that no necessary connection exists between access and *copyrights*. Congress could not have intended such a broad reading of the DMCA. *Accord Corley*, 273 F.3d at 435 (explaining that Congress passed the DMCA's anti-trafficking provisions to help copyright owners protect their works *from piracy* behind a digital wall). . . .

Chamberlain's proposed construction of the DMCA ignores the significant differences between defendants whose accused products enable copying and those, like Skylink, whose accused products enable only legitimate uses of copyrighted software. Chamberlain's repeated reliance on language targeted at defendants trumpeting their "electronic civil disobedience," [*Reimerdes*] at 303, 312, apparently led it to misconstrue significant portions of the DMCA. . . .

. . . Were §1201 (a) to allow copyright owners to use technological measures to block *all* access to their copyrighted works, it would effectively create two distinct copyright regimes. In the first regime, the owners of a typical work protected by copyright would possess only the rights enumerated in 17 U.S.C. §106, subject to the additions, exceptions, and limitations outlined throughout the rest of the Copyright Act—notably but not solely the fair use provisions of §107.[14] Owners

---

14. We do not reach the relationship between §107 fair use and violations of §1201. The District Court in *Reimerdes* rejected the DeCSS defendants' argument that fair use was a *necessary* defense to §1201(a), *Reimerdes*, 111 F. Supp. 2d at 317; because *any* access enables some fair uses, any act of circumvention would embody its own defense. We leave open the question as to when §107 might serve as an affirmative defense to a prima facie violation of §1201. . . .

who feel that technology has put those rights at risk, and who incorporate technological measures to protect those rights from technological encroachment, gain the additional ability to hold traffickers in circumvention devices liable under §1201(b) for putting their rights back at risk by enabling circumventors who use these devices to infringe.

Under the second regime that Chamberlain's proposed construction implies, the owners of a work protected by *both* copyright *and* a technological measure that effectively controls access to that work per §1201(a) would possess *unlimited* rights to hold circumventors liable under §1201(a) *merely for accessing that work*, even if that access enabled *only* rights that the Copyright Act grants to the public. This second implied regime would be problematic for a number of reasons. First, as the Supreme Court recently explained, "Congress' exercise of its Copyright Clause authority must be rational." *Eldred v. Ashcroft*, 537 U.S. 186, 205 n.10, (2003). In determining whether a particular aspect of the Copyright Act "is a rational exercise of the legislative authority conferred by the Copyright Clause . . . we defer substantially to Congress. It is Congress that has been assigned the task of defining the scope of the limited monopoly that should be granted to authors . . . *in order to give the public appropriate access* to their work product." *Id.* at 204-05 (citation omitted) (emphasis added). Chamberlain's proposed construction of §1201(a) implies that in enacting the DMCA, Congress attempted to "give the public appropriate access" to copyrighted works by allowing copyright owners to deny all access to the public. Even under the substantial deference due Congress, such a redefinition borders on the irrational.

That apparent irrationality, however, is not the most significant problem that this second regime implies. Such a regime would be hard to reconcile with the DMCA's statutory prescription that "[n]othing in this section shall affect rights, remedies, limitations, or defenses to copyright infringement, including fair use, under this title." 17 U.S.C. §1201(c)(1). A provision that prohibited access without regard to the rest of the Copyright Act would clearly affect rights and limitations, if not remedies and defenses. . . . Chamberlain's proposed construction of §1201(a) would flatly contradict §1201(c)(1)—a simultaneously enacted provision of the same statute. We are therefore bound, if we can, to obtain an alternative construction that leads to no such contradiction. . . .

In a similar vein, Chamberlain's proposed construction would allow any manufacturer of any product to add a single copyrighted sentence or software fragment to its product, wrap the copyrighted material in a trivial "encryption" scheme, and thereby gain the right to restrict consumers' rights to use its products in conjunction with competing products. In other words, Chamberlain's construction of the DMCA would allow virtually any company to attempt to leverage its sales into aftermarket monopolies—a practice that both the antitrust laws, *see Eastman Kodak Co. v. Image Tech. Servs.*, 504 U.S. 451, 455 (1992), and the doctrine of copyright misuse, *Assessment Techs. of WI, LLC v. WIREdata, Inc.*, 350 F.3d 640, 647 (7th Cir. 2003), normally prohibit. . . .

Finally, the requisite "authorization," on which the District Court granted Skylink summary judgment, points to yet another inconsistency in Chamberlain's proposed construction. The notion of authorization is central to understanding

§1201(a). *See, e.g.*, S. Rep. 105-90 at 28 (1998) ("Subsection (a) applies when a person has not obtained authorized access to a copy or a phonorecord that is protected under the Copyright Act and for which the copyright owner has put in place a technological measure that effectively controls access to his or her work."). Underlying Chamberlain's argument on appeal that it has not granted such authorization lies the necessary assumption that Chamberlain is entitled to prohibit legitimate purchasers of its embedded software from "accessing" the software by using it. Such an entitlement, however, would go far beyond the idea that the DMCA allows copyright owner[s] to prohibit "fair uses . . . as well as foul." *Reimerdes*, 111 F. Supp. 2d at 304. Chamberlain's proposed construction would allow copyright owners to prohibit *exclusively fair* uses even in the absence of any feared foul use. It would therefore allow any copyright owner, through a combination of contractual terms and technological measures, to repeal the fair use doctrine with respect to an individual copyrighted work—or even selected copies of that copyrighted work. Again, this implication contradicts §1201(c)(1) directly. Copyright law itself authorizes the public to make certain uses of copyrighted materials. Consumers who purchase a product containing a copy of embedded software have the inherent legal right to use that copy of the software. What the law authorizes, Chamberlain cannot revoke.[17] . . .

We therefore reject Chamberlain's proposed construction in its entirety. We conclude that 17 U.S.C. §1201 prohibits only forms of access that bear a reasonable relationship to the protections that the Copyright Act otherwise affords copyright owners. While such a rule of reason may create some uncertainty and consume some judicial resources, it is the only meaningful reading of the statute. Congress attempted to balance the legitimate interests of copyright owners with those of consumers of copyrighted products. . . .

. . . Were we to interpret Congress' words in a way that eliminated all balance and granted copyright owners carte blanche authority to preclude all use, Congressional intent would remain unrealized. . . .

. . . The courts must decide where the balance between the rights of copyright owners and those of the broad public tilts subject to a fact-specific rule of reason. Here, Chamberlain can point to no protected property right that Skylink imperils. The DMCA cannot allow Chamberlain to retract the most fundamental right that the Copyright Act grants consumers: the right to use the copy of Chamberlain's embedded software that they purchased.

G. Chamberlain's DMCA Claim . . .

. . . A plaintiff alleging a violation of §1201(a)(2) must prove: (1) ownership of a valid *copyright* on a work, (2) effectively controlled by a *technological measure*, which

---

17. It is not clear whether a consumer who circumvents a technological measure controlling access to a copyrighted work in a manner that enables uses permitted under the Copyright Act but prohibited by contract can be subject to liability under the DMCA. Because Chamberlain did not attempt to limit its customers' use of its product by contract, however, we do not reach this issue.

has been circumvented, (3) that third parties can now *access* (4) *without authorization*, in a manner that (5) infringes or facilitates infringing a right *protected* by the Copyright Act, because of a product that (6) the defendant either (i) *designed or produced* primarily for circumvention; (ii) made available despite only *limited commercial significance* other than circumvention; or (iii) *marketed* for use in circumvention of the controlling technological measure. A plaintiff incapable of establishing any one of elements (1) through (5) will have failed to prove a prima facie case. A plaintiff capable of proving elements (1) through (5) need prove only one of (6)(i), (ii), or (iii) to shift the burden back to the defendant. At that point, the various affirmative defenses enumerated throughout §1201 become relevant. . . .

Chamberlain . . . has failed to show not only the requisite lack of authorization, but also the necessary fifth element of its claim, the critical nexus between access and protection. . . . The Copyright Act authorized Chamberlain's customers to use the copy of Chamberlain's copyrighted software embedded in the GDOs that they purchased. Chamberlain's customers are therefore immune from §1201(a)(1) circumvention liability. In the absence of allegations of either copyright infringement or §1201(a)(1) circumvention, Skylink cannot be liable for §1201(a)(2) trafficking. . . .

NOTES AND QUESTIONS

1. Examine the list of elements that the Federal Circuit says a §1201(a)(2) plaintiff must prove. What part of §1201(a)(2) gives rise to the fifth element? With regard to the fourth element, how might a copyright owner seek to establish the types of access that are unauthorized?

2. The *Chamberlain* court refers to the "rights of the public." What exactly are those rights in the context of §1201? In the context of copyright law generally? Who should identify the "rights of the public," Congress or the courts?

3. According to the *Chamberlain* court, interpreting §1201 to bar access without infringement would be "problematic for a number of reasons." The Ninth Circuit has rejected that conclusion as "contrary to the plain reading of the statute." *MDY Industries, LLC v. Blizzard Entertainment, Inc.*, 629 F.3d 928, 950 (9th Cir. 2011). The *MDY* court contrasted §1201(a)'s reference to "a work protected under this title" with §1201(b)'s reference to "a right of a copyright owner under this title" and concluded that §1201(a) extends "a new form of protection, i.e., the right to prevent circumvention of access controls" to copyrighted works independent of copyright infringement. *Id.* at 945. According to the Ninth Circuit, neither §1201(a)(1) nor (a)(2) explicitly refers to "traditional copyright infringement under §106." *Id.* Which court's interpretation is more faithful to the statutory text? Which court's approach to §1201(a) makes more sense with respect to the goals of copyright law?

≣
Lexmark International, Inc. v. Static Control Components, Inc.
387 F.3d 522 (6th Cir. 2005)

SUTTON, J.: . . .

The Parties.   Headquartered in Lexington, Kentucky, Lexmark is a leading manufacturer of laser and inkjet printers and has sold printers and toner cartridges for its printers since 1991. . . .

Static Control Components [SCC] is a privately held company headquartered in Sanford, North Carolina. . . . [SCC] makes a wide range of technology products, including microchips that it sells to third-party companies for use in remanufactured toner cartridges.

The Two Computer Programs.   The first program at issue is Lexmark's "Toner Loading Program," which measures the amount of toner remaining in the cartridge. . . . The Toner Loading Program relies upon eight program commands. . . . To illustrate the modest size of this computer program, the phrase "Lexmark International, Inc. vs. Static Control Components, Inc." in ASCII format would occupy more memory than either version of the Toner Loading Program. The Toner Loading Program is located on a microchip contained in Lexmark's toner cartridges.

The second program is Lexmark's "Printer Engine Program." The Printer Engine Program occupies far more memory than the Toner Loading Program and translates into over 20 printed pages of program commands. The program controls a variety of functions on each printer—e.g., paper feed and movement, and printer motor control. Unlike the Toner Loading Program, the Printer Engine Program is located within Lexmark's printers.

Lexmark obtained Certificates of Registration from the Copyright Office for both programs. Neither program is encrypted and each can be read (and copied) directly from its respective memory chip.

Lexmark's Prebate and Non-Prebate Cartridges.   Lexmark markets two types of toner cartridges for its laser printers: "Prebate" and "Non-Prebate." Prebate cartridges are sold to business consumers at an up-front discount. In exchange, consumers agree to use the cartridge just once, then return the empty unit to Lexmark; a "shrink-wrap" agreement on the top of each cartridge box spells out these restrictions and confirms that using the cartridge constitutes acceptance of these terms. Non-Prebate cartridges are sold without any discount, are not subject to any restrictive agreements and may be re-filled with toner and reused by the consumer or a third-party remanufacturer. . . .

To ensure that consumers adhere to the Prebate agreement, Lexmark uses an "authentication sequence" that performs a "secret handshake" between each Lexmark printer and a microchip on each Lexmark toner cartridge. . . . [If the handshake is not properly performed], the printer returns an error message and will not operate, blocking consumers from using toner cartridges that Lexmark has not authorized.

SCC's Competing Microchip. SCC sells its own microchip—the "SMARTEK" chip—that permits consumers to satisfy Lexmark's authentication sequence each time it would otherwise be performed, *i.e.*, when the printer is turned on or the printer door is opened and shut. SCC's advertising boasts that its chip breaks Lexmark's "secret code" (the authentication sequence), which "even on the fastest computer available today . . . would take **Years** to run through all of the possible 8-byte combinations to break." SCC sells these chips to third-party cartridge remanufacturers, permitting them to replace Lexmark's chip with the SMARTEK chip on refurbished Prebate cartridges. These recycled cartridges are in turn sold to consumers as a low-cost alternative to new Lexmark toner cartridges.

Each of SCC's SMARTEK chips also contains a copy of Lexmark's Toner Loading Program, which SCC claims is necessary to make its product compatible with Lexmark's printers. The SMARTEK chips thus contain an identical copy of the Toner Loading Program that is appropriate for each Lexmark printer, and SCC acknowledges that it "slavishly copied" the Toner Loading Program "in the exact format and order" found on Lexmark's cartridge chip. A side-by-side comparison of the two data sequences reveals no differences between them. . . .

The Lawsuit. . . . Lexmark alleged that SCC violated the copyright statute, 17 U.S.C. §106, by reproducing the Toner Loading Program on its SMARTEK chip[;] . . . that SCC violated the DMCA by selling a product that circumvents access controls on the Toner Loading Program[;] . . . [and] that SCC violated the DMCA by selling a product that circumvents access controls on the Printer Engine Program. . . .

[After an evidentiary hearing, the district court decided that Lexmark had shown a likelihood of success on each claim and entered a preliminary injunction against SCC.]

III. . . .

Generally speaking, "lock-out" codes fall on the functional-idea rather than the original-expression side of the copyright line. Manufacturers of interoperable devices such as computers and software, game consoles and video games, printers and toner cartridges, or automobiles and replacement parts may employ a security system to bar the use of unauthorized components. To "unlock" and permit operation of the primary device (i.e., the computer, the game console, the printer, the car), the component must contain either a certain code sequence or be able to respond appropriately to an authentication process. To the extent compatibility requires that a particular code sequence be included in the component device to permit its use, the merger and scenes a faire doctrines generally preclude the code sequence from obtaining copyright protection. . . .

. . . [I]f any single byte of the Toner Loading Program is altered, the printer will not function.

> **LOOKING BACK**
>
> As you learned in Chapter 4.C, copyright protection for computer software is complicated by the exclusion of functional subject matter mandated by §102(b).

On this record, pure compatibility requirements justified SCC's copying of the Toner Loading Program . . .

IV. . . .

We initially consider Lexmark's DMCA claim concerning the Printer Engine Program, which (the parties agree) is protected by the general copyright statute. In deciding that Lexmark's authentication sequence "effectively controls access to a work protected under [the copyright provisions]," the district court relied on a definition in the DMCA saying that a measure "effectively controls access to a work" if, "in the ordinary course of operation," it "requires the application of information, or a process or treatment, with the authority of the copyright owner, to gain access to the work." 17 U.S.C. §1201(a)(3). Because Congress did not explain what it means to "gain access to the work," the district court relied on the "ordinary, customary meaning" of "access": "the ability to enter, to obtain, or to make use of," D. Ct. Op. at 41 (quoting *Merriam-Webster's Collegiate Dictionary* 6 (10th ed. 1999)). Based on this definition, the court concluded that "Lexmark's authentication sequence effectively 'controls access' to the Printer Engine Program because it controls the consumer's ability to *make use of* these programs." D. Ct. Op. at 41 (emphasis added).

We disagree. It is not Lexmark's authentication sequence that "controls access" to the Printer Engine Program. *See* 17 U.S.C. §1201(a)(2). It is the purchase of a Lexmark printer that allows "access" to the program. Anyone who buys a Lexmark printer may read the literal code of the Printer Engine Program directly from the printer memory, with or without the benefit of the authentication sequence, and the data from the program may be translated into readable source code after which copies may be freely distributed. No security device, in other words, protects access to the Printer Engine Program Code and no security device accordingly must be circumvented to obtain access to that program code.

The authentication sequence, it is true, may well block one form of "access"— the "ability to . . . make use of" the Printer Engine Program by preventing the printer from functioning. But it does not block another relevant form of "access"—the "ability to [ ] obtain" a copy of the work or to "make use of" the literal elements of the program (its code). Because the statute refers to "control[ling] access to a work protected under this title," it does not naturally apply when the "work protected under this title" is otherwise accessible. Just as one would not say that a lock on the back door of a house "controls access" to a house whose front door does not contain a lock and just as one would not say that a lock on any door of a house "controls access" to the house after its purchaser receives the key to the lock, it does not make sense to say that this provision of the DMCA applies to otherwise-readily-accessible copyrighted works. Add to this the fact that the DMCA not only requires the technological measure to "control[ ] access" but also requires the measure to control that access "effectively," 17 U.S.C. §1201(a)(2), and it seems clear that this provision does not naturally extend to a technological measure that restricts one form of access but leaves another route wide open. *See also id.*

§1201(a)(3) (technological measure must "*require*[ ] the application of information, or a process or a treatment . . . to gain access to the work") (emphasis added). . . .

In the essential setting where the DMCA applies, the copyright protection operates on two planes: in the literal code governing the work and in the visual or audio manifestation generated by the code's execution. For example, the encoded data on CDs translates into music and on DVDs into motion pictures, while the program commands in software for video games or computers translate into some other visual and audio manifestation. In the cases upon which Lexmark relies, restricting "use" of the work means restricting consumers from making use of the copyrightable expression in the work. *See 321 Studios*, 307 F. Supp. 2d at 1095 (movies contained on DVDs protected by an encryption algorithm cannot be watched without a player that contains an access key); *Reimerdes*, 111 F. Supp. 2d at 303 (same); *Gamemasters*, 87 F. Supp. 2d at 981 (Sony's game console prevented operation of unauthorized video games). As shown above, the DMCA applies in these settings when the product manufacturer prevents all access to the copyrightable material and the alleged infringer responds by marketing a device that circumvents the technological measure designed to guard access to the copyrightable material.

The copyrightable expression in the Printer Engine Program, by contrast, operates on only one plane: in the literal elements of the program, its source and object code. Unlike the code underlying video games or DVDs, "using" or executing the Printer Engine Program does not in turn create any protected expression. Instead, the program's output is purely functional: the Printer Engine Program "controls a number of operations" in the Lexmark printer such as "paper feed[,] paper movement[,] [and] motor control." Lexmark Br. at 9; *cf. Lotus Dev.*, 49 F.3d at 815 (determining that menu command hierarchy is an "uncopyrightable method of operation"). And unlike the code underlying video games or DVDs, no encryption or other technological measure prevents access to the Printer Engine Program. . . .

[The court concluded that the DMCA claim regarding the Toner Loading Program failed for the same reason, and also failed to the extent that the Toner Loading Program was not a work protected under the Copyright Act.]

The district court also rejected SCC's interoperability defense—that its replication of the Toner Loading Program data is a "technological means" that SCC may make "available to others" "solely for the purpose of enabling interoperability of an independently created computer program with other programs." 17 U.S.C. §1201(f)(3). In rejecting this defense, the district court said that "SCC's SMARTEK microchips cannot be considered independently created computer programs. [They] serve no legitimate purpose other than to circumvent Lexmark's authentication sequence and . . . cannot qualify as independently created when they contain exact copies of Lexmark's Toner Loading Programs." D. Ct. Op. ¶94, at 47.

Because the issue could become relevant at the permanent injunction stage of this dispute, we briefly explain our disagreement with this conclusion. In particular, the court did not explain why it rejected SCC's testimony that the SMARTEK chips do contain other functional computer programs beyond the copied Toner Loading Program data. . . .

Also unavailing is Lexmark's final argument that the interoperability defense in §1201(f)(3) does not apply because distributing the SMARTEK chip constitutes infringement and violates other "applicable law" (including tortious interference with prospective economic relations or contractual relations). Because the chip contains only a copy of the thus-far unprotected Toner Loading Program and does not contain a copy of the Printer Engine Program, infringement is not an issue. And Lexmark has offered no independent, let alone persuasive, reason why SCC's SMARTEK chip violates any state tort or other state law. . . .

MERRITT, J., concurring: . . . I write separately to emphasize that our holding should not be limited to the narrow facts surrounding either the Toner Loading Program or the Printer Engine Program. We should make clear that in the future companies like Lexmark cannot use the DMCA in conjunction with copyright law to create monopolies of manufactured goods for themselves just by tweaking the facts of this case: by, for example, creating a Toner Loading Program that is more complex and "creative" than the one here, or by cutting off other access to the Printer Engine Program. The crucial point is that the DMCA forbids anyone from trafficking in any technology that "is primarily designed or produced for the purpose of circumventing a technological measure that effectively controls access to a [protected] work." 17 U.S.C. §1201(2)(A). The key question is the "purpose" of the circumvention technology. The microchip in SCC's toner cartridges is intended not to reap any benefit from the Toner Loading Program—SCC's microchip is not designed to measure toner levels— but only for the purpose of making SCC's competing toner cartridges work with printers manufactured by Lexmark.

. . . If we were to adopt Lexmark's reading of the statute, manufacturers could potentially create monopolies for replacement parts simply by using similar, but more creative, lock-out codes. Automobile manufacturers, for example, could control the entire market of replacement parts for their vehicles by including lock-out chips. Congress did not intend to allow the DMCA to be used offensively in this manner, but rather only sought to reach those who circumvented protective measures "for the purpose" of pirating works protected by the copyright statute. Unless a plaintiff can show that a defendant circumvented protective measures for such a purpose, its claim should not be allowed to go forward. If Lexmark wishes to utilize DMCA protections for (allegedly) copyrightable works, it should not use such works to prevent competing cartridges from working with its printer.

. . . [W]e should be wary of shifting the burden to a rival manufacturer to demonstrate that its conduct falls under such an exception in cases where there is no indication that it has any intention of pirating a protected work. . . . [T]he potential cost of extended litigation and discovery where the burden of proof shifts to the defendant is itself a deterrent to innovation and competition. . . .

AFTERMATH

On remand SCC counterclaimed, alleging that Lexmark had engaged in false or misleading advertising in violation of §43(a) of the Lanham Act. Specifically, SCC alleged that Lexmark purposefully misled end users to believe that they were legally required to return the Prebate cartridges to Lexmark after a single use. The district court ruled that SCC lacked standing to assert the Lanham Act claim. Subsequently, the Supreme Court held that SCC comes within the class of plaintiffs Congress authorized to sue under §43(a). *Lexmark Int'l, Inc. v. Static Control Components, Inc.*, 134 S. Ct. 1377 (2014). As of this writing, the litigation continues.

NOTES AND QUESTIONS

1. The *Lexmark* court holds that §1201(a)(2) does not apply to "otherwise-readily-accessible copyrighted works." What made the Toner Loading Program and the Printer Engine Program readily accessible? Could Lexmark have designed the software differently to eliminate this deficiency in its §1201 claim? If unauthorized copies of a work are readily available on the Internet, does that make the work "otherwise-readily-accessible"?

2. Does the court's explanation of what it means for a technological measure to control access make sense? In a portion of the opinion not reproduced here, the *Lexmark* court acknowledged that §1201(a)(2) liability is not dependent on the "creation of an impervious shield" around the copyrighted work. What factors should a court consider in determining whether a technological measure is effective?

3. Industry practice and consumer expectations influenced the courts' decisions in *Chamberlain* and *Lexmark*. We all expect to be able to use universal garage door openers if we lose our original garage door openers and to be able to purchase off-brand printer cartridges for our computer printers. Can shrink-wrap licenses, EULAs, Terms of Use, or even notices on product packaging shape consumer expectations about what they may do with purchased products? Would the presence of a shrinkwrap license restriction have changed the result in *Chamberlain*? Should Lexmark's "Prebate" business model have changed the result in *Lexmark*?

4. Should a maker of a video game be able to assert a violation of §1201(a)(2) when someone offers a technology that is meant to help game players gain an advantage in gameplay? In *MDY Industries, LLC v. Blizzard Entertainment, Inc.*, 629 F.3d 928 (9th Cir. 2011), MDY developed and sold a software robot (or "bot") called Glider that allowed automated play of early levels of Blizzard's multi-player online role-playing game, World of Warcraft (WoW). Blizzard subsequently developed its own software technology, Warden, to prevent WoW players who use unauthorized bots from connecting to WoW's servers. When Blizzard Entertainment added the Warden component to its multiplayer platform it also changed its

Terms of Use to prohibit the use of bots to play the game. The Ninth Circuit held that distribution of the Glider bot violated §1201(a)(2). Do you agree with that conclusion?

5. Do we all expect to be able to play prerecorded movies using any DVD player we choose? In *Reimerdes*, Section 14.B.2 *supra*, the court addressed a technology that the defendants asserted was distributed to facilitate the creation of a different player on which authorized copies of DVDs could be played. Can the *Chamberlain* or *Lexmark* analysis be applied to the facts of *Reimerdes*? Does the statutory language support using different analyses in the different situations?

6. In the *Reimerdes* case the defendants argued that publication of DeCSS was a necessary step in the development of a DVD player for the Linux operating system. The court rejected that argument, which relied on the exemption contained in §1201(f). Examine again that portion of the *Reimerdes* opinion and the statutory language. Would §1201(f) provide a more satisfactory basis for resolution of the disputes in *Chamberlain* and *Lexmark*? Note that in the 2003 rulemaking on exemptions to the circumvention ban, the Copyright Office rejected a proposal (submitted by SCC) to exempt the circumvention of access controls in printers and toner cartridges. It opined that "an existing exemption in section §1201(f) addresses the concerns of remanufacturers." 68 Fed. Reg. at 62,017. Do you agree? Would reliance on the §1201(f) exemption address Judge Merritt's concerns?

D. PROTECTION FOR COPYRIGHT MANAGEMENT INFORMATION

The DMCA also established legal protection for "copyright management information" (CMI) that is attached to a copy of a work, such as information about the copyright owner and the terms of use. The copyright industries argued that such protection would reduce online infringement by ensuring that those who accessed and used copyrighted works online would have accurate information about the works' copyright status.

Both in Congress and in international negotiations over the WCT, the initial U.S. proposals for protecting CMI would have prohibited, among other things, knowingly removing or altering CMI attached to a work and knowingly providing false CMI. The provision ultimately adopted as Article 12 of the WCT, however, contemplates a closer connection to infringement before a penalty may be imposed. Section 1202 of the Copyright Act, which implements Article 12, was influenced significantly by the international debates about the appropriate scope of protection and tracks the WCT's language. Read WCT art. 12 and §1202 now, and then consider the following cases.

Murphy v. Millennium Radio Group, LLC
650 F.3d 295 (3rd Cir. 2011)

FUENTES, J.: . . .

I.

Background

In 2006, Murphy was hired by the magazine *New Jersey Monthly* ("*NJM*") to take a photo of Craig Carton and Ray Rossi, who at the time were the hosts of a show on the New Jersey radio station WKXW, which is owned by Millennium Radio Group. *NJM* used the photo to illustrate an article in its "Best of New Jersey" issue naming Carton and Rossi "best shock jocks" in the state. The photo ("the Image") depicted Carton and Rossi standing, apparently nude, behind a WKXW sign. Murphy retained the copyright to the Image.

An unknown employee of WKXW then scanned in the Image from *NJM* and posted the resulting electronic copy to the WKXW website and to another website, myspacetv.com. The resulting image, as scanned and posted to the Internet, cut off part of the original *NJM* caption referring to the "Best of New Jersey" award. It also eliminated *NJM's* gutter credit (that is, a credit placed in the inner margin, or "gutter," of a magazine page, ordinarily printed in a smaller type and running perpendicular to the relevant image on the page) identifying Murphy as the author of the Image. The WKXW website invited visitors to alter the Image using photo-manipulation software and submit the resulting versions to WKXW. A number of visitors eventually submitted their versions of the photo to WKXW, and it posted 26 of those submissions to its site. The Station Defendants never received Murphy's permission to make use of the Image. . . .

In April 2008, Murphy sued the Station Defendants for violations of §1202 of the Digital Millennium Copyright Act of 1998 ("DMCA"), [and] copyright infringement. . . .

II.

Discussion

A. DMCA claim

Murphy argues that, by reproducing the Image on the two websites without the *NJM* credit identifying him as the author, the Station Defendants violated the Digital Millennium Copyright Act. . . .

Murphy's argument is straightforward. He contends that the *NJM* gutter credit identifying him as the author of the Image is CMI because it is "the name of . . . the author of [the Image]" and was "conveyed in connection with copies of [the Image]." By posting the Image on the two websites without the credit, therefore, the Station Defendants "remove[d] or alter[ed]" CMI and "distribute [d]" a work knowing that its CMI had been "removed or altered" in violation of §1202.

The Station Defendants, on the other hand, insist that one cannot read §1202 in isolation, but must interpret it in conjunction with §1201 and in light of the legislative history of the DMCA to impose an additional limitation on the definition of CMI. They argue that the chapter as a whole protects various kinds of automated systems which protect and manage copyrights. Specifically, §1201 covers the systems . . . that *protect* copyrighted materials and §1202 covers the systems that *manage* copyrighted materials (such as the name of the author of a work). Therefore, they conclude, despite the apparently plain language of §1202, information like the name of the author of a work is not CMI unless it also functions as part of an "automated copyright protection or management system." In other words, to remove, as the Station Defendants did, a printed credit from a magazine photograph which was then posted to a website does not violate §1202, because the credit, although apparently meeting the definition of §1202(c)(2), was not part of an "automated copyright protection or management system." They claim that both the legislative history of the DMCA and the language of the World Intellectual Property Organization treaties which the DMCA implemented support such a reading. Viewed thus, the Station Defendants argue, §1202 will be seen not to apply to Murphy's name as it appeared in the gutter credit near the Image.

We are not aware of any other federal appellate courts which have considered whether the definition of "copyright management information" should be restricted to the context of "automated copyright protection or management systems." We begin, as we must, with the text of §1202. . . .

There is nothing particularly difficult about the text of §1202. Even the Station Defendants, and the courts whose decisions they cite, do not contend that §1202 is, in itself, ambiguous or unclear. Read in isolation, §1202 simply establishes a cause of action for the removal of (among other things) the name of the author of a work when it has been "conveyed in connection with copies of" the work. The statute imposes no explicit requirement that such information be part of an "automated copyright protection or management system," as the Station Defendants claim. In fact, it appears to be extremely broad, with no restrictions on the context in which such information must be used in order to qualify as CMI. If there is a difficulty here, it is a problem of policy, not of logic. Such an interpretation might well provide an additional cause of action under the DMCA in many circumstances in which only an action for copyright infringement could have been brought previously. Whether or not this result is desirable, it is not *absurd,* as might compel us to make a more restrictive reading of §1202's scope.

The Station Defendants argue that to read §1202 by itself is to take too narrow a view of the "plain language" of the statutory text. When interpreting statutory language, we must examine the statute as a whole, rather than considering provisions in isolation. However, nothing in §1201, the provision regarding circumvention of "technological measures" . . . to which the Station Defendants point most insistently, restricts the meaning of CMI in §1202 to information contained in "automated copyright protection or management systems." Section 1201 does not mention "copyright management information"; in fact, it does not refer to §1202 at all. Neither does it contain the phrase "automated copyright protection or management systems." Similarly, §1202 does not refer to §1201, and the definition of CMI is located squarely in §1202.

If, in fact, §1201 and §1202 were meant to have such interrelated interpretations, it is peculiar that there is no explicit indication of this in the text of either provision. Instead, to all appearances, §1201 and §1202 establish independent causes of action which arise from different conduct on the part of defendants, albeit with similar civil remedies and criminal penalties. It may strike some as more intellectually harmonious to interpret the prohibition of removal of CMI in §1202 as restricted to the context of §1201, but nothing in the text of §1201 actually dictates that it should be taken to limit the meaning of "copyright management information."

As for the purpose of the statute as a whole, it is undisputed that the DMCA was intended to expand—in some cases, as discussed above, significantly—the rights of copyright owners. The parties here differ only as to their conclusions regarding the *extent* to which the DMCA expanded those rights. Murphy's definition of CMI provides for a significantly broader cause of action than the Station Defendants' does. However, the Station Defendants can point to nothing in the statute as a whole which compels the adoption of their reading instead of Murphy's. In short, considering the purpose of the statute does not provide us with meaningful guidance in this case.

. . . [I]n accordance with *In re Philadelphia Newspapers,* we must look to the legislative history of the DMCA only for that "extraordinary showing of contrary intentions" which would justify rejecting a straightforward reading of §1202. 599 F. 3d [298, 314 (3d Cir. 2010)]. The Station Defendants rely on the survey of the legislative history undertaken by the courts in *IQ Group v. Wiesner Pub., LLC,* 409 F. Supp. 2d 587 (D.N.J.2006) and *Textile Secrets Int'l, Inc. v. Ya–Ya Brand, Inc.,* 524 F. Supp. 2d. 1184, 1198 (C.D.Cal.2007). The *IQ Group* decision placed most emphasis on a "white paper" of the working group of the Information Infrastructure Task Force (IITF), the organization that produced the first draft of §§1201 and 1202. This white paper reported that

> [a] combination of file- and system-based access controls using encryption technologies, digital signatures and steganography are . . . employed by owners of works to address copyright management concerns. . . . To implement these rights management functions, information will likely be included in digital versions of a work (i.e., *copyright management information*) to inform the user about the authorship and ownership of a work. . . .

409 F. Supp. 2d at 594 (emphasis added). Thus, the *IQ Group* court concluded, the paper "understood 'copyright management information' to be information . . . that is included in digital versions of the work so as to implement 'rights management functions' of 'rights management systems.'" *Id.* at 595. And, as the text of §1202 was not altered before its adoption by Congress, the court found that this gave a clear indication of Congressional intent. *Id.* at 594-95. Additionally, the Senate Committee Report to §[1202] describes CMI as including "such items as the title of the work, the author . . . CMI need not be in digital form, but CMI in digital form is expressly included." *Id.* at 596.

The *Textile Secrets* court also looked to the [WIPO] treaties that the DMCA was intended to implement. The WIPO treaties use a term "rights management information" and define it as "information which identifies the work, the author of the work . . . when any of these items of information is attached to a copy of a work or appears in connection with the communication of a work to the public." They require that parties to the treaties provide adequate remedies against the "remov[al] or alter[ation of] any *electronic* rights management information without authority."

> ### KEEP IN MIND
>
> United States ratification of a treaty does not give copyright owners a private cause of action based on the treaty's provisions. Any cause of action must be grounded in the domestic legislation implementing the treaty. And while international copyright treaties typically establish a "floor" of minimum obligations, countries are free, in their domestic legislation, to expand upon those minimum obligations.

The *Textile Secrets* court concluded that "electronic rights management information" as used in the WIPO treaties and "copyright management information" as used in §1202 must be coterminous in meaning. 524 F. Supp. 2d at 1198. Therefore, it found, "copyright management information" must be electronic. *Id.*

. . . [I]n the end, the strongest case which the Station Defendants can make is that the legislative history of the DMCA is *consistent* with its interpretation, not that it actually *contradicts* the reading advocated by Murphy. The IITF white paper describes CMI as "information [that] will likely be included in digital versions of a work . . . to inform the user about the authorship and ownership of a work." *IQ Group*, 409 F. Supp. 2d at 594. This description leaves the question of just how that information will be included—that is, whether it *must* be used in some form of "an automated copyright protection or management system" or whether it can be conveyed by other means—entirely open.

Similarly, the WIPO treaties' definition of "electronic rights management information" is "information [that] will likely be included in digital versions of a work . . . to inform the user about the authorship and ownership of a work." Although this definition occurs in the context of a broader discussion of systems that control access to copyrighted works, it does not require that "electronic rights management information" be embedded in such systems. In addition, neither the WIPO treaties nor the DMCA indicate the precise relationship between the concepts of CMI and "electronic rights management information" as discussed in the treaties. The Station Defendants argue that their meanings must be identical, but Congress was certainly free, in implementing the WIPO treaties, to define "copyright management information" more broadly than "electronic rights management information."

Thus, while it is possible to read the legislative history to support the Station Defendants' interpretation of CMI, that history does not provide the "extraordinary showing of contrary intentions" which would compel us to disregard the plain language of the statute. This is especially so because the Station Defendants are essentially asking us to rewrite §1202 to insert a term—that is, "automated copyright protection or management system"—which appears nowhere in the text of the DMCA and which lacks a clear definition. We would need compelling justification indeed to adopt such a statutorily unmoored interpretation.

Therefore, we find that CMI, as defined in §1202(c), is *not* restricted to the context of "automated copyright protection or management systems." Rather, a cause of action under §1202 of the DMCA potentially lies whenever the types of information listed in §1202(c)(1)–(8) and "conveyed in connection with copies . . . of a work . . . including in digital form" is falsified or removed, regardless of the form in which that information is conveyed. In this case, the mere fact that Murphy's name appeared in a printed gutter credit near the Image rather than as data in an "automated copyright protection or management system" does not prevent it from qualifying as CMI or remove it from the protection of §1202. . . .

[The court vacated the district court's grant of summary judgment in favor of the Station defendants on the §1202 claim, as well as on the copyright infringement claim and the defendants' fair use defense.]

Kelly v. Arriba Soft Corp.
77 F. Supp. 2d 1116 (C.D. Cal. 1999), aff'd in part and rev'd in part on other grounds, 336 F.3d 811 (9th Cir. 2003)

[Arriba Soft, an image search engine, linked to a website containing Kelly's copyrighted photographs and created "thumbnail" images of the photographs to display as search results. Users who clicked on a thumbnail would see the full-size image via a direct link to Kelly's site, but Arriba framed the full-size images with its own content. Applying a test later identified as the "display" test (see Note 1, Chapter 6.B.1.d, *supra*), the Ninth Circuit initially held that Arriba Soft had infringed Kelly's exclusive right of public display. *Kelly v. Arriba Soft Corp.*, 280 F.3d 934, 947 (9th Cir. 2002). On a motion for rehearing, however, the court withdrew that portion of its opinion, stating that it should "not be cited as precedent." The court ruled that Arriba Soft's creation of the thumbnail images was fair use. *Kelly v. Arriba Soft Corp.*, 336 F.3d 811, 815 (9th Cir. 2003). Kelly also asserted a claim for violation of §1202. That portion of the court's opinion follows.]

TAYLOR, J.: . . . Defendant Ditto (formerly known as Arriba) operates a "visual search engine" on the Internet. . . .

During the period when most of the relevant events in this case occurred, Defendant's visual search engine was known as the Arriba Vista Image Searcher. By "clicking" on the desired thumbnail, an Arriba Vista user could view the "image attributes" window displaying the full-size version of the image, a description of its dimensions, and an address for the Web site where it originated.[1] By clicking on the address, the user could link to the originating Web site for the image.[2]

---

1. This full-size image was not technically located on Defendant's Web site. It was displayed by opening a link to its originating Web page. But only the image itself, and not any other part of the originating Web page, was displayed on the image attributes page. From the user's perspective, the source of the image matters less than the context in which it is displayed.

2. Defendant's current search engine, ditto.com, operates in a slightly different manner. When a ditto.com user clicks on a thumbnail, two windows open simultaneously. One window contains the full-size image; the other contains the originating Web page in full.

Ditto's search engine . . . works by maintaining an indexed database of approximately two million thumbnail images. These thumbnails are obtained through the operation of Ditto's "crawler,"—a computer program that travels the Web in search of images to be converted into thumbnails and added to the index. Ditto's employees conduct a final screening to rank the most relevant thumbnails and eliminate inappropriate images.

Plaintiff Kelly is a photographer specializing in photographs of California gold rush country and related to the works of Laura Ingalls Wilder. . . . Plaintiff . . . maintains two Web sites, one of which . . . provides a "virtual tour" of California's gold rush country and promotes Plaintiff's book on the subject, and the other . . . markets corporate retreats in California's gold rush country.

In January 1999, around thirty five of Plaintiff's images were indexed by the Ditto crawler and put in Defendant's image database. As a result, these images were made available in thumbnail form to users of Defendant's visual search engine.

After being notified of Plaintiff's objections, Ditto removed the images from its database. . . . Meanwhile Plaintiff, having sent Defendant a notice of copyright infringement in January, filed this action in April. Plaintiff argues its copyrights in the images were infringed by Defendant's actions and also alleges Defendant violated the Digital Millennium Copyright Act (DMCA) by removing or altering the copyright management information associated with Plaintiff's images. . . .

Plaintiff argues Defendant violated §1202(b) by displaying thumbnails of Plaintiff's images without displaying the corresponding copyright management information consisting of standard copyright notices in the surrounding text. Because these notices do not appear in the images themselves, the Ditto crawler did not include them when it indexed the images. As a result, the images appeared in Defendant's index without the copyright management information, and any users retrieving Plaintiff's images while using Defendant's Web site would not see the copyright management information.

Section 1202(b)(1) does not apply to this case. Based on the language and structure of the statute, the Court holds this provision applies only to the removal of copyright management information on a plaintiff's product or original work. Moreover, even if §1202(b)(1) applied, Plaintiff has not offered any evidence showing Defendant's actions were intentional, rather than merely an unintended side effect of the Ditto crawler's operation.

Here, where the issue is the absence of copyright management information from *copies* of Plaintiff's works, the applicable provision is §1202(b)(3). To show a violation of that section, Plaintiff must show Defendant makes available to its users the thumbnails and full-size images, which were copies of Plaintiff's work separated from their copyright management information, even though it knows or should know this will lead to infringement of Plaintiff's copyrights. There is no dispute the Ditto crawler removed Plaintiff's images from the context of Plaintiff's Web sites where their copyright management information was located, and converted them to thumbnails in Defendant's index. There is also no dispute the Arriba Vista search engine allowed full-size images to be viewed without their copyright management information.

Defendant's users could obtain a full-sized version of a thumbnailed image by clicking on the thumbnail. A user who did this was given the name of the Web site from which Defendant obtained the image, where any associated copyright management information would be available, and an opportunity to link there.[12] . . .

Based on all of this, the Court finds Defendant did not have "reasonable grounds to know" it would cause its users to infringe Plaintiff's copyrights. Defendant warns its users about the possibility of use restrictions on the images in its index, and instructs them to check with the originating Web sites before copying and using those images, even in reduced thumbnail form.

Plaintiff's images are vulnerable to copyright infringement because they are displayed on Web sites. Plaintiff has not shown users of Defendant's site were any more likely to infringe his copyrights, any of these users did infringe, or Defendant should reasonably have expected infringement. . . .

NOTES AND QUESTIONS

1. Do you agree with the *Murphy* court that there is no basis in the language of §1202 for a narrower interpretation that would align the provision's coverage with that of §1201? If, as the court observed, the different interpretations offered by the parties were both consistent with the legislative history of the DMCA, is the plain meaning rule the best interpretive tool for determining the scope of §1202? Many defendants in copyright infringement cases remove identifying information. The *Murphy* court's interpretation, which reflects the prevailing view, opens the door to §1202 claims in all those cases. In your opinion, is that the right result?

2. Do you agree with the *Kelly* court that Arriba Soft did all that it needed to do to protect the plaintiff's copyright management information? How do you think the plaintiff wanted §1202(b)(3) interpreted? What kind of obligation to protect CMI should be imposed on defendants like Arriba Soft?

3. Under the *Kelly* court's interpretation of §1202(b)(3), what kind of evidence would you need to establish the requisite *mens rea*? What constitutes "reasonable grounds to know" about infringement? What kinds of allegations would be needed to overcome a motion to dismiss a §1202(b) claim on Rule 12(b)(6) grounds? *See, e.g., Leveyfilm, Inc. v. Fox Sports Interactive Media, LLC,* 999 F. Supp. 2d 1098, 1103 (N.D. Ill. 2014) (discussing this question).

4. The combined effect of anticircumvention laws and CMI protection has important implications for users' liberty interests. In 1996, Prof. Julie Cohen observed that "some copyright owners may use the transaction records generated by their copyright management systems to learn more about their customers through a process known as 'profiling,'" and argued that "[t]ogether [§1201 and §1202] authorize copyright owners to implement the full range of 'smart' copyright management technologies . . . and prevent readers from taking measures

___

12. Through Defendant's current search engine, ditto.com, the user can no longer open a full-sized image without also opening the site where its copyright management information is located.

to protect themselves against intrusive monitoring of their activities." Julie E. Cohen, *A Right to Read Anonymously: A Closer Look at "Copyright Management" in Cyberspace,* 28 Conn. L. Rev. 981, 985, 990 (1996). Just how much information should copyright owners be entitled to collect regarding users' activities? Read §1201(i). Would that provision allow the user of a work to employ technological means to prevent the collection of personal information by a copyright owner?

PRACTICE EXERCISES

Which of the following constitute a violation of §1202 under the reasoning in *Murphy*?

1. An author decides to make her work available under a Creative Commons license. She "attaches" the license to the work by embedding code that will generate the license symbol, a short description of the license, and a hyperlink to the full license. Samantha downloads the work, removes the information, and posts the work on her website. Does it matter which Creative Commons license the author selected? (Review the descriptions of the various Creative Commons licenses, Chapter 12.C.2, *supra.*)
2. To discourage online news aggregators from linking to its articles and framing the articles with their own advertisements, Bulletin Co. attaches metadata to each article that specify ownership information and usage rights. According to the metadata, in-line linking and framing are prohibited without a license from Bulletin Co. The *Daily Times*, an online news aggregator, continues its preexisting practice of linking to and framing occasional Bulletin Co. articles. The *Daily Times* leaves the metadata undisturbed.
3. The publisher of a newspaper removes the copyright notice affixed on the articles it accepts for publication from freelance journalists (*see* Question 2, Chapter 12.A.3, *supra*).

E. THE DEBATE OVER DIGITAL TELEVISION

Technological protection for broadcast and cable content is an especially complex topic for a number of reasons. First, as you have already learned, some view the Supreme Court's *Sony* decision, and Congress' refusal to overrule it, as having created a relatively stable set of fair use entitlements with respect to such content. Second, the debate over technological control of broadcast and cable content involves an additional government entity – the Federal Communications Commission (FCC). The FCC regulates under the authority expressly granted by Congress and under its more amorphous ancillary jurisdiction to regulate in covered subject matter areas in order to perform its statutory responsibilities effectively. The FCC generally has regulated consumer electronic technologies only when Congress has expressly authorized it to do so (as in the case of the so-called V-chip, which enables television owners to filter incoming programming based on encoded content ratings). It has, however, from time to time invoked its ancillary jurisdiction to address technological questions that it views as affecting its core statutory mandates. Third, the means by which consumers obtain video content have been changing rapidly in recent years. While many consumers receive video content via cable or satellite subscriptions, increasing numbers have "cut the cord" and watch audiovisual content via the Internet, streaming it from sites like Hulu or Netflix, using devices ranging from computers and iPads to Blu-Ray players and televisions with built-in Internet browsers. The sheer speed of technological change has outpaced a number of policy proposals and actions originally intended to address issues associated with digital television (DTV) distributed by broadcast networks and cable and satellite providers.

Early in the development of DTV, the FCC asserted jurisdiction over the DTV standards development process to coordinate development of a single, commonly accepted standard, and promulgated rules to phase in digital-only broadcasts and equipment. At the same time, the copyright industries argued that DTV equipment needed to include technological content controls so that digital content, and especially high-definition content, could not be broadcast "in the clear" (i.e., unrestricted) into millions of homes. They asserted that without such technological protection, they would be unwilling to provide content in digital formats. Consumer electronics companies feared that technological protection would make expensive DTV equipment even less attractive to consumers, but worried they might be judged facilitators of widespread copyright infringement in its absence. Eventually, the FCC issued an order requiring use of a technical protection protocol called a "broadcast flag" based in part on an industry proposal. The broadcast flag would have provided some protection against redistribution, but in *American Library Ass'n v. FCC,* 406 F.3d 689 (D.C. Cir. 2005), the court held the FCC lacked jurisdiction to issue the order. In 2009, the FCC-supervised transition to DTV was completed without a broadcast flag component in place.

A number of private sector efforts to develop protection measures that would apply from the content's source all the way through to the device ultimately receiving the signal are ongoing. *See, e.g.,* http://www.digital-cp.com/ (last visited Dec. 26, 2014) (describing the "High-bandwidth Digital Content Protection system and listing its adopters); www.dtcp.com (last visited Dec. 26, 2014) (discussing the "Digital Transmission Content Protection" system and describing it as widely adopted . . . in consumer electronics products from set top boxes and [DTVs] to Blu-Ray and DVD recorders; in voluntary standards groups; by a spectrum of cable, satellite, and media services; and over a variety of wireless and wired interfaces"); support.apple.com/en-us/HT201310 (last visited Dec. 26, 2014) (explaining that "Apple TV supports [the High-bandwidth Digital Content Protection copy protection standard] but all devices in the HDMI connection, including the TV, must also support this digital copy protection for successful video playback"). Concerns over lack of compatibility between and across systems and standards remain.

Unlike broadcast programming, cable and satellite programming are encrypted at the source and decrypted, or demodulated, by the "set-top box" furnished by the provider. In DMCA parlance, this system restricts access to programming to paid subscribers. With appropriate standards coordination, DTV technology could eliminate the need for a set-top box from the user's cable provider, allowing viewers to plug their DTV receivers directly into their cable systems. This would enable users to access all of the provider's cable and broadcast programming channels using a single remote control, and to use their DVR or equivalent device with most channels. The FCC viewed this so-called plug and play capability as important to smoothing the transition to DTV and encouraging innovation in the design of delivery devices. Therefore, with input from industry, the FCC promulgated a "cable plug and play" rule in 2003. In *Echostar Satellite LLC v. FCC*, 704 F.3d 992 (D.C. Cir. 2013), however, the court held that the FCC lacked statutory authority to issue the rule, and vacated it in its entirety. Regardless, by the time of *Echostar*, the FCC's attempt to establish a universal cable plug and play standard was widely acknowledged a failure, because it did not support two-way features required by increasingly popular video-on-demand services. Cable providers designed their set-top boxes to incorporate those features, again raising compatibility issues.

NOTES AND QUESTIONS

1. Jurisdictional questions aside, is government oversight of technological measures to protect video content desirable? For different perspectives on that question, see generally Susan P. Crawford, *The Biology of the Broadcast Flag*, 25 Hastings Comm. & Ent. L.J. 559 (2004), and Molly Shaffer Van Houweling, *Communications' Copyright Policy*, 4 J. Telecomm. & High Tech. L. 97 (2005). What are the pros and cons of leaving development of technological protection standards to private industry?

2. Would you support an audio broadcast flag requirement for digital radio? Are the policy considerations identical for video and audio digital content?

15

State Law Theories of Protection and Their Limits

Positioning the Copyright Act within the system of laws that bear on copyright law's subject matter and policy goals is no simple task. In this chapter, we focus primarily on the relationship between copyright law and state law causes of action that relate to copyrighted works. In some circumstances, federal copyright law and policy will preempt state law. We begin by introducing the two kinds of preemption analysis that may be relevant in copyright cases and then explore some topics that have raised particularly difficult preemption problems.

A. FEDERAL INTELLECTUAL PROPERTY PREEMPTION: AN OVERVIEW

1. Introduction to Preemption

Article VI, cl. 2 of the Constitution states:

> This Constitution, and the Laws of the United States which shall be made in pursuance thereof; and all Treaties made, or which shall be made, under the Authority of the United States, shall be the supreme Law of the Land; and the Judges in every State shall be bound thereby, any Thing in the Constitution or Laws of any State to the contrary notwithstanding.

This provision, known as the Supremacy Clause, sets forth the general principle that governs conflicts between state and federal law: Federal law is supreme and will override—or "preempt"—inconsistent state law. The Supreme Court, in turn, has developed a set of interpretive rules to determine when that principle is implicated both generally and in the specific context of intellectual property.

There are three types of federal preemption. First, a federal law may expressly preempt particular state laws or causes of action. Thus, the starting reference point for determining whether a law has preemptive effect is the text of the federal statute. The Copyright Act contains an express preemption provision that prohibits state law claims concerning subject matter "within the general scope of copyright" that are "equivalent to" copyright infringement claims. 17 U.S.C. §301(a). The federal Patent Act, in contrast, contains no such express language.

The second and third types of preemption are implied from a federal statute's scope, purpose, and legislative history. One type of implied preemption, known as "occupation of the field," occurs when federal law completely excludes the states from acting in the covered area. Congressional intent to exclude the states entirely from a particular field "may be inferred from a 'scheme of federal regulation . . . so pervasive as to make reasonable the inference that Congress left no room for the States to supplement it,' or where an Act of Congress 'touch[es] a field in which the federal interest is so dominant that the federal system will be assumed to preclude enforcement of state laws on the same subject.'" *English v. Gen. Elec. Co.*, 496 U.S. 72, 79 (1990) (quoting *Rice v. Santa Fe Elevator Corp.*, 331 U.S. 218, 230 (1947)). An example of this sort of preemption is found in the federal statutes that regulate public safety and health issues relating to nuclear power. *Pacific Gas & Electric Co. v. State Energy Res. Conservation & Dev. Comm'n*, 461 U.S. 190, 205-13 (1983).

Another type of implied preemption, often called "conflict preemption," is narrower. Even when federal law has not completely occupied the covered field, particular state enactments or common law claims for relief may nonetheless conflict with the purpose of the federal statutory scheme. In such cases, the state law will be preempted to the extent of the conflict. For example, in *Geier v. American Honda Motor Co.*, 529 U.S. 861 (2000), the Supreme Court held a state tort action alleging negligent failure to equip a car with a driver's side airbag preempted because it conflicted with federal regulations governing the implementation of airbags and other passive restraints. To determine whether a particular state law or cause of action creates an unacceptable conflict with a federal statutory scheme, courts must inquire whether the state law "stands as an obstacle to the accomplishment and execution of the full purposes and objectives of Congress." *Hines v. Davidowitz*, 312 U.S. 52, 67 (1941).

To complicate matters further, express and implied preemption may coexist in the same statute. A federal statute containing an express preemption provision that covers some state laws may also impliedly preempt other state laws. The express provision establishes an inference that Congress did not intend the statute to have broader preemptive effect, but that inference may be overcome by other evidence of congressional intent. *See Geier*, 529 U.S. at 869-74 ("[T]he principles underlying this Court's preemption doctrine . . . make clear that the express preemption provision imposes no unusual, 'special burden' against [implied] pre-emption."); *Freightliner Corp. v. Myrick*, 514 U.S. 280, 288 (1995). The significance of this rule for our purposes is that the presence of an express preemption provision in the Copyright Act does not necessarily exhaust the possibilities for federal copyright preemption.

Although preemption usually refers to displacement of state law by federal statutory law, a species of preemption also can be accomplished by federal constitutional provisions. The varieties of constitutional preemption parallel those already discussed. Thus, for example, Art. I, §10, which forbids the states from making treaties, expressly excludes the states from the field of foreign relations; the Commerce Clause, Art. I, §8, cl. 3, which gives Congress the power to regulate interstate and foreign commerce, impliedly excludes the states from regulating in those fields; the Fourteenth Amendment expressly forbids the states from taking actions that conflict with the federal principles of due process and equal protection; and the Due Process Clause of the Fourteenth Amendment impliedly forbids the states from taking actions that conflict with the federal principles set forth in the Bill of Rights. The extent to which implied preemption of state law flows from the Intellectual Property Clause itself, rather than from the Patent Act or the Copyright Act, is an unresolved question.

Finally, preemptive effects flowing from the language of constitutional provisions also can constrain Congress from acting in particular ways. For example, the Bankruptcy Clause, Art. I, §8, cl. 4, which requires that federal bankruptcy legislation be uniform, prohibits Congress from enacting individualized grants of bankruptcy relief. The extent to which the language of the Intellectual Property Clause constrains Congress in its exercise of the more general commerce power also is unresolved.

> **LOOKING BACK**
>
> Recall *U.S. v. Martignon*, which you read in Chapter 8.B.1. That case addressed whether Congress could protect certain unfixed works and criminalize bootleg recordings under the Commerce Clause when it could not do so under the Intellectual Property Clause.

2. Intellectual Property and Implied Preemption

In 1964, the Supreme Court decided two patent preemption cases: *Sears, Roebuck & Co. v. Stiffel Co.*, 376 U.S. 225 (1964), and *Compco Corp. v. Day-Brite Lighting, Inc.*, 376 U.S. 234 (1964). Both cases held that the states may not use unfair competition law to prohibit the copying of items failing to meet the standards for patent protection (both cases involved lighting fixtures). The opinions suggested that intellectual property law cuts a broad preemptive swath through state law. According to the *Compco* Court:

> [W]hen an article is unprotected by a patent or a copyright, state law may not forbid others to copy that article. To forbid copying would interfere with the federal policy, found in Art. I, §8, cl. 8 of the Constitution and in the implementing federal statutes, of allowing free access to copy whatever the patent and copyright laws leave in the public domain.

Compco, 476 U.S. at 237.

With this precedent in the background, the Court, in the following case, addressed a claim that the 1909 Copyright Act preempted state regulation of sound recordings. (Unlike the 1976 Act, the 1909 Act did not contain an express preemption provision.)

≣ *Goldstein v. California*
412 U.S. 546 (1972)

BURGER, C.J.: . . .

Petitioners were engaged in what has commonly been called "record piracy" or "tape piracy"—the unauthorized duplication of recordings of performances by major musical artists. Petitioners would purchase from a retail distributor a single tape or phonograph recording of the popular performances they wished to duplicate. . . . At petitioners' plant, the recording was reproduced on blank tapes. . . . The tape was then wound on a cartridge. A label was attached, stating the title of the recorded performance—the same title as had appeared on the original recording, and the name of the performing artists. After final packaging, the tapes were distributed to retail outlets for sale to the public. . . .

The challenged California statute [§653h of the California Penal Code] forbids petitioners to transfer any performance fixed on a tape or record onto other records or tapes with the intention of selling the duplicates, unless they have first received permission from those who, under state law, are the owners of the master recording. Although the protection afforded to each master recording is substantial, lasting for an unlimited time, the scope of the proscribed activities is narrow. No limitation is placed on the use of the music, lyrics, or arrangement employed in making the master recording. Petitioners are not precluded from hiring their own musicians and artists and recording an exact imitation of the performance embodied on the master recording. Petitioners are even free to hire the same artists who made the initial recording in order to duplicate the performance. In essence, the statute thus provides copyright protection solely for the specific expressions which compose the master record or tape.

Petitioners' attack on the constitutionality of §653h has many facets. First, they contend that the statute establishes a state copyright of unlimited duration, and thus conflicts with Art. I, §8, cl. 8, of the Constitution. Second, petitioners claim that the state statute interferes with the implementation of federal policies inherent in the federal copyright statutes. 17 U.S.C. §1 et seq. According to petitioners, it was the intention of Congress, as interpreted by this Court in *Sears, Roebuck & Co. v. Stiffel Co.*, 376 U.S. 225 (1964), and *Compco Corp. v. Day-Brite Lighting*, 376 U.S. 234 (1964), to establish a uniform law throughout the United States to protect original writings. As part of the federal scheme, it is urged that Congress intended to allow individuals to copy any work which was not protected by a federal copyright. Since §653h effectively prohibits the copying of works which are not entitled to federal protection, petitioners contend that it conflicts directly with congressional policy and must fall under the Supremacy Clause of the Constitution. . . .

II . . .

A

. . . The clause of the Constitution granting to Congress the power to issue copyrights does not provide that such power shall vest exclusively in the Federal

Government. Nor does the Constitution expressly provide that such power shall not be exercised by the States. . . .

The question whether exclusive federal power must be inferred is not a simple one, for the powers recognized in the Constitution are broad and the nature of their application varied. . . .

The objective of the Copyright Clause was clearly to facilitate the granting of rights national in scope. While the debates on the clause at the Constitutional Convention were extremely limited, its purpose was described by James Madison in the Federalist:

> The utility of this power will scarcely be questioned. The copyright of authors has been solemnly adjudged, in Great Britain, to be a right of common law. The right to useful inventions seems with equal reason to belong to the inventors. The public good fully coincides in both cases with the claims of individuals. The States cannot separately make effectual provision for either of the cases, and most of them have anticipated the decision of this point, by laws passed at the instance of Congress.

The difficulty noted by Madison relates to the burden placed on an author or inventor who wishes to achieve protection in all States when no federal system of protection is available. To do so, a separate application is required to each state government; the right which in turn may be granted has effect only within the granting State's borders. The national system which Madison supported eliminates the need for multiple applications and the expense and difficulty involved. In effect, it allows Congress to provide a reward greater in scope than any particular State may grant to promote progress in those fields which Congress determines are worthy of national action.

Although the Copyright Clause recognizes the potential benefits of a national system, it does not indicate that all writings are of national interest or that state legislation is, in all cases, unnecessary or precluded. The patents granted by the States in the 18th century show, to the contrary, a willingness on the part of the States to promote those portions of science and the arts which were of local importance. Whatever the diversity of people's backgrounds, origins, and interests, and whatever the variety of business and industry in the 13 Colonies, the range of diversity is obviously far greater today in a country of 210 million people in 50 States. In view of that enormous diversity, it is unlikely that all citizens in all parts of the country place the same importance on works relating to all subjects. Since the subject matter to which the Copyright Clause is addressed may thus be of purely local importance and not worthy of national attention or protection, we cannot discern such an unyielding national interest as to require an inference that state power to grant copyright has been relinquished to exclusive federal control.

. . . [I]n the case of state copyrights, except as to individuals willing to travel across state lines in order to purchase records or other writings protected in their own State, each State's copyrights will still serve to induce new artistic creations within that State—the very objective of the grant of protection. . . .

Similarly, it is difficult to see how the concurrent exercise of the power to grant copyrights by Congress and the States will necessarily and inevitably lead to difficulty. At any time Congress determines that a particular category of "writing" is worthy of national protection and the incidental expense of federal administration, federal copyright protection may be authorized. Where the need for free and unrestricted distribution of a writing is thought to be required by the national interest, the Copyright Clause and the Commerce Clause would allow Congress to eschew all protection. In such cases, a conflict would develop if a State attempted to protect that which Congress intended to be free from restraint or to free that which Congress had protected. However, where Congress determines that neither federal protection nor freedom from restraint is required by the national interest, it is at liberty to stay its hand entirely. Since state protection would not then conflict with federal action, total relinquishment of the States' power to grant copyright protection cannot be inferred. . . .

III

Our conclusion that California did not surrender its power to issue copyrights does not end the inquiry. We must proceed to determine whether the challenged state statute is void under the Supremacy Clause. . . .

While the area in which Congress *may* act is broad, the enabling provision of [the Intellectual Property Clause] does not require that Congress act in regard to all categories of materials which meet the constitutional definitions. Rather, whether any specific category of "Writings" is to be brought within the purview of the federal statutory scheme is left to the discretion of the Congress. The history of federal copyright statutes indicates that the congressional determination to consider specific classes of writings is dependent, not only on the character of the writing, but also on the commercial importance of the product to the national economy. . . .

. . . According to petitioners, Congress addressed the question of whether recordings of performances should be granted protection in 1909; Congress determined that any individual who was entitled to a copyright on an original musical composition should have the right to control to a limited extent the use of that composition on recordings, but that the record itself, and the performance which it was capable of reproducing were not worthy of such protection. . . . [The Court rejected this argument, noting that when Congress granted composers a right to remuneration for "mechanical" reproductions of their works, it was focusing solely on rights in musical compositions and did not "consider[ ] records as anything but a component part of a machine."]

[Petitioners also] argue that Congress so occupied the field of copyright protection as to pre-empt all comparable state action. . . .

Sears and *Compco*, on which petitioners rely, do not support their position. In those cases, the question was whether a State could, under principles of a state unfair competition law, preclude the copying of mechanical configurations which did not possess the qualities required for the granting of a federal design or mechanical patent. The Court stated:

> [T]he patent system is one in which uniform federal standards are carefully used to promote invention while at the same time preserving free competition. Obviously a State could not, consistently with the Supremacy Clause of the Constitution, extend

the life of a patent beyond its expiration date or give a patent on an article which lacked the level of invention required for federal patents. To do either would run counter to the policy of Congress of granting patents only to true inventions, and then only for a limited time. Just as a State cannot encroach upon the federal patent laws directly, it cannot, under some other law, such as that forbidding unfair competition, give protection of a kind that clashes with the objective of the federal patent laws.

Sears, Roebuck & Co. v. Stiffel Co., 376 U.S., at 230—231 (footnotes omitted).

In regard to mechanical configurations, Congress had balanced the need to encourage innovation and originality of invention against the need to insure competition in the sale of identical or substantially identical products. The standards established for granting federal patent protection to machines thus indicated not only which articles in this particular category Congress wished to protect, but which configurations it wished to remain free. The application of state law in these cases to prevent the copying of articles which did not meet the requirements for federal protection disturbed the careful balance which Congress had drawn and thereby necessarily gave way under the Supremacy Clause. No comparable conflict between state law and federal law arises in the case of recordings of musical performances. In regard to this category of "Writings," Congress has drawn no balance; rather, it has left the area unattended, and no reason exists why the State should not be free to act. . . .

DOUGLAS, J., dissenting. . . .

An unpatentable article is "in the public domain and may be made and sold by whoever chooses to do so." [*Sears*], at 231. In that case we did not allow a State to use its unfair competition law to prevent copying of an article which lacked such novelty that it could not be patented. In a companion case, *Compco Corp. v. Day-Brite Lighting*, 376 U.S. 234, 237, where an unfair competition charge was made under state law, we made the same ruling, stating:

> "Today we have held in *Sears, Roebuck & Co. v. Stiffel Co.*, *supra*, that when an article is unprotected by a patent or a copyright, state law may not forbid others to copy that article. To forbid copying would interfere with the federal policy, found in Art. I, s 8, cl. 8, of the Constitution and in the implementing federal statutes, of allowing free access to copy whatever the federal patent and copyright laws leave in the public domain."

Prior to February 25, 1972, copyright protection was not extended to sound recordings. *Sears* and *Compco* make clear that the federal policy expressed in Art. I, §8, cl. 8, is to have "national uniformity in patent and copyright laws," 376 U.S., at 231 n.7, a policy bolstered by Acts of Congress which vest "exclusive jurisdiction to hear patent and copyright cases in federal courts . . . and that section of the Copyright Act which expressly saves state protection of unpublished writings but does not include published writings." *Ibid.*

Prior to February 15, 1972, sound recordings had no copyright protection. And even under that Act the copyright would be effective "only to sound recordings fixed, published, and copyrighted on and after the effective date of this Act [Feb. 15, 1972] . . . ."

California's law promotes monopoly; the federal policy promotes monopoly only when a copyright is issued, and it fosters competition in all other instances.

Moreover, federal law limits its monopoly to 28 years plus a like renewal period, which California extends her monopoly into perpetuity.

Cases like *Sears* were surcharged with "unfair competition" and the present one with "pirated recordings." But free access to products on the market is the consumer interest protected by the failure of Congress to extend patents or copyrights into various areas. . . .

I would reverse the judgment below.

NOTES AND QUESTIONS

1. Is *Goldstein* consistent with *Sears* and *Compco*, as the majority argues? How do *Sears* and *Compco* define the public domain? How does the *Goldstein* Court define it?

2. Does *Goldstein* hold that copyright preemption is different from patent preemption? If so, how? If not, what explains the difference in outcomes? When is congressional silence an indication that subject matter should not be protected and when is Congress leaving room for the states to regulate?

3. Would the *Goldstein* Court have decided the case the same way if the sound recordings at issue had been created in 1973, after the effective date of the legislation extending federal copyright protection to sound recordings?

4. Is Chief Justice Burger's reasoning persuasive regarding the lack of uniformity likely to result when states provide protection? Why, or why not? Would state-created rights in intellectual goods pose a greater threat to the integrity of the federal scheme today than the Court identified in 1972? If the Framers of the Constitution and the first patent and copyright statutes did not perceive such rights as a threat, should the modern realities of interstate trade in intellectual goods influence the preemption analysis?

PRACTICE EXERCISE: COUNSEL A CLIENT

You are an aide to a state legislator in Oregon representing a district that encompasses downtown Portland. The legislator has been approached by a group of chefs that desires to attract more talent to the thriving food scene in Portland. The group wants the legislator to introduce a law that would grant a two-year period of exclusivity to chefs for their "original presentations of food dishes for human consumption." The legislator has asked you to prepare a presentation on whether such state law would be preempted by copyright law. If it would be, she would like the presentation to include other ideas for attracting top chef talent to the state.

Goldstein presented a more promising view of the viability of state law protections for intellectual goods than the Court had in its earlier *Sears* and *Compco* opinions. The Supreme Court's next preemption opinion also upheld a state law against a preemption challenge.

Kewanee Oil Co. v. Bicron Corp.
416 U.S. 470 (1974)

BURGER, C.J.: We granted certiorari to resolve a question on which there is a conflict in the courts of appeals: whether state trade secret protection is pre-empted by operation of the federal patent law. . . .

III

. . . [I]n *Goldstein v. California*, . . . we held that the cl. 8 grant of power to Congress was not exclusive and that, at least in the case of writings, the States were not prohibited from encouraging and protecting the efforts of those within their borders by appropriate legislation. . . .

Just as the States may exercise regulatory power over writings so may the States regulate with respect to discoveries. . . .

IV

The question of whether the trade secret law of Ohio is void under the Supremacy Clause involves a consideration of whether that law "stands as an obstacle to the accomplishment and execution of the full purposes and objectives of Congress." . . .

The stated objective of the Constitution in granting the power to Congress to legislate in the area of intellectual property is to "promote the Progress of Science and useful Arts." The patent laws promote this progress by offering a right of exclusion for a limited period as an incentive to inventors to risk the often enormous costs in terms of time, research, and development. . . . In return for the right of exclusion . . . the patent laws impose upon the inventor a requirement of disclosure. . . . [S]uch additions to the general store of knowledge are of such importance to the public weal that the Federal Government is willing to pay the high price of 17 years[*] of exclusive use for its disclosure, which disclosure, it is assumed, will stimulate ideas and the eventual development of further significant advances in the art. The Court has also articulated another policy of the patent law: that which is in the public domain cannot be removed therefrom by action of the States. . . .

The maintenance of standards of commercial ethics and the encouragement of invention are the broadly stated policies behind trade secret law. "The necessity of good faith and honest, fair dealing, is the very life and spirit of the commercial world." . . .

Having now in mind the objectives of both the patent and trade secret law, we turn to an examination of the interaction of these systems of protection of intellectual property. . . .

As we noted earlier, trade secret law protects items which would not be proper subjects for consideration for patent protection under 35 U.S.C. §101. As in the

---

[*] [The term of a patent is now 20 years from the date of filing.—Eds.]

case of the recordings in *Goldstein v. California*, Congress, with respect to non-patentable subject matter, "has drawn no balance; rather, it has left the area unattended, and no reason exists why the State should not be free to act." . . .

. . . [T]he holder of such a discovery would have no reason to apply for a patent whether trade secret protection existed or not. Abolition of trade secret protection would, therefore, not result in increased disclosure to the public of discoveries in the area of nonpatentable subject matter. . . . [K]eeping such items secret encourages businesses to initiate new and individualized plans of operation, and constructive competition results. . . .

. . . The question remains whether those items which are proper subjects for consideration for a patent may also have available the alternative protection accorded by trade secret law.

Certainly the patent policy of encouraging invention is not disturbed by the existence of another form of incentive to invention. In this respect the two systems are not and never would be in conflict. Similarly, the policy that matter once in the public domain must remain in the public domain is not incompatible with the existence of trade secret protection. By definition a trade secret has not been placed in the public domain.

The more difficult objective of the patent law to reconcile with trade secret law is that of disclosure, the *quid pro quo* of the right to exclude. . . . [It is] useful, in determining whether inventors will refrain because of the existence of trade secret law from applying for patents, thereby depriving the public from learning of the invention, to distinguish between three categories of trade secrets. . . .

. . . [T]he extension of trade secret protection to patentable subject matter that the owner knows will not meet the standards of patentability will . . . encourage invention in areas where patent law does not reach. . . .

[The Court reasoned that extension of trade secret protection to this category of material decreases costly reliance on self-help and encourages innovators to license their secrets for purposes of manufacturing and marketing. It further noted:] In addition to the increased costs for protection from burglary, wire-tapping, bribery, and the other means used to misappropriate trade secrets, there is the inevitable cost to the basic decency of society when one firm steals from another. . . .

The next category of patentable subject matter to deal with is the invention whose holder has a legitimate doubt as to its patentability. The risk of eventual patent invalidity by the courts and the costs associated with that risk may well impel some with a good-faith doubt as to patentability not to take the trouble to seek to obtain and defend patent protection for their discoveries. . . . Trade secret protection would assist those inventors in the more efficient exploitation of their discoveries and not conflict with the patent law. . . .

[A]n invalid patent [i]s so serious a threat to the free use of ideas already in the public domain that . . . [b]etter had the invalid patent never issued. More of those patents would likely issue if trade secret law were abolished. . . .

The final category of patentable subject matter to deal with is the clearly patentable invention, *i.e.*, that invention which the owner believes to meet the standards of patentability. It is here that the federal interest in disclosure is at its peak. . . . In the case of trade secret law no reasonable risk of deterrence from patent application by those who can reasonably expect to be granted patents exists.

Trade secret law provides far weaker protection in many respects than the patent law. While trade secret law does not forbid the discovery of the trade secret by fair and honest means, *e.g.*, independent creation or reverse engineering, patent law operates "against the world," forbidding any use of the invention for whatever purpose for a significant length of time. . . . Where patent law acts as a barrier, trade secret law functions relatively as a sieve. The possibility that an inventor who believes his invention meets the standards of patentability will sit back, rely on trade secret law, and after one year of use forfeit any right to patent protection, 35 U.S.C. §102(b),[*] is remote indeed.

Nor does society face much risk that scientific or technological progress will be impeded by the rare inventor with a patentable invention who chooses trade secret protection over patent protection. The ripeness-of-time concept of invention, developed from the study of the many independent multiple discoveries in history, predicts that if a particular individual had not made a particular discovery others would have, and in probably a relatively short period of time. . . .

We conclude that the extension of trade secret protection to clearly patentable inventions does not conflict with the patent policy of disclosure. . . .

MARSHALL, J., concurring in the result: . . . State trade secret laws and the federal patent laws have co-existed for many, many years. During this time, Congress has repeatedly demonstrated its full awareness of the existence of the trade secret system, without any indication of disapproval. . . .

DOUGLAS, J., with whom BRENNAN, J. concurs, dissenting: Today's decision is at war with the philosophy of *Sears* and *Compco*. . . . We held that when an article is unprotected by a patent, state law may not forbid others to copy it, because every article not covered by a valid patent is in the public domain. . . .

A suit to redress theft of a trade secret is grounded in tort damages for breach of a contract—a historic remedy. Damages for breach of a confidential relation are not pre-empted by this patent law, but an injunction against use is pre-empted because the patent law states the only monopoly over trade secrets that is enforceable by specific performance; and that monopoly exacts as a price full disclosure. A trade secret can be protected only by being kept secret. Damages for breach of a contract are one thing; an injunction barring disclosure does service for the protection accorded valid patents and is therefore pre-empted.

While *Sears* and *Compco* appeared to require broad preemption of state laws protecting intellectual goods, *Goldstein* and *Kewanee* focused more narrowly on the purpose and scope of the contested state laws. Can the two approaches be reconciled? Consider the following case.

---

[*] [At the time of this decision, §102(b) of the Patent Act provided that if an invention has been on sale or in use for more than one year prior to the filing of a patent application, the patent was barred.— Eds.]

Bonito Boats, Inc. v. Thunder Craft Boats, Inc.
489 U.S. 141 (1989)

O'CONNOR, J.: . . .

I

In May 1983 . . . the Florida Legislature enacted Fla. Stat. §559.94 (1987). The statute makes "[i]t . . . unlawful for any person to use the direct molding process to duplicate for the purpose of sale any manufactured vessel hull or component part of a vessel made by another without the written permission of that other person." §559.94(2). The statute also makes it unlawful for a person to "knowingly sell a vessel hull or component part of a vessel duplicated in violation of subsection (2)." §559.94(3). . . .

[Bonito Boats, a Florida corporation, sued Thunder Craft, a Tennessee corporation, for copying its popular 5VBR boat hull design. The Florida courts held that the statute was preempted by the federal patent laws.]

II

. . . The federal patent system . . . embodies a carefully crafted bargain for encouraging the creation and disclosure of new, useful, and nonobvious advances in technology and design in return for the exclusive right to practice the invention for a period of years. . . .

The attractiveness of such a bargain, and its effectiveness in inducing creative effort and disclosure of the results of that effort, depend almost entirely on a backdrop of free competition in the exploitation of unpatented designs and innovations. The novelty and nonobviousness requirements of patentability embody a congressional understanding, implicit in the Patent Clause itself, that free exploitation of ideas will be the rule, to which the protection of a federal patent is the exception. . . .

[O]ur decision in *Sears* clearly indicates that the States may place limited regulations on the circumstances in which such designs are used in order to prevent consumer confusion as to source. Thus, while *Sears* speaks in absolutist terms, its conclusion that the States may place some conditions on the use of trade dress indicates an implicit recognition that all state regulation of potentially patentable but unpatented subject matter is not *ipso facto* pre-empted by the federal patent laws. . . .

[T]he *Kewanee* Court emphasized that "[t]rade secret law provides far weaker protection in many respects than the patent law." . . . This point was central to the Court's conclusion that trade secret protection did not conflict with either the encouragement or disclosure policies of the federal patent law. . . .

[W]e believe that the *Sears* Court correctly concluded that the States may not offer patent-like protection to intellectual creations which would otherwise remain unprotected as a matter of federal law. . . .

III

We believe that the Florida statute at issue in this case so substantially impedes the public use of the otherwise unprotected design and utilitarian ideas embodied in unpatented boat hulls as to run afoul of the teaching of our decisions in *Sears* and *Compco*. It is readily apparent that the Florida statute does not operate to prohibit "unfair competition" in the usual sense that the term is understood. The law of unfair competition has its roots in the common-law tort of deceit: its general concern is with protecting *consumers* from confusion as to source. . . .

In contrast to the operation of unfair competition law, the Florida statute is aimed directly at preventing the exploitation of the design and utilitarian conceptions embodied in the product itself. The sparse legislative history surrounding its enactment indicates that it was intended to create an inducement for the improvement of boat hull designs. . . . To accomplish this goal, the Florida statute endows the original boat hull manufacturer with rights against the world, similar in scope and operation to the rights accorded a federal patentee. . . . The Florida scheme offers this protection for an unlimited number of years to all boat hulls and their component parts, without regard to their ornamental or technological merit. Protection is available for subject matter for which patent protection has been denied or has expired, as well as for designs which have been freely revealed to the consuming public by their creators. . . .

That the Florida statute does not remove all means of reproduction and sale does not eliminate the conflict with the federal scheme. . . . In essence, the Florida law prohibits the entire public from engaging in a form of reverse engineering of a product in the public domain. This is clearly one of the rights vested in the federal patent holder, but has never been a part of state protection under the law of unfair competition or trade secrets. *See Kewanee*, 416 U.S. at 476. . . .

Appending the conclusionary label "unscrupulous" to such competitive behavior merely endorses a policy judgment which the patent laws do not leave the States free to make. . . .

NOTES AND QUESTIONS

1. Do you agree with the *Kewanee* Court that inventors of patentable subject matter meeting patent standards for protection will not routinely opt for trade secret protection instead? As noted in Chapter 2.A.2, *supra*, the Patent & Trademark Office conducts an examination before granting a patent. There are many opportunities during that process for examiners to err – by granting protection when none should be forthcoming or denying it when the invention in fact meets the statutory standards. Given the difficulty in obtaining a patent, is it accurate to conceive of inventors deciding *ex ante* between trade secret protection and certain patent protection?

2. Do you agree that the risk associated with inadvertent disclosure of trade secrets is high enough to encourage patent protection as an alternative? Certainly, there are companies that take that risk successfully: The formula for Coca-Cola has been held as a secret for over a century. What considerations do you think motivated the Coca-Cola Company not to apply for a patent on this formula?

3. Are *Kewanee* and *Bonito Boats* consistent with the other cases discussed in this section? How is state trade secrecy law different from the prohibitions on copying rejected in *Sears* and *Compco*? How was the Florida direct-molding statute different from (a) state trade secret protection at issue in *Kewanee*; and (b) the California record piracy statute at issue in *Goldstein*? How does the *Bonito Boats* Court define the public domain? How does the *Kewanee* Court define it?

> **LOOKING BACK**
>
> Recall the Vessel Hull Design Protection Act, *supra*, Chapter 4.A.2 (Note on Alternative Modes of Protection). It was adopted in part in response to the *Bonito Boats* decision.

4. After *Bonito Boats*, would a state law prohibiting reverse engineering of trade secrets be enforceable? Why, or why not?

B. EXPRESS PREEMPTION UNDER THE 1976 ACT: AN OVERVIEW

As noted above, the Copyright Act of 1976 includes an express preemption provision. In relevant part, §301 states:

> **§301. Preemption with respect to other laws**
> (a) On and after January 1, 1978, all legal or equitable rights that are equivalent to any of the exclusive rights within the general scope of copyright as specified by section 106 in works of authorship that are fixed in a tangible medium of expression and come within the subject matter of copyright as specified by sections 102 and 103, whether created before or after that date and whether published or unpublished, are governed exclusively by this title. Thereafter, no person is entitled to any such right or equivalent right in any such work under the common law or statutes of any State.

17 U.S.C. §301(a).

According to the legislative history, Congress sought to: (1) promote national uniformity both to relieve authors from having to secure protection on a state-by-state basis and to improve the U.S. position in international intellectual property negotiations; (2) eliminate the significance of publication, in light of varying judicial interpretations and the artificiality of the concept; and (3) realize the "limited times" aspect of the protection contemplated by the Intellectual Property Clause by foreclosing the possibility of perpetual protection for unpublished works. *See* H.R. Rep. No. 94-1476, 94th Cong., 2d Sess. 129-30 (1976), *reprinted in* 1976 U.S.C.A.A.N. 5659, 5745-46.

As you will see, §301 leaves a number of questions unanswered, and courts have come to inconsistent results.

1. Basic Cases

Harper & Row, Publishers, Inc. v. Nation Enterprises
723 F.2d 195 (2d Cir. 1983), rev'd on other grounds, 471 U.S. 539 (1985)

[Review the facts of this case in Chapter 10.A.1. In addition to its copyright infringement claim against *The Nation*, Harper & Row also asserted state law claims for conversion and tortious interference with contract. The district court dismissed those claims as preempted under §301(a) of the Copyright Act.]

KAUFMAN, J.: . . . With regard to the issue of conversion, cross-appellants seem unable to decide how to plead the factual elements supporting their claim. Their amended complaint asserted conversion based on the unauthorized publication of *The Nation* article. In this court, they propound a theory which rests the tort upon the unlawful possession of the physical property of the Ford manuscript. In doing so, they have placed themselves neatly upon the horns of a dilemma. If unauthorized publication is the gravamen of their claim, then it is clear that the right they seek to protect is coextensive with an exclusive right already safeguarded by the Act—namely, control over reproduction and derivative use of copyrighted material. As such, their conversion claim is necessarily preempted.

Alternatively, Harper & Row and Reader's Digest suggest it is the possession of the papers themselves which lays the foundation for their claim. Conversion, as thus described, is a tort involving acts—possession and control of chattels—which are qualitatively different from those proscribed by copyright law, and which therefore are not subject to preemption. Cross-appellants have failed, however, to state a conversion claim. Conversion requires not merely temporary interference with property rights, but the exercise of unauthorized dominion and control to the complete exclusion of the rightful possessor. . . . Merely removing one of a number of copies of a manuscript (with or without permission) for a short time, copying parts of it, and returning it undamaged, constitutes far too insubstantial an interference with property rights to demonstrate conversion. . . .

With respect to the claim of tortious interference with contractual relations, cross-appellants' statement of the cause of action in their complaint suggests its infirmity. They allege that cross-appellees have committed a tort "by destroying the exclusive right of an author and his licensed publishers to exercise and enjoy the benefit of the pre-book publication serialization rights." If there is a qualitative difference between the asserted right and the exclusive right under the Act of preparing derivative works based on the copyrighted work, we are unable to discern it. In both cases, it is the act of unauthorized publication which causes the violation. The enjoyment of benefits from derivative use is so intimately bound up with the right itself that it could not possibly be deemed a separate element. . . . As the trial court noted, the fact that cross-appellants pleaded additional elements of awareness and intentional interference, not part of a copyright infringement claim, goes merely to the scope of the right; it does not establish qualitatively different conduct on the part of the infringing party, nor a fundamental non-equivalence between the state and federal rights implicated. . . .

≡ *Video Pipeline, Inc. v. Buena Vista Home*
≡ *Entertainment, Inc.*
  210 F. Supp. 2d 552 (D.N.J. 2002)

[Review the facts of this case in Chapter 12.D. In responding to Video Pipeline's declaratory judgment complaint, Buena Vista Home Entertainment (BVHE) asserted counterclaims involving alleged violations of various state laws by Video Pipeline. What follows is the district court's decision regarding whether the Copyright Act preempts any or all of those claims.]

SIMANDLE, J.: . . .

F. Federal Preemption of State Law Claims

. . . Under the Copyright Act . . . a state common law or statutory claim is preempted if: (1) the particular work to which the state law claim is being applied falls within the type of works protected by the Copyright Act under Sections 102 and 103; and (2) the state law seeks to vindicate "legal or equitable rights that are equivalent" to one of the bundle of exclusive rights already protected by copyright law under 17 U.S.C. §106. Thus, the preemption analysis encompasses both a "subject matter requirement," and a "general scope" or "equivalency" requirement, respectively. . . .

. . . [N]either party contests the applicability of the first prong. . . . The issue here is whether the state laws asserted by defendant BVHE in its counterclaims create rights which are "equivalent to" any of the exclusive rights granted to the copyright holder under §106. If so, they are preempted. The inquiry performed under the second prong of the §301 preemption analysis is as follows: [A] right which is "equivalent to copyright" is one which is infringed by the mere act of reproduction, performance, distribution or display. . . . If, under state law, the act of reproduction, performance, distribution or display . . . will in itself infringe the state created right, then such right is preempted. But if other elements are required, in addition to or instead of, the acts of reproduction, performance, distribution or display, in order to constitute a state created cause of action, then the right does not lie "within the general scope of copyright," and there is no preemption. . . .

1. Unfair Competition Claim

Plaintiff contends that defendant BVHE's state law unfair competition claim is preempted because it is based on misappropriation. . . . Plaintiff alleges that "[a]ll of defendant's state law claims are based upon the premise that the Promotional Previews furnished to Video Pipeline belong to Defendant and were misappropriated by Video Pipeline." Misappropriation, or "reverse passing off," is grounded in the alleged unauthorized copying and use of another's copyrighted expression, and thus fails the extra element test. And, as the Second Circuit in *Moody's Investors* determined, "'[S]tate law claims that rely on the misappropriation branch of unfair competition are preempted.'" [*Financial Info., Inc. v. Moody's Investors,*] 808 F.2d [204] at 208 (quoting *Warner Bros., Inc. v. American Broad. Cos., Inc.,* 720 F.2d 231, 247 (2d Cir. 1983)). In other words, reverse passing off occurs when one markets, sells, and represents the goods or services of another as its very own, and thus gives rise to an actionable claim for reproducing, distributing, or displaying copyrighted works.

. . . Defendant essentially maintains that plaintiff "passed off" its clip previews, which contain defendant's trademarks, as having been created and produced by defendant. . . .

Unfair competition claims involving "passing off" are generally not preempted by federal copyright law. . . . As defendant BVHE correctly contends, passing off claims are not preempted primarily because such claims include the extra element of deception or misrepresentation which is not an element of a copyright claim. . . .

Accordingly, defendant BVHE's counterclaim specifically asserting that plaintiff engaged in "passing off" under state law unfair competition can be construed to encompass the allegation that Video Pipeline is distributing its own products, here clip previews, and representing to the public that they are those of defendant BVHE. This necessarily involves the extra element of misrepresentation or deception which is not an element for copyright infringement. As such, the "passing off" claim is an actionable claim not preempted by the federal Copyright Act. . . .

3. *Unjust Enrichment Claim*

Defendant BVHE argues that its unjust enrichment claim is not federally preempted because such claim requires "extra elements" that renders it qualitatively different from a claim for copyright infringement. . . .

The foundation of defendant's claim is that plaintiff has exploited BVHE's intellectual property without compensating BVHE for the benefits derived from such use. Here, BVHE alleges that "BVHE voluntarily conferred upon Video Pipeline the benefits flowing from use of BVHE's valuable intellectual property," and that plaintiff Video Pipeline "would be unjustly enriched if it were permitted to retain the benefits it has reaped from the unauthorized use of BVHE's intellectual property. . . ." Although defendant BVHE refers to the terms of the Master Clip License Agreement, its claim that plaintiff Video Pipeline is "exploiting" defendant BVHE's works necessarily involves plaintiff's acts in reproducing, distributing and displaying defendant's works, all of which are encompassed in rights protected under copyright law. . . .

. . . In this case, where a claim for breach of implied contract is absent, defendant BVHE's claim for unjust enrichment is . . . duplicative of the relief sought under copyright law.

Because the rights asserted under the unjust enrichment claim in the circumstances of this case generally are equivalent to those protected by federal copyright law, and because defendant BVHE fails to assert an extra element that would render its claim qualitatively distinct from a claim seeking compensation for copyright infringement, defendant's unjust enrichment claim is preempted under federal copyright law. . . .

4. Conversion and Replevin Claims

Defendant BVHE asserts that its conversion and replevin claims are not preempted because these claims involve rights to tangible property not equivalent to the exclusive rights protected by copyright law. "The torts of conversion and trespass relate to interference with tangible rather than intangible property, and hence should be held immune from preemption." 1 Nimmer on Copyright ¶1.01[B][1][i], at 1-41 (2001). . . .

Here, as discussed above, defendant BVHE's conversion claim seeks return of "its tangible property . . . *i.e.*, each of the original Trailers BVHE provided to Video Pipeline." Defendant's replevin claim alleges that "BVHE . . . ha[s] an immediate right of possession to the original Trailers, their tangible property, previously provided to Video Pipeline, which Video Pipeline continues to wrongly hold." . . . Defendant BVHE's claim thus involves tangible, physical property, the rights to which are distinctly different from those rights involved in defendant's copyright counterclaims. To the extent that BVHE seeks the return of such items and alleges that plaintiff continues to wrongly hold such items, the rights it asserts under its state law conversion and replevin claims are not equivalent to those protected by the federal copyright laws, which govern the reproduction, performance, distribution, and display of copyrighted works. Accordingly, defendant's state law conversion and replevin claims are not preempted. . . .

NOTES AND QUESTIONS

1. As *Harper & Row* and *Video Pipeline* illustrate, §301(a) is designed to separate those state law claims that are fundamentally about copying (or one of the other rights enumerated in §106) from those that are fundamentally about something else. What is the two-pronged test the *Video Pipeline* court identifies? Is it consistent with the wording of §301?

2. Would *Goldstein* have been decided differently if the case had arisen under the 1976 Act? Why, or why not? (Make sure to read §301(c) before you answer).

3. Although state law claims for ·relief are often joined with copyright infringement claims, sometimes the plaintiff does not assert a copyright claim. Unless the case presents an independent ground for federal subject matter jurisdiction, lawsuits in this latter group will be filed in state court. Relying on the "complete preemption" doctrine, which applies when a federal statute substitutes an exclusive federal remedy in place of the remedies formerly afforded under state law, several federal courts have allowed removal on the theory that the

> **KEEP IN MIND**
>
> Failure to comply with the statutory deadlines for removal, *see* 28 U.S.C. §1446, effectively means that defendants would have to present their preemption arguments to the state courts, which are much less familiar than the federal courts with copyright jurisprudence.

claim, however styled in the complaint, is "really" a copyright infringement claim even when there is no independent basis (e.g., diversity jurisdiction) for removal. *See Ritchie v. Williams*, 395 F.3d 283 (6th Cir. 2005); *Briarpatch Ltd., L.P. v. Phoenix Pictures, Inc.*, 373 F.3d 296 (2d Cir. 2004), *cert. denied*, 544 U.S. 949 (2005); *Rosciszewski v. Arete Assoc., Inc.*, 1 F.3d 225 (4th Cir. 1993). Completely preempted claims generally are dismissed by the federal court immediately following removal. Alternatively, the claims may be treated as copyright infringement claims and evaluated as such. *See Ritchie*, 395 F.3d at 289 (dismissing as completely preempted contract and tort claims because once recast as copyright claims, they were barred by the three-year statute of limitations in §507(b)).

CONSIDER WHETHER §301 WOULD PREEMPT THE CAUSE OF ACTION IN EACH HYPOTHETICAL

1. The Cool Chicks, a rock band, sue Dave, their former manager, for unjust enrichment. As the basis for this claim, the Cool Chicks allege that Dave improperly retained certain master recordings belonging to the band and exploited these recordings for his own benefit.

2. The Cool Chicks, a rock band, sue Dave, their former manager, for unjust enrichment. As the basis for this claim, the Cool Chicks allege that Dave improperly managed the band's artistic properties and has failed to account for royalties due from the band's recordings.

3. The Cool Chicks, a rock band, sue Dave, their former manager, for conversion. As the basis for this claim, the Cool Chicks allege that Dave has improperly retained certain master recordings belonging to the band.

4. Hilltop, a software company, sues Valley Software, its main rival, for unfair competition. As the basis for this claim, Hilltop alleges that Valley has approached its main customers and falsely represented that Valley's own software program, which costs less than Hilltop's, will perform the same functions as Hilltop's program.

5. Hilltop, a software company, sues Valley Software, its main rival, for unfair competition. As the basis for this claim, Hilltop alleges that Valley has approached its main customers and offered to sell them a program that will perform the same functions in the same way as Hilltop's program, but for a lower price. In fact, Valley's program does perform the same functions in the same way as Hilltop's program.

6. Jack and Jill, the principals of Hilltop, decide to dissolve their business partnership. Jill, who managed the financial side of the business, sues Jack, who managed the technical side of the business, for breach of fiduciary duty. As the basis for this claim, Jill alleges that Jack sold hundreds of copies of Hilltop's software "out the back door" without reporting the sales. Jack responds that he is the sole author of the program in question and that Jill's claim is preempted by §101 of the Copyright Act, which defines the requirements for joint authorship.

2. Diving Deeper: State Laws Expressly Permitted by Section 301

Section 301 not only describes the types of state law causes of action that Congress intended to preempt, but also lists several types of causes of action that Congress did not intend to preempt:

(b) Nothing in this title annuls or limits any rights or remedies under the common law or statutes of any State with respect to —

(1) subject matter that does not come within the subject matter of copyright as specified by sections 102 and 103, including works of authorship not fixed in any tangible medium of expression; or

(2) any cause of action arising from undertakings commenced before January 1, 1978; or

(3) activities violating legal or equitable rights that are not equivalent to any of the exclusive rights within the general scope of copyright as specified by section 106; . . .

17 U.S.C. §301(b).

Section 301 separately addresses in more detail the parameters of state law authority related to protection of moral rights and sound recordings. When Congress enacted the Visual Artists Rights Act in 1990 (VARA), it amended §301 to specify that federal law expressly preempts "all legal or equitable rights that are equivalent to any of the rights conferred by section 106A with respect to works of visual art to which the rights conferred by section 106A apply." 17 U.S.C. §301(f)(1). As you learned in Chapter 8, VARA rights have a different duration than the §106 rights generally—VARA rights extend only for the life of the author. Section 301(f) addresses this difference by providing that "any rights or remedies under the common law or statutes of any State" relating to "activities violating legal or equitable rights [under §106A] which extend beyond the life of the author" are *not* preempted. *Id.* §301(f)(2)(C). Recall that the Berne Convention requires protection for authors' moral rights, but Congress did not amend the Copyright Act to provide moral rights protection when the United States joined Berne. It relied instead on the existence of alternative methods, including state law, to provide the required protection. The Berne Convention requires that moral rights protection last at least as long as protection for the economic rights of authors (in the case of the United States, generally life + 70 years). Berne Conv., art. 6(2). Thus, even after Congress passed VARA, some members felt that international obligations required the preservation of state law *post mortem* protection for moral rights. 136 Cong. Rec. H13314 (daily ed. Oct. 27, 1990) (statement of Rep. Kastenmeier). Additionally, note that the wording of §301(f) seems to permit states to grant moral rights protection to other types of works beyond "works of visual art."

Moreover, §301 expressly permits state law protection for sound recordings fixed before February 15, 1972, the date on which federal copyright protection for sound recordings became available. In recent years, state law protection for pre-1972 sound recordings has generated a fair amount of litigation. In 2014, a federal district court ruled that California's statute granting a right of "exclusive ownership" to authors of pre-1972 sound recordings, Cal. Civ. Code §980(a)(2), included the right to control the public performance of those sound recordings. *Flo & Eddie Inc. v. Sirius XM Radio Inc.*, 2014 WL 4725382 (C.D. Cal. 2014). Recall from Chapter 7 that the Copyright Act does not grant copyright owners of sound recordings a general public performance right, but rather it grants only a limited right to control public performances by means of digital audio transmissions. Authors of pre-1972 sound recording therefore have broader rights under California law than they would if their sound recordings were eligible for federal copyright protection. Moreover, a work need not have originated in a state to be protected there. *See Capitol Records, Inc. v. Naxos of America, Inc.*, 830 N.E.2d 250, 265 (N.Y. 2005) (holding that UK recordings were entitled to protection under New York common law, notwithstanding expiration of the statutory copyrights in the United Kingdom).

NOTES AND QUESTIONS

1. Consider the safe harbor provisions of §512 that provide protection from copyright infringement liability for ISPs, Chapter 9.C, *supra*. Should those safe harbors extend to nonpreempted state law protections for works of authorship? *See UMG Recordings, Inc. v. Escape Media Group, Inc.*, 964 N.Y.S.2d 106 (N.Y. App. Div. 2013) (holding that §512 does not protect ISPs from claims under New York common law protecting pre-1972 sound recordings).

2. If a state adopted a statute providing authors of literary works a right of attribution, would it be preempted under §301? Would it be impliedly preempted by the federal intellectual property scheme?

C. MORE DIFFICULT PREEMPTION PROBLEMS

Review the first prong of the test for §301 preemption described in *Video Pipeline*, above. Section 301 applies only if the work "come[s] within the subject matter of copyright." Can states therefore provide copyright-like protection for works excluded from federal protection, such as ideas or unfixed works? Be sure to read §301(b) before you answer.

Now look again at the second prong of the test. Outside of the most obvious examples, what does it mean for a state law claim to be "qualitatively different" from a copyright one? As introduced in Congress, §301 contained guidance on the types of causes of action Congress did not intend to preempt:

> (b) Nothing in this title annuls or limits any rights or remedies under the common law or statutes of any State with respect to . . .
>> (3) . . . rights against misappropriation not equivalent to any of [the §106] exclusive rights, breaches of contract, breaches of trust, trespass, conversion,

invasion of privacy, defamation, and deceptive trade practices such as passing off and false representation . . .

Howard B. Abrams, *Copyright, Misappropriation, and Preemption: Constitutional and Statutory Limits of State Law Protection*, 1983 Sup. Ct. Rev. 509, 541 (1983), *citing* S. 22, 94th Cong., 1st Sess. §301 (1975); H.R. 2223, 94th Cong., 1st Sess. (1975). Section 301(b)(3) was, however, struck during the floor discussion, ostensibly because the Justice Department objected to the inclusion of misappropriation in §301(b)(3)'s list. *Id.* at 546-47. Unfortunately, the legislative history is sparse, so little can be said about Congress's actual intent. *See id.* at 548.

We consider now some of the more difficult contexts in which courts have addressed §301's test and its interaction with background principles of implied preemption.

1. The Right of Publicity

The state law right of publicity had its genesis in privacy-related concerns, but the right has evolved separately from the right of privacy and rests on a different policy basis. While the right of privacy protects against certain intrusions on a person's dignity, the right of publicity protects individuals against unauthorized (and uncompensated) appropriation of their identities for commercial purposes. Some states have codified the right in statutes, while in others it remains a common law doctrine. In some states, such as California, individuals may have rights under both the relevant statute and common law.

Although all individuals have rights of publicity, most disputes involve celebrities. Such suits illustrate the difference between the rights of privacy and publicity:

> Well-known personalities connected with [the entertainment] industries do not seek . . . "solitude and privacy." . . . Their concern is rather with publicity, which may be regarded as the reverse side of the coin of privacy. . . . [A]lthough the well-known personality does not wish to hide his light under a bushel of privacy, neither does he wish to have his name, photograph, and likeness reproduced and publicized without his consent or without remuneration to him.

Melville B. Nimmer, *The Right of Publicity*, 19 Law & Contemp. Probs. 203, 203-04 (1968), *cited in* 4 J. Thomas McCarthy, McCarthy on Trademarks and Unfair Competition, §28:4 at 28-6 (2003).

Courts have recognized the right of publicity as a type of intellectual property right and its infringement as a commercial tort. In general, to sustain a cause of action for infringement of the right of publicity, the plaintiff must show that she has a right in the identity (often also called "persona") at issue and that right was infringed by unauthorized use likely to cause damage to the identity's commercial value.

Recall the two requirements of §301(a) that must be satisfied before the Copyright Act will preempt a state law cause of action. On its face, a right of publicity claim seems to survive a preemption analysis because the "work" that is the subject of the action is not a "work[] of authorship . . . fixed in a tangible medium of expression and . . . within the subject matter of copyright." 17 U.S.C. §301(a).

Instead, the work is a person's persona. Unfortunately, matters are not so simple. The persona is often portrayed using copyrightable expression, and the right of publicity may effectively create a property right against the world in the means of portrayal. Consider the following cases.

Brown v. Ames
201 F.3d 654 (5th Cir. 2000)

JONES, J.: Appellants Collectibles and Ames principally appeal the district court's determination that appellees' state law claims for violation of their rights of publicity are not preempted by the Copyright Act. The misappropriation consisted of appellants' unauthorized use of appellees' names and likenesses to market appellees' musical performances on CD's and audio cassettes for which appellants also lacked copyrights. Because a person's name and likeness in themselves are not copyrightable, and because the state law tort for misappropriation does not conflict with federal copyright law, appellees' claims are not preempted. . . .

I. Factual and Procedural History

Collectibles is a record label that distributes and sells music recordings, especially repackaged vintage recordings. Ames is a music producer specializing in Texas blues. Appellees are individual blues musicians, songwriters, music producers or heirs of such.

Around 1990, Ames, d/b/a Home Cooking Records, licensed to Collectibles for commercial exploitation master recordings that included performances by appellees. The written license agreements also purported to give Collectibles the right to use the names, photographs, likenesses and biographical material of all those whose performances were on the master recordings. . . . Using the master recordings, Collectibles manufactured and distributed cassettes and CD's, as well as music catalogs, with the names and sometimes the likenesses of the performers on or in them. . . .

In 1994, appellees sued Ames, Collectibles and Jerry and Nina Greene, the owners of Collectibles. . . . Appellees' actions for copyright infringement, violations of the Lanham Act and for misappropriation of name or likeness under Texas state law proceeded to a jury trial. . . .

The jury . . . found that the defendants had misappropriated the names and likenesses of the appellees and had infringed (in the case of Collectibles, innocently) copyrights held by some of the appellees. . . .

Collectibles and Ames have appealed. . . . [T]hey assert [*inter alia*] that the Copyright Act preempts the misappropriation claims. . . .

II. Discussion . . .

In Texas, the tort of misappropriation provides protection from the unauthorized appropriation of one's name, image or likeness. It is best understood as a species of the right of publicity or of privacy. To prevail, a plaintiff must prove that (1) the defendant misappropriated the plaintiff's name or likeness for the value associated with it and not in an incidental manner or for a newsworthy purpose; (2) the plaintiff can be identified from the publication; and (3) the defendant derived some advantage or benefit.

Appellants argue strenuously that appellees have not presented an independent action for misappropriation. Because appellees' names and/or likenesses were used to identify their musical works in Collectibles' CD's, tapes and catalogs, appellants assert that the core of the misappropriation and copyright infringement claims is the same, compelling preemption under section 301 of the misappropriation claims.

Appellants' argument ignores, however, that the content of the right protected by the misappropriation tort does not fall into the subject matter of copyright, as section 301 requires. As the district court correctly recognized, the tort for misappropriation of name or likeness protects "the interest of the individual in the exclusive use of his own identity, in so far as it is represented by his name or likeness, and in so far as the use may be of benefit to him or to others." Restatement (Second) of Torts §652C (1977). In other words, the tort of misappropriation of name or likeness protects a person's *persona*. A *persona* does not fall within the subject matter of copyright—it does not consist of "a 'writing' of an 'author' within the meaning of the Copyright Clause of the Constitution." Nimmer, *supra*, §1.01[B][1][c]; *Jarvis v. A&M Records*, 827 F. Supp. 282, 297 (D.N.J. 1993); *Bi-Rite Enterprises, Inc. v. Button Master*, 555 F. Supp. 1188, 1201 (S.D.N.Y. 1983); *Apigram Publishing Co. v. Factors, Etc., Inc.*, 1980 WL 2047 (N.D. Ohio July 30, 1980); *Lugosi v. Universal Pictures*, 25 Cal. 3d 813, 849 (1979) (Bird, C.J., dissenting). Furthermore, contrary to appellants' implications, appellees' names and likenesses do not become copyrightable simply because they are used to identify the source of a copyrighted work. Therefore, their misappropriation claims do not fit the terms of §301 preemption. . . .

One arguably analogous case has held to the contrary. In *Baltimore Orioles v. Major League Baseball Players Ass'n*, 805 F.2d 663 (7th Cir. 1986), the Seventh Circuit held that the Copyright Act preempted baseball players' rights of publicity in their performances. The court's conclusion turned on its controversial decision that performances in a baseball game were within the subject matter of copyright because the videotape of the game fixed the players' performances in tangible form. *See id.* at 674-76. *Baltimore Orioles*, however, has been heavily criticized for holding that a baseball game is a protectable work of authorship simply because the performance was recorded on videotape that was itself copyrightable. In any event, *Baltimore Orioles* is distinguishable from this case because the right of publicity claimed by the baseball players was essentially a right to prevent rebroadcast of games whose broadcast rights were already owned by the clubs. . . . The case before us offers no such complication, as the appellee performers did not give permission to the appellants to market their recordings or photographs. We decline appellants' invitation to find name or likeness copyrightable simply because they are placed on CD's and tapes or in catalogs that have copyrightable subject matter recorded on them.

The fact that section 301 does not apply does not end the inquiry, however. Although section 301 preemption is not appropriate, conflict preemption might be. The Supremacy Clause dictates that a state law that obstructs the accomplishment of the full purposes and objectives of Congress is preempted. *See Hines v. Davidowitz,* 312 U.S. 52, 67 . . . (1941). . . .

Although appellants argue vigorously that not preempting appellees' misappropriation claims would undermine the copyright system, several considerations belie this claim. First, the right of publicity that the misappropriation tort protects promotes the major objective of the Copyright Act—to support and encourage artistic and scientific endeavors. Second, the record here indicates that industry practice may be to transfer rights in a performer's name or likeness when the copyright is transferred. If that is the case, right of publicity claims will rarely interfere with a copyright holder's use of the creator's name or likeness in connection with the copyright. Third, common law on the right of publicity appears ordinarily to permit an authorized publisher or distributor to use name or likeness to identify truthfully the author or creator of the goods.

Only if states allowed similar claims against authorized publishers or distributors of a work (whether through copyright or the public domain) would the purposes and objectives of the Copyright Act be adversely affected. Such suits would interfere to some extent with the uniformity of the copyright system and the exploitation of works in the public domain. Currently, however, no state seems to have such a law, and the general rule is as described above. Thus, because the tort would currently not be sustainable against valid copyright holders, allowing the claim in this context does not impede the transfer of copyrights or the uniformity of the copyright system.

Supreme Court precedent suggesting that courts should steer a middle ground in considering Copyright Act preemption cases supports our conclusion that appellees' misappropriation claims are not preempted. The leading Supreme Court case on preemption in the intellectual property field, *Bonito Boats, Inc. v. Thunder Craft Boats, Inc.,* 489 U.S. 141 (1989), found that a state statute providing patent-like protection for ideas deemed unprotected under federal patent law was preempted, but warned that "the States remain free to promote originality and creativity in their own domains." *Id.* at 165. The Court went on to state that: "the case for federal preemption is particularly weak where Congress has indicated its awareness of the operation of state law in a field of federal interest, and has nonetheless decided to 'stand by both concepts and to tolerate whatever tension there [is] between them.'" *Id.* at 166-67. As noted in the legislative history of section 301, Congress was aware of the operation of state law on the rights of privacy and publicity, and indicated its intention that such state law causes of action remain. *See* House Report at 132, *reprinted in* 1976 U.S.C.C.A.N. at 5748.

Since appellees' misappropriation claims neither fall within the subject matter of copyright nor conflict with the purposes and objectives of the Copyright Act, the claims were not preempted. . . .

≡ *Toney v. L'Oreal USA, Inc.*
≡ *406 F.3d 905 (7th Cir. 2005)*

KANNE, J.: . . .

I. Background

In November 1995, June Toney, a model who has appeared in print advertisements, commercials, and runway shows, authorized Johnson Products Company to use her likeness on the packaging of a hair-relaxer product called "Ultra Sheen Supreme" from November 1995 until November 2000. In addition, Toney authorized the use of her likeness in national magazine advertisements for the relaxer from November 1995 until November 1996. . . .

In her complaint filed in state court, Toney asserted that [the defendants] used her likeness in connection with the packaging and promotion of the Ultra Sheen Supreme relaxer product beyond the authorized time period. Specifically, she claimed that the defendants thereby violated[, *intera alia*,] her right to publicity in her likeness as protected under the Illinois Right of Publicity Act, 765 Ill. Comp. Stat. 1075/1–60 ("IRPA") . . . .

II. Analysis

The question we must address is whether Toney's claim, brought under the IRPA, is preempted by the Copyright Act. We review this legal question and the district court's decision to grant the defendants' motion to dismiss *de novo*.

The IRPA grants an individual the "right to control and to choose whether and how to use an individual's identity for commercial purposes." 765 Ill. Comp. Stat. 1075/10. Moreover, the IRPA provides that "[a] person may not use an individual's identity for commercial purposes during the individual's lifetime without having obtained previous written consent from the appropriate person . . . ." 765 Ill. Comp. Stat. 1075/30. . . .

B. Toney's Claim Survives Preemption

The IRPA . . . [defines identity] to mean "any attribute of an individual that serves to identify that individual to an ordinary, reasonable viewer or listener, including but not limited to (i) name, (ii) signature, (iii) photograph, (iv) image, (v) likeness, or (vi) voice." 765 Ill. Comp. Stat. 1075/5. In short, the IRPA protects a person's right to publicity. The subject matter of such a claim "is *not* a particular picture or photograph of plaintiff. Rather, what is protected by the right of publicity is the very identity or persona of the plaintiff as a human being." J. Thomas McCarthy, 2 Rts. Of Publicity & Privacy §11:52 (2d ed.2004) A photograph "is merely one copyrightable 'expression' of the underlying 'work,' which is the plaintiff as a human being. There is only one underlying 'persona' of a person protected by the right of publicity." *Id.* In contrast, "[t]here may be dozens or hundreds of photographs which fix certain moments in that person's life. Copyright in each of these photographs might be separately owned by dozens or hundreds of photographers." *Id.* A persona, defined in this way, "can hardly be said to constitute a 'writing' of an 'author' within the meaning of the copyright clause of the Constitution." *Downing v. Abercrombie & Fitch*, 265 F.3d 994, 1003–04 (9th Cir.2001). . . .

Applying the facts of this case to the requirements for preemption, we find that Toney's identity is not fixed in a tangible medium of expression. There is no "work of authorship" at issue in Toney's right of publicity claim. A person's likeness—her persona—is not authored and it is not fixed. The fact that an image of the person might be fixed in a copyrightable photograph does not change this. From this we must also find that the rights protected by the IRPA are not "equivalent" to any of the exclusive rights within the general scope of copyright that are set forth in §106. Copyright laws do not reach identity claims such as Toney's. Identity, as we have described it, is an amorphous concept that is not protected by copyright law; thus, the state law protecting it is not preempted.

We also note that the purpose of the IRPA is to allow a person to control the commercial value of his or her identity. Unlike copyright law, "commercial purpose" is an element required by the IRPA. The phrase is defined to mean "the public use or holding out of an individual's identity (i) on or in connection with the offering for sale or sale of a product, merchandise, goods, or services; (ii) for purposes of advertising or promoting products, merchandise, goods, or services; or (iii) for the purpose of fundraising." 765 Ill. Comp. Stat. 1075/5. Clearly the defendants used Toney's likeness without her consent for their commercial advantage. The fact that the photograph itself could be copyrighted, and that defendants owned the copyright to the photograph that was used, is irrelevant to the IRPA claim. The basis of a right of publicity claim concerns the message—whether the plaintiff endorses, or appears to endorse the product in question. One can imagine many scenarios where the use of a photograph without consent, in apparent endorsement of any number of products, could cause great harm to the person photographed. The fact that Toney consented to the use of her photograph originally does not change this analysis. The defendants did not have her consent to continue to use the photograph, and therefore, they stripped Toney of her right to control the commercial value of her identity.

C. Conflicting Precedent

Our decision in *Baltimore Orioles v. Major League Baseball Players Ass'n*, 805 F.2d 663 (7th Cir. 1986), has been widely criticized by our sister circuits and by several commentators. Many interpret the case as holding that the right of publicity as protected by state law is preempted by §301 in all instances. We take this opportunity to clarify our holding. The case simply does not stand for the proposition that the right of publicity as protected by state law is preempted in all instances by federal copyright law; it does not sweep that broadly.

Baltimore Orioles holds that state laws that intrude on the domain of copyright are preempted even if the particular expression is neither copyrighted nor copyrightable. Such a result is essential in order to preserve the extent of the public domain established by copyright law. Therefore, states may not create rights in material that was published more than 75 years ago, even though that material is not subject to federal copyright. Also, states may not create copyright-like protections in materials that are not original enough for federal protection, such as a telephone book with listings in alphabetical order. *See Feist Publ'ns, Inc. v. Rural Tel. Serv. Co.*, 499 U.S. 340 (1991). *Baltimore Orioles* itself makes clear that "[a] player's right of publicity in his name or likeness would not be preempted if a company, without the consent of the player, used the player's name to advertise its product." 805 F.2d at 666 n.24. Therefore, the bottom line is that Toney's claim under the Illinois right of publicity statute is not preempted by federal copyright law. . . .

Laws v. Sony Music Entertainment
294 F. Supp. 2d 1160 (C.D. Cal. 2003)

BAIRD, J.: . . .

II. Factual and Procedural Background

Plaintiff [Debra Laws] alleges that she is a professional vocalist and recording artist who has achieved international acclaim. She first recorded the song "Very Special" in 1981 for Elektra Records. Since that time, she has continued to perform the song throughout the United States and internationally.

In 1979, Debra Laws entered into a recording agreement with Spirit Productions . . . [which, in turn,] entered into a production agreement with Elektra Records, a division of Warner Communications. Spirit Productions agreed to produce master recordings of Debra Laws for Elektra. The agreement specifically gave Elektra the right to copyright the productions, which Elektra did in 1981. The agreement also granted Elektra the right to license the productions.

On November 26, 2002, Warner licensed to Sony Music a non-exclusive license and right to use a portion of Debra Law's recording of "Very Special" in the song "All I Have" performed by Jennifer Lopez. The agreement required Sony to include a credit stating "Featuring samples from the Debra Laws recording 'Very Special.'"

Sony subsequently released both a music recording and a music video incorporating portions of "Very Special" into "All I Have." Plaintiff alleges that "All I Have" has been a hugely successful recording and music video. Sony did not receive permission from either Spirit or Laws, and neither have received compensation.

Laws filed an action against Sony on February 20, 2003, in Superior Court for Los Angeles County. Plaintiff brings [a number of] causes of action against Defendant Sony [including]: (1) statutory misappropriation of a name or voice for commercial purpose (under California Civil Code §3344); [and] (2) common law invasion of privacy (misappropriation of name or voice) . . . .

IV. Analysis . . .

A. Preemption . . .

Plaintiff contends that her state claims fall outside the scope of the Copyright Act because she is challenging Defendant's unauthorized use of her name and voice, not the use of the sound recordings. Defendant asserts that Plaintiff's voice was fixed in a sound recording, and as such is copyrightable. Therefore, the court must determine whether Defendant's use of Plaintiff's song "Very Special" constituted the use of her voice/name/persona or a sound recording.

The Ninth Circuit has held that the use of a person's voice does not fall under copyright protection and that state law claims are not preempted. *See, Midler v. Ford Motor Co.*, 849 F.2d 460 (9th Cir.1988); *Waits v. Frito–Lay, Inc.*, 978 F.2d 1093, 1098-1100 (9th Cir. 1992). However, in those cases, the expropriator had imitated the person's voice without permission. The courts found that a person's voice is more personal than a work of authorship. *Id*. Both courts associated a person's voice with part of her identity. *Id*. In neither case was the voice "fixed" in a work of authorship. *Id*. . . .

However, when a person's "identity" claims are essentially claims regarding the use of a copyrighted work, then courts have found the state claims to be preempted. In *Motown Record*, the defendants had run an advertisement which capitalized upon the tune of a Supreme's song and the group's image. *Motown*, 657 F. Supp. 1236. The court held that the state law claims revolved around the unauthorized use of a copyrighted work. *Id*. The state law claims were merely claims for the reproduction, performance, distribution or display of a copyrighted work within the scope of the Act. *Id*. As such, the state law claims were preempted. *Id*. . . .

The court finds that the facts in this case are more similar to those in . . . *Motown* than to the facts in the other identity cases. Although Plaintiff claims that Defendant's use of the song is without permission, Defendant did receive permission (in the form of a license) from the rightful copyright owner. Plaintiff's complaint revolves around the use of her voice in a sound recording. Sound recordings are protected by copyright. 17 U.S.C. §102. Defendant used Plaintiff's original voice from the sound recording of "Very Special." According to Plaintiff, Defendant used the *original recordings* to avoid compensating Plaintiff for her performance. In other words, Defendant used Plaintiff's voice by using the copyrightable sound recording that captured that voice.

Although Defendant credits Plaintiff on the song jacket, the court finds that the one, inconspicuous line does not constitute exploitation of Plaintiff's image or identity. In fact, Defendant was complying with its license agreement by including the credit. Therefore, the addition of the name in the credit cannot remove the fact that Plaintiff is essentially contesting the use of a sound recording which is protected by the Copyright Act.

In essence, Plaintiff has failed to show that the use of her voice in a sound recording amounted to the use of her identity. As such, Plaintiff's state law claims are all preempted by the Copyright Act. Indeed were the court to come to the contrary conclusion, then any vocal sound recording would fall outside the parameters of the Copyright Act because of the use of a person's "voice." This contradicts the express intent of Congress to preempt common law or state statutes that extend to works within the Federal Copyright Law. . . .

. . . The court finds that 1) the subject matter of the state law claims fall within the subject matter specified by the Copyright Act and 2) the rights are equivalent to those found in the Copyright Act (reproduction and distribution). Accordingly, Plaintiff's state law claims are preempted. . . .

NOTES AND QUESTIONS

1. Are these cases consistent with each other in interpreting the two requirements for preemption?

2. Note that both *Brown* and *Toney* refer to the *Baltimore Orioles* case. There, major league baseball players had claimed that broadcasts of major league games made without their express consent violated their rights of publicity in their performances. The court held the claim preempted:

> . . . The Players' performances are embodied in a copy, *viz*[.], the videotape of the telecast, from which the performances can be perceived, reproduced, and otherwise communicated indefinitely. Hence, their performances are fixed in tangible form, and any property rights in the performances that are equivalent to any of the rights encompassed in a copyright are preempted. . . .
>
> . . . Because the [allegation is that] the exercise of the Clubs' right to broadcast telecasts of the games infringes the Players' rights of publicity in their performances, the Players' rights of publicity are equivalent to at least one of the rights encompassed by copyright, *viz.*, the right to perform an audiovisual work. Since the works in which the Players claim rights are fixed in tangible form and come within the subject matter of copyright, the Players' rights of publicity in their performance are preempted.

Baltimore Orioles, Inc. v. Major League Baseball Players Ass'n, 805 F.2d 663, 675, 677 (7th Cir. 1986). Do you agree with the *Baltimore Orioles* court? Why, or why not?

3. How would the *Brown* court have analyzed the claims made in *Laws*? In *Laws*, the defendants had a license to the sound recording. In *Brown*, the defendants never had any copyright rights in the recordings or photographs to begin with. Should this matter to the analysis? Did it matter in the *Toney* case that the defendants owned the copyright in the photograph?

4. The *Laws* court referenced the decision in *Midler v. Ford Motor Co.*, 849 F.2d 460, 463 (9th Cir. 1988), *cert. denied sub nom. Midler v. Young & Rubicam, Inc.*, 503 U.S. 951 (1992). There, the Ninth Circuit recognized a right of publicity claim "when a distinctive voice of a professional singer is widely known and is deliberately imitated in order to sell a product." According to the court, Midler did not seek to prevent damages for use of the particular song but rather for use of her voice: "A voice is not copyrightable. The sounds are not 'fixed.' What is put forward as protectible here is more personal than any work of authorship." *Id*. at 462. Are *Laws* and *Midler* consistent?

PRACTICE EXERCISE: COUNSEL A CLIENT

Ted has a very distinctive voice, and several years ago a local TV station hired him to narrate an annual show featuring the highlights from the area's high school football games. The arrangement between Ted and the station was quite casual, with no contract between them. The station later partnered with a software firm to develop software that high schools can use to simulate football plays. The station believes that there is a large market for the software, and has begun advertising, using some of the clips narrated by Ted. Ted has sued for violation of his right of publicity, and the station consults you to determine how to respond. Is Ted's claim preempted? Assume that the TV station decides it no longer wishes to deal with Ted and has hired Marty to do its narration. What advice would you give the station as it deals with Marty?

---

2. Misappropriation

As discussed above, there is some evidence suggesting that the list of causes of action Congress did not intend to preempt under §301 was deleted because the Justice Department objected to the inclusion of misappropriation on that list. At the root of the controversy over misappropriation was the Supreme Court's celebrated opinion in *International News Service v. Associated Press*, 248 U.S. 215 (1918), an excerpt from which follows. During the drafting of the 1976 Act, some argued that the misappropriation theory recognized in *INS* interfered with federal copyright policy and should not survive under a modernized copyright law. Others argued that the misappropriation theory had an important role to play in a world in which collections of information were increasingly valuable. Following the excerpt from *INS* we consider a more recent case addressing a misappropriation claim in light of §301.

≡ *International News Service v. Associated Press*
248 U.S. 215 (1918)

[The parties were competing wire subscription services that transmitted news items to their member newspapers. The dispute arose during World War I. The INS, a service founded by William Randolph Hearst to provide news to Hearst-owned newspapers, had incurred the displeasure of the British High Command for taking positions "strongly sympathetic to the German cause. . . . In retaliation, the British and French authorities cut INS personnel off from the front lines and barred them from using the entire European cable system." Richard A. Epstein, International News Service v. Associated Press: *Custom and Law as Sources of Property Rights in News*, 78 Va. L. Rev. 85, 92 (1992). Left with no direct means of gathering news of the war to transmit to its members, the INS sought to gather the news from the AP instead. Among other things, it copied news items from publicly accessible bulletin boards maintained by AP member newspapers and from early editions of AP member newspapers on the East Coast and transmitted the copied material to Hearst newspapers. Because of the time difference, Hearst newspapers on the West Coast were able to publish these items at the same time as AP member newspapers.]

PITNEY, J.: . . . We need spend no time . . . upon the general question of property in news matter at common law, or the application of the copyright act, since it seems to us the case must turn upon the question of unfair competition in business. And, in our opinion, this does not depend upon any general right of property analogous to the common-law right of the proprietor of an unpublished work to prevent its publication without his consent; nor is it foreclosed by showing that the benefits of the copyright act have been waived. We are dealing here not with restrictions on publication but with the very facilities and processes of publication. The peculiar value of the news is in the spreading of it while it is fresh. . . . [T]he news of current events may be regarded as common property. What we are concerned with is the business of making it known to the world. . . . The parties are competitors in this field; and, on fundamental principles, applicable here as elsewhere, when the rights and privileges of the one are liable to conflict with those of the other, each party is under a duty so as to conduct its own business as not unnecessarily or unfairly to injure that of the other. . . .

. . . [A]lthough we may and do assume that neither party has any remaining property interest as against the public in uncopyrighted news matter after the moment of its first publication, it by no means follows that there is no remaining property interest in it as between themselves. For, to both of them alike, news matter, however little susceptible of ownership or dominion in the absolute sense, is stock in trade, to be gathered at the cost of enterprise, organization, skill, labor, and money, and to be distributed and sold to those who will pay money for it, as for any other merchandise. Regarding the news, therefore, as but the material out of which both parties are seeking to make profits at the same time and in the same field, we hardly can fail to recognize that for this purpose, and as between them, it must be regarded as quasi property, irrespective of the rights of either as against the public. . . .

. . . [D]efendant, by its very act, admits that it is taking material that has been acquired by complainant as the result of organization and the expenditure of labor, skill, and money, and which is salable by complainant for money, and that defendant in appropriating it and selling it as its own is endeavoring to reap where it has not sown, and by disposing of it to newspapers that are competitors of complainant's members is appropriating to itself the harvest of those who have sown. Stripped of all disguises, the process amounts to an unauthorized interference with the normal operation of complainant's legitimate business precisely at the point where the profit is to be reaped, in order to divert a material portion of the profit from those who have earned it to those who have not; with special advantage to the defendant in the competition because of the fact that it is not burdened with any part of the expense of gathering the news. The transaction speaks for itself, and a court of equity ought not to hesitate long in characterizing it as unfair competition in business. . . .

The contention that the news is abandoned to the public for all purposes when published in the first newspaper is untenable. Abandonment is a question of intent, and the entire organization of the Associated Press negatives such a purpose.

The cost of the service would be prohibitive if the reward were to be so limited. No single newspaper, no small group of newspapers, could sustain the expenditure. Indeed, it is one of the most obvious results of defendant's theory that, by permitting indiscriminate publication by anybody and everybody for purposes of profit in competition with the news-gatherer, it would render publication profitless, or so little profitable as in effect to cut off the service. . . .

HOLMES, J., dissenting: . . . Property, a creation of law, does not arise from value, although exchangeable—a matter of fact. Many exchangeable values may be destroyed intentionally without compensation. Property depends upon exclusion by law from interference, and a person is not excluded from using any combination of words merely because someone has used it before. . . . If a given person is to be prohibited from making the use of words that his neighbors are free to make some other ground must be found. . . . [Justice Holmes argued that INS should be enjoined only from publishing copied news items without giving express credit to AP for having gathered them.]

BRANDEIS J., dissenting: . . . [T]he fact that a product of the mind has cost its producer money and labor, and has a value for which others are willing to pay, is not sufficient to ensure to it this legal attribute of property. The general rule of law is, that the noblest of human productions—knowledge, truths ascertained, conceptions, and ideas—became, after voluntary communication to others, free as the air to common use. Upon these incorporeal productions the attribute of property is continued after such communication only in certain classes of cases where public policy has seemed to demand it. These exceptions are confined to productions which, in some degree, involve creation, invention, or discovery. . . .

. . . [W]ith the increasing complexity of society, the public interest tends to become omnipresent; and the problems presented by new demands for justice cease to be simple. Then the creation or recognition by courts of a new private right may work serious injury to the general public, unless the boundaries of the right are definitely established and wisely guarded. In order to reconcile the new private right with the public interest, it may be necessary to prescribe limitations and rules for its enjoyment; and also to provide administrative machinery for enforcing the rules. It is largely for this reason that, in the effort to meet the many new demands for justice incident to a rapidly changing civilization, resort to legislation has latterly been had with increasing frequency. . . .

. . . [L]egislators dealing with the subject might conclude, that the right to news values should be protected to the extent of permitting recovery of damages for any unauthorized use, but that protection by injunction should be denied, just as courts of equity ordinarily refuse (perhaps in the interest of free speech) to restrain actionable libels. . . .

Or again, a legislature might conclude that . . . a news agency should, on some conditions, be given full protection of its business; and to that end a remedy by injunction as well as one for damages should be granted . . . [but] it might declare that, in such cases, news should be protected against appropriation, only if the gatherer assumed the obligation of supplying it at reasonable rates, and without discrimination, to all papers which applied therefor. . . .

National Basketball Ass'n v. Motorola, Inc.
105 F.3d 841 (2d Cir. 1997)

WINTER, J.: Motorola, Inc. and Sports Team Analysis and Tracking Systems ("STATS") appeal from a permanent injunction. . . . The injunction concerns a handheld pager sold by Motorola and marketed under the name "SportsTrax," which displays updated information of professional basketball games in progress. . . .

I. Background

The facts are largely undisputed. Motorola manufactures and markets the SportsTrax paging device while STATS supplies the game information that is transmitted to the pagers. The product became available to the public in January 1996, at a retail price of about $200. SportsTrax's pager has an inch-and-a-half by inch-and-a-half screen and operates in four basic modes: "current," "statistics," "final scores," and "demonstration." It is the "current" mode that gives rise to the present dispute. In that mode, SportsTrax displays the following information on NBA games in progress: (i) the teams playing; (ii) score changes; (iii) the team in possession of the ball; (iv) whether the team is in the free-throw bonus; (v) the quarter of the game; and (vi) time remaining in the quarter. The information is updated every two to three minutes, with more frequent updates near the end of the first half and the end of the game. There is a lag of approximately two or three minutes between events in the game itself and when the information appears on the pager screen.

SportsTrax's operation relies on a "data feed" supplied by STATS reporters who watch the games on television or listen to them on the radio. The reporters key into a personal computer changes in the score and other information such as successful and missed shots, fouls, and clock updates. The information is relayed by modem to STATS's host computer, which compiles, analyzes, and formats the data for retransmission. The information is then sent to a common carrier, which then sends it via satellite to various local FM radio networks that in turn emit the signal received by the individual SportsTrax pagers. . . .

> **KEEP IN MIND**
>
> The claim of unfair competition that the Supreme Court recognized in *INS* was founded on federal common law. Subsequent opinions of the Court rejected the existence of a general federal common law. *Erie R.R. Co. v. Tompkins*, 304 U.S. 64 (1938). Today, misappropriation claims are brought under state unfair competition law (both common law and state statutes).

[The district court dismissed the NBA's federal claims for relief, including a copyright infringement claim, but granted a permanent injunction on the NBA's claim for misappropriation under New York law.]

II. The State Law Misappropriation Claim

[The court observed, first, that the underlying basketball games were not protected by copyright, but that the broadcasts of those games were protected.

Nonetheless, it held that the district court properly dismissed the NBA's copyright claims based on the broadcasts because Motorola and STATS reproduced only unprotected facts. The court then turned to the question of preemption.]

a. Summary

. . . [A] state law claim is preempted when (i) the state law claim seeks to vindicate "legal or equitable rights that are equivalent" to one of the bundle of exclusive rights already protected by copyright law under 17 U.S.C. §106—styled the "general scope requirement"; and (ii) the particular work to which the state law claim is being applied falls within the type of works protected by the Copyright Act under Sections 102 and 103—styled the "subject matter requirement." . . .

b. "Partial Preemption" and the Subject Matter Requirement

The subject matter requirement is met when the work of authorship being copied or misappropriated "fall[s] within the ambit of copyright protection." *Harper & Row, Publishers, Inc. v. Nation Enter.*, 723 F.2d 195, 200 (1985), *rev'd on other grounds*, 471 U.S. 539 (1985). We believe that the subject matter requirement is met in the instant matter and that the concept of "partial preemption" is not consistent with Section 301 of the Copyright Act. Although game broadcasts are copyrightable while the underlying games are not, the Copyright Act should not be read to distinguish between the two when analyzing the preemption of a misappropriation claim based on copying or taking from the copyrightable work. . . . *Baltimore Orioles*, 805 F.2d at 675.

Copyrightable material often contains uncopyrightable elements within it, but Section 301 preemption bars state law misappropriation claims with respect to uncopyrightable as well as copyrightable elements. . . . The legislative history supports this understanding of Section 301(a)'s subject matter requirement. The House Report stated:

> As long as a work fits within one of the general subject matter categories of sections 102 and 103, the bill prevents the States from protecting it even if it fails to achieve Federal statutory copyright because it is too minimal or lacking in originality to qualify, or because it has fallen into the public domain.

H.R. No. 94-1476 at 131, *reprinted in* 1976 U.S.C.C.A.N. at 5747.

Adoption of a partial preemption doctrine—preemption of claims based on misappropriation of broadcasts but no preemption of claims based on misappropriation of underlying facts—would expand significantly the reach of state law claims and render the preemption intended by Congress unworkable. It is often difficult or impossible to separate the fixed copyrightable work from the underlying uncopyrightable events or facts. Moreover, Congress, in extending copyright protection only to the broadcasts and not to the underlying events, intended that the latter be in the public domain. Partial preemption turns that intent on its head by allowing state law to vest exclusive rights in material that Congress intended to be in the public domain and to make unlawful conduct that Congress intended to allow. . . .

c. The General Scope Requirement . . .

We turn . . . to the question of the extent to which a "hot-news" misappropriation claim based on *INS* involves extra elements and is not the equivalent of exclusive rights under a copyright. Courts are generally agreed that some form of such a claim survives preemption. This conclusion is based in part on the legislative history of the 1976 amendments. . . .

The theory of the New York misappropriation cases relied upon by the district court is considerably broader than that of *INS*. For example, the district court quoted at length from *Metropolitan Opera Ass'n v. Wagner-Nichols Recorder Corp.*, 199 Misc. 786, 101 N.Y.S.2d 483 (N.Y. Sup. Ct. 1950), *aff'd*, 279 A.D. 632, 107 N.Y.S.2d 795 (1st Dep't 1951). *Metropolitan Opera* described New York misappropriation law as standing for the "broader principle that property rights of commercial value are to be and will be protected from any form of commercial immorality"; that misappropriation law developed "to deal with business malpractices offensive to the ethics of [] society"; and that the doctrine is "broad and flexible." 939 F. Supp. at 1098-1110 (quoting *Metropolitan Opera*, 101 N.Y.S.2d at 492, 488-89).

However, we believe that *Metropolitan Opera*'s broad misappropriation doctrine based on amorphous concepts such as "commercial immorality" or society's "ethics" is preempted. Such concepts are virtually synonymous for wrongful copying and are in no meaningful fashion distinguishable from infringement of a copyright. . . .

Our conclusion, therefore, is that only a narrow "hot-news" misappropriation claim survives preemption for actions concerning material within the realm of copyright.[7]

In our view, the elements central to an *INS* claim are: (i) the plaintiff generates or collects information at some cost or expense; (ii) the value of the information is highly time-sensitive; (iii) the defendant's use of the information constitutes free-riding on the plaintiff's costly efforts to generate it; (iv) the defendant's use of the information is in direct competition with a product or service offered by the plaintiff; (v) the ability of other parties to free-ride on the efforts of the plaintiff would so reduce the incentive to produce the product or service that its existence or quality would be substantially threatened.

INS is not about ethics; it is about the protection of property rights in time-sensitive information so that the information will be made available to the public by

---

7. Quite apart from Copyright Act preemption, *INS* has long been regarded with skepticism by many courts and scholars and often confined strictly to its facts. In particular, Judge Learned Hand was notably hostile to a broad reading of the case. He wrote:

> [W]e think that no more was covered than situations substantially similar to those then at bar. The difficulties of understanding it otherwise are insuperable. We are to suppose that the court meant to create a sort of common-law patent or copyright for reasons of justice. Either would flagrantly conflict with the scheme which Congress has for more than a century devised to cover the subject-matter.

Cheney Bros. v. Doris Silk Corp., 35 F.2d 279, 280 (2d Cir. 1929), *cert. denied*, 281 U.S. 728 (1930). . . .

profit seeking entrepreneurs. If services like AP were not assured of property rights in the news they pay to collect, they would cease to collect it. . . .

We therefore find the extra elements—those in addition to the elements of copyright infringement—that allow a "hot-news" claim to survive preemption are: (i) the time-sensitive value of factual information, (ii) free-riding by a defendant, and (iii) the threat to the very existence of the product or service provided by the plaintiff.

2. The Legality of SportsTrax

We conclude that Motorola and STATS have not engaged in unlawful misappropriation under the "hot-news" test set out above. To be sure, some of the elements of a "hot-news" *INS* claim are met. The information transmitted to SportsTrax is not precisely contemporaneous, but it is nevertheless time-sensitive. Also, the NBA does provide, or will shortly do so, information like that available through SportsTrax. . . .

However, there are critical elements missing in the NBA's attempt to assert a "hot-news" *INS*-type claim. As framed by the NBA, their claim compresses and confuses three different informational products. The first product is generating the information by playing the games; the second product is transmitting live, full descriptions of those games; and the third product is collecting and retransmitting strictly factual information about the games. The first and second products are the NBA's primary business: producing basketball games for live attendance and licensing copyrighted broadcasts of those games. The collection and retransmission of strictly factual material about the games is a different product: e.g., box-scores in newspapers, summaries of statistics on television sports news, and real-time facts to be transmitted to pagers. In our view, the NBA has failed to show any competitive effect whatsoever from SportsTrax on the first and second products and a lack of any free-riding by SportsTrax on the third. . . .

An indispensable element of an *INS* "hot-news" claim is free-riding by a defendant on a plaintiff's product, enabling the defendant to produce a directly competitive product for less money because it has lower costs. SportsTrax is not such a product. The use of pagers to transmit real-time information about NBA games requires: (i) the collecting of facts about the games; (ii) the transmission of these facts on a network; (iii) the assembling of them by the particular service; and (iv) the transmission of them to pagers or an on-line computer site. Appellants are in no way free-riding on Gamestats. Motorola and STATS expend their own resources to collect purely factual information generated in NBA games to transmit to SportsTrax pagers. They have their own network and assemble and transmit data themselves.

To be sure, if appellants in the future were to collect facts from an enhanced Gamestats pager to retransmit them to SportsTrax pagers, that would constitute free-riding and might well cause Gamestats to be unprofitable because it had to bear costs to collect facts that SportsTrax did not. If the appropriation of facts from one pager to another pager service were allowed, transmission of current information on NBA games to pagers or similar devices would be substantially deterred because any potential transmitter would know that the first entrant would quickly encounter a lower cost competitor free-riding on the originator's transmissions.

However, that is not the case in the instant matter. . . .

NOTES AND QUESTIONS

1. Do you agree with the *NBA* court's analysis of the "subject matter requirement" of §301? Is the court's rejection of a partial preemption rule consistent with the legislative history of §301? Is it consistent with the *Sears*-to-*Bonito Boats* line of cases, *supra*, Section A? Per *Goldstein*, are facts a type of subject matter that Congress has "left . . . unattended"? How does the text of §301 bear on this question?

2. Is each of the elements that the Second Circuit identifies as "extra"—time sensitivity, free riding, and a threat to incentives—sufficiently distinct from the elements necessary to allege a claim of copyright infringement? Are either of the elements that the court did *not* identify as extra—cost or expense and direct competition—sufficiently distinct? Does the Second Circuit's reliance on an "extra-element" test for equivalence make sense in the *NBA* case?

3. The Second Circuit observes that "*INS* is not about ethics." Based on the excerpts from the *INS* opinion reproduced above, do you agree? Was the *INS* Court concerned solely with the likely incentive effects of the challenged conduct?

4. How would the analysis announced in *NBA* apply to a misappropriation claim grounded in the facts of *Feist*, Chapter 2.A.2.b, *supra*? How would it apply to misappropriation claims grounded in the facts of *CCC Info Servs., Inc. v. Maclean Hunter Mkt. Reps.*, or *Matthew Bender & Co. v. West Publ'ing Co.*, Chapter 2.B.2.a, *supra*?

5. The term "misappropriation" also is used in trade secrecy law. The Uniform Trade Secrets Act (UTSA) defines misappropriation as:

> (i) acquisition of a trade secret of another by a person who knows or has reason to know that the trade secret was acquired by improper means; or
> (ii) disclosure or use of a trade secret of another without express or implied consent by a person who
>> (A) used improper means to acquire knowledge of the trade secret; or
>> (B) at the time of disclosure or use, knew or had reason to know that his knowledge of the trade secret was
>>> (I) derived from or through a person who had utilized improper means to acquire it;
>>> (II) acquired under circumstances giving rise to a duty to maintain its secrecy or limit its use; or
>>> (III) derived from or through a person who owed a duty to the person seeking relief to maintain its secrecy or limit its use; or
>> (C) before a material change of his [or her] position, knew or had reason to know that it was a trade secret and that knowledge of it had been acquired by accident or mistake.

U.T.S.A. §1 (1985). The UTSA defines "improper means" to "include[] theft, bribery, misrepresentation, breach or inducement of a breach of a duty to maintain secrecy, or espionage through electronic or other means." *Id.* Recall from *Kewanee, supra,* Section A, that the Supreme Court has held that federal patent law does not preempt state trade secret law because trade secret protection does not interfere with patent law's goals. The Supreme Court has never addressed the question whether copyright law preempts state protection for trade secrets. Does it?

PRACTICE EXERCISES: ADVOCACY

SmartShop.com is a comparison shopping website. SmartShop obtains pricing information by sending software tools called "spiders" to crawl the Web to collect product and pricing data from other sites. JCPenneysues SmartShop.com for misappropriation for taking such information from its website. JCPenney also sues for trespass to chattels. Generally, a cause of action for trespass to chattels requires showing, *inter alia*, that the defendant intentionally interfered with the plaintiff's use or possession of a chattel and thereby damaged it. JCPenney claims that SmartShop exceeded the bounds of any real or implied consent to public access to its website and that SmartShop's spiders, by occupying its servers, caused damage. SmartShop has moved for summary judgment, arguing that both claims are preempted. Outline JCPenney's arguments in opposition to the motion.

---

3. Contract

As you know, contracts are ubiquitous in many of the copyright industries. Historically, claims for breach of contract generally have survived preemption challenges. Because contracts create rights only between their parties, the conventional wisdom holds that state enforcement of their terms does not, as a rule, create a system of entitlements inconsistent with those established by the federal intellectual property system. More recently, however, mass-market licenses have tested the boundaries of the conventional wisdom, raising difficult questions about both the application of §301 and the use of implied preemption analysis.

a. Negotiated Agreements

When applying §301 to contracts covering subject matter within the general scope of copyright, some courts analyze the act that allegedly constitutes the breach. If that act violates one of the exclusive rights under §106 (such as the reproduction right), the court will hold the breach of contract claim preempted. If the allegedly breaching act does not also infringe a §106 right, the court will hold the breach of contract claim not preempted. For example, in *National Car Rental System, Inc. v. Computer Associates International, Inc.*, 991 F.2d 426 (8th Cir.), *cert. denied*, 510 U.S. 861 (1993), the court held that a claim alleging that the defendant breached a software license agreement by using the program to process data for third parties was not preempted:

> CA [i.e., Computer Associates,] does not claim that National is doing something that the copyright laws reserve exclusively to the copyright holder, or that the use restriction is breached "by the mere act of reproduction, performance, distribution or display." Instead . . . CA must be read to claim that National's or EDS's processing of data for third parties is the . . . act [prohibited under their contract]. None of the exclusive copyright rights grant CA that right of their own force. Absent the parties' agreement, this restriction would not exist. Thus, CA is alleging that the contract creates a right not existing under the copyright law, a right based upon National's promise, and that it is suing to protect that contractual right.

Id. at 433. To similar effect is *Kabehie v. Zoland*, 102 Cal. App. 4th, 513 (2002). There, the court explained:

> A right that is qualitatively different from copyright includes a right to payment, a right to royalties, or any other independent covenant. . . . If, however, the promise is equivalent to copyright, the breach of the promise is not the extra element making the action qualitatively different from copyright. In such a case, there is simply no consideration for the promise. The promisor has merely agreed to do that which the promisor is already obligated to do under federal copyright law.

Id. at 528.

Some courts take a different approach, focusing not so much on the act that constitutes the breach but rather on the existence of the contract itself. These courts hold that the distinguishing characteristics of a contract—i.e., existence of a promise, mutual assent, and consideration—render a cause of action for breach of contract qualitatively different from one for copyright infringement. *See, e.g., Taquino v. Teledyne Monarch Rubber*, 893 F.2d 1488, 1501 (5th Cir. 1990) (holding that "contract promise" renders breach of contract action qualitatively different from copyright infringement claim, although also noting that a "right is equivalent if the mere act of reproduction, distribution, or display infringes it"); *Architectronics, Inc. v. Control Sys., Inc.*, 935 F. Supp. 425, 438-39 (S.D.N.Y. 1996). Under this type of analysis, contract claims are rarely preempted.

KEEP IN MIND

A legal challenge to a breach of contract claim based on preemption differs from arguments that, for example, a contract has not been formed or that some of its terms are unenforceable under contract law doctrines like unconscionability. A defense based on preemption argues that even if there is an otherwise enforceable contract, a court may not entertain the state law claim of breach of contract because it is preempted by the Copyright Act.

NOTES AND QUESTIONS

1. Which of the approaches identified above do you prefer? Why? Should the approach vary depending on whether a contract seeks to limit privileges (e.g., resale) that the recipient otherwise would have under copyright law or seeks to create rights (e.g., to payment) that the copyright owner otherwise would not have under

copyright law? For a more detailed discussion of judicial approaches to preemption, see Christina Bohannon, *Copyright Preemption of Contracts*, 67 Md. L. Rev. 616 (2008); Daniel E. Wanat, *Copyright Law, Contract Law, and Preemption Under §301(a) of the Copyright Act of 1976: A Study in Judicial Labeling or Mislabeling and a Proposed Alternative*, 31 Vt. L. Rev. 707 (2007).

2. Companies in many industries require their employees to sign confidentiality agreements obligating them to protect the firms' trade secrets against disclosure. Trade secrets are often embodied in copyrighted works. For example, an employee might breach a confidentiality agreement by disclosing the printed version of a copyrighted marketing plan, making copies in the process. The employer may sue for both trade secret misappropriation and breach of contract. Would the breach of contract claim be preempted?

3. *Rano v. Sipa Press Inc.*, 987 F.2d 580 (9th Cir. 1993), and *Walthal v. Rusk*, 172 F.3d 481 (7th Cir. 1999), both concerned efforts by authors to terminate oral licenses of unspecified duration that they had granted to distributors of their works. In both cases, the authors argued that the applicable state law allowed termination at will, while the distributors argued that this rule of state law was preempted by §203 of the Copyright Act, which governs termination of transfers. According to the distributors' argument, because §203 expressly provides that an author may terminate a grant after 35 years, the author may not terminate sooner even if state law otherwise would allow it. The Ninth Circuit accepted this argument, but the Seventh Circuit rejected it, reasoning that because §203 was intended to protect authors, a state law rule that allowed some authors to terminate even earlier created no conflict. *Rusk*, 172 F.3d at 484-85. The court further observed, however, that §203 would preempt a state law that required a contract to be enforced for longer than 35 years. *Id*. at 486. Thus, both courts implicitly accepted that the Copyright Act might exert preemptive effect even absent an equivalent state law claim.

PRACTICE EXERCISE: ADVOCACY

Acme Publishing Co. licenses its copyrights in several ebooks to Basic Booksellers. Basic Booksellers agrees to pay a per unit royalty for each ebook sold. It also agrees not to install the ebooks on more than two servers and to refrain from criticizing the content of any of Acme's ebooks. Basic Booksellers breaches all of these contractual provisions and Acme Publishing sues. You represent Basic Booksellers in a jurisdiction that has not yet identified its preferred approach to preemption analysis for contract claims. In preparation for a motion to dismiss, outline the arguments for preemption of Acme's breach of contract claim.

---

b. Standard Form Agreements

The argument against preemption of contract claims is more convincing in the context of negotiated agreements than when non-negotiated, boilerplate, mass-market contracts are involved. In the latter context, state enforcement of the "contract" begins to resemble state creation of rights against the world because all purchasers are subject to the restrictive license. As you know from other chapters, much software and digital content now is distributed under shrinkwrap or clickwrap agreements, also referred to as "End User License Agreements" (EULAs), containing terms that limit privileges the recipient otherwise would have under copyright law. Should EULAs be treated the same way as traditional contracts in a preemption analysis?

In *ProCD, Inc. v. Zeidenberg*, 86 F.3d 1447 (7th Cir. 1996), the court addressed a preemption challenge to a contract action based on a shrinkwrap EULA. ProCD marketed a database that contained a white-pages directory that the court assumed was not copyrightable. ProCD charged one price to commercial users and a lower one to consumers. Those who purchased the consumer package were prohibited from engaging in commercial use of the database under the terms of a license "encoded on [] CD-ROM disks as well as printed in the manual, and which appear[ed] on a user's screen every time the software [ran]." *Id.* at 1450. Zeidenberg purchased the consumer version and used it commercially by marketing the database on the Internet for a lower price than ProCD charged for its commercial version. The court held the license an enforceable contract and the breach of contract action not preempted. Although the *ProCD* court rested its holding on §301 of the Copyright Act and cited *National Car Rental* favorably, it did not emphasize either the nature of the act constituting the breach or the existence of a promise, mutual assent, and consideration. The court stated:

> Rights "equivalent to any of the exclusive rights within the general scope of copyright" are rights established *by law*— rights that restrict the options of persons who are strangers to the author. Copyright law forbids duplication, public performance, and so on, unless the person wishing to copy or perform the work gets permission; silence means a ban on copying. A copyright is a right against the world. Contracts, by contrast, generally affect only their parties; strangers may do as they please, so contracts do not create "exclusive rights."

Id. at 1454.

Thus, the *ProCD* ruling extended to EULAs the traditional view that breach of contract actions are not preempted because they bind only their parties and therefore cannot create an unacceptable conflict with federal intellectual property law. At the same time, the *ProCD* court "refrain[ed] from adopting a rule that anything with the label 'contract' is necessarily outside the preemption clause: the variations and possibilities are too numerous to foresee. . . . [S]ome applications of the law of contract could interfere with the attainment of national objectives and therefore come within the domain of §301(a). But general enforcement of shrinkwrap licenses . . . does not create such interference." *Id.* at 1455.

In contrast, in *Vault Corp. v. Quaid Software Ltd.*, 847 F.2d 255 (5th Cir. 1988), the court addressed a copyright preemption challenge to Louisiana's Software License Enforcement Act, which allowed software providers to enforce certain terms so long as they were contained in a license that accompanied the software. At issue specifically was whether Vault could enforce a shrinkwrap license's statutorily authorized prohibition against decompilation and disassembly. The Fifth Circuit stated:

In *Sears, Roebuck & Co. v. Stiffel Co.*, 376 U.S. 225 (1964), the Supreme Court held that "[w]hen state law touches upon the area of [patent or copyright statutes], it is 'familiar doctrine' that the federal policy 'may not be set at naught, or its benefits denied' by the state law." Section 117 of the Copyright Act permits an owner of a computer program to make an adaptation of that program [under certain circumstances]. The provision in Louisiana's License Act, which permits a software producer to prohibit the adaptation of its licensed computer program by decompilation or disassembly, conflicts with the rights of computer program owners under §117 and clearly "touches upon an area" of federal copyright law. For this reason . . . we hold that at least this provision of Louisiana's License Act is preempted by federal law, and thus that the restriction in Vault's license agreement against decompilation or disassembly is unenforceable.

Id. at 269-70.

As you learned in Chapter 10.B.1, over time courts began to consider decompilation for reverse engineering a fair use under certain circumstances. Given *Vault* and *Sega*, many thought a copyright preemption challenge to a breach of contract claim based on a EULA provision banning reverse engineering likely would succeed, despite *ProCD*. Consider the following case.

Bowers v. Baystate Technologies, Inc.
320 F.3d 1317 (Fed. Cir.), cert. denied, 539 U.S. 928 (2003)

[Bowers marketed patented software under a license that prohibited reverse engineering. Baystate marketed competing patented software and sued Bowers for a declaratory judgment of noninfringement, invalidity, or unenforceability of the Bowers patent. Bowers counterclaimed for, *inter alia*, copyright infringement and breach of contract, alleging that Baystate had reverse engineered Bowers's software in violation of the agreement. The jury found Baystate had infringed Bowers's copyright and breached the contract. Baystate appealed.]

RADER, J.: . . . Baystate contends that the Copyright Act preempts the prohibition of reverse engineering embodied in Mr. Bowers' shrink-wrap license agreements. . . . This court holds that, under First Circuit law,[*] the Copyright Act does not preempt or narrow the scope of Mr. Bowers' contract claim.

Courts respect freedom of contract and do not lightly set aside freely-entered agreements. . . . The First Circuit does not interpret [§301] to require preemption as long as "a state cause of action requires an extra element, beyond mere copying, preparation of derivative works, performance, distribution or display." *Data Gen. Corp. v. Grumman Sys. Support Corp.*, 36 F.3d 1147, 1164 (1st Cir. 1994) . . .

The First Circuit has not addressed expressly whether the Copyright Act preempts a state law contract claim that restrains copying. . . . [M]ost courts to examine

---

[*] [When dealing with issues that are outside the exclusive jurisdiction of the Federal Circuit, the court applies the law of the circuit from which the appeal is taken, here, the First Circuit.—Eds.]

this issue have found that the Copyright Act does not preempt contractual constraints on copyrighted articles. *See, e.g., ProCD, Inc. v. Zeidenberg,* 86 F.3d 1447 . . . (7th Cir. 1996).

. . . This court believes that the First Circuit would follow the reasoning of *ProCD* and the majority of other courts to consider this issue. This court, therefore, holds that the Copyright Act does not preempt Mr. Bowers' contract claims.

In making this determination, this court has left untouched the conclusions reached in *Atari Games v. Nintendo* regarding reverse engineering as a statutory fair use exception to copyright infringement. *Atari Games Corp. v. Nintendo of America, Inc.,* 975 F.2d 832 (Fed. Cir. 1992). In *Atari,* this court stated that . . . "[t]he legislative history of section 107 suggests that courts should adapt the fair use exception to accommodate new technological innovations." *Atari,* 975 F.2d at 843. This court noted "[a] prohibition on all copying whatsoever would stifle the free flow of ideas without serving any legitimate interest of the copyright holder." *Id.* Therefore, this court held "reverse engineering object code to discern the unprotectable ideas in a computer program is a fair use." *Id.* Application of the First Circuit's view distinguishing a state law contract claim having additional elements of proof from a copyright claim does not alter the findings of *Atari.* Likewise, this claim distinction does not conflict with the expressly defined circumstances in which reverse engineering is not copyright infringement under 17 U.S.C. §1201(f) (section of the Digital Millennium Copyright Act) and 17 U.S.C. §906 (section directed to mask works).

Moreover, while the Fifth Circuit has held a state law prohibiting all copying of a computer program is preempted by the federal Copyright Act, *Vault Corp. v. Quaid Software, Ltd.,* 847 F.2d 255 (5th Cir. 1988), no evidence suggests the First Circuit would extend this concept to include private contractual agreements supported by mutual assent and consideration. The First Circuit recognizes contractual waiver of affirmative defenses and statutory rights. Thus, case law indicates the First Circuit would find that private parties are free to contractually forego the limited ability to reverse engineer a software product under the exemptions of the Copyright Act. Of course, a party bound by such a contract may elect to efficiently breach the agreement in order to ascertain ideas in a computer program unprotected by copyright law. Under such circumstances, the breaching party must weigh the benefits of breach against the arguably de minimus [*sic*] damages arising from merely discerning non-protected code. . . .

In this case, the contract unambiguously prohibits "reverse engineering." . . . The record amply supports the jury's finding of a breach of that agreement. . . .

DYK, J., concurring in part and dissenting in part.

I join the majority opinion except insofar as it holds that the contract claim is not preempted by federal law. . . . The majority's approach permits state law to eviscerate an important federal copyright policy reflected in the fair use defense, and the majority's logic threatens other federal copyright policies as well. I respectfully dissent.

I . . .

The test for preemption by copyright law, like the test for patent law preemption, should be whether the state law "substantially impedes the public use of the otherwise unprotected" material. *Bonito Boats, Inc. v. Thunder Craft Boats, Inc.,* 489 U.S. 141, 157, 167 (1989) (state law at issue was preempted because it "substantially restrict[ed] the public's ability to exploit ideas that the patent system mandates shall be free for all to use"); *Sears, Roebuck & Co. v. Stiffel Co.,* 376 U.S. 225, 231-32 (1964). *See also Eldred v. Ashcroft,* 537 U.S. 186 (2003) (applying patent precedent in copyright case). In the copyright area, the First Circuit has adopted an "equivalent in substance" test to determine whether a state law is preempted by the Copyright Act. *Data Gen. Corp. v. Grumman Sys. Support Corp.* 36 F.3d 1147, 1164-65 (1st Cir. 1994). . . . "[A]n action is equivalent in substance to a copyright infringement claim [and thus preempted by the Copyright Act] where the additional element merely concerns *the extent to which* authors and their licensees can prohibit unauthorized copying by third parties." *Id.* at 1165 (emphasis in original).

II . . .

We correctly held in *Atari Games Corp. v. Nintendo of America, Inc.,* 975 F.2d 832, 843 (Fed. Cir. 1992), that reverse engineering constitutes a fair use under the Copyright Act. The Ninth and Eleventh Circuits have also ruled that reverse engineering constitutes fair use. *Bateman v. Mnemonics, Inc.,* 79 F.3d 1532, 1539 n.18 (11th Cir.1996); *Sega Enters. Ltd. v. Accolade, Inc.,* 977 F.2d 1510, 1527-28 (9th Cir. 1992). No other federal court of appeals has disagreed.

We emphasized in *Atari* that an author cannot achieve protection for an idea simply by embodying it in a computer program. . . . [T]he fair use defense for reverse engineering is necessary so that copyright protection does not "extend to any idea, procedure, process, system, method of operation, concept, principle, or discovery, regardless of the form in which it is described, explained, illustrated, or embodied in such work," as proscribed by the Copyright Act. 17 U.S.C. §102(b) (2000).

III

A state is not free to eliminate the fair use defense. Enforcement of a total ban on reverse engineering would conflict with the Copyright Act itself by protecting otherwise unprotectable material. If state law provided that a copyright holder could bar fair use of the copyrighted material by placing a black dot on each copy of the work offered for sale, there would be no question but that the state law would be preempted. A state law that allowed a copyright holder to simply label its products so as to eliminate a fair use defense would "substantially impede" the public's right to fair use and allow the copyright holder, through state law, to protect material that the Congress has determined must be free to all under the Copyright Act. *See Bonito Boats,* 489 U.S. at 157.

I nonetheless agree with the majority opinion that a state can permit parties to contract away a fair use defense or to agree not to engage in uses of copyrighted material that are permitted by the copyright law, if the contract is freely negotiated. A freely negotiated agreement represents the "extra element" that prevents preemption of a state law claim that would otherwise be identical to the infringement claim barred by the fair use defense of reverse engineering. *See Data Gen.,* 36 F.3d at 1164-65.

However, state law giving effect to shrinkwrap licenses is no different in substance from a hypothetical black dot law. Like any other contract of adhesion, the only choice offered to the purchaser is to avoid making the purchase in the first place. State law thus gives the copyright holder the ability to eliminate the fair use defense in each and every instance at its option. In doing so, as the majority concedes, it authorizes "shrinkwrap agreements . . . [that] are far broader than the protection afforded by copyright law."

IV

There is, moreover, no logical stopping point to the majority's reasoning. . . . If by printing a few words on the outside of its product a party can eliminate the fair use defense, then it can also, by the same means, restrict a purchaser from asserting the "first sale" defense, embodied in 17 U.S.C. §109(a), or any other of the protections Congress has afforded the public in the Copyright Act. That means that, under the majority's reasoning, state law could extensively undermine the protections of the Copyright Act.

V

The Fifth Circuit's decision in *Vault* directly supports preemption of the shrinkwrap limitation. The majority . . . [misreads *Vault*. There,] the Fifth Circuit held that the specific provision of state law that authorized contracts prohibiting reverse engineering, decompilation, or disassembly of computer programs was preempted by federal law because it conflicted with a portion of the Copyright Act and because it "'touche[d] upon an area' of federal copyright law." 847 F.2d at 269-70 (quoting *Sears, Roebuck,* 376 U.S. at 229). From a preemption standpoint, there is no distinction between a state law that explicitly validates a contract that restricts reverse engineering (*Vault*) and general common law that permits such a restriction (as here). On the contrary, the preemption clause of the Copyright Act makes clear that it covers "any such right or equivalent right in any such work *under the common law or statutes of any State.*" 17 U.S.C. §301(a) (2000) (emphasis added).

I do not read *ProCD, Inc. v. Zeidenberg,* 86 F.3d 1447 (7th Cir. 1996), the only other court of appeals shrinkwrap case, as being to the contrary . . . . The court saw the licensor as legitimately seeking to distinguish between personal and commercial use. . . . The court also emphasized that the license "would not withdraw any information from the public domain" because all of the information on the CD-ROM was publicly available. *Id.* at 1455.

The case before us is different from *ProCD*. The Copyright Act does not confer a right to pay the same amount for commercial and personal use. It does, however, confer a right to fair use, 17 U.S.C. §107, which we have held encompasses reverse engineering.

ProCD and the other contract cases are also careful not to create a blanket rule that all contracts will escape preemption. The court in that case emphasized that "we think it prudent to refrain from adopting a rule that anything with the label 'contract' is necessarily outside the preemption clause." . . .

I conclude that *Vault* states the correct rule; that state law authorizing shrink-wrap licenses that prohibit reverse engineering is preempted; and that the First Circuit would so hold because the extra element here "merely concerns *the extent to which* authors and their licensees can prohibit unauthorized copying by third parties." *Data Gen.*, 36 F.3d at 1165 (emphasis in original). I respectfully dissent.

NOTES AND QUESTIONS

1. Do you find the majority or the dissent in *Bowers* more convincing? Why?

2. Should the distinction between standard-form and negotiated agreements matter in the preemption analysis? Why, or why not?

3. In Chapter 10.B.1 you read *Sega Enterprises Ltd. v. Accolade, Inc.*, 977 F.2d 1510 (9th Cir. 1992), in which the court held that §117 did not authorize disassembly of object code because such a use goes "far beyond that contemplated by CONTU and authorized by section 117." *Id.* at 1520. The court did, however, determine that in certain circumstances fair use permits the reproduction of computer software that occurs in the course of disassembly. Should it make a difference in the preemption analysis if the contractual clause at issue negates an express limitation of the Copyright Act, such as §117, or instead forecloses a judicial application of the fair use doctrine? In *Bowers*, the jury concluded that Baystate's product, allegedly created after disassembling Bowers's copyrighted software, infringed the plaintiff's copyrights. Should the merits of that infringement claim affect the analysis of the preemption question?

4. Fair use encompasses many acts in addition to reverse engineering. In practice, very few contracts literally prohibit "fair use," perhaps because fair use is so hard to define in advance of litigation. Instead, firms employ contract terms that spell out permitted and prohibited uses in detail (e.g., restrictions that purport to prevent a purchaser from criticizing the copyrighted work). Some of the prohibited acts might involve using the copyrighted work in a way that would be fair under certain circumstances; others may not implicate §106 at all. How should a court analyze a preemption challenge to a claim of breach of such a clause?

5. Recall the copyright misuse doctrine, which you studied in Chapter 12.D. Which doctrine do you think is better adapted to addressing restrictive contractual provisions, copyright misuse or preemption? What are the differences in analysis and result?

Table of Cases

Principal cases are indicated by italics.

Table of Statutes and Other Laws

967

CODE OF FEDERAL REGULATIONS

TREATIES

EUROPEAN UNION DIRECTIVES

Table of Authorities

Principal texts are indicated by italics.

Abrams, *Copyright, Misappropriation, and Preemption: Constitutional and Statutory Limits of State Law Protection,* 1983 Sup. Ct. Rev. 509 (1983), 932

Alford, To Steal a Book Is an Elegant Offense (1995), *21*

Arewa, *From J.C. Bach to Hip Hop: Musical Borrowing, Copyright, and Cultural Context,* 84 N.C. L. Rev. 547 (2006), 429

Ayres & Talley, *Solomonic Bargaining: Dividing a Legal Entitlement to Facilitate Coasean Trade,* 104 Yale L.J. 1027 (1995), 120

Benkler, *Sharing Nicely: On Shareable Goods and the Emergence of Sharing as a Modality of Economic Production,* 114 Yale L.J. 273 (2004), 551

Bessen & Meurer, Patent Failure: How Judges, Bureaucrats, and Lawyers Put Innovators at Risk (2008), 242

Birnhack, *Who Owns Bratz? The Integration of Copyright and Employment Law,* 20 Fordham Intell. Prop., Media & Ent. L.J. 95 (2009), 160

Black & Page, *Add-On Infringements,* 15 Hastings Comm/Ent. L.J. 615 (1993), 331

Blair & Cotter, *The Elusive Logic of Standing Doctrine in Intellectual Property Law,* 74 Tul. L. Rev. 1323 (2000), 768

Bohannon, *Copyright Preemption of Contracts,* 67 Md. L. Rev. 616 (2008), 951

Bosman, *Library E-Books Live Longer, So Publisher Limits Shelf Life,* N.Y. Times, Mar. 15, 2011, 741

Bracha, *The Ideology of Authorship Revisited: Authors, Markets, and Liberal Values in Early American Copyright,* 108 Yale L.J. 186 (2008), 140

Brandeis & Warren, *The Right to Privacy,* 4 Harv. L. Rev. 193 (1890), 567

Bridy, *Graduated Response American Style: "Six Strikes" Measured Against Five Norms,* 23 Fordham Intell. Prop., Media & Ent. L.J. 1 (2012), 536

Burk, *Patenting Speech,* 79 Tex. L. Rev. 99 (2000), 72

Burk & Cohen, *Fair Use Infrastructure for Rights Management Systems,* 15 Harv. J.L. & Tech. 41 (2001), 884

Casey & Sawicki, *Copyright in Teams,* 80 U. Chi. L. Rev. 1683 (2014), 159

Chafee, *Reflections on the Law of Copyright,* 45 Colum. L. Rev. 503 (1945), 102, 324

Chisum, Chisum on Patents (2001), 120

Clapes et al., *Silicon Epics and Binary Bards: Determining the Proper Scope of Copyright Protection for Computer Programs,* 34 UCLA L. Rev. 1493 (1987), 206

Index